Get Connected.

Finance Prep Courses

Do your students struggle with prerequisite material from accounting, math, statistics, MS Excel, and economics? With the Finance Prep Courses, students will view a video to refresh them on these topics, and then answer questions to test their understanding. You can either assign as homework or include for optional practice. This product gives you more time in class to cover finance topics, and ensures that students do not get left behind.

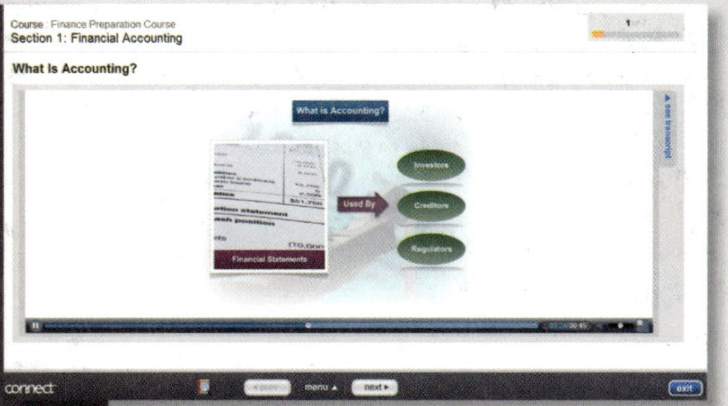

Guided Examples

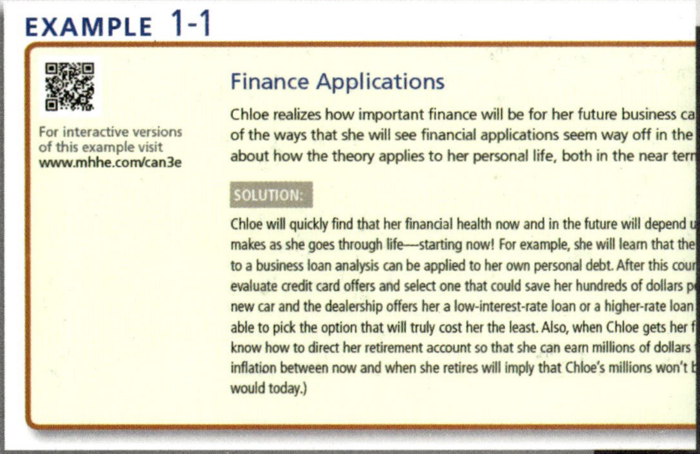
EXAMPLE 1-1

For interactive versions of this example visit www.mhhe.com/can3e

Finance Applications

Chloe realizes how important finance will be for her future business ca of the ways that she will see financial applications seem way off in the about how the theory applies to her personal life, both in the near tern

SOLUTION:

Chloe will quickly find that her financial health now and in the future will depend u makes as she goes through life—starting now! For example, she will learn that the to a business loan analysis can be applied to her own personal debt. After this cour evaluate credit card offers and select one that could save her hundreds of dollars p new car and the dealership offers her a low-interest-rate loan or a higher-rate loan able to pick the option that will truly cost her the least. Also, when Chloe gets her f know how to direct her retirement account so that she can earn millions of dollars inflation between now and when she retires will imply that Chloe's millions won't b would today.)

Guided Examples provide students with narrated and animated video tutorials and step-by-step walkthroughs of exercises and examples from the text. Students appreciate the Guided Examples because they can learn to solve a problem when they get stuck doing their homework. There are multiple tutorials for each example, including a tutorial with decision points and walkthroughs using different calculators and Excel.

Get Engaged.

eBooks

Connect Plus includes a media-rich eBook that allows you to share your notes with your students. Your students can insert and review their own notes, highlight the text, search for specific information, and interact with media resources. Using an eBook with *Connect Plus* gives your students a complete digital solution that allows them to access their materials from any computer.

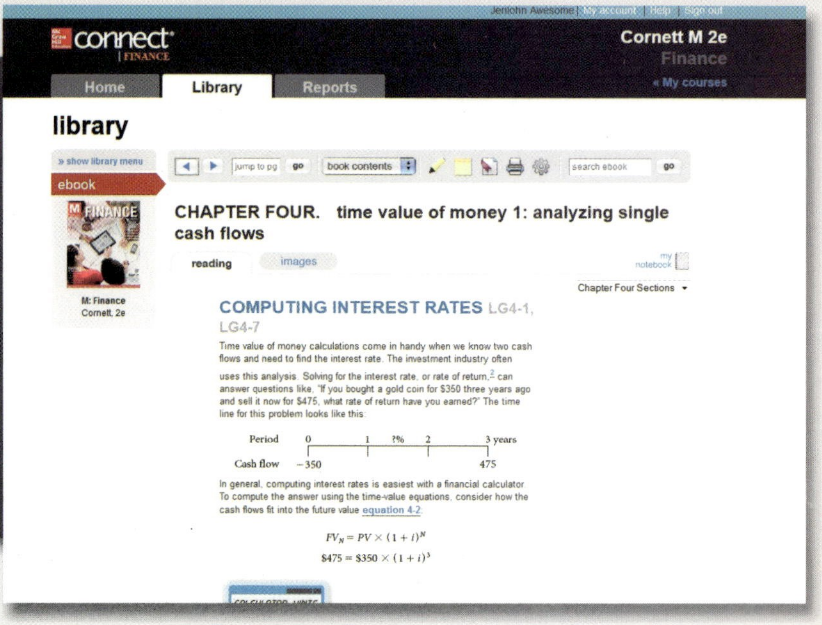

End-of-Chapter and Test Bank Content

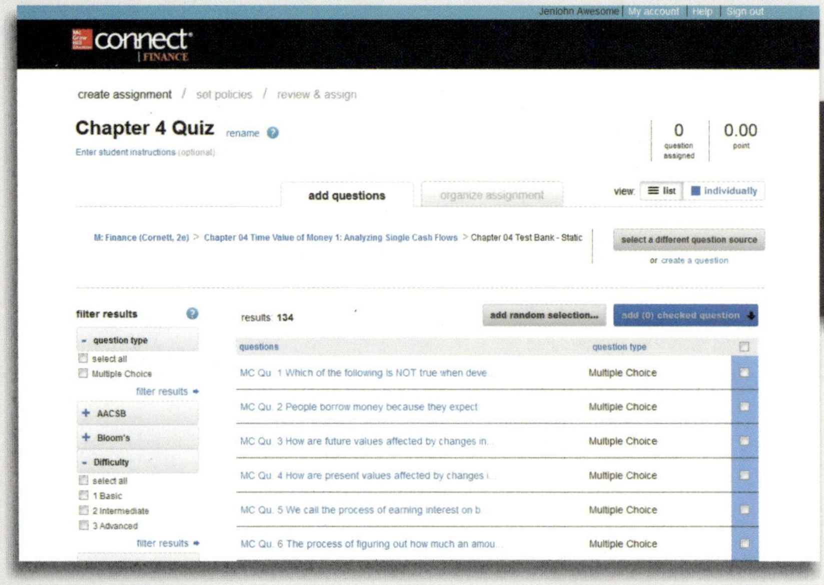

Connect Finance includes both static and algorithmic versions of end-of-chapter problems and static and algorithmic test bank questions.

finance
applications & theory

The McGraw-Hill/Irwin Series in Finance, Insurance and Real Estate

Stephen A. Ross, Franco Modigliani Professor of Finance and Economics
Sloan School of Management Massachusetts Institute of Technology, Consulting Editor

FINANCIAL MANAGEMENT

Block, Hirt, and Danielsen
Foundations of Financial Management
Fifteenth Edition

Brealey, Myers, and Allen
Principles of Corporate Finance
Eleventh Edition

Brealey, Myers, and Allen
Principles of Corporate Finance, Concise
Second Edition

Brealey, Myers, and Marcus
Fundamentals of Corporate Finance
Seventh Edition

Brooks
FinGame Online 5.0

Bruner
Case Studies in Finance: Managing for Corporate Value Creation
Seventh Edition

Cornett, Adair, and Nofsinger
Finance: Applications and Theory
Third Edition

Cornett, Adair, and Nofsinger
M: Finance
Second Edition

DeMello
Cases in Finance
Second Edition

Grinblatt (editor)
Stephen A. Ross, Mentor: Influence through Generations

Grinblatt and Titman
Financial Markets and Corporate Strategy
Second Edition

Higgins
Analysis for Financial Management
Tenth Edition

Kellison
Theory of Interest
Third Edition

Ross, Westerfield, and Jaffe
Corporate Finance
Tenth Edition

Ross, Westerfield, Jaffe, and Jordan
Corporate Finance: Core Principles and Applications
Fourth Edition

Ross, Westerfield, and Jordan
Essentials of Corporate Finance
Eighth Edition

Ross, Westerfield, and Jordan
Fundamentals of Corporate Finance
Tenth Edition

Shefrin
Behavioral Corporate Finance: Decisions that Create Value
First Edition

White
Financial Analysis with an Electronic Calculator
Sixth Edition

INVESTMENTS

Bodie, Kane, and Marcus
Essentials of Investments
Ninth Edition

Bodie, Kane, and Marcus
Investments
Tenth Edition

Hirt and Block
Fundamentals of Investment Management
Tenth Edition

Jordan and Miller
Fundamentals of Investments: Valuation and Management
Seventh Edition

Stewart, Piros, and Heisler
Running Money: Professional Portfolio Management
First Edition

Sundaram and Das
Derivatives: Principles and Practice
First Edition

FINANCIAL INSTITUTIONS AND MARKETS

Rose and Hudgins
Bank Management and Financial Services
Ninth Edition

Rose and Marquis
Financial Institutions and Markets
Eleventh Edition

Saunders and Cornett
Financial Institutions Management: A Risk Management Approach
Eighth Edition

Saunders and Cornett
Financial Markets and Institutions
Fifth Edition

INTERNATIONAL FINANCE

Eun and Resnick
International Financial Management
Seventh Edition

REAL ESTATE

Brueggeman and Fisher
Real Estate Finance and Investments
Fourteenth Edition

Ling and Archer
Real Estate Principles: A Value Approach
Fourth Edition

FINANCIAL PLANNING AND INSURANCE

Allen, Melone, Rosenbloom, and Mahoney
Retirement Plans: 401(k)s, IRAs, and Other Deferred Compensation Approaches
Eleventh Edition

Altfest
Personal Financial Planning
First Edition

Harrington and Niehaus
Risk Management and Insurance
Second Edition

Kapoor, Dlabay, and Hughes
Focus on Personal Finance: An Active Approach to Help You Develop Successful Financial Skills
Fourth Edition

Kapoor, Dlabay, and Hughes
Personal Finance
Eleventh Edition

Walker and Walker
Personal Finance: Building Your Future
First Edition

finance
applications & theory
third edition

Marcia Millon Cornett
Bentley University

Troy A. Adair Jr.
Berkeley College

John Nofsinger
Washington State University

Mc Graw Hill Education

FINANCE: APPLICATIONS & THEORY, THIRD EDITION

Published by McGraw-Hill Education, 2 Penn Plaza, New York, NY 10121.

Some ancillaries, including electronic and print components, may not be available to customers outside the United States.

This book is printed on acid-free paper.

1 2 3 4 5 6 7 8 9 0 DOW/DOW 1 0 9 8 7 6 5 4

ISBN 978-0-07-786168-1
MHID 0-07-786168-X

Senior Vice President, Products & Markets: *Kurt L. Strand*
Vice President, Content Production & Technology Services: *Kimberly Meriwether David*
Managing Director: *Douglas Reiner*
Executive Brand Manager: *Chuck Synovec*
Executive Director of Development: *Ann Torbert*
Development Editor: *Noelle Bathurst*
Director of Digital Content: *Doug Ruby*
Digital Development Editor: *Meg B. Maloney*
Digital Development Editor: *Kevin Shanahan*
Executive Marketing Manager: *Melissa S. Caughlin*
Director, Content Production: *Terri Schiesl*
Content Project Manager: *Danielle Clement*
Senior Buyer: *Carol A. Bielski*
Design: *Srdjan Savanovic*
Cover Image: © *ewg3D*
Senior Content Licensing Specialist: *Jeremy Cheshareck*
Typeface: *10.5/13 PalatinoLTStd-Roman*
Compositor: *Laserwords Private Limited*
Printer: *R. R. Donnelley*

All credits appearing on page or at the end of the book are considered to be an extension of the copyright page.

Library of Congress Cataloging-in-Publication Data

Cornett, Marcia Millon.
Finance : applications & theory/Marcia Millon Cornett, Bentley University, Troy A. Adair Jr., Berkeley College, John Nofsinger, Washington State University.—Third edition.
pages cm.—(The McGraw-Hill/Irwin series in finance, insurance and real estate)
Includes index.
ISBN 978-0-07-786168-1 (alk. paper)
ISBN 0-07-786168-X (alk. paper)
1. Finance. I. Adair, Troy A. (Troy Alton), 1964- II. Nofsinger, John R. III. Title.
HG173.C679 2015
332—dc23

2013038214

www.mhhe.com

dedicated

to my parents, Tom and Sue—Marcia Millon Cornett

to Kieran, the love of my life—Troy A. Adair Jr.

to Anna, my wife and best friend—John Nofsinger

about the authors

Marcia Millon Cornett ***Professor of Finance in the School of Management at Bentley University.*** She received her BS degree in economics from Knox College in Galesburg, Illinois, and her MBA and PhD degrees in finance from Indiana University in Bloomington, Indiana. Dr. Cornett has written and published several articles in the areas of bank performance, bank regulation, corporate finance, and investments. Articles authored by Dr. Cornett have appeared in such academic journals as the *Journal of Finance;* the *Journal of Money, Credit, and Banking;* the *Journal of Financial Economics; Financial Management;* and the *Journal of Banking and Finance.* In 2008, Dr. Cornett was ranked the 124th most-published out of 17,600 and the number five female author in finance literature over the last 50 years. Along with Anthony Saunders (John M. Schiff Professor of Finance at the Stern School of Business at New York University), Dr. Cornett has just completed writing the 8th edition of *Financial Institutions Management* (McGraw-Hill/Irwin) and the 5th edition of *Financial Markets and Institutions* (McGraw-Hill/Irwin). She serves as an associate editor for the *Journal of Financial Services Research,* the *Review of Financial Economics, Financial Review,* and *Multinational Finance Journal.* Dr. Cornett has served as a member of the board of directors, the executive committee, and the finance committee of the SIU Credit Union. Dr. Cornett has also taught at Southern Illinois University at Carbondale, the University of Colorado, Boston College, and Southern Methodist University. She is a member of the Financial Management Association, the American Finance Association, and the Western Finance Association.

Troy Alton Adair Jr. ***Associate Vice President for Institutional Effectiveness at Berkeley College.*** He received his BS degree in computers/information science from the University of Alabama at Birmingham, his MBA from the University of North Dakota, and his PhD in finance from Indiana University. Dr. Adair has written articles on bank regulator self-interest, analyst earnings per share forecasting, and capital budgeting in continuous time and is the author of *Corporate Finance Demystified, Excel Applications in Corporate Finance,* and *Excel Applications in Investments* (all McGraw-Hill/Irwin). He has also served as a consultant on financial data information systems and business intelligence to a number of international banks and insurance companies, and as the faculty representative to the board of trustees investments committee at Alma College. Dr. Adair has also taught at the University of Michigan, Alma College, Hofstra University, Indiana University, and the University of North Carolina at Chapel Hill. He is a member of the Financial Management Association, the American Finance Association, and the Southern Finance Association.

John Nofsinger ***Professor of Finance at Washington State University.*** He earned his BS degree in electrical engineering from Washington State University, his MBA degree from Chapman University, and his PhD degree in finance from Washington State University. Dr. Nofsinger has written dozens of articles in the areas of investments, corporate finance, and behavioral finance. These papers have appeared in the scholarly journals, the *Journal of Finance, Journal of Business, Journal of Financial and Quantitative Analysis, Financial Management, Journal of Corporate Finance, Journal of Banking and Finance, Journal of Behavioral Decision Making,* among others. Dr. Nofsinger has also authored (or coauthored) six trade books and textbooks that have been translated into six different languages. The most prominent of these books are the industry book, *The Psychology of Investing,* and a textbook, *Investments: Analysis and Behavior* (McGraw-Hill/Irwin, coauthored with Mark Hirschey, the Anderson W. Chandler Professor of Business at the University of Kansas). Dr. Nofsinger is a leading expert in behavioral finance and is a frequent speaker on this topic at industry conferences, universities, and academic conferences. He has often been quoted or appeared in the financial media, including *The Wall Street Journal, Financial Times, Fortune, Bloomberg BusinessWeek, Smart Money, Washington Post,* and *CNBC,* and other media from *The Dolans* to *The Street.com.*

a note from the authors

"There is a lot to cover in this course so I focus on the core concepts, theories, and problems."

"I like to teach the course by using examples from their own individual lives."

"My students come into this course with varying levels of math skills."

How many of these quotes might you have said while teaching the undergraduate corporate finance course? Our many years of teaching certainly reflect such sentiments, and as we prepared to write this book, we conducted many market research studies that confirm just how much these statements—or ones similar—are common across the country. This critical course covers so many crucial topics that instructors need to focus on core ideas to ensure that students are getting the preparation they need for future classes—and for their lives beyond college.

We did not set out to write this book to change the way finance is taught, but rather to parallel and support the way that instructors from across the country currently teach finance. Well over 600 instructors teaching this course have shared their class experiences and ideas via a variety of research methods that we used to develop the framework for this text. We are excited to have authored a book that we think you will find fits your classroom style perfectly.

KEY THEMES

This book's framework emphasizes three themes. See pages xiii to xvi for a description of features in our book that support these themes.

- **Finance is about connecting core concepts.** We all struggle with fitting so many topics into this course, so this text strives to make it easier for you by getting back to the core concepts, key research, and current topics. We realize that today's students expect to learn more in class from lectures than in closely studying their textbooks, so we've created brief chapters that clearly lead students to crucial material that they need to review if they are to understand how to approach core financial concepts. The text is also organized around learning goals, making it easier for you to prep your course and for students to study the right topics.
- **Finance can be taught using a personal perspective.** Most long-term finance instructors have often heard students ask "How is this course relevant to me?" on the first day of class. We no longer teach classes dedicated solely to finance majors; many of us now must teach the first finance course to a mix of business majors. We need to give finance majors the rigor they need while not overwhelming class members from other majors. For years, instructors have used individual examples to help teach these concepts, but this is the first text to integrate this personal way of teaching into the chapters.
- **Finance focuses on solving problems and decision making.** This isn't to say that concepts and theories aren't important, but students will typically need to solve some kind of mathematical problem—or at least understand

the impact of different numerical scenarios—to make the right decision on common finance issues. If you, as an instructor, either assign problems for homework or create exams made up almost entirely of mathematical material, you understand the need for good problems (and plenty of them). You also understand from experience the number of office hours you spend tutoring students and grading homework. Students have different learning styles, and this text aims to address that challenge to allow you more time in class to get through the critical topics.

CHANGES IN THE THIRD EDITION

Based on feedback from users and reviewers, we undertook an ambitious revision in order to make the book follow your teaching strategy even more closely. Below are the changes we made for this third edition, broken out by chapter.

Overall

- Simplified figures where appropriate and added captions to emphasize the main "takeaways"
- Updated data, company names, and scenarios to reflect latest available data and real-world changes
- Cross-referenced numbered examples with similar end-of-chapter problems and self-test problems so students can easily model their homework
- Updated the numbers in the end-of-chapter problems to provide variety and limit the transfer of answers from previous classes

Chapter 1: Introduction to Financial Management

- Expanded discussion of agency relationships and problems between managers and stakeholders

Chapter 2: Reviewing Financial Statements

- Added discussion of earnings before interest, taxes, depreciation, and assets (EBITDA) and net operating profit after taxes (NOPAT)
- Added discussion of EPS dilution, including new in-chapter example and end-of-chapter problem
- Added discussion of where to find financial statements for a firm
- Added a new Finance at Work on American Apparel delisting letter
- Added Appendix with financial statements in Excel format

Chapter 3: Analyzing Financial Statements

- Added discussion of gross profit margin and operating profit margin
- Added explanation of debt-to-asset ratio transformed to equity multiplier and debt-to-equity ratios
- Expanded definition of debt management ratios to include coverage ratios
- Added additional end-of-chapter problems on interactions between ratios
- Added Excel file for calculating ratios from financial statements

Chapter 4: Time Value of Money 1: Analyzing Single Cash Flows

- Expanded introductory discussion
- Converted all tables to spreadsheet layout
- Clarified discussion of payment to cash flow

- Added PV and FV labels to all time line diagrams
- Updated Mini-Case data

Chapter 5: Time Value of Money 2: Analyzing Annuity Cash Flows

- Converted all tables to spreadsheet layout
- Added PV and FV labels to all time line diagrams
- Updated and revised Finance at Work boxes
- Reduced derivation part of an equation
- Added new Math Coach to compute amortization in TVM calculators

Chapter 6: Understanding Financial Markets and Institutions

- Updated all figures, tables, and examples
- Added Finance at Work box on JPMorgan, "London whale," and derivative losses
- Added discussion on financial institutions move away from risk measurement and management to servicers of mortgages and other risky assets
- Added discussion of shadow banks
- Added new example on determinants of interest rates in individual securities
- Added new self-test problem and end-of-chapter problems
- Updated Appendix

Chapter 7: Valuing Bonds

- Updated real data, real bonds, and real companies in examples and figures
- Converted all tables to spreadsheet layout
- Added a discussion of convertible bonds with margin definition
- Added PV and FV labels to all time line diagrams
- Added TVM calculator to Example 7-6
- Clarified and expanded discussion of the call price
- Updated Greek tragedy Finance at Work box
- Added a new self-test problem on capital gains and losses in bonds

Chapter 8: Valuing Stocks

- Updated real data, real stocks, and real companies in examples and figures
- Converted all tables to spreadsheet layout
- Changed specialist to designated market maker
- New Example 8-1
- Clarified description of equation 8-6
- Simplified variable growth figure, equation, and discussion
- Added discussion of P/CF and P/B relative price ratios
- Updated Mini-Case

Chapter 9: Characterizing Risk and Return

- Updated real data, real indexes, and real companies in examples, discussions, and tables
- Converted all tables to spreadsheet layout
- Improved discussion of dollar returns and percentage returns

- Moved geometric mean return equation from footnote into the text
- Updated Mini-Case

Chapter 10: Estimating Risk and Return

- Updated real data, indexes, betas, and companies in examples, discussions, and tables
- Converted all tables to spreadsheet layout
- Clarified description of equations 10-1 and 10-2
- Changed example from Boeing to General Electric
- New table and description for spreadsheet computation of computing beta
- Updated the Mini-Case

Chapter 11: Calculating the Cost of Capital

- Expanded discussion of WACC for projects versus WACC for firm
- Added discussion of WACC from the viewpoint of the investor versus that of the firm
- Expanded discussion of intuition underlying calculation of project WACC
- Enhanced intuitive explanation for the use of divisional WACCs
- Added details concerning flotation costs to the corporation

Chapter 12: Estimating Cash Flows on Capital Budgeting Projects

- Enhanced intuitive explanation of why accelerated depreciation is preferred
- Added additional explanation of adjusting the project's initial cash flow to account for flotation costs
- Added additional end-of-chapter problems dealing with replacement projects' cash flows

Chapter 13: Weighing Net Present Value and Other Capital Budgeting Criteria

- Changed calculation and discussion of profitability index to reflect a benchmark of 1
- Enhanced explanation of calculation of MIRR
- Enhanced discussion of payback
- Added additional clarifications concerning use of NPV profiles

Chapter 14: Working Capital Management and Policies

- Added discussion of relationship between working capital management and operations management
- Enhanced explanation and example concerning use of Miller-Orr model

Chapter 15: Financial Planning and Forecasting

- Updated examples of naïve approach to forecasting sales, average approach, adjusting for seasonality and trend, and calculating additional funds needed using pro forma balance sheets

Chapter 16: Assessing Long-Term Debt, Equity, and Capital Structure

- Added coverage of operating leverage and total leverage to discussion of financial leverage
- Enhanced discussion of break-even EBIT

Chapter 17: Sharing Firm Wealth: Dividends, Share Repurchases, and Other Payouts

- Revised discussion of residual dividend model to reflect firms' responses to changing economic conditions
- Enhanced discussion of extraordinary dividends
- Updated dividend policy examples

Chapter 18: Issuing Capital and the Investment Banking Process

- Revised/simplified Figure 18.1
- Added Finance at Work box and discussion of Facebook IPO
- Added discussion of Dutch auction IPO and direct IPO

Chapter 19: International Corporate Finance

- Updated the real data and companies in examples, discussions, and tables
- Converted all tables to spreadsheet layout

Chapter 20: Mergers and Acquisitions and Financial Distress

- Added Herfindahl-Hirschman Index (HHI)
- Added new end-of-chapter problems
- Increased discussion of debtor in possession and cramdown
- New Finance at Work box on American Airline bankruptcy
- Added M&A calculation in Excel format

Chapter Features

CONNECTING CORE CONCEPTS

Learning Goals appear at the beginning of each chapter and are indicated throughout the text next to headings, examples, summary, and end-of-chapter problems to which they relate. These outcomes help instructors structure their classes and assign readings and homework. The accompanying test bank provides instructors with hundreds of questions organized by level and learning goals to make customization even easier!

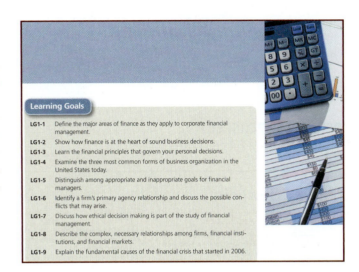

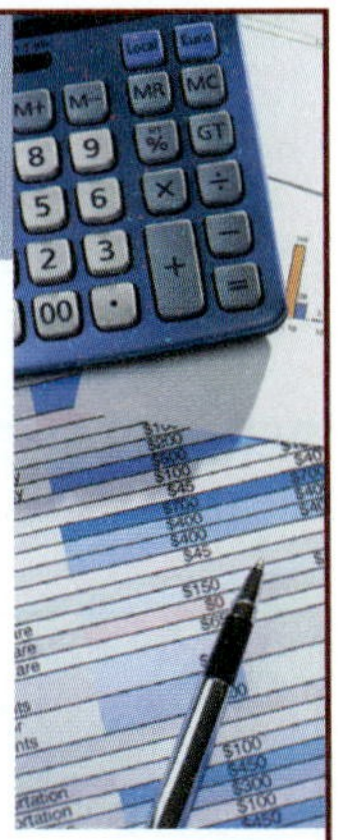

Learning Goals

- **LG1-1** Define the major areas of finance as they apply to corporate financial management.
- **LG1-2** Show how finance is at the heart of sound business decisions.
- **LG1-3** Learn the financial principles that govern your personal decisions.
- **LG1-4** Examine the three most common forms of business organization in the United States today.
- **LG1-5** Distinguish among appropriate and inappropriate goals for financial managers.
- **LG1-6** Identify a firm's primary agency relationship and discuss the possible conflicts that may arise.
- **LG1-7** Discuss how ethical decision making is part of the study of financial management.
- **LG1-8** Describe the complex, necessary relationships among firms, financial institutions, and financial markets.
- **LG1-9** Explain the fundamental causes of the financial crisis that started in 2006.

finance at work — markets

JP MORGAN'S $2 BILLION BLUNDER

A massive trading bet boomeranged on JPMorgan Chase & Co., leaving the bank with at least $2 billion in trading losses and its chief executive, Jamie Dimon, with a rare black eye following a long run as what some called the "King of Wall Street." The losses stemmed from wagers gone wrong in the bank's Chief Investment Office, which manages risk for the New York company . . . Large positions taken in that office by a trader nicknamed "the London whale" had roiled a sector of the debt markets. The bank, betting on a continued economic recovery with a complex web of trades tied to the values of corporate bonds, was hit hard when prices moved against it starting last month, causing losses in many of its derivative positions. The losses occurred while JPMorgan tried to scale back the trade.

The bank's strategy was "flawed, complex, poorly reviewed, poorly executed, and poorly monitored," Mr. Dimon said Thursday in a hastily arranged conference call with analysts and investors after the stock-market close. He called the mistake "egregious, self-inflicted," and said: "We will admit it, we will fix it and move on." . . . JPMorgan, the nation's largest bank by assets, said in its quarterly filing with regulators Thursday that the plan it has been using to hedge risks "has proven to be riskier, more volatile, and less effective as an economic hedge than the firm previously believed." . . . Mr. Dimon said the trading losses were "slightly more" than $2 billion so far in the second quarter. . . The *Journal* reported in April that hedge funds and other investors were making bets in the market for insurance-like products called credit-default swaps, or CDS, to try to take advantage of trades done by a London-based trader named Bruno Michel Iksil who worked out of the Chief Investment Office, or CIO. . . On Thursday he admitted the bank acted "defensively" when news reports surfaced. "With hindsight we should have been paying more attention to it," he said. "This not how we want to run a business."

The CIO group once had a large trade designed to protect the company from a downturn in the economy. Earlier this year, it began reducing that position and taking a bullish stance on the financial health of certain companies and selling protection that would compensate buyers if those companies defaulted on debts. Mr. Iksil was a heavy seller of CDS contracts tied to a basket, or index, of companies. In April the cost of protection began to rise, contributing to the losses. Mr. Iksil's group had roughly $350 billion of investment securities at December 31, according to company filings, or about 15 percent of the bank's total assets . . . Mr. Dimon said the bank has an extensive review underway of what went wrong, which he said included "many errors," "sloppiness," and "bad judgment."

Source: Dan Fitzpatrick, Gregory Zuckerman, and Liz Rappaport, "J.P. Morgan's $2 Billion Blunder," *The Wall Street Journal Online*, May 11, 2012. Reprinted by permission of *The Wall Street Journal*. www.wsj.com

want to know more? **Key Words to Search for Updates:** JPMorgan, London whale, derivative trading losses

Finance at Work boxes highlight current events and hot topics noted in the news. The *Want to know more?* feature in each box contains suggested words to use for searching the Internet for updates. These features are great to use for class discussion or as homework assignments.

Time Out boxes, featured at the end of sections, test students' understanding of the key terms and core concepts just presented. Answers to the Time Out questions appear at the end of each chapter.

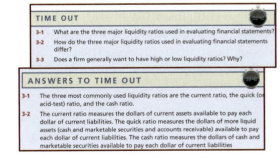

TIME OUT

- **3-1** What are the three major liquidity ratios used in evaluating financial statements?
- **3-2** How do the three major liquidity ratios used in evaluating financial statements differ?
- **3-3** Does a firm generally want to have high or low liquidity ratios? Why?

ANSWERS TO TIME OUT

- **3-1** The three most commonly used liquidity ratios are the current ratio, the quick (or acid-test) ratio, and the cash ratio.
- **3-2** The current ratio measures the dollars of current assets available to pay each dollar of current liabilities. The quick ratio measures the dollars of more liquid assets (cash and marketable securities and accounts receivable) available to pay each dollar of current liabilities. The cash ratio measures the dollars of cash and marketable securities available to pay each dollar of current liabilities

Research It! projects, perfect for individual assignments or as group projects, are included at the end of each chapter and require students to search the Web for data and other information to answer the questions.

research it! **Analyzing Financial Statements**

Go to the website of Walmart Stores, Inc., at **www.walmartstores.com** and get the latest financial statements from the annual report using the following steps.

Click on "Investors." Click on "Financial Information." Click on "Annual Reports." Click on the most recent date. This will bring the file onto your computer that contains the relevant data.

Using the most recent balance sheet and income statement, calculate the financial ratios for the firm, including the internal and sustainable growth rates.

PERSONAL PERSPECTIVE

viewpoints

Business Application

The managers of DPH Tree Farm, Inc., have released public statements that the firm's performance surpasses that of other firms in the industry. They cite the firm's liquidity and asset management positions as particularly strong. DPH's superior performance in these areas has resulted in superior overall returns for their stockholders. What are the key financial ratios that DPH Tree Farm, Inc., needs to calculate and evaluate in order to justify these statements? **(See solution on p. 99)**

Personal Application

Chris Ryan is looking to invest in DPH Tree Farm, Inc. Chris has the most recent set of financial statements from DPH Tree Farm's annual report but is not sure how to evaluate them or measure the firm's performance relative to other firms in the industry. What are the financial ratios with which Chris should measure the performance of DPH Tree Farm, Inc.? How can Chris use these ratios to evaluate the firm's performance? **(See solution on p. 99)**

So how can these financial ratios work in your life?

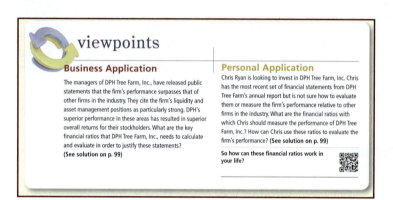

Viewpoints, a unique feature presented at the beginning of each chapter, pose both a business and a personal problem using key chapter topics. These Viewpoints scenarios immediately set a context for the chapter and allow instructors to take class discussion in multiple directions to make key concepts clearer. **Viewpoints Revisited** at the end of the chapter show how these problems are solved. **Viewpoints Extended** leverage a variety of media to provide an extended look at each personal application raised. These are accessible online at **www.mhhe.com/can3e** or through the QR code shown at the bottom of the column.

Numbered examples in each chapter feature various perspectives, so students gain practice in solving problems in both business and individual contexts. Each example contains a list of end-of-chapter problems that are similar, in order to better model the solution process. The QR codes in the top corner of each example link to the interactive video guided examples.

LG4-4 **EXAMPLE 4-3**

Buy Now and Don't Pay for Two Years

For interactive versions of this example visit www.mhhe.com/can3e

Suppose that a marketing manager for a retail furniture company proposes a sale. Customers can buy now but don't have to pay for their furniture purchases for two years. From a time value of money perspective, selling furniture at full price with payment in two years is equivalent to selling furniture at a sale, or discounted, price with immediate payment. If interest rates are 7.5 percent per year, what is the equivalent sale price of a $1,000 sleeper-sofa when the customer takes the full two years to pay for it?

SOLUTION: The time line for this problem is:

Period	0	7.5%	1	2 years
Cash flow	PV=?			FV=1,000

Using equation 4-5, the present value computation is

$$PV = \frac{FV_N}{(1+i)^N} = \frac{\$1{,}000}{1.075^2} = \frac{\$1{,}000}{1.1556} = \$865.33$$

CALCULATOR HINTS
N = 2
I = 7.5
PMT = 0
FV = 1000
CPT PV = −865.33

In this case, the marketing proposal for delaying payment for two years is equivalent to selling the $1,000 sleeper-sofa for a sale price of $865.33, or a 13.5 percent discount. When stores promote such sales, they often believe that customers will not be able to pay the full amount at the end of the two years and then must pay high interest rate charges and late fees. Customers who do pay on time are getting a good deal.

Similar to Problems 4-9, 4-10, 4-11, 4-12, self-test problem 2

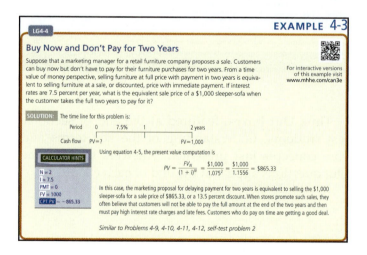

PROBLEM-SOLVING AND LEARNING STYLES

Each numbered example is accompanied by a **video guided example.** These exciting, unique features detail the solution to a key problem or concept within each chapter. For each example, students can scan the accompanying QR code or go to the book's website at **www.mhhe.com/can3e** to find the following additional support. **(See inside back cover for more information.)**

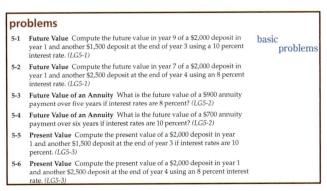

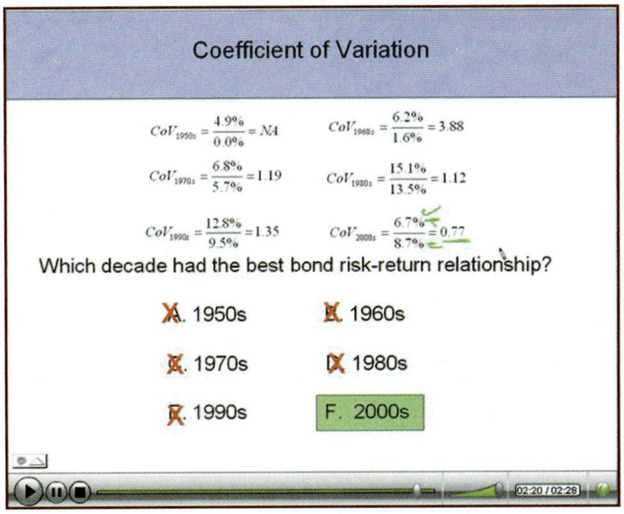

- The exact example in the book is worked out in a visual, narrated format.
- A similar example is presented in a video format, which stops at decision points in the problem and asks the students to identify the next step. The video continues, explaining why the student is correct or incorrect, and continues solving the problem. This feature allows students to apply and check their learning before doing homework.
- The solution to the example in the book is demonstrated using the TI-83, HP, and BA II Plus Professional calculators—reducing the class time needed to teach students how to use their calculators.
- The solution to the example in the book is demonstrated using Excel, to help you and your students get a basic understanding of how to set up the spreadsheets.

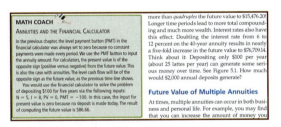

MATH COACH

ANNUITIES AND THE FINANCIAL CALCULATOR

In the previous chapter, the level payment button (PMT) in the financial calculator was always set to zero because no constant payments were made every period. We use the PMT button to input the annuity amount. For calculators, the present value is of the opposite sign (positive versus negative) from the future value. This is also the case with annuities. The level cash flow will be of the opposite sign as the future value, as the previous time line shows.

You would use the financial calculator to solve the problem of depositing $100 for five years via the following inputs: N = 5, I = 8, PV = 0, PMT = −100. In this case, the input for present value is zero because no deposit is made today. The result of computing the future value is 586.66.

more than *quadruples* the future value to $15,476.20! Longer time periods lead to more total compounding and much more wealth. Interest rates also have this effect. Doubling the interest rate from 6 to 12 percent on the 40-year annuity results in nearly a five-fold increase in the future value to $76,709.14. Think about it: Depositing only $100 per year (about 25 lattes per year) can generate some serious money over time. See Figure 5.1. How much would $2,000 annual deposits generate?

Future Value of Multiple Annuities

At times, multiple annuities can occur in both business and personal life. For example, you may find that you can increase the amount of money you

Math Coach boxes are featured in many chapters to help avoid the most common mathematical mistakes in a particular problem.

you are able to increase your investment in the retirement program to $6,000 per year (your contribution plus the company match). What would be the future value of your retirement wealth from this program if investments are compounded at 7 percent?

CALCULATOR HINTS

Add to previous answer
N = 20
I = 7
PV = 0
PMT = −1500
CPT FV = 61,493.24

SOLUTION:

You can compute the future value using two annuities. The first annuity is one with payments of $4,500 that lasts 40 years. The second is a $1,500 (= $6,000 − $4,500) annuity that lasts only 20 years. We already computed the future value of the first annuity in the previous example: $898,358. The future value of the second annuity is:

$$FVA_{20} = \$1{,}500 \times \frac{(1 + 0.07)^{20} - 1}{0.07} = \$1{,}500 \times 40.9955 = \$61{,}493.24$$

So, your retirement wealth from this program would be $959,851 (= $898,358 + $61,493).

Similar to Problems 5-19, 5-20, self-test problem 1

Calculator keystroke hints are included in the margin and next to key examples, if applicable, showing a quick snapshot of how to solve the problem using a financial calculator. These can easily be skipped if calculators are not used for your class.

End-of-chapter problems are grouped according to level of difficulty and are structured so that every odd-numbered problem is mirrored by a similar even-numbered problem. Therefore, instructors can assign two different sets of similar problems to different sections. Alternatively, instructors can use one set of problems to work in class and use the other as homework.

problems

basic problems

5-1 **Future Value** Compute the future value in year 9 of a $2,000 deposit in year 1 and another $1,500 deposit at the end of year 3 using a 10 percent interest rate. *(LG5-1)*

5-2 **Future Value** Compute the future value in year 7 of a $2,000 deposit in year 1 and another $2,500 deposit at the end of year 4 using an 8 percent interest rate. *(LG5-1)*

5-3 **Future Value of an Annuity** What is the future value of a $900 annuity payment over five years if interest rates are 8 percent? *(LG5-2)*

5-4 **Future Value of an Annuity** What is the future value of a $700 annuity payment over six years if interest rates are 10 percent? *(LG5-2)*

5-5 **Present Value** Compute the present value of a $2,000 deposit in year 1 and another $1,500 deposit at the end of year 3 if interest rates are 10 percent. *(LG5-3)*

5-6 **Present Value** Compute the present value of a $2,000 deposit in year 1 and another $2,500 deposit at the end of year 4 using an 8 percent interest rate. *(LG5-3)*

Self-Test Problems with Solutions appear before the gradable problem sets so students can test themselves before diving into their homework.

self-test problems with solutions

LG4-2,4-3,4-5

1 **Two Future Values** You have entered a consulting deal with a company. You are to complete two projects. The first project will take one year to finish. The second project will take two years and must be started immediately following the first one. The deal includes a provision in which the company will make a $10,000 payment to your retirement plan after the first project and $20,000 after the second project. You have 20 years until retirement and will earn 9 percent per year on your retirement plan money. How much money will you have for retirement from these two payments?

integrated mini-case Working with Financial Statements

Listed are the 2015 financial statements for Garners' Platoon Mental Health Care, Inc. Spread the balance sheet and income statement. Calculate the financial ratios for the firm, including the internal and sustainable growth rates. Using the DuPont system of analysis and the industry ratios reported, evaluate the performance of the firm.

Integrated Mini-Cases at the end of each chapter combine the chapter's key concepts into a more complex problem to help students understand how concepts and methods tie together.

Numbered equations are presented throughout and summarized at the end of each chapter. A concerted effort has been made to reduce the number of different variables used in equations in order to simplify some of the critical financial formulas. Where possible, equations are also presented in "word form" at the same time they are presented in "number form" to address alternate learning styles.

3-1 $$\text{Current ratio} = \frac{\text{Current assets}}{\text{Current liabilities}}$$

3-2 $$\text{Quick ratio (acid-test ratio)} = \frac{\text{Current assets} - \text{Inventory}}{\text{Current liabilities}}$$

3-3 $$\text{Cash ratio} = \frac{\text{Cash and marketable securities}}{\text{Current liabilities}}$$

3-4 $$\text{Inventory turnover} = \frac{\text{Sales or cost of goods sold}}{\text{Inventory}}$$

SUPPLEMENTS FOR THE INSTRUCTOR

ONLINE LEARNING CENTER

www.mhhe.com/can3e

A wealth of information is available online at our website. You will have access to study materials specifically created for this text, such as:

- **Test Bank** Hundreds of questions complement the material presented in the book. The Test Bank is tagged by level of difficulty, learning goal, AACSB knowledge categories, and Bloom's taxonomy—making it easy for instructors to customize exams to reflect the material stressed in class. The test bank is available in Word files and in McGraw-Hill's flexible electronic test creation and testing program, ***EZ Test Online.***

  In EZ Test Online, instructors can select questions from multiple McGraw-Hill test banks or compose their own, and then either print the test for paper distribution or administer it online. The test bank is also available in McGraw-Hill's dynamic online homework management system, ***Connect*** (see page xviii for details).
- **Solutions Manual** Developed by authors Marcia Cornett, Troy Adair, and John Nofsinger, this resource contains the worked-out solutions to all the end-of-chapter problems, in the consistent voice and method of the book. The solutions have been class-tested and checked by multiple instructors to ensure accuracy.
- **PowerPoint Presentation** The PowerPoint presentations have been carefully updated for the third edition. These slides contain lecture notes, which closely follow the book content, enhanced with the tables and figures from the chapters. Several chapters are also supplemented with additional presentations that contain notes and examples using financial calculators. Instructors can easily customize these slides to suit their classroom needs and various presentation styles.

ASSURANCE OF LEARNING

Many educational institutions today are focused on the notion of assurance of learning, an important element of some accreditation standards. *Finance: Applications and Theory* is designed specifically to support your assurance of learning initiatives with a simple, yet powerful, solution.

Each test bank and end-of-chapter question for *Finance: Applications and Theory* maps to a specific chapter learning goal listed in the text. You can use the test bank software to easily query for learning goals that directly relate to the learning objectives for your course. You can then use the reporting features of the software to aggregate student results in similar fashion, making the collection and presentation of assurance of learning data simple and easy.

AACSB STATEMENT

The McGraw-Hill Companies is a proud corporate member of AACSB International. Understanding the importance and value of AACSB accreditation, *Finance: Applications and Theory,* has sought to recognize the curricula guidelines detailed in the AACSB standards for business accreditation by connecting selected questions in the test bank to the general knowledge and skill guidelines found in the AACSB standards.

The statements contained in *Finance: Applications and Theory,* are provided only as a guide for the users of this text. The AACSB leaves content coverage and assessment within the purview of individual schools, the mission of the school, and the faculty. While *Finance: Applications and Theory,* and the teaching package make no claim of any specific AACSB qualification or evaluation, we have, within *Finance: Applications and Theory,* labeled selected questions according to the six general knowledge and skills areas.

FOR THE STUDENT

ONLINE LEARNING CENTER

www.mhhe.com/can3e

Students will have access to study materials specifically created for this text, such as:

- **Guided Examples** Each numbered example featured within the book has a series of five different tutorials that accompany it: a narrated example, a related example with interactive solutions and decision points that need to be made by the student, an example using the BA II Plus calculator, another example using the TI-83 calculator, and an example using Excel.
- **Practice Quizzes** These online quizzes offer a quick way to review concepts presented in the chapter. Ten multiple-choice questions are included for each chapter so students can test their knowledge related to specific chapter content.

Instructors have access to all the material that students can view but will also have password-protected access to the teaching support materials.

PACKAGING OPTIONS

Please contact your McGraw-Hill/Irwin sales representative to find out more about these exciting packaging options now available for your class.

MCGRAW-HILL *CONNECT FINANCE*

Less Managing. More Teaching. Greater Learning.

McGraw-Hill *Connect Finance* is an online assignment and assessment solution that connects students with the tools and resources they'll need to achieve success.

McGraw-Hill *Connect Finance* helps prepare students for their future by enabling faster learning, more efficient studying, and higher retention of knowledge.

McGraw-Hill *Connect Finance* features

Connect Finance offers a number of powerful tools and features to make managing assignments easier, so faculty can spend more time teaching. With *Connect Finance,* students can engage with their coursework anytime and anywhere, making the learning process more accessible and efficient. *Connect Finance* to accompany *Finance: Applications and Theory,* third edition, makes homework more intuitive.

- Guided examples walk students step-by-step through a problem similar to the one they are working on
- Feedback offers the option to present worked-out solutions to the problem, showing the students each step of the process

Simple assignment management

With *Connect Finance,* creating assignments is easier than ever, so you can spend more time teaching and less time managing. The assignment management function enables you to:

- Create and deliver assignments easily with selectable end-of-chapter questions and test bank items.
- Streamline lesson planning, student progress reporting, and assignment grading to make classroom management more efficient than ever.

- Go paperless with the eBook and online submission and grading of student assignments.

Smart grading

When it comes to studying, time is precious. *Connect Finance* helps students learn more efficiently by providing feedback and practice material when they need it, where they need it. When it comes to teaching, your time also is precious. The grading function enables you to:

- Have assignments scored automatically, giving students immediate feedback on their work and side-by-side comparisons with correct answers.
- Access and review each response; manually change grades or leave comments for students to review.
- Reinforce classroom concepts with practice tests and instant quizzes.

Instructor Library

The *Connect Finance* Instructor Library is your repository for additional resources to improve student engagement in and out of class. You can select and use any asset that enhances your lecture. The *Connect Finance* Instructor Library includes all of the instructor supplements for this text.

Student Study Center

The *Connect Finance* Student Study Center is the place for students to access additional resources. The Student Study Center:

- Offers students quick access to lectures, practice materials, eBooks, and more.
- Provides instant practice material and study questions, easily accessible on the go.

Diagnostic and Adaptive Learning of Concepts: LearnSmart

Students want to make the best use of their study time. The LearnSmart adaptive self-study technology within *Connect Finance* provides students with a seamless combination of practice, assessment, and remediation for every concept in the textbook. LearnSmart's intelligent software adapts to every student response and automatically delivers concepts that advance students' understanding while reducing time devoted to the concepts already mastered. The result for every student is the fastest path to mastery of the chapter concepts. LearnSmart:

- Applies an intelligent concept engine to identify the relationships between concepts and to serve new concepts to each student only when he or she is ready.
- Adapts automatically to each student, so students spend less time on the topics they understand and practice more those they have yet to master.
- Provides continual reinforcement and remediation, but gives only as much guidance as students need.
- Integrates diagnostics as part of the learning experience.
- Enables you to assess which concepts students have efficiently learned on their own, thus freeing class time for more applications and discussion.

Student progress tracking

Connect Finance keeps instructors informed about how each student, section, and class is performing, allowing for more productive use of lecture and office hours. The progress-tracking function enables you to:

- View scored work immediately and track individual or group performance with assignment and grade reports.

- Access an instant view of student or class performance relative to learning objectives.
- Collect data and generate reports required by many accreditation organizations, such as AACSB and AICPA.

McGraw-Hill *Connect Plus Finance*

McGraw-Hill reinvents the textbook learning experience for the modern student with *Connect Plus Finance.* A seamless integration of an eBook and *Connect Finance, Connect Plus Finance* provides all of the *Connect Finance* features plus the following:

- An integrated eBook, allowing for anytime, anywhere access to the textbook.
- Dynamic links between the problems or questions you assign to your students and the location in the eBook where that problem or question is covered.
- A powerful search function to pinpoint and connect key concepts in a snap.

In short, *Connect Finance* offers you and your students powerful tools and features that optimize your time and energies, enabling you to focus on course content, teaching, and student learning. *Connect Finance* also offers a wealth of content resources for both instructors and students. This state-of-the-art, thoroughly tested system supports you in preparing students for the world that awaits.

For more information about *Connect,* go to www.mcgrawhillconnect.com, or contact your local McGraw-Hill sales representative.

TEGRITY CAMPUS: LECTURES 24/7

Tegrity Campus is a service that makes class time available 24/7 by automatically capturing every lecture in a searchable format for students to review when they study and complete assignments. With a simple one-click start-and-stop process, you capture all computer screens and corresponding audio. Students can replay any part of any class with easy-to-use browser-based viewing on a PC or Mac.

Educators know that the more students can see, hear, and experience class resources, the better they learn. In fact, studies prove it. With Tegrity Campus, students quickly recall key moments by using Tegrity Campus's unique search feature. This search helps students efficiently find what they need, when they need it, across an entire semester of class recordings. Help turn all your students' study time into learning moments immediately supported by your lecture.

To learn more about Tegrity, watch a two-minute Flash demo at http://tegritycampus.mhhe.com.

MCGRAW-HILL CUSTOMER CARE CONTACT INFORMATION

At McGraw-Hill, we understand that getting the most from new technology can be challenging. That's why our services don't stop after you purchase our products. You can e-mail our Product Specialists 24 hours a day to get product training online. Or you can search our knowledge bank of Frequently Asked Questions on our support website. For Customer Support, call **800-331-5094,** e-mail **hmsupport@mcgraw-hill.com**, or visit **www.mhhe.com/support**. One of our Technical Support Analysts will be able to assist you in a timely fashion.

acknowledgments

Development of this book series started with a course survey that was completed by 400 instructors across the country. The following is a list of the reviewers that became part of the many review stages, focus groups, and class-testing—all of which were invaluable to us during the development of this book.

Rebecca Abraham
Nova Southeastern University

Benjamin Abugri
Southern Connecticut State University

Paul Adams
University of Cincinnati at Cincinnati

Pankaj Agrrawal
University of Maine

Aigbe Akhigbe
University of Akron

Anne Anderson
Lehigh University

Murat Aydogdu
Bryant University

Robert Balik
Western Michigan University

Marvin Ball
East Oregon University

Brian Barczyk
University of Akron

Laura Beal
University of Nebraska, Omaha

Jaclyn Beierlein
East Carolina University

Ronald Benson
University of Maryland University College

Eli Beracha
East Carolina University

Robert Boldin
Indiana University of Pennsylvania

Denis Boureaux
University of Louisiana

David Bourff
Boise State University

Walter Boyle
Fayetteville Tech Community College

Joe Bracato
Tarleton State University

Cheryl A. Broyler
Preston University

Celso Brunetti
Johns Hopkins University

Sarah K. Bryant
Shippensburg University

James Buck
East Carolina University

Steven Burris
Kennedy-King College

Steven Byers
Idaho State University

Cynthia Campbell
Iowa State University

Stephen Caples
University of Houston, Clear Lake

Bob Castaneda
Robert Morris University

Su-Jane Chen
Metro State College of Denver

Samuel Chinnis
Guilford Tech Community College

Andreas Christofi
Monmouth University

Cetin Ciner
University of North Carolina, Wilmington

Thomas Coe
Quinnipiac University

Julie Dahlquist
University of Texas, San Antonio

Kenneth Daniels
Virginia Commonwealth University

Natalya Delcoure
Sam Houston State University

James DeLoach
Troy University

Michael Devaney
Southeast Missouri State University

Anne Drougas
Dominican University

David Dumpe
Kent State University

Alan Eastman
Indiana University of Pennsylvania

Scott Ehrhorn
Liberty University

Zekeriya Eser
Eastern Kentucky University

Angelo Esposito
University of North Florida

Joe Farinella
University of North Carolina, Wilmington

John Farlin
Ohio Dominican University

John Fay
Santa Clara University

David Fehr
Southern New Hampshire University

Calvin Fink
Bethune-Cookman College

Barbara Fischer
Cardinal Stritch University

Susan Flaherty
Towson University

Frank Flanegin
Robert Morris University

Sharon Garrison
University of Arizona

Victoria Geyfman
Bloomsburg University

Charmaine Glegg
East Carolina University

Cameron Gordon
University of Canberra

Ed Graham
University of North Carolina, Wilmington

Greg Gregoriou
SUNY, Plattsburgh

Richard Gregory
East Tennessee State University, Johnson City

Keshav Gupta
Kutztown University

Neeraj Gupta
Elon University

Matthew Haertzen
Northern Arizona University

Christine Harrington
State University of New York, Oneonta

James Harriss
Campbell University

Travis Hayes
Chattanooga State University

Heikki Heino
Governors State University

Susan Hendrickson
Robert B. Miller College

Steve Henry
Sam Houston State University

Rodrigo Hernandez
Radford University

James Howard
University of Maryland

Bharat Jain
Towson University

Joel Jankowski
University of Tampa

Domingo Joaquin
Illinois State University

Martin S. St. John
Westmoreland County Community College

Steve Johnson
University of Northern Iowa

Jacqueline Griffith Jonnard
Berkeley College

Daniel Jubinski
Saint Joseph's University

Dongmin Ke
Kean University

Francis E. Laatsch
Bowling Green State University

Stephen Lacewell
Murray State University

Miranda Lam
Salem State University

Baeyong Lee
Fayetteville State University

Adam Lei
Midwestern State University

Fei Leng
University of Washington, Tacoma

Denise Letterman
Robert Morris University

Ralph Lim
Sacred Heart University

Bing-Xuan Lin
University of Rhode Island

Leng Ling
Georgia College and State University

Scott W. Lowe
James Madison University

Balasundram Maniam
Sam Houston State University

Kelly Manley
Gainesville State College

Peter Martino
Johnson & Wales University

Mario Mastrandrea
Cleveland State University

Leslie Mathis
University of Memphis

Christine McClatchey
University of Northern Colorado

Bruce L. McManis
Nicholls State University

Kathleen S. McNichol
LaSalle University

James A. Milanese
University of North Carolina, Greensboro

Banamber Mishra
McNeese State University

Helen Moser
St. Cloud State University

Tarun Mukherjee
University of New Orleans

Elisa Muresan
Long Island University

James Nelson
East Carolina University

Tom C. Nelson
Leeds School of Business

Tom Nelson
University of Colorado, Boulder

Terry Nixon
Miami University of Ohio, Oxford

Vivian Okere
Providence College

Brett Olsen
University of Northern Iowa

Elisabeta Pana
Illinois Wesleyan University

Jeff Parsons
California State University, Fullerton

Robert Pavlik
Elon University

Ivelina Pavlova
University of Houston, Clear Lake

Anil Pawar
San Diego State University

Glenn Pettengill
Grand Valley State University

Ted Pilger
Southern Illinois University, Carbondale

Wendy Pirie
Valparaiso University

Gary E. Porter
John Carroll University

Franklin Potts
Baylor University

Eric Powers
University of South Carolina

Robert Prati
East Carolina University

Lora Reinholz
Marquette University

Nivine Richie
University of North Carolina, Wilmington

Tammy Rogers
University of Central Arkansas

Philip Romero
University of Oregon

Philip Russel
Philadelphia University

Benito Sanchez
Kean University

Oliver Schnusenberg
University of North Florida

Andrew Spieler
Hofstra University

Jim Sprow
Corban College

Gikenn L. Stevens
Franklin & Marshall College

Gordon Stringer
University of Colorado, Colorado Springs

Don Stuhlman
Wilmington University

Jennifer O'Sullivan
Hardin-Simmons University

Mike Sullivan
University of Nevada, Las Vegas

Janikan Supanvanji
St. Cloud State University

Arun Tandon
University of South Florida, Lakeland

Heidi Toprac
University of Texas, Austin

Kudret Topyan
Manhattan College

Michael Toyne
Northeastern State University

Jack Trifts
Bryant University

Gary Tripp
Southern New Hampshire University

Kuo-Cheng Tseng
California State University, Fresno

James A. Turner
Weber State University

John Upstrom
Loras College

Victor Wakeling
Kennesaw State University

Michael C. Walker
University of Cincinnati

Peggy Ward
Wichita State University

Gwendolyn Webb
Baruch College

Paul Weinstock
Ohio State University

Kyle Wells
University of New Mexico

John B. White
Georgia Southern University

Susan White
University of Maryland

George Young
Liberty University

Zhong-Guo Zhou
California State University, Northridge

Feifei Zhu
Hawaii Pacific University, Honolulu

Emily Norman Zietz
Middle Tennessee State University

We are also indebted to the talented staff at McGraw-Hill/Irwin for their expertise and guidance, specifically Noelle Bathurst, development editor; Chuck Synovec, executive brand manager; Melissa Caughlin, marketing manager; Jennifer Jelinski, marketing specialist; Danielle Clement, content project manager; Meg Maloney and Kevin Shanahan, digital development editors; and Srdjan Savanovic, senior designer. We would also like to thank Blerina Reca, Weicheng Wang, and Hongyan Fang.

We hope you like the outcome of this text. Research and development is always ongoing, and we are interested in your feedback on how this text has worked for you!

Marcia Millon Cornett
Troy A. Adair Jr.
John Nofsinger

brief table of contents

PART ONE: INTRODUCTION 2

1 Introduction to Financial Management *2*

PART TWO: FINANCIAL STATEMENTS 32

2 Reviewing Financial Statements *32*
Appendix 2A: Various Formats for Financial Statements (located at www.mhhe.com/can3e)

3 Analyzing Financial Statements *76*

PART THREE: VALUING OF FUTURE CASH FLOWS 118

4 Time Value of Money 1: Analyzing Single Cash Flows *118*

5 Time Value of Money 2: Analyzing Annuity Cash Flows *148*

PART FOUR: VALUING OF BONDS AND STOCKS 188

6 Understanding Financial Markets and Institutions *188*
Appendix 6A: The Financial Crisis: The Failure of Financial Institution Specialness (located at www.mhhe.com/can3e)

7 Valuing Bonds *232*

8 Valuing Stocks *272*

PART FIVE: RISK AND RETURN 306

9 Characterizing Risk and Return *306*

10 Estimating Risk and Return *338*

PART SIX: CAPITAL BUDGETING 372

11 Calculating the Cost of Capital *372*

12 Estimating Cash Flows on Capital Budgeting Projects *404*
Appendix 12A: MACRS Depreciation Tables *434*

13 Weighing Net Present Value and Other Capital Budgeting Criteria *438*

PART SEVEN: WORKING CAPITAL MANAGEMENT AND FINANCIAL PLANNING 474

14 Working Capital Management and Policies *474*
Appendix 14A: The Cash Budget *505*

15 Financial Planning and Forecasting *512*

PART EIGHT: CAPITAL STRUCTURE ISSUES 544

16 Assessing Long-Term Debt, Equity, and Capital Structure *544*
17 Sharing Firm Wealth: Dividends, Share Repurchases, and Other Payouts *578*
18 Issuing Capital and the Investment Banking Process *602*

PART NINE: OTHER TOPICS IN FINANCE 630

19 International Corporate Finance *630*
20 Mergers and Acquisitions and Financial Distress *660*

table of contents

PART ONE: Introduction 2

1 Introduction to Financial Management 2

1.1 Finance in Business and in Life *4*

What Is Finance? *4*

Subareas of Finance *7*

Application and Theory for Financial Decisions *9*

Finance versus Accounting *11*

1.2 The Financial Function *11*

The Financial Manager *11*

Finance in Other Business Functions *11*

Finance in Your Personal Life *12*

1.3 Business Organization *13*

Sole Proprietorships *13*

Partnerships *13*

Corporations *14*

Hybrid Organizations *14*

1.4 Firm Goals *16*

1.5 Agency Theory *17*

Agency Problem *17*

Corporate Governance *18*

The Role of Ethics *20*

1.6 Financial Markets, Intermediaries, and the Firm *21*

1.7 The Financial Crisis *22*

What Started It *22*

Why It Got Worse *23*

The Effect on the Public Sector *23*

Looking Ahead *23*

Summary of Learning Goals *24*

Self-Test Problems with Solutions *27*

Questions *27*

Research It! *28*

Integrated Mini-Case *28*

Answers to Time Out *30*

PART TWO: Financial Statements *32*

2 Reviewing Financial Statements *32*

2.1 Balance Sheet *34*

Assets *34*

Liabilities and Stockholders' Equity *35*

Managing the Balance Sheet *36*

2.2 Income Statement *39*

Debt versus Equity Financing *41*

Corporate Income Taxes 41

2.3 Statement of Cash Flows *45*

GAAP Accounting Principles *45*

Noncash Income Statement Entries *45*

Sources and Uses of Cash *46*

2.4 Free Cash Flow *49*

2.5 Statement of Retained Earnings *51*

2.6 Cautions in Interpreting Financial Statements *52*

Summary of Learning Goals *55*

Self-Test Problems with Solutions *58*

Questions *63*

Problems *64*

Research It! *72*

Integrated Mini-Case *72*

Answers to Time Out *74*

Appendix 2A: Various Formats for Financial Statements (located at www.mhhe.com/can3e)

3 Analyzing Financial Statements *76*

3.1 Liquidity Ratios *78*

3.2 Asset Management Ratios *79*

Inventory Management *79*

Accounts Receivable Management *80*

Accounts Payable Management *81*

Fixed Asset and Working Capital Management *81*

Total Asset Management *82*

3.3 Debt Management Ratios *84*

Debt versus Equity Financing *84*

Coverage Ratios *85*

3.4 Profitability Ratios *86*

3.5 Market Value Ratios *89*

3.6 DuPont Analysis *90*
3.7 Other Ratios *94*
Spreading the Financial Statements *94*
Internal and Sustainable Growth Rates *95*
3.8 Time Series and Cross-Sectional Analysis *96*
3.9 Cautions in Using Ratios to Evaluate Firm Performance *97*
Summary of Learning Goals *100*
Self-Test Problems with Solutions *103*
Questions *105*
Problems *106*
Research It! *113*
Integrated Mini-Case *113*
Answers to Time Out *114*

PART THREE: Valuing of Future Cash Flows *118*

4 Time Value of Money 1: Analyzing Single Cash Flows *118*

4.1 Organizing Cash Flows *120*
4.2 Future Value *120*
Single-Period Future Value *121*
Compounding and Future Value *122*
4.3 Present Value *128*
Discounting *128*
4.4 Using Present Value and Future Value *130*
Moving Cash Flows *130*
4.5 Computing Interest Rates *133*
Return Asymmetries *134*
4.6 Solving for Time *135*
Summary of Learning Goals *137*
Self-Test Problems with Solutions *138*
Questions *140*
Problems *141*
Research It! *144*
Integrated Mini-Case *144*
Answers to Time Out *146*

5 Time Value of Money 2: Analyzing Annuity Cash Flows *148*

5.1 Future Value of Multiple Cash Flows *149*
Finding the Future Value of Several Cash Flows *150*
Future Value of Level Cash Flows *151*
Future Value of Multiple Annuities *152*

5.2 Present Value of Multiple Cash Flows *155*
Finding the Present Value of Several Cash Flows *155*
Present Value of Level Cash Flows *155*
Present Value of Multiple Annuities *159*
Perpetuity—A Special Annuity *160*
5.3 Ordinary Annuities versus Annuities Due *160*
5.4 Compounding Frequency *162*
Effect of Compounding Frequency *162*
5.5 Annuity Loans *166*
What Is the Interest Rate? *166*
Finding Payments on an Amortized Loan *167*
Summary of Learning Goals *173*
Self-Test Problems with Solutions *175*
Questions *178*
Problems *179*
Combined Chapter 4 and Chapter 5 Problems *184*
Research It! *185*
Integrated Mini-Case *185*
Answers to Time Out *186*

PART FOUR: Valuing of Bonds and Stocks *188*

6 Understanding Financial Markets and Institutions *188*

6.1 Financial Markets *189*
Primary Markets versus Secondary Markets *190*
Money Markets versus Capital Markets *192*
Other Markets *195*
6.2 Financial Institutions *197*
Unique Economic Functions Performed by Financial Institutions *199*
6.3 Interest Rates *203*
Factors That Influence Interest Rates for Individual Securities *205*
Theories Explaining the Shape of the Term Structure of Interest Rates *211*
Forecasting Interest Rates *217*
Summary of Learning Goals *219*
Self-Test Problems with Solutions *221*
Questions *223*
Problems *224*
Research It! *228*
Integrated Mini-Case *228*
Answers to Time Out *229*
Appendix 6A: The Financial Crisis: The Failure of Financial Institution Specialness (located at www.mhhe.com/can3e)

7 Valuing Bonds *232*

7.1 Bond Market Overview *233*
Bond Characteristics *233*
Bond Issuers *235*
Other Bonds and Bond-Based Securities *236*
Reading Bond Quotes *239*
7.2 Bond Valuation *242*
Present Value of Bond Cash Flows *242*
Bond Prices and Interest Rate Risk *243*
7.3 Bond Yields *247*
Current Yield *247*
Yield to Maturity *247*
Yield to Call *249*
Municipal Bonds and Yield *251*
Summarizing Yields *252*
7.4 Credit Risk *253*
Bond Ratings *253*
Credit Risk and Yield *255*
7.5 Bond Markets *256*
Following the Bond Market *257*
Summary of Learning Goals *259*
Self-Test Problems with Solutions *262*
Questions *264*
Problems *265*
Research It! *269*
Integrated Mini-Case *269*
Answers to Time Out *270*

8 Valuing Stocks *272*

8.1 Common Stock *274*
8.2 Stock Markets *274*
Tracking the Stock Market *277*
Trading Stocks *279*
8.3 Basic Stock Valuation *281*
Cash Flows *281*
Dividend Discount Models *283*
Preferred Stock *284*
Expected Return *286*
8.4 Additional Valuation Methods *287*
Variable-Growth Techniques *287*
The P/E Model *291*
Estimating Future Stock Prices *293*

Summary of Learning Goals *295*
Self-Test Problems with Solutions *298*
Questions *299*
Problems *300*
Research It! *304*
Integrated Mini-Case *304*
Answers to Time Out *304*

PART FIVE: Risk and Return *306*

9 Characterizing Risk and Return *306*

9.1 Historical Returns *307*
- Computing Returns *307*
- Performance of Asset Classes *310*

9.2 Historical Risks *311*
- Computing Volatility *312*
- Risk of Asset Classes *314*
- Risk versus Return *315*

9.3 Forming Portfolios *316*
- Diversifying to Reduce Risk *316*
- Modern Portfolio Theory *318*

Summary of Learning Goals *325*
Self-Test Problems with Solutions *327*
Questions *329*
Problems *330*
Research It! *335*
Integrated Mini-Case *335*
Answers to Time Out *337*

10 Estimating Risk and Return *338*

10.1 Expected Returns *340*
- Expected Return and Risk *340*
- Risk Premiums *342*

10.2 Market Risk *343*
- The Market Portfolio *343*
- Beta, a Measure of Market Risk *345*
- The Security Market Line *346*
- Finding Beta *349*
- Concerns about Beta *350*

10.3 Capital Market Efficiency *352*
- Efficient Market Hypothesis *353*
- Behavioral Finance *355*

10.4 Implications for Financial Managers *355*
Using the Constant-Growth Model for Required Return *357*
Summary of Learning Goals *359*
Self-Test Problems with Solutions *361*
Questions *363*
Problems *364*
Research It! *369*
Integrated Mini-Case *369*
Answers to Time Out *370*

PART SIX: Capital Budgeting *372*

11 Calculating the Cost of Capital *372*

11.1 The WACC Formula *374*
Calculating the Component Cost of Equity *374*
Calculating the Component Cost of Preferred Stock *376*
Calculating the Component Cost of Debt *376*
Choosing Tax Rates *377*
Calculating the Weights *378*
11.2 Firm WACC versus Project WACC *379*
Project Cost Numbers to Take from the Firm *380*
Project Cost Numbers to Find Elsewhere: The Pure-Play Approach *381*
11.3 Divisional WACC *383*
Pros and Cons of a Divisional WACC *383*
Subjective versus Objective Approaches *386*
11.4 Flotation Costs *389*
Adjusting the WACC *389*
Summary of Learning Goals *391*
Self-Test Problems with Solutions *394*
Questions *397*
Problems *397*
Research It! *401*
Integrated Mini-Case *401*
Answers to Time Out *402*

12 Estimating Cash Flows on Capital Budgeting Projects *404*

12.1 Sample Project Description *405*
12.2 Guiding Principles for Cash Flow Estimation *406*
Opportunity Costs *406*
Sunk Costs *407*
Substitutionary and Complementary Effects *407*
Stock Dividends and Bond Interest *408*

12.3 Total Project Cash Flow *408*

Calculating Depreciation *408*

Calculating Operating Cash Flow *409*

Calculating Changes in Gross Fixed Assets *410*

Calculating Changes in Net Working Capital *411*

Bringing It All Together *412*

12.4 Accelerated Depreciation and the Half-Year Convention *413*

MACRS Depreciation Calculation *414*

Section 179 Deductions *414*

Impact of Accelerated Depreciation *415*

12.5 "Special" Cases Aren't Really That Special *416*

12.6 Choosing between Alternative Assets with Differing Lives: EAC *418*

12.7 Flotation Costs Revisited *421*

Summary of Learning Goals *423*

Self-Test Problems with Solutions *425*

Questions *428*

Problems *428*

Research It! *431*

Integrated Mini-Case *431*

Answers to Time Out *432*

Appendix 12A: MACRS Depreciation Tables *434*

13 Weighing Net Present Value and Other Capital Budgeting Criteria *438*

13.1 The Set of Capital Budgeting Techniques *439*

13.2 The Choice of Decision Statistic Format *440*

13.3 Processing Capital Budgeting Decisions *441*

13.4 Payback and Discounted Payback *441*

Payback Statistic *442*

Payback Benchmark *442*

Discounted Payback Statistic *443*

Discounted Payback Benchmark *443*

Payback and Discounted Payback Strengths and Weaknesses *445*

13.5 Net Present Value *446*

NPV Statistic *446*

NPV Benchmark *448*

NPV Strengths and Weaknesses *449*

13.6 Internal Rate of Return and Modified Internal Rate of Return *449*

Internal Rate of Return Statistic *450*

Internal Rate of Return Benchmark *450*

Problems with Internal Rate of Return *451*

IRR and NPV Profiles with Non-Normal Cash Flows *452*

Differing Reinvestment Rate Assumptions of NPV and IRR *453*

Modified Internal Rate of Return Statistic *453*

IRRs, MIRRs, and NPV Profiles with Mutually Exclusive Projects *455*
MIRR Strengths and Weaknesses *460*
13.7 Profitability Index *460*
Profitability Index Statistic *461*
Profitability Index Benchmark *461*
Summary of Learning Goals *462*
Self-Test Problem with Solution *465*
Questions *467*
Problems *468*
Research It! *472*
Integrated Mini-Case *472*
Answers to Time Out *473*

PART SEVEN: Working Capital Management and Financial Planning *474*

14 Working Capital Management and Policies *474*

14.1 Revisiting the Balance-Sheet Model of the Firm *476*
14.2 Tracing Cash and Net Working Capital *476*
The Operating Cycle *477*
The Cash Cycle *477*
14.3 Some Aspects of Short-Term Financial Policy *478*
The Size of the Current Assets Investment *479*
Alternative Financing Policies for Current Assets *480*
14.4 The Short-Term Financial Plan *482*
Unsecured Loans *482*
Secured Loans *483*
Other Sources *483*
14.5 Cash Management *484*
Reasons for Holding Cash *484*
Determining the Target Cash Balance: The Baumol Model *485*
Determining the Target Cash Balance: The Miller-Orr Model *486*
Other Factors Influencing the Target Cash Balance *489*
14.6 Float Control: Managing the Collection and Disbursement of Cash *490*
Accelerating Collections *490*
Delaying Disbursements *490*
Ethical and Legal Questions *491*
14.7 Investing Idle Cash *492*
Why Firms Have Surplus Cash *492*
What to Do with Surplus Cash *492*
14.8 Credit Management *492*
Credit Policy: Terms of the Sale *492*

Credit Analysis *493*
Collection Policy *493*
Summary of Learning Goals *495*
Self-Test Problems with Solutions *497*
Questions *499*
Problems *500*
Research It! *502*
Integrated Mini-Case *503*
Answers to Time Out *503*
Appendix 14A: The Cash Budget *505*

15 Financial Planning and Forecasting *512*

15.1 Financial Planning *513*
15.2 Forecasting Sales *514*
The Naïve Approach *514*
The Average Approach *516*
Estimating Sales with Systematic Variations: Adjusting for Trends and Seasonality *518*
15.3 External Financing *521*
The Simple Approach to Estimating Necessary External Financing: Additional Funds Needed *521*
Forecasting Financial Statements *525*
Summary of Learning Goals *533*
Self-Test Problems with Solutions *534*
Questions *538*
Problems *538*
Research It! *542*
Integrated Mini-Case *542*
Answers to Time Out *543*

PART EIGHT: Capital Structure Issues *544*

16 Assessing Long-Term Debt, Equity, and Capital Structure *544*

16.1 Active versus Passive Capital Structure Changes *545*
16.2 Capital Structure Theory: The Effect of Financial Leverage *546*
Modigliani and Miller's "Perfect World" *547*
M&M with Corporate Taxes *551*
The Choice to Re-Leverage *554*
Break-Even EBIT and EBIT Expectations *557*
16.3 M&M with Corporate Taxes and Bankruptcy *559*
Types of Bankruptcies in the United States *559*
Costs of Financial Distress *560*
The Value of the Firm with Taxes *and* Bankruptcy *563*

16.4 Capital Structure Theory versus Reality *565*
Optimal Theoretical Capital Structure *565*
Observed Capital Structures *565*
Summary of Learning Goals *566*
Self-Test Problems with Solutions *568*
Questions *571*
Problems *572*
Research It! *576*
Integrated Mini-Case *576*
Answers to Time Out *576*

17 Sharing Firm Wealth: Dividends, Share Repurchases, and Other Payouts *578*

17.1 Dividends versus Capital Gains *579*
Dividend Irrelevance Theorem *580*
Why Some Investors Favor Dividends *581*
Why Some Investors Favor Capital Gains *581*
17.2 Other Dividend Policy Issues *582*
The Information Effect *582*
The Clientele Effect *582*
Corporate Control Issues *583*
17.3 Real-World Dividend Policy *583*
The Residual Dividend Model *584*
Extraordinary Dividends *585*
17.4 Dividend Payment Logistics *586*
Payment Procedures *587*
Effect of Dividends on Stock Prices *587*
17.5 Stock Dividends and Stock Splits *591*
Stock Dividends *591*
Stock Splits *591*
Effect of Splits and Stock Dividends on Stock Prices *591*
17.6 Stock Repurchases *592*
Advantages of Repurchases *593*
Disadvantages of Repurchases *593*
Effect of Repurchases on Stock Prices *594*
Summary of Learning Goals *595*
Self-Test Problems with Solutions *597*
Questions *597*
Problems *598*
Research It! *600*
Integrated Mini-Case *600*
Answers to Time Out *601*

18 Issuing Capital and the Investment Banking Process *602*

18.1 Sources of Capital for New and Small Firms *603*

Debt Financing *604*

Equity Financing and Expertise *608*

The Choice to Go Public *609*

18.2 Public Firms' Capital Sources *611*

Debt Financing *612*

Equity Financing *616*

Summary of Learning Goals *621*

Self-Test Problems with Solutions *623*

Questions *624*

Problems *625*

Research It! *628*

Integrated Mini-Case *628*

Answers to Time Out *629*

PART NINE: Other Topics in Finance *630*

19 International Corporate Finance *630*

19.1 Global Business *632*

International Opportunities *632*

Corporate Expansion into Other Countries *634*

19.2 Foreign Currency Exchange *636*

Exchange Rates *636*

Exchange Rate Risk *638*

The Forward Exchange Rate and Hedging *640*

Interest Rate Parity *641*

Purchasing Power Parity and Future Exchange Rates *642*

19.3 Political Risks *645*

19.4 International Capital Budgeting *647*

Summary of Learning Goals *648*

Self-Test Problems with Solutions *651*

Questions *652*

Problems *653*

Research It! *656*

Integrated Mini-Case *657*

Answers to Time Out *658*

20 Mergers and Acquisitions and Financial Distress *660*

20.1 Mergers and Acquisitions *661*

Types of Mergers *663*

Motives for Mergers and Acquisitions *663*

Valuing a Merger *670*

20.2 Financial Distress *672*

Types and Causes of Financial Distress *672*

Informal Resolutions of Financial Distress *673*

Federal Bankruptcy Laws *674*

Predicting Bankruptcy *679*

Summary of Learning Goals *685*

Self-Test Problems with Solutions *687*

Questions *691*

Problems *692*

Research It! *701*

Integrated Mini-Case *701*

Answers to Time Out *702*

Appendix A *Present Value and Future Value Tables* *704*

Appendix B *Selected Answers to End-of-Chapter Problems* *708*

Photo Credits *715*

Index *717*

finance

applications & theory

PART ONE

1 Introduction to Financial Management

viewpoints

Business Application

Caleb has worked very hard to create and expand his juice stand at the mall. He has finally perfected his products and feels that he is offering the right combination of juice and food. As a result, the stand is making a nice profit. Caleb would like to open more stands at malls all over his state and eventually all over the country.

Caleb knows he needs more money to expand. He needs money to buy more equipment, buy more inventory, and hire and train more people. How can Caleb get the capital he needs to expand? **(See solution on p. 24)**

Personal Application

Dagmar is becoming interested in investing some of her money. However, she has heard about several corporations in which the investors lost all of their money. In the past decade, Dagmar has heard that Lehman Brothers (2008), Chrysler (2009), and Six Flags (2009) have all filed for bankruptcy. These firms' stockholders lost their entire investments in these firms.

Many of the stockholders who lost money were employees of these companies who had invested some of their retirement money in the company stock. Dagmar wonders what guarantee she has as an investor against losing her money. **(See solution on p. 24)**

What is the best way for Dagmar to ensure a happy retirement?

Learning Goals

LG1-1 Define the major areas of finance as they apply to corporate financial management.

LG1-2 Show how finance is at the heart of sound business decisions.

LG1-3 Learn the financial principles that govern your personal decisions.

LG1-4 Examine the three most common forms of business organization in the United States today.

LG1-5 Distinguish among appropriate and inappropriate goals for financial managers.

LG1-6 Identify a firm's primary agency relationship and discuss the possible conflicts that may arise.

LG1-7 Discuss how ethical decision making is part of the study of financial management.

LG1-8 Describe the complex, necessary relationships among firms, financial institutions, and financial markets.

LG1-9 Explain the fundamental causes of the financial crisis that started in 2006.

Do you know: What finance entails? How financial management functions within the business world? Why you might benefit from studying financial principles? This chapter is the ideal place to get answers to those questions. **Finance** is the study of *applying specific value* to things we own, services we use, and decisions we make. Examples are as varied as shares of stock in a company, payments on a home mortgage, the purchase of an entire firm, and the personal decision to retire early. In this text, we focus primarily on one area of finance, **financial management,** which concentrates on valuing things from the perspective of a company, or firm.

Financial management is critically important to the success of any business organization, and throughout the text we concentrate on describing the key financial concepts in corporate finance. As a bonus, you will find that many tools and techniques for handling the financial management of a firm also apply to broader types of financial problems, such as personal finance decisions.

In finance, *cash flow* is the term that describes the process of paying and receiving money. It makes sense to start our discussion of finance with an illustration of various financial cash flows. We use simple graphics to help explain the nature of finance and to demonstrate the different *subareas* of the field of finance.

After we have an overall picture of finance, we will discuss four important variables in the business environment that can and do have significant impact on the firm's financial decisions. These are (1) the organizational form of the business, (2) the agency relationship between the managers and owners of a firm, (3) ethical considerations as finance is applied in the real world, and (4) the source and implications of the current financial crisis.

LG1-1

1.1 • Finance in Business and in Life

finance

The study of applying specific value to things we own, services we use, and decisions we make.

financial management

The process for and the analysis of making financial decisions in the business context.

As you begin this course, what is your first impression of the world of finance? No doubt you've experienced the current economic recession firsthand and read, perhaps in detail, about the financial crisis that peaked in the fall of 2008. An understanding of cause, effect, and future impact will be important as we go forward, so please see the nearby Finance at Work reading and Section 1.7 of this chapter for brief background information and some analyses to set the stage for more complete explanations to come. But setting aside thoughts of recession and indulging in a quick look at popular culture, you'll recognize that other influences have been at work for some time. Your opinions already may have been negatively skewed by entertainment. Many movies have portrayed finance professionals as greedy and unethical (see, for example, *Wall Street,* 1987; *Barbarians at the Gate,* 1993; *Boiler Room,* 2000; and *Wall Street: Money Never Sleeps,* 2010). While colorful characters make for good entertainment, fictional depictions do not reflect reality when it comes to what finance professionals actually do and how they contribute to society. The more you study managerial finance, the more you'll appreciate this discipline's broad potential to power the managerial decision making that moves our economy forward.

And what exactly makes up this engine of financial decision making? Successful application of *financial theories* helps money flow from individuals who want to improve their financial future to businesses that want to expand the scale or scope of their operations. These exchanges lead to a growing economy and more employment opportunities for people at all income levels. So, two important things result from this simple exchange: the economy will be more productive as a result, and individuals' wealth will grow into the future.

In this first section, we develop a comprehensive description of finance and its subareas, and we look at the specific decisions that professionals in each subarea must make. As you will see, all areas of finance share a common set of ideas and application tools.

What Is Finance?

To get the clearest possible picture of how finance works, let's begin by grouping all of an economy's participants along two dimensions. The first dimension is made up of those who may have "extra" money (i.e., money above and beyond their current spending needs) for investment. The second dimension is made up of those who have an ability to develop viable business ideas, a sense of business creativity. Both money and ideas are fuel for the financial engine. In our simple model, these two dimensions result in four groups representing economic roles in society, as shown in Figure 1.1. Of course, people can move from one group to another over time.

figure 1.1

Participants in Our Hypothetical Economy

Four groups form according to the availability of money and ideas.

	No Extra Money	Extra Money
No Economically Viable Business Ideas	Type 1: No money and no ideas	Type 2: Money but no ideas
Economically Viable Business Ideas	Type 3: No money but ideas	Type 4: Both money and ideas

finance at work — markets

THE FINANCIAL CRISIS: INTRODUCTION AND OVERVIEW

At the time of this writing, the world economy has been reeling for over six years from the effects of the worst financial crisis since the Great Depression of the 1930s. By mid-March 2009, the Dow Jones Industrial Average (DJIA) had fallen in value 53.8 percent in less than 1½ years' time, larger than the decline during the market crash of 1937–1938 when it fell 49 percent. Though the Dow has since recovered much of those losses, the markets continue to be very volatile and unsettled: On May 6, 2010, just after 2:30 pm EST, the Dow plunged by 998.50 points, a loss of 9.2 percent and the biggest one-day fall ever.

The commonly accepted cause of the crisis was the collapse of U.S. home prices in late 2006 and early 2007, but the problem has since spread to affect every part of the economy: The investment banking industry saw the failure or acquisition of all but two of its major firms (Goldman Sachs and Morgan Stanley), and these two firms converted to commercial bank holding companies (i.e., banks much like your neighborhood bank that tend to be safer and less profitable than investment banks). AIG, one of the largest insurance companies in the United States, survived only because of a federal government bailout. Commercial banking giant Citigroup required a massive government guarantee against losses and an injection of cash to prevent failure. The crisis spread internationally, too. Real estate markets fell in many countries across the world. The crisis had a profound impact on the financial health of banks, especially in Europe. In 2010, the unemployment rate had risen to over 10 percent. By 2012, it was still over 8 percent.

The exact mechanisms by which falling home prices led to such dramatic changes in the economic landscape are complicated and have yet to be covered in this book, so we will delay an in-depth discussion of the crisis until later, but we did feel that this is a good place to touch upon the ways that the fallout from the financial crisis are going to affect you, the student, in the years and decades to come.

First, those of you who hoped to fund your education with student loans may be finding it difficult to obtain such loans, especially at favorable rates. If so, thank the financial crisis: Lenders are much more leery about lending money due to the uncertain economic future they (and you, in your hopeful future employment) face. (And we won't even get into the whole idea of your parents taking out a home equity loan to help you through . . .)

Second, as you've no doubt noticed, jobs are scarce, primarily due to companies' uncertainty about the future. We expect it to stay this way for a while, though the impending retirement of the baby boomers will eventually benefit you.

Third, once you do make it through school and start your career, you may want to hold off on buying a home for a while. Most of the reasons are probably obvious, but compounding the uncertainty about being able to eventually unload any house you buy is the fact that lenders have greatly cut back on the availability of credit, asking for substantial down payments and loan servicing fees when they *do* lend.

By now, you're probably starting to wonder if you missed the part about Eeyore (the gloomy donkey in the Winnie-the-Pooh books) being one of the coauthors of this book. Don't despair: The current financial crisis *does* have potential silver linings to offer to those who are prepared and educated enough to take advantage of them.

After the extent of the crisis had started to become evident to everyone, one of the authors of this book was asked by a television reporter, "Why would anyone want to study finance *now?!?!*" Well, on the one hand, and in the words of the Spanish-born American philosopher and poet George Santayana, "Those who do not learn from history are doomed to repeat it." You *really* don't want to go through this type of thing again, do you?

Another reason to study finance is that some of those silver linings we referred to are beginning to peek through the clouds: For example, in the aftermath of the crisis, more firms in general (and financial institutions in particular) are much more focused on the concepts of measuring and managing risks than ever before, and to effectively do so they need a trained and informed workforce.

! want to know more? Key Words to Search for Updates: housing bubble, subprime lending, mortgage-backed securities, AIG, Countrywide Financial

Type 1 people in our model do not lend significant sums of money (*capital*) or spend much money in a business context, so they play no direct role in **financial markets,** the mechanisms by which capital is exchanged. Although these people probably play indirect roles by providing labor to economic enterprises or by consuming their products, for simplicity we focus on those who play direct roles. Therefore, type 1 participants will be asked to step aside.

financial markets
The places and processes that facilitate the trading of financial assets between investors.

Type 4 people use financial tools to evaluate their own business concepts and then choose the ideas with the most potential. From there, they create their own enterprises to implement their best ideas efficiently and effectively. Type 4 individuals, however, are self-funded and do not need financial markets. The

figure 1.2

Capital Flow from Investors to Companies
Investors are people or groups who need ideas to make more money, and companies are groups who need money to develop the ideas they do have.

financial tools they use and the types of decisions they make are narrowly focused or specific to their own purposes. For our discussion, then, type 4 individuals also are asked to move to the sidelines.

Now for our financial role players, the type 2 and type 3 people. Financial markets and financial institutions allow these people to participate in a mutually advantageous exchange. Type 2 people temporarily lend their money to type 3 people, who put that money to use with their good business ideas.

In most developed economies, type 2 participants are usually individual **investors.** *You* will likely be an individual investor for most of your life. Each of us separately may not have a lot of extra money at any one time, but by aggregating our available funds, we can provide sizable amounts for investment.

investors
Those who buy securities or other assets in hopes of earning a return and getting more money back in the future.

Type 3 participants, the idea generators, may be individuals, but they are more commonly corporations or other types of companies with research and development (R&D) departments dedicated to developing innovative ideas. It's easy to see that investors and companies can help one another. If investors lend their "extra" capital to companies, as shown in Figure 1.2, then companies can use this capital to fund expansion projects. Economically successful projects will eventually be able to repay the money (plus profit) to investors, as Figure 1.3 shows.

figure 1.3

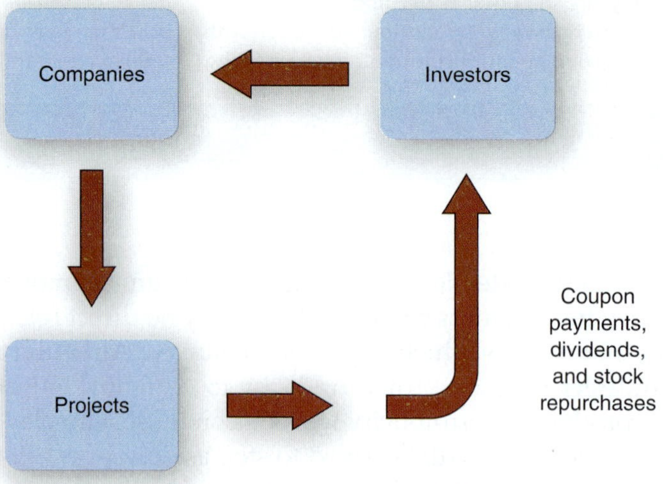

Return of Capital to Investors
In this basic process, the company can expand its business, hire more employees, and create a promising future for its own growth. Meanwhile, the investor can increase wealth for the future.

figure 1.4

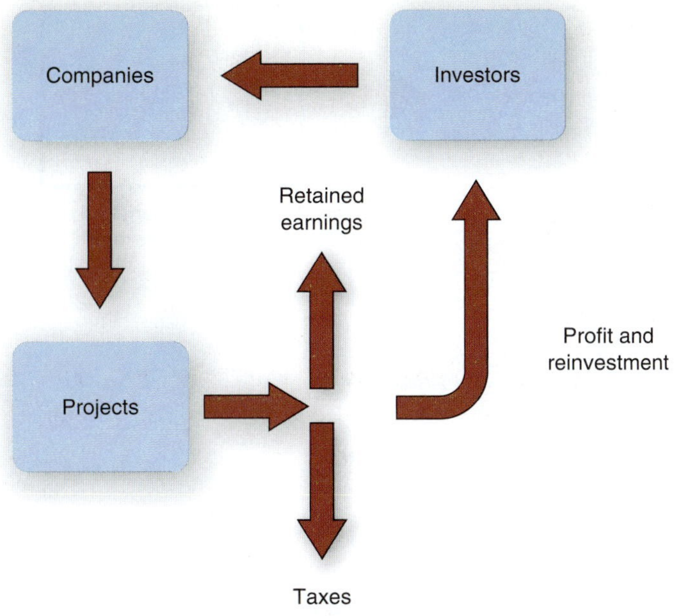

The Complete Cash Flows of Finance

All the subareas of the financial system interact, with retained earnings and taxes playing a role in the flows.

Of course, not all of the cash will return to the investors. In reality, sources of friction arise in this system, and the amount of capital returned to investors is reduced. Two primary sources of friction are **retained earnings,** which are basically funds the firm keeps for its ongoing operations, and *taxes,* which the government imposes on the company and individuals to help fund public services. Figure 1.4 shows an analysis of cash flows with the associated retained earnings and tax payments. In a very simple way, this figure provides an intuitive overall explanation of finance and of its major subareas. For example, individuals must assess which investment opportunities are right for their needs and risk tolerance; financial institutions and markets must efficiently distribute the capital; and companies must evaluate their potential projects and wisely decide which projects to fund, what kind of capital to use, and how much capital to return to investors. All of these types of decisions deal with the basic cash flows of finance shown in Figure 1.4, but from different perspectives.

retained earnings

The portion of company profits that are kept by the company rather than distributed to the stockholders as cash dividends.

Subareas of Finance

Investments is the subarea of finance that involves methods and techniques for making decisions about what kinds of *securities* to own (e.g., bonds or stocks), which firms' securities to buy, and how to pay the investor back in the form that the investor wishes (e.g., the timing and certainty of the promised cash flows). Figure 1.5 models cash flows from the investor's perspective. The concerns of the investments subarea of finance are shown (with the movement of red arrows) from the investor's viewpoint (seen as the blue box).

investments

The analysis and process of choosing securities and other assets to purchase.

Financial management is the subarea that deals with a firm's decisions in acquiring and using the cash that is received from investors or from retained earnings. Figure 1.6 depicts the financial management process very simply. As

figure 1.5

Investments
Investors mark the start and end of the financial process; they put money in and reap the rewards (or take the risk).

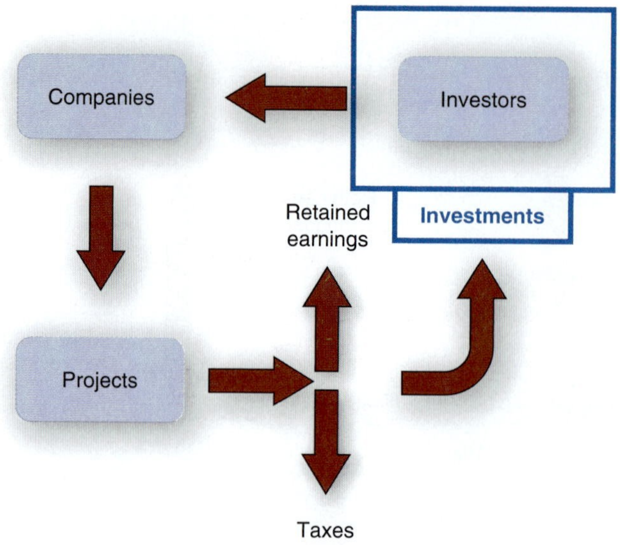

we know, this text focuses primarily on financial management. We'll see that this critical area of finance involves decisions about:

- How to organize the firm in a manner that will attract capital.
- How to raise capital (e.g., bonds versus stocks).
- Which projects to fund.
- How much capital to retain for ongoing operations and new projects.
- How to minimize taxation.
- How to pay back capital providers.

figure 1.6

Financial Management
Financial managers make decisions that should benefit both the company and the investor.

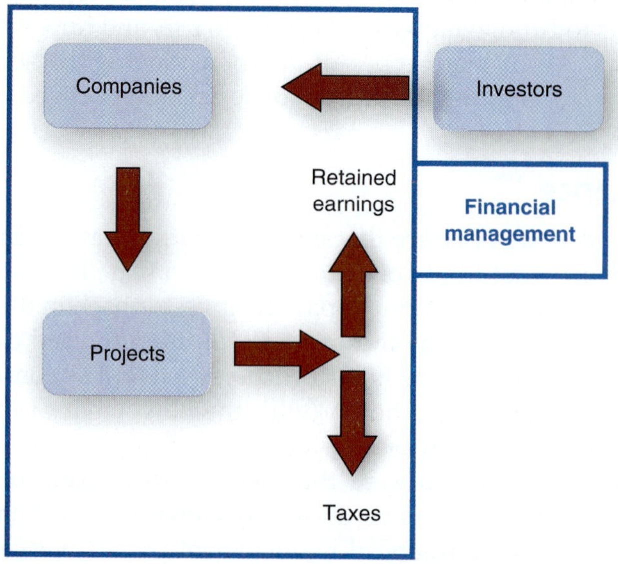

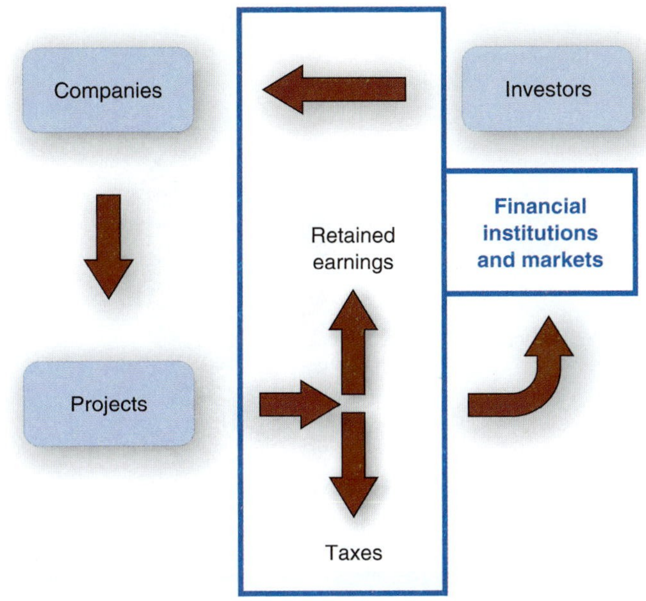

figure 1.7

Financial Institutions and Markets
Financial institutions and markets facilitate the flows of money between investors and companies.

All of these decisions are quite involved, and we will discuss them throughout later chapters.

Financial institutions and markets make up another major subarea of finance. These two dynamic entities work in different ways to facilitate capital flows between investors and companies. Figure 1.7 illustrates the process in which the firm acquires capital and investors take part in ongoing securities trading to increase that capital. Financial institutions, such as banks and pension administrators, are vital players that contribute to the dynamics of interest rates.

financial institutions and markets
The organizations that facilitate the flow of capital between investors and companies.

International finance is the final major subarea of finance we will study. As the world has transformed into a global economy, finance has had to become much more innovative and sensitive to changes in other countries. Investors, companies, business operations, and capital markets may all be located in different countries. Adapting to this environment requires understanding of international dynamics, as Figure 1.8 shows. In the past, international financial decisions were considered to be a straightforward application of the other three financial subareas. But experience has shown that the uncertainty about future exchange rates, political risk, and changing business laws across the globe adds enough complexity to these decisions to classify international finance as a subarea of finance in its own right.

international finance
The use of finance theory in a global business environment.

Application and Theory for Financial Decisions

Cash flows are neither instantaneous nor guaranteed. We need to keep this in mind as we begin to apply finance theory to real decisions. Future cash flows are uncertain in terms of both timing and size, and we refer to this uncertainty as **risk.** Investors experience risk about the return of their capital. Companies experience risk in funding and operating their business projects. Most financial decisions involve comparing the rewards of a decision to the risks that decision may generate.

risk
A potential future negative impact to value and/or cash flows. It is often discussed in terms of the probability of loss and the expected magnitude of the loss.

figure 1.8

International Finance
Laws, risks, and business relationships are variable across different countries but can interact profitably.

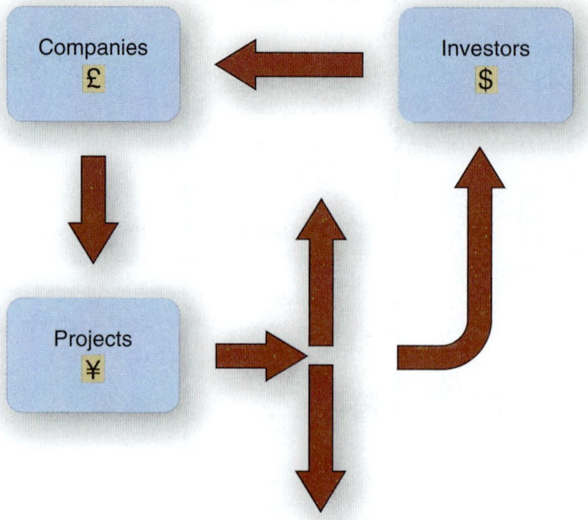

financial asset

A general term for securities like stocks, bonds, and other assets that represent ownership in a cash flow.

asset classes

A group of securities that exhibit similar characteristics, behave similarly in the marketplace, and are subject to the same laws and regulations.

real assets

Physical property like gold, machinery, equipment, or real estate.

real markets

The places and processes that facilitate the trading of real assets.

time value of money (TVM)

The theory and application of valuing cash flows at various points in time.

Comparing rewards with risks frequently involves assessing the value today of cash flows that we expect to receive in the future. For example, the price of a **financial asset,** something worth money, such as a stock or a bond, should depend on the cash flows you expect to receive from that asset in the future. A stock that's expected to deliver high cash flows in the future will be more valuable today than a stock with low expected future cash flows. Of course, investors would like to buy stocks whose market prices are currently lower than their actual values. They want to get stocks on sale! Similarly, a firm's goal is to fund projects that will give them more value than their costs.

Financial assets are normally grouped into **asset classes** according to their risk and return characteristics. The most commonly accepted groups of asset classes are stocks, bonds, money market instruments, real estate, and derivative securities, all of which we will discuss in more detail later in the book. As the risk and return profiles of each of these asset classes differ widely between classes, the mathematical models, terminology, and expertise of each class tend to be very specialized and trading tends to happen in distinct, separate financial markets for each asset class.

Despite the large number of stories about investors who've struck it rich in the stock market, it's actually more likely that a firm will find "bargain" projects, projects that may yield profit for a reasonable investment, than investors will find underpriced stocks. Firms can find bargains because business projects involve **real assets** trading in **real markets** (markets in tangible assets). In the real environment, some level of monopoly power, special knowledge, and expertise possibly can make such projects worth more than they cost. Investors, however, are trading financial assets in financial markets, where the assets are more likely to be worth, on average, exactly what they cost.

The method for relating expected or future cash flows to today's value, called *present value,* is known as **time value of money (TVM).** Chapters 4 and 5 cover this critical financial concept in detail and apply it to the financial world (as well as daily life). Since the expected cash flows of either a business project or an investment are likely to be uncertain, any TVM analysis must account for both the timing and the risk level of the cash flows.

Finance versus Accounting

In most companies, the financial function is usually closely associated with the accounting function. In a very rough sense, the accountant's job is to keep track of what happened *in the past* to the firm's money, while the finance job uses these historical figures with current information to determine what should happen *now and in the future* with the firm's money. The results of financial decisions will eventually appear in accounting statements, so this close association makes sense. Nevertheless, accounting tends to focus on and characterize the past, while finance focuses on the present and future.

TIME OUT

1-1 What are the main subareas of finance and how do they interact?

1.2 • The Financial Function

LG1-2

As we said previously, this text focuses primarily on financial management, so we will discuss the particular functions and responsibilities of the firm's financial manager. We will also explain how the financial function fits in and interacts with the other areas of the firm. Finally, to make this study as interesting and as relevant as possible, we will make the connections that allow you to see how the concepts covered in this book are important in your own personal finances.

The Financial Manager

The firm's highest-level financial manager is usually the chief financial officer, or CFO. Both the company treasurer and the controller report to the CFO. The treasurer is typically responsible for:

- Managing cash and credit.
- Issuing and repurchasing financial securities such as stocks and bonds.
- Deciding how and when to spend capital for new and existing projects.
- Hedging (reducing the firm's potential risk) against changes in foreign exchange and interest rates.

In larger corporations, the treasurer may also oversee other areas, such as purchasing insurance or managing the firm's pension fund investments. The controller oversees the accounting function, usually managing the tax, cost accounting, financial accounting, and data processing functions.

Finance in Other Business Functions

Although the CFO and treasurer positions tend to be the firm's most visible finance-related positions, finance affects the firm in many ways and throughout all levels of a company's organizational chart. Finance permeates the entire business organization, providing guidance for both strategic and day-to-day decisions of the firm and collecting information for control and feedback about the firm's financial decisions.

Operational managers use finance daily to determine how much overtime labor to use, or to perform cost/benefit analysis when they consider new production lines or methods. Marketing managers use finance to assess the cost effectiveness of doing follow-up marketing surveys. Human resource managers use finance to evaluate the company's cost for various employee benefit packages. No matter where you work in business, finance can help you do your job better.

defined benefit plan

A retirement plan in which the employer funds a pension generally based on each employee's years of service and salary.

LG1-3

defined contribution plan

A retirement plan in which the employee contributes money and directs its investment. The amount of retirement benefits are directly related to the amount of money contributed and the success of its investment.

401k plan

A defined contribution plan that is sponsored by corporate employers.

Individual Retirement Account (IRA)

A self-sponsored retirement program.

Finance in Your Personal Life

Finance can help you make good financial decisions in your personal life. Consider these common activities you will probably face in your life:

- Borrowing money to buy a new car.
- Refinancing your home mortgage at a lower rate.
- Making credit card or student loan payments.
- Saving for retirement.

You will be able to perform all of these tasks better after learning about finance. Recent changes throughout our economy and the U.S. business environment make knowledge of finance even more valuable to you than before. For example, most companies have switched from providing **defined benefit** retirement plans to employees to offering **defined contribution** plans (such as **401k** plans) and self-funded plans like **Individual Retirement Accounts (IRAs).** Tax changes in the early 1980s made this switch more or less inevitable. It appears that each of us will have to ensure adequate funds for our own retirement—much more so than previous generations.

EXAMPLE 1-1

LG1-3

For interactive versions of this example visit www.mhhe.com/can3e

Finance Applications

Chloe realizes how important finance will be for her future business career. However, some of the ways that she will see financial applications seem way off in the future. She is curious about how the theory applies to her personal life, both in the near term and in the long term.

SOLUTION:

Chloe will quickly find that her financial health now and in the future will depend upon many decisions she makes as she goes through life—starting now! For example, she will learn that the same tools that she applies to a business loan analysis can be applied to her own personal debt. After this course, Chloe will be able to evaluate credit card offers and select one that could save her hundreds of dollars per year. When she buys a new car and the dealership offers her a low-interest-rate loan or a higher-rate loan with cash back, she will be able to pick the option that will truly cost her the least. Also, when Chloe gets her first professional job, she will know how to direct her retirement account so that she can earn millions of dollars for her future. (Of course, inflation between now and when she retires will imply that Chloe's millions won't be worth as much as they would today.)

TIME OUT

1-2 How might the application of finance improve your professional and personal decisions?

1.3 • Business Organization

LG1-4

In the United States, people can structure businesses in any of several ways; the number of owners is the key to how business structures are classified. Traditionally, single owners, partners, and corporations operate businesses. We can express the advantages and disadvantages of each organizational form through several dimensions:

- Who controls the firm.
- Who owns the firm.
- What are the owners' risks.
- What access to capital exists.
- What are the tax ramifications.

Recently, small businesses have adopted hybrid structures that capture the benefits from multiple organizational forms, and we'll discuss those hybrid structures after we cover the more common, traditional types of business organizations.

sole proprietorship
A business entity that is not legally separate from its owner.

unlimited liability
A situation in which a person's personal assets are at risk from a business liability.

equity
An ownership interest in a business enterprise.

angel investors
Individuals who provide small amounts of capital and expert business advice to small firms in exchange for an ownership stake in the firm.

venture capitalists
Similar to angel investors except that they are organized as groups of investors and can provide larger amounts of capital.

general partnership
A form of business organization where the partners own the business together and are personally liable for legal actions and debts of the firm.

Sole Proprietorships

The **sole proprietorship** represents, by far, the most common type of business in the United States.[1] A sole proprietorship is defined as any unincorporated business owned by a single individual.[2] Perhaps these businesses are so popular because they are relatively easy to start, and they're subject to a much lighter regulatory and paperwork burden than other business forms. The owner, or sole proprietor, of the business has complete control of the firm's activities. The owner also receives all of the firm's profits and is solely responsible for all losses.

The biggest disadvantage that sole proprietorships carry relative to other organizational forms is that they have **unlimited liability** for their companies' debts and actions. The owner's personal assets may be confiscated if the business fails. The law recognizes no distinction between the owner's business assets and personal assets. The income of the business is also added to the owner's personal income and taxed by the government at the appropriate personal tax rate. Finally, sole proprietors have a difficult time obtaining capital to expand their business operations. Banks and other lenders are not typically interested in lending much money to sole proprietors because small firms have only one person liable for paying back the debt. A sole proprietor could raise capital by issuing **equity** to another investor. **Angel investors** and **venture capitalists** exchange capital for ownership in a business. But this requires re-forming the business as a partnership and the sole proprietor must give up some of the ownership (and thus control) of the firm. Table 1.1 summarizes sole proprietorships' characteristics, along with those of the three other business organizations we will study.

Partnerships

A **general partnership,** or as it is more commonly known, a *partnership,* is an organizational form that features multiple individual owners. Each partner can own a different percentage of the firm. Firm control is typically determined by

[1]According to the IRS' *SOI Tax Stats—Integrated Business Data* for 2007, 78.21 percent of all businesses in the U.S. were sole proprietorships.
[2]However, if you are the sole member of a domestic limited liability company (LLC, discussed below), you are not a sole proprietor if you elect to treat the LLC as a corporation.

table 1.1 | **Characteristics of Business Organization**

	Ownership	Control	Ownership Risk	Access to Capital	Taxes
Sole Proprietor	Single individual	Proprietor	Unlimited liability	Very limited	Paid by owner
Partnership	Multiple people	Shared by partners	Unlimited liability	Limited	Paid by partners
Corporation	Public investors who own the stock	Company managers	Stockholders can only lose their investment in the firm	Easy access	Corporation pays income tax and stockholders pay taxes on dividends
Hybrids: S-corp, LLP, LLC, LP	Partners or shareholders	Shared	Mostly limited	Limited by firm size restrictions	Paid by partners or shareholders

the size of partners' ownership stakes. Business profits are split among the partners according to a prearranged agreement, usually by the percentage of firm ownership. Received profits are added to each partner's personal income and taxed at personal income tax rates.

The partners jointly share unlimited personal liability for the debts of the firm and all are obligated for contracts agreed to by any one of the partners. Banks are more willing to lend to partnerships than to sole proprietorships, because all partners are liable for repaying the debt. Partners would have to give up some ownership and control in the firm to raise more equity capital. In order to raise enough capital for substantial growth, a partnership often changes into a public corporation.

Corporations

public corporation

A company owned by a large number of stockholders from the general public.

double taxation

A situation in which two taxes must be paid on the same income.

limited liability

Limitation of a person's financial liability to a fixed sum or investment.

A **public corporation** is a legally independent entity entirely separate from its owners. This independence dramatically alters the firm's characteristics. Corporations hold many rights and obligations of individual persons, such as the ability to own property, sign binding contracts, and pay taxes. Federal and state governments tax corporate income once at the corporate level. Then shareholders pay taxes again at the personal level when corporate profits are paid out as dividends. This practice is generally known as **double taxation.**

Corporate owners are stockholders, also called *shareholders.* Public corporations typically have thousands of stockholders. The firm must hire managers to direct the firm, since thousands of individual shareholders could not direct day-to-day operations under any sort of consensus. As a result, managers control the company. Strong possibilities of conflicts of interests arise when one group of people owns the business, but another group controls it. We'll discuss conflicts of interest and their resolution later in the chapter.

As individual legal entities, corporations assume liability for their own debts, so the shareholders have only **limited liability.** That is, corporate shareholders cannot lose more money than they originally paid for their shares of stock. This limited liability is one reason that many people feel comfortable owning stock. Corporations are thus able to raise incredible amounts of money by selling stock (equity) and borrowing money. The largest businesses in the world are organized as corporations.

Hybrid Organizations

To promote the growth of small businesses, the U.S. government allows for several types of business organizations that simultaneously offer limited personal liability for the owners *and* provide a pass-through of all firm earnings to the owners, so that the earnings are subject only to single taxation.

finance at work — corporate

GOOGLE BUYS YOUTUBE

In November 2006, Web search leader Google purchased the online video-sharing phenomenon YouTube for $1.65 billion. Google bought the firm by giving YouTube owners shares of Google stock in exchange for their ownership in YouTube. YouTube was a private corporation owned primarily by cofounders Chad Hurley and Steve Chen, who each received over $300 million of Google stock. Venture capital firm Sequoia Capital had backed YouTube and received $442 million of Google stock. Two dozen YouTube employees also had ownership stakes; some of them became millionaires from the deal.

YouTube was founded in February 2005. Imagine starting a business that was purchased for $1.65 billion less than two years later! Consider how many finance people and applications were needed to organize the buyout. Google's CFO George Reyes and team had to determine the value that YouTube could bring to Google. They also had to convince their own Google stockholders that Google did not overpay for the purchase. To do so, auditors had to evaluate YouTube's cash flows and the riskiness of those cash flows. The CFO, along with investment banker advisors, had to decide how to pay for YouTube. Google swapped its own stock for the firm but could have paid all cash or used a combination of cash and stock.

YouTube owners also had to assess the value of their stock to ensure that they received a fair price. Google's offer had to be compared to alternatives. For example, YouTube could have waited for a better offer from Google or sought an offer from another firm. Or YouTube owners could have decided to take the company public and sold shares to public investors.

This chapter illustrates the kinds of issues that finance addresses. The rest of the book describes the theories and tools needed to make these judgments. The practice of finance isn't just about numbers—the results of financial analysis are very dynamic and exciting!

! want to know more? Key Words to Search for Updates: Google, YouTube

Hybrid organizations offer single taxation and limited liability to all owners. Examples are *S corporations, limited liability partnerships (LLPs),* and *limited liability companies (LLCs).* Others, called *limited partnerships (LPs),* offer single taxation and limited liability to the *limited partners,* but also have *general partners,* who benefit from single taxation but also must bear personal liability for the firm's debts.

hybrid organizations
Business forms that have some attributes of corporations and some of proprietorships/partnerships.

The U.S. government typically restricts hybrid organization status to relatively small firms. The government limits the maximum number of shareholders or partners involved,[3] the maximum amount of investment capital allowed, and the lines of business permitted. These restrictions are consistent with the government's stated reason for allowing the formation of these forms of business organization—to encourage the formation and growth of small businesses.

TIME OUT

1-3 Why must an entrepreneur give up some control of the business as it grows into a public corporation?

1-4 What advantages does the corporate form of organization hold over a partnership?

[3]For example, current federal regulations limit the number of shareholders in an S corporation to no more than 100.

1.4 • Firm Goals

LG1-5

maximization of shareholder wealth

A view that management should first and foremost consider the interests of shareholders in its business decisions.

stakeholder

A person or organization that has a legitimate interest in a corporation.

invisible hand

A metaphor used to illustrate how an individual pursuing his own interests also tends to promote the good of the community.

Tens of thousands of public corporations operate in the United States. Many of them are the largest business organizations in the world. Because U.S. corporations are so large and because there are so many of them, corporations have a tremendous impact on society. Given the power that these huge firms wield, many people question what the corporate goals should be. Two different, well-developed viewpoints have arisen concerning what the goal of the firm should be. The owners' perspective holds that the only appropriate goal is to **maximize shareholder wealth.** The competing viewpoint is from the **stakeholders'** perspective, which emphasizes social responsibility over profitability. This view maintains that managers must maximize the total satisfaction of all stakeholders in a business. These stakeholders include the owners and shareholders, but also include the business's customers, employees, and local communities.

While strong arguments speak in favor of both perspectives, financial practitioners and academics now tend to believe that the manager's primary responsibility should be to maximize shareholder wealth and give only secondary consideration to other stakeholders' welfare. One of the first, and most well-known, proponents of this viewpoint was Adam Smith, an 18th-century economist who argued that, in capitalism, an individual pursuing his own interests tends also to promote the good of his community.[4]

Smith argued that the **invisible hand** of the market, acting through competition and the free price system, would ensure that only those activities most efficient and beneficial to society as a whole would survive in the long run. Thus, those same activities would also profit the individual most. When companies try to implement a goal other than profit maximization, their efforts tend to backfire. Consider the firm that tries to maximize employment. The high number of employees raises costs. Soon the firm will find that its costs are too high to allow it to compete against more efficient firms, especially in a global business environment. When the firm fails, all employees are let go and employment ends up being minimized, not maximized.

Regardless of whether you believe Smith's assertion or not, a more pragmatic reason supports the argument that maximizing owners' wealth is an admirable goal. As we will discuss, the owners of the firm hire managers to work on their behalf, so the manager is morally, ethically, and legally required to act in the owners' best interests. Any relationships between the manager and other firm stakeholders are necessarily secondary to the goal that shareholders give to their hired managers.

Maximizing owners' equity value means carefully considering:

- How best to bring additional funds into the firm.
- Which projects to invest in.
- How best to return the profits from those projects to the owners over time.

For corporations, maximizing the value of owners' equity can also be stated as *maximizing the current value per share, or* ***stock price,*** *of existing shares.* To the extent that the current stock price can be expected to include the present value of any future expected cash flows accruing to the owners, the goal of maximizing stock price provides us with a single, concrete, measurable gauge of value. You may be tempted to choose several other potential goals over maximizing the value of owners' equity. Common alternatives are:

- Maximizing net income or profit.
- Minimizing costs.
- Maximizing market share.

[4]See Book IV of his *The Wealth of Nations.*

Although these may look appealing, each of these goals has some potentially serious shortcomings. For example, net income is measured on a year-by-year or quarter-by-quarter basis. When we say that we want to maximize profits, to *which* net income figure are we referring? We can maximize this year's net income in several legitimate ways, but many of these ways impose costs which will reduce future income. Or, current net income can be pushed into future years. Neither of these two extremes will likely encourage the firm's short-term and long-term stability. One more likely goal would be to maximize today's value of *all* future years of net income. Of course, this possible goal is very close to maximizing the current stock price, without the convenient market-oriented measure of the stock price. Another problem with considering maximizing all future profits as the goal is that net income (for reasons we'll go into later) does not really measure how much money the firm is actually earning.

Minimizing costs and *maximizing market share* also have fundamental problems as potential goals. Certainly minimizing costs would not make some stakeholders, such as employees, very happy. In addition, without spending the money on R&D and new product development, many companies would not survive long in the ever-evolving economy without improving their products. A firm can always increase market share by lowering price. But if a firm loses money on every product sold, then selling more products will simply drive the firm into fiscal distress.

TIME OUT

1-5 Describe why the primary objective of maximizing shareholder value may actually be the most beneficial for society in the long run.

1.5 • Agency Theory

LG1-6

Whenever one party (the *principal*) hires someone else (the *agent*) to work for him or her, their interaction is called an *agency relationship.* The agent is always supposed to act in the principal's best interests. For example, an apartment complex manager should ensure that tenants aren't doing willful damage to the property, that fire codes are enforced, and that the vacancy rate is kept as low as possible, because these are best for the apartment owner.

Agency Problem

In the context of a public corporation, we have already noted that stockholders hire managers to run the firm. Ideally, managers will operate the firm so that the shareholders realize maximum value for their equity. But managers may be tempted to operate the firm to serve their own best interests. Managers could spend company money to improve their own lifestyle instead of earning more profits for shareholders. Sometimes the manager's best interest does not necessarily align with shareholder goals. This creates a situation that we refer to as the **agency problem.**

For example, suppose it is time to buy a new corporate car for the firm's **chief executive officer (CEO).** Assuming that the CEO has no extraordinary driving requirements, shareholders might wish for the CEO to buy a nice, conservative domestic sedan. But suppose that the CEO demands the newest, biggest luxury car available. It's tempting to say that the shareholders could just tell the CEO which car to buy. But remember, the CEO has most of the control in a public corporation. Organizational behavior specialists have identified three basic approaches to minimize this conflict of interest. First, ignore it. If the amount of money involved is small enough relative to the firm's cash flows, or if the suitability of

agency problem

The difficulties that arise when a principal hires an agent and cannot fully monitor the agent's actions.

chief executive officer (CEO)

The highest-ranking corporate manager.

the purchase in question is ambiguous enough, shareholders might be best served to simply overlook the problem. A good deal of research literature suggests that allowing the manager a certain amount of such **perks (perquisites)** might actually enhance owner value, in that such items may boost managers' productivity.[5]

perks/perquisites

Nonwage compensation, often in the form of company car, golf club membership, etc.

The second approach to mitigating this conflict is to monitor managers' actions. Monitoring at too fine a level of detail is probably counterproductive and prohibitively expensive. However, major firm decisions are usually monitored at least roughly through the accounting auditing process.

In addition, concentrated ownership in the firm by large stakeholders such as financial institutions, investment companies, individual block holders, or debt holders give those large stakeholders increased incentives to monitor the activities of management. These incentives are often driven by both **economies of scale** in monitoring and by the claim of the stakeholder having a different risk/return profile than the claim of other stakeholders.

economies of scale

Cost advantages when fixed costs are spread over a large number of units.

To see the impact of economies of scale in monitoring costs, consider a simple example: Suppose that it costs $3.00 each way (i.e., $6.00 round-trip) for a shareholder in a firm to hop on the subway and ride down to the firm's offices in order to go through the firm's financial statements, and that the most savings to shareholders that could possibly result from this monitoring would be $5.00 per share. Would anyone owning a single share ever take the ride to check up on the firm? No, because it would cost a certain $6.00 in order to save a possible $5.00. However, someone owning 100 shares in the firm would find it worthwhile to pay for the subway ride, assuming that the chance of saving $5.00 × 100 = $500 is large enough.

To envision the effect of one stakeholder having a different claim than others, consider the position of a bondholder in a firm where there isn't much free cash flow in the firm above and beyond that which is needed to make the interest payments on her bond. If the manager of the firm is going to spend an extra $20,000 to buy an unnecessarily luxurious company car, that $20,000 is very likely to come out of the bondholder's pocket, so she will definitely have a heightened incentive to monitor the manager's company car purchase. On the other hand, if the firm had so much free cash flow available that the expenditure of the extra $20,000 is unlikely to affect the payment of the bond interest, then the bondholder would have much less incentive to monitor.[6]

option

The opportunity to buy stock at a fixed price over a specific period of time.

The final approach for aligning managers' personal interests with those of owners is to make the managers owners—that is, to offer managers an equity stake in the firm so that management participates in any equity value increase. Many corporations take this approach, either through explicitly granting shares to managers, by awarding them **options** on the firm's stock, or by allowing them to purchase shares at a subsidized price through an **employee stock option plan (ESOP).** When firm managers are also firm owners, their incentives are more likely to align with stockholders' best interests.

employee stock option plan (ESOP)

An incentive program that grants options to employees (typically managers) as compensation.

Corporate Governance

We refer to the process of monitoring managers and aligning their incentives with shareholder goals as **corporate governance.** Theoretically, managers work for shareholders. In reality, because shareholders are usually inactive, the

corporate governance

The set of laws, policies, incentives, and monitors designed to handle the issues arising from the separation of ownership and control.

[5]See, for example, Raghuram Rajan and Julie Wulf, "Are Perks Really Managerial Excess?" *Journal of Financial Economics* 79(1), 2006, 1–33.

[6]In case you are wondering why the stockholders—who would be the eventual recipients of such "extra" free cash flow—wouldn't then have increased incentives to monitor, they would. But, considering that the typical bond sells for $1,000 or more while the typical share of stock sells for much less, and taking into account that bond ownership tends to be much more concentrated than stock ownership in many firms, ask yourself whether bondholders or stockholders are more likely to enjoy economies of scale in monitoring.

firm actually seems to belong to management. Generally speaking, the investing public does not know what goes on at the firm's operational level. Managers handle day-to-day operations, and they know that their work is mostly unknown to investors. This lack of supervision demonstrates the need for monitors. Figure 1.9 shows the people and organizations that help monitor corporate activities.

The monitors inside a public firm are the **board of directors,** who are appointed to represent shareholders' interests. The board hires the CEO, evaluates management, and can also design compensation contracts to tie management's salaries to firm performance.

The monitors outside the firm include auditors, analysts, investment banks, and credit rating agencies. **Auditors** examine the firm's accounting systems and comment on whether financial statements fairly represent the firm's financial position. **Investment analysts** follow a firm, conduct their own evaluations of the company's business activities, and report to the investment community. **Investment banks,** which help firms access capital markets and advise managers about how to interact with those capital markets, also monitor firm performance. **Credit analysts** examine a firm's financial strength for its debt holders. The government also monitors business activities through the Securities and Exchange Commission (SEC) and the Internal Revenue Service (IRS).

board of directors
The group of directors elected by stockholders to oversee management in a corporation.

auditor
A person who performs an independent assessment of the fairness of a firm's financial statements.

investment analyst
A person who analyzes a company's business prospects and gives opinions about its future success.

investment banks
Banks that help companies and governments raise capital.

credit analyst
A person who analyzes a company's ability to repay its debts and reports the findings as a grade.

figure 1.9 Corporate Governance Monitors

Corporate governance balances the needs of stockholders and managers. Inside the public firm, the members of the board of directors monitor how the firm is run. Outside the firm, auditors, analysts, investment banks, and credit rating agencies act as monitors.

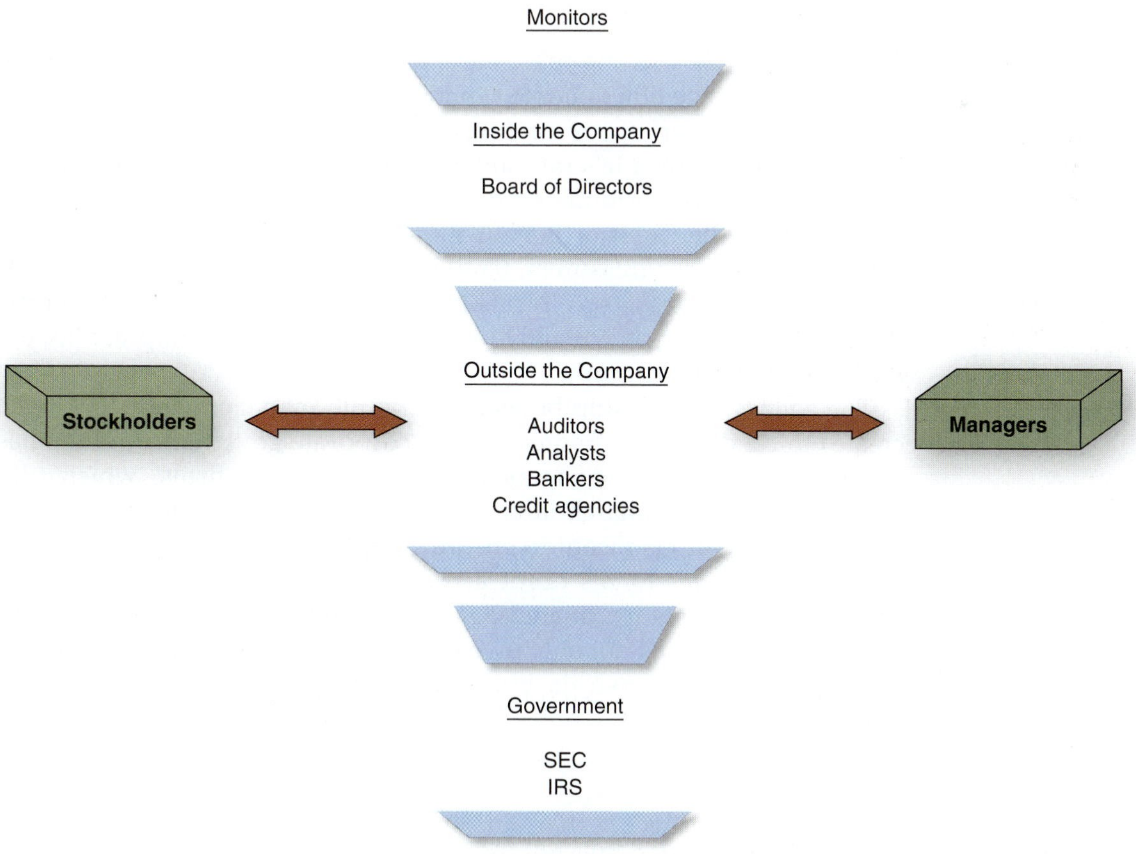

EXAMPLE 1-2

LG1-6

For interactive versions of this example visit www.mhhe.com/can3e

Executive Compensation

In 2005, firms in the Standard & Poor's 500 Index paid their CEOs, on average, $13.51 million—a 16.1 percent increase over the previous year. So the average CEO compensation was 411 times the average employee's compensation. In 2006, the increase in CEO pay was 8.9 percent. Every year, the controversy over CEO pay arises again. What arguments could be made for each side?

SOLUTION:

Many people believe that CEOs are paid too much for the services they provide. They receive compensation that is far higher than workers' pay within their firms. Over the years, executive compensation has also increased at a faster and higher rate than has the value of the stockholders' wealth. For example, the return for stockholders of the S&P 500 Index firms was 15.6 percent in 2006 and 4.9 percent in 2005, compared to CEO pay increases of 8.9 percent and 16.1 percent, respectively. Each firm's board of directors sets CEO compensation. However, CEOs may have undue influence over director selection, tenure, and committee assignments—even over selecting the compensation advisors. This practice creates an unhealthy conflict of interest.

Others believe that a skilled CEO can positively affect company performance and that, therefore, the firm needs to offer high compensation and a bundle of perquisites to attract the best talent. To overcome agency problems, managers must be given incentives that pay very well when the company performs very well. If CEOs create a substantial amount of shareholder wealth, then who is to say that they are overpaid?

The Role of Ethics

LG1-7

ethics
The study of values, morals, and morality.

fiduciary
A legal duty between two parties where one party must act in the interest of the other party.

Ethics must play a strong role in any practice of finance. Finance professionals commonly manage other people's money. For example, corporate managers control the stockholder's firm, bank employees manage deposits, and investment advisors manage people's investment portfolios. These **fiduciary** relationships create tempting opportunities for finance professionals to make decisions that either benefit the client or benefit the advisors themselves. Professional associations (such as for treasurers, bank executives, investment professionals, etc.) place a strong emphasis on ethical behavior and provide ethics training and standards. Nevertheless, as with any profession with millions of practitioners, a few are bound to act unethically.

The agency relationship between corporate managers and stockholders can create ethical dilemmas. Sometimes the corporate governance system has failed to prevent unethical managers from stealing from firms, which ultimately means stealing from shareholders. Governments all over the world have passed laws and regulations meant to ensure compliance with ethical codes of behavior.[7] And if professionals don't act appropriately, governments have set up strong punishments for financial malfeasance. In the end, financial managers must realize that they not only owe their shareholders the very best decisions to further shareholder interests, but they also have a broader obligation to society as a whole.

[7]The Sarbanes-Oxley Act of 2002 was passed in response to a number of recent major corporate accounting scandals including those affecting Enron, Tyco International, and WorldCom. The goal of the act was to make the accounting and auditing procedures more transparent and trustworthy.

finance at work — corporate

THE AMAZING STORY OF APPLE INC. AND STEVE JOBS

Steven Jobs and Stephen Wozniak started Apple Computer in 1976 as an equal partnership. Together, they built 50 computers in a garage using money borrowed from family, the proceeds from the sale of a VW bus, and credit from the parts distributor.

Jobs and Wozniak then designed the Apple II computer. But a higher production level to make more than 50 computers required more space and employees. They needed much more capital. They could not get a loan until angel investor Mike Markkula (an Intel executive) became a partner in the firm. He invested $92,000 and his personal guarantee induced a bank to loan Apple $250,000. As production ramped up in 1977, Apple Computer incorporated. Most shares were owned by Jobs, Wozniak, and Markkula, but the principals made some shares available to employees. They also hired an experienced manager (Mike Scott) to be the CEO and run the firm. Note that as the firm expanded, Jobs' ownership level and control got diluted. By 1980, Apple Computer had sold a total of 121,000 computers—against a potential demand of millions more. Apple needed even more capital.

At the end of 1980, Apple became a public corporation and sold $65 million worth of stock to public investors. Steve Jobs, cofounder of Apple, still owned more shares than anyone else (7.5 million), but he owned less than half of the firm. He gave up a great deal of ownership to new investors in exchange for the capital to expand the firm. Unhappy with Mike Scott's leadership, Steve Jobs also became CEO of Apple.

After a couple of years, Apple's board of directors felt that Jobs was not experienced enough to steer the firm through its rapid expansion. They hired John Sculley as CEO in 1983. In 1985, a power struggle ensued for control of the firm, and the board backed Sculley over Jobs. Jobs was forced out of Apple and no longer had a say in business operations, even though he was the largest shareholder and an original cofounder of the firm.

So, Steve Jobs bought Pixar in 1986 for $5 million and founded NeXT Computer. Over the next 10 years, Jobs' Pixar produced mega hit movies like *Toy Story, A Bug's Life,* and *Monsters, Inc.* This time, he kept 53 percent ownership of Pixar to ensure keeping full control. In the meantime, Apple Computer began to struggle, with losses of $800 million in 1996 and $1 billion in 1997. To get Steve Jobs back into the firm, Apple bought NeXT for $400 million and hired him as Apple's CEO. Over the next few years, Jobs introduced the iMac, iPod, and iTunes, and Apple became very profitable again! Jobs was given the use of a $90 million Gulfstream jet as a perk. To realign his incentives, he became an Apple owner again via compensation that included options on 10 million shares of stock and 30 million shares of **restricted stock.** Then in 2006, Disney bought Pixar by swapping $7.4 billion worth of Disney stock for Pixar stock. When the deal closed, Steve Jobs became the largest owner of Disney stock (7 percent) and joined Disney's board of directors.

Wow! What a story of accessing capital, business organizational form, company control, and corporate governance.

want to know more? Key Words to Search for Updates: Steve Jobs, Apple Computer, Pixar

TIME OUT

1-6 What unethical activities might managers engage in because of the agency problem?

1-7 Explain how the corporate governance system reduces the agency problem.

restricted stock
A special type of stock that is not transferable from the current holder to others until specific conditions are satisfied.

1.6 • Financial Markets, Intermediaries, and the Firm

LG1-8

Astute readers will note that our emphasis on the role of financial markets and intermediaries grew throughout this chapter. This emphasis is intentional, as we feel that you must understand the role and impact of these institutions on the firm if you are to grasp the context in which professionals make financial management decisions.

We want to emphasize one other important point about these financial institutions (FI). Very astute readers may wonder how, if financial markets are competitive, investment banks and other financial institutions are able to make such impressive profits. Although FIs assist others with transactions involving financial assets in the financial markets, they do so as paid services. Successful

figure 1.10 **Financial Institutions' Cash Flows**

The unique services and products that financial institutions provide allow them to make money.

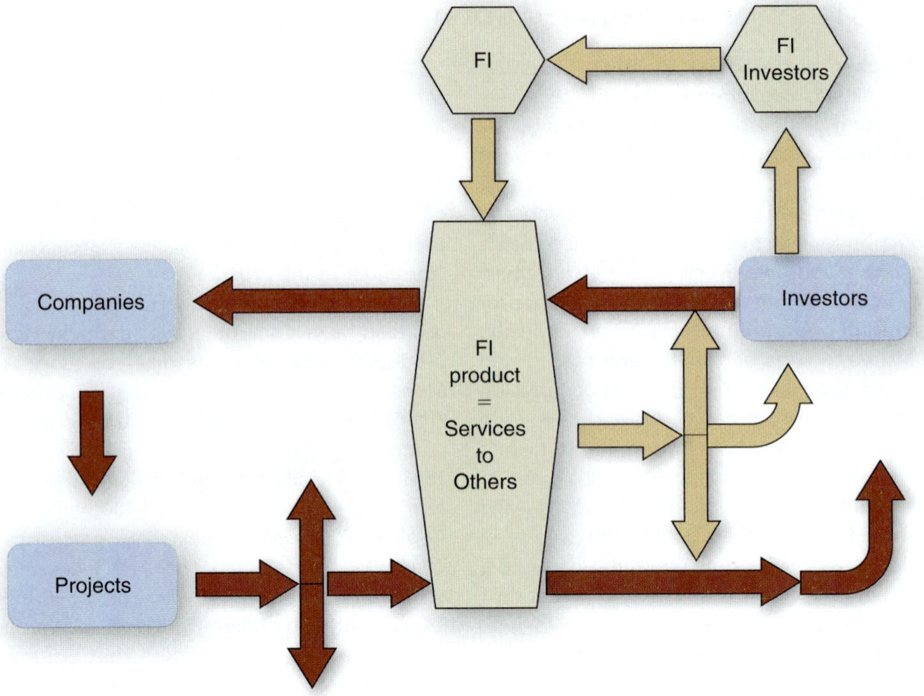

execution of those services takes unique assets and expertise. As shown in Figure 1.10, it's the use of those unique assets and expertise that provides financial institutions with their high profit margins.

TIME OUT

1-8 What is the role of financial institutions in a capitalist economy?

LG1-9

1.7 • The Financial Crisis

It would be impossible to write a new edition of this book without mentioning the 800-pound gorilla in the room that is the financial crisis. We will be discussing aspects of the crisis throughout the book, but we give you a little bit of insight concerning the causes of the crisis here to provide a foundation that we can refer to later.

What Started It

Signs of significant problems in the U.S. economy arose in late 2006 and the first half of 2007, when home prices plummeted and defaults by **subprime mortgage borrowers** (i.e., those borrowers charged higher interest rates because of their higher chance of default) began to affect the mortgage lending industry as a whole, as well as other parts of the economy noticeably. Mortgage delinquencies, particularly on subprime mortgages, surged in the last quarter of 2006 through 2008 as home owners who stretched themselves financially to buy a home or

subprime mortgage borrowers

Borrowers charged higher interest rates because of their higher chance of default.

refinance a mortgage in the early 2000s fell behind on their loan payments. Foreclosure filings jumped 93 percent in July 2007 over July 2006. Between August 2007 and October 2008, an additional 936,439 homes were lost to foreclosure.

These problems arose after one of the largest periods of home-ownership growth in U.S. history, with the seasonally adjusted home ownership rate reaching a peak of 69.2 percent in the first quarter of 2005. To fund this unprecedented growth, mortgage lenders had increasingly started to sell the rights to the payments on the loans they had originated to other financial institutions or investors. This process is called **securitization.**

securitization

A process where loan originators sell the rights to the payments on the loans to other financial institutions or investors.

As a result, when mortgage borrowers started to default on their mortgages in late 2006, it was not just the lenders who had originated the mortgages who were affected, but also the broad variety of individual investors, pension funds, insurance companies, and many others who had invested heavily in such **mortgage-backed securities.**

mortgage-backed securities

Securities that represent a claim against the cash flows from a pool of mortgage loans.

Why It Got Worse

The widespread effects of the collapse of the housing bubble damaged financial institutions severely, raising questions about solvency even for those institutions which survived the bubble. As a result, the surviving institutions tightened their lending standards, making credit less available for both consumers and businesses in the economy.

This decreased availability of credit, along with damaged investor confidence, led businesses to reduce their forecasted sales and revenue figures. In turn, lower forecasted demand for products in the economy led employers to reduce their workforces, resulting in double-digit unemployment figures and further eroding consumer confidence.

The Effect on the Public Sector

In the aftermath of the housing bubble collapse, the federal government took extensive steps to stimulate the economy to provide for an economic "soft landing." The American Recovery and Reinvestment Act, passed by the U.S. Congress on February 13, 2009, devoted $308.3 billion to appropriations spending, including $120 billion on infrastructure and science and more than $30 billion on energy-related infrastructure projects. Another $267 billion would go for direct spending, including increased unemployment benefits and food stamps. Finally, $212 billion was set aside for tax breaks for individuals and businesses.

By the summer and fall of 2009, the economy appeared to be slowly beginning to recover. Pending home sales and residential construction both posted significant increases, the unemployment rate dropped below 10 percent, GDP was once again increasing, and consumer spending was once again on the rise. Unfortunately, state and local governments have continued to struggle with the aftermath of the crisis, enduring both reduced income tax revenues and decreasing property tax revenues caused by property reappraisals. So the economy never experienced the typical post-recession high-growth rebound and has been sputtering ever since.

Looking Ahead

At the time of this writing, the financial crisis appears to be starting to get somewhat better. Increasing consumer demand and diminishing unemployment point to better times ahead. However, both lenders' and consumers' tendencies to be more cautious, along with the continuing fiscal problems facing state and local municipalities in the foreseeable future, are likely to make the road to recovery a long and slow one.

viewpoints REVISITED

Business Application Solution

Because Caleb is a sole proprietor of a small business, he will have trouble getting loans for large amounts of money if he wants to expand. Caleb should consider the following options.

First, Caleb can expand slowly. He can get a small loan or self-fund an expansion into one other mall. Once the new juice stand is making a profit, he can expand again. The advantage of this slow expansion is that he retains full ownership and control of his business. One significant risk is that others may copy his idea and open their own stands, thus taking the prime spots in malls before he gets there.

In order to obtain the capital to expand more quickly, Caleb may have to take on a partner. Forming a partnership with an angel investor or a venture capitalist who can provide business expertise and substantial amounts of capital would allow for much faster expansion. The disadvantage of this option is that Caleb will have to give up some ownership of his business.

Personal Application Solution

Dagmar should know that the market gives no guarantees against losing money investing in company stocks. These companies failed for different reasons. Lehman Brothers failed because it adopted too-risky business practices, the Chrysler bankruptcy has been blamed on speculation by a small group of investors, and Six Flags' bankruptcy was caused by commitments to pay dividends that it couldn't honor.

Dagmar should also know that the collapse of these firms, and others, has led to a strengthened corporate governance system for monitoring managerial actions. We all hope that this new governance system will reduce the number of company failures due to managerial malfeasance. Nevertheless, she can minimize her loss from a corporate bankruptcy by not putting all her "eggs in one basket." Diversification is a finance principle discussed in detail later in this book.

summary of learning goals

Finance is largely about the determination and evaluation of cash flows and value. Financial management is critically important to the success of any business organization. This book describes the key finance concepts central to corporate finance. The organizational form of a business may impact its cash flow and value. The firm's organizational structure influences managerial goals, incentives, and the agency relationship between management and the firm's owners. Most of these finance principles can be successfully applied to one's personal life.

LG1-1 Define the major areas of finance as they apply to corporate financial management. Subareas or concentrations within finance include investments, financial management, financial institutions and markets, and international finance. Individuals must assess what investment opportunities best meet their needs and their risk tolerances. Financial institutions and markets must efficiently distribute capital between investors and companies. Companies use financial management to evaluate potential projects and decide which to fund, what capital to use, and what kind and amount of capital to return to investors. Finance in a global context is more than just an extension of domestic finance activities. International finance deals with the special risks and opportunities of moving cash flows in a global business.

LG1-2 Show how finance is at the heart of sound business decisions. Finance permeates entire business organizations, providing guidance for the firm's strategic (long-term) and day-to-day decisions. Many nonfinance professionals within a firm can use financial concepts to improve their decisions.

LG1-3 Learn the financial principles that govern your personal decisions. Knowing finance theory and applying financial tools will help you make better personal decisions.

LG1-4 Examine the three most common forms of business organization in the United States today. Sole proprietors own and control their own businesses. The owner receives all profits and pays taxes at a personal income tax rate. The sole proprietor has unlimited liability for the firm's actions and often may have difficulty obtaining capital for expansion. Similar businesses with multiple owners are known as partnerships. The partners share ownership, control, and the profits. A public corporation has thousands of owners—its stockholders. The firm hires managers who control the day-to-day firm operations. Corporations have virtually unlimited access to capital—much more so than other business organizational forms. Corporate profits are taxed twice—first at the corporate level and then again at stockholders' personal tax rate when dividends are paid. Stockholders have limited liability and can only lose the amount of money they originally invested in the stock.

LG1-5 Distinguish among appropriate and inappropriate goals for financial managers. Most finance professionals agree that maximizing the value of stockholders' equity, as measured by stock price, ensures a financially successful and stable firm for the long run. Financially stable firms are good for stakeholders, such as employees, managers, customers, and local communities. Other goals, like maximizing employment, market share, or profits, do not ensure firm viability over the long run.

LG1-6 Identify a firm's primary agency relationship and discuss the possible conflicts that may arise. Theoretically, managers work for shareholders. In reality, because shareholders aren't involved in day-to-day firm activities, managers control the firm. Managers might be tempted to operate the firm in such a way as to benefit themselves more than the shareholders. Corporate governance is the system of incentives and monitors that tries to overcome this agency problem. Shareholders can align managers' interests with stockholder interests by making managers part owners of the firm. Then, various monitors follow the firm and report on its activities.

LG1-7 Discuss how ethical decision making is part of the study of financial management. Because finance professionals commonly manage other people's money in a fiduciary capacity, ethics are of primary importance in finance.

LG1-8 Describe the complex, necessary relationships among firms, financial institutions, and financial markets. Financial institutions assist companies and individuals with transactions involving financial assets in the financial markets. Firms' ability to acquire capital is particularly important.

LG1-9 Explain the fundamental causes of the financial crisis that started in 2006. The crisis was sparked by the collapse of U.S. home prices in late 2006 and 2007, spread to other financial institutions via affected mortgage-backed securities, and resulted in a tightening of credit by financial institutions and a loss of confidence by consumers.

key terms

agency problem, The difficulties that arise when a principal hires an agent and cannot fully monitor the agent's actions. *p. 17*

angel investors, Individuals who provide small amounts of capital and expert business advice to small firms in exchange for an ownership stake in the firm. *p. 13*

auditor, A person who performs an independent assessment of the fairness of a firm's financial statements. *p. 19*

asset classes, A group of securities that exhibit similar characteristics, behave similarly in the marketplace, and are subject to the same laws and regulations. *p. 10*

board of directors, The group of directors elected by stockholders to oversee management in a corporation. *p. 19*

chief executive officer (CEO), The highest-ranking corporate manager. *p. 17*

corporate governance, The set of laws, policies, incentives, and monitors designed to handle the issues arising from the separation of ownership and control. *p. 18*

credit analyst, A person who analyzes a company's ability to repay its debts and reports the findings as a grade. *p. 19*

defined benefit plan, A retirement plan in which the employer funds a pension generally based on each employee's years of service and salary. *p. 12*

defined contribution plan, A retirement plan in which the employee contributes money and directs its investment. The amount of retirement benefits are directly related to the amount of money contributed and the success of its investment. *p. 12*

double taxation, A situation in which two taxes must be paid on the same income. *p. 14*

economies of scale, Cost advantages when fixed costs are spread over a large number of units. *p. 18*

employee stock option plan (ESOP), An incentive program that grants options to employees (typically managers) as compensation. *p. 18*

equity, An ownership interest in a business enterprise. *p. 13*

ethics, The study of values, morals, and morality. *p. 20*

fiduciary, A legal duty between two parties where one party must act in the interest of the other party. *p. 20*

finance, The study of applying specific value to things we own, services we use, and decisions we make. *p. 4*

financial asset, A general term for securities like stocks, bonds, and other assets that represent ownership in a cash flow. *p. 10*

financial institutions and markets, The organizations that facilitate the flow of capital between investors and companies. *p. 9*

financial management, The process for and the analysis of making financial decisions in the business context. *p. 4*

financial market, The places and processes that facilitate the trading of financial assets between investors. *p. 5*

401k plan, A defined contribution plan that is sponsored by corporate employers. *p. 12*

general partnership, A form of business organization where the partners own the business together and are personally liable for legal actions and debts of the firm. *p. 13*

hybrid organizations Business forms that have some attributes of corporations and some of proprietorships/partnerships. *p. 15*

Individual Retirement Account (IRA), A self-sponsored retirement program. *p. 12*

international finance, The use of finance theory in a global business environment. *p. 9*

investment analyst, A person who analyzes a company's business prospects and gives opinions about its future success. *p. 19*

investment banks, Banks that help companies and governments raise capital. *p. 19*

investment, The analysis and process of choosing securities and other assets to purchase. *p. 7*

investors, Those who buy securities or other assets in hopes of earning a return and getting more money back in the future. *p. 6*

invisible hand, A metaphor used to illustrate how an individual pursuing his own interests also tends to promote the good of the community. *p. 16*

limited liability, Limitation of a person's financial liability to a fixed sum or investment. *p. 14*

maximization of shareholder wealth, A view that management should first and foremost consider the interests of shareholders in its business decisions. *p. 16*

mortgage-backed securities, Securities that represent a claim against the cash flows from a pool of mortgage loans. *p. 23*

option, The opportunity to buy stock at a fixed price over a specific period of time. *p. 18*

perks/perquisites, Nonwage compensation, often in the form of company car, golf club membership, etc. *p. 18*

public corporation, A company owned by a large number of stockholders from the general public. *p. 14*

real assets, Physical property like gold, machinery, equipment, or real estate. *p. 10*

real markets, The places and processes that facilitate the trading of real assets. *p. 10*

restricted stock, A special type of stock that is not transferable from the current holder to others until specific conditions are satisfied. *p. 21*

retained earnings, The portion of company profits that are kept by the company rather than distributed to the stockholders as cash dividends. *p. 7*

risk, A potential future negative impact to value and/or cash flows. It is often discussed in terms of the probability of loss and the expected magnitude of the loss. *p. 9*

securitization, A process where loan originators sell the rights to the payments on the loans to other financial institutions or investors. *p. 23*

sole proprietorship, A business entity that is not legally separate from its owner. *p. 13*

stakeholder, A person or organization that has a legitimate interest in a corporation. *p. 16*

subprime mortgage borrowers, Borrowers charged higher interest rates because of their higher chance of default. *p. 22*

time value of money (TVM), The theory and application of valuing cash flows at various points in time. *p. 10*

unlimited liability, A situation in which a person's personal assets are at risk from a business liability. *p. 13*

venture capitalists, Similar to angel investors except that they are organized as groups of investors and can provide larger amounts of capital. *p. 13*

self-test problems with solutions

1 Organizational Form: Titus founded his own construction wholesale business many years ago. After building a successful firm that supplies materials to real estate developers in his region, he joined with a partner who provided the capital to expand throughout the state. They changed the business to a privately-owned corporation of which Titus owns 60 percent of the shares. The partner owns 30 percent of the shares and 10 percent were set aside to give to some employees in a stock ownership plan. The statewide expansion has been a big success. Financial advisors have suggested to Titus that he take the company public. What issues should he consider when thinking about it?

Solution:

Some big advantages accrue to a public corporation. By going public, he could raise much more capital and expand the firm nationally. Being a larger national firm might give him more ability to buy his products at lower costs. Also, the owners (himself, the partner, and some employees) would have greater ability to sell their shares to "cash out" of the firm—or at least to sell some shares and diversify their wealth. This also allows an older entrepreneur both to keep the business wealth he generated and to transition into retirement. Some disadvantages also arise when a firm goes public. Titus will have to give up some fraction of his ownership and thus may eventually lose control of the firm. The profits of the firm will be taxed twice, once at the firm level and then again at the shareholder level. Titus will have to evaluate these advantages and disadvantages to decide whether to go public.

questions

1. Describe the type of people who use the financial markets. *(LG1-1)*
2. What is the purpose of financial management? Describe the kinds of activities that financial management involves. *(LG1-1)*
3. What is the difference in perspective between finance and accounting? *(LG1-2)*
4. What personal decisions can you think of that will benefit from your learning finance? *(LG1-3)*
5. What are the three basic forms of business ownership? What are the advantages and disadvantages to each? *(LG1-4)*

6. Among the three basic forms of business ownership, describe the ability of each form to access capital. *(LG1-4)*
7. Explain how the founder of a business can eventually lose control of the firm. How can the founder ensure this will not happen? *(LG1-4)*
8. Explain the shareholder wealth maximization goal of the firm and how it can be measured. Make an argument for why it is a better goal than maximizing profit. *(LG1-5)*
9. Name and describe as many corporate stakeholders as you can. *(LG1-5)*
10. What conflicts of interest can arise between managers and stockholders? *(LG1-6)*
11. Figure 1.9 shows firm monitors. In your opinion, which group is in the best position to monitor the firm? Explain. Which group has the potential to be the weakest monitor? Explain. *(LG1-6)*
12. In recent years, governments all over the world have passed laws that increased the penalties for executives' crimes. Do you think this will deter unethical corporate managers? Explain. *(LG1-6)*
13. Every year, the media report on the vast amounts of money (sometimes hundreds of millions of dollars) that some CEOs earn from the companies they manage. Are these CEOs worth it? Give examples. *(LG1-6)*
14. Why is ethical behavior so important in the field of finance? *(LG1-7)*
15. Does the goal of shareholder wealth maximization conflict with behaving ethically? Explain. *(LG1-7)*
16. Describe how financial institutions and markets facilitate the expansion of a company's business. *(LG1-8)*

research it! Corporate Governance

The corporate governance system continues to evolve. After the very visible governance failures in the early 2000s, national focus was placed on this issue. The U.S. government passed new laws regarding auditing, board of directors' composition, and executive behavior. Directors also began to change the form of executive incentive compensation. Some believe the changes went too far and have placed a costly burden on public corporations. Others believe that some new laws did not go far enough to rein in the extreme levels of executive compensation. For information on this ongoing debate, visit the leading independent source for U.S. corporate governance and executive compensation, The Corporate Library, at **www.thecorporatelibrary.com**.

integrated mini-case Corporate Citizenship

What is a company's responsibility to society? Proponents of the modern view of stakeholder theory argue that companies have a social obligation to operate in ethically, socially, and environmentally responsible ways. This active approach is referred to as *corporate social responsibility (CSR)* or *corporate citizenship*. The idea of corporate citizenship is that a firm should conduct its business in a manner that meets its economic, legal, ethical, and philanthropic expectations.

The economic responsibilities have the highest priority. A firm must be efficient and survive over the long term in order to be useful to society. It

figure 1.11

Top Three CSR Topics Getting Attention in Your Firm

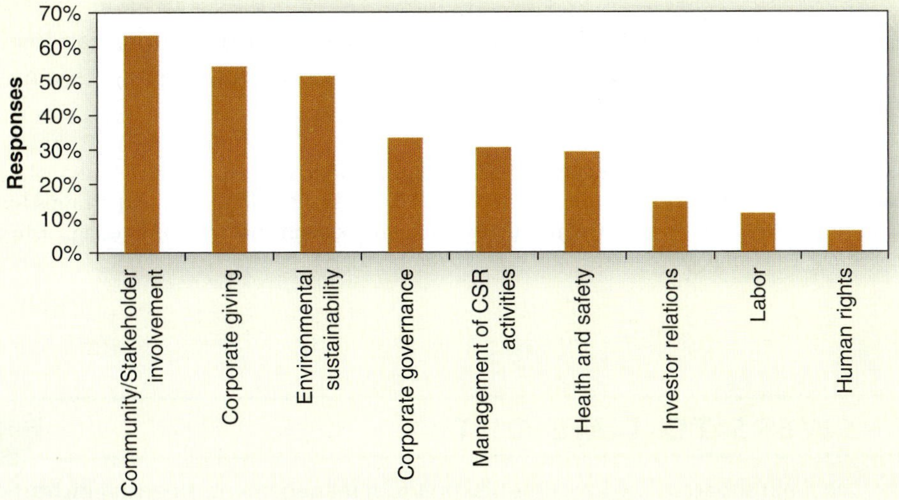

must also execute its business activities in a legal and ethical way. These responsibilities are over and above the ones codified in laws and are in line with societal norms and customs. They are expected by society even though they may be ill-defined. This could include things such as environmental ethics. Philanthropy is the least important priority. The corporate citizenship concept focuses more on engagement with stakeholders to achieve mutual goals.

Some corporations have responded to this trend by including CSR-oriented statements in their corporate goals. These statements recognize that CSR has value in a code of conduct or ethics, a commitment to local communities, an interest in employee health and education, an environmental consciousness, and recognition of social issues (diversity, social fairness, etc.). In October 2006, The Conference Board surveyed large U.S. firms on corporate citizenship issues and 198 firms responded. Figure 1.11 shows the results of the survey when firms were asked about the top three CSR topics receiving attention at the company.

What is the motivation for these companies to fund CSR programs? When asked, 92 percent stated that enhancing corporate reputation was very important. Other popular responses were for recruiting and retention (78 percent) and reducing risk (65 percent).

a. Walmart generates over $11 billion in profits per year and is the largest corporate employer in the U.S., with 1.4 million employees. But Walmart also seems to be coming under increasing pressure from different social groups for its business practices. Community groups have worked to keep Walmart from coming to their towns. Walmart claims that its low prices help everyone in the community. Also by giving over $270 million to charity last year, it is the largest corporate cash contributor in the U.S. Go to **www.wakeupwalmart.com** and describe the current stakeholder problems with Walmart. Also go to **www.walmart.com** and describe what Walmart is doing to engage these stakeholders. What is your opinion?

b. What activities might companies engage in to satisfy the four components of corporate citizenship: economic, legal, ethical, and philanthropic?

c. By embracing citizenship goals, assess whether corporations can insulate themselves from many activist actions, thereby avoiding negative media events.

References: Archie B. Carroll, "Corporate Social Responsibility: Evolution of a Definitional Construct," *Business & Society* 38, no. 3 (1999): 268–295, and David Vidal, "Reward Trumps Risk: How Business Perspectives on Corporate Citizenship and Sustainability Are Changing," *Executive Action Series,* The Conference Board, No. 216, November 2006.

ANSWERS TO TIME OUT

1-1 The main subareas are investments, financial management, financial institutions and markets, and international finance. Investors interact with the other groups by buying and selling securities through financial markets, being influenced by what to buy and sell by the quality of firms' financial management, and assessing international opportunities for investment and for firm prospects. Financial management acquires and repays capital from investors through financial institutions and markets. Financial managers must also run their businesses in an increasingly internationally integrated economy. Financial institutions and markets facilitate the allocation of capital between the investment and financial management subareas.

1-2 Finance knowledge and tools help people to understand, evaluate, and deal with financial risks in both their professional and personal lives. In addition, the application of finance helps people manage cash flow and valuation decisions. Making good cash flow and value decisions will help make business operations more successful and personal wealth grow.

1-3 In order for a business to grow very large, it needs a lot of capital. Banks and other lenders do not lend large amounts of money to individual small business owners. This leaves equity, the only other source of capital left to grow. People who provide equity capital become part owners. Owners of a business demand some control of that business. Thus, an entrepreneur must give up some control of the firm in order to access equity capital and become much larger.

1-4 The corporation can have any number of owners (stockholders) and thus can acquire vast amounts of capital. In addition, corporations have an easier time borrowing money from banks and public bond holders. Corporations also hire professional managers.

1-5 Maximizing shareholder value provides many advantages for society. For example, more people will be willing to offer their capital through buying stocks when they believe companies are trying to maximize their value. Since more capital will be offered, then more business, expansion, and employment will result. In addition, this goal gives the best opportunity for long-term existence and stability of the firm, which benefits employees and local communities.

1-6 The most common activity is to use the company's resources to benefit themselves at the expense of the shareholders. Examples include low-interest loans and unnecessary or personal use of a corporate jet, homes, or apartments. However, managers may also use their influence to get friends and relatives hired by the company or to steer them business.

1-7 The corporate governance system reduces the agency problem by monitoring management activities through many different groups and people. These people witness and report on different aspects of managers' activities. In addition, incentives may be created to align the manager's own interests with those of the shareholders.

1-8 Financial institutions are critical to the function of a capitalist society. Capitalism requires the flow of capital from those with excess funds to those with good uses for it. There are far more ideas on how to use money than there are sources of money. In other words, money is a scarce resource. The existing money must be able to flow to the best ideas and projects in order to maximize the benefit to the economy and to society. Financial institutions and markets make this happen.

PART TWO

2 Reviewing Financial Statements

viewpoints

Business Application

The managers of DPH Tree Farm, Inc., believe the firm could double its sales if it had additional factory space and acreage. If DPH purchased the factory space and acreage in 2016, these new assets would cost $27 million to build and would require an additional $1 million in cash, $5 million in accounts receivable, $6 million in inventory, and $4 million in accounts payable. In addition to accounts payable, DPH Tree Farm would finance the new assets with the sale of a combination of long-term debt (40 percent of the total) and common stock (60 percent of the total). Assuming all else stays constant, what will these changes do to DPH Tree Farm's 2016 balance sheet assets, liabilities, and equity? (See 2015 balance sheet on p. 35) **(See solution on p. 54)**

Personal Application

Chris Ryan is looking to invest in DPH Tree Farm, Inc. Chris has the most recent set of financial statements from DPH Tree Farm's annual report but is not sure how to read them or what they mean. What are the four financial statements that Chris should pay most attention to? What information will these key financial statements contain? **(See solution on p. 54)**

Thinking of starting your own business? Learn more . . .

*See Appendix 2A: Various Formats for Financial Statements online at **www.mhhe.com/can3e.**

Learning Goals

LG2-1 Recall the major financial statements that firms must prepare and provide.

LG2-2 Differentiate between book (or accounting) value and market value.

LG2-3 Explain how taxes influence corporate managers' and investors' decisions.

LG2-4 Differentiate between accounting income and cash flows.

LG2-5 Demonstrate how to use a firm's financial statements to calculate its cash flows.

LG2-6 Observe cautions that should be taken when examining financial statements.

Corporate managers must issue many reports to the public. Most stockholders, analysts, government entities, and other interested parties pay particular attention to annual reports. An annual report provides four basic *financial statements:* the balance sheet, the income statement, the statement of cash flows, and the statement of retained earnings. A **financial statement** provides an accounting-based picture of a firm's financial position.

Whereas accountants use reports to present a picture of what happened in the past, finance professionals use financial statements to draw inferences about the future. The four statements function to provide key information to managers, who make financial decisions, and to investors, who will accept or reject possible future investments in the firm. When you encountered these four financial statements in accounting classes, you learned how they function to place the right information in the right places. In this chapter, you will see how understanding these statements, which are the "right places" for crucial information, creates a solid base for your understanding of decision-making processes in managerial finance.

Financial statements of publicly traded firms can be found in a number of places. For example, all quarterly and annual financial statements can be found at a firm's website (often under a section titled "investor relations"). Financial statements of publicly traded companies are reported to the Securities and Exchange Commission (SEC), who makes them publicly available at their website (www.sec.gov); annual reports are listed under the term 10-K, and quarterly financial statements are listed as 10-Qs. Finally, a number of websites exist (e.g., finance.yahoo.com) where one can view and download financial statements of publicly traded companies. Nonpublic firms are not required to submit financial statements to the SEC. Thus, it can be quite difficult to find detailed financial information about these firms. This is one reason why some large firms (Cargill, Toys "R" Us, Fidelity) hesitate to become publicly traded; they prefer to keep their financial statement information private.

It should also be noted that this chapter presents a basic set of financial statements; enough so that, from a financial manager's viewpoint, we can identify the basic categories on each statement and relationships

financial statement

Statement that provides an accounting-based picture of a firm's financial position.

across statements. Individual firms' financial statements may look different from those presented in the chapter, depending on the level of detail and accounting methods used. Further, financial statements may be presented in various formats, e.g., in a pdf file or in an Excel spreadsheet. Appendix 2A to the chapter (located at the book's website, www.mhhe.com/can3e) presents the 2012 financial statements for Colgate-Palmolive Company as listed in its Annual Report, in its 10-K statement, and in an Excel spreadsheet. Note that while the numbers are the same in all formats, the presentation of the numbers can vary greatly.

This chapter examines each statement to clarify its major features and uses. We highlight the differences between the accounting-based (book) value of a firm (reflected in these statements) and the true market value of a firm, which we will come to understand more fully. We also make a clear distinction between accounting-based income and actual cash flows, a topic further explored in Chapter 3, where we see how important cash flows are to the study of finance.

We also open a discussion in this chapter about how firms choose to represent their earnings. We'll see that managers have substantial discretion in preparing their firms' financial statements, depending on strategic plans for the organization's future. This is worth looking into as we keep the discipline of finance grounded in a real-world context. Finally, leading into Chapter 3, we discuss some cautions to bear in mind when reviewing and analyzing financial statements.

LG2-1

2.1 • Balance Sheet

balance sheet

The financial statement that reports a firm's assets, liabilities, and equity at a particular point in time.

The **balance sheet** reports a firm's assets, liabilities, and equity at a particular point in time. It is a picture of the assets the firm owns and who has claims on these assets as of a given date, for example, December 31, 2015. A firm's assets must equal (balance) the liabilities and equity used to purchase the assets (hence the term *balance sheet*):

$$\text{Assets} = \text{Liabilities} + \text{Equity} \tag{2-1}$$

liquidity

The ease of conversion of an asset into cash at a fair value.

Figure 2.1 illustrates a basic balance sheet and Table 2.1 presents a simple balance sheet for DPH Tree Farm, Inc., as of December 31, 2015 and 2014. The left side of the balance sheet lists assets of the firm and the right side lists liabilities and equity. Both assets and liabilities are listed in descending order of **liquidity,** that is, the time and effort needed to convert the accounts to cash. The most liquid assets—called *current assets*—appear first on the asset side of the balance sheet. The least liquid, called *fixed assets,* appear last. Similarly, current liabilities—those obligations that the firm must pay within a year—appear first on the right side of the balance sheet. Stockholders' equity, which never matures, appears last on the balance sheet.

current assets

Assets that will normally convert to cash within one year.

Assets

marketable securities

Short-term, low-rate investment securities held by the firm for liquidity purposes.

fixed assets

Assets with a useful life exceeding one year.

Figure 2.1 shows that assets fall into two major categories: current assets and fixed assets. **Current assets** will normally convert to cash within one year. They include cash and **marketable securities** (short-term, low-rate investment securities held by the firm for liquidity purposes), accounts receivable, and inventory. **Fixed assets** have a useful life exceeding one year. This class of assets includes physical (tangible) assets, such as net plant and equipment, and other, less tangible, long-term assets, such as patents and trademarks. We find the value of net plant and equipment by taking the difference between gross plant and

figure 2.1

The Basic Balance Sheet

Total Assets	Total Liabilities and Equity
Current assets	Current liabilities
Cash and marketable securities	Accrued wages and taxes
Accounts receivable	Accounts payable
Inventory	Notes payable
Fixed assets	Long-term debt
Gross plant and equipment	
Less: Depreciation	Stockholders' equity
Net plant and equipment	Preferred stock
Other long-term assets	Common stock and paid-in surplus
	Retained earnings

table 2.1 | **Balance Sheet for DPH Tree Farm, Inc.**

DPH TREE FARM, INC.
Balance Sheet as of December 31, 2015 and 2014
(in millions of dollars)

	2015	2014		2015	2014
Assets			**Liabilities and Equity**		
Current assets			Current liabilities		
Cash and marketable securities	$ 24	$ 25	Accrued wages and taxes	$ 20	$ 15
Accounts receivable	70	65	Accounts payable	55	50
Inventory	111	100	Notes payable	45	45
Total	$205	$190	Total	$120	$110
Fixed assets			Long-term debt	195	190
Gross plant and equipment	$368	$300	Total debt	315	300
Less: Depreciation	53	40	Stockholders' equity		
Net plant and equipment	$315	$260	Preferred stock (5 million shares)	$ 5	$ 5
Other long-term assets	50	50	Common stock and paid-in surplus (20 million shares)	40	40
			Retained earnings	210	155
Total	$365	$310	Total	$255	$ 200
Total assets	$570	$500	Total liabilities and equity	$570	$ 500

equipment (or the fixed assets' original value) and the depreciation accumulated against the fixed assets since their purchase. Likewise, other long-term assets would be listed net of amortization.

liabilities

Funds provided by lenders to the firm.

Liabilities and Stockholders' Equity

Lenders provide funds, which become **liabilities,** to the firm. Liabilities fall into two categories as well: current or long-term. **Current liabilities** constitute the firm's obligations due within one year, including accrued wages and taxes, accounts payable, and notes payable. **Long-term debt** includes long-term loans and bonds with maturities of more than one year.

current liabilities

Obligations of the firm that are due within one year.

long-term debt

Obligations of the firm that are due in more than one year.

The difference between total assets and total liabilities of a firm is the stockholders' (or owners') equity. The firm's preferred and common stock owners provide the funds known as **stockholders' equity. Preferred stock** is a hybrid

stockholders' equity

Funds provided by the firm's preferred and common stock owners.

preferred stock

A hybrid security that has characteristics of both long-term debt and common stock.

common stock and paid-in surplus

The fundamental ownership claim in a public or private company.

retained earnings

The cumulative earnings the firm has reinvested rather than pay out as dividends.

security that has characteristics of both long-term debt and common stock. Preferred stock is similar to common stock in that it represents an ownership interest in the issuing firm but, like long-term debt, it pays a fixed periodic (dividend) payment. Preferred stock appears on the balance sheet as the cash proceeds when the firm sells preferred stock in a public offering. **Common stock and paid-in surplus** is the fundamental ownership claim in a public or private company. The proceeds from common stock and paid-in surplus appear as the other component of stockholders' equity. If the firm's managers decide to reinvest cumulative earnings (recorded on the firm's income statement) rather than pay the dividends to stockholders, the balance sheet will record these funds as **retained earnings.**

Managing the Balance Sheet

Managers must monitor a number of issues underlying items reported on their firms' balance sheets. We examine these issues in detail throughout the text. In this chapter, we briefly introduce them. These issues include:

- The accounting method for fixed asset depreciation.
- The level of net working capital.
- The liquidity position of the firm.
- The method for financing the firm's assets—equity or debt.
- The difference between the book value reported on the balance sheet and the true market value of the firm.

ACCOUNTING METHOD FOR FIXED ASSET DEPRECIATION Managers can choose the accounting method they use to record depreciation against their fixed assets. Recall from accounting that *depreciation* is the charge against income that reflects the estimated dollar cost of the firm's fixed assets. The straight-line method and the MACRS (modified accelerated cost recovery system) are two choices. Companies commonly choose MACRS when computing the firm's taxes and the straight-line method when reporting income to the firm's stockholders. The MACRS method accelerates depreciation, which results in higher depreciation expenses and lower taxable income, thus lower taxes, in the early years of a project's life. Regardless of the depreciation method used, over time both the straight-line and MACRS methods result in the same amount of depreciation and therefore tax (cash) outflows. However, because the MACRS method defers the payment of taxes to later periods, firms often favor it over the straight-line method of depreciation. We discuss this choice further in Chapter 12.

net working capital

The difference between a firm's current assets and current liabilities.

NET WORKING CAPITAL We arrive at a **net working capital** figure by taking the difference between a firm's current assets and current liabilities.

$$\text{Net working capital} = \text{Current assets} - \text{Current liabilities} \quad \textbf{(2-2)}$$

So, clearly, net working capital is positive when the firm has more current assets than current liabilities. Table 2.1 shows the 2015 and 2014 year-end balance sheets for DPH Tree Farm, Inc. At year-end 2015, the firm had $205 million of current assets and $120 million of current liabilities. So the firm's net working capital was $85 million. A firm needs cash and other liquid assets to pay its bills as expenses come due. As described in more detail in Chapter 14, liability holders monitor net working capital as a measure of a firm's ability to pay its obligations. Positive net working capital values are usually a sign of a healthy firm.

LIQUIDITY As we noted previously, any firm needs cash and other liquid assets to pay its bills as debts come due. Liquidity actually refers to two dimensions: the ease with which the firm can convert an asset to cash, and the degree to which such a conversion takes place at a fair market value. You can convert any asset to cash quickly if you price the asset low enough. But clearly, you will wish to convert the asset without giving up a great portion of its value. So a highly liquid asset can be sold quickly at its fair market value. An illiquid asset, on the other hand, cannot be sold quickly unless you reduce the price far below fair value.

Current assets, by definition, remain relatively liquid, including cash and assets that will convert to cash within the next year. Inventory is the least liquid of the current assets. Fixed assets, then, remain relatively illiquid. In the normal course of business, the firm would have no plans to liquefy or convert these tangible assets such as buildings and equipment into cash.

Liquidity presents a double-edged sword on a balance sheet. The more liquid assets a firm holds, the less likely the firm will be to experience financial distress. However, liquid assets generate little or no profits for a firm. For example, cash is the most liquid of all assets, but it earns little, if any, for the firm. In contrast, fixed assets are illiquid, but provide the means to generate revenue. Thus, managers must consider the trade-off between the advantages of liquidity on the balance sheet and the disadvantages of having money sit idle rather than generating profits.

DEBT VERSUS EQUITY FINANCING You learned in your high school physics class that levers are very useful and powerful machines—given a long enough lever, you can move almost anything. **Financial leverage** is likewise very powerful. Leverage in the financial sense refers to the extent to which a firm chooses to finance its ventures or assets by issuing debt securities. The more debt a firm issues as a percentage of its total assets, the greater its financial leverage. We discuss in later chapters why financial leverage can greatly magnify the firm's gains *and* losses for the firm's stockholders.

financial leverage

The extent to which debt securities are used by a firm.

When a firm issues debt securities—usually bonds—to finance its activities and assets, debt holders usually demand first claim to a fixed amount of the firm's cash flows. Their claims are fixed because the firm must only pay the interest owed to bondholders and any principal repayments that come due within any given period. Stockholders—who buy equity securities or stocks—claim any cash flows left after debt holders are paid. When a firm does well, financial leverage increases shareholders' rewards, since the share of the firm's profits promised to debt holders is set and predictable.

However, financial leverage also increases risk. Leverage can create the potential for the firm to experience financial distress and even bankruptcy. If the firm has a bad year and cannot make its scheduled debt payments, debt holders can force the firm into bankruptcy. But managers generally prefer to fund firm activities using debt, precisely because they can calculate the cost of doing business without giving away too much of the firm's value. As described in more detail in Chapter 16, managers often walk a fine line as they decide upon the firm's **capital structure**—the amount of debt versus equity financing held on the balance sheet—because it can determine whether the firm stays in business or goes bankrupt.

capital structure

The amount of debt versus equity financing held on the balance sheet.

book (or historical cost) value

Assets are listed on the balance sheet at the amount the firm paid for them.

LG2-2

BOOK VALUE VERSUS MARKET VALUE Beginning finance students usually have already taken accounting, so they are familiar with the accounting point of view. For example, a firm's balance sheet shows its **book (or historical cost) value** based on generally accepted accounting principles (GAAP). Under GAAP, assets appear on the balance sheet at what the firm paid for them, regardless of what those assets might be worth today if the firm were to sell them. Inflation and market forces make many assets worth more now than they were worth when the firm bought them. So in many cases, book values differ widely from **market values** for the same assets—the amount that the assets would fetch if the

market value

Assets are listed at the amount the firm would get if it sold them.

firm actually sold them. For the firm's current assets—those that mature within a year—the book value and market value of any particular asset will remain very close. For example, the balance sheet lists cash and marketable securities at their market value. Similarly, firms acquire accounts receivable and inventory and then convert these short-term assets into cash fairly quickly, so the book value of these assets is generally close to their market value.

The "book value versus market value" issue really arises when we try to determine how much a firm's fixed assets are worth. In this case, book value is often very different from market value. For example, if a firm owns land for 100 years, this asset appears on the balance sheet at its historical cost (of 100 years ago). Most likely, the firm would reap a much higher price on the land upon its sale than the historical price would indicate.

Again, accounting tools reflect the past: Balance sheet assets are listed at historical cost. Managers would thus see little relation between the total asset value listed on the balance sheet and the current market value of the firm's assets. Similarly, the stockholders' equity listed on the balance sheet generally differs from the true market value of the equity. In this case, the market value may be higher or lower than the value listed on the firm's accounting books. So financial managers and investors often find that balance sheet values are not always the most relevant numbers. The following example illustrates the difference between the book value and the market value of a firm's assets.

EXAMPLE 2-1

LG2-2

For interactive versions of this example visit www.mhhe.com/can3e

Calculating Book versus Market Value

EZ Toy, Inc., lists fixed assets of $25 million on its balance sheet. The firm's fixed assets were recently appraised at $32 million. EZ Toy, Inc.'s, balance sheet also lists current assets at $10 million. Current assets were appraised at $11 million. Current liabilities' book and market values stand at $6 million and the firm's long-term debt is $15 million. Calculate the book and market values of the firm's stockholders' equity. Construct the book value and market value balance sheets for EZ Toy, Inc.

SOLUTION:

Recall the balance sheet identity in equation 2-1: Assets = Liabilities + Equity. Rearranging this equation: Equity = Assets − Liabilities. Thus, the balance sheets would appear as follows:

	Book Value	Market Value		Book Value	Market Value
Assets			**Liabilities and Equity**		
Current assets	$ 10m	$ 11m	Current liabilities	$ 6m	$ 6m
Fixed assets	25m	32m	Long-term debt	15m	15m
			Stockholders' equity	14m	22m
Total	$ 35m	$ 43m	Total	$ 35m	$ 43m

Similar to Problems 2-17, 2-18, self-test problem 2

TIME OUT

2-1 What is a balance sheet?

2-2 Which are the most liquid assets and liabilities on a balance sheet?

2.2 • Income Statement

You will recall that **income statements** show the total revenues that a firm earns and the total expenses the firm incurs to generate those revenues over a specific period of time, for example, the year 2015. Remember that while the balance sheet reports a firm's position at a point in time, the income statement reports performance over a period of time, for example, over the last year. Figure 2.2 illustrates a basic income statement and Table 2.2 shows a simple income statement for DPH Tree Farm, Inc., for the years ended December 31, 2015 and 2014. DPH's revenues (or net sales) appear at the top of the income statement. The income statement then shows various expenses (cost of goods sold, other operating expenses, depreciation, interest, and taxes) subtracted from revenues to arrive at profit or income measures.

income statement

Financial statement that reports the total revenues and expenses over a specific period of time.

The top part of the income statement reports the firm's operating income. First, we subtract the cost of goods sold (the direct costs of producing the firm's product) from net sales to get **gross profit** (so, DPH Tree Farm enjoyed gross profits of \$155 million in 2014 and \$182 million in 2015). Next, we deduct other operating expenses from gross profits to get earnings before interest, taxes, depreciation, and amortization (**EBITDA**); DPH Tree Farm's EBITDA was \$140 million in 2014 and \$165 million in 2015. Other operating expenses include marketing and selling expenses as well as general and administrative expenses. Finally, we subtract depreciation and amortization from EBITDA to get operating profit or earnings before interest and taxes (**EBIT**) (so DPH Tree Farm's EBIT was \$128 million in 2014 and \$165 million in 2015). The EBIT figure represents the profit earned from the sale of the product without any financing cost or tax considerations.

gross profit

Net sales minus cost of goods sold.

EBITDA

Earnings before interest, taxes, depreciation, and amortization.

EBIT

Earnings before interest and taxes.

The bottom part of the income statement summarizes the firm's financial and tax structure. First, we subtract interest expense (the cost to service the firm's debt) from EBIT to get earnings before taxes (**EBT**). So, as we follow our sample income statement, DPH Tree Farm had EBT of \$110 million in 2014 and \$136 million in 2015. Of course, firms differ in their financial structures and tax situations. These differences can cause two firms with identical operating income to report differing levels of net income. For example, one firm may finance its assets with only debt, while another finances with only common equity. The company with no debt would have no interest expense. Thus, even though EBIT for the two firms is identical, the firm with all-equity financing and no debt would report higher net income. We subtract taxes from EBT to get the last item on the income

EBT

Earnings before taxes.

figure 2.2

The Basic Income Statement

Net sales	Operating income
Less: Cost of goods sold	
Gross profits	
Less: Other operating expenses	
Earnings before interest, taxes, depreciation, and amortization (EBITDA)	
Less: Depreciation and amortization	
Earnings before interest and taxes (EBIT)	
Less: Interest	Financing and tax considerations
Earnings before taxes (EBT)	
Less: Taxes	
Net income before preferred dividends	
Less: Preferred stock dividends	
Net income available to common stockholders	

table 2.2 | **Income Statement for DPH Tree Farm, Inc.**

DPH TREE FARM, INC. Income Statement for Years Ending December 31, 2015 and 2014 (in Millions of Dollars)		
	2015	**2014**
Net sales (all credit)	$ 315	$ 275
Less: Cost of goods sold	133	120
Gross profits	$ 182	$ 155
Less: Other operating expenses	17	15
Earnings before interest, taxes, depreciation, and amortization (EBITDA)	$ 165	$ 140
Less: Depreciation and amortization	13	12
Earnings before interest and taxes (EBIT)	$ 152	$ 128
Less: Interest	16	18
Earnings before taxes (EBT)	$ 136	$ 110
Less: Taxes	46	40
Net income	$ 90	$ 70
Less: Preferred stock dividends	$ 10	$ 10
Net income available to common stockholders	$ 80	$ 60
Less: Common stock dividends	25	25
Addition to retained earnings	$ 55	$ 35
Per (common) share data:		
Earnings per share (EPS)	$ 4.00	$ 3.00
Dividends per share (DPS)	$ 1.25	$ 1.25
Book value per share (BVPS)	$ 12.50	$ 9.75
Market value (price) per share (MVPS)	$ 17.25	$ 15.60

net income

The bottom line on the income statement.

statement (the "bottom line"), or **net income.** DPH Tree Farm, Inc., reported net income of $70 million in 2014 and $90 million in 2015.

Below the net income, or bottom line, on the income statement, firms often report additional information summarizing income and firm value. For example, with its $90 million of net income in 2015, DPH Tree Farm, Inc., paid its preferred stockholders cash dividends of $10 million and its common stockholders cash dividends of $25 million, and added the remaining $55 million to retained earnings. Table 2.1 shows that retained earnings on the balance sheet increased from $155 million in 2014 to $210 million in 2015. Other items reported below the bottom line include:

$$\text{Earnings per share } (EPS) = \frac{\text{Net income available to common stockholders}}{\text{Total shares of common stock outstanding}} \quad \textbf{(2-3)}$$

$$\text{Dividends per share } (DPS) = \frac{\text{Common stock dividends paid}}{\text{Number of shares of common stock outstanding}} \quad \textbf{(2-4)}$$

$$\text{Book value per share } (BVPS) = \frac{\text{Common stock} + \text{Paid-in surplus} + \text{Retained earnings}}{\text{Number of shares of common stock outstanding}} \quad \textbf{(2-5)}$$

$$\text{Market value per share } (MVPS) = \text{Market price of the firm's common stock} \quad \textbf{(2-6)}$$

We discuss these items further in Chapter 3.

Debt versus Equity Financing

As mentioned earlier, when a firm issues debt to finance its assets, it gives the debt holders first claim to a fixed amount of its cash flows. Stockholders are entitled to any residual cash flows, or net income. Thus, when a firm alters its capital structure to include more or less debt (and, in turn, less or more equity), it impacts the residual cash flows available for the stockholders, i.e., the numerator of the EPS equation. Further, as the firm alters its capital structure, it will issue more shares of stock when it increases equity to reduce debt, or it will buy back shares of stock when it decreases equity to increase debt, i.e., the denominator of the EPS equation. Thus, a change in capital structure will cause a firm's stockholders' EPS to change. The question is: Will the reduction (increase) in financial distress and bankruptcy risk from the reduction (increase) in financial leverage appease the stockholders who have lost (gained) earnings per share?

EXAMPLE 2-2

LG2-1

Impact of Capital Structure on a Firm's EPS

Consider a firm with an EBIT of $750,000. The firm finances its assets with $1,600,000 debt (costing 5 percent) and 200,000 shares of stock selling at $6.00 per share. To reduce the firm's risk associated with this financial leverage, the firm is considering reducing its debt by $600,000 by selling an additional 100,000 shares of stock. The firm is in the 40 percent tax bracket. The change in capital structure will have no effect on the operations of the firm. Thus, EBIT will remain at $750,000. Calculate the dilution in the firm's EPS from this change in capital structure.

For interactive versions of this example visit www.mhhe.com/can3e

SOLUTION:

The EPS before and after this change in capital structure is illustrated below:

Change		Before Capital Structure Change		After Capital Structure Change
EBIT		$750,000		$750,000
Less: Interest	($1,600,000 × 0.05)	80,000	($1,000,000 × 0.05)	50,000
EBT		670,000		700,000
Less: Taxes (40%)		268,000		280,000
Net income		$402,000		$420,000
Divided by # of shares		200,000		300,000
EPS		$2.01		$1.40

The change in capital structure would dilute the stockholders' EPS by $0.61.

Similar to Problems 2-5, 2-6, 2-23, 2-24

Corporate Income Taxes

LG2-3

Firms pay out a large portion of their earnings in taxes. For example, in 2012, Walmart had EBT of $24.40 billion. Of this amount, Walmart paid $6.74 billion (over 27 percent of EBT) in taxes. Firms may also defer taxes, e.g., in 2012, Walmart listed a provision for deferred taxes of $1.20 billion. Deferred taxes occur when a company postpones paying taxes on profits earned in a particular period. For example, some expenses, such as those associated with research and development or incurred in mergers, may be written off over a fixed number of years. In these cases, the firm's current year profits for tax purposes would be lower than the profits computed for accounting purposes. Thus, the company ends up postponing part of its tax liability on this year's profits to future years.

table 2.3 Corporate Tax Rates as of 2015

Taxable Income	Pay this Amount on Base Income	Plus this Percentage on Anything Over the Base
$0–$50,000	$ 0	15%
$50,001–$75,000	7,500	25
$75,001–$100,000	13,750	34
$100,001–$335,000	22,250	39
$335,001–$10,000,000	113,900	34
$10,000,001–$15,000,000	3,400,000	35
$15,000,001–$18,333,333	5,150,000	38
Over $18,333,333	6,416,667	35

Congress oversees the U.S. tax code, which determines corporate tax obligations. Corporate taxes can thus change with changes of administration or other changes in the business or public environment. As you might expect, the U.S. tax system is extremely complicated, so we do not attempt to cover it in detail here. However, firms recognize taxes as a major expense item and many financial decisions arise from tax considerations. In this section we provide a general overview of the U.S. corporate tax system.

The 2015 corporate tax schedule appears in Table 2.3. Note from this table that the U.S. tax structure is progressive, meaning that the larger the income, the higher the taxes assessed. However, corporate tax rates do not increase in any kind of linear way based on this progressive nature: They rise from a low of 15 percent to a high of 39 percent, then drop to 34 percent, rise to 38 percent, and finally drop to 35 percent.

average tax rate

The percentage of each dollar of taxable income that the firm pays in taxes.

marginal tax rate

The amount of additional taxes a firm must pay out for every additional dollar of taxable income it earns.

In addition to calculating their tax liability, firms also want to know their **average tax rate** and **marginal tax rate.** You can figure the average tax rate as the percentage of each dollar of taxable income that the firm pays in taxes.

$$\text{Average tax rate} = \frac{\text{Tax liability}}{\text{Taxable income}} \quad \textbf{(2-7)}$$

From your economics classes, you can probably guess that the firm's marginal tax rate is the amount of additional taxes a firm must pay out for every additional dollar of taxable income it earns.

EXAMPLE 2-3

LG2-3

For interactive versions of this example visit www.mhhe.com/can3e

Calculation of Corporate Taxes

Indian Point Kennels, Inc., earned $16.5 million taxable income (EBT) in 2015. Use the tax schedule in Table 2.3 to determine the firm's 2015 tax liability, its average tax rate, and its marginal tax rate.

SOLUTION:

From Table 2.3, the $16.5 million of taxable income puts Indian Point Kennels in the 38 percent marginal tax bracket. Thus

$$\begin{aligned}\text{Tax liability} &= \text{Tax on base amount} + \text{Tax rate (Amount over base)}\\ &= \$5{,}150{,}000 + 0.38(\$16{,}500{,}000 - \$15{,}000{,}000) = \$5{,}720{,}000\end{aligned}$$

Note that the base amount is the maximum dollar value listed in the previous tax bracket. In this example, we take the highest dollar value ($15,000,000) in the preceding tax bracket (35 percent). The additional percentage owed results from multiplying the income above and beyond the $15,000,000 (or $1,500,000) by the marginal tax rate (38 percent). The *average* tax rate for Indian Point Kennels, Inc., comes to:

$$\text{Average tax rate} = \frac{\text{Tax liability}}{\text{Taxable income}}$$

$$= \$5,720,000 / \$16,500,000 = 34.67\%$$

If Indian Point Kennels earned $1 more of taxable income, it would pay 38 cents (its tax rate of 38 percent) more in taxes. Thus, the firm's marginal tax rate is 38 percent.

Similar to Problems 2-7, 2-8, 2-25, 2-26, self-test problem 3

INTEREST AND DIVIDENDS RECEIVED BY CORPORATIONS Any interest that corporations receive is taxable, although a notable exception arises: Interest on state and local government bonds is exempt from federal taxes. The U.S. tax code allows this exception to encourage corporations to be better community citizens by supporting local governments. Another exception of sorts arises when one corporation owns stock in another corporation. Seventy percent of any dividends received from other corporations is tax exempt. Only the remaining 30 percent is taxed at the receiving corporation's tax rate.[1]

EXAMPLE 2-4

LG2-3

Corporate Taxes with Interest and Dividend Income

In the previous example, suppose that in addition to the $16.5 million of taxable income, Indian Point Kennels, Inc., received $250,000 of interest on state-issued bonds and $500,000 of dividends on common stock it owns in DPH Tree Farm, Inc. How do these items affect Indian Point Kennel's tax liability, average tax rate, and marginal tax rate?

For interactive versions of this example visit www.mhhe.com/can3e

SOLUTION:

In this case, interest on the state-issued bonds is not taxable and should not be included in taxable income. Further, the first 70 percent of the dividends received from DPH Tree Farm is not taxable. Thus, only 30 percent of the dividends received are taxed, so:

$$\text{Taxable income} = \$16,500,000 + (0.3)\$500,000 = \$16,650,000$$

Now Indian Point Kennel's tax liability will be:

$$\text{Tax liability} = \$5,150,000 + 0.38(\$16,650,000 - \$15,000,000) = \$5,777,000$$

The $500,000 of dividend income increased Indian Point Kennel's tax liability by $57,000. Indian Point Kennels, Inc.'s resulting average tax rate is now:

$$\text{Average tax rate} = \$5,777,000 / \$16,650,000 = 34.70\%$$

Finally, if Indian Point Kennels earned $1 more of taxable income, it would still pay 38 cents (based upon its marginal tax rate of 38 percent) more in taxes.

Similar to Problems 2-8, 2-25, 2-26

[1]This tax code provision prevents or reduces any triple taxation that could occur: Income could be taxed at three levels: (1) on the income from the dividend-paying firm, (2) as income for the dividend-receiving firm, and (3) finally, on the personal income of stockholders who receive dividends.

INTEREST AND DIVIDENDS PAID BY CORPORATIONS Corporate interest payments appear on the income statement as an expense item, so we deduct interest payments from operating income when the firm calculates taxable income. But any dividends paid by corporations to their shareholders are not tax deductible. This is one factor that encourages managers to finance projects with debt financing rather than to sell more stock. Suppose one firm uses mainly debt financing and another firm, with identical operations, uses mainly equity financing. The equity-financed firm will have very little interest expense to deduct for tax purposes. Thus, it will have higher taxable income and pay more taxes than the debt-financed firm. The debt-financed firm will pay fewer taxes and be able to pay more of its operating income to asset funders, that is, its bondholders and stockholders. So even stockholders prefer that firms finance assets primarily with debt rather than with stock. However, as mentioned earlier, increasing the amount of debt financing of the firm's assets also increases risks. So these affects must be balanced when selecting the optimal capital structure for a firm. The debt-versus-equity financing issue is called *capital structure,* which we address more fully in Part Eight of the book.

EXAMPLE 2-5

LG2-1

For interactive versions of this example visit www.mhhe.com/can3e

Effect of Debt-versus-Equity Financing on Funders' Returns

Suppose that you are considering a stock investment in one of two firms (AllDebt, Inc., and AllEquity, Inc.), both of which operate in the same industry and have identical operating incomes of $5 million. AllDebt, Inc., finances its $12 million in assets with $11 million in debt (on which it pays 10 percent interest) and $1 million in equity. AllEquity, Inc., finances its $12 million in assets with no debt and $12 million in equity. Both firms pay 30 percent tax on their taxable income. Calculate the income that each firm has available to pay its debt and stockholders (the firms' asset funders) and the resulting returns to these asset funders for the two firms.

SOLUTION:

	AllDebt	AllEquity
Operating income	$5.00m	$5.00m
Less: Interest	1.10m	0.00m
Taxable income	$3.90m	$5.00m
Less: Taxes (30%)	1.17m	1.50m
Net income	$2.73m	$3.50m
Income available for asset funders (= Operating income − Taxes)	$3.83m	$3.50m
Return on asset-funders' investment	$3.83m/$12.00m = 31.92%	$3.50m/$12.00m = 29.17%

By financing most of its assets with debt and receiving the associated tax benefits from the interest paid on this debt, AllDebt, Inc., is able to pay more of its operating income to the funders of its assets, i.e., its debt holders and stockholders, than AllEquity, Inc.

Similar to Problems 2-19, 2-20

TIME OUT

2-3 What is an income statement?

2-4 When a corporation owns stock in another corporation, what percentage of dividends received on the stock is taxed?

2.3 • Statement of Cash Flows

LG2-4

Income statements and balance sheets are the most common financial documents available to the public. However, managers who make financial decisions need more than these two statements—reports of past performance—on which to base their decisions for today and into the future. A very important distinction between the accounting point of view and the finance point of view is that financial managers and investors are *far more interested in actual cash flows* than in the backward-looking profit listed on the income statement.

The **statement of cash flows** is a financial statement that shows the firm's cash flows over a given period of time. This statement reports the amounts of cash the firm has generated and distributed during a particular time period. The bottom line on the statement of cash flows—the difference between cash sources and uses—equals the change in cash and marketable securities on the firm's balance sheet from the previous year's balance. That is, the statement of cash flows reconciles noncash balance sheet items and income statement items to show changes in the cash and marketable securities account on the balance sheet over the particular analysis period.

statement of cash flows
Financial statement that shows the firm's cash flows over a period of time.

To clarify why this statement is so crucial, it helps to understand that figures on an income statement may not represent the actual cash inflows and outflows for a firm during a given period of time. There are two main issues, GAAP accounting principles and non-cash income statement entries.

GAAP Accounting Principles

Company accountants must prepare firm income statements following GAAP principles. GAAP procedures require that the firm recognize revenue at the time of sale. But sometimes the company receives the cash before or after the time of sale. Likewise, GAAP counsels the firm to show production and other expenses on the income statement as the sales of those goods take place. So production and other expenses associated with a particular product's sale appear on the income statement (for example, cost of goods sold and depreciation) only when that product sells. Of course, just as with revenue recognition, actual cash outflows incurred with production may occur at a very different point in time—usually much earlier than GAAP principles allow the firm to formally recognize the expenses.

Noncash Income Statement Entries

Further, income statements contain several noncash entries, the largest of which is depreciation. Depreciation attempts to capture the noncash expense incurred as fixed assets deteriorate from the time of purchase to the point when those assets must be replaced.

Let's illustrate the effect of depreciation: Suppose a firm purchases a machine for $100,000. The machine has an expected life of five years and at the end of those five years, the machine will have no expected salvage value. The firm incurs a $100,000 cash outflow at the time of purchase. But the entire $100,000 does not appear on the income statement in the year that the firm purchases the machine—in accounting terms, the machine is not expensed in the year of purchase. Rather, if the firm's accounting department uses the straight-line depreciation method, it deducts only $100,000/5, or $20,000, each year as an expense. This $20,000 equipment expense is not a cash outflow for the firm. The person in charge of buying the machine knows that the cash flow occurred at the time of purchase—and it totaled $100,000 rather than $20,000.

In conclusion, finance professionals know that the firm needs cash, not accounting profits, to pay the firm's obligations as they come due, to fund the firm's operations and growth, and to compensate the firm's ultimate owners: its shareholders.

LG2-5

Sources and Uses of Cash

In general, some activities increase cash (cash sources) and some decrease cash (cash uses). Figure 2.3 classifies the firm's basic cash sources and uses. Cash sources include decreasing noncash assets or increasing liabilities (or equity). For example, a drop in accounts receivable means that the firm has collected cash from its credit sales—a cash source. Likewise, if a firm sells new common stock, the firm has used primary markets to raise cash. In contrast, a firm uses cash when it increases noncash assets (buying inventory) or decreases a liability (paying off a bank loan). The statement of cash flows separates these cash flows into three categories or sections:

1. Cash flows from operating activities.
2. Cash flows from investing activities.
3. Cash flows from financing activities.
4. Net change in cash and marketable securities.

The basic setup of a statement of cash flows is shown in Figure 2.4 and a more detailed statement of cash flows for DPH Tree Farm for the year ending December 31, 2015, appears as Table 2.4.

cash flows from operations

Cash flows that are the direct result of the production and sale of the firm's products.

Cash flows from operations (Section A in Figure 2.4 and Table 2.4) are those cash inflows and outflows that result directly from producing and selling the firm's products. These cash flows include:

- Net income (adding back depreciation,[2] a noncash expense item that is included in net income).
- Working capital accounts other than cash and operations-related short-term debt.

Most finance professionals consider this top section of the statement of cash flows to be the most important. It shows quickly and compactly the firm's cash flows generated by and used for the production process. For example, DPH Tree Farm,

figure 2.3

Sources and Uses of Cash

Sources of Cash	Uses of Cash
Net income	Net losses
Depreciation	Increase a noncash current asset
Decrease a noncash current asset	Increase a fixed asset
Decrease a fixed asset	Decrease a current liability
Increase a current liability	Decrease long-term debt
Increase long-term debt	Repurchase common or preferred stock
Sell common or preferred stock	Pay dividends

[2]Any other noncash expense (e.g., amortization) would also be added back to net income and any noncash revenue would be subtracted.

figure 2.4

The Statement of Cash Flows

Section A. Cash flows from operating activities
- Net income
- Additions (sources of cash):
  - Depreciation
  - Decrease in noncash current assets (e.g., decrease in accounts receivable)
  - Increase in accrued wages and taxes
  - Increase in accounts payable
- Subtractions (uses of cash):
  - Increase in noncash current assets (e.g., increase in inventory)
  - Decrease in accrued wages and taxes
  - Decrease in accounts payable

Section B. Cash flows from investing activities
- Additions:
  - Decrease in fixed assets
  - Decrease in other long-term assets
- Subtractions:
  - Increase in fixed assets
  - Increase in other long-term assets

Section C. Cash flows from financing activities
- Additions:
  - Increase in notes payable
  - Increase in long-term debt
  - Increase in common and preferred stock
- Subtraction:
  - Decrease in notes payable
  - Decrease in long-term debt
  - Decrease in common and preferred stock
  - Dividends paid

Section D. Net change in cash and marketable securities

Inc., generated $97 million in cash flows from its 2015 production. That is, producing and selling the firm's product resulted in a net cash inflow for the firm. Managers and investors look for positive cash flows from operations as a sign of a successful firm—positive cash flows from the firm's operations is precisely what gives the firm value. Unless the firm has a stable, healthy pattern in its cash flows from operations, it is not financially healthy no matter what its level of cash flow from investing activities or cash flows from financing activities.

Cash flows from investing activities (Section B in Figure 2.4 and Table 2.4) are cash flows associated with buying or selling of fixed or other long-term assets. This section of the statement of cash flows shows cash inflows and outflows from long-term investing activities—most significantly the firm's investment in fixed assets. For example, DPH Tree Farm, Inc., used $68 million in cash to purchase fixed and other long-term assets in 2015. DPH funded this $68 million cash outflow with the $97 million cash surplus DPH Tree Farm produced from its operations.

cash flows from investing activities

Cash flows associated with the purchase or sale of fixed or other long-term assets.

Cash flows from financing activities (Section C in Figure 2.4 and Table 2.4) are cash flows that result from debt and equity financing transactions. These include raising cash by:

- Issuing short-term debt
- Issuing long-term debt
- Issuing stock

cash flows from financing activities

Cash flows that result from debt and equity financing transactions.

table 2.4 | **Statement of Cash Flows for DPH Tree Farm, Inc.**

DPH TREE FARM, INC. Statement of Cash Flows for Year Ending December 31, 2015 (in millions of dollars)	2015
Section A. Cash flows from operating activities	
Net income	$ 90
Additions (sources of cash):	
Depreciation	13
Increase in accrued wages and taxes	5
Increase in accounts payable	5
Subtractions (uses of cash):	
Increase in accounts receivable	−5
Increase in inventory	−11
Net cash flow from operating activities	$ 97
Section B. Cash flows from investing activities	
Subtractions:	
Increase in fixed assets	−$ 68
Increase in other long-term assets	0
Net cash flow from investing activities	−$ 68
Section C. Cash flows from financing activities	
Additions:	
Increase in notes payable	$ 0
Increase in long-term debt	5
Increase in common and preferred stock	0
Subtractions:	
Preferred stock dividends paid	−10
Common stock dividends paid	−25
Net cash flow from financing activities	−$ 30
Section D. Net change in cash and marketable securities	−$ 1

or using cash to:

- Pay dividends
- Pay off debt
- Buy back stock

In 2015, DPH Tree Farm, Inc.'s, financing activities produced a net cash outflow of $30 million. As we saw with cash flows from financing activities, this $30 million cash outflow was funded (at least partially) with the $97 million cash surplus DPH Tree Farm produced from its operations. Managers, investors, and analysts normally expect the cash flows from financing activities to include small amounts of net borrowing along with dividend payments. If, however, a firm is going through a major period of expansion, net borrowing could reasonably be much higher.

net change in cash and marketable securities

The sum of the cash flows from operations, investing activities, and financing activities.

Net change in cash and marketable securities (Section D in Figure 2.4 and Table 2.4), the bottom line of the statement of cash flows, shows the sum of cash flows from operations, investing activities, and financing activities. This sum will reconcile to the net change in cash and marketable securities account on the balance sheet over the period of analysis. For example, the bottom line of the statement of cash flows for DPH Tree Farm is −$1 million. This is also the change in the cash and marketable securities account on the balance sheet (in Table 2.1) between 2014 and 2015 ($24 million − $25 million = −$1 million). In this case, the firm's operating, investing, and financing activities combined to produce a net drain on the firm's cash during 2015—cash outflows were greater than cash inflows, largely because of the $68 million investment in long-term and fixed assets. Of course, when the bottom line is positive, a firm's cash inflows exceed cash outflows for the period.

Even though a company may report a large amount of net income on its income statement during a year, the firm may actually receive a positive, negative, or zero amount of cash. For example, DPH Tree Farm, Inc., reported net income of \$90 million on its income statement (in Table 2.2), yet reported a net change in cash and marketable securities of −\$1 million on its statement of cash flows (in Table 2.4). Accounting rules under GAAP create this sense of discord: Net income is the result of accounting rules, or GAAP, that do not necessarily reflect the firm's cash flows. While the income statement shows a firm's accounting-based income, the statement of cash flows more often reflects reality today and is thus more important to managers and investors as they seek to answer such important questions as:

- Does the firm generate sufficient cash to pay its obligations, thus avoiding financial distress?
- Does the firm generate sufficient cash to purchase assets needed for sustained growth?
- Does the firm generate sufficient cash to pay down its outstanding debt obligations?

2.4 • Free Cash Flow

The statement of cash flows measures net cash flow as net income plus noncash adjustments. However, to maintain cash flows over time, firms must continually replace working capital and fixed assets and develop new products. Thus, firm managers cannot use the available cash flows any way they please. Specifically, the value of a firm's operations depends on the future expected **free cash flows,** defined as after-tax operating profit minus the amount of new investment in working capital, fixed assets, and the development of new products. Thus, free cash flow represents the cash that is actually available for distribution to the investors in the firm—the firm's debt holders and stockholders—after the investments that are necessary to sustain the firm's ongoing operations are made.

free cash flows

The cash that is actually available for distribution to the investors in the firm after the investments that are necessary to sustain the firm's ongoing operations are made.

To calculate free cash flow (FCF), we use the mathematical equation that appears below:

$$\begin{aligned} FCF &= [EBIT\,(1 - \text{Tax rate}) + \text{Depreciation}] - [\Delta\text{Gross fixed assets} \\ &\qquad + \Delta\text{Net operating working capital}] \\ &= [NOPAT + \text{Depreciation}] - \text{Investment in operating capital} \\ &= \text{Operating cash flow} - \text{Investment in operating capital} \end{aligned} \quad \textbf{(2-8)}$$

Notice from this equation that free cash flow merges information from the income statement (performance) with information from the balance sheet (resources used to produce performance).

To calculate free cash flow, we start with operating cash flow. Firms generate operating cash flow (OCF) after they have paid necessary operating expenses and taxes. This **net operating profit after taxes (NOPAT)** is the net profit a firm earns after taxes, but before any financing costs. It is the profit available for debt holders and stockholders if the firm does not replace existing or invest in new working capital or fixed assets. Depreciation, a noncash charge, is added back to NOPAT to determine total OCF. We add other relevant noncash charges, such as amortization and depletion, back as well. Firms either buy physical assets or earmark funds for eventual equipment replacement to sustain firm operations; this is called *investment in operating capital (IOC).* In accounting terms, IOC includes the firm's gross investments (or changes) in fixed assets, current

net operating profit after taxes (NOPAT)

Net profit a firm earns after taxes but before any financing costs.

assets, and spontaneous current liabilities (such as accounts payable and accrued wages). Thus, free cash flow measures how well managers utilize the resources of the company to increase firm performance and, thus, enhance shareholder wealth.

EXAMPLE 2-6

LG2-5

For interactive versions of this example visit www.mhhe.com/can3e

Calculating Free Cash Flow

From Tables 2.1 and 2.2, in 2015, DPH Tree Farm, Inc., had EBIT of $152 million, a tax rate of 33.82 percent ($46m/$136m), and depreciation expense of $13 million. Therefore, DPH Tree Farm's operating cash flow was:

$$\begin{aligned} OCF &= EBIT\,(1 - \text{Tax rate}) + \text{Depreciation} \\ &= \$152\text{m}\,(1 - 0.3382) + \$13\text{m} = \$114\text{m} \end{aligned}$$

DPH Tree Farm's gross fixed assets increased by $68 million between 2014 and 2015. The firm's current assets increased by $15 million and spontaneous current liabilities increased by $10 million ($5 million in accrued wages and taxes and $5 million in accounts payable). Therefore, DPH's investment in operating capital for 2015 was:

$$\begin{aligned} IOC &= \Delta\text{Gross fixed assets} + \Delta\text{Net operating working capital} \\ &= \$68\text{m} + (\$15\text{m} - \$10\text{m}) = \$73\text{m} \end{aligned}$$

Accordingly, what was DPH Tree Farm's free cash flow for 2015?

SOLUTION:

$$\begin{aligned} FCF &= \text{Operating cash flow} - \text{Investment in operating capital} \\ &= \$114\text{m} - \$73\text{m} = \$41\text{m} \end{aligned}$$

In other words, in 2015, DPH Tree Farm, Inc., had cash flows of $41 million available to pay its stockholders and debt holders.

Similar to Problems 2-11, 2-12, self-test problem 4

Like the bottom line shown on the statement of cash flows, the level of free cash flow can be positive, zero, or negative. A positive free cash flow value means that the firm may distribute funds to its investors (debt holders and stockholders.) When the firm's free cash flows come in as zero or negative, however, the firm's operations produce no cash flows available for investors. Of course, if free cash flow is negative because operating cash flow is negative, investors are likely to take up the issue with the firm's management. Negative free cash flows as a result of negative operating cash flows generally indicate that the firm is experiencing operating or managerial problems. A firm with positive operating cash flows, but negative free cash flows, however, is not necessarily a poorly managed firm. Firms that invest heavily in operating capital to support growth often have positive operating cash flows but negative free cash flows. But in this case, the negative free cash flow will likely result in growing future profits.

TIME OUT

2-5 What is a statement of cash flows?

2-6 What are the main sections on the statement of cash flows?

table 2.5 | **Statement of Retained Earnings for DPH Tree Farm, Inc.**

DPH TREE FARM, INC. Statement of Retained Earnings as of December 31, 2015 (in millions of dollars)		
		2015
Balance of retained earnings, December 31, 2014		$155
Plus: Net income for 2015		90
Less: Cash dividends paid		
Preferred stock	$10	
Common stock	25	
Total cash dividends paid		35
Balance of retained earnings, December 31, 2015		$210

2.5 • Statement of Retained Earnings

The **statement of retained earnings** provides additional details about changes in retained earnings during a reporting period. This financial statement reconciles net income earned during a given period and any cash dividends paid within that period on one side with the change in retained earnings between the beginning and ending of the period on the other. Table 2.5 presents DPH Tree Farm, Inc.'s, statement of retained earnings as of December 31, 2015. The statement shows that DPH Tree Farms brought in a net income of $90 million during 2015. The firm paid out $10 million in dividends to preferred stockholders and another $25 million to common stockholders. The firm then had $55 million to reinvest back into the firm, which shows as an increase in retained earnings. Thus, the retained earnings account on the balance sheet (Table 2.1) increased from $155 million at year-end 2014 to $210 million at year-end 2015.

statement of retained earnings

Financial statement that reconciles net income earned during a given period and any cash dividends paid with the change in retained earnings over the period.

Increases in retained earnings occur not just because a firm has net income, but also because the firm's common stockholders agree to let management reinvest net income back into the firm rather than pay it out as dividends. If the shareholders disagreed with the firm's policy, they would simply sell their shares. Reinvesting earnings is less expensive than raising capital from outside sources (debt and equity markets). Further, reinvesting net income into retained earnings allows the firm to grow by providing additional funds that can be spent on plant and equipment, inventory, and other assets needed to generate even more profit. So, retained earnings represent a claim against all of the firm's assets and not against a particular asset.

LG2-1

EXAMPLE 2-7

Statement of Retained Earnings

Indian Point Kennels, Inc., earned net income in 2015 of $10.78 million. The firm paid out $1 million in cash dividends to its preferred stockholders and $2.5 million in cash dividends to its common stockholders. The firm ended 2014 with $135.75 million in retained earnings. Construct a statement of retained earnings to calculate the year-end 2015 balance of retained earnings.

For interactive versions of this example visit www.mhhe.com/can3e

SOLUTION:

The statement of retained earnings for 2015 is as follows:

INDIAN POINT KENNELS, INC. Statement of Retained Earnings as of December 31, 2015 (in millions of dollars)		
Balance of retained earnings, December 31, 2014		$135.75
Plus: Net income for 2015		10.78
Less: Cash dividends paid		
Preferred stock	$1.0	
Common stock	2.5	
Total cash dividends paid		3.50
Balance of retained earnings, December 31, 2015		$143.03

Similar to Problems 2-13, 2-14, self-test problem 1

TIME OUT

2-7 What is a statement of retained earnings?

2-8 If, during a given period, a firm pays out more in dividends than it has net income, what happens to the firm's retained earnings?

LG2-6

2.6 • Cautions in Interpreting Financial Statements

As we mentioned earlier in the chapter, firms must prepare their financial statements according to GAAP. GAAP provides a common set of standards intended to produce objective and precise financial statements. But recall also that managers have significant discretion over their reported earnings. Managers and financial analysts have recognized for years that firms use considerable latitude in using accounting rules to manage their reported earnings in a wide variety of contexts. Indeed, within the GAAP framework, firms can "smooth" earnings. That is, firms often take steps to over- or understate earnings at various times. Managers may choose to smooth earnings to show investors that firm assets are growing steadily. Similarly, one firm may be using straight-line depreciation for its fixed assets, while another is using a modified accelerated cost recovery method (MACRS), which causes depreciation to accrue quickly. If the firm uses MACRS accounting methods, its managers write fixed asset values down quickly; assets will thus have lower book values than if the firm used straight-line depreciation methods.

earnings management

The process of controlling a firm's earnings.

Sarbanes-Oxley Act of 2002

Requires that a firm's senior management must sign off on the financial statements of the firm, certifying the statements as accurate and representative of the firm's financial condition during the period covered.

This process of controlling a firm's earnings is called **earnings management.** At the extreme, earnings management has resulted in some widely reported accounting scandals involving Enron, Merck, WorldCom, and other major U.S. corporations that tried to artificially influence their earnings by manipulating accounting rules. Congress responded to the spate of corporate scandals that emerged after 2001 with the **Sarbanes-Oxley Act,** passed in June 2002. Sarbanes-Oxley requires public companies to ensure that their corporate boards' audit committees have considerable experience applying generally accepted accounting principles (GAAP) for financial statements. The act also requires that a firm's senior management must sign off on the financial statements of the firm, certifying the

finance at work — markets

AMERICAN APPAREL RECEIVES NYSE AMEX DELISTING LETTERS RELATING TO LATE FILING OF 10-QS AND 10-K

American Apparel (APP), a vertically integrated manufacturer, distributor, and retailer of branded fashion basic apparel, is an extreme example of a firm that failed to comply with SEC and Sarbanes-Oxley Act requirements three times over a period of less than one year. The result each time was a notice of delisting sent to the firm by the SEC. APP was eventually able to address the issues and is still an exchange-listed company.

On May 19, 2010, APP announced its preliminary first quarter 2010 financial results. In the announcement, American Apparel stated that, "While the financial results reported herein are preliminary and subject to adjustment, American Apparel is working to complete the preparation and review of the financial statements, and related disclosures, for the quarter ended March 31, 2010. The company is still reviewing certain items, including retail store impairment, inventory reserves and the provision for income taxes. Until the review of these items is completed, the company is not in a position to complete the preparation of the financial statements and certain related information required to be included in its Quarterly Report on Form 10-Q for the quarter ended March 31, 2010 . . . No assurances can be given as to when the Form 10-Q will ultimately be filed, or that the financial statements contained therein will not differ materially from those presented in this preliminary earnings release" (Press Release, May 19, 2010).

On May 18, 2010, APP received a letter from the NYSE Amex stating that the company's failure to timely file the Form 10-Q is a material violation of the company's listing agreement with the Exchange. The letter stated that by June 1, 2010, the company must submit a plan to the Exchange outlining how it would bring the company into compliance by no later than August 16, 2010. APP submitted their plan of compliance and on June 23, 2010, the Exchange announced the plan as accepted. APP filed its first quarter 2010 10-Q on August 17, 2010.

This was not the end, however, as APP had yet to file its second quarter 10-Q. On August 23, 2010, APP announced that it received a second letter from the NYSE Amex stating that the company's failure to timely file the Form 10-Q is a material violation of the company's listing agreement with the Exchange. APP stated that the delay in filing had been caused by the resignation of Deloitte & Touche, APP's auditor. Deloitte said it found material weaknesses in internal controls over financial reporting and that, consequently, the company's 2009 financial statements may not be reliable. Subsequently, the company was again threatened with being delisted for failing to submit a quarterly earnings report. This time the Exchange accepted AAPP's plan to file the second quarter 10-Q no later than November 15, 2010. APP filed its second quarter 2010 10-Q on November 1, 2010.

Still facing trouble, on March 22, 2011, APP announced that it could not meet an SEC deadline to file its annual report. The company received a third notice of delisting in less than a year. In this case, because of the issues that arose regarding the 2009 annual report, the company was in violation for both its 2009 and 2010 annual reports. The letter from the Exchange stated that the filing of a complete 2009 10-K, which included audited financials, was a condition for the company's continued listing on the Exchange. APP filed an amended 2009 10-K on February 7, 2011, and its 2010 10-K on March 31, with amendments on May 2, May 3, and May 17.

! want to know more? Key Words to Search For Updates: Sarbanes-Oxley Act of 2002, stock delistings, 10Q filing, 10K filing

statements as accurate and representative of the firm's financial condition during the period covered. If a firm's board of directors or senior managers fail to comply with Sarbanes-Oxley (SOX), the firm may be delisted from stock exchanges.

As illustrated in the Finance at Work reading, American Apparel failed to file quarterly and annual reports in 2010 and 2011 in a timely manner. As a result, the firm's common stock became subject to delisting. Congress's goal in passing SOX was to prevent deceptive accounting and management practices and to bring stability to jittery stock markets battered in 2002 by accounting and managerial scandals that cost employees their life savings and harmed many innocent shareholders as well. See also the discussion of the role of ethics in finance in Chapter 1.

TIME OUT

2-9 What is earnings management?

viewpoints REVISITED

Business Application Solution

If the managers of DPH Tree Farm increase the firm's fixed assets by $27 million and net working capital by $8 million in 2016, the balance sheet would look like the following one (Table 2.6). That is, gross fixed assets increase by $27 million, to $395 million; cash, accounts receivable, and inventory would increase by $1 million, $5 million, and $6 million, respectively. DPH Tree Farm's total assets will thus grow by $39 million to $609 million by year-end 2016. This growth in assets would be financed with $4 million in accounts payable, and the remaining $35 million will be financed with 40 percent long-term debt ($0.4 \times \$35m = \$14m$) and 60 percent with common stock ($0.6 \times \$35m = \$21m$).

Personal Application Solution

As Chris Ryan examines the 2015 financial statements for DPH Tree Farm, Inc., she needs to remember that the balance sheet reports a firm's assets, liabilities, and equity at a particular point in time, the income statement reports the total revenues and expenses over a specific period of time, the statement of cash flows shows the firm's cash flows over a period of time, and the statement of retained earnings reconciles net income earned during a given period and any cash dividends paid with the change in retained earnings over the period.

GAAP procedures dictate how each financial statement is prepared. GAAP requires that the firm recognizes revenue when the firm sells the product, which is not necessarily when the firm receives the cash. Likewise, under GAAP, expenses appear on the income statement as they match sales. That is, the income statement recognizes production and other expenses associated with sales when the firm sells the product. Again, the actual cash outflow associated with producing the goods may actually occur at a very different time than that reported.

(continued)

table 2.6 | **Revised Balance Sheet for DPH Tree Farm, Inc.**

DPH TREE FARM, INC.
Balance Sheet as of December 31, 2016
(in millions of dollars)

	2016			2016	
Assets			**Liabilities and Equity**		
Current assets:			Current liabilities:		
Cash	$ 25	($24 + $1)	Accrued wages and taxes	$ 20	
Accounts receivable	75	($70 + $5)	Accounts payable	59	($55 + $4)
Inventory	117	($111 + $6)	Notes payable	45	
Total	$ 217		Total	$ 124	
Fixed assets:					
Gross plant and equipment	$ 395	($368 + $27)	Long-term debt:	$ 209	($195 + 0.4($39 − $4))
Less: Depreciation	53		Stockholders' equity:		
Net plant and equipment	$ 342		Preferred stock (5 million shares)	$ 5	
Other long-term assets	50		Common stock and paid-in surplus (20 million shares)	61	($40 + 0.6($39 − $4))
			Retained earnings	210	
Total	$ 392		Total	$ 276	
Total assets	$ 609	($570 + $39)	Total liabilities and equity	$ 609	($570 + $39)

viewpoints REVISITED

Personal Application Solution (concluded)

In addition, the income statement contains several noncash items, the largest of which is depreciation. As a result, figures shown on an income statement may not be representative of the actual cash inflows and outflows for a firm during any particular period.

For investors like Chris Ryan, the actual cash flows are often more important than the accounting profit listed on the income statement. Cash, not accounting profit, is needed to pay the firm's obligations as they come due: to fund the firm's operations and growth, and to compensate the firm's owners. So Chris is more likely to find the answers she seeks in the statement of cash flows, which shows the firm's cash flows over a given period of time. The statement of cash flows reports the amounts of cash generated and cash distributed by a firm during the time period analyzed.

Finally, Chris must remember that firms are required to prepare their financial statements according to GAAP. GAAP allows managers to have significant discretion over their reported earnings, in other words, to *manage earnings.* Indeed, managers can report their results in a way that indicates to investors that the firm's assets are growing more steadily than may really be the case. Similarly, the choice of depreciation method—straight-line or MACRS—for fixed assets may make two firms with identical fixed assets appear to have very different results. Thus, Chris may need to delve more deeply into research about this firm's—or any firm's—financial condition before she makes any final investment decision.

summary of learning goals

This chapter reviewed the four basic financial statements. We examined each statement's major features. The chapter also discussed cautions that readers of financial statements should take when reviewing the documents.

LG2-1 **Recall the major financial statements that firms must prepare and provide.** In any annual report, you will find the four basic financial statements—the balance sheet, the income statement, the statement of cash flows, and the statement of retained earnings. These four statements provide an accounting-based picture of a firm's financial position. These statements often provide a key source of information for firm managers to make financial decisions and for investors to decide whether to invest in the firm.

LG2-2 **Differentiate between book (or accounting) value and market value.** A firm's balance sheet shows its book (or historical cost) value based on generally accepted accounting principles (GAAP). Under GAAP, assets are listed on the balance sheet at the amount the firm paid for them, regardless of what they might be worth today. Market value is the amount the firm would get if it actually sold an asset. The book value and market value of a firm's current assets are generally very close in value. However, the book value of a firm's fixed assets is often very different from the market value.

LG2-3 **Explain how taxes influence corporate managers' and investors' decisions.** Firms pay out a large portion of their earnings as taxes. The U.S. Congress sets (and often changes) the U.S. tax code, which in turn determines corporate tax obligations. The U.S. tax system is extremely complicated and we do not attempt to cover it in detail here. However, taxes are a major expense item for a firm and they are a crucial part of many financial decisions.

LG2-4 Differentiate between accounting income and cash flows. The income statement is prepared using GAAP. Following GAAP, revenue is recognized at the time of sale, which is not necessarily when cash is received. Likewise, under GAAP, expenses appear on the income statement as they match sales. That is, production and other expenses associated with the sales reported on the income statement (for example, cost of goods sold and depreciation) are recognized at the time the product is sold. Again, the actual cash outflow associated with these expenses may occur at a very different point in time.

In addition, the income statement contains several noncash items. The largest is depreciation. As a result, figures shown on an income statement may not represent the actual cash inflows and outflows for a firm during a particular period. For the financial manager and investors, however, these cash flows are precisely the most important information available among the financial documents—more important than the accounting profit listed on the income statement. Cash, not accounting profit, is needed to pay the firm's obligations as they come due, to fund operations and growth, and to compensate firm owners.

LG2-5 Demonstrate how to use a firm's financial statements to calculate its cash flows. The statement of cash flows is the financial statement that shows the firm's cash flows over a given period of time. The statement of cash flows reports how much cash the firm generates and distributes during the time period analyzed. The bottom line of the statement of cash flows—the difference between cash sources and cash uses—equals the change in cash and marketable securities on the firm's balance sheet. That is, the statement of cash flows reconciles income statement items and noncash balance sheet items to get to the change in the cash and marketable securities account on the balance sheet over the period of analysis.

LG2-6 Observe cautions that should be taken when examining financial statements. Firms must prepare their financial statements according to GAAP, which provides a common set of standards intended to produce financial statements that are objective and precise. However, GAAP also allows managers significant discretion over the firm's reported earnings. Managers and financial analysts have recognized for years that firms use considerable latitude in accounting rules to manage their reported earnings in a wide variety of contexts.

chapter equations

2-1 $$\text{Assets} = \text{Liabilities} + \text{Equity}$$

2-2 $$\text{Net working capital} = \text{Current assets} - \text{Current liabilities}$$

2-3 $$\text{Earnings per share } (EPS) = \frac{\text{Net income available to common stockholders}}{\text{Total shares of common stock outstanding}}$$

2-4 $$\text{Dividends per share } (DPS) = \frac{\text{Common stock dividends paid}}{\text{Number of shares of common stock outstanding}}$$

2-5 $$\text{Book value per share } (BVPS) = \frac{\text{Common stock} + \text{Paid-in surplus} + \text{Retained earnings}}{\text{Number of shares of common stock outstanding}}$$

2-6 $$\text{Market value per share } (MVPS) = \text{Market price of the firm's common stock}$$

2-7 $$\text{Average tax rate} = \frac{\text{Tax liability}}{\text{Taxable income}}$$

2-8 $$\begin{aligned} FCF &= [EBIT(1 - \text{Tax rate}) + \text{Depreciation}] - [\Delta\text{Gross fixed assets} \\ &\quad + \Delta\text{Net operating working capital}] \\ &= [NOPAT + \text{Depreciation}] - \text{Investment in operating capital} \\ &= \text{Operating cash flow} - \text{Investment in operating capital} \end{aligned}$$

key terms

average tax rate, The percentage of each dollar of taxable income that the firm pays in taxes. *p. 42*

balance sheet, The financial statement that reports a firm's assets, liabilities, and equity at a particular point in time. *p. 34*

book (or historical cost) value, Assets are listed on the balance sheet at the amount the firm paid for them. *p. 37*

capital structure, The amount of debt versus equity financing held on the balance sheet. *p. 37*

cash flows from financing activities, Cash flows that result from debt and equity financing transactions. *p. 47*

cash flows from investing activities, Cash flows associated with the purchase or sale of fixed or other long-term assets. *p. 47*

cash flows from operations, Cash flows that are the direct result of the production and sale of the firm's products. *p. 46*

common stock and paid-in surplus, The fundamental ownership claim in a public or private company. *p. 36*

current assets, Assets that will normally convert to cash within one year. *p. 34*

current liabilities, Obligations of the firm that are due within one year. *p. 35*

earnings management, The process of controlling a firm's earnings. *p. 52*

EBIT, Earnings before interest and taxes. *p. 39*

EBITDA, Earnings before interest, taxes, depreciation, and amortization. *p. 39*

EBT, Earnings before taxes. *p. 39*

financial leverage, The extent to which debt securities are used by a firm. *p. 37*

financial statement, Statement that provides an accounting-based picture of a firm's financial position. *p. 33*

fixed assets, Assets with a useful life exceeding one year. *p. 34*

free cash flows, The cash that is actually available for distribution to the investors in the firm after the investments that are necessary to sustain the firm's ongoing operations are made. *p. 49*

gross profit, Net sales minus cost of goods sold. *p. 39*

income statement, Financial statement that reports the total revenues and expenses over a specific period of time. *p. 39*

liabilities, Funds provided by lenders to the firm. *p. 35*

liquidity, The ease of conversion of an asset into cash at a fair value. *p. 34*

long-term debt, Obligations of the firm that are due in more than one year. *p. 35*

marginal tax rate, The amount of additional taxes a firm must pay out for every additional dollar of taxable income it earns. *p. 42*

marketable securities, Short-term, low-rate investment securities held by the firm for liquidity purposes. *p. 48*

market value, Assets are listed at the amount the firm would get if it sold them. *p. 37*

net change in cash and marketable securities, The sum of the cash flows from operations, investing activities, and financing activities. *p. 48*

net income, The bottom line on the income statement. *p. 40*

net operating profit after taxes (NOPAT), Net profit a firm earns after taxes but before any financing costs. *p. 49*

net working capital, The difference between a firm's current assets and current liabilities. *p. 36*

preferred stock, A hybrid security that has characteristics of both long-term debt and common stock. *p. 35*

retained earnings, The cumulative earnings the firm has reinvested rather than pay out as dividends. *p. 36*

Sarbanes-Oxley Act of 2002, Requires that a firm's senior management must sign off on the financial statements of the firm, certifying the statements as accurate and representative of the firm's financial condition during the period covered. *p. 52*

statement of cash flows, Financial statement that shows the firm's cash flows over a period of time. *p. 45*

statement of retained earnings, Financial statement that reconciles net income earned during a given period and any cash dividends paid with the change in retained earnings over the period. *p. 51*

stockholders' equity, Funds provided by the firm's preferred and common stock owners. *p. 35*

self-test problems with solutions

LG2-1

1 Financial Statements Listed below are partial financial statements for Marion & Carter, Inc. Complete each of these statements. Fill in the blanks on the four financial statements.

MARION & CARTER, INC.
Balance Sheet as of December 31, 2015 and 2014
(in millions of dollars)

	2015	**2014**		**2015**	**2014**
Assets			**Liabilities and Equity**		
Current assets:			Current liabilities:		
Cash and marketable securities	$ 165	$ 155	Accrued wages and taxes	$ 124	$ 95
Accounts receivable		400	Accounts payable	340	
Inventory	690	620	Notes payable	342	280
Total	$ 1,290	$ 1,175	Total	$ 806	$ 685
Fixed assets:			Long-term debt:	$ 1,210	$
Gross plant and equipment	$	$ 1,860	Stockholders' equity:		
Less: Depreciation	330	250	Preferred stock (25 million shares)	$25	$ 25
Net plant and equipment	$ 1,950	$ 1,610	Common stock and paid-in surplus	250	
			(200 million shares)		
Other long-term assets	350	310	Retained earnings	1,299	957
Total	$	$ 1,920	Total	$ 1,574	$ 1,232
Total assets	$ 3,590	$ 3,095	Total liabilities and equity	$ 3,590	$

MARION & CARTER, INC.
Income Statement for Years Ending December 31, 2015 and 2014
(in millions of dollars)

	2015	**2014**
Net sales	$	$ 1,705
Less: Cost of goods sold	830	
Gross profits	$ 1,123	$ 958
Less: Other operating expenses	100	90
Earnings before interest, taxes, depreciation, and amortization (EBITDA)	$ 1,023	$ 868
Less: Depreciation	80	75
Earnings before interest and taxes (EBIT)	$ 943	$ 793
Less: Interest		112
Earnings before taxes (EBT)	$ 844	$ 681
Less: Taxes		248
Net income	$ 559	$ 433
Less: Preferred stock dividends	$ 62	$ 62
Net income available to common stock holders	$ 497	$ 371
Less: Common stock dividends	155	
Addition to retained earnings	$ 342	$ 216
Per (common) share data:		
Earnings per share (EPS)	$	$ 1.855
Dividends per share (DPS)	$ 0.775	$
Book value per share (BVPS)	$	$ 6.035
Market value (price) per share (MVPS)	$22.970	$21.470

MARION & CARTER, INC.
Statement of Cash Flows for Year Ending December 31, 2015
(in millions of dollars)

Section A. Cash flows from operating activities

Net income	$ ☐
Additions (sources of cash):	
Depreciation	80
Increase in accrued wages and taxes	☐
Increase in accounts payable	30
Subtractions (uses of cash):	
Increase in accounts receivable	−35
Increase in inventory	☐
Net cash flow from operating activities:	$ ☐

Section B. Cash flows from investing activities

Subtractions:	
Increase in fixed assets	−$ 420
Increase in other long-term assets	☐
Net cash flow from investing activities:	$ ☐

Section C. Cash flows from financing activities

Additions:	
Increase in notes payable	$ ☐
Increase in long-term debt	32
Increase in common and preferred stock	0
Subtractions:	
Pay preferred stock dividends	☐
Pay common stock dividends	☐
Net cash flow from financing activities:	$ ☐

Section D. Net change in cash and marketable securities | $ 10

MARION & CARTER, INC.
Statement of Retained Earnings as of December 31, 2015
(in millions of dollars)

Balance of retained earnings, December 31, 2014		$ 957
Plus: Net income for 2015		☐
Less: Cash dividends paid		
Preferred stock	$ ☐	
Common stock	☐	
Total cash dividends paid		☐
Balance of retained earnings, December 31, 2015		$1,299

Solution:

MARION & CARTER, INC.
Balance Sheet as of December 31, 2015 and 2014
(in millions of dollars)

Assets	2015	2014	Liabilities and Equity	2015	2014
Current assets:			Current liabilities:		
Cash and marketable securities	$ 165	$ 155	Accrued wages and taxes	$124	$ 95
Accounts receivable	1,290 − 690 − 165 = 435	400	Accounts payable	340	685 − 280 − 95 = 310
Inventory	690	620	Notes payable	342	280
Total	$ 1,290	$1,175	Total	$806	$ 685

(continued)

	2015	2014		2015	2014
Fixed assets:			Long-term debt:	$ 1,210	3,095 − 1,232 − 685 = $1,178
Gross plant and equipment	1,950 + 330 = $2,280	$1,860	Stockholders' equity:		
Less: Depreciation	330	250	Preferred stock (25 million shares)	$ 25	$ 25
Net plant and equipment	$1,950	$1,610	Common stock and paid-in surplus (200 million shares)	250	1,232 − 957 − 25 = 250
Other long-term assets	350	310	Retained earnings	1,299	957
Total	1,950 + 350 = $2,300	$1,920	Total	$ 1,574	$1,232
Total assets	$3,590	$3,095	Total liabilities and equity	$ 3,590	$3,095

MARION & CARTER, INC.
Income Statement for Years Ending December 31, 2015 and 2014
(in millions of dollars)

	2015	2014
Net sales	1,123 + 830 = $ 1,953	$ 1,705
Less: Cost of goods sold	830	1705 − 958 = 747
Gross profits	$ 1,123	$ 958
Less: Other operating expenses	100	90
Earnings before interest, taxes, depreciation, and amortization (EBITDA)	$ 1,023	$ 868
Less: Depreciation	80	75
Earnings before interest and taxes (EBIT)	$ 943	$ 793
Less: Interest	943 − 844 = 99	112
Earnings before taxes (EBT)	$ 844	$ 681
Less: Taxes	844 − 559 = 285	248
Net income	$ 559	$ 433
Less: Preferred stock dividends	$ 62	$ 62
Net income available to common stockholders	$ 497	$ 371
Less: Common stock dividends	155	371 − 216 = 155
Addition to retained earnings	$ 342	$ 216
Per (common) share data:		
Earnings per share (EPS)	497/200 = $ 2.485	$ 1.855
Dividends per share (DPS)	$ 0.775	155/200 = $ 0.775
Book value per share (BVPS)	(1,574 − 25)/200 = $ 7.745	$ 6.035
Market value (price) per share (MVPS)	$22.970	$21.470

MARION & CARTER, INC.
Statement of Cash Flows for Year Ending December 31, 2015
(in millions of dollars)

Section A. Cash flows from operating activities	
Net income	$559
Additions (sources of cash):	
Depreciation	80
Increase in accrued wages and taxes	124 − 95 = 29
Increase in accounts payable	30
Subtractions (uses of cash):	
Increase in accounts receivable	−35
Increase in inventory	−(690 − 620) = −70
Net cash flow from operating activities:	559 + 80 + 29 + 30 − 35 − 70 = $593

(continued)

Section B. Cash flows from investing activities	
Subtractions:	
Increase in fixed assets	−$420
Increase in other long-term assets	−(350 − 310) = −40
Net cash flow from investing activities:	−420 − 40 = −$460
Section C. Cash flows from financing activities	
Additions:	
Increase in notes payable	342 − 280 = $62
Increase in long-term debt	32
Increase in common and preferred stock	0
Subtractions:	
Pay dividends	62 + 155 = $217
Net cash flow from financing activities:	62 + 32 − 217 = −$123
Section D. Net change in cash and marketable securities	$ 10

MARION & CARTER, INC.
Statement of Retained Earnings as of December 31, 2015
(in millions of dollars)

Balance of retained earnings, December 31, 2014		$ 957
Plus: Net income for 2015		559
Less: Cash dividends paid		
Preferred stock	$ 62	
Common stock	155	
Total cash dividends paid		217
Balance of retained earnings, December 31, 2015		$1,299

2 **Market Value versus Book Value** Little Carrie's SpinBall Corp. lists fixed assets of $16 million on its balance sheet. The firm's fixed assets have recently been appraised at $20 million. Little Carrie's SpinBall Corp.'s balance sheet also lists current assets at $6.25 million. Current assets were appraised at $7.50 million. Current liabilities' book and market values stand at $3.75 million and the firm's book and market values of long-term debt are $8.75 million. Calculate the book and market values of the firm's stockholders' equity. Construct the book value and market value balance sheets for Little Carrie's SpinBall Corp. LG2-2

Solution:

Recall the balance sheet identity in equation 2-1: Assets = Liabilities + Equity. Rearranging this equation: Equity = Assets − Liabilities. Thus, the balance sheets would appear as follows:

	Book Value	Market Value		Book Value	Market Value
Assets			**Liabilities and Equity**		
Current assets	$ 6.25m	$ 7.50m	Current liabilities	$ 3.75m	$ 3.75m
Fixed assets	16.00m	20.00m	Long-term debt	8.75m	8.75m
			Stockholders' equity	9.75m	15.00m
Total	$22.25m	$27.50m	Total	$22.25m	$27.50m

LG2-3

3 Corporate Taxes The Talley Corporation had a 2015 taxable income of \$365,000 from operations after all operating costs but before: (1) interest expense of \$50,000, (2) dividends received of \$15,000, (3) dividends paid of \$25,000, and (4) income taxes.

a. Calculate Talley's taxable income.

b. Calculate Talley's income tax liability for 2015.

c. Calculate Talley's after-tax income for 2015.

d. What are the company's average and marginal tax rates on taxable income?

Solution:

a. $$\text{Taxable income} = EBIT - \text{Interest expense} + \text{Taxable portion of dividends received}$$
$$= \$365{,}000 - \$50{,}000 + \$15{,}000\,(1 - 0.7) = \$319{,}500$$

b. $$\text{Tax liability} = \text{Tax on base amount} + \text{Tax rate (amount over base)}$$
$$= \$22{,}250 + 0.39\,(\$319{,}500 - \$100{,}000) = \$107{,}855$$

c. $$\text{After-tax income} = \$365{,}000 - \$50{,}000 + \$15{,}000 - \$107{,}855 = \$222{,}145$$

d. The resulting average tax rate for Talley Corporation is:

$$\text{Average tax rate} = \frac{\text{Tax liability}}{\text{Taxable income}} = \frac{\$107{,}855}{\$319{,}500} = 33.76\%$$

$$\text{Marginal tax rate} = 39\%$$

LG2-5

4 Free Cash Flow In 2015, McSweeney Power, Inc., earned an EBIT of \$675 million, had a tax rate of 33.48 percent, and computed its depreciation expense as \$57 million. McSweeney Power's gross fixed assets increased by \$58 million from 2014 to 2015. The firm's current assets increased by \$30 million and spontaneous current liabilities increased by \$15 million (\$5 million in accrued wages and taxes and \$10 million in accounts payable).

a. Calculate McSweeney Power's operating cash flow for 2015.

b. Calculate McSweeney Power's investment in operating capital for 2015.

c. Calculate McSweeney Power's free cash flow for 2015.

Solution:

a. Operating cash flow for 2015 is:

$$OCF = EBIT\,(1 - \text{Tax rate}) + \text{Depreciation}$$
$$= \$675\text{m}\,(1 - 0.3348) + \$57\text{m} = \$506\text{m}$$

b. Investment in operating capital for 2015 is:

$$IOC = \Delta\text{Gross fixed assets} + \Delta\text{Net operating working capital}$$
$$= \$58\text{m} + (\$30\text{m} - \$15\text{m}) = \$73\text{m}$$

c. Free cash flow for 2015 is:

$$FCF = \text{Operating cash flow} - \text{Investment in operating capital}$$
$$= \$506\text{m} - \$73\text{m} = \$433\text{m}$$

In other words, in 2015, McSweeney Power, Inc., had cash flows of \$433 million available to pay its stockholders and debt holders.

questions

1. List and describe the four major financial statements. *(LG2-1)*
2. On which of the four major financial statements (balance sheet, income statement, statement of cash flows, or statement of retained earnings) would you find the following items? *(LG2-1)*
   a. Earnings before taxes.
   b. Net plant and equipment.
   c. Increase in fixed assets.
   d. Gross profits.
   e. Balance of retained earnings, December 31, 20xx.
   f. Common stock and paid-in surplus.
   g. Net cash flow from investing activities.
   h. Accrued wages and taxes.
   i. Increase in inventory.
3. What is the difference between current liabilities and long-term debt? *(LG2-1)*
4. How does the choice of accounting method used to record fixed asset depreciation affect management of the balance sheet? *(LG2-1)*
5. What are the costs and benefits of holding liquid securities on a firm's balance sheet? *(LG2-1)*
6. Why can the book value and market value of a firm differ? *(LG2-1)*
7. From a firm manager's or investor's point of view, which is more important—the book value of a firm or the market value of the firm? *(LG2-2)*
8. What do we mean by a progressive tax structure? *(LG2-3)*
9. What is the difference between an average tax rate and a marginal tax rate? *(LG2-3)*
10. How does the payment of interest on debt affect the amount of taxes the firm must pay? *(LG2-3)*
11. The income statement is prepared using GAAP. How does this affect the reported revenue and expense measures listed on the balance sheet? *(LG2-4)*
12. Why do financial managers and investors find cash flows to be more important than accounting profit? *(LG2-4)*
13. Which of the following activities result in an increase (decrease) in a firm's cash? *(LG2-5)*
    a. Decrease fixed assets.
    b. Decrease accounts payable.
    c. Pay dividends.
    d. Sell common stock.
    e. Decrease accounts receivable.
    f. Increase notes payable.
14. What is the difference between cash flows from operating activities, cash flows from investing activities, and cash flows from financing activities? *(LG2-5)*

15. What are free cash flows for a firm? What does it mean when a firm's free cash flow is negative? *(LG2-5)*
16. What is earnings management? *(LG2-6)*
17. What does the Sarbanes-Oxley Act require of firm managers? *(LG2-6)*

problems

basic problems

2-1 Balance Sheet You are evaluating the balance sheet for Goodman's Bees Corporation. From the balance sheet you find the following balances: cash and marketable securities = \$400,000, accounts receivable = \$1,200,000, inventory = \$2,100,000, accrued wages and taxes = \$500,000, accounts payable = \$800,000, and notes payable = \$600,000. Calculate Goodman Bees' net working capital. *(LG2-1)*

2-2 Balance Sheet Casello Mowing & Landscaping's year-end 2015 balance sheet lists current assets of \$435,200, fixed assets of \$550,800, current liabilities of \$416,600, and long-term debt of \$314,500. Calculate Casello's total stockholders' equity. *(LG2-1)*

2-3 Income Statement The Fitness Studio, Inc.'s, 2015 income statement lists the following income and expenses: EBIT = \$538,000, interest expense = \$63,000, and net income = \$435,000. Calculate the 2015 taxes reported on the income statement. *(LG2-1)*

2-4 Income Statement The Fitness Studio, Inc.'s, 2015 income statement lists the following income and expenses: EBIT = \$773,500, interest expense = \$100,000, and taxes = \$234,500. The firm has no preferred stock outstanding and 100,000 shares of common stock outstanding. Calculate the 2015 earnings per share. *(LG2-1)*

2-5 Income Statement Consider a firm with an EBIT of \$850,000. The firm finances its assets with \$2,500,000 debt (costing 7.5 percent) and 400,000 shares of stock selling at \$5.00 per share. To reduce the firm's risk associated with this financial leverage, the firm is considering reducing its debt by \$1,000,000 by selling an additional 200,000 shares of stock. The firm is in the 40 percent tax bracket. The change in capital structure will have no effect on the operations of the firm. Thus, EBIT will remain at \$850,000. Calculate the change in the firm's EPS from this change in capital structure. *(LG2-1)*

2-6 Income Statement Consider a firm with an EBIT of \$550,000. The firm finances its assets with \$1,000,000 debt (costing 5.5 percent) and 200,000 shares of stock selling at \$12.00 per share. The firm is considering increasing its debt by \$900,000, using the proceeds to buy back 75,000 shares of stock. The firm is in the 40 percent tax bracket. The change in capital structure will have no effect on the operations of the firm. Thus, EBIT will remain at \$550,000. Calculate the change in the firm's EPS from this change in capital structure. *(LG2-1)*

2-7 Corporate Taxes Oakdale Fashions, Inc., had \$245,000 in 2015 taxable income. Using the tax schedule in Table 2.3, calculate the company's 2015 income taxes. What is the average tax rate? What is the marginal tax rate? *(LG2-3)*

2-8 **Corporate Taxes** Hunt Taxidermy, Inc., is concerned about the taxes paid by the company in 2015. In addition to $42.4 million of taxable income, the firm received $2,975,000 of interest on state-issued bonds and $1,000,000 of dividends on common stock it owns in Oakdale Fashions, Inc. Calculate Hunt Taxidermy's tax liability, average tax rate, and marginal tax rate. *(LG2-3)*

2-9 **Statement of Cash Flows** Ramakrishnan, Inc., reported 2015 net income of $15 million and depreciation of $2,650,000. The top part of Ramakrishnan, Inc.'s 2015 and 2014 balance sheets is reproduced below (in millions of dollars).

	2015	2014		2015	2014
Current assets:			Current liabilities:		
Cash and marketable securities	$ 20	$ 15	Accrued wages and taxes	$ 19	$ 18
Accounts receivable	84	75	Accounts payable	51	45
Inventory	121	110	Notes payable	45	40
Total	$225	$ 200	Total	$115	$103

Calculate the 2015 net cash flow from operating activities for Ramakrishnan, Inc. *(LG2-4)*

2-10 **Statement of Cash Flows** In 2015, Usher Sports Shop had cash flows from investing activities of −$4,364,000 and cash flows from financing activities of −$5,880,000. The balance in the firm's cash account was $1,615,000 at the beginning of 2015 and $1,742,000 at the end of the year. Calculate Usher Sports Shop's cash flow from operations for 2015. *(LG2-4)*

2-11 **Free Cash Flow** You are considering an investment in Fields and Struthers, Inc., and want to evaluate the firm's free cash flow. From the income statement, you see that Fields and Struthers earned an EBIT of $62 million, had a tax rate of 30 percent, and its depreciation expense was $5 million. Fields and Struthers' NOPAT gross fixed assets increased by $32 million from 2014 and 2015. The firm's current assets increased by $20 million and spontaneous current liabilities increased by $12 million. Calculate Fields and Struthers' NOPAT operating cash flow, investment in operating capital, and free cash flow for 2015. *(LG2-5)*

2-12 **Free Cash Flow** Tater and Pepper Corp. reported free cash flows for 2015 of $39.1 million and investment in operating capital of $22.1 million. Tater and Pepper incurred $13.6 million in depreciation expense and paid $28.9 million in taxes on EBIT in 2015. Calculate Tater and Pepper's 2015 EBIT. *(LG2-5)*

2-13 **Statement of Retained Earnings** Mr. Husker's Tuxedos Corp. began the year 2015 with $256 million in retained earnings. The firm earned net income of $33 million in 2015 and paid dividends of $5 million to its preferred stockholders and $10 million to its common stockholders. What is the year-end 2015 balance in retained earnings for Mr. Husker's Tuxedos? *(LG2-1)*

2-14 **Statement of Retained Earnings** Use the following information to find dividends paid to common stockholders during 2015. *(LG2-1)*

Balance of retained earnings, December 31, 2014		$462m
Plus: Net income for 2015		15m
Less: Cash dividends paid		
Preferred stock	$ 1m	
Common stock	☐	
Total cash dividends paid		☐
Balance of retained earnings, December 31, 2015		$470m

intermediate problems

2-15 Balance Sheet Brenda's Bar and Grill has total assets of $15 million, of which $5 million are current assets. Cash makes up 10 percent of the current assets and accounts receivable makes up another 40 percent of current assets. Brenda's gross plant and equipment has a book value of $11.5 million and other long-term assets have a book value of $500,000. Using this information, what is the balance of inventory and the balance of depreciation on Brenda's Bar and Grill's balance sheet? *(LG2-1)*

2-16 Balance Sheet Glen's Tobacco Shop has total assets of $91.8 million. Fifty percent of these assets are financed with debt of which $28.9 million is current liabilities. The firm has no preferred stock but the balance in common stock and paid-in surplus is $20.4 million. Using this information, what is the balance for long-term debt and retained earnings on Glen's Tobacco Shop's balance sheet? *(LG2-1)*

2-17 Market Value versus Book Value Muffin's Masonry, Inc.'s, balance sheet lists net fixed assets as $14 million. The fixed assets could currently be sold for $19 million. Muffin's current balance sheet shows current liabilities of $5.5 million and net working capital of $4.5 million. If all the current accounts were liquidated today, the company would receive $7.25 million cash after paying the $5.5 million in current liabilities. What is the book value of Muffin's Masonry's assets today? What is the market value of these assets? *(LG2-2)*

2-18 Market Value versus Book Value Ava's SpinBall Corp. lists fixed assets of $12 million on its balance sheet. The firm's fixed assets have recently been appraised at $16 million. Ava's SpinBall Corp.'s balance sheet also lists current assets at $5 million. Current assets were appraised at $6 million. Current liabilities' book and market values stand at $3 million and the firm's book and market values of long-term debt are $7 million. Calculate the book and market values of the firm's stockholders' equity. Construct the book value and market value balance sheets for Ava's SpinBall Corp. *(LG2-2)*

2-19 Debt versus Equity Financing You are considering a stock investment in one of two firms (NoEquity, Inc., and NoDebt, Inc.), both of which operate in the same industry and have identical operating income of $32.5 million. NoEquity, Inc., finances its $65 million in assets with $64 million in debt (on which it pays 10 percent interest annually) and $1 million in equity. NoDebt, Inc., finances its $65 million in assets with no debt and $65 million in equity. Both firms pay a tax rate of 30 percent on their taxable income. Calculate the net income and return on assets for the two firms. *(LG2-1)*

2-20 Debt versus Equity Financing You are considering a stock investment in one of two firms (AllDebt, Inc., and AllEquity, Inc.), both of which operate in the same industry and have identical operating income of $12.5 million. AllDebt, Inc., finances its $25 million in assets with

$24 million in debt (on which it pays 10 percent interest annually) and $1 million in equity. AllEquity, Inc., finances its $25 million in assets with no debt and $25 million in equity. Both firms pay a tax rate of 30 percent on their taxable income. Calculate the income available to pay the asset funders (the debt holders and stockholders) and resulting return on assets for the two firms. *(LG2-1)*

2-21 Income Statement You have been given the following information for Corky's Bedding Corp.:

a. Net sales = $11,250,000.

b. Cost of goods sold = $7,500,000.

c. Other operating expenses = $250,000.

d. Addition to retained earnings = $1,000,000.

e. Dividends paid to preferred and common stockholders = $495,000.

f. Interest expense = $850,000.

The firm's tax rate is 35 percent. Calculate the depreciation expense for Corky's Bedding Corp. *(LG2-1)*

2-22 Income Statement You have been given the following information for Moore's HoneyBee Corp.:

a. Net sales = $32,000,000.

b. Gross profit = $18,700,000.

c. Other operating expenses = $2,500,000.

d. Addition to retained earnings = $4,700,000.

e. Dividends paid to preferred and common stockholders = $2,900,000.

f. Depreciation expense = $2,800,000.

The firm's tax rate is 35 percent. Calculate the cost of goods sold and the interest expense for Moore's HoneyBee Corp. *(LG2-1)*

2-23 Income Statement Consider a firm with an EBIT of $1,000,000. The firm finances its assets with $4,500,000 debt (costing 8 percent) and 200,000 shares of stock selling at $16.00 per share. To reduce risk associated with this financial leverage, the firm is considering reducing its debt by $2,500,000 by selling additional shares of stock. The firm is in the 40 percent tax bracket. The change in capital structure will have no effect on the operations of the firm. Thus, EBIT will remain at $1,000,000. Calculate the change in the firm's EPS from this change in capital structure. *(LG2-1)*

2-24 Income Statement Consider a firm with an EBIT of $10,500,000. The firm finances its assets with $50,000,000 debt (costing 6.5 percent) and 10,000,000 shares of stock selling at $10.00 per share. The firm is considering increasing its debt by $25,000,000, using the proceeds to buy back shares of stock. The firm is in the 40 percent tax bracket. The change in capital structure will have no effect on the operations of the firm. Thus, EBIT will remain at $10,500,000. Calculate the change in the firm's EPS from this change in capital structure. *(LG2-1)*

2-25 Corporate Taxes The Dakota Corporation had a 2015 taxable income of $33,365,000 from operations after all operating costs but before (1) interest charges of $8,500,000; (2) dividends received of $750,000; (3) dividends paid of $5,250,000; and (4) income taxes. *(LG2-3)*

a. Use the tax schedule in Table 2.3 to calculate Dakota's income tax liability.

b. What are Dakota's average and marginal tax rates on taxable income?

2-26 **Corporate Taxes** Suppose that in addition to $17.85 million of taxable income, Texas Taco, Inc., received $1,105,000 of interest on state-issued bonds and $760,000 of dividends on common stock it owns in Arizona Taco, Inc. *(LG2-3)*

a. Use the tax schedule in Table 2.3 to calculate Texas Taco's income tax liability.

b. What are Texas Taco's average and marginal tax rates on taxable income?

2-27 **Statement of Cash Flows** Use the balance sheet and income statement below to construct a statement of cash flows for Clancy's Dog Biscuit Corporation. *(LG2-5)*

CLANCY'S DOG BISCUIT CORPORATION
Balance Sheet as of December 31, 2015 and 2014
(in millions of dollars)

	2015	2014		2015	2014
Assets			**Liabilities and Equity**		
Current assets:			Current liabilities:		
Cash and marketable securities	$ 5	$ 5	Accrued wages and taxes	$ 10	$ 6
Accounts receivable	20	19	Accounts payable	16	15
Inventory	36	29	Notes payable	14	13
Total	$ 61	$ 53	Total	$ 40	$ 34
Fixed assets:			Long-term debt:	$ 57	$ 53
Gross plant and equipment	$106	$ 88	Stockholders' equity:		
Less: Depreciation	15	11	Preferred stock (2 million shares)	$ 2	$ 2
	$ 91	$ 77	Common stock and paid-in surplus		
Net plant and equipment			(5 million shares)	11	11
Other long-term assets	15	15	Retained earnings	57	45
Total	$106	$ 92	Total	$ 70	$ 58
Total assets	$167	$145	Total liabilities and equity	$167	$145

CLANCY'S DOG BISCUIT CORPORATION
Income Statement for Years Ending December 31, 2015 and 2014
(in millions of dollars)

	2015	2014
Net sales	$ 76	$ 80
Less: Cost of goods sold	38	34
Gross profits	$ 38	$ 46
Less: Other operating expenses	6	5
Earnings before interest, taxes, depreciation, and amortization (EBITDA)	$ 32	$ 41
Less: Depreciation	4	4
Earnings before interest and taxes (EBIT)	$ 28	$ 37
Less: Interest	5	5
Earnings before taxes (EBT)	$ 23	$ 32
Less: Taxes	7	10
Net income	$ 16	$ 22
Less: Preferred stock dividends	$ 1	$ 1
Net income available to common stockholders	$ 15	$ 21
Less: Common stock dividends	3	3
Addition to retained earnings	$ 12	$ 18
Per (common) share data:		
Earnings per share (EPS)	$ 3.00	$ 4.20
Dividends per share (DPS)	$ 0.60	$ 0.60
Book value per share (BVPS)	$ 13.60	$ 11.20
Market value (price) per share (MVPS)	$ 14.25	$ 14.60

2-28 Statement of Cash Flows Use the balance sheet and income statement below to construct a statement of cash flows for Valium's Medical Supply Corporation. *(LG2-5)*

VALIUM'S MEDICAL SUPPLY CORPORATION
Balance Sheet as of December 31, 2015 and 2014
(in thousands of dollars)

	2015	2014		2015	2014
Assets			**Liabilities and Equity**		
Current assets:			Current liabilities:		
Cash and marketable securities	$ 74	$ 73	Accrued wages and taxes	$ 58	$ 45
Accounts receivable	199	189	Accounts payable	159	145
Inventory	322	291	Notes payable	131	131
Total	$ 595	$ 553	Total	$ 348	$ 321
Fixed assets:			Long-term debt:	$ 565	$ 549
Gross plant and equipment	$ 1,084	$ 886	Stockholders' equity:		
Less: Depreciation	153	116	Preferred stock (6 thousand shares)	$ 6	$ 6
Net plant and equipment	$ 931	$ 770	Common stock and paid-in surplus (100 thousand shares)	120	120
Other long-term assets	130	130	Retained earnings	617	457
Total	$ 1,061	$ 900	Total	$ 743	$ 583
Total assets	$ 1,656	$ 1,453	Total liabilities and equity	$1,656	$1,453

VALIUM'S MEDICAL SUPPLY CORPORATION
Income Statement for Years Ending December 31, 2015 and 2014
(in thousands of dollars)

	2015	2014
Net sales	$ 888	$ 798
Less: Cost of goods sold	387	350
Gross profits	$ 501	$ 448
Less: Other operating expenses	48	42
Earnings before interest, taxes, depreciation, and amortization (EBITDA)	$ 453	$ 406
Less: Depreciation	37	35
Earnings before interest and taxes (EBIT)	$ 416	$ 371
Less: Interest	46	40
Earnings before taxes (EBT)	$ 370	$ 331
Less: Taxes	129	112
Net income	$ 241	$ 219
Less: Preferred stock dividends	$ 6	$ 6
Net income available to common stockholders	$ 235	$ 213
Less: Common stock dividends	75	75
Addition to retained earnings	$ 160	$ 138
Per (common) share data:		
Earnings per share (EPS)	$ 2.35	$ 2.13
Dividends per share (DPS)	$ 0.75	$ 0.75
Book value per share (BVPS)	$ 7.37	$ 5.77
Market value (price) per share (MVPS)	$ 8.40	$ 6.25

2-29 Statement of Cash Flows Chris's Outdoor Furniture, Inc., has net cash flows from operating activities for the last year of $340 million. The income statement shows that net income is $315 million and depreciation expense is $46 million. During the year, the change in inventory on the balance sheet was $38 million, change in accrued wages and taxes was $15 million, and change in accounts payable was $20 million. At the beginning of the year, the balance of accounts receivable was $50 million. Calculate the end-of-year balance for accounts receivable. *(LG2-5)*

2-30 Statement of Cash Flows Dogs 4 U Corporation has net cash flow from financing activities for the last year of $34 million. The company paid $178 million in dividends last year. During the year, the change in notes payable on the balance sheet was $39 million and change in common and preferred stock was $0. The end-of-year balance for long-term debt was $315 million. Calculate the beginning-of-year balance for long-term debt. *(LG2-5)*

2-31 Free Cash Flow The 2015 income statement for Duffy's Pest Control shows that depreciation expense was $197 million, EBIT was $494 million, and the tax rate was 30 percent. At the beginning of the year, the balance of gross fixed assets was $1,562 million and net operating working capital was $417 million. At the end of the year, gross fixed assets was $1,803 million. Duffy's free cash flow for the year was $424 million. Calculate the end-of-year balance for net operating working capital. *(LG2-5)*

2-32 Free Cash Flow The 2015 income statement for Egyptian Noise Blasters shows that depreciation expense is $85 million, NOPAT is $246 million. At the end of the year, the balance of gross fixed assets was $655 million. The change in net operating working capital during the year was $73 million. Egyptian's free cash flow for the year was $190 million. Calculate the beginning-of-year balance for gross fixed assets. *(LG2-5)*

2-33 Statement of Retained Earnings Thelma and Louie, Inc., started the year with a balance of retained earnings of $543 million and ended the year with retained earnings of $589 million. The company paid dividends of $35 million to the preferred stockholders and $88 million to common stockholders. Calculate Thelma and Louie's net income for the year. *(LG2-1)*

2-34 Statement of Retained Earnings Jamaica Tours, Inc., started the year with a balance of retained earnings of $1,780 million. The company reported net income for the year of $284 million and paid dividends of $17 million to the preferred stockholders and $59 million to common stockholders. Calculate Jamaica Tour's end-of-year balance in retained earnings. *(LG2-1)*

advanced problems

2-35 Income Statement Listed below is the 2015 income statement for Tom and Sue Travels, Inc.

TOM AND SUE TRAVELS, INC.
Income Statement for Year Ending December 31, 2015
(in millions of dollars)

Net sales	$16.500
Less: Cost of goods sold	7.100
Gross profits	$ 9.400
Less: Other operating expenses	3.200
Earnings before interest, taxes, depreciation, and amortization (EBITDA)	$ 6.200
Less: Depreciation	2.900
Earnings before interest and taxes (EBIT)	$ 3.300
Less: Interest	0.950
Earnings before taxes (EBT)	$ 2.350
Less: Taxes	0.705
Net income	$ 1.645

The CEO of Tom and Sue's wants the company to earn a net income of $2.250 million in 2016. Cost of goods sold is expected to be 60 percent of net sales, depreciation and other operating expenses are not expected to change, interest expense is expected to increase to $1.050 million, and the firm's tax rate will be 30 percent. Calculate the net sales needed to produce net income of $2.250 million. *(LG2-1)*

2-36 **Income Statement** You have been given the following information for PattyCake's Athletic Wear Corp. for the year 2015:

 a. Net sales = $38,250,000.

 b. Cost of goods sold = $22,070,000.

 c. Other operating expenses = $5,300,000.

 d. Addition to retained earnings = $1,195,500.

 e. Dividends paid to preferred and common stockholders = $1,912,000.

 f. Interest expense = $1,785,000.

 g. The firm's tax rate is 30 percent.

 In 2016:

 h. Net sales are expected to increase by $9.75 million.

 i. Cost of goods sold is expected to be 60 percent of net sales.

 j. Depreciation and other operating expenses are expected to be the same as in 2015.

 k. Interest expense is expected to be $2,004,286.

 l. The tax rate is expected to be 30 percent of EBT.

 m. Dividends paid to preferred and common stockholders will not change.

 Calculate the addition to retained earnings expected in 2016. *(LG2-1)*

2-37 **Free Cash Flow** Rebecky's Flowers 4U, Inc., had free cash flows during 2015 of $43 million, NOPAT of $85 million, and depreciation of $14 million. Using this information, fill in the blanks on Rebecky's balance sheet below. *(LG2-5)*

REBECKY'S FLOWERS 4U, INC. Balance Sheet as of December 31, 2015 and 2014 (in millions of dollars)						
Assets	**2015**	**2014**	**Liabilities and Equity**		**2015**	**2014**
Current assets:			Current liabilities:			
Cash and marketable securities	$ 28	$ 25	Accrued wages and taxes		$ 17	$ 15
Accounts receivable	75	65	Accounts payable		☐	50
Inventory	118	100	Notes payable		45	45
Total	$ 221	$ 190	Total		$ ☐	$ 110
Fixed assets:			Long-term debt:		$ ☐	$ 190
Gross plant and equipment	$ 333	$ 300	Stockholders' equity:			
Less: Depreciation	54	40	Preferred stock (5 million shares)		$ 5	$ 5
Net plant and equipment	$ 279	$ 260	Common stock and paid-in surplus (20 million shares)		40	40
Other long-term assets	50	50	Retained earnings		192	155
Total	$ 329	$ 310	Total		$ 237	$ 200
Total assets	$ 550	$ 500	Total liabilities and equity		$ 550	$ 500

2-38 Free Cash Flow Vinny's Overhead Construction had free cash flow during 2015 of $25.4 million. The change in gross fixed assets on Vinny's balance sheet during 2015 was $7.0 million and the change in net operating working capital was $8.4 million. Using this information, fill in the blanks on Vinny's income statement below. *(LG2-5)*

VINNY'S OVERHEAD CONSTRUCTION, CORP. Income Statement for Year Ending December 31, 2015 (in millions of dollars)	
Net sales	$____
Less: Cost of goods sold	116.10
Gross profits	$66.00
Less: Other operating expenses	12.40
Earnings before interest, taxes, depreciation, and amortization (EBITDA)	$53.60
Less: Depreciation	10.20
Earnings before interest and taxes (EBIT)	
Less: Interest	____
Earnings before taxes (EBT)	$____
Less: Taxes	____
Net income	$27.64

research it! Reviewing Financial Statements

Go to the website of Walmart Stores, Inc., and get the latest financial statements from the annual report using the following steps.

Go to **www.walmartstores.com**. Click on Investors, then select Financial Information; next choose Annual Reports; finally, click on the most recent date. This will bring the file onto your computer that contains the relevant data.

Locate the total assets, total equity, net sales, net income, dividends paid, cash flows from operating activities, and cash flows from investing activities for the last two years. How have these items changed over the last two years?

integrated mini-case Working with Financial Statements

Shown below are partial financial statements for Garners' Platoon Mental Health Care, Inc. Fill in the blanks on the four financial statements.

GARNERS' PLATOON MENTAL HEALTH CARE, INC. Balance Sheet as of December 31, 2015 and 2014 (in millions of dollars)					
	2015	**2014**		**2015**	**2014**
Assets			**Liabilities and Equity**		
Current assets:			Current liabilities:		
Cash and marketable securities	$ 421	$____	Accrued wages and taxes	$ 316	$ 242
Accounts receivable	____	1,020	Accounts payable	867	791
Inventory	1,760	1,581	Notes payable	____	714
Total	$3,290	$____	Total	$2,055	$1,747

	2015	2014		2015	2014
Fixed assets:			Long-term debt:	$ 3,090	$
Gross plant and equipment	$	$4,743	Stockholders' equity:		
Less: Depreciation	840	640	Preferred stock (30 million shares)	$ 60	$ 60
Net plant and equipment	$4,972	$	Common stock and paid-in surplus (200 million shares)	637	
Other long-term assets		790	Retained earnings	3,312	2,440
Total	$5,864	$4,893	Total	$ 4,009	$ 3,137
Total assets	$	$7,889	Total liabilities and equity	$ 9,154	$ 7,889

GARNERS' PLATOON MENTAL HEALTH CARE, INC.
Income Statement for Years Ending December 31, 2015 and 2014
(in millions of dollars)

	2015	2014
Net sales	$ 4,980	$
Less: Cost of goods sold		2,035
Gross profits	$ 2,734	$ 2,313
Less: Other operating expenses	125	100
Earnings before interest, taxes, depreciation, and amortization (EBITDA)	$ 2,609	$ 2,213
Less: Depreciation	200	191
Earnings before interest and taxes (EBIT)	$ 2,409	$
Less: Interest		285
Earnings before taxes (EBT)	$ 2,094	$ 1,737
Less: Taxes		
Net income	$ 1,327	$ 1,105
Less: Preferred stock dividends	$ 60	$
Net income available to common stockholders	$ 1,267	$ 1,045
Less: Common stock dividends	395	395
Addition to retained earnings	$ 872	$
Per (common) share data:		
Earnings per share (EPS)	$	$
Dividends per share (DPS)	$	$
Book value per share (BVPS)	$	$
Market value (price) per share (MVPS)	$ 26.850	$ 22.500

GARNERS' PLATOON MENTAL HEALTH CARE, INC.
Statement of Cash Flows for Year Ending December 31, 2015
(in millions of dollars)

Section A. Cash flows from operating activities	
Net income	$
Additions (sources of cash):	
Depreciation	
Increase in accrued wages and taxes	
Increase in accounts payable	
Subtractions (uses of cash):	
Increase in accounts receivable	
Increase in inventory	
Net cash flow from operating activities	$

Section B. Cash flows from investing activities

Subtractions:

Increase in fixed assets	$	☐
Increase in other long-term assets		☐
Net cash flow from investing activities	$	☐

Section C. Cash flows from financing activities

Additions:

Increase in notes payable	$	☐
Increase in long-term debt		☐
Increase in common and preferred stock		☐

Subtractions:

Dividends paid		☐
Net cash flow from financing activities	$	☐
Section D. Net change in cash and marketable securities	$	26

GARNERS' PLATOON MENTAL HEALTH CARE, INC.
Statement of Retained Earnings as of December 31, 2015
(in millions of dollars)

Balance of retained earnings, December 31, 2014		$ 2,440
Plus: Net income for 2015		☐
Less: Cash dividends paid		
Preferred stock	$ ☐	
Common stock	☐	
Total cash dividends paid		☐
Balance of retained earnings, December 31, 2015		$ ☐

ANSWERS TO TIME OUT

2-1 The balance sheet reports a firm's assets, liabilities, and equity at a particular point in time. A firm's assets must equal (balance) the liabilities and equity used to purchase the assets (hence the term *balance sheet*).

2-2 The most liquid assets—called current assets—appear first on the asset side of the balance sheet. The most liquid liabilities—called current liabilities—appear first on the liabilities and equity side of the balance sheet.

2-3 An income statement shows the total revenues that a firm earns and the total expenses the firm incurs to generate those revenues over a specific period of time—generally one year. Remember that while the balance sheet reports a firm's position at a point in time, the income statement reports performance over a period of time, for example, over the last year.

2-4 When one corporation owns stock in another corporation, 70 percent of any dividends received from other corporations is tax exempt. Only the remaining 30 percent is taxed at the receiving corporation's tax rate.

2-5 The statement of cash flows is a financial statement that shows the firm's cash flows over a given period of time. This statement reports the amounts of cash that the firm generates and distributes during a particular time period. The bottom line on the statement of cash flows—the difference between cash sources and uses—equals the change in cash and marketable securities on the firm's balance sheet from the previous year's balance. That is, the statement of cash flows reconciles income statement items and noncash balance sheet items to show changes in the cash and marketable securities account on the balance sheet over the particular analysis period.

2-6 The statement of cash flows separates cash flows into four categories or sections: cash flows from operating activities; cash flows from investing activities; cash flows from financing activities; and net change in cash and marketable securities.

2-7 The statement of retained earnings provides additional details about changes in retained earnings during a reporting period. This financial statement reconciles net income earned during a given period and any cash dividends paid within that period on one side with the change in retained earnings between the beginning and ending of the period on the other.

2-8 If a firm pays out more in dividends than it has net income, retained earnings will decrease.

2-9 Managers have significant discretion over their reported earnings. Managers and financial analysts have recognized for years that firms use considerable latitude in using accounting rules to manage their reported earnings in a wide variety of contexts. Indeed, within the GAAP framework, firms can "smooth" earnings. That is, firms often take steps to over- or understate earnings at various times. Managers may choose to smooth earnings to show investors that firm assets are growing steadily. Similarly, one firm may be using straight-line depreciation for its fixed assets, while another is using a modified accelerated cost recovery method (MACRS), which causes depreciation to accrue quickly. If the firm uses MACRS accounting methods, it writes fixed asset values down quickly; assets will thus have lower book values than if the firm used straight-line depreciation methods. This process of controlling a firm's earnings is called *earnings management.*

3 Analyzing Financial Statements

viewpoints

Business Application

The managers of DPH Tree Farm, Inc., have released public statements that the firm's performance surpasses that of other firms in the industry. They cite the firm's liquidity and asset management positions as particularly strong. DPH's superior performance in these areas has resulted in superior overall returns for their stockholders. What are the key financial ratios that DPH Tree Farm, Inc., needs to calculate and evaluate in order to justify these statements? **(See solution on p. 99)**

Personal Application

Chris Ryan is looking to invest in DPH Tree Farm, Inc. Chris has the most recent set of financial statements from DPH Tree Farm's annual report but is not sure how to evaluate them or measure the firm's performance relative to other firms in the industry. What are the financial ratios with which Chris should measure the performance of DPH Tree Farm, Inc.? How can Chris use these ratios to evaluate the firm's performance? **(See solution on p. 99)**

So how can these financial ratios work in your life?

Learning Goals

LG3-1 Calculate and interpret major liquidity ratios.
LG3-2 Calculate and interpret major asset management ratios.
LG3-3 Calculate and interpret major debt ratios.
LG3-4 Calculate and interpret major profitability ratios.
LG3-5 Calculate and interpret major market value ratios.
LG3-6 Appreciate how various ratios relate to one another.
LG3-7 Understand the differences between time series and cross-sectional ratio analysis.
LG3-8 Explain cautions that should be taken when examining financial ratios.

We reviewed the major financial statements in Chapter 2. These financial statements provide information on a firm's financial position at a point in time or its operations over some past period of time. But these financial statements' real value lies in the fact that managers, investors, and analysts can use the information the statements contain to analyze the current financial performance or condition of the firm. More importantly, managers can use this information to plan changes that will improve the firm's future performance and, ultimately, its market value. Managers, investors, and analysts universally use ratios to evaluate financial statements. **Ratio analysis** involves calculating and analyzing financial ratios to assess a firm's performance and to identify actions that could improve firm performance. The most frequently used ratios fall into five groups: (1) liquidity ratios, (2) asset management ratios, (3) debt management ratios, (4) profitability ratios, and (5) market value ratios. Each of the five groups focuses on a specific area of the financial statements that managers, investors, and analysts assess.

In this chapter, we review these ratios, describe what each ratio means, and identify the general trend (higher or lower) that managers and investment analysts look for in each ratio. Note as we review the ratios that the number calculated for a ratio is not always good or bad and that extreme values (either high or low) can be a bad sign for a firm. We will discuss how a ratio that seems too good can actually be bad for a company. We will also see how ratios interrelate—how a change in one ratio may affect the value of several ratios. It is often hard to make sense of a set of performance ratios. Thus, when managers or investors review a firm's financial position through ratio analysis, they often start by evaluating trends in the firm's financial ratios over time and by comparing their firm's ratios with that of other firms in the same industry. Finally, we discuss cautions that you should take when using ratio analysis to evaluate firm performance. As we go through the chapter, we show sample ratio analysis using the financial statements for DPH Tree Farm, Inc., listed in Tables 2.1 and 2.2.

LG3-1

3.1 • Liquidity Ratios

ratio analysis

The process of calculating and analyzing financial ratios to assess the firm's performance and to identify actions needed to improve firm performance.

liquidity ratios

Measure the relation between a firm's liquid (or current) assets and its current liabilities.

As we stated in Chapter 2, firms need cash and other liquid assets (or current assets) to pay their bills (or current liabilities) as they come due. **Liquidity ratios** measure the relationship between a firm's liquid (or current) assets and its current liabilities. The three most commonly used liquidity ratios are the current ratio, the quick (or acid-test) ratio, and the cash ratio.

$$\text{Current ratio} = \frac{\text{Current assets}}{\text{Current liabilities}} \qquad \textbf{(3-1)}$$

The broadest liquidity measure, the current ratio, measures the dollars of current assets available to pay each dollar of current liabilities.

$$\text{Quick ratio (acid-test ratio)} = \frac{\text{Current assets} - \text{Inventory}}{\text{Current liabilities}} \qquad \textbf{(3-2)}$$

Inventories are generally the least liquid of a firm's current assets. Further, inventory is the current asset for which book values are the least reliable measures of market value. In practical terms, what this means is that if the firm must sell inventory to pay upcoming bills, the firm will most likely have to discount inventory items in order to liquidate them, and therefore, they are the current assets on which losses are most likely to occur. Therefore, the quick (or acid-test) ratio measures a firm's ability to pay off short-term obligations without relying on inventory sales. The quick ratio measures the dollars of more liquid assets (cash and marketable securities and accounts receivable) available to pay each dollar of current liabilities.

$$\text{Cash ratio} = \frac{\text{Cash and marketable securities}}{\text{Current liabilities}} \qquad \textbf{(3-3)}$$

If the firm sells accounts receivable to pay upcoming bills, the firm must often discount the accounts receivable to sell them—the assets once again bring less than their book value. Therefore, the cash ratio measures a firm's ability to pay short-term obligations with its available cash and marketable securities.

Of course, liquidity on the balance sheet is important. The more liquid assets a firm holds, the less likely the firm is to experience financial distress. Thus, the higher the liquidity ratios, the less liquidity risk a firm has. But as with everything else in business, high liquidity represents a painful trade-off for the firm. Liquid assets generate little, if any, profits for the firm. In contrast, fixed assets are illiquid, but generate revenue for the firm. Thus, extremely high levels of liquidity guard against liquidity crises, but at the cost of lower returns on assets. High liquidity levels may actually show bad or indecisive firm management. Thus, in deciding the appropriate level of current assets to hold on the balance sheet, managers must consider the trade-off between the advantages of being liquid versus the disadvantages of reduced profits. Note that a company with very predictable cash flows can maintain low levels of liquidity without incurring much liquidity risk.

EXAMPLE 3-1

LG3-1

For interactive versions of this example visit www.mhhe.com/can3e

Calculating Liquidity Ratios

Use the balance sheet (Table 2.1) and income statement (Table 2.2) for DPH Tree Farm, Inc., to calculate the firm's 2015 values for the liquidity ratios.

SOLUTION:

The liquidity ratios for DPH Tree Farm, Inc., are calculated as follows. The industry average is reported alongside each ratio.

$$\text{Current ratio} = \frac{\$205\text{m}}{\$120\text{m}} = 1.71 \text{ times} \qquad \text{Industry average} = 1.50 \text{ times}$$

$$\text{Quick ratio (acid-test ratio)} = \frac{\$205\text{m} - \$111\text{m}}{\$120\text{m}} = 0.78 \text{ times} \qquad \text{Industry average} = 0.50 \text{ times}$$

$$\text{Cash ratio} = \frac{\$24\text{m}}{\$120\text{m}} = 0.20 \text{ times} \qquad \text{Industry average} = 0.15 \text{ times}$$

All three liquidity ratios show that DPH Tree Farm, Inc., has more liquidity on its balance sheet than the industry average (we discuss the process used to develop an industry average in section 3.8). Thus, DPH Tree Farm has more cash and other liquid assets (or current assets) available to pay its bills (or current liabilities) as they come due than does the average firm in the tree farm industry.

Similar to Problems 3-1, 3-2, self-test problem 1

TIME OUT

3-1 What are the three major liquidity ratios used in evaluating financial statements?

3-2 How do the three major liquidity ratios used in evaluating financial statements differ?

3-3 Does a firm generally want to have high or low liquidity ratios? Why?

3.2 • Asset Management Ratios

LG3-2

asset management ratios

Measure how efficiently a firm uses its assets (inventory, accounts receivable, and fixed assets), as well as its accounts payable.

Asset management ratios measure how efficiently a firm uses its assets (inventory, accounts receivable, and fixed assets), as well as how efficiently the firm manages its accounts payable. The specific ratios allow managers and investors to evaluate whether a firm is holding a reasonable amount of each type of asset and whether management uses each type of asset to effectively generate sales. The most frequently used asset management ratios are listed in the following sections, grouped by type of asset.

Inventory Management

As they decide the optimal inventory level to hold on the balance sheet, managers must consider the trade-off between the advantages of holding sufficient levels of inventory to keep the production process going versus the costs of holding large amounts of inventory. Two frequently used ratios are the inventory turnover and days' sales in inventory.

$$\text{Inventory turnover} = \frac{\text{Sales or cost of goods sold}}{\text{Inventory}} \tag{3-4}$$

The inventory turnover measures the number of dollars of sales produced per dollar of inventory. Cost of goods sold is used in the numerator when managers want to emphasize that inventory is listed on the balance sheet at cost, that is, the cost of sales generated per dollar of inventory.

$$\text{Days' sales in inventory} = \frac{\text{Inventory} \times 365 \text{ days}}{\text{Sales or cost of goods sold}}$$
$$= \frac{365 \text{ days}}{\text{Inventory turnover}} \quad \textbf{(3-5)}$$

The days' sales in inventory ratio measures the number of days that inventory is held before the final product is sold.

In general, a firm wants to produce a high level of sales per dollar of inventory; that is, it wants to turn inventory over (from raw materials to finished goods to sold goods) as quickly as possible. A high level of sales per dollar of inventory implies reduced warehousing, monitoring, insurance, and any other costs of servicing the inventory. So, a high inventory turnover ratio or a low days' sales in inventory is generally a sign of good management.

However, if the inventory turnover ratio is extremely high and the days' sales in inventory is extremely low, the firm may not be holding sufficient inventory to prevent running out (or stocking out) of the raw materials needed to keep the production process going. Thus, production and sales stop, which wastes the firm's fixed resources. So, extremely high levels for the inventory turnover ratio and low levels for the days' sales in inventory ratio may actually be a sign of bad firm or production management. Note that companies with very good supply chain relations can maintain lower levels of inventory without incurring as much risk of stockouts.

Accounts Receivable Management

As they decide what level of accounts receivable to hold on the firm's balance sheet, managers must consider the trade-off between the advantages of increased sales by offering customers better terms versus the disadvantages of financing large amounts of accounts receivable. Two ratios used here are the accounts receivable turnover and average collection period.

$$\text{Accounts receivable turnover} = \frac{\text{Credit sales}}{\text{Accounts receivable}} \quad \textbf{(3-6)}$$

The accounts receivable turnover measures the number of dollars of sales produced per dollar of accounts receivable.

$$\text{Average collection period } (ACP) = \frac{\text{Accounts receivable} \times 365 \text{ days}}{\text{Credit sales}}$$
$$= \frac{365 \text{ days}}{\text{Accounts receivable turnover}} \quad \textbf{(3-7)}$$

The average collection period (ACP) measures the number of days accounts receivable are held before the firm collects cash from the sale. This ratio is also sometimes termed the days' sales outstanding (DSO).

In general, a firm wants to produce a high level of sales per dollar of accounts receivable; that is, it wants to collect its accounts receivable as quickly as possible to reduce any cost of financing accounts receivable, including interest expense on liabilities used to finance accounts receivable and defaults associated with accounts receivable. In general, a high accounts receivable turnover or a low ACP is a sign of good management, which is well aware of financing costs and customer remittance habits.

However, if the accounts receivable turnover is extremely high and the ACP is extremely low, the firm's accounts receivable policy may be so strict that customers prefer to do business with competing firms. Firms offer accounts receivable terms as an incentive to get customers to buy products from their firm rather than a competing firm. By offering customers the accounts receivable privilege, management allows them to buy (more) now and pay later. Without this incentive, customers may choose to buy the goods from the firm's competitors who offer better credit terms. So extremely high accounts receivable turnover levels and low ACP levels may be a sign of bad firm management.

Accounts Payable Management

As they decide the accounts payable level to hold on the balance sheet, managers must consider the trade-off between maximizing the use of free financing that raw material suppliers offer versus the risk of losing the opportunity to buy on account. Two ratios commonly used are the accounts payable turnover and average payment period.

$$\text{Accounts payable turnover} = \frac{\text{Cost of goods sold}}{\text{Accounts payable}} \qquad \textbf{(3-8)}$$

The accounts payable turnover ratio measures the dollar cost of goods sold per dollar of accounts payable.

$$\text{Average payment period } (APP) = \frac{\text{Accounts payable} \times 365 \text{ days}}{\text{Cost of goods sold}}$$

$$= \frac{365 \text{ days}}{\text{Accounts payable turnover}} \qquad \textbf{(3-9)}$$

The average payment period (APP) measures the number of days that the firm holds accounts payable before it has to extend cash to pay for its purchases.

In general, a firm wants to pay for its purchases as slowly as possible. The slower the firm pays for its supply purchases, the longer it can avoid obtaining other costly sources of financing such as notes payable or long-term debt. Thus, a low accounts payable turnover or a high APP is generally a sign of good management.

However, if the accounts payable turnover is extremely low and the APP is extremely high, the firm may be abusing the credit terms that its raw materials suppliers offer. At some point, the firm's suppliers may revoke its ability to buy raw materials on account and the firm will lose this source of free financing. If this situation is developing, extremely low levels for the accounts receivable turnover and high levels for the APP may point to bad firm management.

Fixed Asset and Working Capital Management

Two ratios that summarize the efficiency in a firm's overall asset management are the fixed asset turnover and sales to working capital ratios.

$$\text{Fixed asset turnover} = \frac{\text{Sales}}{\text{Net fixed assets}} \qquad \textbf{(3-10)}$$

The fixed asset turnover ratio measures the number of dollars of sales produced per dollar of net fixed assets.

$$\text{Sales to working capital} = \frac{\text{Sales}}{\text{Working capital}} \qquad \textbf{(3-11)}$$

Similarly, the sales to working capital ratio measures the number of dollars of sales produced per dollar of net working capital (current assets minus current liabilities).

In general, the higher the level of sales per dollar of fixed assets and working capital, the more efficiently the firm is being run. Thus, high fixed asset turnover and sales to working capital ratios are generally signs of good management. However, if either the fixed asset turnover or sales to working capital ratio is extremely high, the firm may be close to its maximum production capacity. If capacity is hit, the firm cannot increase production or sales. Accordingly, extremely high fixed asset turnover and sales to working capital ratio levels may actually indicate bad firm management if managers have allowed the company to approach maximum capacity without making any accommodations for growth.

Note a word of caution here. The age of a firm's fixed assets will affect the fixed asset turnover ratio level. A firm with older fixed assets, listed on its balance sheet at historical cost, will tend to have a higher fixed asset turnover ratio than will a firm that has just replaced its fixed assets and lists them on its balance sheet at a (most likely) higher value. Accordingly, the firm with newer fixed assets would have a lower fixed asset turnover ratio. But this is because it has updated its fixed assets, while the other firm has not. It is *not* correct to conclude that the firm with new assets is underperforming relative to the firm with older fixed assets listed on its balance sheet. Similarly, for firms that are in an expansion phase, a lower fixed asset turnover is actually a good sign. It is *not* correct to conclude that a firm with expanding assets is underperforming relative to a firm with no growth.

Total Asset Management

The final two asset management ratios put it all together. They are the total asset turnover and capital intensity ratios.

$$\text{Total asset turnover} = \frac{\text{Sales}}{\text{Total assets}} \qquad \textbf{(3-12)}$$

The total asset turnover ratio measures the number of dollars of sales produced per dollar of total assets.

$$\text{Capital intensity} = \frac{\text{Total assets}}{\text{Sales}} \qquad \textbf{(3-13)}$$

Similarly, the capital intensity ratio measures the dollars of total assets needed to produce a dollar of sales.

In general, a well-managed firm produces many dollars of sales per dollar of total assets, or uses few dollars of assets per dollar of sales. Thus, in general, the higher the total asset turnover and lower the capital intensity ratio, the more efficient the overall asset management of the firm will be. However, if the total asset turnover is extremely high and the capital intensity ratio is extremely low, the firm may actually have an asset management problem. As described above, inventory stockouts, capacity problems, or tight account receivables policies can all lead to a high total asset turnover and may actually be signs of poor firm management.

EXAMPLE 3-2

LG3-2

Calculating Asset Management Ratios

For interactive versions of this example visit www.mhhe.com/can3e

Use the balance sheet (Table 2.1) and income statement (Table 2.2) for DPH Tree Farm, Inc., to calculate the firm's 2015 values for the asset management ratios.

SOLUTION:

We calculate the asset management ratios for DPH Tree Farm, Inc., as follows. The industry average is reported alongside each ratio.

i. Inventory turnover $= \dfrac{\$315m}{\$111m} = 2.84$ times Industry average = 2.15 times

ii. Days' sales in inventory $= \dfrac{\$111m \times 365 \text{ days}}{\$315m} = \dfrac{365 \text{ days}}{2.84 \text{ times}} = 129$ days Industry average = 170 days

iii. Accounts receivable turnover $= \dfrac{\$315m}{\$70m} = 4.50$ times Industry average = 3.84 times

iv. Average collection period $= \dfrac{\$70m \times 365 \text{ days}}{\$315m} = \dfrac{365 \text{ days}}{4.50 \text{ times}} = 81$ days Industry average = 95 days

v. Accounts payable turnover $= \dfrac{\$133m}{\$55m} = 2.42$ times Industry average = 3.55 times

vi. Average payment period $= \dfrac{\$55m \times 365 \text{ days}}{\$133m} = \dfrac{365 \text{ days}}{2.42 \text{ times}} = 151$ days Industry average = 102 days

vii. Fixed asset turnover $= \dfrac{\$315m}{\$315m} = 1.00$ times Industry average = 0.85 times

viii. Sales to working capital $= \dfrac{\$315m}{\$205m - \$120m} = 3.71$ times Industry average = 3.20 times

ix. Total assets turnover $= \dfrac{\$315m}{\$570m} = 0.55$ times Industry average = 0.40 times

x. Capital intensity $= \dfrac{\$570m}{\$315m} = 1.81$ times Industry average = 2.50 times

In all cases, asset management ratios show that DPH Tree Farm, Inc., is outperforming the industry average. The firm is turning over its inventory faster than the average firm in the tree farm industry, thus producing more dollars of sales per dollar of inventory. It is also collecting its accounts receivable faster and paying its accounts payable slower than the average firm. Further, DPH Tree Farm is producing more sales per dollar of fixed assets, working capital, and total assets than the average firm in the industry.

Similar to Problems 3-3, 3-4, self-test problem 1

TIME OUT

3-4 What are the major asset management ratios?

3-5 Does a firm generally want to have high or low values for each of these ratios?

3-6 Explain why many of these ratios are mirror images of one another.

LG3-3

3.3 • Debt Management Ratios

debt management ratios

Measure the extent to which the firm uses debt (or financial leverage) versus equity to finance its assets as well as how well the firm can pay off its debt.

As we discussed in Chapter 2, financial leverage refers to the extent to which the firm uses debt securities in its capital structure. The more debt a firm uses as a percentage of its total assets, the greater is its financial leverage. **Debt management ratios** measure the extent to which the firm uses debt (or financial leverage) versus equity to finance its assets as well as how well the firm can pay off its debt. The specific ratios allow managers and investors to evaluate whether a firm is financing its assets with a reasonable amount of debt versus equity financing, as well as whether the firm is generating sufficient earnings or cash to make the promised payments on its debt. The most commonly used debt management ratios are listed in the following sections.

Debt versus Equity Financing

capital structure

The amount of debt versus equity held on the balance sheet.

Managers' choice of **capital structure**—the amount of debt versus equity to issue—affects the firm's viability as a long-term entity. In deciding the level of debt versus equity financing to hold on the balance sheet, managers must consider the trade-off between maximizing cash flows to the firm's stockholders versus the risk of being unable to make promised debt payments. Ratios that are commonly used are the debt ratio, debt-to-equity, and equity multiplier.

$$\text{Debt ratio} = \frac{\text{Total debt}}{\text{Total assets}} \tag{3-14}$$

The debt ratio measures the percentage of total assets financed with debt.

$$\text{Debt-to-equity} = \frac{\text{Total debt}}{\text{Total equity}} \tag{3-15}$$

The debt-to-equity ratio measures the dollars of debt financing used for every dollar of equity financing.

$$\text{Equity multiplier} = \frac{\text{Total assets}}{\text{Total equity}} \text{ or } \frac{\text{Total assets}}{\text{Common stockholders' equity}} \tag{3-16}$$

The equity multiplier ratio measures the dollars of assets on the balance sheet for every dollar of equity (or just common stockholders' equity) financing.

As you might suspect, all three measures are related.[1] Specifically,

$$\text{Debt ratio} = 1 - \frac{1}{\text{Equity multiplier}} = \frac{1}{(1/\text{Debt-to-equity}) + 1}$$

$$\text{Debt-to-equity} = \frac{1}{(1/\text{Debt ratio}) - 1} = \text{Equity multiplier} - 1$$

$$\text{Equity multiplier} = \frac{1}{1 - \text{Debt ratio}} = \text{Debt-to-equity} + 1$$

So, the lower the debt, debt-to-equity, or equity multiplier, the less debt and more equity the firm uses to finance its assets (i.e., the bigger the firm's equity cushion).

When a firm issues debt to finance its assets, it gives the debt holders first claim to a fixed amount of its cash flows. Stockholders are entitled to any residual

[1]To see this remember the balance sheet identity is Assets (A) = Debt (D) + Equity (E). Dividing each side of this equation by assets, we get $A/A = D/A + E/A$. Rearranging this equation, $D/A = A/A - E/A = 1 - E/A = 1 - [1/(A/E)]$. Also, $D/A = (A - E)/A = 1/[A/(A - E)] = 1/[(A - E + E)/(A - E)] = 1/[(E/(A - E) + (A - E)/(A - E)] = 1/[E/D + 1] = 1/[1/(D/E) + 1]$. Dividing each side of the balance sheet identity equation by equity, we get $A/E = D/E + E/E$, or $A/E = D/E + 1$. Also, rearranging this equation, $D/E = A/E - 1$.

cash flows—those left after debt holders are paid. When a firm does well, financial leverage increases the reward to shareholders since the amount of cash flows promised to debt holders is constant and capped. So when firms do well, financial leverage creates more cash flows to share with stockholders—it magnifies the return to the stockholders of the firm (recall Example 2-5). This magnification is one reason that stockholders encourage the use of debt financing.

However, financial leverage also increases the firm's potential for financial distress and even failure. If the firm has a bad year and cannot make promised debt payments, debt holders can force the firm into bankruptcy. Thus, a firm's current and potential debt holders (and even stockholders) look at equity financing as a safety cushion that can absorb fluctuations in the firm's earnings and asset values and guarantee debt service payments. Clearly, the larger the fluctuations or variability of a firm's cash flows, the greater the need for an equity cushion.

Coverage Ratios

Three additional debt management ratios are the times interest earned, fixed-charge coverage, and cash coverage ratios. These ratios are different measures of a firm's ability to meet its debt obligations.

$$\text{Times interest earned} = \frac{EBIT}{\text{Interest}} \tag{3-17}$$

The times interest earned ratio measures the number of dollars of operating earnings available to meet each dollar of interest obligations on the firm's debt.

$$\text{Fixed-charge coverage} = \frac{\text{Earnings available to meet fixed charges}}{\text{Fixed charges}} \tag{3-18}$$

The fixed-charge coverage ratio measures the number of dollars of operating *earnings* available to meet the firm's interest obligations and other fixed charges.

$$\text{Cash coverage} = \frac{EBIT + \text{Depreciation}}{\text{Fixed charges}} \tag{3-19}$$

The cash coverage ratio measures the number of dollars of operating *cash* available to meet each dollar of interest and other fixed charges that the firm owes.

With the help of the times interest earned, fixed-charge coverage, and cash coverage ratios, managers, investors, and analysts can determine whether a firm has taken on a debt burden that is too large. These ratios measure the dollars available to meet debt and other fixed-charge obligations. A value of one for these ratios means that $1 of earnings or cash is available to meet each dollar of interest or fixed-charge obligations. A value of less (greater) than one means that the firm has less (more) than $1 of earnings or cash available to pay each dollar of interest or fixed-charge obligations.[2] Further, the higher the times interest earned, fixed-charge coverage, and cash coverage ratios, the more equity and less debt the firm uses to finance its assets. Thus, low levels of debt will lead to a dilution of the return to stockholders due to increased use of equity as well as to not taking advantage of the tax deductibility of interest expense.

[2]The fixed-charge and cash coverage ratios can be tailored to a particular firm's situation, depending on what really constitutes fixed charges that must be paid. One version of it follows: (EBIT + Lease payments)/[Interest + Lease payments + Sinking fund/$(1 - t)$], where t is the firm's marginal tax rate. Here, it is assumed that sinking fund payments must be made. They are adjusted by the division of $(1 - t)$ into a before-tax cash outflow so they can be added to other before-tax cash outflows.

EXAMPLE 3-3

LG3-3

For interactive versions of this example visit www.mhhe.com/can3e

Calculating Debt Management Ratios

Use the balance sheet (Table 2.1) and income statement (Table 2.2) for DPH Tree Farm, Inc., to calculate the firm's 2015 values for the debt management ratios.

SOLUTION:

The debt management ratios for DPH Tree Farm, Inc., are calculated as follows. The industry average is reported alongside each ratio.

i. Debt ratio $= \frac{\$120m + \$195m}{\$570m} = 55.26\%$ Industry average = 68.50%

ii. Debt-to-equity $= \frac{\$120m + \$195m}{\$255m} = 1.24$ times Industry average = 2.17 times

iii. Equity multiplier $= \frac{\$570m}{\$255m} = 2.24$ times Industry average = 4.10 times

or $\frac{\$570m}{\$255m - \$5m} = 2.28$ times Industry average = 4.14 times

iv. Times interest earned $= \frac{\$152m}{\$16m} = 9.50$ times Industry average = 5.15 times

v. Fixed-charge coverage $= \frac{\$152m}{\$16m} = 9.50$ times Industry average = 5.70 times

vi. Cash coverage $= \frac{\$152m + \$13m}{\$16m} = 10.31$ times Industry average = 7.78 times

In all cases, debt management ratios show that DPH Tree Farm, Inc., holds less debt on its balance sheet than the average firm in the tree farm industry. Further, the firm has more dollars of operating earnings and cash available to meet each dollar of interest obligations (there are no other fixed charges listed on DPH Tree Farm's income statement) on the firm's debt. This lack of financial leverage decreases the firm's potential for financial distress and even failure, but may also decrease equity shareholders' chance for magnified earnings. If the firm has a bad year, it has promised relatively few payments to debt holders. Thus, the risk of bankruptcy is small. However, when DPH Tree Farm, Inc., does well, the low level of financial leverage dilutes the return to the stockholders of the firm. This dilution of profit is likely to upset common stockholders of the firm.

Similar to Problems 3-5, 3-6, self-test problem 1

profitability ratios

Ratios that show the combined effect of liquidity, asset management, and debt management on the firm's overall operating results.

TIME OUT

3-7 What are the major debt management ratios?

3-8 Does a firm generally want to have high or low values for each of these ratios?

3-9 What is the trade-off between using too much financial leverage and not using enough leverage? Who is likely to complain the most in each case?

LG3-4

3.4 • Profitability Ratios

The liquidity, asset management, and debt management ratios examined so far allow for an isolated or narrow look at a firm's performance. **Profitability ratios** show the combined effects of liquidity, asset management, and debt management on the overall operating results of the firm. Profitability ratios are among the most watched and best known of the financial ratios. Indeed, firm values (or stock prices) react quickly to unexpected changes in these ratios. The most commonly used profitability ratios are listed below.

$$\text{Gross profit margin} = \frac{\text{Sales} - \text{Cost of goods sold}}{\text{Sales}} \tag{3-20}$$

The gross profit margin is the percent of sales left after costs of goods sold are deducted.

$$\text{Operating profit margin} = \frac{EBIT}{\text{Sales}} \tag{3-21}$$

The operating profit margin is the percent of sales left after all operating expenses are deducted.

$$\text{Profit margin} = \frac{\text{Net income available to common stockholders}}{\text{Sales}} \tag{3-22}$$

The profit margin is the percentage of sales left after all firm expenses are deducted. Thus, this ratio provides the net profit margin of the firm, as opposed to the gross profit or operating profit margin.

$$\text{Basic earnings power } (BEP) = \frac{EBIT}{\text{Total assets}} \tag{3-23}$$

The basic earnings power ratio measures the operating return on the firm's assets, regardless of financial leverage and taxes. This ratio measures the operating profit (EBIT) earned per dollar of assets on the firm's balance sheet.

$$\text{Return on assets } (ROA) = \frac{\text{Net income available to common stockholders}}{\text{Total assets}} \tag{3-24}$$

Return on assets (ROA) measures the overall return on the firm's assets, including financial leverage and taxes. This ratio is the net income earned per dollar of assets on the firm's balance sheet.

$$\text{Return on equity } (ROE) = \frac{\text{Net income available to common stockholders}}{\text{Common stockholders' equity}} \tag{3-25}$$

Return on equity (ROE) measures the return on the common stockholders' investment in the assets of the firm. ROE is the net income earned per dollar of common stockholders' equity. The value of a firm's ROE is affected not only by net income, but also by the amount of financial leverage or debt that firm uses. As stated previously, financial leverage magnifies the return to the stockholders of the firm. However, financial leverage also increases the firm's potential for financial distress and even failure. Generally, a high ROE is considered to be a positive sign of firm performance. However, if performance comes from a high degree of financial leverage, a high ROE can indicate a firm with an unacceptably high level of bankruptcy risk as well.

$$\text{Dividend payout} = \frac{\text{Common stock dividends}}{\text{Net income available to common stockholders}} \tag{3-26}$$

Finally, the dividend payout ratio is the percentage of net income available to common stockholders that the firm actually pays as cash to these investors.

For all but the dividend payout, the higher the value of the ratio, the higher the profitability of the firm. But just as has been the case previously in this chapter, high profitability ratio levels may result from poor management in other areas of the firm as much as superior financial management. A high profit (and gross profit or operating profit) margin means that the firm has low expenses relative to sales. The BEP reflects how much the firm's assets earn from operations, regardless of financial leverage and taxes. It follows logically that managers, investors, and analysts find BEP a useful ratio when they compare firms that differ in financial leverage and taxes. In contrast, ROA measures the firm's overall performance. It shows how the firm's assets generate a return that includes financial leverage and tax decisions made by management.

ROE measures the return on common stockholders' investment. Since managers seek to maximize common stock price, managers, investors, and analysts monitor ROE above all other ratios. The dividend payout ratio measures how much of the profit the firm retains versus how much it pays out to common stockholders as dividends. The lower the dividend payout ratio, the more profits the firm retains for future growth or other projects. A profitable firm that retains its earnings increases its level of equity capital as well as its own value.

EXAMPLE 3-4

LG3-4

For interactive versions of this example visit www.mhhe.com/can3e

Calculating Profitability Ratios

Use the balance sheet (Table 2.1) and income statement (Table 2.2) for DPH Tree Farm, Inc., to calculate the firm's 2015 values for the profitability ratios.

SOLUTION:

The profitability ratios for DPH Tree Farm, Inc., are calculated as follows. The industry average is reported alongside each ratio.

i. $\text{Gross profit margin} = \dfrac{\$182\text{m}}{\$315\text{m}} = 57.78\%$ Industry average = 56.65%

ii. $\text{Operating profit margin} = \dfrac{\$152\text{m}}{\$315\text{m}} = 48.25\%$ Industry average = 46.88%

iii. $\text{Profit margin} = \dfrac{\$80\text{m}}{\$315\text{m}} = 25.40\%$ Industry average = 23.25%

iv. $\text{Basic earnings power } (BEP) = \dfrac{\$152\text{m}}{\$570\text{m}} = 26.67\%$ Industry average = 22.85%

v. $\text{Return on assets } (ROA) = \dfrac{\$80\text{m}}{\$570\text{m}} = 14.04\%$ Industry average = 9.30%

vi. $\text{Return on equity } (ROE) = \dfrac{\$80\text{m}}{\$40\text{m} + \$210\text{m}} = 32.00\%$ Industry average = 38.00%

vii. $\text{Dividend payout} = \dfrac{\$25\text{m}}{\$80\text{m}} = 31.25\%$ Industry average = 30.90%

These ratios show that DPH Tree Farm, Inc., is more profitable than the average firm in the tree farm industry. The profit margin, gross profit margin, operating profit margin, BEP, and ROA are all higher than industry figures. Despite this, the ROE for DPH Tree Farm is much lower than the industry average. DPH's low debt level and high equity level relative to the industry is the main reason for DPH's strong figures relative to the industry. As we mentioned above, DPH's managerial decisions about capital structure dilute its returns, which will likely upset its common stockholders. To counteract common stockholders' discontent, DPH Tree Farm pays out a slightly larger percentage of its income to its common stockholders as cash dividends. Of course, this slightly high dividend payout ratio means that DPH Tree Farm retains less of its profits to reinvest into the business. A profitable firm that retains its earnings increases its equity capital level as well as its own value.

Similar to Problems 3-7, 3-8, self-test problem 1

TIME OUT

3-10 What are the major profitability ratios?

3-11 Does a firm generally want to have high or low values for each of these ratios?

3-12 What are the trade-offs to having especially high or low values for ROE?

3.5 • Market Value Ratios

LG3-5

As noted, ROE is a most important financial statement ratio for managers and investors to monitor. Generally, a high ROE is considered to be a positive sign of firm performance. However, if a high ROE results from a highly leveraged position, it can signal a firm with a high level of bankruptcy risk. While ROE does not directly incorporate this risk, for publicly traded firms, market prices of the firm's stock do. (We look at stock valuation in Chapter 8.) Since the firm's stockholders earn their returns primarily from the firm's stock market value, ratios that incorporate stock market values are equally, and arguably more, important than other financial statement ratios.

The final group of ratios is market value ratios. **Market value ratios** relate a firm's stock price to its earnings and its book value. For publicly traded firms, market value ratios measure what investors think of the company's future performance and risk.

market value ratios
Ratios that relate a firm's stock price to its earnings and book value.

$$\text{Market-to-book ratio} = \frac{\text{Market price per share}}{\text{Book value per share}} \quad \textbf{(3-27)}$$

The market-to-book ratio measures the amount that investors will pay for the firm's stock per dollar of equity used to finance the firm's assets. Book value per share is an accounting-based number reflecting the firm's assets' historical costs, and hence historical value. The market-to-book ratio compares the market (current) value of the firm's equity to its historical cost. In general, the higher the market-to-book ratio, the better the firm. If liquidity, asset management, debt management, and accounting profitability are good for a firm, then the market-to-book ratio will be high. A market-to-book ratio greater than one (or 100 percent) means that stockholders will pay a premium over book value for their equity investment in the firm.

$$\text{Price-earnings } (PE) \text{ ratio} = \frac{\text{Market price per share}}{\text{Earnings per share}} \quad \textbf{(3-28)}$$

One of the best known and most often quoted figures, the price-earnings (or PE) ratio measures how much investors are willing to pay for each dollar the firm earns per share of its stock. PE ratios are often quoted in multiples—the number of dollars per share—that fund managers, investors, and analysts compare within industry classes. Managers and investors often use PE ratios to evaluate the relative financial performance of the firm's stock. Generally, the higher the PE ratio, the better the firm's performance. Analysts and investors, as well as managers, expect companies with high PE ratios to experience future growth, to have rapid future dividend increases, or both, because retained earnings will support the company's goals. However, for value-seeking investors, high-PE firms indicate expensive companies. Further, higher PE ratios carry greater risk because investors are willing to pay higher prices today for a stock in anticipation of higher earnings in the future. These earnings may or may not materialize. Low-PE firms are generally companies with little expected growth or low earnings. However, note that earnings depend on many factors (such as financial leverage or taxes) that have nothing to do directly with firm operations.

EXAMPLE 3-5

LG3-5

For interactive versions of this example visit www.mhhe.com/can3e

Calculating Market Value Ratios

Use the balance sheet (Table 2.1) and income statement (Table 2.2) for DPH Tree Farm, Inc., to calculate the firm's 2015 values for the market value ratios.

SOLUTION:

The market value ratios for DPH Tree Farm, Inc., are calculated as follows. The industry average is reported alongside each ratio.

i. Market-to-book ratio $= \dfrac{\$17.25}{\$12.50} = 1.38$ times   Industry average = 2.15 times

ii. Price-earnings (*PE*) ratio $= \dfrac{\$17.25}{\$4.00} = 4.31$ times   Industry average = 6.25 times

These ratios show that DPH Tree Farm's investors will not pay as much for a share of DPH's stock per dollar of book value and earnings as the average for the industry. DPH's low leverage level and high reliance on equity relative to the industry are likely the main reason for investors' disinterest. As mentioned previously, DPH's seemingly intentional return dilution will likely upset the firm's common stockholders. Accordingly, stockholders lower the amount they are willing to invest per dollar of book value and EPS.

Similar to Problems 3-9, 3-10, self-test problem 1

TIME OUT

3-13 What are the major market value ratios?

3-14 Does a firm generally want to have high or low values for each of these ratios?

3-15 Discuss the price-earnings ratio and explain why it assumes particular importance among all of the other ratios we have presented.

LG3-6

3.6 • DuPont Analysis

DuPont system of analysis

An analytical method that uses the balance sheet and income statement to break the ROA and ROE ratios into component pieces.

Table 3.1 (on page 92) lists the ratios we discuss, their values for DPH Tree Farm, Inc., as of 2015, and the corresponding values for the tree farm industry. The value of each ratio for DPH Tree Farm is highlighted in green if it is generally stronger than the industry and is highlighted in red if it is generally a negative sign for the firm. As we noted in this chapter's introduction, many of the ratios we have discussed thus far are interrelated. So a change in one ratio may well affect the value of several ratios. Often these interrelations can help evaluate firm performance. Managers and investors often perform a detailed analysis of ROA (return on assets) and ROE (return on equity) using the **DuPont system of analysis**. Popularized by the DuPont Corporation, the DuPont system of analysis uses the balance sheet and income statement to break the ROA and ROE ratios into component pieces.

The basic DuPont equation looks at ROA as the product of the profit margin and the total asset turnover ratios:

$$\text{ROA} = \text{Profit margin} \times \text{Total asset turnover}$$

$$\frac{\text{Net income available to common stockholders}}{\text{Total assets}} = \frac{\text{Net income available to common stockholders}}{\text{Sales}} \times \frac{\text{Sales}}{\text{Total assets}} \quad \textbf{(3-29)}$$

The basic DuPont equation looks at the firm's overall profitability as a function of the profit the firm earns per dollar of sales (operating efficiency) and the dollar of sales produced per dollar of assets on the balance sheet (efficiency in asset use). With this tool, managers can see the reason for any changes in ROA in more detail. For example, if ROA increases, the DuPont equation may show that the net profit margin was constant, but the total asset turnover (efficiency in using assets) increased, or that total asset turnover remained constant, but profit margins (operating efficiency) increased. Managers can identify the reasons for an ROA change more specifically by using the ratios described above to further break down operating efficiency and efficiency in asset use.

Next, the DuPont system looks at ROE as the product of ROA and the equity multiplier.

$$\text{ROE} = \text{ROA} \times \text{Equity multiplier}$$

$$\frac{\text{Net income available to common stockholders}}{\text{Common stockholders' equity}} = \text{ROA} \times \frac{\text{Total assets}}{\text{Common stockholders' equity}} \quad \textbf{(3-30)}$$

Notice that this version of the equity multiplier uses the return to common stockholders (the firm's owners) only. So the DuPont equity multiplier uses common stockholders' equity only, rather than total equity (which includes preferred stock).

Taking this breakdown one step further, the DuPont system breaks ROE into the product of the profit margin, the total asset turnover, and the equity multiplier.

$$\text{ROE} = \text{Profit margin} \times \text{Total asset turnover} \times \text{Equity multiplier}$$

$$\frac{\text{Net income available to common stockholders}}{\text{Common stockholders' equity}} = \frac{\text{Net income available to common stockholders}}{\text{Sales}} \times \frac{\text{Sales}}{\text{Total assets}} \times \frac{\text{Total assets}}{\text{Common stockholders' equity}} \quad \textbf{(3-31)}$$

This presentation of ROE allows managers, analysts, and investors to look at the return on equity as a function of the net profit margin (profit per dollar of sales from the income statement), the total asset turnover (efficiency in the use of assets from the balance sheet), and the equity multiplier (financial leverage from the balance sheet). Again, we can break these components down to identify possible causes for a ROE change more specifically. Figure 3.1 illustrates the DuPont system of analysis breakdown of ROA and ROE. The figure highlights how many of the ratios discussed in this chapter are linked.

table 3.1 | **Summary of Ratios and Their Values for DPH Tree Farm, Inc., and the Tree Farm Industry**

Ratio	Value for DPH Tree Farm, Inc.	Value for the Tree Farm Industry
Liquidity ratios:		
Current ratio $= \frac{\text{Current assets}}{\text{Current liabilities}}$	1.71 times	1.50 times
Quick ratio (acid-test ratio) $= \frac{\text{Current assets} - \text{Inventory}}{\text{Current liabilities}}$	0.78 times	0.50 times
Cash ratio $= \frac{\text{Cash and marketable securities}}{\text{Current liabilities}}$	0.20 times	0.15 times
Asset management ratios:		
Inventory turnover $= \frac{\text{Sales or cost of goods sold}}{\text{Inventory}}$	2.84 times	2.15 times
Days' sales in inventory $= \frac{\text{Inventory} \times 365 \text{ days}}{\text{Sales or cost of goods sold}}$	129 days	170 days
Accounts receivable turnover $= \frac{\text{Credit sales}}{\text{Accounts receivable}}$	4.50 times	3.84 times
Average collection period $= \frac{\text{Accounts receivable} \times 365 \text{ days}}{\text{Credit sales}}$	81 days	95 days
Accounts payable turnover $= \frac{\text{Cost of goods sold}}{\text{Accounts payable}}$	2.42 times	3.55 times
Average payment period (*APP*) $= \frac{\text{Accounts payable} \times 365 \text{ days}}{\text{Cost of goods sold}}$	151 days	102 days
Fixed asset turnover $= \frac{\text{Sales}}{\text{Net fixed assets}}$	1.00 times	0.85 times
Sales to working capital $= \frac{\text{Sales}}{\text{Working capital}}$	3.71 times	3.20 times

(Continued)

figure 3.1

DuPont System Analysis Breakdown of ROA and ROE

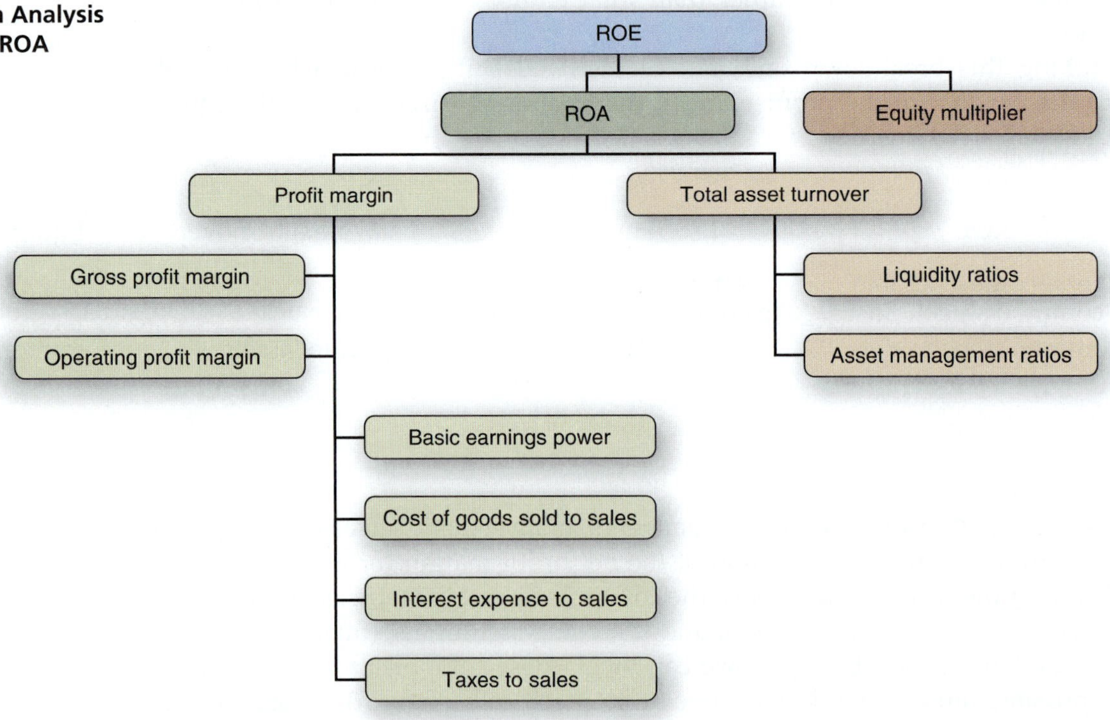

Ratio	Value for DPH Tree Farm, Inc.	Value for the Tree Farm Industry
Total assets turnover $= \dfrac{\text{Sales}}{\text{Total assets}}$	0.55 times	0.40 times
Capital intensity $= \dfrac{\text{Total assets}}{\text{Sales}}$	1.81 times	2.50 times
Debt management ratios:		
Debt ratio $= \dfrac{\text{Total debt}}{\text{Total assets}}$	55.26%	68.50%
Debt-to-equity $= \dfrac{\text{Total debt}}{\text{Total equity}}$	1.24 times	2.17 times
Equity multiplier $= \dfrac{\text{Total assets}}{\text{Total equity}}$	2.24 times	4.10 times
or $\dfrac{\text{Total assets}}{\text{Common stockholders' equity}}$	2.28 times	4.14 times
Times interest earned $= \dfrac{EBIT}{\text{Interest}}$	9.50 times	5.15 times
Fixed-charge coverage $= \dfrac{\text{Earnings available to meet fixed charges}}{\text{Fixed charges}}$	9.50 times	5.70 times
Cash coverage $= \dfrac{EBIT + \text{Depreciation}}{\text{Fixed charges}}$	10.31 times	7.78 times
Profitability ratios:		
Gross profit margin $= \dfrac{\text{Sales} - \text{Cost of goods sold}}{\text{Sales}}$	57.78%	56.65%
Operating profit margin $= \dfrac{EBIT}{\text{Sales}}$	48.25%	46.88%
Profit margin $= \dfrac{\text{Net income available to common stockholders}}{\text{Sales}}$	25.40%	23.25%
Basic earnings power $= \dfrac{EBIT}{\text{Total assets}}$	26.67%	22.85%
Return on assets $= \dfrac{\text{Net income available to common stockholders}}{\text{Total assets}}$	14.04%	9.30%
Return on equity $= \dfrac{\text{Net income available to common stockholders}}{\text{Common stockholders' equity}}$	32.00%	38.00%
Dividend payout $= \dfrac{\text{Common stock dividends}}{\text{Net income available to common stockholders}}$	31.25%	30.90%
Market value ratios:		
Market-to-book ratio $= \dfrac{\text{Market price per share}}{\text{Book value per share}}$	1.38 times	2.15 times
Price-earnings ratio $= \dfrac{\text{Market price per share}}{\text{Earnings per share}}$	4.31 times	6.25 times

EXAMPLE 3-6

LG3-6

Application of DuPont Analysis

Use the balance sheet (Table 2.1) and income statement (Table 2.2) for DPH Tree Farm, Inc., to calculate the firm's 2015 values for the ROA and ROE DuPont equations.

For interactive versions of this example visit www.mhhe.com/can3e

SOLUTION:

The ROA and ROE DuPont equations for DPH Tree Farm, Inc., are calculated as follows. The industry average is reported below each ratio.

i.

$$ROA = \text{Profit margin} \times \text{Total asset turnover}$$

$$14.04\% = 25.39683\% \times 0.55263 \text{ times}$$

$$\text{Industry average: } 9.30\% = 23.25\% \times 0.40 \text{ times}$$

$$\frac{\text{Net income available to common stockholders}}{\text{Total assets}} = \frac{\text{Net income available to common stockholders}}{\text{Sales}} \times \frac{\text{Sales}}{\text{Total assets}}$$

$$\frac{\$80m}{\$570m} = \frac{\$80m}{\$315m} \times \frac{\$315m}{\$570m}$$

ii.

$$ROE = \text{Profit margin} \times \text{Total asset turnover} \times \text{Equity multiplier}$$

$$32.00\% = 25.39683\% \times 0.55263 \text{ times} \times 2.28 \text{ times}$$

$$\text{Industry average: } 38.50\% = 23.25\% \times 0.40 \text{ times} \times 4.13978 \text{ times}$$

$$\frac{\text{Net income available to common stockholders}}{\text{Common stockholders' equity}} = \frac{\text{Net income available to common stockholders}}{\text{Sales}} \times \frac{\text{Sales}}{\text{Total assets}} \times \frac{\text{Total assets}}{\text{Common stockholders' equity}}$$

$$\frac{\$80m}{\$40m + \$210m} = \frac{\$80m}{\$315m} \times \frac{\$315m}{\$570m} \times \frac{\$570m}{\$40m + \$210m}$$

As we saw with profitability ratios, DPH Tree Farm, Inc., is more profitable than the average firm in the tree farm industry when it comes to overall efficiency expressed as return on assets, or ROA. The DuPont equation highlights that this superior performance comes from both profit margin (operating efficiency) and total asset turnover (efficiency in asset use). Despite this, the ROE for DPH Tree Farm lags the average industry ROE. The DuPont equation highlights that this inferior performance is due solely to the low level of debt and high level of equity used by DPH Tree Farm relative to the industry.

Similar to Problems 3-11, 3-12

TIME OUT

3-16 What are the DuPont ROA and ROE equations?

3-17 How do each of these equations help to explain firm performance and pinpoint areas for improvement?

LG3-6

3.7 • Other Ratios

Spreading the Financial Statements

common-size financial statements

Dividing all balance sheet amounts by total assets and all income statement amounts by net sales.

In addition to the many ratios listed, managers, analysts, and investors can also compute additional ratios by dividing all balance sheet amounts by total assets and all income statement amounts by net sales. These calculations, sometimes called *spreading the financial statements,* yield what we call **common-size financial statements** that correct for sizes. Year-to-year growth rates in common-size balance sheets and income statement balances provide useful ratios for identifying trends. They also allow for an easy comparison of balance sheets and income statements across firms in the industry. Common-size financial statements may provide quantitative clues about the direction that the firm (and perhaps the industry) is moving. They may thus provide roadmaps for managers' next moves.

Internal and Sustainable Growth Rates

Remember again that any firm manager's job is to maximize the firm's market value. The firm's ROA and ROE can be used to evaluate the firm's ability to grow and its market value to be maximized. Specifically, managers, analysts, and investors use these ratios to calculate two growth measures: the internal growth rate and the sustainable growth rate.

The **internal growth rate** is the growth rate a firm can sustain if it uses only internal financing—that is, retained earnings—to finance future growth. Mathematically, the internal growth rate is:

internal growth rate

The growth rate a firm can sustain if it finances growth using only internal financing, that is, retained earnings growth.

$$\text{Internal growth rate} = \frac{ROA \times RR}{1 - (ROA \times RR)} \quad \textbf{(3-32)}$$

where RR is the firm's earnings retention ratio. The retention ratio represents the portion of net income that the firm reinvests as retained earnings:

$$\text{Retention ratio } (RR) = \frac{\text{Addition to retained earnings}}{\text{Net income available to common stockholders}} \quad \textbf{(3-33)}$$

Since a firm either pays its net income as dividends to its stockholders or reinvests those funds as retained earnings, the dividend payout and the retention ratios must always add to one:

$$\text{Retention ratio} = 1 - \text{Dividend payout ratio} \quad \textbf{(3-34)}$$

A problem arises when a firm relies only on internal financing to support asset growth: Through time, its debt ratio will fall because as asset values grow, total debt stays constant—only retained earnings finance asset growth. If total debt remains constant as assets grow, the debt ratio decreases. As we noted above, shareholders often become disgruntled if, as the firm grows, a decreasing debt ratio (increasing equity financing) dilutes their return. So as firms grow, managers must often try to maintain a debt ratio that they view as optimal. In this case, managers finance asset growth with new debt *and* retained earnings. The maximum growth rate that can be achieved this way is the **sustainable growth rate**. Mathematically, the sustainable growth rate is:

sustainable growth rate

The growth rate a firm can sustain if it finances growth using both debt and internal financing such that the debt ratio remains constant.

$$\text{Sustainable growth rate} = \frac{ROE \times RR}{1 - (ROE \times RR)} \quad \textbf{(3-35)}$$

Maximizing the sustainable growth rate helps firm managers maximize firm value. When applying the DuPont ROE equation (3-31) here (i.e., ROE = Profit margin × Total asset turnover × Equity multiplier), notice that a firm's sustainable growth depends on four factors:

1. The profit margin (operating efficiency).
2. The total asset turnover (efficiency in asset use).
3. Financial leverage (the use of debt versus equity to finance assets).
4. Profit retention (reinvestment of net income into the firm rather than paying it out as dividends).

Increasing any of these factors increases the firm's sustainable growth rate and hence helps to maximize firm value. Managers, analysts, and investors will want to focus on these areas as they evaluate firm performance and market value.

EXAMPLE 3-7

LG3-7

For interactive versions of this example visit www.mhhe.com/can3e

Calculating Internal and Sustainable Growth Rates

Use the balance sheet (Table 2.1) and income statement (Table 2.2) for DPH Tree Farm, Inc., to calculate the firm's 2015 internal and sustainable growth rates.

SOLUTION:

The internal and sustainable growth rates for DPH Tree Farm, Inc., are calculated as follows. The industry average is reported alongside each ratio.

$$\text{Retention rate } (RR) = \frac{\$210\text{m} - \$155\text{m}}{\$80\text{m}} = 0.6875 \text{ or } 68.75\%$$

$$\text{Industry RR} = 1 - \text{Industry dividend payout ratio} = 1 - 0.3090 = 0.6910$$

$$\text{i. Internal growth rate} = \frac{0.1404 \times 0.6875}{1 - (0.1404 \times 0.6875)} = 0.1068 \text{ or } 10.68\%$$

$$\text{Industry average internal growth rate} = \frac{0.0930 \times 0.6910}{1 - (0.0930 \times 0.6910)} = 0.0687 \text{ or } 6.87\%$$

$$\text{ii. Sustainable growth rate} = \frac{0.3200 \times 0.6875}{1 - (0.3200 \times 0.6875)} = 0.2821 \text{ or } 28.21\%$$

$$\text{Industry average sustainable growth rate} = \frac{0.3800 \times 0.6910}{1 - (0.3800 \times 0.6910)} = 0.3561 \text{ or } 35.61\%$$

MATH COACH

When putting values into the equation, enter them in decimal format, not percentage format

CORRECT 1 − (0.1404 × 0.6875)

NOT CORRECT 1 − (14.04 × 68.75)

These ratios show that DPH Tree Farm, Inc., can grow faster than the industry if the firm uses only retained earnings to finance the growth. However, if DPH grows while keeping the debt ratio constant (e.g., both debt and retained earnings are used to finance the growth), industry firms can grow much faster than DPH Tree Farm. Once again, DPH's low debt level and high equity level relative to the industry creates this disparity. Therefore, DPH Tree Farm limits its growth as a result of its managerial decisions.

Similar to Problems 3-13, 3-14, self-test problem 2

TIME OUT

3-18 What does "spreading the financial statements" mean?

3-19 What are retention rates and internal and sustainable growth rates?

3-20 What factors enter into sustainable growth rates?

LG3-7

3.8 • Time Series and Cross-Sectional Analysis

time series analysis
Analyzing firm performance by monitoring ratio trends.

cross-sectional analysis
Analyzing the performance of a firm against one or more companies in the same industry.

We have explored many ratios that allow managers and investors to examine firm performance. But to really analyze performance in a meaningful way, we must interpret our ratio results against some kind of standard or benchmark. To interpret financial ratios, managers, analysts, and investors use two major types of benchmarks: (1) performance of the firm over time (**time series analysis**) and (2) performance of the firm against one or more companies in the same industry (**cross-sectional analysis**).

Analyzing ratio trends over time, along with absolute ratio levels, gives managers, analysts, and investors information about whether a firm's financial condition is improving or deteriorating. For example, ratio analysis may reveal that the days' sales in inventory is increasing. This suggests that inventories, relative to the sales they support, are not being used as well as they were in the past. If this increase is the result of a deliberate policy to increase inventories to offer customers a wider choice and if it results in higher future sales volumes or increased margins that more than compensate for increased capital tied up in inventory, the increased relative size of the inventories is good for the firm. Managers and investors should be concerned, on the other hand, if increased inventories result from declining sales but steady purchases of supplies and production.

Looking at one firm's financial ratios, even through time, gives managers, analysts, and investors only a limited picture of firm performance. Ratio analysis almost always includes a comparison of one firm's ratios relative to the ratios of other firms in the industry, or cross-sectional analysis. The key to cross-sectional analysis is identifying similar firms that compete in the same markets, have similar asset sizes, and operate in a similar manner to the firm being analyzed. Since no two firms are identical, obtaining such a comparison group is no easy task. Thus, the choice of companies to use in cross-sectional analysis is at best subjective. Note that as we calculated the financial ratios for DPH Tree Farm, Inc., throughout the chapter, we compared them to the industry average. Comparative ratios that can be used in cross-sectional analysis are available from many sources. For example, Value Line Investment Surveys, Robert Morris Associates, Hoover's Online (at www.hoovers.com), and MSN Money website (at moneycentral.msn.com) are examples of four major sources of financial ratios for numerous industries that operate within the United States and worldwide.

TIME OUT

3-21 What is time series analysis of a firm's operations?

3-22 What is cross-sectional analysis of a firm's operations?

3-23 How do time series and cross-sectional analyses differ, and what information would you expect to gain from each?

3.9 • Cautions in Using Ratios to Evaluate Firm Performance

LG3-8

Financial statement analysis allows managers, analysts, and investors to better understand a firm's performance. However, data from financial statements should not be received without certain cautions. These include:

1. Financial statement data are historical. Historical data may not reflect future performance. While we can make projections using historical data, we must also remember that projections may be inaccurate if historical performance does not persist.
2. As we discussed in Chapter 2, firms use different accounting procedures. For example, inventory methods can vary. One firm may use FIFO (first-in, first-out), transferring inventory at the first purchase price, while another uses LIFO (last-in, first-out), transferring inventory at the last purchase price. Likewise, the depreciation method used to value a firm's fixed assets over time may vary across firms. One firm may use straight-line depreciation, while another may use an accelerated depreciation method (e.g., MACRS). Particularly, when reviewing cross-sectional ratios, differences in accounting rules can affect balance sheet values and financial ratios. It is important to know which accounting rules the firms under consideration

are using before making any conclusions about their performance from ratio analysis.

3. Similarly, a firm's cross-sectional competitors may often be located around the world. Financial statements for firms based outside the United States do not necessarily conform to GAAP. Even beyond inventory pricing and depreciation methods, different accounting standards and procedures make it hard to compare financial statements and ratios of firms based in different countries.
4. Sales and expenses vary throughout the year. Managers, analysts, and investors need to note the timing of these fund flows when performing cross-sectional analysis. Otherwise they may draw conclusions from comparisons that are actually the result of seasonal cash flow differences. Similarly, firms end their fiscal years at different dates. For cross-sectional analysis, this complicates any comparison of balance sheets during the year. Likewise, one-time events, such as a merger, may affect a firm's financial performance. Cross-sectional analysis involving these events can result in misleading conclusions.
5. Large firms often have multiple divisions or business units engaged in different lines of business. In this case, it is difficult to truly compare a set of firms with which managers and investors can perform cross-sectional analysis.
6. Firms often window dress their financial statements to make annual results look better. For example, to improve liquidity ratios calculated with year-end balance sheets, firms often delay payments for raw materials, equipment, loans, and so on to build up their liquid accounts and thus their liquidity ratios. If possible, it is often more accurate to use something other than year-end financial statements to conduct ratio analysis.
7. Individual analysts may calculate ratios in modified forms. For example, one analyst may calculate ratios using year-end balance sheet data, while another may use the average of the beginning- and end-of-year balance sheet data. If the firm's balance sheet has changed significantly during the year, this difference in the way the ratio is calculated can cause large variations in ratio values for a given period of analysis and large variations in any conclusions drawn from these ratios regarding the financial health of the firm.

Financial statement ratio analysis is a major part of evaluating a firm's performance. If managers, analysts, or investors ignore the issues noted here, they may well draw faulty conclusions from their analysis. However, used intelligently and with good judgment, ratio analysis can provide useful information on a firm's current position and hint at future performance.

TIME OUT

3-24 What cautions should managers and investors take when using ratio analysis to evaluate a firm?

viewpoints REVISITED

Business Application Solution

The managers of DPH Tree Farm, Inc., have stated that its performance surpasses that of other firms in the industry. Particularly strong are the firm's liquidity and asset management positions. The superior performance in these areas has resulted in superior overall returns for the stockholders of DPH Tree Farm, Inc., according to DPH management. Having analyzed the financial statements using ratio analysis, we could conclude that these statements are partially true. All three liquidity ratios show that DPH Tree Farm holds more liquidity on its balance sheet than the industry average. Thus, DPH Tree Farm has more cash and other liquid assets (or current assets) available to pay its bills (or current liabilities) as they come due than the average firm in the tree farm industry. In all cases, the asset management ratios show that DPH Tree Farm, Inc., is outperforming the industry average in its asset management. The firm is turning over its inventory faster than the average firm in the tree farm industry, thus producing more dollars of sales per dollar of inventory. It is also collecting its accounts receivable faster and paying its accounts payable slower than the average firm. Further, DPH Tree Farm is producing more sales per dollar of fixed assets, working capital, and total assets than the average firm in the industry. The profitability ratios show that DPH Tree Farm, Inc., is more profitable than the average firm in the tree farm industry. The profit margin, BEP, and ROA are all higher than the industry. Despite this, the ROE for DPH Tree Farm is much lower than the average for the industry.

What the managers do not state is that the debt management ratios show that DPH Tree Farm, Inc., holds less debt on its balance sheet than the average firm in the tree farm industry. This is a good sign in that this lack of financial leverage decreases the firm's potential for financial distress and even failure. If the firm has a bad year, it has promised relatively few payments to debt holders. Thus, the risk of bankruptcy is small. Further, the firm has more dollars of operating earnings and cash available to meet each dollar of interest obligations on the firm's debt.

(continued)

Personal Application Solution

To evaluate DPH Tree Farm, Inc.'s, financial statements, Chris Ryan would want to perform ratio analysis in which she uses the financial statements to calculate the most commonly used ratios. These include liquidity ratios, asset management ratios, debt management ratios, profitability ratios, and market value ratios. The value of these ratios for DPH Tree Farms and the tree farming industry are presented in Table 3.1. Chris might also want to spread the financial statements. These calculations yield common-size, easily compared financial statements that can be used to identify changes in corporate performance as well as how DPH Tree Farm compares to other firms in the industry. Having calculated these ratios, Chris can identify any interrelationships in the ratios by performing a detailed analysis of ROA and ROE using the DuPont system of analysis. A critical part of performance analysis lies in the interpretation of these numbers against some benchmark. To interpret the financial ratios, Chris will also want to evaluate the performance of the firm over time (time series analysis) and the performance of the firm against one or more companies in the same industry (cross-sectional analysis). Finally, Chris needs to exercise some cautions when reviewing data from financial statements. For example, the financial statement data are historical and may not be representative of future performance. Further, she needs to know what accounting rules DPH Tree Farm uses before making any comparisons or conclusions about its performance from ratio analysis. Finally, DPH Tree Farm's managers may have window dressed their financial statements to make them look better.

viewpoints REVISITED

Business Application Solution (concluded)

However, when DPH Tree Farm, Inc., does well, the low level of financial leverage dilutes the return to the stockholders of the firm. This profit dilution will likely upset the firm's common stockholders. Indeed, the market value ratios show that DPH Tree Farm's investors will not pay as much for a share of the firm's stock per dollar of book value and earnings as the average for the industry. The low debt level and high equity level used by DPH Tree Farm relative to the industry is likely a main reason for this unenthusiastic response by DPH investors.

summary of learning goals

Ratio analysis involves the process of calculating and analyzing financial ratios to assess a firm's performance and to identify actions needed to improve firm performance. The most commonly used ratios for ratio analysis fall into five groups: (1) liquidity ratios, (2) asset management ratios, (3) debt management ratios, (4) profitability ratios, and (5) market value ratios. This chapter reviewed these ratios, described what each ratio means, and identified the general trend (higher or lower) managers and investors look for in each ratio.

LG3-1 **Calculate and interpret major liquidity ratios.** Liquidity ratios measure the relation between a firm's liquid (or current) assets and its current liabilities.

LG3-2 **Calculate and interpret major asset management ratios.** Asset management ratios measure how efficiently a firm uses its assets (inventory, accounts receivable, and fixed assets), as well as its accounts payable.

LG3-3 **Calculate and interpret major debt ratios.** Debt management ratios measure the extent to which the firm uses debt (or financial leverage) versus equity to finance its assets as well as how well the firm can pay off its debt.

LG3-4 **Calculate and interpret major profitability ratios.** Profitability ratios show the combined effect of liquidity, asset management, and debt management on the overall operating results of the firm.

LG3-5 **Calculate and interpret major market value ratios.** Market value ratios relate a firm's stock price to its earnings and book value.

LG3-6 **Appreciate how various ratios relate to one another.** Many of the ratios we review are interrelated. That is, a change in one ratio may affect the value of several ratios. To see how these interrelations help evaluate firm performance, managers, analysts and investors often perform a detailed analysis of ROA and ROE using the DuPont system of analysis. DuPont system of analysis uses the balance sheet and income statement to break the ROA and ROE ratios into component pieces.

LG3-7 **Understand the differences between time series and cross-sectional ratio analysis.** When managers, analysts, or investors review a firm's financial position through ratio analysis, they often start by evaluating trends in the firm's financial position over time (time series analysis) and by comparing the firm's performance with that of other firms in the same industry (cross-sectional analysis).

LG3-8 **Explain cautions that should be taken when examining financial ratios.** The analysis of financial statements allows managers and investors to better understand a firm's performance. However, some cautions should be remembered when reviewing data from financial statements.

chapter equations

3-1 $$\text{Current ratio} = \frac{\text{Current assets}}{\text{Current liabilities}}$$

3-2 $$\text{Quick ratio (acid-test ratio)} = \frac{\text{Current assets} - \text{Inventory}}{\text{Current liabilities}}$$

3-3 $$\text{Cash ratio} = \frac{\text{Cash and marketable securities}}{\text{Current liabilities}}$$

3-4 $$\text{Inventory turnover} = \frac{\text{Sales or cost of goods sold}}{\text{Inventory}}$$

3-5 $$\text{Days' sales in inventory} = \frac{\text{Inventory} \times \text{365 days}}{\text{Sales or cost of goods sold}} = \frac{\text{365 days}}{\text{Inventory turnover}}$$

3-6 $$\text{Accounts receivable turnover} = \frac{\text{Credit sales}}{\text{Accounts receivable}}$$

3-7 $$\text{Average collection period } (ACP) = \frac{\text{Accounts receivable} \times \text{365 days}}{\text{Credit sales}} = \frac{\text{365 days}}{\text{Accounts receivable turnover}}$$

3-8 $$\text{Accounts payable turnover} = \frac{\text{Cost of goods sold}}{\text{Accounts payable}}$$

3-9 $$\text{Average payment period } (APP) = \frac{\text{Accounts payable} \times \text{365 days}}{\text{Cost of goods sold}} \text{ or } \frac{\text{365 days}}{\text{Accounts payable turnover}}$$

3-10 $$\text{Fixed asset turnover} = \frac{\text{Sales}}{\text{Net fixed assets}}$$

3-11 $$\text{Sales to working capital} = \frac{\text{Sales}}{\text{Working capital}}$$

3-12 $$\text{Total asset turnover} = \frac{\text{Sales}}{\text{Total assets}}$$

3-13 $$\text{Capital intensity} = \frac{\text{Total assets}}{\text{Sales}}$$

3-14 $$\text{Debt ratio} = \frac{\text{Total debt}}{\text{Total assets}}$$

3-15 $$\text{Debt-to-equity} = \frac{\text{Total debt}}{\text{Total equity}}$$

3-16 $$\text{Equity multiplier} = \frac{\text{Total assets}}{\text{Total equity}} \text{ or } \frac{\text{Total assets}}{\text{Common stockholders' equity}}$$

3-17 $$\text{Times interest earned} = \frac{EBIT}{\text{Interest}}$$

3-18 $$\text{Fixed-charge coverage} = \frac{\text{Earnings available to meet fixed charges}}{\text{Fixed charges}}$$

3-19 $$\text{Cash coverage} = \frac{EBIT + \text{Depreciation}}{\text{Fixed charges}}$$

3-20 Gross profit margin $= \dfrac{\text{Sales} - \text{Cost of goods sold}}{\text{Sales}}$

3-21 Operating profit margin $= \dfrac{EBIT}{\text{Sales}}$

3-22 Profit margin $= \dfrac{\text{Net income available to common stockholders}}{\text{Sales}}$

3-23 Basic earnings power $(BEP) = \dfrac{EBIT}{\text{Total assets}}$

3-24 Return on assets $(ROA) = \dfrac{\text{Net income available to common stockholders}}{\text{Total assets}}$

3-25 Return on equity $(ROE) = \dfrac{\text{Net income available to common stockholders}}{\text{Common stockholders' equity}}$

3-26 Dividend payout $= \dfrac{\text{Common stock dividends}}{\text{Net income available to common stockholders}}$

3-27 Market-to-book ratio $= \dfrac{\text{Market price per share}}{\text{Book value per share}}$

3-28 Price-earnings (PE) ratio $= \dfrac{\text{Market price per share}}{\text{Earnings per share}}$

3-29
$$ROA = \text{Profit margin} \times \text{Total asset turnover}$$
$$\frac{\text{Net income available to common stockholders}}{\text{Total assets}} = \frac{\text{Net income available to common stockholders}}{\text{Sales}} \times \frac{\text{Sales}}{\text{Total assets}}$$

3-30
$$ROE = ROA \times \text{Equity multiplier}$$
$$\frac{\text{Net income available to common stockholders}}{\text{Common stockholders' equity}} = ROA \times \frac{\text{Total assets}}{\text{Common stockholders' equity}}$$

3-31
$$ROE = \text{Profit margin} \times \text{Total asset turnover} \times \text{Equity multiplier}$$
$$\frac{\text{Net income available to common stockholders}}{\text{Common stockholders' equity}} = \frac{\text{Net income available to common stockholders}}{\text{Sales}} \times \frac{\text{Sales}}{\text{Total assets}} \times \frac{\text{Total assets}}{\text{Common stockholders' equity}}$$

3-32 Internal growth rate $= \dfrac{ROA \times RR}{1 - (ROA \times RR)}$

3-33 Retention ratio $(RR) = \dfrac{\text{Addition to retained earnings}}{\text{Net income available to common stockholders}}$

3-34 Retention ratio $= 1 -$ Dividend payout ratio

3-35 Sustainable growth rate $= \dfrac{ROE \times RR}{1 - (ROE \times RR)}$

key terms

asset management ratios, Measure how efficiently a firm uses its assets (inventory, accounts receivable, and fixed assets), as well as its accounts payable. *p. 79*

capital structure, The amount of debt versus equity held on the balance sheet. *p. 84*

common-size financial statements, Dividing all balance sheet amounts by total assets and all income statement amounts by net sales. *p. 94*

cross-sectional analysis, Analyzing the performance of a firm against one or more companies in the same industry. *p. 96*

debt management ratios, Measure the extent to which the firm uses debt (or financial leverage) versus equity to finance its assets as well as how well the firm can pay off its debt. *p. 84*

DuPont system of analysis, An analytical method that uses the balance sheet and income statement to break the ROA and ROE ratios into component pieces. *p. 90*

internal growth rate, The growth rate a firm can sustain if it finances growth using only internal financing, that is, retained earnings growth. *p. 95*

liquidity ratios, Measure the relation between a firm's liquid (or current) assets and its current liabilities. *p. 78*

market value ratios, Ratios that relate a firm's stock price to its earnings and book value. *p. 89*

profitability ratios, Ratios that show the combined effect of liquidity, asset management, and debt management on the firm's overall operating results. *p. 86*

ratio analysis, The process of calculating and analyzing financial ratios to assess the firm's performance and to identify actions needed to improve firm performance. *p. 77*

sustainable growth rate, The growth rate a firm can sustain if it finances growth using both debt and internal financing such that the debt ratio remains constant. *p. 95*

time series analysis, Analyzing firm performance by monitoring ratio trends. *p. 96*

self-test problems with solutions

1 Calculating Ratios Listed below are the balance sheet and income statement for Marion & Carter, Inc. Use these financial statements to calculate liquidity, asset management, debt management, profitability, and market value ratios for 2015. LG3-1 through LG3-5

MARION & CARTER, INC.
Balance Sheet as of December 31, 2015 and 2014
(in millions of dollars)

	2015	2014		2015	2014
Assets			**Liabilities and Equity**		
Current assets:			Current liabilities:		
Cash and marketable securities	$ 165	$ 155	Accrued wages and taxes	$ 124	$ 95
Accounts receivable	475	400	Accounts payable	360	310
Inventory	650	620	Notes payable	322	280
Total	$ 1,290	$ 1,175	Total	$ 806	$ 685
Fixed assets:			Long term debt:	$ 1,210	$ 1,178
Gross plant and equipment	$ 2,280	$ 1,860	Stockholders' equity:		
Less: Depreciation	330	250	Preferred stock (25 million shares)	$ 25	$ 25
Net plant and equipment	$ 1,950	$ 1,610	Common stock and paid in surplus (200 million shares)	250	250
Other long term assets	350	310	Retained earnings	1,299	957
Total	$ 2,300	$ 1,920	Total	$ 1,574	$ 1,232
Total assets	$ 3,590	$ 3,095	Total liabilities and equity	$ 3,590	$ 3,095

MARION & CARTER, INC.
Income Statement for Years Ending December 31, 2015 and 2014
(in millions of dollars)

	2015	2014
Net sales (all credit)	$ 2,053	$ 1,705
Less: Cost of goods sold	941	755
Gross profits	$ 1,112	$ 950
Less: Depreciation	80	75
Other operating expenses	89	82
Earnings before interest and taxes (EBIT)	$ 943	$ 793
Less: Interest	99	112
Earnings before taxes (EBT)	$ 844	$ 681
Less: Taxes	285	248
Net income	$ 559	$ 433
Less: Preferred stock dividends	$ 62	$ 62
Net income available to common stockholders	$ 497	$ 371
Less: Common stock dividends	155	155
Addition to retained earnings	$ 342	$ 216
Per (common) share data:		
Earnings per share (EPS)	$ 2.485	$ 1.855
Dividends per share (DPS)	$ 0.775	$ 0.775
Book value per share (BVPS)	$ 7.745	$ 6.035
Market value (price) per share (MVPS)	$ 22.970	$ 21.470

Solution:

Liquidity ratios:

$$\text{Current ratio} = \frac{\$1{,}290\text{m}}{\$806\text{m}} = 1.60 \text{ times}$$

$$\text{Quick ratio (acid-test ratio)} = \frac{\$1{,}290\text{m} - \$650\text{m}}{\$806\text{m}} = 0.79 \text{ times}$$

$$\text{Cash ratio} = \frac{\$165\text{m}}{\$806\text{m}} = 0.20 \text{ times}$$

Asset management ratios:

$$\text{Inventory turnover} = \frac{\$2{,}053\text{m}}{\$650\text{m}} = 3.16 \text{ times}$$

$$\text{Days' sales in inventory} = \frac{\$650\text{m} \times 365 \text{ days}}{\$2{,}053\text{m}} = 115.56 \text{ days}$$

$$\text{Accounts receivable turnover} = \frac{\$2{,}053\text{m}}{\$475\text{m}} = 4.32 \text{ times}$$

$$\text{Average collection period} = \frac{\$475\text{m} \times 365 \text{ days}}{\$2{,}053\text{m}} = 84.45 \text{ days}$$

$$\text{Accounts payable turnover} = \frac{\$941\text{m}}{\$360\text{m}} = 2.61 \text{ times}$$

$$\text{Average payment period} = \frac{\$360\text{m} \times 365 \text{ days}}{\$941\text{m}} = 139.64 \text{ days}$$

$$\text{Fixed asset turnover} = \frac{\$2{,}053\text{m}}{\$1{,}950\text{m}} = 1.05 \text{ times}$$

$$\text{Sales to working capital} = \frac{\$2{,}053\text{m}}{\$1{,}290\text{m} - \$806\text{m}} = 4.24 \text{ times}$$

$$\text{Total asset turnover} = \frac{\$2{,}053\text{m}}{\$3{,}590\text{m}} = 0.57 \text{ times}$$

$$\text{Capital intensity} = \frac{\$3{,}590\text{m}}{\$2{,}053\text{m}} = 1.75 \text{ times}$$

Debt management ratios:

$$\text{Debt ratio} = \frac{\$806\text{m} + \$1{,}210\text{m}}{\$3{,}590\text{m}} = 56.16\%$$

$$\text{Debt-to-equity} = \frac{\$806\text{m} + \$1{,}210\text{m}}{\$1{,}574\text{m}} = 1.28 \text{ times}$$

$$\text{Equity multiplier} = \frac{\$3{,}590\text{m}}{\$1{,}574\text{m}} = 2.28 \text{ times}$$

$$\text{Times interest earned} = \frac{\$943\text{m}}{\$99\text{m}} = 9.53 \text{ times}$$

$$\text{Fixed-charge coverage} = \frac{\$943\text{m}}{\$99\text{m}} = 9.53 \text{ times}$$

$$\text{Cash coverage} = \frac{\$943\text{m} + \$80\text{m}}{\$99\text{m}} = 10.33 \text{ times}$$

Profitability ratios:

$$\text{Profit margin} = \frac{\$497\text{m}}{\$2{,}053\text{m}} = 24.21\%$$

$$\text{Gross profit margin} = \frac{\$1{,}112\text{m}}{\$2{,}053\text{m}} = 54.16\%$$

$$\text{Operating profit margin} = \frac{\$943\text{m}}{\$2{,}053\text{m}} = 45.93\%$$

$$\text{Basic earnings power} = \frac{\$943\text{m}}{\$3{,}590\text{m}} = 26.27\%$$

$$\text{Return on assets} = \frac{\$497\text{m}}{\$3{,}590\text{m}} = 13.84\%$$

$$\text{Return on equity} = \frac{\$497\text{m}}{\$250\text{m} + \$1{,}299\text{m}} = 32.09\%$$

$$\text{Divident payout} = \frac{\$155\text{m}}{\$497\text{m}} = 31.19\%$$

Market value ratios:

$$\text{Market-to-book ratio} = \frac{\$22.970}{\$7.745} = 2.97 \text{ times}$$

$$\text{Price-earnings ratio} = \frac{\$22.970}{\$2.485} = 9.24 \text{ times}$$

2 Internal and Sustainable Growth Rates Calculate the internal growth rate and sustainable growth rate for Marion & Carter, Inc., using the 2015 financial statements. LG3-6

Solution:

$$\text{Retention rate } (RR) = \frac{\$1{,}299\text{m} - \$957\text{m}}{\$497\text{m}} = 0.6881, \text{ or } 68.81\%$$

$$\text{Internal growth rate} = \frac{0.1384 \times 0.6881}{1 - (0.1384 \times 0.6881)} = 0.1053, \text{ or } 10.53\%$$

$$\text{Sustainable growth rate} = \frac{0.3209 \times 0.6881}{1 - (0.3209 \times 0.6881)} = 0.2834, \text{ or } 28.34\%$$

questions

1. Classify each of the following ratios according to a ratio category (liquidity ratio, asset management ratio, debt management ratio, profitability ratio, or market value ratio). *(LG3-1 through LG3-5)*
   - **a.** Current ratio
   - **b.** Inventory turnover
   - **c.** Return on assets
   - **d.** Average payment period
   - **e.** Times interest earned
   - **f.** Capital intensity
   - **g.** Equity multiplier
   - **h.** Basic earnings power
2. For each of the following actions, determine what would happen to the current ratio. Assume nothing else on the balance sheet changes and that net working capital is positive. *(LG3-1)*
   - **a.** Accounts receivable are paid in cash
   - **b.** Notes payable are paid off with cash
   - **c.** Inventory is sold on account
   - **d.** Inventory is purchased on account
   - **e.** Accrued wages and taxes increase
   - **f.** Long-term debt is paid with cash
   - **g.** Cash from a short-term bank loan is received
3. Explain the meaning and significance of the following ratios. *(LG3-1 through LG3-5)*
   - **a.** Quick ratio
   - **b.** Average collection period

c. Return on equity

d. Days' sales in inventory

e. Debt ratio

f. Profit margin

g. Accounts payable turnover

h. Market-to-book ratio

4. A firm has an average collection period of 10 days. The industry average ACP is 25 days. Is this a good or poor sign about the management of the firm's accounts receivable? *(LG3-2)*

5. A firm has a debt ratio of 20 percent. The industry average debt ratio is 65 percent. Is this a good or poor sign about the management of the firm's financial leverage? *(LG3-3)*

6. A firm has an ROE of 20 percent. The industry average ROE is 12 percent. Is this a good or poor sign about the management of the firm? *(LG3-4)*

7. Why is the DuPont system of analysis an important tool when evaluating firm performance? *(LG3-6)*

8. A firm has an ROE of 10 percent. The industry average ROE is 15 percent. How can the DuPont system of analysis help the firm's managers identify the reasons for this difference? *(LG3-6)*

9. What is the difference between the internal growth rate and the sustainable growth rate? *(LG3-6)*

10. What is the difference between time series analysis and cross-sectional analysis? *(LG3-7)*

11. What information does time series and cross-sectional analysis provide for firm managers, analysts, and investors? *(LG3-7)*

12. Why is it important to know a firm's accounting rules before making any conclusions about its performance from ratios analysis? *(LG3-8)*

13. What does it mean when a firm window dresses its financial statements? *(LG3-8)*

basic problems

problems

3-1 Liquidity Ratios You are evaluating the balance sheet for PattyCake's Corporation. From the balance sheet you find the following balances: cash and marketable securities = \$400,000; accounts receivable = \$1,200,000; inventory = \$2,100,000; accrued wages and taxes = \$500,000; accounts payable = \$800,000; and notes payable = \$600,000. Calculate PattyCake's current ratio, quick ratio, and cash ratio. *(LG3-1)*

3-2 Liquidity Ratios The top part of Ramakrishnan, Inc.'s, 2015 and 2014 balance sheets is listed below (in millions of dollars).

	2015	2014		2015	2014
Current assets:			Current liabilities:		
Cash and marketable securities	$ 34	$ 25	Accrued wages and taxes	$ 32	$ 31
Accounts receivable	143	128	Accounts payable	87	76
Inventory	206	187	Notes payable	76	68
Total	$ 383	$ 340	Total	$ 195	$ 175

Calculate Ramakrishnan, Inc.'s, current ratio, quick ratio, and cash ratio for 2015 and 2014. *(LG3-1)*

3-3 **Asset Management Ratios** Tater and Pepper Corp. reported sales for 2015 of $23 million. Tater and Pepper listed $5.6 million of inventory on its balance sheet. Using a 365-day year, how many days did Tater and Pepper's inventory stay on the premises? How many times per year did Tater and Pepper's inventory turn over? *(LG3-2)*

3-4 **Asset Management Ratios** Mr. Husker's Tuxedos Corp. ended the year 2015 with an average collection period of 32 days. The firm's credit sales for 2015 were $56.1 million. What is the year-end 2015 balance in accounts receivable for Mr. Husker's Tuxedos? *(LG3-2)*

3-5 **Debt Management Ratios** Tiggie's Dog Toys, Inc., reported a debt-to-equity ratio of 1.75 times at the end of 2015. If the firm's total debt at year-end was $25 million, how much equity does Tiggie's have on its balance sheet? *(LG3-3)*

3-6 **Debt Management Ratios** You are considering a stock investment in one of two firms (LotsofDebt, Inc., and LotsofEquity, Inc.), both of which operate in the same industry. LotsofDebt, Inc., finances its $30 million in assets with $29 million in debt and $1 million in equity. LotsofEquity, Inc., finances its $30 million in assets with $1 million in debt and $29 million in equity. Calculate the debt ratio, equity multiplier, and debt-to-equity ratio for the two firms. *(LG3-3)*

3-7 **Profitability Ratios** Maggie's Skunk Removal Corp.'s 2015 income statement listed net sales of $12.5 million, gross profit of $6.9 million, EBIT of $5.6 million, net income available to common stockholders of $3.2 million, and common stock dividends of $1.2 million. The 2015 year-end balance sheet listed total assets of $52.5 million and common stockholders' equity of $21 million with 2 million shares outstanding. Calculate the gross profit margin, operating profit margin, profit margin, basic earnings power, ROA, ROE, and dividend payout. *(LG3-4)*

3-8 **Profitability Ratios** In 2015, Jake's Jamming Music, Inc., announced an ROA of 8.56 percent, ROE of 14.5 percent, and profit margin of 20.5 percent. The firm had total assets of $9.5 million at year-end 2015. Calculate the 2015 values of net income available to common stockholders, common stockholders' equity, and net sales for Jake's Jamming Music, Inc. *(LG3-4)*

3-9 **Market Value Ratios** You are considering an investment in Roxie's Bed & Breakfast Corp. During the last year, the firm's income statement listed an addition to retained earnings of $4.8 million and common stock dividends of $2.2 million. Roxie's year-end balance sheet shows common stockholders' equity of $35 million with 10 million shares of common stock outstanding. The common stock's market price per share was $9.00. What is Roxie's Bed & Breakfast's book value per share and earnings per share? Calculate the market-to-book ratio and PE ratio. *(LG3-5)*

3-10 **Market Value Ratios** Dudley Hill Golf Club's market-to-book ratio is currently 2.5 times and the PE ratio is 6.75 times. If Dudley Hill Golf Club's common stock is currently selling at $22.50 per share, what is the book value per share and earnings per share? *(LG3-5)*

3-11 **DuPont Analysis** If Silas 4-Wheeler, Inc., has an ROE of 18 percent, equity multiplier of 2, and a profit margin of 18.75 percent, what is the total asset turnover and the capital intensity? *(LG3-6)*

3-12 **DuPont Analysis** Last year, Hassan's Madhatter, Inc., had an ROA of 7.5 percent, a profit margin of 12 percent, and sales of $25 million. Calculate Hassan's Madhatter's total assets. *(LG3-6)*

3-13 **Internal Growth Rate** Last year, Lakesha's Lounge Furniture Corporation had an ROA of 7.5 percent and a dividend payout ratio of 25 percent. What is the internal growth rate? *(LG3-6)*

3-14 **Sustainable Growth Rate** Last year Lakesha's Lounge Furniture Corporation had an ROE of 17.5 percent and a dividend payout ratio of 20 percent. What is the sustainable growth rate? *(LG3-6)*

intermediate problems

3-15 **Liquidity Ratios** Brenda's Bar and Grill has current liabilities of $15 million. Cash makes up 10 percent of the current assets and accounts receivable makes up another 40 percent of current assets. Brenda's current ratio is 2.1 times. Calculate the value of inventory listed on the firm's balance sheet. *(LG3-1)*

3-16 **Liquidity and Asset Management Ratios** Mandesa, Inc., has current liabilities of $8 million, current ratio of 2 times, inventory turnover of 12 times, average collection period of 30 days, and credit sales of $64 million. Calculate the value of cash and marketable securities. *(LG3-1, LG3-2)*

3-17 **Asset Management and Profitability Ratios** You have the following information on Els' Putters, Inc.: Sales to working capital is 4.6 times, profit margin is 20 percent, net income available to common stockholders is $5 million, and current liabilities are $6 million. What is the firm's balance of current assets? *(LG3-2, LG3-4)*

3-18 **Asset Management and Debt Management Ratios** Use the following information to complete the following balance sheet. Sales are $8.8 million, capital intensity ratio is 2.10 times, debt ratio is 55 percent, and fixed asset turnover is 1.2 times. *(LG3-2, LG3-3)*

Assets		Liabilities and Equity	
Current assets	$_____	Total liabilities	$_____
Fixed assets	_____	Total equity	_____
Total assets	$_____	Total liabilities and equity	$_____

3-19 **Debt Management Ratios** Tiggie's Dog Toys, Inc., reported a debt-to-equity ratio of 1.75 times at the end of 2015. If the firm's total assets at year-end were $25 million, how much of their assets are financed with debt and how much with equity? *(LG3-3)*

3-20 **Debt Management Ratios** Calculate the times interest earned ratio for LaTonya's Flop Shops, Inc., using the following information. Sales are $1.5 million, cost of goods sold is $600,000, depreciation expense is $150,000, other operating expenses is $300,000, addition to retained earnings is $146,250, dividends per share is $1, tax rate is 30 percent, and number of shares of common stock outstanding is 90,000. LaTonya's Flop Shops has no preferred stock outstanding. *(LG3-3)*

3-21 **Profitability and Asset Management Ratios** You are thinking of investing in Nikki T's, Inc. You have only the following information on the firm at year-end 2015: Net income is $250,000, total debt is $2.5 million, and debt ratio is 55 percent. What is Nikki T's ROE for 2015? *(LG3-2, LG3-4)*

3-22 **Profitability Ratios** Rick's Travel Service has asked you to help piece together financial information on the firm for the most current year. Managers give you the following information: sales are $8.2 million, total debt is $2.1 million, debt ratio is 40 percent, and ROE is 18 percent. Using this information, calculate Rick's ROA. *(LG3-4)*

3-23 **Market Value Ratios** Leonatti Labs' year-end price on its common stock is $35. The firm has total assets of $50 million, debt ratio of 65 percent, no preferred stock, and 3 million shares of common stock outstanding. Calculate the market-to-book ratio for Leonatti Labs. *(LG3-5)*

3-24 **Market Value Ratios** Leonatti Labs' year-end price on its common stock is $15. The firm has a profit margin of 8 percent, total assets of $42 million, a total asset turnover of 0.75, no preferred stock, and 3 million shares of common stock outstanding. Calculate the PE ratio for Leonatti Labs. *(LG3-5)*

3-25 **DuPont Analysis** Last year, Stumble-on-Inn, Inc., reported an ROE of 18 percent. The firm's debt ratio was 55 percent, sales were $15 million, and the capital intensity was 1.25 times. Calculate the net income for Stumble-on-Inn last year. *(LG3-6)*

3-26 **DuPont Analysis** You are considering investing in Nuran Security Services. You have been able to locate the following information on the firm: total assets are $24 million, accounts receivable are $3.3 million, ACP is 25 days, net income is $3.5 million, and debt-to-equity is 1.2 times. Calculate the ROE for the firm. *(LG3-6)*

3-27 **Internal Growth Rate** Dogs R Us reported a profit margin of 10.5 percent, total asset turnover of 0.75 times, debt-to-equity of 0.80 times, net income of $500,000, and dividends paid to common stockholders of $200,000. The firm has no preferred stock outstanding. What is Dogs R Us's internal growth rate? *(LG3-6)*

3-28 **Sustainable Growth Rate** You have located the following information on Webb's Heating & Air Conditioning: debt ratio is 54 percent, capital intensity is 1.10 times, profit margin is 12.5 percent, and the dividend payout is 25 percent. Calculate the sustainable growth rate for Webb. *(LG3-6)*

Use the following financial statements for Lake of Egypt Marina, Inc., to answer Problems 3-29 through 3-33.

LAKE OF EGYPT MARINA, INC. Balance Sheet as of December 31, 2015 and 2014 (in millions of dollars)					
	2015	**2014**		**2015**	**2014**
Assets			**Liabilities and Equity**		
Current assets:			Current liabilities:		
Cash and marketable securities	$ 75	$ 65	Accrued wages and taxes	$ 40	$ 43
Accounts receivable	115	110	Accounts payable	90	80
Inventory	200	190	Notes payable	80	70
Total	$ 390	$ 365	Total	$ 210	$ 193
Fixed assets:			Long term debt:	$ 300	$ 280
Gross plant and equipment	$ 580	$ 471	Stockholders' equity:		
Less: Depreciation	110	100	Preferred stock (5 million shares)	$ 5	$ 5
Net plant and equipment	$ 470	$ 371	Common stock and paid in surplus	65	65
			(65 million shares)		
Other long term assets	50	49	Retained earnings	330	242
Total	$ 520	$ 420	Total	$ 400	$ 312
Total assets	$ 910	$ 785	Total liabilities and equity	$ 910	$ 785

LAKE OF EGYPT MARINA, INC. Income Statement for Years Ending December 31, 2015 and 2014 (in millions of dollars)		
	2015	**2014**
Net sales (all credit)	$ 515	$ 432
Less: Cost of goods sold	230	175
Gross profits	$ 285	$ 257
Less: Other operating expenses	30	25
Earnings before interest, taxes, depreciation, and amortization (EBITDA)	$ 255	$ 232
Less: Depreciation	22	20
Earnings before interest and taxes (EBIT)	$ 233	$ 212
Less: Interest	33	30
Earnings before taxes (EBT)	$ 200	$ 182
Less: Taxes	57	55
Net income	$ 143	$ 127
Less: Preferred stock dividends	$ 5	$ 5
Net income available to common stockholders	$ 138	$ 122
Less: Common stock dividends	65	65
Addition to retained earnings	$ 73	$ 57
Per (common) share data:		
Earnings per share (EPS)	$ 2.123	$ 1.877
Dividends per share (DPS)	$ 1.000	$ 1.000
Book value per share (BVPS)	$ 6.077	$ 4.723
Market value (price) per share (MVPS)	$14.750	$12.550

3-29 Spreading the Financial Statements Spread the balance sheets and income statements of Lake of Egypt Marina, Inc., for 2015 and 2014. *(LG3-6)*

3-30 Calculating Ratios Calculate the following ratios for Lake of Egypt Marina, Inc., as of year-end 2015. *(LG3-1 through LG3-5)*

	Lake of Egypt Marina, Inc.	Industry
a. Current ratio		2.00 times
b. Quick ratio		1.20 times
c. Cash ratio		0.25 times
d. Inventory turnover		3.60 times
e. Days' sales in inventory		101.39 days
f. Average collection period		32.50 days
g. Average payment period		45.00 days
h. Fixed asset turnover		1.25 times
i. Sales to working capital		4.25 times
j. Total asset turnover		0.85 times
k. Capital intensity		1.18 times
l. Debt ratio		62.50%
m. Debt-to-equity		1.67 times
n. Equity multiplier		2.67 times
o. Times interest earned		8.50 times
p. Cash coverage		8.75 times
q. Profit margin		28.75%
r. Gross profit margin		56.45%
s. Operating profit margin		46.78%
t. Basic earnings power		32.50%
u. ROA		19.75%
v. ROE		36.88%
w. Dividend payout		35.00%
x. Market-to-book ratio		2.55 times
y. PE ratio		15.60 times

3-31 **DuPont Analysis** Construct the DuPont ROA and ROE breakdowns for Lake of Egypt Marina, Inc. *(LG3-6)*

3-32 **Internal and Sustainable Growth Rates** Calculate the internal and sustainable growth rate for Lake of Egypt Marina, Inc. *(LG3-6)*

3-33 **Cross-Sectional Analysis** Using the ratios from Problem 3-30 for Lake of Egypt Marina, Inc., and the industry, what can you conclude about Lake of Egypt Marina's financial performance for 2015? *(LG3-7)*

advanced problems

3-34 **Ratio Analysis** Use the following information to complete the balance sheet below. *(LG3-1 through LG3-5)*

Current ratio = 2.5 times

Profit margin = 10%

Sales = $1,200m

ROE = 20%

Long-term debt to Long-term debt and equity = 55%

Current assets	$______	Current liabilities	$210m
Fixed assets	______	Long-term debt	______
		Stockholders' equity	______
Total assets	$______	Total liabilities and equity	$______

3-35 Ratio Analysis Use the following information to complete the balance sheet. *(LG3-1 through LG3-5)*

Current ratio = 2.20 times

Credit sales = $1,200m

Average collection period = 60 days

Inventory turnover = 1.50 times

Total asset turnover = 0.75 times

Debt ratio = 60%

Cash	$ ______		
Accounts receivable	______	Current liabilities	$ 500m
Inventory	______	Long-term debt	______
Current assets	$ ______	Total debt	$ ______
Fixed assets	______	Stockholders' equity	______
Total assets	$ ______	Total liabilities and equity	$ ______

3-36 DuPont Analysis Last year, K9 WebbWear, Inc., reported an ROE of 20 percent. The firm's debt ratio was 55 percent, sales were $20 million, and the capital intensity was 1.25 times. Calculate the net income and profit margin for K9 WebbWear last year. This year, K9 WebbWear plans to increase its debt ratio to 60 percent. The change will not affect sales or total assets, however, it will reduce the firm's profit margin to 11 percent. By how much will the change in K9 WebbWear's debt ratio affect its ROE? *(LG3-6)*

3-37 DuPont Analysis You are considering investing in Dakota's Security Services. You have been able to locate the following information on the firm: Total assets are $32 million, accounts receivable are $4.4 million, ACP is 25 days, net income is $4.66 million, and debt-to-equity is 1.2 times. All sales are on credit. Dakota's is considering loosening its credit policy such that ACP will increase to 30 days. The change is expected to increase credit sales by 5 percent. Any change in accounts receivable will be offset with a change in debt. No other balance sheet changes are expected. Dakota's profit margin will remain unchanged. How will this change in accounts receivable policy affect Dakota's net income, total asset turnover, equity multiplier, ROA, and ROE? *(LG3-6)*

3-38 Internal Growth Rate Last year, Marly Brown, Inc., reported an ROE of 20 percent. The firm's debt-to-equity was 1.50 times, sales were $20 million, the capital intensity was 1.25 times, and dividends paid to common stockholders were $1,000,000. The firm has no preferred stock outstanding. This year, Marly Brown plans to decrease its debt-to-equity ratio to 1.20 times. The change will not affect sales, total assets, or dividends paid, however, it will reduce the firm's profit margin to 9.85 percent. Use the DuPont equation to determine how the change in Marly Brown's debt ratio will affect its internal growth rate. *(LG3-6)*

3-39 Sustainable Growth Rate You are considering investing in Annie's Eatery. You have been able to locate the following information on the firm: Total assets are $40 million, accounts receivable are $6.0 million, ACP is 30 days, net income is $4.75 million, debt-to-equity is 1.5 times, and dividend payout ratio is 45 percent. All sales are on credit. Annie's is considering loosening its credit policy such that ACP will increase to 35 days. The change is expected to increase credit sales by 5 percent. Any change in accounts receivable will be offset with a change in debt. No other balance sheet changes are expected. Annie's profit margin and dividend payout ratio will remain unchanged. Use the DuPont equation to determine how this change in accounts receivable policy will affect Annie's sustainable growth rate. *(LG3-6)*

research it! Analyzing Financial Statements

Go to the website of Walmart Stores, Inc., at **www.walmartstores.com** and get the latest financial statements from the annual report using the following steps.

Click on "Investors." Click on "Financial Information." Click on "Annual Reports." Click on the most recent date. This will bring the file onto your computer that contains the relevant data.

Using the most recent balance sheet and income statement, calculate the financial ratios for the firm, including the internal and sustainable growth rates.

integrated mini-case Working with Financial Statements

Listed are the 2015 financial statements for Garners' Platoon Mental Health Care, Inc. Spread the balance sheet and income statement. Calculate the financial ratios for the firm, including the internal and sustainable growth rates. Using the DuPont system of analysis and the industry ratios reported, evaluate the performance of the firm.

GARNERS' PLATOON MENTAL HEALTH CARE, INC.
Balance Sheet as of December 31, 2015
(in millions of dollars)

Assets		**Liabilities and Equity**	
Current assets:		Current liabilities:	
Cash and marketable securities	$ 421	Accrued wages and taxes	$ 316
Accounts receivable	1,109	Accounts payable	867
Inventory	1,760	Notes payable	872
Total	$ 3,290	Total	$ 2,055
Fixed assets:		Long term debt:	$ 3,090
Gross plant and equipment	$ 5,812	Stockholders' equity:	
Less: Depreciation	840	Preferred stock (30 million shares)	$ 60
Net plant and equipment	$ 4,972	Common stock and paid in surplus (200 million shares)	637
Other long term assets	892	Retained earnings	3,312
Total	$ 5,864	Total	$ 4,009
Total assets	$ 9,154	Total liabilities and equity	$ 9,154

GARNERS' PLATOON MENTAL HEALTH CARE, INC.
Income Statement for Year Ending December 31, 2015
(in millions of dollars)

Net sales (all credit)	$ 4,980
Less: Cost of goods sold	2,246
Gross profits	$ 2,734
Less: Other operating expenses	125
Earnings before interest, taxes, depreciation, and amortization (EBITDA)	$ 2,609
Less: Depreciation	200
Earnings before interest and taxes (EBIT)	$ 2,409
Less: Interest	315
Earnings before taxes (EBT)	$ 2,094
Less: Taxes	767
Net income	$ 1,327

(continued)

Less: Preferred stock dividends	$ 60
Net income available to common stockholders	$ 1,267
Less: Common stock dividends	395
Addition to retained earnings	$ 872
Per (common) share data:	
Earnings per share (EPS)	$ 6.335
Dividends per share (DPS)	$ 1.975
Book value per share (BVPS)	$19.745
Market value (price) per share (MVPS)	$26.850

	Garners' Platoon Mental Health Care, Inc.	Industry
Current ratio		2.00 times
Quick ratio		1.20 times
Cash ratio		0.25 times
Inventory turnover		2.50 times
Days' sales in inventory		146.00 days
Average collection period		91.00 days
Average payment period		100.00 days
Fixed asset turnover		1.25 times
Sales to working capital		4.00 times
Total asset turnover		0.50 times
Capital intensity		2.00 times
Debt ratio		50.00%
Debt-to-equity		1.00 times
Equity multiplier		2.00 times
Times interest earned		7.25 times
Cash coverage		8.00 times
Profit margin		18.75%
Gross profit margin		49.16%
Operating profit margin		42.02%
Basic earnings power		19.90%
ROA		9.38%
ROE		18.75%
Dividend payout		35.00%
Market-to-book ratio		1.30 times
PE ratio		4.10 times

ANSWERS TO TIME OUT

3-1 The three most commonly used liquidity ratios are the current ratio, the quick (or acid-test) ratio, and the cash ratio.

3-2 The current ratio measures the dollars of current assets available to pay each dollar of current liabilities. The quick ratio measures the dollars of more liquid assets (cash and marketable securities and accounts receivable) available to pay each dollar of current liabilities. The cash ratio measures the dollars of cash and marketable securities available to pay each dollar of current liabilities

3-3 The more liquid assets a firm holds, the less likely it is that the firm will experience financial distress. Thus, the higher the liquidity ratios, the less liquidity risk a firm has. But liquid assets generate little, if any, profits for the firm. In contrast, fixed assets are illiquid, but generate revenue for the firm. Thus, extremely high levels of liquidity guard against liquidity crises but at the cost of lower returns on assets.

3-4 The major asset management ratios are the inventory turnover, the days' sales in inventory, the accounts receivable turnover, the average collection period (ACP), the accounts payable turnover, the average payment period (APP), the fixed asset turnover, the sales to working capital, the total asset turnover, and the capital intensity.

3-5 In general, a firm wants to produce a high level of sales per dollar of inventory. That is, it wants to turn inventory over as quickly as possible. However, if the inventory turnover ratio is extremely high and the days' sales in inventory is extremely low, the firm may not be holding sufficient inventory to prevent running out of the raw materials needed to keep the production process going.

In general, a firm wants to collect its accounts receivable as quickly as possible. However, if the accounts receivable turnover ratio is extremely high and the ACP is extremely low, the firm's accounts receivable policy may be so strict that customers prefer to do business with competing firms.

In general, a firm wants to pay for its purchases as slowly as possible. Thus, a high APP or a low accounts payable turnover is generally a sign of good management. However, if the APP is extremely high and the accounts payable turnover is extremely low, the firm may be abusing the credit terms that its raw materials suppliers offer. At some point, the firm's suppliers may revoke its ability to buy raw materials on account and the firm will lose this source of free financing.

In general, high fixed asset turnover and sales to working capital are signs of good management. However, if either the fixed asset turnover or sales to working capital is extremely high, the firm may be close to its maximum production capacity.

In general, the higher the total asset turnover and lower the capital intensity, the more efficient the overall asset management of the firm will be. However, as described above, inventory stockouts, capacity problems, or tight account receivables policies can all lead to a high total asset turnover and may actually be signs of poor firm management.

3-6 Many of the ratios are mirror images of one another because one ratio might be the inverse of another ratio. For example, the inventory turnover ratio measures the number of times per year that inventory is turned over, while the days' sales in inventory ratio measures the number of days that inventory is held before the final product is sold.

3-7 The major debt management ratios are the debt ratio, the debt-to-equity, the equity multiplier, the times interest earned, the fixed-charge coverage, and the cash coverage.

3-8 Low levels of debt will lead to a dilution of the return to stockholders due to a greater increased use of equity as well as not taking advantage of the tax deductibility of interest expense. However, high levels of debt increase a firm's potential for financial distress and even failure. If the firm has a bad year and cannot make its promised debt payments, debt holders can force the firm into bankruptcy.

3-9 In deciding the level of debt versus equity financing to hold on the balance sheet, managers must consider the trade-off between maximizing cash flows to the firm's stockholders versus the risk of being unable to make promised debt payments. When firms do well, financial leverage creates more cash flows to share with stockholders—it magnifies the return to the stockholders of the firm. This magnification is one reason that firm stockholders encourage the use of debt financing. However, financial leverage also increases the firm's potential for financial distress and even failure. If the firm has a bad year and cannot make promised debt payments, debt holders can force the firm into bankruptcy. Thus, a firm's current and potential debt holders (and even stockholders) look at equity financing as a safety cushion that can absorb fluctuations in the firm's earnings and asset values and guarantee debt service payments.

3-10 The major profitability ratios are the gross profit margin, operating profit margin, profit margin, the basic earnings power, the return on assets (ROA), the return on equity (ROE), and the dividend payout.

3-11 For all but the dividend payout, the higher the value of the ratio, the higher the profitability of the firm. But just as has been the case previously in this chapter, high profitability ratio levels may result from poor management in other areas of the firm as much as superior financial management.

3-12 Generally, a high ROE is considered to be a positive sign of firm performance. However, if performance comes from a high degree of financial leverage, a high ROE can indicate a firm with an unacceptably high level of bankruptcy risk as well.

3-13 The major market value ratios are the market-to-book ratio and the price-earnings (or PE) ratio.

3-14 Generally, the higher the market-to-book and PE ratios, the better the firm's performance. However, for value seeking investors, high market-to-book and PE firms indicate expensive companies. Further, higher PE ratios carry greater risk because investors are willing to pay higher prices today for a stock in anticipation of higher earnings in the future. These earnings may or may not materialize. Low-PE firms are generally companies with little expected growth or low earnings.

3-15 The price-earnings (or PE) ratio measures how much investors are willing to pay for each dollar the firm earns per share of its stock. PE ratios are often quoted in multiples—the number of dollars per share—which fund managers, investors, and analysts compare within industry classes. Managers and investors often use PE ratios to evaluate the relative financial performance of the firm's stock.

3-16 The basic DuPont equation looks at ROA as the product of the profit margin and the total asset turnover ratios. The DuPont ROE equation looks at ROE as a product of the profit margin, the total asset turnover, and the equity multiplier.

3-17 This presentation of ROA and ROE allows managers, analysts, and investors to look at the return on assets and return on equity as a function of the net profit margin (profit per dollar of sales from the income statement), total asset turnover (efficiency in the use of assets from the balance sheet), and the equity multiplier (financial leverage from the balance sheet).

3-18 Managers, analysts, and investors can compute additional ratios by dividing all balance sheet amounts by total assets and all income statement amounts by net sales. These calculations, sometimes called "spreading the financial statements," yield what we call "common-size" financial statements that adjust for sizes.

3-19 The internal growth rate is the growth rate a firm can sustain if it uses only internal financing—that is, retained earnings—to finance future growth. The retention ratio represents the portion of net income that the firm reinvests as retained earnings. Since a firm either pays its net income as dividends to its stockholders or reinvests those funds as retained earnings, the dividend payout and the retention ratios must always add to one. The sustainable growth rate is the maximum growth rate that can be achieved when managers finance asset growth with new debt *and* retained earnings.

3-20 A firm's sustainable growth depends on four factors: (1) the profit margin (operating efficiency), (2) the total asset turnover (efficiency in asset use), (3) financial leverage (the use of debt versus equity to finance assets), and (4) profit retention (reinvestment of net income into the firm rather than paying it out as dividends).

3-21 Time series analysis involves analyzing ratio trends over time, along with absolute ratio levels. It gives managers, analysts, and investors information about whether a firm's financial condition is improving or deteriorating.

3-22 Cross-sectional analysis involves a comparison of one firm's ratios relative to the ratios of other firms in the industry. Key to cross-sectional analysis is identifying similar firms in that they compete in the same markets, have similar asset sizes, and operate in a similar manner to the firm being analyzed.

3-23 Analyzing ratio trends over time, along with absolute ratio levels, gives managers, analysts, and investors information about whether a firm's financial condition is improving or deteriorating. Cross-sectional analysis gives the manager a comparison of one firm's ratios relative to the ratios of other firms in the industry.

3-24 Data from financial statements should not be received without certain cautions. These include: (1) Financial statement data are historical; historical data may not reflect future performance. (2) Firms use different accounting procedures. (3) A firm's cross-sectional competitors may often be located around the world; financial statements for firms based outside the U.S. do not necessarily conform to GAAP. (4) Sales and expenses vary throughout the year. Managers, analysts, and investors need to note the timing of these fund flows when performing cross-sectional analysis. Similarly, firms end their fiscal years at different dates. Likewise, one-time events, such as a merger, may affect a firm's financial performance. (5) Large firms often have multiple divisions or business units engaged in different lines of business. (6) Firms often window dress their financial statements to make annual results look better. (7) Individual analysts may calculate ratios in modified forms.

PART THREE

4 Time Value of Money 1: Analyzing Single Cash Flows

viewpoints

Business Application

As the production manager of Head Phone Gear, Inc., you have received an offer from the supplier who provides the wires used in headsets. Due to poor planning, the supplier has an excess amount of wire and is willing to sell $500,000 worth for only $450,000. You already have one year's supply on hand. It would cost you $2,000 to store the wire until Head Phone Gear needs it next year. What implied interest rate would you be earning if you purchased and stored the wire? Should you make the purchase? **(See solution on p. 136)**

Personal Application

Payday lending has become a multibillion-dollar industry across the United States in just a few years. It provides people with short-term loans and gets its name from the fact that the loan is to be paid back at the borrower's next payday. Anthony is short a few hundred dollars and his next paycheck is two weeks away. For a $300 loan, Anthony must pay a $50 "fee" in advance and repay the $300 loan in two weeks. What implied interest rate would Anthony pay for this two-week period? Is this a good deal? **(See solution on p. 136)**

But what if Anthony can't pay the loan back on time?

Learning Goals

LG4-1 Create a cash flow time line.

LG4-2 Compute the future value of money.

LG4-3 Show how the power of compound interest increases wealth.

LG4-4 Calculate the present value of a payment made in the future.

LG4-5 Move cash flows from one year to another.

LG4-6 Apply the Rule of 72.

LG4-7 Compute the rate of return realized on selling an investment.

LG4-8 Calculate the number of years needed to grow an investment.

In business and personal life, cash flows of different types are paid and received in the future. Your company can contract to build and ship its product to a foreign buyer for a $10 million single payment in two years. You may have a car loan and a $300 per month level payment over the next four years. It may be that you will pay a series of uneven tuition payments over the next couple of years as tuition changes. Whether the future entails single, level, or uneven cash flows, we need a method for comparing them when paid at different points in time.

Both this chapter and the next illustrate time value of money (TVM) calculations, which we will use throughout the rest of this book. We hope you will see what powerful tools they are for making financial decisions. Whether you're managing the financial or other functional area of a business or making decisions in your personal life, being able to make TVM calculations will help you make financially sound decisions.

This background will also allow you to understand why CEOs, CFOs, and other professionals make the decisions that they do. Together, this chapter and the next will present all aspects of TVM. Since some students find this topic intimidating, we split the topic into two chapters as a way of providing more examples and practice opportunities. As you see the examples and work the practice problems, we believe that you will find that TVM is not difficult.

Factors to consider when making time value of money decisions include:

- Size of the cash flows.
- Time between the cash flows.
- Rate of return we can earn.

The title of this chapter refers to the time value of money. But why might money change values, and why does it depend on time? Consider that $100 can buy you an assortment of food and drinks today. Will you be able to buy those same items in five years with the same $100? Probably not. Inflation might cause these items to cost $120. If so, in terms of buying "stuff," the dollar would have lost value over the five years. If you don't need to spend your money today, putting it in your mattress will only cause it to lose value over time. Instead, there are banks that would like to use your money and pay you back later, with interest. This interest is your compensation to offset the money's decline in value. Each dollar will be worth less in the future, but you'll get more dollars. So you'll be able to buy the same items as before.

The basic idea behind the time value of money is that $1 today is worth more than $1 promised next year. But how much more? Is $1 today worth $1.05 next year? $1.08? $1.12? The answer varies depending on current interest rates. This chapter describes the time value of money concept and provides the tools needed to analyze single cash flows at different points in time.

4.1 • Organizing Cash Flows

LG4-1

time line

A graphical representation showing the size and timing of cash flows through time.

inflow

Cash received, often from income or sale of an investment.

outflow

Cash payment, often a cost or the price of an investment or deposit.

interest rate

The cost of borrowing money denoted as a percent.

Managing cash flow timing is one of the most important tasks in successfully operating a business. A helpful tool for organizing our analysis is the **time line,** which shows the magnitude of cash flows at different points in time, such as monthly, quarterly, semiannually, or yearly. Cash we receive is called an **inflow,** and we denote it with a positive number. Cash that leaves us, such as a payment or contribution to a deposit, is an **outflow** designated with a negative number.

The following time line illustrates a $100 deposit you made at a bank that pays 5 percent interest. In one year, the $100 has become $105. *Given that interest rate,* having $100 now (in year 0) has the same value as having $105 in one year.

Here's a simple example: Suppose you allowed the bank to rent your $100 for a year at a cost of 5 percent, or $5. This cost is known as the **interest rate.**

Period	0	5%	1	2 years
Cash flow	−100		105	

Interest rates will affect you throughout your life, both in business and in your personal life. Companies borrow money to build factories and expand into new locations and markets. They expect the future revenues generated by these activities to more than cover the interest payments and repay the loan. People borrow money on credit cards and obtain loans for cars and home mortgages. They expect their purchases to give them the satisfaction in the future that compensates them for the interest payments charged on the loan. Understanding the dynamics between interest rates and cash inflows and outflows over time is key to financial success. The best place to start learning these concepts lies in understanding how money grows over time.

TIME OUT

4-1 Why is a dollar worth more today than a dollar received one year from now?

4-2 Drawing on your past classes in accounting, explain why time lines must show one negative cash flow and one positive cash flow.

4-3 Set up a time line, given a 6 percent interest rate, with a cash inflow of $200 today and a cash outflow of $212 in one year.

4.2 • Future Value

future value (FV)

The value of an investment after one or more periods.

The $105 one-time cash flow that your bank credits to your account in one year is known as a **future value (FV)** of $100 in one year at a 5 percent annual interest rate. If interest rates were higher than 5 percent, then the future value of your $100 would also be higher. If you left your money in the bank for more than one year, then its future value would continue to grow over time. Let's see why.

Single-Period Future Value

LG4-2

Computing the future value of a sum of money one year from today is straightforward: Add the interest earned to today's cash flow. In this case:

$$\text{Value in 1 year} = \text{Today's cash flow} + \text{Interest earned}$$
$$\$105 = \$100 + \$5$$

We computed the \$5 interest figure by multiplying the interest rate by today's cash flow (\$100 × 5%). Note that in equations, interest rates appear in decimal format. So we use 0.05 for 5 percent:

$$\$100 + (\$100 \times 0.05) = \$105.$$

Note that this is the same as:

$$\$100 \times (1 + 0.05) = \$105$$

We need the 1 in the parentheses to recapture the original deposit and the 0.05 is for the interest earned. We can generalize this computation to any amount of today's cash flow. In the general form of the future value equation, we call cash today **present value,** or **PV.** We compute the future value one year from now, called FV_1, using the interest rate, i:

present value (PV)

The amount a future cash flow is worth today.

$$\text{Value in 1 year} = \text{Today's value} \times (1 + \text{Interest rate})$$
$$FV_1 = PV \times (1 + i) \quad \textbf{(4-1)}$$

Notice that this is the same equation we used to figure the future value of your \$100. We've simply made it generic so we can use it over and over again. The 1 subscript means that we are calculating for only one period—in this case, one year. If interest rates were 6 percent instead of 5 percent per year, for instance, we could use equation 4-1 to find that the future value of \$100 in one year is \$106 [= \$100 × (1 + 0.06)].

Of course, the higher the interest rate, the larger the future value will be. Table 4.1 shows the interest cost and future value for a sample of different cash flows and interest rates. Notice from the first two lines of the table that, while the difference in interest earned between 5 percent and 6 percent (\$1) doesn't seem like much on a \$100 deposit, the difference on a \$15,000 deposit (the following two lines) is substantial (\$150).

table 4.1 | **Higher Interest Rates and Cash Flows Lead to Higher Future Values**

	A	B	C	D
1	**Higher Interest Rates Lead to Higher Future Values**			
2	**Today's Cash Flow**	**Interest Rate**	**Interest Cost**	**Next Year's Future Value**
3	\$100.00	5%	\$5.00	\$105.00
4	\$100.00	6%	\$6.00	\$106.00
5	\$15,000.00	5%	\$750.00	\$15,750.00
6	\$15,000.00	6%	\$900.00	\$15,900.00
7				
8	**Higher Cash Flows Today Lead to Higher Future Values**			
9	**Today's Cash Flow**	**Interest Rate**	**Interest Cost**	**Next Year's Future Value**
10	\$500.00	7.50%	\$37.50	\$537.50
11	\$750.00	7.50%	\$56.25	\$806.25

LG4-3

Compounding and Future Value

After depositing \$100 for one year, you must decide whether to take the \$105 or leave the money at the bank for another year to earn another 5 percent (or whatever interest rate the bank currently pays). In the second year at the bank, the deposit earns 5 percent on the \$105 value, which is \$5.25 (= \$105 × 0.05). Importantly, you get more than the \$5 earned the first year, which would be a simple total of \$110. The extra 25 cents earned in the second year is interest *on interest that was earned in the first year.* We call this process of earning interest both on the original deposit and on the earlier interest payments **compounding.**

compounding

The process of adding interest earned every period on both the original investment and the reinvested earnings.

So, let's illustrate a \$100 deposit made for two years at 5 percent in the following time line:

Period	0	5%	1	5%	2 years
Cash flow	PV = −100				FV = ?

LG4-1

The question mark denotes the amount we want to solve for. As with all TVM problems, we simply have to identify what element we're solving for; in this case, we're looking for the FV. To compute the two-year compounded future value, simply use the 1-year equation (4-1) twice.

$$\$100 \times (1 + 0.05) \times (1 + 0.05) = \$110.25$$

So the future value of \$100 deposited today at 5 percent interest is \$110.25 in period 2. You can see that this represents \$10 of interest payments generated from the original \$100 (\$5 each year) and \$0.25 of interest earned in the second year on previously earned interest payments. The \$5 of interest earned every year on the original deposit is called **simple interest.** Any amount of interest earned above the \$5 in any given year comes from compounding. Over time, the new interest payments earned from compounding can become substantial. The multiyear form of equation 4-1 is the future value in year *N*, shown as:

simple interest

Interest earned only on the original deposit.

$$\text{Future value in } N \text{ years} = \text{Present value} \times N \text{ years of compounding}$$

$$FV_N = PV \times (1 + i)^N \qquad \textbf{(4-2)}$$

We can solve the 2-year deposit problem more directly using equation 4-2 as \$110.25 = \$100 × $(1.05)^2$. Here, solving for FV in the equation requires solving for only one unknown. In fact, all TVM equations that you will encounter only require figuring out what is unknown in the situation and solving for that one unknown factor.

We can easily adapt equation 4-2 to many different future value problems. What is the future value in 30 years of that \$100 earning 5 percent per year? Using equation 4-2, we see that the future value is \$100 × $(1.05)^{30}$ = \$432.19. The money has increased substantially! You have made a profit of \$332.19 over and above your original \$100. Of this profit, only \$150 (= \$5 × 30 years) came from simple interest earned on the original deposit. The rest, \$182.19 (= \$332.19 − \$150), is from the compounding effect of earning interest on previously earned interest.

Remember that the difference between earning 5 percent and 6 percent in interest on the \$100 was only \$1 the first year. So what is the future value difference after 15 years? Is it \$15? No, as Figure 4.1 shows, the difference in future value substantially increases over time. The difference is \$31.76 in year 15 and \$142.15 in year 30.

figure 4.1

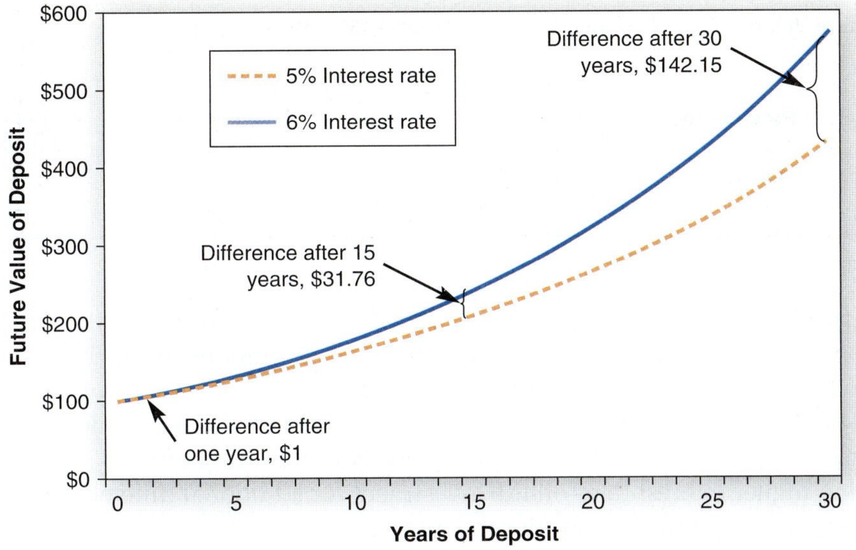

The Future Value of $100

Small differences in interest rates can really add up over time!

LG4-3

THE POWER OF COMPOUNDING Compound interest is indeed a powerful tool for building wealth. Albert Einstein, the German-born American physicist who developed the special and general theories of relativity and won the Nobel Prize for Physics in 1921, is supposed to have said, "The most powerful force in the universe is compound interest."[1] Figure 4.2 illustrates this point. It shows the original

figure 4.2

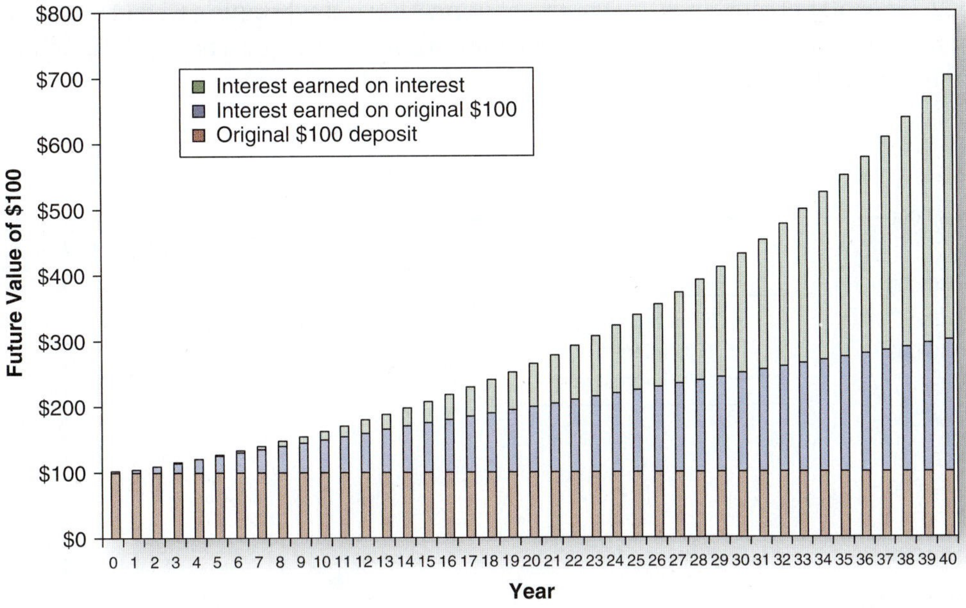

Interest Earned on Prior Interest at a 5 Percent Rate

The money from interest-on-interest will eventually exceed the interest from the original deposit.

[1]No one seems to know exactly what he said, when he said it, or to whom. Similar statements commonly attributed to Einstein are: (1) compound interest is the greatest wonder of the universe, (2) compound interest is the ninth wonder of the world, and (3) it is the greatest mathematical discovery of all time. If he did not say any of these things, he (or someone else) should have!

table 4.2 | **Compounding Builds Wealth Over Time**

	A	B	C	D	E
1	**Future Value of $100 Deposited at 5%, 10%, and 15% Interest Rates**				
2					
3			**Future Value**		
4	**Interest Rate Earned**	**5 years**	**10 years**	**20 years**	**30 years**
5	5%	$127.63	$162.89	$265.33	$432.19
6	10%	$161.05	$259.37	$672.75	$1,744.94
7	15%	$201.14	$404.56	$1,636.65	$6,621.18

$100 deposited, the cumulative interest earned on that deposit, and the cumulative interest-on-interest earned. By the 27th year, the money from the interest-on-interest exceeds the interest earned on the original deposit. By the 40th year, interest-on-interest contributes more than double the interest on the deposit. The longer money can earn interest, the greater the compounding effect.

Earning higher interest rates on the investment for additional time periods magnifies compounding power. Consider the future value of $100 deposited at different interest rates and over different time periods as shown in Table 4.2. The future value of $100 earning 5 percent per year for five years is $127.63, for a gain of $27.63. Would you double your gain by simply investing that same $100 at double the interest rate, 10 percent? No, because compounding changes the nature of the investment so that your money grows exponentially, not in a simple linear relationship. The future value of $100 in five years at 10 percent is $161.05. The $61.05 gain is *more* than double the gain of $27.63 earned at 5 percent. Tripling the interest rate to 15 percent shows a gain of $101.14 that is nearly *quadruple* the gain earned at 5 percent.

The same effect occurs when we increase the time. When the deposit earns 10 percent per year for five years, the gain is $61.05. When we double the amount of time to 10 years, the gain more than doubles to $159.37. If we double the time again to 20 years, the gain increases not to just $318.74 (= $159.37 × 2) but to $572.75. At 10 percent for 30 years, the gain on $100 is a whopping $1,644.94. Interest rates and time *are both* important factors in compounding! These relationships are illustrated in Figure 4.3.

figure 4.3

The Impact of Time and the Magnitude of the Interest Rate

The future value differences between compounding interest rates expand exponentially over time.

Future value of $100 deposited at 5%, 10%, and 15% interest rates

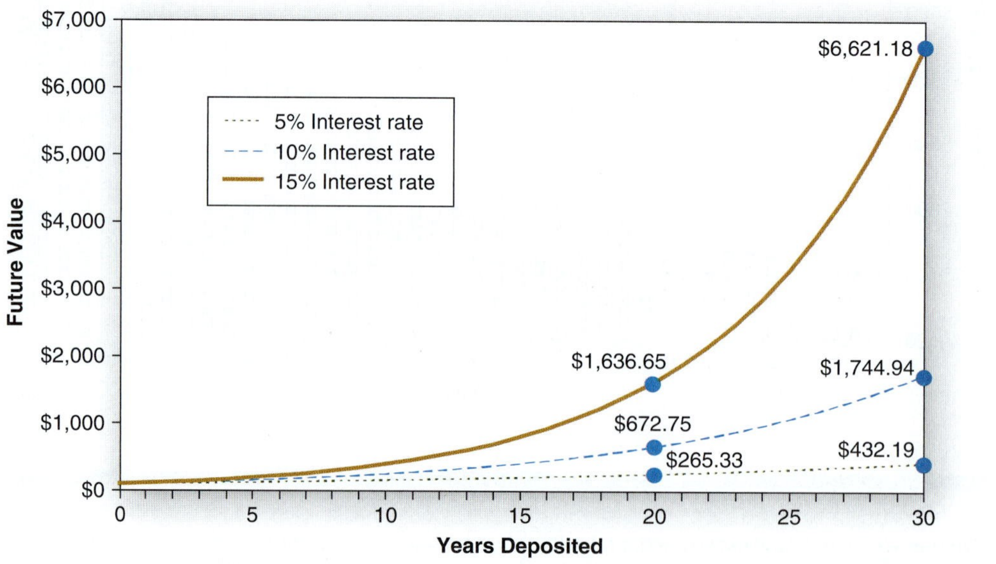

TIME OUT

4-4 How does compounding help build wealth (or increase debt) over time?

4-5 Why does doubling the interest rate or time quickly cause more than a doubling of the future value?

LG4-3

COMPOUNDING AT DIFFERENT INTEREST RATES OVER TIME Interest rates have varied over time. In the past half-century, banks have offered depositors rates lower than 1 percent and as high as double digits. They've also charged interest from about 5.5 percent to 21.6 percent to consumers for various kinds of loans. Let's look at how to compute future value when rates change, so that money earns interest at multiple interest rates over time. In our first example in this chapter, your deposit of \$100 earned 5 percent interest. Now consider the future value when the bank announces it will pay 6 percent interest in the second year. How much will you earn now? We can illustrate the question with this time line:

Period	0	5%	1	6%	2 years
Cash flow	PV = −100				FV =?

LG4-4

EXAMPLE 4-1

LG4-3

Graduation Celebration Loan

Dominic is a fourth-year business student who wants to go on a graduation celebration/vacation in Mexico but he has no money to pay for the trip. After the vacation, Dominic will start his career. His job will require moving to a new town and buying professional clothes. He asked his parents to lend him \$1,500, which he figures he will be able to pay back in three years. His parents agree to lend him the money, but they will charge 7 percent interest per year. What amount will Dominic need to pay back? How much interest will he pay? How much of what he pays is interest-on-interest?

For interactive versions of this example visit www.mhhe.com/can3e

SOLUTION:

Dominic will have to pay:

$$FV_3 = \$1{,}500 \times (1.07)^3 = \$1{,}500 \times 1.225 = \$1{,}837.56$$

Of the \$1,837.56 he owes his parents, \$337.56 (= \$1,837.56 − \$1,500) is interest. We can illustrate this time-value problem in the following time line.

Period	0	7%	1	7%	2	7%	3 years
Cash flow	PV=1,500						FV=−1,837.56

CALCULATOR HINTS

N = 3
I = 7
PV = 1500
PMT = 0
CPT FV = −1837.56

LG1

Compare this compound interest with simple interest. Simple interest would be 7 percent of \$1,500 (which is \$105) per year. The 3-year cost would then be \$315 (= 3 × \$105). The difference between the compound interest of \$337.56 and the total simple interest of \$315 is the interest-on-interest of \$22.56.

Similar to Problems 4-3, 4-4, 4-5, 4-6, 4-21, 4-22, 4-33, 4-34, self-test problem 1

MATH COACH

USING A FINANCIAL CALCULATOR

Financial, or business, calculators are programmed to perform the time value of money equations we develop in this chapter and the next. The two most common types of inexpensive financial calculators that can perform such functions are the Hewlett-Packard 10B II Business Calculator and the Texas Instruments BA II (Plus or Professional). Among many useful financial shortcuts these calculators have five specific financial buttons. The relevant financial buttons for time value of money (TVM) calculations are listed below. The HPIOBII calculator buttons look like this:

1. N (for the number of periods),
2. I/YR (for the interest rate),
3. PV (for present value),
4. PMT (for a constant payment every period), and
5. FV (for future value).

Notice that the TI BA II Plus financial calculator buttons appear to be very similar:

A common, more sophisticated and expensive calculator is the TI-83. This calculator has a menu system that includes the financial functions as shown:

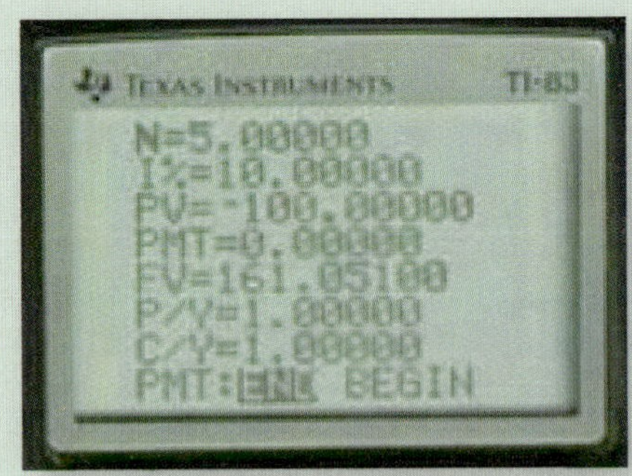

To get to the TVM menu, select APPLICATIONS and then choose FINANCE, and finally 1 TVM SOLVER on the previous screens.

Setting Up Your Calculator

These calculators come from the factory with specific settings. You will find it useful to change two of them. The first is to set the number of digits shown after the

We already know that the \$100 deposit will grow to \$105 at the end of the first year. This \$105 will then earn 6 percent in the second year and have a value of \$111.30 (= \$105 × 1.06). If we put the two steps together into one equation, the solution appears as \$111.30 = \$100 × 1.05 × 1.06. From this you should not be surprised that a general equation for future value of multiple interest rates is:

Future value in N periods = Today's value × Each period's compounding

$$FV_N = PV \times (1 + i_{\text{period 1}}) \times (1 + i_{\text{period 2}}) \times (1 + i_{\text{period 3}}) \times \cdots \times (1 + i_{\text{period } N}) \quad \textbf{(4-3)}$$

Note that the future value equation 4-2 is a special case of the more general equation 4-3. If the interest rate every period is the same, we can write equation 4-3 as equation 4-2.

EXAMPLE 4-2

LG4-3

For interactive versions of this example visit www.mhhe.com/can3e

Celebration Loan with Payback Incentive

Reexamine the loan Dominic was seeking from his parents in the previous example. His parents want to give him an incentive to pay off the loan as quickly as possible. They structure the loan so they charge 7 percent interest the first year and increase the rate 1 percent each decimal point on the calculator display. The factory setting is for two digits. However, consider a problem in which we use a 5.6 percent interest rate. The decimal version of this percentage is 0.056, which a two-digit display would round to 0.06. It's less worrisome to set the calculator to display the number of digits necessary to show the right number; this is called a *floating point display*. To set a floating point display for the HP calculator, press the color button, then the DISP button, and finally the decimal (.) button. To set the display for a floating point decimal on the TI calculator, push the 2ND button, followed by the FORMAT button, followed by the 9 button, and finally the ENTER button.

The second change you'll want to make is to set the number of times the calculator compounds each period. The settings may be preset to 12 times per period. Reset this to one time per period. To change the HP calculator to compound once per period, push the 1 button, then the color button, and finally the P/YR button. On the TI calculator, simply push the 2ND button, the P/Y button, the number one, and the ENTER button. These new settings will remain in the calculator until you either change them or remove the calculator's batteries.

Using Your Calculator

The calculators compute time-value problems in similar ways. Enter the cash flows into the time-value buttons (PV, PMT, and FV) consistent with the way they are shown in a time line. In other words, cash inflows should be positive and cash outflows negative. Thus, PV and FV cash flows are nearly always opposite in sign. Enter interest rates (I) in the percentage form, not the decimal form. Also enter the number of periods in the problem (N).

Consider our earlier example of the $100 deposit for two years earning a 5 percent interest rate.

1. To set the number of years, press 2 and then the N button.
2. To set the interest rate, press 5 and then the I button. (Note that interest rates are in percentage format for using a financial calculator and in decimal format for using the equations.)
3. To enter the current cash flow: press 100, then make it negative by pressing the +/− button, then press the PV button.
4. We won't use the PMT button, so enter 0 and then the PMT button.
5. To solve for future value, press the compute button (CPT) [for the TI] and then the FV button [press the FV button only for the HP].
6. Solution: the display should show FV = 110.25

Note that the answer is positive, consistent with an inflow and the time line diagram. These values remain in the TVM registers even after the calculator is turned off. So when you start a new problem, you should clear out old values first. For the HP calculator, clear the registers by pressing the shift/orange key before pressing C. You can clear the BAII Plus calculator using 2ND and CLR TVM.

You'll notice that throughout this book we use the equations in the main text to solve time value of money problems. We provide the calculator solutions in the margins.

year until the loan is paid. How much will Dominic owe if he waits three years to pay off the loan? Say that in the third year he considers whether to pay off the loan or wait one more year. How much more will he pay if he waits one more year?

SOLUTION:

For a payment in the third year, Dominic will pay interest of 7 percent the first year, 8 percent the second year, and 9 percent the third year. He will have to pay:

$$FV_3 = \$1{,}500 \times 1.07 \times 1.08 \times 1.09 = \$1{,}500 \times 1.2596 = \$1.889.41$$

The cash flow time line is:

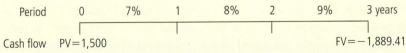

Period	0	7%	1	8%	2	9%	3 years
Cash flow	PV=1,500						FV=−1,889.41

Even worse, if he waits until the fourth year, he will pay one year of interest at 10 percent. The total payment will be

$$FV_4 = \$1{,}889.41 \times 1.10 = \$2{,}078.35$$

Because of both the escalating interest rate and the compounding effect, Dominic must make timely and increasing payments the longer he delays in paying off the loan. Deciding in the third year to put off the payment an extra year would cost him an additional $188.94 (= $2,078.35 − $1,889.41).

Similar to Problems 4-7, 4-8

LG4-4

4.3 • Present Value

We asked earlier what happens when you deposit $100 cash in the bank to earn 5 percent interest for one year—the bank pays you a $105 future value. However, we could have asked the question in reverse. That is, if the bank will pay $105 in one year and interest rates are 5 percent, how much would you be willing to deposit now, to receive that payment in a year? Here, we start with a future value and must find the present value—a different kind of calculation called discounting.

Discounting

discounting

The process of finding present value by reducing future values using the discount, or interest, rate.

While the process of a present value growing over time into the future is called *compounding*, the process of figuring out how much an amount that you expect to receive in the future is worth today is **discounting.** Just as compounding significantly increases the present value into the future, discounting significantly decreases the value of a future amount to the present. Since discounting is the reverse of compounding, we can rearrange equation 4-1 to solve for the present value of a cash flow received one year in the future.

Present value of next period's cash flow = Next period's value ÷ One period of discounting

$$PV = \frac{FV_1}{(1+i)} \tag{4-4}$$

Suppose the bank is going to pay $105 in one year and interest rates are 5 percent. Then the present value of the payment is $105/1.05 = $100. Present values are always smaller than future values (as long as interest rates are greater than zero!), and the difference between what an investment is worth today and what it's worth when you're supposed to redeem it gets larger as the interest rate increases. Likewise, if the amount of time until the expected payment date increases, the difference will also increase in value.

DISCOUNTING OVER MULTIPLE PERIODS Discounting over multiple periods is the reverse process of compounding over multiple periods. Knowing this, we can find the general equation for present value by rearranging the terms in equation 4-2 to form:

discount rate

The interest rate used to discount future cash flow(s) to the present.

PV of cash flow made in N years = Cash flow in year $N \div N$ years of discounting

$$PV = \frac{FV_N}{(1+i)^N} \tag{4-5}$$

The interest rate, *i*, which we use to calculate present value, is often referred to as the **discount rate.** How much is a $100 payment to be made in the future worth today? Of course, it depends on how far into the future you expect to receive the payment and the discount rate used. If you receive a $100 cash flow in five years, then its present value is $78.35, discounted at 5 percent:

CALCULATOR HINTS

N = 5
I = 5
PMT = 0
FV = 100
CPT PV = −78.35

$$PV = \$100/(1.05)^5 = \$100/1.2763 = \$78.35$$

The time line looks like this:

LG4-1

Period	0	5%	1	5%	2	5%	3	5%	4	5%	5 years
Cash flow	PV = −78.35										FV = 100

figure 4.4

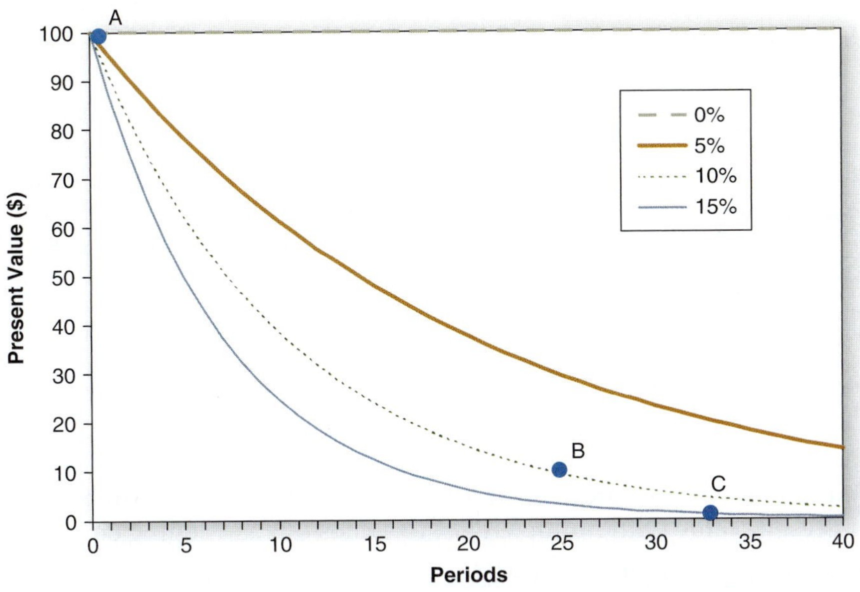

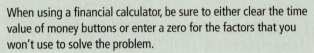

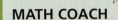

Present Value of a $100 Cash Flow Made in the Future

The higher the discount rate, the more quickly the cash flow value falls.

If the discount rate rises to 10 percent, the present value of our $100 to be paid to us in five years is only $62.09 today. At a 15 percent interest rate, the present value declines to less than half the future cash flow: $49.72. Higher interest rates discount future cash flows more quickly and dramatically. You can see this principle illustrated in Figure 4.4.

> **MATH COACH**
>
> When using a financial calculator, be sure to either clear the time value of money buttons or enter a zero for the factors that you won't use to solve the problem.

Moving right from point A in the figure, notice that if interest rates are 0 percent, the present value will equal the future value. Also note from the curved lines that when the discount rate is greater than zero, the discounting to present value is not linear through time. The higher the discount rate, the more quickly the cash flow value falls. If the discount rate is 10 percent, a $100 cash flow that you would receive in 25 years is worth less than $10 today, as shown at point B in the figure. With a 15 percent discount rate, the $100 payment to be received in 33 years, at point C, is worth less than $1 today.

EXAMPLE 4-3

LG4-4

Buy Now and Don't Pay for Two Years

Suppose that a marketing manager for a retail furniture company proposes a sale. Customers can buy now but don't have to pay for their furniture purchases for two years. From a time value of money perspective, selling furniture at full price with payment in two years is equivalent to selling furniture at a sale, or discounted, price with immediate payment. If interest rates are 7.5 percent per year, what is the equivalent sale price of a $1,000 sleeper-sofa when the customer takes the full two years to pay for it?

For interactive versions of this example visit www.mhhe.com/can3e

SOLUTION:

The time line for this problem is:

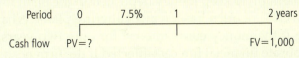

Period	0	7.5%	1	2 years
Cash flow	PV=?			FV=1,000

CALCULATOR HINTS

N = 2
I = 7.5
PMT = 0
FV = 1000
CPT PV = −865.33

Using equation 4-5, the present value computation is

$$PV = \frac{FV_N}{(1 + i)^N} = \frac{\$1,000}{1.075^2} = \frac{\$1,000}{1.1556} = \$865.33$$

In this case, the marketing proposal for delaying payment for two years is equivalent to selling the $1,000 sleeper-sofa for a sale price of $865.33, or a 13.5 percent discount. When stores promote such sales, they often believe that customers will not be able to pay the full amount at the end of the two years and then must pay high interest rate charges and late fees. Customers who do pay on time are getting a good deal.

Similar to Problems 4-9, 4-10, 4-11, 4-12, self-test problem 2

LG4-4

DISCOUNTING WITH MULTIPLE RATES We can also discount a future cash flow at different interest rates per period. We find the general form of the equation for present value with multiple discount rates by rearranging equation 4-3:

Present value with different discount rates = Future cash flow ÷ Each period's discounting

$$PV = \frac{FV_N}{(1 + i_{\text{period }1}) \times (1 + i_{\text{period }2}) \times (1 + i_{\text{period }3}) \times \cdots \times (1 + i_{\text{period }N})} \qquad \textbf{(4-6)}$$

Suppose that we expect interest rates to increase over the next few years, from 7 percent this year, to 8 percent next year, to 8.5 percent in the third year. In this environment, how would we work out the present value of a future $2,500 cash flow in year 3? The time line for this problem is

LG4-1

Period	0	7%	1	8%	2	8.5%	3 years
Cash flow	PV=?						FV=2,500

Using equation 4-6 shows that the present value is $1,993.90:

$$PV = \frac{\$2,500}{1.07 \times 1.08 \times 1.085} = \frac{\$2,500}{1.2538} = \$1,993.90$$

TIME OUT

4-6 How are interest rates in the economy related to the way people value future cash payments?

4-7 Explain how discounting is the reverse of compounding.

4.4 • Using Present Value and Future Value

Moving Cash Flows

LG4-5

As managers analyze investment projects, debt management, and cash flow, they frequently find it useful to move cash flows to different points in time. While you may be planning to keep money deposited in the bank for three years when you will buy a car, life often has a way of altering plans. What type of car might you purchase if the money earns interest for only two years, or for four years? How is a corporate financial forecast affected if the firm needs to remodel a factory two years sooner than planned? Moving cash flows around in time is

table 4.3 | **Equivalent Cash Flows in Time**

When Interest Rates Are	A Cash Flow of	In Year	Can be Moved to Year	With Equation	Equivalent Cash Flow
Moving Later versus Moving Earlier					
8%	$1,000	5	10	$FV_{10} = PV_5 \times (1+i)^5 = \$1{,}000 \times (1.08)^5 =$	$1,469.33
8	1,000	5	2	$PV_2 = FV_5 / (1+i)^3 = \$1{,}000 / (1.08)^3 =$	793.83
Moving Earlier					
10	500	9	8	$PV_8 = FV_9 / (1+i)^1 = \$500 / (1.10)^1 =$	454.55
10	500	9	0	$PV_0 = FV_9 / (1+i)^9 = \$500 / (1.10)^9 =$	212.05
Moving Later					
12	100	4	20	$FV_{20} = PV_4 \times (1+i)^{16} = \$100 \times (1.12)^{16} =$	613.04
12	100	4	30	$FV_{30} = PV_4 \times (1+i)^{26} = \$100 \times (1.12)^{26} =$	1,904.01

important to businesses and individuals alike for sound financial planning and decision making.

Moving cash flows from one point in time to another requires us to use both present value and future value equations. Specifically, we use the present value equation for moving cash flows *earlier* in time, and the future value cash flows for moving cash flows *later* in time. For example, what's the value in year 2 of a $200 cash flow to be received in three years, when interest rates are 6 percent? This problem requires moving the $200 payment in the third year to a value in the second year, as shown in the time line:

LG4-1

Since the cash flow is to be moved one year *earlier* in time, we use the present value equation:

$$PV_2 = FV_3/(1+i)^1 = \$200/(1.06)^1 = \$188.68$$

CALCULATOR HINTS

N = 1
I = 6
PMT = 0
FV = 200
CPT PV = −188.68

When interest rates are 6 percent, a $188.68 payment in year 2 equates to a $200 payment in year 3.

What about moving the $200 cash flow to year 5? Since this requires moving the cash flow later in time by two years, we use the future value equation. In this case, the equivalent of $200 in the third year is a fifth-year payment of:

$$FV_5 = PV_3 \times (1+i)^2 = \$200 \times (1.06)^2 = \$200 \times 1.1236 = \$224.72$$

CALCULATOR HINTS

N = 2
I = 6
PV = 200
PMT = 0
CPT PV = −224.72

Table 4.3 illustrates how we might move several cash flows. At an 8 percent interest rate, a $1,000 cash flow due in year 5 compounded to year 10 equals $1,469.33. We could also discount that same $1,000 cash flow to a value of $793.83 in year 2. At an 8 percent interest rate, the three cash flows ($793.83 in year 2, $1,000 in year 5, and $1,469.33 in year 10) become equivalent. Table 4.3 illustrates the movement of other cash flows given different interest rates and time periods.

Moving cash flows from one year to another creates an easy way to compare or combine two cash flows. Would you rather receive $150 in year 2 or $160 in year 2? Since both cash flows occur in the same year, the comparison is straightforward. But we can't directly add or compare cash flows in different years until we consider their time value. We can compare cash flows in different years by moving one cash flow to the same time as the other using the present value or future value equations. Once you have the value of each cash flow in the same year, you can directly compare or combine them.

LG4-6

Rule of 72

An approximation for the number of years needed for an investment to double in value.

RULE OF 72 Albert Einstein is also credited with popularizing compound interest by introducing a simple mathematical approximation for the number of years required to double an investment. It's called the **Rule of 72.**

$$\text{Approximate number of years to double an investment} = \frac{72}{\text{Interest rate}} \quad \textbf{(4-7)}$$

The Rule of 72 illustrates the power of compound interest. How many years will it take to double money deposited at 6 percent per year? Using the Rule of 72, we find the answer is 12 years (= 72/6). A higher interest rate causes faster increases in future value. A 9 percent interest rate allows money to double in just eight years (= 72/9). Remember that this rule provides only a mathematical approximation. It's more accurate with lower interest rates. After all, with a 72 percent interest rate, the rule predicts that it will take one year to double the money (= 72/72). However, we know that it actually takes a 100 percent rate to double money in one year.

We can also use the Rule of 72 to approximate the interest rate needed to double an investment in a specific amount of time. What rate do we need to double an investment in 5 years? Rearranging equation 4-7 shows that the rate needed is 14.4 percent (= 72/5) per year.

EXAMPLE 4-4

LG4-5

For interactive versions of this example visit www.mhhe.com/can3e

Pay Damages or Appeal?

Timber, Inc., lost a lawsuit in a business dispute. The judge ordered the company to pay the plaintiff $175,000 in one year. Timber's attorney advises Timber to appeal the ruling. If so, Timber will likely lose again and will still have to pay the $175,000. But by appealing, Timber moves the $175,000 payment to year 2, along with the attorney's fee of $20,000 for the extra work. The interest rate is 7 percent. What decision should Timber make?

SOLUTION:

Timber executives must decide whether to pay $175,000 in one year or $195,000 in two years. To compare the two choices more directly, move the payment in year 2 to year 1 and then compare it to $175,000. Timber should choose to make the smaller payment. The computation is:

$$PV_1 = FV_2/(1 + i)^1 = \$195{,}000/(1.07)^1 = \$182{,}242.99$$

The value in year 1 of a year 2 payment of $195,000 is $182,242.99, which is clearly more than the $175,000 year 1 payment. So Timber should *not* appeal and should pay the plaintiff $175,000 in one year (and may want to look for another attorney).

Similar to Problems 4-23, 4-24, 4-25, 4-26, 4-27, 4-28, 4-41

CALCULATOR HINTS

N = 1
I = 7
PMT = 0
FV = 195000
CPT PV = −182,242.99

TIME OUT

4-8 In Example 4-4, could Timber, Inc., have performed its analysis by moving the $175,000 to year 2 and comparing? Would the firm then have made the same decision?

4-9 At what interest rate (and number of years) does the Rule of 72 become too inaccurate to use?

finance at work — investments

TVM CAVEAT EMPTOR

Not making your payments on time can get very expensive. Reconsider the furniture selling experience in Example 4-3. The store has given customers the opportunity to buy the sleeper-sofa today and not pay the $1,000 price for two years. But what happens if you forget to pay on time? Indeed, many people do forget. Others simply haven't saved $1,000 and can't make the payment. The fine print in these deals provides the penalties for late payment. For example, the late clause might require a 10 percent annually compounded interest rate to apply to any late payment—retroactive to the sale date. Thus, being one day late with the payment will automatically incur an interest charge for the entire two years of $210 (= $\$1{,}000 \times 1.1^2 - \$1{,}000$), which is in addition to the original $1,000 still owed, of course.

The impact of making late payments can also show up later when you apply for credit cards, auto loans, and other credit. Credit rating agencies gather information on us from companies, banks, and landlords to grade our payment history. If you consistently make late payments on your apartment, credit card, or electric bill, these agencies will give you a poor grade. The higher your grade, called a credit score, the more likely you are to be able to get a loan and pay a lower interest rate on that loan. People with lower credit scores may not be able to borrow money and when they can, they will pay higher interest rates on their credit cards and auto loans. Paying a higher interest rate can really cost you a lot of money. Remember the future value differences between interest rates illustrated in Table 4.2 and Figure 4.3. Those people who have really bad credit scores can't get loans from banks and merchants and have to rely on payday lending places that charge enormously high rates, as highlighted in this chapter's Personal Application Viewpoint.

Making a late payment might not seem like a big deal at the time, but it can really cost you!

want to know more? Key Words to Search for Updates: credit report, credit ratings, credit score

4.5 • Computing Interest Rates

LG4-7

Time value of money calculations come in handy when we know two cash flows and need to find the interest rate. The investment industry often uses this analysis. Solving for the interest rate, or rate of return,[2] can answer questions like, "If you bought a gold coin for $350 three years ago and sell it now for $475, what rate of return have you earned?" The time line for this problem looks like this:

Period	0	1	?%	2	3 years
Cash flow	PV = −350				FV = 475

LG4-1

In general, computing interest rates is easiest with a financial calculator. To compute the answer using the time-value equations, consider how the cash flows fit into the future value equation 4-2:

CALCULATOR HINTS
N = 3
PV = −350
PMT = 0
FV = 475
CPT I = 10.716

$$FV_N = PV \times (1 + i)^N$$

$$\$475 = \$350 \times (1 + i)^3$$

Rearranging gives:

$$\$475/\$350 = (1 + i)^3, \text{ or } 1.357 = (1 + i)^3$$

[2] The terms *interest rate* and *rate of return* are referring to the same thing. However, it is a common convention to refer to interest rate when you are the one paying the cash flows and refer to rate of return when you are the one receiving the cash flows.

table 4.4 | **Interest Rate per Year to Double an Investment**

LG4-6

	A	B	C
1	**Number of Years to Double Investment**	**Precise Annual Interest Rate**	**Rule of 72 Interest Rate Estimate**
2	1	100.00%	72.00%
3	2	41.42%	36.00%
4	3	25.99%	24.00%
5	4	18.92%	18.00%
6	5	14.87%	14.40%
7	6	12.25%	12.00%
8	7	10.41%	10.29%
9	8	9.05%	9.00%
10	9	8.01%	8.00%
11	10	7.18%	7.20%
12	15	4.73%	4.80%
13	20	3.53%	3.60%
14	25	2.81%	2.88%
15	30	2.34%	2.40%

To solve for the interest rate, *i*, take the third root of both sides of the equation. To do this, take 1.357 to the 1/3 power using the y^x button on your calculator.[3] Doing this leads to:

$$1.107 = (1 + i), \text{ or } i = 0.107 = 10.7\%$$

If you buy a gold coin for $350 and sell it three years later for $475, you earn a 10.7 percent return per year.

Time is an important factor in computing the return that you're earning per year. Turning a $100 investment into $200 is a 100 percent return. If your investments earn this much in two years, then they earned a 41.42 percent rate of return per year [$\$100 \times (1.4142)^2 = \$200$]. Table 4.4 shows the annual interest rate earned for doubling an investment over various time periods. Notice how compounding complicates the solution: It's not as simple as just dividing by the number of years. Getting a 100 percent return in two years means earning 41.42 percent per year, not 50 percent per year. Table 4.4 also shows the Rule of 72 interest rate estimate.

MATH COACH

When using a financial calculator to compute an interest rate between two cash flows, you must enter one cash flow as a negative number. This is because you must inform the calculator which payments are cash inflows and which are cash outflows. If you input all the cash flows as the same sign, the calculator will show an error when asked to compute the interest rate.

Return Asymmetries

Suppose you bought a gold coin for $700 last year and now the market will pay you only $350. Clearly, the investment earned a negative rate of return. Use a financial calculator or a time-value equation to verify that this is a return of −50 percent. You lost half your money! So, in order to break even and get back to $700, you need to earn a positive 50 percent, right? Wrong. Note that to get from $350 to $700, your money needs to double! You need a 100 percent return to make up for a 50 percent decline. Similarly, you need a gain of 33.33 percent to make up for a 25 percent decline. If your investment declines by 10 percent, you'll need an 11.11 percent gain to offset the loss. In general, only a higher positive return can offset any given negative return.

[3]The general equation for computing the interest rate is $i = \left(FV_N/PV\right)^{\frac{1}{N}} - 1$.

TIME OUT

4-10 Say you double your money in three years. Explain why the rate of return is NOT 33.3 percent per year.

4-11 Show that you must earn a 25 percent return to offset a 20 percent loss.

4.6 • Solving for Time

LG4-8

Sometimes you may need to determine the time period needed to accumulate a specific amount of money. If you know the starting cash flow, the interest rate, and the future cash flow (the sum you will need), you can solve the time value equations for the number of years that you will need to accumulate that money. Just as with solving for different interest rates, solving for the number of periods is complicated and requires using natural logarithms.[4] Many people prefer to use a financial calculator to solve for the number of periods.

LG4-7

When interest rates are 9 percent, how long will it take for a $5,000 investment to double? Finding the solution with a financial calculator entails entering

- I = 9
- PV = −5,000
- PMT = 0
- FV = 10,000

The answer is 8.04 years, or eight years and two weeks. The Rule of 72 closely approximates the answer, which predicts eight years (= 72/9).

MATH COACH

SIMPLE TVM SPREADSHEET FUNCTIONS

Common spreadsheet programs include time value of money functions. The functions are:

Compute a future value	=	FV(rate,nper,pmt,pv,type)
Compute a present value	=	PV(rate,nper,pmt,fv,type)
Compute the number of periods	=	NPER(rate,pmt,pv,fv,type)
Compute an interest rate	=	RATE(nper,pmt,pv,fv,type)
Compute a repeating payment	=	PMT(rate,nper,pv,fv,type)

The five input/outputs (FV, PV, NPER, RATE, PMT) work similarly to the five TVM buttons on a business calculator. The *type* input defaults to 0 for normal situations, but can be set to 1 for computing annuity due problems (see Chapter 5). Different spreadsheet programs might have slightly different notations for these five functions.

Consider the future value problem of Example 4-1. The spreadsheet solution is the same as the TVM calculator solution. Note that since the PV is listed as a positive number, the FV output is a negative number.

	A	B	C	D
1				
2	Present Value =	$1,500		
3	Future Cash Flow =	-$1,837.56 =FV(B4,B5,0,B2,0)		
4	Interest Rate =	7%		
5	# of Periods =	3		

The inputs to the function can be directed to other cells, like the *rate, nper,* and *pv* in the this illustration. Or the input can be the actual number, like *pmt* and *type*.

	A	B	C	D
1				
2	Present Value =	-$350		
3	Future Cash Flow =	$475		
4	Interest Rate =	10.72% =RATE(B5,0,B2,B3,0)		
5	# of Periods =	3		

This spreadsheet solves for the interest rate in the preceding example in the text. Just like using the TVM calculator, the PV and FV must be of opposite signs to avoid getting an error message.

See this textbook's online student center to watch instructional videos on using spreadsheets. Also note that the solution for all the examples in the book are illustrated using spreadsheets in videos that are also available on the textbook website, www.mhhe.com/can3e.

[4]The equation for solving for the number of periods is $N = \dfrac{\ln\left(FV_N/PV\right)}{\ln(1+i)}$.

EXAMPLE 4-5

LG4-8

For interactive versions of this example visit www.mhhe.com/can3e

Growth in Staffing Needs

Say that you are the sales manager of a company that produces software for human resource departments. You are planning your staffing needs, which depend on the volume of sales over time. Your company currently sells \$350 million of merchandise per year and has grown 7 percent per year in the past. If this growth rate continues, how long will it be before the firm reaches \$500 million in sales? How long before it reaches \$600 million?

SOLUTION:

You could set up the following time line to illustrate the problem:

Period	0	1	7% ...	2	? years
Cash flow	PV = −350				FV = 500

As shown in the margin, \$350 million of sales growing at 7 percent per year will reach \$500 million in five years and three months. To reach \$600 million will take just two weeks short of eight years.

Similar to Problems 4-31, 4-32, self-test problem 4

CALCULATOR HINTS

I = 7
PV = −350
PMT = 0
FV = 500
CPT N = 5.27

TIME OUT

4-12 In Example 4-5, how long will it take your company to double its sales?

4-13 In what other areas of business can these time-value concepts be used?

viewpoints REVISITED

Business Application Solution

You must compare the cash flows of buying the wire now at a discount, or waiting one year. The cost of the wire should include both the supplier's bill and the storage cost, for a total of \$452,000. What interest rate is implied by a \$452,000 cash flow today versus \$500,000 in one year? Using equation 4-2:

$$FV_N = PV \times (1 + i)^N$$
$$\$500{,}000 = \$452{,}000 \times (1 + i)^1$$
$$i = \$500{,}000/\$452{,}000 - 1 = 0.1062 \text{ or } 10.62\%$$

CALCULATOR HINTS

N = 1
PV = −452000
PMT = 0
FV = 500000
CPT I = 10.62

Whether your company should purchase the wire today depends on the cost of the firm's capital (discussed in Chapter 11). If it costs the firm less than 10.6 percent to obtain cash, then you should purchase the wire today. Otherwise, you should not.

Personal Application Solution

Since Anthony's loan of \$300 requires an immediate \$50 payment, the actual cash flow is \$250 (= \$300 − \$50). He then must repay the full \$300. Use equation 4-2 to compute the interest rate you pay for the period:

$$FV_N = PV \times (1 + i)^N$$
$$\$300 = \$250 \times (1 + i)^1$$
$$i = \$300/\$250 - 1 = 0.20 \text{ or } 20\%$$

CALCULATOR HINTS

N = 1
PV = −250
PMT = 0
FV = 300
CPT I = 20.00

Anthony is paying 20 percent for a loan of only two weeks! This is equivalent to paying 11,348 percent per year (this is shown in Chapter 5). He will never be able to build wealth if he continues to pay interest rates like this. Indeed, many people get trapped in a continuing cycle, obtaining one payday loan after another.

WARNING: Payday loans are almost always terrible deals for the borrower!

summary of learning goals

In this chapter, we introduce the concept of the time value of money. We describe the tools used to determine how money today grows over time. The same tools, once rearranged, also can determine the value of a future cash flow today, as $100 paid in the future is worth less than $100 today. Other useful applications of the time-value equations include determining the rate earned on an investment or figuring out the time needed for an investment to reach a specific amount of money. The next chapter continues with this topic and introduces intrayear compounding and how to handle multiple cash flows.

LG4-1 **Create a cash flow time line.** The first step in analyzing a time-value problem is to identify the cash inflows and outflows, the time when they occur, and the pertinent interest rate. Organizing the specific factors that appear in TVM equations makes finding the answers more straightforward.

LG4-2 **Compute the future value of money.** Money deposited today at a bank will grow to a larger amount next year. The higher the interest rate, or the longer the money is left to grow, the greater the final amount will be. Future values are larger than present values given a positive interest rate.

LG4-3 **Show how the power of compound interest increases wealth.** The interest payment earned in the first year adds to the deposit for the second year. In the second year of the deposit with compounding, both the original deposit and the interest earned in the first year will earn interest. Over time, compound interest earned on prior interest payments can become substantial. At times, different interest rates may apply to compound future value over time.

Earning just 1 percent more in interest rate every year results in much higher future values over time. Doubling the interest rate can mean triple or even quadruple earnings over 20 or 30 years. Time has the same effect. Doubling the time that money is invested more than doubles the amount of profits earned.

LG4-4 **Calculate the present value of a payment made in the future.** A dollar paid (or received) in the future is not worth as much as a dollar paid (or received) today. Computing the present value of a payment made in the future is called *discounting*. The interest rate used to determine the present value is the discount rate. As long as the discount rate is positive, present values are smaller than future values. Higher discount rates cause the value of the future value to decline more quickly and dramatically.

LG4-5 **Move cash flows from one year to another.** A cash flow may actually occur in a year other than originally planned. To evaluate the effect, we use the future value equation to move cash flows later in time and the present value equation to move cash flows earlier in time until all cash flows are expressed in the same period. By moving one cash flow to the same year as the other, we can directly compare them.

LG4-6 **Apply the Rule of 72.** To approximate the length of time needed to double a sum of money, simply divide 72 by the interest rate. The Rule of 72 is useful for estimating interest rates at or below 15 percent but deviates too much from true values at higher interest rates.

LG4-7 **Compute the rate of return realized on selling an investment.** The number of years between the present and future cash flows is an important factor in determining the annual rate earned. Because we compute rates of return using the beginning-period value of an investment, investments that feature gains and losses may become asymmetric between gains and losses. You double your investment with a 100 percent return but lose all your profits with a subsequent 50 percent decline in price.

LG4-8 **Calculate the number of years needed to grow an investment.** You can use the time-value equations and a business calculator to compute the number of years to reach a specific level of desired growth. The higher the interest rate, the shorter the time period needed to achieve the growth.

chapter equations

4-1 Future value in 1 year $= FV_1 = PV \times (1 + i)$

4-2 Future value in N years $= FV_N = PV \times (1 + i)^N$

4-3 Future value in N periods $= FV_N = PV \times (1 + i_{\text{period 1}}) \times (1 + i_{\text{period 2}}) \times (1 + i_{\text{period 3}}) \times \cdots \times (1 + i_{\text{period } N})$

4-4 Present value of next period's cash flow $= PV = FV_1/(1 + i)$

4-5 Present value of cash flow made in N years $= PV = FV_N/(1 + i)^N$

4-6 Present value with different discount rates

$$= PV = \frac{FV_N}{(1 + i_{\text{period 1}}) \times (1 + i_{\text{period 2}}) \times (1 + i_{\text{period 3}}) \times \cdots \times (1 + i_{\text{period } N})}$$

4-7 Approximate number of years to double an investment $= \dfrac{72}{\text{Interest rate}}$

key terms

compounding, The process of adding interest earned every period on both the original investment and the reinvested earnings. *p. 122*

discounting, The process of finding present value by reducing future values using the discount, or interest, rate. *p. 128*

discount rate, The interest rate used to discount future cash flow(s) to the present. *p. 128*

future value (FV), The value of an investment after one or more periods. *p. 120*

inflow Cash received, often from income or sale of an investment. *p. 120*

interest rate, The cost of borrowing money denoted as a percent. *p. 120*

outflow, Cash payment, often a cost or the price of an investment or deposit. *p. 120*

present value (PV), The amount a future cash flow is worth today. *p. 121*

Rule of 72, An approximation for the number of years needed for an investment to double in value. *p. 132*

simple interest, Interest earned only on the original deposit. *p. 122*

time line, A graphical representation showing the size and timing of cash flows through time. *p. 120*

self-test problems with solutions

LG4-2,4-3,4-5

1 **Two Future Values** You have entered a consulting deal with a company. You are to complete two projects. The first project will take one year to finish. The second project will take two years and must be started immediately following the first one. The deal includes a provision in which the company will make a $10,000 payment to your retirement plan after the first project and $20,000 after the second project. You have 20 years until retirement and will earn 9 percent per year on your retirement plan money. How much money will you have for retirement from these two payments?

Solution:

The future value of each payment can be computed and then added together in year 20. The $10,000 payment will be paid in one year and compounded for 19 years:

$$FV_N = PV_1 \times (1 + i)^N$$
$$FV_{20} = \$10{,}000 \times (1 + 0.09)^{19}$$
$$= \$10{,}000 \times 5.1417$$
$$= \$51{,}416.61$$

CALCULATOR HINTS
N = 19
I = 9
PV = −10000
PMT = 0
CPT FV = 51,416.61

So the first payment will grow to $51,416.61 by your planned retirement.

The $20,000 payment will be paid in three years and compounded for 17 years:

$$FV_N = PV_3 \times (1 + i)^N$$
$$FV_{20} = \$20{,}000 \times (1 + 0.09)^{17}$$
$$= \$20{,}000 \times 4.328$$
$$= \$86{,}552.67$$

CALCULATOR HINTS
N = 17
I = 9
PV = −20000
PMT = 0
CPT FV = 86,552.67

So the second payment will grow to $86,552.67. Because both payments are now moved to year 20, they can be combined. The money available in 20 years will be $137,969.28 (= $51,416.61 + $86,552.67).

2 Present Value You have decided to leave the small advertising firm where you are a partner. The partnership agreement among the partners states that if a partner leaves, that person's ownership in the firm is "cashed out" with an immediate payment consisting of 5 percent of last year's revenue. Last year the firm had revenue of $1 million. But your partners would rather not have to pay out this big cash flow to you this year because they are expecting much more business soon. In fact, they believe that they will be earning revenues of $1.5 million in just two years. So, they offer you a choice between taking 5 percent of last year's revenue now, or taking 4 percent of expected revenue in two years. If you believe an appropriate discount rate is 10 percent, which cash out payment should you accept? LG4-4

Solution:

You should find the present value of the alternative and compare it to the deal to receive payment now. If things go as expected, waiting two years would result in a payment of $60,000 (= $1.5 million × 0.04). The present value of this future payment can be computed as:

$$PV = FV_N/(1 + i)^N$$
$$PV = \$60{,}000/(1 + 0.10)^2$$
$$= \$60{,}000/1.21$$
$$= \$49{,}586.78$$

CALCULATOR HINTS
N = 2
I = 10
PMT = 0
FV = 60000
CPT PV = 49.566.78

The present value of the "wait two years" alternative is $49,586.78. Getting a cash out payment now would be $50,000 (= $1 million × 0.05). Because the immediate cash-out is worth more, on a time-value basis, you should take it now. Also note that the waiting alternative is risky. You might get less if the firm does not grow as expected.

3 Computing Rates of Return Say that you invested $1,000 and found two years later that the investment had fallen to $600. Your hopes are that the investment will get back to even during the next two years. What was the annual rate of return earned in the first two years? What rate would need to be earned in the next two years to break even? Show a time line of the problem. LG4-1,4-7

Solution:

The time line for the problem is shown below. The single question mark (?) and double question mark (??) show the two rates to be computed.

Period	0	?%	1	?%	2	??%	3	??%	4 years
Cash flow	−1,000				600				1,000

To solve for the first 2-year annual rate, use the future value equation:

$$FV_N = PV \times (1 + i)^N$$

$$\$600 = \$1{,}000 \times (1 + i)^2$$

Rearranging gives:

$$0.6 = (1 + i)^2$$

$$i = -0.2254, \text{ or } -22.54 \text{ percent}$$

The annual return for the first two years was −22.54 percent.

CALCULATOR HINTS
N = 2
PV = −1000
PMT = 0
FV = 600
CPT I = 22.54

To solve for the next 2-year annual rate, use the future value equation again:

$$FV_N = PV \times (1 + i)^N$$

$$\$1{,}000 = \$600 \times (1 + i)^2$$

Rearranging gives:

$$1.67 = (1 + i)^2$$

$$i = 0.2910, \text{ or } 29.10 \text{ percent}$$

Notice the asymmetry: It will take you two years of 29.10 percent returns to offset two years of −22.54 percent returns.

CALCULATOR HINTS
N = 2
PV = −600
PMT = 0
FV = 1000
CPT I = 29.10

LG4-8

4 Computing Time Periods Consider that you, a college student, have recently been given a trust fund from your grandparents. The grandparents were concerned about giving a large amount of money to a young person with no experience earning, managing, or investing money. Therefore, they set up the trust so that the $1 million inheritance would have to triple in value to $3 million before you can have access to it. They figured this would give you time to learn more about finance. Now you want to estimate how long it will be before you can start spending some of the money. How long will you have to wait if the fund earns an interest rate of 4 percent, 6 percent, or 9 percent per year?

Solution:

Using the financial calculator, you can solve for the number of years. This is done for the 4 percent interest rate; refer to the calculator hint in the margin. Earning 4 percent per year, it will take 28 years for the trust fund to triple in size. You could easily compute the time it will take earning 6 percent by entering 6 into the interest rate (I) button and recomputing the periods. Earning 6 percent, it will take 18 years, 10 months and 2 weeks. If the fund earns 9 percent, it will take 12 years and 9 months to triple. It looks like you are going to have plenty of time to learn about money!

CALCULATOR HINTS
I = 4
PV = −1
PMT = 0
FV = 3
CPT N = 28.01

questions

1. List and describe the purpose of each part of a time line with an initial cash inflow and a future cash outflow. Which cash flows should be negative and which positive? Why? *(LG4-1)*

2. How are the present value and future value related? *(LG4-2)*
3. Would you prefer to have an investment earning 5 percent for 40 years or an investment earning 10 percent for 20 years? Explain. *(LG4-3)*
4. How are present values affected by changes in interest rates? *(LG4-4)*
5. What do you think about the following statement? "I am going to receive $100 two years from now and $200 three years from now, so I am getting a $300 future value." How could the two cash flows be compared or combined? *(LG4-5)*
6. Show how the Rule of 72 can be used to approximate the number of years to quadruple an investment. *(LG4-6)*
7. Without making any computations, indicate which of each pair has a higher interest rate: *(LG4-7)*
   a. $100 doubles to $200 in five years *or* seven years.
   b. $500 increases in four years to $750 *or* to $800.
   c. $300 increases to $450 in two years *or* increases to $500 in three years.
8. A $1,000 investment has doubled to $2,000 in eight years because of a 9 percent rate of return. How much longer will it take for the investment to reach $4,000 if it continues to earn a 9 percent rate? *(LG4-8)*

problems

basic problems

4-1 **Time Line** Show the time line for a $500 cash inflow today, a $605 cash outflow in year 2, and a 10 percent interest rate. *(LG4-1)*

4-2 **Time Line** Show the time line for a $400 cash outflow today, a $518 cash inflow in year 3, and a 9 percent interest rate. *(LG4-1)*

4-3 **One Year Future Value** What is the future value of $500 deposited for one year earning an 8 percent interest rate annually? *(LG4-2)*

4-4 **One Year Future Value** What is the future value of $400 deposited for one year earning an interest rate of 9 percent per year? *(LG4-2)*

4-5 **Multiyear Future Value** How much would be in your savings account in 11 years after depositing $150 today if the bank pays 8 percent per year? *(LG4-3)*

4-6 **Multiyear Future Value** Compute the value in 25 years of a $1,000 deposit earning 10 percent per year. *(LG4-3)*

4-7 **Compounding with Different Interest Rates** A deposit of $350 earns the following interest rates:

a. 8 percent in the first year.

b. 6 percent in the second year.

c. 5.5 percent in the third year.

What would be the third year future value? *(LG4-3)*

4-8 **Compounding with Different Interest Rates** A deposit of $750 earns interest rates of 9 percent in the first year and 12 percent in the second year. What would be the second year future value? *(LG4-3)*

4-9 **Discounting One Year** What is the present value of a $350 payment in one year when the discount rate is 10 percent? *(LG4-4)*

4-10 **Discounting One Year** What is the present value of a $200 payment in one year when the discount rate is 7 percent? *(LG4-4)*

4-11 **Present Value** What is the present value of a $1,500 payment made in nine years when the discount rate is 8 percent? *(LG4-4)*

4-12 **Present Value** Compute the present value of an $850 payment made in ten years when the discount rate is 12 percent. *(LG4-4)*

4-13 **Present Value with Different Discount Rates** Compute the present value of $1,000 paid in three years using the following discount rates: 6 percent in the first year, 7 percent in the second year, and 8 percent in the third year. *(LG4-4)*

4-14 **Present Value with Different Discount Rates** Compute the present value of $5,000 paid in two years using the following discount rates: 8 percent in the first year and 7 percent in the second year. *(LG4-4)*

4-15 **Rule of 72** Approximately how many years are needed to double a $100 investment when interest rates are 7 percent per year? *(LG4-6)*

4-16 **Rule of 72** Approximately how many years are needed to double a $500 investment when interest rates are 10 percent per year? *(LG4-6)*

4-17 **Rule of 72** Approximately what interest rate is needed to double an investment over five years? *(LG4-6)*

4-18 **Rule of 72** Approximately what interest rate is earned when an investment doubles over 12 years? *(LG4-6)*

4-19 **Rates over One Year** Determine the interest rate earned on a $1,400 deposit when $1,800 is paid back in one year. *(LG4-7)*

4-20 **Rates over One Year** Determine the interest rate earned on a $2,300 deposit when $2,900 is paid back in one year. *(LG4-7)*

intermediate problems

4-21 **Interest-on-Interest** Consider a $2,000 deposit earning 8 percent interest per year for five years. What is the future value, and how much total interest is earned on the original deposit versus how much is interest earned on interest? *(LG4-3)*

4-22 **Interest-on-Interest** Consider a $5,000 deposit earning 10 percent interest per year for ten years. What is the future value, how much total interest is earned on the original deposit, and how much is interest earned on interest? *(LG4-3)*

4-23 **Comparing Cash Flows** What would be more valuable, receiving $500 today or receiving $625 in three years if interest rates are 7 percent? Why? *(LG4-5)*

4-24 **Comparing Cash Flows** Which cash flow would you rather pay, $425 today or $500 in two years if interest rates are 10 percent? Why? *(LG4-5)*

4-25 **Moving Cash Flows** What is the value in year 3 of a $700 cash flow made in year 6 if interest rates are 10 percent? *(LG4-5)*

4-26 **Moving Cash Flows** What is the value in year 4 of a $1,000 cash flow made in year 6 if interest rates are 8 percent? *(LG4-5)*

4-27 **Moving Cash Flows** What is the value in year 10 of a $1,000 cash flow made in year 3 if interest rates are 9 percent? *(LG4-5)*

4-28 **Moving Cash Flows** What is the value in year 15 of a $250 cash flow made in year 3 if interest rates are 11 percent? *(LG4-5)*

4-29 **Solving for Rates** What annual rate of return is earned on a $1,000 investment when it grows to $1,800 in six years? *(LG4-7)*

4-30 **Solving for Rates** What annual rate of return is earned on a $5,000 investment when it grows to $9,500 in five years? *(LG4-7)*

4-31 **Solving for Time** How many years *(and months)* will it take $2 million to grow to $5 million with an annual interest rate of 7 percent? *(LG4-8)*

4-32 **Solving for Time** How long will it take $2,000 to reach $5,000 when it grows at 10 percent per year? *(LG4-8)*

advanced problems

4-33 **Future Value** At age 30 you invest $1,000 that earns 8 percent each year. At age 40 you invest $1,000 that earns 12 percent per year. In which case would you have more money at age 60? *(LG4-2)*

4-34 **Future Value** At age 25 you invest $1,500 that earns 8 percent each year. At age 40 you invest $1,500 that earns 11 percent per year. In which case would you have more money at age 65? *(LG4-2)*

4-35 **Solving for Rates** You invested $2,000 in the stock market one year ago. Today, the investment is valued at $1,500. What return did you earn? What return would you need to get next year to break even overall? *(LG4-7)*

4-36 **Solving for Rates** You invested $3,000 in the stock market one year ago. Today, the investment is valued at $3,750. What return did you earn? What return would you suffer next year for your investment to be valued at the original $3,000? *(LG4-7)*

4-37 **Solving for Rates** What annual rate of return is earned on a $4,000 investment made in year 2 when it grows to $6,500 by the end of year 7? *(LG4-7)*

4-38 **Solving for Rates** What annual rate of return is implied on a $2,500 loan taken next year when $3,500 must be repaid in year 4? *(LG4-7)*

4-39 **General TVM** Ten years ago, Hailey invested $2,000 and locked in a 9 percent annual interest rate for 30 years (ending 20 years from now). Aidan can make a 20-year investment today and lock in a 10 percent interest rate. How much money should he invest now in order to have the same amount of money in 20 years as Hailey? *(LG4-2, LG4-4)*

4-40 **General TVM** Ten years ago, Hailey invested $3,000 and locked in an 8 percent annual interest rate for 30 years (ending 20 years from now). Aidan can make a 20-year investment today and lock in a 10 percent interest rate. How much money should he invest now in order to have the same amount of money in 20 years as Hailey? *(LG4-2, LG4-4)*

4-41 **Moving Cash Flows** You are scheduled to *receive* a $500 cash flow in one year, a $1,000 cash flow in two years, and *pay* an $800 payment in three years. If interest rates are 10 percent per year, what is the combined present value of these cash flows? *(LG4-5)*

4-42 **Spreadsheet Problem** Oil prices have increased a great deal in the last decade. The following table shows the average oil price for each year since 1949. Many companies use oil products as a resource in their own business operations (like airline firms and manufacturers of plastic products). Managers of these firms will keep a close watch on how rising oil prices will impact their costs. The interest rate in the PV/FV equations can also be interpreted as a growth rate in sales, costs, profits, and so on (see Example 4-5).

a. Using the 1949 oil price and the 1969 oil price, compute the annual growth rate in oil prices during those 20 years.

b. Compute the annual growth rate between 1969 and 1989 and between 1989 and 2012.

c. Given the price of oil in 2012 and your computed growth rate between 1989 and 2012, compute the future price of oil in 2015 and 2020.

Average Oil Prices					
Year	Per Barrel	Year	Per Barrel	Year	Per Barrel
1949	$2.54	1970	$ 3.18	1991	$16.54
1950	$2.51	1971	$ 3.39	1992	$15.99
1951	$2.53	1972	$ 3.39	1993	$14.25
1952	$2.53	1973	$ 3.89	1994	$13.19
1953	$2.68	1974	$ 6.87	1995	$14.62
1954	$2.78	1975	$ 7.67	1996	$18.46
1955	$2.77	1976	$ 8.19	1997	$17.23
1956	$2.79	1977	$ 8.57	1998	$10.87
1957	$3.09	1978	$ 9.00	1999	$15.56
1958	$3.01	1979	$12.64	2000	$26.72
1959	$2.90	1980	$21.59	2001	$21.84
1960	$2.88	1981	$31.77	2002	$22.51
1961	$2.89	1982	$28.52	2003	$27.54
1962	$2.90	1983	$26.19	2004	$38.93
1963	$2.89	1984	$25.88	2005	$46.47
1964	$2.88	1985	$24.09	2006	$58.30
1965	$2.86	1986	$12.51	2007	$64.67
1966	$2.88	1987	$15.40	2008	$91.48
1967	$2.92	1988	$12.58	2009	$53.48
1968	$2.94	1989	$15.86	2010	$71.21
1969	$3.09	1990	$20.03	2011	$87.04
				2012	$93.02

research it! Stock Market Returns

What kind of returns might you expect in the stock market? One way to measure how the stock market has performed is to examine the rate of return of the S&P 500 Index. To see historical prices of the S&P 500 Index, go to Yahoo! Finance (**finance.yahoo.com**) and click on the "S&P" link on the top left-hand side. Then click "Historical Prices" on the left menu, select "Monthly" prices, and click the "Get Prices" button.

Compute the 1-year, 5-year, and 10-year returns over time. What do you conclude about the returns during each of these periods?

integrated mini-case Investing in Gold

People have had a fascination with gold for thousands of years. Archaeologists have discovered gold jewelry in Southern Iraq dating to 3000 BC and gold ornaments in Peru dating to 1200 BC. The ancient Egyptians were masters in the use of gold for jewelry, ornaments, and economic exchange. By 1000 BC, squares of gold were a legal form of money in China. The Romans issued a popular gold coin called the Aureus (*aureus* is the Latin word for gold). By AD 1100, gold coins had been issued by several European countries. Gold has been a highly sought-after asset all over the world and has always retained at least some economic value over thousands of years.

The United States has had a very chaotic history with gold. For example, in the Great Depression, President Franklin D. Roosevelt banned the export of gold and ordered U.S. citizens to hand in all the gold they possessed. It was not until the end of 1974 that the ban on gold ownership by U.S. citizens was lifted. By 1986, the U.S. government's attitude on gold ownership had completely turned around, as evidenced by the resumption of the U.S. Mint's production of gold coins with the American Eagle. However, U.S. investors have little more than 30 years of gold-investing experience. Figure 4.5 shows how the price of gold per ounce has changed since 1974.

These end-of-December prices do not illustrate the true magnitude of the bubble in gold prices that occurred in 1980. The price of gold increased from $512 at the end of 1979 to a peak of $870 on January 21, 1980. The subsequent crash in the price of gold was just as spectacular. The annual returns of gold are shown in Table 4.5. Gold prices have been very volatile, increasing dramatically for one or two years and then experiencing significant declines the next year or two.

a. Compute the rate of return in gold prices that occurred during the three weeks between the last day of 1979 and the January 21, 1980 peak.

b. By the end of 1980, gold had dropped to $589.75 per ounce. Compute the rate of return from the peak to the end of 1980.

c. Imagine that you invested $1,000 in gold at the end of 1999. Use the returns in Table 4.5 to determine the value of the investment at the end of 2012.

figure 4.5 **December Gold Prices since 1974**

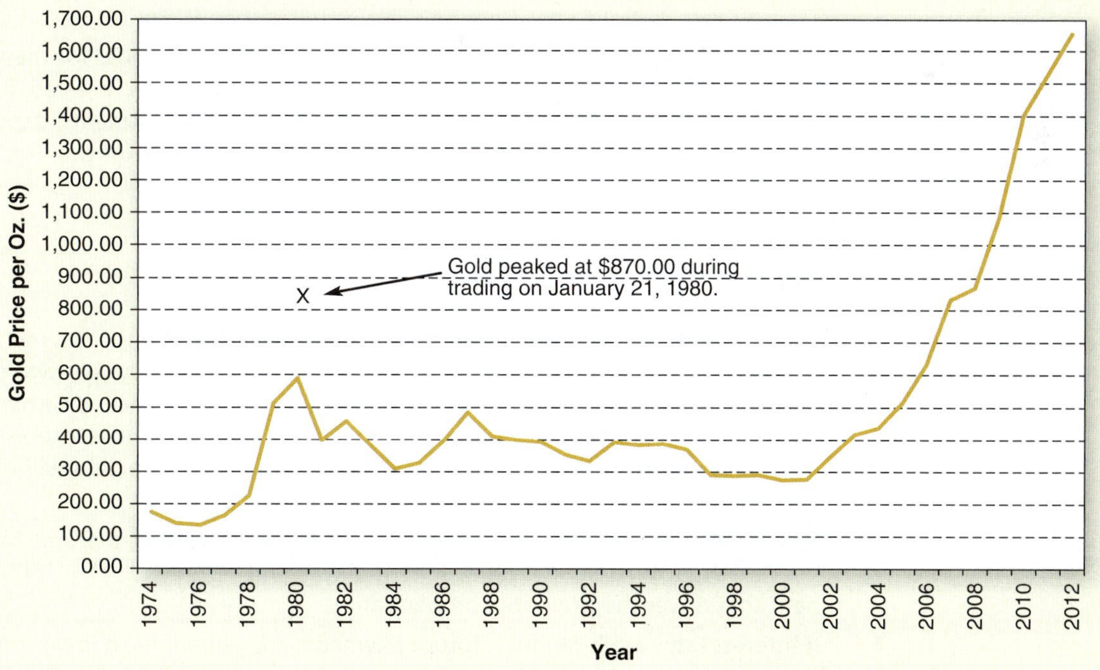

Data Source: Kitco (www.kitco.com)

table 4.5 | **Annual Gold Returns Since 1975**

	A	C	D	E	G
1	**Year**	**Annual Gold Return**		**Year**	**Annual Gold Return**
2	1975	−19.86%		1994	−2.17%
3	1976	−4.10%		1995	0.98%
4	1977	22.64%		1996	−4.59%
5	1978	37.01%		1997	−21.41%
6	1979	126.55%		1998	−0.83%
7	1980	15.19%		1999	0.85%
8	1981	−32.60%		2000	−5.44%
9	1982	14.94%		2001	0.75%
10	1983	−16.31%		2002	25.57%
11	1984	−19.19%		2003	19.89%
12	1985	5.68%		2004	4.65%
13	1986	21.31%		2005	17.77%
14	1987	22.21%		2006	23.20%
15	1988	−15.26%		2007	31.92%
16	1989	−2.84%		2008	4.32%
17	1990	−1.47%		2009	25.04%
18	1991	−10.07%		2010	29.24%
19	1992	−5.75%		2011	8.93%
20	1993	17.68%		2012	8.26%

ANSWERS TO TIME OUT

4-1 Positive interest rates in the economy mean that $1 deposited today would return more than $1 in the future. To return $1 in the future, deposit less than $1 today. Thus, $1 received one year from now is worth less than $1 today.

4-2 Cash flow accounting labels money spent as a negative cash flow for the firm. This type of cash flow is put in the debit column. When cash is received, it is added as a positive cash flow and registered as a credit. Investments, deposits, and loans all include one cash flow where money leaves your (or the firm's) hands and one cash flow where money goes into your hands.

4-3

Period	0	6%	1 year
Cash flow	$200		−$212

4-4 The principal in an investment or debt increases over time by the interest rate. However, compounding causes interest to be earned on money that was previously earned as interest. So, wealth is built from both the principal earning profits and prior profits earning additional profits. If this is a debt whose interest payments are not being paid but added to the principal, then the debt will increase in the same way.

4-5 Future value increases quickly when either the interest rate or the time increases because the future value is an exponential function, $PV \times (1 + i)^N$. It is the exponent that drives the dramatic compounding.

4-6 If interest rates are high, then future payments are valued much lower today than they would be if interest rates were low.

4-7 Compounding increases present values into the future while discounting does the opposite. Discounting reduces future values into the present. The TVM equations show the relationship between a present value and a future value. When moving cash flows forward in time, we call it *compounding.* When moving cash flows back in time, we call it *discounting.*

4-8 Yes, the $175,000 could be moved from year 1 to year 2 using the 7 percent interest rate and compared with the $195,000 year 2 payment. The two procedures are equivalent mathematically and will lead to the same decision.

4-9 This depends on what level of accuracy is needed. Interest rates that are too low or too high cause less accurate Rule of 72 estimates. Consider the following interest rates with associated years to double using the Rule of 72 and the TVM equations:

Interest Rate (percent)	Rule Estimate (years)	TVM (years)
3	24.0	23.4
5	14.4	14.2
7	10.3	10.2
9	8.0	8.0
11	6.5	6.6
13	5.5	5.7
15	4.8	5.0
17	4.2	4.4

4-10 The 33.3 percent estimate misses the effect of compounding. Earning interest-on-interest allows money to double in three years at a 26 percent rate.

4-11 Consider a $100 investment that loses 20 percent to $80. This $80 would have to earn $20 to reach $100 again. A $20 profit on an $80 investment is a $20 ÷ $80 = 0.25, or 25 percent return.

4-12 To double the sales at a 7 percent growth rate takes 10.24 years (using a TVM calculator with PV of −350, FV of 700, and PMT of 0.).

4-13 TVM concepts can be used in many business areas. Moving cash flows, investment, debt, and growth are important in fields such as accounting, entrepreneurship, marketing, management, and manufacturing.

PART THREE

5 Time Value of Money 2: Analyzing Annuity Cash Flows

viewpoints

Business Application

Walkabout Music, Inc., issued $20 million in debt ten years ago to finance its factory construction. The debt allows Walkabout to make interest-only payments at a 7 percent coupon rate, paid semiannually for 30 years. Debt issued today would carry only 6 percent interest. The company's CFO is considering whether or not to issue new debt (for 20 years) to pay off the old debt. To pay off the old debt early, Walkabout would have to pay a special "call premium" totaling $1.4 million to its debt holders. To issue new debt, the firm would have to pay investment bankers a fee of $1.2 million. Should the CFO replace the old debt with new debt? **(See solution on p. 172)**

Personal Application

Say that you obtained a mortgage for $150,000 three years ago when you purchased your home. You've been paying monthly payments on the 30-year mortgage with a fixed 8 percent interest rate and have $145,920.10 of principal left to pay. Recently, your mortgage broker called to mention that interest rates on new mortgages have declined to 7 percent. He suggested that you could save money every month if you refinanced your mortgage. You could find a 27-year mortgage at the new interest rate for a $1,000 fee. Should you refinance your mortgage? **(See solution p. 172)**

But what if you want to move in the next few years? Is it still a good idea?

Learning Goals

LG5-1 Compound multiple cash flows to the future.

LG5-2 Compute the future value of frequent, level cash flows.

LG5-3 Discount multiple cash flows to the present.

LG5-4 Compute the present value of an annuity.

LG5-5 Figure cash flows and present value of a perpetuity.

LG5-6 Adjust values for beginning-of-period annuity payments.

LG5-7 Explain the impact of compound frequency and the difference between the annual percentage rate and the effective annual rate.

LG5-8 Compute the interest rate of annuity payments.

LG5-9 Compute payments and amortization schedules for car and mortgage loans.

LG5-10 Calculate the number of payments on a loan.

We explained basic time value computations in the previous chapter. Those TVM equations covered moving a single cash flow from one point in time to another. While this circumstance does describe *some* problems that businesses and individuals face, most debt and investment applications of time value of money feature multiple cash flows. In fact, *most* situations require many equal payments over time. Since these situations require a bit more complicated analysis, this chapter continues the TVM topic for applications that require many equal payments over time. For example, car loans and home mortgage loans require the borrower to make the same monthly payment for many months or years. People save for the future through monthly contributions to their pension portfolios. People in retirement must convert their savings into monthly income. Companies also make regular payments. Johnson & Johnson (ticker: JNJ) will pay level semiannual interest payments through 2033 on money it borrowed. General Motors (ticker: GM) paid a $0.50 per share quarterly dividend to stockholders for six straight years until 2006, when it switched to a $0.25 dividend. These examples require payments (and compounding) over different time intervals (monthly for car loans and semiannually for company debt). How are we to value these payments into common or comparable terms? In this chapter, we illustrate how to value multiple cash flows over time, including many equal payments, and how to incorporate different compounding frequencies.

5.1 • Future Value of Multiple Cash Flows

Chapter 4 illustrated how to take single payments and compound them into the future. To save enough money for a down payment on a house or for retirement, people typically make many contributions over time to their savings accounts. We can add the future value of each contribution together to see what the total will be worth at some future point in time—such as age 65 for retirement or in two years for a down payment on a house.

LG5-1

Finding the Future Value of Several Cash Flows

Consider the following contributions to a savings account over time. You make a \$100 deposit today, followed by a \$125 deposit next year, and a \$150 deposit at the end of the second year. If interest rates are 7 percent, what's the future value of your deposits at the end of the third year? The time line for this problem is illustrated as:

Period	0	1	7%	2	3 years
Cash flow	−100	−125		−150	FV = ?

CALCULATOR HINTS

FV of 1st deposit:
N = 3
I = 7
PV = −100
PMT = 0
CPT FV = 122.50

FV of 2nd deposit:
N = 2
I = 7
PV = −125
PMT = 0
CPT FV = 143.11

FV of 3rd deposit:
N = 1
I = 7
PV = −150
PMT = 0
CPT FV = 160.50

Add the 3 FVs.

Note that the first deposit will compound for three years. That is, the future value in year 3 of a cash flow in year 0 will compound 3 (= 3 − 0) times. The deposit at the end of the first year will compound twice (= 3 − 1). In general, a deposit in year m will compound $N - m$ times for a future value in year N. We can find the total amount at the end of three years by computing the future value of each deposit and then adding them together. Using the future value equation from Chapter 4, the future value of today's deposit is $\$100 \times (1 + 0.07)^3 = \$122.50$. Similarly, the future value of the next two deposits are $\$125 \times (1 + 0.07)^2 = \$143.11$ and $\$150 \times (1 + 0.07)^1 = \$160.50$, respectively.

Putting these three individual future value equations together would yield:

$$FV_3 = \$100 \times (1 + 0.07)^3 + \$125 \times (1 + 0.07)^2 + \$150 \times (1 + 0.07)^1 = \$426.11$$

The general equation for computing the future value of multiple and varying cash flows (or payments) is:

$$FV_N = \text{Future value of first cash flow} + \text{Future value of second cash flow} + \cdots + \text{Future value of last cash flow}$$
$$= PMT_m \times (1 + i)^{N-m} + PMT_n \times (1 + i)^{N-n} + \cdots + PMT_p \times (1 + i)^{N-p} \quad \textbf{(5-1)}$$

In this equation, the letters m, n, and p denote when the cash flows occur in time. Each deposit can be different from the others.

EXAMPLE 5-1

LG 5-1

For interactive versions of this example visit www.mhhe.com/can3e

Saving for a Car

Say that as a freshman in college, you will be working as a house painter for each of the next three summers. You intend to set aside some money from each summer's paycheck to buy a car for your senior year. If you can deposit \$2,000 from the first summer, \$2,500 in the second summer, and \$3,000 in the last summer, how much money will you have to buy a car if interest rates are 5 percent?

CALCULATOR HINTS

FV of 1st cash flow:
N = 2
I = 5
PV = −2000
PMT = 0
CPT FV = 2,205

SOLUTION:

The time line for the forecast is:

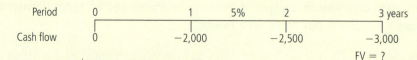

Period	0	1	5%	2	3 years
Cash flow	0	−2,000		−2,500	−3,000
					FV = ?

The first cash flow, which occurs at the end of the first year, will compound for two years. The second cash flow will be invested for only one year. The last contribution will not have any time to grow before the purchase of the car. Using equation 5-1, the solution is

$$FV_3 = [\$2{,}000 \times (1 + 0.05)^{3-1}] + [\$2{,}500 \times (1 + 0.05)^{3-2}] + [\$3{,}000 \times (1 + 0.05)^{3-3}]$$
$$= (\$2{,}000 \times 1.1025) + (\$2{,}500 \times 1.05) + (\$3{,}000 \times 1) = \$7{,}830$$

You will have $7,830 in cash to purchase a car for your senior year.

Similar to Problems 5-1, 5-2, 5-17, 5-18, 5-43, 5-44

FV of 2nd cash flow:
N = 1
I = 5
PV = −2500
PMT = 0
CPT FV = 2,625

FV total = 2,205
+ 2,625 + 3,000
= $7,830

Future Value of Level Cash Flows

LG5-2

Now suppose that each cash flow is the same and occurs every year. Level sets of frequent cash flows are common in finance—we call them **annuities.** The first cash flow of an annuity occurs at the end of the first year (or other time period) and continues every year to the last year. We derive the equation for the future value of an annuity from the general equation for future value of multiple cash flows, equation 5-1. Since each cash flow is the same, and the cash flows are every period, the equation appears as:

annuity
A stream of level and frequent cash flows paid at the end of each time period—often referred to as an *ordinary annuity.*

$$FVA_N = \text{Future value of first payment} + \text{Future value of second payment} + \cdots + \text{Last payment}$$
$$= PMT \times (1 + i)^{N-1} + PMT \times (1 + i)^{N-2} + PMT \times (1 + i)^{N-3} + \cdots + PMT(1 + i)^0$$

The term *FVA* is used to denote that this is the future value of an annuity. Factoring out the common level cash flow, PMT, we can summarize and reduce the equation as:

Future value of an annuity = Payment × Annuity compounding

$$FVA_N = PMT \times \frac{(1 + i)^N - 1}{i} \qquad \textbf{(5-2)}$$

Suppose that $100 deposits are made at the end of each year for five years. If interest rates are 8 percent per year, the future value of this annuity stream is computed using equation 5-2 as:

$$FVA_5 = \$100 \times \frac{(1 + 0.08)^5 - 1}{0.08} = \$100 \times 5.8666 = \$586.66$$

We can show these deposits and future value on a time line as:

LG5-2

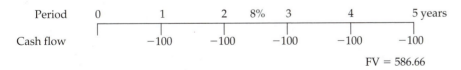

Period	0	1	2 (8%)	3	4	5 years
Cash flow		−100	−100	−100	−100	−100
						FV = 586.66

Five deposits of $100 each were made. So, the $586.66 future value represents $86.66 of interest paid. As with almost any TVM problem, the length of time of the annuity and the interest rate for compounding are very important factors in accumulating wealth within the annuity. Consider the examples in Table 5.1. A $50 deposit made every year for 20 years will grow to $1,839.28 with a 6 percent interest rate. Doubling the annual deposits to $100 also doubles the future value to $3,678.56. However, making $100 deposits for *twice* the amount of time, 40 years,

table 5.1 **Magnitude of Periodic Payments, Number of Years Invested, and Interest Rate on FV of Annuity**

	A	B	C	D
1	Annuity Cash Flow	Number of Years	Interest Rate	Future Value
2	$ 50	20	6%	$ 1,839.28
3	100	20	6	3,678.56
4	100	40	6	15,476.20
5	100	40	12	76,709.14

MATH COACH

ANNUITIES AND THE FINANCIAL CALCULATOR

In the previous chapter, the level payment button (PMT) in the financial calculator was always set to zero because no constant payments were made every period. We use the PMT button to input the annuity amount. For calculators, the present value is of the opposite sign (positive versus negative) from the future value. This is also the case with annuities. The level cash flow will be of the opposite sign as the future value, as the previous time line shows.

You would use the financial calculator to solve the problem of depositing $100 for five years via the following inputs: N = 5, I = 8, PV = 0, PMT = −100. In this case, the input for present value is zero because no deposit is made today. The result of computing the future value is 586.66.

more than *quadruples* the future value to $15,476.20! Longer time periods lead to more total compounding and much more wealth. Interest rates also have this effect. Doubling the interest rate from 6 to 12 percent on the 40-year annuity results in nearly a five-fold increase in the future value to $76,709.14. Think about it: Depositing only $100 per year (about 25 lattes per year) can generate some serious money over time. See Figure 5.1. How much would $2,000 annual deposits generate?

Future Value of Multiple Annuities

At times, multiple annuities can occur in both business and personal life. For example, you may find that you can increase the amount of money you

figure 5.1 **Future Value of a $100 Annuity at 6 Percent**

Longer time periods lead to more total compounding and much more wealth.

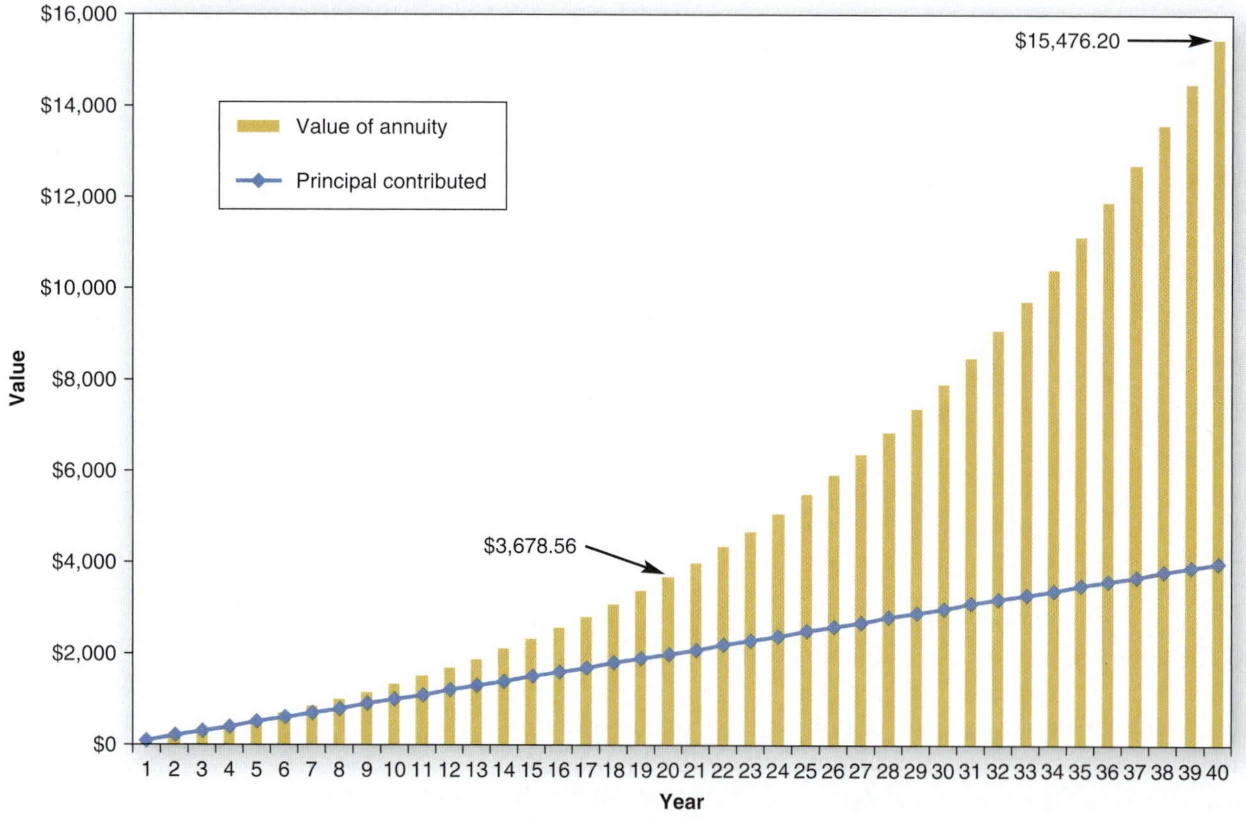

save each year because of a promotion or a new and better job. As an illustration, reconsider the annual $100 deposits made for five years at 8 percent per year. This time, the deposit can be increased to $150 for the fourth and fifth years. How can we use the annuity equation to compute the future value when we have two levels of cash flows? In this case, the cash flow can be categorized as two annuities. The first annuity is a $100 cash flow for five years. The second annuity is a $50 cash flow for two years. We demonstrate this as:

LG5-2

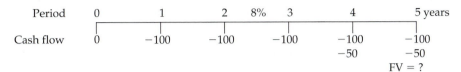

Period	0	1	2	8% 3	4	5 years
Cash flow	0	−100	−100	−100	−100	−100
					−50	−50
						FV = ?

To determine the future value of these two annuities, compute the future value of each one separately, and then simply add them together. The future value of the $100 annuity is the same as computed before, $586.66. The future value of the $50 annuity, using the TVM equation for the future value of a cash stream, is:

MATH COACH

Solving Multiple Annuities

The trick to solving multiple annuity problems is to disentangle cash flows into groups of level payments ending in the future value year that we've designated.

$$FVA_N = \$50 \times \frac{(1 + 0.08)^2 - 1}{0.08}$$
$$= \$50 \times 2.08 = \$104$$

So, the future value of both of the annuities is $690.66 (= $586.66 + $104). In the same way, we could easily compute the future value if the last two cash flows are $50 *lower* ($50 each), instead of $50 higher ($150 each). To solve this alternative version, we would simply *subtract* the $104 future value instead of adding it.

EXAMPLE 5-2

LG5-2

Saving in the Company Pension Plan

You started your first job after graduating from college. Your company offers a retirement plan for which the company contributes 50 percent of what you contribute each year. So, if you contribute $3,000 per year from your salary, the company adds another $1,500. You get to decide how to invest the total annual contribution from several portfolio choices that the plan administrator provides. Suppose that you pick a mixture of stocks and bonds that is expected to earn 7 percent per year. If you plan to retire in 40 years, how big will you expect that retirement account to be? If you could earn 8 percent per year, how much money would be available?

For interactive versions of this example visit www.mhhe.com/can3e

SOLUTION:

Every year, you and your employer will set aside a total of $4,500 for your retirement. Using equation 5-2 shows that the future value of this annuity is:

$$FVA_{40} = \$4{,}500 \times \frac{(1 + 0.07)^{40} - 1}{0.07} = \$4{,}500 \times 199.6351 = \$898{,}358.00$$

Note that you can build a substantial amount of wealth ($898,358) through your pension plan at work. If you can earn just 1 percent more each year, 8 percent total, you could be a millionaire!

$$FVA_{40} = \$4{,}500 \times \frac{(1 + 0.08)^{40} - 1}{0.08} = \$4{,}500 \times 259.0565 = \$1{,}165{,}754.33$$

Similar to Problems 5-3, 5-4, self-test problem 1

CALCULATOR HINTS

N = 40
I = 7
PV = 0
PMT = −4500
CPT FV = 898,358.00

NOW CHANGE TO:
I = 8
CPT FV = 1,165,754.33

finance at work — personal

WHO WILL SAVE FOR THEIR FUTURE?

Though it seems way too early for you to think about planning for your "golden years," financially wise people realize that it's never too early to start. Unfortunately, most people save little for their retirement years. Seventy percent of workers surveyed report that they have saved less than $50,000. How far does that get you? Using a 6 percent investment return, $50,000 can generate a monthly income of only $299.78 for 30 years, at which time it is used up. That is less than $3,600 per year! The average Social Security monthly benefit is just over $1,230 per month, or about $13,400 per year. While seventy percent of workers have saved less than $50,000, only 10 percent have saved over $250,000.

This chapter illustrates that much higher amounts of wealth can be accumulated if you start early! One easy way to do this is through a retirement plan at work. Most company and government employers offer employees defined contribution plans. (The corporate version is called a 401(k) plan; a nonbusiness plan is usually referred to as a 403(b) plan—both named after the legislation that created the plans.) These plans place all of the responsibility on employees to provide for their retirement. Employees contribute from their own paychecks and decide how to invest. Employees' decisions about how much to contribute and how early to start contributing have a dramatic impact on retirement wealth. Consider employees who earn $50,000 annually for 40 years and then retire. Note that if the employees contribute for 40 years, they must start by age 25 or so—starting early is vitally important! Contributing 5 percent of their salaries ($2,500) to the 401(k) plan every year and having it earn a 4 percent return will generate $237,564 for retirement. A 10 percent contribution ($5,000) would create $475,128 for retirement. Finally, investment decisions that yield an 8 percent return would yield $1.3 million with a 10 percent contribution. This is quite a range of retirement wealth generated from just three important decisions each employee must make—how much to contribute, how to invest the funds, and when to start! Unfortunately, too many people make poor decisions. The average 401(k) account value for people in their 60s is only $136,400—often because people start 401(k) contributions too late to allow the funds to compound much.

Saving and investing money through a defined contribution plan is a good way to build wealth for retirement. But you must follow these rules: Start Early, Save Much, and Don't Touch!

Sources: "Preparing for Retirement in America," 2012 Retirement Confidence Survey Fact Sheet #3. http://www.ebri.org/pdf/surveys/rcs/2012/fs-03-rcs-12-fs3-saving.pdf.

want to know more? Key Words to Search for Updates: Employee Benefit Research Institute (go to www.ebri.org), retirement income

EXAMPLE 5-3

LG5-2

For interactive versions of this example visit www.mhhe.com/can3e

Growing Retirement Contributions

In the previous example, you are investing a total of $4,500 per year for 40 years in your employer's retirement program. You believe that with raises and promotions, you will eventually be able to contribute more money each year. Consider that halfway through your career, you are able to increase your investment in the retirement program to $6,000 per year (your contribution plus the company match). What would be the future value of your retirement wealth from this program if investments are compounded at 7 percent?

SOLUTION:

You can compute the future value using two annuities. The first annuity is one with payments of $4,500 that lasts 40 years. The second is a $1,500 (= $6,000 − $4,500) annuity that lasts only 20 years. We already computed the future value of the first annuity in the previous example: $898,358. The future value of the second annuity is:

$$FVA_{20} = \$1,500 \times \frac{(1 + 0.07)^{20} - 1}{0.07} = \$1,500 \times 40.9955 = \$61,493.24$$

So, your retirement wealth from this program would be $959,851 (= $898,358 + $61,493).

Similar to Problems 5-19, 5-20, self-test problem 1

CALCULATOR HINTS

Add to previous answer
N = 20
I = 7
PV = 0
PMT = −1500
CPT FV = 61,493.24

TIME OUT

5-1 Describe how compounding affects the future value computation of an annuity.

5-2 Reconsider your original retirement plan example to invest $4,500 per year for 40 years. Now consider the result if you don't contribute anything for four years (years 19 to 22) while your child goes to college. How many annuity equations will you need to find the future value of your 401(k) in this situation?

5.2 • Present Value of Multiple Cash Flows

The future value concept is very useful to understand how to build wealth for the future. The present value concept will help you most particularly for personal applications such as evaluating loans (like car and mortgage loans) and business applications (like determining the value of business opportunities).

LG5-3

Finding the Present Value of Several Cash Flows

Consider the cash flows that we showed at the very beginning of the chapter: You deposit $100 today, followed by a $125 deposit next year, and a $150 deposit at the end of the second year. In the previous situation, we sought the future value when interest rates are 7 percent. Instead of future value, we compute the present value of these three cash flows. The time line for this problem appears as:

Period	0	1	7%	2 years
Cash flow	−100	−125		−150
	PV = ?			

CALCULATOR HINTS

PV of 1st cash flow is $100.

PV of 2nd cash flow:
N = 1
I = 7
PMT = 0
FV = −125
CPT PV = 116.82

PV of 3rd cash flow:
N = 2
I = 7
PMT = 0
FV = −150
CPT PV = 131.02

Add the 3 PVs.

The first cash flow is already in year zero, so its value will not change. We will discount the second cash flow one year and the third cash flow two years. Using the present value equation from the previous chapter, the present value of today's payment is simply $100 ÷ (1 + 0.07)^0 = $100. Similarly, the present value of the next two cash flows are $125 ÷ (1 + 0.07)^1 = $116.82 and $150 ÷ (1 + 0.07)^2 = $131.02, respectively. Therefore, the present value of these cash flows is $347.84 (= $100 + $116.82 + $131.02).

Putting these three individual present value equations together would yield:

$$PV = [\$100 \div (1 + 0.07)^0] + [\$125 \div (1 + 0.07)^1] + [\$150 \div (1 + 0.07)^2] = \$347.84$$

CALCULATOR HINTS

Use the CF registers to solve:
CF
CF0 = 100
C01 = 125
F01 = 1
C02 = 150
F02 = 1

NPV
I = 7
CPT NPV = 347.84

The general equation for discounting multiple and varying cash flows is:

$$PV = \text{Present value of first cash flow} + \text{Present value of second cash flow} + \cdots + \text{Present value of last cash flow}$$

$$= \frac{PMT_m}{(1+i)^m} + \frac{PMT_n}{(1+i)^n} + \cdots + \frac{PMT_p}{(1+i)^p} \quad \textbf{(5-3)}$$

In this equation, the letters m, n, and p denote when the cash flows occur in time. Each deposit can differ from the others in terms of size and timing.

Present Value of Level Cash Flows

LG5-4

You will find that this present value of an annuity concept will have many business and personal applications throughout your life. Most loans are set up so that the amount borrowed (the present value) is repaid through level payments made every

MATH COACH

Using a Financial Calculator—Part 2

The five TVM buttons/functions in financial calculators have been fine, so far, for the types of TVM problems we've been solving. Sometimes we had to use them two or three times for a single problem, but that was usually because we needed an intermediate calculation to input into another TVM equation.

Luckily, most financial calculators also have built-in worksheets specifically designed for computing TVM in problems with multiple nonconstant cash flows.

To make calculator worksheets as flexible as possible, they are usually divided into two parts: one for input, which we'll refer to as the CF (cash flow) worksheet, and one or more for showing the calculator solutions. We'll go over the conventions concerning the CF worksheet here, and we'll discuss the output solutions in Chapter 13.

The CF worksheet is usually designed to handle inputting sets of multiple cash flows as quickly as possible. As a result, it normally consists of two sets of variables or cells—one for the cash flows and one to hold a set of frequency counts for the cash flows, so that we can tell it we have seven $1,500 cash flows in a row instead of having to enter $1,500 seven times.

Using the frequency counts to reduce the number of inputs is handy, but you must take care. Frequency counts are only good for embedded annuities of identical cash flows. You have to ensure that you don't mistake another kind of cash flow for an annuity.

Also, using frequency counts will usually affect the way that the calculator counts time periods. As an example, let's talk about how we would put the set of cash flows shown here into a CF worksheet:

Period	0	1	2	3	4	5	6	7	8
(10%)									
Cash flow	−$800	$150	$200		$150	$150	$150	$75	$75

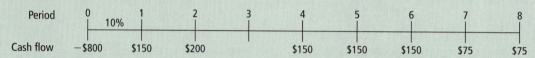

To designate which particular value we'll place into each particular cash flow cell in this worksheet, we'll note the value and the cell identifier, such as CF0, CF1, and so forth. We'll do the same for the frequency cells, using F1, F2, etc., to identify which CF cell the

period (the annuity). Lenders will examine borrowers' budgets and determine how much each borrower can afford as a payment. The maximum loan offered will be the present value of that annuity payment. The equation for the present value of an annuity can be derived from the general equation for the present value of multiple cash flows, equation 5-3. Since each cash flow is the same, and the borrower pays the cash flows every period, the present value of an annuity, PVA, can be written as:

Present value = Payment × Annuity discount

$$PVA_N = PMT \times \left[\frac{1 - \dfrac{1}{(1+i)^N}}{i} \right] \qquad \textbf{(5-4)}$$

Suppose that someone makes $100 payments at the end of each year for five years. If interest rates are 8 percent per year, the present value of this annuity stream is computed using equation 5-4 as:

$$PVA_5 = \$100 \times \left[\frac{1 - \dfrac{1}{(1+0.08)^5}}{0.08} \right] = \$100 \times 3.9927 = \$399.27$$

CALCULATOR HINTS

N = 5
I = 8
PMT = −100
FV = 0
CPT PV = 399.27

The time line for these payments and present value appears as:

Period	0	1	2	3	4	5 years
(8%)						
Cash flow		−100	−100	−100	−100	−100
	399.27					

frequency cell goes with. (Note that, in most calculators, CF0 is treated as a unique value with an unalterable frequency of 1; we're going to make the same assumption here so you'll never see a listing for F0.) For this sample timeline, our inputs would be:

−$800	[CF0]		
$150	[CF1]	1	[F1]
$200	[CF2]	1	[F2]
$ 0	[CF3]	1	[F3]
$150	[CF4]	3	[F4]
$ 75	[CF5]	2	[F5]

To compute the present value of these cash flows, use the NPV calculator function. The NPV function computes the present value of all the future cash flows and then adds the year 0 cash flow. Then, on the NPV worksheet, you would simply need to enter the interest rate and solve for the NPV:

10%	[I]
[CPT]	[NPV] = − $144.61

Note a few important things about this example:

1. We had to manually enter a value of $0 for CF3. If we hadn't, the calculator wouldn't have known about it and would have implicitly assumed that CF4 came one period after CF2.
2. Once we use a frequency cell for one cash flow, all numbering on any subsequent cash flows that we enter into the calculator is going to be messed up, at least from our point of view. For instance, the first $75 isn't what we would call "CF5," is it? We'd call it "CF7" because it comes at time period 7; but calculators usually treat CF5 as "the fifth set of cash flows," so we'll just have to try to do the same to be consistent.
3. If we really don't need to use frequency cells, we will usually just leave them out of the guidance instructions in this chapter to save space.

table 5.2 | **Magnitude of the Annuity, Number of Years Invested, and Interest Rate on PV**

	A	B	C	D
1	Annuity Cash Flow	Number of Years	Interest Rate	Present Value
2	$ 50	20	6%	$ 573.50
3	100	20	6	1,146.99
4	100	40	6	1,504.63
5	100	40	12	824.38

LG5-4

Notice that although five payments of $100 each were made, $500 total, the present value is only $399.27. As we've noted previously, the span of time over which the borrower pays the annuity and the interest rate for discounting strongly affect present value computations. When you borrow money from the bank, the bank views the amount it lends as the present value of the annuity it receives over time from the borrower. Consider the examples in Table 5.2.

A $50 deposit made every year for 20 years is discounted to $573.50 with a 6 percent discount rate. Doubling the annual cash flow to $100 also doubles the present value to $1,146.99. But extending the time period does not impact the present value as much as you might expect. Making $100 payments for twice the amount of time—40 years—does not double the present value. As you can see in Table 5.2, the present value increases less than 50 percent to only $1,504.63! If the discount rate increases from 6 percent to 12 percent on the 40-year annuity, the present value will shrink to $824.38.

The present value of a cash flow made far into the future is not very valuable today, as Figure 5.2 illustrates. That's why doubling the number of years

figure 5.2

Present Value of Each Annuity Cash Flow

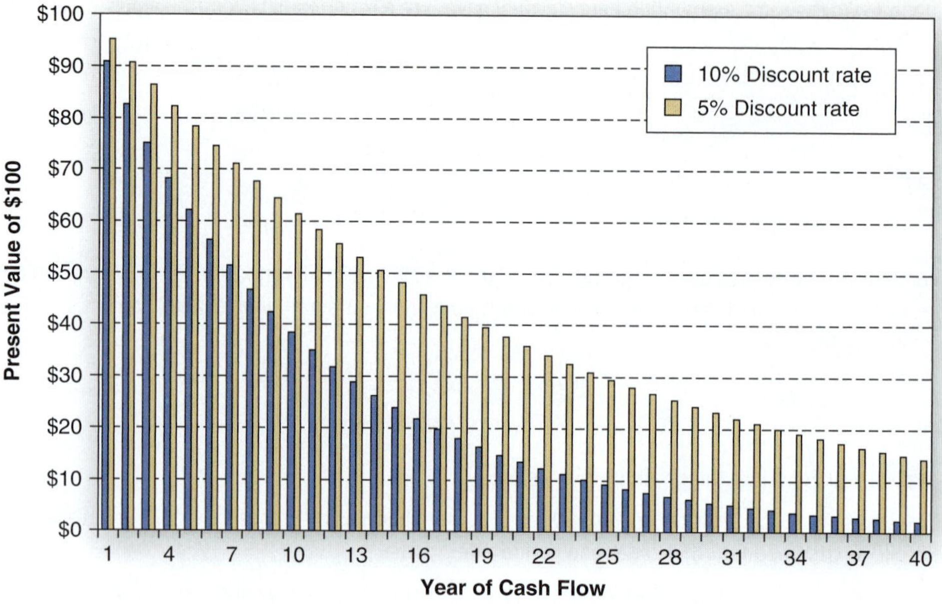

in the table from 20 to 40 only increased the present value by approximately 30 percent. Notice how the present value of $100 annuity payments declines for the cash flows made later in time, especially at higher discount rates. The $100 cash flow in year 20 is worth less than $15 today if we use a 10 percent discount rate; they're worth more than double, at nearly $38 today, if we use a discount rate of 5 percent. The figure also shows how quickly present value declines with a higher discount rate relative to a lower rate. As we showed above, the present values of the annuities in the figure are the sums of the present values shown. Since the present values for the 10 percent discount rate are smaller, the present value of an annuity is smaller as interest rates rise.

EXAMPLE 5-4

LG5-4

For interactive versions of this example visit www.mhhe.com/can3e

Value of Payments

Your firm needs to buy additional physical therapy equipment that costs $20,000. The equipment manufacturer will give you the equipment now if you will pay $6,000 per year for the next four years. If your firm can borrow money at a 9 percent interest rate, should you pay the manufacturer the $20,000 now or accept the 4-year annuity offer of $6,000?

SOLUTION:

We can find the cost of the 4-year, $6,000 annuity in present value terms using equation 5-4:

$$PVA_4 = \$6{,}000 \times \left[\frac{1 - \dfrac{1}{(1+0.09)^4}}{0.09}\right] = \$6{,}000 \times 3.2397 = \$19{,}438.32$$

The cost of paying for the equipment over time is $19,438.32. This is less, in present value terms, than paying $20,000 cash. The firm should take the annuity payment plan.

Similar to Problems 5-7, 5-8, self-test problem 2

CALCULATOR HINTS

N = 4
I = 9
PMT = −6000
FV = 0
CPT PV = 19,438.32

Present Value of Multiple Annuities

Just as we can combine annuities to solve various future value problems, we can also combine annuities to solve some present value problems with changing cash flows. Consider Alex Rodriguez's (A-Rod's) baseball contract in 2000 with the Texas Rangers. This contract made A-Rod into the "$252 million man." The contract was structured so that the Rangers paid A-Rod a $10 million signing bonus, $21 million per year in 2001 through 2004, $25 million per year in 2005 and 2006, and $27 million per year in 2007 through 2010.[1] Note that adding the signing bonus to the annual salary equals the $252 million figure. However, Rodriguez would receive the salary in the future. Using an 8 percent discount rate, what is the present value of A-Rod's contract?

We begin by showing the salary cash flows with the time line:

LG5-4

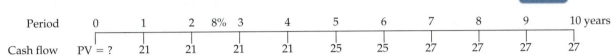

Period	0	1	2	8% 3	4	5	6	7	8	9	10 years
Cash flow	PV = ?	21	21	21	21	25	25	27	27	27	27

First create a $27 million, 10-year annuity. Here are the associated cash flows:

Period	0	1	2	8% 3	4	5	6	7	8	9	10 years
Cash flow	PV = ?	27	27	27	27	27	27	27	27	27	27
		−6	−6	−6	−6	−2	−2				

Now create a −$2 million, six-year annuity:

Period	0	1	2	8% 3	4	5	6	7	8	9	10 years
Cash flow	PV = ?	27	27	27	27	27	27	27	27	27	27
		−2	−2	−2	−2	−2	−2				
		−4	−4	−4	−4						

Notice that creating the −$2 million annuity also resulted in the third annuity of −$4 million for four years. This time line shows three annuities. If you add the cash flows in any year, the sum is A-Rod's salary for that year. Now we can find the present value of each annuity using equation 5-4 three times.

$$PVA_{10} = \$27\text{m} \times \left[\frac{1 - \dfrac{1}{(1+0.08)^{10}}}{0.08}\right] = \$27\text{m} \times 6.7101 = \$181.17 \text{ million}$$

$$PVA_{6} = -\$2\text{m} \times \left[\frac{1 - \dfrac{1}{(1+0.08)^{6}}}{0.08}\right] = -\$2\text{m} \times 4.6228 = \$-9.25 \text{ million}$$

$$PVA_{4} = -\$4\text{m} \times \left[\frac{1 - \dfrac{1}{(1+0.08)^{4}}}{0.08}\right] = -\$4\text{m} \times 3.3121 = -13.25 \text{ million}$$

CALCULATOR HINTS

N = 10
I = 8
PMT = −27
FV = 0
CPT PV = 181.17

Now change to
N = 6
PMT = 2
CPT PV = −9.25

Now change to
N = 4
PMT = 4
CPT PV = −13.25

[1]The contract actually contains some complications like incentives to play well and salary deferral. We ignore those complicating factors here.

Adding the value of the three annuities reveals that the present value of A-Rod's salary was \$158.67 million (= \$181.17m − \$9.25m − \$13.25m). Adding in the \$10 million signing bonus produces a contract value of \$168.67 million. So, the present value of A-Rod's contract turns out to be quite considerable, but you might not call him the \$252 million man![2]

LG5-5

Perpetuity—A Special Annuity

perpetuity
An annuity with cash flows that continue forever.

consols
Investment assets structured as perpetuities.

A perpetuity is a special type of annuity with a stream of level cash flows that are paid forever. These arrangements are called **perpetuities** because payments are perpetual. Assets that offer investors perpetual payments are preferred stocks and British 2½% Consolidated Stock, a debt referred to as **consols.**

The value of an investment like this is the present value of all future annuity payments. As the cash flow continues indefinitely, we can't use equation 5-4. Luckily, mathematicians have figured out that when the number of periods, *N*, in equation 5-4 goes to infinity, the equation reduces to a very simple one:

$$\text{Present value of a perpetuity} = \text{Payment} \div \text{Interest rate}$$

$$PV \text{ of a perpetuity} = \frac{PMT}{i} \qquad \textbf{(5-5)}$$

For example, the present value of an annual \$100 perpetuity discounted at 10 percent is \$1,000 (= \$100 ÷ 0.10). Compare this to the present value of a \$100 annuity of 40 years as shown in Table 5.2. The 40-year annuity's value is \$977.91. You'll see that extending the payments from 40 years to an infinite number of years adds only \$22.09 (= \$1,000 − \$977.91) of value. This demonstrates once again how little value today is placed on cash flows paid many years into the future.

TIME OUT

5-3 How important is the magnitude of the discount rate in present value computations? Do significantly higher interest rates lead to significantly higher present values?

5-4 Reconsider the physical therapy equipment example. If interest rates are only 7 percent, should you pay the up-front fee or the annuity?

5.3 • Ordinary Annuities versus Annuities Due

annuity due
An annuity in which cash flows are paid at the beginning of each time period.

So far, we've assumed that every cash flow comes in at the end of every period. But in many instances, cash flows come in at the beginning of each period. An annuity in which the cash flows occur at the beginning of each period is called an **annuity due.**

Consider the 5-year \$100 annuity due. The cash flow in the beginning of year 1 looks like it's actually a cash flow today.

LG5-6

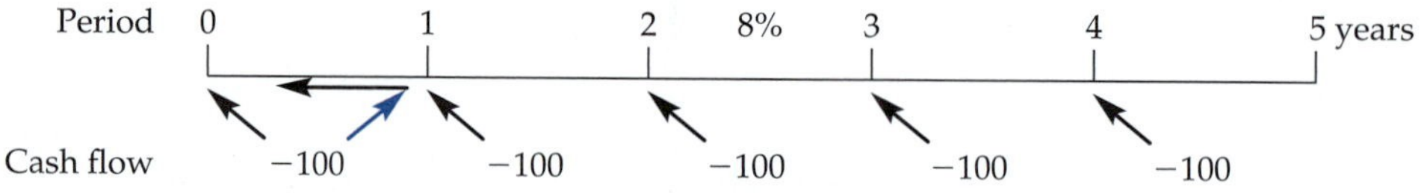

Note that these five annuity-due cash flows are essentially the same as a payment today and a four-year ordinary annuity.

[2]Rodriguez opted out of the contract after the 2007 season and then re-signed with the New York Yankees with a new contract.

finance at work — behavioral

TAKE YOUR LOTTERY WINNINGS NOW OR LATER?

On March 31, 2012, three lottery players co-won a record Powerball jackpot of \$640 million. The winners had two choices for payment: They could split a much-discounted lump sum cash payment immediately or take 30 annuity payments (one immediately and then one every year for 29 years, which is a 30-year annuity due). The annuity payment to be split would be \$24.61 million (= \$640 million ÷ 26) for 26 years. The immediate lump sum offered to be split was \$462.3 million. One way to decide between the two alternatives would be to use the time value of money concepts. The winners might have computed the present value of the annuity and compared it to the lump sum cash payment.

At the time, long-term interest rates were 3.2 percent. The present value of the annuity offered was \$443.85 million. (Compute this yourself.) Notice that winning \$640 million does not deliver \$640 million of value! If the decision was made from this perspective, the group should take the lump sum choice because it has more value than the annuity alternative, and that is what the three winners did. In fact, most winners do. Financial advisors tend to recommend that lottery winners take the lump sum because they believe that the money can earn a higher return than the 3.2 percent interest rate.

Good reasons arise for taking the annuity, however. To earn the higher return on the lump sum, the advisor (and the group of owners) would have to take risks. In addition, most of the lump sum would have to be invested. But most people who choose the lump sum end up spending much of it in the first couple of years. Stories abound about lottery winners who declare bankruptcy a few years after receiving their money. Choosing the annuity helps instill financial discipline, since the winners can't waste money today that they won't receive for years.

Source: Ronald D. Orol, "3 Winning Tickets Sold in \$640 Million Lottery," *Market Watch,* March 31, 2012, http://articles.marketwatch.com/2012-03-31/general/31265196_1_million-lottery-kansas-lottery-ticket.

! want to know more? Key Words to Search for Updates: Powerball winners (go to www.powerball.com)

FUTURE VALUE OF AN ANNUITY DUE So, how do we calculate the future value of the 5-year annuity due shown in the time line? The first cash flow of an ordinary 5-year annuity can compound for four years. The last cash flow does not compound at all. From the time line, you can see that the first cash flow of the annuity due essentially occurs in year zero, or today. So the first cash flow compounds for five years. The last cash flow of an annuity due compounds one year. The main difference between an annuity due and an ordinary annuity is that all the cash flows of the annuity due compound one more year than the ordinary annuity. The future value of the annuity due will simply be the future value of the ordinary annuity multiplied by $(1 + i)$: LG5-6

$$\text{Future value of an annuity due} = \text{Future value of an annuity} \times \text{One year of compounding}$$

$$FVA_N \text{ due} = FVA_N \times (1 + i) \qquad \textbf{(5-6)}$$

Earlier in the chapter, the future value of this ordinary annuity was shown to be \$586.66. Therefore, the future value of the annuity due is \$633.59 (= \$586.66 × 1.08).

PRESENT VALUE OF AN ANNUITY DUE What is a five-year annuity due, shown previously, worth today? Remember that we discount the first cash flow of an ordinary five-year annuity one year. We discount the last cash flow for the full five years. But since the first cash flow of the annuity due is already paid today, we don't

MATH COACH

SETTING FINANCIAL CALCULATORS FOR ANNUITY DUE

Financial calculators can be set for beginning-of-period payments. Once set, you compute future and present values of annuities due just as you would the ordinary annuity. To set the HP calculator, press the color button followed by the BEG/END button. To set the TI calculator for an annuity due, push the 2ND button, followed by the BGN button, followed by the 2ND button again, followed by the SET button, and followed by the 2ND button a third time, finally the QUIT button. To set the HP and TI calculators back to end-of-period cash flows, repeat these procedures.

LG5-6

discount it at all. We discount the last cash flow of an annuity due only four years. Indeed, we discount all the cash flows of the annuity due one year less than we would discount the ordinary annuity. Therefore, the present value of the annuity due is simply the present value of the ordinary annuity multiplied by $(1 + i)$:

$$PVA_N \text{ due} = PVA_N \times (1 + i) \qquad \textbf{(5-7)}$$

Earlier in the chapter, we discovered that the present value of this ordinary annuity was $399.27. So the present value of the annuity due is $431.21 (= $399.27 × 1.08).

Interestingly, we make the same adjustment, $(1 + i)$, to both the ordinary annuity present value and future value to compute the annuity due value.

CALCULATOR HINTS

Change to BGN
N = 5
I = 8
PMT = −100
FV = 0
CPT PV = 431.21

TIME OUT

5-5 In what situations might you need to use annuity due analysis instead of an ordinary annuity analysis?

5-6 Reconsider your retirement plan earlier in this chapter. What would your retirement wealth grow to be if you started contributing today?

5.4 • Compounding Frequency

So far, all of our examples and illustrations have used annual payments and annual compounding or discounting periods. But many situations that use cash flow time-value-of-money analysis require more frequent or less frequent time periods than simple yearly entries. Bonds make semiannual interest payments; stocks pay quarterly dividends. Most consumer loans require monthly payments. Monthly payments require monthly compounding. In this section, we'll discuss the implications of compounding more than once a year.

MATH COACH

ANNUITY COMPUTATIONS IN SPREADSHEETS

The TVM functions in a spreadsheet handle annuity payments similar to financial calculators. The spreadsheet Math Coach in Chapter 4 shows the functions. The functions have an annuity input.

The example illustrated earlier in this chapter asks for the FV of annual $100 deposits earning 8 percent. The spreadsheet solution is the same as the equation and calculator solutions. If you want the FV of an annuity due, just change the *type* from 0 to 1.

	A	B	C	D
1				
2	Present Value =	$0		
3	Future Value =	$586.66 =FV(B5,B6,B4,B2,0)		
4	Annuity Payment =	-$100.00		
5	Interest Rate =	8%		
6	# of Periods =	5		

See this textbook's online student center to watch instructional videos on using spreadsheets.

Effect of Compounding Frequency

Consider a $100 deposit made today with a 12 percent annual interest rate. What's the future value of this deposit in one year? Equation 4-2 from the previous chapter shows that the answer is $112. What would happen if the bank compounded the interest every six months instead of at the end of the year? Halfway through the year, the bank would compute that the deposit has grown 6 percent (half the annual 12 percent rate) to $106. At the end of the year, the bank would compute another 6 percent interest payment. However, this 6 percent is earned on $106, not the original $100 deposit. The end-of-year value is therefore $112.36 (= $106 × 1.06). By compounding twice per year instead of just once, the future value is $0.36 higher. Though this amount may seem negligible, you might be surprised to see how quickly the difference becomes significant.

table 5.3 | **Future Value in One Year and Compounding Frequency of $100 at 12 percent**

	A	B	C	D
1	**Frequency**	**Period Interest Rate**	**Future Value Equation**	**Future Value**
2	Annual	12%	$\$100 \times 1.12^{1}$	$ 112.00
3	Semiannual	6	100×1.06^{2}	112.36
4	Quarterly	3	100×1.03^{4}	112.55
5	Monthly	1	100×1.01^{12}	112.68
6	Daily	0.032877	$100 \times 1.00032877^{365}$	112.748
7	Hourly	0.00136986	$100 \times 1.0000136986^{8760}$	112.749

The higher the compound frequency, the higher the future value will be.

LG5-7

Instead of compounding annually or semiannually, what might happen if compounding were quarterly? Since each year contains four quarters, the interest rate per quarter would be 3 percent (= 12 percent ÷ 4 quarters). The future value in one year, compounded quarterly, is \$112.55 ($= \$100 \times 1.03^4$). Again, the compounding frequency increased and so did the future value.

Table 5.3 shows the effect of various compounding frequencies. We'd like to draw your attention to two important points in the table. First, the higher the compound frequency, the higher the future value will be. Second, the relative increase in value from increasing compounding frequency seems to diminish with increasing frequencies. For example, increasing frequency from annual to semiannual increased the future value by 36 cents. However, increasing frequency from daily to hourly compounding increases the future value by only 0.1 cent.[3]

EXAMPLE 5-5

LG5-4

Car Loan Debt

Now you would like to buy a car. You have reviewed your budget and determined that you can afford to pay \$500 per month as a car payment. How much can you borrow if interest rates are 9 percent and you pay the loan over four years? How much could you borrow if you agree to pay for six years instead?

For interactive versions of this example visit www.mhhe.com/can3e

SOLUTION:

The loan amount is the present value of the 48-month, \$500 annuity. Note that the loan term will be 48 (= 4 × 12) months and the interest rate is 0.75 (= 9 ÷ 12) percent. Using equation 5-4, you discover that you can borrow up to \$20,092 to buy a car:

$$PVA_{48} = \$500 \times \left[\frac{1 - \dfrac{1}{(1 + 0.0075)^{48}}}{0.0075} \right] = \$500 \times 40.1848 = \$20,092.39$$

If you are willing to borrow money for six years instead of four, the small change to the equation results in your ability to borrow \$27,738. Although this would allow you to buy a more expensive car, it would also require two more years of \$500 payments (an additional \$12,000 of payments!).

Similar to Problems 5-25, 5-26, self-test problem 4

CALCULATOR HINTS

N = 48
I = 0.75
PMT = −500
FV = 0
CPT PV = 20,092.39

Then change N to 72
CPT PV = 27,738.42

[3] It is also possible to continuously compound. The future value of a continuously compounded deposit is $FV_N = PV \times e^{(i \times N)}$, where e has a value of 2.7183.

When we work with annuity cash flows, the compound frequency used is the same as the timing of the cash flows. When annuity cash flows are paid monthly, then interest is also compounded monthly, as seen in Examples 5-5 and 5-6.

EXAMPLE 5-6

LG5-7

For interactive versions of this example visit www.mhhe.com/can3e

Making Monthly Pension Contributions

Reexamine your original plan to contribute to your company retirement plan. Instead of a total contribution of $4,500 per year for 40 years, you are able to contribute monthly. Given your expected 7 percent per year investment return, how much money can you expect in your retirement account?

SOLUTION:

Now your total monthly contribution will be $375 (= $4,500 ÷ 12), which will continue for 480 months and earn a 0.58333 (= 7 ÷ 12) percent monthly return. The results of equation 5-2 show that the future value of this annuity is:

$$FVA_{40} = \$375 \times \frac{[1 + (0.07/12)]^{480} - 1}{0.07/12} = \$375 \times 2{,}624.8135 = \$984{,}305.02$$

When you made contributions annually, the future value was $898,358 (Example 5-2). By changing to monthly contributions, your retirement nest egg increased by nearly $86,000 to $984,305!

Similar to Problems 5-51, 5-52, self-test problem 3

CALCULATOR HINTS

N = 480
I = 7 ÷ 12
PV = 0
PMT = −375
CPT FV = 984,305.02

LG5-7

EARs AND APRs If you borrowed $100 at a 12 percent interest rate, you would expect to pay $112 in one year. If the loan compounded monthly, then you would owe $112.68 at the end of the year, as Table 5.3 shows. So a 12 percent loan compounded monthly means that you really pay more than 12 percent. In fact, you would pay 12.68 percent. In this example, the 12 percent rate is called the **annual percentage rate (APR).** The higher rate, 12.68 percent, is called the **effective annual rate (EAR)**—a more accurate measurement of what you will actually pay.

Lenders are legally required to show potential borrowers the APR on any loan offered. While the difference in APR and EAR is not that large in this example, it's interesting that the law requires only the less accurate (and lower) one to be shown. Since the EAR is a more accurate measure of what you will pay, it's useful to know how to convert a stated APR to an EAR. Equation 5-8 shows this conversion with a compounding frequency of m times per year:

$$EAR = \left(1 + \frac{APR}{m}\right)^{m} - 1 \qquad \textbf{(5-8)}$$

Table 5.4 shows various EAR conversions. If compounding occurs annually, you will see that the EAR and the APR will be the same. If compounding

MATH COACH

COMMON MISTAKES

As you figure present and future values of annuity cash flows, check that all terms are consistent: the number of payments, interest rate, and payment size all need to use common terms. If your payments are monthly, then the number of payments must reflect the number of months; the interest rate must be stated as a per-month rate, and the payment register must reflect that monthly payment.

annual percentage rate (APR)
The interest rate per period times the number of periods in a year.

effective annual rate (EAR)
An interest rate that reflects annualizing with compounding figured in.

table 5.4 | **The EAR Is Higher than the APR**

	A	B	C	D
1	**APR**	**Compounding Periods**	**Equation**	**= EAR**
2	*Varying the Compounding Periods*			
3	5%	1	$(1 + 0.05/1)^1 - 1$	5.00%
4	5	4	$(1 + 0.05/4)^4 - 1$	5.09
5	5	12	$(1 + 0.05/12)^{12} - 1$	5.12
6	*Varying APR and Compounding Periods*			
7	9	4	$(1 + 0.09/4)^4 - 1$	9.31
8	9	12	$(1 + 0.09/12)^{12} - 1$	9.38
9	12	4	$(1 + 0.12/4)^4 - 1$	12.55
10	12	12	$(1 + 0.12/12)^{12} - 1$	12.68

Note: This compound frequency effect grows substantially for higher interest rates or longer term loans.

happens more than once a year, then the EAR will be higher than the APR. The table also demonstrates that the compound frequency effect grows substantially for higher interest rates or longer term loans. Compounded quarterly, the EAR is hardly different at all from a 5 percent APR: 5.09 percent versus 5 percent. The difference is larger when the APR is 12 percent. Compounded quarterly, the EAR is higher at 12.55 percent.

EXAMPLE 5-7

LG5-7

Evaluating Credit Card Offers

For interactive versions of this example visit www.mhhe.com/can3e

As a college student, you probably receive many credit card offers in the mail. Consider these two offers. The first card charges a 16 percent APR. An examination of the footnotes reveals that this card compounds monthly. The second credit card charges 15.5 percent APR and compounds weekly. Which card has a lower effective annual rate?

SOLUTION:

Compute the EAR of each card to compare them in common (and realistic) terms. The first card has an EAR of:

$$EAR = \left(1 + \frac{0.16}{12}\right)^{12} - 1 = 0.1732, \text{ or } 17.23\%$$

The EAR of the second card is:

$$EAR = \left(1 + \frac{0.155}{52}\right)^{52} - 1 = 0.1674, \text{ or } 16.74\%$$

You should pick the second credit card because it has a lower effective annual rate. But note also that you will always be better off if you pay your credit card balance whenever the bill comes due.

Similar to Problems 5-15, 5-16, self-test problem 3

TIME OUT

5-7 Why is EAR a more accurate measure of the rate actually paid than APR?

5-8 What would have a smaller present value: a future sum discounted annually or one discounted monthly?

5.5 • Annuity Loans

In this chapter, we've focused on computing the future and present value of annuities. But in many situations, these values are already known and what we really need to compare are the payments or implied interest rate—usually, the highest interest rate offered.

What Is the Interest Rate?

LG5-8 Many business and personal applications already state the cost of an investment, as well as the annuity cash flows and time period. We need, then, to solve for the implied interest rate of this investment. Unfortunately, we have no general, easy equation to solve for the interest rate. Even financial calculators use an iterating process, which causes them to "think" a little longer before displaying the estimated interest rate result.

Consider the plight of a manager of a small doctor's office who has the opportunity to buy a piece of imaging equipment for $100,000. The equipment will allow the office to generate $25,000 in profits for six years, at which time the equipment will be worn out and without value in the United States.[4] What rate of return does this purchase offer the doctor's office? The time line for this problem appears as:

Period	0	1	2	3 I = ?	4	5	6 years
Cash flow	−100,000	25,000	25,000	25,000	25,000	25,000	25,000

For the financial calculator solution, input N = 6, PV = −100000, PMT = 25000, and FV = 0. The interest rate result is then 12.98 percent. So, if this is a high enough return relative to other uses of the $100,000, the doctor's office should seriously consider purchasing the imaging machine.

EXAMPLE 5-8

LG5-8

For interactive versions of this example visit www.mhhe.com/can3e

Computing Interest Rate Needed

After saving diligently throughout your entire career, you and your spouse are finally ready to retire with a nest egg of $800,000. You need to invest this money in a mix of stocks and bonds that will allow you to withdraw $6,000 per month for 30 years. What interest rate do you need to earn?

SOLUTION:

Use a financial calculator and input N = 360, PV = −800000, PMT = 6000, and FV = 0. The interest rate result is 0.6860 percent. But remember, since the periods and payments are in months, the interest rate is too. It is customary to report this as an APR: 8.23 percent (= 0.6860 percent × 12). However, the EAR more accurately reflects the true interest rate, 8.55 percent (= $1.00686^{12} - 1$). In order for your money to last for 30 years while funding a $6,000 per month income, you must earn at least an 8.23 APR per year return.

If you have uneven cash flows, use the calculator CF worksheet and then solve with the IRR function.

Similar to Problems 5-33, 5-34, 5-35, 5-36

[4]Some charities are now gathering "obsolete" U.S. medical equipment and sending the materials to less developed countries—a situation in which everybody wins.

Finding Payments on an Amortized Loan

MATH COACH

COMMON MISTAKES

As we noted in Chapter 4, when computing the interest rate, make sure that the present value and the annuity payments are of different signs (positive versus negative). Otherwise, the calculator will show an error.

Many consumers and small business owners already know how much money they want to borrow and the level of current interest rates. Usually, they need to translate this information into the actual payments to determine if they can really afford the purchase. A loan structured for annuity payments that completely pay off the debt is called an **amortized loan.** To compute the annuity cash flow of an amortized loan, rearrange the present value of an annuity formula, equation 5-4, to solve for the payment:

LG5-9

amortized loan

A loan in which the borrower pays interest and principal over time.

Payment = Present value × Amortization

$$PMT_N = PV \times \left[\frac{i}{1 - \dfrac{1}{(1+i)^N}}\right] \quad \textbf{(5-9)}$$

Most car loans require monthly payments for three to five years. Assume that you need a $10,000 loan to buy a car. The loan is for four years and interest rates are 9 percent per year APR. To implement equation 5-9, use an interest rate of 0.75 percent (= 9 percent/12) and 48 periods (= 4 × 12) as:

$$PMT_{48} = \$10{,}000 \times \left[\frac{0.0075}{1 - \dfrac{1}{(1+0.0075)^{48}}}\right] = \$10{,}000 \times 0.024885 = \$248.85$$

CALCULATOR HINTS

N = 48
I = 0.75
PV = 10000
FV = 0
CPT PMT = −248.85

So, when interest rates are 9 percent, it takes monthly payments of $248.85 to pay off a $10,000 loan in four years.

Interest rate levels and loan length strongly affect how large your payments will be. Table 5.5 shows the monthly payments needed to pay off a mortgage debt at various interest rates and lengths of time. (Try computing the payments yourself!) Note that as the interest rate declines, the monthly payment also declines. This is why people rush to refinance their mortgages after interest rates fall. A decline of 1 or 2 percent can save a homeowner hundreds of dollars every month. You will also see from the table that paying off a mortgage in only 15 years requires larger payments, but generally saves thousands in interest.

table 5.5 | **Monthly Payments on a $225,000 Loan**

	A	B	C
1	**Annual Percentage Rate (APR)**	**Years to Repay Loan**	**Monthly Payment**
2	*30-Year Mortgage*		
3	10%	30	$1,974.54
4	8	30	1,650.97
5	7	30	1,496.93
6	6	30	1,348.99
7	*15-Year Mortgage*		
8	8	15	2,150.22
9	7	15	2,022.36
10	6	15	1,898.68

table 5.6 | Amortization Schedule over Four Years (9 percent APR)

	A	B	C	D	E	F	G	H	I	J	K	L
1	Month	Beginning Balance	Total Payment	Interest Paid	Principal Paid	Ending Balance	Month	Beginning Balance	Total Payment	Interest Paid	Principal Paid	Ending Balance
2	1	$10,000.00	$248.85	$75.00	$173.85	$9,826.15	25	$5,447.13	$248.85	$40.85	$208.00	$5,239.14
3	2	9,826.15	248.85	73.70	175.15	9,651.00	26	5,239.14	248.85	39.29	209.56	5,029.58
4	3	9,651.00	248.85	72.38	176.47	9,474.53	27	5,029.58	248.85	37.72	211.13	4,818.45
5	4	9,474.53	248.85	71.06	177.79	9,296.74	28	4,818.45	248.85	36.14	212.71	4,605.74
6	5	9,296.74	248.85	69.73	179.12	9,117.61	29	4,605.74	248.85	34.54	214.31	4,391.43
7	6	9,117.61	248.85	68.38	180.47	8,937.15	30	4,391.43	248.85	32.94	215.91	4,175.52
8	7	8,937.15	248.85	67.03	181.82	8,755.32	31	4,175.52	248.85	31.32	217.53	3,957.99
9	8	8,755.32	248.85	65.66	183.19	8,572.14	32	3,957.99	248.85	29.68	219.17	3,738.82
10	9	8,572.14	248.85	64.29	184.56	8,387.58	33	3,738.82	248.85	28.04	220.81	3,518.01
11	10	8,387.58	248.85	62.91	185.94	8,201.64	34	3,518.01	248.85	26.39	222.46	3,295.55
12	11	8,201.64	248.85	61.51	187.34	8,014.30	35	3,295.55	248.85	24.72	224.13	3,071.41
13	12	8,014.30	248.85	60.11	188.74	7,825.56	36	3,071.41	248.85	23.04	225.81	2,845.60
14	13	7,825.56	248.85	58.69	190.16	7,635.40	37	2,845.60	248.85	21.34	227.51	2,618.09
15	14	7,635.40	248.85	57.27	191.58	7,443.81	38	2,618.09	248.85	19.64	229.21	2,388.88
16	15	7,443.81	248.85	55.83	193.02	7,250.79	39	2,388.88	248.85	17.92	230.93	2,157.94
17	16	7,250.79	248.85	54.38	194.47	7,056.32	40	2,157.94	248.85	16.18	232.67	1,925.28
18	17	7,056.32	248.85	52.92	195.93	6,860.40	41	1,925.28	248.85	14.44	234.41	1,690.87
19	18	6,860.40	248.85	51.45	197.40	6,663.00	42	1,690.87	248.85	12.68	236.17	1,454.70
20	19	6,663.00	248.85	49.97	198.88	6,464.12	43	1,454.70	248.85	10.91	237.94	1,216.76
21	20	6,464.12	248.85	48.48	200.37	6,263.75	44	1,216.76	248.85	9.13	239.72	977.04
22	21	6,263.75	248.85	46.98	201.87	6,061.88	45	977.04	248.85	7.33	241.52	735.51
23	22	6,061.88	248.85	45.46	203.39	5,858.49	46	735.51	248.85	5.52	243.33	492.18
24	23	5,858.49	248.85	43.94	204.91	5,653.58	47	492.18	248.85	3.69	245.16	247.02
25	24	5,653.58	248.85	42.40	206.45	5,447.13	48	247.02	248.87	1.85	247.02	0.00
26												
27								Total interest paid =		1,944.82		

LG5-9

loan principal

The balance yet to be paid on a loan.

amortization schedule

A table detailing the periodic loan payment, interest payment, and debt balance over the life of the loan.

AMORTIZED LOAN SCHEDULES When you pay a car loan or home mortgage, you will often find it useful to know how much of the debt, or **loan principal,** you still owe. For example, consider a case wherein you bought a car two years ago using a 4-year loan. In order to sell the car now, the loan balance will have to be paid off. Being able to compute this principal balance may influence your chances of selling the car.

An interest-only loan allows the borrower to make payments that consist totally of interest payments, so none of the debt is reduced. A $10,000 interest-only loan with a 9 percent APR paid monthly will cost $75 per month (= $10,000 × 0.09 ÷ 12). Amortizing this loan over four years requires monthly payments of $248.85 (see earlier car loan problem). The difference in the first month's payment on the two loans is $173.85 (= $248.85 − $75) and represents the amount of the regular amortized loan's payment that goes to reducing the principal balance. So after the first month's payment, the amortized loan's balance has fallen to $9,826.15, while the interest-only loan still has a balance of $10,000.

In the second month, the interest incurred on the regular amortized loan is $73.70 (= $9,826.15 × 0.09 ÷ 12), so the $248.85 second-month payment represents principal payment of $175.15. These numbers are shown in the **amortization schedule** of Table 5.6. The table will show you that the early payments on a car loan go mostly to paying the interest rather than reducing the principal. That interest component declines over time, and then the principal balance declines.

The amortization schedule shows that if you wish to sell the car after two years, you will have to pay the loan company a car loan (principal) debt of

$5,447.13. Of course, if you had an interest-only loan, you would still owe the full principal of $10,000 after two years. Amortization schedules are also useful for determining other things, like the total amount of interest that you will pay over the life of the loan. In this case, if you take a regular loan in which you pay both principal and interest, you pay $10,000 in principal and nearly $1,945 in interest during the four years of the loan. The interest component is an even larger component of longer-term loans, like 30-year mortgages. Depending on the interest rate charged, the first payment in a mortgage consists of 75 percent to 95 percent interest. The home mortgage principal balance falls very slowly in the first years of the loan.

We construct amortization schedules by showing the loan's principal balance at the beginning of the month. This is the same as the balance at the end of the previous month (except for the very first payment). Then we compute the interest owed on that balance for the month. After paying that interest, what's left of the monthly payment reduces the loan balance for the next month. Because of these repetitive computations, spreadsheets make amortization schedules easy to construct.

EXAMPLE 5-9

LG5-9

Monthly Mortgage Payments

For interactive versions of this example visit www.mhhe.com/can3e

Say that you have your heart set on purchasing a beautiful, old Tudor-style house for $250,000. A mortgage broker says that you can qualify for a mortgage for 80 percent (or $200,000) of the price. If you get a 15-year mortgage, the interest rate will be 6.1 percent APR. A 30-year mortgage costs 6.4 percent. One of the factors that will help you decide which mortgage to take is the magnitude of the monthly payments. What will they be?[5]

SOLUTION:

To pay off the mortgage in only 15 years, the payments would have to be larger than for the 30-year mortgage. The higher payment will be eased somewhat because the interest rate is lower on the 15-year mortgage. The payment for the 15-year mortgage is:

$$PMT_{180} = \$200,000 \times \left[\frac{0.0050833}{1 - \dfrac{1}{(1 + 0.0050833)^{180}}}\right] = \$200,000 \times 0.0084927 = \$1,698.54$$

The payment for the 30-year mortgage would be:

$$PMT_{360} = \$200,000 \times \left[\frac{0.0053333}{1 - \dfrac{1}{(1 + 0.0053333)^{360}}}\right] = \$200,000 \times 0.00625506 = \$1,251.01$$

So, the payments on the 15-year mortgage are nearly $450 more each month than the 30-year mortgage payments. You must decide whether the cost of paying the extra $450 each month is worth it to own the house with no debt 15 years sooner. The decision would depend on your financial budget and the strength of your desire to be debt free.

Similar to Problems 5-39, 5-40, self-test problems 1 and 4

CALCULATOR HINTS

N = 180
I = 6.1 ÷ 12
PV = 200000
FV = 0
CPT PMT = −1,698.54

For 30-year mortgage:
N = 360
I = 6.4 ÷ 12
CPT PMT = −1,251.01

[5]Most homeowners are actually most interested in their total payment, which will include hazard insurance for the home and property taxes. Such payments are referred to as PITI—principal, interest, taxes, and insurance. For simplicity, we use only PI payments here—principal and interest.

MATH COACH

USING THE AMORT FUNCTION IN TVM CALCULATORS

TVM calculators have preprogrammed functions to compute the amount of principal paid part way through a mortgage. For example, if you took out a 30-year, $200,000 mortgage at a 6 percent APR, how much principal have you paid after five years? How much do you still owe? How much interest have you paid?

To answer these questions, first enter the mortgage information to compute the monthly payments. Then use the AMORT function. This example uses the Texas Instruments BA II+ as an example. The Hewlett-Packard and other TVM calculators have similar functions. The AMORT function allows you to compute the loan balance at any time during the mortgage period. It also computes the amount of principal and interest that has been paid during any time period. To answer the questions above:

CALCULATOR HINTS

N = 360
I = 0.5
PV = 200000
FV = 0
CPT PMT = −1,199.10

1. Press 2nd AMORT and P1 = 1 appears. (This refers to the first payment of the mortgage.)
2. Press the down arrow ↓, P2 = appears. (This refers to the last payment made.)
3. The question refers to 5 years of payments, which is 60 months. Enter 60 and press ENTER.

The calculator has now computed the loan balance after the 60th payment and the amount of principal and interest that have been paid between the first and the 60th payment.

4. Press the down arrow ↓, displayed is BAL = 186,108.71, which is the loan balance.
5. Press the down arrow ↓, displayed is PRN = 13,891.29, which is the principal paid in the first 5 years.
6. Press the down arrow ↓, displayed is INT = −58,054.78, which is the interest paid in the first 5 years.

Note that in the beginning of a mortgage, far more interest is paid than principal.

COMPUTE THE TIME PERIOD You might also find it useful to know how long it will take to pay off a loan with specific annuity payments. To find the number of periods, you can solve equation 5-9 for *N*—the number of payments—but the equation becomes quite complicated.[6] Many people just use a financial calculator or spreadsheet. We can check to see if the $248.85 monthly payment would indeed pay off the $10,000, 9 percent car loan in four years. Finding the solution with a financial calculator entails entering I = 0.75, PV = 10000, PMT = −248.85, and FV = 0. The answer is 48 months.

EXAMPLE 5-10

LG5-10

For interactive versions of this example visit www.mhhe.com/can3e

Time to Pay Off a Credit Card Balance

Through poor financial management, your friend has racked up $5,000 in debt on his credit card. The card charges a 19 percent APR and compounds monthly. His latest bill shows that he must pay a minimum of $150 this month. At this rate, how long will it take your friend to pay off his credit card debt?

[6]The equation for solving for the number of periods in an annuity is:

$$N = \frac{\ln\left({}^{PMT}\!/_{(PMT - PVA_N \times i)} \right)}{\ln(1 + i)}$$

SOLUTION:

Using the financial calculator, input I = 1.58333 (= 19/12), PV = 5000, PMT = −150, FV = 0. The answer is 48 months, or 4 years. If the friend pays the minimum payment, then it will be a long time before he will be out of debt. The credit card company is very content to continue to earn the high return for many years—essentially, the interest on the loan and a very small portion of the principal. Your friend should pay more than the minimum charge to reduce his debt quicker.

Similar to Problems 5-41, 5-42, self-test problem 4

TIME OUT

5-9 How might credit card companies keep their cardholders in debt for a long time? What payment do the credit card companies expect your friend to make so that he never pays down the debt?

5-10 Can you find the interest rate if you know the annuity payments and a future value? Under what circumstances might you want to solve this kind of problem? Which equation would you use?

ADD-ON INTEREST One method of calculating payments of a loan that is popular in payday lending is called **add-on interest.** This method computes the amount of the interest payable at the beginning of the loan, which is then added to the principal of the loan. This total is then divided into the number of payments to be made. Consider a loan of $1,000 to be paid with 9 percent add-on interest and repaid in six monthly payments.

add-on interest

A calculation of the amount of interest determined at the beginning of the loan and then added to the principal.

The total interest for this loan is computed as 9 percent of $1,000 for 6 months, or $45 (= 0.09 × $1,000 × ½). This is added to the principal for a total of $1,045. Each of the six monthly payments is then $1,045 ÷ 6 = $174.17. Be alert that the add-on interest method seriously understates the real interest rate that is being paid! If you borrow $1,000 and repay a $174.17 monthly annuity for six months, the monthly interest rate is 1.27 percent. This is a 15.27 percent APR (= 1.27% × 12) and a 16.39 percent EAR ($= 1.0127^{12} - 1$)—both much higher than the advertised 9 percent interest rate of this loan.

CALCULATOR HINTS

N = 6
PV = 1000
PMT = −174.17
FV = 0
CPT I = 1.27

viewpoints REVISITED

Business Application Solution

Walkabout Music, Inc., pays $700,000 (= $20 million × 0.07 ÷ 2) in interest every six months on its existing debt. The new debt would require payments of $600,000 (= $20 million × 0.06 ÷ 2) every six months, which represents a $100,000 savings semiannually.

The present value of these savings over the next 20 years is computed using 40 semiannual periods and a 3 percent interest rate per period:

$$PVA_N = \$100{,}000 \times \left[\frac{1 - \dfrac{1}{(1+0.03)^{40}}}{0.03}\right] = \$2{,}311{,}477.20$$

CALCULATOR HINTS

N = 20 × 2 = 40
I/Y = 6 ÷ 2 = 3
PMT = 100000
FV = 0
CPT PV = −2,311,477.20

Since this savings is less than the $2.6 million cost of refinancing, the CFO should not refinance the old debt at this time. The company should wait until it can find more favorable terms.

Personal Application Solution

Should you switch to a new home mortgage with a lower interest rate? To answer this question, first find the monthly savings with the new mortgage. Then compare the present value of the savings to the cost of getting the new mortgage.

The current monthly mortgage payments are:

$$PMT_N = \$150{,}000 \times \left[\frac{0.00667}{1 - \dfrac{1}{(1+0.00667)^{360}}}\right] = \$1{,}100.65$$

CALCULATOR HINTS

N = 30 × 12 = 360
I/Y = 8 ÷ 12 = 0.667
PV = 150000
FV = 0
CPT PMT = −1,100.65

CALCULATOR HINTS

N = 27 × 12 = 324
I/Y = 7 ÷ 12 = 0.5833
PV = 145920.10
FV = 0
CPT PMT = −1,003.66

The new mortgage payments would be:

$$PMT_N = \$145{,}920.10 \times \left[\frac{0.00583}{1 - \dfrac{1}{(1+0.00583)^{324}}}\right] = \$1{,}003.66$$

The new mortgage would save you $96.99 per month for the next 27 years.

The present value of these savings at the current 7 percent interest rate is:

$$PVA_N = \$96.99 \times \left[\frac{1 - \dfrac{1}{(1+0.00583)^{324}}}{0.00583}\right] = \$14{,}101.18$$

CALCULATOR HINTS

N = 27 × 12 = 324
I/Y = 7 ÷ 12 = 0.5833
PMT = 96.99
FV = 0
CPT PV = $14,101.18

Since the present value of the monthly savings is greater than the $1,000 broker fee, you should refinance the mortgage.

summary of learning goals

In this chapter, we extend the concept of the time value of money to multiple cash flows and traditional types of loans and investment plans. Common loans and investment programs are in the form of frequent, consistent, and level cash flows, called *annuities*. We've introduced and illustrated the tools used to describe the dynamics of present and future value of annuity payments. You might find other useful applications of annuity equations to determine loan payments, the interest rate associated with an annuity stream, or how long it will take to repay a debt.

LG5-1 **Compound multiple cash flows to the future.** In Chapter 4, we illustrated how a deposit today increases in value over time. But many situations include multiple deposits over time. Each of these deposits compounds and they can be added together at some future point in time.

LG5-2 **Compute the future value of frequent, level cash flows.** We call any frequent, consistent, series of level cash flows an annuity. Many retirement savings plans include contributing the same amount of money every month to a portfolio. We can compute the future value of your retirement nest egg if the portfolio is invested to earn a specific interest rate. We describe and work through many future value of an annuity tools that you can use in many applications.

Compounding makes the magnitude of the interest rate earned have a distinct impact on future value. Higher interest rates lead to more interest earnings, which in turn lead to more interest-on-interest growth. The number of annuity cash flows also strongly affects the size of the future value of a stream of cash flows.

LG5-3 **Discount multiple cash flows to the present.** You will find that you will often need to figure the present value of many cash flows. First, compute the present value of each individual cash flow using the appropriate discount rate. Once each cash flow is discounted to the present, they will be in common terms and thus can be added together.

LG5-4 **Compute the present value of an annuity.** You'll find that the present value of an annuity concept has many applications. Most car and home mortgage loans are set up so that the amount borrowed (the present value) is repaid through level payments made every period (the annuity). Given the amount of money a borrower can afford to pay (the annuity), lenders will compute its present value to determine the amount of a loan they are willing to offer. Your credit rating and current economic conditions will determine the interest rate that the lender will offer.

Borrowers can borrow more money when interest rates are lower. The present value of an annuity declines quickly for higher (interest) discount rates. Indeed, the present value of annuity payments made far into the future are worth very little today.

LG5-5 **Figure cash flows and present value of a perpetuity.** The perpetuity, a special form of annuity, pays cash flows forever. The present value of perpetuities has some applications in the investment industry.

LG5-6 **Adjust values for beginning-of-period annuity payments.** Most ordinary annuities assume that cash flows are paid at the end of each period. Many people who want to start investing for their future want to start today, not at the end of the month or year. Starting today implies an annuity stream that is paid at the beginning of the period. Beginning-of-period cash flows are referred to as *annuities due*. You can compute the present or future value of an annuity due by computing the value of an ordinary annuity and then multiplying by $(1 + i)$.

LG5-7 **Explain the impact of compound frequency and the difference between the annual percentage rate and the effective annual rate.** Many cash flows are made monthly, quarterly, or semiannually. In these cases, the interest rate is compounded multiple times within the year. When computing the future value of an annuity, the higher the compound frequency, the higher will be the future value. While the future value will increase as compounding frequency increases, the size of each increase in future value diminishes as compounding frequencies increase.

So, the future value of a 12 percent interest rate compounded annually is lower than if it were compounded monthly. This simple form of an annualized interest rate is called the *annual percentage rate (APR)*. Compounding monthly causes the interest rate to be effectively higher, and thus the future value grows. This *effective annual rate (EAR)* is a more accurate measure of the interest rate paid. The law requires lenders to show potential borrowers the APR. While the difference in APR and EAR is not that large, note that the law requires the less accurate (and lower) one to be shown except for large and extended loans such as mortgages.

LG5-8 **Compute the interest rate of annuity payments.** If you can compute the implied rate of return in a series of cash flows, you can more easily evaluate investment opportunities for both business and individual applications. This computation typically requires the use of a financial calculator or spreadsheet.

LG5-9 **Compute payments and amortization schedules for car and mortgage loans.** When you take out a loan for a car or home mortgage, you usually already know the amount (or present value) you want to borrow. You will usually find the monthly payment at today's interest rates more relevant for your budget. Obviously, lower interest rates require lower payments. This is why people refinance their home mortgage when rates fall. People also frequently try to lower the periodic payments by extending the time period (or term) of the loan. Loan amortization schedules show the principal balance and interest paid per period.

LG5-10 **Calculate the number of payments on a loan.** When you get your credit card bill, it will offer a minimum payment, which usually only pays the accrued interest and a small amount of principal. If you want to pay down credit card debt, you can use the TVM tools we illustrate in the chapter and this minimum payment to figure the time period it will take to pay off the credit card. Making larger payments will reduce this payoff time. Better yet, paying the balance in full every period will keep you from accumulating large credit card balances. Pay the most you can every month.

chapter equations

5-1 $$FV_N = \text{Future value of first cash flow} + \text{Future value of second cash flow} + \cdots + \text{Future value of last cash flow}$$
$$= PMT_m \times (1+i)^{N-m} + PMT_n \times (1+i)^{N-n} + \cdots + PMT_p \times (1+i)^{N-p}$$

5-2 $$FVA_N = PMT \times \frac{(1+i)^N - 1}{i}$$

5-3 $$PV = \text{Present value of first cash flow} + \text{Present value of second cash flow} + \cdots + \text{Present value of last cash flow}$$
$$= \frac{PMT_m}{(1+i)^m} + \frac{PMT_n}{(1+i)^n} + \cdots + \frac{PMT_p}{(1+i)^p}$$

5-4 $$PVA_N = PMT \times \left[\frac{1 - \frac{1}{(1+i)^N}}{i}\right]$$

5-5 $$PV \text{ of a perpetuity} = \frac{PMT}{i}$$

5-6 $$FVA_N \text{ due} = FVA_N \times (1+i)$$

5-7 $PVA_N \text{ due} = PVA_N \times (1 + i)$

5-8 $EAR = \left(1 + \frac{APR}{m}\right)^m - 1$

5-9 $PMT_N = PV \times \left[\frac{i}{1 - \frac{1}{(1 + i)^N}}\right]$

key terms

add-on interest, A calculation of the amount of interest determined at the beginning of the loan and then added to the principal. *p. 171*

amortized loan, A loan in which the borrower pays interest and principal over time. *p. 167*

amortization schedule, A table detailing the periodic loan payment, interest payment, and debt balance over the life of the loan. *p. 168*

annual percentage rate (APR), The interest rate per period times the number of periods in a year. *p. 164*

annuity, A stream of level and frequent cash flows paid at the end of each time period—often referred to as an *ordinary annuity*. *p. 151*

annuity due, An annuity in which cash flows are paid at the beginning of each time period. *p. 160*

consols, Investment assets structured as perpetuities. *p. 160*

effective annual rate (EAR), An interest rate that reflects annualizing with compounding figured in. *p. 164*

loan principal, The balance yet to be paid on a loan. *p. 168*

perpetuity, An annuity with cash flows that continue forever. *p. 160*

self-test problems with solutions

1 Future Value and Annuity Payments Chandler and Monica are trying to decide if they will have enough money to retire early in 12 years, at age 60. Their current assets are \$300,000 in retirement plans and they have \$100,000 in other investments. Together, they contribute \$28,000 per year to their retirement plans and another \$6,000 to other investments. If their assets grow at 8 percent per year, how much money will they have when they turn 60? After they retire, they will invest their wealth more conservatively and it will earn 5 percent per year. Is this enough to fund a \$100,000 per year retirement for 40 years?

LG 5-2, 5-9

Solution:

Chandler and Monica's current assets of \$400,000 will grow to \$1,007,268 (= $\$400,000 \times 1.08^{12}$) in 12 years. Their annuity contributions of \$34,000 (= \$28,000 + \$6,000) will add another:

$$FVA_{12} = \$34,000 \times \frac{(1 + 0.08)^{12} - 1}{0.08} = \$34,000 \times 18.977126 = \$645,222$$

CALCULATOR HINTS

Future wealth:

N = 12
I = 8
PV = −400000
PMT = −34000
CPT FV = 1,652,490

Income annuity:

N = 40
I = 5
PV = −1652490
FV = 0
CPT PMT = 96,304

So their total retirement wealth is \$1,652,490 (= \$1,007,268 + \$645,222). To determine the income this wealth generates over 40 years, compute the annual annuity payments as:

$$PMT_{40} = \$1{,}652{,}490 \times \left[\frac{0.05}{1 - \dfrac{1}{(1 + 0.05)^{40}}}\right] = \$1{,}652{,}490 \times 0.058278$$

$$= \$96{,}304$$

It appears that Chandler and Monica would not quite make their \$100,000 income requirement. However, a few years after they retire, they would be eligible for Social Security. Though relatively meager, the Social Security payments will be enough to comfortably put their income over the \$100,000 level.

LG5-4

2 Present Value of an Annuity Kevin and Kody are identical twins, have identical jobs, and earn the same salary. However, Kody has been far more financially responsible. He pays his bills on time and pays off his credit card debt quickly. Kevin has been less financially responsible. He often forgets to pay bills and has allowed his credit card balance to balloon. If he is short on cash for the month, he simply decides not to pay even the minimum balance. Now Kevin and Kody are each looking to buy houses. They both decide that they can afford a \$1,000 monthly mortgage payment. On Kody's trip to the mortgage broker, he learns that he can obtain a mortgage for a 7 percent APR. Because of Kevin's bad credit rating, he will be charged 10 percent. How is Kevin's bad credit going to impact his house search?

Solution:

With \$1,000 monthly payments, a 7 percent interest rate, and a 30-year loan, Kody uses the present value of an annuity equation and computes the amount he can borrow. The 7 percent APR is 0.58333 percent (= 7 ÷ 12).

CALCULATOR HINTS

For Kody

N = 360
I = 0.58333
PMT = −1000
FV = 0
CPT PV = 150,307.57

For Kevin

I = 0.83333
CPT PV = 113,950.82

$$PVA_{360} = \$1{,}000 \times \left[\frac{1 - \dfrac{1}{(1 + 0.0058333)^{360}}}{0.0058333}\right] = \$1{,}000 \times 150.3076$$

$$= \$150{,}308$$

With a 20 percent down payment on the house, Kody can look for houses that cost about \$187,900 (= \$150,308 ÷ 0.8). Kevin must pay a higher interest rate and computes that he can borrow a total of:

$$PVA_{360} = \$1{,}000 \times \left[\frac{1 - \dfrac{1}{(1 + 0.008333)^{360}}}{0.008333}\right] = \$1{,}000 \times 113.9509$$

$$= \$113{,}951$$

If Kevin can find a 20 percent down payment, he can look for houses in the price range of \$142,400. Because of Kevin's poor credit management, he must buy a house that is over \$45,000 less expensive than Kody can buy, even though Kevin is paying exactly the same monthly mortgage payment as Kody.

LG5-7

3 Compound Frequency Say that you own a small business, which you plan to expand. Your expansion plans include borrowing \$50,000 from the bank with a 3-year, amortized loan. The bank has given you these loan choices:

Annual payments, 10 percent APR
Quarterly payments, 9.8 percent APR
Monthly payments, 9.5 percent APR

Which loan would have a lower effective annual rate?

Solution:

The effective annual rate for the annual payment loan is:

$$EAR = \left(1 + \frac{0.10}{1}\right)^1 - 1 = 0.10 = 10\%$$

The effective annual rate for the quarterly payment loan is:

$$EAR = \left(1 + \frac{0.098}{4}\right)^4 - 1 = 0.1017 = 10.17\%$$

The effective annual rate for the monthly payment loan is:

$$EAR = \left(1 + \frac{0.095}{12}\right)^{12} - 1 = 0.0992 = 9.92\%$$

So, the lowest cost loan is the monthly one.

4 Annuity Payments and Amortization Schedule Consider Rachel and Ross, a young couple who wish to buy their first home. To do this, they will need to borrow $20,000 from her parents to fund some of the down payment. Rachel's parents will charge them a 7 percent rate. They will make monthly payments over three years to repay the loan. Ross wants to deduct the loan's interest from his taxes, so they need to know how much in interest they will pay each year. Compute monthly payments and create an amortization schedule to determine the interest paid each year.

LG5-9, 5-10

Solution:

The loan will be repaid over 36 months and use a 0.5833 percent (= 7 percent ÷ 12) monthly interest rate. Therefore, the monthly payments will be:

$$PMT_{36} = \$20{,}000 \times \left[\frac{0.005833}{1 - \dfrac{1}{(1 + 0.005833)^{36}}}\right] = \$20{,}000 \times 0.030877$$

$$= \$617.54$$

CALCULATOR HINTS

N = 36
I = 0.5833
PV = 20000
FV = 0
CPT PMT = −617.54

The following table shows the amortization schedule.

	A	B	C	D	E	F
1	Month	(1) Beginning Balance [(5) of Prior Month]	(2) Total Payment	(3) Interest Paid [= (1) × 7%/12]	(4) Principal Paid [= (2) − (3)]	(5) Ending Balance [= (1) − (4)]
2	1	$20,000.00	$617.54	$116.67	$500.87	$19,499.13
3	2	19,499.13	617.54	113.74	503.80	18,995.33
4	3	18,995.33	617.54	110.81	506.73	18,488.60
5	4	18,488.60	617.54	107.85	509.69	17,978.91
6	5	17,978.91	617.54	104.88	512.66	17,466.24
7	6	17,466.24	617.54	101.89	515.65	16,950.59
8	7	16,950.59	617.54	98.88	518.66	16,431.93

(continued)

	A	B	C	D	E	F
1	Month	(1) Beginning Balance [(5) of Prior Month]	(2) Total Payment	(3) Interest Paid [= (1) × 7%/12]	(4) Principal Paid [= (2) – (3)]	(5) Ending Balance [= (1) – (4)]
9	8	$16,431.93	$617.54	$95.85	$521.69	$15,910.24
10	9	15,910.24	617.54	92.81	524.73	15,385.51
11	10	15,385.51	617.54	89.75	527.79	14,857.72
12	11	14,857.72	617.54	86.67	530.87	14,326.85
13	12	14,326.85	617.54	83.57	533.97	13,792.88
14	13	13,792.88	617.54	80.46	537.08	13,255.80
15	14	13,255.80	617.54	77.33	540.21	12,715.59
16	15	12,715.59	617.54	74.17	543.37	12,172.22
17	16	12,172.22	617.54	71.00	546.54	11,625.69
18	17	11,625.69	617.54	67.82	549.72	11,075.96
19	18	11,075.96	617.54	64.61	552.93	10,523.03
20	19	10,523.03	617.54	61.38	556.16	9,966.88
21	20	9,966.88	617.54	58.14	559.40	9,407.48
22	21	9,407.48	617.54	54.88	562.66	8,844.82
23	22	8,844.82	617.54	51.59	565.95	8,278.87
24	23	8,278.87	617.54	48.29	569.25	7,709.62
25	24	7,709.62	617.54	44.97	572.57	7,137.06
26	25	7,137.06	617.54	41.63	575.91	6,561.15
27	26	6,561.15	617.54	38.27	579.27	5,981.88
28	27	5,981.88	617.54	34.89	582.65	5,399.24
29	28	5,399.24	617.54	31.50	586.04	4,813.19
30	29	4,813.19	617.54	28.08	589.46	4,223.73
31	30	4,223.73	617.54	24.64	592.90	3,630.83
32	31	3,630.83	617.54	21.18	596.36	3,034.47
33	32	3,034.47	617.54	17.70	599.84	2,434.63
34	33	2,434.63	617.54	14.20	603.34	1,831.29
35	34	1,831.29	617.54	10.68	606.86	1,224.43
36	35	1,224.43	617.54	7.14	610.40	614.04
37	36	614.04	617.62	3.58	614.04	0.00
38						
39				Year 1 Interest =	$1,203.36	
40				Year 2 Interest =	$754.65	
41				Year 3 Interest =	$273.50	

Ross and Rachel will pay $1,203.36 in interest the first year, $754.65 in the second year, and $273.50 in the third year.

questions

1. How can you add a cash flow in year 2 and a cash flow in year 4? In year 7? *(LG5-1)*
2. People can become millionaires in their retirement years quite easily if they start saving early in employer 401(k) or 403(b) programs (or even if their employers don't offer such programs). Demonstrate the growth of a $250 monthly contribution for 40 years earning 9 percent APR. *(LG5-2)*
3. When you discount multiple cash flows, how does the future period that a cash flow is paid affect its present value and its contribution to the value of all the cash flows? *(LG5-3)*
4. How can you use the present value of an annuity concept to determine the price of a house you can afford? *(LG5-4)*

5. Since perpetuity payments continue forever, how can a present value be computed? Why isn't the present value infinite? *(LG5-5)*

6. Explain why you use the same adjustment factor, $(1 + i)$, when you adjust annuity due payments for both future value and present value. *(LG5-6)*

7. Use the idea of compound interest to explain why EAR is larger than APR. *(LG5-7)*

8. Would you rather pay $10,000 for a 5-year, $2,500 annuity or a 10-year, $1,250 annuity? Why? *(LG5-8)*

9. The interest on your home mortgage is tax deductible. Why are the early years of the mortgage more helpful in reducing taxes than in the later years? *(LG5-9)*

10. How can you use the concepts illustrated in computing the number of payments in an annuity to figure how to pay off a credit card balance? How does the magnitude of the payment impact the number of months? *(LG5-10)*

problems

basic problems

5-1 Future Value Compute the future value in year 9 of a $2,000 deposit in year 1 and another $1,500 deposit at the end of year 3 using a 10 percent interest rate. *(LG5-1)*

5-2 Future Value Compute the future value in year 7 of a $2,000 deposit in year 1 and another $2,500 deposit at the end of year 4 using an 8 percent interest rate. *(LG5-1)*

5-3 Future Value of an Annuity What is the future value of a $900 annuity payment over five years if interest rates are 8 percent? *(LG5-2)*

5-4 Future Value of an Annuity What is the future value of a $700 annuity payment over six years if interest rates are 10 percent? *(LG5-2)*

5-5 Present Value Compute the present value of a $2,000 deposit in year 1 and another $1,500 deposit at the end of year 3 if interest rates are 10 percent. *(LG5-3)*

5-6 Present Value Compute the present value of a $2,000 deposit in year 1 and another $2,500 deposit at the end of year 4 using an 8 percent interest rate. *(LG5-3)*

5-7 Present Value of an Annuity What's the present value of a $900 annuity payment over five years if interest rates are 8 percent? *(LG5-4)*

5-8 Present Value of an Annuity What's the present value of a $700 annuity payment over six years if interest rates are 10 percent? *(LG5-4)*

5-9 Present Value of a Perpetuity What's the present value, when interest rates are 7.5 percent, of a $50 payment made every year forever? *(LG5-5)*

5-10 Present Value of a Perpetuity What's the present value, when interest rates are 8.5 percent, of a $75 payment made every year forever? *(LG5-5)*

5-11 **Present Value of an Annuity Due** If the present value of an ordinary, 7-year annuity is $6,500 and interest rates are 7.5 percent, what's the present value of the same annuity due? *(LG5-6)*

5-12 **Present Value of an Annuity Due** If the present value of an ordinary, 6-year annuity is $8,500 and interest rates are 9.5 percent, what's the present value of the same annuity due? *(LG5-6)*

5-13 **Future Value of an Annuity Due** If the future value of an ordinary, 7-year annuity is $6,500 and interest rates are 7.5 percent, what is the future value of the same annuity due? *(LG5-6)*

5-14 **Future Value of an Annuity Due** If the future value of an ordinary, 6-year annuity is $8,500 and interest rates are 9.5 percent, what's the future value of the same annuity due? *(LG5-6)*

5-15 **Effective Annual Rate** A loan is offered with monthly payments and a 10 percent APR. What's the loan's effective annual rate *(EAR)*? *(LG5-7)*

5-16 **Effective Annual Rate** A loan is offered with monthly payments and a 13 percent APR. What's the loan's effective annual rate *(EAR)*? *(LG5-7)*

intermediate problems

5-17 **Future Value** Given a 4 percent interest rate, compute the year 6 future value of deposits made in years 1, 2, 3, and 4 of $1,100, $1,200, $1,200, and $1,500. *(LG5-1)*

5-18 **Future Value** Given a 5 percent interest rate, compute the year 6 future value of deposits made in years 1, 2, 3, and 4 of $1,000, $1,300, $1,300, and $1,400. *(LG5-1)*

5-19 **Future Value of Multiple Annuities** Assume that you contribute $200 per month to a retirement plan for 20 years. Then you are able to increase the contribution to $300 per month for another 30 years. Given a 7 percent interest rate, what is the value of your retirement plan after the 50 years? *(LG5-2)*

5-20 **Future Value of Multiple Annuities** Assume that you contribute $150 per month to a retirement plan for 15 years. Then you are able to increase the contribution to $350 per month for the next 25 years. Given an 8 percent interest rate, what is the value of your retirement plan after the 40 years? *(LG5-2)*

5-21 **Present Value** Given a 6 percent interest rate, compute the present value of payments made in years 1, 2, 3, and 4 of $1,000, $1,200, $1,200, and $1,500. *(LG5-3)*

5-22 **Present Value** Given a 7 percent interest rate, compute the present value of payments made in years 1, 2, 3, and 4 of $1,000, $1,300, $1,300, and $1,400. *(LG5-3)*

5-23 **Present Value of Multiple Annuities** A small business owner visits her bank to ask for a loan. The owner states that she can repay a loan at $1,000 per month for the next three years and then $2,000 per month for two years after that. If the bank is charging customers 7.5 percent APR, how much would it be willing to lend the business owner? *(LG5-4)*

5-24 **Present Value of Multiple Annuities** A small business owner visits his bank to ask for a loan. The owner states that he can repay a loan at $1,500 per month for the next three years and then $500 per month for two years after that. If the bank is charging customers 8.5 percent APR, how much would it be willing to lend the business owner? *(LG5-4)*

5-25 **Present Value** You are looking to buy a car. You can afford $450 in monthly payments for four years. In addition to the loan, you can make a $1,000 down payment. If interest rates are 5 percent APR, what price of car can you afford? *(LG5-4)*

5-26 **Present Value** You are looking to buy a car. You can afford $650 in monthly payments for five years. In addition to the loan, you can make a $750 down payment. If interest rates are 8 percent APR, what price of car can you afford? *(LG5-4)*

5-27 **Present Value of a Perpetuity** A perpetuity pays $100 per year and interest rates are 7.5 percent. How much would its value change if interest rates increased to 9 percent? Did the value increase or decrease? *(LG5-5)*

5-28 **Present Value of a Perpetuity** A perpetuity pays $50 per year and interest rates are 9 percent. How much would its value change if interest rates decreased to 7.5 percent? Did the value increase or decrease? *(LG5-5)*

5-29 **Future and Present Value of an Annuity Due** If you start making $50 monthly contributions today and continue them for five years, what's their future value if the compounding rate is 10 percent APR? What is the present value of this annuity? *(LG5-6)*

5-30 **Future and Present Value of an Annuity Due** If you start making $75 monthly contributions today and continue them for four years, what is their future value if the compounding rate is 12 percent APR? What is the present value of this annuity? *(LG5-6)*

5-31 **Compound Frequency** Payday loans are very short-term loans that charge very high interest rates. You can borrow $225 today and repay $300 in two weeks. What is the compounded *annual* rate implied by this 33.33 percent rate charged for only two weeks? *(LG5-7)*

5-32 **Compound Frequency** Payday loans are very short-term loans that charge very high interest rates. You can borrow $500 today and repay $590 in two weeks. What is the compounded *annual* rate implied by this 18 percent rate charged for only two weeks? *(LG5-7)*

5-33 **Annuity Interest Rate** What's the interest rate of a 6-year, annual $5,000 annuity with present value of $20,000? *(LG5-8)*

5-34 **Annuity Interest Rate** What's the interest rate of a 7-year, annual $4,000 annuity with present value of $20,000? *(LG5-8)*

5-35 **Annuity Interest Rate** What annual interest rate would you need to earn if you wanted a $1,000 per month contribution to grow to $75,000 in six years? *(LG5-8)*

5-36 **Annuity Interest Rate** What annual interest rate would you need to earn if you wanted a $600 per month contribution to grow to $45,000 in six years? *(LG5-8)*

5-37 **Add-On Interest Payments** To borrow $500, you are offered an add-on interest loan at 8 percent. Two loan payments are to be made, one at six months and the other at the end of the year. Compute the two equal payments. *(LG5-8)*

5-38 Add-On Interest Payments To borrow $800, you are offered an add-on interest loan at 7 percent. Three loan payments are to be made, one at four months, another at eight months, and the last one at the end of the year. Compute the three equal payments. *(LG5-8)*

5-39 Loan Payments You wish to buy a $25,000 car. The dealer offers you a 4-year loan with a 9 percent APR. What are the monthly payments? How would the payment differ if you paid interest only? What would the consequences of such a decision be? *(LG5-9)*

5-40 Loan Payments You wish to buy a $10,000 dining room set. The furniture store offers you a 3-year loan with an 11 percent APR. What are the monthly payments? How would the payment differ if you paid interest only? What would the consequences of such a decision be? *(LG5-9)*

5-41 Number of Annuity Payments Joey realizes that he has charged too much on his credit card and has racked up $5,000 in debt. If he can pay $150 each month and the card charges 17 percent APR (compounded monthly), how long will it take him to pay off the debt? *(LG5-10)*

5-42 Number of Annuity Payments Phoebe realizes that she has charged too much on her credit card and has racked up $6,000 in debt. If she can pay $200 each month and the card charges 18 percent APR (compounded monthly), how long will it take her to pay off the debt? *(LG5-10)*

advanced problems

5-43 Future Value Given an 8 percent interest rate, compute the year 7 future value if deposits of $1,000 and $2,000 are made in years 1 and 3, respectively, and a withdrawal of $700 is made in year 4. *(LG5-10)*

5-44 Future Value Given a 9 percent interest rate, compute the year 6 future value if deposits of $1,500 and $2,500 are made in years 2 and 3, respectively, and a withdrawal of $600 is made in year 5. *(LG5-1)*

5-45 EAR of Add-On Interest Loan To borrow $2,000, you are offered an add-on interest loan at 10 percent with 12 monthly payments. First compute the 12 equal payments and then compute the EAR of the loan. *(LG5-7, LG5-8)*

5-46 EAR of Add-On Interest Loan To borrow $700, you are offered an add-on interest loan at 9 percent with 12 monthly payments. First compute the 12 equal payments and then compute the EAR of the loan. *(LG5-7, LG5-8)*

5-47 Low Financing or Cash Back? A car company is offering a choice of deals. You can receive $500 cash back on the purchase or a 3 percent APR, 4-year loan. The price of the car is $15,000 and you could obtain a 4-year loan from your credit union, at 6 percent APR. Which deal is cheaper? *(LG5-4, LG5-9)*

5-48 Low Financing or Cash Back? A car company is offering a choice of deals. You can receive $1,000 cash back on the purchase, or a 2 percent APR, 5-year loan. The price of the car is $20,000 and you could obtain a 5-year loan from your credit union, at 7 percent APR. Which deal is cheaper? *(LG5-4, LG5-9)*

5-49 **Amortization Schedule** Create the amortization schedule for a loan of $15,000, paid monthly over three years using a 9 percent APR. *(LG5-9)*

5-50 **Amortization Schedule** Create the amortization schedule for a loan of $5,000, paid monthly over two years using an 8 percent APR. *(LG5-9)*

5-51 **Investing for Retirement** Monica has decided that she wants to build enough retirement wealth that, if invested at 8 percent per year, will provide her with $3,500 of monthly income for 20 years. To date, she has saved nothing, but she still has 30 years until she retires. How much money does she need to contribute per month to reach her goal? *(LG5-4, LG5-9)*

5-52 **Investing for Retirement** Ross has decided that he wants to build enough retirement wealth that, if invested at 7 percent per year, will provide him with $3,000 of monthly income for 30 years. To date, he has saved nothing, but he still has 20 years until he retires. How much money does he need to contribute per month to reach his goal? *(LG5-4, LG5-9)*

5-53 **Loan Balance** Rachel purchased a $15,000 car three years ago using an 8 percent, 4-year loan. She has decided that she would sell the car now, if she could get a price that would pay off the balance of her loan. What is the minimum price Rachel would need to receive for her car? *(LG5-9)*

5-54 **Loan Balance** Hank purchased a $20,000 car two years ago using a 9 percent, 5-year loan. He has decided that he would sell the car now, if he could get a price that would pay off the balance of his loan. What's the minimum price Hank would need to receive for his car? *(LG5-9)*

5-55 **Teaser Rate Mortgage** A mortgage broker is offering a $183,900 30-year mortgage with a teaser rate. In the first two years of the mortgage, the borrower makes monthly payments on only a 4 percent APR interest rate. After the second year, the mortgage interest rate charged increases to 7 percent APR. What are the monthly payments in the first two years? What are the monthly payments after the second year? *(LG5-9)*

5-56 **Teaser Rate Mortgage** A mortgage broker is offering a $279,000 30-year mortgage with a teaser rate. In the first two years of the mortgage, the borrower makes monthly payments on only a 4.5 percent APR interest rate. After the second year, the mortgage interest rate charged increases to 7.5 percent APR. What are the monthly payments in the first two years? What are the monthly payments after the second year? *(LG5-9)*

5-57 **Spreadsheet Problem** Consider a person who begins contributing to a retirement plan at age 25 and contributes for 40 years until retirement at age 65. For the first ten years, she contributes $3,000 per year. She increases the contribution rate to $5,000 per year in years 11 through 20. This is followed by increases to $10,000 per year in years 21 through 30 and to $15,000 per year for the last ten years. This money earns a 9 percent return. First compute the value of the retirement plan when she turns age 65. Then compute the annual payment she would receive over the next 40 years if the wealth was converted to an annuity payment at 8 percent. *(LG5-2, LG5-9)*

combined chapter 4 and chapter 5 problems

4&5-1 **Future Value** Consider that you are 35 years old and have just changed to a new job. You have $80,000 in the retirement plan from your former employer. You can roll that money into the retirement plan of the new employer. You will also contribute $3,600 each year into your new employer's plan. If the rolled-over money and the new contributions both earn a 7 percent return, how much should you expect to have when you retire in 30 years?

4&5-2 **Future Value** Consider that you are 45 years old and have just changed to a new job. You have $150,000 in the retirement plan from your former employer. You can roll that money into the retirement plan of the new employer. You will also contribute $7,200 each year into your new employer's plan. If the rolled-over money and the new contributions both earn an 8 percent return, how much should you expect to have when you retire in 20 years?

4&5-3 **Future Value and Number of Annuity Payments** Your client has been given a trust fund valued at $1 million. He cannot access the money until he turns 65 years old, which is in 25 years. At that time, he can withdraw $25,000 per month. If the trust fund is invested at a 5.5 percent rate, how many months will it last your client once he starts to withdraw the money?

4&5-4 **Future Value and Number of Annuity Payments** Your client has been given a trust fund valued at $1.5 million. She cannot access the money until she turns 65 years old, which is in 15 years. At that time, she can withdraw $20,000 per month. If the trust fund is invested at a 5 percent rate, how many months will it last your client once she starts to withdraw the money?

4&5-5 **Present Value and Annuity Payments** A local furniture store is advertising a deal in which you buy a $3,000 dining room set and do not need to pay for two years (no interest cost is incurred). How much money would you have to deposit now in a savings account earning 5 percent APR, compounded monthly, to pay the $3,000 bill in two years? Alternatively, how much would you have to deposit in the savings account each month to be able to pay the bill?

4&5-6 **Present Value and Annuity Payments** A local furniture store is advertising a deal in which you buy a $5,000 living room set with three years before you need to make any payments (no interest cost is incurred). How much money would you have to deposit now in a savings account earning 4 percent APR, compounded monthly, to pay the $5,000 bill in three years? Alternatively, how much would you have to deposit in the savings account each month to be able to pay the bill?

4&5-7 **House Appreciation and Mortgage Payments** Say that you purchase a house for $200,000 by getting a mortgage for $180,000 and paying a $20,000 down payment. If you get a 30-year mortgage with a 7 percent interest rate, what are the monthly payments? What would the loan balance be in ten years? If the house appreciates at 3 percent per year, what will be the value of the house in ten years? How much of this value is your equity?

4&5-8 **House Appreciation and Mortgage Payments** Say that you purchase a house for $150,000 by getting a mortgage for $135,000 and paying a $15,000 down payment. If you get a 15-year mortgage with a 7 percent interest rate, what are the monthly payments? What would the loan balance be in five years? If the house appreciates at 4 percent per year, what will be the value of the house in five years? How much of this value is your equity?

4&5-9 **Construction Loan** You have secured a loan from your bank for two years to build your home. The terms of the loan are that you will borrow $200,000 now and an additional $100,000 in one year. Interest of 10 percent APR will be charged on the balance monthly. Since no payments will be made during the 2-year loan, the balance will grow at the 10 percent compounded rate. At the end of the two years, the balance will be converted to a traditional 30-year mortgage at a 6 percent interest rate. What will you be paying as monthly mortgage payments (principal and interest only)?

4&5-10 **Construction Loan** You have secured a loan from your bank for two years to build your home. The terms of the loan are that you will borrow $100,000 now and an additional $50,000 in one year. Interest of 9 percent APR will be charged on the balance monthly. Since no payments will be made during the 2-year loan, the balance will grow. At the end of the two years, the balance will be converted to a traditional 15-year mortgage at a 7 percent interest rate. What will you pay as monthly mortgage payments (principal and interest only)?

research it! Retirement Income Calculators

The Internet provides some excellent retirement income calculators. You can find one by Googling "retirement income calculator." Many of the calculators allow you to determine your predicted annual income from a retirement nest egg under different assumptions. For example, you can spend only the investment income generated from the nest egg. Most retirees try not to touch the principal. Or, you can spend both the income and the nest egg itself. These calculators let you input the size of the retirement wealth and the investment return to be earned. They then make time value computations to determine the annual income the nest egg will provide.

Go to a retirement income calculator like the one at MSN Money. Use the calculator to create a retirement scenario. Use the TVM equations or a financial calculator to check the Internet results.
(http://money.msn.com/retirement/retirement-calculator.aspx)

integrated mini-case Paying on your Stafford Loan

Consider Gavin, a new freshman who has just received a Stafford student loan and started college. He plans to obtain the maximum loan from Stafford at the beginning of each year. Although Gavin does not have to make any payments while he is in school, the (unsubsidized) 6.8 percent interest owed (compounded monthly) accrues and is added to the balance of the loan. After graduation, Gavin gets a 6-month grace period. This means that monthly payments are still not required, but interest is still accruing. After the grace period, the standard repayment plan is to amortize the debt using monthly payments for ten years.

a. Show a time line of when the loans will be taken.

Unsubsidized Stafford Loan Limits	
Freshman	$6,000
Sophomore	6,000
Junior	7,000
Senior	7,000

b. What will be the loan balance when Gavin graduates after his fourth year of school?

c. What is the loan balance six months after graduation?

d. Using the standard repayment plan and a 6.8 percent APR interest rate, compute the monthly payments Gavin owes after the grace period.

ANSWERS TO TIME OUT

5-1 Compounding allows for the earning of interest on the interest that was earned earlier in time. When this occurs more often, more money will be built. So, the greater the compounding frequency, the higher the future value of the annuity.

5-2 You can solve this several ways. First, you can use one annuity of $4,500 for the entire period. Then use a second annuity of $4,500 starting in year 19 and continuing to the end. The future value of this second annuity would be subtracted from the first annuity. Last, add a third annuity of $4,500 starting in year 23. Another way to solve this problem is to start with the $4,500 annuity for the entire period. Then subtract the future values of each of the four individual nonpayments of $4,500.

5-3 The magnitude of the discount rate is very important in the present value computation. The longer the discount period, the more important the interest rate magnitude becomes. No, higher interest rates lead to lower present values.

5-4 The present value of the annuity at 7 percent is $20,323. In this case, the fee of $20,000 appears cheaper.

5-5 Annuity due is good to use in cases where one of the annuity payments is made immediately instead of waiting to the end of the period (year, month, etc.).

5-6 It is easy to switch from the regular annuity future value to the future value of this annuity due. You simply multiply the future value previously found by (1 + i).

5-7 The APR is an easy number to compute and understand, but it does not account for the extra money paid because of compounding. EAR is more difficult to compute, but does incorporate the compounding effect.

5-8 If both discounting examples have the same APR, then the one discounted monthly will result in a smaller present value. This is because it will have a higher EAR.

5-9 Credit card companies allow a small minimum payment each month. This small payment is often mostly interest and entails little principal. Therefore, the cardholder does not pay down very much of the debt and remains in debt for a long time. If the minimum payment is only interest, then the debt will never be paid off.

5-10 If you know the annuity payments, the future value, and the number of payments, then you can determine the implied interest rate. You should solve for the interest rate using a financial calculator as it is quite difficult using the TVM equations.

PART FOUR

6 Understanding Financial Markets and Institutions*

viewpoints

Business Application

DPH Corporation needs to issue new bonds either this year or in two years. DPH Corp. is a profitable firm, but if the U.S. economy were to experience a downturn, the company would see a big drop in sales over the next two years as its products are very sensitive to changes in the overall economy. DPH Corp. currently has $10 million in public debt outstanding, but its bonds are not actively traded. What questions must DPH Corp. consider as its managers decide whether to issue bonds today or in two years? How can DPH Corp. get these bonds to potential buyers and thus raise the needed capital? **(See solution on p. 218)**

Personal Application

John Adams wants to invest in one of two corporate bonds issued by separate firms. One bond yields 8.00 percent with a 10-year maturity; the other offers a 10.00 percent yield and a 9-year maturity. The second bond *seems* to be the better deal. Is it necessarily the bond in which John should invest? Once he decides which bond represents the better investment, how can John go about buying the bond? **(See solution on p. 218)**

Should John consider bonds from other countries?

*See Appendix 6A: The Financial Crisis: The Failure of Financial Institution Specialness online at **www.mhhe.com/can3e**.

How do funds flow throughout the economy? How do financial markets operate and relate to one another? As an individual investor or a financial manager you need to know. Your future decision-making skills depend on it. Investors' funds flow through financial markets such as the New York Stock Exchange and mortgage markets. Financial institutions—commercial banks (e.g., Bank of America), investment banks (e.g., Morgan Stanley), and mutual funds (e.g., Fidelity)—act as intermediaries to channel funds from individual savers or investors through financial markets. This chapter looks at the nature and operations of financial markets and discusses the financial institutions (FIs) that participate in those markets. Bonds, stocks, and other securities that trade in the markets are covered in Chapters 7 and 8.

In this chapter we also examine how significant changes in the way financial institutions deliver services played a major role in forming the severe financial crisis that began in late 2008. We examine some of the crisis's underlying causes, review some of the major events that occurred during that time, and discuss some resulting regulatory and industry changes that are in effect today in Appendix 6A, which is located on the book's website (www.mhhe.com/can3e).

Learning Goals

- **LG6-1** Differentiate between primary and secondary markets and between money and capital markets.
- **LG6-2** List the types of securities traded in money and capital markets.
- **LG6-3** Identify different types of financial institutions and the services that each provides.
- **LG6-4** Analyze specific factors that influence interest rates.
- **LG6-5** Offer different theories that explain the shape of the term structure of interest rates.
- **LG6-6** Demonstrate how forward interest rates derive from the term structure of interest rates.

6.1 • Financial Markets

Financial markets exist to manage the flow of funds from investors to borrowers as well as from one investor to another. We generally differentiate financial markets by their primary financial instruments' characteristics (such as bond maturities) or the market's location. Specifically, we can distinguish markets along two major dimensions:

- Primary versus secondary markets.
- Money versus capital markets.

LG6-1

Primary Markets versus Secondary Markets

financial markets

The arenas through which funds flow.

primary markets

Markets in which corporations raise funds through new issues of securities.

investment banks

Financial institutions that arrange primary market transactions for businesses.

Primary markets provide a forum in which demanders of funds (e.g., corporations such as IBM or government entities such as the U.S. Treasury) raise funds by issuing new financial instruments, such as stocks and bonds. Corporations or government entities continually have new projects or expanded production needs, but do not have sufficient internally generated funds (such as retained earnings) to support their capital needs. Thus, corporations and governments issue securities in external primary markets to raise additional funds. These entities sell the new financial instrument issues to initial fund suppliers (e.g., households) in exchange for the funds (money) that the issuer requires.

In the United States, financial institutions called **investment banks** arrange most primary market transactions for businesses. Some of the best-known examples of U.S. investment banks include Morgan Stanley, Goldman Sachs, or Merrill Lynch (owned by Bank of America, a commercial bank). These firms intermediate between issuing parties (fund demanders) and investors (fund suppliers). Investment banks provide fund demanders with a number of services, including advising the company or government agency about the securities issue (such as an appropriate offer price and number of securities to issue) and attracting initial public purchasers of the customer's securities offerings. Firms that need funds are seldom expert at raising capital themselves, so they avert risk and lower their costs by turning to experts at investment banks to issue their primary market securities.

The initial (or primary market) sale of securities occurs either through a public offering or as a private placement to a small group of investors. An investment bank serves as a security underwriter in a public offering. In a private placement, the security issuer engages the group of buyers (usually fewer than 10) to purchase the whole issue. Buyers are typically financial institutions. To protect smaller individual investors against a lack of disclosure, publicly traded securities must be registered with the Securities and Exchange Commission (SEC). Private placements, on the other hand, can be unregistered and resold to large, financially sophisticated investors only. Large investors supposedly possess the resources and expertise to analyze a security's risk. Privately placed bonds and stocks traditionally have been among the most illiquid securities in the securities markets; only the very largest financial institutions or institutional investors are able or willing to buy and hold them in the absence of an active secondary market. Issuers of privately placed securities tend to be less well known (e.g., medium-sized municipalities and corporations). Because of this lack of information and its associated higher risk, returns paid to holders of privately placed securities tend to be higher than those on publicly placed securities issues.

Figure 6.1 illustrates a time line for the primary market exchange of funds for a new issue of corporate bonds or equity. We will further discuss how companies, the U.S. Treasury, and government agencies that market primary government securities, such as Ginnie Mae and Freddie Mac, go about selling primary market securities in Chapter 8. Throughout this text, we focus on government securities from the *buyer's,* rather than the seller's, point of view. You can find in-depth discussions of government securities from the sellers' point of view in a public finance text.

initial public offerings (IPOs)

The first public issue of financial instruments by a firm.

Primary market financial instruments include stock issues from firms initially going public (e.g., allowing their equity shares to be publicly traded on stock markets for the first time). We usually refer to these first-time issues as **initial public offerings (IPOs)**. For example, on May 17, 2012, Facebook announced a $16 billion IPO of its common stock. Facebook used several investment banks, including

figure 6.1

Primary Market Transfer of Funds

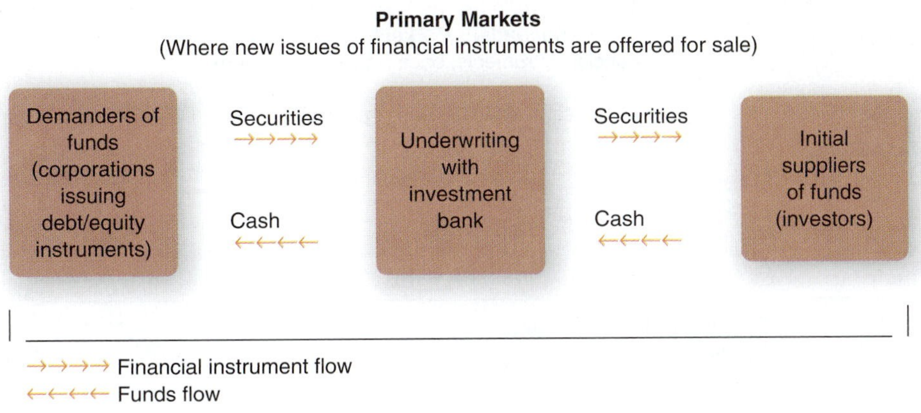

Morgan Stanley, JPMorgan, and Goldman Sachs, to underwrite the company's stock. Publicly traded firms may issue additional bonds or stocks as primary market securities. For example, on June 5, 2012, Dollar General announced that it would sell an additional 30 million shares of common stock (at $46.75 per share) underwritten by investment banks such as Citigroup, Goldman Sachs, KKR, Barclays, and JPMorgan. These funds augmented Dollar General's existing capital (equity) of $4,591 million.

SECONDARY MARKETS Once firms issue financial instruments in primary markets, these same stocks and bonds are then traded—that is, bought and resold—in **secondary markets**. The New York Stock Exchange (NYSE) and the NASDAQ are two well-known examples of secondary markets for trading stocks (see Chapters 7 and 8). In addition to stocks and bonds, secondary markets also exist for financial instruments backed by mortgages and other assets, foreign exchange, and futures and options (i.e., derivative securities, discussed later in the chapter).

secondary markets

Markets that trade financial instruments once they are issued.

Buyers find sellers of secondary market securities in economic agents that need funds (fund demanders). Secondary markets provide a centralized marketplace where economic agents know that they can buy or sell most securities quickly and efficiently. Secondary markets, therefore, save economic agents the search costs of finding buyers or sellers on their own. Figure 6.2 illustrates a secondary market transfer of funds. Secondary market buyers often use securities brokers such as Charles Schwab or other brokerage firms to act as intermediaries as they exchange funds for securities (see Chapter 8). An important note: The firm that originally issued the stock or bond is not involved in secondary market transactions in any way—no money accrues to the company itself when its stock trades in a secondary market.

Secondary markets offer benefits to both investors (fund suppliers) and issuers (fund demanders). Investors gain liquidity and diversification benefits (see Chapter 10). Although corporate security issuers are not directly involved in secondary market transactions, issuers do gain information about their securities' current market value. Publicly traded firms can thus observe how investors perceive their corporate value and their corporate decisions by tracking their firms' securities' secondary market prices. Such price information allows issuers to evaluate how well they are using internal funds as well as the funds

figure 6.2

Secondary Market Transfer of Funds

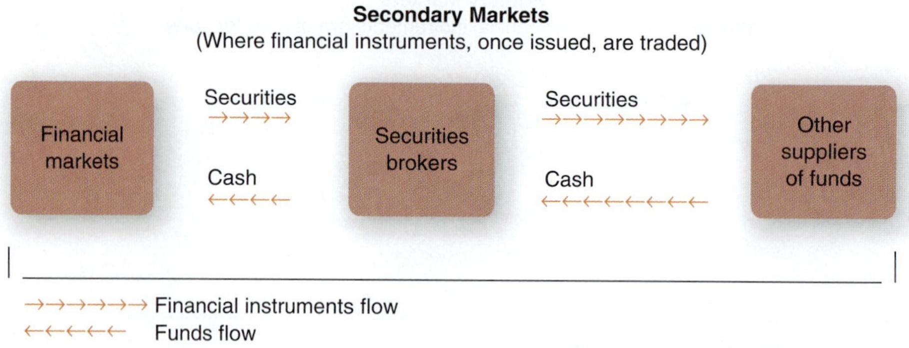

generated from previously issued stocks and bonds and provides indications about how well any subsequent bond or stock offerings might be received—and at what price.

trading volume

The number of shares of a security that are simultaneously bought and sold during a period.

Secondary market **trading volume** can be quite large. Trading volume is defined as the number of shares of a security that are simultaneously bought and sold during a given period. Each seller and each buyer actually contract with the exchange's clearinghouse, which then matches sell and buy orders for each transaction. The clearinghouse is a company whose stock trades on the exchange, and the clearinghouse runs on a for-profit basis.

The exchange and the clearinghouse can process many transactions in a single day. For example, on October 28, 1997, NYSE trading volume exceeded 1 billion shares for the first time ever. On October 10, 2008 (at the height of the financial crisis), NYSE trading volume topped 7.3 billion shares, the highest level to date. In contrast, during the mid-1980s, a NYSE trading day during which 250 million shares traded was considered a high-volume day.

LG6-1

Money Markets versus Capital Markets

We noted that financial markets are differentiated in part by the maturity dates of the instruments traded. This distinction becomes important when we differentiate money markets from capital markets. Both of these markets deal in debt securities (capital markets also deal in equity securities); the question becomes one of when the securities come due.

money markets

Markets that trade debt securities or instruments with maturities of less than one year.

over-the-counter market

Markets that do not operate in a specific fixed location—rather, transactions occur via telephones, wire transfers, and computer trading.

MONEY MARKETS **Money markets** feature debt securities or instruments with maturities of one year or less (see Figure 6.3). In money markets, agents with excess short-term funds can lend (or supply) to economic agents who need (or demand) short-term funds. The suppliers of funds buy money market instruments and the demanders of funds sell money market instruments. Because money market instruments trade for only short periods of time, fluctuations in secondary-market prices are usually quite small. With less volatility, money market securities are thus less risky than longer-term instruments. In the United States, many money market securities do not trade in a specific location; rather, transactions occur via telephones, wire transfers, and computer trading. Thus, most U.S. money markets are said to be **over-the-counter (OTC) markets**.

figure 6.3

Money versus Capital Market Maturities

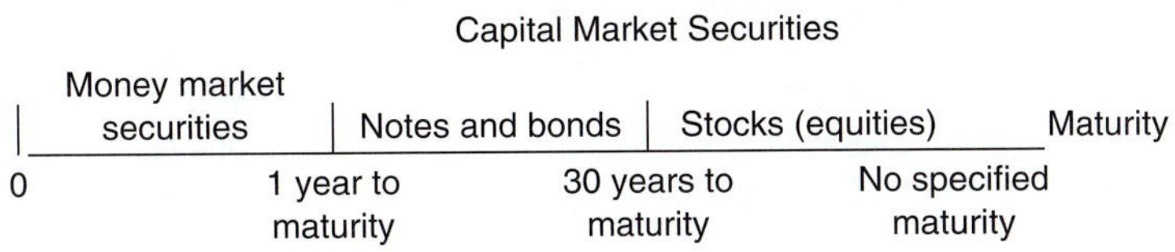

table 6.1 | Money Market Instruments

Treasury bills: Short-term U.S. government obligations.

Federal funds: Short-term funds transferred between financial institutions, usually for no more than one day.

Repurchase agreements (repos): Agreements involving security sales by one party to another, with the promise to reverse the transaction at a specified date and price, usually at a discounted price.

Commercial paper: Short-term unsecured promissory notes that companies issue to raise short-term cash (sometimes called Paper).

Negotiable certificates of deposit: Bank-issued time deposits that specify an interest rate and maturity date and are negotiable—that is, traded on an exchange. Their face value is usually at least $100,000.

Banker acceptances (BAs): Bank-guaranteed time drafts payable to a vendor of goods.

MONEY MARKET INSTRUMENTS Corporations and government entities issue a variety of money market securities to obtain short-term funds. These securities include:

LG6-2

- Treasury bills.
- Federal funds and repurchase agreements.
- Commercial paper.
- Negotiable certificates of deposit.
- Banker's acceptances.

Table 6.1 lists and defines each money market security. Figure 6.4 graphically depicts the proportion of U.S. money market instruments outstanding across three decades. Notice that, in 2013, Treasury bills commanded the highest dollar value of all money market instruments, followed by negotiable CDs, federal funds and repurchase agreements, and commercial paper.

capital markets

Markets that trade debt (bonds) and equity (stock) instruments with maturities of more than one year.

CAPITAL MARKETS **Capital markets** are markets in which parties trade equity (stocks) and debt (bonds) instruments that mature in more than one year (see Figure 6.3). Given their longer maturities, capital market instruments are subject to wider price fluctuations than are money market instruments (see the term structure discussion below and in Chapter 7).

LG6-1

CAPITAL MARKET INSTRUMENTS Capital market securities include:

LG6-2

- U.S. Treasury notes and bonds.
- U.S. government agency bonds.
- State and local government bonds.
- Mortgages and mortgage-backed securities.
- Corporate bonds.
- Corporate stocks.

figure 6.4 Money Market Instruments Outstanding

Here we see how the percentage of each money market instrument traded changes across three decades.

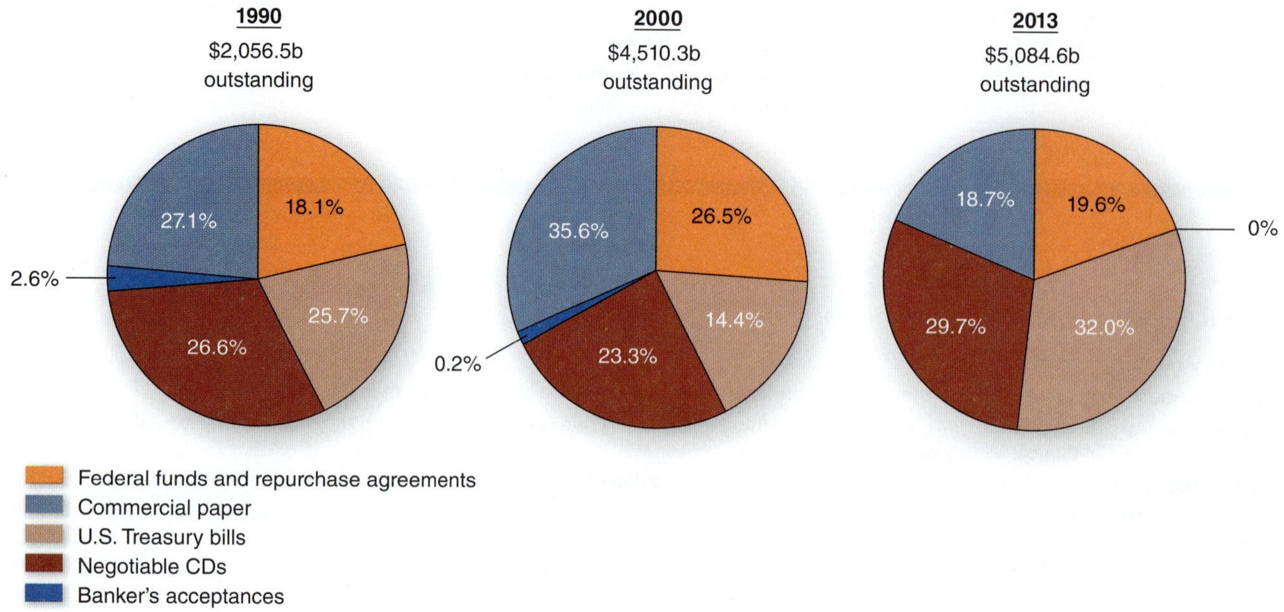

Source: Federal Reserve Board, "Flow of Fund Accounts," *Statistical Releases,* Washington, DC, various issues. www.federalreserve.gov

table 6.2 Capital Market Instruments

Treasury notes and bonds: U.S. Treasury long-term obligations issued to finance the national debt and pay for other federal government expenditures.

U.S. government agency bonds: Long-term debt securities collateralized by a pool of assets and insured by agencies of the U.S. government.

State and local government bonds: Debt securities issued by state and local (e.g., county, city, school) governments, usually to cover capital (long-term) improvements.

Mortgages: Long-term loans issued to individuals or businesses to purchase homes, pieces of land, or other real property.

Mortgage-backed securities: Long-term debt securities that offer expected principal and interest payments as collateral. These securities, made up of many mortgages, are gathered into a pool and are thus "backed" by promised principal and interest cash flows.

Corporate bonds: Long-term debt securities issued by corporations.

Corporate stocks: Long-term equity securities issued by public corporations; stock shares represent fundamental corporate ownership claims.

Table 6.2 lists and defines each capital market security. Figure 6.5 graphically depicts U.S. capital market instruments outstanding over three decades. Note that corporate stocks (equities) represent the largest capital market instrument, followed by mortgages and mortgage-backed securities and then corporate bonds. The relative size of capital markets depends on two factors: the number of securities issued and their market prices. The 1990s saw consistently rising bull markets; hence the sharp increase in equities' dollar value outstanding. Stock values fell in the early 2000s as the U.S. economy experienced a downturn—partly because of 9/11 and partly because interest rates began to rise—and stock prices fell. Stock prices in most sectors subsequently recovered and, by 2007, even surpassed their 1999 levels. Stock prices fell precipitously during the financial crisis of 2008 and 2009. As of mid-March 2009, the Dow Jones Industrial Average (DJIA) had fallen in value 53.8 percent in less than 1½ year's time. This was greater than the decline during the market crash of 1937 and 1938, when it fell 49 percent. However, stock prices recovered along with the economy in the last

figure 6.5 Capital Market Instruments Outstanding

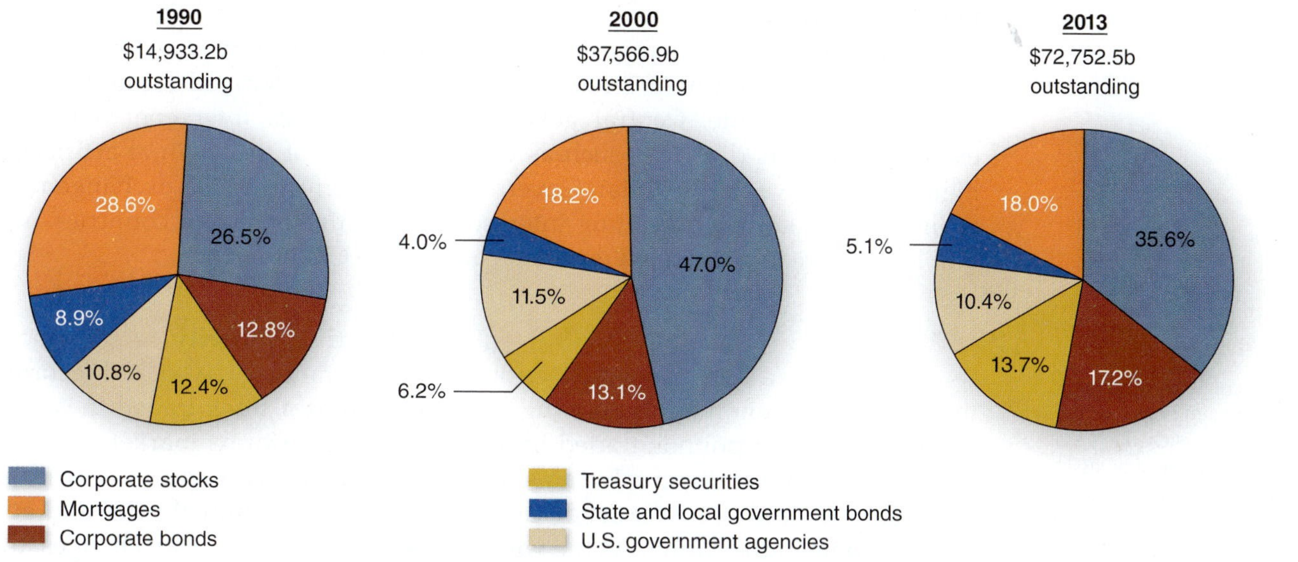

Source: Federal Reserve Board, "Flow of Fund Accounts," *Statistical Releases*, Washington, DC, various issues. www.federalreserve.gov

half of 2009 and first half of 2010, rising 71.1 percent between March 2009 and April 2010. However, it took until March 5, 2013 for the DJIA to surpass its pre-crisis high of 14,164.53, closing at 14,253.77 for the day.

Other Markets

FOREIGN EXCHANGE MARKETS Today, most U.S.-based companies operate globally. Competent financial managers understand how events and movements in financial markets in other countries can potentially affect their own companies' profitability and performance. For example, in 2012, IBM experienced a drop in revenue of 3 percent due to foreign exchange trends. Coca-Cola, which gets the majority of its sales from outside the United States, also saw revenues decrease by approximately 5 percent as the U.S. dollar strengthened relative to foreign currencies.

Foreign exchange markets trade currencies for immediate (also called "spot") or some future stated delivery. When a U.S. corporation sells securities or goods overseas, the resulting cash flows denominated in a foreign currency expose the firm to **foreign exchange risk**. This risk arises from the unknown value at which foreign currency cash flows can be converted into U.S. dollars. Foreign currency exchange rates vary day to day with worldwide demand and supply of foreign currency and U.S. dollars. Investors who deal in foreign-denominated securities face the same risk.

foreign exchange markets
Markets in which foreign currency is traded for immediate or future delivery.

foreign exchange risk
Risk arising from the unknown value at which foreign currency cash flows can be converted into U.S. dollars.

The actual number of U.S. dollars that a firm receives on a foreign investment depends on the exchange rate between the U.S. dollar and the foreign currency just as much as it does on the investment's performance. Firms will have to convert the foreign currency into U.S. dollars at the prevailing exchange rate. If the foreign currency depreciates (falls in value) relative to the U.S. dollar (say from 0.1679 dollar per unit of foreign currency to 0.1550 dollar per unit of foreign currency) over the investment period (i.e., the period between when a foreign investment is made and the time it comes to fruition), the dollar value of cash flows received will fall. If the foreign currency appreciates, or rises in value, relative to the U.S. dollar, the dollar value of cash flows received from the foreign investment will increase.

Foreign currency exchange rates are variable. They vary day to day with demand for and supply of foreign currency and with demand for and supply of dollars worldwide. Central governments sometimes intervene in foreign exchange markets directly—such as China's valuing of the yuan at artificially high rates relative to the dollar. Governments also affect foreign exchange rates indirectly by altering prevailing interest rates within their own countries. You will learn more about foreign exchange markets in Chapter 19.

derivative security

A security formalizing an agreement between two parties to exchange a standard quantity of an asset at a predetermined price on a specified date in the future.

DERIVATIVE SECURITIES MARKETS A **derivative security** is a financial security (such as a futures contract, option contract, or mortgage-backed security) that is linked to another, underlying security, such as a stock traded in capital markets or British pounds traded in foreign exchange (forex) markets. Derivative securities generally involve an agreement between two parties to exchange a standard quantity of an asset or cash flow at a predetermined price and at a specified date in the future. As the value of the underlying security changes, the value of the derivative security changes.

While derivative security contracts, especially for physical commodities like corn or gold, have existed for centuries, derivative securities markets grew increasingly popular in the 1970s, 1980s, and 1990s as traders, firms, and academics figured out how to spread risk for more and more underlying commodities and securities by using derivative contracts. Derivative contracts generally feature a high degree of leverage; that is, the investor only has to put up a very small portion of the underlying commodity or security's value to affect or control the underlying commodity or security.

Derivative securities traders can be either users of derivative contracts (for hedging and other purposes) or dealers (such as banks) that act as counterparties in customer trades for fees. An example of hedging involves commodities such as corn, wheat, or soybeans. For example, suppose you run a flour mill and will need to buy either soft wheat (Chicago) or hard red winter wheat (Kansas City) in the future. If you are concerned that the price of wheat will rise, you might lock in a price today to meet your needs six months from now by buying wheat futures on a commodities exchange. If you are correct and wheat prices rise over the six months, you may purchase the wheat by closing out your futures positions, buying the wheat at the futures price rather than the higher market price. Likewise, if you know that you will be delivering a large shipment to, say, Europe, in three months, you might take an offsetting position in euro futures contracts to lock in the exchange rate between the dollar and the euro as it stands today—and (you hope) eliminate foreign exchange risk from the transaction.

Derivative securities markets are the newest—and potentially the riskiest—of the financial security markets. Losses associated with off-balance-sheet mortgage-backed securities created and held by FIs were at the very heart of the financial crisis. Signs of significant problems in the U.S. economy first appeared in late 2006 and early 2007 when home prices plummeted and defaults began to affect the mortgage lending industry as a whole, as well as other parts of the economy noticeably. Mortgage delinquencies, particularly on subprime mortgages, surged in the last quarter of 2006 through 2008 as homeowners who had stretched themselves to buy or refinance a home in the early 2000s fell behind on their loan payments. As mortgage borrowers defaulted, the financial institutions that held their mortgages and credit derivative securities (in the form of mortgage-backed securities) started announcing huge losses on them. These losses reached $700 billion worldwide by early 2009. The situation resulted in the finance at work | markets

JP MORGAN'S $2 BILLION BLUNDER

A massive trading bet boomeranged on JPMorgan Chase & Co., leaving the bank with at least $2 billion in trading losses and its chief executive, Jamie Dimon, with a rare black eye following a long run as what some called the "King of Wall Street." The losses stemmed from wagers gone wrong in the bank's Chief Investment Office, which manages risk for the New York company . . . Large positions taken in that office by a trader nicknamed "the London whale" had roiled a sector of the debt markets. The bank, betting on a continued economic recovery with a complex web of trades tied to the values of corporate bonds, was hit hard when prices moved against it starting last month, causing losses in many of its derivative positions. The losses occurred while JPMorgan tried to scale back the trade.

The bank's strategy was "flawed, complex, poorly reviewed, poorly executed, and poorly monitored," Mr. Dimon said Thursday in a hastily arranged conference call with analysts and investors after the stock-market close. He called the mistake "egregious, self-inflicted," and said: "We will admit it, we will fix it and move on." . . . JPMorgan, the nation's largest bank by assets, said in its quarterly filing with regulators Thursday that the plan it has been using to hedge risks "has proven to be riskier, more volatile, and less effective as an economic hedge than the firm previously believed." . . . Mr. Dimon said the trading losses were "slightly more" than $2 billion so far in the second quarter . . . The *Journal* reported in April that hedge funds and other investors were making bets in the market for insurance-like products called credit-default swaps, or CDS, to try to take advantage of trades done by a London-based trader named Bruno Michel Iksil who worked out of the Chief Investment Office, or CIO . . . On Thursday he admitted the bank acted "defensively" when news reports surfaced. "With hindsight we should have been paying more attention to it," he said. "This not how we want to run a business."

The CIO group once had a large trade designed to protect the company from a downturn in the economy. Earlier this year, it began reducing that position and taking a bullish stance on the financial health of certain companies and selling protection that would compensate buyers if those companies defaulted on debts. Mr. Iksil was a heavy seller of CDS contracts tied to a basket, or index, of companies. In April the cost of protection began to rise, contributing to the losses. Mr. Iksil's group had roughly $350 billion of investment securities at December 31, according to company filings, or about 15 percent of the bank's total assets . . . Mr. Dimon said the bank has an extensive review underway of what went wrong, which he said included "many errors," "sloppiness," and "bad judgment."

Source: Dan Fitzpatrick, Gregory Zuckerman, and Liz Rappaport, "J.P. Morgan's $2 Billion Blunder," *The Wall Street Journal Online,* May 11, 2012. Used with permission of Dow Jones & Company, Inc. via Copyright Clearance Center, Inc.

! want to know more? **Key Words to Search for Updates:** JPMorgan, London whale, derivative trading losses

failure, acquisition, or bailout of some of the largest FIs and a near meltdown of the world's financial and economic systems. More recently, the Finance at Work box above highlights huge losses experienced by JPMorgan Chase from positions in the derivative securities markets.

TIME OUT

6-1 How do primary and secondary markets differ?

6-2 What are foreign exchange markets?

6-3 What are derivatives securities?

6.2 • Financial Institutions

LG6-3

financial institutions Institutions that perform the essential function of channeling funds from those with surplus funds to those with shortages of funds.

Financial institutions (e.g., banks, thrifts, insurance companies, mutual funds) perform vital functions to securities markets of all sorts. They channel funds from those with surplus funds (suppliers of funds) to those with shortages of funds (demanders of funds). In other words, FIs operate financial markets. FIs allow financial markets to function by providing the least costly and most efficient way to channel funds to and from these markets. FIs play a second crucial role by spreading risk among market participants. This risk-spreading function is vital to entrepreneurial efforts, for few firms or individuals could afford the risk of launching an expensive new product or process by themselves. Individual investors take on pieces of the risk by buying shares in risky enterprises. Investors then mitigate their own risks by diversifying their holdings into appropriate portfolios, which we cover in Chapters 9 and 10. Table 6.3 lists and summarizes the various types of FIs.

To understand just how important FIs are to the efficient operation of financial markets, imagine a simple world in which FIs did not exist. In such a world, suppliers of funds (e.g., households), generating excess savings by consuming less than they earn, would have a basic choice. They could either hold cash as an asset or invest that cash in the securities issued by users of funds (e.g., corporations, governments, or retail borrowers). In general, demanders (users) of funds issue financial claims (e.g., equity and debt securities) to finance the gap between their investment expenditures and their internally generated savings, such as retained earnings or tax funds. As shown in Figure 6.6, in a world without financial institutions, we would have **direct transfers** of funds from fund suppliers to fund users. In return, financial claims would flow directly from fund users to fund suppliers.

direct transfer

The process used when a corporation sells its stock or debt directly to investors without going through a financial institution.

In this economy without FIs, the amount of funds flowing between fund suppliers and fund users through financial markets would likely be quite low for several reasons:

- Once they have lent money in exchange for financial claims, fund suppliers would need to continually monitor the use of their funds. Fund suppliers must ensure that fund users neither steal the funds outright nor waste the funds on projects that have low or negative returns, since either theft or waste would lower fund suppliers' chances of being repaid and/or earning a positive return on their investments (such as through the receipt of dividends or interest). Monitoring against theft, misuse, or underuse of their funds would cost any given fund supplier a lot of time and effort, and of course each fund supplier, regardless of the dollar value of the investment, would have to carry out the same costly and time-consuming process. Further, many investors do not have the financial training to understand the necessary business information to assess whether a securities issuer is making the best use of their funds. In fact, so many

table 6.3 | **Types of Financial Institutions**

Commercial banks: Depository institutions whose major assets are loans and whose major liabilities are deposits. Commercial bank loans cover a broader range, including consumer, commercial, and real estate loans, than do loans from other depository institutions. Because they are larger and more likely to have access to public securities markets, commercial bank liabilities generally include more nondeposit sources of funds than do those of other depository institutions.

Thrifts: Depository institutions including savings associations, savings banks, and credit unions. Thrifts generally perform services similar to commercial banks, but they tend to concentrate their loans in one segment, such as real estate loans or consumer loans. Credit unions operate on a not-for-profit basis for particular groups of individuals, such as a labor union or a particular company's employees.

Insurance companies: Protect individuals and corporations (policyholders) from financially adverse events. Life insurance companies provide protection in the event of untimely death or illness, and help in planning retirement. Property casualty insurance protects against personal injury and liability due to accidents, theft, fire, and so on.

Securities firms and investment banks: Underwrite securities and engage in related activities such as securities brokerage, securities trading, and making markets in which securities trade.

Finance companies: Make loans to both individuals and businesses. Unlike depository institutions, finance companies do not accept deposits, but instead rely on short- and long-term debt for funding, and many of their loans are collateralized with some kind of durable good, such as washer/dryers, furniture, carpets, and the like.

Mutual funds: Pool many individuals' and companies' financial resources and invest those resources in diversified asset portfolios.

Pension funds: Offer savings plans through which fund participants accumulate savings during their working years. Participants then withdraw their pension resources (which have presumably earned additional returns in the interim) during their retirement years. Funds originally invested in and accumulated in a pension fund are exempt from current taxation. Participants pay taxes on distributions taken after age 55, when their tax brackets are (presumably) lower.

figure 6.6

Flow of Funds in a World without FIs

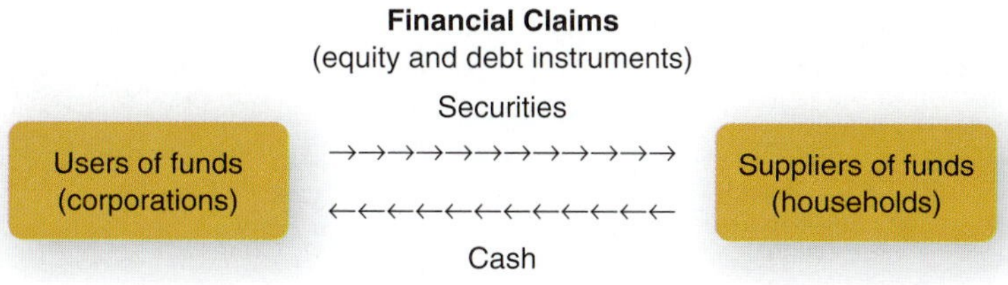

investment opportunities are available to fund suppliers, that even those trained in financial analysis rarely have the time to monitor how their funds are used in all of their investments. The resulting lack of monitoring increases the risk of directly investing in financial claims. Given these challenges, fund suppliers would likely prefer to delegate the task of monitoring fund borrowers to ensure good performance to others.

- Many financial claims feature a long-term commitment (e.g., mortgages, corporate stock, and bonds) for fund suppliers, but suppliers may not wish to hold these instruments directly. Specifically, given the choice between holding cash or long-term securities, fund suppliers may choose to hold cash for its **liquidity**. This is especially true if the suppliers plan to use their savings to finance consumption expenditures before their creditors expect to repay them. Fund suppliers may also fear that they will not find anyone to purchase their financial claim and free up their funds. When financial markets are not very developed, or deep, in terms of the number of active buyers and sellers in the market, such liquidity concerns arise.
- Even though real-world financial markets provide some liquidity services by allowing fund suppliers to trade financial securities among themselves, fund suppliers face **price risk** when they buy securities—fund suppliers may not get their principal back, let alone any return on their investment. Trading securities on secondary markets involves various transaction costs. The price at which investors can sell a security on secondary markets such as the New York Stock Exchange (NYSE) or NASDAQ may well differ from the price they initially paid for the security. The investment community as a whole may change the security's valuation between the time the fund supplier bought it and the time the fund supplier sold it. Also, dealers, acting as intermediaries between buyers and sellers, charge transaction costs for completing a trade. So even if an investor bought a security and then sold it the next day, the investor would likely lose money from transaction and other costs.

liquidity
The ease with which an asset can be converted into cash.

price risk
The risk that an asset's sale price will be lower than its purchase price.

Unique Economic Functions Performed by Financial Institutions

LG6-3

Because of (1) monitoring costs, (2) liquidity costs, and (3) price risk, most average investors may well view direct investment in financial claims and markets as an unattractive proposition and, as fund suppliers, they will likely prefer to hold cash. As a result, financial market activity (and therefore savings and investment) would likely remain quite low. However, the financial system has developed an alternative, indirect way for investors (or fund suppliers) to channel funds to users of funds: financial intermediaries **indirectly transfer** funds to ultimate

indirect transfer
A transfer of funds between suppliers and users of funds through a financial institution.

figure 6.7

Flow of Funds in a World with FIs

Financial institutions stand between fund suppliers and users.

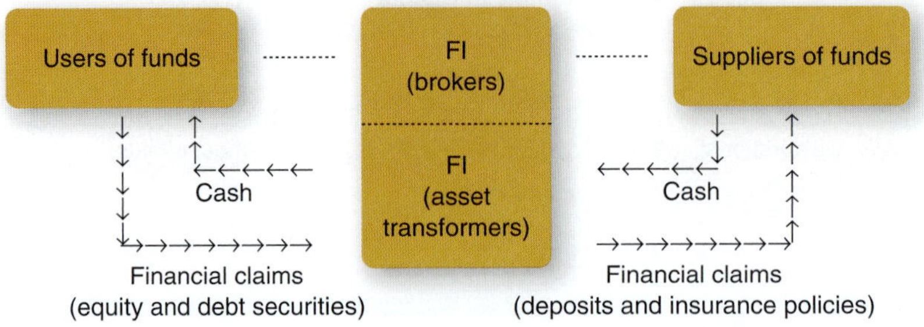

fund users. Because of monitoring, liquidity risk, and price risk costs, fund suppliers often prefer to hold financial intermediaries' financial claims rather than those directly issued by the ultimate fund users. Consider Figure 6.7, which more closely represents the way that funds flow in the U.S. financial system than does Figure 6.6. Notice how financial institutions stand—or intermediate—between fund suppliers and fund users. That is, FIs channel funds from ultimate suppliers to ultimate fund users. Fund suppliers and users use these FIs to channel funds because of financial intermediaries' unique ability to measure and manage risk, and thus reduce monitoring costs, liquidity costs, and price risk.

MONITORING COSTS As we noted above, a fund suppler who directly invests in a fund user's financial claims faces a high cost of comprehensively monitoring the fund user's actions in a timely way. One solution to this problem is that a large number of small investors can group their funds together by holding claims issued by an FI. In turn, the FI will invest in direct financial claims that fund users issue. Financial institutions' aggregation of funds from fund suppliers resolves a number of problems:

- First, large FIs now have much greater incentive to collect information and monitor the ultimate fund user's actions, because the FI has far more at stake than any small individual fund supplier would have.
- Second, the FI performs the necessary monitoring function via its own internal experts. In an economic sense, fund suppliers appoint the FI as a **delegated monitor** to act on their behalf. For example, full-service securities firms such as Bank of America Merrill Lynch carry out investment research on new issues and make investment recommendations for their retail clients (investors), while commercial banks collect deposits from fund suppliers and lend these funds to ultimate users, such as corporations. An important part of these FIs' functions is their ability and incentive to monitor ultimate fund users.

delegated monitor
An economic agent appointed to act on behalf of smaller investors in collecting information and/or investing funds on their behalf.

asset transformer
Service provided by financial institutions in which financial claims issued by an FI are more attractive to investors than are the claims directly issued by corporations.

secondary securities
Packages or pools of primary claims.

LIQUIDITY AND PRICE RISK In addition to providing more and better information about fund users' activities, financial intermediaries provide additional liquidity to fund suppliers, acting as **asset transformers** as follows: FIs purchase the financial claims that fund users issue—primary securities such as mortgages, bonds, and stocks—and finance these purchases by selling financial claims to household investors and other fund suppliers as deposits, insurance policies, or other **secondary securities**. The secondary securities—packages or pools of primary claims—that FIs collect and then issue are often more liquid than are the primary securities themselves. For example, banks and thrift institutions (e.g., savings associations) offer draft deposit accounts with fixed principal values and (often) guaranteed interest rates. Fund suppliers can generally access the funds in those accounts on demand. Money market mutual funds issue shares to household savers that allow the savers to maintain almost fixed principal amounts while earning somewhat higher interest rates than on bank deposits. Further, savers can also withdraw these funds on demand whenever the saver writes a check on the account. Even life insurance companies allow policyholders to borrow against their company-held policy balances with very short notice.

THE SHIFT AWAY FROM RISK MEASUREMENT AND MANAGEMENT AND THE FINANCIAL CRISIS Certainly, a major event that changed and reshaped the financial services industry was the financial crisis of the late 2000s. As FIs adjusted to regulatory changes brought about in the 1980s and 1990s, one result was a dramatic increase in systemic risk of the financial system, caused in large part by a shift in the banking model from that of "originate and hold" to "originate to distribute." In the traditional model, banks take short-term deposits and other sources of funds and use them to fund longer term loans to businesses and consumers. Banks typically hold these loans to maturity, and thus have an incentive to screen and monitor borrower activities even after a loan is made. However, the traditional banking model exposes the institution to potential liquidity, interest rate, and credit risk. In attempts to avoid these risk exposures and generate improved return-risk trade-offs, banks have shifted to an underwriting model in which they originate or warehouse loans, and then quickly sell them. Figure 6.8 shows the growth in bank loan secondary market trading from 1991 through 2012. Note the huge growth in bank loan trading even during the financial crisis of 2008 and 2009. When loans trade, the secondary market produces information that can substitute for the information and monitoring of banks.[1] Further, banks

figure 6.8

Bank Loan Secondary Market Trading

Bank loan sales have increased dramatically over the last twenty years.

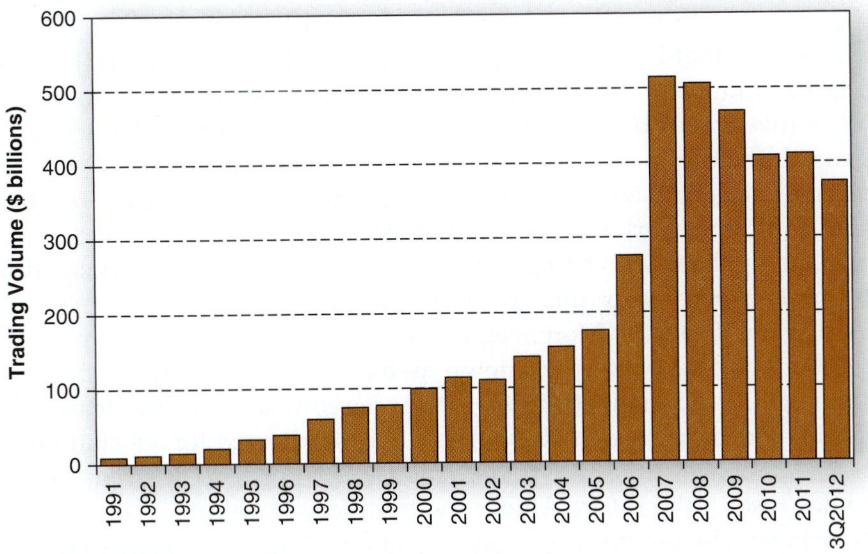

[1]Gande and Saunders, "Are Banks Still Special When There Is a Secondary Market for Loans?" *Journal of Finance*, 2012, pp. 1649–1684, find that equity of borrowers whose bank loans trade on secondary markets for the first time receive positive announcement period returns. Further, the announcement by a bank of new loans to a borrower after the borrower's loans begin trading in the secondary markets show positive announcment period returns.

may have lower incentives to collect information and monitor borrowers if they sell loans rather than keep them as part of the bank's portfolio of assets. Indeed, most large banks are organized as financial service holding companies to facilitate these new activities.

More recently activities of shadow banks, nonfinancial service firms that perform banking services, have facilitated the change from the "originate and hold" model of commercial banking to the "originate and distribute" banking model. Participants in the shadow banking system include structured investment vehicles (SIVs), special purpose vehicles (SPVs), asset-backed commercial paper (ABCP) conduits, limited-purpose finance companies, money market mutual funds (MMMFs), and credit hedge funds. In the shadow banking system, savers place their funds with money market mutual[2] and similar funds, which invest these funds in the liabilities of other shadow banks. Borrowers get loans and leases from shadow banks such as finance companies rather than from banks. Like the traditional banking system, the shadow banking system intermediates the flow of funds between net savers and net borrowers. However, instead of the bank serving as the middleman, it is the nonbank financial service firm, or shadow bank, that intermediates. Further, unlike the traditional banking system, where the complete credit intermediation is performed by a single bank, in the shadow banking system it is performed through a series of steps involving many nonbank financial service firms.

These innovations remove risk from the balance sheet of financial institutions and shift risk off the balance sheet and to other parts of the financial system. Since the FIs, acting as underwriters, are not exposed to the credit, liquidity, and interest rate risks of traditional banking, they have little incentive to screen and monitor activities of borrowers to whom they originate loans. Thus, FIs' role as specialists in risk measurement and management is reduced.

Adding to FIs' move away from risk measurement and management was the boom ("bubble") in the housing markets, which began building in 2001, particularly after the terrorist attacks of 9/11. The immediate response by regulators to the terrorist attacks was to create stability in the financial markets by providing liquidity to FIs. For example, the Federal Reserve lowered the short-term interest rate that banks and other financial institutions pay in the federal funds market and even made lender of last resort funds available to nonbank FIs such as investment banks. Perhaps not surprisingly, low interest rates and the increased liquidity provided by central banks resulted in a rapid expansion in consumer, mortgage, and corporate debt financing. Demand for residential mortgages and credit card debt rose dramatically. As the demand for debt grew, especially among those who had previously been excluded from participating in the debt markets because of their poor credit ratings, FIs began lowering their credit quality cutoff points. Moreover, to boost their earnings in that part of the mortgage market now popularly known as the "subprime market," banks and other mortgage-supplying institutions often offered relatively low "teaser" rates on adjustable rate mortgages (ARMs). These ARMs allowed for substantial step-ups in rates after the initial rate period expired two or three years later and if market rates rose in the future. Under the traditional banking structure, banks might have been reluctant to so aggressively pursue low credit quality borrowers for fear that the loans would default. However, under the originate to distribute model of banking, asset securitization and loan syndication allowed banks to

[2]Recent regulatory proposals recognize that MMMFs are operating as "banks," including requirements that MMMFs maintain capital levels similar to banks and/or be backed by a private deposit insurance scheme.

retain little or no part of the loans, and hence the default risk on loans that they originated. Thus, as long as the borrower did not default within the first few months after a loan's issuance and the loans were sold or securitized without recourse back to the bank, the issuing bank could ignore longer term credit risk concerns. The result was deterioration in credit quality, at the same time as there was a dramatic increase in consumer and corporate leverage.

Eventually, in 2006, housing prices started to fall. At the same time, the Federal Reserve started to raise interest rates as it began to fear inflation. Since many subprime mortgages originated in the 2001 to 2005 period had adjustable rates, the cost of meeting mortgage commitments rose to unsustainable levels for many low-income households. The confluence of falling house prices, rising interest rates, and rising mortgage costs led to a wave of mortgage defaults in the subprime market and foreclosures that only reinforced the downward trend in house prices. The number of subprime mortgages that were more than 60 days behind on their payments was 17.1 percent in June 2007 and over 20 percent in August 2007. As this happened, the poor quality of the collateral and credit quality underlying subprime mortgage pools became apparent, with default rates far exceeding those apparently anticipated by the rating agencies in setting their initial subprime mortgage securitizations ratings. In 2007, the percentage of subprime mortgage-backed securities delinquent by 90 days or more was 10.09 percent, substantially higher than the 5.37 percent rate in May 2005. The financial crisis began. Appendix 6A to this chapter (located on the book's website, www.mhhe.com/can3e) provides a detailed discussion of the causes of, major events during, and regulatory and industry changes resulting from the financial crisis.

The economy relies on financial institutions to act as specialists in risk measurement and management. The importance of this was demonstrated during the global financial crisis. When FIs failed to perform their critical risk measurement and management functions, a crisis of confidence that disrupted financial markets ensued. The result was a worldwide breakdown in credit markets, as well as an enhanced level of equity market volatility.

TIME OUT

6-4 List the major types of financial institutions.

6-5 What three main issues would deter fund suppliers from directly purchasing securities?

6-6 What events resulted in banks' shift from the traditional banking model of "originate and hold" to a model of "originate and distribute"?

6.3 • Interest Rates

We often speak of "the interest rate" as if only one rate applies to all financial situations or transactions. In fact, we can list tens or hundreds of interest rates that are appropriate in various conditions or situations within the U.S. economy on any particular day. Let's explore a bit how the financial sector sets these rates and how the rates relate to one another. We actually observe **nominal interest rates** in financial markets—these are the rates most often quoted by financial news services. As we will see in Chapters 7 and 8, nominal interest rates (or, simply, interest rates) directly affect most tradable securities' value or price. Since

nominal interest rates
The interest rates actually observed in financial markets.

figure 6.9 Key U.S. Interest Rates, 1972–2013

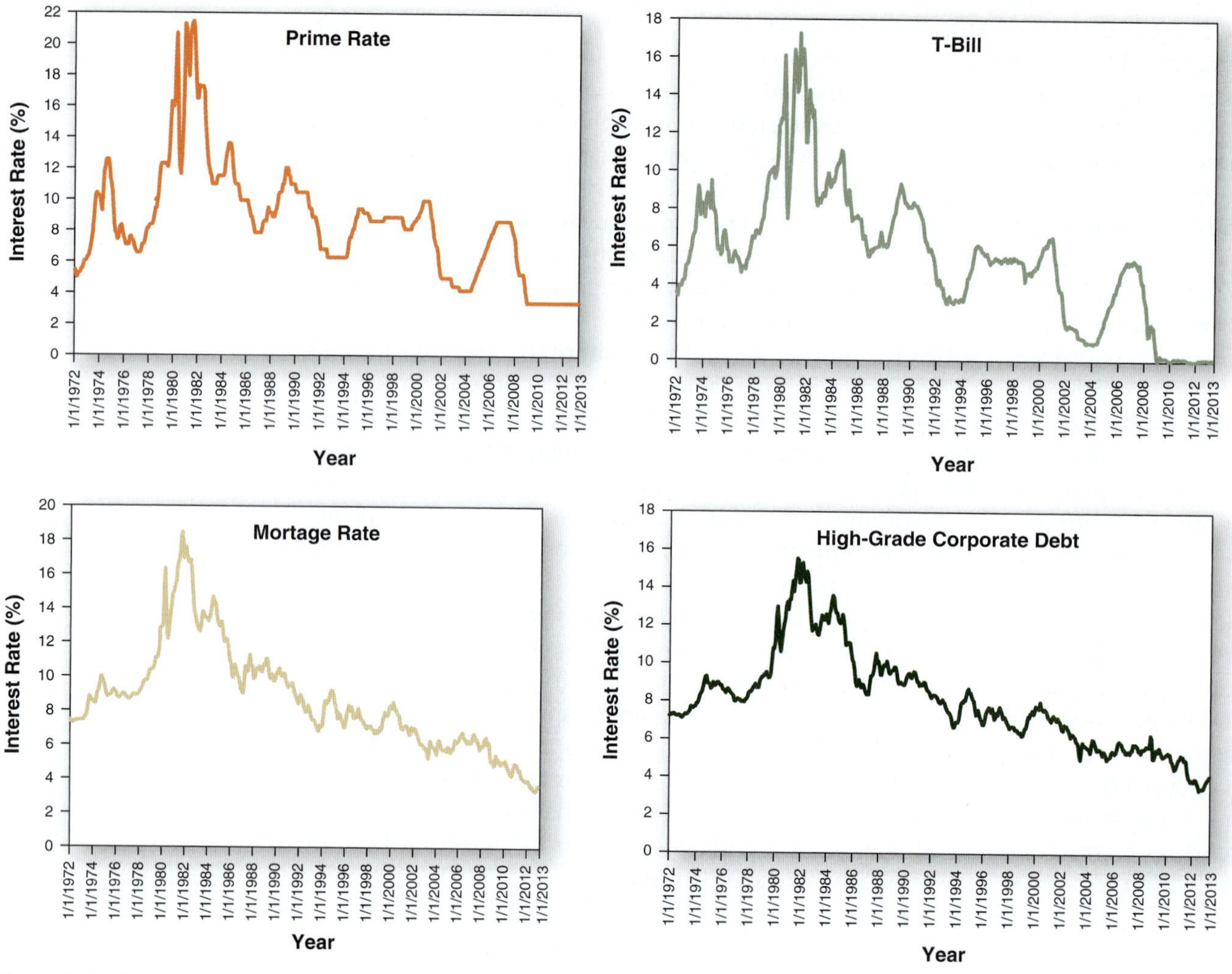

Source: Federal Reserve Board, website, various dates. www.federalreserve.gov

any change in nominal interest rates has such profound effects on security prices, financial managers and individual investors spend a lot of time and effort trying to identify factors that may influence future interest rate levels.

Of course, interest rate changes influence investment performance and trigger buy or sell decisions for individual investors, businesses, and governmental units alike. For example, in 2008 and 2009, the Federal Reserve, in an effort to address the severe financial crisis, unexpectedly announced that it would drop its target fed funds rate to a range between 0 and 0.25 percent and lowered its discount window rate to 0.5 percent, the lowest level since the 1940s. These rates remained at historically low levels into 2013.

Figure 6.9 illustrates the movement of several key U.S. interest rates over the past 41 years:

- The prime commercial loan rate.
- The 3-month T-bill rate.
- The home mortgage rate.
- The high-grade corporate bond rate.

Figure 6.9 shows how interest rates vary over time. For example, the prime rate hit highs of over 20 percent in the early 1980s, yet fell as low as 4.75 percent in the early 1970s. The prime rate stayed below 10 percent throughout much of the 1990s, fell back further to 4.00 percent in the early 2000s, then rose to as high as 8.25 percent in the mid-2000s. During the financial crisis of 2008 and 2009, the Fed took aggressive actions to stimulate the economy, including dropping interest rates to historic lows. As a result, the prime rate fell to 3.25 percent and stayed there through 2013.

Factors That Influence Interest Rates for Individual Securities

LG6-4

Specific factors that affect nominal interest rates for any particular security include:

- Inflation.
- The real risk-free rate.
- Default risk.
- Liquidity risk.
- Special provisions regarding the use of funds raised by a particular security issuer.
- The security's term to maturity.

We will discuss each of these factors after summarizing them in Table 6.4.

INFLATION The first factor that influences interest rates is the economy-wide *actual or expected inflation rate.* Specifically, the higher the level of actual or expected inflation, the higher will be the level of interest rates. We define **inflation** of the general price index of goods and services (or the inflation premium, IP) as the (percentage) increase in the price of a standardized basket of goods and services over a given period of time. The U.S. Department of Commerce measures inflation using indexes such as the consumer price index (CPI) and the producer price index (PPI). For example, the annual inflation rate using the CPI index between years t and $t + 1$ would be equal to:

inflation
The continual increase in the price level of a basket of goods and services.

$$IP = \frac{CPI_{t+1} - CPI_t}{CPI_t} \times 100 \tag{6-1}$$

The positive relationship between interest rates and inflation rates is fairly intuitive: When inflation raises the general price level, investors who buy financial assets must earn a higher interest rate (or inflation premium) to compensate for continuing to hold the investment. Holding on to their investments means that they incur higher costs of forgoing consumption of real goods and services today, only to have to buy these same goods and services at higher prices in the future. In other words, the higher the rate of inflation, the more expensive the same basket of goods and services will be in the future.

table 6.4 | **Factors Affecting Nominal Interest Rates**

Inflation: A continual increase in the price level of a basket of goods and services throughout the economy as a whole.

Real risk-free rate: Risk-free rate adjusted for inflation; generally lower than nominal risk-free rates at any particular time.

Default risk: Risk that a security issuer will miss an interest or principal payment or continue to miss such payments.

Liquidity risk: Risk that a security cannot be sold at a price relatively close to its value with low transaction costs on short notice.

Special provisions: Provisions (e.g., taxability, convertibility, and callability) that impact a security holder beneficially or adversely and as such are reflected in the interest rates on securities that contain such provisions.

Time to maturity: Length of time until a security is repaid; used in debt securities as the date upon which the security holders get their principal back.

real risk-free rate

The interest rate that would exist on a risk-free security if no inflation were expected.

REAL RISK-FREE RATES A **real risk-free rate** is the rate that a risk-free security would pay if no inflation were expected over its holding period (e.g., a year). As such, it measures only society's relative time preference for consuming today rather than tomorrow. The higher society's preference to consume today (i.e., the higher its time value of money or rate of time preference), the higher the real risk-free rate (RFR) will be.

Fisher Effect Economists often refer to the relationship among real risk-free rates (RFR), expected inflation (expected IP), and nominal risk-free rates (i), described previously, as the Fisher effect, named for Irving Fisher, who identified these economic relationships early last century. The Fisher effect theorizes that nominal risk-free rates that we observe in financial markets (e.g., the 1-year Treasury bill rate) must compensate investors for:

- Any inflation-related reduction in purchasing power lost on funds lent or principal due.
- An additional premium above the expected rate of inflation for forgoing present consumption (which reflects the real risk-free rate issue discussed previously).

$$i = \text{Expected } IP + RFR \quad \textbf{(6-2)}$$

Thus, the nominal risk-free rate will equal the real risk-free rate only when market participants expect inflation to be zero: Expected $IP = 0$. Similarly, the nominal risk-free rate will equal the expected inflation rate only when the real risk-free rate is zero. We can rearrange the nominal risk-free rate equation to show what determines the real interest rate:[3]

$$RFR = i - \text{Expected } IP \quad \textbf{(6-3)}$$

It needs to be noted that the expected inflation rate is difficult to estimate accurately, so the real risk-free rate can be difficult to measure accurately. Investors' expectations are not always realized either.

EXAMPLE 6-1

LG6-4

For interactive versions of this example visit www.mhhe.com/can3e

Calculating Real Risk-Free Rates

One-year Treasury bill rates in 2007 averaged 4.53 percent and inflation (measured by the consumer price index) for the year was 4.10 percent. If investors had expected the same inflation rate as that actually realized, calculate the real risk-free rate for 2007 according to the Fisher effect.

SOLUTION:

4.53% − 4.10% = 0.43%

Similar to Problems 6-1, 6-2, self-test problem 1

[3]Often the Fisher effect formula is written as $(1 + i) = (1 + IP) \times (1 + RFR)$, which, when solved for i, becomes: $i = \text{Expected } IP + RFR + (\text{Expected } IP \times RFR)$, where Expected $IP \times RFR$ is the inflation premium for the loss of purchasing power on the promised nominal interest rate payments due to inflation. For small values of Expected IP and RFR this term is negligible. The approximation formula used here assumes these values are small.

figure 6.10

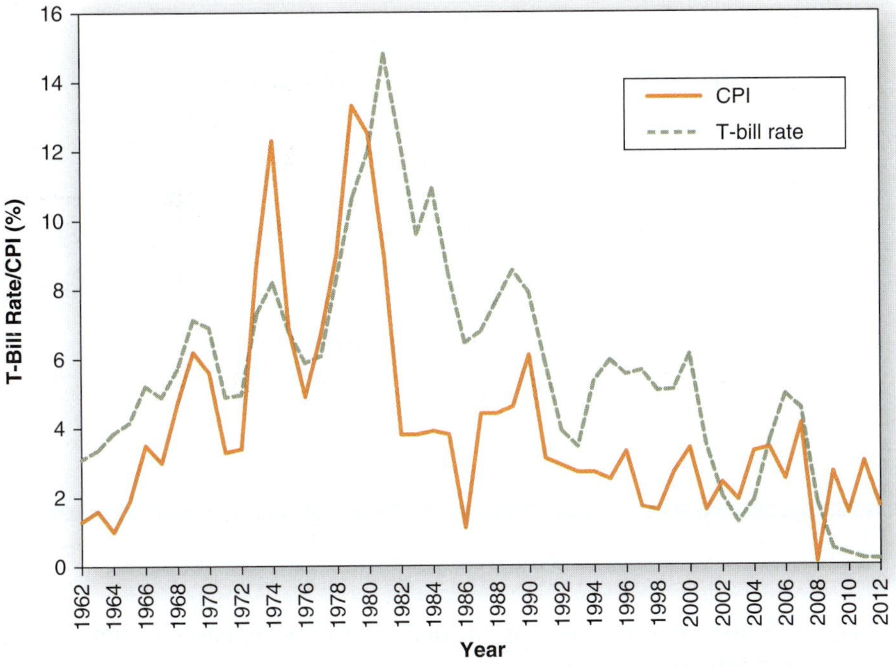

Nominal Interest Rates versus Inflation

Notice the difference between the nominal risk-free rate and the change in CPI over the last several decades.

Source: Federal Reserve Board and U.S. Department of Labor websites, various dates. www.federalreserve.gov and www.states.bls.gov/cpi/home.htm

The 1-year T-bill rate in 2012 was 0.17 percent, while the CPI for the year was 1.70 percent, which implies a real risk-free rate of −1.53 percent—that is, the real risk-free rate was actually negative. Thus, the real value of investments actually decreased in that year.

Figure 6.10 shows the nominal risk-free rate (1-year T-bill rate) versus the change in the CPI from 1962 through 2012. Note that generally the T-bill rate is greater than the CPI, that is, the real risk-free rate earned on securities is positive. It is during periods of economic slowdowns that the T-bill rate is less than the CPI, that is, real risk-free rates are negative.

DEFAULT OR CREDIT RISK **Default risk** is the risk that a security issuer may fail to make its promised interest and principal payments to its bondholders (or its dividend in the case of preferred stockholders). The higher the default risk, the higher the interest rate that security buyers will demand to compensate them for this default (or credit) risk relative to default-risk-free U.S. Treasury securities. Since the U.S. government has taxation powers and can print currency, the risk of its defaulting on debt payments is practically zero. But some borrowers, such as corporations or individuals, have less predictable cash flows (and no powers to tax anyone to raise funds immediately). So investors must charge issuers other than the U.S. government a premium for any perceived probability of default and the cost of potentially recovering the amount loaned built into their regular interest rate premium. The difference between a quoted interest rate on a security (security j) and a Treasury security with similar maturity, liquidity, tax, and other features is called a *default* or *credit risk premium* (DRP_j). That is:

default risk

The risk that a security issuer will default on that security by being late on or missing an interest or principal payment.

$$DRP_j = i_{jt} - i_{Tt} \quad \textbf{(6-4)}$$

figure 6.11

Default Risk Premiums on Corporate Bonds

Source: Federal Reserve Board website, various dates. www.federalreserve.gov

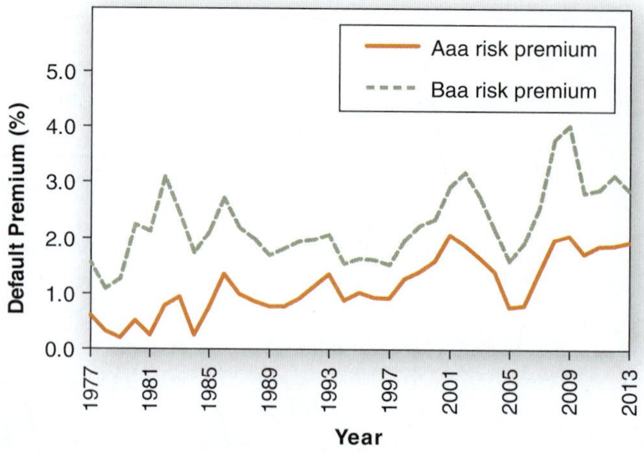

where i_{jt} = Interest rate on a security issued by a non-Treasury issuer (issuer j) of maturity m at time t.

i_{Tt} = Interest rate on a security issued by the U.S. Treasury of maturity m at time t.

Various rating agencies, including Moody's and Standard & Poor's, evaluate and categorize the potential default risk on many corporate bonds, some state and municipal bonds, and some stocks. We cover these ratings in more detail in Chapter 8. For example, in 2013, the 10-year Treasury rate was 1.97 percent. Moody's Aaa-rated and Baa-rated corporate debt carried interest rates of 3.90 percent and 4.84 percent, respectively. Thus, the average default risk premiums on the Aaa-rated and Baa-rated corporate debt were:

$$DRP_{\text{Aaa}} = 3.90\% - 1.97\% = 1.93\%$$

$$DRP_{\text{Baa}} = 4.84\% - 1.97\% = 2.87\%$$

Figure 6.11 presents these risk premiums for the stated creditworthiness categories of bonds from 1977 through 2013. Notice from this figure and Figure 6.10 that default risk premiums tend to increase when the economy is contracting and decrease when the economy is expanding. For example, from 2007 to 2008, real risk-free rates (T-bills − CPI in Figure 6.10) increased from 0.43 percent to 1.73 percent. Over the same period, default risk premiums on Aaa-rated bonds increased from 1.39 percent to 1.97 percent. Baa-rated bonds showed a default risk premium increase from 2.55 percent to 3.78 percent.

LIQUIDITY RISK A highly liquid asset can be sold at a predictable price with low transaction costs. That is, the holder can convert the asset at its fair market value on short notice. The interest rate on a security reflects its relative liquidity, with highly liquid assets carrying the lowest interest rates (all other characteristics remaining the same). Likewise, if a security is illiquid, investors add a **liquidity risk** premium (LRP) to the interest rate on the security. In the United States, most government securities sell in liquid markets, as do large corporations' stocks and bonds. Securities issued by smaller companies trade in relatively less liquid markets.

liquidity risk

The risk that a security cannot be sold at a predictable price with low transaction costs on short notice.

A different type of liquidity risk premium may also exist if investors dislike long-term securities because their prices (present values, as discussed below and in Chapters 4 and 7) react more to interest rate changes than short-term securities do. In this case, a higher liquidity risk premium may be added to a security with a longer maturity because of its greater exposure to price risk (loss of capital value) on the longer-term security as interest rates change.

SPECIAL PROVISIONS OR COVENANTS Sometimes a security's issuing party attaches special provisions or covenants to the security issued. Such provisions affect the interest rates on these securities relative to securities without such provisions attached to them. Some of these special provisions include the security's taxability, convertibility, and callability. For example, investors pay no federal taxes on interest payments received from municipal securities. So a municipal bond holder may demand a lower interest rate than that demanded on a comparable taxable bond—such as a Treasury bond (which is taxable at the federal level but not at the state or local levels) or a corporate bond (the interest on which is taxable at the state, local, and federal levels).

Another special covenant is convertibility: A convertible bond offers the holder the opportunity to exchange the bond for another type of the issuer's securities—usually preferred or common stock—at a preset price (see Chapter 7). This conversion option can be valuable to purchasers, so convertible security buyers require lower interest rates than a comparable nonconvertible security holder would require (all else equal). In general, special provisions that benefit security holders (e.g., tax-free status and convertibility) bring with them lower interest rates, and special provisions that benefit security issuers (e.g., callability, by which an issuer has the option to retire, or call, the security prior to maturity at a preset price) require higher interest rates to encourage purchase.

TERM TO MATURITY Interest rates also change—sometimes daily—because of a bond's term to maturity. Financial professionals refer to this daily or even hourly changeability in interest rates as the **term structure of interest rates**, or the yield curve. The shape of the yield curve derives directly from time value of money principles. The term structure of interest rates compares interest rates on debt securities based on their time to maturity, assuming that all other characteristics (i.e., default risk, liquidity risk) are equal. Interest rates change as the maturity of a debt security changes; in general, the longer the term to maturity, the higher the required interest rate buyers will demand. This addition to the required interest rate is the maturity premium (MP). The MP, which is the difference between the required yield on long- versus short-term securities of the same characteristics except maturity, can be positive, negative, or zero.

term structure of interest rates

A comparison of market yields on securities, assuming all characteristics except maturity are the same.

The financial industry most often reports and analyzes the yield curve for U.S. Treasury securities. The yield curve for U.S. Treasury securities has taken many shapes over the years, but the three most common shapes appear in Figure 6.12. In graph (a), the yield curve on February 26, 2013, yields rise steadily with maturity when the yield curve slopes upward. This is the most common yield curve. On average, the MP is positive, as you might expect. Graph (b) shows an inverted, or downward-sloping, yield curve, reported on November 24, 2000, in which yields decline as maturity increases. Inverted yield curves do not generally last very long. In this case, the yield curve inverted as the U.S. Treasury began retiring long-term (30-year) bonds as the country began to pay off the national debt. Finally, graph (c) shows a flat yield curve, reported on June 4, 2007, when the yield to maturity is virtually unaffected by the term to maturity.

Note that yield curves may reflect factors other than investors' preferences for the maturity of a security. In reality, liquidity differences may arise among the securities traded at different points along the yield curve. For example, newly issued 20-year Treasury bonds offer a lower rate of return than previously issued

figure 6.12 Common Shapes for Yield Curves on Treasury Securities

Three common yield curve shapes are (a) upward sloping, (b) downward sloping, and (c) a flat slope.

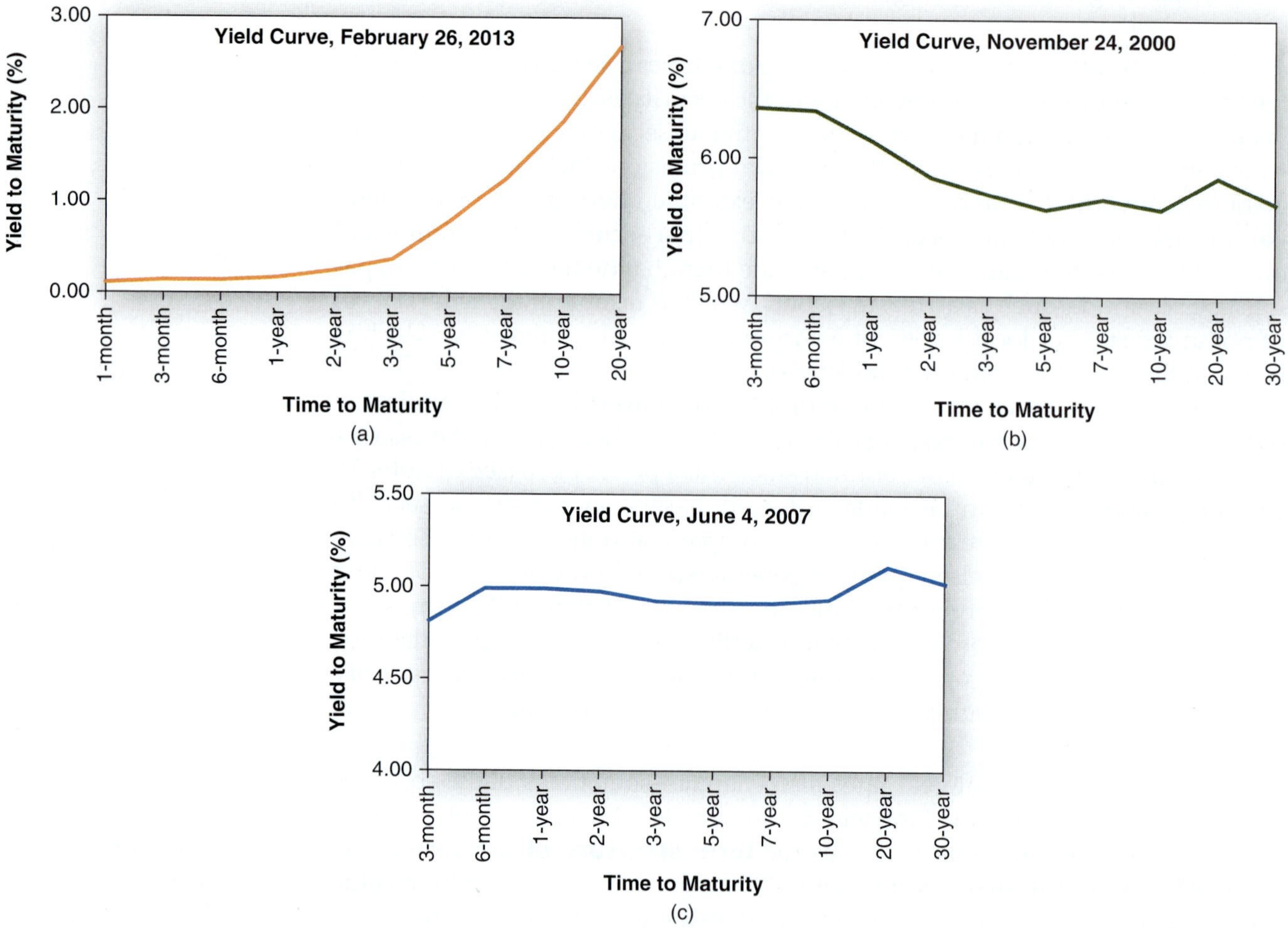

Source: U.S. Treasury, Office of Debt Management, Daily Treasury Yield Curves, various dates. www.ustreas.gov

Treasury bonds (so-called seasoned issues), all else being equal. Ten-year Treasury bonds may be more liquid if investors prefer new ("on the run") securities to previously issued ("off the run") securities. Specifically, since the U.S. Treasury has historically issued new 10-year notes and 20-year bonds only at the long end of the maturity spectrum, a seasoned 10-year Treasury bond would have to have been issued 10 years previously (i.e., it was originally a 20-year bond when it was issued 10 years previously). Increased demand for previously issued (and thus more liquid) 20-year Treasury bonds relative to the newly issued but less liquid 10-year Treasury bonds can be large enough to push the equilibrium interest rate on the 20-year Treasury bonds below that for the 10-year Treasury bonds and even below short-term rates. In the next section, we will review three major theories that financial analysts often use to explain the shape of the yield-to-maturity curve (or the shape of the term structure of interest rates).

Putting together the factors that affect interest rates in different markets, we can use the following general equation to note the influence of the factors that functionally impact the fair interest rate—the rate necessary to compensate investors for all security risks—(i_j^*) on an individual (jth) financial security.

$$i_j^* = f(IP, RFR, DRP_j, LRP_j, SCP_j, MP_j) \quad \textbf{(6-5)}$$

where

IP = Inflation premium.

RFR = Real risk-free rate.

DRP_j = Default risk premium on the jth security.

LRP_j = Liquidity risk premium on the jth security.

SCP_j = Special covenant premium on the jth security.

MP_j = Maturity premium on the jth security.

The first two factors, IP and RFR, are common to all financial securities, while the other factors can uniquely influence the price of a single security.

LG6-4

EXAMPLE 6-2

Determinants of Interest Rates for Individual Securities

Morningstar Corp.'s 8-year bonds are currently yielding a return of 6.85 percent. The expected inflation premium is 1.15 percent annually and the real risk-free rate is expected to be 2.25 percent annually over the next 8 years. The default risk premium on Morningstar's bonds is 1.35 percent. The maturity risk premium is 0.50 percent on 2-year securities and increases by 0.05 percent for each additional year to maturity. Calculate the liquidity risk premium on Morningstar's 8-year bonds.

For interactive versions of this example visit www.mhhe.com/can3e

SOLUTION:

$$6.85\% = 1.15\% + 2.25\% + 1.35\% + LRP + (0.50\% + (0.05\% \times 6))$$

$$= > DRP = 6.85\% - (1.15\% + 2.25\% + 1.35\% + (0.50\% + (0.05\% \times 6))) = 1.30\%$$

Similar to Problems 6-3, 6-4, self-test problem 2

TIME OUT

6-7 What is the difference between nominal and real risk-free rates?

6-8 What does "the term structure of interest rates" mean?

6-9 What shape does the term structure usually take? Why?

Theories Explaining the Shape of the Term Structure of Interest Rates

LG6-5

We just explained the necessity of a maturity premium, the relationship between a security's interest rate and its remaining term to maturity. We can illustrate these issues by showing that the term structure of interest rates can take a number of different shapes. As you might expect, economists and financial theorists with various viewpoints differ among themselves in theorizing why the yield curve takes different shapes. Explanations for the yield curve's shape fall predominantly into three categories:

- The unbiased expectations theory.
- The liquidity premium theory.
- The market segmentation theory.

figure 6.13

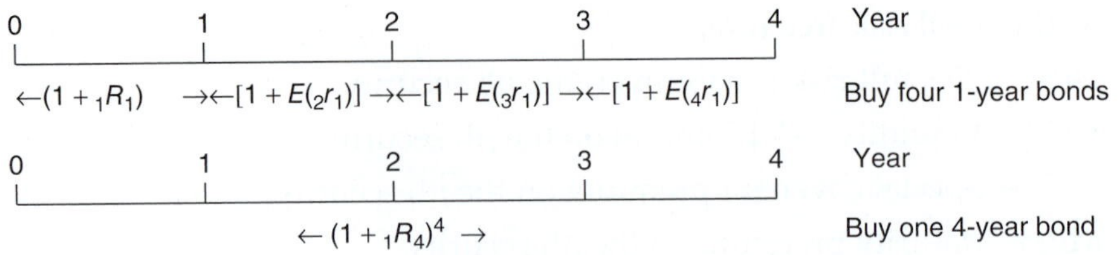

Unbiased Expectations Theory of the Term Structure of Interest Rates

Return from buying four 1-year maturity bonds versus buying one 4-year maturity bond.

Look again at Figure 6.12 (a), which presents the Treasury yield curve as of February 26, 2013. We see that the yield curve on this date reflected the normal upward-sloping relationship between yield and maturity. Now let's turn to explanations for this shape based on the three predominant theories noted above.

UNBIASED EXPECTATIONS THEORY According to the unbiased expectations theory of the term structure of interest rates, at any given point in time, the yield curve reflects the *market's current expectations of future short-term rates.* As illustrated in Figure 6.13, the intuition behind the unbiased expectations theory is this: If investors have a 4-year investment horizon, they could either buy current 4-year bonds and earn the current (or spot) yield on a 4-year bond (${}_1R_4$, if held to maturity) each year, or they could invest in four successive 1-year bonds [of which they know only the current 1-year spot rate (${}_1R_1$)]. But investors also expect what the unknown future 1-year rates [$E({}_2r_1)$, $E({}_3r_1)$, and $E({}_4r_1)$] will be. Note that each interest rate term has two subscripts, e.g., ${}_1R_4$. The first subscript indicates the period in which the security is bought, so that 1 represents the purchase of a security in period 1. The second subscript indicates the maturity on the security. Thus, 4 represents the purchase of a security with a 4-year life. Similarly, $E({}_3r_1)$ is the expected return on a security with a 1-year life purchased in period 3.

According to the unbiased expectations theory, the return for holding a 4-year bond to maturity should equal the expected return for investing in four successive 1-year bonds (as long as the market is in equilibrium). If this equality does not hold, an arbitrage opportunity exists. That is, if investors could earn more on the 1-year bond investments, they could short (or sell) the 4-year bond, use the proceeds to buy the four successive 1-year bonds, and earn a guaranteed profit over the 4-year investment horizon. So, according to the unbiased expectations theory, if the market expects future 1-year rates to rise each successive year into the future, then the yield curve will slope upward. Specifically, the current 4-year T-bond rate or return will exceed the 3-year bond rate, which will exceed the 2-year bond rate, and so on. Similarly, if the market expects future 1-year rates to remain constant each successive year into the future, then the 4-year bond rate will equal the 3-year bond rate. That is, the term structure of interest rates will remain constant (flat) over the relevant time period. Specifically, the unbiased expectation theory states that current long-term interest rates are geometric averages of current and expected *future* short-term interest rates. The mathematical equation representing this relationship is:

$$(1 + {}_1R_N)^N = (1 + {}_1R_1)[1 + E({}_2r_1)]\cdots[1 + E({}_Nr_1)] \quad \textbf{(6-6)}$$

therefore:

$${}_1R_N = \{[1 + {}_1R_1][1 + E({}_2r_1)]\cdots[1 + E({}_Nr_1)]\}^{1/N} - 1 \quad \textbf{(6-7)}$$

where ${}_1R_N$ = Actual N-period rate today (i.e., the first day of year 1).
N = Term to maturity.

$_1R_1$ = Actual 1-year rate today.

$E(_ir_1)$ = Expected 1-year rates for years 2, 3, 4, . . . , N in the future.

Notice that uppercase interest rate terms, $_1R_t$, are the actual current interest rates on securities purchased today with a maturity of t years. Lowercase interest rate terms, $_tr_1$, represent estimates of future 1-year interest rates starting t years into the future.

EXAMPLE 6-3

LG6-5

Calculating Yield Curves

For interactive versions of this example visit www.mhhe.com/can3e

Suppose that the current 1-year rate (1-year spot rate) and expected 1-year T-bond rates over the following three years (i.e., years 2, 3, and 4, respectively) are as follows:

$$_1R_1 = 2.94\% \quad E(_2r_1) = 4\% \quad E(_3r_1) = 4.74\% \quad E(_4r_1) = 5.10\%$$

Construct a yield curve using the unbiased expectations theory.

SOLUTION:

Using the unbiased expectations theory, current (or today's) rates for 1-, 2-, 3-, and 4-year maturity Treasury securities should be:

$_1R_1 = 2.94\%$ (Expected return of security with 1-year life purchased in period 1)

$_1R_2 = [(1 + 0.0294)(1 + 0.04)]^{1/2} - 1 = 3.47\%$

$_1R_3 = [(1 + 0.0294)(1 + 0.04)(1 + 0.0474)]^{1/3} - 1 = 3.89\%$

$_1R_4 = [(1 + 0.0294)(1 + 0.04)(1 + 0.0474)(1 + 0.051)]^{1/4} - 1 = 4.19\%$

and the current yield to maturity curve will be upward sloping as shown:

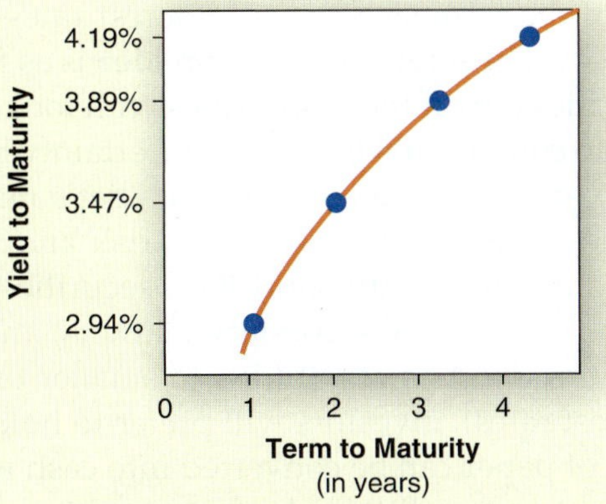

This upward-sloping yield curve reflects the market's expectation of persistently rising 1-year (short-term) interest rates over the future horizon.[4]

Similar to Problems 6-5, 6-6, 6-7, 6-8, self-test problem 3

MATH COACH

When putting interest rates into the equation, enter them in decimal format, not percentage format.
Correct: (1 + 0.0294)
Not correct: (1 + 2.94)

[4]That is, $E(_4r_1) > E(_3r_1) > E(_2r_1) > {_1R_1}$.

figure 6.14

Yield Curve Using the Unbiased Expectation Theory (UET) versus the Liquidity Premium Theory (LPT)

Notice the differences in the shape of the yield curve under the UET and the LPT.

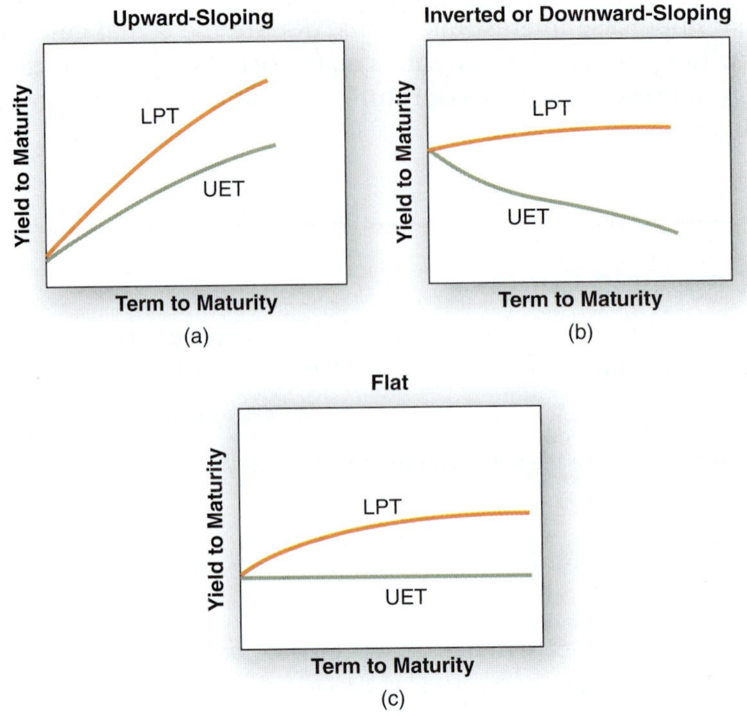

LIQUIDITY PREMIUM THEORY The second popular explanation—the liquidity premium theory of the term structure of interest rates—builds on the unbiased expectations theory. The liquidity premium idea is as follows: Investors will hold long-term maturities only if these securities with longer term maturities are offered at a premium to compensate for future uncertainty in the security's value. Of course, uncertainty or risk increases with an asset's maturity. This theory is thus consistent with our discussions of market risk and liquidity risk, above. Specifically, in a world of uncertainty, short-term securities provide greater marketability (due to their more active secondary markets) and have less price risk than long-term securities do. As a result (due to smaller price fluctuations for a given change in interest rates), investors will prefer to hold shorter-term securities because this kind of paper can be converted into cash with little market risk. Said another way, investors face little risk of a capital loss, i.e., a fall in the price of the security below its original purchase price. So, investors must be offered a liquidity premium to buy longer-term securities that carry higher capital loss risk. This difference in market and liquidity risk can be directly related to the fact that longer-term securities are more sensitive to interest rate changes in the market than are shorter-term securities—Chapter 7 discusses bond interest rate sensitivity and the link to a bond's maturity. Because longer maturities on securities mean greater market and liquidity risk, the liquidity premium increases as maturity increases.

The liquidity premium theory states that long-term rates are equal to geometric averages of current and expected short-term rates (like the unbiased expectations theory), plus liquidity risk premiums that increase with the security's maturity (this is the extension of the liquidity premium added to the unbiased expectations theory). Figure 6.14 illustrates the differences in the shape of the yield curve under the unbiased expectations theory versus the liquidity premium theory. For example, according to the liquidity premium theory, an upward-sloping yield curve may reflect investors' expectations that future short-term rates will be flat, but because liquidity premiums increase with maturity, the yield curve will nevertheless slope upward. Indeed, an upward-sloping yield curve may reflect expectations that future interest rates will rise, be flat, or even fall as long as the liquidity premium increases with maturity fast enough to produce an upward-sloping yield curve. The liquidity premium theory can be mathematically represented as

$$ {}_1R_N = \{[1 + {}_1R_1][1 + E({}_2r_1) + L_2]\cdot\cdot[1 + E({}_Nr_1) + L_N]\}^{1/N} - 1 \qquad \textbf{(6-8)} $$

where L_t = Liquidity premium for a period t and $L_2 < L_3 < L_N$.

LG6-5

EXAMPLE 6-4

Calculating Yield Curves Using the Liquidity Premium Theory

Suppose that the current 1-year rate (1-year spot rate) and expected 1-year T-bond rates over the following three years (i.e., years 2, 3, and 4, respectively) are as follows:

$$ {}_1R_1 = 2.94\%,\ E({}_2r_1) = 4.00\%,\ E({}_3r_1) = 4.74\%\ E({}_4r_1) = 5.10\% $$

In addition, investors charge a liquidity premium on longer-term securities such that:

$$ L_2 = 0.10\%\ L_3 = 0.20\%,\ L_4 = 0.30\% $$

Using the liquidity premium theory, construct the yield curve.

For interactive versions of this example visit www.mhhe.com/can3e

SOLUTION:

Using the liquidity premium theory, current rates for 1-, 2-, 3-, and 4-year maturity Treasury securities should be:

${}_1R_1$ = 2.94%

${}_1R_2 = [(1 + 0.0294)(1 + 0.04 + 0.001)]^{1/2} - 1 = 3.52\%$

${}_1R_3 = [(1 + 0.0294)(1 + 0.04 + 0.001)(1 + 0.0474 + 0.002)]^{1/3} - 1 = 3.99\%$

${}_1R_4 = [(1 + 0.0294)(1 + 0.04 + 0.001)(1 + 0.0474 + 0.002)(1 + 0.051 + 0.003)]^{1/4} - 1 = 4.34\%$

and the current yield to maturity curve will be upward sloping as shown:

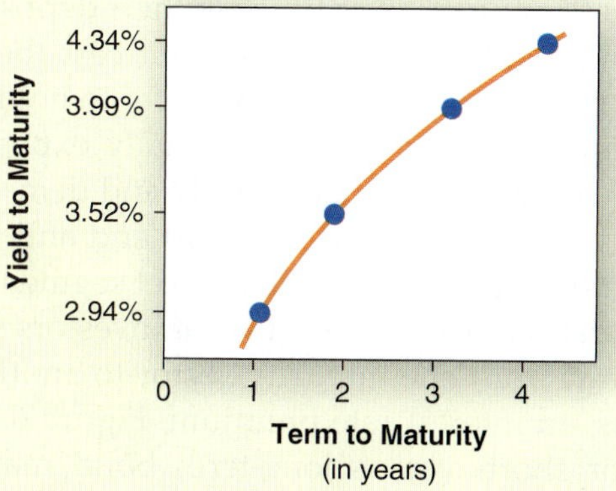

Similar to Problems 6-9, 6-10, self-test problem 3

Let's compare the yield curves in Examples 6-3 (using the unbiased expectations theory) and 6-4. Notice that the liquidity premium in year 2 (L_2 = 0.10%) produces a 0.05 (= 3.52% − 3.47%) percent premium on the yield to maturity on a 2-year T-note, the liquidity premium for year 3 (L_3 = 0.20%) produces a

figure 6.15

Market Segmentation and Determination of the Slope of Yield Curve

The higher the demand for securities, the higher the yield on those securities.

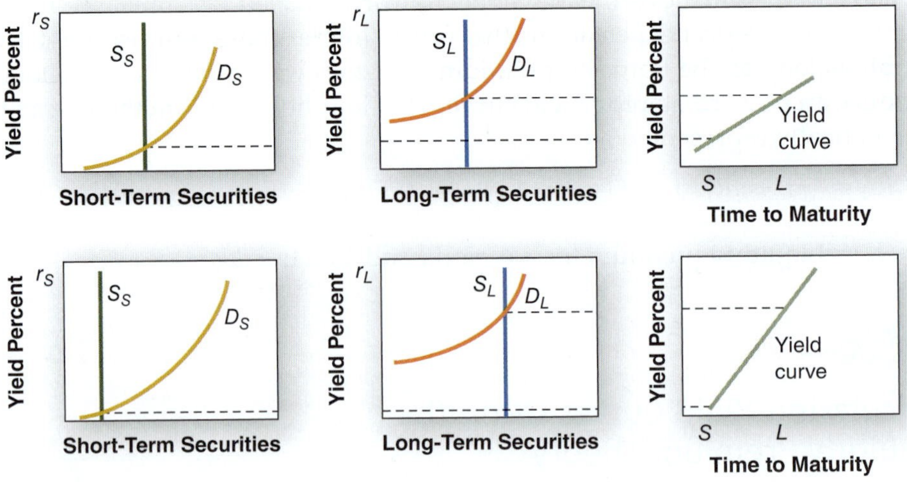

0.10 (= 3.99% − 3.89%) percent premium on the yield to maturity on the 3-year T-note, and the liquidity premium for year 4 (L_4 = 0.30%) produces a 0.15 (= 4.34% − 4.19%) percent premium on the yield to maturity on the 4-year T-note.

MARKET SEGMENTATION THEORY The market segmentation theory does not build on the unbiased expectations theory or the liquidity premium theory, but rather argues that individual investors and FIs have specific maturity preferences, and convincing them to hold securities with maturities other than their most preferred requires a higher interest rate (maturity premium). The main thrust of the market segmentation theory is that investors do not consider securities with different maturities as perfect substitutes. Rather, individual investors and FIs have distinctly preferred investment horizons dictated by the dates when their liabilities will come due. For example, banks might prefer to hold relatively short-term U.S. Treasury bonds because their deposit liabilities also tend to be short-term—recall that bank customers can access their funds on demand. Insurance companies, on the other hand, may prefer to hold long-term U.S. Treasury bonds because life insurance contracts usually expose insurance firms to long-term liabilities. Accordingly, distinct supply and demand conditions within a particular maturity segment—such as the short end and long end of the bond market—determine interest rates under the market segmentation theory.

The market segmentation theory assumes that investors and borrowers generally do not want to shift from one maturity sector to another without adequate compensation—that is, an interest rate premium. Figure 6.15 demonstrates how changes in supply for short- versus long-term bond market segments result in changing shapes of the yield to maturity curve. Specifically, as shown in Figure 6.15, the higher the demand for securities is, the higher the yield on those securities.[5] Further, as the supply of securities decreases in the short-term market and increases in the long-term market, the slope of the yield curve becomes

[5]In general, the price and yield on a bond are inversely related. Thus, as the price of a bond falls (becomes cheaper), the demand for the bond will rise. This is the same as saying that as the yield on a bond rises, it becomes cheaper and the demand for it increases. See Chapter 7.

steeper. If the supply of short-term securities had increased while the supply of long-term securities had decreased, the yield curve would have a flatter slope and might even have sloped downward. Indeed, the U.S. Treasury's large-scale repurchases of long-term Treasury bonds (i.e., reductions in supply) in early 2000 has been viewed as the major cause of the inverted yield curve that appeared in February 2000.

TIME OUT

6-10 What three theories explain the shape of the yield curve?

6-11 Explain how arbitrage plays a role in the unbiased expectations explanation of the shape of the yield curve.

Forecasting Interest Rates

LG6-6

We noted in the time value of money (TVM) chapters (Chapters 4 and 5) that as interest rates change, so do the values of financial securities. Accordingly, both individual investors and public corporations want to be able to predict or forecast interest rates if they wish to trade profitably. For example, if interest rates rise, the value of investment portfolios of individuals and corporations will fall, resulting in a loss of wealth. So, interest rate forecasts are extremely important for the financial wealth of both public corporations and individuals.

Recall our discussion of the unbiased expectations theory in the previous section of this chapter. That theory indicated that the market's expectation of future short-term interest rates determines the shape of the yield curve. For example, an upward-sloping yield curve implies that the market expects future short-term interest rates to rise. So, we can use the unbiased expectations theory to forecast (short-term) interest rates in the future (i.e., forward 1-year interest rates). A **forward rate** is an expected, or implied, rate on a short-term security that will originate at some point in the future. Using the equations in the unbiased expectations theory, we can directly derive the market's expectation of forward rates from existing or actual rates on spot market securities.

forward rate

An expected rate (quoted today) on a security that originates at some point in the future.

To find an implied forward rate on a 1-year security to be issued one year from today, we can rewrite the unbiased expectations theory equation as follows:

$$ {}_1R_2 = [(1 + {}_1R_1)(1 + {}_2f_1)]^{1/2} - 1 \qquad \textbf{(6-9)} $$

where ${}_2f_1$ = expected 1-year rate for year 2, or the implied forward 1-year rate for next year.

Saying that ${}_2f_1$ is the expected 1-year rate for year 2 is the same as saying that, once we isolate the ${}_2f_1$ term, the equation will give us the market's estimate of the expected 1-year rate for year 2. Solving for ${}_2f_1$ we get:

$$ {}_2f_1 = [(1 + {}_1R_2)^2/(1 + {}_1R_1)] - 1 \qquad \textbf{(6-10)} $$

In general, we can find the forward rate for any year, N, into the future using the following generalized equation derived from the unbiased expectations theory:

$$ {}_Nf_1 = [(1 + {}_1R_N)^N/(1 + {}_1R_{N-1})^{N-1}] - 1 \qquad \textbf{(6-11)} $$

EXAMPLE 6-5

LG6-6

For interactive versions of this example visit www.mhhe.com/can3e

Estimating Forward Rates

In the mid-2000s, the existing or current (spot) 1-, 2-, 3-, and 4-year zero coupon Treasury security rates were as follows:

$$_1R_1 = 5.00\%,\ _1R_2 = 4.95\%,\ _1R_3 = 4.93\%,\ _1R_4 = 4.94\%$$

Using the unbiased expectations theory, calculate 1-year forward rates on zero coupon Treasury bonds for years 2, 3, and 4.

SOLUTION:

$$_2f_1 = [(1.0495)^2/(1.0500)] - 1 = 4.90\%$$
$$_3f_1 = [(1.0493)^3/(1.0495)^2] - 1 = 4.89\%$$
$$_4f_1 = [(1.0494)^4/(1.0493)^3] - 1 = 4.97\%$$

Similar to Problems 6-15, 6-16, self-test problem 4

TIME OUT

6-12 What is a forward rate?

6-13 How can we obtain an implied forward rate from current short- and long-term interest rates?

6-14 Why is it useful to calculate forward rates?

View Appendix 6A: The Financial Crisis: The Failure of Financial Institution Specialness at the website for this textbook (www.mhhe.com/can3e)

viewpoints REVISITED

Business Application Solution

In deciding when to issue new debt, DPH Corporation needs to consider two main factors. First, what might happen to specific factors that affect interest rates on any debt the firm may issue? Such specific factors include changes in the firm's default risk, liquidity risk, any special provisions regarding the use of funds raised by the firm's security issuance, and the debt's term to maturity. An increase (decrease) in any of these risks over the next two years would increase (decrease) the rate of interest DPH Corp. would be required to pay to holders of the new debt and would potentially make the debt issue in two years

(continued)

Personal Application Solution

In deciding which corporate bond to buy, John Adams needs to consider specific factors that affect differences in interest rates on debt. These specific factors include the general level of inflation and the real risk-free rate in the U.S. economy, as well as the default risk, liquidity risk, any special provisions regarding the use of funds raised by a security issuance, and the term to maturity of the two debt issues. While one bond earns more (10.00 percent) than the other (8.00 percent), it may be that the higher-yielding bond has more default, liquidity, or other risk than the lower-yielding bond. Thus, the higher yield brings with

(continued)

viewpoints REVISITED

Business Application Solution (concluded)

less (more) attractive. Second, what might happen to the general level of interest rates in the U.S. economy over the next two years? This involves an analysis of any changes in inflation or the real risk-free rate. DPH can estimate how interest rates may change by examining the term structure of interest rates or the current yield curve. In addition to any internal analysis of these factors, DPH Corp. can get expert advice about the timing of its debt issue and get the new debt to the capital market with help from an investment bank. These financial institutions underwrite securities and engage in related activities, such as making a market in which securities can trade.

Personal Application Solution (concluded)

it more risk. John Adams must consider whether he is willing to incur higher risk to get higher returns. In addition to his own analysis of these factors, John Adams can get expert advice about which bond to buy and then buy the bond with a securities firm's help. These financial institutions engage in activities such as securities brokerage, securities trading, and making markets in which securities can trade.

summary of learning goals

In this chapter, we reviewed the basic operations of financial markets and institutions. We described the ways in which funds flow through an economic system from lenders to borrowers and outlined the markets and instruments that lenders and borrowers employ to complete this process. We also reviewed factors that determine nominal interest rates and interest rates' effects on security prices and values in financial markets. We described how interest rate levels change over time and how these changes are determined. Finally, the chapter introduced theories regarding the determination of the shape of the term structure of interest rates. The learning goals for the chapter included:

LG6-1 **Differentiate between primary and secondary markets and between money and capital markets.** Primary markets are markets in which demanders of funds (e.g., corporations) raise funds through new issues of financial instruments, such as stocks and bonds. Once financial instruments such as stocks are issued in primary markets, they are then traded—that is, rebought and resold in secondary markets. Money markets are markets that trade debt securities or instruments with maturities of one year or less. Capital markets are markets that trade equity (stocks) and debt (bonds) instruments with maturities of more than one year.

LG6-2 **List the types of securities traded in money and capital markets.** A variety of money market securities are issued by corporations and government units to obtain short-term funds. These securities include Treasury bills, federal funds and repurchase agreements, commercial paper, negotiable certificates of deposit, and banker's acceptances. Capital market securities include Treasury notes and bonds, state and local government bonds, U.S government agency bonds, mortgages and mortgage-backed securities, corporate bonds, and corporate stocks.

LG6-3 Identify different types of financial institutions and the services that each provides. Financial institutions (banks, thrifts, insurance companies, securities firms and investment banks, finance companies, mutual funds, and pension funds) perform the essential function of channeling funds from those with surplus funds (suppliers of funds) to those with shortages of funds (demanders of funds).

LG6-4 Analyze specific factors that influence interest rates. Specific factors that affect differences in interest rates include inflation, the real risk-free rate, default risk, liquidity risk, special provisions that impact a security holder beneficially or adversely, and the term to maturity of the security.

LG6-5 Offer different theories that explain the shape of the term structure of interest rates. Explanations for the shape of the yield curve fall predominantly into three theories: the unbiased expectations theory, the liquidity premium theory, and the market segmentation theory.

LG6-6 Demonstrate how forward interest rates derive from the term structure of interest rates. A forward rate is an expected, or implied, rate on a short-term security that is to be originated at some point in the future. Using the equations representing unbiased expectations theory, the market's expectation of forward rates can be derived directly from existing or actual rates on securities currently traded in the spot market.

chapter equations

6-1 $$IP = \frac{CPI_{t+1} - CPI_t}{CPI_t} \times 100$$

6-2 $$i = \text{Expected } IP + RFR$$

6-3 $$RFR = i - \text{Expected } IP$$

6-4 $$DRP_j = i_{jt} - i_{Tt}$$

6-5 $$i_j^* = f(IP, RFR, DRP_j, LRP_j, SCP_j, MP_j)$$

6-6 $$(1 + {}_1R_N)^N = (1 + {}_1R_1)[1 + E({}_2r_1)] \ldots [1 + E({}_Nr_1)]$$

6-7 $${}_1R_N = \{[1 + {}_1R_1][1 + E({}_2r_1)] \ldots [1 + E({}_Nr_1)]\}^{1/N} - 1$$

6-8 $${}_1R_N = \{[1 + {}_1R_1][1 + E({}_2r_1) + L_2] \ldots [1 + E({}_Nr_1) + L_N]\}^{1/N} - 1$$

6-9 $${}_1R_2 = [(1 + {}_1R_1)(1 + {}_2f_1)]^{1/2} - 1$$

6-10 $${}_2f_1 = [(1 + {}_1R_2)^2/(1 + {}_1R_1)] - 1$$

6-11 $${}_Nf_1 = [(1 + {}_1R_N)^N/(1 + {}_1R_{N-1})^{N-1}] - 1$$

key terms

asset transformer, Service provided by financial institutions in which financial claims issued by an FI are more attractive to investors than are the claims directly issued by corporations. *p. 200*

capital markets, Markets that trade debt (bonds) and equity (stock) instruments with maturities of more than one year. *p. 193*

default risk, The risk that a security issuer will default on that security by being late on or missing an interest or principal payment. *p. 207*

delegated monitor, An economic agent appointed to act on behalf of smaller investors in collecting information and/or investing funds on their behalf. *p. 200*

derivative security, A security formalizing an agreement between two parties to exchange a standard quantity of an asset at a predetermined price on a specified date in the future. *p. 196*

direct transfer, The process used when a corporation sells its stock or debt directly to investors without going through a financial institution. *p. 198*

financial institutions, Institutions that perform the essential function of channeling funds from those with surplus funds to those with shortages of funds. *p. 197*

financial markets, The arenas through which funds flow. *p. 189*

foreign exchange markets, Markets in which foreign currency is traded for immediate or future delivery. *p. 195*

foreign exchange risk, Risk arising from the unknown value at which foreign currency cash flows can be converted into U.S. dollars. *p. 195*

forward rate, An expected rate (quoted today) on a security that originates at some point in the future. *p. 217*

indirect transfer, A transfer of funds between suppliers and users of funds through a financial institution. *p. 199*

inflation, The continual increase in the price level of a basket of goods and services. *p. 205*

initial public offerings (IPOs), The first public issue of financial instruments by a firm. *p. 190*

investment banks, Financial institutions that arrange primary market transactions for businesses. *p. 190*

liquidity, The ease with which an asset can be converted into cash. *p. 199*

liquidity risk, The risk that a security cannot be sold at a predictable price with low transaction costs on short notice. *p. 208*

money markets, Markets that trade debt securities or instruments with maturities of less than one year. *p. 192*

nominal interest rates, The interest rates actually observed in financial markets. *p. 203*

over-the-counter market, Markets that do not operate in a specific fixed location—rather, transactions occur via telephones, wire transfers, and computer trading. *p. 192*

price risk, The risk that an asset's sale price will be lower than its purchase price. *p. 199*

primary markets, Markets in which corporations raise funds through new issues of securities. *p. 190*

real risk-free rate, The interest rate that would exist on a default-free security if no inflation were expected. *p. 206*

secondary markets, Markets that trade financial instruments once they are issued. *p. 191*

secondary securities, Packages or pools of primary claims. *p. 200*

term structure of interest rates, A comparison of market yields on securities, assuming all characteristics except maturity are the same. *p. 209*

trading volume, The number of shares of a security that are simultaneously bought and sold during a period. *p. 192*

self-test problems with solutions

1 Calculating Real Risk-Free Rates One-year Treasury bill rates in 20XX averaged 3.25 percent and inflation (measured by the consumer price index) for the year was 2.10 percent. If investors had expected the same inflation rate as that actually realized, calculate the real risk-free rate for 20XX according to the Fisher effect. LG6-4

Solution:

3.25% − 2.10% = 1.15%

2 Determinants of Interest Rates for Individual Securities NikkiG's, Inc.'s, 10-year bonds are currently yielding a return of 7.25 percent. The expected inflation premium is 1.25 percent annually and the real risk-free rate is expected to be 2.60 percent annually over the next 10 years. The liquidity risk premium on NikkiG's bonds is 1.25 percent. The maturity risk premium is 0.40 percent on 2-year securities and increases by 0.03 percent for each additional year to maturity. Calculate the default risk premium on NikkiG's 10-year bonds. LG6-4

Solution:

$7.25\% = 1.25\% + 2.60\% + DRP + 1.25\% + (0.40\% + (0.03\% \times 8))$
$=> DRP = 7.25\% - (1.25\% + 2.60\% + 1.25\% + (0.40\% + (0.03\% \times 8))) = 1.51\%$

LG6-5

3 Unbiased Expectations Theory versus Liquidity Premium Theory Suppose that the current one-year rate (one-year spot rate) and expected one-year T-bond rates over the following three years (i.e., years 2, 3, and 4, respectively) are as follows:

$$_1R_1 = 1.94\%,\ E(_2r_1) = 2.5\%,\ E(_3r_1) = 3.74\%,\ E(_4r_1) = 4.10\%$$

In addition, investors charge a liquidity premium on longer-term securities such that:

$$L_2 = 0.05\%,\ L_3 = 0.10\%,\ L_4 = 0.20\%$$

Construct a yield curve using the unbiased expectations theory and using the liquidity premium theory.

Solution:

Using the unbiased expectations theory, current (or today's) rates for 1-, 2-, 3-, and 4-year maturity Treasury securities should be:

$$_1R_1 = 1.94\%$$
$$_1R_2 = [(1 + 0.0194)(1 + 0.025)]^2 - 1 = 2.22\%$$
$$_1R_3 = [(1 + 0.0194)(1 + 0.025)(1 + 0.0374)]^{1/3} - 1 = 2.72\%$$
$$_1R_4 = [(1 + 0.0194)(1 + 0.025)(1 + 0.0374)(1 + 0.041)]^{1/4} - 1 = 3.07\%$$

and the current yield to maturity curve will be upward sloping as shown as the curve UET in the following figure.

Using the liquidity premium theory, current rates for 1-, 2-, 3-, and 4-year maturity Treasury securities should be:

$$_1R_1 = 1.94\%$$
$$_1R_2 = [(1 + 0.0194)(1 + 0.025 + 0.0005)]^{½} - 1 = 2.24\%$$
$$_1R_3 = [(1 + 0.0194)(1 + 0.025 + 0.0005)(1 + 0.0374 + 0.001)]^{1/3} - 1 = 2.77\%$$
$$_1R_4 = [(1 + 0.0194)(1 + 0.025 + 0.0005)(1 + 0.0374 + 0.001)(1 + 0.041 + 0.002)]^{1/4} - 1 = 3.15\%$$

and the current yield to maturity curve will be upward sloping as shown as the curve LPT in the following figure.

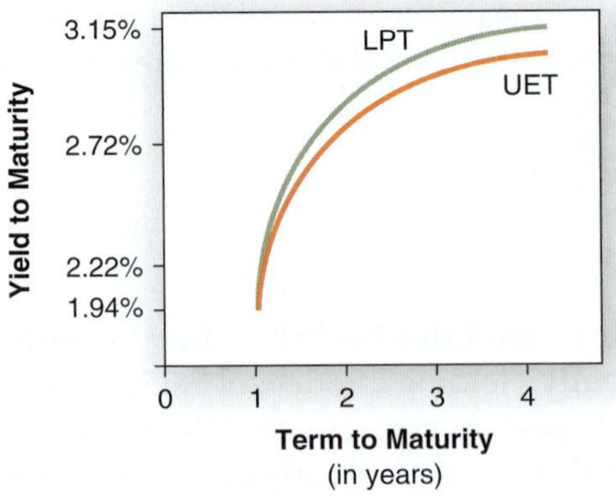

Comparing the yield curves in the graph above, notice that the liquidity premium in year 2 ($L_2 = 0.05\%$) produces a 0.02 percent premium on the yield to maturity on a 2-year T-note, the liquidity premium for year 3 ($L_3 = 0.10\%$) produces a 0.05 percent premium on the yield to maturity on the 3-year T-note, and the liquidity premium for year 4 ($L_4 = 0.20\%$) produces a 0.08 percent premium on the yield to maturity on the 4-year T-note.

4 Estimating Forward Rates *The Wall Street Journal* reports that the existing or current (spot) 1-, 2-, 3-, and 4-year Treasury security rates are as follows: LG6-6

$$_1R_1 = 1.94\%, \quad _1R_2 = 2.25\%, \quad _1R_3 = 2.75\%, \quad _1R_4 = 3.15\%$$

Using the unbiased expectations theory, calculate 1-year forward rates on Treasury bonds for years 2, 3, and 4.

Solution:

$_2f_1 = [(1.0225)^2/(1.0194)] - 1 = 2.56\%$
$_3f_1 = [(1.0275)^3/(1.0225)^2] - 1 = 3.76\%$
$_4f_1 = [(1.0315)^4/(1.0275)^3] - 1 = 4.36\%$

questions

1. Classify the following transactions as taking place in the primary or secondary markets *(LG6-1):*
   a. IBM issues $200 million of new common stock.
   b. The New Company issues $50 million of common stock in an IPO.
   c. IBM sells $5 million of GM preferred stock out of its marketable securities portfolio.
   d. The Magellan Fund buys $100 million of previously issued IBM bonds.
   e. Prudential Insurance Co. sells $10 million of GM common stock.

2. Classify the following financial instruments as money market securities or capital market securities *(LG6-2):*
   a. Federal funds
   b. Common stock
   c. Corporate bonds
   d. Mortgages
   e. Negotiable certificates of deposit
   f. U.S. Treasury bills
   g. U.S. Treasury notes
   h. U.S. Treasury bonds
   i. State and government bonds

3. What are the different types of financial institutions? Include a description of the main services offered by each. *(LG6-3)*

4. How would economic transactions between suppliers of funds (e.g., households) and users of funds (e.g., corporations) occur in a world without FIs? *(LG6-3)*

5. Why would a world limited to the direct transfer of funds from suppliers of funds to users of funds likely result in quite low levels of fund flows? *(LG6-3)*

6. How do FIs reduce monitoring costs associated with the flow of funds from fund suppliers to fund users? *(LG6-3)*

7. How do FIs alleviate the problem of liquidity risk faced by investors wishing to invest in securities of corporations? *(LG6-3)*

8. What are six factors that determine the nominal interest rate on a security? *(LG6-4)*

9. What should happen to a security's equilibrium interest rate as the security's liquidity risk increases? *(LG6-4)*

10. Discuss and compare the three explanations for the shape of the yield curve. *(LG6-5)*

11. Are the unbiased expectations and liquidity premium theories explanations for the shape of the yield curve completely independent theories? Explain why or why not. *(LG6-5)*

12. What is a forward interest rate? *(LG6-6)*

13. If we observe a 1-year Treasury security rate that is higher than the 2-year Treasury security rate, what can we infer about the 1-year rate expected one year from now? *(LG6-6)*

problems

basic problems

6-1 **Determinants of Interest Rates for Individual Securities** A particular security's default risk premium is 2 percent. For all securities, the inflation risk premium is 1.75 percent and the real risk-free rate is 3.5 percent. The security's liquidity risk premium is 0.25 percent and maturity risk premium is 0.85 percent. The security has no special covenants. Calculate the security's equilibrium rate of return. *(LG6-4)*

6-2 **Determinants of Interest Rates for Individual Securities** You are considering an investment in 30-year bonds issued by Moore Corporation. The bonds have no special covenants. *The Wall Street Journal* reports that 1-year T-bills are currently earning 1.25 percent. Your broker has determined the following information about economic activity and Moore Corporation bonds:

Real risk-free rate = 0.75%

Default risk premium = 1.15%

Liquidity risk premium = 0.50%

Maturity risk premium = 1.75%

a. What is the inflation premium? *(LG6-4)*

b. What is the fair interest rate on Moore Corporation 30-year bonds? *(LG6-4)*

6-3 **Determinants of Interest Rates for Individual Securities** Dakota Corporation 15-year bonds have an equilibrium rate of return of 8 percent. For all securities, the inflation risk premium is 1.75 percent and the real risk-free rate is 3.50 percent. The security's liquidity risk premium is 0.25 percent and maturity risk premium is 0.85 percent. The security has no special covenants. Calculate the bond's default risk premium. *(LG6-4)*

6-4 **Determinants of Interest Rates for Individual Securities** A 2-year Treasury security currently earns 1.94 percent. Over the next two years, the real risk-free rate is expected to be 1.00 percent per year and the inflation premium is expected to be 0.50 percent per year. Calculate the maturity risk premium on the 2-year Treasury security. *(LG6-4)*

6-5 **Unbiased Expectations Theory** Suppose that the current 1-year rate (1-year spot rate) and expected 1-year T-bill rates over the following three years (i.e., years 2, 3, and 4, respectively) are as follows:

$$_1R_1 = 6\%, \; E(_2r_1) = 7\%, \; E(_3r_1) = 7.5\%, \; E(_4r_1) = 7.85\%$$

Using the unbiased expectations theory, calculate the current (long-term) rates for 1-, 2-, 3-, and 4-year-maturity Treasury securities. Plot the resulting yield curve. *(LG6-5)*

6-6 **Unbiased Expectations Theory** Suppose that the current 1-year rate (1-year spot rate) and expected 1-year T-bill rates over the following three years (i.e., years 2, 3, and 4, respectively) are as follows:

$$_1R_1 = 1\%, \; E(_2r_1) = 3.75\%, \; E(_3r_1) = 4.25\%, \; E(_4r_1) = 5.75\%$$

Using the unbiased expectations theory, calculate the current (long-term) rates for 1-, 2-, 3-, and 4-year-maturity Treasury securities. Plot the resulting yield curve. *(LG6-5)*

6-7 **Unbiased Expectations Theory** One-year Treasury bills currently earn 1.45 percent. You expect that one year from now, 1-year Treasury bill rates will increase to 1.65 percent. If the unbiased expectations theory is correct, what should the current rate be on 2-year Treasury securities? *(LG6-5)*

6-8 **Unbiased Expectations Theory** One-year Treasury bills currently earn 2.15 percent. You expect that one year from now, 1-year Treasury bill rates will increase to 2.65 percent and that two years from now, 1-year Treasury bill rates will increase to 3.05 percent. If the unbiased expectations theory is correct, what should the current rate be on 3-year Treasury securities? *(LG6-6-5)*

6-9 **Liquidity Premium Theory** One-year Treasury bills currently earn 3.45 percent. You expect that one year from now, 1-year Treasury bill rates will increase to 3.65 percent. The liquidity premium on 2-year securities is 0.05 percent. If the liquidity premium theory is correct, what should the current rate be on 2-year Treasury securities? *(LG6-5)*

6-10 **Liquidity Premium Theory** One-year Treasury bills currently earn 2.25 percent. You expect that one year from now, 1-year Treasury bill rates will increase to 2.45 percent and that two years from now, 1-year Treasury bill rates will increase to 2.95 percent. The liquidity premium on 2-year securities is 0.05 percent and on 3-year securities is 0.15 percent. If the liquidity premium theory is correct, what should the current rate be on 3-year Treasury securities? *(LG6-5)*

6-11 **Liquidity Premium Theory** Based on economists' forecasts and analysis, 1-year Treasury bill rates and liquidity premiums for the next four years are expected to be as follows:

$$R_1 = 0.65\%$$
$$E(_2r_1) = 1.75\% \qquad L_2 = 0.05\%$$
$$E(_3r_1) = 1.85\% \qquad L_3 = 0.10\%$$
$$E(_4r_1) = 2.15\% \qquad L_4 = 0.12\%$$

Using the liquidity premium theory, plot the current yield curve. Make sure you label the axes on the graph and identify the four annual rates on the curve both on the axes and on the yield curve itself. *(LG6-5)*

6-12 Liquidity Premium Theory Based on economists' forecasts and analysis, 1-year Treasury bill rates and liquidity premiums for the next four years are expected to be as follows:

$R_1 = 1.25\%$

$E({}_2r_1) = 2.15\%$ $\quad L_2 = 0.08\%$

$E({}_3r_1) = 2.55\%$ $\quad L_3 = 0.10\%$

$E({}_4r_1) = 3.00\%$ $\quad L_4 = 0.15\%$

Using the liquidity premium theory, plot the current yield curve. Make sure you label the axes on the graph and identify the four annual rates on the curve both on the axes and on the yield curve itself. (*LG6-5*)

intermediate problems

6-13 Determinants of Interest Rates for Individual Securities Tom and Sue's Flowers, Inc.'s, 15-year bonds are currently yielding a return of 8.25 percent. The expected inflation premium is 2.25 percent annually and the real risk-free rate is expected to be 3.50 percent annually over the next 15 years. The default risk premium on Tom and Sue's Flowers' bonds is 0.80 percent. The maturity risk premium is 0.75 percent on 5-year securities and increases by 0.04 percent for each additional year to maturity. Calculate the liquidity risk premium on Tom and Sue's Flowers, Inc.'s, 15-year bonds. *(LG6-4)*

6-14 Determinants of Interest Rates for Individual Securities NikkiG's Corporation's 10-year bonds are currently yielding a return of 6.05 percent. The expected inflation premium is 1.00 percent annually and the real risk-free rate is expected to be 2.10 percent annually over the next ten years. The liquidity risk premium on NikkiG's bonds is 0.25 percent. The maturity risk premium is 0.10 percent on 2-year securities and increases by 0.05 percent for each additional year to maturity. Calculate the default risk premium on NikkiG's 10-year bonds. *(LG6-4)*

6-15 Unbiased Expectations Theory Suppose we observe the following rates: ${}_1R_1 = 8\%$, ${}_1R_2 = 10\%$. If the unbiased expectations theory of the term structure of interest rates holds, what is the 1-year interest rate expected one year from now, $E({}_2r_1)$? *(LG6-5)*

6-16 Unbiased Expectations Theory *The Wall Street Journal* reports that the rate on 4-year Treasury securities is 1.60 percent and the rate on 5-year Treasury securities is 2.15 percent. According to the unbiased expectations theories, what does the market expect the 1-year Treasury rate to be four years from today, $E({}_5r_1)$? *(LG6-5)*

6-17 Liquidity Premium Theory *The Wall Street Journal* reports that the rate on 3-year Treasury securities is 5.25 percent and the rate on 4-year Treasury securities is 5.50 percent. The 1-year interest rate expected in three years is, $E({}_4r_1)$, is 6.10 percent. According to the liquidity premium hypotheses, what is the liquidity premium on the 4-year Treasury security, L_4? *(LG6-5)*

6-18 Liquidity Premium Theory Suppose we observe the following rates: ${}_1R_1 = 0.75\%$, ${}_1R_2 = 1.20\%$, and $E({}_2r_1) = 0.907\%$. If the liquidity premium theory of the term structure of interest rates holds, what is the liquidity premium for year 2, L_2? *(LG6-5)*

6-19 **Forecasting Interest Rates** You note the following yield curve in *The Wall Street Journal.* According to the unbiased expectations theory, what is the 1-year forward rate for the period beginning one year from today, $_2f_1$? *(LG6-6)*

Maturity	Yield
One day	2.00%
One year	5.50
Two years	6.50
Three years	9.00

6-20 **Forecasting Interest Rates** On March 11, 20XX, the existing or current *(spot)* 1-, 2-, 3-, and 4-year zero coupon Treasury security rates were as follows:

$$_1R_1 = 0.75\%,\ _1R_2 = 1.35\%,\ _1R_3 = 1.75\%,\ _1R_4 = 1.90\%$$

Using the unbiased expectations theory, calculate the 1-year forward rates on zero coupon Treasury bonds for years 2, 3, and 4 as of March 11, 20XX. *(LG6-6)*

advanced problems

6-21 **Determinants of Interest Rates for Individual Securities** *The Wall Street Journal* reports that the current rate on 10-year Treasury bonds is 7.25 percent, on 20-year Treasury bonds is 7.85 percent, and on a 20-year corporate bond issued by MHM Corp. is 8.75 percent. Assume that the maturity risk premium is zero. If the default risk premium and liquidity risk premium on a 10-year corporate bond issued by MHM Corp. are the same as those on the 20-year corporate bond, calculate the current rate on MHM Corp.'s 10-year corporate bond. *(LG6-4)*

6-22 **Determinants of Interest Rates for Individual Securities** *The Wall Street Journal* reports that the current rate on 8-year Treasury bonds is 5.85 percent, the rate on 15-year Treasury bonds is 6.25 percent, and the rate on a 15-year corporate bond issued by MHM Corp. is 7.35 percent. Assume that the maturity risk premium is zero. If the default risk premium and liquidity risk premium on an 8-year corporate bond issued by MHM Corp. are the same as those on the 15-year corporate bond, calculate the current rate on MHM Corp.'s 8-year corporate bond. *(LG6-4)*

6-23 **Determinants of Interest Rates for Individual Securities** *The Wall Street Journal* reports that the current rate on 5-year Treasury bonds is 1.85 percent and on 10-year Treasury bonds is 3.35 percent. Assume that the maturity risk premium is zero. Calculate the expected rate on a 5-year Treasury bond purchased five years from today, $E(_5r_5)$. *(LG6-4)*

6-24 **Determinants of Interest Rates for Individual Securities** *The Wall Street Journal* reports that the current rate on 10-year Treasury bonds is 2.25 percent and the rate on 20-year Treasury bonds is 4.50 percent. Assume that the maturity risk premium is zero. Calculate the expected rate on a 10-year Treasury bond purchased ten years from today, $E(_{10}r_{10})$. *(LG6-4)*

6-25 **Unbiased Expectations Theory** Suppose we observe the 3-year Treasury security rate ($_1R_3$) to be 8 percent, the expected 1-year rate next year—$E(_2r_1)$—to be 4 percent, and the expected one-year rate the following year—$E(_3r_1)$—to be 6 percent. If the unbiased expectations theory of the term structure of interest rates holds, what is the 1-year Treasury security rate, $_1R_1$? *(LG6-5)*

6-26 **Unbiased Expectations Theory** *The Wall Street Journal* reports that the rate on 3-year Treasury securities is 1.20 percent and the rate on 5-year Treasury securities is 2.15 percent. According to the unbiased expectations theory, what does the market expect the 2-year Treasury rate to be three years from today, $E({}_3r_2)$? *(LG6-5)*

6-27 **Forecasting Interest Rates** Assume the current interest rate on a 1-year Treasury bond (${}_1R_1$) is 4.50 percent, the current rate on a 2-year Treasury bond (${}_1R_2$) is 5.25 percent, and the current rate on a 3-year Treasury bond (${}_1R_3$) is 6.50 percent. If the unbiased expectations theory of the term structure of interest rates is correct, what is the 1-year forward rate expected on Treasury bills during year 3, ${}_3f_1$? *(LG6-6)*

6-28 **Forecasting Interest Rates** A recent edition of *The Wall Street Journal* reported interest rates of 1.25 percent, 1.60 percent, 1.98 percent, and 2.25 percent for 3-, 4-, 5-, and 6-year Treasury security yields, respectively. According to the unbiased expectation theory of the term structure of interest rates, what are the expected 1-year forward rates for years 4, 5, and 6? *(LG6-6)*

research it! Spreads

Go to the Federal Reserve Board's website at **www.federalreserve.gov** and get the latest rates on 10-year T-bills and Aaa- and Baa-rated corporate bonds using the following steps.

Go to the Federal Reserve's website at **www.federalreserve.gov**. Click on "Economic Research and Data," then click on "Selected Interest Rates-H.15." Click on the most recent date. This will bring the file onto your computer that contains the relevant data. Click on "Historical Data" and then "10-Year" under "Treasury Constant Maturities," or "Aaa" and "Baa" under "Corporate Bonds" to get past data. Calculate the current spread of Aaa- and Baa-rated bonds over the 10-year Treasury-bond rate. How have these spreads changed over the last two years?

integrated mini-case: Calculating Interest Rates

From discussions with your broker, you have determined that the expected inflation premium is 1.35 percent next year, 1.50 percent in year 2, 1.75 percent in year 3, and 2.00 percent in year 4 and beyond. Further, you expect that real risk-free rates will be 3.20 percent next year, 3.30 percent in year 2, 3.75 percent in year 3, and 3.80 percent in year 4 and beyond. You are considering an investment in either 5-year Treasury securities or 5-year bonds issued by PeeWee Corporation. The bonds have no special covenants. Your broker has determined the following information about economic activity and PeeWee Corporation 5-year bonds:

Default risk premium = 2.10%
Liquidity risk premium = 1.75
Maturity risk premium = 0.75

Further, the maturity risk premium on PeeWee bonds is 0.1875 percent per year starting in year 2. PeeWee's default risk premium and liquidity risk premium do not change with bond maturity.

a. What is the fair interest rate on 5-year Treasury securities?

b. What is the fair interest rate on PeeWee Corporation 5-year bonds?

c. Plot the 5-year yield curve for the Treasury securities.

d. Plot the 5-year yield curve for the PeeWee Corporation bonds.

ANSWERS TO TIME OUT

6-1 Primary markets provide a forum in which demanders of funds (e.g., corporations such as IBM or government entities such as the U.S. Treasury) raise funds by issuing new financial instruments, such as stocks and bonds. Corporations or government entities continually have new projects or expanded production needs, but do not have sufficient internally generated funds (such as retained earnings) to support their capital needs. Thus, corporations and governments issue securities in external primary markets to raise additional funds. Once firms issue financial instruments in primary markets, these same stocks and bonds are then traded—that is, bought and resold—in secondary markets.

6-2 Foreign exchange markets trade currencies for immediate (also called *spot*) or for some future stated delivery.

6-3 A derivative security is a financial security (such as a futures contract, option contract, or swap contract) that is linked to another underlying security, such as a stock traded in capital markets or British pounds traded in foreign exchange (forex) markets. Derivative securities generally involve an agreement between two parties to exchange a standard quantity of an asset or cash flow at a predetermined price and at a specified date in the future. As the value of the underlying security changes, the value of the derivative security changes.

6-4 The major types of financial institutions are:

Commercial banks are depository institutions whose major assets are loans and whose major liabilities are deposits.

Thrifts are depository institutions, including savings associations, savings banks, and credit unions, that generally perform services similar to commercial banks but tend to concentrate their loans in one segment, such as real estate loans or consumer loans.

Insurance companies protect individuals and corporations (policyholders) from financially adverse events, such as untimely death, illness, retirement, and personal injury and liability due to accidents, theft, fire, and so on.

Securities firms and investment banks underwrite securities and engage in related activities such as securities brokerage, securities trading, and making markets in which securities trade.

Finance companies make loans to both individuals and businesses. The loans are funded by short- and long-term debt, and many are collateralized with some kind of durable good, such as washer/dryers, furniture, carpets, and the like.

Mutual funds pool many individuals' and companies' financial resources and invest those resources in diversified asset portfolios.

Pension funds offer savings plans through which fund participants accumulate savings during their working years.

6-5 First, once they have lent money in exchange for financial claims, fund suppliers would need to continually monitor the use of their funds to guard against theft and waste. Second, many financial claims feature a long-term commitment (e.g., mortgages, corporate stock, and bonds) for fund suppliers, thus creating another disincentive for fund suppliers to hold direct financial claims that fund users may issue. Third, even though real-world financial markets provide some liquidity services by allowing fund suppliers to trade financial securities among themselves, fund suppliers face price risk when they buy securities—fund suppliers may not get their principal back, let alone any return on their investment.

6-6 A major event that changed and reshaped the financial services industry was the financial crisis of the late 2000s. As FIs adjusted to regulatory changes brought about in the 1980s and 1990s, one result was a dramatic increase in systemic risk of the financial system, caused in large part by a shift in the banking model from that of "originate and hold" to "originate to distribute." In the traditional model, banks take short-term deposits and other sources of funds and use them to fund longer term loans to businesses and consumers. Banks typically hold these loans to maturity, and thus have an incentive to screen and monitor borrower activities even after a loan is made. However, the traditional banking model exposes the institution to potential liquidity, interest rate, and credit risk. In attempts to avoid these risk exposures and generate improved return-risk trade-offs, banks shifted to an underwriting model in which they originated or warehoused loans, and then quickly sold them. Indeed, most large banks organized as financial service holding companies to facilitate these new activities. More recently activities of shadow banks, nonfinancial service firms that perform banking services, have facilitated the change from the originate-and-hold model of commercial banking to the originate-and-distribute banking model. In the shadow banking system, savers place their funds with money market mutual and similar funds, which invest these funds in the liabilities of other shadow banks. Like the traditional banking system, the shadow banking system intermediates the flow of funds between net savers and borrowers. However, instead of the bank serving as the middleman, it is the nonbank financial service firm, or shadow bank, that intermediates. Further, unlike the traditional banking system where the complete credit intermediation is performed by a single bank, in the shadow banking system, it is performed through a series of steps involving many nonbank financial service firms. These innovations remove risk from the balance sheet of financial institutions and shift risk off the balance sheet and to other parts of the financial system. Since the FIs, acting as underwriters, are not exposed to the credit, liquidity, and interest rate risks of traditional banking, they have little incentive to screen and monitor activities of borrowers to whom they originate loans. Thus, FIs role as specialists in risk measurement and management is reduced.

6-7 We actually observe nominal risk-free rates in financial markets—these are the rates most often quoted by financial news services. Real risk-free rates are interest rate adjusted for inflation; generally lower than nominal risk-free rates at any particular time.

6-8 The term structure of interest rates compares interest rates on debt securities based on their time to maturity, assuming that all other characteristics (i.e., default risk, liquidity risk) are equal.

6-9 The yield curve for U.S. Treasury securities has taken many shapes over the years, but the three most common shapes are: (1) the upward-sloping yield curve (most common) where yields rise steadily with maturity; (2) an inverted or downward-sloping yield curve in which yields decline as maturity increases; and (3) a flat yield curve, when the yield to maturity is virtually unaffected by the term to maturity.

6-10 Explanations for the yield curve's shape fall predominantly into three categories: the unbiased expectations theory, the liquidity premium theory, and the market segmentation theory.

6-11 According to the unbiased expectations theory, the return for holding a 4-year bond to maturity should equal the expected return for investing in four successive 1-year bonds (as long as the market is in equilibrium). If this equality does not hold, an arbitrage opportunity exists. That is, if investors could earn more on the 1-year bond investments, they could short (or sell) the 4-year bond, use the proceeds to buy the four successive 1-year bonds, and earn a guaranteed profit over the 4-year investment horizon.

6-12 A forward rate is an expected, or implied, rate on a short-term security that will originate at some point in the future.

6-13 To find an implied forward rate on a 1-year security to be issued one year from today, we can rewrite the unbiased expectations theory equation as follows:

$$_1R_2 = [(1 + {_1R_1})(1 + {_2f_1})]^{1/2} - 1 \qquad \textbf{(6-9)}$$

where $_2f_1$ = Expected 1-year rate for year 2, or the implied forward 1-year rate for next year. Saying that $_2f_1$ is the expected 1-year rate for year 2 is the same as saying that, once we isolate the $_2f_1$ term, the equation will give us the market's estimate of the expected 1-year rate for year 2.

6-14 As interest rates change, so do the values of financial securities. Accordingly, both individual investors and public corporations want to be able to predict or forecast interest rates if they wish to trade profitably. For example, if interest rates rise, the value of investment portfolios of individuals and corporations will fall, resulting in a loss of wealth. So, interest rate forecasts are extremely important for the financial wealth of both public corporations and individuals.

7 Valuing Bonds

viewpoints

Business Application

You are the chief financial officer (CFO) for Beach Sand Resorts. The firm needs $150 million of new capital to renovate a hotel property. As you discuss the firm's plans with a credit rating agency, you learn that if 15-year bonds are used to raise this capital, the bonds will be rated BB and will have to offer a 7 percent return. How many bonds will you have to issue to raise the necessary capital? What semiannual interest payments will Beach Sand have to make? **(See solution on p. 259)**

Personal Application

You would like to invest in bonds. Your broker suggests two different bonds. The first, issued by Trust Media, will mature in 2018. Its price is quoted at 96.21 and it pays a 5.7 percent coupon. The second bond suggested, issued by Abalon, Inc., also matures in 2018. This bond's price is 101.94 and pays a 5.375 percent coupon. To help you decide between the bonds, you want to know how much money it will cost to buy 10 bonds, what interest payments you will receive, and what return the bonds offer if purchased today. Also, you want to understand the differences between what the two bonds imply about their risk. **(See solution on p. 259)**

How do you even purchase a bond in the first place?

Learning Goals

LG7-1 Describe bond characteristics.

LG7-2 Identify various bond issuers and their motivation for issuing debt.

LG7-3 Read and interpret bond quotes.

LG7-4 Compute bond prices using present value concepts.

LG7-5 Explain the relationship between bond prices and interest rates.

LG7-6 Compute bond yields.

LG7-7 Find bond ratings and assess credit risk's effects on bond yields.

LG7-8 Assess bond market performance.

How important are bonds and the bond market to a capitalist economy? Those unfamiliar with the financial markets may have the impression that the stock market dominates capital markets in the United States and in other countries. Stock market performance appears constantly on 24-hour TV news channels and on the evening news. By contrast, we seldom hear any mention of the bond market. While bonds may not generate the same excitement that stocks do, they are an even more important capital source for companies, governments, and other organizations. The bond market is actually larger than the stock market. At the end of 2012, the U.S. bond market represented roughly $38 trillion in outstanding debt obligations. At the same time, the market value of all common stock issues was worth less than half of the value of the bond market, at roughly $15.8 trillion.

Bonds also trade in great volume and frequency. During 2012, the total average daily trading in all types of U.S. bonds reached over $840 billion. Investors are often attracted to the stock market because it offers the potential for high investor returns—but great risks come with that high potential return. While some bonds offer safer and more stable returns than stocks, other bonds also offer high potential rewards and, consequently, higher risk.

In this chapter, we will explore bond characteristics and their price dynamics. You will see that bond pricing uses many time value of money principles that we've used in the preceding chapters.

7.1 • Bond Market Overview

Bond Characteristics

Bonds are debt obligation securities that corporations, the federal government or its agencies, or states and local governments issue to fund various projects or operations. All of these organizations periodically need to raise capital for various reasons, which was formally discussed in Chapter 6. Bonds are also known as **fixed-income securities** because bondholders (investors) know both how much they will receive in interest payments and when their principal will be returned. From the bond issuer's point of view, the bond is a loan that requires regular interest payments and an eventual repayment of the borrowed **principal.** Investors—often pension funds, banks, and mutual funds—buy bonds to earn investment returns. Most bonds follow a relatively standard structure. A legal contract called the **indenture agreement** outlines the precise terms between the issuer and the bondholders. Any bond's main characteristics include:

bond
Publicly traded form of debt.

fixed-income securities
Any securities that make fixed payments.

principal
Face amount, or par value, of debt.

indenture agreement
Legal contract describing the bond characteristics and the bondholder and issuer rights.

table 7.1 | **Typical Bond Features**

Characteristic	Description	Common Values
Par value	The amount of the loan to be repaid. This is often referred to as the *principal* of the bond.	$1,000
Time to maturity	The number of years left until the maturity date.	1 year to 30 years
Call	The opportunity for the issuer to repay the principal before the maturity date, usually because interest rates have fallen or issuer's circumstances have changed. When calling a bond, the issuer commonly pays the principal and one year of interest payments.	Many bonds are not callable. For those that are, a common feature is that the bond can be called any time after 10 years of issuance.
Coupon rate	The interest rate used to compute the bond's interest payment each year. Listed as a percentage of par value, the actual payments usually are paid twice per year.	2 to 10 percent
Bond price	The bond's market price reported as a percentage of par value.	80 to 120 percent of par value

maturity date

The calendar date on which the bond principal comes due.

par value

Amount of debt borrowed to be repaid; face value.

- The date the principal will be repaid (the **maturity date**).
- The **par value,** or face value, of each bond, which is the principal loan amount that the borrower must repay.
- The coupon (interest) rate.
- A description of any property to be pledged as collateral.
- Steps that the bondholder can take in the event that the issuer fails to pay the interest or principal.

time to maturity

The length of time (in years) until the bond matures and the issuer repays the par value.

Table 7.1 describes par value and other bond characteristics. Most bonds have a par value of $1,000. This is the amount of principal the issuer has promised to repay. Bonds have fixed lives. The bond's life ends when the issuer repays the par value to the buyer on the bond's maturity date. Although a bond will mature on a specific calendar date, the bond is usually referenced by its **time to maturity,** that is, 2 years, 5 years, 20 years, and so on. In fact, the market groups bonds together by their time to maturity and classifies them as short-term bonds, medium-term bonds, or long-term bonds, regardless of issuer. Long-term bonds carry 20 or 30 years to maturity. Of course, over time, the 30-year bond becomes a 20-year bond, 10-year bond, and eventually matures. But other time periods to maturity do exist. For example, in 2011, the railroad company Norfolk Southern Corp. issued $400 million of bonds with 100 years to maturity. The bonds have a coupon (interest) rate of 6 percent and mature in 2111.

LG7-1

When interest rates economywide fall several percentage points (which often takes several years), homeowners everywhere seek to refinance their home mortgages. They want to make lower interest payments (and sometimes want to pay down their mortgage principal) every month. Corporations that have outstanding bond debt will also want to refinance those bonds. Sometimes the indenture contract (the legal contract between a bond issuer and bondholders) allows companies to do so; sometimes the indenture prohibits refinancing. Bonds that can be refinanced have a **call** feature, which means that the issuer can "call" the bonds back and repay the principal before the maturity date. To compensate the bondholders for getting the bond called, the issuer pays the principal and a **call premium.** The most common call premium is one year's worth of interest payments. In some indentures, the call premium declines over time.

call

An issuer redeeming the bond before the scheduled maturity date.

call premium

The amount in addition to the par value paid by the issuer when calling a bond.

coupon rate

The annual amount of interest paid expressed as a percentage of the bond's par value.

The bond's **coupon rate** determines the dollar amount of interest paid to bondholders. The coupon rate appears on the bond and is listed as a percentage of the par value. So a 5 percent coupon rate means that the issuer will pay 5 percent of $1,000, or $50, in interest every year, usually divided into two equal semiannual payments. So a 5 percent coupon bond will pay $25 every six months. Companies set the coupon rate as the prevailing market interest rate at the time of bond issue. The name *coupon* is a holdover from the past, when bonds were actually issued with a coupon book. Every six months a bondholder would tear out a coupon and mail it to the issuer, who would then make the interest payment. These are sometimes referred to as *bearer bonds* (often a feature of spy or mystery movies), because whoever held the coupon book could receive the payments. Nowadays, issuers register bond owners and automatically wire interest payments to the owner's bank or brokerage account. Nevertheless, the term *coupon* persists today.

> **MATH COACH**
>
> **PERCENT-TO-DECIMAL CONVERSIONS**
>
> When discussing interest rates or using them in calculator or spreadsheet time value of money functions, the value should be in percent (%) form, like 2.5%, 7%, and 11%. When using interest rates in formulas, the value needs to be in decimal form, like 0.025, 0.07, and 0.11.
>
> To convert between the two forms of representing an interest rate, use
>
> $$\text{Decimal} = \frac{\text{Percent (\%)}}{100}$$

At original issue, bonds typically sell at par value, unless interest rates are very volatile. Bondholders recoup the par value on the bond's maturity date. However, at all times in between these two dates, bonds might trade among investors in the secondary bond market. The **bond's price** as it trades in the secondary market will not likely be the par value. Bonds trade for higher and lower prices than their par values. We'll thoroughly demonstrate the reasons for bond pricing in a later section of this chapter. Bond prices are quoted in terms of percent of par value rather than in dollar terms. Sources of trading information list a bond that traded at $1,150 as 115, and a bond that traded for $870 as 87.

bond price
Current price that the bond sells for in the bond market.

EXAMPLE 7-1

LG7-1

Bond Characteristics

Consider a bond issued 10 years ago with an at-issue time to maturity of 30 years. The bond's coupon rate is 8 percent and it currently trades in the bond market for 109. Assuming a par value of $1,000, what is the bond's current time to maturity, semiannual interest payment, and bond price in dollars?

For interactive versions of this example visit www.mhhe.com/can3e

SOLUTION:

Time to maturity = 30 years − 10 years = 20 years

Annual payment = 0.08 × $1,000 = $80, so semiannual payment is $40

Bond price = 1.09 × $1,000 = $1,090

Similar to Problems 7-1, 7-2, 7-3, 7-4, self-test problem 1

Bond Issuers

LG7-2

For many years, bonds were considered stodgy, overly conservative investments. Not anymore! The fixed-income industry has seen tremendous innovation in the past couple of decades. The financial industry has created and issued many new types of bonds and fixed-income securities, some with odd-sounding acronyms, like TIGRs, CATS, COUGRs, and PINEs, all of which are securities based on U.S. Treasuries. Even with all the innovation, the traditional three main bond issuers remain: U.S. Treasury bonds, corporate bonds, and municipal bonds. Figure 7.1 shows the amount of money that these bond issuers have raised each year.

LG7-2

TREASURY BONDS Treasury bonds carry the "full-faith-and-credit" backing of the U.S. government and investors have long considered them among the safest fixed-income investments in the world. The federal government sells Treasury securities through public auctions to finance the federal deficit. When the deficit is large, more bonds come to auction. In addition, the Federal Reserve System (the Fed) uses Treasury securities to implement monetary policy. Technically,

figure 7.1

Amount of Capital Raised Yearly from Bonds Issued by Local and Federal Government and Corporations

Local or municipal governments, the U.S. Treasury, and corporations have issued many new types of bonds and fixed-income securities over the past two decades.

Data Source: Securities Industry and Financial Markets Association

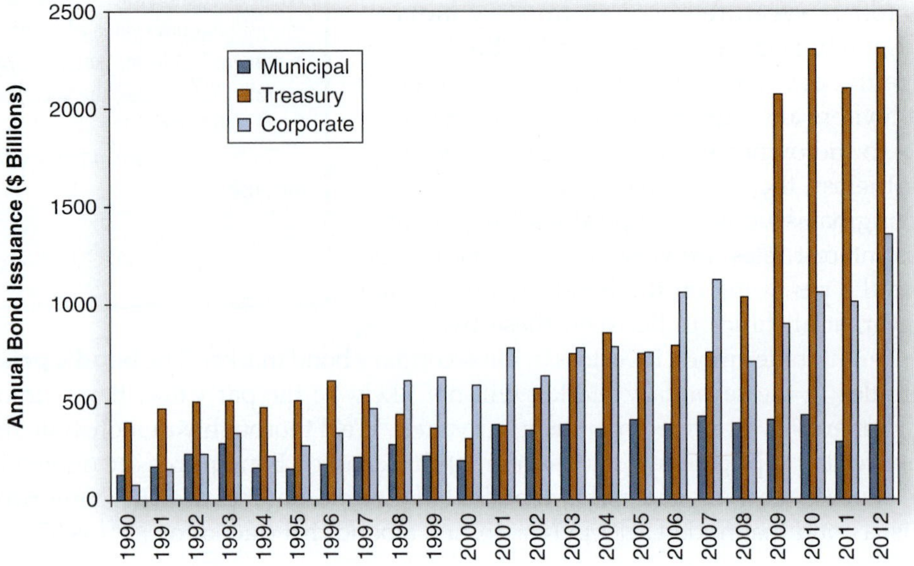

Treasury securities issued with 1 to 10 years until maturity are Treasury notes. Securities issued with 10 to 30 years until maturity are Treasury bonds. Figure 7.1 shows that the number of new Treasuries being offered actually declined in the late 1990s as the federal budget deficit declined. However, this reversed in 2002 and then dramatically accelerated in 2009 after the global financial crisis.

CORPORATE BONDS Corporations raise capital to finance investments in inventory, plant and equipment, research and development, and general business expansion. As managers decide how to raise capital, corporations can issue debt, equity (stocks), or a mixture of both. The driving force behind a corporation's financing strategy is the desire to minimize its total capital costs. Through much of the 1990s, corporations tended to issue equity (stocks) to raise capital. Beginning in 1998 and through 2012, corporations switched to raising capital by issuing bonds to take advantage of low interest rates and issued $12.8 trillion in new bonds. You can see this rise in capital reflected in Figure 7.1.

MUNICIPAL BONDS State and local governments borrow money to build, repair, or improve streets, highways, hospitals, schools, sewer systems, and so on. The interest and principal on these municipal bonds are repaid in two ways. Projects that benefit the entire community, such as courthouses, schools, and municipal office buildings, are typically funded by general obligation bonds and repaid using tax revenues. Projects that benefit only certain groups of people, such as toll roads and airports, are typically funded by revenue bonds and repaid from user fees. Interest payments paid to municipal bondholders are not taxed at the federal level, or by the state for which the bond is issued.

Treasury Inflation-Protected Securities

TIPS are U.S. government bonds where the par value changes with inflation.

LG7-2

Other Bonds and Bond-Based Securities

Treasury Inflation-Protected Securities (TIPS) have proved one of the most successful recent innovations in the bond market. The U.S. Treasury began issuing this new type of Treasury bond, which is indexed to inflation, in 1997.

TIPS have fixed coupon rates like traditional Treasuries. The new aspect is that the federal government adjusts the par value of the TIPS bond for inflation. Specifically, it increases at the rate of inflation (measured by the consumer price index, CPI). As the bond's par value changes over time, interest payments also change. At maturity, investors receive an inflation-adjusted principal amount. If inflation has been high, investors will expect that the adjusted principal amount will be substantially higher than the original $1,000. Consider a 10-year TIPS issued on January 15, 2009, that pays a 2⅛ percent coupon. The reference CPI for these bonds is 214.69971. Four years later (on January 15, 2013) the reference CPI was 230.22100. So the par value of the TIPS in early 2013 was $1,072.29 (= $1,000 × 230.22100 ÷ 214.69971). Therefore, the 2⅛ percent coupon (paid semiannually) would be $11.39 = (0.02125 × $1,072.29 ÷ 2). A TIPS' total return comes from both the interest payments and the inflation adjustment to the par value.

EXAMPLE 7-2

LG7-2

TIPS Payments

A TIPS bond was issued on July 15, 2006, that pays a 2½ percent coupon. The reference CPI at issue was 201.95. The reference CPI for the following interest payments were:

January 2009	214.70
July 2009	213.52
January 2010	216.25

Given these numbers, what is the par value and interest payment of the TIPS on the three interest-payment dates? What is the total return from January 2009 to January 2010?

SOLUTION:

Compute the TIPS index ratio for each period as current CPI divided by the at-issue CPI: The par value for January 2009 is $1,000 × 214.70 ÷ 201.95 = $1,063.13, so the interest payment is 0.025 × $1,063.13 ÷ 2 = $13.29. The answers for the next two dates are:

July 2009	Par value = $1,057.29	Interest payment = $13.22
January 2010	Par value = $1,070.81	Interest payment = $13.39

The capital gain between January 2009 and January 2010 is $1,070.81 − $1,063.13 = $7.68. Adding the two interest payments together results in $26.61 (= $13.22 + $13.39). Thus, the total return is 3.23% = ($7.68 + $26.61)/$1,063.13.

Similar to Problems 7-7, 7-8, 7-19, 7-20, 7-33, 7-34

For interactive versions of this example visit www.mhhe.com/can3e

U.S. government agency securities are debt securities issued to provide low-cost financing for desirable private-sector activities such as home ownership, education, and farming. Fannie Mae, Freddie Mac, Student Loan Marketing Association (Sallie Mae), Federal Farm Credit System, Federal Home Loan Banks, and the Small Business Administration, among others, issue these **agency bonds** to support particular sectors of the economy. Agency securities do not carry the federal government's full-faith-and-credit guarantee, but the government has never let one of its agencies fail. Because investors believe that the federal government will continue in this watchdog role, agency bonds are thought to be very safe and may provide a slightly higher return than Treasury securities do.

agency bonds
Bonds issued by U.S. government agencies.

finance at work — personal finance

BUY TREASURIES DIRECT!

Treasury bonds are U.S. government-issued debt securities that investors trade on secondary markets. The government also issues nonmarketable debt, called "savings bonds," directly to investors. The common EE savings bonds, introduced in 1980, do not pay regular interest payments. Instead, interest accrues and adds to the bond's value. After a 1-year holding period, they can be redeemed at almost any bank or credit union. You can now purchase savings bonds and other Treasury securities (bills, notes, bonds, and TIPS) electronically through the U.S. Treasury's website, treasurydirect.gov. You can set up an account in minutes and buy savings bonds with cash from your bank account. You can also redeem your bonds and transfer the proceeds back to your bank account. Bonds can be purchased 24 hours a day, 7 days a week at no cost.

When bondholders redeem savings bonds, they receive the original value paid plus the accrued interest. Paper bonds sell at half of the face value; if investors hold them for the full 30 years, they receive the par value. Investors buy electronic bonds at face value and earn interest in addition to the par value. Unlike other bonds, savers need not report income from these interest payments to the IRS until they actually redeem the bonds. So savings bonds count as tax-deferred investments.

About one in six Americans owns savings bonds. Savings bonds are used for a variety of purposes, such as personal savings instruments or gifts from grandparents to grandchildren. After the September 11, 2001, terrorist attacks, many Americans wanted to show support for the government. In December 2001, banks selling government EE savings bonds began printing "Patriot bond" on them. So EE savings bonds are now often called Patriot Bonds.

want to know more? Key Words to Search for Updates: TreasuryDirect (go to www.treasurydirect.gov)

U.S. government agencies invented one popular type of debt security: **mortgage-backed securities** (MBSs). Fannie Mae and Freddie Mac offer subsidies or mortgage guarantees for people who wouldn't otherwise qualify for mortgages, especially first-time homeowners. Fannie Mae started out as a government-owned enterprise in 1938 and became a publicly held corporation in 1968. Freddie Mac was chartered as a publicly held corporation at its inception in 1970. Since 2008, both have been in government conservatorship and run by the Federal Housing Finance Agency. To increase the amount of money available (liquidity) for the home mortgage market, Fannie Mae and Freddie Mac purchase home mortgages from banks, credit unions, and other lenders. They combine the mortgages into diversified portfolios of such loans and then issue mortgage-backed securities, which represent a share in the mortgage debt, to investors. As homeowners pay off or refinance the underlying portfolio of mortgage loans, MBS investors receive interest and principal payments. After selling mortgages to Fannie Mae or Freddie Mac, mortgage lenders have "new" cash to provide more mortgage loans. This process worked well for decades until the late 2000s, when subprime mortgages were given to people who couldn't afford them. As you know, defaults on these loans were the underpinnings of the financial crisis.

mortgage-backed securities Debt securities whose interest and par value payments originate from real estate mortgage payments.

We could apply the same concept to any type of loan; indeed, the financial markets have already invented many such pooled-debt securities. Typical examples include credit card debt, auto loans, home equity loans, and equipment leases. Like mortgage-backed securities, investors receive interest and principal from **asset-backed securities** as borrowers pay off their consumer loans. The asset-backed securities market is one of the fastest-growing areas in the financial services sector.

asset-backed securities Debt securities whose payments originate from other loans, such as credit card debt, auto loans, and home equity loans.

On the bond's maturity date, the bondholder receives the par value, which is typically $1,000. However, some corporate bonds give the bondholder a choice between the par value and a specified number of shares of stock. This type of bond is referred to as a **convertible bond** because it can be converted to

convertible bond A debt security that can be converted to shares of stock or another type of security.

finance at work — markets

MORTGAGE-BACKED SECURITIES AND FINANCIAL CRISIS

In the old days, a bank with $100,000 to lend would fund a mortgage and charge a fee for originating the loan. The bank would then collect interest on the loan over time. In the past few decades, the process changed to where that bank could sell that mortgage to investment banks and get the $100,000 back. The bank could then originate another mortgage and collect another fee. Bank revenue transitioned from interest earnings to fee earnings. This worked pretty well for several decades because the bank made more profits and more money was funneled into the community for home buyers. It is the securitization of debt that makes this possible. Financial institutions like Fannie Mae and investment banks bought up these mortgages, pooled them, and issued bonds against them (called mortgage-backed securities, or MBSs) to sell to investors. In effect, buyers of the MBSs are the actual lenders of the mortgage and banks simply earned fees for servicing the loans.

Note that this lending model gives banks and mortgage brokers the incentive to initiate as many mortgage loans as they can resell to maximize fee income. Then in 2000 to early 2004, the Federal Reserve kept adjusting interest rates on federal funds downward and kept them low. This both made home ownership more affordable, sparking a housing bubble, and drove investors to look for bonds that paid higher yields. Consequently, many loans were granted to individuals with poor creditworthiness (subprime borrowers). These subprime borrowers were charged higher interest rates. When these subprime mortgages were packed into the pool of mortgages, the MBSs offered higher yields. Thus, there was a high demand from investors for these MBSs, which fostered more poor credit quality loan originations.

Then from July 2004 to July 2006, the Federal Reserve started increasing interest rates. This placed some downward pressure on housing prices because it made homes less affordable. At the same time, most subprime mortgages originating from 2005 and 2006 were written on adjustable rates, and those interest rates adjusted upward too, making the payments too high for many borrowers. The subprime borrowers soon began to fall behind on their monthly payments leading to foreclosures and additional downward pressure on housing prices. The devaluation of housing prices eroded the home equity of homeowners and led to further foreclosures and further price decreases. The MBSs also devalued quickly.

Who owned MBSs? It turns out that the owners of these securities were financial firms, such as investment banks, commercial banks, insurance companies, mutual funds and pension funds all over the world. Their weakened financial strength led to bank failures, bailouts and a global credit crisis.

Source: Yuliya Demyanyk, and Otto Van Hemert, "Understanding the Subprime Mortgage Crisis," *Review of Financial Studies,* 2009.

want to know more? Key Words to Search for Updates: subprime, MBS, financial crisis

company stock. The number of shares of stock for which the bond can be converted is specified when the bond is originally issued. Thus, the bondholder will want to receive the shares when the stock price has risen since bond issuance, and they will want the $1,000 when the stock has declined in value.

Reading Bond Quotes

LG7-3

To those familiar with bond terminology, bond quotes provide all of the information needed to make informed investment decisions. The volume of Treasury securities traded each day is substantial. Treasury bonds and notes average more than a half billion dollars in trading daily. Investors exhibit much less enthusiasm for corporate or municipal bonds, perhaps because the markets for each particular bond or bonds with the same maturity, coupon rate, and credit ratings are much thinner and, therefore, less liquid. Most bond quote tables report only a small fraction of the outstanding bonds on any given day. Bond quotes can be found in *The Wall Street Journal* and online at places like Yahoo! Finance (yahoo.finance.com) and BondsOnline (www.bonds-online.com). Table 7.2 shows three bond quote examples.

A typical listing for Treasury bonds appears first. Here, this Treasury bond pays bondholders a coupon of 2.375 percent. On a $1,000 par value bond, this interest income would be $23.75 annually, paid as $11.875 every six months per bond. The bond will mature in February of 2015—since this is fairly soon, the

table 7.2 | **Bond Quote Examples**

Treasury Securities					
COUPON RATE	**MO/YR**	**BID**	**ASKED**	**CHG**	**ASK YLD**
2.375	Feb 15	104.2188	104.2266	−0.0313	0.294
Corporate Bond					
COMPANY	**COUPON**	**MATURITY**	**LAST PRICE**	**YIELD**	
Anheuser-Busch InBev	2.50	July 2022	91.470	2.56	
Municipal Bond					
ISSUE	**COUPON**	**MATURITY**	**PRICE**		**BID YLD**
NYC Muni Wtr Fin Auth	4.500	06-15-37	97.570		4.66

bond is considered a short-term bond. Both the bid and the ask quotes for the bond appear, expressed as percentages of the bond's par value of $1,000. The bid price is the price at which investors can sell the bond. A bid of 104.2188 means that an investor could sell for $1,042.188. Investors can buy this bond at the ask price of 104.2266, or $1,042.266. Since the price is higher than the par value of the bond, the bond is selling at a premium to par because its coupon rate is higher than current rates. Thus, investors call this kind of security a **premium bond.**

premium bond

A bond selling for greater than its par value.

Notice that the ask price is higher than the bid price. The difference is known as the bid-ask spread. Investors buy at the higher price and sell at the lower price. The bid-ask spread is thus the cost of actively trading bonds. Investors buy and sell with a bond dealer. Since the bond dealer takes the opposite side of the transaction, the dealer buys at the low price and sells at the higher price. The bid-ask spread is part of the dealer's compensation for taking on risk. An investor who bought this bond and held it to maturity would experience a $42.27 (= $1,042.27 − $1,000) capital loss (−4.06 percent [= −$42.27/$1,042.27]). The bond lost 0.0313 percent of its value during the day's trading—a change of −$0.31 for a $1,000 par value bond. Last, the bond is offering investors who purchase it at the ask price and hold it to maturity a 0.294 percent annual return.

Corporate bond quotes provide similar information. The table shows the quote for a Anheuser-Busch bond that offers bondholders a coupon of 2.50 percent, or $12.50 semiannually (= $1,000 × 0.025 ÷ 2). The bond would be considered a mid-term bond (usually 5 years to maturity), since it matures in the year 2022. Corporate bonds are also quoted in percentage of par value. The price quote of 97.470 indicates that the last trade occurred at a price of $974.70 per bond. Since the bond is selling for a price lower than its $1,000 par value, it's called a **discount bond.** An investor who bought this bond would reap a $25.30 (= $1,000 − $974.70) capital gain if the bond were held to maturity. The Anheuser-Busch bond represents an annual return of 2.56 percent for the investor who purchases the bond at $974.70.

discount bond

A bond selling for lower than its par value.

Companies set a bond's coupon rate when they originally issue the bond. A number of factors determine that coupon rate:

- The amount of uncertainty about whether the company will be able to make all the payments.
- The term of the loan.
- The level of interest rates in the overall economy at the time.

Bonds from different companies carry different coupon rates because some, or all, of these determining factors differ. Even a single company that has raised capital through bond issues many times may carry very different coupon rates on its various issues, because the bond issues would be offered in different years when the overall economic condition and interest rates differ.

Table 7.2 also shows a quote for a municipal bond issued by the New York City Municipal Water Finance Authority. This city government agency has raised capital by issuing municipal bonds to build reservoir facilities to provide water to New York City. The bond pays a 4.500 percent coupon, and since it matures in 2037, it's considered a long-term bond. According to Table 7.2, the bond is trading at a price just below par value—97.57 percent. Most municipal bonds, unlike other bonds, feature a $5,000 face value rather than the typical par value of $1,000. So, the 97.57 percent price quote represents a dollar amount of $4,878.50 (= 0.9757 × $5,000). The low rate of return relative to Treasury bonds with similar maturities also has an explanation. Municipal bondholders do not have to pay federal income taxes on the interest payments that they receive from those securities. We explore this (sometimes) substantial advantage further in a later section of this chapter.

EXAMPLE 7-3

LG7-3

Bond Quotes

You note the following bond quotes and wish to determine each bond's price, term, and interest payments.

For interactive versions of this example visit www.mhhe.com/can3e

Treasury Securities

MATURITY RATE	MO/YR	BID	ASKED	CHG	ASK YLD
9.00	Nov 18	137.5938	137.6250	−0.1563	4.80

Corporate Bond

COMPANY	COUPON	MATURITY	LAST PRICE	LAST YIELD
Kohls Corp	7.375	Oct 15, 2011	110.01	4.991

Municipal Bond

ISSUE	COUPON	MATURITY	PRICE	YLD TO MAT
Florida St Aquis & Bridge Constr	5.00	July 1, 2025	106.78	4.458

SOLUTION:

The Treasury bond matures in November of 2018 and pays 9 percent interest. Investors receive cash interest payment of $45 (= 0.09 × $1,000 ÷ 2) semiannually. Since the bond matures in less than ten years but more than one year, we would consider it a mid-term bond. Since no "n" appears next to the maturity date, we can also tell that the security was issued as a bond that would mature in 30 years. Investors could sell this bond for $1,375.94 (= 137.594 × $1,000) and buy it for $1,376.25 (= 1.37625 × $1,000). The price fell on this particular day by $1.56 (= −0.0015625 × $1,000). The dealer earned $0.31 (× $1,376.25 − $1,375.94) on each trade of these premium bonds.

The Kohls corporate bond pays a semiannual interest payment of $36.88 (= 0.07375 × $1,000 ÷ 2) and its price is $1,100.10 (= 1.1001 × $1,000). This premium bond's 7.375 percent rate is likely well above market rates, which is why an investor would be willing to pay a premium for it.

The state of Florida issued the muni bond to fund bridge construction. With a $5,000 par value, the interest payments are $125 (= 0.05 × $5,000 ÷ 2) every six months. The bonds are priced at $5,339.00 (= 1.0678 × $5,000).

Similar to Problems 7-9, 7-10, self-test problem 1

TIME OUT

7-1 Describe the different reasons that the U.S. government, local governments, and corporations would issue bonds.

7-2 What is the following bond's price and what dollar amount will the bond pay for its semiannual interest payment?

COMPANY	COUPON	MATURITY	PRICE	YIELD
Home Depot Inc.	5.40	Mar 1, 2018	100.06	5.391

7.2 • Bond Valuation

Present Value of Bond Cash Flows

LG7-4

Any bond's value computation directly applies time value of money concepts. Bondholders know the interest payments that they are scheduled to receive and the repayment of the par value at maturity. The current price of a bond is, therefore, the *present value of these future cash flows discounted at the prevailing market interest rate.* The prevailing market interest rate will depend on the bond's term to maturity, credit quality, and tax status.

zero coupon bond
A bond that does not make interest payments but generally sells at a deep discount and then pays the par value at the maturity date.

The simplest type of bond for time value of money calculations is a **zero coupon bond.** As you might guess from its name, a zero coupon bond makes no interest payments. Instead, the bond pays only the par value payment at its maturity date. So a zero coupon bond sells at a substantial discount from its par value. For example, a bond with a par value of $1,000, maturing in 20 years, and priced to yield 6 percent, might be purchased for about $306.56. At the end of 20 years, the bond investor will receive $1,000. The difference between $1,000 and $306.56 (which is $693.44) represents the interest income received over the 20 years based upon the discount rate of 6 percent. The time line for this zero coupon bond valuation appears as:

Period	0	5	6%	10	15	20 years
Cash flow	PV=?					1,000

We compute the zero's price by finding the present value of the $1,000 cash flow received in 20 years. However, to be consistent with regular coupon-paying bonds, zero coupon bonds are priced using semiannual compounding. So the formula and calculator valuation would use 40 semiannual periods at a 3 percent interest rate rather than 20 periods at 6 percent. Using the present value equation of Chapter 4 results in

CALCULATOR HINTS
N = 40
I = 3
PMT = 0
FV = 1000
CPT PV = −306.56

$$PV = \frac{FV_N}{(1+i)^N} = \frac{\$1{,}000}{1.03^{40}} = \frac{\$1{,}000}{3.262} = \$306.56$$

So the zero coupon bond's price is indeed a steep discount to its par value. This makes sense because investors would only buy a security that pays $1,000 in many years for a price that is much lower to make enough profit to make up for the forgone semiannual interest payments. For comparison's sake, instead of the 20-year zero, consider a 20-year bond with a 7 percent coupon. So this 20-year maturity bond pays $35 in interest payments every six months. We can think of these interest payments as an annuity stream. If the market discount rate is 6 percent annually, the time line appears as

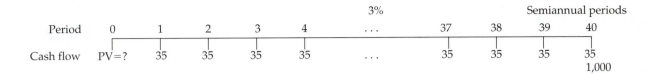

						3%			Semiannual periods	
Period	0	1	2	3	4	...	37	38	39	40
Cash flow	PV=?	35	35	35	35	...	35	35	35	35 1,000

LG7-4

The time line shows the 40 semiannual payments (with the accompanying semiannual interest rate at 3 percent) of \$35 and the par value payment at the bond's maturity. Think through this: When bonds pay semiannual payments, the discount rate must be a semiannual rate. Thus, the 6 percent annual rate becomes a 3 percent semiannual rate. So we then compute the price of this bond by adding the present value of the interest payment annuity cash flow to the present value of the future par value. A combination of the present value equations for the annuity cash flows and the value of the par redemption appear in the bond valuation equation 7-1:

Present value of bond = Present value of interest payments + Present value of par value

$$= PMT \times \left[\frac{1 - \frac{1}{(1+i)^N}}{i}\right] + \frac{\$1{,}000}{(1+i)^N} \qquad \textbf{(7-1)}$$

where *PMT* is the interest payment, *N* is the number of periods until maturity, and *i* is the market interest rate per period on securities with the same bond characteristics. If this bond paid interest annually, then these variables would take yearly period values. Since this bond pays semiannually, *PMT*, *N*, and *i* are all denoted in semiannual periods. The price of this coupon bond should be:

$$\text{Bond price} = \$35 \times \left[\frac{1 - \frac{1}{(1+0.03)^{40}}}{0.03}\right] + \frac{\$1{,}000}{(1+0.03)^{40}}$$

$$= \$809.017 + \$306.557 = \$1{,}115.57$$

Of the \$1,115.57 bond price, most of the value comes from the semiannual \$35 coupon payments (\$809.017) and not the value from the future par value payment (\$306.557).

Because equation 7-1 is quite complex, we usually compute bond prices using a financial calculator or computer program. An investor would compute the bond value using a financial calculator by entering $N = 40$, $I = 3$, $PMT = 35$, $FV = 1000$, and computing the present value (*PV*). The calculator solution is \$1,115.57.[1]

CALCULATOR HINTS

N = 40
I = 3
PMT = 35
FV = 1000
CPT PV = −1,115.57

Bond Prices and Interest Rate Risk

LG7-5

At the time of purchase, the bond's interest payments and par value expected at maturity are fixed and known. Over time, economywide interest rates change, but the bond's coupon rate remains fixed. A rise in prevailing interest rates (also called *increasing the discount rate*) reduces all bonds' values. If interest rates fall, all bonds will enjoy rising values. Consider that when interest rates rise, newly

[1]In order to focus on the valuation concepts, we present these examples with the full six months until the bond's next interest payment. However, bonds can be sold anytime between interest payments. When this occurs, we simply add the interest accrued since the last payment to the price.

EXAMPLE 7-4

LG7-4

For interactive versions of this example visit www.mhhe.com/can3e

Find the Value of a Bond

Consider a 15-year bond that has a 5.5 percent coupon, paid semiannually. If the current market interest rate is 6.5 percent, and the bond is priced at $940, should you buy this bond?

SOLUTION:

Compute the value of the bond using equation 7-1. Use semiannual compounding ($N = 2 \times 15 = 30$, $I = 6.5 \div 2 = 3.25$, and $PMT = 0.055 \times \$1{,}000 \div 2 = \$27.50$) as:

$$\text{Bond value} = \$27.50 \times \left[\frac{1 - \dfrac{1}{(1+0.0325)^{30}}}{0.0325}\right] + \frac{\$1{,}000}{(1+0.0325)^{30}} = \$522.00 + \$383.09 = \$905.09$$

CALCULATOR HINTS

N = 30
I = 3.25
PMT = 27.50
FV = 1000
CPT PV = −905.09

So this bond's value is $905.09, which is less than the $940 price. The bond is overvalued in the market and you should not buy it.

Similar to Problems 7-21, 7-22, 7-23, 7-24, self-test problem 1

MATH COACH

Bond Pricing and Periods

Since most bonds have semiannual interest payments, we must use semiannual periods to discount the cash flows. Most errors in computing a bond price occur in the adjustment for semiannual periods. The errors happen whether you are using either the bond pricing equation or a financial calculator. To convert to semiannual periods, be sure to adjust the three variables: number of periods, interest rate, and payments.

The number of years needs to be multiplied by 2 for the number of semiannual periods. The interest rate should be divided by 2 for a 6-month rate. Divide the annual coupon payment by 2 for the 6-month payment. Remember to adjust all three inputs for the semiannual periods.

A coupon-paying bond's price should hover reasonably around the par value of the bond. For a $1,000 par value bond, we could expect a price in the range of $700 to $1,300. If you compute a price outside this range, check to see whether you made the semiannual period adjustments correctly.

issued bonds offer to pay higher interest rates than the rates offered on existing bonds. So to sell an existing bond with its lower coupon rate, its market price must fall so that the buyer can expect a profit similar to that offered by newly issued bonds. Similarly, when prevailing interest rates fall, market prices for outstanding bonds rise to bring the offered return on older bonds with higher coupon rates into line with new issues. So market interest rates and bond prices are *inversely* related. That is, they move in opposite directions.

Figure 7.2 demonstrates how the price of a 30-year Treasury bond may change over time. The 10.69 percent coupon exactly matched prevailing interest rates when the bond was issued in 1983. Consequently, the bond sells for its par value of $1,000. Shortly thereafter, interest rates quickly rose to very high levels (over 15 percent) in the economy. As interest rates rose, bond prices had to decline. Then in 1984, interest rates started a prolonged descent to near 0 in 2009 and again in 2012. Note that while a bond is issued at $1,000 and returns $1,000 at maturity, its price can vary a great deal in between. Bond investors must be aware that bond prices fluctuate on a day-to-day basis as interest rates fluctuate. The determinates

figure 7.2

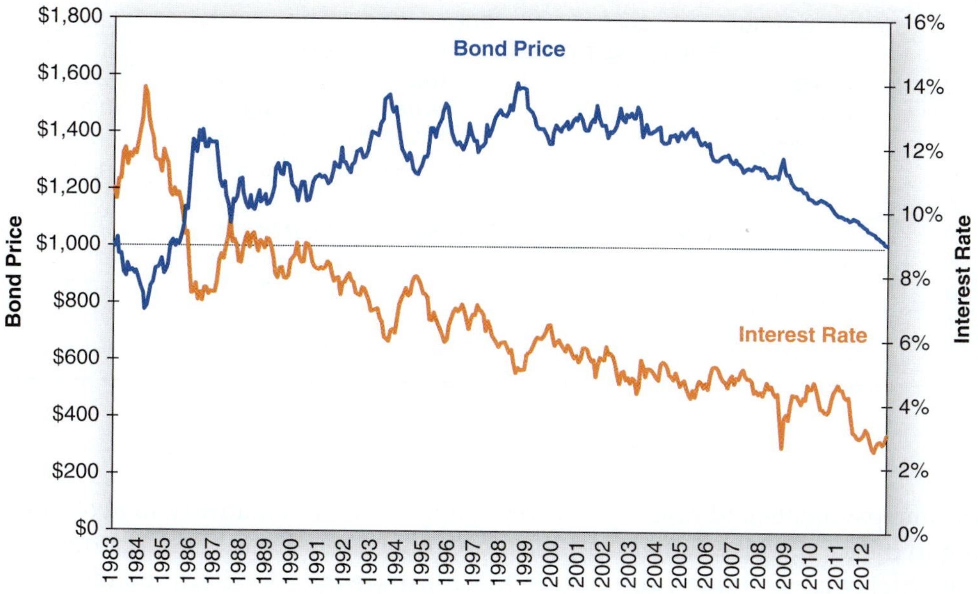

A Demonstration of the Price and Market Interest Rate over Time of a 30-Year Treasury Bond Issued in 1983 with a Coupon of 10.69 Percent

As interest rates rise, bond prices fall. Here you can see great variance in the economy over 30 years. Long-term bondholders experience substantial interest rate risk.

Data source: Yahoo! Finance, finance.yahoo.com.

of market interest rate levels and changes are discussed in Chapter 6. Bondholders can incur large capital gains or capital losses.

The fact that, as prevailing interest rates change, the prices of existing bonds will change has a specific name in the financial industry—interest rate risk. **Interest rate risk** means that during periods when interest rates change substantially (and quickly), bondholders experience distinct gains and losses in their bond inventories. But interest rate risk does not affect all bonds exactly the same. Very short-term bonds experience little or no fluctuation in their prices, and thus expose the bondholder to little interest rate risk. Long-term bondholders experience substantial interest rate risk. Table 7.3 illustrates the impact of interest rate risk on bonds with different coupons and times to maturity.

interest rate risk

The chance of a capital loss due to interest rate fluctuations.

The first four rows show the prices and price changes for 30-year bonds with different coupon rates. Notice that the bonds with higher coupon rates also have higher prices. Bondholders as a rule find it more valuable to receive the large annuity payments. Also notice that a 1 percent increase in interest rates from 6 percent to 7 percent causes bond prices to fall. Bondholders with higher coupon bonds are not affected as much by interest rate increases because they can take the large coupon payments and reinvest those cash flows in new bonds that offer higher returns.

The price decline is greater for bonds with lower coupons because of **reinvestment rate risk.** When interest rates increase, bondholders' cash flows—both periodic payments and final payoff at maturity—are discounted at a higher rate, decreasing a bond's value. Because the cash flows from low-coupon bonds are smaller, the holder of such bonds will have less money available from interest payments to buy the new, higher coupon bonds. Thus bondholders of lower coupon bonds have their capital tied up in assets that are not making them as much money. They face a bad dilemma: They can sell their lower coupon bonds and take a greater capital loss, using the (smaller) proceeds to buy new bonds with higher coupon rates. Or they can continue to receive the small

reinvestment rate risk

The chance that future interest payments will have to be reinvested at a lower interest rate.

table 7.3 | **Interest Rate Risk**

	A	B	C	D	E
1	**Time to Maturity**	**Coupon**	**Price at 6%**	**Price at 7%**	**Change**
2	**THE IMPACT OF THE COUPON RATE ON PRICE**				
3	30 years	0%	$ 169.73	$ 126.93	–25.2%
4	30 years	5	861.62	750.55	–12.9
5	30 years	7	1,138.38	1,000.00	–12.2
6	30 years	10	1,553.51	1,374.32	–11.5
7					
8	**THE IMPACT OF TIME TO MATURITY ON PRICE**				
9	20 years	5	884.43	786.45	–11.1
10	10 years	5	925.61	857.88	–7.3
11	5 years	5	957.35	916.83	–4.2
12	2 years	5	981.41	963.27	–1.8

income payments and hold their lower coupon bonds to maturity to avoid locking in the capital loss. Either way, they lose money relative to those bondholders with higher coupon rates. You can see this illustrated in the 30-year bonds shown in Table 7.3. Reinvestment rates tend to help partially offset changing discount rates for higher coupon paying bonds.

LG7-5

Another factor that influences the amount of reinvestment risk bondholders face is their bonds' time to maturity. The last four bonds in the table all have a 5 percent coupon but have different times to maturity. Note that when interest rates increase, the bond prices of longer-term bonds decline more than shorter-term bonds. This shows that bonds with longer maturities and lower coupons have the highest interest rate risk. Short-term bonds with high coupons have the lowest interest rate risk. High interest rate risk bonds experience considerable price declines when interest rates are rising. However, these bonds also experience dramatic capital gains when interest rates are falling. While a 1 percent change in market interest rates is not commonly seen on a daily or monthly basis, such a change is not unusual over the course of several months or a year.

EXAMPLE 7-5

LG7-5

For interactive versions of this example visit www.mhhe.com/can3e

Capital Gains in the Bond Market

Say that you anticipate falling long-term interest rates from 6 percent to 5.5 percent during the next year. If this occurs, what will be the total return for a 20-year, 6.5 percent coupon bond through the interest rate decline?

SOLUTION:

To determine the total return, compute the capital gain or loss and the interest paid over the year. The capital gain or loss is determined from the change in price. The current bond price is:

$$\text{Bond price} = \$32.50 \times \left[\frac{1 - \dfrac{1}{(1+0.03)^{40}}}{0.03}\right] + \frac{\$1{,}000}{(1+0.03)^{40}} = \$751.230 + \$306.557 = \$1{,}057.79$$

The price in one year would be:

$$\text{Bond price} = \$32.50 \times \left[\frac{1 - \dfrac{1}{(1 + 0.0275)^{38}}}{0.0275}\right] + \frac{\$1,000}{(1 + 0.0275)^{38}} = \$760.276 + \$356.690 = \$1,116.97$$

So, the capital gain is \$59.18 (= \$1,116.97 − \$1,057.79). The interest payment during the year is \$65 (= 0.065 × \$1,000). If interest rates fall to 5.5 percent, then this bond should provide a total return of \$124.18, which would be an 11.74 percent return (= \$124.18 ÷ \$1,057.79). Of course, this is only an anticipated interest rate change and it may not occur.

Similar to Problems 7-25, 7-26, 7-35, 7-36, self-test problem 5

CALCULATOR HINTS

N = 40
I = 3
PMT = 32.50
FV = 1000

CPT PV = −1,057.79

Then change

N = 38
I = 2.75

CPT PV = −1,116.97

TIME OUT

7-3 Show the time line and compute the present value for an 8.5 percent coupon bond (paid semiannually) with 12 years left to maturity and a market interest rate of 7.5 percent.

7-4 Describe the relationship between interest rate changes and bond prices.

7.3 • Bond Yields

Current Yield

LG7-6

Although we speak about "the prevailing interest rate," bond relationships reflect many interest rates (also called *yields*). Some rates are difficult to calculate but accurately reflect the return the bond is offering. Others, like the **current yield,** are easy to compute but only approximate the bond's true return. A bond's current yield is defined as the bond's annual coupon rate divided by the bond's current market price. Current yield measures the rate of return a bondholder would earn annually from the coupon interest payments alone if the bond were purchased at a stated price. Current yield does not measure the total expected return because it does not account for any capital gains or losses that will occur from purchasing the bond at a discount or premium to par.

current yield
Return from interest payments; computed as the annual interest payment divided by the current bond price.

Yield to Maturity

LG7-6

Yield to maturity is a more meaningful equation for investors than the simple current yield calculation. The yield to maturity calculation tells bond investors the total rate of return that they might expect if the bond were bought at a particular price and held to maturity. While the yield to maturity calculation provides more information than the current yield calculation, it's also more difficult to compute, because we must compute the bond's cash flows' internal rate of return. This calculation seeks to equate the bond's current market price with the value of all anticipated future interest and par value payments. In other words, it is the discount rate that equates the present value of all future cash flows with

yield to maturity
The total return the bond offers if purchased at the current price and held to maturity.

the current price of the bond. To calculate yield to maturity, investors must solve for the interest rate, i, in equation 7-2, or solve for i in:

$$\text{Bond price} = \text{PV of annuity } (PMT, i, N) + PV(FV, i, N) \quad \textbf{(7-2)}$$

Investors commonly compute the yield to maturity using financial calculators. For example, consider a 7 percent coupon bond (paid semiannually) with eight years to maturity and a current price of $1,150. The return that the bond offers investors, the yield to maturity, is computed as $N = 16$, $PV = -1150$, $PMT = 35$, and $FV = 1000$. Computing the interest rate (I) gives us 2.363 percent. We must remember, however, that 2.363 percent is only the return for six months because the bond pays semiannually. Yield to maturity always means an annual return. So, this bond's yield to maturity is 4.73 percent (2×2.363 percent).

EXAMPLE 7-6

LG7-6

For interactive versions of this example visit www.mhhe.com/can3e

Computing Current Yield and Yield to Maturity

You have identified a 3.5 percent Treasury bond with four years left to maturity and a quoted price of 96:09. Calculate the bond's current yield and yield to maturity.

SOLUTION:

(1) First, identify that the bond's price is $962.81 (= 96 09/32% × $1,000 = 0.9628125 × $1,000).

(2) The annual $35 in interest payments is paid in two $17.50 semiannual payments. Therefore, the current yield of the bond is 3.64 percent (= $35 ÷ $962.81).

(3) The yield to maturity is computed using equation 7-2 and the financial calculator as $N = 8$, $PV = -962.81$, $PMT = 17.50$, and $FV = 1{,}000$. Computing the interest rate (I) results in 2.263 percent and multiplying by 2 gives the yield to maturity of 4.53 percent.

(4) Note that the current yield is less than the yield to maturity because it does not account for the capital gain to be earned if held to maturity.

CALCULATOR HINTS

N = 8
PV = −962.81
PMT = 17.50
FV = 1000
CPT I = 2.263
so YTM = 2.263 × 2
= 4.53%

Similar to Problems 7–13, 7–14, 7–27, 7–28, self-test problem 2

MATH COACH

BOND YIELDS AND FINANCIAL CALCULATORS

People computing a bond's yield to maturity make three common mistakes. To avoid the first mistake, ensure that the bond price (PV) is a different sign than the interest and par value cash flows (PMT and FV). The second mistake: People forget to make the number of periods (N) and the per-period interest payment (PMT) consistent. Both should be in semiannual terms if the coupon payment is paid semiannually. Last, many people forget to multiply the resulting calculator interest rate (I) output by 2 to convert the semiannual rate back to an annual rate.

Notice the link between a bond's yield to maturity and the prevailing market interest rates used to determine a bond's price as we discussed in the previous section. We use the market interest rate to compute the bond's value. We use the actual bond price to compute its yield to maturity. If the bond is correctly priced at its economic value, then the market interest rate will equal the yield to maturity. Thus, the relationship that we previously identified between bond prices and market interest rates applies to yields as well. This shows the inverse relationship between bond prices and bond yields. As a bond's price falls, its yield to maturity increases and a rising bond price accompanies a falling yield. Look back at Figure 7.2 and you will see this relationship clearly.

Yield to Call

The yield to maturity computation assumes that the bondholder will hold the bond to its maturity. But remember that some bonds have call provisions that allow the issuers to repay the bondholder's par value prior to its scheduled maturity. Issuers often call bonds after large drops in market interest rates. In such cases, issuers commonly pay bondholders the bond's par value plus one year of interest payments. The reasons behind early bond redemptions are obvious. When interest rates fall, issuers can sell new bonds at lower interest rates. Companies want to refinance their debt—just as homeowners do—to reduce their interest payments.

Issuers gain important advantages with call provisions because they allow refinancing opportunities. Of course, the same provisions are disadvantages for bond investors. When bonds are called, investors receive the par value and call premium, but then investors must seek equally profitable bonds to buy with the proceeds. You will recall that investors can face reinvestment risk—the available bonds aren't as profitable because interest rates have declined. Bonds are called away at the worst time for investors. In addition, bond prices will rise as market interest rates fall, which could provide issuers opportunities to sell the bonds at a profit. But the price increases will be limited by the fact that the bond will likely be called early. As partial compensation, bond investors receive the call price, which is the par value of the bond plus the call premium (typically one year of interest payments). The possibility that bonds can be called early dampens their upside price potential. We can even compute the price of a bond that's likely to be called from the equation: LG7-6

Price of a callable bond = Present value of interest payments to call date + Present value of call price

$$= PMT \times \left[\frac{1 - \frac{1}{(1+i)^N}}{i} \right] + \frac{\text{Call price}}{(1+i)^N} \qquad \textbf{(7-3)}$$

In this case, N is the number of periods until the bond can be called and i is the prevailing market rate. The prevailing market interest rate will probably differ from the rate for a noncallable bond. The previous section demonstrated via the yield curve that bonds with different maturities have different yields. A bond that matures in 20 years, but is likely to be called in five years, will carry a yield appropriate for a 5-year bond.

Now, reconsider the 20-year bond with a 7 percent coupon that we discussed previously (see pp. 242–243). If the bond can be called in five years with a call price of \$1,070, the appropriate discount rate happens to be 5.75 percent annually at that time (instead of the 6 percent in the original problem). This time line would be LG7-6

2.875%; Semiannual periods

Period	0	1	2	3	4	. . .	7	8	9	10
Cash flow	PV=?	35	35	35	35	. . .	35	35	35	35
										1,070

The changes in this time line are only 10 semiannual payments of \$35 (rather than 40 such semiannual payments), a 2.875 percent semiannual discount rate, and the call price payment of \$1,070. The price of this callable bond would be:

$$\text{Bond price} = \$35 \times \left[\frac{1 - \frac{1}{(1+0.02875)^{10}}}{0.02875} \right] + \frac{\$1{,}070}{(1+0.02875)^{10}}$$

$$= \$300.47 + \$805.91 = \$1{,}106.38$$

CALCULATOR HINTS

N = 10
I = 2.875
PMT = 35
FV = 1070
CPT PV = −1,106.38

In this example, the callable bond would be priced at $1,106.38, which is slightly lower than an identical bond that was not callable, priced at $1,115.57.

yield to call

The total return that the bond offers if purchased at the current price and held until the bond is called.

If a bond is likely to be called, then the yield to maturity calculation does not give investors a good estimate of their return. Bondholders can use instead a **yield to call** calculation, which differs from the yield to maturity only in that its calculation assumes that the investor will receive the par value and call premium at the earliest call date. For example, reconsider the 7 percent coupon bond (paid semiannually) with 8 years to maturity, which we examined previously (see p. 248). The current bond price is $1,130 (which is slightly lower than the yield to maturity bond price of $1,150). If the bond can be called in three years at a specific call price of the par value plus one annual coupon, then what is the yield to call? The yield to call is computed as $N = 6$, $PV = -1130$, $PMT = 35$, and $FV = 1070$. The resulting interest rate (I) is 2.26 percent. The yield to call for this bond is thus 4.52 percent ($= 2 \times 2.26\%$).

MATH COACH

SPREADSHEETS AND BOND PRICING

Common spreadsheet programs have functions that can compute the price or yield to maturity of a bond. The functions are:

Compute a bond price =
PRICE(settlement,maturity,rate,yld,redemption,frequency,basis)

Compute a yield to maturity =
YIELD(settlement,maturity,rate,pr,redemption,frequency,basis)

Settlement is the bond's settlement date. This is the purchase date of the bond; typically it is today. *Maturity* is the bond's maturity date. *Rate* is the bond's annual coupon rate. *Pr* is the bond's price per $100 face value. Note that the par value of a bond is typically $1,000, so an adjustment is needed for this input. *Redemption* is the bond's redemption value per $100 face value. *Frequency* is the number of coupon payments per year. For semiannual, frequency = 2. *Basis* is the type of day count basis to use.

Consider the bond valuation problem of Example 7-4. The spreadsheet solution is the same as the TVM calculator solution and the pricing equation.

	A	B	C	D	E
1					
2	Settlement date	11/15/2011	=DATE(2011,11,15)		
3	Maturity date	11/15/2026	=DATE(2026,11,15)		
4	Coupon Rate	5.50%			
5	Interest rate (Yld)	6.50%			
6	Redemption	100			
7	Frequency	2			
8					
9	Bond price (per $100 par value) =	$90.51	=PRICE(B2,B3,B4,B5,B6,B7,1)		
10	Bond price (per $1000 par value) =	$905.09	=10*B9		

Also consider the yield to maturity problem in Example 7-6. This spreadsheet solves for the yield to maturity.

	A	B	C	D	E
1					
2	Settlement date	11/15/2011	=DATE(2011,11,15)		
3	Maturity date	11/15/2015	=DATE(2015,11,15)		
4	Coupon Rate	3.50%			
5	Bond Price	96.28			
6	Redemption	100			
7	Frequency	2			
8					
9	Yield to Maturity =	4.53%	=YIELD(B2,B3,B4,B5,B6,B7,1)		

See this textbook's online student center to watch instructional videos on using spreadsheets. Also note that the solutions for all the examples in the book are illustrated using spreadsheets in videos that are also available on the textbook website.

Municipal Bonds and Yield

LG7-6

Municipal bonds (munis) seem to offer low yields to maturity compared to the return that corporate bonds and Treasury securities offer. Munis offer lower rates because the interest income they generate for investors is tax-exempt—at least at the federal level.[2] Specifically, income from municipal bonds is not subject to taxation by the federal government or the state government where the bonds are issued. As a result, municipal bond investors willingly accept lower yields than those they can obtain from taxable bonds. Generally speaking, investors compare the after-tax interest income earned on taxable bonds against the return earned on municipal bonds. For example, suppose an investor in the 35 percent *marginal* income tax bracket has $100,000 to invest in either corporate or municipal bonds. The $100,000 investment would earn a taxable $7,000 annually from 7 percent corporate bonds or $5,000 from tax-exempt 5 percent municipal bonds. After taxes, the corporate bond leaves the investor with $4,550 [=(1 − 0.35) × $7,000]. Obviously, this is less than the tax-free income of $5,000 generated by the muni bond.

A common way to compare yields from muni bonds versus those from taxable bonds is to convert the yield to maturity of the muni to a **taxable equivalent yield,** as shown in equation 7-4.

taxable equivalent yield

Modification of a municipal bond's yield to maturity used to compare muni bond yields to taxable bond yields.

$$\text{Equivalent taxable yield} = \frac{\text{Muni yield}}{1 - \text{Tax rate}} \qquad \textbf{(7-4)}$$

For high-income investors (in the 35 percent marginal tax bracket) a 5 percent muni bond has an equivalent taxable yield of 7.69 percent [= 0.05 ÷ (1 − 0.35)]. The 5 percent muni is more attractive for this investor than a 7 percent corporate bond. However, for an investor with lower income (in the 28 percent marginal tax bracket) the equivalent taxable yield is only 6.94 percent. The corporate bond

EXAMPLE 7-7

LG7-6

Which Bond Has a Better After-Tax Yield?

For interactive versions of this example visit www.mhhe.com/can3e

Imagine a time when you have a high income, placing you in the 31 percent marginal tax bracket. You are interested in investing some money in a bond issue and have three alternatives. The first is a corporate bond with a 6.4 percent yield to maturity. The second bond is a Treasury that offers a 5.7 percent yield. The third choice is a municipal bond priced at a yield to maturity of 4.0 percent. Which bond gives you the highest after-tax yield?

SOLUTION:

The Treasury and corporate bonds are both taxable, so we can compare them directly with each other. The yield of 6.4 percent on the corporate is clearly higher than the 5.7 percent yield offered by the Treasury bond. To include a comparison with the nontaxable municipal bond, compute its equivalent taxable yield as in equation 7-4:

$$\text{Equivalent taxable yield} = \frac{4.0\%}{1 - 0.31} = 5.80\%$$

The municipal bond's equivalent taxable yield of 5.80 percent is higher than the Treasury but lower than the corporate bond.

Similar to Problems 7-15, 7-16, 7-31, 7-32, 7-37, 7-38, self-test problem 3

[2]States have differing rules about whether they tax the income from a particular municipal bond—they will generally tax income from munis issued out of state. Further, capital gains arising from municipal bond sales may be taxed, and the income from municipal bonds must be added to overall income when determining the Alternative Minimum Tax consequences.

table 7.4 | **Summary of Interest Rates**

Interest Rate	Purpose	Description
Coupon rate	Compute bond cash interest payments	The coupon rate is reported as a bond characteristic. It is reported as a percentage and is multiplied by the par value of the bond to determine the annual cash interest payment. The coupon rate will not change through the life of the bond.
Current yield	Quick assessment of the interest rate a bond is offering	Computed as the annual interest payment divided by the current price of the bond. It measures the return to be expected from just the interest payments if the bond was purchased at the current price. Since the bond price may change daily, the current yield will change daily.
Yield to maturity	Accurate measurement of the interest rate a bond is offering	The return offered by the bond if purchased at the current price. This return includes both the expected income and capital gain/loss if held to the maturity date. The yield to maturity will change daily as the bond price changes.
Yield to call	Interest rate obtained if the bond is called	Same as the yield to maturity except that it is assumed that the bond will be called at the earliest date it can be called.
Taxable equivalent yield	Comparison of nontaxable bond yields to taxable bond yields	Investors must pay taxes on most types of bonds. However, municipal bonds are tax free. To compare the muni's nontaxable yield to maturity to that of taxable bonds, divide the yield by one minus the investor's marginal tax rate.
Market interest rate	Comparison of prices of all bonds	The interest rate determined by the bond prices of actual trades between buyers and sellers. The market interest rate will be different for bonds of different times to maturity and different levels of risk.
Total return	Determine realized performance of an investment	Realized return that includes both income and capital gain/loss profits.

provides more after-tax profit than the muni for this investor. It's easy to see why muni bonds are popular among high-income investors (those with substantial marginal tax rates).

LG7-6

Summarizing Yields

In this section, we have presented several different types of interest rates, or yields, associated with bonds. See a summary in Table 7.4. Many of these yields relate to one another. Consider the bonds and associated yields reported in Table 7.5. Treasury bonds (1) to (3) show how coupon rates, current yield, and yield to maturity relate. When a bond trades at its par value (usually $1,000), then the coupon rate, current yield, and yield to maturity are all the same. When that bond is priced at a premium (bond 2), then both the current yield and the yield to maturity will be lower than the coupon rate. They are both higher than the coupon rate when the bond trades at a discount. Notice that yield to maturity is higher than current yield for discount bonds, and that yield to maturity is lower than current yield for premium bonds. In other words, the current yield always lies between the coupon rate and the yield to maturity. Both the current yield and the yield to maturity move in the opposite direction to the bond's price.

Bonds (4) to (6) are callable corporate bonds. Recall that all the yields (current yield, yield to maturity, and yield to call) are identical when the bond trades at par value. When interest rates fall and bond prices increase, as with bond (5), the issuing corporation has a strong incentive to call the bond after five years, as allowed in the indenture agreement. So investors should base their purchase decisions on the yield to call. When interest rates increase, bond prices decline (as bond (6) shows). In this case, investors could compute the yield to call (as shown), but the information isn't useful because the company will not likely call the bond while interest rates are high.

The last three bonds shown in the table are municipal bonds. Recall that these bonds typically offer lower yields because the income from munis is tax exempt. It is easier to compare municipal bonds with Treasuries and corporate bonds if you compute the municipal bond's taxable equivalent yield first. Here, we use a marginal tax rate of 35 percent in the calculation. The last column of the table

table 7.5 | **Price, Coupon, and Yield Relationships of a 10-Year Bond**

	A	B	C	D	E	F	G
1		Price	Coupon Rate	Current Yield	Yield to Maturity	Yield to Call (in 5 Years)	Taxable Equivalent Yield (35% Tax Rate)
2	(1) Treasury	$1,000.00	5%	5%	5%		5%
3	(2) Treasury	1,100.00	5	4.55	3.79		3.79
4	(3) Treasury	900.00	5	5.56	6.37		6.37
5	(4) Corporate	1,000.00	6	6	6	6%	6
6	(5) Corporate	1,100.00	6	5.41	4.61	4.59	4.61
7	(6) Corporate	900.00	6	6.67	7.44	9.52	7.44
8	(7) Muni	1,000.00	4	4	4		6.15
9	(8) Muni	1,100.00	4	3.64	2.84		4.37
10	(9) Muni	900.00	4	4.44	5.30		8.16

Call price = Par value + One year's interest

shows that the taxable equivalent yield of the municipal bonds is really quite competitive with corporate bond yields. Any investor with income taxed at the 35 percent marginal tax bracket would prefer the municipal bond over the corporate bond if the muni's taxable equivalent yield is higher than the yield to maturity (or yield to call) of the corporate bond.

The table also shows that Treasury securities offer lower yields than corporate bonds with similar terms to maturity. The difference (or spread) between Treasury and corporate yields gives rise to a discussion of bond credit risk, which follows.

TIME OUT

7-5 Calculate the yield to maturity for a zero coupon bond with a price of $525 and ten years left to maturity.

7-6 Which is higher for a discount bond, the yield to maturity or the coupon rate? Why?

7.4 • Credit Risk

LG7-7

Bond Ratings

Will a bond issuer make the promised interest and par value payments over the next 10, 20, or even 30 years? **Credit quality risk** is the chance that the bond issuer will not be able to make timely payments. To assess this risk, independent **bond rating** agencies, such as Moody's and Standard & Poor's, monitor corporate, U.S. agency, or municipal developments during the bond's lifetime and report their findings as a grade or rating. The U.S. government issues the highest credit quality debt, though that consensus has recently come into doubt as the U.S. debt and budget deficit have ballooned.

credit quality risk
The chance that the issuer will not make timely interest payments or even default.

bond rating
A grade of credit quality as reported by credit rating agencies.

Bond credit rating agencies in the United States include Moody's Investors Service, Standard & Poor's Corporation, Fitch IBCA Inc., Dominion Bond Rating Service, and A.M. Best Co. Each of these credit analysis firms assigns similar ratings based on detailed analyses of issuers' financial condition, general economic and credit market conditions, and the economic value of any underlying collateral. The Standard & Poor's ratings are shown in Table 7.6. Their highest credit-quality rating is AAA. Bonds rated AAA, AA, A, or BBB are considered **investment grade** bonds. The issuers of these securities have the highest chance of making all interest and par value payments promised in the indenture agreement.

investment grade
High credit quality corporate bonds.

table 7.6 | **Standard & Poor's Bond Credit Ratings**

Credit Risk	Credit Rating	Description
Investment Grade		
Highest quality	AAA	The obligor's (issuer's) capacity to meet its financial commitment on the obligation is extremely strong.
High quality	AA	The obligor's capacity to meet its financial commitment on the obligation is very strong.
Upper medium grade	A	The obligor's capacity to meet its financial commitment on the obligation is still strong, though somewhat susceptible to the adverse effects of changes in circumstances and economic conditions.
Medium grade	BBB	The obligor exhibits adequate protection. However, adverse economic conditions or changing circumstances are more likely to lead to a weakened capacity to meet its financial commitment.
Below Investment Grade		
Somewhat speculative	BB	Faces major ongoing uncertainties or exposure to adverse business, financial, or economic conditions which could lead to the obligor's inadequate capacity to meet its financial commitment.
Speculative	B	Adverse business, financial, or economic conditions will likely impair the obligor's capacity or willingness to meet its financial commitment.
Highly speculative	CCC	Currently vulnerable to nonpayment, and is dependent upon favorable business, financial, and economic conditions for the obligor to meet its financial commitment.
Most speculative	CC	Currently highly vulnerable to nonpayment.
Imminent default	C	Bankruptcy petition has been filed or similar action taken, but payments on this obligation are being continued.
Default	D	Obligations are in default or the filing of a bankruptcy petition has occurred and payments are jeopardized.

Source: Standard & Poor's web page.

The investment community considers bonds rated BB and below to be below-investment grade bonds, and some investors, such as pension funds or other fiduciaries, cannot purchase these securities for their portfolios. These bonds are considered to be speculative because they carry a significant risk that the issuer will not make current or future payments. Speculative bonds are sometimes called **junk bonds** because of this risk. In order to attract buyers, issuers sell these bonds at a considerable discount from par and a high associated yield to maturity. Agencies often enhance ratings from "AA" to "CCC" with the addition of a plus (+) or minus (−) sign to show relative standing within the major rating categories. For example, Dave & Buster's, Inc., a restaurant and entertainment company, saw its bonds upgraded from B+ to BB− by Standard & Poor's on February 15, 2013. On the other hand, the day before, Moody's downgraded McGraw-Hill Cos. from A3 to Baa2. These rating changes impact not only the current prices of these bonds, but also the interest rate Dave & Buster and McGraw-Hill would have to pay if they issued new bonds.

junk bonds

Low credit quality corporate bonds, also called speculative bonds or high-yield bonds.

Standard & Poor's signals that it's considering a rating change by placing an individual bond, or all of a given issuer's bonds, on CreditWatch (S&P). Rating agencies make their ratings information available to the public through their ratings information desks. In addition to published reports, ratings are made available in many public libraries and over the Internet.

LG7-7

Credit rating agencies conduct general economic analyses of companies' business and analyze firms' specific financial situations. A single company may carry several outstanding bond issues. If these issues feature fundamental differences, then they may have different credit level risks. For example, **unsecured corporate bonds**, or **debentures,** are backed only by the reputation and financial stability of the corporation. A **senior bond** has a priority claim over junior (more recently issued) securities in the event of default or bankruptcy. So, senior

unsecured corporate bonds

Corporate debt not secured by collateral such as land, buildings, or equipment.

debentures

Unsecured bonds.

senior bonds

Older bonds that carry a higher claim to the issuer's assets.

figure 7.3

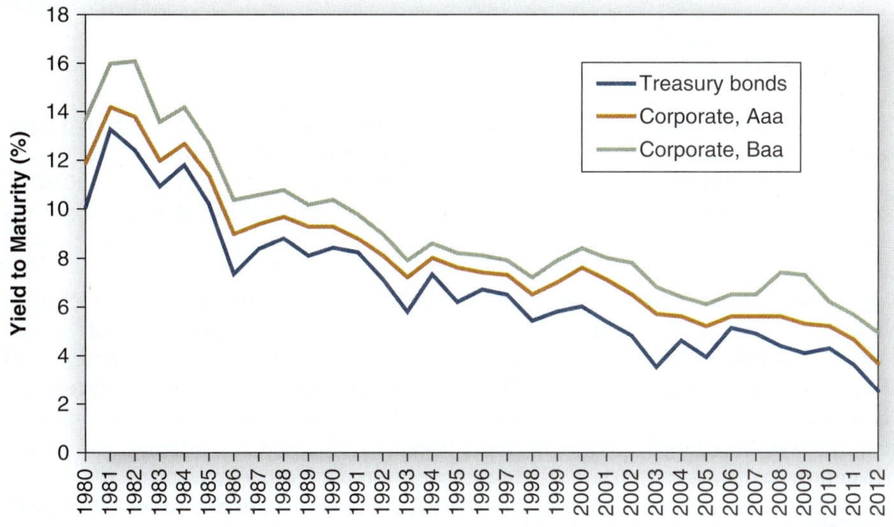

Yield to Maturity on Long-Term Bonds of Different Credit Risk, 1980–2012

Looking at the historical yields for long-term Treasury and corporate bonds, notice how the yield spread between high- and low-quality bonds varies substantially over time.

bonds carry less credit risk than junior bonds. Some bonds are secured with collateral. When you buy a car using a loan, the car is collateral for that loan. If you don't make the loan payments, the bank will repossess the car. Companies can also offer collateral when issuing bonds. When a firm uses collateral such as real estate or factory equipment, the bonds are called **mortgage bonds** or **equipment trust certificates,** respectively. Bonds issued with no collateral generally carry higher credit risk.

mortgage bonds

Bonds secured with real estate as collateral.

equipment trust certificates

Bonds secured with factory and equipment as collateral.

Credit Risk and Yield

LG7-7

Investors will only purchase higher risk bonds if those securities offer higher returns. Therefore, issuers price bonds with high credit risk to offer high yields to maturity. So another common name for junk bonds is **high-yield bonds.** Differences in credit risk are a prime source of differences in yields between government and various corporate bonds. Figure 7.3 shows the historical average annual yields for long-term Treasury bonds and corporate bonds with credit ratings of Aaa and Baa since 1980. Riskier low-quality bonds always offer a higher yield than the higher quality bonds. However, the yield spread between high- and low-quality bonds varies substantially over time. The yield difference between Baa bonds and Treasuries was as high as 3.7 percent and 3.3 percent in 1982 and 2003, respectively. The spread has been as narrow as 1.3 percent and 1.4 percent in 1994 and 2006, respectively.

high-yield bonds

Bonds with low credit quality that offer a high yield to maturity, also called junk bonds.

How do some corporations' debt obligations become junk bonds? Some companies that aren't economically sound or those that use a high degree of financial leverage issue junk bonds. In other cases, financially strong companies issue investment grade bonds and then, over time, begin to have trouble. Eventually a company's bonds can be downgraded to junk status. For example, General Motors (GM) bonds were considered of the highest quality from the 1950s through the 1980s and much of the 1990s. On May 9, 2005, Standard & Poor's downgraded GM bonds to junk status. Junk bonds that were originally issued at investment grade status are called *fallen angels.* GM eventually filed for bankruptcy protection in June 2009.

finance at work — markets

A GREEK TRAGEDY: DEBT CRISIS

Greece joined the European monetary union in 2000, which means the euro replaced drachmas as the national currency. The euro was a much stronger currency than the drachma because it was backed by the economic prosperity of the whole European Union. Hence, the Greek government was able to borrow from foreign investors at much lower interest rates. This contributed to the ensuing economic boom and expansion of government spending in Greece.

The Greek government has long been operating on high budget deficits and borrowing. But the problems really began in the Fall of 2009 when the new elected government found that it had inherited a financial burden that was much larger than previously reported. The budget deficit was revised to be larger than 13 percent of the size of the economy. The revelation of these huge government deficits and debts cast enormous doubt on the ability of the Greek government to pay its debts.

This increase in risk was reflected on December 8, 2009, by the downgrade to BBB (lowest in the Euro Zone) of the Sovereign bond of Greece by the Fitch credit rating firm. Standard & Poor's and Moody's both downgraded Greece Sovereigns to junk bond status in May and June of 2010. As a consequence, Greece found that it was difficult to borrow more money and had to offer lenders yields of as much as 12 percent and a financial crisis developed.

In order to restore investor confidence, the Greek government has pledged to an austerity plan that cuts spending and reduces the budget deficit. However, the success of the plans has been undermined by strong domestic opposition as illustrated by strikes and even riots. As a temporary solution, the European Union and the International Monetary Fund together offered a large loan package to help out Greece. This calmed the bond market and Greek bond yields fell, but they are still high. Unfortunately, the severe economic depression in Greece has caused further problems with its ability to pay its debt. In 2011 and 2012, Greece enacted several bond restructurings which mandated changes in the terms. They are considered selective bond defaults.

want to know more? **Key Words to Search for Updates:** Greek bonds, Greek debt crisis

Bonds that experience credit-rating downgrades must offer a higher yield. As all the future cash flows are fixed, the bond price must fall to create a higher yield to maturity. Alternatively, bonds that are upgraded experience price increases and yield decreases. Bond upgrades often occur during strong economic periods because corporate issuers tend to perform better financially at these times. In a weak economy, high-yield bonds lose their luster because the default risk rises. More credit downgrades occur during economic recessions.

TIME OUT

7-7 Explain why a change in a bond's credit rating will cause its price to change.

7-8 One company has issued two bond classes. One issue is a mortgage bond and the other is a debenture. Which issue will have a higher bond rating and which will offer a higher yield?

LG7-8

7.5 • Bond Markets

The majority of trading volume in the bond market occurs in a decentralized, over-the-counter market. Most trades occur between bond dealers and large institutions (like mutual funds, pension funds, and insurance companies). Dealers bid for bonds that investors seek to sell and offer bonds from their own inventory when investors want to buy. This is especially true for the very active Treasury securities market. However, a small number of corporate bonds are listed on centralized exchanges.

figure 7.4 Most Active Investment Grade Bonds, February 19, 2013

This is an example of the most actively traded bonds for a given day on the New York Stock Exchange.

CUSIP	ISSUER NAME	COUPON	MATURITY	BID SIZE	BID	OFFER	OFFER SIZE
36962G5M2	General Electric Cap Corp.	2.150%	09 Jan 2015	31	$102.760	$102.920	50
36962G5C4	General Electric Cap Corp.	2.950%	09 May 2016	101	$105.780	$106.020	50
06740L8C2	Barclays Bank PLC	7.625%	21 Nov 2022	500	$100.700	$100.950	333
38141EA74	Goldman Sachs Group Inc.	3.700%	01 Aug 2015	368	$105.570	$105.820	40
06051GER6	Bank of America Corp.	1.500%	09 Oct 2015	50	$100.220	$100.500	50
38143USC6	Goldman Sachs Group Inc.	3.625%	07 Feb 2016	100	$106.020	$106.320	100

Source: NYSE Euronext, https://bonds.nyx.com/bonds-informer

The NYSE operates the largest centralized U.S. bond market. The majority of bond volume at the NYSE is in corporate debt. The most actively traded bonds for the day are shown in Figure 7.4. Even the most active corporate bonds experience relatively low trading volume. Note that some of the bonds traded are short-term, like General Electric, Goldman Sachs, and Bank of America. Other bonds have many years to maturity, like the Barclay's Bank bond that matures in November 2022.

Following the Bond Market

LG7-8

The entire bond market encompasses a wide variety of securities with varying credit quality from different issuers. Large differences also arise among bonds in terms of their characteristics such as term to maturity and size of the coupon. The biggest factor associated with changes in bond prices is changes in interest rates. So, one common way to describe the direction of bond prices is simply to report the change in interest rates, since we know that interest rate changes will affect all bonds the same way. The interest rate referenced is the yield to maturity and daily yield change for the 10-year Treasury. Knowing how this interest rate changed today gives bond investors a good idea of the general price movement of all types of bonds.

Bond indexes track specific segments of the bond market. Various securities firms, such as Barclays Capital or Merrill Lynch, maintain these indexes that capture bond price and yield changes in particular segments. You can find information about major bond indexes on the Internet and in publications like *The Wall Street Journal* (both in print and online). Figure 7.5 shows indexes that track bonds by type of issuer (federal government, corporation, local government, etc.) and time to maturity (short, intermediate, and long).

TIME OUT

7-9 Why can we use various interest rates to describe the performance of the entire bond market?

7-10 What bond segments are measured by which bond indexes?

figure 7.5 Major Bond Indexes as Reported in *The Wall Street Journal* and on the Internet, February 15, 2013

Here are indexes that track bonds by type of issuer (federal government, corporation, local government, etc.) and time to maturity (short, intermediate, and long).

Index	Close	% Chg	YTD total return	52-wk % Chg	YIELD (%), 52-WEEK RANGE Latest	Low	High	SPREAD, 52-WEEK RANGE (●) Latest — Latest	Low	High
Broad Market Barclays Capital										
U.S. Government/Credit	1997.51	-0.06	-0.77	3.14	1.650	1.490	2.080	n.a.	49.00	79.00
Barclays Aggregate	1732.40	-0.03	-0.65	2.71	1.920	1.560	2.350	n.a.	45.00	87.00
Hourly Treasury Indexes Barclays Capital										
Composite (Price Return)	1458.40	-0.04	-1.20	-1.59	1.140	0.800	1.340	-6.00	-6.00	-6.00
Composite (Total Return)	12895.88	-0.04	-1.00	0.58	1.140	0.800	1.340	-6.00	-6.00	-6.00
Intermediate (Price Return)	1287.78	-0.02	-0.80	-1.25	0.890	0.570	1.090	-6.00	-6.00	-6.00
Intermediate (Total Return)	10759.36	-0.02	-0.60	0.75	0.890	0.570	1.090	-6.00	-6.00	-6.00
Long-Term (Price Return)	2198.87	-0.22	-3.84	-3.86	2.810	2.190	3.000	-6.00	-6.00	-5.00
Long-Term (Total Return)	23604.97	-0.22	-3.56	-0.58	2.810	2.190	3.000	-6.00	-6.00	-5.00
U.S. Corporate Indexes Barclays Capital										
U.S. Corporate	2325.02	-0.10	-0.83	6.24	2.820	2.640	3.510	n.a.	131.00	215.00
Intermediate	2279.59	-0.08	-0.21	5.78	2.140	1.990	2.900	n.a.	116.00	201.00
Long-term	2946.44	-0.15	-2.40	7.48	4.650	4.260	5.210	n.a.	168.00	251.00
Double-A-rated (AA)	485.03	-0.12	-0.92	3.60	2.020	1.760	2.710	n.a.	62.00	132.00
Triple-B-rated (Baa)	576.85	-0.10	-0.74	7.26	3.330	3.160	4.120	n.a.	175.00	262.00
High Yield Bonds Merrill Lynch										
High Yield Constrained*	n.a.	n.a.	n.a.	n.a.	n.a.	n.a.	n.a.	n.a.	n.a.	n.a.
Triple-C-rated (CCC)	n.a.	n.a.	n.a.	n.a.	n.a.	n.a.	n.a.	n.a.	n.a.	n.a.
High Yield 100	n.a.	n.a.	n.a.	n.a.	n.a.	n.a.	n.a.	n.a.	n.a.	n.a.
Europe High Yield Constrained	n.a.	n.a.	n.a.	n.a.	n.a.	n.a.	n.a.	n.a.	n.a.	n.a.
Global High Yield Constrained	n.a.	n.a.	n.a.	n.a.	n.a.	n.a.	n.a.	n.a.	n.a.	n.a.
Mortgage-Backed Merrill Lynch										
Ginnie Mae (GNMA)	n.a.	n.a.	n.a.	n.a.	n.a.	n.a.	n.a.	n.a.	n.a.	n.a.
Fannie Mae (FNMA)	n.a.	n.a.	n.a.	n.a.	n.a.	n.a.	n.a.	n.a.	n.a.	n.a.
Freddie Mac (FHLMC)	n.a.	n.a.	n.a.	n.a.	n.a.	n.a.	n.a.	n.a.	n.a.	n.a.
Tax-Exempt Merrill Lynch										
Muni Master	n.a.	n.a.	n.a.	n.a.	n.a.	n.a.	n.a.	n.a.	n.a.	n.a.
7-12 years	n.a.	n.a.	n.a.	n.a.	n.a.	n.a.	n.a.	n.a.	n.a.	n.a.
12-22 years	n.a.	n.a.	n.a.	n.a.	n.a.	n.a.	n.a.	n.a.	n.a.	n.a.
22-plus years	n.a.	n.a.	n.a.	n.a.	n.a.	n.a.	n.a.	n.a.	n.a.	n.a.
Bond Buyer 6% Muni	131.22	0.05	0.94	5.29	4.040	3.890	4.690	...	...	...

Source: *The Wall Street Journal* Online. Major Bond Indexes web page.

viewpoints REVISITED

Business Application Solution

To raise $150 million, Beach Sand Resorts would need to issue 150,000 bonds at the customary $1,000 par value (= $150 million ÷ $1,000). The bonds will have to offer a 7 percent coupon. This means that Beach Sand Resorts will pay $35 in interest every six months for each bond issued (= 0.07 × $1,000 ÷ 2). So for all 150,000 bonds, they will pay $5.25 million semiannually (= $35 × 150,000).

Personal Application Solution

You can calculate that buying 10 of the Trust Media bonds at the quoted price of 96.21 will cost $9,621 (= 0.9621 × $1,000 × 10) and would generate $285 (= 0.057 × $1,000 × 10 ÷ 2) in interest payments every six months. Buying the bond in 2012, it is priced to offer a 6.47 percent yield to maturity. Ten of the Abalon bonds would cost $10,194 (= 1.0194 × $1,000 × 10) and pay $268.75 (= 0.05375 × $1,000 × 10 ÷ 2) in interest payments every six months. This bond is priced to offer a 5.0 percent yield to maturity. The Trust bonds cost less to purchase, pay more in interest, and offer a higher return than the Abalon bonds. This is because the Trust bonds have higher credit risk. You must decide if the higher return of the Trust bonds is worth taking the extra risk.

CALCULATOR HINTS

N = 12
PV = −1019.40
PMT = 26.875
FV = 1000

CPT I = 2.50
2.50 × 2 = 5.0

summary of learning goals

This chapter describes the bond market. Debt is an important source of capital for companies and governments. A well-functioning bond market contributes to a successful economy. Investors can benefit from bond ownership. Before buying bonds, people should understand how they work.

LG7-1 Describe bond characteristics. Bonds are debt securities that pay a rate of interest called the *coupon rate.* The dollar amount of interest is based on the par value (typically $1,000) of the bond. Interest is usually paid semiannually throughout the time to maturity. At the bond's maturity date, the par value is repaid in full. The bond's legal contract, the indenture agreement, states whether the bond has a call provision that allows the issuer to redeem the bond prior to scheduled maturity. If the bond is called, the issuer pays the bondholder the par value and a call premium.

LG7-2 Identify various bond issuers and their motivations for issuing debt. Treasury securities are obligations of the U.S. government. The U.S. government uses this debt to fund spending that exceeds its revenue. Treasury bills are extremely short term, usually 30 to 90 days until maturity. Treasury notes are issued with 1 to 10 years to maturity, while Treasury bonds are issued with 10 to 30 years. Corporations borrow money by issuing bonds as a source of capital to invest in expansion and new business opportunities. State and local governments borrow money by issuing municipal bonds. The interest income from municipal bonds is, for the most part, tax exempt and therefore appeals to investors in the highest tax brackets.

LG7-3 **Read and interpret bond quotes.** A bond's price and coupon rate are expressed as percentages of the bond's par value. The bid price is the price at which investors can sell the bond and the ask price is the price at which investors buy a bond. When a quoted price is higher than the par value of the bond, the bond can be referred to as a *premium bond.* A bond that carries a price lower than 100 percent of par value is called a *discount bond.*

LG7-4 **Compute bond prices using present value concepts.** The current price of a bond is computed by discounting the future cash flows received: interest payments and par value repayment. The prevailing market interest rate for a bond with similar term to maturity, credit quality, and tax status is used as the discount rate.

LG7-5 **Explain the relationship between bond prices and interest rates.** As prevailing interest rates change in the economy, bond prices also change. Interest rates and bond prices move in opposite directions. A rise in interest rates increases the discount rate and thus reduces a bond's value. The value of a bond will rise when interest rates fall. Changes in interest rates create risk factors for bonds called *reinvestment risk* and *interest rate risk.*

LG7-6 **Compute bond yields.** The simplest bond yield computation is the current yield—simply one year of interest payments divided by the current bond price. Current yield measures the return earned from the interest payments of the bond. However, many bondholders will experience a capital gain or loss in addition to the return from interest payments. The total rate that would be earned if a bond is purchased and held to maturity is the bond's yield to maturity. If a bond is callable, investors may compute the yield to call to assess the return earned if the bond ends up being called. Since municipal bonds pay tax-exempt interest payments, investors commonly compute a taxable equivalent yield to properly compare municipal returns to taxable bond returns.

LG7-7 **Find bond ratings and assess credit risk's effects on bond yields.** Credit quality risk measures the possibility that the bond issuer will fail to make timely interest and principal payments or that the issuer may even default on the debt. Credit rating agencies grade bond risks and report bond ratings. High-quality corporate bonds are considered investment grade, while higher credit risk bonds are speculative, also called *junk bonds* and *high-yield bonds.*

LG7-8 **Assess bond market performance.** Investors can follow the bond market through prevailing market interest rates because interest rates and bond prices move in the opposite direction. Bond indexes track specific segments of the bond market. Popular bond segments are short-term bonds, long-term bonds, Treasuries, high-grade corporate bonds, high-yield bonds, and municipal bonds.

chapter equations

7-1 $$\text{Present value of bond} = PMT \times \left[\frac{1 - \frac{1}{(1+i)^N}}{i}\right] + \frac{\$1{,}000}{(1+i)^N}$$

7-2 $$\text{Bond price} = PV \text{ of annuity } (PMT, i, N) + PV\ (FV, i, N)$$

7-3 $$\text{Price of a callable bond} = PMT \times \left[\frac{1 - \frac{1}{(1+i)^N}}{i}\right] + \frac{\text{Call price}}{(1+i)^N}$$

7-4 $$\text{Equivalent taxable yield} = \frac{\text{Muni yield}}{1 - \text{Tax rate}}$$

key terms

agency bonds, Bonds issued by U.S. government agencies. *p. 237*

asset-backed securities, Debt securities whose payments originate from other loans, such as credit card debt, auto loans, and home equity loans. *p. 238*

bond, Publicly traded form of debt. *p. 233*

bond price, Current price that the bond sells for in the bond market. *p. 234*

bond rating, A grade of credit quality as reported by credit rating agencies. *p. 253*

call, An issuer redeeming the bond before the scheduled maturity date. *p. 234*

call premium, The amount in addition to the par value paid by the issuer when calling a bond. *p. 234*

convertible bond, A debt security that can be converted to shares of stock or another type of security. *p. 238*

coupon rate, The annual amount of interest paid expressed as a percentage of the bond's par value. *p. 234*

credit quality risk, The chance that the issuer will not make timely interest payments or even default. *p. 253*

current yield, Return from interest payments; computed as the annual interest payment divided by the current bond price. *p. 247*

debentures, Unsecured bonds. *p. 254*

discount bond, A bond selling for lower than its par value. *p. 240*

equipment trust certificates, Bonds secured with factory and equipment as collateral. *p. 255*

fixed-income securities, Any securities that make fixed payments. *p. 233*

high-yield bonds, Bonds with low credit quality that offer a high yield to maturity, also called junk bonds. *p. 255*

indenture agreement, Legal contract describing the bond characteristics and the bondholder and issuer rights. *p. 233*

interest rate risk, The chance of a capital loss due to interest rate fluctuations. *p. 245*

investment grade, High credit quality corporate bonds. *p. 253*

junk bonds, Low credit quality corporate bonds, also called speculative bonds or high-yield bonds. *p. 254*

maturity date, The calendar date on which the bond principal comes due. *p. 233*

mortgage-backed securities, Debt securities whose interest and par value payments originate from real estate mortgage payments. *p. 238*

mortgage bonds, Bonds secured with real estate as collateral. *p. 255*

par value, Amount of debt borrowed to be repaid; face value. *p. 233*

premium bond, A bond selling for greater than its par value. *p. 240*

principal, Face amount, or par value, of debt. *p. 233*

reinvestment rate risk, The chance that future interest payments will have to be reinvested at a lower interest rate. *p. 245*

senior bonds, Older bonds that carry a higher claim to the issuer's assets. *p. 254*

taxable equivalent yield, Modification of a municipal bond's yield to maturity used to compare muni bond yields to taxable bond yields. *p. 251*

time to maturity, The length of time (in years) until the bond matures and the issuer repays the par value. *p. 234*

Treasury Inflation-Protected Securities, TIPS are U.S. government bonds where the par value changes with inflation. *p. 236*

unsecured corporate bonds, Corporate debt not secured by collateral such as land, buildings, or equipment. *p. 254*

yield to call, The total return that the bond offers if purchased at the current price and held until the bond is called. *p. 250*

yield to maturity, The total return the bond offers if purchased at the current price and held to maturity. *p. 247*

zero coupon bond, A bond that does not make interest payments but generally sells at a deep discount and then pays the par value at the maturity date. *p. 242*

self-test problems with solutions

LG7-1, 7-3, 7-4

1 Bond Quotes and Value Sheila's broker has given her the following bond quote for a bond issued by Delvin Hardware. What is the price she would pay to buy this bond? Before buying the bond, Sheila notices that other bonds with the same time to maturity and credit rating are offering a 5.08 yield to maturity. What is the bond price at the 5.08 yield? Should Sheila buy this bond? The date is March 2, 2014.

Price	Coupon (%)	Maturity	YTM (%)	Current Yield (%)	Fitch Ratings	Callable
101.57	5.200	1-Mar-2018	4.777	5.119	AA	No

Solution:

Sheila knows that the bond quote means that it would cost her $1,015.70 (= 1.0157 × $1,000) to purchase now. However, this bond is priced to offer a lower yield to maturity (4.777%) than that offered by similar bonds (5.08%), so it appears mispriced. The value of this bond using the 5.08 percent market interest rate can be computed using equation 7-1. The semiannual interest payment is $26 (= 0.052 × $1,000 ÷ 2) and will be paid eight more times. The bond's value is:

CALCULATOR HINTS

N = 8
I = 2.54
PMT = 26.00
FV = 1000

CPT PV = −1004.29

$$\text{Bond value} = \$26.00 \times \left[\frac{1 - \dfrac{1}{(1+0.0254)^8}}{0.0254}\right] + \frac{\$1{,}000}{(1+0.0254)^8}$$

$$= \$186.10 + \$818.19 = \$1{,}004.29$$

Since the bond's value is $1,004.29 and the price is $1,015.70, it appears to be overpriced by $11.41. Sheila may want to consider other bonds that offer an appropriate yield for their level of risk.

LG7-6

2 Yield to Maturity and Yield to Call Kaito is considering a bond issued from All Satellite Radio. The bond has a 9.625 percent coupon and will mature on August 1, 2018. The current market price for the bond is 101.50 and the date is February 2, 2012. Kaito wants to know the current yield and yield to maturity that the bond is offering. In addition, the bond can be called on August 1, 2014, at a price of 104.813. So he wants to know the yield to call as well.

Solution:

The Radio bond pays $48.125 (= 0.09625 × $1,000 ÷ 2) in interest every six months and has 6½ years until it matures. At a price of 101.50, the bond's current yield is 9.48 percent ($96.25 ÷ $1,015.00). The yield to maturity can be found with equation 7-2 and the financial calculator as N = 13, PV = −1015, PMT = 48.125, and FV = 1000. Computing the interest rate (I) results in 4.656 percent and multiplying by 2 gives the yield to maturity of 9.31 percent. Kaito knows that Radio could call the bond early. To compute the yield to call, the number of periods and the future price need to be changed. In that case, the yield to call would be computed as N = 5, PV = −1015, PMT = 48.125, and FV = 1048.13 Computing the interest rate (I) results in 5.33 percent and multiplying by 2 gives the yield call of 10.66 percent.

LG7-6

3 Municipal Bonds and Income Tax Brackets Shane is a securities broker with many clients. His company has acquired a large number of municipal bonds issued for the Atlanta, Georgia, airport. These bonds pay a coupon of 5 percent, mature on January 1, 2034, have an AAA credit rating, and carry a price of 107.091. Assume that it is January 2, 2013, and that the par value of the bond is $5,000. As an alternative, corporate bonds with similar risk and time to maturity offer a 6.35 percent yield to maturity. Shane is trying to determine which of his clients these bonds would benefit the most.

Solution:

Since these municipal bonds are issued in the state of Georgia, the bondholders in Georgia will not have to pay either federal or state income tax on the interest payments. Therefore, Shane should focus on his clients who live in Georgia. This bond offers investors a yield to maturity that can be computed using equation 7-2. Using the financial calculator, enter N = 44, PV = −5354.55, PMT = 125, and FV = 5000. Computing the interest rate (I) results in 2.245 percent and multiplying by 2 gives the yield to maturity of 4.49 percent. The tax savings provide a larger benefit for people in a higher marginal tax bracket. Investors in the 35 percent tax bracket can compare the muni bond yield to a taxable corporate yield by converting the muni to an equivalent taxable yield as in equation 7-4:

$$\text{Equivalent taxable yield} = \frac{4.49\%}{1 - 0.35} = 6.91\%$$

So people in the highest tax bracket will prefer this municipal bond to the similar corporate bonds offering only 6.35 percent. The following table shows the equivalent taxable yield for the marginal tax brackets of 2009. Shane notes that in this case, his clients in the upper two marginal tax brackets would benefit from these municipal bonds. Investors in the lower brackets would do better purchasing the corporate bonds.

Marginal Tax Bracket (%)	10	15	25	28	33	35
Equivalent Taxable Yield (%)	4.99	5.28	5.99	6.19	6.70	6.91

4 **Credit Risk and Bond Costs** Monica is CFO of a manufacturing company that wants to raise capital for several new business projects. The firm's current bonds are rated A. Monica is working closely with the credit rating agencies to determine what the credit rating would be on new bonds issued under two different circumstances. In the first case, the firm would issue $50 million in new bonds to fund a project. In the second case, the firm would issue $150 million to fund two new projects. The credit rating agency says that the first alternative would result in a BBB rating and the second case would result in a BB rating. Monica uses the following current market yield table to assess the interest cost of the two alternatives. What would the interest rate cost (in dollars) be in each case? LG7-7

Credit Rating	AAA	AA	A	BBB	BB	B
20-Year Average Yield	5.7	5.9	6.1	6.5	7.1	8.4

Solution:

If Monica goes with the first case and raises $50 million with a bond issue, the bonds will be rated BBB, the lowest investment grade rating. She would issue the bonds with the market rate 6.5 percent as the coupon rate. This means that she will have to pay $3.25 million (= 0.065 × $50 million) every year in interest payments. If she decides to issue $150 million in bonds instead, they will be rated BB, and be known as junk bonds. She will need to offer the higher interest rate of 7.1 percent as the coupon rate. Therefore, she will have to pay \$10.65 million (= 0.071 × \$150 million) every year in interest payments. The difference in the two options is due to both the difference in coupon rate and the amount of money borrowed. One other issue Monica may want to consider is the reputation impact of having bonds rated in the junk bond range. Other people in the industry often use bond ratings as a signal about the financial stability of the firm. Her suppliers may begin to worry about the firm if it has a BB rating and may not be willing to extend credit. In other words, the second case may create some financial problems in other parts of the company.

LG7-5,7-7

5 Capital Gains and Losses in Bonds Microcasm, Inc., a pharmaceutical company, has issued bonds that now have 15 years to maturity. The bonds have a coupon rate of 4.4 percent and a recent bond quote of 102.35. The bond has a credit rating of BBB and is priced to provide a 4.187 yield to maturity. A news announcement today discloses that Microcasm has been named in a lawsuit that could become a serious program for the firm. As a response, Standard & Poor's lowered its credit rating to BB+. The bonds with this credit rating and maturity have a yield to maturity of 5.08. What is the price change experienced by the bonds (in dollars and percentage)?

CALCULATOR HINTS

N = 30
I = 2.54
PMT = 22
FV = 1000

CPT PV = −929.22

Solution:

The bond price before the announcement can be computed from the bond quote of 102.35, which indicates a price of \$1,023.50. The price after the announcement can be computed using semiannual compounding:

$$\text{Bond Price} = \$22 \times \left[\frac{1 - \dfrac{1}{(1 + 0.0254)^{30}}}{0.0254} \right] + \frac{1{,}000}{(1 + 0.0254)^{30}} = \$458.02 + \$471.19 = \$929.21$$

Therefore, the bond changed −\$94.29 [= \$1,023.50 − \$929.21], or −9.21 percent [= −\$94.29/\$1,023.50] of its value.

questions

1. What does a call provision allow issuers to do, and why would they do it? *(LG7-1)*
2. List the differences between the new TIPS and traditional Treasury bonds. *(LG7-2)*
3. Explain how mortgage-backed securities work. *(LG7-2)*
4. Provide the definitions of a discount bond and a premium bond. Give examples. *(LG7-3)*
5. Describe the differences in interest payments and bond price between a 5 percent coupon bond and a zero coupon bond. *(LG7-4)*
6. All else equal, which bond's price is more affected by a change in interest rates, a short-term bond or a longer-term bond? Why? *(LG7-5)*
7. All else equal, which bond's price is more affected by a change in interest rates, a bond with a large coupon or a small coupon? Why? *(LG7-5)*

8. Explain how a bond's interest rate can change over time even if interest rates in the economy do not change. *(LG7-5)*

9. Compare and contrast the advantages and disadvantages of the current yield computation versus yield to maturity calculations. *(LG7-6)*

10. What is the yield to call and why is it important to a bond investor? *(LG7-6)*

11. What is the purpose of computing the equivalent taxable yield of a municipal bond? *(LG7-6)*

12. Explain why high-income and wealthy people are more likely to buy a municipal bond than a corporate bond. *(LG7-6)*

13. Why does a Treasury bond offer a lower yield than a corporate bond with the same time to maturity? Could a corporate bond with a different time to maturity offer a lower yield? Explain. *(LG7-7)*

14. Describe the difference between a bond issued as a high-yield bond and one that has become a "fallen angel." *(LG7-7)*

15. What is the difference in the trading volume between Treasury bonds and corporate bonds? Give examples and/or evidence. *(LG7-8)*

problems

basic problems

7-1 **Interest Payments** Determine the interest payment for the following three bonds: 3½ percent coupon corporate bond (paid semiannually), 4.25 percent coupon Treasury note, and a corporate zero coupon bond maturing in ten years. (Assume a $1,000 par value.) *(LG7-1)*

7-2 **Interest Payments** Determine the interest payment for the following three bonds: 4½ percent coupon corporate bond (paid semiannually), 5.15 percent coupon Treasury note, and a corporate zero coupon bond maturing in 15 years. (Assume a $1,000 par value.) *(LG7-1)*

7-3 **Time to Maturity** A bond issued by Ford on May 15, 1997 is scheduled to mature on May 15, 2097. If today is November 16, 2014, what is this bond's time to maturity? *(LG7-1)*

7-4 **Time to Maturity** A bond issued by IBM on December 1, 1996, is scheduled to mature on December 1, 2096. If today is December 2, 2015, what is this bond's time to maturity? *(LG7-1)*

7-5 **Call Premium** A 6 percent corporate coupon bond is callable in five years for a call premium of one year of coupon payments. Assuming a par value of $1,000, what is the price paid to the bondholder if the issuer calls the bond? *(LG7-1)*

7-6 **Call Premium** A 5.5 percent corporate coupon bond is callable in ten years for a call premium of one year of coupon payments. Assuming a par value of $1,000, what is the price paid to the bondholder if the issuer calls the bond? *(LG7-1)*

7-7 **TIPS Interest and Par Value** A 2¾ percent TIPS has an original reference CPI of 185.4. If the current CPI is 210.7, what is the current interest payment and par value of the TIPS? *(LG7-2)*

7-8 **TIPS Interest and Par Value** A 3⅛ percent TIPS has an original reference CPI of 180.5. If the current CPI is 206.8, what is the current interest payment and par value of the TIPS? *(LG7-2)*

7-9 **Bond Quotes** Consider the following three bond quotes: a Treasury note quoted at 97:27, a corporate bond quoted at 103.25, and a municipal bond quoted at 101.90. If the Treasury and corporate bonds have a par value of $1,000 and the municipal bond has a par value of $5,000, what is the price of these three bonds in dollars? *(LG7-3)*

7-10 **Bond Quotes** Consider the following three bond quotes: a Treasury bond quoted at 106:14, a corporate bond quoted at 96.55, and a municipal bond quoted at 100.95. If the Treasury and corporate bonds have a par value of $1,000 and the municipal bond has a par value of $5,000, what is the price of these three bonds in dollars? *(LG7-3)*

7-11 **Zero Coupon Bond Price** Calculate the price of a zero coupon bond that matures in 20 years if the market interest rate is 3.8 percent. *(LG7-4)*

7-12 **Zero Coupon Bond Price** Calculate the price of a zero coupon bond that matures in 15 years if the market interest rate is 5.75 percent. *(LG7-4)*

7-13 **Current Yield** What's the current yield of a 3.8 percent coupon corporate bond quoted at a price of 102.08? *(LG7-6)*

7-14 **Current Yield** What's the current yield of a 5.2 percent coupon corporate bond quoted at a price of 96.78? *(LG7-6)*

7-15 **Taxable Equivalent Yield** What's the taxable equivalent yield on a municipal bond with a yield to maturity of 3.5 percent for an investor in the 33 percent marginal tax bracket? *(LG7-6)*

7-16 **Taxable Equivalent Yield** What's the taxable equivalent yield on a municipal bond with a yield to maturity of 2.9 percent for an investor in the 28 percent marginal tax bracket? *(LG7-6)*

7-17 **Credit Risk and Yield** Rank from highest credit risk to lowest risk the following bonds, with the same time to maturity, by their yield to maturity: Treasury bond with yield of 5.55 percent, IBM bond with yield of 7.49 percent, Trump Casino bond with yield of 8.76 percent, and Banc One bond with a yield of 5.99 percent. *(LG7-7)*

7-18 **Credit Risk and Yield** Rank the following bonds in order from lowest credit risk to highest risk all with the same time to maturity, by their yield to maturity: Treasury bond with yield of 4.65 percent, United Airline bond with yield of 9.07 percent, Bank of America bond with a yield of 6.25 percent, and Hewlett-Packard bond with yield of 6.78 percent. *(LG7-7)*

intermediate problems

7-19 **TIPS Capital Return** Consider a 3.5 percent TIPS with an issue CPI reference of 185.6. At the beginning of this year, the CPI was 193.5 and was at 199.6 at the end of the year. What was the capital gain of the TIPS in dollars and in percentage terms? *(LG7-2)*

7-20 **TIPS Capital Return** Consider a 2.25 percent TIPS with an issue CPI reference of 187.2. At the beginning of this year, the CPI was 197.1 and was at 203.8 at the end of the year. What was the capital gain of the TIPS in dollars and in percentage terms? *(LG7-2)*

7-21 **Compute Bond Price** Compute the price of a 3.8 percent coupon bond with 15 years left to maturity and a market interest rate of 6.8 percent. (Assume interest payments are semiannual.) Is this a discount or premium bond? *(LG7-4)*

7-22 **Compute Bond Price** Compute the price of a 5.6 percent coupon bond with ten years left to maturity and a market interest rate of 7.0 percent.

(Assume interest payments are semiannual.) Is this a discount or premium bond? *(LG7-4)*

7-23 **Compute Bond Price** Calculate the price of a 5.2 percent coupon bond with 18 years left to maturity and a market interest rate of 4.6 percent. (Assume interest payments are semiannual.) Is this a discount or premium bond? *(LG7-4)*

7-24 **Compute Bond Price** Calculate the price of a 5.7 percent coupon bond with 22 years left to maturity and a market interest rate of 6.5 percent. (Assume interest payments are semiannual.) Is this a discount or premium bond? *(LG7-4)*

7-25 **Bond Prices and Interest Rate Changes** A 5.75 percent coupon bond with ten years left to maturity is priced to offer a 6.5 percent yield to maturity. You believe that in one year, the yield to maturity will be 5.8 percent. What is the change in price the bond will experience in dollars? *(LG7-5)*

7-26 **Bond Prices and Interest Rate Changes** A 6.5 percent coupon bond with 14 years left to maturity is priced to offer a 7.2 percent yield to maturity. You believe that in one year, the yield to maturity will be 6.8 percent. What is the change in price the bond will experience in dollars? *(LG7-5)*

7-27 **Yield to Maturity** A 5.65 percent coupon bond with 18 years left to maturity is offered for sale at $1,035.25. What yield to maturity is the bond offering? (Assume interest payments are semiannual.) *(LG7-6)*

7-28 **Yield to Maturity** A 4.30 percent coupon bond with 14 years left to maturity is offered for sale at $943.22. What yield to maturity is the bond offering? (Assume interest payments are semiannual.) *(LG7-6)*

7-29 **Yield to Call** A 6.75 percent coupon bond with 26 years left to maturity can be called in six years. The call premium is one year of coupon payments. It is offered for sale at $1,135.25. What is the yield to call of the bond? (Assume interest payments are semiannual.) *(LG7-6)*

7-30 **Yield to Call** A 5.25 percent coupon bond with 14 years left to maturity can be called in four years. The call premium is one year of coupon payments. It is offered for sale at $1,075.50. What is the yield to call of the bond? (Assume interest payments are semiannual.) *(LG7-6)*

7-31 **Comparing Bond Yields** A client in the 39 percent marginal tax bracket is comparing a municipal bond that offers a 4.5 percent yield to maturity and a similar-risk corporate bond that offers a 6.45 percent yield. Which bond will give the client more profit after taxes? *(LG7-6)*

7-32 **Comparing Bond Yields** A client in the 28 percent marginal tax bracket is comparing a municipal bond that offers a 4.5 percent yield to maturity and a similar-risk corporate bond that offers a 6.45 percent yield. Which bond will give the client more profit after taxes? *(LG7-6)*

advanced problems

7-33 **TIPS Total Return** Reconsider the 3.5 percent TIPS discussed in problem 7-19. It was issued with CPI reference of 185.6. The bond is purchased at the beginning of the year (after the interest payment), when the CPI was 193.5. For the interest payment in the middle of the year, the CPI was 195.1. Now, at the end of the year, the CPI is 199.6 and the interest payment has been made. What is the total return of the TIPS in dollars and in percentage terms for the year? *(LG7-2)*

7-34 **TIPS Total Return** Reconsider the 2.25 percent TIPS discussed in problem 7-20. It was issued with CPI reference of 187.2. The bond is purchased at the beginning of the year (after the interest payment), when the CPI was 197.1. For the interest payment in the middle of the year, the CPI was 200.1. Now, at the end of the year, the CPI is 203.8 and the interest payment has been made. What is the total return of the TIPS in dollars and in percentage terms for the year? *(LG7-2)*

7-35 **Bond Prices and Interest Rate Changes** A 6.25 percent coupon bond with 22 years left to maturity is priced to offer a 5.5 percent yield to maturity. You believe that in one year, the yield to maturity will be 6.0 percent. If this occurs, what would be the total return of the bond in dollars and percent? *(LG7-5)*

7-36 **Bond Prices and Interest Rate Changes** A 7.5 percent coupon bond with 13 years left to maturity is priced to offer a 6.25 percent yield to maturity. You believe that in one year, the yield to maturity will be 7.0 percent. If this occurs, what would be the total return of the bond in dollars and percentage terms? *(LG7-5)*

7-37 **Yields of a Bond** A 2.50 percent coupon municipal bond has 12 years left to maturity and has a price quote of 98.45. The bond can be called in four years. The call premium is one year of coupon payments. Compute and discuss the bond's current yield, yield to maturity, taxable equivalent yield (for an investor in the 35 percent marginal tax bracket), and yield to call. (Assume interest payments are semiannual and a par value of $5,000.) *(LG7-6)*

7-38 **Yields of a Bond** A 3.85 percent coupon municipal bond has 18 years left to maturity and has a price quote of 103.20. The bond can be called in eight years. The call premium is one year of coupon payments. Compute and discuss the bond's current yield, yield to maturity, taxable equivalent yield (for an investor in the 35 percent marginal tax bracket), and yield to call. (Assume interest payments are semiannual and a par value of $5,000.) *(LG7-6)*

7-39 **Bond Ratings and Prices** A corporate bond with a 6.5 percent coupon has 15 years left to maturity. It has had a credit rating of BBB and a yield to maturity of 7.2 percent. The firm has recently gotten into some trouble and the rating agency is downgrading the bonds to BB. The new appropriate discount rate will be 8.5 percent. What will be the change in the bond's price in dollars and percentage terms? (Assume interest payments are semiannual.) *(LG7-7)*

7-40 **Bond Ratings and Prices** A corporate bond with a 6.75 percent coupon has ten years left to maturity. It has had a credit rating of BB and a yield to maturity of 8.2 percent. The firm has recently become more financially stable and the rating agency is upgrading the bonds to BBB. The new appropriate discount rate will be 7.1 percent. What will be the change in the bond's price in dollars and percentage terms? (Assume interest payments are semiannual.) *(LG7-7)*

7-41 **Spreadsheet Problem** Say that in June of 2014, a company issued bonds that are scheduled to mature in June of 2017. The coupon rate is 5.75 percent and is semiannually. The bond issue was rated AAA.

a. Build a spreadsheet that shows how much money the firm pays for each interest rate payment and when those payments will occur if the bond issue sells 50,000 bonds.

b. If the bond issue rating would have been BBB, then the coupon rate would have been 6.30 percent. Show the interest payments with this rating. Explain why bond ratings are important to firms issuing capital debt.

c. Consider that interest rates in the economy increased in the first half of 2012. If the firm would have issued the bonds in January of 2012, then the coupon rate would have only been 5.40 percent. How much extra money per year is the firm paying because it issued the bonds in June instead of January?

research it! Bond Information Online

Information on the bond market is widely available in papers like *The Wall Street Journal* and *Barron's*. Bond information can also be found online at financial websites like **finance.yahoo.com** and **www.finra.org.** The bond credit rating agencies also maintain websites with their own bond market news.

You can follow the bond market easily at places like the Yahoo! Finance website. Click on the Bond link in the menu to go to their Bond Center. Bond yields for various maturity Treasury securities are shown for today and for previous days. The Bond Composite Rates link shows similar comparisons for municipal and corporate bonds too.

Bond calculators are also available free on the Web. Compare a bond price result from your calculator or the price equation with the online bond calculator result at Investopedia. (**www.investopedia.com/calculator/BondPrice.aspx**)

integrated mini-case Corporate Bond Credit Risk Changes and Bond Prices

Land'o'Toys is a profitable, medium-sized, retail company. Several years ago it issued a 6½ percent coupon bond, which pays interest semiannually. The bond will mature in ten years and is currently priced in the market as $1,037.19. The average yields to maturity for 10-year corporate bonds are reported in the following table by bond rating.

Bond Rating	Yield (%)	Bond Rating	Yield (%)
AAA	5.4	BB	7.3
AA	5.7	B	8.2
A	6.0	CCC	9.2
BBB	6.5	CC	10.5
		C	12.0
		D	14.5

Periodically, one company will purchase another by buying all of the target firm's stock. The bonds of the target firm continue to exist. The debt obligation is assumed by the new firm. The credit risk of the bonds often changes because of this type of an event.

Suppose that the firm Treasure Toys makes an announcement that it is purchasing Land'o'Toys. Due to Treasure Toys' projected financial structure after the purchase, Standard & Poor's states that the bond rating for Land'o'Toys bonds will change to BB.

a. Compute the yield to maturity of Land'o'Toys bonds before the purchase announcement and use it to determine the likely bond rating.

b. Assume the bond's price changes to reflect the new credit rating. What is the new price? Did the price increase or decrease?

c. What is the dollar change and percentage change in the bond price?

d. How do the bond investors feel about the announcement?

ANSWERS TO TIME OUT

7-1 The federal government issues bonds to fund its annual spending deficit and to refund old bonds that are maturing. Local governments and corporations issue bonds to raise the capital needed to fund projects. For local governments, those projects might be the building of roads, bridges, sewer systems, schools, airports, etc. For companies, the projects tend to be expansions of their businesses, which might entail a large factory, new facilities in different geographical locations, and even the purchase of existing business lines from other companies.

7-2 The current price is 100.06 percent of \$1,000, which is \$1,000.60. It will pay a semiannual payment of 5.40% × \$1,000 ÷ 2 = \$27.

7-3

3.75% — Semiannual periods

Period	0	1	2	3	4	. . .	21	22	23	24
Cash flow	?	42.5	42.5	42.5	42.5	. . .	42.5	42.5	42.5	42.5 1,000

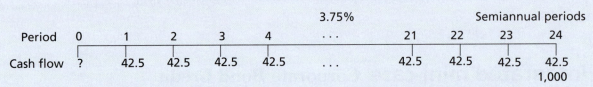

$$\text{Bond price} = \$42.50 \times \left[\frac{1 - \dfrac{1}{(1 + 0.0375)^{24}}}{0.0375}\right] + \frac{\$1{,}000}{(1 + 0.0375)^{24}} = \$664.90 + \$413.32 = \$1{,}078.22$$

7-4 The relationship is one of opposite directions. Increases in market interest rates are associated with decreases in the price of existing bonds. Decreases in interest rates accompany increases in bond prices.

7-5 Using the calculator with settings of N = 20, PV = −525, PMT = 0, FV = 1000, solving for I gives 3.274 percent. Multiplying this semiannual yield by 2 gives a 6.55 percent yield to maturity.

7-6 The yield to maturity is higher than the coupon rate for a discount bond. By definition, bonds become discount bonds when the market interest rate (known as the yield to maturity for a bond) rises above the fixed coupon rate.

7-7 A credit rating change will change the appropriate discount for the bond. An increase in the rating calls for a lower discount rate to be used while a decrease in the rating calls for a higher discount rate. This change in the discount rate directly impacts the bond price.

7-8 The mortgage bond has real estate collateral whereas the debenture has no collateral. Therefore, the mortgage bond is considered a safer security for investors and will be given a higher rating. With the lower bond rating, the debenture will have to offer a higher yield.

7-9 Since bond prices move in the opposite direction to interest rates, the change in interest rates provides much of the information for knowing the change in bond prices.

7-10 Figure 7.5 illustrates many of the popular bond indexes. For example, Barclays Capital reports various broad market and U.S. Treasury bond indexes. For corporate bonds, Merrill Lynch reports indexes for medium-term investment grade, long-term investment grade, and speculative grade. Merrill Lynch also has municipal bond indexes.

8 Valuing Stocks

viewpoints

Business Application

As CEO of your firm, Dawa Tech, which makes computer components, you have been able to grow its dividends by 8 percent per year to a recent $2 per share. You expect this growth to continue. As a result, the stock price has risen to $65 and has a P/E ratio of 16.25.

Tomorrow, you are scheduled to meet with some stockholders and financial analysts. To prepare for the meeting, you should know what return the shareholders seem to expect and estimate where the Dawa stock price may be in three years. How will you go about preparing for this meeting? **(See solution on p. 295)**

Personal Application

You are impressed with the news and entertainment firm CBC Newscorp. The per-share dividends have increased from $1.25 per year three years ago to the recent $1.68 annual dividend. Then you discover that 15 analysts are following the firm and that their mean growth estimate for the future is 10.1 percent. Now you want to know if the current selling price of $54 seems like a good deal if the appropriate required return for the stock is 13.5 percent. **(See solution on p. 295)**

Who are these "analysts," and where can you find their opinions?

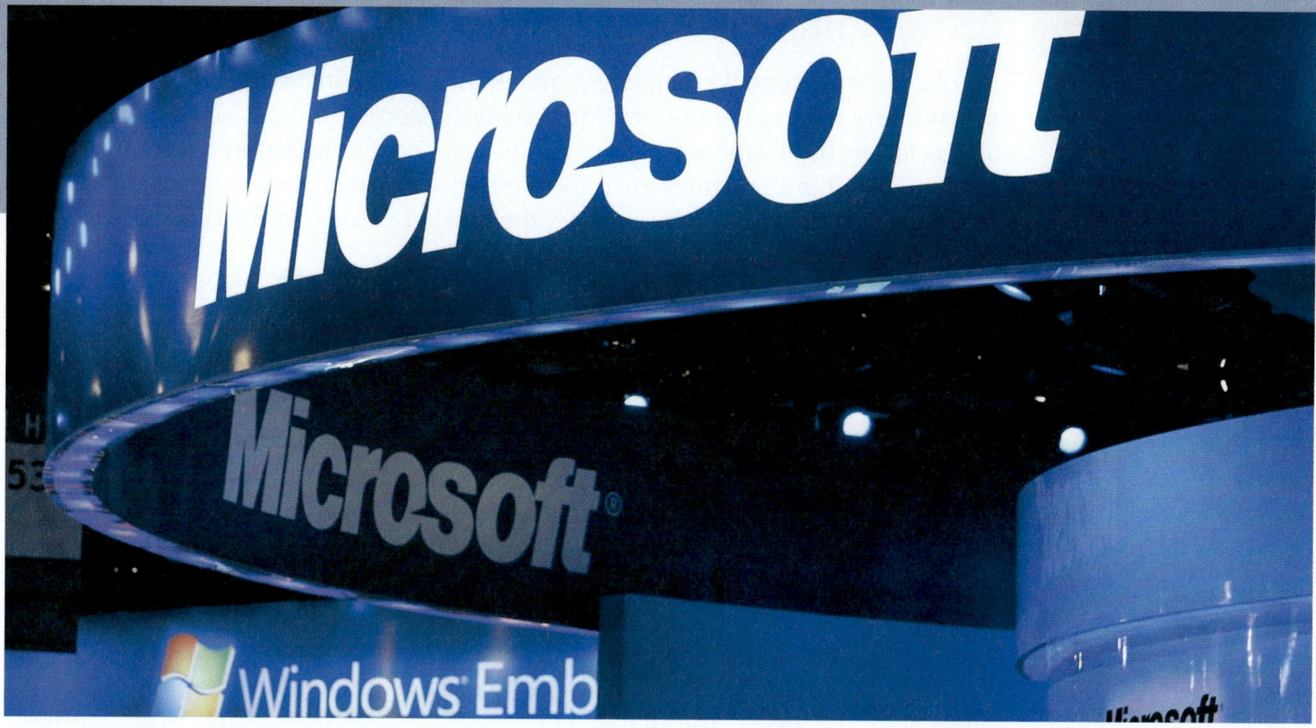

Businesses need capital to start up operations, expand product lines and services, and serve new markets. In the last chapter, we discussed debt, which is one source of financial capital upon which businesses can draw. Their other source of capital is called *equity*, or *business ownership*. Public corporations share business ownership and raise money by issuing stocks to investors. When the company sells this form of equity ownership to raise money, it gives up some ownership—and thus some control—over the business. Investors buy stock to receive the benefits of business ownership. Most citizens do not have the time or expertise to operate their own businesses. Buying stock allows them to participate in the profits of economic activities. Access to equity capital has allowed entrepreneurs like Bill Gates of Microsoft and Larry Page of Google to take their companies public so that their businesses can become large corporations. Both the company founders and the new owners (stock investors) have amassed much wealth over the years under this arrangement. One very important reason that investors are willing to buy company stock as an investment is that they know that they can sell the stock during any trading day. Investors buy and sell stocks among themselves in stock markets. Well-functioning stock markets are critical to any capitalistic economy. In this chapter, we'll discuss stock market operations and stock valuation.

Learning Goals

LG8-1 Understand the rights and returns that come with common stock ownership.

LG8-2 Know how stock exchanges function.

LG8-3 Track the wider stock market with stock indexes and differentiate among the kinds of information each index provides.

LG8-4 Know the terminology of stock trading.

LG8-5 Compute stock values using dividend discount and constant-growth models.

LG8-6 Calculate the stock value of a variable-growth-rate company.

LG8-7 Assess relative stock values using the P/E ratio model.

LG8-1

8.1 • Common Stock

common stock

An ownership stake in a corporation.

Equity securities (stocks) represent ownership shares in a corporation. **Common stock** offers buyers the potential for current income from dividends and capital appreciation from any stock price increases. Over time, some corporate profits are reinvested in the firm, which increases the value of each shareholder's stake in the business. At any point in time, the market value of a firm's common stock depends on many factors, including:

- The company's profitability.
- Growth prospects for the future.
- Current market interest rates.
- Conditions in the overall stock market.

Over periods of 30 to 40 years, stocks have offered investors the best opportunities to increase wealth. Since stocks are also susceptible to price declines and stock price fluctuations can be very volatile over short periods of time, stock investing requires a longer-term outlook.

Virtually any business firm that is organized as a corporation (see Chapter 1) may choose to issue publicly traded stock. Common stockholders vote to elect the board of directors; they also vote on various other proposals requested by other shareholders or the management team. As owners of the firm, common stockholders are considered to be **residual claimants.** This means that common stockholders have the right to claim any cash flows or value after all other claimants have received what they are owed. As a company earns cash flows, it must pay suppliers, employees, expenses, taxes, and debt interest payments. Stockholders claim the leftover (or residual) cash flow. These profits can be used to reinvest in the firm to foster growth, pay dividends to shareholders, or a combination of the two.

residual claimants

Ownership of cash flows and value after other claimants are paid.

Stocks of growing firms are valuable. Stocks in firms that pay dividends to shareholders are also valuable. Stocks issued by firms that have greater amounts of residual cash flow are more valuable. The value is reflected in the stock price. *Therefore, stock price values arise from the company's underlying business success.* Many different investors and analysts may estimate a stock's fundamental value based upon some outlook or theory. But the actual stock price is determined on stock exchanges when investors seek to trade with one another. Let's discuss this trading process and then explore how stocks are valued.

LG8-2

8.2 • Stock Markets

In general, people will invest significant amounts of their wealth in stocks only if they know that they can convert their shares into cash at any time. Stock exchanges provide this liquidity, allowing buyers and sellers the means to transact stock trades with each other. This liquidity gives many people the confidence to invest in the first place and makes stocks (as well as bonds) attractive investments relative to less-liquid assets like real estate or fine collectibles—which can be difficult to sell quickly at full value.

New York Stock Exchange (NYSE)

Large and prestigious stock exchange with a trading floor.

The most well-known stock exchange in the world is the **New York Stock Exchange (NYSE).** The New York Stock Exchange, located in New York City on the corner of Wall Street and Broad Street, is the largest U.S. stock exchange as measured by the value of companies listed and the dollar value of trading activity. The NYSE is the largest equities marketplace in the world and is home to approximately 2,300 companies (many with multiple securities listed). While other exchanges may boast more companies listed, the largest companies in the world tend to list in New York. The holding company that owns the NYSE, NYSE Euronext, also operates Euronext N.V., a Europe-based electronic exchange market. Together, the NYSE and the Euronext list more than 8,000 equity, derivate, fixed-income, and exchanged-traded securities.

Much of the stock buying and selling at the NYSE occurs at 17 stations, called **trading posts,** on the trading floor. Each post is staffed by a designated market maker (formerly known as specialists), who oversees the orderly trading of the specific stocks assigned to that post. **Brokers,** located around the perimeter of the floor, act as agents for those buying and selling stocks. Brokers execute orders by matching buy and sell orders. Once the buy and sell orders match, the transaction is completed and the trade appears on trading screens viewed by people all over the world.

trading posts
Trading location on the floor of a stock exchange.

brokers
Floor traders who execute orders for others and themselves.

Consider this scenario. You decide to buy shares of McDonald's stock because of new menu items and other initiatives. You place a buy order for 100 shares with your broker—either with a simple phone call or through an online brokerage service. The broker then sends the order to the NYSE electronically via the NYSE Super Display Book system to the trading post assigned for McDonald's stock. At the trading post, the specialist makes sure the transaction is executed in a fair and orderly manner. Your buy order competes with other orders at the point of sale for the best price and an on-floor broker executes your purchase. You will receive a trade confirmation from your broker describing the trade and noting the exact amount you owe for the 100 shares of McDonald's plus any applicable commissions. The NYSE reports the transaction and it appears within seconds on displays across the country and around the world. Note that buy and sell orders are electronically routed from all over the world to the NYSE, which then routes trade results back. Since most of the trade orders are already in electronic form, why not electronically match buy and sell orders and bypass any human intervention in floor trading? Indeed, the NYSE has joined many other exchanges in becoming increasingly electronic. Some floor specialist firms can see a time when no human intervention will be a part of floor trading at the NYSE. Their claim that human intervention can detect and prevent problems with electronic trades has been widely questioned.

The NYSE will trade hundreds of thousands, even millions, of McDonald's stock shares in a given day. An intraday (during trading hours) stock quote for McDonald's stock, **ticker symbol** MCD, is shown in Figure 8.1. On March 13, 2013, more than 2 million McDonald's shares traded by early afternoon. The stock traded at $99.15 per share, which was $0.39 higher than the closing price of the previous day. At this price, McDonald's stock is currently much closer to its 52-week high of $99.50 than to its 52-week low of $83.31.

ticker symbol
Unique code for a company consisting of one to five letters.

To list its stock on the NYSE, a company must meet minimum requirements for its:

- Total number of stockholders.
- Level of trading volume.
- Corporate earnings.
- Firm size.

The exchange also charges an initial list fee and an annual fee. Listing standards and fees are higher for the NYSE than for other stock exchanges, so many firms cannot (or choose not to) list their stocks there. Right down the street is the **American Stock Exchange (AMEX).** It also uses a specialist trading system like the NYSE.

American Stock Exchange (AMEX)
Stock exchange with a trading floor; owned by the NYSE.

figure 8.1

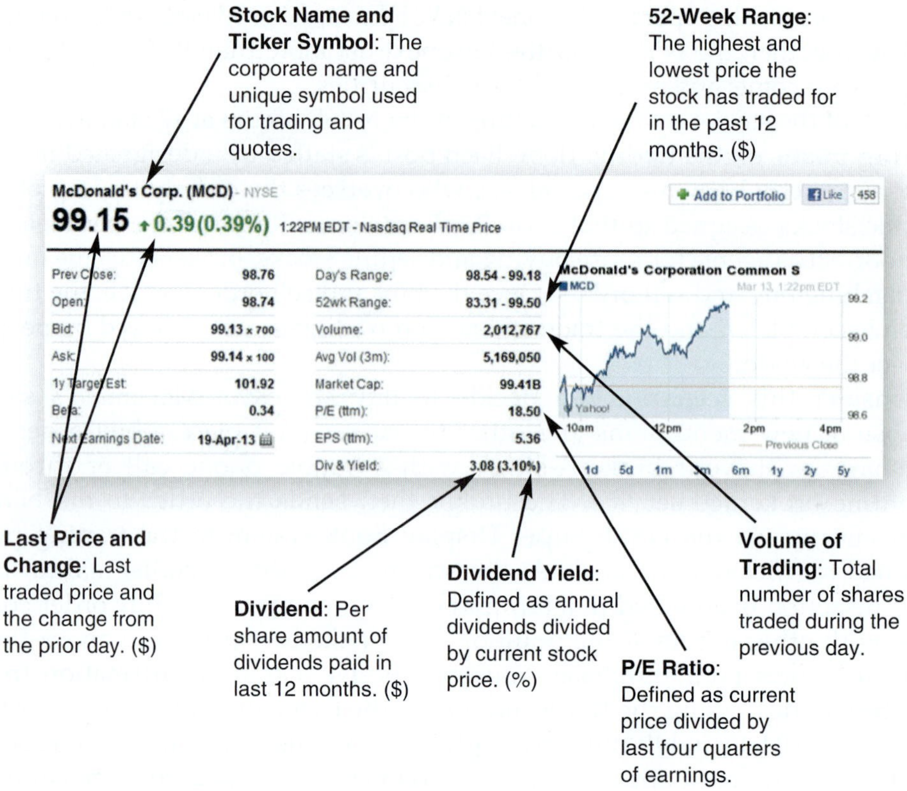

Read a Stock Quote, March 13, 2013, Yahoo! Finance

If you know what to look for, reading a stock quote is not as complicated as it first may appear.

NASDAQ Stock Market

Large electronic stock exchange.

Another popular stock trading system is the **NASDAQ Stock Market,** an electronic stock market without a physical trading floor. Today, NASDAQ features many of the big-name high-tech companies investors have come to know, like Apple Computer (ticker: AAPL), Intel (ticker: INTC), Microsoft (ticker: MSFT), and Qualcomm (ticker: QCOM). Many newer high-tech companies like Google (ticker: GOOG), Netflix (ticker: NFLX), and Adobe Systems Inc. (ticker: ADBE), are also listed on NASDAQ. In 2007, NASDAQ purchased OMX, which owned seven Nordic and Baltic stock exchanges, and became NASDAQ OMX. NASDAQ ranks second, behind the NYSE, among the world's equity markets in terms of total dollar volume. NASDAQ lists approximately 3,600 domestic and foreign companies.

market makers

Dealers and specialists who oversee an orderly trading process.

dealers

NASDAQ market makers who use their own capital to trade with investors

Instead of having a trading floor, NASDAQ uses a vast electronic trading system that executes trades via computer rather than in person. Instead of one designated market maker overseeing the process for an individual stock on a trading floor, Nasdaq's system uses multiple **market makers,** or **dealers.** Market makers use their own stock inventory and capital to compete with other dealers to buy and sell the stocks they represent. When an investor places an order through a stockbroker for a NASDAQ-listed stock, the electronic system routes the order and the investor buys shares from the dealer offering the best (lowest) price. Typical NASDAQ stocks support ten market makers actively competing with one another for investor trades.

Table 8.1 shows trading activity on the three main stock exchanges for one day in March 2013. The NYSE and NASDAQ each show a high amount of trading, with a total volume of over 3 billion for the NYSE and over 1.5 billion for NASDAQ. Trading on the AMEX is much smaller at less than 81 million shares traded.

table 8.1 | **Trading on the NYSE, NASDAQ, and AMEX, March 13, 2013**

	NYSE	AMEX	NASDAQ
Advancing issues	2,147 (52%)	178 (37%)	1,379 (54%)
Declining issues	1,832 (45%)	264 (55%)	1,059 (42%)
Unchanged issues	131 (3%)	37 (8%)	113 (4%)
New highs	419	11	157
New lows	37	6	20
Total volume	3,176,421,849	80,693,143	1,542,404,769

Source: Yahoo! Finance

The business of providing platforms or forums for investors and speculators to trade stocks and other financial assets has been changing rapidly. Many exchanges that previously used physical floor trading systems with specialists and open outcry to establish stock prices are shifting to electronic systems with no trading floors. Long-standing, traditional exchanges are also merging with other domestic and international exchanges to create fewer, but larger, forums that focus not just on U.S. securities but on many more internationally focused financial assets. The wider range of represented securities allows traders new opportunities to explore trading relationships among securities traded across the world. This worldwide trading will establish economically sound prices and additional financial stability around the world.

TIME OUT

8-1 What are three primary stock exchanges in the United States and where are they located? For which of the exchanges does physical location matter? Why?

8-2 Describe differences in trading procedures on the NYSE versus the NASDAQ. Which do you think is most fair to investors? Why?

Tracking the Stock Market

LG8-3

With thousands of stocks trading every minute, many stock prices rise while others fall. Table 8.1 also shows that, throughout the trading day, 2,147 stocks increased in price on the NYSE while 1,832 stocks decreased in price. While the NASDAQ also experienced more stocks with increases in price than declines, the AMEX saw more declines. In addition to the number of stocks advancing and declining, the table also shows the number of stocks that hit new 52-week price highs (419 listed on the NYSE) and new lows (37 on the NYSE) on that day. So, was this a good day or a bad day in the stock market?

To say anything about the *general* direction of the stock market, **stock indexes** are useful. Dozens of stock indexes are designed to track the overall market; many more track different market segments. The three most recognized indexes are the **Dow Jones Industrial Average (DJIA)**, the **Standard & Poor's 500 Index (S&P 500)**, and the **NASDAQ Composite Index.**

Charles H. Dow invented the first stock average in 1884. At the turn of the 20th century, railroads were the first major corporations. So he began with 11 stocks, mostly railroads. Dow created a price average by simply adding up 11 stock prices and dividing by the number 11. Two years later, Dow began tracking a 12-stock industrial average. This industrial average would eventually evolve into the modern DJIA, which is a price average of 30 large, industry-leading stocks that together represent roughly 30 percent of the total

stock index
Index of market prices of a particular group of stocks. The index is used to measure those stocks' performance.

Dow Jones Industrial Average (DJIA)
A popular index of 30 large, industry-leading firms.

Standard & Poor's 500 Index (S&P 500)
A stock index of 500 large companies

NASDAQ Composite Index
A technology-firm weighted index of stocks listed on the NASDAQ Stock Exchange.

stock value of all U.S. equities. DJIA level changes describe how the largest companies that participate in the stock market performed over a given period. The DJIA was at 14,455.28, a change of +5.22 (or 0.4 percent), on the day illustrated in Table 8.1.

The Standard & Poor's Corp. introduced its 500-stock index in 1957. Standard & Poor's chooses companies to include in the S&P 500 Index to represent the 10 sectors of the economy:

- Financial
- Information technology
- Health care
- Industrials
- Consumer discretionary
- Consumer staples
- Energy
- Telecom services
- Utilities
- Materials

market capitalization

The size of the firm measured as the current stock price multiplied by the number of shares outstanding.

S&P uses **market capitalization** (a measure of company size using stock price times shares outstanding), not just stock prices, of the largest 500 U.S. firms to compute the index. These 500 firms represent roughly 80 percent of the overall stock market capitalization (number of shares times share price). Although the DJIA is a long-time favorite with the media and individual investors, the S&P 500 is much preferred in the investment industry because of its broader representation of the market as a whole. S&P 500 performance provides a standard against which most U.S. money managers and pension plan sponsors can compare their investment performance. During trading on March 13, 2013, the S&P 500 gained 2.04 (0.13 percent) to close at 1,554.52.

The NASDAQ Composite Index measures the market capitalization of all common stocks listed on the NASDAQ stock exchange. Since the NASDAQ lists so many large, technology-oriented companies, many investors and analysts consider this index to reflect the tech sector performance more than that of the overall stock market. The NASDAQ Composite gained 2.80 to 3,245.12 on March 13, 2013, a gain of 0.09 percent. Because all three popular indexes were up on this day, most reports would reflect a good day for the stock market.

Figure 8.2 shows the levels of all these stock indexes since 1980. The DJIA (maroon line) level appears on the left-hand axis. Both the S&P 500 (green line) and the NASDAQ Composite (orange line) run from the right-hand axis. The rapid price appreciation for NASDAQ stocks during the late 1990s—the tech boom years—is unprecedented for such a large and widely followed market index. The NASDAQ Composite soared from 817 in March 1995 to peak on March 10, 2000, at 5,048.62, for a 518 percent total return in only five years—a 43.9 percent annual rate of share-price appreciation for NASDAQ stocks. The NASDAQ index performed much better than did the DJIA (19.0 percent per year) or the S&P 500 (22.7 percent per year). The NASDAQ "price bubble" set the stage for one of the most dramatic stock price declines in history: The NASDAQ Composite Index plunged to 1,114.11 on October 9, 2002, losing 78 percent of its value. The other index values also fell during this period, albeit not as sharply. Note that the DJIA didn't climb back to its 2000 high until March 2006. The S&P 500 Index finally recovered in May 2007. The NASDAQ Composite still has a long way to go to recover from its fall from pre-2000 levels.

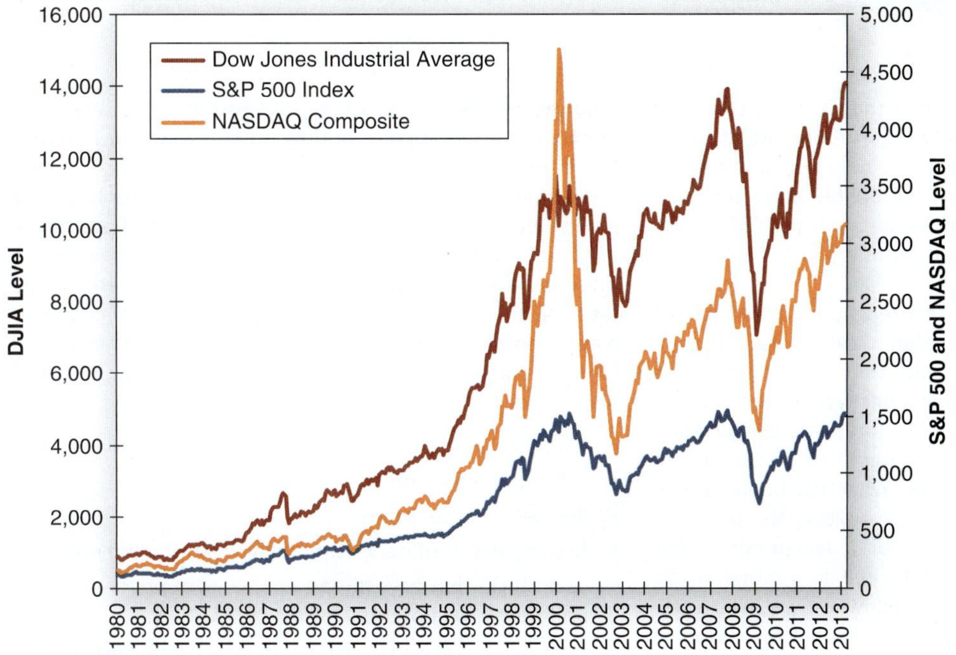

figure 8.2

Stock Market Index Levels Since 1980

This graph comparing the DJIA, S&P 500, and NASDAQ Composite indexes gives you a picture of their magnitude, as well as their patterns.

The figure also shows the stock market reaction to the financial crisis that began in 2008. There were sharp declines in all three indexes. After closing at a new high of 14,093.08 on October 12, 2007, the DJIA then fell to close at only 6,547.05 on March 9, 2009. The DJIA fully recovered in early 2013 and closed above 15,000 for the first time on May 7, 2013.

TIME OUT

8-3 Discuss why the day's market return may be different when measured by the DJIA, S&P 500 Index, and NASDAQ Composite taken separately.

8-4 Why might the "market bubble" phenomenon appear more dramatic because it occurred in the NASDAQ Composite rather than by the DJIA or S&P 500 Index?

8-5 If you followed the market regularly, to which index would you give the most credence? Why?

Trading Stocks

LG8-4

People who wish to buy and sell stocks need to open stock brokerage accounts. Traditional, full-service stockbrokers (e.g., Morgan Stanley Smith Barney, Merrill Lynch, UBS, Edward Jones) provide clients with research and advice in addition to executing trades. Their clients pay for this research and advice: Commission fees for these services may run well over $100 per trade. Discount brokerage firms (e.g., Charles Schwab, E-trade, Scottrade, TD Ameritrade) charge a much lower commission, $5 to $30 per trade, but do not provide the additional services. Investors at discount brokerages usually place trades through the brokerage's Internet sites.

Buy and sell orders go through the brokerage firm to a market maker (a dealer or a specialist) at a stock exchange. The quoted **bid** is the highest price at

bid
The quoted price investors are likely to receive when they sell stock.

finance at work — behavioral

INVESTOR PSYCHOLOGY

To us today, it may seem ludicrous that in the years 1634 to 1636, the people of Holland were in the midst of "Tulip Mania," and the price for a single rare tulip bulb approached the equivalent of $35,000. Then the bubble burst and tulip prices quickly plunged to less than the equivalent of $1. We may call those people who invested in a $35,000 tulip bulb irrational or even "crazy."

But this type of story seems to repeat itself throughout history. Investors paid extremely high prices for the new computer stocks in the 1960s, the "nifty fifty" companies in the 1970s, Japanese stocks during the 1980s, and Internet stocks during the late 1990s. The mania for stocks like Iomega drove its price from an equivalent of $1 per share in January of 1995 to over $75 in just 16 months. When the bubble burst, the price fell hard. Many years later, in 2008, the company was purchased by EMC Corporation for dollars per share. But that's just one company. A portfolio full of Internet stocks experienced a similar price mania followed by a severe fall. Investors created a stock index (TheStreet.com Internet Index) designed to track Internet stocks in late 1998, but by that time, part-time investors and veterans alike were already well into the craze. The Internet index started at 250, quickly rose to 1,270 by March of 2000, and subsequently fell to a low of 63 in October of 2002. Of course, the tech stock bubble was followed by the real estate bubble. In retrospect, irrational bubble-like prices are not confined to tulips and the 17th century in Holland.

Seemingly irrational behavior may not occur only during highly emotional periods of a price bubble. Recently, a growing recognition has arisen that "normal" investors often behave in a way that might not be described as fully rational. Investors, being human, are subject to cognitive biases and emotions. Studies of investor behavior have discovered that investors commonly succumb to psychological biases and:

- Trade too much.
- Sell winners too soon.
- Refuse to realize losses.
- Become overconfident—especially when trading online.
- Seek stocks that have already increased in price—perhaps up to their full potential price.
- Consider and react to what's happening with each stock in isolation, rather than remembering the purpose for forming an overall portfolio.

Investors who succeed in the long run are those who learn to avoid these psychological biases.

want to know more? Key Words to Search for Updates: irrational exuberance, price bubble, mania

which the market maker offers to pay for the stock. Investors have little choice but to accept this selling price, because regardless of the broker used, the market maker offers the only place to sell the stock. The quoted **ask** price is the lowest price at which a market maker will sell a stock—so investors buy at the ask price. The difference between the bid and the ask price may be only $0.01 for high-volume stocks and can be as high as $0.20 for less-often traded companies. The spread between the bid and the ask price is a cost to the investor and a profit for the market maker. This profit compensates the market maker for providing a market and liquidity for that stock.

ask

The quoted price investors are likely to pay when they buy stock.

Investors can place a buy or sell **market order.** A market order to buy stock will be filled immediately at the current ask price when routed to the stock exchange. A sell market order will be filled at the current bid price. The advantage of a market order is that it executes immediately at the best available price. The disadvantage of a market order is that the investor does not know in advance what that fill price will be. Investors can name their own prices by using **limit orders,** in which investors specify the price at which they are willing to execute the buy or sell order. With a buy limit order, a trade is executed if the ask quote is at or below the price target. For a sell limit order, a trade is executed if the bid quote moves through the specified price. If the current quote does not meet the price cited in the limit order, the trade is not executed. The advantage of a limit order is that the investor makes the trade at the desired price; the disadvantage is that the trade might not be executed at all.

market order

A stock buy or sell order to be immediately executed at the current market price.

limit order

A stock buy or sell order at a specific price. It will only be executed if the market price meets the specified price.

Consider a quote of McDonald's stock with a bid price of $99.00 and an ask price of $99.05. An investor placing a market buy order would purchase the stock at $99.05. A market sell order would execute as the price rises through $99.00. Note that an investor who simultaneously bought and sold 100 shares would pay $9,905 and receive $9,900—losing $5. An investor who places a buy limit order at $98.75 will only purchase the shares if the ask price falls to $98.75 or lower. If the ask does not fall, the order will not execute. Bid and ask prices tell investors at what prices the stock can currently be traded in general. But being able to buy at the ask price does not guarantee that the stock should be *valued* at that price. We'll discuss various ways to arrive at reasonable per-share stock values in the next section.

TIME OUT

8-6 Explain how the difference in the bid and ask prices might be considered a hidden cost to the investor.

8-7 The bid and ask prices for Amazon.com are $37.79 and $37.85. If these quotes occur when a trade order is made, at what price would a market buy order execute? Would a limit sell order execute with a target price of $37.75?

8.3 • Basic Stock Valuation

Cash Flows

In the previous chapter, we showed how we value bonds by finding the present value of the future interest payments and the future par value. Stock valuation uses the same concept of finding the present value of future dividends and the future selling price. But of course uncertainty about both price appreciation and future dividend payment streams complicate stock valuation. Consider the simple case of valuing a stock to be held for one year shown in the time line. LG8-5

Period	0	i	1 year
Cash flow	PV = ?		D_1+P_1

The value of such a stock today, P_0, is the present value of the dividend to be received in the first year, D_1, plus the present value of the expected sales price in one year, P_1. The interest rate used to discount the cash flows is shown as i. Using the present value equation from Chapter 4 results in:

Today's value = Present value of next year's dividend and price

$$P_0 = \frac{D_1 + P_1}{1 + i} \qquad \textbf{(8-1)}$$

Whenever investors deal with future stock prices and future dividend payments, they must use expected values, not certain ones. Companies rarely decrease their dividends; most companies' dividends either remain constant or slowly grow. Examining a firm's dividend history over the past few years will give clues to that company's future dividend policy. For example, The Coca-Cola Company (ticker: KO) paid a $0.155 per share dividend for each quarter in 2006. The firm then raised the quarterly dividend to $0.17 for each quarterly dividend in 2007. The company paid quarterly dividends in 2008, 2009, 2010, 2011, and 2012 of $0.19, $0.205, $0.22, $0.235, and $0.255, respectively. This increase of $0.015 to $0.02 in the dividend every year seems fairly stable.

Stock prices, though, show much more volatility than dividend histories do. We face much uncertainty in trying to predict stock prices in the short term.

Using a longer holding period to estimate stock value reduces *some,* but by no means all, of the uncertainty. A 2-year holding period appears like this:

Period	0	i	1	2 years
Cash flow	PV = ?		D_1	D_2+P_2

The present value of the cash flows in years 1 and 2 is today's stock value:

Today's value = Present value of next year's dividend, the second year's dividend, and the future price

$$P_0 = \frac{D_1}{1+i} + \frac{D_2 + P_2}{(1+i)^2} \quad \textbf{(8-2)}$$

Notice that the divisor for the second term on the right-hand side of equation 8-2 is raised to the second power. This reflects the two years over which those cash flows must be discounted. You can do this analysis over any holding period. For a holding period of n years, the value of a stock is measured by the present value of dividends over the n years, and the eventual sale price, P_n.

P_0 = Sum of the present value of each payment received

$$P_0 = \frac{D_1}{1+i} + \frac{D_2}{(1+i)^2} + \cdots + \frac{D_n + P_n}{(1+i)^n} \quad \textbf{(8-3)}$$

This formula incorporates both dividend income and capital appreciation or capital loss. It fully includes both major components of the investor's total return from investment.

EXAMPLE 8-1

LG8-5

For interactive versions of this example visit www.mhhe.com/can3e

CALCULATOR HINTS

1ST CASH FLOW:
N = 1. I = 11.5
PMT = 0, FV = 1.10
CPT PV = −0.987
2ND CASH FLOW:
N = 2. I = 11.5
PMT = 0, FV = 1.18
CPT PV = −0.949
3RD CASH FLOW:
N = 3. I = 11.5
PMT = 0, FV = 52.03
CPT PV = −37.534

VALUE = \$0.987 + \$0.949 + \$37.534 = \$39.47

Valuing Coca-Cola Stock

In March 2013, you are valuing Coca-Cola stock to compare its value to its market price. The current market price is \$38.79. Given the history of Coca-Cola's dividends, you believe that the company will pay total dividends in 2013 of \$1.10 (= 4 × \$0.275). Your analysis indicates that the total dividends in 2014 and 2015 will be \$1.18 and \$1.28, respectively. In addition, you believe that the price of Coca-Cola stock at the end of 2015 will be \$50.75 per share. If the appropriate discount rate is 11.5 percent, what is the value of Coca-Cola stock?

SOLUTION:

To organize your data, you first create the following timeline:

Period	0	11.5%	1	2	3 years
Cash flow	PV = ?		\$1.10	\$1.18	\$1.28 + \$50.75

Using equation 8-3, you compute the stock value as:

$$P_0 = \frac{\$1.10}{1+0.115} + \frac{\$1.18}{(1+0.115)^2} + \frac{\$1.28 + \$50.75}{(1+0.115)^3} = \$0.987 + \$0.949 + \$37.534 = \$39.47$$

Since your analysis shows that Coca-Cola's stock should be valued at \$39.47 while it's selling for only \$38.79, the stock appears to be slightly undervalued. You believe that this might be a good time to buy some Coca-Cola stock.

Similar to Problems 8-15, 8-16, 8-27, 8-28, self-test problem 1

figure 8.3

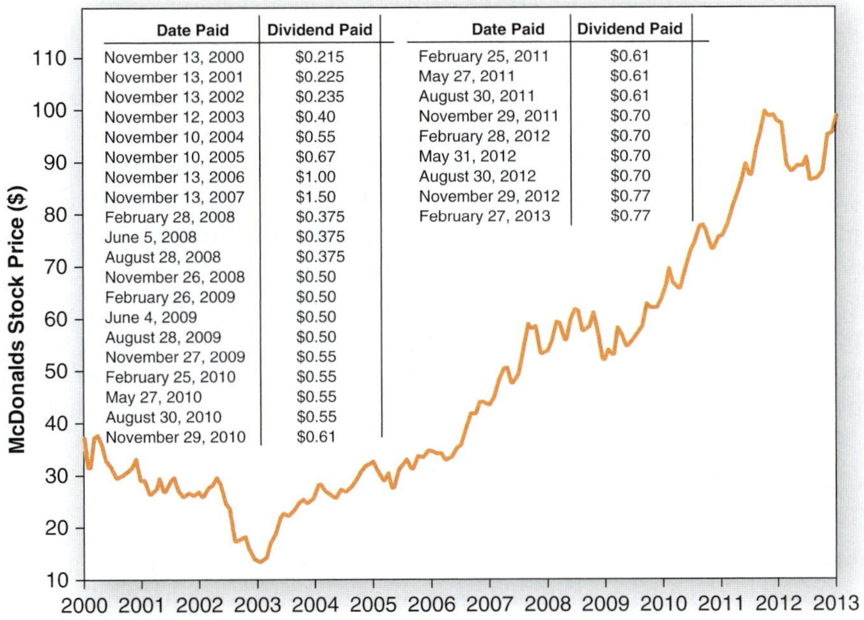

Date Paid	Dividend Paid	Date Paid	Dividend Paid
November 13, 2000	$0.215	February 25, 2011	$0.61
November 13, 2001	$0.225	May 27, 2011	$0.61
November 13, 2002	$0.235	August 30, 2011	$0.61
November 12, 2003	$0.40	November 29, 2011	$0.70
November 10, 2004	$0.55	February 28, 2012	$0.70
November 10, 2005	$0.67	May 31, 2012	$0.70
November 13, 2006	$1.00	August 30, 2012	$0.70
November 13, 2007	$1.50	November 29, 2012	$0.77
February 28, 2008	$0.375	February 27, 2013	$0.77
June 5, 2008	$0.375		
August 28, 2008	$0.375		
November 26, 2008	$0.50		
February 26, 2009	$0.50		
June 4, 2009	$0.50		
August 28, 2009	$0.50		
November 27, 2009	$0.55		
February 25, 2010	$0.55		
May 27, 2010	$0.55		
August 30, 2010	$0.55		
November 29, 2010	$0.61		

Dividends and Stock Price of McDonald's since 2000

Dividends rarely decline, but stock prices often do!

As is often the case in finance, implementing equation 8-3 presents problems for some firms in practical terms. What will the future dividends of the firm be? What will the stock price be in three, five, or ten years? While it seems that the dividend growth of Coca-Cola will be constant, consider the actual dividends and stock price of McDonald's Corp. since 2000 shown in Figure 8.3.

McDonald's paid an annual dividend from 2000 to 2007. Some increases were small, like the $0.01 increase from 2000 to 2001 and again to 2002. Other increases were quite large, like the $0.50 increase between 2006 and 2007. Then McDonald's changed to the more common quarterly dividend in 2008. The figure also shows that McDonald's stock price has been very volatile. The price fell from $37 in 2000 to nearly $12 in 2003 and then rapidly increased to $60 in 2007. The stock went sideways during the financial crisis and then shot up to $100 in late 2011. An investor in 2000 would have had a very difficult time accurately forecasting these future dividends and stock prices. Indeed, short-term stock price changes seem almost random. Stock valuation can really only be viewed from a long-term perspective. Because predicting future dividends is uncertain at best, it's better to project valuation as a likely range of prices under reasonable assumptions rather than as a single price. After all, this computed price is an estimate of the firm's intrinsic value. This intrinsic value may differ from the stock price trading in the market. This possibility is discussed as a market efficiency topic in Chapter 10.

Dividend Discount Models

LG8-5

We can extend the discounted cash flow approach in equation 8-3 for an infinite stream of dividends, $n \rightarrow \infty$, and no final future selling price. If stockholders receive all future cash flows as future dividends, the stock's value to the investor is the present value of all these future dividends. In other words, embedded in any stock price is the value of all future dividends. We can demonstrate this value as:

$$P_0 = \frac{D_1}{1+i} + \frac{D_2}{(1+i)^2} + \frac{D_3}{(1+i)^3} + \cdots \tag{8-4}$$

dividend discount model

A valuation approach based on future dividend income.

This equation shows the general case of the **dividend discount model.** The dividend discount model provides a useful theoretical basis because it illustrates the importance of dividends as a fundamental stock price determinant.

But, again, finance professionals find it difficult to apply the dividend discount model because it requires that they estimate an infinite number of future dividends. To use the model in practice, analysts make simplifying assumptions to make the model workable. One common assumption: The firm has a constant dividend growth rate, g. If this is the case, next year's dividend is simply this year's dividend that grew one year at the growth rate, that is, $D_1 = D_0 \times (1 + g)$. In fact, we can express each dividend as a function of D_0 and we can rewrite equation 8-4 as:

$$P_0 = \frac{D_0(1+g)}{1+i} + \frac{D_0(1+g)^2}{(1+i)^2} + \frac{D_0(1+g)^3}{(1+i)^3} + \cdots \tag{8-5}$$

So, with this version of the model, we need not forecast an infinite string of dividends; D_0 and g take care of that. However, we must still compute an infinite sum of numbers. Luckily, mathematicians know equations like these; they are known as power series. This power series can be simplified to the **constant-growth model,** and it assumes that the growth rate is smaller than the discount rate (i.e., for $g < i$):

constant-growth model

A valuation method based on constantly growing dividends.

Stock value = Next year's dividend ÷ (Discount rate − Growth rate)

$$\text{Constant growth model} = P_0 = \frac{D_0(1+g)}{i-g} = \frac{D_1}{i-g} \tag{8-6}$$

If $g \geq i$, then the denominator would be zero or negative. Economically and mathematically, this is a nonsensical result. In the short run, a firm can grow very quickly. In the long run, no company can grow faster than the overall economic growth rate forever. You may hear the constant-growth model referred to as the *Gordon growth model,* after financial economist Myron J. Gordon.

Investors use several methods to estimate a firm's growth rate for this model. They can project the dividend trend into the future and determine the implied growth rate, compute the past growth rate, or even consider a financial analyst's growth rate predictions. Consider Coca-Cola's dividend behavior. If the 2012 dividend was $1.02 and the projected dividends will grow to $1.38 in 2015, the implied projected dividend growth rate is therefore 7.85 percent (N = 4, PV = −1.02, PMT = 0, FV = 1.38, CPT I = 7.85) annually. The growth rate in dividend changes from 2008 to 2012 was 7.63 percent (N = 4, PV = −0.76, PMT = 0, FV = 1.02, CPT I = 7.63) per year. You can find analyst forecasts many places online. The Yahoo! Finance web page for Coca-Cola has an Analyst Estimates link, which shows the average analysts' forecast for the firm's growth in the next five years at 8.95 percent.

LG8-5

Preferred Stock

preferred stock

A class of stock with fixed dividends.

A special case of the constant-growth model occurs when the dividend does not grow but is the same every year. This zero-growth rate case describes a **preferred stock.** The term *preferred* comes from the fact that this type of stock takes preference over common stock in bankruptcy proceedings. Preferred stockholders have a higher priority for receiving proceeds from bankruptcy proceedings than do common stockholders. Preferred stock is largely owned by other companies, rather

EXAMPLE 8-2

LG8-3

Constant Growth and Coca-Cola Stock

For interactive versions of this example visit www.mhhe.com/can3e

Assume that you are valuing Coca-Cola stock again. This time you are using the constant-growth model, assuming a discount rate of 11.5 percent.

SOLUTION:

You have a choice of three growth rates to use. The implied projected dividend growth rate is 7.85 percent. Past dividend growth has been 7.63 percent and analysts forecast an 8.95 percent growth. Compute the stock value using all three growth rates.

Using a dividend growth rate of 7.85 percent and equation 8-6, the stock value is \$30.14:

$$P_0 = \frac{\$1.02 \times (1 + 0.0785)}{0.115 - 0.0785} = \$30.14$$

Using a dividend growth rate of 8.95 percent, the stock value is \$43.58:

$$P_0 = \frac{\$1.02 \times (1 + 0.0895)}{0.115 - 0.0895} = \$43.58$$

Using a dividend growth rate of 7.63 percent, the stock value is \$28.37:

$$P_0 = \frac{\$1.02 \times (1 + 0.0763)}{0.115 - 0.0763} = \$28.37$$

Notice how a small change in the growth rate has a large impact on the stock value in this model. At a current price of \$38.79 per share, Coca-Cola could be considered undervalued or overvalued depending on the growth rate used.

Similar to Problems 8-19, 8-20, 8-29, 8-30, 8-31, 8-32, self-test problem 2

than by individual investors, because its dividends are mostly nontaxable income (70 percent of the income is exempt from taxes) to other corporations. Preferred stockholders do not have voting rights like common stockholders, though, which prevents one company from controlling another through preferred stock ownership.

MATH COACH

USING THE CONSTANT-GROWTH-RATE MODEL

The distinction between the recent year's dividends, D_0, and next year's dividends, D_1, can be confusing in the constant-growth-rate model. The model's equation presents two different numerators. If you are given information about dividends last year or just paid, use the $D_0(1 + g)$ version of the equation. If you have information about expected dividends or next year's dividend, use the D_1 version of the equation.

An interesting characteristic of preferred stock is that it pays a constant dividend. Because the dividend does not change, the preferred stock can be valued using the constant-growth-rate model with a zero growth rate expressed as $P = D/i$. What would Coca-Cola's stock be worth if its dividend stayed at \$1.02 and never grew? Using the same 11.5 percent discount rate, the stock would be valued at \$8.87 (= \$1.02 ÷ 0.115). Given Coca-Cola's current stock price of \$38.79, over 77.1 percent [= (\$38.79 − \$8.87)/\$38.79] of its stock value comes from the expectation that Coca-Cola's dividend will grow. In other words, investors highly value a growing firm.

Most companies issue only common stock, but nearly 1,000 preferred stock issues still exist. Table 8.2 compares the common stock and preferred stock for 10 firms. Many of the preferred stocks come from the finance, energy, and real estate sectors. Notice that the **dividend yield** for preferred stock is higher than for the common stock, because preferred stock investors should expect a return from dividend payments only. Common stockholders will also expect a return from capital appreciation over time. Common stocks also trade much more frequently than preferred stocks do.

dividend yield
Last four quarters of dividend income expressed as a percentage of the current stock price.

table 8.2 | **Common and Preferred Stock, March 13, 2013**

Company	Ticker	Price	Annual Dividend (Yield%)	Volume	Ticker	Price	Annual Dividend (Yield%)	Volume
	COMMON STOCK				PREFERRED STOCK			
Alcoa Inc.	AA	$8.62	$0.12(1.4)	13,091,073	AA.PR	$89.00	$3.75(4.2)	2,242
El Du Pont de Nemours & Co.	DD	$49.59	$1.72(3.5)	5,100,209	DDPRA	$87.50	$3.50(4.0)	5,153
Ford Motor Co.	F	$13.40	$0.40(3.1)	26,454,559	FPRA	$25.55	$1.88(7.3)	97,959
National Healthcare	NHC	$46.09	$1.20(2.6)	2,205	NHCA	$15.52	$0.80(5.1)	634
PG&E Corp.	PCG	$43.30	$1.82(4.3)	1,783,689	PCG.PRA	$30.15	$1.50(5.0)	1,025
Public Storage Inc.	PSA	$146.68	$4.40(2.9)	767,965	PSAPRL	$25.17	$1.68(6.7)	12,331

Source: New York Stock Exchange **(www.nyse.com)**

The zero-growth-rate version of the constant-growth valuation model shows that, since dividends are fixed, a preferred stock's price changes because of changes in the discount rate, *i*. When interest rates throughout the economy change, the discount rate also changes. Preferred stock prices thus tend to act like bond prices. When interest rates rise, preferred stock prices fall. When interest rates decline, preferred stock prices rise. Preferred stock is usually categorized with bonds in the fixed-income security group because it acts so much like debt securities, even though a preferred stock represents equity ownership, like common stock.

LG8-5

Expected Return

Stock valuation models require a discount rate, *i*, in order to compute the present value of the future cash flows. The discount rate used should reflect the investment risk level. Higher risk investments should be evaluated using higher interest rates. For example, the previous chapter on bonds demonstrated that higher risk bonds, such as junk bonds, offer higher rates of return. Similarly, investors demand higher returns from higher risk stocks than they do from lower risk stocks. We discuss stock risk measurement and appropriate expected returns in the next section of this book.

However, one method for determining what return stock investors require from a stock is to use the constant-growth-rate model. If the current stock price fairly reflects its value, then the discount rate, *i*, in equation 8-6 should be the expected return for the stock. Solving for this expected return results in equation 8-7:

$$\text{Expected return} = i = \frac{D_1}{P_0} + g = \text{Dividend yield} + \text{Capital gain} \qquad \textbf{(8-7)}$$

Note that the expected return comes again from two sources: dividend yield and expected appreciation of the stock price, or capital gain. For example, consider that Coca-Cola's dividend in 2013, D_1, is expected to be \$1.10 per share. At a current price of \$38.79, Coca-Cola offers a dividend yield of 2.84 percent (= \$1.10 ÷ \$38.79). Since analysts believe that the firm's stock price will grow at 8.95% percent in the future, investors expect a total return of 11.79 percent (= 2.84% + 8.95%). Dividend yield can represent a substantial portion of the profits for an investor. Many people get too enamored of high **growth stocks** that do not pay dividends and therefore miss out on an important source of stable returns.

growth stocks

Companies expected to have above-average rates of growth in revenue, earnings and/or dividends.

Corporate managers conduct an important application of the expected return concept to determine the return that their shareholders expect of them. We will discuss this application in detail in Part Six: Capital Budgeting.

finance at work — investments

FINANCIAL ANALYSTS' PREDICTIONS AND OPINIONS

Financial analysts examine a firm's business and financial success and assess long-term prospects and management effectiveness. They combine this microeconomic analysis with a macroeconomic view of the conditions of the economy, financial markets, and industry outlooks. Their evaluation results in earnings predictions, stock price targets, and opinions about whether investors should buy the stock. Such recommendations can help investors decide whether to buy, hold, or sell the stock.

Analysts hired by brokerage firms and investment banks are called *sell-side analysts* because their firms make money by selling stocks and bonds. These analysts publicize their predictions and opinions publicly and in company "tip sheets" that are passed along to clients. Keep in mind that sell-side analysts often have incentives to be optimistic. Pension funds and mutual funds often hire analysts to give fund managers private opinions about securities. These analysts are referred to as *buy-side analysts* because they are hired by investment firms looking for advice on what stocks to buy for their portfolios. Because this is private, little buy-side research is made public.

Consider the 18 sell-side analysts' predictions reported for Coca-Cola on the Yahoo! Finance website. The average 5-year share price growth prediction from these analysts is 8.95 percent. This is lower than the growth prediction for the industry (12.97 percent) and sector (13.75 percent). Last, analysts give opinions on whether investors should buy, sell, or hold Coca-Cola stock. Recommendations come in five levels: Strong Buy, Buy, Hold, Sell, and Strong Sell. Of the 18 analysts, five recommend a Strong Buy, six recommend a Buy, and six recommend a Hold. Note that even though the analysts predict lower than average growth for the industry and sector, and that the analysts provide meager price targets, only one of the analysts recommend a Sell or Strong Sell of the stock. This optimism in analysts' opinions is common. Knowledgeable investors know that a "hold" recommendation is as negative as most public or sell-side analysts get, and therefore a "hold" may actually represent a signal to sell.

! want to know more? Key Words to Search for Updates: analyst opinion, financial analyst bias

TIME OUT

8-8 Explain how valuable a firm's (and therefore its stock's) growth is. Demonstrate this with growth and no-growth examples.

8-9 What proportion of the 11.79 percent of Coca-Cola's expected return above comes from dividend yield?

8.4 • Additional Valuation Methods

Variable-Growth Techniques

LG8-6

Some companies grow at such a high rate that we cannot use the constant-growth-rate model to forecast their value. High growth rates might be sustainable for several years, but cannot continue forever. Consider what happens to a high-growth firm. Other companies will surely notice the market potential for high-growth rates and will enter those product markets to compete with the high-growth firm. The competition will soon drive down the growth rates for all companies in that product market. Companies that experience unusually high-growth tend to see that growth become only average in the future unless they possess some kind of entry barrier such as a patent or government regulation due to economies of scale.

Remember that the constant-growth-rate model does not work for companies where $g > i$. And of course, we do not really expect the growth rate for these fast-growing firms to remain constant. To value these firms, we must use a **variable-growth-rate** technique. The variable-growth-rate method combines the present-value cash flow from equation 8-3 and the constant-growth-rate model from equation 8-6.

variable growth rate
A valuation technique used when a firm's current growth rate is expected to change some time in the future.

First, the investor chooses two different growth rates for two stages of the analysis. The first and higher growth rate, g_1, is the current growth rate, which

figure 8.4

Variable Dividend Growth

Divide into two stages at the first year of the new growth rate.

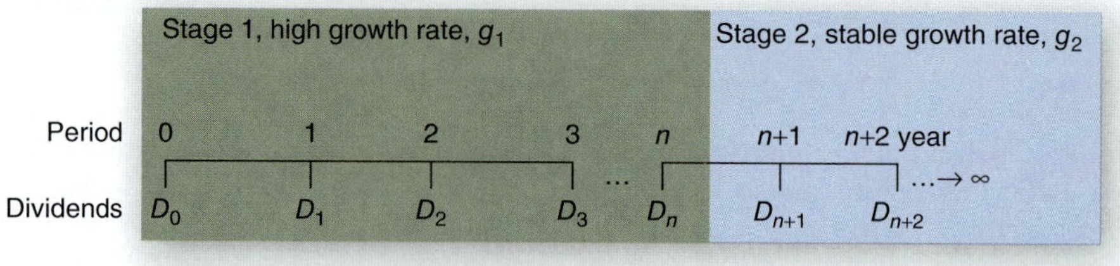

figure 8.5

Stage 1 Dividends

Calculate the dividends in the first stage.

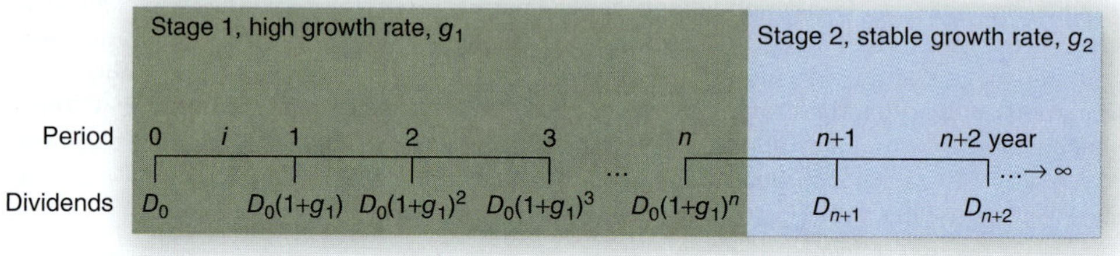

we expect to last only a few years. A few years from now, we expect the firm to grow at a slower but more sustainable rate of growth, g_2. Figure 8.4 shows the cash flow time line when the first growth rate applies for the first n years, followed by the second growth rate, which applies forever.

When we analyze a variable-growth-rate stock like the one in the figure, we know the recent dividend, D_0, and the two expected growth rates. Therefore, we can calculate each of the dividends shown in general terms (i.e., D_1). For example, the dividend in the first year (D_1) is the year zero dividend that grows at g_1, specifically $D_1 = D_0 \times (1 + g_1)$. The dividend then grows at g_1 again for the second year dividend, $D_2 = D_0 \times (1 + g_1)^2$. The dividend continues to grow through the first stage to year n at $D_n = D_0 \times (1 + g_1)^n$. Figure 8.5 shows the first-stage dividends.

At this point, the company starts to move into stage 2 at the more modest growth rate, g_2, and the dividends reflect that slower growth rate. So $D_n +_1$ is the dividend Dn that grew at the rate g_2, or $Dn +_1 = D_0 \times (1 + g_1)^n \times (1 + g_2)$. Similarly, the dividend in year $n + 2$ is $Dn +_2 = D_0 \times (1 + g_1)^n \times (1 + g_2)^2$. We can now substitute the known dividends as presented in Figure 8.5 into Figure 8.6.

Once we have calculated all of the dividends, we can begin finding the value of the variable-growth stock by focusing on Stage 2 of the problem. Assume that the dividends in Stage 2 are growing at a modest rate, g_2, forever. As long as $g_2 < i$, Stage 2 can use the constant-growth model, equation 8-6. Remember that the constant-growth model, $P_0 = D_1/(i - g)$, replaces all future dividends with one value in the previous period. In previous applications, the growth began in year 1, so the value used for all future dividends came from the year 0 dividend. In this case, the change in the dividend rate occurs in year $n + 1$, so we will use the value from year n. So, using the constant-growth model, we can replace all the cash flows in Stage 2 with one value from year n, as:

$$P_n = \frac{D_{n+1}}{i - g_2} = \frac{D_0(1 + g_1)^n(1 + g_2)}{i - g_2}$$

figure 8.6

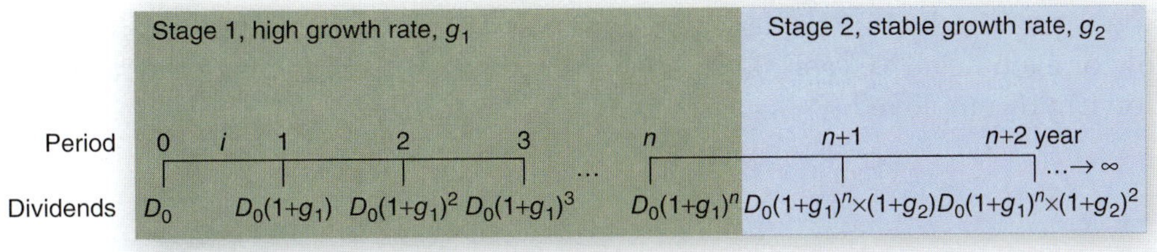

Details of the Variable Growth Dividends

Compute the dividends in the second stage.

figure 8.7

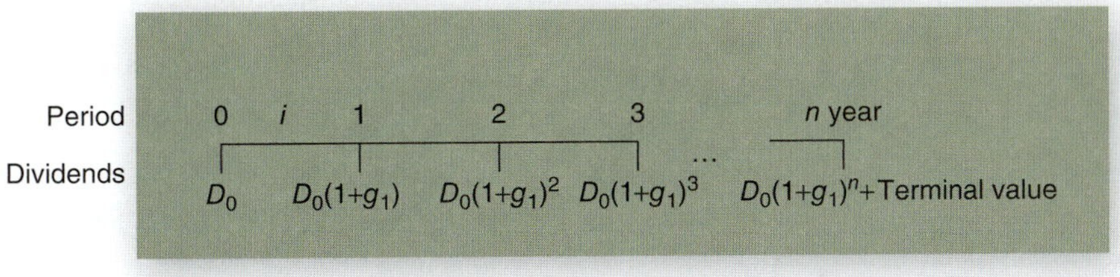

New Stage 1 of the Variable Growth Dividend Technique

Replace all of the dividends to infinity with the price (terminal value) in year *n*. Stage 2 disappears.

The cash flows from Figure 8.6 now appear as shown in Figure 8.7.

By replacing all the Stage 2 cash flows that continued indefinitely with one terminal price in year *n*, we reduce the problem to a fixed number of cash flows. The value of this variable-growth stock is finally computed as the present value of these cash flows, as solved with equation 8-3. Substituting the cash flows shown in Figure 8.7 into equation 8-3 gives us the general formula for finding the value of a variable-growth stock:

General two-stage growth valuation model:

Stock value = Present value of each dividend during the first growth stage + Present value of the second stage growth

$$P_0 = \frac{D_0(1+g_1)}{1+i} + \frac{D_0(1+g_1)^2}{(1+i)^2} + \frac{D_0(1+g_1)^3}{(1+i)^3} + \cdots + \frac{D_0(1+g_1)^n + \text{Terminal value}}{(1+i)^n} \qquad \textbf{(8-8)}$$

$$\text{where Terminal value} = \frac{D_0(1+g_1)^n(1+g_2)}{i-g_2}$$

The practical application of the variable-growth valuation technique requires the investor to decide how long the current high-growth rate will last before declining to a more stable rate.

The constant-growth-rate model is most useful for large, mature companies that grow in a stable manner. The variable-growth-rate model works well for dividend paying companies that have an unusually fast rate of growth in the near future but are expected to enter a more stable growth rate environment soon. But there are still many firms that do not fit these two descriptions of firm growth. For example, many firms pay no dividends. To value firms with no dividends, replace the dividends in the models with cash flows. When you do this, you are valuing the entire firm, not just the stock value, because cash flows go to both stockholders and debt holders. In the case where a firm has low or even negative cash flows, then the valuation techniques in the next section can be employed.

EXAMPLE 8-3

LG8-6

For interactive versions of this example visit www.mhhe.com/can3e

Variable Growth and McDonald's Stock

The dividend has grown from \$1.00 per share on November 13, 2006 to \$2.80 during 2012. This represents an annual growth rate of 18.7 percent (N = 6, PV = −1.00, PMT = 0, FV = 2.80, CPT I = 18.7). You think this growth rate will continue for three years and then fall to the long-term growth rate of 9.29 percent predicted by analysts. You assume a 13 percent discount rate.

SOLUTION:

Figure 8.3 shows a \$2.80 (= 4 × \$0.70) per share recent annual dividend. Modify equation 8-8 for a Stage 1 length of three years and then substitute $i = 0.13$, $g_1 = 0.187$, $g_2 = 0.0929$, and $D_0 = \$2.80$. The valuation equation and solution becomes:

Period	0	1	2	3
Dividends	$D_0 = \$2.80$	$D_1 = \$2.80 \times (1.187)$	$D_2 = \$2.80 \times (1.187)^2$	$D_3 = \$2.80 \times (1.187)^3$
				$P_3 = \$2.80 \times (1.187)^3 \times (0.0929) \div (0.14 - 0.0929)$

$$P_0 = \frac{\$2.80(1 + 0.187)}{1 + 0.13} + \frac{\$2.80(1 + 0.187)^2}{(1 + 0.13)^2} + \frac{\$2.80(1 + 0.187)^3 + \text{Terminal value}}{(1 + 0.13)^3}$$

$$\text{where Terminal value} = \frac{\$2.80(1 + 0.187)^3(1 + 0.0929)}{0.13 - 0.0929} = \$137.95$$

$$= \$2.94 + \$3.09 + \frac{\$4.68 + \$137.95}{1.443}$$

$$= \$104.88$$

Given these parameters, McDonald's stock is worth nearly \$105 per share. Figure 8.3 shows that the stock price in early 2013 was around \$99. Comparing the stock's value to its market price, the stock is undervalued.

Similar to Problems 8-33, 8-34, self-test problem 3

TIME OUT

8-10 Explain how the variable-growth-rate technique could be used for a firm whose dividend is not expected to grow for three years and then will grow at 5 percent indefinitely.

8-11 Set up and solve the McDonald's valuation problem assuming that the first stage growth will last only two years.

The P/E Model

LG8-7

The valuation models that we've presented thus far help investors attempt to compute a stock's fundamental value based upon its cash flows to the investor. Another common approach is to assess a stock's **relative value.** This approach compares one company's stock valuation to other firms' stock values to evaluate whether your target company's stock is appropriately priced. The price of a stock taken in isolation doesn't give us a good measure of how expensive it is. Let's use an analogy: At the grocery store, we are less concerned with the total price of a bag of sugar than we are with the price per pound. Similarly, the price of the stock matters less than its price per one dollar of earnings.

relative value

A stock's priceyness measured relative to other stocks.

Consider one company that earned \$5 per share in profits for the year. Its stock sells for \$100. Another company earned \$2 per share and its stock price is \$50 per share. At first glance, the first stock appears to be more expensive because its price is a high \$100 compared to the lower \$50 price of the second stock. However, the first company generated higher per-share profits than did the second company. Buying the first stock means that you purchase \$5 in earnings. The \$100 stock price implies a cost of \$20 for every \$1 in earnings (= \$100 ÷ \$5) generated. The \$50 price of the second stock implies a cost of \$25 for every \$1 in earnings (= \$50 ÷ \$2). So in this regard, the second company becomes more expensive. The **price-earnings (P/E) ratio** represents the most common valuation yardstick in the investment industry; it allows investors to quickly compare the cost of earnings. The P/E ratio is simply the current price of the stock divided by the last four quarters of earnings per share:

price-earnings (P/E) ratio

Current stock price divided by four quarters of earnings per share.

$$P/E = \frac{\text{Current stock price}}{\text{Per-share earnings for last 12 months}} \quad \textbf{(8-9)}$$

More accurately, this figure is the **trailing P/E ratio** and it is often denoted as P/E_0, where the 0 subscript denotes the past (or trailing) earnings.

trailing P/E ratio

The P/E ratio computed using the *past* four quarters of earnings per share.

Figure 8.8 shows two companies' trailing P/E ratios: Coca-Cola and McDonald's, as well as the Dow Jones Industrial Average's trailing P/E ratio over a 16-year period. The P/E ratio for the DJIA changes slowly and mostly stays in the 18 to 27 range until the recent drop to 15. Historically, the DJIA's P/E ratio has fallen

figure 8.8

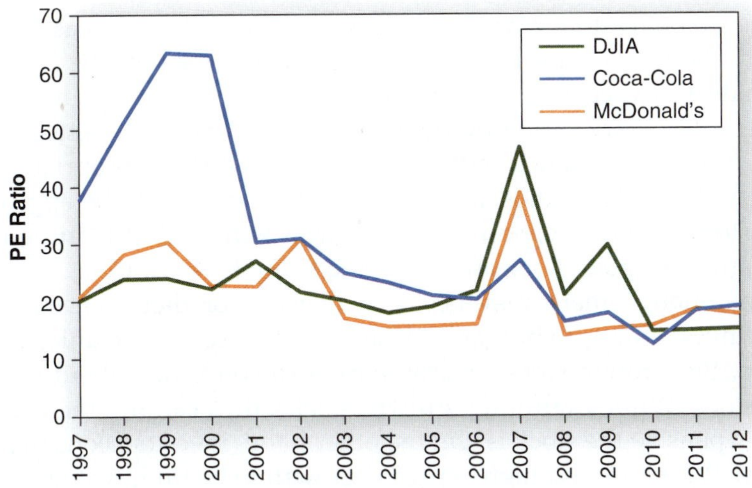

Historical P/E Ratio of the DJIA, Coca-Cola, and McDonald's

P/E ratios of large, successful companies can vary considerably over time. Here, you see that investors valued Coca-Cola over McDonald's in the late 1990s, but by the beginning of 2008 this preference had evened out.

as low as single digits and climbed to over 30. The figure also shows that the P/E ratio for McDonald's has varied more than has the index's P/E ratio. The P/E ratio for Coca-Cola has experienced wild changes—as high as 63 and as low as 18. Figure 8.8 shows that investors valued Coca-Cola more than McDonald's in the late 1990s, but valued them nearly the same by the beginning of 2008.

Variations in P/E ratios between popular companies can be quite large. For example, in March of 2013, the P/E ratio for Google was 25.6, while the ratio for ConocoPhillips was only 8.7. Google stock is much more expensive than ConocoPhillips. But this does not mean the ConocoPhillips stock is a better deal than Google stock. Investors are willing to pay much more in relative terms for Google because they expect Google will grow much faster than ConocoPhillips. Indeed, analysts predict an annual growth rate of 13.58 percent per year for Google over the next five years, while they expect a growth rate of only 2.93 percent for ConocoPhillips. Remember that Example 8-2 shows how small changes in growth can result in large stock value changes. The large difference in expected growth between Google and ConocoPhillips causes a large difference in their relative value.

We can more directly see the impact that growth can have on the P/E ratio by modifying the constant-growth model. Begin with the model, $P_0 = D_1 \div (i - g)$. Dividing both sides by the firm's earnings results in $P_0/E_0 = (D_1/E_0) \div (i - g)$. Note that the dividend payout ratio of the firm (D/E), the discount rate (i), and the growth rate (g), taken together, determine the P/E ratio. All else held equal, larger growth rates will lead to larger P/E ratios. Also, firms that have higher payout ratios will have higher P/E ratios. Of course, if a firm pays out a high portion of its earnings as dividends, then it may not have the cash to fund high growth. Thus, high dividend payout firms tend not to be priced the same as high growth firms.

The value of a stock, and thus its price, relates directly to its future success. Note that valuation models use estimates of future dividends and growth rates. Because of this focus on the future, many people prefer to use a P/E ratio that also looks forward rather than trailing. A **forward P/E ratio** uses analyst estimates of the earnings in the next 12 months instead of the past 12 months and can be denoted as P/E_1. The forward P/E ratio has the advantage over the trailing P/E ratio in that it incorporates investors' expectations of the firm's upcoming profits. A disadvantage is that expected earnings are harder to estimate and thus less accurate than past earnings. The media uses the trailing P/E ratio, while financial managers and investors use the forward P/E ratio more.

forward P/E ratio

The P/E ratio computed using the *estimated* next four quarters of earnings per share.

Knowledgeable investors who use the P/E ratio as a relative measure of value compare it to the firm's expected growth rate. Table 8.3 shows the forward P/E ratio and analysts' expected growth rates for the 30 Dow Jones Industrial Average firms. The firms are sorted by their forward P/E ratios. Investors consider companies with high P/E ratios and high growth rates to be appropriately priced. Companies with low P/E ratios and low growth also seem to be appropriately priced. Investors should be concerned about firms with high P/E ratios and only single-digit growth rates. As such, Procter & Gamble, Coca-Cola, McDonald's, and Verizon, among others, may be too expensive for their expected growth rates. Many investors like to buy growth stocks. They seek companies with high growth rates. But growth stock investors are also concerned about paying too much for a stock. While examining growth stocks, they can use the P/E ratio to assess how expensive the stock is. On the other hand, investors consider companies with low P/E ratios and high expected growth to be undervalued, and they are often referred to as **value stocks.** Caterpillar and Bank of America would qualify as value stocks. Many investors like to buy value stocks because they feel they are getting a bargain price for a stable company.

value stocks

Companies considered to be temporarily undervalued.

table 8.3 | **P/E Ratios and Analyst Growth Estimates of DJIA Firms, March 13, 2013**

	A	B	C	D	E
1	**Ticker**	**Company Name**	**Stock Price**	**Forward P/E Ratio**	**Next 5 Year's Growth (%)**
2	HD	Home Depot	$70.76	18.32	16.42
3	PG	Procter & Gamble	76.8	17.33	7.93
4	KO	Coca-Cola Company	38.59	16.19	8.95
5	MCD	McDonald's Corporation	99.38	15.14	8.89
6	VZ	Verizon Communication	47.94	14.56	6.33
7	DIS	Walt Disney	57.34	13.81	11.26
8	MMM	3M Company	105.09	13.55	9.83
9	JNJ	Johnson & Johnson	78.55	13.12	6.41
10	T	AT&T Inc.	36.6	13.03	5.50
11	UTX	United Technologies	93.08	12.68	13.63
12	GE	General Electric	23.49	12.4	11.00
13	WMT	Wal-Mart Stores	73.65	11.98	8.83
14	AXP	American Express	65.3	11.66	10.94
15	PFE	Pfizer	28.02	11.37	2.69
16	MRK	Merck & Company	44.59	11.19	2.73
17	XOM	Exxon Mobil	89.26	10.8	1.79
18	IBM	International Business Machines	212.06	10.7	9.86
19	TRV	The Travelers Company	82.12	10.61	10.05
20	DD	E.I. du Pont de Nemours	49.59	10.55	6.08
21	BA	Boeing Company	84.75	10.36	10.67
22	AA	Alcoa, Inc.	8.54	9.82	6.50
23	CSCO	Cisco Systems	21.58	9.79	8.40
24	INTC	Intel Corporation	21.66	9.72	12.33
25	CAT	Caterpillar	89.28	9.46	14.00
26	CVX	Chevron Corporation	118.36	9.16	0.08
27	UNH	UnitedHealth Group	54.48	9.11	10.94
28	MSFT	Microsoft Corporation	27.92	8.69	8.38
29	BAC	Bank of America	12.06	8.55	18.76
30	JPM	JPMorgan Chase	50.16	8.25	7.16
31	HPQ	Hewlett-Packard	21.32	5.34	0.25

Source: Yahoo! Finance Screener

There are some cases when a P/E ratio is not useful for relative valuation. For example, sometimes, a firm will lose money. That is, the earnings are negative. In other cases, a firm will take a large "write-off" that will temporarily suppress earnings. In these cases, the P/E ratio would be negative or temporarily large. Therefore, other common relative value techniques are to utilize cash flow (CF) or book value (B) instead of earnings. The P/CF ratio is useful when firms take accounting write-offs that temporarily and dramatically impact earnings. The P/B ratio is useful in all cases but is particularly useful when a firm loses money and has negative cash flows. The book value of a firm is a very stable measure of accounting value, and it is therefore useful when earnings are volatile.

Estimating Future Stock Prices

We can often find it useful to estimate a stock's future price. Consider equation 8-3's cash flow discount valuation model. The model requires estimates of future dividends and a future price. How can investors estimate this future price? They can use the P/E ratio model for this purpose. Upon reflection, you will see that multiplying the P/E ratio by earnings results in a stock price. So, in order to estimate a future price, simply multiply the expected P/E ratio by the expected earnings. This concept is captured in the following equation:

$$\text{Future price} = \text{Future P/E ratio} \times \text{Future earnings per share}$$

$$\begin{aligned} P_n &= (^P/_E)_n \times E_n \\ &= (^P/_E)_n \times E_0 \times (1 + g)^n \end{aligned} \quad \textbf{(8-10)}$$

As the formula shows, we can use assumptions about the earnings growth rate to estimate earnings in year n. Many investors believe the firm's P/E ratio in year n is best estimated using today's P/E ratio. However, if today's P/E ratio seems unusual compared with similar firms or even compared with a stock index, then adjustments might be wise.

TIME OUT

8-12 Consider two firms with the same P/E ratio. Explain how one could be described as expensive compared to the other.

8-13 Compute the stock price for Chevron in five years if you expect the P/E ratio to decline to 6 and the earnings per share is \$8.41.

EXAMPLE 8-4

For interactive versions of this example visit www.mhhe.com/can3e

The P/E Ratio Model for Caterpillar

Look at Table 8.3 and notice that the P/E ratio for Caterpillar seems low at 9.46 relative to the growth (14 percent) that analysts expect. Caterpillar earned \$8.48 per share and paid a \$2.08 dividend last year. You decide to explore this apparent anomaly and figure out what Caterpillar's stock price might reach in five years.

SOLUTION:

Compute the expected future price in five years under two different scenarios. The first assumption is that Caterpillar's P/E ratio will be the same in five years as it is today. But since this P/E ratio seems a bit low, the second scenario allows for a rise in the P/E ratio to 11. Under these two scenarios, the future price estimates are:

$$P_5 = (^P/_E)_n \times E_0 \times (1 + g)^n = 9.46 \times \$8.48 \times (1 + 0.14)^5 = \$154.46$$

$$P_5 = (^P/_E)_n \times E_0 \times (1 + g)^n = 11 \times \$8.48 \times (1 + 0.14)^5 = \$179.60$$

Note that if the P/E ratio increases from 9.46 to 11 in five years, the future price could be more than 16 percent higher than analysts expect without the change.

Similar to Problems 8-25, 8-26, 8-35, 8-36

viewpoints REVISITED

Business Application Solution

You can compute the expected return using equation 8-7 as,

$$i = \frac{\$2 \times (1 + 0.08)}{\$65} + 0.08 = 0.0332 + 0.08 = 0.1132$$

Investors expect an 11.32 percent return.

The P/E ratio of 16.25 and the stock price of \$65 indicates that earnings were \$4.00 per share (= \$65 ÷ 16.25). If the P/E ratio of 16.25 continues, then the price of the stock in three years may be \$81.88 [$= 16.25 \times \$4 \times (1.08)^3$]. However, a P/E ratio of 16.25 may seem a little high for a firm with an 8 percent growth rate. So the P/E ratio might decline a bit to 15. If so, the stock price in three years would be \$75.58. On the other hand, P/E ratios in the stock market may increase in general, thereby inflating this firm's ratio to 17. In this case, the price would be \$85.66.

You should report an expected stock price range of \$75.58 to \$85.66 with a target of \$81.88.

Personal Application Solution

The information provided allows for two growth rate estimates for stock valuation. The dividend growth from \$1.25 to \$1.68 in three years implies a 10.36 percent historical growth rate (N = 3, PV = −1.25, PMT = 0, FV = 1.68, CPT I = 10.36). Since analysts' mean growth estimate is 10.1 percent, you can use either, or both, rates in the constant-growth-rate model using a 13.5 percent discount rate:

$$P_0 = \frac{\$1.68 \times (1 + 0.1036)}{0.135 - 0.1036} = \$59.05$$

$$P_0 = \frac{\$1.68 \times (1 + 0.101)}{0.135 - 0.101} = \$54.40$$

Both valuation estimates exceed the current price of \$54. The current stock price does not appear overvalued, so you can consider the purchase.

summary of learning goals

This chapter describes stock ownership and discusses why efficient and fair stock markets are vital in capitalist economies. Investors can benefit from owning common stock. The existence of the stock exchanges allows for easy transfer of stock from one investor to another, providing much more liquidity than would investments with similar returns on investment. The media commonly reports stock market performance using stock indexes. Before buying or selling a stock, investors should determine the stock's value. Many stock valuation methods apply time value of money principles.

LG8-1 **Understand the rights and returns that come with common stock ownership.** Common stockholders own the corporations in which they hold stock. Stockholders earn investment returns from receiving dividends and from stock price appreciation. As residual claimants, common stockholders claim any cash flows to the firm that remain after the firm pays all other claims—creditors, bondholders, and preferred stockholders. When residual cash flows are high (low), stock values will be high (low).

LG8-2 **Know how stock exchanges function.** Stock exchanges allow investors to quickly and inexpensively buy and sell thousands of stock shares. Trading at physical exchanges like the New York Stock Exchange and the American Stock Exchange takes place at brokers' trading posts on the floor by open outcry. Specialists and/or market makers oversee brokers and trades to ensure smooth trading in the stocks for which the specialists or dealers are responsible. Dealers create market liquidity in the Nasdaq's electronic stock market; the AMEX and the NYSE process increasing percentages of their trades electronically as open outcry trading becomes increasingly rare. Billions of shares of stock trade every day on each of the exchanges.

LG8-3 Track the wider stock market with stock indexes, and differentiate among the kinds of information each index provides. General stock market performance is measured with popular stock indexes like the Dow Jones Industrial Average, the Standard & Poor's 500 Index, and the NASDAQ Composite. The DJIA includes 30 of the largest (market capitalization) and most active companies in the U.S. economy. The S&P 500 Index combines the 500 firms that are the largest in their respective economic sectors. The NASDAQ Composite includes all the stock listed on the NASDAQ Stock Exchange. Because so many very large technology firms trade on the NASDAQ, investors consider this index's performance a bellwether of the tech sector.

LG8-4 Know the terminology of stock trading. Investors buy stock at the quoted ask price and sell at the bid price. The difference between the bid and ask price is the spread—usually a small amount that reimburses the specialist or dealer for expenses. A market order will be immediately executed at quoted prices when the order arrives at the exchange. A limit order will be executed only if the order's price conditions are met; if the price conditions don't materialize, a limit order will not be executed and the trade will not take place.

LG8-5 Compute stock values using dividend discount and constant-growth models. We can estimate a stock's value by discounting the future dividends and future stock price appreciation using an appropriate required rate of return as the discount rate. Because future dividends and future stock prices are highly uncertain, we simplify the models if we can reasonably assume conditions such as a constant-dividend-growth rate. We value preferred stock as a special zero-growth case of the constant-growth model. Valuation model dynamics make clear that lower discount rates lead to higher valuations. Higher growth rates also lead to higher valuations.

LG8-6 Calculate the stock value of a variable-growth-rate company. Many companies grow very fast at first; we can expect slower future growth. We call such companies "variable-growth-rate" firms. We value these firms using a two-stage process with both the constant-growth model and the discounted cash flow model.

LG8-7 Assess relative stock values using the P/E ratio model. Many investors use the P/E ratio as the most popular relative stock valuation measure. Both individual firm and overall market P/E ratios fluctuate over time. High P/E ratios are associated with high-growth stocks. Firms with high P/E ratios but low growth rates are considered relatively expensive. However, firms with low P/E ratios and high growth are considered cheap and we thus refer to them as value stocks. We often use the P/E ratio model with the firm's growth rate to estimate a stock's future price.

chapter equations

8-1 $$P_0 = \frac{D_1 + P_1}{1 + i}$$

8-2 $$P_0 = \frac{D_1}{1 + i} + \frac{D_2 + P_2}{(1 + i)^2}$$

8-3 $$P_0 = \frac{D_1}{1 + i} + \frac{D_2}{(1 + i)^2} + \cdots + \frac{D_n + P_n}{(1 + i)^n}$$

8-4 $$P_0 = \frac{D_1}{1 + i} + \frac{D_2}{(1 + i)^2} + \frac{D_3}{(1 + i)^3} + \cdots$$

8-5 $$P_0 = \frac{D_0(1 + g)}{1 + i} + \frac{D_0(1 + g)^2}{(1 + i)^2} + \frac{D_0(1 + g)^3}{(1 + i)^3} + \cdots$$

8-6 $$\text{Constant-growth model} = P_0 = \frac{D_0(1 + g)}{i - g} = \frac{D_1}{i - g}$$

8-7 $$\text{Expected return} = i = \frac{D_1}{P_0} + g = \text{Dividend yield} + \text{Capital gain}$$

$$8\text{-}8 \quad P_0 = \frac{D_0(1+g_1)}{1+i} + \frac{D_0(1+g_1)^2}{(1+i)^2} + \frac{D_0(1+g_1)^3}{(1+i)^3} + \cdots + \frac{D_0(1+g_1)^n + \dfrac{D_0(1+g_1)^n(1+g_2)}{i-g_2}}{(1+i)^n}$$

$$8\text{-}9 \quad P/E = \frac{\text{Current stock price}}{\text{Per-share earnings for last 12 months}}$$

$$8\text{-}10 \quad P_n = ({}^{P}/_{E})_n \times E_n = ({}^{P}/_{E})_n \times E_0 \times (1+g)^n$$

key terms

American Stock Exchange (AMEX), Stock exchange with a trading floor; owned by the NYSE. *p. 275*

ask, The quoted price investors are likely to pay when they buy stock. *p. 280*

bid, The quoted price investors are likely to receive when they sell stock. *p. 279*

brokers, Floor traders who execute orders for others and themselves. *p. 275*

common stock, An ownership stake in a corporation. *p. 274*

constant-growth model, A valuation method based on constantly growing dividends. *p. 284*

dealers, NASDAQ market makers who use their own capital to trade with investors. *p. 276*

dividend discount model, A valuation approach based on future dividend income. *p. 284*

dividend yield, Last four quarters of dividend income expressed as a percentage of the current stock price. *p. 285*

Dow Jones Industrial Average (DJIA), A popular index of 30 large, industry-leading firms. *p. 277*

financial analyst, Industry professional who makes predictions about a firm's future earnings and growth, and who may provide buy/sell/hold opinions to investors. *p. 287*

forward P/E ratio, The P/E ratio computed using the *estimated* next four quarters of earnings per share. *p. 292*

growth stocks, Companies expected to have above-average rates of growth in revenue, earnings and/or dividends. *p. 286*

limit order, A stock buy or sell order at a specific price. It will only be executed if the market price meets the specified price. *p. 280*

market capitalization, The size of the firm measured as the current stock price multiplied by the number of shares outstanding. *p. 278*

market makers, Dealers and specialists who oversee an orderly trading process. *p. 276*

market order, A stock buy or sell order to be immediately executed at the current market price. *p. 280*

NASDAQ Composite Index, A technology-firm weighted index of stocks listed on the NASDAQ Stock Exchange. *p. 277*

NASDAQ Stock Market, Large electronic stock exchange. *p. 276*

New York Stock Exchange (NYSE), Large and prestigious stock exchange with a trading floor. *p. 274*

preferred stock, A class of stock with fixed dividends. *p. 284*

price-earnings (P/E) ratio, Current stock price divided by four quarters of earnings per share. *p. 291*

relative value, A stock's priceyness measured relative to other stocks. *p. 291*

residual claimants, Ownership of cash flows and value after other claimants are paid. *p. 274*

Standard & Poor's 500 Index (S&P 500), A stock index of 500 large companies. *p. 277*

stock index, Index of market prices of a particular group of stocks. The index is used to measure those stocks' performance. *p. 277*

ticker symbol, Unique code for a company consisting of one to five letters. *p. 275*

trading posts, Trading location on the floor of a stock exchange. *p. 275*

trailing P/E ratio, The P/E ratio computed using the *past* four quarters of earnings per share. *p. 291*

value stocks, Companies considered to be temporarily undervalued. *p. 292*

variable growth rate, A valuation technique used when a firm's current growth rate is expected to change some time in the future. *p. 287*

self-test problems with solutions

LG8-5

1 Discounting Dividends and Future Price You are checking a financial analyst's recommendation. The analyst projects a company's stock price to be \$72 per share in three years. The most recent annual dividend was \$1.68 per share. The analyst expects that dividend to grow at 9.8 percent annually. Given a 13.5 percent required return, the analyst claims the stock is undervalued at the current price of \$54; thus he strongly urges investors to buy it. Using these assumptions, is the stock really undervalued?

Solution:

Using the \$72 target price and expected dividends, you can use equation 8-3 to value the cash flows. Since the dividends grow at 9.8 percent, the next three annual dividends will be $D_1 = \$1.84$ (= \$1.68 × 1.098), $D_2 = \$2.03$ (= \$1.84 × 1.098), and $D_3 = \$2.22$ (= \$2.03 × 1.098). Discounting these cash flows results in a value of \$53.96:

$$P_0 = \frac{\$1.84}{1 + 0.135} + \frac{\$2.03}{(1 + 0.135)^2} + \frac{\$2.22 + \$72}{(1 + 0.135)^3} = \$1.63 + \$1.58 + \$50.76$$

$$= \$53.96$$

At the current \$54 per share price, the stock does not appear undervalued. It appears fairly valued.

LG8-5

2 Growth Rates, Required Return, and Value Consider that a company is about to embark on a large high-risk project. You believe that when this news is publicly announced, shareholders will react by requiring a higher return from the company and by expecting faster growth. The company is expected to pay a \$1.75 per share dividend next year. You think that the current price of \$70 is fair, given the expected 9 percent growth rate. However, after the announcement investors will expect a 10 percent growth rate and increase the required return by 1.2 percent. If this occurs as you predict, how will the stock price change because of the announcement?

Solution:

It's not initially clear whether this will be good or bad news for the stock price. A rise in the growth rate increases the stock's value. But a higher required return lowers the value. The two changes somewhat offset one another. Since the current \$70 stock price is fair, investors require a return of 11.5 percent (= \$1.75 ÷ \$70 + 0.09) before the announcement. After the announcement, investors will require a 12.7 percent return (= 0.115 + 0.012) and expect a 10 percent growth rate. Therefore, the new stock price should be \$64.81 per share, a decline of \$5.19 (−7.4 percent).

$$P_0 = \frac{\$1.75}{0.127 - 0.10} = \$64.81$$

This was bad news for the stock price.

LG8-6

3 Variable Growth Rates Years Young Match is an online dating firm that finds matches for active people over 55. It has seen substantial growth in revenue and profits as the baby-boom generation ages. The firm will pay its first-ever dividend of \$0.20 per share (\$0.05 per quarter) next year. The dividend is expected to grow at 20 percent per year for the next four years. In the fifth year and afterwards, the Years Young dividend will grow at a steady 9.5 percent per year. If the appropriate discount rate for Years Young is 11 percent, what is the value of the stock?

Solution:

The variable-growth-rate technique should be used to value this stock. First, calculate the dividends for the first four years. The first dividend is given as $D_1 = \$0.20$. Using the 20 percent growth rate, the rest of the first stage dividends are $D_2 = \$0.24$ (= \$0.20 × 1.20), $D_3 = \$0.288$ (= \$0.24 × 1.20), and $D_4 = \$0.346$ (= \$0.288 × 1.20). The first dividend in the second growth stage is $D_5 = \$0.378$ (= \$0.346 × 1.095). Next, use the constant-growth-rate model and the 11 percent discount rate to convert the rest of the dividends to a terminal price in year four:

$$\text{Terminal value} = P_4 = \frac{\$0.378}{0.11 - 0.095} = \$25.23$$

Finally, equation 8-3 can be used to discount all the cash flows as:

$$P_0 = \frac{\$0.20}{1 + 0.11} + \frac{\$0.24}{(1 + 0.11)^2} + \frac{\$0.288}{(1 + 0.11)^3} + \frac{\$0.346 + \$25.23}{(1 + 0.11)^4}$$
$$= \$0.180 + \$0.195 + \$0.211 + \$16.847 = \$17.43$$

The stock for the Years Young Match company is valued at \$17.43.

4 The P/E Ratio and Relative Value Home Shop (HS) has a stock price of \$31.79 and is expected to grow at 14.1 percent per year. HS's P/E ratio is 14.3. Three other firms are also expected to grow at a similar rate: General Electronic, Almo, and Cisko. The P/E ratios of these firms range from 11.16 to 12.91, with an average of 12.0. If investors decided that HS should be equally expensive as these other firms, what price would the stock fall to in order for it to have a P/E ratio of 12.0? What return would result from this change in price? LG8-7

Solution:

Since the price of HS is \$31.79 and the P/E ratio is 14.3, then the expected earnings of HS are \$2.22 per share (= \$31.79 ÷ 14.3). For the P/E ratio to be 12.0, the price would have to fall to \$26.64 (= 12.0 × \$2.22). The \$5.15 decrease would represent a 16.2 percent (= −\$5.15 ÷ \$31.79) capital loss in the price.[1]

questions

1. As owners, what rights and advantages do shareholders obtain? *(LG8-1)*
2. Describe how being a residual claimant can be very valuable. *(LG8-1)*
3. Obtain a current quote of McDonald's (MCD) from the Internet. Describe what has changed since the quote in Figure 8.1. *(LG8-2)*
4. Get the trading statistics for the three main U.S. stock exchanges. Compare the trading activity to that of Table 8.1. *(LG8-2)*
5. Why might the Standard & Poor's 500 Index be a better measure of stock market performance than the Dow Jones Industrial Average? Why is the DJIA more popular than the S&P 500? *(LG8-3)*
6. Explain how it is possible for the DJIA to increase one day while the NASDAQ Composite decreases during the same day. *(LG8-3)*
7. Which is higher, the ask quote or the bid quote? Why? *(LG8-4)*

[1]An alternative solution is to recognize that a change in the P/E ratio from 14.3 to 12.0 represents a −16.1 percent change. Thus the price would have to change by the same proportion.

8. Illustrate through examples how trading commission costs impact an investor's return. *(LG8-4)*

9. Describe the difference in the timing of trade execution and the certainty of trade price between market orders and limit orders. *(LG8-4)*

10. What are the differences between common stock and preferred stock? *(LG8-5)*

11. How important is growth to a stock's value? Illustrate with examples. *(LG8-5)*

12. Under what conditions would the constant-growth model *not* be appropriate? *(LG8-5)*

13. The expected return derived from the constant-growth-rate model relies on dividend yield and capital gain. Where do these two parts of the return come from? *(LG8-5)*

14. Describe, in words, how to use the variable-growth-rate technique to value a stock. *(LG8-6)*

15. Can the variable-growth-rate model be used to value a firm that has a negative growth rate in Stage 1 and a stable and positive growth in Stage 2? Explain. *(LG8-6)*

16. Explain why using the P/E relative value approach may be useful for companies that do not pay dividends. *(LG8-7)*

17. How is a firm's changing P/E ratio reflected in the stock price? Give examples. *(LG8-7)*

18. Differentiate the characteristics of growth stocks and value stocks. *(LG8-7)*

19. What's the relationship between the P/E ratio and a firm's growth rate? *(LG8-7)*

20. Describe the process for using the P/E ratio to estimate a future stock price. *(LG8-7)*

problems

basic problems

8-1 Stock Index Performance On March 5, 2013, the Dow Jones Industrial Average set a new high. The index closed at 14,253.77, which was up 125.95 that day. What was the return (in percent) of the stock market that day? *(LG8-3)*

8-2 Stock Index Performance On March 9, 2009, the Dow Jones Industrial Average reached a new low. The index closed at 6,547.05, which was down 79.89 that day. What was the return (in percent) of the stock market that day? *(LG8-3)*

8-3 Buying Stock with Commissions Your discount brokerage firm charges $7.95 per stock trade. How much money do you need to buy 200 shares of Pfizer, Inc. (PFE), which trades at $31.40? *(LG8-4)*

8-4 Buying Stock with Commissions Your discount brokerage firm charges $9.50 per stock trade. How much money do you need to buy 300 shares of Time Warner, Inc. (TWX), which trades at $22.62? *(LG8-4)*

8-5 Selling Stock with Commissions Your full-service brokerage firm charges $140 per stock trade. How much money do you receive after selling 200 shares of Nokia Corporation (NOK), which trades at $20.13? *(LG8-4)*

8-6 Selling Stock with Commissions Your full-service brokerage firm charges $135 per stock trade. How much money do you receive after selling 250 shares of International Business Machines (IBM), which trades at $96.17? *(LG8-4)*

8-7 Buying Stock with a Market Order You would like to buy shares of Sirius Satellite Radio (SIRI). The current ask and bid quotes are $3.96 and $3.93, respectively. You place a market buy order for 500 shares that executes at these quoted prices. How much money did it cost to buy these shares? *(LG8-4)*

8-8 Buying Stock with a Market Order You would like to buy shares of Coldwater Creek, Inc. (CWTR). The current ask and bid quotes are $20.70 and $20.66, respectively. You place a market buy order for 200 shares that executes at these quoted prices. How much money did it cost to buy these shares? *(LG8-4)*

8-9 Selling Stock with a Limit Order You would like to sell 200 shares of Xenith Bankshares, Inc. (XBKS). The current ask and bid quotes are $4.66 and $4.62, respectively. You place a limit sell order at $4.65. If the trade executes, how much money do you receive from the buyer? *(LG8-4)*

8-10 Selling Stock with a Limit Order You would like to sell 100 shares of Echo Global Logistics, Inc. (ECHO). The current ask and bid quotes are $15.33 and $15.28, respectively. You place a limit sell order at $15.31. If the trade executes, how much money do you receive from the buyer? *(LG8-4)*

8-11 Value of a Preferred Stock A preferred stock from Duquesne Light Company (DQUPRA) pays $3.55 in annual dividends. If the required return on the preferred stock is 6.7 percent, what's the value of the stock? *(LG8-5)*

8-12 Value of a Preferred Stock A preferred stock from Hecla Mining Co. (HLPRB) pays $3.50 in annual dividends. If the required return on the preferred stock is 6.8 percent, what is the value of the stock? *(LG8-5)*

8-13 P/E Ratio and Stock Price Ultra Petroleum (UPL) has earnings per share of $1.56 and a P/E ratio of 32.48. What's the stock price? *(LG8-7)*

8-14 P/E Ratio and Stock Price JPMorgan Chase Co. (JPM) has earnings per share of $3.53 and a P/E ratio of 13.81. What is the price of the stock? *(LG8-7)*

intermediate problems

8-15 Value of Dividends and Future Price A firm is expected to pay a dividend of $1.35 next year and $1.50 the following year. Financial analysts believe the stock will be at their price target of $68 in two years. Compute the value of this stock with a required return of 10 percent. *(LG8-5)*

8-16 Value of Dividends and Future Price A firm is expected to pay a dividend of $2.05 next year and $2.35 the following year. Financial analysts believe the stock will be at their price target of $110 in two years. Compute the value of this stock with a required return of 12 percent. *(LG8-5)*

8-17 Dividend Growth Annual dividends of AT&T Corp (T) grew from $0.96 in 2000 to $1.76 in 2012. What was the annual growth rate? *(LG8-5)*

8-18 Dividend Growth Annual dividends of General Electric (GE) grew from $0.66 in 2001 to $1.03 in 2006. What was the annual growth rate? *(LG8-5)*

8-19 Value a Constant Growth Stock Financial analysts forecast Safeco Corp.'s (SAF) growth rate for the future to be 8 percent. Safeco's recent dividend was $0.88. What is the value of Safeco stock when the required return is 12 percent? *(LG8-5)*

8-20 Value a Constant Growth Stock Financial analysts forecast Limited Brands (LTD) growth rate for the future to be 12.5 percent. LTD's recent dividend was $0.60. What is the value of Limited Brands stock when the required return is 14.5 percent? *(LG8-5)*

8-21 **Expected Return** Ecolap Inc. (ECL) recently paid a $0.46 dividend. The dividend is expected to grow at a 14.5 percent rate. At a current stock price of $44.12, what is the return shareholders are expecting? *(LG8-5)*

8-22 **Expected Return** Paychex Inc. (PAYX) recently paid an $0.84 dividend. The dividend is expected to grow at a 15 percent rate. At a current stock price of $40.11, what is the return shareholders are expecting? *(LG8-5)*

8-23 **Dividend Initiation and Stock Value** A firm does not pay a dividend. It is expected to pay its first dividend of $0.20 per share in three years. This dividend will grow at 11 percent indefinitely. Using a 12 percent discount rate, compute the value of this stock. *(LG8-6)*

8-24 **Dividend Initiation and Stock Value** A firm does not pay a dividend. It is expected to pay its first dividend of $0.25 per share in two years. This dividend will grow at 10 percent indefinitely. Using an 11.5 percent discount rate, compute the value of this stock. *(LG8-6)*

8-25 **P/E Ratio Model and Future Price** Kellogg Co. (K) recently earned a profit of $2.52 earnings per share and has a P/E ratio of 13.5. The dividend has been growing at a 5 percent rate over the past few years. If this growth rate continues, what would be the stock price in five years if the P/E ratio remained unchanged? What would the price be if the P/E ratio declined to 12 in five years? *(LG8-7)*

8-26 **P/E Ratio Model and Future Price** New York Times Co. (NYT) recently earned a profit of $1.21 per share and has a P/E ratio of 19.59. The dividend has been growing at a 7.25 percent rate over the past six years. If this growth rate continues, what would be the stock price in five years if the P/E ratio remained unchanged? What would the price be if the P/E ratio increased to 22 in five years? *(LG8-7)*

advanced problems

8-27 **Value of Future Cash Flows** A firm recently paid a $0.45 annual dividend. The dividend is expected to increase by 10 percent in each of the next four years. In the fourth year, the stock price is expected to be $80. If the required return for this stock is 13.5 percent, what is its value? *(LG8-5)*

8-28 **Value of Future Cash Flows** A firm recently paid a $0.60 annual dividend. The dividend is expected to increase by 12 percent in each of the next four years. In the fourth year, the stock price is expected to be $110. If the required return for this stock is 14.5 percent, what is its value? *(LG8-5)*

8-29 **Constant Growth Stock Valuation** Waller Co. paid a $0.137 dividend per share in 2000, which grew to $0.55 in 2012. This growth is expected to continue. What is the value of this stock at the beginning of 2013 when the required return is 13.7 percent? *(LG8-5)*

8-30 **Constant Growth Stock Valuation** Campbell Soup Co. (CPB) paid a $0.632 dividend per share in 2003, which grew to $0.76 in 2006. This growth is expected to continue. What is the value of this stock at the beginning of 2007 when the required return is 8.7 percent? *(LG8-5)*

8-31 **Changes in Growth and Stock Valuation** Consider a firm that had been priced using a 10 percent growth rate and a 12 percent required return.

The firm recently paid a $1.20 dividend. The firm just announced that because of a new joint venture, it will likely grow at a 10.5 percent rate. How much should the stock price change (in dollars and percentage)? *(LG8-5)*

8-32 Changes in Growth and Stock Valuation Consider a firm that had been priced using an 11.5 percent growth rate and a 13.5 percent required return. The firm recently paid a $1.50 dividend. The firm has just announced that because of a new joint venture, it will likely grow at a 12 percent rate. How much should the stock price change (in dollars and percentage)? *(LG8-5)*

8-33 Variable Growth A fast-growing firm recently paid a dividend of $0.35 per share. The dividend is expected to increase at a 20 percent rate for the next three years. Afterwards, a more stable 12 percent growth rate can be assumed. If a 13 percent discount rate is appropriate for this stock, what is its value? *(LG8-6)*

8-34 Variable Growth A fast-growing firm recently paid a dividend of $0.40 per share. The dividend is expected to increase at a 25 percent rate for the next four years. Afterwards, a more stable 11 percent growth rate can be assumed. If a 12.5 percent discount rate is appropriate for this stock, what is its value? *(LG8-6)*

8-35 P/E Model and Cash Flow Valuation Suppose that a firm's recent earnings per share and dividend per share are $2.50 and $1.30, respectively. Both are expected to grow at 8 percent. However, the firm's current P/E ratio of 22 seems high for this growth rate. The P/E ratio is expected to fall to 18 within five years. Compute a value for this stock by first estimating the dividends over the next five years and the stock price in five years. Then discount these cash flows using a 10 percent required rate. *(LG8-5, LG8-7)*

8-36 P/E Model and Cash Flow Valuation Suppose that a firm's recent earnings per share and dividend per share are $2.75 and $1.60, respectively. Both are expected to grow at 9 percent. However, the firm's current P/E ratio of 23 seems high for this growth rate. The P/E ratio is expected to fall to 19 within five years. Compute a value for this stock by first estimating the dividends over the next five years and the stock price in five years. Then discount these cash flows using an 11 percent required rate. *(LG8-5, LG8-7)*

8-37 Spreadsheet Problem Spreadsheets are especially useful for computing stock value under different assumptions. Consider a firm that is expected to pay the following dividends:

Year 1	2	3	4	5	6	
$1.20	$1.20	$1.50	$1.50	$1.75	$1.90	and grow at 5% thereafter

a. Using an 11 percent discount rate, what would be the value of this stock?

b. What is the value of the stock using a 10 percent discount rate? A 12 percent discount rate?

c. What would the value be using a 6 percent growth rate after year 6 instead of the 5 percent rate using each of these three discount rates?

d. What do you conclude about stock valuation and its assumptions?

research it! Stock Screener

Investors can choose from many thousands of stocks. The large number to choose from can be quite daunting to new investors. Fortunately, some good stock screeners are available for free on the Internet that will find only the kinds of companies the investor is looking for. Looking for small value companies? A stock screen at Yahoo! Finance will show all the stocks that meet the three criteria of (1) market capitalization between $250 million and $1 billion, (2) P/E ratio less than or equal to 10, and (3) a quick ratio greater or equal to 1.0. In March of 2013, 45 firms met all three of these criteria. Yahoo! Finance provides 18 screens like this one to choose from. Pick one of these preset screens. Discuss the kinds of stocks the screen will find and report on those companies. **(http://screener.finance.yahoo.com/presetscreens.html)**

integrated mini-case: Valuing Carnival Corporation

Carnival Corp. provides cruises to major vacation destinations. Carnival operates 100 cruise ships with a total capacity of 180,746 passengers in North America, Europe, the United Kingdom, Germany, Australia, and New Zealand. The company also operates hotels, sightseeing motor coaches and rail cars, and luxury day boats. These activities generated earnings per share of $1.67 for 2012. The stock price at the end of 2012 was $36.77. The previous stock prices and dividends are shown in the following table.

	2005	2006	2007	2008	2009	2010	2011	2012
Annual dividend	$ 0.80	$ 1.025	$ 1.375	$ 1.20	$ 0.00	$ 0.40	$1.00	$1.00
Stock price in the following January	$51.76	$51.56	$44.40	$18.19	$33.33	$38.80	$32.64	$36.77

Carnival is a firm in the General Entertainment industry, which is in the Services sector. The following table shows some key statistics for Carnival, the industry, and the sector.

Key Statistic	Carnival	General Entertainment	Services Sector
P/E ratio	21.17	15.30	12.65
Dividend yield	2.80%	3.05%	1.69%
Next 5-year growth	12.91%	18.74%	14.23%

Use the various valuation models and relative value measures to assess whether Carnival stock is correctly valued. Compute value estimates from multiple models. The appropriate required rate of return is 11 percent.

ANSWERS TO TIME OUT

8-1 The New York Stock Exchange (NYSE) has a physical location in New York City near the American Exchange. NASDAQ is an electronic network and therefore does not have a specific location per se.

8-2 The NYSE uses a specialist at each trading post on the floor to manage the trading in the stocks assigned to that post. Orders come to the floor through stock brokers worldwide. The trades are executed through an auction system with the floor brokers. NASDAQ uses an electronic network that ties together many dealers that are interested in trading the stock. These dealers compete with each other to offer the best price. Orders come in from stock brokers and are executed with the dealer that has the best price. Both of these systems are good and each exchange works diligently to make their system effective and efficient for investors.

8-3 First, these indexes are composed of different stocks. Second, the type of stocks in each index may be weighted toward different industries. Last, the indexes are computed using different methodologies.

8-4 The bubble mostly occurred in the Internet and other technology-oriented firms. These firms, especially the smaller ones, made up a much larger portion of the NASDAQ Composite than the DJIA or the S&P 500. Therefore, the dramatic price rise and fall for these companies had a bigger impact on NASDAQ. This is visually seen in the figure.

8-5 Of the popular indexes, the S&P 500 Index includes the largest portion of the market capitalization and therefore gives the best indication of what is happening in the stock market.

8-6 An investor buys at the higher ask price and sells at the lower bid price. Thus, the difference between the bid and ask price is a cost to the trader. If the bid-ask spread is \$0.05, this cost seems small for an \$80 stock and high for a \$5 stock.

8-7 A market buy order would execute at the ask price of \$37.85. Yes, the limit sell order at \$37.75 executes if the bid is at \$37.75 or higher. So, the order would execute at the bid of \$37.79.

8-8 Firm growth is very valuable to the value of a stock. Consider three firms with the same \$1 dividend and 12 percent discount rate but with growth of 10 percent, 5 percent, and zero percent, respectively. Using the Gordon growth model, the stock price estimates are:

$$P_0 = \frac{\$1 \times (1 + 0.1)}{0.12 - 0.10} = \$55 \quad P_0 = \frac{\$1 \times (1 + 0.05)}{0.12 - 0.05} = \$15 \quad P_0 = \frac{\$1 \times (1 + 0)}{0.12 - 0} = \$8.33$$

Note how dramatically different the price estimates are.

8-9 The dividend yield for Coca-Cola was 2.84 percent. This is a 24.09 percent (= 2.84 ÷ 11.79) proportion of the total expected return. The rest comes from growth expectations.

8-10 The variable-growth model was demonstrated using an initially high growth rate that reduced to a long-term growth rate. However, it is valid with any initial growth rate (high, low, zero, and even negative). The key is that it must settle into a long-term constant-growth rate that is lower than the discount rate.

8-11
$$P_0 = \frac{\$2.20(1 + 0.218)}{1 + 0.14} + \frac{\$2.20(1 + 0.218)^2 + \dfrac{\$2.20(1 + 0.218)^2(1 + 0.102)}{0.14 - 0.102}}{(1 + 0.14)^2}$$
$$= \$2.351 + \frac{\$3.264 + \$94.649}{1.2996}$$
$$= \$77.69$$

8-12 Rearranging the Gordon growth model, $P_0/E_0 = (D_1/E_0) \div (i - g)$, we see that the P/E ratio is related to the firm's growth rate. Higher P/E ratios are expected for firms with higher growth rates. If two firms have the same P/E ratio, the one with the higher growth rate might be described as cheap compared to the firm with the lower growth rate.

8-13 $P_5 = (P/E) \times E_0 \times (1 + g)^5 = 6 \times \$8.41 \times (1 + 0.18)^5 = \$115.44$

PART FIVE

9 Characterizing Risk and Return

viewpoints

Business Application

Managers from the production and marketing departments have proposed some risky new business projects for your firm. These new ideas appear to be riskier than the firm's current business operations.

You know that diversifying the firm's product offerings could reduce the firm's overall risk. However, you are concerned that taking on these new projects will make the firm's stock too risky. How can you determine whether these project ideas would make the firm's stock riskier or less risky? **(See solution on p. 325)**

Personal Application

Suppose an investor owns a portfolio of 100 percent long-term Treasury bonds because the owner prefers low risk. The investor has avoided owning stocks because of their high volatility.

The investor's stockbroker claims that putting 10 percent of the portfolio in stocks would actually reduce total risk and increase the portfolio's expected return. The investor knows that stocks are riskier than bonds. How can adding the risky stocks to the bond portfolio reduce the risk level? **(See solution on p. 325)**

Is there such a thing as a high-reward, zero-risk investment?

Learning Goals

LG9-1 Compute an investment's dollar and percentage return.

LG9-2 Find information about the historical returns and volatility for the stock, bond, and cash markets.

LG9-3 Measure and evaluate the total risk of an investment using several methods.

LG9-4 Recognize the risk-return relationship and its implications.

LG9-5 Plan investments that take advantage of diversification and its impact on total risk.

LG9-6 Find efficient and optimal portfolios.

LG9-7 Compute a portfolio's return.

You can invest your money very safely by opening a savings account at a bank or by buying Treasury bills. So why would you invest your money on risky stocks and bonds if you can take advantage of low-risk opportunities? The answer: Very low risk investments also provide a very low return. Investors take on higher risk investments in expectation of earning higher returns. Likewise, businesses also take on risky capital investments only if they expect to earn higher returns that at least cover their costs, including investors' required return. Both investor and business sentiments create a positive relationship between risk and expected return. Of course, taking risk means that you get no guarantee that you will recoup your investment. In the short run, higher risk investments often significantly underperform lower risk investments. Companies and investors should expect higher risk investments to earn higher returns only over the long term (many years). In addition, not all forms of risk are rewarded. In this chapter, you'll see how the risk-return relationship fundamentally affects finance theory. We focus on using historical information to characterize past returns and risks. We show how you can diversify to eliminate some risk and expect the highest return possible for your desired risk level. In Chapter 10, we'll turn to estimating the risks and returns you should expect in the future.

9.1 • Historical Returns

Let's begin our discussion of risk and return by characterizing the concept of return. First, we need a method for calculating returns. After computing a return, investors need to assess whether it was a good, average, or bad investment return. Examining returns from the past gives us a general idea of what we might expect to see in the future. We should think in terms of return for the long run because a return for any one year can be quite different from the average returns from the past couple of decades.

Computing Returns

How much have you earned on each of your investments? Two ways to determine this are to compute the actual dollar return or compute the dollar return as a percentage of the money invested.

dollar return

The amount of profit or loss from an investment denoted in dollars.

DOLLAR RETURN The **dollar return** earned includes any capital gain (or loss) that occurred as well as any income that you received over the period. Equation 9-1 illustrates the dollar return calculation:

$$\begin{aligned}\text{Dollar return} &= \text{Capital gain or loss} + \text{Income} \\ &= (\text{Ending value} - \text{Beginning value}) + \text{Income} \qquad \textbf{(9-1)}\end{aligned}$$

For example, say you held 200 shares of Mattel Inc. (MAT) stock. The stock price of the toy and game producer had a market price of $29.88 per share at the end of 2011. Mattel also paid $1.24 in dividends per share during 2012. At the end of 2012, Mattel's stock price was $37.63. For the whole of 2012, you earned a capital gain of ($37.63 − $29.88) × 200 shares, or $1,550, and received a dividend payment of 200 shares × $1.24, or $248. So the total dollar return on your investment was $1,798 (= $1,550 + $248) for 2012.

In Mattel's case, the stock price increased, so you experienced a capital gain. On the other hand, the consumer electronic goods retailer RadioShack Corp. (RSH) started the year at $7.39 per share, paid a $0.25 dividend, and ended 2012 at $3.29. If you owned 200 shares of RadioShack, you would have experienced a capital loss of $820. This loss would have been partially offset by the $50 of dividends received. However, the total dollar return would still have been −$770. Stock prices can fluctuate substantially and cause large positive or negative dollar returns.

Does your dollar return depend on whether you continue to hold the Mattel and RadioShack stock or sell it? No. In general, finance deals with *market* values. Mattel stock was worth $37.63 at the end of 2012 regardless of whether you held the stock or sold it. If you sell it, then we refer to your gains as "realized" gains. If you continue to hold the stock, the gains are "unrealized" gains.

percentage return

The dollar return characterized as a percentage of money invested.

PERCENTAGE RETURN We usually find it more useful to characterize investment earnings as **percentage returns** so that we can easily compare one investment's return to other alternatives' returns. We calculate percentage return by dividing the dollar return by the investment's value at the beginning of the time period.

$$\text{Percentage return} = \frac{\text{Ending value} - \text{Beginning value} + \text{Income}}{\text{Beginning value}} \times 100\% \qquad \textbf{(9-2)}$$

Because it's standardized, we can use percentage returns for almost any type of investment. We can use beginning and ending values for stock positions, bond prices, real estate values, and so on. Investment income may be stock dividends, bond interest payments, or other receipts. The percentage return for holding the Mattel stock during calendar year 2012 was 25.9 percent, computed as:

$$\begin{aligned}\text{Mattel percentage return} &= \frac{(\$37.63 \times 200) - (\$29.88 \times 200) + (\$1.24 \times 200)}{\$29.88 \times 200} \\ &= 0.259, \text{ or } 25.9\%\end{aligned}$$

The return for the RadioShack position during the same period was a whopping −52.11 percent:

$$\begin{aligned}\text{RadioShack percentage return} &= \frac{(\$3.29 \times 200) - (\$7.39 \times 200) + (\$0.25 \times 200)}{\$7.39 \times 200} \\ &= -0.5211, \text{ or } -52.11\%\end{aligned}$$

Both firms belong to the S&P 500 Index, which earned 16.0 percent in 2012.

EXAMPLE 9-1

LG9-1

Computing Returns

You are evaluating a stock's short-term performance. On August 16, 2010, technology firm 3PAR saw its stock price surge on news of a takeover battle between Dell and Hewlett-Packard. 3PAR stock had closed the previous trading day at \$9.65 and was up to \$18.00 by the end of the day. 3PAR had ended 2009 at \$11.85 and does not pay a dividend. What is the dollar return and percentage return of 300 shares of 3PAR for the day and year to date?

For interactive versions of this example visit www.mhhe.com/can3e

SOLUTION:

For the day, realize that no income is paid. Therefore, the dollar return is \$2,505 = 300 × (\$18.00 − \$9.65) + 0 and the percent return is 86.53% = \$2,505 ÷ (300 × \$9.65). The year to date (YTD) return also does not include dividend income. So the dollar YTD return is \$1,845 = 300 × (\$18.00 − \$11.85). The 3PAR YTD percentage return is:

$$\text{3PAR YTD return} = \frac{(\$18.00 \times 300) - (\$11.85 \times 300) + (\$0)}{\$11.85 \times 300} = 0.5190, \text{ or } 51.90\%$$

Hewlett-Packard eventually won the bidding war and purchased 3PAR for \$33 per share!

Similar to Problems 9-1, 9-2, 9-3, 9-4, self-test problem 1

Are the 2012 returns for Mattel and RadioShack typical? We look to **average returns** to examine performance over time. The arithmetic average return provides an estimate for how the investment has performed over longer periods of time. The formula for the average return is:

average returns

A measure summarizing the past performance of an investment.

$$\text{Average return} = \text{Sum of all returns} \div \text{Number of returns}$$

$$= \frac{\sum_{t=1}^{N} \text{Return}_t}{N} \qquad \textbf{(9-3)}$$

where the return for each subperiod is summed up and divided by the number of subperiods. You can state the returns in either percentage or decimal format. Table 9.1 shows the annual returns for Mattel and RadioShack from 1985 to 2012. First, notice that over time, the returns are quite varied for both firms. The stock return for Mattel has ranged from a low of −52.4 percent in 1999 to a high of 82.6 percent in 1991. RadioShack's stock return varied between −52.4 percent (2012) to 84.3 percent (1993). Also note that the returns appear unpredictable or random. Sometimes a large negative return is followed by another bad year, like Mattel's returns in 2007 and 2008. Other times, a poor year is followed by a very good year, like 2008 and 2009 for RadioShack. The table also reports average annual returns for Mattel and RadioShack of 16.7 percent and 6.1 percent, respectively. Over the years, the annual returns for these stocks have been quite different from their average returns.

The average returns shown in this chapter are more precisely called arithmetic average returns. These average returns are appropriate for statistical analysis. However, they do not accurately illustrate the historical performance of a stock or portfolio. To see this, consider the \$100 stock that earned a 50 percent return one year (to \$150) and then earned a −50 percent return the next year (to \$75). The arithmetic average return is therefore (50% + −50%) ÷ 2 = 0%. Do

table 9.1 **Annual and Average Returns for Mattel and RadioShack, 1985 to 2012**

	A	B	C	D	E	F
1		Mattel	RadioShack		Mattel	RadioShack
2	1985	−7.4%	38.0%	1999	−52.4%	81.9%
3	1986	5.7	19.8	2000	47.4	13.1
4	1987	−40.3	−25.6	2001	28.8	−42.4
5	1988	45.1	25.1	2002	5.5	−36.1
6	1989	64.0	−15.4	2003	−3.5	64.8
7	1990	26.5	−11.3	2004	5.4	2.4
8	1991	82.6	−19.0	2005	−12.6	−32.3
9	1992	33.0	10.5	2006	52.1	1.0
10	1993	6.9	84.3	2007	−10.5	−20.4
11	1994	15.5	−5.9	2008	−28.5	−32.3
12	1995	59.8	−12.3	2009	44.3	72.7
13	1996	10.5	20.5	2010	24.0	−21.4
14	1997	46.6	73.5	2011	35.6	−50.5
15	1998	−43.0	40.5	2012	25.9	−52.1
16				Average =	16.7%	6.1%

Note the range of returns. Few annual returns are close to the average return.

Data Source: Yahoo! Finance

you believe the average return was zero percent per year? If you started with a $100 stock and ended with a $75 stock, did you earn zero percent? No, you lost money. A measure of that performance should illustrate a negative return. The accurate measure to be used in performance analysis is called the **geometric mean return,** or the mean return computed by finding the equivalent return that is compounded for N periods. In this example, the mean return is $[(1 + 0.50) \times (1 + -0.50)]^{1/2} - 1 = -0.134$, or −13.4 percent. Given the loss of $25 over two years, this −13.4 percent per year mean return seems more reasonable than the zero percent average return.

geometric mean return

The mean return computed by finding the equivalent return that is compounded for *N* periods.

The general formula for the geometric mean return is

$$\text{Geometric mean return} = \left[\prod_{t=1}^{N}\left(1 + \frac{\text{Return}_t}{100}\right)\right]^{\frac{1}{N}} - 1 \qquad \textbf{(9-4)}$$

LG9-2

Performance of Asset Classes

During any given year, the stock market may perform better than the bond market, or it may perform worse. Over longer time periods, how do stocks, bonds, or cash securities perform? Historically, stocks have performed better than either bonds or cash. Table 9.2 shows the average returns for these three asset classes over the period 1950 to 2012, as well as over various subperiods. Over the entire period, stocks (as measured by the S&P 500 Index) earned an average 12.4 percent return per year. This is double the 6.8 percent return earned by long-term Treasury bonds. Cash securities, measured by U.S. Treasury bills, earned an average 4.6 percent return.

The table also shows each asset class's average return for each decade since 1950. The best decade for the stock market was the 1950s, when stocks earned an average 20.9 percent per year. The 1990s ran a close second with a 19 percent per year return. The best decade for the bond market was the 1980s, when it earned an average 13.5 percent per year return due to capital gains as interest rates fell.

table 9.2 | Annual and Average Returns for Stocks, Bonds, and T-Bills, 1950 to 2012

	A	B	C	D	E
1			Stocks	Long-Term Treasury Bonds	T-Bills
2	1950 to 2012	Average	12.4%	6.8%	4.6%
3	1950 to 1959	Average	20.9	0.0	2.0
4	1960 to 1969	Average	8.7	1.6	4.0
5	1970 to 1979	Average	7.5	5.7	6.3
6	1980 to 1989	Average	18.2	13.5	8.9
7	1990 to 1999	Average	19.0	9.5	4.9
8	2000	Annual Return	−9.1	20.1	5.9
9	2001	Annual Return	−11.9	4.6	3.5
10	2002	Annual Return	−22.1	17.2	1.6
11	2003	Annual Return	28.7	2.1	1.0
12	2004	Annual Return	10.9	7.7	1.4
13	2005	Annual Return	4.9	6.5	3.1
14	2006	Annual Return	15.8	1.9	4.7
15	2007	Annual Return	3.5	9.8	3.4
16	2008	Annual Return	−35.5	22.7	1.5
17	2009	Annual Return	23.5	−12.2	0.2
18	2000 to 2009	Average	0.9	8.0	2.7
19	2010	Annual Return	15.1	9.4	0.01
20	2011	Annual Return	2.1	29.9	0.02
21	2012	Annual Return	16.0	3.6	0.02
22					

Returns have been very different among decades.

Stocks have outperformed bonds in every decade since 1950 except the recent 2000s. Notice that the average return in the stock and bond markets has not been negative during any decade since 1950. But average stock returns do not really paint a very accurate picture of annual returns. Individual annual returns from 2000 to 2009 show that returns can vary strongly and be quite negative in any particular year. Indeed, this annual variability defines risk. The stock market return in 2008 was particularly poor because of the financial crisis. However, not all stocks fell the same amount. Notice that Mattel and RadioShack declined by only 28.5 and 32.3 percent while the stock market in general declined 35.5 percent. Financial company stocks fell the most during the crisis.

TIME OUT

9-1 How important were dividend payments to the total returns that Mattel and RadioShack offered investors?

9-2 Using the average returns shown in Table 9.2, compute how much a $10,000 investment made in each asset class at the beginning of each decade would become at the end of each decade.

9.2 • Historical Risks

When you purchase a U.S. Treasury bill, you know exactly what your dollar and percentage return are going to be. Many people find comfort in the certainty from this safe investment. On the other hand, when you purchase a stock, you do not know what your return is going to be—either in the short term or in the long run. This uncertainty is precisely what makes stock investing risky. It's useful to evaluate this uncertainty quantitatively so that we can compare risk among different stocks and asset classes.

LG9-3

Computing Volatility

standard deviation

A measure of past return volatility, or risk, of an investment.

total risk

The volatility of an investment, which includes current portions of firm-specific risk and market risk.

Financial theory suggests that investors should look at an investment's historical returns to assess how much uncertainty to expect in the future. If you see high variability in historical returns, you should expect a high degree of future uncertainty. Table 9.2 shows that between 2000 and 2009, the stock market experienced a range of −35.5 percent return in 2008 to a 28.7 percent return in 2003. Bonds experienced a smaller variability: −12.2 percent return in 2009 to 22.7 percent return in 2008. Examining the range of historical returns provides just one way to express the return volatility that we can expect. In practical terms, the finance industry uses a statistical return volatility measure known as the **standard deviation** of percentage returns. We calculate standard deviation as the square root of the variance, and this figure represents the security's or portfolio's **total risk.** We'll discuss other risk measurements in the next chapter.

Our process of computing standard deviation starts with the average return over the period. The average annual return for the stock market since 1950 is 12.4 percent. How much can the return in any given year deviate from this average? We compute the actual annual deviation by subtracting the return each year from this average return: $\text{Return}_{(1950)} - \text{Average return}$; $\text{Return}_{(1951)} - \text{Average return}$; $\text{Return}_{(1952)} - \text{Average return}$, and so on. Note that many of these deviations will be negative (from a lower-than-average return that year) and others will be positive (from a higher-than-average return). If we computed the *average* of these return deviations, our result would be zero. Large positive deviations cancel out large negative deviations and hide the variability. To really see the size of the variations without the distractions that come with including a positive or negative sign, we square each deviation before adding them up. Dividing by the number of returns in the sample minus one provides the return *variance.*[1] The square root of the return variance is the standard deviation:

$$\text{Standard deviation} = \text{Square root of the average squared deviation of returns}$$

$$= \sqrt{\frac{\sum_{t=1}^{N}(\text{Return}_t - \text{Average return})^2}{N-1}} \qquad \textbf{(9-5)}$$

A large standard deviation indicates greater return volatility—or high risk. Table 9.3 shows the standard deviations of Mattel stock returns over 28 years. The Deviation column shows the annual return minus Mattel's average return of 16.7 percent. The last column squares each deviation. Then we sum up these squared deviations and divide the result by the number of observations less one (27) to compute the return variance. If we want to use a measure that makes sense in the real world (how would you interpret a squared percentage, anyway?), we take

[1]We use the denominator of $N-1$ to compute a sample's standard deviation, which is the most common for finance applications. We would divide the standard deviation of a population simply by N.

table 9.3 | **Computation of Mattel Stock Return Standard Deviation**

	A	B	C	D
1		**Mattel Return**	**Deviation**	**Squared Deviation**
2	1985	−7.4%	−7.4%	0.5%
3	1986	5.7	5.7	0.3
4	1987	−40.3	−40.3	16.3
5	1988	45.1	45.1	20.3
6	1989	64.0	64.0	40.9
7	1990	26.5	26.5	7.0
8	1991	82.6	82.6	68.3
9	1992	33.0	33.0	10.9
10	1993	6.9	6.9	0.5
11	1994	15.5	15.5	2.4
12	1995	59.8	59.8	35.8
13	1996	10.5	10.5	1.1
14	1997	46.6	46.6	21.7
15	1998	−43.0	−43.0	18.5
16	1999	−52.4	−52.4	27.4
17	2000	47.4	47.4	22.5
18	2001	28.8	28.8	8.3
19	2002	5.5	5.5	0.3
20	2003	−3.5	−3.5	0.1
21	2004	5.4	5.4	0.3
22	2005	−12.6	−12.6	1.6
23	2006	52.1	52.1	27.1
24	2007	−10.5	−10.5	1.1
25	2008	−28.5	−28.5	8.1
26	2009	44.3	44.3	19.7
27	2010	24.0	24.0	5.8
28	2011	35.6	35.6	12.7
29	2012	25.9	25.9	6.7
30	**Average =**	**16.7%**	**Sum =**	**386.1%**
31			**Variance =**	**14.3%**
32			**Std Dev =**	**37.8%**
33				

Investors use standard deviation as a measure of risk; the higher the standard deviation, the riskier the asset.
Data Source: Yahoo! Finance

the square root of the variance to get the standard deviation. Mattel's standard deviation of returns during this sample period comes to 33.8 percent. In comparison, the standard deviation of RadioShack stock returns for this same period is 41.0 percent. Since RadioShack's standard deviation is higher, its stock features more total risk than Mattel's stock does.

Although analysts and investors use a stock return's standard deviation as an important and common measure of risk, it's laborious to compute by hand. Most people use a spreadsheet or statistical software to calculate stock return standard deviations.

EXAMPLE 9-2

LG9-1, 9-3

Risk and Return

Find the average return and risk (as measured by standard deviation) for Mattel since 2003. Table 9.3 shows the annual returns for years 2003 to 2012.

For interactive versions of this example visit www.mhhe.com/can3e

SOLUTION:

First, *compute the average annual return* for the period. Using equation 9-3:

$$\frac{-3.5\% + 5.4\% - 12.6\% + 52.1\% - 10.5\% - 28.5\% + 44.3\% + 24.0\% + 35.6\% + 25.9\%}{10} = \frac{132\%}{10} = 13.2\%$$

Mattel has averaged a 13.2 percent return per year since 2002. To compute the risk, use the standard deviation equation 9-5. First, find the deviations of return for each year:

Year 2003	2004	2005	2006	2007	2008	2009	2010	2011	2012
−3.5% − 13.2%	5.4% − 13.2%	−12.6% − 13.2%	52.1% − 13.2%	−10.5% − 13.2%	−28.5% − 13.2%	44.3% − 13.2%	24.0% − 13.2%	35.6% − 13.2%	25.9% − 13.2%

Square those deviations:

Year 2003	2004	2005	2006	2007	2008	2009	2010	2011	2012
$(-3.5\% - 13.2\%)^2$	$(5.4\% - 13.2\%)^2$	$(-12.6\% - 13.2\%)^2$	$(52.1\% - 13.2\%)^2$	$(-10.5\% - 13.2\%)^2$	$(-28.5\% - 13.2\%)^2$	$(44.3\% - 13.2\%)^2$	$(24.0\% - 13.2\%)^2$	$(35.6\% - 13.2\%)^2$	$(25.9\% - 13.2\%)^2$

Then add them up, divide by $n-1$, and take the square root:

$$= \sqrt{\frac{278.7 + 61.8 + 667.3 + 1509.1 + 564.7 + 1740.0 + 968.3 + 116.6 + 501.6 + 161.5}{9}} = \sqrt{6569.5} = 27.0\%$$

Mattel stock has averaged a 13.2 percent return with a standard deviation of 27.0 percent since 2003.

Similar to Problems 9-15, 9-16, 9-17, 9-18, 9-33, 9-34, self-test problem 2

table 9.4 | **Annual Standard Deviation of Returns for Stocks, Bonds, and T-Bills, 1950 to 2012**

	Stocks	Long-Term Treasury Bonds	T-Bills
1950 to 2012	17.5%	10.8%	2.9%
1950 to 1959	19.8	4.9	0.8
1960 to 1969	14.4	6.2	1.3
1970 to 1979	19.2	6.8	1.8
1980 to 1989	12.7	15.1	2.6
1990 to 1999	14.2	12.8	1.2
2000 to 2009	20.4	10.3	1.9

Some decades experience higher risk than others in each asset class.

LG9-2

Risk of Asset Classes

We report the standard deviations of return for stocks, bonds, and T-bills in Table 9.4 for 1950 to 2012 and for each decade since 1950. Over the entire sample, the stock market returns' standard deviation is 17.5 percent. As we would expect, stock market volatility is higher than bond market volatility (10.8 percent) or for T-bills (2.9 percent). These volatility estimates are consistent with our previously stated position that the stock market carries more risk than the bond or cash markets do. Every decade since 1950 has seen a lot of stock market volatility. The bond market experienced the most volatility in the 1980s and 1990s as interest rates varied.

You will recall from Chapter 7 that since any bond's par value and coupon rate are fixed, bond prices must fluctuate to adjust for changes in interest rates. Bond prices respond inversely to interest rate changes: As interest rates rise, bond prices fall, and if interest rates fall, bond prices rise. T-bill returns have experienced very low volatility over each decade. Indeed, T-bills are commonly considered to be one of the only risk-free assets. Higher-risk investments offer higher returns over time. But short-term fluctuations in the value of higher risk investments can be substantial. The stock market is risky—while it has offered a good annual return of 12.4 percent, that return comes with volatility of 17.5 percent standard deviation. Many investors may intellectually understand that this high risk means that they may receive very poor returns in the short term. Investors really felt the full force of this risk when the stock market declined three years in a row (2000 to 2002). Some investors even decided that this was too much risk for them and they sold out of the stock market before the 2003 rally. Other investors got out of the stock market after it plunged to lows in March 2009. Market volatility can cause investors to make emotionally based decisions—selling at low prices.

The stock market returns' standard deviations that appear in Table 9.4 are all considerably lower than the standard deviations of Mattel and of RadioShack stocks (33.8 percent and 41.0 percent, respectively). In this case, we measure stock market return and standard deviation using the S&P 500 Index. Mattel and RadioShack are both included in the S&P 500 Index. Why do these two large firms have measures of total risk—standard deviations—that are at least twice as large as the standard deviations on the stock market returns? Are Mattel and RadioShack just two of the most risky firms in the Index? Actually, no. The differences in standard deviations between these individual companies and the entire market have much more to do with *diversification.* Owning 500 companies, such as all of those included in the S&P 500 Index, generates much less risk than owning just one company. This phenomenon appears in the standard deviation measure. We'll discuss the effects of diversification in detail later in this chapter.

Risk versus Return

LG9-4

Investors can buy very safe T-bills. Or they can take some risk to seek higher returns. How much extra return can you expect for taking more risk? This is known as the *trade-off between risk and return.* The **coefficient of variation** (CoV) is a common *relative* measure of this risk-vs-reward relationship. The equation for the coefficient of variation is simply the standard deviation divided by average return. It is interpreted as the amount of risk (measured by volatility) per unit of return:

coefficient of variation
A measure of risk to reward (standard deviation divided by average return) earned by an investment over a specific period of time.

$$\text{Coefficient of variation} = \text{Amount of risk} \div \text{Return}$$

$$= \frac{\text{Standard deviation}}{\text{Average return}} \quad \textbf{(9-6)}$$

As an investor, you would want to receive a very high return (the denominator in the equation) with a very low risk (the numerator). So, a smaller CoV indicates a better risk-reward relationship. Since the average return and standard deviation for Mattel stock are 16.7 percent and 33.8 percent, its CoV is 2.02 (= 33.8 ÷ 16.7). This is better than RadioShack's CoV of 6.72 (= 41.0 ÷ 6.1). For all asset classes for the period 1950 to 2009, the stock market earned a higher return than bonds and was also riskier. But which one had a better risk-return relationship? The CoV for common stock is 1.41 (= 17.5 ÷ 12.4). For Treasury bonds, the coefficient of variation is 1.59 (= 10.8 ÷ 6.8). Even though stocks are riskier than bonds, they involve a somewhat better risk-reward trade-off.

EXAMPLE 9-3

LG 9-4

For interactive versions of this example visit www.mhhe.com/can3e

Risk versus Return

You are interested in the risk-return relationship of stocks in each decade since 1950. Obtain the average returns and risks in Tables 9.2 and 9.4.

SOLUTION:

Using the coefficient of variation, the average returns, and standard deviation of return, compute the following risk-return relationships:

$$CoV_{1950s} = \frac{19.8\%}{20.9\%} = 0.95 \quad CoV_{1960s} = \frac{14.4\%}{8.7\%} = 1.66$$

$$CoV_{1970s} = \frac{19.2\%}{7.5\%} = 2.56 \quad CoV_{1980s} = \frac{12.7\%}{18.2\%} = 0.70$$

$$CoV_{1990s} = \frac{14.2\%}{19.0\%} = 0.75 \quad CoV_{2000s} = \frac{20.4\%}{0.9\%} = 22.67$$

Note that over short time periods, the stock risk-return relationship varies significantly.

Similar to Problems 9-7, 9-8, 9-19, 9-20, 9-33, and 9-34, self-test problem 3

TIME OUT

9-3 What volatility measure can we use to evaluate and compare risk among different investment alternatives?

9-4 Explain why the coefficients of variation for Mattel and RadioShack are so much higher than the CoV for the stock market as a whole.

portfolio

A combination of investment assets held by an investor.

diversification

The process of putting money in different types of investments for the purpose of reducing the overall risk of the portfolio.

firm-specific risk

The portion of total risk that is attributable to firm or industry factors. Firm-specific risk can be reduced through diversification.

9.3 • Forming Portfolios

As we noted previously, Mattel and RadioShack stocks' risk as measured by their standard deviations appear quite high compared to the standard deviation of the S&P 500 Index. This is by no means a coincidence. Combining stocks into **portfolios** can reduce many sources of stock risk. **Diversification** reduces risk. The S&P 500 Index, for example, tracks 500 companies, which allows for a great deal of diversification.

LG9-5

Diversifying to Reduce Risk

Think about a stock's total risk as having two components. The first component includes risks that are both specific to that company and common to other companies in the same industry. We call this risk **firm-specific risk.** The stock's other risk component is general risk that all firms—and all individuals, for that

table 9.5 Combining Stocks Can Greatly Reduce Risk

	A	B	C	D
1		**RadioShack**	**Mattel**	**Portfolio of RadioShack and Mattel**
2	1985	−7.4%	38.0%	15.3%
3	1986	5.7	19.8	12.7
4	1987	−40.3	−25.6	−32.9
5	1988	45.1	25.1	35.1
6	1989	64.0	−15.4	24.3
7	1990	26.5	−11.3	7.6
8	1991	82.6	−19.0	31.8
9	1992	33.0	10.5	21.7
10	1993	6.9	84.3	45.6
11	1994	15.5	−5.9	4.8
12	1995	59.8	−12.3	23.8
13	1996	10.5	20.5	15.5
14	1997	46.6	73.5	60.0
15	1998	−43.0	40.5	−1.2
16	1999	−52.4	81.9	14.8
17	2000	47.4	13.1	30.3
18	2001	28.8	−42.4	−6.8
19	2002	5.5	−36.1	−15.3
20	2003	−3.5	64.8	30.7
21	2004	5.4	2.4	3.9
22	2005	−12.6	−32.3	−22.4
23	2006	52.1	1.0	26.5
24	2007	−10.5	−20.4	−15.5
25	2008	−28.5	−32.3	−30.4
26	2009	44.3	72.7	58.5
27	2010	24.0	−21.4	1.3
28	2011	35.6	−50.5	−7.4
29	2012	25.9	−52.1	−13.1
30	**Average =**	**16.7**	**6.1**	**11.4**
31	**Std Dev =**	**33.8**	**41.0**	**24.4**
32				

The risk-reducing power of diversification! Note that the risk of the portfolio is lower than the risk of the two stocks individually.

Data Source: Yahoo! Finance

matter—face based upon economic strength both domestically and globally. We call this type of risk **market risk.** These risks appear in the equation

market risk

The portion of total risk that is attributable to overall economic factors.

$$\text{Total risk} = \text{Firm-specific risk} + \text{Market risk} \qquad \textbf{(9-7)}$$

Standard deviations measure total risk. Individual stocks are subject to many firm-specific risks. We can reduce firm-specific risk by combining stocks into a portfolio. Since we can reduce firm-specific risk by diversifying, this risk is sometimes referred to as **diversifiable risk.** If RadioShack announces lower-than-expected profits, its stock price will decline. However, since this news is *specific* to RadioShack, the news should not affect Mattel stock's price. On the other hand, if the government announces a change in unemployment, both stocks' prices will change to some degree. Macroeconomic events represent market risks because such events—unemployment claims, interest rate changes, national budget deficits or surpluses—affect all companies.

diversifiable risk

Another term for firm-specific risk.

Suppose that you own only RadioShack stock and have earned the annual returns shown in Table 9.5. Then someone suggests that you add Mattel to your RadioShack stock to form a two-stock portfolio. Both Mattel and RadioShack stocks carry a lot of total risk. But look at the risk and return characteristics of a portfolio consisting of 50 percent RadioShack stock and 50 percent Mattel

figure 9.1

Adding Stocks to a Portfolio Reduces Risk

The total portfolio risk is greatly reduced by adding the first few stocks to a portfolio.

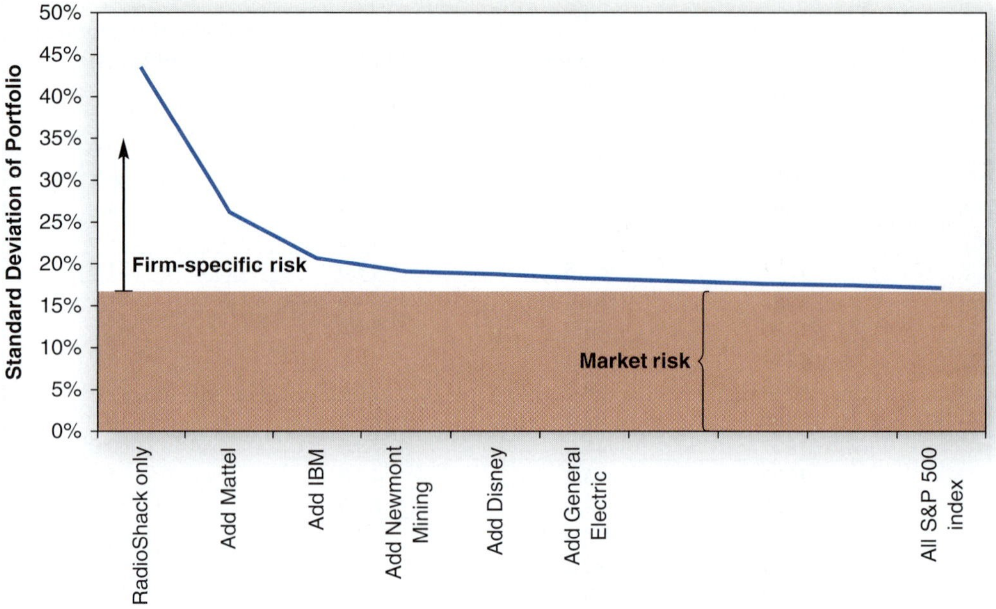

stock. You start with RadioShack stock, which provided an average return of 6.1 percent with a risk of 41.0 percent. The two-stock portfolio earns an average 11.4 percent return with a standard deviation of only 24.4 percent. You added a high-risk stock to a high-risk stock and you ended up with a portfolio with much lower risk! This is a hallmark of most portfolios, which pool market risk but often provide offsetting, reduced firm-specific risks overall.

Next, add IBM stock to your Mattel and RadioShack stock portfolio. Figure 9.1 shows that the total risk of this three-stock portfolio declines to 20.8 percent. Note that adding Newmont Mining, Disney, and General Electric also reduces the total risk of the stock portfolio. As you add more stocks, the firm-specific risk portion of the total portfolio risk declines. The total risk falls rapidly as we add the first few stocks. Diversification's power to reduce firm-specific risk weakens for the later stocks added to the portfolio, because we have already eliminated much of the firm-specific risk. We could continue to add stocks until the portfolio comprises all S&P 500 Index firms, in which case the standard deviation of the portfolio would be 17.9 percent. At this point, virtually all of the firm-specific risk has been purged and the portfolio carries only market risk, which is sometimes called **nondiversifiable risk.**

nondiversifiable risk
Another term for market risk.

LG9-6

Modern Portfolio Theory

modern portfolio theory
A concept and procedure for combining securities into a portfolio to minimize risk.

optimal portfolio
The best portfolio of securities for the investor's level of risk aversion.

The concept that diversification reduces risk was formalized in the early 1950s by Harry Markowitz, who eventually won the Nobel Prize in Economics for his work. Markowitz's **modern portfolio theory** shows how risk reduction occurs when securities are combined. The theory also describes how to combine stocks to achieve the lowest total risk possible for a given expected return. Or, said differently, it describes how to achieve the highest expected return for the desired risk level. The combination of securities that achieves the highest expected return for a given risk level is called the investor's **optimal portfolio.**

In our Mattel and RadioShack portfolio example, we allocated 50 percent of the portfolio to Mattel and 50 percent to RadioShack. Is this the best allocation

finance at work — personal

INVESTOR DIVERSIFICATION PROBLEMS

Experts have examined investor behavior using detailed datasets of stock brokerage accounts, employee pension plans, and the Survey of Consumer Finances. Studies have identified many investor behaviors that are inconsistent with the principle of full diversification:

- Many households own relatively few individual stocks—they held a median number of two stocks until 2001, when it rose to three. Of course, many households own equity indirectly, through mutual funds or retirement accounts, and these indirect holdings tend to be much better diversified.
- Ten to 15 percent of households with between $100,000 and $1 million in financial asset wealth own no stocks (neither directly nor indirectly through funds).
- Investors seem to prefer securities of local firms. Many geographic regions feature companies that are heavily concentrated in few industries. Thus, a local preference could reduce diversification opportunities.
- Many employees hold mostly their employers' stocks (more than 50 percent of employee holdings), particularly within their 401(k) retirement savings accounts. Holding a lot of a single stock creates a "portfolio" with high total risk.

Finance professionals and the investment industry have established diversification concepts for many decades and can help investors maximize their returns with appropriate risk levels. But many investors do not consult professionals; they fail to diversify and thus take unnecessary diversifiable risk.

Sources: John Y. Campbell, "Household Finance," *Journal of Finance* 61 (2006): 1553–1604; Valery Polkovichenko, "Household Portfolio Diversification: A Case for Rank-Dependent Preferences," *Review of Financial Studies* 18 (2005): 1467–1500; and Shlomo Benartzi, Richard Thaler, Stephen Utkus, and Cass Sunstein, "The Law and Economics of Company Stock in 401(k) Plans," *Journal of Law and Economics* 50 (2007):45–79.

want to know more? Key Words to Search for Updates: diversification, pension plan choices, asset allocation

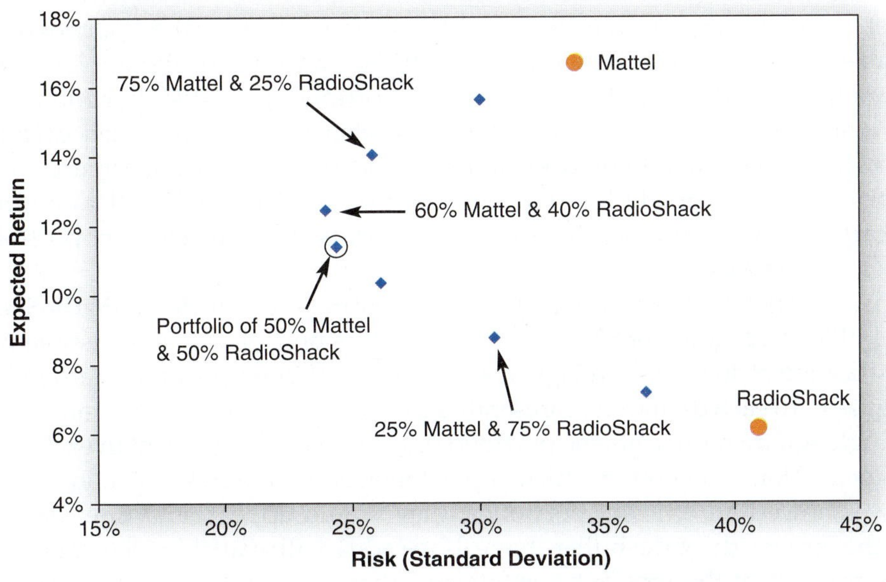

figure 9.2

Risk and Return Ramifications of Portfolio Allocations to Mattel and RadioShack

Investors only value the portfolios at the top of the graph because they offer the same risk as the lower portfolios but with higher expected return!

for the portfolio? Consider the different allocations shown in Figure 9.2 for the two stocks. The graph shows the expected return (computed as average return) and risk (computed as standard deviation) of various portfolios. It would be terrific if you could find a portfolio located in the upper left-hand corner. That is, investors would like a high expected return with low risk. One large dot shows

figure 9.3

Efficient Portfolios from Four Stocks

The efficient portfolios dominate all of the individual stocks.

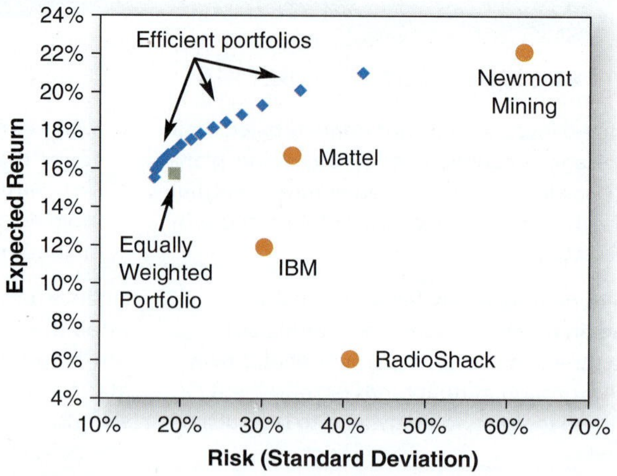

the risk-return point for owning only Mattel. The other large dot shows owning only RadioShack. The smaller diamonds show 10/90, 25/75, 40/60, 50/50, 60/40, 75/25, and 90/10 allocations of Mattel/RadioShack stocks.

While all these portfolios are possible, not all are desirable. For example, the portfolio of 25 percent Mattel and 75 percent RadioShack is not desirable. Other portfolios provide *both* higher return and lower risk. We say that one portfolio dominates the other if it has higher expected return for the same (or less) risk, or the same (or higher) expected return with lower risk. The dominating portfolios appear higher and to the left in the figure. One such portfolio consists of 75 percent Mattel stock and 25 percent RadioShack stock. The 50/50 portfolio (circled in the figure) is also better than the 25/75 portfolio. However, the 50/50 portfolio isn't desirable because a portfolio with slightly higher return and slightly lower risk appears above and to the left of the 50/50 portfolio: the 60/40 portfolio. Portfolios with the highest return possible for each risk level are called **efficient portfolios.** Notice that if you drew a line connecting the dots, the figure would appear like the end of a bullet. The portfolios on the top of the bullet dominate the portfolios on the bottom; the top portfolio dots show the efficient portfolios for these two stocks.

efficient portfolios

The set of portfolios that have the maximum expected return for each level of risk.

Figure 9.3 shows efficient portfolios for combining the four stocks: RadioShack, Mattel, IBM, and Newmont Mining. We used this portfolio to demonstrate how diversification reduces risk in Figure 9.1. These portfolios appear as diamonds in the figure with each diamond representing a different allocation of the four stocks. The single square represents the portfolio that consists of 25 percent in each of the four stocks. Notice that other, efficient portfolios dominate this portfolio.

If we showed all efficient portfolios, they would appear as a line that connects the upper side of the bullet shape. If we added all available securities to the graph, then all of the efficient portfolios of those securities form the **efficient frontier.** Efficient frontier portfolios dominate all other possible stock portfolios. The shape of the efficient frontier implies that diminishing returns apply to risk-taking in the investment world. To gain ever-higher expected rates of return, investors must be willing to take on ever-increasing amounts of risk. The optimal portfolio for you is one on the efficient frontier that reflects the amount of risk that you're willing to take. Clearly, optimal portfolio choice depends on individual risk preferences. Highly risk-averse investors will select low-risk portfolios on the efficient frontier, while more adventuresome investors will select

efficient frontier

The combination of all efficient portfolios.

figure 9.4

Efficient Portfolios from Four Stocks

Combining stocks that move together over time does not offer much risk reduction. Combining stocks that do not move together provides a lot of risk reduction.

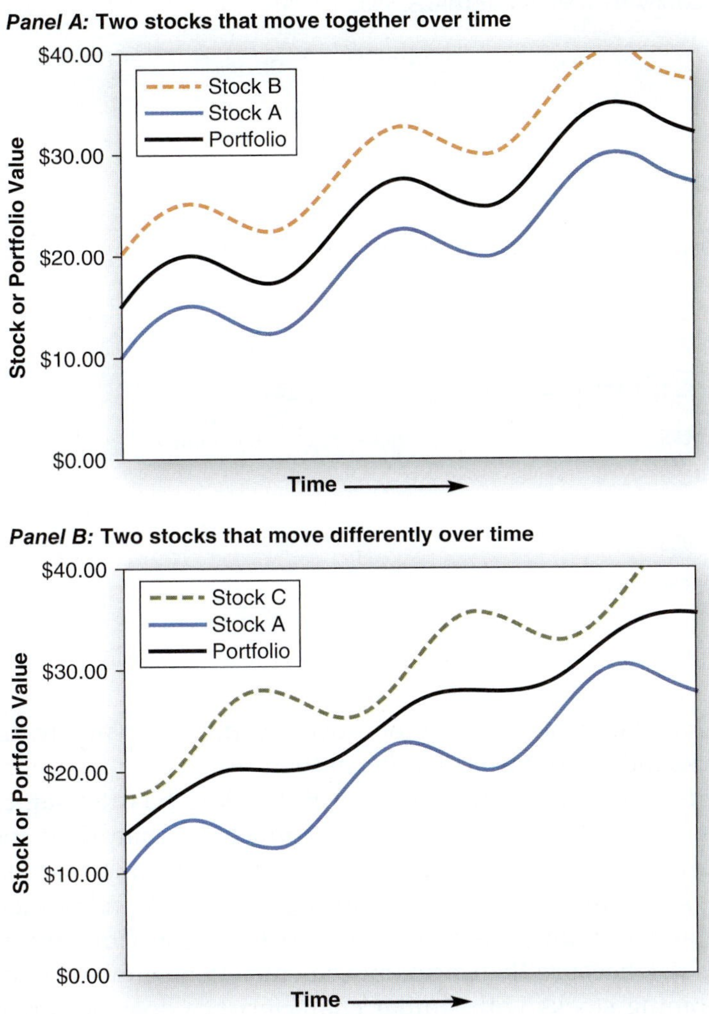

higher-risk portfolios. Any choice may be appropriate, given differences in individual risk preferences.

Investors can further diversify by adding foreign stocks and commodities to their portfolio. For example, a U.S. investor can lower total risk by adding stocks from emerging market countries and gold.

LG9-5

HOW DOES DIVERSIFICATION WORK? Will combining any two stocks greatly reduce total risk as much as combining RadioShack and Mattel did? The answer is no. If two stocks are subject to exactly the same kinds of events such that their returns always behave the same way over time, then we have no need to own both stocks—simply pick the one that performs better. Diversification comes when two stocks are subject to different kinds of events such that their returns differ over time.

Consider the illustration in Figure 9.4. You own Stock A in Panel A of the figure. The stock features risk, as demonstrated by its price volatility over time. You would like to reduce the risk by combining your position in Stock A with an equal position in Stock B. In this case, the alternative stock, Stock B, moves the same way over time as Stock A does. When Stock A goes up, so does Stock B. They also decline together. A portfolio of both stocks is illustrated. Notice how

table 9.6 | **Correlation between Various Stocks and Asset Classes**

PANEL A: COMPANY ANNUAL RETURNS, 1985 TO 2012							
	RadioShack	**Mattel**	**IBM**	**Newmont Mining**	**Disney**	**General Electric**	**Citigroup**
RadioShack	1						
Mattel	−0.157	1					
IBM	0.338	−0.125	1				
Newmont Mining	−0.029	−0.130	−0.199	1			
Disney	0.325	0.352	0.004	0.228	1		
General Electric	0.565	0.238	0.337	0.002	0.542	1	
Citigroup	0.400	0.348	0.042	−0.126	0.321	0.784	1
Bank of New York	0.269	0.472	0.071	−0.306	0.438	0.644	0.649

PANEL B: ASSET CLASS ANNUAL RETURNS, 1950 TO 2012			
	Stocks	**Long-Term Treasury Bonds**	**T-Bills**
Stocks	1		
Long-term Treasury bonds	−0.014	1	
T-bills	−0.053	0.132	1

Correlation shows that some stocks move together and some do not.

the portfolio has the same volatility of Stocks A and B separately. Combining these two stocks did not reduce volatility, or total risk.

Now consider Stock C, shown in Panel B. Stock C has the same volatility as Stock A, but its price moves in different directions than does the price of Stock A. When Stock A's price increases, Stock C's price increases sometimes and decreases sometimes. As shown, a portfolio of Stock A and Stock C features much lower volatility than either Stock A or Stock C alone. Combining Stocks A and C reduces risk because their price movements often counteract one another. In short, combining stocks with similar characteristics does not provide much diversification and thus risk reduction. Combining stocks with many differences does provide diversification and thus lowers risk.

correlation

A measurement of the co-movement between two variables that ranges between −1 and +1.

The ways that stocks co-move over time determines how much diversification and thus risk reduction we can achieve by combining them. So what we need is some measure of co-movement to help investors form diversified portfolios. That measure, called **correlation,** is denoted by the Greek letter ρ (rho). Correlation is a statistical measure with some very useful characteristics that makes it easy to interpret. Its value is bounded between −1 and +1. A correlation value of +1 means that returns from two different securities move perfectly in sync. They change lock-step up and down together. A value of −1 means that returns from two securities are perfectly inversely correlated—they move exactly opposite. A value of 0 means that the movements of the two returns over time are unrelated to one another. Investors seeking diversification look for stocks where the returns have low or negative correlations with each other.

What return correlations are common between stocks? Panel A of Table 9.6 shows the correlations between many companies. One high correlation shown is the 0.649 correlation between Citigroup and the Bank of New York. This shouldn't be surprising, because these are two similar firms in the same industry. Combining these two stocks wouldn't reduce risk very much in a portfolio. The largest negative correlation is the correlation of −0.306 between Newmont Mining and the Bank of New York. These firms practice in very different industries and provide large risk reduction possibilities. Note that the correlation between RadioShack and Mattel is −0.157. This negative correlation gives us an

finance at work — markets

INTERNATIONAL OPPORTUNITIES FOR DIVERSIFICATION

The U.S. stock market represents nearly 47 percent of all stock value worldwide. Japanese and U.K. stock markets represent 11 percent and 8 percent of the worldwide stock market value, respectively. Many investment and diversification opportunities present themselves internationally! However, most people allocate very little or none of their portfolios to international securities. If worldwide opportunities can create greater diversification, then those who don't invest in international stocks miss out on an important opportunity to reduce risk in their portfolios.

MSCI Barra is the leading provider of global stock market indexes. Some MSCI Barra indexes follow individual countries. In addition, MSCI Barra compiles composite indexes for groups of companies in developed markets, emerging markets, frontier markets, and by geographic regions. Investment managers use the MSCI World Index, the MSCI EAFE (Europe, Australasia, Far East) Index, and the MSCI Emerging Markets Index as premier benchmarks to measure global stock market performance.

The following table shows the average annual returns and standard deviations for the U.S. stock market, Treasury bonds, and the MSCI EAFE and MSCI Emerging Markets indexes for the period 1988 to 2012. Note that both the EAFE and the Emerging Markets indexes feature higher risk than the S&P 500 Index. The Emerging Markets return has been high, but the EAFE return has been low compared to the U.S. stock and bond markets.

	S&P 500	Bonds	EAFE	Emerging Markets
Average	11.2%	9.8%	5.7%	15.7%
Std. Deviation	18.0	11.1	20.2	34.9

The correlations among these markets appear as follows:

	S&P 500	Bonds	EAFE	Emerging Markets
S&P 500	1			
Bonds	−0.11	1		
EAFE	0.73	−0.39	1	
Emerging Markets	0.51	−0.40	0.76	1

The correlation between the S&P 500 Index and the MSCI EAFE is 0.73 and between the Emerging Markets is 0.51. These correlations indicate that diversification might work. Even better diversification appears to be possible between the U.S. Treasury Bond Market and the EAFE and Emerging Markets indexes—look at the negative correlations!

Source: www.mscibarra.com

want to know more? Key Words to Search for Updates: international diversification, global asset allocation

answer to the question of why total risk (in the form of standard deviations) fell so much when we combined the two stocks relative to their individual standard deviations as shown in Figure 9.2. Most of the correlations in Table 9.6 are positive. Because most stocks are positively correlated, we typically add many stocks together to fully eliminate all the firm-specific risk in the portfolio, as we showed in Figure 9.1.

Panel B of Table 9.6 shows correlations between stocks, bonds, and T-bills. At −0.014, the correlation between stocks and bonds is small. The small correlation allows for the possibility of good risk reduction by adding bonds to a stock portfolio. Therefore, a well-diversified portfolio will contain both stocks and bonds. LG9-2

PORTFOLIO RETURN A portfolio's return calculation is straightforward. A portfolio's return comes directly from the returns of the portfolio securities and the proportion of the portfolio invested in each security. For example, General Electric stock earned −1.9 percent. The Newmont Mining earned 17.3 percent over the same period. If you had invested a quarter of your money in General Electric stock and three quarters of it in Newmont Mining stock, then your portfolio return would be: LG9-7

$$\text{Return contribution from GE} + \text{Contribution from NEM}$$
$$= (0.25 \times -1.9\%) + (0.75 \times 17.3\%) = 12.50\%$$

To calculate the return on a three-stock portfolio, you will need the proportion of each stock in the portfolio and each stock's return. We typically call these proportions *weights*, signified by w. So, a portfolio with n securities will have a return of

$$R_p = (\text{Proportion of portfolio in first stock} \times \text{That stock's return}) + (\text{Second stock portion} \times \text{Second stock return}) + \cdots$$

$$= (w_1 \times R_1) + (w_2 \times R_2) + (w_3 \times R_3) + \cdots + (w_n \times R_n) = \sum_{i=1}^{n} w_i R_i \quad \textbf{(9-8)}$$

MATH COACH

When computing portfolio returns, use the decimal format for the portfolio weights and the percentage format for the security returns. The result of equation 9-8 will then be in percentage format.

where the sum of the weights, w, must equal one. The portfolio's rate of return is a simple weighted sum of the returns of each stock in the portfolio. Investors choose portfolio weights by determining how much of each stock they want in their portfolios. Ideally, investors will choose weights for their portfolios located on the efficient frontier (shown in Figure 9.3).

EXAMPLE 9-4

LG 9-7

For interactive versions of this example visit www.mhhe.com/can3e

Computing Portfolio Returns

At the beginning of the year, you owned $5,000 of Disney stock, $10,000 of Bank of New York stock, and $15,000 of IBM stock. During the year, Disney, Bank of New York, and IBM returned −4.8 percent, 19.4 percent, and 12.8 percent, respectively. What is your portfolio's return?

SOLUTION:

First determine your portfolio weights. The three stocks make up a $30,000 portfolio. Disney makes up a 16.67 percent (= $5,000 ÷ $30,000) portion of the portfolio. Bank of New York stock makes up a 33.33 percent (=$10,000 ÷ $30,000) portion, and IBM a 50.0 percent (=$15,000 ÷ $30,000) portion. The portfolio return can now be computed as:

$$R_P = (0.1667 \times -4.8\%) + (0.3333 \times 19.4\%) + (0.50 \times 12.8\%) = -0.80\% + 6.47\% + 6.40\% = 12.07\%$$

Similar to Problems 9-11, 9-12, 9-13, 9-14, 9-23, 9-24, 9-25, 9-26, 9-29, 9-30, 9-31, 9-32, self-test problem 1

TIME OUT

9-5 Describe characteristics of companies that would be good to combine into a portfolio.

9-6 Explain why one portfolio made up of the same companies (but not in the same proportions) as another portfolio can be undesirable in comparison.

9-7 Combining which two companies in Table 9.6 would reduce risk the most? Combining which two would create the least diversification?

viewpoints REVISITED

Business Application Solution

We can apply diversification concepts and modern portfolio theory to many more applications than just investment portfolios. For example, a manufacturing facility can be more efficient by producing different products during the year as demand dictates the need for one product over another. Salespeople can reduce the volatility of their commission incomes by having many different products to sell.

Although new project ideas have more risk, they could actually reduce the firm's overall risk if the projects diversify the firm's current business operations. You could evaluate this possibility by determining the correlation between the expected cash flows from each project idea with the expected cash flows of the firm's current business operations. A low or negative correlation would mean that the new projects could actually reduce risk for the firm. Note that some firms may find that their position is too conservative and that they wish to increase their risk to increase the possibility of earning a higher return.

Personal Application Solution

Since 1950, Tables 9.2 and 9.4 show that the bond market experienced an average return and standard deviation of 6.8 percent and 10.8 percent, respectively. Stocks earned a 12.4 percent return with a 17.5 percent standard deviation. The investor is correct in the belief that the stock market is riskier than the bond market.

However, Table 9.6 shows that the correlation between the stock and bond market is very low, at −0.014. This result allows some diversification opportunity. Indeed, a portfolio of 10 percent stocks and 90 percent bonds would have experienced an average annual return of 7.3 percent with a standard deviation of 9.9 percent since 1950. The broker is correct; adding a small portion of stocks to a bond portfolio actually reduces total risk!

summary of learning goals

In this chapter, we described how to measure investment risk and return. In the long run, higher risk should be associated with higher returns. In the short term, though, high-risk investments experience a great deal of volatility and produce extreme returns. Recall that the market does not reward all risks. We can, for example, reduce firm-specific risk by diversifying our holdings. We get the best diversification opportunities when we combine securities that have very different return characteristics.

LG9-1 Compute an investment's dollar and percentage return. Dollar returns on an investment include both the capital gain (or loss) from any price change in the investment and any income received. Stocks pay dividend income and fixed income securities, such as bonds, pay regularly scheduled interest payments as income. We can find the percentage return by dividing the dollar return by the investment's value at the beginning of the period. Percentage return is a more useful measure to compare performance among different securities. To make meaningful comparisons, we typically average annual percentage returns to assess the investment's historical performance.

LG9-2 Find information about the historical returns and volatility for the stock, bond, and cash markets. Stocks have earned an average 12.4 percent return per year since 1950. However, stock market performance can be very volatile. Investors have frequently seen double-digit percentage stock price declines as well as spectacular increases. This high volatility is illustrated by the stock market's standard deviation of 17.5 percent on average returns of 12.4 percent.

Bonds have earned lower average returns of 6.8 percent annually, but have also experienced less risk (standard deviation of 10.8 percent). The cash market, as measured by T-bill performance, shows an average return and standard deviation of 4.6 percent and 2.9 percent, respectively.

LG9-3 **Measure and evaluate the total risk of an investment using several methods.** An investment's total risk encompasses the total range of expected outcomes. We measure the likelihood of any particular expected outcome by the past return volatility of the security. We calculate volatility using the statistical concept of the standard deviation of returns. A larger standard deviation indicates higher total risk.

LG9-4 **Recognize the risk-return relationship and its implications.** When low-return, safe investments are available, why would an investor take risk? The motivation for taking on riskier investments is that they offer a higher return. The performance and risk of the stock and bond markets over a long period of time illustrate the direct risk-return relationship that lies at the heart of investment philosophy. Recognize that this relationship can be interpreted in the reverse. When an investment achieves a high return, know that it must be risky.

We commonly measure the risk-return relationship using the coefficient of variation (CoV). The CoV is the standard deviation of an investment's returns divided by its average return. The CoV reports the amount of risk taken for every 1 percent of return earned. So lower CoV values indicate more favorable risk-return relationships.

LG9-5 **Plan investments that take advantage of diversification and its impact on total risk.** Recall that an investment's total risk comprises firm-specific risk and market risk. Combining stocks can potentially reduce firm-specific risk in the portfolio. Firms whose returns differ from each other offer the best diversification possibilities. A correlation measures how two different stocks have performed over time relative to one another. Correlations range between −1 and +1. Combining stocks with low or negative correlations can significantly reduce firm-specific risk and thus reduce total risk in an investor's portfolio.

LG9-6 **Find efficient and optimal portfolios.** Investors want the highest return possible for their preferred risk level. If two portfolios have the same risk level, the one that gives the higher expected return dominates the other. A portfolio that has the highest expected return for its risk level dominates all other portfolios with same risk level; we call this dominating mix an efficient portfolio. The set of all efficient portfolios forms the efficient frontier. Investors pick the efficient portfolio with their own desired risk level to find their optimal portfolios.

LG9-7 **Compute a portfolio's return.** A portfolio's return comes directly from the returns of the securities in the portfolio and the proportions, or weights, of each investment in the portfolio. In other words, the portfolio return is the weighted average of the portfolio's securities' returns.

chapter equations

9-1 $$\text{Dollar return} = (\text{Capital gain or loss}) + \text{Income} = (\text{Ending value} - \text{Beginning value}) + \text{Income}$$

9-2 $$\text{Percentage return} = \frac{\text{Ending value} - \text{Beginning value} + \text{Income}}{\text{Beginning value}} \times 100\%$$

9-3 $$\text{Average return} = \frac{\sum_{t=1}^{N} \text{Return}_t}{N}$$

9-4 $$\text{Geometric mean return} = \left[\prod_{t=1}^{N}\left(1 + \frac{\text{Return}_t}{100}\right)\right]^{\frac{1}{N}} - 1$$

9-5 $$\text{Standard deviation} = \sqrt{\frac{\sum_{t=1}^{N}(\text{Return}_t - \text{Average return})^2}{N-1}}$$

9-6 $$\text{Coefficient of variation} = \frac{\text{Standard deviation}}{\text{Average return}}$$

$$\textbf{9-7} \quad \text{Total risk} = \text{Firm-specific risk} + \text{Market risk}$$

$$\textbf{9-8} \quad R_p = (w_1 \times R_1) + (w_2 \times R_2) + (w_3 \times R_3) + \cdots + (w_n \times R_n) = \sum_{i=1}^{n} w_i R_i$$

key terms

average returns, A measure summarizing the past performance of an investment. *p. 309*

coefficient of variation, A measure of risk to reward (standard deviation divided by average return) earned by an investment over a specific period of time. *p. 315*

correlation, A measurement of the co-movement between two variables that ranges between −1 and +1. *p. 322*

diversification, The process of putting money in different types of investments for the purpose of reducing the overall risk of the portfolio. *p. 316*

diversifiable risk, Another term for firm-specific risk. *p. 317*

dollar return, The amount of profit or loss from an investment denoted in dollars. *p. 308*

efficient frontier, The combination of all efficient portfolios. *p. 320*

efficient portfolios, The set of portfolios that have the maximum expected return for each level of risk. *p. 320*

firm-specific risk, The portion of total risk that is attributable to firm or industry factors. Firm-specific risk can be reduced through diversification. *p. 316*

geometric mean return, The mean return computed by finding the equivalent return that is compounded for *N* periods. *p. 310*

market risk, The portion of total risk that is attributable to overall economic factors. *p. 317*

modern portfolio theory, A concept and procedure for combining securities into a portfolio to minimize risk. *p. 318*

nondiversifiable risk, Another term for market risk. *p. 318*

optimal portfolio, The best portfolio of securities for the investor's level of risk aversion. *p. 318*

percentage return, The dollar return characterized as a percentage of money invested. *p. 308*

portfolio, A combination of investment assets held by an investor. *p. 316*

standard deviation, A measure of past return volatility, or risk, of an investment. *p. 312*

total risk, The volatility of an investment, which includes current portions of firm-specific risk and market risk. *p. 312*

self-test problems with solutions

LG 9-1, 9-7

1 Computing Returns Consider that you own the following position at the beginning of the year: 200 shares of US Bancorp at \$29.89 per share, 300 shares of Micron Technology at \$13.31 per share, and 250 shares of Hilton Hotels at \$24.11 per share. During the year, US Bancorp and Hilton Hotels both paid a dividend of \$1.39 and \$0.16, respectively. At the end of the year, the stock prices of US Bancorp, Micron, and Hilton Hotels were \$36.19, \$13.12, and \$34.90, respectively. What are the dollar and percentage return of the stocks and the return of the portfolio?

Solution:

You can compute the dollar and percentage returns as:

$$\begin{aligned}
\text{US Bancorp dollar return} &= 200 \times (\$36.19 - \$29.89 + \$1.39) = \$1{,}538.00 \\
\text{Percent return} &= \$1{,}538.00 \div (200 \times \$29.89) = 25.73\% \\
\text{Micron dollar return} &= 300 \times (\$13.12 - \$13.31) = \$\,-57.00 \\
\text{Percent return} &= \$\,-57.00 \div (300 \times \$13.31) = -1.43\% \\
\text{Hilton Hotels dollar return} &= 250 \times (\$34.90 - \$24.11 + \$0.16) = \$2{,}737.50 \\
\text{Percent return} &= \$2{,}737.50 \div (250 \times \$24.11) = 45.42\%
\end{aligned}$$

Now you need the portfolio weights of each stock. The total value of the portfolio at the beginning of the year was:

$$\text{Beginning of year value} = 200 \times \$29.89 + 300 \times \$13.31 + 250 \times \$24.11 = \$15{,}998.50$$

So the stock weights are:

$$\text{US Bancorp weight} = 200 \times \$29.89 \div \$15{,}998.50 = 0.3737$$
$$\text{Micron weight} = 300 \times \$13.31 \div \$15{,}998.50 = 0.2496$$
$$\text{Hilton Hotels weight} = 250 \times \$24.11 \div \$15{,}998.50 = 0.3768$$

Now compute the portfolio return as:

$$\text{Portfolio return} = 0.3737 \times 25.73\% + 0.2496 \times -1.43\% + 0.3768 \times 45.42\% = 26.37\%$$

LG 9-3, 9-5

2 **Risk and Returns** The annual returns for GlaxoSmithKline and for Aetna are show in the table.

	GlaxoSmithKline	Aetna
Year 1	7.94%	−8.34%
Year 2	9.87	51.28
Year 3	5.63	84.70
Year 4	28.73	64.49
Year 5	−21.59	24.70

What is the average return and standard deviation of returns for these two firms? What is the average return and risk of a portfolio consisting of 75 percent of GlaxoSmithKline and 25 percent Aetna?

Solution:

Using the average and standard deviation equations for the GlaxoSmithKline returns results in:

$$\text{Average} = \frac{7.94\% + 9.87\% + 5.63\% + 28.73\% - 21.59\%}{5} = \frac{30.58\%}{5} = 6.12\%$$

Standard deviation =

$$\sqrt{\frac{(7.94\% - 6.12\%)^2 + (9.87\% - 6.12\%)^2 + (5.63\% - 6.12\%)^2 + (28.73\% - 6.12\%)^2 + (-21.59\% - 6.12\%)^2}{5 - 1}}$$
$$= \sqrt{324.00} = 18.00\%$$

For the portfolio, to compute the return for the portfolio each year, use the 75 percent and 25 percent weights:

$$0.75 \times 7.94\% + 0.25 \times -8.34\% = 3.87\%.$$

The risk and return of these two stocks and the portfolio are:

	GlaxoSmithKline	Aetna	75/25 Portfolio
Year 1	7.94%	−8.34%	3.87%
Year 2	9.87	51.28	20.22
Year 3	5.63	84.70	25.40
Year 4	28.73	64.49	37.67
Year 5	−21.59	24.70	−10.02
Average	6.12	43.37	15.43
Std. deviation	18.00	36.19	18.70

This combination of the two stocks forms a portfolio that is only slightly riskier than GlaxoSmithKline alone, but earns more than twice the return of GlaxoSmithKline.

3 **Risk versus Return** You have gathered average return and standard deviation data for five stocks (A–E). How have these stocks performed on a risk-versus-return basis? Compute the coefficient of variation for each one. LG9-4

Annual Return	Company A	B	C	D	E
Average	13%	14%	9%	11%	9%
Standard deviation	35	44	18	25	30

Solution:

Compute the CoVs as:

$$CoV_A = \frac{35\%}{13\%} = 2.69 \quad CoV_B = \frac{44\%}{14\%} = 3.14$$

$$CoV_C = \frac{18\%}{9\%} = 2.00 \quad CoV_D = \frac{25\%}{11\%} = 2.27$$

$$CoV_E = \frac{30\%}{9\%} = 3.33$$

Since lower values represent a better risk-reward trade-off, the stocks can be ordered from best to worst as C, D, A, B, and E.

4 **Diversification Opportunities** You have also computed the correlation between each of the five stocks in ST-3. These correlations are reported in the following table. Assess which stocks should be combined into a portfolio. LG9-5

Correlations	A	B	C	D
B	0.45			
C	0.32	0.25		
D	0.11	−0.18	0.33	
E	0.20	−0.07	0.35	0.95

Solution:

First, note that stocks D and E do not seem to provide much diversification potential with each other because they have a correlation of nearly 1, at 0.95. They also have similar correlations with the other stocks. For example, stock D has a correlation with stock C of 0.33 while stock E has a correlation with stock C of 0.35. Realize that you gain very little in owning both stock D and stock E. Therefore, select stock D for the portfolio because it has exhibited a better risk-reward relationship (see ST-3). Also note that all of the other stocks appear to have reasonably low correlations with one another and therefore would benefit a portfolio. You should look into forming a portfolio of stocks A, B, C, and D.

questions

1. Why is the percentage return a more useful measure than the dollar return? *(LG9-1)*
2. Characterize the historical return, risk, and risk-return relationship of the stock, bond, and cash markets. *(LG9-2)*
3. How do we define risk in this chapter and how do we measure it? *(LG9-3)*

4. What are the two components of total risk? Which component is part of the risk-return relationship? Why? *(LG9-3)*
5. What's the source of firm-specific risk? What's the source of market risk? *(LG9-3)*
6. Which company is likely to have lower total risk, General Electric or Coca-Cola? Why? *(LG9-3)*
7. Can a company change its total risk level over time? How? *(LG9-3)*
8. What does the coefficient of variation measure? Why is a lower value better for the investor? *(LG9-4)*
9. You receive an investment newsletter advertisement in the mail. The letter claims that you should invest in a stock that has doubled the return of the S&P 500 Index over the last three months. It also claims that this stock is a surefire safe bet for the future. Explain how these two claims are inconsistent with finance theory. *(LG9-4)*
10. What does diversification do to the risk and return characteristics of a portfolio? *(LG9-5)*
11. Describe the diversification potential of two assets with a −0.8 correlation. What's the potential if the correlation is +0.8? *(LG9-5)*
12. You are a risk-averse investor with a low-risk portfolio of bonds. How is it possible that adding some stocks (which are riskier than bonds) to the portfolio can lower the total risk of the portfolio? *(LG9-5)*
13. You own only two stocks in your portfolio but want to add more. When you add a third stock, the total risk of your portfolio declines. When you add a tenth stock to the portfolio, the total risk declines. Adding which stock, the third or the tenth, likely reduced the total risk more? Why? *(LG9-5)*
14. Many employees believe that their employer's stock is less likely to lose half of its value than a well-diversified portfolio of stocks. Explain why this belief is erroneous. *(LG9-5)*
15. Explain what we mean when we say that one portfolio dominates another portfolio. *(LG9-6)*
16. Explain what the efficient frontier is and why it is important to investors. *(LG9-6)*
17. If an investor's desired risk level changes over time, should the investor change the composition of his or her portfolio? How? *(LG9-6)*
18. Say you own 200 shares of Mattel and 100 shares of RadioShack. Would your portfolio return be different if you instead owned 100 shares of Mattel and 200 shares of RadioShack? Why? *(LG9-7)*

problems

basic problems

9-1 **Investment Return** FedEx Corp. stock ended the previous year at $103.39 per share. It paid a $0.35 per share dividend last year. It ended last year at $106.69. If you owned 200 shares of FedEx, what was your dollar return and percent return? *(LG9-1)*

9-2 **Investment Return** Sprint Nextel Corp. stock ended the previous year at $23.36 per share. It paid a $2.37 per share dividend last year. It ended last year at $18.89. If you owned 500 shares of Sprint, what was your dollar return and percent return? *(LG9-1)*

9-3 **Investment Return** A corporate bond that you own at the beginning of the year is worth $975. During the year, it pays $35 in interest payments and ends the year valued at $965. What was your dollar return and percent return? *(LG9-1)*

9-4 **Investment Return** A Treasury bond that you own at the beginning of the year is worth $1,055. During the year, it pays $35 in interest payments and ends the year valued at $1,065. What was your dollar return and percent return? *(LG9-1)*

9-5 **Total Risk** Rank the following three stocks by their level of total risk, highest to lowest. Rail Haul has an average return of 12 percent and standard deviation of 25 percent. The average return and standard deviation of Idol Staff are 15 percent and 35 percent; and of Poker-R-Us are 9 percent and 20 percent. *(LG9-3)*

9-6 **Total Risk** Rank the following three stocks by their total risk level, highest to lowest. Night Ryder has an average return of 12 percent and standard deviation of 32 percent. The average return and standard deviation of WholeMart are 11 percent and 25 percent; and of Fruit Fly are 16 percent and 40 percent. *(LG9-3)*

9-7 **Risk versus Return** Rank the following three stocks by their risk-return relationship, best to worst. Rail Haul has an average return of 12 percent and standard deviation of 25 percent. The average return and standard deviation of Idol Staff are 15 percent and 35 percent; and of Poker-R-Us are 9 percent and 20 percent. *(LG9-4)*

9-8 **Risk versus Return** Rank the following three stocks by their risk-return relationship, best to worst. Night Ryder has an average return of 13 percent and standard deviation of 29 percent. The average return and standard deviation of WholeMart are 11 percent and 25 percent; and of Fruit Fly are 16 percent and 40 percent. *(LG9-4)*

9-9 **Dominant Portfolios** Determine which one of these three portfolios dominates another. Name the dominated portfolio and the portfolio that dominates it. Portfolio Blue has an expected return of 12 percent and risk of 18 percent. The expected return and risk of portfolio Yellow are 15 percent and 17 percent, and for the Purple portfolio are 14 percent and 21 percent. *(LG9-6)*

9-10 **Dominant Portfolios** Determine which one of the three portfolios dominates another. Name the dominated portfolio and the portfolio that dominates it. Portfolio Green has an expected return of 15 percent and risk of 21 percent. The expected return and risk of portfolio Red are 13 percent and 17 percent, and for the Orange portfolio are 13 percent and 16 percent. *(LG9-6)*

9-11 **Portfolio Weights** An investor owns $6,000 of Adobe Systems stock, $5,000 of Dow Chemical, and $5,000 of Office Depot. What are the portfolio weights of each stock? *(LG9-7)*

9-12 **Portfolio Weights** An investor owns $3,000 of Adobe Systems stock, $6,000 of Dow Chemical, and $7,000 of Office Depot. What are the portfolio weights of each stock? *(LG9-7)*

9-13 **Portfolio Return** Year-to-date, Oracle had earned a −1.34 percent return. During the same time period, Valero Energy earned 7.96 percent and McDonald's earned 0.88 percent. If you have a portfolio made up of 30 percent Oracle, 25 percent Valero Energy, and 45 percent McDonald's, what is your portfolio return? *(LG9-7)*

9-14 **Portfolio Return** Year-to-date, Yum Brands had earned a 3.80 percent return. During the same time period, Raytheon earned 4.26 percent and Coca-Cola earned −0.46 percent. If you have a portfolio made up of 30 percent Yum Brands, 30 percent Raytheon, and 40 percent Coca-Cola, what is your portfolio return? *(LG9-7)*

intermediate problems

9-15 **Average Return** The past five monthly returns for Kohls are 4.11 percent, 3.62 percent, −1.68 percent, 9.25 percent, and −2.56 percent. What is the average monthly return? *(LG9-1)*

9-16 **Average Return** The past five monthly returns for PG&E are −3.17 percent, 3.88 percent, 3.77 percent, 6.47 percent, and 3.58 percent. What is the average monthly return? *(LG9-1)*

9-17 **Standard Deviation** Compute the standard deviation of Kohls' monthly returns shown in problem 9-15. *(LG9-3)*

9-18 **Standard Deviation** Compute the standard deviation of PG&E's monthly returns shown in problem 9-16. *(LG9-3)*

9-19 **Risk versus Return in Bonds** Assess the risk-return relationship of the bond market (see Tables 9.2 and 9.4) during each decade since 1950. *(LG9-2, LG9-4)*

9-20 **Risk versus Return in T-bills** Assess the risk-return relationship in T-bills (see Tables 9.2 and 9.4) during each decade since 1950. *(LG9-2, LG9-4)*

9-21 **Diversifying** Consider the characteristics of the following three stocks:

	Expected Return	Standard Deviation
Thumb Devices	13%	23%
Air Comfort	10	19
Sport Garb	10	17

The correlation between Thumb Devices and Air Comfort is −0.12. The correlation between Thumb Devices and Sport Garb is −0.21. The correlation between Air Comfort and Sport Garb is 0.77. If you can pick only two stocks for your portfolio, which would you pick? Why? *(LG9-4, LG9-5)*

9-22 **Diversifying** Consider the characteristics of the following three stocks:

	Expected Return	Standard Deviation
Pic Image	11%	19%
Tax Help	9	19
Warm Wear	14	25

The correlation between Pic Image and Tax Help is 0.88. The correlation between Pic Image and Warm Wear is −0.21. The correlation between Tax Help and Warm Wear is −0.19. If you can pick only two stocks for your portfolio, which would you pick? Why? *(LG9-4, LG9-5)*

9-23 **Portfolio Weights** If you own 200 shares of Alaska Air at $42.88, 350 shares of Best Buy at $51.32, and 250 shares of Ford Motor at $8.51, what are the portfolio weights of each stock? *(LG9-7)*

9-24 **Portfolio Weights** If you own 400 shares of Xerox at $17.34, 500 shares of Qwest at $8.15, and 350 shares of Liz Claiborne at $44.73, what are the portfolio weights of each stock? *(LG9-7)*

9-25 **Portfolio Return** At the beginning of the month, you owned $5,500 of General Dynamics, $7,500 of Starbucks, and $8,000 of Nike. The monthly returns for General Dynamics, Starbucks, and Nike were 7.44 percent, −1.36 percent, and −0.54 percent. What is your portfolio return? *(LG9-7)*

9-26 **Portfolio Return** At the beginning of the month, you owned $6,000 of News Corp, $5,000 of First Data, and $8,500 of Whirlpool. The monthly returns for News Corp, First Data, and Whirlpool were 8.24 percent, −2.59 percent, and 10.13 percent. What's your portfolio return? *(LG9-7)*

advanced problems

9-27 **Asset Allocation** You have a portfolio with an asset allocation of 50 percent stocks, 40 percent long-term Treasury bonds, and 10 percent T-bills. Use these weights and the returns in Table 9.2 to compute the return of the portfolio in the year 2000 and each year since. Then compute the average annual return and standard deviation of the portfolio and compare them with the risk and return profile of each individual asset class. *(LG9-2, LG9-5)*

9-28 **Asset Allocation** You have a portfolio with an asset allocation of 35 percent stocks, 55 percent long-term Treasury bonds, and 10 percent T-bills. Use these weights and the returns in Table 9.2 to compute the return of the portfolio in the year 2000 and each year since. Then compute the average annual return and standard deviation of the portfolio and compare them with the risk and return profile of each individual asset class. *(LG9-2, LG9-5)*

9-29 **Portfolio Weights** You have \$15,000 to invest. You want to purchase shares of Alaska Air at \$42.88, Best Buy at \$51.32, and Ford Motor at \$8.51. How many shares of each company should you purchase so that your portfolio consists of 30 percent Alaska Air, 40 percent Best Buy, and 30 percent Ford Motor? Report only whole stock shares. *(LG9-7)*

9-30 **Portfolio Weights** You have \$20,000 to invest. You want to purchase shares of Xerox at \$17.34, Qwest at \$8.15, and Liz Claiborne at \$44.73. How many shares of each company should you purchase so that your portfolio consists of 25 percent Xerox, 40 percent Qwest, and 35 percent Liz Claiborne? Report only whole stock shares. *(LG9-7)*

9-31 **Portfolio Return** The following table shows your stock positions at the beginning of the year, the dividends that each stock paid during the year, and the stock prices at the end of the year. What is your portfolio dollar return and percentage return? *(LG9-7)*

Company	Shares	Beginning of Year Price	Dividend Per Share	End of Year Price
US Bank	300	\$43.50	\$2.06	\$43.43
PepsiCo	200	59.08	1.16	62.55
JDS Uniphase	500	18.88		16.66
Duke Energy	250	27.45	1.26	33.21

9-32 **Portfolio Return** The following table shows your stock positions at the beginning of the year, the dividends that each stock paid during the year, and the stock prices at the end of the year. What is your portfolio dollar return and percentage return? *(LG9-7)*

Company	Shares	Beginning of Year Price	Dividend Per Share	End of Year Price
Johnson Controls	350	\$72.91	\$1.17	\$85.92
Medtronic	200	57.57	0.41	53.51
Direct TV	500	24.94		24.39
Qualcomm	250	43.08	0.45	38.92

9-33 **Risk, Return, and Their Relationship** Consider the following annual returns of Estee Lauder and Lowe's Companies:

	Estee Lauder	Lowe's Companies
Year 1	23.4%	−6.0%
Year 2	−26.0	16.1
Year 3	17.6	4.2
Year 4	49.9	48.0
Year 5	−16.8	−19.0

Compute each stock's average return, standard deviation, and coefficient of variation. Which stock appears better? Why? *(LG9-3, LG9-4)*

9-34 Risk, Return, and Their Relationship Consider the following annual returns of Molson Coors and International Paper:

	Molson Coors	International Paper
Year 1	16.3%	4.5%
Year 2	−9.7	−17.5
Year 3	36.5	−0.2
Year 4	−6.9	26.6
Year 5	16.2	−11.1

Compute each stock's average return, standard deviation, and coefficient of variation. Which stock appears better? Why? *(LG9-3, LG9-4)*

9-35 Spreadsheet Problem Following are the monthly returns for October 2007 to March 2013 of three international stock indices: All Ordinaries of Australia, Nikkei 225 of Japan, and FTSE 100 of England.

Date	All Ordinaries	NIKKEI 225	FTSE	Date	All Ordinaries	NIKKEI 225	FTSE
Mar-13	−2.74%	7.25%	0.80%	Jun-10	−2.89%	−3.95%	−5.23%
Feb-13	4.48	3.78	1.34	May-10	−7.87	−11.65	−6.57
Jan-13	5.07	7.15	6.43	Apr-10	−1.21	−0.29	−2.22
Dec-12	3.24	10.05	0.53	Mar-10	5.20	9.52	6.07
Nov-12	−0.38	5.80	1.45	Feb-10	1.18	−0.71	3.20
Oct-12	2.93	0.66	0.71	Jan-10	−5.85	−3.30	−4.15
Sep-12	1.55	0.34	0.54	Dec-09	3.55	12.85	4.28
Aug-12	1.16	1.67	1.35	Nov-09	1.48	−6.87	2.90
Jul-12	3.72	−3.46	1.15	Oct-09	−1.95	−0.97	−1.74
Jun-12	0.04	5.43	4.70	Sep-09	5.69	−3.42	4.58
May-12	−7.47	−10.27	−7.27	Aug-09	5.52	1.31	6.52
Apr-12	1.07	−5.58	−0.53	Jul-09	7.64	4.00	8.45
Mar-12	0.73	3.71	−1.75	Jun-09	3.53	4.58	−3.82
Feb-12	1.44	10.46	3.34	May-09	1.83	7.86	4.10
Jan-12	5.22	4.11	1.96	Apr-09	6.01	8.86	8.09
Dec-11	−1.76	0.25	1.22	Mar-09	7.14	7.15	2.51
Nov-11	−4.03	−6.16	−0.70	Feb-09	−5.21	−5.32	−7.70
Oct-11	7.13	3.31	8.11	Jan-09	−4.95	−9.77	−6.42
Sep-11	−6.86	−2.85	−4.93	Dec-08	−0.36	4.08	3.41
Aug-11	−2.90	−8.93	−7.23	Nov-08	−7.78	−0.75	−2.04
Jul-11	−3.42	0.17	−2.19	Oct-08	−14.00	−23.83	−10.71
Jun-11	−2.70	1.26	−0.74	Sep-08	−11.20	−13.87	−13.02
May-11	−2.25	−1.58	−1.32	Aug-08	3.22	−2.27	4.15
Apr-11	−0.60	0.97	2.73	Jul-08	−5.26	−0.78	−3.80
Mar-11	0.10	−8.18	−1.42	Jun-08	−7.64	−5.98	−7.06
Feb-11	1.52	3.77	2.24	May-08	2.07	3.53	−0.56
Jan-11	0.06	0.09	−0.63	Apr-08	4.57	10.57	6.76
Dec-10	3.65	2.94	6.72	Mar-08	−4.67	−7.92	−3.10
Nov-10	−1.20	7.98	−2.59	Feb-08	−0.39	0.08	0.08
Oct-10	2.08	−1.78	2.28	Jan-08	−11.28	−11.21	−8.94
Sep-10	4.46	6.18	6.19	Dec-07	−2.62	−2.38	0.38
Aug-10	−1.52	−7.48	−0.62	Nov-07	−2.74	−6.31	−4.30
Jul-10	4.22	1.65	6.94	Oct-07	3.01	−0.29	3.94

a. Compute and compare each index's monthly average return and standard deviation.

b. Compute the correlation between (1) All Ordinaries and Nikkei 225, (2) All Ordinaries and FTSE 100, and (3) Nikkei 225 and FTSE 100, and compare them.

c. Form a portfolio consisting of one-third of each of the indexes and show the portfolio return each year, and the portfolio's return and standard deviation.

research it! Following a Portfolio

Following stocks in a portfolio is easier than ever. Many financial websites have the capability to follow the stocks in your portfolio over time. Just enter your stocks, the number of shares, your purchase price, and your commission cost and you can see how your portfolio is doing. These portfolio managers will update your portfolio as stock prices change, minute to minute. Yahoo! Finance has a portfolio management tool. Go to the site and start a portfolio to watch (which requires free registration). Try entering symbols EBAY, T, LMT, DUK, and GSK. As a start, assume you own 200 shares of each. You can watch the value of the portfolio change and see how each stock is doing every day. (**http://finance.yahoo.com**)

integrated mini-case: Diversifying with Other Asset Classes

Many more types of investments are available besides stocks, bonds, and cash securities. Many people invest in real estate and in precious metals, primarily gold. What are the risk and return characteristics of these investments and do they provide diversification opportunities to the typical stock investor?

You can invest in real estate in many ways. You can build properties, own rental units, and trade raw land. These activities take enormous time and expertise. One of the easiest ways to invest in real estate is through *real estate investment trusts* (REITs) that trade like stocks on the stock exchanges. A REIT represents ownership in a portfolio consisting of a pool of real estate assets. An index of all REITs is a good measure of the performance of the real estate market. The following table shows the annual returns for the All REITs Index alongside the returns of the S&P 500 Index.

	S&P 500 Index	All REITs Index	Gold Price Changes
1975	37.2%	36.3%	−19.9%
1976	23.8	49.0	−4.1
1977	−7.2	19.1	22.6
1978	6.6	−1.6	37.0
1979	18.4	30.5	126.5
1980	32.4	28.0	15.2
1981	−4.9	8.6	−32.6
1982	21.4	31.6	14.9

(continued)

	S&P 500 Index	All REITs Index	Gold Price Changes
1983	22.5	25.5	−16.3
1984	6.3	14.8	−19.2
1985	32.2	5.9	5.7
1986	18.5	19.2	21.3
1987	5.2	−10.7	22.2
1988	16.8	11.4	−15.3
1989	31.5	−1.8	−2.8
1990	−3.2	−17.3	−1.5
1991	30.6	35.7	−10.1
1992	7.7	12.2	−5.7
1993	10.0	18.5	17.7
1994	1.3	0.8	−2.2
1995	37.4	18.3	1.0
1996	23.1	35.8	−4.6
1997	33.4	18.9	−21.4
1998	28.6	−18.8	−0.8
1999	21.0	−6.5	0.9
2000	−9.1	25.9	−5.4
2001	−11.9	15.5	0.7
2002	−22.1	5.2	25.6
2003	28.7	38.5	19.9
2004	10.9	30.4	4.6
2005	4.9	8.3	17.8
2006	15.8	34.4	24.0
2007	3.5	−17.8	31.1
2008	−35.5	−40.0	4.3
2009	23.5	20.9	25.0
2010	15.1	22.8	25.3
2011	2.1	3.6	8.9
2012	16.0	15.5	8.3

Gold has been a highly sought-after asset all over the world, and has retained at least some economic value over thousands of years. The United States has had a very chaotic history with gold. Americans have sought to "strike it rich" through gold rushes in North Carolina (early 1800s), California and Nevada (mid-1800s), and Alaska (late 1800s). Struggling in the Great Depression, President Franklin D. Roosevelt ordered U.S. citizens to hand in all the gold they possessed. The ban on U.S. citizens owning gold was not lifted until the end of 1974. The table also shows the return from gold prices.

The returns for stocks, real estate, and gold are all volatile. However, during many years, the return of one asset is up while the others are down. This looks promising for diversification opportunities.

a. Using a spreadsheet, compute the average return and standard deviation of each of the three asset classes.

b. Compute the annual returns of a portfolio consisting of 50 percent stocks/40 percent real estate/10 percent gold. What is the average return and standard deviation of this portfolio? Also compute the average return and standard deviation of the following portfolios: 75 percent/20 percent/5 percent and 80 percent/5 percent/15 percent. How do these portfolios perform compared to owning just stocks?

c. Plot the average return and standard deviation of the three assets and the three portfolios on a risk-return graph like Figure 9.3.

ANSWERS TO TIME OUT

9-1 Dividends are a large portion of the return realized by stockholders in the long run. In any given year, the capital gain or loss may dominate the dividend. In many years, the capital gain is low and thus the dividend is a larger portion of the return. Since the capital gain is frequently negative and the dividend is always positive, the dividend plays an important role over time.

9-2 Use the future value equation. For example, for stocks $FV_{\text{end of 1950 s}} = \$10{,}000 \times (1 + 0.209)^{10} = \$66{,}721$.

Answers are:

	In Stocks	In Bonds	In Cash
1950s	$66,721	$10,000	$12,190
1960s	23,030	11,720	14,802
1970s	20,610	17,408	18,422
1980s	53,232	35,478	23,457
1990s	56,947	24,782	16,134
2000s	10,937	21,589	13,180

9-3 Standard deviation of returns measures the variability of returns over time. This variability gives investors an idea of the likely range of potential returns.

9-4 The standard deviation (the numerator in the CoV equation) for individual companies is much higher than for the stock market as a whole. This is because it is a measure of total risk, which includes much firm-specific risk for firms. But firm-specific risk is diversified away in the overall market.

9-5 It is useful to find companies whose returns behave differently from each other over time. This comes about from companies that have different businesses. This is measured by a statistical tool, correlation. It is also good if these companies have high expected returns.

9-6 The return on a portfolio depends on the proportions of each asset owned in the portfolio and the returns that each of those assets generates. If the first portfolio is weighted toward poor-performing stocks and the second owns more of the high-performing stocks, the first portfolio will be undesirable in comparison.

9-7 The lowest correlation in Table 9.6 is between the Bank of New York and Newmont Mining. So this combination has the best chance of reducing risk. The least opportunity for diversification is between General Electric and Citigroup because they have the highest correlation.

PART FIVE

10 Estimating Risk and Return

viewpoints

Business Application

Consider that you work in the finance department of a large corporation. Your team is analyzing several new projects the firm can pursue. To complete the analysis, the team needs to know what return stockholders require from the firm.

You are to estimate this required return. Shareholders' expected return will depend on your company's risk level. What information do you need to gather and how might you compute this return? **(See solution on p. 358)**

Personal Application

You have just started your first job in the corporate world and need to make some retirement plan decisions. The company's 401(k) retirement plan offers three investment choices: a stock portfolio, a bond portfolio, and a money market account. For your allocation, you decide to contribute $200 per month to the stock portfolio, $100 to the bond portfolio, and $50 to the money market account.

What risk level are you taking in your retirement portfolio and what return should you expect over the long run? **(See solution on p. 358)**

Investing mainly in my own company's stock is safer, right? Maybe not . . .

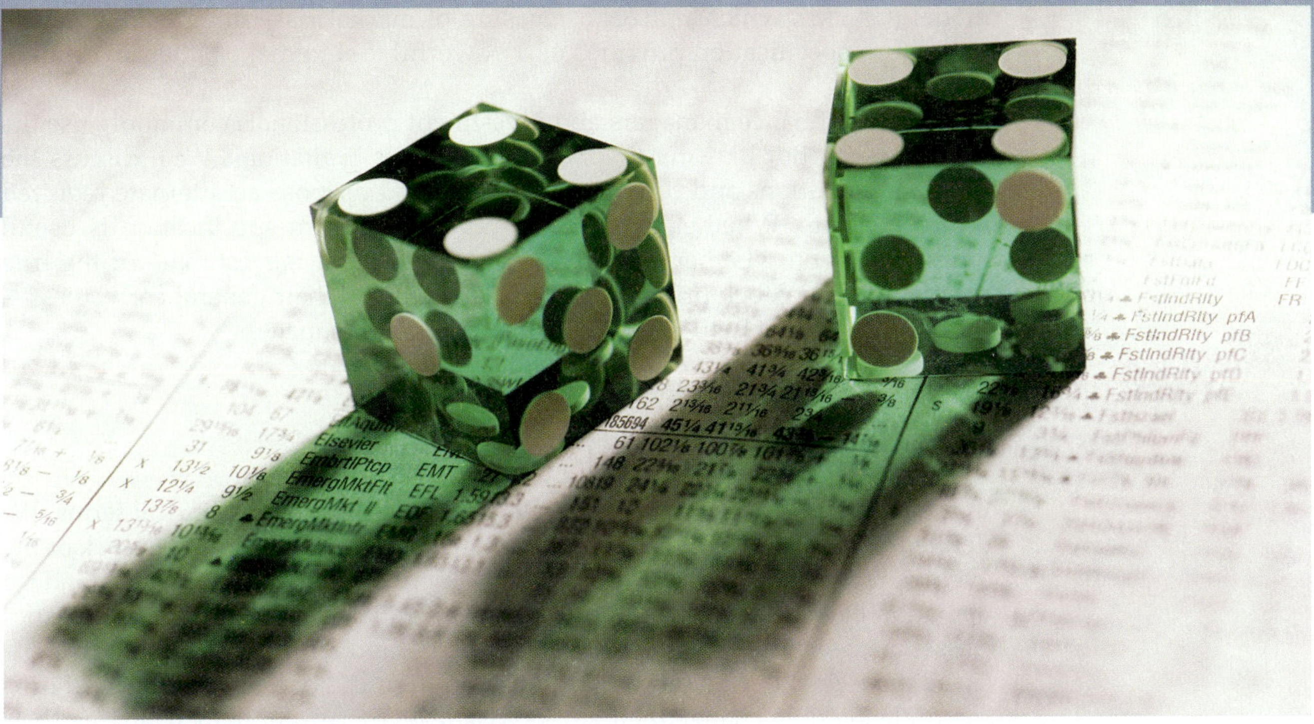

Is it possible for investors to know the exact risk they have to take? In Chapters 9 and 10, we explore methods to find the return that individual or institutional investors require to make a particular investment attractive. In the previous chapter, we established a positive relationship between risk and return using historical data. Risk and return play an undeniable role as investors seek the best return for the least risk. But until there's some way to forecast the future, financial managers and investors must make investment decisions armed only with their *expectations* about future risk and return. We need an exact specification that shows directly the amount of reward required for investors to take the level of risk in a given firm's stock or portfolio of securities. In this chapter we will also see how investors get the information they need to make risk-reward decisions.

Investors need to know how much risk they have to take to confidently expect a 10 percent return. Managers also want to know what return shareholders require so that they can decide how to meet those expectations. In Chapter 11, we'll explore how managers conduct financial analysis to find the shareholders' required return. If we want to specify the exact risk-return relationship, we need to develop a better measure of *risk* for individuals and institutional investors. As we saw in Chapter 9, any firm's total risk is specific to that particular firm. But the market doesn't reward firm-specific risk because investors can easily diversify away any single firm's specific risks by owning other offsetting firms' stocks to create a portfolio subject only to market or undiversifiable risk. So, we need to find just the market risk portion of total risk for investors. The theory to find the market risk portion of stock ownership extends modern portfolio theory. Our search to find market risk will lead us to the capital asset pricing

Learning Goals

LG10-1 Compute forward-looking expected return and risk.

LG10-2 Understand risk premiums.

LG10-3 Know and apply the capital asset pricing model (CAPM).

LG10-4 Calculate and apply beta, a measure of market risk.

LG10-5 Differentiate among the different levels of market efficiency and their implications.

LG10-6 Calculate and explain investors' required return and risk.

LG10-7 Use the constant-growth model to compute required return.

model (CAPM), which utilizes a measure of market risk called beta. CAPM's risk-return specification provides us a powerful tool to make better investment decisions.

Corporate finance managers and investment professionals commonly use the beta measure. But like any theory, CAPM has its limitations. We'll discuss the CAPM's limitations and concerns about beta and propose an alternate required return measure. Whether beta or any other risk-return specification is useful relies in part on whether a stock's price represents a fair estimate of the true company value. Stock price validity and reliability—their general correctness—is vitally important both to investors and corporate managers.

LG10-1 10.1 • Expected Returns

In the previous chapter, we characterized risk and return in historical terms. We defined a stock's return as the actual profit realized while holding the stock or the average return over a longer period. We described risk simply as the standard deviation of those returns—a term already familiar to you from your statistics classes. So, we did a good job describing the risk and return that the stock experienced *in the past.* But do those risk and return figures hold into the future? Firms can quite possibly change their stocks' risk level by substantially changing their business. If a firm takes on riskier new projects over time, or changes the nature of its business, the firm itself will become riskier. Similarly, firms can reduce their risk level—and hence, their stock's riskiness—by choosing low-risk new projects. Both investors and firms find *expected return,* a forward-looking return calculation that includes risk measures, very useful to estimate future stock performance.

LG10-1 Expected Return and Risk

We can attribute a company's business success over a year partly to its management talent, strategies, and other firm-specific activities. Overall economic conditions will also affect a firm's level of success or failure. Consider a steel manufacturer—Nucor Corp. The steel business closely follows economic trends. In a good economy, demand for steel is strong as builders and manufacturers step up building and production. During economic recessions, demand for steel falls off quickly. So, if we want to assess Nucor's probabilities for success next year, we know that we must look partly at Nucor's managerial ability and partly at the economic outlook.

Unfortunately, we cannot accurately predict what the economy will be like next year. Predicting economic activity is like predicting the weather—forecasts give the **probability** of rain or sunshine. Economists cannot say for sure whether the economy will be good or bad next year. Instead, they may forecast a 70 percent chance that the economy will be good and a 30 percent chance of a recession. Similarly, analysts might say that given Nucor's managerial talent, if the economy is good, Nucor will perform well and the stock will increase 20 percent. If the economy goes into a recession, then Nucor's stock will fall 10 percent. So what return do you expect from Nucor? The return still depends on the state of the economy.

probability

The likelihood of occurrence.

This leads us directly to a key concept: **expected return.** We compute expected return by multiplying each possible return by the probability, p, of that return occurring. We then sum them (recall that all probabilities must add to one). Let's place Nucor in an economy with only two states: good and recession. In this scenario, Nucor's expected return would be 11 percent [= (0.7 × 20%) + (0.3 × −10%)]. Of course, nothing is quite that simple. Economists

expected return

The average of the possible returns weighted by the likelihood of those returns occurring.

seldom predict simple two-state views of the economy as in the previous example. Rather, economists give much more detailed forecasts (such as three states: red-hot economy, average expansion, and recession). So our general equation for a stock's expected return with S different conditions of the economy is:

$$\text{Expected return} = \text{Sum of (Each return} \times \text{Probability of that return)} \quad \textbf{(10-1)}$$
$$= (p_1 \times \text{Return}_1) + (p_2 \times \text{Return}_2) + (p_3 \times \text{Return}_3)$$
$$+ \cdots + (p_s \times \text{Return}_s) = \sum_{j=1}^{s} p_j \times \text{Return}_j$$

The result of this expected return calculation has some interesting properties. First, the expected return figure expresses what the average return would be over time if the probabilistic states of the economy occur as predicted. For example, the 70/30 **probability distribution** for good-recession economic states suggests that the economy will be good in 7 of the next 10 years, earning Nucor shareholders a 20 percent return in each of those years. Shareholders would lose 10 percent in each of the three recession years. So the *average return* over those 10 years would be 11 percent, the same as the expected return. The second interesting property: The expected return itself will not likely occur during any one year. Remember that Nucor will earn either a return of 20 percent or −10 percent. Yet its expected return is 11 percent, a value that it cannot earn because we have no economic condition for which the return is 11 percent. Again, this illustration seems extreme because we used only two economic states. Any real economic forecast would instead include a probability distribution of many potential economic conditions.

probability distribution
The set of probabilities for all possible occurrences.

We can also characterize risk via this expected return figure. The expected return procedure shows potential return possibilities, but we don't know which one will actually occur, so we face uncertainty. In the last chapter, we measured risk using the standard deviation of returns over time. We can use the same principle to measure risk for expected returns. What range of different expected returns will Nucor exhibit from the expected return of 11 percent? In our two-state description of the economy, the deviation could be either 9 percent (= 20% − 11%) or −21 percent (= −10% − 11%). We compute the standard deviation of expected returns the same way we did for historical returns. We square the deviations, then multiply by the probability of that deviation occurring, and then sum them all up. So Nucor's return variance is 189.0 [= $(0.7 \times 9^2) + (0.3 \times -21^2)$]. As a final step, we take the square root of our result to put the figure back into sensible terms. The standard deviation for Nucor is 13.75 percent (= $\sqrt{189}$). The general equation for the standard deviation of S different economic states is:

> **MATH COACH**
>
> **EXPECTED RETURN AND STANDARD DEVIATION**
>
> When you compute expected return and standard deviation, you'll find it helpful to use the decimal format for the probability of the economic state and percentages to state the return in each state.

$$\text{Standard deviation} = \text{Square root of the sum of (Probability of a return}$$
$$\times \text{ Each return's squared deviation from the average)}$$
$$= \sqrt{p_1 \times (\text{Return}_1 - \text{Expected return})^2 + p_2 \times (\text{Return}_2 - \text{Expected return})^2 + \cdots} \quad \textbf{(10-2)}$$
$$= \sqrt{\sum_{j=1}^{s} p_j \times (\text{Return}_j - \text{Expected return})^2}$$

EXAMPLE 10-1

LG10-1

For interactive versions of this example visit www.mhhe.com/can3e

Expected Return and Risk

Bailey has a probability distribution for four possible states of the economy, as shown below. She has also calculated the return that Motor Music stock would earn in each state. Given this information, what's Motor Music's expected return and risk?

Economic State	Probability	Return
Fast growth	0.15	25%
Slow growth	0.60	15%
Recession	0.20	−5%
Depression	0.05	−20%

SOLUTION:

Bailey can compute the expected return using equation 10-1:

$$\text{Expected return} = (0.15 \times 25\%) + (0.60 \times 15\%) + (0.20 \times -5\%) + (0.05 \times -20\%) = 10.75\%$$

Then Bailey can compute the expected return by computing the standard deviation using equation 10-2:

$$\text{Standard deviation} = \sqrt{\begin{array}{l}0.15 \times (25\% - 10.75\%)^2 + 0.60 \times (15\% - 10.75\%)^2 + 0.20 \\ \times (-5\% - 10.75\%)^2 + 0.05 \times (-20\% - 10.75\%)^2\end{array}}$$

$$= \sqrt{30.46 + 10.84 + 49.61 + 47.28} = 11.76\%$$

The expected return and standard deviation are 10.75 percent and 11.76 percent, respectively. We could also show these equations in a table, such as:

Economic State	Probability	Return	$p \times$ Return	Deviation	Squared Dev.	$\times p$
Fast growth	0.15	25%	3.75%	14.25%	203.06	30.46
Slow growth	0.60	15	9.00	4.25	18.06	10.84
Recession	0.20	−5	−1.00	−15.75	248.06	49.61
Depression	0.05	−20	−1.00	−30.75	945.56	47.28
Sum =	1.0		10.75%			138.19
				Square root =		11.76%

Similar to Problems 10-1, 10-2, 10-17, 10-18, 10-23, 10-24, self-test problem 1

LG10-2

Risk Premiums

Throughout the book, we have mentioned the positive relationship between expected return and risk. Consider this key question: You have a riskless investment available to you. The short-term government debt security, the T-bill, offers you a low return with no risk. Why would you invest in anything risky, when you could simply buy T-bills? The answer, of course, is that some investors want a higher return and are willing to take some risk to raise their returns. Investors who take on a little risk should expect a slightly higher return than the T-bill rate. People who take on higher risk levels should expect higher returns. Indeed, it's only logical that investors require this extra return to willingly take the added risk.

The expected return of an investment is often expressed in two parts, a risk-free return and a risky contribution. The return investors require for the risk level they take is called the **required return:**

required return

The level of total return needed to be compensated for the risk taken. It is made up of a risk-free rate and a risk premium.

$$\text{Required return} = \text{Risk-free rate} + \text{Risk premium} \qquad \textbf{(10-3)}$$

table 10.1 | **The Realized Average Annual Risk Premium for Stocks**

	1950 to 2012	1950 to 1959	1960 to 1969	1970 to 1979	1980 to 1989	1990 to 1999	2000 to 2009	2010 to 2012
Risk premium	7.9%	18.8%	4.7%	1.2%	9.3%	14.1%	−1.8%	11.0%

Realized risk premiums were very different in each decade. The recent decade even had a negative risk premium!
Source: S&P 500 Index and T-bill rate data.

The *risk-free rate* is typically considered the return on U.S. government bonds and bills and equals the real interest rate and the expected inflation premium that we discussed in Chapter 6. The **risk premium** is the reward investors require for taking risk. How large are the rewards for taking risk? As we discussed in the previous chapter, the market doesn't reward all risks. The firm-specific portion of total risk for any stock can be diversified away, and since the investor takes on such risk out of ignorance or by mistake, an efficient market will not reward anyone for taking on this "superfluous" risk. So as we examine historical risk premiums, we do so with a diversified portfolio that contains no firm-specific risk.

risk premium
The portion of the required return that represents the reward for taking risk.

Table 10.1 shows the average annual return on the S&P 500 Index minus the T-bill rate for different time periods. The remainder after we subtract the T-bill rate is the risk premium; in this case, it's the **market risk premium**—the reward for taking general (unsystematic) stock market risk. Since 1950, the average market risk premium has been 7.9 percent per year. Over the long run, this is the reward for taking stock market risk. The actual, realized risk premium during particular decades has varied. The average risk premium has been as high as 18.8 percent for the 1950s and as low as −1.8 percent during the 2000s. The performance in the 2000s is unusual; the stock market return has been so poor that it has not beaten the risk-free rate. Investors require a risk premium for taking on market risk. But taking that risk also means that they will periodically experience poor returns.

market risk premium
The return on the market portfolio minus the risk-free rate. Risk premiums for specific firms are based on the market risk premium.

TIME OUT

10-1 Describe the similarities between computing average return and expected return. Also, describe the similarities between expected return risk and historical risk.

10-2 Why would people take risks by investing their hard-earned money?

10.2 • Market Risk

How much risk should you take to achieve the return you want over time? In the previous chapter, we demonstrated that individual stocks and different portfolios exhibit different levels of total risk. Recall that the rewards for carrying risk apply only to the market risk (or undiversifiable) portion of total risk. But how do investors know how much of the 33.8 percent standard deviation of returns for Mattel Inc. is firm-specific risk and how much of that deviation is market risk? The answer to this important question will determine how much of a risk premium investors should require for Mattel. The attempt to specify an equation that relates a stock's required return to an appropriate risk premium is known as **asset pricing.**

asset pricing
The process of directly specifying the relationship between required return and risk.

The Market Portfolio

The best-known asset pricing equation is the **capital asset pricing model**, typically referred to as **CAPM.** Though many theorists formulated theories that, in the end, supported the CAPM's effectiveness, credit for the model goes to William

capital asset pricing model (CAPM)
An asset pricing theory based on a beta, a measure of market risk.

figure 10.1

Maximizing Expected Return

In MPT, investors want to be on the efficient frontier (Panel A) because it gives them the highest expected return for each level of risk. However, after adding a riskless asset (Panel B), investors can then get portfolios on the straight line (shown), which offers a higher expected return for each level of risk than the efficient frontier.

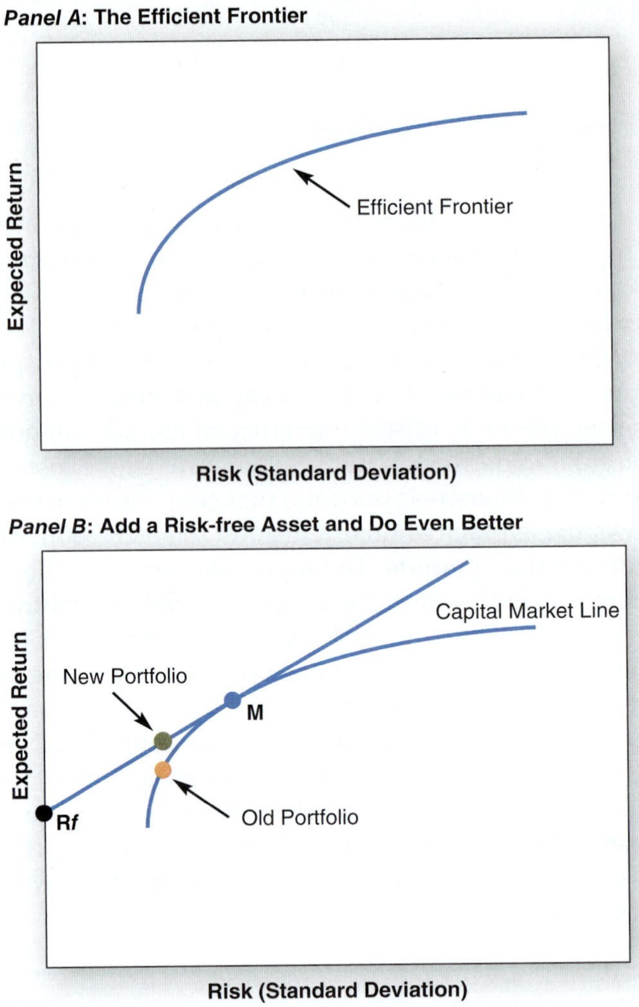

Sharpe and John Lintner. Sharpe eventually won a Nobel Prize for his work in 1990. (Lintner died in 1983, and Nobel Prizes are not awarded posthumously.) Today, both investors and corporate finance professionals use CAPM widely. In developing the CAPM, Lintner and Sharpe sought to emphasize the individual investor's best strategy to maximize returns for a given amount of market risk.

CAPM starts with modern portfolio theory. Remember from the previous chapter that when you combine securities into a portfolio, you can find a set of portfolios that dominate all others. The best combinations possible use all the risky securities available (but not the risk-free asset) to create efficient frontier portfolios, as shown by the curved line in Figure 10.1, panel A. These portfolios represent combinations of various risky securities that give the highest expected return for each potential level of risk.

capital market line (CML)

The line on a graph of return and risk (standard deviation) from the risk-free rate through the market portfolio.

The idea of a risk premium in equation 10-3 implies a risk-free investment, like T-bills. Panel B shows where the risk-free asset would appear on the **capital market line (CML).** The risk-free asset must lie on the *y*-axis precisely because it carries no risk. Now we draw a line from the risk-free security to a point tangent to the efficient frontier. The CML relationship appears as a line because investments show a direct risk-reward relationship. You may recall from your economics classes that only one tangency point will be possible between this kind of curve and a straight line. The spot where the tangency occurs is called the **market portfolio,** which has a special significance. The market portfolio represents ownership in all traded assets in the economy, so this portfolio provides maximum diversification. You can locate your optimal portfolio on this line by owning various combinations of the risk-free security and the market portfolio. If most of your money is invested in the market portfolio, then you will have a portfolio on the line that lies just to the left of the market portfolio dot in the graph. If you own just a little of the market portfolio and hold mostly risk-free securities, then your portfolio will lie on the line near the risk-free security dot. For your investments to lie on the line to the right of the market portfolio, you would have to invest all your money in the market portfolio, then borrow more money and invest these additional funds in the market portfolio. Borrowing money to invest is known as using **financial leverage.** Using financial leverage increases the overall risk of the portfolio.

market portfolio

In theory, the market portfolio is the combination of securities that places the portfolio on the efficient frontier and on a line tangent from the risk-free rate. In practice, the S&P 500 Index is used to proxy for the market portfolio.

financial leverage

The use of debt to increase an investment position.

Notice that if you had a portfolio on the efficient frontier (labeled "old portfolio"), you could do better. Instead of owning the old portfolio, you can put some of your money in the market portfolio and some in the risk-free security to obtain the "new portfolio." See how the new portfolio dominates that old one? It carries the same risk level, but offers a higher return. In fact, notice that the line drawn between the risk-free investment and the market portfolio dominates all of the efficient frontier portfolios (except the market portfolio itself). All portfolio allocations between the risk-free security and the market portfolio constitute the capital market line. All investors should want to locate their portfolios on the CML, rather than the efficient frontier. Portfolios on the CML offer the highest expected return for any level of desired risk, which the investor controls by deciding how much of the market portfolio and how much of the risk-free asset to hold. Risk-averse investors can put more of their money in T-bills and less into the market portfolio. Investors willing to take on higher risk for larger returns can put more of their money in the market portfolio.

Beta, a Measure of Market Risk

LG10-4

The CML demonstrates that the market portfolio is crucial. Indeed, its return less the risk-free rate represents the expected average market risk premium. The market portfolio features no firm-specific risk; all such risk is diversified away. So the market portfolio carries only market risk. So the market portfolio's risk factor allows us to compute a measure of firm-specific risk for any individual stock or portfolio. We can now examine the question posed at the beginning of this section: "How much of Mattel's total risk is attributable to market risk?" The standard deviation of returns includes all of Mattel stock's risk—it quantifies how much the stock price rises and falls. The market risk portion will rise and fall along with the market portfolio. If we subtract the market risk portion from the total risk measure, we're left with firm-specific risk. This part of risk rises and falls in ways unrelated to market changes.

Remember that portfolio theory describes a measure—correlation—that measures how two stocks move together through time. Instead of measuring how any two stocks or portfolios move together, we now want to know how a stock or portfolio moves relative to market portfolio movements. This measure is known as **beta (β).** Beta measures the comovement between a stock and the market portfolio.

beta (β)

A measure of the sensitivity of a stock or portfolio to market risk.

If Mattel's total risk level is measured by its standard deviation, σ_{Mattel}, then we can find the portion of this risk that is attributable to the market in general by multiplying Mattel's total risk by its correlation with the market portfolio, $\sigma_{\text{Mattel}} \times \rho_{\text{Mattel, Market}}$. The beta computation is scaled so that the market portfolio itself has a beta of one. The scaling is done by dividing by standard deviation of

table 10.2 | **Dow Jones Industrial Average Stock Betas**

Company	Beta	Company	Beta
3M Company	1.08	Home Depot	1.01
Alcoa	1.86	International Business Machines	0.65
American Express	1.03	Intel	0.98
AT&T	0.38	Johnson & Johnson	0.47
Boeing	1.04	JPMorgan Chase	1.63
Bank of America	1.78	McDonald's	0.34
Caterpillar	1.80	Merck	0.38
Cisco Systems	1.41	Microsoft	1.17
Chevron	1.18	Pfizer	0.81
Coca-Cola	0.37	Procter & Gamble	0.31
Disney	1.09	Travelers	0.83
Du Pont de Nemours	1.47	United Technologies	1.14
Exxon Mobil	0.86	UnitedHealth Group	0.57
General Electric	1.41	Verizon Communications	0.34
Hewlett-Packard	1.54	Walmart Stores	0.41

Data Source: Yahoo! Finance, April 6, 2013

the market portfolio: $\rho_{\text{Mattel}} \times \rho_{\text{Mattel,Market}} \div \rho_{\text{Market}}$.[1] Stocks with betas larger than one are considered riskier than the market portfolio, while betas of less then one indicate lower risk. Mattel has a beta of 0.65, meaning that Mattel has low sensitivity to market risk. When the market portfolio moves, you can expect Mattel stock to move in the same direction. Technically, you should expect Mattel's realized risk premium to be 35 percent less than the realized market risk premium.

Table 10.2 shows the beta for each of the 30 companies in the Dow Jones Industrial Average. Investors consider many of these companies high risk, like Alcoa ($\beta = 1.86$) and Bank of America (1.78). These firms' stocks carry high market risk because the demand for their products is very sensitive to the overall economy's strength. The financial crisis and its aftermath have put Bank of America in a risky position. Investors consider other companies safe bets with low risk, like Procter & Gamble (0.31), McDonald's (0.34), and Verizon (0.34). Many lower-beta firms sell consumer goods that we consider the necessities of life, which we will buy whether the economy is in recession or expansion. The demand for these products is price inelastic and not sensitive to economic conditions. Some companies have nearly the same risk as the market portfolio, like Home Depot (1.01) and Intel (0.98).

LG10-3 The Security Market Line

security market line

Similar to the capital market line except risk is characterized by beta instead of standard deviation.

Beta indicates the market risk that each stock represents to investors. So the higher the beta, the higher the risk premium investors will demand to undertake that security's market risk. Since beta sums up precisely what investors want to know about risk, we often replace the standard deviation risk measure shown in Figure 10.1 with beta. Figure 10.2 shows required return versus beta risk. We call the line in this figure the **security market line** (SML), which illustrates how required return relates to risk at any particular time, all else held equal. The SML also shows the market portfolio's risk premium or any stock's risk premium.

[1]A mathematically equivalent equation for beta is $\beta = \text{cov}(R_s, R_M)/\text{var}(R_M)$, where cov() is the covariance between the stock and market portfolio returns, and var() is the variance of the market portfolio.

figure 10.2

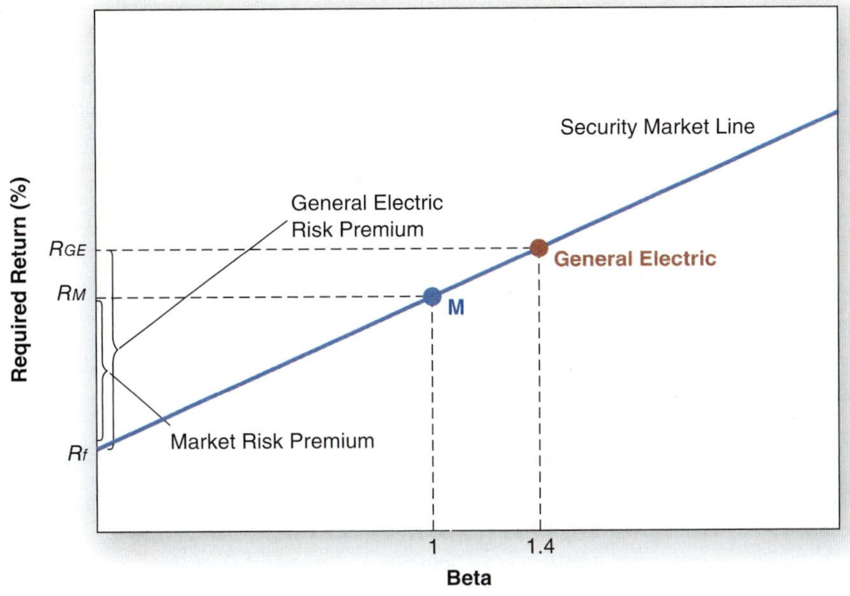

The Security Market Line Uses Beta as the Risk Measure

General Electric has higher risk than the overall stock market, so it should require a higher return.

When a stock like General Electric carries a beta greater than one, then its risk premium must be larger than the market risk premium. A stock like Johnson & Johnson carries a lower beta than does the overall market; therefore Johnson & Johnson would offer a lower risk premium to investors.

We can use the SML to show the relationship between risk and return for any stock or portfolio. To precisely quantify this relationship, we need the equation for the SML. The equation of any line can be defined as $y = b + m\,x$, were b is the intercept and m is the slope. In this case, the y axis is required return and the x axis is beta. The intercept is R_f. You may remember that the slope is the "rise over run" between two points on the line. The rise between the risk-free security and the market portfolio is $R_M - R_f$ and the run is $1 - 0$. Substituting into the line equation results in the CAPM:

$$\begin{aligned} \text{Expected return} &= \text{Risk-free rate} + \text{Beta} \times \text{Market risk premium} \\ &= R_f + \beta(R_M - R_f) \end{aligned} \quad \textbf{(10-4)}$$

So, we have determined a way to estimate any stock's required return once we have determined its beta. Consider this: We expect the market portfolio to earn 12 percent and T-bill yields are 5 percent. Then General Electric's required return, with a $\beta = 1.41$, is $5\% + 1.41 \times (12\% - 5\%) = 14.87$ percent. Table 10.3 shows the 30 Dow Jones Industrial Average stocks' required return, using these same market and risk-free rate assumptions. Higher-risk companies have higher betas, and thus require higher returns.

EXAMPLE 10-2

LG10-3

CAPM and Under- or Overvalued Stock

Say that you are a corporate CFO. You know that the risk-free rate is currently 4.5 percent and you expect the market to earn 11 percent this year. Through your own analysis of the firm, you think it will earn a 13.5 percent return this year. If the beta of the company is 1.2, should you consider the firm undervalued or overvalued?

For interactive versions of this example visit www.mhhe.com/can3e

SOLUTION:

You can compute shareholders' required return with CAPM as 4.5% + 1.2 × (11% − 4.5%) = 12.3%. Since you think the firm will actually earn more than this required return, the firm appears to be currently undervalued. That is, its price must rise more then predicted by CAPM to obtain the return you estimated in your original analysis.

Similar to Problems 10-7, 10-8, 10-19, 10-20, self-test problem 3

table 10.3 | **Required Returns for DJIA Stocks**

Company	Required Return	Company	Required Return
3M Company	12.56%	Home Depot	12.07%
Alcoa	18.02	International Business Machines	9.55
American Express	12.21	Intel	11.86
AT&T	7.66	Johnson & Johnson	8.29
Boeing	12.28	JPMorgan Chase	16.41
Bank of America	17.46	McDonald's	7.38
Caterpillar	17.60	Merck	7.66
Cisco Systems	14.87	Microsoft	13.19
Chevron	13.26	Pfizer	10.67
Coca-Cola	7.59	Procter & Gamble	7.17
Disney	12.63	Travelers	10.81
Du Pont de Nemours	15.29	United Technologies	12.98
Exxon Mobil	11.02	UnitedHealth Group	8.99
General Electric	14.87	Verizon Communications	7.38
Hewlett-Packard	15.78	Walmart Stores	7.87

Higher beta stocks require higher expected returns.
Assumptions: market return = 12% and risk-free rate = 5%.

portfolio beta

The combination of the individual company beta's in an investor's portfolio.

PORTFOLIO BETA As you might expect, a stock **portfolio's beta** is the weighted average of the portfolio stocks' betas. The portfolio beta equation resembles equation 9-7, which gives the return of a portfolio:

$$\beta_p = \text{Sum of the beta of each stock} \times \text{Its weight in the portfolio}$$

$$= (w_1 \times \beta_1) + (w_2 \times \beta_2) + (w_3 \times \beta_3) + \cdots + (w_n \times \beta_n) = \sum_{j=1}^{n} w_j\beta_j \qquad \textbf{(10-5)}$$

With this equation, you can easily determine whether adding a particular stock to the portfolio will increase or decrease the portfolio's total market risk. If you add a stock with a higher beta than the existing portfolio, then the new portfolio will carry higher market risk than the old one did. Although we can find the effects on total portfolio risk of adding particular stocks using beta, the same is not necessarily true if we use standard deviations as our risk measure. The new stock, however risky, might have low correlations with the other stocks in the portfolio—offsetting (negative) correlations would reduce total risk.

LG10-4

EXAMPLE 10-3

Portfolio Beta

You have a portfolio consisting of 20 percent Boeing stock ($\beta = 1.04$), 40 percent Hewlett-Packard stock ($\beta = 1.54$), and 40 percent McDonald's stock ($\beta = 0.34$). How much market risk does the portfolio have?

For interactive versions of this example visit www.mhhe.com/can3e

SOLUTION:

Compute a beta for the portfolio. Using equation 10-5, the portfolio beta is $0.2 \times 1.04 + 0.4 \times 1.54 + 0.4 \times 0.34 = 0.96$. Note that this portfolio carries 4 percent less market risk than the general market does.

Similar to Problems 10-11, 10-12, 10-21, 10-22, 10-27, 10-28, self-test problem 2

Finding Beta

LG10-4

The CAPM is an elegant explanation that relates the return you should require for taking on various levels of market risk. Although CAPM provides many practical applications, you need a company's beta to use those applications. Where or how can you obtain a beta? You have two ways. First, given the returns of the company and the market portfolio, you can compute the beta yourself. Second, you can find the beta that others have computed through financial information data providers.

Many financial outlets publish company betas. Websites that provide company betas for free include MSN Money, Yahoo! Finance, and Zacks, to name just a few. For example, in April 2013, the beta these websites listed for AT&T were: MSN Money (0.53), Yahoo! Finance (0.38), and Zacks (0.54). Note that these reported betas have some differences. To know why differences might arise, consider how you would go about gathering information and computing beta yourself.

To compute your own beta, first obtain historical returns for the company of interest and of the market portfolio. Then run a regression of the company return as the dependent variable and the market portfolio return as the independent variable. The resulting market portfolio return coefficient is beta. Many important questions may come to mind. First, what do you use as the market portfolio? People typically use a major stock index like the S&P 500 Index to proxy for the market portfolio. Second, what time frame should you use? You can use daily, weekly, monthly, or even annual returns. Using monthly returns is the most common. How long a time series is needed? As you will recall, statistical estimates become more reliable and valid as more data are used. But you will have to weigh those statistical advantages against the fact that companies change their business enterprises and thus their risk levels over time. Using data from too long ago reflects risks that may no longer apply. Generally speaking, using time series data of three to five years is common. Whatever decisions you make to address these questions, be consistent by making the same decisions for all the company betas you compute. Table 10.4 shows the spreadsheet of a stock's beta calculation. In this case, monthly returns from five years are used for the stock return and a market index. The SLOPE() function of the spreadsheet directly computes the regression coefficient of interest. The beta estimation using the spreadsheet function is 0.83.

table 10.4 | **Compute Beta Using a Spreadsheet**

	A	B	C	D	E
1	**Date**	**Stock Return**	**Market Return**		
2	Apr	−4.13%	−1.01%		
3	Mar	0.84	3.60	beta =	
4	Feb	−0.46	1.11	=SLOPE(B2:B60,C2:C60) =	0.83
5	Jan	5.83	5.04		
6	Dec	−0.47	0.71		
7	Nov	8.23	0.28		
8	Oct	−8.43	−1.98		
9	Sep	2.44	2.42		
10	Aug	6.42	1.98		
11	Jul	2.17	1.26		
12	Jun	7.25	3.96		
13	May	−8.19	−6.27		
14	Apr	14.51	−0.75		
15	Mar	12.70	3.13		
16	Feb	−7.59	4.06		
17	Jan	12.33	4.36		
18	Dec	−9.98	0.85		
19	Nov	−9.94	−0.51		
20	Oct	−1.26	10.77		
21	Sep	0.46	−7.18		
22	Aug	−3.28	−5.68		
49	May	−3.14	5.31		
50	Apr	9.64	9.39		
51	Mar	13.35	8.54		
52	Feb	10.15	−10.99		
53	Jan	14.70	−8.57		
54	Dec	20.09	0.78		
55	Nov	−25.40	−7.48		
56	Oct	−21.33	−16.94		
57	Sep	−9.96	−9.08		
58	Aug	5.86	1.22		
59	Jul	4.10	−0.99		
60	Jun	−10.16	−8.60		

The spreadsheet function SLOPE() finds the statistical relationship between a stock's return and the market return. Considering these monthly returns for a stock and a market index, the beta of this stock is 0.83.

LG10-4

Concerns about Beta

Consider the estimation choices just mentioned. Say you estimate a firm's beta using monthly data for five years and the Dow Jones Industrial Average return as the market portfolio. Suppose that the result is a beta of 1.3. Then you try again using weekly returns for three years and the return from the S&P 500 Index as the market portfolio's yield, resulting in a beta of 0.9. These estimates are quite different and would create a large variation in required return if you plugged them into the CAPM. So, which is the more accurate estimate? Unfortunately, we may not be able to determine which is most representative, or "true." In general, you may estimate a little different beta using different market portfolio proxies, different return intervals (like monthly returns versus annual returns), and different time periods. A problem at the end of this chapter explores these differences.

In addition to these estimation problems, a company can change its risk level, and thus its beta, by changing the way it operates within its business,

finance at work — markets

ARE STOCKS REALLY GOOD OR BAD?

One of the basic financial theories tells us how we should view the relationship between risk and expected returns. In a nutshell, risk and expected return are positively related. A high-risk investment needs to have a high expected return, or no one would want to buy that investment. With this lack of demand, the investment's price would drop until it offers new buyers a high expected return for the future. The higher return is the reward for taking the extra risk. Similarly, low-risk investments offer low expected returns.

To quantify risk, the finance industry tends to use two measures; volatility of returns and beta. The volatility, measured by variance or standard deviation, tells us how much a return can deviate from the average return. Beta tells us how much market risk an investment has. These measures are very useful in assessing the risk of an investment or portfolio and what return premium should be expected for taking risk.

However, people do not naturally think of risk within this financial theory framework. First, investors care less about how an investment's return deviates from expectations and more about how the return may be lower than expected. In other words, a higher return than expected is not considered risky, only a lower return, or even, gulp, a loss, is viewed as risk.

Also, real people do not think in terms of the high risk/return versus the low risk/return scale. Instead, people think in terms of better or worse. For example, three financial economists ran an experiment in which they asked high net worth individuals for either their expected return predictions or their risk assessment (both on a 0 to 10 scale) of over 200 of the Fortune 500 companies. When they compiled all the responses, they found the relationship in this figure. Notice anything odd? This shows that firms with low risk are expected to earn a high return. People act as if expected return and risk are negatively related! This is the opposite of financial theory. Instead of evaluating firms within the framework that high expected return goes with high risk and low return goes with low risk, people seem to think in terms of good versus bad stocks. What are the characteristics of a "good" stock? Characteristics that seem good are high expected return and low risk. When an investor feels a stock is good, then it is attributed with high return and low risk. When an investor feels the stock is bad, then it is attributed with low return and high risk. Psychologists call this perception or belief an "affect."

Beliefs about Performance and Risk of Fortune 500 Firms

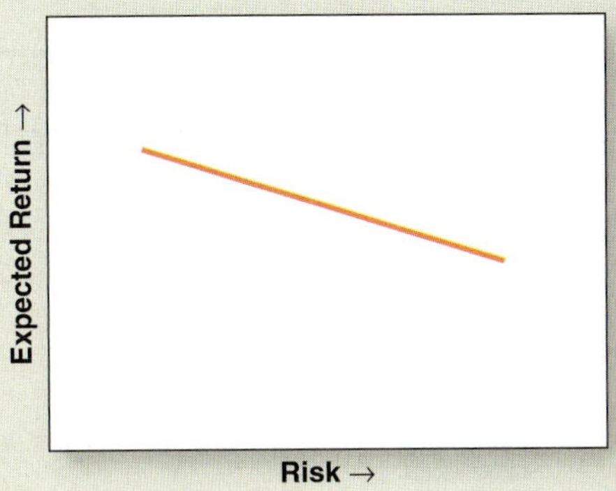

Unfortunately, thinking about risk and return from the affect framework causes investors to misunderstand the underlying dynamics of actual expected return and risk. Thus, they may make poor decisions regarding risk and return.

Source: Meir Statman, Kenneth L. Fisher, and Deniz Anginer, "Affect in a Behavioral Asset-Pricing Model," *Financial Analysts Journal*, March/April 2008, Figure 3: Relationship between Expected Return Scores and Risk Scores. Reproduced with permission from the CFA Institute.

want to know more? **Key Words to Search for Updates:** affect, measuring investment risk, risk and behavioral finance

by expanding into new businesses, and/or by changing its debt load. So even if beta is an accurate measure of what the firm's risk level was in the past, does it apply to the future? Beta's applicability will depend on the firm's future plans.

Both financial managers and investors share these concerns about beta. In the end, beta's usefulness depends on its reliability. Unfortunately, beta's empirical record is not as good as we would like. We should expect that companies with high betas yield higher returns than companies with low betas. On average, though, this does not turn out to be the case. A company's beta does not appear to predict its future return very well. Since characterizing the risk-return relationship is so important, finance researchers have introduced other asset pricing models. One promising model adds more risk factors to the predictive relationship other than just market risk. Firm size and book-to-market ratio have had some success predicting returns, so new models often include factors derived from these characteristics along with beta as a measure of market risk.

TIME OUT

10-3 Explain why portfolios that lie on the capital market line offer better risk-return trade-offs than those that lie on the efficient frontier.

10-4 Examine the betas in Table 10.2. Which seem about right to you and which seem to indicate too much or too little risk for that firm?

LG10-5

10.3 • Capital Market Efficiency

The risk and return relationship rests on an underlying assumption that stock prices are generally "correct"—they are not predictably too high or too low. Imagine having a system that identified undervalued stocks with low risks (i.e., relatively high returns with a low beta). Because those stocks are undervalued, they will earn you a high return, on average, as their stock prices rise to their correct value. Note that the CAPM's risk-return relationship would be incorrect. You would be consistently getting high returns with low risk. On the other hand, if you consistently picked overvalued stocks, you wouldn't be earning enough return to compensate you for the risks you are taking. Investors move their money to the best alternatives by selling overvalued stocks and buying undervalued stocks. This causes the prices of the overvalued stocks to drop and the prices of the undervalued stocks to rise until both stocks' returns stand more in line with their riskiness. Thus, the risk-return relationship relies on the idea that prices are generally accurate.

efficient market

A securities market in which prices fully reflect available information on each security.

What conditions are necessary for an **efficient market?** Efficient, or perfectly competitive, markets feature:

- Many buyers and sellers.
- No prohibitively high barriers to entry.
- Free and readily available information available to all participants.
- Low trading or transaction costs.

Are these conditions met for the U.S. stock market? Certainly millions of stock investors trade every day, buying and selling securities. With discount brokers and online traders, the costs to trade are fairly minimal and present no real barriers to enter the market. Information is increasingly accessible from many sources and trading philosophies, and commission costs and bid-ask spreads have steadily declined. With millions of the larger companies' shares (say the S&P 500) of stock trading every day, the U.S. stock exchanges appear to meet efficiency conditions. But other segments of the market, like those exchanges that trade in **penny stocks,** feature very thin trading. The prices of these very small companies' stock may not be fair and these equities may be manipulated in fraudulent scams. In the 1970s and 1980s, penny stock king Meyer Blinder and his firm Blinder-Robinson was known as "blind 'em and rob 'em" as they practiced penny stock price manipulation to rob many small investors of their entire investments in these small markets. These days, penny stock price manipulation is typically conducted through e-mail and Web posting scams.

penny stocks

The stocks of small companies that are priced below $1 per share.

Efficient Market Hypothesis

LG10-5

Our concept of market efficiency provides a good framework for understanding how stock prices change over time. This theory is described in the **efficient market hypothesis (EMH),** which states that *security prices fully reflect all available information.* At any point in time, the price for any stock or bond reflects the collective wisdom of market participants about the company's future prospects. Security prices change as new information becomes available. Since we cannot predict whether new information about a company will be good news or bad news, we cannot predict whether its stock price will go up or go down. This makes short-term stock-price movements unpredictable. But in the longer run, stock prices will adjust to their proper level as market participants gather and digest all available information.

efficient market hypothesis (EMH)

A theory that describes what types of information are reflected in current stock prices.

The EMH brings us to the question of what type of information is embedded within current stock prices. Segmenting information into three categories leads to the three basic levels of market efficiency, described as:

1. Weak-form efficiency—current prices reflect all information derived from trading. This stock market information generally includes current and past stock prices and trading volume.
2. Semistrong-form efficiency—current prices reflect all **public information.** This includes all information that has already been revealed to the public, like financial statements, news, analyst opinions, and so on.
3. Strong-form efficiency—current prices reflect *all* information. In addition to public information, prices reflect the **privately held information** that has not yet been released to the public, but may be known to some people, like managers, accountants, auditors, and so on.

public information

The set of information that has been publicly released. Public information includes data on past stock prices and volume, financial statements, corporate news, analyst opinion, etc.

privately held information

The set of information that has not been released to the public, but is known by few individuals, likely company insiders.

Each of the EMH's three forms rests on different assumptions regarding the extent of information that is incorporated into stock prices at any point in time. A fourth possibility—that markets may not be efficient and prices may not reflect all the information known about a company—also arises.

The *weak-form* efficiency level involves the lowest information hurdle, stating that stock prices reflect all past price and trading volume activity. If true, this level of efficiency would have important ramifications. A segment of the investment industry uses price and volume charts to make investment timing decisions. Technical analysis has a large following and its own vocabulary of patterns and trends (resistance, support, breakout, momentum, etc.). If the market is at least weak-form efficient, then prices already reflect this information and these activities would not result in useful predictions about future price changes, and thus would be a waste of time. Indeed, the people who make the most money from price charting services are the people who sell the services, not the investors who buy and use those services.

The *semistrong-form* efficiency level assumes that stock prices include all public information. Notice that past stock prices and volumes are publicly available information, so this level includes the weak form as a subset. Important investment implications arise if markets are efficient to public information. Many investors conduct security analysis in which they obtain financial data and other public information to assess whether a company's stock is undervalued or overvalued. But in a semistrong-form efficient market, stock prices already reflect this information and are thus "correct." Using only public information, you would not be able to determine whether a stock is misvalued because that information is already reflected in the price.

If prices reflect all public information, then those prices will react as traders hear new (or private) information. Consider a company that announces

figure 10.3

Potential Price Reaction to a Good News Announcement

Stock prices react quickly to news, but do they react accurately?

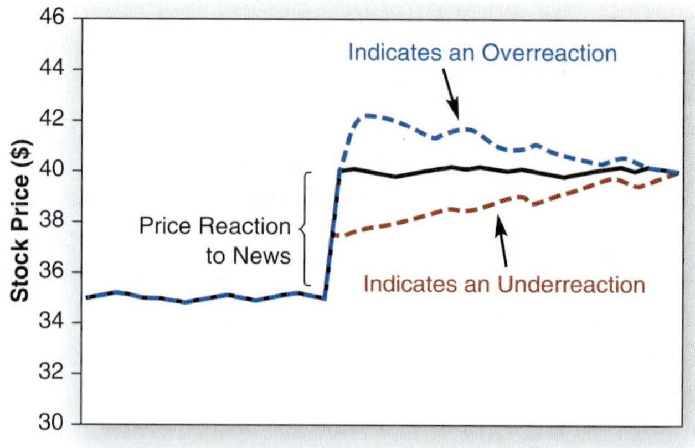

surprisingly good quarterly profits. Traders and investors will have factored the old profit expectations into the stock price. As they incorporate the new information, the stock price will quickly rise to a new and accurate price as shown in the solid black line in Figure 10.3. Note that the stock price was $35 before the announcement and $40 immediately following. If you tried to buy the stock after hearing the news, then you would have bought at $40 and not received any benefit of the good quarterly profit news. On the other hand, if the market is not semistrong-form efficient, then the price might react quickly, but not accurately. The dashed green line shows a reaction in a non-semistrong efficient market where the price continues to drift up well after the announcement. This gradual drift to the "correct" price indicates that the market initially underreacted to the news. In this case, you could have bought the stock after the announcement and still earned a profit. The dotted blue line shows an overreaction to the firm's better-than-expected profits announcement. If markets either consistently underreact or consistently overreact to announcements that would change stock prices (earnings, stock split, dividend, etc.), then we would believe that the market is not semistrong efficient.

The *strong-form* market efficiency level presents the highest hurdle to test market reaction to information. The strong-form level includes information considered by the weak-form, the semistrong-form, as well as privately known information. People within firms, like CEOs and CFOs, know information that has not yet been released to the public. They may trade on this privately held, or insider, information and their trading may cause stock prices to change as it reflects that private information. In this way, stock prices could reflect even privately known information. Note that the firm managers, accountants, and auditors know several days in advance that a firm has earned unexpectedly high quarterly profits. If the stock price already incorporated this closely held private knowledge, then the big price reaction shown in Figure 10.3 would not occur.

So, is the stock market efficient? If it is, at what level? This has been a hotly debated topic for decades and continues to be. It is not likely that the market is strong-form efficient. Since insider trading is punished, insider information must be valuable. However, much evidence suggests that the market could be weak-form or semistrong-form efficient. Of course, we also have evidence that the market is not efficient at any of the three levels. We will explore this more in the following section.

Behavioral Finance

LG10-5

The argument for the market being efficient works as follows: Many individual and professional investors constantly look for mispriced stocks. If they find a stock that is undervalued, they will buy it and drive up its price until it's correctly priced. Likewise, investors would sell an overpriced stock, driving down its price until it's correctly valued. With so many investors looking for market "mistakes," it's unlikely that any mispriced stock opportunities will be left in the market.

The argument against the market being efficient is equally convincing. The market comprises many people transacting with one another. When someone makes trading decisions influenced by emotion or psychological bias, those decisions may not seem rational. When many people fall under such influences, their trading decisions may actually drive stock prices away from the correct price as emotion carries the traders away from rationality. For example, many people believe that investors were "irrationally exuberant" about technology stocks in the late 1990s—and that their buying excitement drove prices to an artificially high level. In 2000, the excitement wore off and tech stock prices plummeted. Whenever a set of stock prices go unnaturally high and subsequently crash down, the market experiences what we call a **stock market bubble.**

stock market bubble

Investor enthusiasm causes an inflated bull market that drives prices too high, ending in a dramatic collapse in prices.

In the past couple of decades, finance researchers have studied **behavioral finance** and found that people often behave in ways that are very likely "irrational." At times, investors appear to be too optimistic, as though they are looking through rose-colored glasses. At other times they appear to be too pessimistic. Common investment decisions aren't necessarily optimal ones, which flies in the face of the economist's expectation of rational economic actors. Perhaps, then, capital markets don't represent perfectly competitive or efficient markets if buyers and sellers do not always make rational choices.

behavioral finance

The study of the cognitive processes and biases associated with making financial and economic decisions.

It may take many biased investors to move a stock's price enough that it would be considered a pricing mistake. However, the important decisions in a company are typically made by just one CEO or a management team. Thus, their biases can have a direct impact on decisions involving hundreds of millions, or even billions of dollars. In other words, the contribution of behavioral finance to economic decision making is likely to be even more important in corporate behavior than market behavior. For example, consider the psychological concept of **overconfidence.** One of the most pervasive biases, overconfidence describes a tendency for people to overestimate the accuracy of their knowledge and underestimate the risks of a decision. These problems can adversely affect important decisions of investment (i.e., acquiring other firms) and financing (i.e., issuing new stock or bonds).

overconfidence

Overconfidence is used to describe three psychological observations. First, people are miscalibrated on understanding the precision of their knowledge. Second, people have a tendency to underestimate risks, and third, people tend to believe that they are better than average at tasks they are familiar with.

TIME OUT

10-5 Can the market be semistrong-form efficient but not weak-form efficient? Explain.

10-6 If the market usually overreacts to bad news announcements, what would your return be like if you bought after you heard the bad news?

10.4 • Implications for Financial Managers

LG10-6

Financial managers must understand the crucial relationship between risk and return for several reasons. First, while the relationship between risk and return is demonstrated here using the capital markets, it equally applies to many business finance at work

markets

BUBBLE TROUBLE

Many professionals criticize the EMH because the overall market sometimes seems too high or too low. A very dramatic example of the market level being artificially high is the market bubble. During a market bubble, the market quickly inflates on rampant speculation and subsequently crashes. Investors who buy near the peak of the bubble risk losing nearly all their investment.

One of the United States' earliest stock market bubbles was the bubble and crash of 1929. Note from the figure that the DJIA started in 1927 at around 160. By October 1929, the DJIA had reached nearly 400 and then crashed. By mid-1932, the DJIA had fallen to the 40s. The sustained fall coincided with an economic depression. Panel A of the figure also shows a price bubble in gold. The price of gold was $230 per ounce in January 1979. The late 1970s and early 1980s saw double-digit inflation throughout the economy, and many investors felt that gold represented a safe and inflation-proof investment. Just one year later, the price had skyrocketed to $870. It then fell below $300 in less than two and a half years. Could gold be in another bubble? In late 2008, gold's price was $750; it shot to $1,500 in late 2011.

See the spectacular tech bubble during the 1990s? The NASDAQ 100, which started in 1985 at 250, soared to a peak of 4,816.35 on March 24, 2000. It then fell to less than 1,000 in two and a half years. The rise and fall of the NASDAQ 100 seems much more pronounced than the Japanese stock bubble of the 1980s. From a January 2, 1985, start at 11,543, the Nikkei 225 soared to a closing high of 38,916 on December 29, 1989. The bubble then burst and the Japanese stock market plummeted. The Nikkei has yet to fully recover, trading today at around the 16,500 level.

EMH critics do not believe that the entire stock market, or a substantial segment of it, can be correctly valued before, during, or after a bubble. It certainly appears to be overvalued during the time the bubble is inflating.

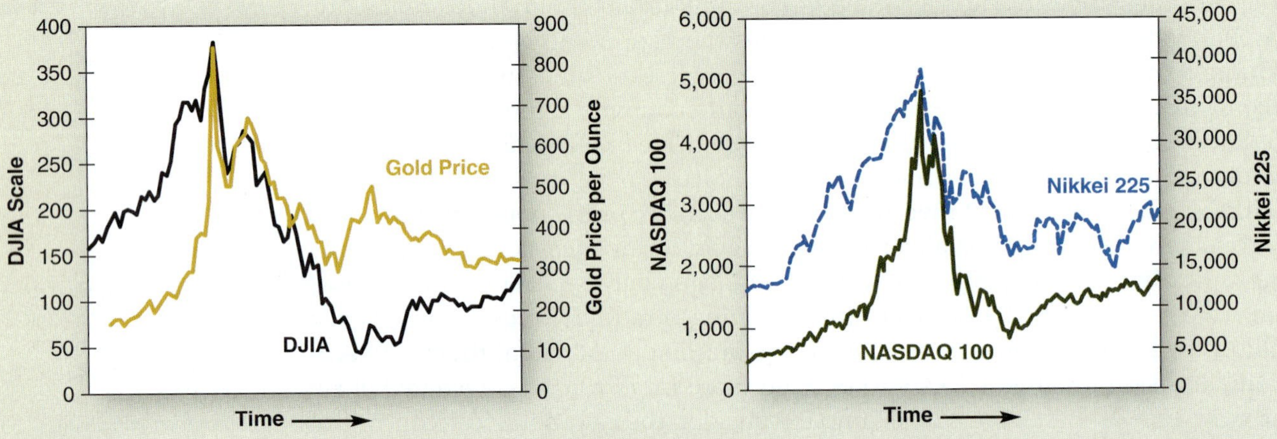

want to know more? Key Words to Search For Updates: stock bubble, irrational exuberance

decisions. A firm's product mix, marketing campaign combination, and research and development programs all entail risk and potential rewards. Being able to understand and characterize these decisions within a risk and return framework can help managers make better decisions. In addition, managers must understand what return their stockholders require at various times of firm operations. After all, a firm must receive enough revenue from its variously risky activities to pay its business and debt costs and reward the owners (the stockholders). Managers must thus include the return to shareholders when they analyze new business opportunities.

Firms and capital markets also interact directly. For example, a good understanding of market efficiency helps managers understand how their stock prices will react to different types of decisions (like dividend changes) and news announcements (like unexpectedly high or low profitability). In fact, many managers own company stock and are thus compensated through programs that rely on the stock price, like **restricted stock** and **executive stock options.** Companies also periodically issue (sell) additional shares of stock to raise more capital, and these sales depend upon market efficiency assumptions. The firm would not want to sell additional shares if the stock price is too low (i.e., undervalued). They *would* want to sell more shares at any time that they thought their shares are overvalued. Other times, firms repurchase (buy back) shares of stock. The firm might want to do this if its shares were undervalued, but not if its shares were overvalued. Of course, valuation is not an issue if security markets are efficient.

restricted stock

Shares of stock issued to executives that have limitations on when they can be sold.

executive stock options

Special rights given to corporate executives to buy a specific number of shares of the company stock at a fixed price during a specific period of time.

Using the Constant-Growth Model for Required Return

LG10-7

For decades, financial managers have used the CAPM to compute shareholders' required return. Given recent concerns about beta's limitations, many see the CAPM as a less useful model for calculating appropriate returns. Some have turned instead to another model useful for computing required return—the constant-growth model discussed in Chapter 8. We can arrange the terms of that model as:

$$i = \text{Dividend yield} + \text{Constant growth}$$

$$= \frac{D_1}{P_0} + g \qquad \textbf{(10-6)}$$

Of course, this model assumes that the stock is efficiently priced. This model holds an advantage in that it uses current firm data (dividend, D_1, and price, P_0) and a simple forward estimate (growth, g) to assess what investors currently expect the stock to return, i. For example, Table 10.2 shows Walmart's beta as 0.41. Using this beta, Table 10.3 shows that shareholders require only 7.87 percent return to hold Walmart stock, given its low risk profile. You may find it hard to believe that Walmart's owners (the shareholders) expect such a low return from one of the world's most profitable firms. So perhaps this is a case in which the CAPM result isn't very useful. Applying the constant-growth model looks something like this: Walmart is expected to pay a \$2.80 dividend this year and say the stock price currently stands at \$76 per share. Financial analysts believe Walmart will grow at 9 percent per year for the next five years. The constant growth rate model suggests that Walmart shareholders expect a 12.68 percent [= (\$2.80 ÷ \$76) + 0.09] return. So, which required return seems more likely, the 7.87 percent computed from CAPM or the 12.68 percent suggested by the constant-growth model? It is likely that Walmart investors are expecting closer to the 13 percent return than the 8 percent estimate.

Financial managers need an estimate of their shareholders' required return in order to make appropriate decisions about their companies' future growth. Good financial managers will compute shareholders' required return using as many methods as they can to determine the most realistic value possible.

EXAMPLE 10-4

LG10-7

Required Return

Note from Table 10.3 that the required returns for 3M, Home Depot, and Hewlett-Packard are 12.56 percent, 12.07 percent, and 15.78 percent, respectively. These expectations may seem quite far apart, considering that all three firms are in the DJIA and are leaders in their market sectors. Use the following information to compute the constant-growth model estimate of the required return:

For interactive versions of this example visit www.mhhe.com/can3e

	Expected Dividend	Current Price	Analyst Growth Estimate
3M Company	$2.54	$105.70	10.4%
Home Depot	1.56	70.10	14.5
Hewlett-Packard	0.53	22.00	0.25

SOLUTION:

You can now use equation 10-6 to find each company's required return as:

$$\text{3M required return} = (\$2.54 \div \$105.70) + 0.104 = 12.80\%$$

$$\text{Home Depot required return} = (\$1.56 \div \$70.10) + 0.145 = 16.73\%$$

$$\text{Hewlett-Packard required return} = (\$0.53 \div \$22.00) + 0.0025 = 2.66\%$$

The 3M estimates using CAPM and the constant-growth rate model are similar. The constant-growth rate model estimate is more than 4 percent higher than the CAPM estimate for Home Depot, but far lower for Hewlett-Packard.

Similar to Problems 10-15, 10-16, 10-29, 10-30, self-test problem 3

TIME OUT

10-7 Why is the shareholders' required return important to corporate managers?

viewpoints REVISITED

Business Application Solution

You need to determine the firm's level of market risk. If you can obtain a beta, then you can make a required return estimate using CAPM. To assess the result, you can use the constant-growth model to check the CAPM estimated required return for comparison's sake.

If you find the beta of the firm to be 1.8, assume a market return of 11 percent, and note a 5 percent T-bill rate, the CAPM computations would be:

$$5\% + 1.8 \times (11\% - 5\%) = 15.8 \text{ percent}$$

The firm will pay a $0.50 dividend next year and the current stock price is $32. Managers believe the company will grow at 13 percent per year for the foreseeable future. The constant-growth model computation gives:

$$\$0.50 \div \$32 + 0.13 = 0.1456, \text{ or } 14.56 \text{ percent}$$

You can now take these estimates to the team.

Personal Application Solution

You are investing 57.1 percent (= $200 ÷ $350) of your monthly contribution in stocks. You are also contributing 28.6 percent in bonds and 14.3 percent into a money market account. The diversified stock portfolio has a beta of 1. The long-term bond portfolio has a beta of 0.18. By definition, the money market account is risk-free and thus has a beta of zero.

The beta of this portfolio is therefore:

$$0.571 \times (1) + 0.286 \times (0.18) + 0.143 \times (0) = 0.62$$

With a portfolio beta of 0.62, a market return of 11 percent, and a risk-free rate of 5 percent, you can expect a return of:

$$5\% + 0.62 \times (11\% - 5\%) = 8.72 \text{ percent}$$

If you want a higher expected return, you will have to take more risk. You can do that by contributing a higher proportion of your funds to the stock portfolio.

summary of learning goals

In this chapter, we explored the theory and application of expected return. As an incentive to take market risk, investors require a commensurate return. We developed more precise specifications of the risk and required return relationship here via the CAPM and then discussed whether the underlying assumptions of the CAPM hold well enough in reality for CAPM required return estimates to give realistic insight into what investors really expect. However, people often think about risk differently from how it is captured by traditional statistical measures, which can lead to misconceptions.

LG10-1 **Compute forward-looking expected return and risk.** A firm's stock return performance relates closely to the strength of the economy. We can compute expected return and risk using the probabilities of various good and bad economic states occurring in the future as predicted by macroeconomists.

LG10-2 **Understand risk premiums.** Investors will take on risk if they are given positive risk premiums. The risk premium of the stock market itself is defined as the market return minus the risk-free rate. The market risk premium provides a basis for us to understand the rewards for taking risk. Any particular stock's risk premium will be jointly determined by the market risk premium and the stock's sensitivity to market risk.

LG10-3 **Know and apply the capital asset pricing model (CAPM).** Adding a risk-free security to any portfolio along the efficient frontier gives the investor a higher required return. Investors should own combinations of the market portfolio and the risk-free security. As we change the amounts of the market portfolio and risk-free securities that investors may choose according to their risk preferences, we derive the security market line. The security market line's equation is known as CAPM, which specifies a direct relationship between required return and market risk. Any stock's required return comprises the risk-free rate plus the stock's risk premium. That risk premium is determined by the amount of market risk to which the stock is subject, as measured by beta.

LG10-4 **Calculate and apply beta, a measure of market risk.** We can use a stock's standard deviation to measure a stock's volatility. The market only rewards investors for taking on the portion of risk or volatility that arises due to general, economywide volatility, as shown in the market portfolio. The market risk portion of total risk is scaled so that a beta of one represents the risk of the overall stock market. A beta of 0.5 means that the stock exhibits only half of the overall stock market risk, while a beta of 2 means that the stock exhibits twice the risk that the overall market shows. A riskless security—such as a U.S. Treasury bill—has a zero beta. We can compute betas using past stock returns and the returns from a market portfolio proxy, like the S&P 500 Index. Many financial publications and financial websites also provide their own beta estimates for particular stocks.

LG10-5 **Differentiate among the different levels of market efficiency and their implications.** Financial risk-reward relationships rely upon the assumption that stock market prices are generally "right," given known company information. Various levels of the efficient market hypothesis (EMH) are characterized by the information types that stock prices reflect. The weak-form level of market efficiency states that stock prices incorporate all trading information, like past prices and trading volume. The semistrong-form efficiency level states that current stock prices reflect all public information. Note that publicly known information includes the weak-form efficiency information and financial statements, analyst opinions, news, etc. Information that is not publicly known, but that is known by some corporate officers and other insiders, is called privately held information. The strong-form market efficiency level of the EMH claims that stock prices incorporate all information, public and private. Note that all U.S. stock exchanges forbid corporate officers and other people privy to closely held information from profiting from such information—an activity known as insider trading. The fourth possibility of the EMH is that stock prices are not efficient and thus are not always correct. If this is the case, investors can profit from mispricings.

LG10-6 Calculate and explain investors' required return and risk. Financial managers—and all managers, for that matter—must have a firm grasp upon the trade-off between risk and return. This trade-off arises in many business decisions involving product mix, marketing campaigns, and research and development. Financial managers in particular must understanding the return that shareholders require from the firm when they analyze new business opportunities.

LG10-7 Use the constant-growth model to compute required return. The constant-growth model provides a useful alternative to the CAPM for computing shareholders' required return. This model requires only the current stock price, an estimate of next year's dividends, and an estimate of the firm's growth rate. To make the best assessment of the required return, compute estimates from both the CAPM and the constant-growth model and compare them, judging which seems more in line with investors' actual expectations.

chapter equations

10-1 $$\text{Expected return} = (p_1 \times \text{Return}_1) + (p_2 \times \text{Return}_2) + (p_3 \times \text{Return}_3) + \cdots + (p_s \times \text{Return}_s) = \sum_{j=1}^{s} p_j \times \text{Return}_j$$

10-2 $$\text{Standard deviation} = \sqrt{p_1 \times (\text{Return}_1 - \text{Expected return})^2 + p_2 \times (\text{Return}_2 - \text{Expected return})^2 + \cdots} = \sqrt{\sum_{j=1}^{s} p_j \times (\text{Return}_j - \text{Expected return})^2}$$

10-3 Required return = Risk-free rate + Risk premium

10-4 $$\text{Expected return} = R_f + \beta(R_M - R_f)$$

10-5 $$\beta_p = (w_1 \times \beta_1) + (w_2 \times \beta_2) + (w_3 \times \beta_3) + \cdots + (w_n \times \beta_n) = \sum_{j=1}^{n} w_j \beta_j$$

10-6 $$i = \text{Dividend yield} + \text{Constant growth} = \frac{D_1}{P_0} + g$$

key terms

asset pricing, The process of directly specifying the relationship between required return and risk. *p. 343*

behavioral finance, The study of the cognitive processes and biases associated with making financial and economic decisions. *p. 355*

beta (β), A measure of the sensitivity of a stock or portfolio to market risk. *p. 345*

capital asset pricing model (CAPM), An asset pricing theory based on a beta, a measure of market risk. *p. 343*

capital market line, The line on a graph of return and risk (standard deviation) from the risk-free rate through the market portfolio. *p. 344*

efficient market, A securities market in which prices fully reflect available information on each security. *p. 352*

efficient market hypothesis (EMH), A theory that describes what types of information are reflected in current stock prices. *p. 353*

executive stock options, Special rights given to corporate executives to buy a specific number of shares of the company stock at a fixed price during a specific period of time. *p. 357*

expected return, The average of the possible returns weighted by the likelihood of those returns occurring. *p. 340*

financial leverage, The use of debt to increase an investment position. *p. 345*

market portfolio, In theory, the market portfolio is the combination of securities that places the portfolio on the efficient frontier and on a line tangent from the risk-free rate. In practice, the S&P 500 Index is used to proxy for the market portfolio. *p. 345*

market risk premium, The return on the market portfolio minus the risk-free rate. Risk premiums for specific firms are based on the market risk premium. *p. 343*

overconfidence, A term used to describe three psychological observations: (1) people are miscalibrated on understanding the precision of their knowledge; (2) people have a tendency to underestimate risks, and (3) people tend to believe that they are better than average at tasks they are familiar with. *p. 355*

penny stocks, The stocks of small companies that are priced below $1 per share. *p. 352*

portfolio beta, The combination of the individual company beta's in an investor's portfolio. *p. 348*

privately held information, The set of information that has not been released to the public, but is known by few individuals, likely company insiders. *p. 353*

probability, The likelihood of occurrence. *p. 340*

probability distribution, The set of probabilities for all possible occurrences. *p. 341*

public information, The set of information that has been publicly released. Public information includes data on past stock prices and volume, financial statements, corporate news, analyst opinion, etc. *p. 353*

required return, The level of total return needed to be compensated for the risk taken. It is made up of a risk-free rate and a risk premium. *p. 342*

restricted stock, Shares of stock issued to executives that have limitations on when they can be sold. *p. 357*

risk premium, The portion of the required return that represents the reward for taking risk. *p. 343*

security market line, Similar to the capital market line except risk is characterized by beta instead of standard deviation. *p. 346*

stock market bubble, Investor enthusiasm causes an inflated bull market that drives prices too high, ending in a dramatic collapse in prices. *p. 355*

self-test problems with solutions

1 Expected Return and Risk An economist has determined that the probability of the economy being in various states is shown in the following table. LG10-1

Economic State	Probability	Return
Fast growth	0.13	40%
Slow growth	0.42	15
No growth	0.25	5
Recession	0.17	−15
Depression	0.03	−30

You have added the return that your firm will achieve in each economic state. Given this information, you can compute the expected return and risk of the firm.

Solution:

Use equations 10-1 and 10-2 to complete the following table:

Economy	Probability	Return	$P \times$ Return	Deviation	Deviation^2	$\times P$
Fast growth	0.13	40%	5.20%	30.70%	942.49	122.52
Slow growth	0.42	15	6.30	5.70	32.49	13.65
No growth	0.25	5	1.25	−4.30	18.49	4.62
Recession	0.17	−15	−2.55	−24.30	590.49	100.38
Depression	0.03	−30	−0.90	−39.30	1544.49	46.33
Sum =	1		9.30%			287.51
					Square root =	16.96%

The expected return for the firm is 9.3 percent and the standard deviation risk is 16.96 percent.

LG10-3, 10-4

2 **Portfolio Beta and Required Return** You have a stock portfolio that consists of the following positions:

	Shares	Price	Beta
Apple Inc.	50	$89.00	2.40
Fiserv	100	55.00	1.34
Monster Worldwide	150	52.00	2.37
Ross Stores	200	34.00	1.27
Whole Foods	100	51.00	1.66

The beta of each stock is also shown. What is the portfolio beta? If the market return is expected to be 12 percent and the risk-free rate is 4 percent, what is the required return of the portfolio?

Solution:

To compute the portfolio beta, you must first calculate the portfolio weights for each stock. The position of each stock is denoted by the number of shares multiplied by the price of the stock. Adding all of the positions results in a total portfolio value of $29,650. The portion that each stock represents in the portfolio is shown as its weight and is computed by dividing each position by the total portfolio value. Once the weights are known, then equation 10-5 can be used. The last column shows the computations for the portfolio beta.

	Share	Price	Position	Weight	Beta	$W \times$ Beta
Apple Inc.	50	$89.00	$4,450	0.15	2.40	0.36
Fiserv	100	55.00	5,500	0.19	1.34	0.25
Monster Worldwide	150	52.00	7,800	0.26	2.37	0.62
Ross Stores	200	34.00	6,800	0.23	1.27	0.29
Whole Foods	100	51.00	5,100	0.17	1.66	0.29
	Sum =		$29,650	1.00		1.81

The beta of this portfolio is 1.81. This is a high-risk portfolio. You can now use the CAPM to compute the required return of the portfolio as

$$4\% + 18.1 \times (12\% - 4\%) = 18.47 \text{ percent}$$

LG10-4, 10-7

3 **Required Return** Compute the required return for three stocks: Molson Coors, Hilton Hotels, and Tribune Co. To be thorough, compute required return using both the CAPM and the constant-growth model.

For the CAPM analysis, see the following market risk information: Molson Coors ($\beta = 0.37$), Hilton Hotels ($\beta = 1.51$), and Tribune ($\beta = 0.46$). Assume that the risk-free rate is 4.5 percent and the market risk premium is 6 percent.

For the constant-growth model, the stock price, dividend, and growth information is:

	Price	Dividend	Growth Rate
Molson Coors	$50.05	$1.20	9.0%
Hilton Hotels	36.70	0.16	15.0
Tribune	30.65	0.76	11.0

Solution:

Start by calculating the required return using CAPM. Note that it was the market risk premium that was given instead of the market return. Since the market risk premium is what goes in the parenthesis of the equation, the results are:

$$\text{Molson Coors: } 4.5\% + 0.37 \times (6\%) = 6.72\%$$

$$\text{Hilton Hotel: } 4.5\% + 1.51 \times (6\%) = 13.56\%$$

$$\text{Tribune: } 4.5\% + 0.46 \times (6\%) = 7.26\%$$

The required returns for Molson Coors and for Tribune seem a little low. So you should also compute the required return using the constant-growth model:

$$\text{Molson Coors: } (\$1.20 \div \$50.05) + 0.09 = 11.40\%$$

$$\text{Hilton Hotel: } (\$0.16 \div \$36.70) + 0.15 = 15.44\%$$

$$\text{Tribune: } (\$0.76 \div \$30.65) + 0.11 = 13.48\%$$

These estimates for the required return seem much better for Molson Coors and Tribune, but the Hilton Hotels estimate may be a little high.

questions

1. Consider an asset that provides the same return no matter what economic state occurs. What would be the standard deviation (or risk) of this asset? Explain. *(LG10-1)*
2. Why is expected return considered "forward-looking"? What are the challenges for practitioners to utilize expected return? *(LG10-1)*
3. In 2000, the S&P 500 Index earned −9.1 percent while the T-bill yield was 5.9 percent. Does this mean the market risk premium was negative? Explain. *(LG10-2)*
4. How might the magnitude of the market risk premium impact people's desire to buy stocks? *(LG10-2)*
5. Describe how adding a risk-free security to modern portfolio theory allows investors to do better than the efficient frontier. *(LG10-3)*
6. Show on a graph like Figure 10.2 where a stock with a beta of 1.3 would be located on the security market line. Then show where that stock would be located if it is undervalued. *(LG10-3)*

www.mhhe.com/can3e

7. Consider that you have three stocks in your portfolio and wish to add a fourth. You want to know if the fourth stock will make the portfolio riskier or less risky. Compare and contrast how this would be assessed using standard deviation versus market risk (beta) as the measure of risk. *(LG10-3)*

8. Describe how different allocations between the risk-free security and the market portfolio can achieve any level of market risk desired. Give examples of a portfolio from a person who is very risk averse and a portfolio for someone who is not so averse to taking risk. *(LG10-3)*

9. Cisco Systems has a beta of 1.25. Does this mean that you should expect Cisco to earn a return 25 percent higher than the S&P 500 Index return? Explain. *(LG10-4)*

10. Note from Table 10.2 that some technology-oriented firms (Intel) in the Dow Jones Industrial Average have high market risk while others (AT&T and Verizon) have low market risk. How do you explain this? *(LG10-4)*

11. Find a beta estimate from three different sources for General Electric (GE). Compare these three values. Why might they be different? *(LG10-4)*

12. If you were to compute beta yourself, what choices would you make regarding the market portfolio, the holding period for the returns (daily, weekly, etc.), and the number of returns? Justify your choices. *(LG10-4)*

13. Explain how the concept of a positive risk-return relationship breaks down if you can systematically find stocks that are overvalued and undervalued. *(LG10-5)*

14. Determine what level of market efficiency each event is consistent with the following:
    - a. Immediately after an earnings announcement the stock price jumps and then stays at the new level. *(LG10-5)*
    - b. The CEO buys 50,000 shares of his company and the stock price does not change. *(LG10-5)*
    - c. The stock price immediately jumps when a stock split is announced, but then retraces half of the gain over the next day. *(LG10-5)*
    - d. An investor analyzes company quarterly and annual balance sheets and income statements looking for undervalued stocks. The investor earns about the same return as the S&P 500 Index. *(LG10-5)*

15. Why do most investment scams conducted over the Internet and e-mail involve penny stocks instead of S&P 500 Index stocks? *(LG10-5)*

16. Describe a stock market bubble. Can a bubble occur in a single stock? *(LG10-5)*

17. If stock prices are not strong-form efficient, then what might be the price reaction to a firm announcing a stock buyback? Explain. *(LG10-6)*

18. Compare and contrast the assumptions that need to be made to compute a required return using CAPM and the constant-growth model. *(LG10-7)*

19. How should you handle a case where required return computations from CAPM and the constant-growth model are very different? *(LG10-7)*

problems

basic problems

10-1 Expected Return Compute the expected return given these three economic states, their likelihoods, and the potential returns: *(LG10-1)*

Economic State	Probability	Return
Fast growth	0.3	40%
Slow growth	0.4	10
Recession	0.3	−25

10-2 **Expected Return** Compute the expected return given these three economic states, their likelihoods, and the potential returns: *(LG10-1)*

Economic State	Probability	Return
Fast growth	0.2	35%
Slow growth	0.6	10
Recession	0.2	−30

10-3 **Required Return** If the risk-free rate is 3 percent and the risk premium is 5 percent, what is the required return? *(LG10-2)*

10-4 **Required Return** If the risk-free rate is 4 percent and the risk premium is 6 percent, what is the required return? *(LG10-2)*

10-5 **Risk Premium** The average annual return on the S&P 500 Index from 1986 to 1995 was 15.8 percent. The average annual T-bill yield during the same period was 5.6 percent. What was the market risk premium during these ten years? *(LG10-2)*

10-6 **Risk Premium** The average annual return on the S&P 500 Index from 1996 to 2005 was 10.8 percent. The average annual T-bill yield during the same period was 3.6 percent. What was the market risk premium during these ten years? *(LG10-2)*

10-7 **CAPM Required Return** Hastings Entertainment has a beta of 0.65. If the market return is expected to be 11 percent and the risk-free rate is 4 percent, what is Hastings' required return? *(LG10-3)*

10-8 **CAPM Required Return** Nanometrics, Inc., has a beta of 3.15. If the market return is expected to be 10 percent and the risk-free rate is 3.5 percent, what is Nanometrics' required return? *(LG10-3)*

10-9 **Company Risk Premium** Netflix, Inc., has a beta of 3.61. If the market return is expected to be 13 percent and the risk-free rate is 3 percent, what is Netflix' risk premium? *(LG10-3)*

10-10 **Company Risk Premium** Paycheck, Inc., has a beta of 0.94. If the market return is expected to be 11 percent and the risk-free rate is 3 percent, what is Paycheck's risk premium? *(LG10-3)*

10-11 **Portfolio Beta** You have a portfolio with a beta of 1.35. What will be the new portfolio beta if you keep 85 percent of your money in the old portfolio and 5 percent in a stock with a beta of 0.78? *(LG10-3)*

10-12 **Portfolio Beta** You have a portfolio with a beta of 1.1. What will be the new portfolio beta if you keep 85 percent of your money in the old portfolio and 15 percent in a stock with a beta of 0.5? *(LG10-3)*

10-13 **Stock Market Bubble** The NASDAQ stock market bubble peaked at 4,816 in 2000. Two and a half years later it had fallen to 1,000. What was the percentage decline? *(LG10-5)*

10-14 **Stock Market Bubble** The Japanese stock market bubble peaked at 38,916 in 1989. Two and a half years later it had fallen to 15,900. What was the percentage decline? *(LG10-5)*

10-15 Required Return Paccar's current stock price is $48.20 and it is likely to pay a $0.80 dividend next year. Since analysts estimate Paccar will have an 8.8 percent growth rate, what is its required return? *(LG10-7)*

10-16 Required Return Universal Forest's current stock price is $57.50 and it is likely to pay a $0.26 dividend next year. Since analysts estimate Universal Forest will have a 9.5 percent growth rate, what is its required return? *(LG10-7)*

intermediate problems

10-17 Expected Return Risk For the same economic state probability distribution in problem 10-1, determine the standard deviation of the expected return. *(LG10-1)*

Economic State	Probability	Return
Fast growth	0.3	40%
Slow growth	0.4	10
Recession	0.3	−25

10-18 Expected Return Risk For the same economic state probability distribution in problem 10-2, determine the standard deviation of the expected return. *(LG10-1)*

Economic State	Probability	Return
Fast growth	0.2	35%
Slow growth	0.6	10
Recession	0.2	−30

10-19 Undervalued/Overvalued Stock A manager believes his firm will earn a 14 percent return next year. His firm has a beta of 1.5, the expected return on the market is 12 percent, and the risk-free rate is 4 percent. Compute the return the firm should earn given its level of risk and determine whether the manager is saying the firm is undervalued or overvalued. *(LG10-3)*

10-20 Undervalued/Overvalued Stock A manager believes his firm will earn a 14 percent return next year. His firm has a beta of 1.2, the expected return on the market is 11 percent, and the risk-free rate is 5 percent. Compute the return the firm should earn given its level of risk and determine whether the manager is saying the firm is undervalued or overvalued. *(LG10-3)*

10-21 Portfolio Beta You own $10,000 of Olympic Steel stock that has a beta of 2.2. You also own $7,000 of Rent-a-Center (beta = 1.5) and $8,000 of Lincoln Educational (beta = 0.5). What is the beta of your portfolio? *(LG10-3)*

10-22 Portfolio Beta You own $7,000 of Human Genome stock that has a beta of 3.5. You also own $8,000 of Frozen Food Express (beta = 1.6) and $10,000 of Molecular Devices (beta = 0.4). What is the beta of your portfolio? *(LG10-3)*

advanced problems

10-23 Expected Return and Risk Compute the expected return and standard deviation given these four economic states, their likelihoods, and the potential returns: *(LG10-1)*

Economic State	Probability	Return
Fast growth	0.30	60%
Slow growth	0.50	13
Recession	0.15	−15
Depression	0.05	−45

10-24 Expected Return and Risk Compute the expected return and standard deviation given these four economic states, their likelihoods, and the potential returns: *(LG10-1)*

Economic State	Probability	Return
Fast growth	0.25	50%
Slow growth	0.55	11
Recession	0.15	−15
Depression	0.05	−50

10-25 Risk Premiums You own $10,000 of Denny's Corp. stock that has a beta of 2.9. You also own $15,000 of Qwest Communications (beta = 1.5) and $5,000 of Southwest Airlines (beta = 0.7). Assume that the market return will be 11.5 percent and the risk-free rate is 4.5 percent. What is the market risk premium? What is the risk premium of each stock? What is the risk premium of the portfolio? *(LG10-3)*

10-26 Risk Premiums You own $15,000 of Opsware, Inc., stock that has a beta of 3.8. You also own $10,000 of Lowe's Companies (beta = 1.6) and $10,000 of New York Times (beta = 0.8). Assume that the market return will be 12 percent and the risk-free rate is 6 percent. What is the market risk premium? What is the risk premium of each stock? What is the risk premium of the portfolio? *(LG10-3)*

10-27 Portfolio Beta and Required Return You hold the positions in the following table. What is the beta of your portfolio? If you expect the market to earn 12 percent and the risk-free rate is 3.5 percent, what is the required return of the portfolio? *(LG10-3)*

	Price	Shares	Beta
Amazon.com	$40.80	100	3.8
Family Dollar Stores	30.10	150	1.2
McKesson Corp.	57.40	75	0.4
Schering-Plough Corp.	23.80	200	0.5

10-28 Portfolio Beta and Required Return You hold the positions in the following table. What is the beta of your portfolio? If you expect the market to earn 12 percent and the risk-free rate is 3.5 percent, what is the required return of the portfolio? *(LG10-3)*

	Price	Shares	Beta
Advanced Micro Devices	$ 14.70	300	4.2
FedEx Corp.	120.00	50	1.1
Microsoft	28.90	100	0.7
Sara Lee Corp.	17.25	150	0.5

10-29 Required Return Using the information in the table, compute the required return for each company using both CAPM and the constant-growth model. Compare and discuss the results. Assume that the market portfolio will earn 12 percent and the risk-free rate is 3.5 percent. *(LG10-3, 10-7)*

	Price	Upcoming Dividend	Growth	Beta
US Bancorp	$36.55	$1.60	10.0%	1.8
Praxair	64.75	1.12	11.0	2.4
Eastman Kodak	24.95	1.00	4.5	0.5

10-30 Required Return Using the information in the table, compute the required return for each company using both CAPM and the constant-growth model. Compare and discuss the results. Assume that the market portfolio will earn 11 percent and the risk-free rate is 4 percent. *(LG10-3, LG10-7)*

	Price	Upcoming Dividend	Growth	Beta
Estee Lauder	$47.40	$0.60	11.7%	0.75
Kimco Realty	52.10	1.54	8.0	1.3
Nordstrom	5.25	0.50	14.6	2.2

10-31 Spreadsheet Problem As discussed in the text, beta estimates for one firm will vary depending on various factors such as the time over which the estimation is conducted, the market portfolio proxy, and the return intervals. You will demonstrate this variation using returns for Microsoft.

a. Using all 45 monthly returns for Microsoft and the two stock market indexes, compute Microsoft's beta using the S&P 500 Index as the market proxy. Then compute the beta using the NASDAQ index as the market portfolio proxy. Compare the two beta estimates.

b. Now estimate the beta using only the most recent 30 monthly returns and the S&P 500 Index. Compare the beta estimate to the estimate in part *(a)* when using the S&P 500 Index and all 45 monthly returns.

	A	B	C	D	E	F	G	H	I	J	K	L
1	Date	MSFT	S&P500	Nasdaq	Date	MSFT	S&P500	Nasdaq	Date	MSFT	Nasdaq	Nasdaq
2	Mar-13	0.31%	–1.01%	–1.95%	Dec-11	13.74%	4.36%	8.01%	Sep-10	8.88%	3.69%	5.86%
3	Feb-13	2.91	3.60	3.40	Nov-11	1.50	0.85	–0.58	Aug-10	4.33	8.76	12.04
4	Jan-13	2.13	1.11	0.57	Oct-11	–3.22	–0.51	–2.39	Jul-10	–8.55	–4.74	–6.24
5	Dec-12	2.76	5.04	4.06	Sep-11	6.97	10.77	11.14	Jun-10	12.17	6.88	6.90
6	Nov-12	0.34	0.71	0.31	Aug-11	–6.40	–7.18	–6.36	May-10	–10.81	–5.39	–6.55
7	Oct-12	–5.95	0.28	1.11	Jul-11	–2.34	–5.68	–6.42	Apr-10	–15.16	–8.20	–8.29
8	Sep-12	–4.13	–1.98	–4.46	Jun-11	5.42	–2.15	–0.62	Mar-10	4.28	1.48	2.64
9	Aug-12	–3.43	2.42	1.61	May-11	3.95	–1.83	–2.18	Feb-10	2.15	5.88	7.14
10	Jul-12	5.28	1.98	4.34	Apr-11	–2.90	–1.35	–1.33	Jan-10	2.20	2.85	4.23
11	Jun-12	–3.65	1.26	0.15	Mar-11	2.08	2.85	3.32	Dec-09	–7.52	–3.70	–5.37
12	May-12	4.77	3.96	3.81	Feb-11	–4.46	–0.10	–0.04	Nov-09	3.62	1.78	5.81
13	Apr-12	–8.23	–6.27	–7.19	Jan-11	–3.57	3.20	3.04	Oct-09	6.53	5.74	4.86
14	Mar-12	–0.73	–0.75	–1.46	Dec-10	–0.65	2.26	1.78	Sep-09	7.81	–1.98	–3.64
15	Feb-12	1.62	3.13	4.20	Nov-10	10.49	6.53	6.19	Aug-09	4.34	3.57	5.64
16	Jan-12	8.22	4.06	5.44	Oct-10	–4.70	–0.23	–0.37	Jul-09	5.41	3.36	1.54

c. Estimate Microsoft's beta using the following quarterly returns. Compare the estimate to the ones from parts (a) and (b).

	A	B	C
1	Date	MSFT	S&P500
2	Q1 2013	8.00%	10.03%
3	Q4 2012	−9.53	−1.01
4	Q3 2012	−2.04	5.76
5	Q2 2012	−4.57	−3.29
6	Q1 2012	25.08	12.00
7	Q4 2011	5.08	11.15
8	Q3 2011	−3.64	−14.33
9	Q2 2011	3.04	−0.39
10	Q1 2011	−8.47	5.42
11	Q4 2010	14.65	10.20
12	Q3 2010	7.02	10.72
13	Q2 2010	−21.09	−11.86
14	Q1 2010	−3.46	4.87
15	Q4 2009	19.01	5.49
16	Q3 2009	8.82	14.98

research it! Find a Beta

Using beta as a risk measure has been fully integrated into corporate finance and the investment industry. You can obtain a beta for most companies at many financial websites. Sites that list a beta include MSN Money (in the Company Report section), Yahoo! Finance (in the Key Statistics section), and Zacks (follow the Detailed Quote link). Obtain the beta for your favorite company from several different websites. Are the values you obtain similar? If they are not, why might they be different?
(moneycentral.msn.com, finance.yahoo.com, www.zacks.com)

integrated mini-case: AT&T's Beta

When you go on the Web to find a firm's beta, you do not know how recently it was computed, what index was used as a proxy for the market portfolio, or which time series of returns the calculations used. Earlier in this chapter, it was shown that when we went on the Web to find a beta for AT&T, we found the following: MSN Money (0.53), Yahoo! Finance (0.38), and Zacks (0.54).

An alternative is to compute beta yourself. A common estimation procedure is to use 60 months of return data and to use the S&P 500 Index as the market portfolio. You can obtain price data for a company and for the S&P 500 Index free from websites like Yahoo! Finance. Using monthly prices, you can compute the monthly returns, as $(P_n - P_{n-1}) \div P_{n-1}$. Below are 60 monthly returns for AT&T and the S&P 500 Index. You can use these returns to compute AT&T's beta. A spreadsheet, like Excel, can run a regression (go to Tool menu, select Data Analysis, and then Regression). Select AT&T returns as the y variable and S&P 500 Index return as the x variable. The coefficient for the x variable is the beta estimate. The regression will provide all the statistical information you might like. However, if you only want beta, you can simply use the SLOPE function in Excel. Or you may have learned to run a regression using statistical software.

	A	B	C	D	E	F	G	H	I
1	**Date**	**AT&T**	**S&P500 Index**	**Date**	**AT&T**	**S&P500 Index**	**Date**	**AT&T**	**S&P500 Index**
2	Apr 13	3.62%	−1.01%	Aug 11	−2.67%	−5.68%	Dec 09	4.02%	1.78%
3	Mar 13	2.17	3.60	Jul 11	−5.56	−2.15	Nov 09	4.97	5.74
4	Feb 13	3.22	1.11	Jun 11	−0.49	−1.83	Oct 09	−3.53	−1.98
5	Jan 13	4.54	5.04	May 11	1.41	−1.35	Sep 09	3.71	3.57
6	Dec 12	−1.25	0.71	Apr 11	3.13	2.85	Aug 09	−0.70	3.36
7	Nov 12	−1.32	0.28	Mar 11	7.86	−0.10	Jul 09	7.41	7.41
8	Oct 12	−7.18	−1.98	Feb 11	3.12	3.20	Jun 09	0.20	0.02
9	Sep 12	2.88	2.42	Jan 11	−4.97	2.26	May 09	−3.25	5.31
10	Aug 12	−3.38	1.98	Dec 10	5.70	6.53	Apr 09	3.26	9.39
11	Jul 12	7.68	1.26	Nov 10	−2.54	−0.23	Mar 09	6.06	8.54
12	Jun 12	4.34	3.96	Oct 10	1.16	3.69	Feb 09	−3.49	−10.99
13	May 12	3.85	−6.27	Sep 10	5.81	8.76	Jan 09	−12.32	−8.57
14	Apr 12	6.87	−0.75	Aug 10	4.20	−4.74	Dec 08	−0.22	0.78
15	Mar 12	2.06	3.13	Jul 10	9.12	6.88	Nov 08	6.70	−7.48
16	Feb 12	4.04	4.06	Jun 10	−0.48	−5.39	Oct 08	−2.61	−16.94
17	Jan 12	−1.34	4.36	May 10	−6.76	−8.20	Sep 08	−12.73	−9.08
18	Dec 11	4.35	0.85	Apr 10	2.53	1.48	Aug 08	3.84	1.22
19	Nov 11	−1.13	−0.51	Mar 10	4.11	5.88	Jul 08	−7.43	−0.99
20	Oct 11	4.37	10.77	Feb 10	−2.15	2.85	Jun 08	−15.55	−8.60
21	Sep 11	0.15	−7.18	Jan 10	−8.16	−3.70	May 08	3.06	1.07

a. Compute AT&T's beta using the listed returns.

b. Compare your estimate with the ones found on the Web as listed.

c. How different will the required returns be using these betas? Compute required return using each beta (assume that the risk-free rate is 5 percent and the market return will be 13 percent).

ANSWERS TO TIME OUT

10-1 Average return is computed using the simple average of historical returns. The expected return is a forward-looking return. However, it is computed using a weighted average (the probabilities) of returns. The returns used in the various economic stages are usually chosen from historical knowledge of how the firm performs in each stage. Thus, both measures use an average of historical returns in one way or another. The historical risk and expected risk are both measured using standard deviation and historical knowledge of returns as well.

10-2 Many people are willing to take market risk because over time they expect to earn a risk premium. This risk premium allows them to build their wealth significantly more than just investing in the risk-free asset. However, because risk is involved, these people should have a long-term focus and recognize that they can lose money in the short term.

10-3 For every point on the efficient frontier (except the market portfolio), you can form a portfolio that has the same level of risk, but a higher expected return through a combination of the market portfolio and the risk-free asset. Thus, the capital market line has a better risk-return trade-off because it has a higher return at every level of risk.

10-4 Procter & Gamble is a diversified firm selling consumer goods that are purchased in good economies and bad. Thus, its low beta of 0.31 seems reasonable. Similarly, Walmart is a discount retailer whose products also seem recession-proof. The low beta of 0.41 seems fine. At this time, Bank of America has struggled through the financial crisis, and what its financial liabilities may ultimately be from the mortgage debacle is unclear. The high and very risky beta of 1.78 seems right. On the other hand, Home Depot operates in the housing industry, which has been declining. Its beta of 1.01 does not seem high enough considering the risks.

10-5 No. Weak-form efficiency is a subset of semistrong-form efficiency. Information about market prices and volumes is public and is thus included in the broader definition of public information in the semistrong-form efficiency hypothesis. Therefore, if a market is semistrong-form efficient, it is also weak-form efficient, by definition.

10-6 Consider a case when the market consistently overreacted to bad news announcements. This means that prices would fall too far after the announcement and eventually partially rebound. If this scenario was predictable, an investor could make money by buying stocks after bad news and capturing the price bounce.

10-7 Consider that you obtained money from the bank and had to pay an 8 percent interest rate. If you invested that money in a project that returned 5 percent to you, then you would not be earning enough to pay back the bank. You need to earn more than 8 percent on your business project in order to be successful. Corporate managers are using the shareholders' equity capital and need to know what return they require. This return is more difficult to estimate than a bank loan. But it helps managers to know what return they must achieve when using the capital to fund business opportunities.

PART SIX

11 Calculating the Cost of Capital

viewpoints

Business Application

MP3 Devices, Inc., is about to launch a new project to create and market a combination MP3 player-video projector. MP3 Devices currently uses a particular mixture of debt, common stock, and preferred shares in its capital structure, but the firm is thinking of using the launch of the new project as an opportunity to change that capital structure.

The new project will be funded with 40 percent debt, 10 percent preferred stock, and 50 percent common stock. MP3 Devices currently has 10 million shares of common stock outstanding, selling at $18.75 per share, and expects to pay an annual dividend of $1.35 one year from now, after which future dividends are expected to grow at a constant 6 percent rate. MP3's debt consists of 20-year, 10-percent annual coupon bonds with a face value of $150 million and a market value of $165 million and the company's capital mix also includes 100,000 shares of 10 percent preferred stock selling at par.

If MP3 Devices faces a marginal tax rate of 34 percent, what weighted average cost of capital should it use as it evaluates this project? **(See solution on p. 391)**

Personal Application

Mackenzie is currently finishing up her bachelor's degree and is considering going back to grad school for a master's degree. She currently has $17,125 in student loans carrying an 8 percent interest rate from her bachelor's degree and estimates that she will need to take out an additional $29,000 in student loans (at the same interest rate) to make it through the master's program she'd like to attend. The IRS allows taxpayers with student loans to deduct the interest on those loans, but only up to a maximum amount of $2,500 per year. Assuming that Mackenzie will face a marginal personal tax rate of 25 percent when she graduates, what will be the average after-tax interest rate that she will be paying on the student loans immediately after she graduates with her master's? **(See solution on p. 391)**

How else can Mackenzie finance her graduate degree? What will happen to her after-tax interest rate?

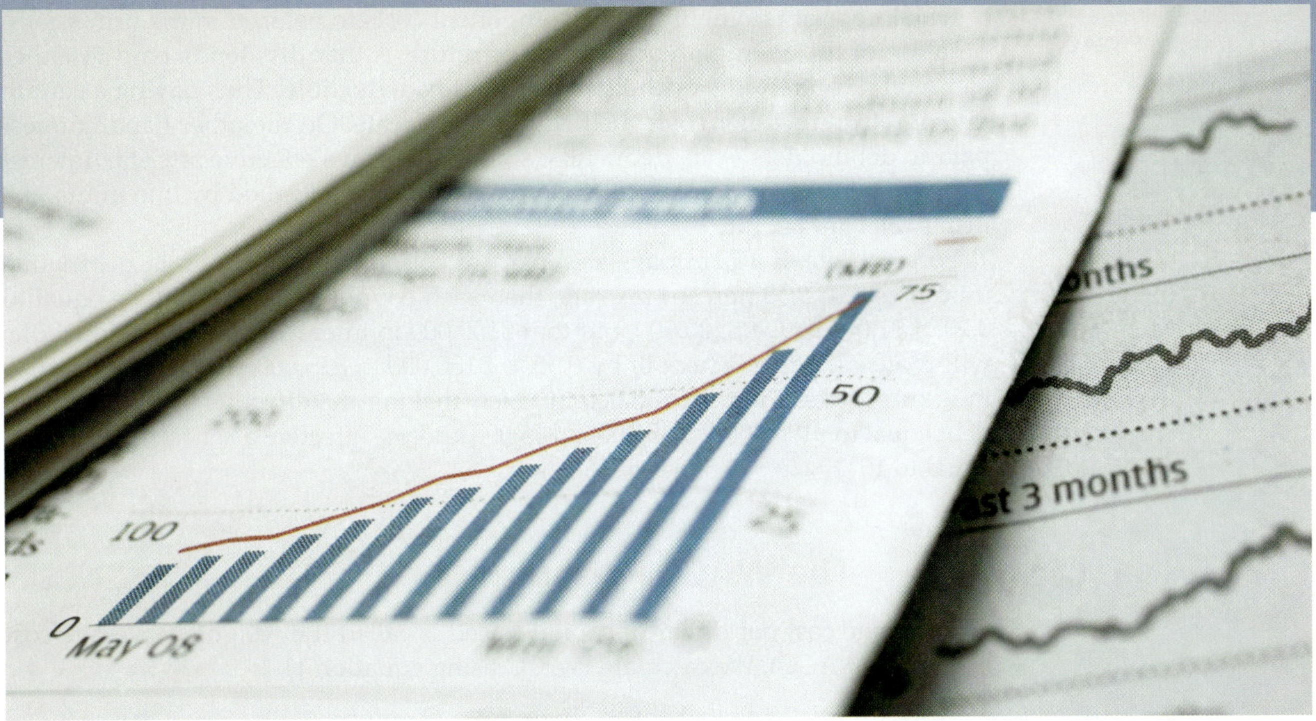

In the previous two chapters, we discussed investors' required return given a particular risk profile. In this chapter, we examine the question from the firm's point of view: How much must the firm pay to finance its operations and expansions using debt and equity sources? Firms use a combination of debt and equity sources to fund their operations, projects, and any expansions they may undertake. In Chapter 14, we'll explore the factors that managers consider as they choose the optimal capital structure mix. For now, we'll assume that management has chosen the optimal mix for us, and that it's our job to implement it.

As we've seen in previous chapters, investors face different kinds of risks associated with debt, preferred stock, and equity. As a result, their required rates of return for each debt or equity source differ as well. So, as the firm uses a combination of different financing sources, we must calculate the investors' *average* required rate of return. Since firms seldom use equal amounts of debt and equity capital sources, we will need to calculate a *weighted* average, with weights based on the proportion of debt and equity capital used.

As we'll see, we can measure such a **weighted-average cost of capital (WACC)** in a variety of situations and for a number of purposes. For example, if we're interested in determining the average rate of return that the firm must earn from existing operations when we don't expect the firm's capital structure to change, we can calculate the WACC using the firm's *current* capital structure and *existing* **component costs**; however, if we're trying to determine the average rate of return that we would need to earn from a new project in order for it to add value to the firm, we would want to use the project's *proposed* capital structure and *its* component costs.

Learning Goals

LG11-1 Understand the relationship of cost of capital to the investor's required return.

LG11-2 Use the weighted-average cost of capital (WACC) formula to calculate a project's cost of capital.

LG11-3 Explain how the firm chooses among estimating costs of equity, preferred stock, and debt.

LG11-4 Calculate the weights used for WACC projections.

LG11-5 Identify which elements of WACC are used to calculate a project-specific WACC.

LG11-6 Evaluate trade-offs between a firmwide WACC and a divisional cost of capital approach.

LG11-7 Distinguish subjective and objective approaches to divisional cost of capital.

LG11-8 Demonstrate how to adjust the WACC to reflect flotation costs.

weighted-average cost of capital (WACC)

The weighted-average after-tax cost of the capital used by a firm, with weights set equal to the relative percentage of each type of capital used.

component costs

The individual costs of each type of capital—bonds, preferred stock, and common stock.

One important point about the component costs to be used in the firm's computation of the average required rate of return is that dividends paid to either common or preferred stockholders are not tax deductible. Thus paying a certain rate of return to either costs the firm that same rate. On the other hand, interest paid to debtholders *is* tax deductible so that the firm's effective after-tax interest cost will be equal to the interest rate paid on debt multiplied by one minus the firm's relevant tax rate.

For example, if a firm pays a 10 percent coupon on \$1 million in debt while it is subject to a 35 percent tax rate, then each coupon payment will be equal to $0.10 \times \$1{,}000{,}000 = \$100{,}000$, but that \$100,000 in interest, being tax deductible, will reduce the firm's tax bill by $0.35 \times \$100{,}000 = \$35{,}000$. So paying \$100,000 in interest saves the firm \$35,000 in taxes, making the effective after-tax cost of debt equal to $\$100{,}000 - \$35{,}000 = \$65{,}000$ and the effective after-tax interest rate equal to $10\% \times (1 - 0.35) = 6.5\%$.

LG11-2

11.1 • The WACC Formula

The average cost per dollar of capital raised is called the weighted-average cost of capital (WACC). We calculate WACC using equation 11-1:

$$
\begin{aligned}
WACC &= \text{Percentage of equity} \times \text{Cost of equity} \\
&\quad + \text{Percentage of preferred stock} \times \text{Cost of preferred stock} \\
&\quad + \text{Percentage of debt} \times \text{After-tax cost of debt} \\
&= \frac{E}{E+P+D} i_E + \frac{P}{E+P+D} i_P + \frac{D}{E+P+D} i_D \times (1 - T_C)
\end{aligned}
\qquad \textbf{(11-1)}
$$

where

E = Market value of equity used in financing the relevant project or firm.

P = Market value of preferred stock used.

D = Market value of debt used.

$\frac{E}{E+P+D}$ = Percentage of financing that is equity.

$\frac{P}{E+P+D}$ = Percentage of financing that is preferred stock.

$\frac{D}{E+P+D}$ = Percentage of financing that is debt.

i_E = Cost of equity.

i_P = Cost of preferred stock.

i_D = Before-tax cost of debt.

T_C = Appropriate corporate tax rate.

Notice that we use weights based on market values rather than book values because market values reflect investors' assessment of what they would be willing to pay for the various types of securities.

Calculating the Component Cost of Equity

We could calculate i_E using the capital asset pricing model:

$$i_E = R_f + \beta(R_M - R_f) \qquad \textbf{(11-2)}$$

Or, we can assume that the equity in question is a constant-growth stock such as the ones we modeled in Chapter 8. Under this assumption, we can solve the constant-growth model for i_E:

$$i_E = \frac{D_1}{P_0} + g \qquad \textbf{(11-3)}$$

Which way is better? Well, theoretically, both should give us the same answer, but depending on the situation, some pragmatic reasons may dictate your choice.

1. In situations where you do not have sufficient historic observations to estimate β (i.e., when the stock is fairly new), or when you suspect that the past level of the stock's systematic (or market) risk might not be a good indicator of the future, you do not want to use the CAPM, where β_E estimates *future* systematic risk, calculated based on *historic* systematic risk.
2. In situations where you can expect constant dividend growth, the constant-growth model is appropriate. But although you can try to adjust the model for stocks without constant dividend growth, doing so may introduce potentially sizable errors, so it is not the best choice for stocks that increase their dividends irregularly.

Overall, we should expect that the CAPM approach to estimating i_E will apply more accurately in most cases. However, if you do encounter a situation in which the constant-growth model applies, then you can certainly use it. If we are really fortunate and happen to have enough information to use both approaches, then we should probably *use* both, taking an average of the resulting estimates of i_E.[1]

LG11-2

EXAMPLE 11-1

Cost of Equity

ADK Industries' common shares sell for $32.75 per share. ADK expects to set its next annual dividend at $1.54 per share. If ADK expects future dividends to grow by 6 percent per year, indefinitely, the current risk-free rate is 3 percent, the expected return on the market is 9 percent, and the stock has a beta of 1.3, what should be firm's cost of equity?

For interactive versions of this example visit www.mhhe.com/can3e

SOLUTION:

The cost of equity using the CAPM will be:

$$\begin{aligned} i_E &= R_f + \beta(R_M - R_f) \\ &= 0.03 + 1.3[0.09 - 0.03] \\ &= 0.1080, \text{ or } 10.80\% \end{aligned}$$

The cost of equity using the constant-growth model will be:

$$\begin{aligned} i_E &= \frac{D_1}{P_0} + g \\ &= \frac{\$1.54}{\$32.75} + .06 \\ &= 0.1070, \text{ or } 10.70\% \end{aligned}$$

Our best estimate of ADK's equity would therefore be: $\dfrac{10.70\% + 10.80\%}{2} = 10.75\%$.

Similar to Problems 11-1, 11-2

[1]Think of taking such an average as being intuitively the same as diversifying our "portfolio" of data across the two different estimation techniques, thereby reducing the average amount of estimation error. Taking this average is intuitively the same as diversifying your portfolio of data across two different estimation techniques. These options allow you to reduce your average amount of estimation error.

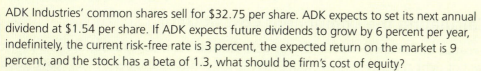

Calculating the Component Cost of Preferred Stock

As we discussed in Chapter 8, preferred stock represents a special case of the constant-growth model, wherein g equals zero. So we can estimate preferred stocks' component cost using a simplified version of equation 11-3:

$$i_P = \frac{D_1}{P_0} \qquad \textbf{(11-4)}$$

EXAMPLE 11-2

LG11-3

For interactive versions of this example visit www.mhhe.com/can3e

Cost of Preferred Stock

Suppose that ADK also has one million shares of 7 percent preferred stock outstanding, trading at $72 per share. What is ADK's component cost for preferred equity?

SOLUTION:

The cost of the preferred stock will equal:

$$\begin{aligned} i_P &= \frac{D_1}{P_0} \\ &= \frac{\$7}{\$72} \\ &= 0.0972, \text{ or } 9.72\% \end{aligned}$$

Similar to Problems 11-7, 11-8

MATH COACH

PREFERRED STOCK DIVIDENDS

The assumed par value of preferred stock is $100. So, a 7 percent preferred stock pays $7 a year in dividends.

Calculating the Component Cost of Debt

Because of the tax deductibility of debt for the firm, computing the component cost of debt actually has two parts. We must estimate the before-tax cost of debt, i_D, and then adjust this figure to convert it to the after-tax rate of return.

To estimate i_D, we need to solve for the yield to maturity (YTM) on the firm's existing debt:

$$\text{Solve}\left\{PV = PMT \times \left[\frac{1 - \frac{1}{(1 + i_D)^N}}{i_D}\right] + \frac{FV}{(1 + i_D)^N}\right\} \text{ for } i_D \qquad \textbf{(11-5)}$$

Solve for the interest rate that makes the price equal to the sum of the present values of the coupons and the face value of the bond.

Intuitively, by using the price on the firm's existing debt in equation 11-5, we are calculating the rate of return expected by investors currently buying the firm's existing bonds. As discussed later when we cover how to calculate project-specific WACCs, the fact that *all* of the firms' bonds get their interest paid out of *all* the firm's cash flows before any of the firm's shareholders get anything implies that this expected rate of return on existing firm debt should also be a good proxy for the rate of return that potential investors would demand on any *new* debt issued by the firm as well.

Finally, if we think of the YTM as the rate that bond investors expect to *get* for investing in the bond, then we need to adjust it for the tax deductibility of debt interest to convert this to a measure of how much it actually costs the firm to *pay* that YTM. We do so by multiplying the YTM by $(1 - T_C)$.

EXAMPLE 11-3

LG11-3

Cost of Debt

ADK has 30,000 20-year, 8 percent annual coupon bonds outstanding. If the bonds currently sell for 97.5 percent of par and the firm pays an average tax rate of 35.92 percent, what will be the before-tax and after-tax component cost for debt?

For interactive versions of this example visit www.mhhe.com/can3e

SOLUTION:

The before-tax cost of debt will be the solution to:

$$\text{Solve}\left\{\$975 = \$80 \times \left[\frac{1 - \frac{1}{(1+i_D)^{20}}}{i_D}\right] + \frac{\$1{,}000}{(1+i_D)^{20}}\right\} \text{for } i_D$$

CALCULATOR HINTS

N = 20
PV = −975
PMT = 80
FV = 1000
CPT I = 8.26

which will equal 8.26 percent. Multiplying this by one minus the tax rate will yield the after-tax cost of debt: $0.0826 \times (1 - 0.3592) = 0.0529$, or 5.29%.

Similar to Problems 11-3, 11-4

table 11.1 | **Corporate Tax Rates**

Taxable Income			Tax Rate
$0	–	$50,000	15%
50,001	–	75,000	25
75,001	–	100,000	34
100,001	–	335,000	39
335,001	–	10,000,000	34
10,000,001	–	15,000,000	35
15,000,001	–	18,333,333	38
18,333,334	+		35

Choosing Tax Rates

The interest paid on debt is tax deductible, but the benefit of that tax deductibility will vary based on the firm's marginal tax rate. The appropriate tax rate to be used in the WACC will be the weighted average of the marginal tax rates that would have been paid on the taxable income shielded by the interest deduction.

For example, if a firm had earnings before interest and taxes (EBIT) of $400,000, taxable interest deductions of $100,000, and faced the corporate tax schedule shown in Table 11.1, then the appropriate tax rate would equal a weighted average of the marginal tax rates from the fourth (i.e., 39%) and fifth (34%) tax brackets. The weights would be determined by the relative impacts of the brackets in the computation of the post-interest tax bill:

$$\frac{\$35{,}000}{\$100{,}000} \times 0.39 + \frac{\$65{,}000}{\$100{,}000} \times 0.34 = 0.3575, \text{ or } 35.75\%$$

EXAMPLE 11-4

LG11-3

For interactive versions of this example visit www.mhhe.com/can3e

Tax Rate

Suppose that ADK expects EBIT to be approximately $20 million per year for the foreseeable future. Given the 30,000, 20-year, 8 percent annual coupon bonds discussed in the previous example, what would the appropriate tax rate be for use in the calculation of the debt component of ADK's WACC?

SOLUTION:

The interest payments on the bonds would total 30,000 × $1,000 × 0.08 = $2,400,000 per year, resulting in earnings before tax (EBT) of $20,000,000 − $2,400,000 = $17,600,000.

As taxable income falls from $20,000,000 to $17,600,000 after the firm pays the interest on the bonds, $1,666,667, or 69.44 percent, of the $2,400,000 reduction would fall in the highest 35 percent bracket, while the remaining $733,333, or 30.56 percent ($733,333/$2,400,000), would occur in the 38 percent tax bracket, making the weighted average applicable tax rate equal to:

$$\begin{aligned} T_C &= (0.6944 \times 0.35) + (0.3056 \times 0.38) \\ &= 0.3592, \text{ or } 35.92\% \end{aligned}$$

Similar to Problems 11-5, 11-6

Calculating the Weights

Calculating the weights to be used in the WACC formula is mathematically very simple: We just calculate the percentages of the funding that come from equity, preferred stock, and debt, respectively.

Sounds easy, right? Well, the tricky part to this lies in determining what we mean by "the funding": If we are calculating WACC for a firm, then "the funding" encompasses all the capital in the firm, and *E, P,* and *D* will be determined by computing the total market value of the firm's common stock, preferred stock, and debt, respectively. However, if we are computing WACC for a project, then "the funding" will only include the financing for the project, and *E, P,* and *D* will be equal to the amount of each used in the financing of that project.[2]

If you think about this for a second, you will realize that this means that projects can wind up having different WACCs than their firm. That is not just OK, it is also exactly right because, as we will see in a later chapter, the firm is like a diversified portfolio of different projects, all with different risks and returns. And one of the things that can contribute to the risk of a project is the choice of how much common stock, preferred stock, and debt is used to finance it.

EXAMPLE 11-5

LG11-4

For interactive versions of this example visit www.mhhe.com/can3e

Capital Structure Weights and WACC

Let us continue the previous examples. Suppose that ADK has issued 3 million shares of common stock, 1 million shares of preferred stock, and the previously mentioned 30,000 bonds outstanding. What will ADK's WACC be, considering ADK as a firm?

[2]We'll discuss more about calculating WACC for a project later in the chapter.

SOLUTION:

Using the securities' prices given in previous examples, ADK's equity, preferred stock, and debt will have the following total market values:

- Equity: 3m × \$32.75 = \$98.25m
- Preferred stock: 1m × \$72 = \$72m
- Debt: 30,000 × \$975 = \$29.25m

The total combined market value for all three capital sources is \$199.5 million. The applicable weights for each capital source will therefore be

$$\text{For common equity: } \frac{E}{E+P+D} = \frac{\$98.25\text{m}}{\$199.5\text{m}} = 0.4925, \text{ or } 49.25\%$$

$$\text{For preferred stock: } \frac{P}{E+P+D} = \frac{\$72\text{m}}{\$199.5\text{m}} = 0.3609, \text{ or } 36.09\%$$

$$\text{For debt: } \frac{D}{E+P+D} = \frac{\$29.25\text{m}}{\$199.5\text{m}} = 0.1466, \text{ or } 14.66\%$$

Tying this all in together with the answers from the previous examples, ADK will have a WACC of:

$$\begin{aligned} WACC &= \frac{E}{E+P+D} i_E + \frac{P}{E+P+D} i_P + \frac{D}{E+P+D} i_D \times (1 - T_C) \\ &= (0.4925 \times 0.1075) + (0.3609 \times 0.0972) + (0.1466 \times 0.0826 \times [1 - 0.3592]) \\ &= 0.0958, \text{ or } 9.58\% \end{aligned}$$

Similar to Problems 11-9 to 11-14, 11-21, 11-22, self-test problem 1

TIME OUT

11-1 Explain why we multiply the component cost of debt by the marginal tax rate, T_D, but don't do so for the component costs of equity or preferred stock.

11-2 How would we compute i_D if a company had multiple bond issues outstanding?

11.2 • Firm WACC versus Project WACC

LG11-5

So far, we have been defining the WACC as a weighted-average cost across the firm's different financing sources. If we think of the firm as a portfolio of different projects and products, we see that the WACC will be a weighted-average cost of capital across the items in that portfolio, too. This way it represents the cost of capital for the "typical" project that the firm is currently undertaking. However, firms grow by taking on new projects. So now the question is: can managers use our firm-wide WACC, calculated previously, to evaluate the firm's newly proposed projects?

The answer is: *It depends.* If a new project is similar enough to existing projects, then yes, managers can use the firm's WACC as the new project's cost of capital. But say that your firm is contemplating undertaking a significantly different project—one far different from any project that the firm is already engaged in. What then? Then we cannot expect the firm's overall WACC to appropriately measure the new project's cost of capital. Let your intuition work on this: If the new project is riskier than the firm's existing projects, then it should be "charged" a higher cost of capital. If it's safer, then the firm should assign the new project a lower cost of capital.

Consider a U.S. firm—let's call it GassUp—that currently owns a chain of gas stations. Firm management is considering a new project: opening up a series of gourmet coffee shops. Given the demand for upscale coffee in the United States, as well as the historically volatile oil markets, it's probably difficult to say exactly whether the coffee shops will be *more* or *less* risky than gas stations. We can probably say, though, that the two enterprises will face *different* risks. For example, if the coffee shops are located within the busiest and most stable gas stations—say the ones that lie along freeways—then the firm faces remodeling of existing buildings rather than starting from scratch. Locating the coffee shops within existing structures would likely mean that the risks will be lower than building new stations or new coffee shops.

So, does this mean that GassUp should calculate a heterogeneous WACC for each new project using purely project-specific numbers? Well, not exactly. As we'll discuss, some inputs to WACC should be project-specific, but others should be consistent with the firmwide values used in calculating a firmwide WACC.

Project Cost Numbers to Take from the Firm

It is tempting to argue that all component inputs for a project-specific WACC should be based on the specific project attributes, but if we created all project-specific numbers, what fundamental issue related to bonds and preferred stock would we be ignoring? That both bonds and preferred stocks create claims on the *firm*, not on any particular group of projects within that firm. Furthermore, debt claims are superior to those of common stockholders. So if the new project *does* significantly increase the firm's overall risk, the increased risk will be borne disproportionately by common stockholders. Debtholders and preferred stockholders will likely face minimal impact on the risk and return that their investments give them, no matter what new project the firm undertakes—even if those claimants own bonds or preferred shares that the firm issued to fund the new project.

For example, suppose GassUp decides to build entirely separate facilities for its coffee shops, which it will name "Bottoms Up." GassUp partially finances its expansion into coffee shops with debt, and the project turns out to be more like "Bottoms Down"—far less successful than the firm had hoped. Though this would be an unfortunate turn of events for GassUp's common shareholders, the firm's creditors and preferred shareholders would likely still collect their usual interest and dividend payments from GassUp's gross revenues from gas station operations.

Creditors understand that their repayment probably comes from continuing operations and take current cash flows into account when a firm comes seeking funds. For example, if a small firm approaches a bank for a loan to finance an expansion, the bank will normally spend more time analyzing *current* cash flows to determine the probability that they will recoup their loan than it will analyzing the potential new cash flows from the proposed expansion.

Note that this situation holds true only as long as the new projects represent fairly small investments compared to ongoing operations. As new projects become *large* relative to ongoing cash-flow producing activities, creditors will have to examine the likelihood of being repaid from the new projects much more closely. New projects, however great their potential, inherently carry more risk than do established current operations. Changes in the proportion of new projects relative to ongoing operations will thus translate into increased risk for the creditor, who will ask for a higher rate of return to offset the risk.

Since most firms tend to grow incrementally, we will assume (unless otherwise indicated) that we're examining situations in which the number of new projects is small relative to ongoing operations. We can therefore assume that using the firm's existing WACC for both debt and preferred stock is appropriate.

Project Cost Numbers to Find Elsewhere: The Pure-Play Approach

Since we have decided not to adjust the firmwide costs of debt or preferred stock for the risk of a project, where *should* we account for the new project risk brought to the firm overall? As with several other questions associated with risk- and profit-sharing that we'll discuss in Chapter 16, the answer lies with *equity.*

The firm's risk changes when it takes on a project that is noticeably different from its existing lines of business. Since debtholders and preferred stockholders will not bear much of this change in risk, the firm spreads the risks that it takes with new projects by transferring most of the risk to the common stockholders.

In response to such a change in the firm's risk profile, stockholders adjust their required rate of return to adjust for the new risk level. Absent any alteration to the firm's capital structure,[3] changes in the firm's risk profile are due to differences in the firm's **business risks** based on the mix of the new and existing product lines. The firm's beta reflects those differences in each product line.

business risk

The risk of a project arising from the line of business it is in; the variability of a firm's or division's cash flows.

Obviously, no proposed new project will have a history of previous returns. Without such data, neither analysts nor investors can calculate a project-specific beta. So what data can we use? To the extent that we can find other firms engaged in the proposed new line of business, we can use their betas as proxies to estimate the project's risk. Ideally, the other firms would be engaged *only* in the proposed new line of business; such monothemed firms are usually referred to as *pure plays,* with this term also in turn being applied to this approach to estimating a project's beta.

An average of n such **proxy betas** will give us a fairly accurate estimate of what the new project's beta will be.[4]

proxy beta

The beta (a measure of the riskiness) of a firm in a similar line of business as a proposed new project.

$$i_E = r_f + \beta_{Avg}[E(r_M) - r_f]$$

where

$$\beta_{Avg} = \frac{\sum_{j=1}^{N} \beta_j}{n} \qquad \textbf{(11-6)}$$

This average will be an estimate, in the strictest statistical sense of the word. You might recall from your statistics classes that we will need to be careful to get as large a sample as possible if we want to get as much statistical power for our estimate as possible. Ideally, we would like to find at least three or four companies from which to draw proxy betas, called *pure-play proxies,* to ensure that we have a large enough sample size to safely make meaningful inferences. In reality, however, two proxies (or even one) might represent a suitable sample if their business line resembles the proposed new project closely enough. In particular, we may want to use betas from industry front-runners, and rely less on betas of any firms that the company really doesn't want to emulate.

What shall we do if we cannot find *any* pure-play proxies? Well, in that case, we may want to use firms that, while not *solely* in the same business as the

financial risk

The risk of a project to equity holders stemming from the use of debt in the financial structure of the firm; refers to the issue of how a firm decides to distribute the business risk between debt and equity holders.

[3]In reality, new projects are often financed with different proportions of equity, debt, and preferred stock than were used to fund the firm's existing operations. As we will discuss in Chapter 16, such a change in capital structure will result in a change in **financial risk**, with increased leverage magnifying β.

[4]As we will also discuss in Chapter 16, we will be able to take a straight average of the proxy firm's betas as the estimate of our beta only if the capital structures of all the proxies are identical to each other and to that of our proposed new project. If not, we will need to adjust the proxies' estimated betas for differences in capital structures before averaging them. Then we will need to readjust the average beta for our project's capital structure before using the estimate.

proposed project's venture, have a sizable proportion of revenues from that line. We may then be able to "back out" the impact of their other lines of business from their firm's beta to leave us with a good enough estimate of what the new project's beta might be.

Be sure to use weights based on the *project's* sources of capital, and not necessarily the *firm's* capital structure. If the new project is going to use more or less debt than the firm's existing projects do, then the risk- and reward-sharing are going to vary across the different types of capital (as discussed in Chapter 16), and we will want to recognize this in our WACC computation.

Finally, we need to consider the appropriate corporate tax rate to use in calculating the WACC for a project. That marginal corporate tax rate will be the average marginal tax rate to which the project's cash flows will be subject. Assume a firm with \$400,000 of EBIT from current operations is considering a new project that will increase EBIT by \$200,000. Since this \$200,000 increase will keep the firm's marginal tax in the fifth bracket of Table 11.1, the appropriate tax rate to compute the project's WACC will simply be 34 percent.

To summarize, the component costs and weights to compute a project-specific WACC should be as shown in equation 11-7, with the source of each part indicated by the appropriate subscript:

$$WACC_{\text{Project}} = \frac{E_{\text{Project}}}{E_{\text{Project}} + P_{\text{Project}} + D_{\text{Project}}} i_{E,\text{ Project}} + \frac{P_{\text{Project}}}{E_{\text{Project}} + P_{\text{Project}} + D_{\text{Project}}} i_{P,\text{ Firm}} + \frac{D_{\text{Project}}}{E_{\text{Project}} + P_{\text{Project}} + D_{\text{Project}}} i_{D,\text{ Firm}} \times (1 - T_{C,\text{ Project}}) \quad \textbf{(11-7)}$$

EXAMPLE 11-6

LG 11-5

For interactive versions of this example visit www.mhhe.com/can3e

Calculation of Project WACC

Suppose that Evita's Subs, a local shipyard, is considering opening up a chain of sandwich shops. Evita's capital structure currently consists of 2 million outstanding shares of common stock, selling for \$83 per share, and a \$50 million bond issue, selling at 103 percent of par. Evita's stock has a beta of 0.72, the expected market risk premium is 7 percent, and the current risk-free rate is 4.5 percent. The bonds pay a 9 percent annual coupon and mature in 20 years. The current operations of the firm produce EBIT of \$100 million per year, and the new sandwich operations would add only an expected \$12 million per year to that. Also, suppose that Evita's management has done some research on the sandwich shop industry, and discovered that such firms have an average beta of 1.23. If the new project will be funded with 50 percent debt and 50 percent equity, what should be the WACC for this new project?

SOLUTION:

First, note that Evita's currently doesn't have any outstanding preferred stock and doesn't plan on using any to finance the new project, so that makes our job a little simpler. Also note that, though we are given enough information to calculate the firm's current capital structure weights and component cost of equity, we won't need those figures, as this new project's capital structure differs from the firm's existing structure. We already know the capital structure weights for the new project (50 percent debt and 50 percent equity), so we just need to calculate the appropriate component costs.

For equity, the appropriate cost will be based upon the average risk of sandwich shops:

$$\begin{aligned} i_E &= R_f + \beta,\text{ Project } (R_M - R_f) \\ &= 0.045 + 1.23[0.07] \\ &= 0.1311,\text{ or } 13.11\% \end{aligned}$$

Since the new sandwich project appears to be small relative to the firm's existing line of business, we will assume that the new bondholders will expect to be repaid out of cash flows to the existing shipyards, and the YTM on the new bonds issued to finance this project will be the same as the YTM on the existing bonds:

$$\text{Solve}\left\{ \$1{,}030 = \$90 \times \left[\frac{1 - \frac{1}{(1+i_D)^{20}}}{i_D}\right] + \frac{\$1{,}000}{(1+i_D)^{20}} \right\} \text{ for } i_D$$

which gives us an i_D of 8.68 percent.

Finally, the current EBIT already puts the firm in the top 35 percent tax bracket, so the additional EBIT generated by the project will also be taxed at this same marginal 35 percent tax rate. Therefore, the WACC of the new project will be:

$$\begin{aligned} WACC_{\text{Project}} &= \frac{E_{\text{Project}}}{E_{\text{Project}} + P_{\text{Project}} + D_{\text{Project}}} i_{E,\text{ Project}} + \frac{D_{\text{Project}}}{E_{\text{Project}} + P_{\text{Project}} + D_{\text{Project}}} i_{D,\text{ Firm}} \times (1 - T_{C,\text{ Project}}) \\ &= 0.5 \times 0.1311 + 0.5 \times 0.0868 \times (1 - 0.35) \\ &= 0.0938,\text{ or } 9.38\% \end{aligned}$$

Similar to Problems 11-16 to 11-21, self-test problem 2

CALCULATOR HINTS

N = 20
PV = −1030
PMT = 90
FV = 1000
CPT I = 8.68

TIME OUT

11-3 For computing a project WACC, why do we take some component costs from the firm, but compute others that are specific for the project being considered?

11-4 It is usually much easier to find proxy firms that are engaged in multiple lines of business than it is to find pure-play proxies. Explain how such firms can be used to estimate the beta for a new project.

11.3 • Divisional WACC

Do firms calculate risk-appropriate WACC for every new project they consider? While this would be ideal, pragmatically it just is not always feasible. In large corporations, managers evaluate dozens or even hundreds of proposed new projects each year. The costs in terms of time and effort of estimating project-specific WACCs individually for each project are simply prohibitive. Instead, large firms often take a middle-of-the-road approach that can achieve many of the of project-specific WACC calculations with much less time and resources. The key to this approach is to calculate a **divisional WACC**.

divisional WACC

An estimated WACC computed using some sort of proxy for the average equity risk of the projects in a particular division.

Pros and Cons of a Divisional WACC

As with most choices in life as well as finance, there are pros and cons to the divisional WACC. Let's first consider the disadvantage of using a firm's WACC to evaluate new, risk-heterogeneous projects. To make things simple, let's assume that we are looking at a firm that uses only equity finance, so that WACC is simply equal to i_E.

figure 11.1

Risk-Appropriate WACCs

In an all-equity firm, WACC is theoretically equal to i_E for each proposed project, which will increase as the risk (i.e., β) of the project increases.

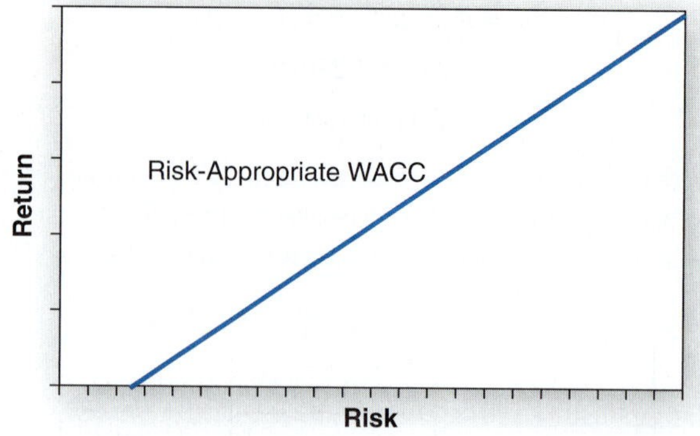

Take a look at Figure 11.1. Similar to our discussion of the security market line in Chapter 10, required rates of return for projects with varying degrees of risk would lie along the sloped line shown in the figure. We could then evaluate projects with various degrees of risk based on the relationship between their expected rate of return and the required rate of return for that risk level. Turning to Figure 11.2, you can see that using risk-appropriate WACCs, projects A and B would be accepted, since their *expected* rates of return would be higher than their respective *required* rates of return. Projects C and D would be rejected because our simple scheme shows that these projects are not expected to return enough to cover market-required returns, given the projects' riskiness.

However, using a firmwide WACC would result in a comparison of the project's expected rates of return to a single, flat, firmwide cost of capital as Figure 11.3 shows. Using a simple firmwide WACC to evaluate new projects would give an unfair advantage to projects that present more risk than the firm's average beta. Using a firmwide WACC would also work against projects that involved less risk than the firm's average beta. Looking at the same sample projects as before, we see that Project A would now be rejected, while Project C would be accepted.

figure 11.2

Sample Projects versus Risk-Sensitive WACC

Projects A and B have expected returns *greater than* their risk-appropriate WACCs. Projects C and D have expected returns *less than* their risk-appropriate WACCs.

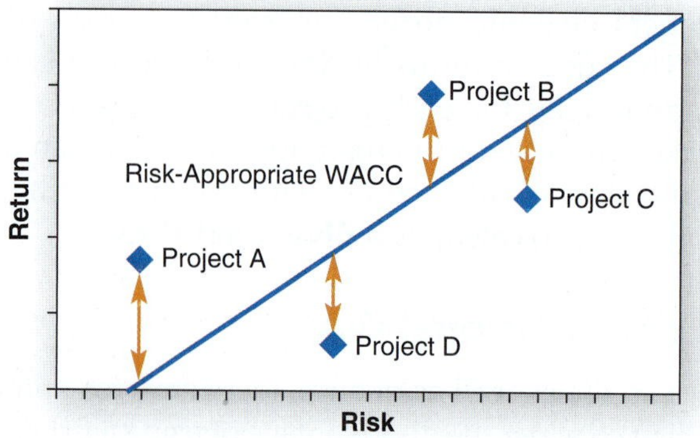

figure 11.3

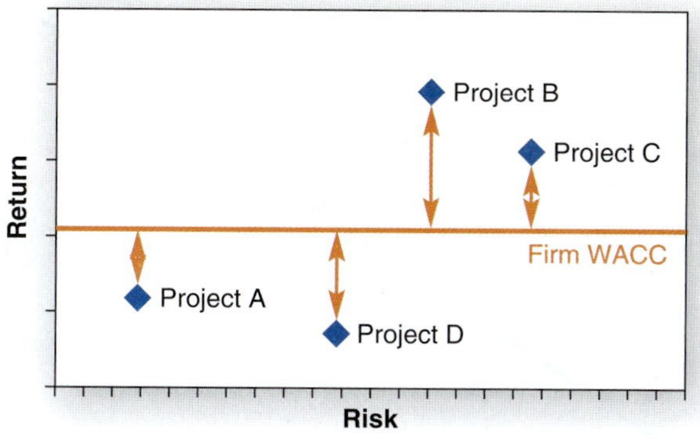

Sample Project versus Firmwide WACC

If we were to mistakenly compare projects bearing different risks to this single firmwide WACC, we would conclude that projects A and D have expected rates of return *less than* the firmwide WACC and Projects B and C have expected returns *greater than* the firmwide WACC.

Using a firmwide WACC in this way, as an inappropriate benchmark for projects of differing risk from the firm's current operations, will result in quite a few incorrect decisions. In fact, the use of a firmwide WACC to evaluate *any* projects with risk-return coordinates lying in the two shaded triangles shown in Figure 11.4 will result in an incorrect accept/reject decision.

Computing a few "risk aware" divisional WACCs instead of just one "risk insensitive" firmwide WACC can greatly reduce the number of projects that get incorrectly accepted or rejected this way. To do so, we divide the firm's existing projects into divisions, where the different divisions proxy for systematically different average project risk levels. Calculating WACCs for each division separately, as Figure 11.5 shows, greatly reduces the problem of basing decisions on inaccurate results from using firmwide WACC for all projects.

figure 11.4

Incorrect Decisions Caused by Inappropriate Use of Firmwide WACC

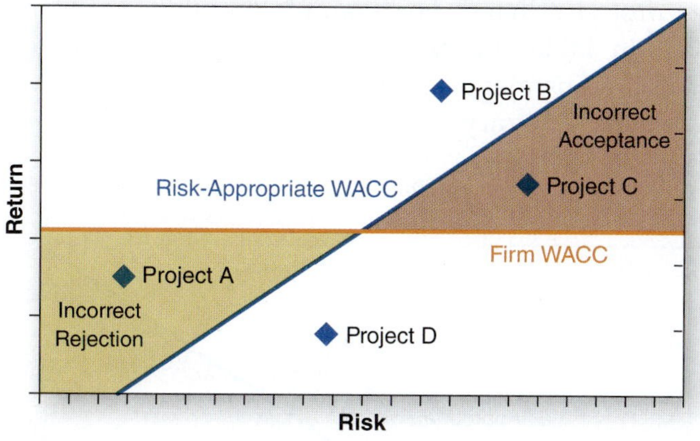

The gold-shaded triangle on the lower left contains projects such as Project A, which is *incorrectly rejected* by a firm. It has risk *less than* the average risk of the firm. Its expected rate of return is *greater than* its correctly calculated risk-appropriate WACC but *less than* an inappropriately calculated firmwide WACC.

The pink-shaded triangle on the upper right contains projects such as Project C, which is *incorrectly accepted* by a firm. It has risk *greater than* the average risk of the firm. Its expected rate of return is *less than* a correctly calculated risk-appropriate WACC but *greater than* an inappropriately calculated firmwide WACC.

figure 11.5

Divisional WACCs

Instead of calculating a single firmwide WACC based on the average risk of all projects in the firm, assume that the firm calculates division-specific WACCs based on the average risk of the projects in each respective division.

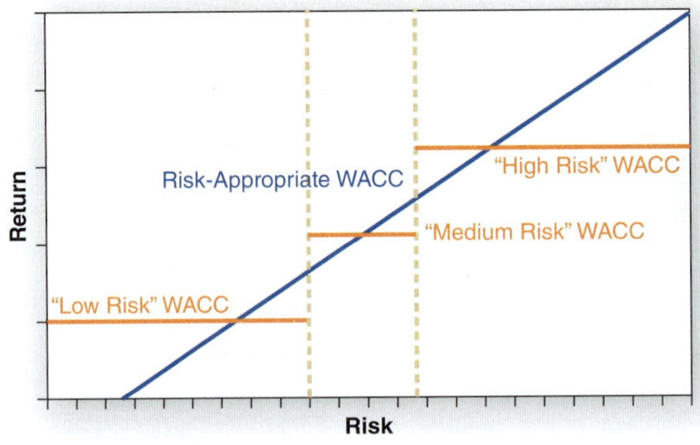

Using divisional WACCs like this will not *eliminate* problems of incorrect acceptance and incorrect rejection, but it will greatly reduce their frequency. Instead of making errors corresponding to the two large triangular areas indicated in Figure 11.4, we will instead have six smaller areas of error shown in Figure 11.6. More acceptance/rejection regions will result in fewer errors.

For example, let's consider our four sample projects from before. We now evaluate them using divisional WACCs as shown in Figure 11.7. We would correctly accept both projects A and B and correctly reject projects C and D.

Subjective versus Objective Approaches

We can form divisional WACCs subjectively by simply considering the project's risk relative to the firm's existing lines of business. If the project is riskier (safer) than the firm average, adjust the firm WACC upward (downward) to account for our subjective opinion of project riskiness. The biggest disadvantage to this approach is that the adjustments are pretty much picked out of thin air and created just for the project at hand. For example, consider the sample subjective divisional WACCs in Table 11.2. Both the project assignments to the divisions and then the WACC adjustments for the very low risk, low risk, high risk, and very high risk are fairly arbitrary.

figure 11.6

Divisional WACC Errors

Total incorrect acceptances/rejections turn out to be less when divisional WACCs are used.

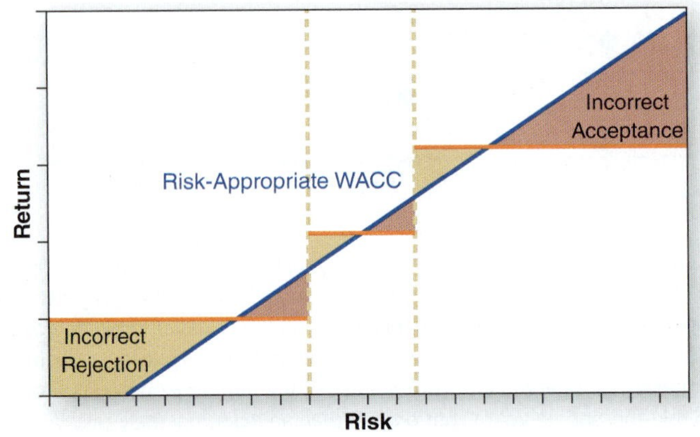

figure 11.7

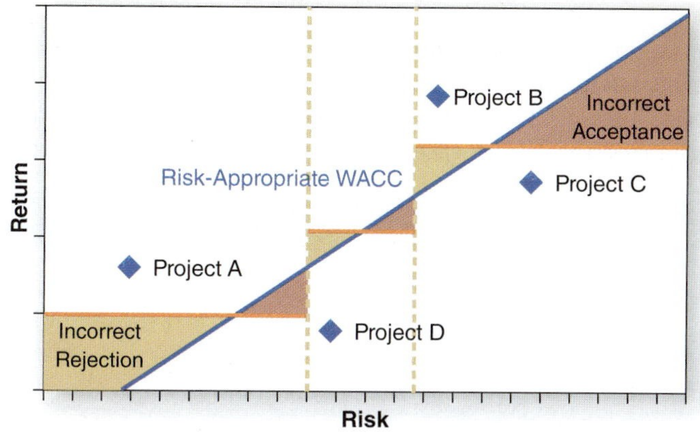

Example Decisions Using Divisional WACCs

Projects A and B here are *correctly accepted,* while projects C and D are *correctly rejected.*

table 11.2 | **Subjective Divisional WACCs**

Risk Level	Discount Rate
Very low risk	Firm WACC − 5%
Low risk	Firm WACC − 2%
Same risk as firm	Firm WACC
High risk	Firm WACC + 3%
Very high risk	Firm WACC + 7%

An objective approach would be to compute the average beta per division, use these figures in the CAPM formula to calculate i_E for each division, and then, in turn, use divisional estimates of i_E to construct divisional WACCs. Though the objective approach would usually be more precise, resulting in fewer incorrect accept/reject decisions, the subjective approach is more frequently used because it is easier to implement.

LG11-7

EXAMPLE 11-7

Divisional Costs of Capital

Assume that BF, Inc., an all-equity firm, has a firmwide WACC of 10 percent, and that the firm is broken into three divisions: Textiles, Accessories, and Miscellaneous. The average Textiles project has a beta of 0.7; the average Accessories project has a beta of 1.3; and the average Miscellaneous project has a beta of 1.1.

The firm is currently considering the projects shown in the following table. The current approach is to use the firm's WACC to evaluate all projects, but management sees the wisdom in adopting a subjective divisional cost of capital approach. Firm management is thus considering a divisional cost of capital scheme in which they will use the firm's WACC for Miscellaneous projects, the firm's WACC minus 1 percent for Textiles projects, and the firm's WACC plus 3 percent for Accessories projects. The current expected return to the market is 12 percent, and the current risk-free rate is 5.75 percent.

For this group of projects, how much better would their accept/reject decisions be if they used this approach rather than if they continued to use the firm's WACC to evaluate all projects? Would switching to an objective divisional cost of capital approach, where the WACC for each division is based on that division's average beta, improve their accept/reject criteria any further?

For interactive versions of this example visit www.mhhe.com/can3e

SOLUTION:

Determine the required rates of return for each project assuming that the firm uses the firmwide WACC and adds the subjective adjustments to construct divisional WACCs. The objective computation of divisional WACCs using each division's average beta and the i_E computed using each project's specific beta is indicated in the following table. In each case, project acceptances appear in blue print, and project rejections appear in red print.

Project	Division	Expected i_E	Beta
A	$\beta_{Accessories}$	17.00%	1.3
B	$\beta_{Accessories}$	15.00	1.2
C	$\beta_{Miscellaneous}$	13.00	1.3
D	$\beta_{Miscellaneous}$	11.00	0.7
E	$\beta_{Textiles}$	9.00	0.8
F	$\beta_{Textiles}$	7.00	0.5

Project	Division	Expected i_E	Beta	Firm WACC	Subjective i_E	Objective i_E	Specific i_E
A	$\beta_{Accessories}$	17.00%	1.3	10.00%	13.00%	13.88%	13.88%
B	$\beta_{Accessories}$	15.00	1.2	10.00	13.00	13.88	13.25
C	$\beta_{Miscellaneous}$	13.00	1.3	10.00	10.00	12.63	13.88
D	$\beta_{Miscellaneous}$	11.00	0.7	10.00	10.00	12.63	10.13
E	$\beta_{Textiles}$	9.00	0.8	10.00	9.00	10.13	10.75
F	$\beta_{Textiles}$	7.00	0.5	10.00	9.00	10.13	8.88

Using the "Specific i_E" yields the "correct" accept/reject decision; that is, these accept/reject decisions would be generated exactly the same if the firm had the time and resources to compute the i_E on a project-by-project basis. In this particular situation, using the firm WACC as a benchmark for all the projects would result in projects E and F being rejected, since they both will return expected rates less than the firm's 10 percent required rate of return. By comparison to the results using the Specific i_E, both of these rejections are appropriate. We would prefer that the accept/reject criteria took account of risk; that is, both projects would be rejected because their expected returns (9 percent and 7 percent, respectively) are less than the required returns (10.75 and 8.88 percent, respectively) based on their specific levels of project risk rather than assuming that both projects carry the same risk as the firm's overall risk. However, using the firm's WACC incorrectly accepts project C.

Using the subjectively adjusted approach to calculating i_E results in required rates of return of 13 percent for Accessories projects, 10 percent for Miscellaneous projects, and 9 percent for Textiles projects. The associated accept/reject decisions actually incorrectly accepts projects C and E, making the subjectively adjusted WACC approach worse (in this specific example) than simply using the firmwide WACC.

Finally, using the objective approach to constructing divisional costs of capital, along with the three divisions' average betas given above, results in required rates of return for the three divisions of:

$$i_E = R_f + \beta(R_M - R_f)$$

$$i_{E,\ Accessories} = 0.0575 + 1.3[0.12 - 0.0575] = 0.1388, \text{ or } 13.88\%$$

$$i_{E,\ Miscellaneous} = 0.0575 + 1.1[0.12 - 0.0575] = 0.1263, \text{ or } 12.63\%$$

$$i_{E,\ Textiles} = 0.0575 + 0.7[0.12 - 0.0575] = 0.1013, \text{ or } 10.13\%$$

As these solutions show, using these divisional cost of capital figures as required rates of return for each project results in correct rejections of projects E and F, but also results in an incorrect rejection of project D and an incorrect acceptance of project C relative to computing i_E on a project-by-project basis.

Overall, using either the objective or subjective approaches to calculating divisional costs of capital will not be as precise as using project-specific WACCs: We will wind up incorrectly accepting and/or rejecting some projects. Making incorrect decisions on some of our project choices may be worth it if the projects in question aren't large enough for project-specific calculations to be cost-effective.

Similar to Problems 11-25 to 11-28

TIME OUT

11-5 Divisions of a corporation are not usually formed based explicitly on differences in risk between the projects in different divisions. Rather, they are normally formed along product-type or geographic differences. Explain how this division scheme may still result in divisions that *do* differ among themselves by average risk. Also explain why calculating divisional WACCs in such a situation will still improve decision making over simply using a firmwide WACC for project acceptance or rejection.

11-6 Explain why, in Example 11-7, using objectively computed divisional WACCs still resulted in an incorrect accept/reject decision for project D.

11.4 • Flotation Costs

LG11-8

We know that firms use varied sources of funding. Until now, our calculations have used retained earnings to fund projects. What if a firm funds a project by issuing externally generated new capital—additional stock, bonds, and so on? Then the firm has to pay the costs of printing the new stock or bond certificates, commissions to the underwriters helping the firm to sell the stocks and bonds, government registration fees, and other associated costs. So to figure project WACCs, we must integrate these **flotation costs** into our component costs as well.

flotation costs
Fees paid by firms to investment banks for issuing new securities.

We can approach the commission costs in two basic ways. We can either increase the project's WACC to incorporate the flotation costs' impact as a percentage of WACC, or we can leave the WACC alone and adjust the project's initial investment upward to reflect the "true" cost of the project. Both approaches have advantages and disadvantages. The first approach tends to understate the component cost of new equity, and the latter approach violates the **separation principle** of capital budgeting, which states that the calculations of cash flows should remain independent of financing. We will discuss the separation principle and the second approach in the next chapter.

separation principle
Theory maintaining that the sources and uses of capital should be decided upon independently.

Adjusting the WACC

The first approach to adjusting for flotation costs is to adjust the issue price of new securities by subtracting flotation cost, *F*, to reflect the net security price. Then use this net price to calculate the component cost of capital. For equity, this approach is most commonly applied to the constant-growth model:

$$i_E = \frac{D_1}{P_0 - F} + g \qquad \textbf{(11-8)}$$

If we instead want to apply this approach to the cost of equity obtained from the CAPM formula, we would adjust it upward by an equivalent amount.

EXAMPLE 11-8

LG11-8

Flotation-Adjusted Cost of Equity

Suppose that, as in Example 11-1, ADK Industries' common shares are selling for \$32.75 per share, and the company expects to set its next annual dividend at \$1.54 per share. All future dividends are expected to grow by 6 percent per year indefinitely. In addition, let us suppose that ADK faces a flotation cost of 20 percent on new equity issues. Calculate the flotation-adjusted cost of equity.

For interactive versions of this example visit www.mhhe.com/can3e

SOLUTION:

Twenty percent of $32.75 will be $6.55, so the flotation-adjusted cost of equity will be:

$$i_E = \frac{D_1}{P_0 - F} + g$$

$$= \frac{\$1.54}{\$32.75 - \$6.55} + 0.06$$

$$= 0.1188, \text{ or } 11.88\%$$

Notice that the result is 1.18 percent above the non-flotation-adjusted cost of equity, 10.70 percent, computed using the constant-growth model in Example 11-1. If we instead wanted to use the CAPM estimate, we would take the non-flotation-adjusted CAPM estimate from the same example, 10.80 percent, and add the same differential of 1.18 percent to it to get the flotation-adjusted value:

$$i_E = 0.1080 + 0.0118 = 0.1198 \text{ or } 11.98\%$$

The adjustments for the component costs of preferred stock and debt will be similar:

$$i_P = \frac{D_1}{P_0 - F} \quad \textbf{(11-9)}$$

$$\text{Solve} \left\{ PV - F = PMT \times \left[\frac{1 - \frac{1}{(1 + i_D)^N}}{i_D} \right] + \frac{FV}{(1 + i_D)^N} \right\} \text{ for } i_D \quad \textbf{(11-10)}$$

Similar to Problems 11-23, 11-24

TIME OUT

11-7 Why should we expect the flotation costs for debt to be significantly lower than those for equity?

11-8 Explain how we should go about computing the WACC for a project which uses both retained earnings and a new equity issue.

viewpoints REVISITED

Business Application Solution

MP3 Devices, Inc., faces current component costs of capital equal to:

$$i_E = \frac{D_1}{P_0} + g \qquad\qquad i_P = \frac{D_1}{P_0}$$

$$= \frac{\$1.35}{\$18.75} + 0.06 \qquad\qquad = \frac{\$10}{\$100}$$

$$= 0.1320, \text{ or } 13.20\% \qquad = 0.1000, \text{ or } 10.00\%$$

$$\text{Solve} \left\{ \$1{,}100 = \$100 \times \left[\frac{1 - \dfrac{1}{(1 + i_D)^{20}}}{i_D} \right] + \frac{\$1{,}000}{(1 + i_D)^{20}} \right\} \text{ for } i_D$$

gives $i_D = 0.0891$, or 8.91%

CALCULATOR HINTS

N = 20
PV = −1,100
PMT = 100
FV = 1000
CPT I = 8.91%

Using the target capital structure weights, MP3's WACC equals:

$$\text{WACC} = 0.5 \times 0.1320 + 0.1 \times 0.10 + 0.4 \times 0.0891 \times (1 - 0.34)$$
$$= 0.0995, \text{ or } 9.95\%$$

Personal Application Solution

Mackenzie can expect a total of \$17,125 + \$29,000 = \$46,125 in student loans when she graduates from her master's program. At an 8 percent rate of interest, the yearly interest charges will be \$3,690 immediately after she graduates (though they will go down once she starts paying off some of the principal). Since the yearly interest will be more than the allowable \$2,500 deduction, we can express her after-tax interest rate as the following weighted average:

$$\text{WACC} = \frac{D_{\text{Nondeductible}}}{D_{\text{Nondeductible}} + D_{\text{Deductible}}} i_D + \frac{D_{\text{Deductible}}}{D_{\text{Nondeductible}} + D_{\text{Deductible}}} i_D \times (1 - T_P)$$

$$= \frac{\$3{,}690 - \$2{,}500}{\$3{,}690} \times 0.08 + \frac{\$2{,}500}{\$3{,}690} \times 0.08 \times (1 - 0.25)$$

$$= 0.3225 \times 0.08 + 0.6775 \times 0.08 \times 0.75$$

$$= 0.0664, \text{ or } 6.64\%$$

summary of learning goals

This chapter covers how to incorporate previous chapters' pricing formulas into weighted-average costs of capital calculations. We also discussed situations in which a firmwide WACC is appropriate for valuing a project, and when we need to calculate a project-specific WACC. We also discussed the trade-offs inherent in using divisional WACCs. Finally, we saw that incorporating flotation costs will increase the WACC above the value it would have if the firm was able to raise all funds internally.

LG11-1 Understand the relationship of cost of capital to the investor's required return. When firms use multiple sources of capital, they need to calculate the appropriate discount rate for valuing their firm's cash flows as a weighted average of the capital component costs.

LG11-2 Use the weighted-average cost of capital (WACC) formula to calculate a project's cost of capital. The WACC formula uses the after-tax costs of capital to compute the firm's weighted-average cost of debt financing. Since interest on a firm's pure debt is paid out of before-tax income, the yield paid on bonds does not really come entirely out of the firm's pockets. If the firm had not paid out the interest owed to debtholders, then those funds would have been taxed. So, effectively, the firm only pays out $(1 - T_C)$ times the yield on debt to the debtholders; the government "pays" the remainder, T_C, times the yield.

LG11-3 Explain how the firm chooses among estimating costs of equity, preferred stock, and debt. We estimate the component costs of capital using pricing formulas we have seen in previous chapters for equity, preferred stock, and debt, reworked to solve for the appropriate interest rate.

LG11-4 Calculate the weights used for WACC projections. Appropriate weights used in calculating a WACC should reflect the relative sizes of the total market capitalizations for each kind of security that the firm issues—debt, preferred stock, and pure equity. Use market values rather than book values to calculate a WACC because market values reflect investors' assessment of what they would be willing to pay for the various types of securities.

LG11-5 Identify which elements of WACC are used to calculate a project-specific WACC. Any debt or preferred stock that a firm issues, regardless of whether the securities will finance new projects or fund existing operations, are rightfully obligations of the entire firm. Thus, any debt and preferred stock components of capital should use firmwide, not project-specific, WACC figures. Therefore, we can expect common stockholders to bear the brunt of the risk of new projects. Accordingly, the component cost of equity should reflect the *project* risk as measured by a proxy beta.

LG11-6 Evaluate trade-offs between a firmwide WACC and a divisional cost of capital approach. Since firms evaluate projects continually, managers need a shortcut to avoid calculating project-specific WACCs for every project that they consider. They may use either a firmwide WACC or a divisional WACC instead, but using the shortcuts involves a trade-off between speed and precision. Using firmwide or divisional WACCS means that the firm can calculate fewer WACCs than it has projects, but doing so will also introduce error into the accept/reject decisions. Decision errors rise further when managers use a single, firmwide WACC for all projects, or when they evaluate projects with significantly different risk than the firm's or division's average risk.

LG11-7 Distinguish subjective and objective approaches to divisional cost of capital. The subjective approach requires only that WACCs for "risky" divisions be adjusted (sometimes arbitrarily so that risky division WACCs will be higher than firm WACCs). Similarly, subjective approaches adjust downward divisional WACCs for relatively safe divisions. An objective approach to computing a divisional WACC uses the average beta of projects in each division to calculate the WACC.

LG11-8 Demonstrate how to adjust the WACC to reflect flotation costs. Flotation costs increase costs if the firm must rely upon externally raised funds for a project. We adjust the WACC for flotation costs by subtracting the flotation costs from the prices of new securities at issue. Then we use the lower adjusted prices to calculate the respective component costs. Since we reduce the price of the securities but not the size of the expected future cash flows due to capital providers, this approach raises each capital source's effective cost.

chapter equations

11-1 $$WACC = \frac{E}{E + P + D}i_E + \frac{P}{E + P + D}i_P + \frac{D}{E + P + D}i_D \times (1 - T_C)$$

11-2 $$i_E = R_f + \beta(R_M - R_f)$$

11-3 $$i_E = \frac{D_1}{P_0} + g$$

11-4 $$i_P = \frac{D_1}{P_0}$$

11-5 $$\text{Solve}\left\{PV = PMT \times \left[\frac{1 - \frac{1}{(1 + i_D)^N}}{i_D}\right] + \frac{FV}{(1 + i_D)^N}\right\} \text{for } i_D$$

11-6 $$i_E = r_f + \beta_{Avg}\,[E(r_M) - r_f]$$

where

$$\beta_{Avg} = \frac{\sum_{j=1}^{N}\beta_j}{n}$$

11-7 $$WACC_{\text{Project}} = \frac{E_{\text{Project}}}{E_{\text{Project}} + P_{\text{Project}} + D_{\text{Project}}}i_{E,\text{ Project}} + \frac{P_{\text{Project}}}{E_{\text{Project}} + P_{\text{Project}} + D_{\text{Project}}}i_{P,\text{ Firm}} + \frac{D_{\text{Project}}}{E_{\text{Project}} + P_{\text{Project}} + D_{\text{Project}}}i_{D,\text{Firm}} \times (1 - T_{C,\text{ Project}})$$

11-8 $$i_E = \frac{D_1}{P_0 - F} + g$$

11-9 $$i_P = \frac{D_1}{P_0 - F}$$

11-10 $$\text{Solve}\left\{PV - F = PMT \times \left[\frac{1 - \frac{1}{(1 + i_D)^N}}{i_D}\right] + \frac{FV}{(1 + i_D)^N}\right\} \text{for } i_D$$

key terms

business risk, The risk of a project arising from the line of business it is in; the variability of a firm's or division's cash flows. *p. 381*

component costs, The individual costs of each type of capital—bonds, preferred stock, and common stock. *p. 373*

divisional WACC, An estimated WACC computed using some sort of proxy for the average equity risk of the projects in a particular division. *p. 383*

financial risk, The risk of a project to equity holders stemming from the use of debt in the financial structure of the firm; refers to the issue of how a firm decides to distribute the business risk between debt and equity holders. *p. 381*

flotation costs, Fees paid by firms to investment banks for issuing new securities. *p. 389*

proxy beta, The beta (a measure of the riskiness) of a firm in a similar line of business as a proposed new project. *p. 381*

separation principle, Theory maintaining that the sources and uses of capital should be decided upon independently. *p. 389*

weighted-average cost of capital (WACC), The weighted-average after-tax cost of the capital used by a firm, with weights set equal to the relative percentage of each type of capital used. *p. 373*

self-test problems with solutions

LG11-3, 11-4

1 Computing Firmwide WACC Sound & Vision Studios (SVS) has 5 million common shares outstanding, which sell for $24 per share. SVS management is expected to set the next annual dividend at $2.25 per share, and investors and analysts expect all future dividends to grow by 8 percent per year, indefinitely. The current risk-free rate is 5.50 percent, the expected return on the market is 11 percent, and the stock has a beta of 2.2. SVS also has 1 million shares of 5 percent preferred stock outstanding, with these shares selling for $44 per share, and 150,000, 15-year, 9 percent annual coupon bonds outstanding, currently selling for 112 percent of par. If SVS is in the 35 percent tax bracket, what is the firm's WACC?

Solution:

The component cost of equity, i_E, computed using the CAPM, will be equal to:

$$0.055 + 2.2(0.11 - 0.055) = 0.1760$$

The component cost of equity computed using the constant-growth model will be equal to:

$$\frac{\$2.25}{\$24.00} + 0.08 = 0.1738$$

Absent any guidance concerning which estimate is most appropriate, our best approach is to take the average of the two as i_E:

$$i_E = \frac{0.1760 + 0.1738}{2} = 0.1749$$

The component cost of preferred stock, i_P, will be equal to:

$$\frac{\$5}{\$44} = 0.1136$$

The component cost of debt, i_D, will be the solution to:

$$\$1{,}120 = \$90 \times \left[\frac{1 - \dfrac{1}{(1 + i_D)^{15}}}{i_D}\right] + \frac{\$1{,}000}{(1 + i_D)^{15}} \Rightarrow i_D = 0.0763$$

The market values of equity, preferred stock, and debt will be:

$$E = 5\text{m} \times \$24.00 = \$120\text{m}$$
$$P = 1\text{m} \times \$44.00 = \$44\text{m}$$
$$D = 150{,}000 \times \$1{,}120 = \$168\text{m}$$

And we can use these proportions to calculate the weights:

$$\frac{E}{E + P + D} = \frac{\$120\text{m}}{\$120\text{m} + \$44\text{m} + \$168\text{m}} = 0.3614$$

$$\frac{P}{E + P + D} = \frac{\$44\text{m}}{\$120\text{m} + \$44\text{m} + \$168\text{m}} = 0.1325$$

$$\frac{E}{E + P + D} = \frac{\$168\text{m}}{\$120\text{m} + \$44\text{m} + \$168\text{m}} = 0.5060$$

Using the weights, the component costs, and the tax rate, we can calculate the WACC as:

$$\begin{aligned} WACC &= 0.3614 \times 0.1749 + 0.1325 \times 0.1136 + 0.5060 \times 0.0763 \times (1 - 0.35) \\ &= 0.1034, \text{ or } 10.34\% \end{aligned}$$

2 Calculating Project WACC Ranks Engineering, a civil engineering firm that has historically gotten most of its revenues from the planning and construction of public works projects, is considering starting a new division that will submit architectural designs for private engineering projects, such as designing shopping malls. Adding the new division is expected to increase the firm's EBIT from $8 million to $10 million. While the civil engineering industry has a fairly low beta of 0.65, the private design market is a bit riskier, and Ranks has commissioned a study that shows that the average beta in that industry is approximately 1.3. Rank's capital structure currently consists of 1 million outstanding shares of common stock, selling for $37 per share, and a $15 million bond issue, selling at 98 percent of par. The expected market risk premium is 8 percent, and the current risk-free rate is 5.7 percent. The bonds pay an 8 percent annual coupon and mature in 10 years. If the new division will be funded with 70 percent equity and 30 percent debt, what should be the WACC for this new division? LG11-5

Solution:

The weights to be used in the calculation of the division's WACC will be the 70 percent equity/30 percent debt specified in the problem and will not be based upon the company's existing capital structure.

The component cost of equity, i_E, will use the beta of the new line of business:

$$0.057 + 1.3(0.08) = 0.1610$$

The component cost of debt, i_D, will be the solution to:

$$\$980 = \$80 \times \left[\frac{1 - \frac{1}{(1 + i_D)^{10}}}{i_D}\right] + \frac{\$1{,}000}{(1 + i_D)^{10}} \Rightarrow i_D = 0.0830$$

The rise in EBIT from $8 million to $10 million will occur entirely in the second 34 percent tax bracket of Table 11.1, so 34 percent will be the appropriate tax rate for computation of the division's WACC, which will be equal to:

$$\begin{aligned} WACC &= 0.70 \times 0.1610 + 0.30 \times 0.0830 \times (1 - 0.34) \\ &= 0.1291, \text{ or } 12.91\% \end{aligned}$$

3 Firmwide WACC Decisions An all-equity firm is considering the projects shown in the following table. The T-bill rate is 6 percent and the market risk premium is 9 percent. If the firm uses its current WACC of 16.8 percent to evaluate these projects, which project(s), if any, will be incorrectly rejected? LG11-6

Project	Expected Return	Beta
A	8.0%	0.2
B	19.0	1.4
C	13.0	0.8
D	17.0	1.3

Solution:

If the firm uses the current WACC of 16.8 percent to evaluate all projects, projects A and C will be rejected. To determine if these rejections are correct or incorrect, we have to calculate what the projects' risk-specific WACCs should be:

$$WACC_A = i_{E,A} = 0.06 + 0.2 \times 0.09 = 0.078, \text{ or } 7.8\%$$

$$WACC_C = i_{E,C} = 0.06 + 0.8 \times 0.09 = 0.132, \text{ or } 13.2\%$$

Based on these numbers, project C *should* be rejected, as its risk-appropriate WACC of 13.2 percent is higher than its expected return of 13 percent. This result indicates that the project is not expected to earn a high enough level of return to compensate for its expected risk.

Project A's risk-appropriate rate of return at 7.8 percent is less than its expected 8 percent return, so it should be accepted. Project A's rejection when using the firmwide WACC is incorrect.

4 **Include Impact of Flotation Costs** Redo ST-1 for a proposed new project in the same line of business as the firm's current operations, but assuming that new equity will have a flotation cost of 15 percent, preferred stock will have a flotation cost of 10 percent, and debt will have a flotation cost of 3 percent.

Solution:

The component cost of equity, i_E, using flotation costs and the constant-growth model, will be:

$$\frac{\$2.25}{\$24.00 - (0.15 \times \$24.00)} + 0.08 = 0.1903$$

Since this is 19.03% − 17.38% = 1.65% higher than the calculated number when we ignored flotation costs, we could also adjust the i_E we had previously calculated using the CAPM of 17.60% by adding 1.65% to it, also: 17.60% + 1.65% = 19.25%, similar to the approach we took in Example 11-8.

Taking an average of the two measures of i_E computed incorporating flotation costs will give us the number we should use in the calculation of the WACC:

$$\frac{0.1903 + 0.1925}{2} = 0.1914$$

The component cost of preferred stock, i_P, will equal:

$$\frac{\$5}{\$44 - (0.1 \times \$44)} = 0.1263$$

The component cost of debt, i_D, will be the solution to:

$$\$1{,}120(1 - 0.03) = \$90 \times \left[\frac{1 - \frac{1}{(1 + i_D)^{15}}}{i_D}\right] + \frac{\$1{,}000}{(1 + i_D)^{15}} \Rightarrow i_D = 0.0799$$

No change in the capital structure weights or in the tax rate will occur, so the WACC for the new project will be:

$$WACC = 0.3614 \times 0.1914 + 0.1325 \times 0.1263 + 0.5060 \times 0.0799 \times (1 - 0.35)$$
$$= 0.1122, \text{ or } 11.22\%$$

questions

1. How would you handle calculating the cost of capital if a firm were planning to issue two different classes of common stock? *(LG11-1)*
2. Why don't we multiply the cost of preferred stock by 1 minus the tax rate, as we do for debt? *(LG11-2)*
3. Expressing WACC in terms of i_E, i_P, and i_D, what is the theoretical minimum for the WACC? *(LG11-2)*
4. Under what situations would you want to use the CAPM approach for estimating the component cost of equity? The constant-growth model? *(LG11-3)*
5. Could you calculate the component cost of equity for a stock with nonconstant expected growth rates in dividends if you didn't have the information necessary to compute the component cost using the CAPM? Why or why not? *(LG11-3)*
6. Why do we use market-based weights instead of book-value-based weights when computing the WACC? *(LG11-4)*
7. Suppose your firm wanted to expand into a new line of business quickly, and that management anticipated that the new line of business would constitute over 80 percent of your firm's operations within three years. If the expansion was going to be financed partially with debt, would it still make sense to use the firm's existing cost of debt, or should you compute a new rate of return for debt based on the new line of business? *(LG11-5)*
8. Explain why the divisional cost of capital approach may cause problems if new projects are assigned to the wrong division. *(LG11-6)*
9. When will the subjective approach to forming divisional WACCs be better than using the firmwide WACC to evaluate all projects? *(LG11-7)*
10. Suppose a new project was going to be financed partially with retained earnings. What flotation costs should you use for retained earnings? *(LG11-8)*

problems

basic problems

11-1 **Cost of Equity** Diddy Corp. stock has a beta of 1.2, the current risk-free rate is 5 percent, and the expected return on the market is 13.5 percent. What is Diddy's cost of equity? *(LG11-3)*

11-2 **Cost of Equity** JaiLai Cos. stock has a beta of 0.9, the current risk-free rate is 6.2 percent, and the expected return on the market is 12 percent. What is JaiLai's cost of equity? *(LG11-3)*

11-3 **Cost of Debt** Oberon, Inc., has a $20 million (face value) 10-year bond issue selling for 97 percent of par that pays an annual coupon of 8.25 percent. What would be Oberon's before-tax component cost of debt? *(LG11-3)*

11-4 **Cost of Debt** KatyDid Clothes has a $150 million (face value) 30-year bond issue selling for 104 percent of par that carries a coupon rate of 11 percent, paid semiannually. What would be Katydid's before-tax component cost of debt? *(LG11-3)*

11-5 **Tax Rate** Suppose that LilyMac Photography expects EBIT to be approximately $200,000 per year for the foreseeable future, and that it has 1,000 10-year, 9 percent annual coupon bonds outstanding. What would the appropriate tax rate be for use in the calculation of the debt component of LilyMac's WACC? *(LG11-3)*

11-6 **Tax Rate** PDQ, Inc., expects EBIT to be approximately $11 million per year for the foreseeable future, and that it has 25,000 20-year, 8 percent annual coupon bonds outstanding. What would the appropriate tax rate be for use in the calculation of the debt component of PDQ's WACC? *(LG11-3)*

11-7 **Cost of Preferred Stock** ILK has preferred stock selling for 97 percent of par that pays an 8 percent annual coupon. What would be ILK's component cost of preferred stock? *(LG11-3)*

11-8 **Cost of Preferred Stock** Marme, Inc., has preferred stock selling for 96 percent of par that pays an 11 percent annual coupon. What would be Marme's component cost of preferred stock? *(LG11-3)*

11-9 **Weight of Equity** FarCry Industries, a maker of telecommunications equipment, has 2 million shares of common stock outstanding, 1 million shares of preferred stock outstanding, and 10,000 bonds. If the common shares are selling for $27 per share, the preferred shares are selling for $14.50 per share, and the bonds are selling for 98 percent of par, what would be the weight used for equity in the computation of FarCry's WACC? *(LG11-4)*

11-10 **Weight of Equity** OMG Inc. has 4 million shares of common stock outstanding, 3 million shares of preferred stock outstanding, and 5,000 bonds. If the common shares are selling for $17 per share, the preferred shares are selling for $26 per share, and the bonds are selling for 108 percent of par, what would be the weight used for equity in the computation of OMG's WACC? *(LG11-4)*

11-11 **Weight of Debt** FarCry Industries, a maker of telecommunications equipment, has 2 million shares of common stock outstanding, 1 million shares of preferred stock outstanding, and 10,000 bonds. If the common shares are selling for $27 per share, the preferred shares are selling for $14.50 per share, and the bonds are selling for 98 percent of par, what weight should you use for debt in the computation of FarCry's WACC? *(LG11-4)*

11-12 **Weight of Debt** OMG Inc. has 4 million shares of common stock outstanding, 3 million shares of preferred stock outstanding, and 5,000 bonds. If the common shares are selling for $27 per share, the preferred shares are selling for $26 per share, and the bonds are selling for 108 percent of par, what weight should you use for debt in the computation of OMG's WACC? *(LG11-4)*

11-13 **Weight of Preferred Stock** FarCry Industries, a maker of telecommunications equipment, has 2 million shares of common stock outstanding, 1 million shares of preferred stock outstanding, and 10,000 bonds. If the common shares sell for $27 per share, the preferred shares sell for $14.50 per share, and the bonds sell for 98 percent of par, what weight should you use for preferred stock in the computation of FarCry's WACC? *(LG11-4)*

11-14 **Weight of Preferred Stock** OMG Inc. has 4 million shares of common stock outstanding, 3 million shares of preferred stock outstanding, and 5,000 bonds. If the common shares sell for $17 per share, the preferred shares sell for $16 per share, and the bonds sell for 108 percent of par, what weight should you use for preferred stock in the computation of OMG's WACC? *(LG11-4)*

intermediate problems

11-15 **WACC** Suppose that TapDance, Inc.'s, capital structure features 65 percent equity, 35 percent debt, and that its before-tax cost of debt is 8 percent, while its cost of equity is 13 percent. If the appropriate weighted average tax rate is 34 percent, what will be TapDance's WACC? *(LG11-2)*

11-16 **WACC** Suppose that JB Cos. has a capital structure of 78 percent equity, 22 percent debt, and that its before-tax cost of debt is 11 percent while its cost of equity is 15 percent. If the appropriate weighted-average tax rate is 25 percent, what will be JB's WACC? *(LG11-2)*

11-17 **WACC** Suppose that B2B, Inc., has a capital structure of 37 percent equity, 17 percent preferred stock, and 46 percent debt. If the before-tax component costs of equity, preferred stock, and debt are 14.5 percent, 11 percent, and 9.5 percent, respectively, what is B2B's WACC if the firm faces an average tax rate of 30 percent? *(LG11-2)*

11-18 **WACC** Suppose that MNINK Industries' capital structure features 63 percent equity, 7 percent preferred stock, and 30 percent debt. If the before-tax component costs of equity, preferred stock, and debt are 11.60 percent, 9.5 percent, and 9 percent, respectively, what is MNINK's WACC if the firm faces an average tax rate of 34 percent? *(LG11-2)*

11-19 **WACC** TAFKAP Industries has 3 million shares of stock outstanding selling at $17 per share, and an issue of $20 million in 7.5 percent annual coupon bonds with a maturity of 15 years, selling at 106 percent of par. If TAFKAP's weighted average tax rate is 34 percent and its cost of equity is 14.5 percent, what is TAFKAP's WACC? *(LG11-3)*

11-20 **WACC** Johnny Cake Ltd. has 10 million shares of stock outstanding selling at $23 per share and an issue of $50 million in 9 percent annual coupon bonds with a maturity of 17 years, selling at 93.5 percent of par. If Johnny Cake's weighted-average tax rate is 34 percent, its next dividend is expected to be $3 per share, and all future dividends are expected to grow at 6 percent per year, indefinitely, what is its WACC? *(LG11-3)*

11-21 **WACC Weights** BetterPie Industries has 3 million shares of common stock outstanding, 2 million shares of preferred stock outstanding, and 10,000 bonds. If the common shares are selling for $47 per share, the preferred shares are selling for $24.50 per share, and the bonds are selling for 99 percent of par, what would be the weights used in the calculation of BetterPie's WACC? *(LG11-4)*

11-22 **WACC Weights** WhackAmOle has 2 million shares of common stock outstanding, 1.5 million shares of preferred stock outstanding, and 50,000 bonds. If the common shares are selling for $63 per share, the preferred shares are selling for $52 per share, and the bonds are selling for 103 percent of par, what would be the weights used in the calculation of WhackAmOle's WACC? *(LG11-4)*

11-23 **Flotation Cost** Suppose that Brown-Murphies' common shares sell for $19.50 per share, that the firm is expected to set their next annual dividend at $0.57 per share, and that all future dividends are expected to grow by 4 percent per year, indefinitely. If Brown-Murphies faces a flotation cost of 13 percent on new equity issues, what will be the flotation-adjusted cost of equity? *(LG11-8)*

advanced problems

11-24 **Flotation Cost** A firm is considering a project that will generate perpetual after-tax cash flows of $15,000 per year beginning next year. The project has the same risk as the firm's overall operations and must be financed externally. Equity flotation costs 14 percent and debt issues cost 4 percent on an after-tax basis. The firm's D/E ratio is 0.8. What is the most the firm can pay for the project and still earn its required return? *(LG11-2)*

11-25 **Firmwide versus Project-Specific WACCs** An all-equity firm is considering the projects shown below. The T-bill rate is 4 percent and the market risk premium is 7 percent. If the firm uses its current WACC of 12 percent to evaluate these projects, which project*(s)*, if any, will be incorrectly rejected? *(LG11-6)*

Project	Expected Return	Beta
A	8.0%	0.5
B	19.0	1.2
C	13.0	1.4
D	17.0	1.6

11-26 **Firmwide versus Project-Specific WACCs** An all-equity firm is considering the projects shown below. The T-bill rate is 4 percent and the market risk premium is 7 percent. If the firm uses its current WACC of 12 percent to evaluate these projects, which project*(s)*, if any, will be incorrectly accepted? *(LG11-6)*

Project	Expected Return	Beta
A	8.0%	0.5
B	19.0	1.2
C	13.0	1.4
D	17.0	1.6

11-27 **Divisional WACCs** Suppose your firm has decided to use a divisional WACC approach to analyze projects. The firm currently has four divisions, A through D, with average betas for each division of 0.6, 1.0, 1.3, and 1.6, respectively. If all current and future projects will be financed with half debt and half equity, and if the current cost of equity (based on an average firm beta of 1.0 and a current risk-free rate of 7 percent) is 13 percent and the after-tax yield on the company's bonds is 8 percent, what will the WACCs be for each division? *(LG11-7)*

11-28 **Divisional WACCs** Suppose your firm has decided to use a divisional WACC approach to analyze projects. The firm currently has four divisions, A through D, with average betas for each division of 0.9, 1.1, 1.3, and 1.5, respectively. If all current and future projects will be financed with 25 percent debt and 75 percent equity, and if the current cost of equity (based on an average firm beta of 1.2 and a current risk-free rate of 4 percent) is 12 percent and the after-tax yield on the company's bonds is 9 percent, what will the WACCs be for each division? *(LG11-7)*

research it! Finding the Before-Tax Cost of Debt, i_D

For component debt costs, we'd like to use the yield to maturity on bonds that resembles the maturity of our potential debt if possible. Let's assume that we want to find a bond issue with approximately ten years until maturity (as of January 2012) for Sears. Luckily, Sears has quite a few outstanding bond issues to choose from, and we can access the information on these issues on the Yahoo! Finance page.

Go to **http://finance.yahoo.com** and start by clicking on "Investing" and then "Bonds." Then enter Sears in the "Bond Lookup" box and click on "Search." You'll be presented with a list of Sears outstanding bonds sorted in order of decreasing maturity. Once you've identified the bond with the maturity closest to the maturity you want, click on the "Issue" entry and look up the Yield to Maturity.

Your turn: Go to the Yahoo! Finance website and find the YTM on the bond with a maturity that's as close as possible to ten years from today's date.

integrated mini-case WACC for a New Project

LilyMac Studios, a national chain of photography studios, is considering opening up a chain of coffee shop/art galleries. While the existing operations of the firm have a beta of 1.17, the new chain is expected to have a beta of 0.8.

LilyMac currently has 500,000 shares of common stock outstanding, which are selling for $63.72 per share, and a $10 million bond issue, selling at 104 percent of par. The expected market risk premium is 6 percent, and the current risk-free rate is 5.5 percent. The bonds pay an 8 percent semiannual coupon and mature in 20 years.

The current operations of the firm produce EBIT of $18 million per year, and the chain's operations are expected to add $25 million per year to that. The new chain will be funded with 65 percent equity and 35 percent debt, and estimated flotation costs are expected to be 12 percent and 5 percent, respectively.

What should be the WACC for the new chain of coffee shops?

ANSWERS TO TIME OUT

11-1 Debt interest is paid out of before-tax earnings, implying that paying $1 in interest really costs the firm only $1 × (1 − T_C); common and preferred stock dividends are paid out of after-tax net income, and so do not have a tax shelter effect.

11-2 We would compute the *weighted-average cost* of debt, using the percentage of total market value of each issue as its weight.

11-3 The costs of debt and preferred stock are *firmwide* obligations, not project-specific ones, because *debtholders* and owners of preferred shares can legally expect to be paid back out of the firm's revenues even if the specific project being funded is not successful.

11-4 We can often "back out" a pure-play beta by adjusting such a firm's beta to offset the impact of the other lines of business. For example, suppose that we are trying to find a proxy beta for a project involving the production of dishwashers. If we can find a potential proxy company with a beta of 0.75 that makes both dishwashers and air conditioners (and which earns approximately half its revenue from each line of business), and we can elsewhere estimate the average beta of an air-conditioning manufacturer to be, say, 0.8, then we extrapolate that the beta for the dishwasher division of that company must be the solution to $0.75 = (0.5 \times 0.8) + (0.5 \times \beta_{\text{Dishwashers}})$, or $\beta_{\text{Dishwashers}} = 0.7$.

11-5 Divisions based on either product type or geographic location will also usually proxy for differences in project risk. For example, many large auto manufacturers use divisional breakdowns based on both product types and geography (e.g., "Ford of North America," or "Dodge Truck Division"). Though these divisions are not explicitly targeted at separating projects by risk, selling a new Ford Focus in Europe is obviously going to have different risks than selling the same car in North America due to the differences in competitive environment, consumer tastes, and so on.

11-6 Project D's beta is lower than average for its division, so the objectively computed divisional WACC for its division will still overstate the project's required rate of return versus a project-specific WACC. Holding the project up to too high of a benchmark will cause it to be incorrectly rejected.

11-7 Debt is easier for the underwriter to sell for several reasons. Debt is safer and therefore more attractive to many groups of potential buyers. It also tends to be sold in larger denominations primarily to large financial institutions, such as mutual funds and pension funds, which requires the underwriter to contact a smaller group of potential buyers than if assisting in a stock issue.

11-8 We would take a weighted average of the flotation cost for new equity and that of retained earnings (which would be equal to zero), where the weights would be equal to the proportion of each type of equity financing used.

PART SIX

12 Estimating Cash Flows on Capital Budgeting Projects

viewpoints

Business Application

Suppose that McDonald's is considering introducing the McTurkey Dinner (MTD). The company anticipates that the MTD will have unit sales, prices, and cost figures as shown in the following table for the next five years, after which the firm will retire the MTD. Introducing the MTD will require $7 million in new assets, which will fall into the MACRS five-year class life. McDonald's expects the necessary assets to be worth $2 million in market value at the end of the project life. In addition, the company expects that NWC requirements at the beginning of each year will be approximately 13 percent of the projected sales throughout the coming year and fixed costs will be $2 million per year. McDonald's uses an 11 percent cost of capital for similar projects and is subject to a 35 percent marginal tax rate. What will be this project's expected cash flows? **(See solution on p. 423)**

Personal Application

Achmed contemplates going back to school part-time to get an MBA. He anticipates that it would take him four years to get his MBA, and the program would cost $15,000 per year in books and tuition (payable at the beginning of each year). He also thinks that he would need to get a new laptop (which he was going to buy anyway as a portable gaming system) for $2,500 when he starts the program, and he just paid $250 to take the GMAT. After graduation, Achmed anticipates that he will be able to earn approximately $10,000 more per year with the MBA, and he thinks he'll work for about another 20 years after getting the MBA. What total cash flows should Achmed consider in his decision? **(See solution on p. 423)**

Thinking about an MBA? What returns can you expect from the investment?

McTurkey Dinner Projections

Year	Estimated Unit Sales	Estimated Selling Price Per Unit	Estimated Variable Cost Per Unit
1	400,000	$7.00	$3.35
2	1,000,000	7.21	3.52
3	1,000,000	7.43	3.70
4	1,000,000	7.65	3.89
5	500,000	7.88	4.08

Learning Goals

LG12-1 Explain why we use pro forma statements to analyze project cash flows.

LG12-2 Identify which cash flows we can incrementally apply to a project and which ones we cannot.

LG12-3 Calculate a project's expected cash flows using the free cash flow approach.

LG12-4 Explain how accelerated depreciation affects project cash flows.

LG12-5 Calculate free cash flows for replacement equipment.

LG12-6 Calculate cash flows associated with cost-cutting proposals.

LG12-7 Demonstrate the EAC approach to choosing among alternative cash streams for recurring projects.

LG12-8 Adjust initial project investments to account for flotation costs.

To evaluate capital budgeting projects, we have to estimate how much cash outflow each project will need and how much cash inflow it will generate, as well as exactly when such outflows and inflows will occur. Estimating these cash flows isn't difficult, but it is *complicated,* as there are lots of little details to keep track of. Accordingly, as you look through this chapter's examples, questions, and problems, you'll notice that these types of problems involve a lot more information than those you've seen elsewhere in the text, such as:

- The particular new product or service's costs and revenues.
- The likely impact that the new service or product will have on the firm's existing products' costs and revenues.
- The impact of using existing assets or employees already employed elsewhere in the firm.
- How to handle charges such as the research and development costs incurred to develop the new product.

One of the keys to this chapter will be making sure that we have a systematic approach to handling and arranging details. In the next few sections, we're going to construct a process which, if we follow it faithfully, will guide us in considering factors such as those listed.

The exact process that we're going to use is more formally referred to as **pro forma analysis.** In particular, we will use a form of *pro forma analysis* that will estimate expected future cash flows of a project using only the necessary parts of the balance sheet and income statements; if a part of either financial statement doesn't change because of the new project, we'll ignore it. This approach will allow us to focus on the question, "What will be this project's impact on the firm's total cash flows if we go forward?"

12.1 • Sample Project Description

Let's suppose that we are working for a game development company, First Strike Software (FSS). FSS is considering leasing a new plant in Gatlinburg, Tennessee, which it will use to produce copies of its new game "FinProf," a role-playing game where the player battles aliens invading a local college's finance department.

FSS will price this game at $39.99, and the firm estimates sales for each of the next three years as shown in Table 12.1. Given buyers' rapidly changing tastes in computer games, FSS does not expect to be able to sell any more copies after year 3.

pro forma analysis

Process of estimating expected future cash flows of a project using only the relevant parts of the balance sheet and income statements.

table 12.1 | **Sample Project Projected Unit Sales**

Year	Unit Sales
1	15,000
2	27,000
3	5,000

Variable costs per game are low ($4.25), and FSS expects fixed costs to total $150,000 per year, including rent. Start-up costs include $75,000 for a software-duplicating machine, plus an additional $2,000 in shipping and installation costs. For our first stab at analyzing this project, we will assume that the duplicating machine will be straight-line depreciated to $5,000 over the life of the project. We'll expect that machine to bring only $2,000 on the market after we're done using it.

FinProf is an updated version of an older game sold by FSS, MktProf. FSS intends to keep selling MktProf but anticipates that FinProf will decrease sales of MktProf by 2,000 units per year throughout the life of the new game. MktProf sells for $19.99 and has variable costs of $3.50 per unit. The decrease in MktProf sales will not affect either NWC or fixed assets.

Development costs totaled $150,000 throughout development of the game, and First Strike estimates its NWC requirements at the beginning of each year will be approximately 10 percent of the projected sales during the coming year. First Strike is in the 34 percent tax bracket and uses a discount rate of 15 percent on projects with risk profiles such as this. The relevant question: Should FSS put FinProf into production or not?

LG12-2

12.2 • Guiding Principles for Cash Flow Estimation

incremental cash flows

Cash flows directly attributable to the adoption of a new project.

When we calculate a project's expected cash flows, we must ensure that we cover all **incremental cash flows,** that is, the cash flow changes that we would expect throughout the entire firm as the new project comes on board. Some incremental cash flow effects are fairly obvious. For example, suppose a firm has to buy a new asset to support a new project but would not be buying the asset if the project were not adopted. Clearly, the cash associated with buying the asset is due to the project, and we should therefore count it when we calculate the cash flows associated with that project. But we can hardly expect *all* incremental cash flows to be so obvious. Other incremental cash flows, as discussed in the following sections, are more subtle, and we'll have to watch for them very carefully.

LG12-2

Opportunity Costs

opportunity cost

The dollar cost or forgone opportunity of using an asset already owned by the firm, or a person already employed by the firm, in a new project.

As you likely remember from your microeconomics classes, an **opportunity cost** exists whenever a firm has to choose how to allocate scarce resources. If those resources go into project A, the firm must forgo using them in any other way. Those forgone choices represent lost opportunities, and we have to account for them when calculating cash flows attributable to project A.

For example, suppose that FSS already owned the piece of software-duplicating machinery discussed previously. If the machinery was already being fully utilized by another project within the company, then obviously switching it over to the FinProf game would require that other project to find another source of software duplication. Therefore, to be fair, the FinProf project should be charged for the use of the machinery.

Even if the machinery was not currently being used in any other projects, it could still possibly have an opportunity cost associated with using it in the

FinProf project. If FSS could potentially sell the machinery on the open market for $75,000, the company would have to give up receiving that $75,000 in order to use the piece of machinery for the FinProf game. In the end, it would not really matter whether the firm had to buy the asset from outside sources or not; either way, the project will be tying up $75,000 worth of capital, and it should be charged for doing so.

The underlying concept behind charging the project for the opportunity cost of using an asset also has broader implications: Overall, we should charge any new project for any assets used by that project as well as any wages and benefits paid to employees working on it. Even if the firm was already employing those people prior to starting work on the new project, they are no longer available to work on any existing projects; and if the firm did not have any new projects, it could have laid those employees off, saving their wages and benefits.

Sunk Costs

LG12-2

If a firm has already paid an expense or is obligated to pay one in the future, regardless of whether a particular project is undertaken, that expense is a **sunk cost.** A firm should *never* count sunk costs in project cash flows.

sunk cost

A cost that has already been incurred and cannot be recovered.

For example, FSS incurred $150,000 in development costs in the previous example. Development costs would presumably include items such as the salaries of the game's programmers, market research costs, and so forth. Since we are not told otherwise, we can sensibly assume that the money is gone, and that FSS will never recoup its development money, even if it decides not to go ahead with publishing the game. Thus those costs are sunk, and FSS should not even consider them as part of its decision about whether to move forward with putting the FinProf game into production.

Substitutionary and Complementary Effects

LG12-2

If a new product or service will either reduce or increase sales, costs, or necessary assets for existing products or services, then those changes are incremental to the project and should rightfully be included in the project cash flows. For example, consider how FSS's FinProf game may affect the existing MktProf game. The gross sales and variable cost figures for the new game might be as shown in Table 12.2.

However, FSS also expects the MktProf game to lose yearly sales of 2,000 × $19.99 = $39,980 when FinProf comes aboard. Further, the decrease in sales of MktProf will also result in a decrease in yearly variable costs of 2,000 × $3.50 = $7,000 per year. So the net incremental sales and variable cost figures for the project will be as shown in Table 12.3.

table 12.2 | **Gross Sales and Variable Costs for FinProf**

Year	Sales	Variable Costs
1	15,000 × $39.99 = $599,850	15,000 × $4.25 = $63,750
2	27,000 × $39.99 = $1,079,730	27,000 × $4.25 = $114,750
3	5,000 × $39.99 = $199,950	5,000 × $4.25 = $21,250

table 12.3 | **Net Incremental and Variable Costs for FinProf**

Year	Sales	Variable Costs
1	$599,850 − $39,980 = $559,870	$63,750 − $7,000 = $56,750
2	$1,079,730 − $39,980 = $1,039,750	$114,750 − $7,000 = $107,750
3	$199,950 − $39,980 = $159,970	$21,250 − $7,000 = $14,250

We see a reduction in both sales and variable costs because FinProf is a partial **substitute** for MktProf. If the new game had been a **complement,** then both sales and variable costs of the existing product would have increased instead.

LG12-2

Stock Dividends and Bond Interest

substitute and complement

Effects that arise from a new product or service either decreasing or increasing sales, respectively, of the firm's existing products and services.

One final, important note concerning incremental project cash flows: We will never count any **financing costs,** including dividends paid on stock or interest paid on debt, as expenses of the project. The costs of capital are already included as component costs in the weighted average cost of capital (WACC) that we will be using to discount these cash flows in the next chapter. If we were to include them in the cash flow figures as well, we would be double-counting them.

financing costs

Interest paid to debt holders or dividends paid to stockholders.

TIME OUT

12-1 Suppose that your manager will be devoting half of her time to a new project, with the other half devoted to currently existing projects. How would you reflect this in your calculation of the incremental cash flows of the project?

12-2 Could a new product have both substitutionary and complementary effects on existing products?

LG12-3

12.3 • Total Project Cash Flow

In Chapter 2, we discussed the concept of free cash flow (FCF), which we defined as

$$\begin{aligned} FCF &= \text{Operating cash flow} - \text{Investment in operating capital} \\ &= [EBIT\,(1 - \text{Tax rate}) + \text{Depreciation}] \\ &\quad - [\Delta\text{Gross fixed assets} + \Delta\text{Net operating working capital}] \end{aligned} \qquad \textbf{(12-1)}$$

In this chapter, we are going to use this variable again as a measure of the total amount of available cash flow from a project. However, we will observe two important differences from how we used it in Chapter 2. First, since we will be considering potential projects rather than a particular firm's actual, historic activities, the FCF numbers we calculate will be, frankly, guesses—informed guesses, surely, but guesses nonetheless. Since we will be "calculating" guesses, we will introduce possible estimation error into our capital budgeting decision statistics, which we will discuss in the next chapter.

Second, we will now calculate FCF on potential projects individually, rather than across the firm as a whole as we did in Chapter 2. In some ways, calculating FCF on individual projects will make our job much easier, since we need not worry about estimating an entire set of balance sheets for the firm. Instead, we will only have to be concerned with the limited subset of pro forma statements necessary to keep track of the assets, expense categories, and so on that a new project will affect. Unfortunately, the elements of that limited set will vary from situation to situation, and the hard part will be identifying which parts of the balance sheets are necessary and which are not.

LG12-3

Calculating Depreciation

Expected depreciation on equipment used during the life of the project will affect both the operating cash flows and the change in gross fixed assets that will occur at the end of the project, so let's start our organizing there.

For First Strike's proposed FinProf project, the firm will depreciate capital assets such as the software-duplicating machine using the straight-line method to an ending book value of $5,000. To calculate the annual depreciation amount, First Strike will first need to compute the machinery's **depreciable basis.** According to the Internal Revenue Service's (IRS) Publication 946, the depreciable basis for real property is:

depreciable basis

An asset's cost plus the amounts you paid for items such as sales tax, freight charges, and installation and testing fees.

- Its cost.
- Amounts paid for items such as sales tax.
- Freight charges.
- Installation and testing fees.

So the depreciable basis for the new project's software-duplicating machine will be the $75,000 purchase price plus the $2,000 shipping and installation cost, for a total depreciable basis of $77,000.

Under straight-line depreciation, the annual depreciation for each year will be equal to the depreciable basis minus the projected ending book value, all over the number of years in the life of the asset:

$$\text{Depreciation} = \frac{\text{Depreciable basis} - \text{Ending book value}}{\text{Life of asset}} \qquad \textbf{(12-2)}$$

We'll discuss later in the chapter why this depreciation assumption is far too simple, and why other, more complicated depreciation methods can be much more advantageous to the company. For now, though, this straight-line depreciation approach will suffice for our initial go at calculating the project's cash flows.

Calculating Operating Cash Flow

We defined operating cash flow (OCF) in Chapter 2 as *EBIT* (*1* − *Tax rate*) + *Depreciation.* We will still calculate OCF as being mathematically equal to *EBIT* (*1* − *Tax rate*) + *Depreciation.* But remember that we will be constructing the FCF components ourselves instead of taking them off an income statement that someone else has already produced. So we will usually find it most helpful to conduct this calculation by using what we will call a "quasi-income statement" that leaves out some components like interest deductions. (Note that the process of leaving out any interest deduction is exactly in line with our discussion of not counting interest on debt as an expense of the project, but the resulting financial statement would *not* make an accountant happy).

Such a statement is shown in Table 12.4 for First Strike's proposed project. The primary benefit of calculating OCF this way instead of as an algebraic formula is that with this format, we have space to expand subcalculations, such as the impact of FinProf being a partial substitute for the MktProf product.

Before we move on, notice that not only is EBIT negative in year 3 of OCF calculations, but we also assume that this negative EBIT, in turn, generates a "negative tax bill" (i.e., a tax credit, when we subtract the negative tax amount of −$9,615 from the negative EBIT). Why do we make this assumption?

Well, the rule for handling negative EBIT is that when calculating the cash flows for a single project for a firm, we assume that any loss by the project in a particular period can be applied against assumed before-tax profits made by the *rest* of the firm in that period. So, while our project is expected to have a loss of $28,280 before taxes during year 3, the assumed ability of the firm to use that loss to shelter $28,280 in before-tax profits *elsewhere* in the firm means that the incremental after-tax net income for this project during year 3 is expected to be −$28,280 − (−$9,615) = −$18,665. This is still negative, but less negative than the EBIT because of this tax-sheltering effect.

table 12.4 | **Calculation of OCF**

	Year 1		Year 2		Year 3	
Sales of FinProf	$599,850		$1,079,730		$199,950	
Less: Reduced sales of MktProf	39,980		39,980		39,980	
Net incremental sales		$559,870		$1,039,750		$159,970
Variable costs of FinProf	$ 63,750		$ 114,750		$ 21,250	
Less: Reduced costs of MktProf	7,000		7,000		7,000	
Less: Incremental variable costs		56,750		107,750		14,250
Less: Fixed costs		150,000		150,000		150,000
Less: Depreciation		24,000		24,000		24,000
Earnings before interest and taxes		$329,120		$ 758,000		−$28,280
Less: Taxes		111,901		257,720		−9,615
Net income		$ 217,219		$ 500,280		−$18,665
Plus: Depreciation		24,000		24,000		24,000
Operating cash flow		$ 241,219		$ 524,280		$ 5,335

What would we do if we expected a negative EBIT during a particular year and this was the only project the firm was undertaking, or if this project was so big that a negative EBIT would overshadow any potential profits elsewhere in the firm? Long story short, we would not get to take the tax credit during that year . . . but we will leave the discussion of just exactly when we *would* get to take it to a more advanced text.

Calculating Changes in Gross Fixed Assets

Gross fixed assets will change in almost every project at both the beginning (when assets are usually purchased) and at the end (when assets are usually sold). First Strike's proposed project is no exception.

Calculating the change in gross fixed assets at the beginning of the project is fairly straightforward—it will simply equal the asset's depreciable basis. So, for FSS's project, we will increase gross fixed assets by $77,000 at time zero.

At the end of a project, the change in gross fixed assets is a little more complicated, because whenever a firm sells any asset, it has to consider the tax consequences of that sale. The IRS treats any sale of assets for more than depreciated book value as taxable gains and any sale for less than book value as taxable losses. In either event, we can calculate the after-tax cash flow (ATCF) from the sale of an asset using the following formula, where T_C is the same appropriate corporate tax rate discussed in the previous chapter.

$$ATCF = \text{Book value} + (\text{Market value} - \text{Book value}) \times (1 - T_C) \qquad \textbf{(12-3)}$$

Since the machinery for FSS's project will be depreciated down to $5,000 but is expected to sell for only $2,000, the ATCF for that asset's sale will equal:

$$\begin{aligned} ATCF &= \$5{,}000 + (\$2{,}000 - \$5{,}000) \times (1 - 0.34) \\ &= \$3{,}020 \end{aligned}$$

Note that this formula would work equally well on an asset sold at a gain.

EXAMPLE 12-1

LG 12-3

ATCF for an Asset Sold at a Gain

Suppose that a firm facing a marginal tax rate of 25 percent sells an asset for $4,000 when its depreciated book value is $2,000. What will be the ATCF from the sale of this asset?

For interactive versions of this example visit www.mhhe.com/can3e

SOLUTION:

The ATCF will equal:

$$\begin{aligned} ATCF &= \$2{,}000 + (\$4{,}000 - \$2{,}000) \times (1 - 0.25) \\ &= \$3{,}500 \end{aligned}$$

Similar to Problems 12-1, 12-8

Calculating Changes in Net Working Capital

We can make several different assumptions concerning the NWC level necessary to support a project. The most straightforward of these would be to simply assume that we add NWC at the beginning of the project and subtract it at the end. This assumption would be valid if the project is expected to have steady sales throughout its life, or if variations in NWC do not affect the project much.

FSS's proposed project, however, features a more typical product life cycle. Its unit sales will follow an approximate bell-shaped curve. When sales are timed in this way, FSS needs to give a little more thought to exactly when the firm needs to set aside net working capital to support high sales volumes and when it can reduce NWC as sales drop off.

The assumption that First Strike's NWC at any particular time will be a function of the *next* year's sales might seem odd at first glance. But a little thought about how we measure balance sheet numbers (such as NWC) and income statement items (such as sales) will show that, really, this assumption makes a lot of sense. Since income statements (and our quasi-income statement discussed previously) measure what happens *during* a period, the sales show up on the statement at the end of the year, even though they actually start accumulating at the *beginning* of the year. The balance sheet "snapshots," on the other hand, capture how much capital sits in NWC accounts *at a particular point in time*. Therefore, for example, the sales figures that appear in the time 1 OCF calculation must be supported when they start occurring, at time zero. The time zero NWC changes need to reflect that activity. Of course, the same argument holds true in general, too: Any sales figure that appears in a time N OCF calculation needs NWC support at the *beginning* of year N, which is actually time $N - 1$. So NWC at time $N - 1$ should vary with time N sales.

Also, note that it is just the *changes* in the level of NWC, not the levels themselves, that will affect our cash flows. To explain why, we need throw a little more intuition into the pot here.

First, we have to admit that we do not really care about the changes in NWC, either, at least not for their own sake; instead, what we are actually measuring is the *investment* in capital necessary to make those changes happen. (And that's why there is a negative sign in front of NWC in our formula for free cash flow: It *costs* us money to make NWC bigger, and vice versa).

Second, we need to think a little about exactly what we are measuring when we talk about using NWC to support sales. Since NWC equals current assets

table 12.5 | **Change in NWC**

Year:	0	1	2	3
Level of NWC	\$59,985	\$107,973	\$19,995	\$0
$NWC_t - NWC_{t-1} = \Delta NWC_t$	\$59,985 − \$0 = \$59,985	\$107,973 − \$59,985 = \$47,988	\$19,995 − \$107,973 = −\$87,978	\$0 − \$19,995 = −\$19,995

minus current liabilities, it's probably easier to think of it as being composed of cash, accounts receivable, and inventory, net of current liabilities. Do these types of assets get used up? Sure, when cash is used to make change, or when someone pays off an account receivable, or when we sell finished goods out of inventory, the respective account will go down. But those accounts go down *because we are bringing in money*, and some of that money can be used to "restock the shelves," so to speak; that is, when someone buys one of our products out of inventory, we assume that part of the purchase price goes toward replenishing the inventory we just sold, and when someone pays off an account receivable, we assume that allows us to turn around and lend that money to someone else and so forth.

The basic point here is that cash, once invested in NWC, pretty much replenishes itself until we manually take it back out. So when we are looking at the levels of NWC throughout the life of a project, it is the *changes* in those levels that we have to finance, not the levels themselves. Once we put a million dollars into inventory, it sort of stays there because of this idea of replenishment, even when we sell some of the inventory. And if we are keeping track of the amount of money that we have to invest in inventory or some other type of NWC account, we will find investment necessary only when we need to *grow* NWC by adding to that million dollars (or when we decide to take some of it back out).

So, we can use the given information for the First Strike project to compute the NWC necessary to support sales throughout the project's life, and then in turn use NWC levels to compute the necessary changes in NWC, as shown in Table 12.5. Notice that the NWC level at each time is simply 10 percent of the following year's sales figures from Table 12.4.

This method for computing changes in NWC levels has several appealing features:

- The changes in NWC at the beginning of a project will always equal the level at time 0, as NWC will be going from a presumed zero level before the project starts up to that new, non-zero level.
- Allowing NWC to vary as a percentage of coming sales like this allows FSS to add NWC during periods when it expects sales to increase (e.g., years 0 and 1 in this example) and to decrease NWC when it expects sales to fall off (e.g., years 2 and 3 in this example). NWC levels fall off the last two years of this project precisely because FSS expects sales to fall off and is adjusting NWC to compensate.
- Finally, one especially nice feature of this approach is that it will always automatically bring NWC back down to a zero level when the project ends. Since sales in the year *after* the project ends are always zero, 10 percent of zero will also be zero. This corresponds to what we would expect to see in the real world: when a project ends, the firm sells off inventory, collects from customers, pays off accounts receivable, and so forth.

Bringing It All Together

Using the numbers that we calculated for OCF, change in gross fixed assets, and change in NWC, First Strike's expected total cash flows from the new project would be as shown in Table 12.6.

table 12.6 | **Total Cash Flows**

Year:	0		1		2		3
OCF		$ 0		$241,219		$524,280		$ 5,335
FA	$77,000		$ 0		$ 0		−$3,020	
NWC	59,985		47,988		−87,978		−19,995	
Less: IOC		136,985		47,988		−87,978		−23,015
FCF		−$136,985		$193,231		$612,258		$28,350

Note, in particular, that correct use of the after-tax cash flow from selling the machinery at the end of the project requires that we change the cash flows' sign to negative when we enter it for year 3. Why? Because the ATCF formula shown in equation 12-3 does a little *too* much work for us. It computes cash flow effects of selling the asset, while the formula we are using for FCF wants us to enter the change in fixed assets. Or, to put it another way, cash flow at the end of the project should go up *because* fixed assets decrease. We subtract that decrease in our $FCF = OCF - (\Delta FA + \Delta NWC)$ calculation, which has the effect of "subtracting a minus." Eventually, then, we increase the final year's FCF above that which we would have generated by just combining OCF with the cash freed up from decreasing NWC.

TIME OUT

12-3 Explain why an increase in NWC is treated as a cash outflow rather than as an inflow.

12-4 Will OCF typically be larger or smaller than net income? Why?

12.4 • Accelerated Depreciation and the Half-Year Convention

LG12-4

Our FCF calculation in the previous section was complete, but we used a rather simplistic assumption concerning depreciation in the calculations. In reality, the IRS requires that depreciation must be calculated using the *half-year convention.* The IRS thus requires that all property placed in service during a given period is assumed to be placed in service at the midpoint of that period.[1] By implication, three years of asset life, such as the machinery in the First Strike example, will extend over *four* calendar years of the firm. Table 12.7 shows an excerpt from the IRS depreciation table for straight-line depreciation using the half-year convention.

table 12.7 | **Excerpt of Straight-Line Depreciation Table with Half-Year Convention**

	Normal Recovery Period				
Year	2.5	3	3.5	4	5
1	20.00%	16.67%	14.29%	12.50%	10.00%
2	40.00	33.33	28.57	25.00	20.00
3	40.00	33.33	28.57	25.00	20.00
4	0.00	16.67	28.57	25.00	20.00
5	0.00	0.00	0.00	12.50	20.00
6	0.00	0.00	0.00	0.00	10.00

[1]There are also midmonth and midquarter conventions, which apply in special circumstances. Please refer to IRS Publication 946 for details.

The percentage figures denote how much of the asset's depreciable basis may be deducted in each respective firm calendar year. For example, an asset with a depreciable basis of $100,000 falling into the 3-year class life would be depreciated $100,000 × 0.1667 = $16,670 during the first calendar year the firm owned it, $33,330 during the second and third years of ownership, and another $16,670 during the fourth year of ownership.

The IRS provides guidance on which categories various assets fall into, so it's usually pretty easy to figure out which column to use. For this text, we will assume that we are always told which column to use.

Note that the IRS's interpretation of the half-year convention is not as direct as simply taking one-half of the first year's depreciation and moving it to the end of the asset's life. For example, the column for 3.5-year depreciation shows that such an asset would have 14.29 percent of its value depreciated during the first year and 28.57 percent during each of the second, third, and fourth years. So, rather than using a formula to compute the depreciation percentage, it's preferable to look the percentages up from the appropriate IRS table. A copy of the entire table for straight-line depreciation using the half-year convention appears as Appendix 12A at the end of this chapter.

LG12-4

MACRS Depreciation Calculation

Though the IRS allows firms to use the straight-line method with the half-year convention to depreciate assets, most businesses probably benefit from using some form of *accelerated depreciation.* Accelerated depreciation allows firms to expense more of an asset's cost earlier in the asset's life. An example of this is the double-declining-balance (DDB or 200 percent declining balance) depreciation method, under which the depreciation rate is double that used in the straight-line method. The IRS also uses the half-year convention with DDB depreciation. MACRS (Modified Accelerated Cost Recovery System) uses DDB for 3- to 10-year property. For 15- to 20-year property, MACRS uses the 150 percent declining balance method. Both of these methods switch to straight-line (SL) depreciation whenever SL becomes more advantageous to the taxpayer. For real estate, MACRS uses straight-line depreciation and the mid-month convention. The good news is that the applicable depreciation percentages are provided for you in the MACRS depreciation tables compiled by the IRS. We have provided this for you in Appendix 12A. An excerpt of the DDB section of the MACRS table appears as Table 12.8. MACRS is generally the depreciation method of choice for firms since it provides the most advantageous method of depreciation.

LG12-4

Section 179 Deductions

Section 179 deduction

A deduction targeted at small businesses that allows them to immediately expense asset purchases up to a certain limit rather than depreciating them over the assets' useful lives.

We can accelerate asset expensing even further by expensing assets immediately in the year of purchase. The IRS allows most businesses to immediately expense up to $500,000 of property placed in service each year under what is referred to as a **Section 179 deduction.** The Section 179 deduction is obviously targeted at helping small businesses, so it places an annual limit on the amount of deductible property. If the cost of qualifying Section 179 property you put into service in a single tax year exceeds the current statutory base of $2 million (as of the 2013 tax year), then you cannot take the full deduction. The maximum deduction is also limited to the annual taxable income from the active conduct of the business.

For example, consider a manufacturer who completely re-equips his facility in 2015, at a cost of $2.1 million. This is $100,000 more than allowed, so he must reduce his eligible deductible limit to $400,000, which is the current $500,000 expensing limit minus the $100,000 excess over the current statutory base limit. To take this deduction, the firm must have at least $400,000 of taxable income for

table 12.8 | **DDB Depreciation with Half-Year Convention**

	Normal Recovery Period			
Year	**3**	**5**	**7**	**10**
1	33.33%	20.00%	14.29%	10.00%
2	44.45	32.00	24.49	18.00
3	14.81	19.20	17.49	14.40
4	7.41	11.52	12.49	11.52
5	0.00	11.52	8.93	9.22
6	0.00	5.76	8.92	7.37
7	0.00	0.00	8.93	6.55
8	0.00	0.00	4.46	6.55
9	0.00	0.00	0.00	6.56
10	0.00	0.00	0.00	6.55
11	0.00	0.00	0.00	3.28
12	0.00	0.00	0.00	0.00
13	0.00	0.00	0.00	0.00
14	0.00	0.00	0.00	0.00
15	0.00	0.00	0.00	0.00
16	0.00	0.00	0.00	0.00
17	0.00	0.00	0.00	0.00
18	0.00	0.00	0.00	0.00
19	0.00	0.00	0.00	0.00
20	0.00	0.00	0.00	0.00
21	0.00	0.00	0.00	0.00

the year. A company that spent $2.5 million (= $2 million + $500,000) or more on qualifying Section 179 property would not be able to take the deduction at all, regardless of its taxable income. Property that does not qualify for a Section 179 deduction can be depreciated using MACRS.

Property eligible for a Section 179 deduction includes:

- Machinery and equipment.
- Furniture and fixtures.
- Most storage facilities.
- Single-purpose agricultural or horticultural structures.
- Off-the-shelf computer software.
- Certain qualified real property (limited to $250,000 of the $500,000 expensing limit).

Ineligible property includes:

- Buildings and their structural components (unless specifically qualified).
- Income-producing property (investment or rental property).
- Property held by an estate or trust.
- Property acquired by gift or inheritance.
- Property used in a passive activity.
- Property purchased from related parties.
- Property used outside of the United States.

Like many IRS deductions, there are several terms and conditions that apply, so be sure to get all the facts if you intend to use this method of depreciation.

Impact of Accelerated Depreciation

LG12-4

So, let's return to our FSS example and FinProf. Remember that our initial, simplistic view of depreciation had us taking $24,000 per year in depreciation for each of the three years of the project's life. If the software reproduction

table 12.9 | **FSS's Yearly Depreciation and Ending Book Values under Alternative Depreciation**

	Year 1	Year 2	Year 3	Ending BV
Straight-line	$77,000 × 16.67% = $12,835.90	$77,000 × 33.33% = $25,664.10	$77,000 × 33.33% = $25,664.10	$12,835.90
DDB	$77,000 × 33.33% = $25,664.10	$77,000 × 44.45% = $34,226.50	$77,000 × 14.81% = $11,403.70	$5,705.70

machinery fell into the 3-year life class, we could instead have taken the following depreciation amounts by using either the straight-line or DDB approaches, as shown in Table 12.9.

If First Strike could take advantage of the Section 179 deduction that would probably be the most advantageous way to deduct the cost of the new machinery —it could deduct the entire $77,000 in year 1. If FSS could not use a Section 179 deduction, the DDB depreciation available under MACRS would result in the next quickest recovery of the tax breaks associated with the machinery purchase.

And why is it better to depreciate the cost of an asset as quickly as possible? Well, taking the depreciation over a longer time span doesn't get you more dollars of depreciation tax shield; it just stretches the same total amount of dollars over that longer time span. So, think about it in the context of time value of money: The present value of $X of total income tax shield will be highest when we get the $X as soon as possible.

TIME OUT

12-5 Explain why, under MACRS, "5-year" depreciation is actually spread over six years, 6-year depreciation spreads into seven years, and so forth.

12-6 If the IRS wanted to encourage businesses to invest in certain types of assets, would it put them into shorter or longer MACRS life-class categories?

LG12-5

12.5 • "Special" Cases Aren't Really That Special

As long as we are consistent in using incremental FCF to calculate total project cash flows, we can handle many project types that are habitually viewed as "special" cases requiring extraordinary treatment with some relatively simple revisions to the methods we used for valuing First Strike's proposed new project.

EXAMPLE 12-2

LG12-5

For interactive versions of this example visit www.mhhe.com/can3e

Replacement Problem

Suppose that Just-in-Time Donuts is considering replacing one of its existing ovens. The original oven cost $100,000 when purchased five years ago and has been depreciated by $9,000 per year since then. Just-in-Time thinks that it can sell the old machine for $65,000 if it sells today, and for $10,000 by waiting another five years until the oven's anticipated life is over. Just-in-Time is considering replacing this oven with a new one, which costs $150,000, partly because the new oven will save $50,000 in costs per year relative to the old oven. The new oven will be subject to 3-year class life DDB depreciation under MACRS, with an anticipated useful life of five years. At the end of the five years, Just-In-Time will abandon the oven as worthless. If Just-in-Time faces a marginal tax rate of 35 percent, what will be the total project cash flows if it replaces the oven?

SOLUTION:

If Just-in-Time Sells the old oven today for \$65,000 when it has a remaining book value of \$55,000 (\$100,000 purchase price − 5 years of \$9,000 per year depreciation), then the ATCF from its sale will equal:

$$\begin{aligned} ATCF &= \text{Book value} + (\text{Market value} - \text{Book value}) \times (1 - T_C) \\ &= \$55{,}000 + (\$65{,}000 - \$55{,}000) \times (1 - 0.35) \\ &= \$61{,}500 \end{aligned}$$

In return for selling the old oven today, however, Just-in-Time will have to forgo both the yearly depreciation that the company would have received for it over the next five years and the \$10,000 that it could get for selling it at the end of the five years. We must reflect both of these factors in our calculation of incremental FCFs so that we are reckoning the true costs of the project. In addition, switching from the old oven to the new one would apparently alter neither sales nor NWC requirements across the 5-year life of the new oven:

Year	Year 0	Year 1	Year 2	Year 3	Year 4	Year 5
Net incremental sales		\$ 0	\$ 0	\$ 0	\$ 0	\$ 0
Less: Net incremental variable costs		−50,000	−50,000	−50,000	−50,000	−50,000
Depreciation on new oven		\$49,995	\$66,675	\$22,215	\$11,115	\$ 0
Forgone depreciation on old oven		−9,000	−9,000	−9,000	−9,000	−9,000
Less: Incremental depreciation		40,995	57,675	13,215	2,115	−9,000
EBIT		\$ 9,005	−\$7,675	\$36,785	\$47,885	\$59,000
Less: Taxes		3,152	−2,686	12,875	16,760	20,650
"Net income"		\$ 5,853	−\$4,989	\$23,910	\$31,125	\$38,350
Plus: Depreciation		40,995	57,675	13,215	2,115	−9,000
OCF		\$46,848	\$52,686	\$37,125	\$33,240	\$29,350
ΔFA for new oven	\$150,000					\$ 0
ΔFA for old oven	−61,500					10,000
ΔFA	\$ 88,500					\$10,000
ΔNWC	0					0
Less: Investment in operating capital	\$88,500	0	0	0	0	10,000
FCF = OCF − IOC	−\$88,500	\$46,848	\$52,686	\$37,125	\$33,240	\$19,350

We usually think that a positive value for ΔFA is associated with the purchase of FA. But note that in this circumstance, the \$10,000 for the forgone sale of the old oven at time 5 is *not* an investment in fixed assets, but rather the opportunity cost of not getting to sell the old oven at that time.

Similar to Problem 12-13

EXAMPLE 12-3

LG12-6

Cost-Cutting Problem

For interactive versions of this example visit www.mhhe.com/can3e

Your company is considering a new computer system that will initially cost \$1 million. It will save your firm \$300,000 a year in inventory and receivables management costs. The system is expected to last for five years and will be depreciated using three-year MACRS. The firm expects that the system will have a salvage value of \$50,000 at the end of year 5. This purchase does not affect net working capital; the marginal tax rate is 34 percent, and the required return is 8 percent. What will be the total project cash flows if this cost-cutting proposal is implemented?

SOLUTION:

Since the new computer falls into the 3-year MACRS category, it will be fully depreciated when the project ends five years from now. As a result, the ATCF from the sale of the computer will be:

$$\begin{aligned} ATCF &= BV + (MV - BV) \times (1 - T_C) \\ &= \$0 + (\$50{,}000 - \$0) \times (1 - 0.34) \\ &= \$33{,}000 \end{aligned}$$

And the FCFs for the cost-cutting proposal will be equal to:

Year	Year 0		Year 1	Year 2	Year 3	Year 4		Year 5
Net incremental sales			$ 0	$ 0	$ 0	$ 0		$ 0
Less: Incremental variable costs			−300,000	−300,000	−300,000	−300,000		−300,000
Less: Incremental depreciation			333,300	444,500	148,100	74,100		0
EBIT			−$33,300	−$144,500	$151,900	$225,900		$300,000
Less: Taxes			−11,322	−49,130	51,646	76,806		102,000
"Net income"			−$21,978	−$95,370	$100,254	$149,094		$198,000
Plus: Depreciation			333,300	444,500	148,100	74,100		0
OCF			$311,322	$349,130	$248,354	$223,194		$198,000
ΔFA	$1,000,000						−$33,000	
ΔNWC	0						0	
Less: Investment in operating capital		$1,000,000	0	0	0	0		−33,000
FCF = OCF − IOC		−$1,000,000	$311,322	$349,130	$248,354	$223,194		$231,000

Similar to Problem 12-9

TIME OUT

12-7 Explain why, in Example 12-2, the investment in operating capital in the last year of the project was positive instead of negative.

12-8 Would it ever be possible to have a project that generated net positive cash flows across all years of a project's life just by buying and depreciating assets?

LG12-7

12.6 • Choosing between Alternative Assets with Differing Lives: EAC

One type of problem that also deserves special mention involves situations where we're asked to choose between two different assets that can be used for the same purpose. Such a problem does not usually require the computation of incremental FCF, but instead will require you to take the two alternatives sets of incremental cash flows associated with the two assets and restructure them so that they can be compared to each other.

For example, suppose a company has decided to go ahead with a project but needs to choose between two alternative assets, where:

- Both assets will result in the same sales.
- Both assets may have different costs and recurring expenses.
- Assets will last different lengths of time.
- When the chosen asset wears out, it will be replaced with an identical machine.

In such a situation, the firm can not really compare one iteration of each machine to the other, since they last different lengths of time. The key here is to use the fact that since the firm will replace each machine with another identical machine when it wears out, it is really being asked to choose between two sets of infinite, but systematically varying, sets of cash flows. To handle such a situation, we need to "smooth out" the variation in each set of cash flows so that each becomes a perpetuity. Then the company can choose between the two machines based on which will generate the highest present value of cash flows.

figure 12.1

Cash Flows of Repeated Purchases of Machine B

Year	0	1	2	3	4	5	6
B	–$12,000	–$3,500	–$3,500	–$3,500			
				–$12,000	–$3,500	–$3,500	–$3,500
							–$12,000
B Total	–$12,000	–$3,500	–$3,500	–$15,500	–$3,500	–$3,500	–$15,500

Since the decision will involve only a subset of a project's cash flows—the purchase of one of a choice of assets—that present value will probably be negative. If the firm were to look at all the benefits deriving from the choice of which asset to use, including expected sales and so forth, the present value of all cash flows would need to be positive for the entire project to be attractive. We will discuss this in much greater depth in the next chapter when we cover the **net present value (NPV)** rule for capital budgeting decisions.

The basic concept behind the EAC approach is to use TVM to turn each iteration of each project into an annuity. Once we have done that, then we can think of the stream of iterations of doing that project again and again as a stream of annuities, all with equal payments—or, to put it another way, as a perpetuity.

To compute and use the EACs of two or more alternative assets:

1. Find the sum of the present values of the cash flows (the net present value, or NPV, which we will cover in great detail in the next chapter) for one iteration of A and one iteration of B.
2. Treat each sum as the present value of an annuity with life equal to the life of the respective asset, and solve for each asset's payment.
3. Choose the asset with the highest (i.e., least negative) EAC.

It may seem that we have just done exactly what we said we should not do: compare the cash flows from one machine A to those from one machine B. In fact, the comparison we just did is actually much broader than that, though it will take a little explanation to see.

Visualize the cash flows to the infinitely repeated purchases of machine B (chosen simply because it has a short life, so it will be easier to see multiple iterations on a time line in the following discussion) as shown in Figure 12.1.

EXAMPLE 12-4

LG12-7

EAC Approach

Suppose that your company has won a bid for a new project—painting highway signs for the local highway department. Based on past experience, you are pretty sure that your company will have the contract for the foreseeable future, and now you have to decide whether to use machine A or machine B to paint the signs: Machine A costs $20,000, lasts five years, and will generate annual after-tax net expenses of $2,500. Machine B costs $12,000, lasts three years, and will have after-tax net expenses of $3,500 per year. Assume that, in either case, each machine will simply be junked at the end of its useful life, and the firm faces a cost of capital of 12 percent. Which machine should you choose?

For interactive versions of this example visit www.mhhe.com/can3e

SOLUTION:

One iteration of each machine will consist of the sets of cash flows shown below:

Year	0	1	2	3	4	5
Machine A CFs	−$20,000	−$2,500	−$2,500	−$2,500	−$2,500	−$2,500
Machine B CFs	−12,000	−3,500	−3,500	−3,500		

The sum of the present values of machine A's cash flows will be:

$$\sum_{t=0}^{5}\frac{CF_t}{(1+i)^t} = \frac{CF_0}{(1+i)^0} + \frac{CF_1}{(1+i)^1} + \frac{CF_2}{(1+i)^2} + \frac{CF_3}{(1+i)^3} + \frac{CF_4}{(1+i)^4} + \frac{CF_5}{(1+i)^5}$$

$$= \frac{-\$20{,}000}{(1.12)^0} + \frac{-\$2{,}500}{(1.12)^1} + \frac{-\$2{,}500}{(1.12)^2} + \frac{-\$2{,}500}{(1.12)^3} + \frac{-\$2{,}500}{(1.12)^4} + \frac{-\$2{,}500}{(1.12)^5}$$

$$= -\$29{,}012$$

CALCULATOR HINTS

N = 5
I = 12
PV = 29,012
FV = 0
CPT PMT = −8,048

Treating this as the present value of a 5-period annuity, setting *i* to 12 percent, and solving for payment will yield a payment of −$8,048, which is machine A's EAC.

The sum of the present values of machine B's cash flows will be

$$\sum_{t=0}^{3}\frac{CF_t}{(1+i)^t} = \frac{CF_0}{(1+i)^0} + \frac{CF_1}{(1+i)^1} + \frac{CF_2}{(1+i)^2} + \frac{CF_3}{(1+i)^3}$$

$$= \frac{-\$12{,}000}{(1.12)^0} + \frac{-\$3{,}500}{(1.12)^1} + \frac{-\$3{,}500}{(1.12)^2} + \frac{-\$3{,}500}{(1.12)^3}$$

$$= -\$20{,}406$$

CALCULATOR HINTS

N = 3
I = 12
PV = 20,406
FV = 0
CPT PMT = 8,496

Treating this as the present value of a 3-period annuity, setting *i* to 12 percent, and solving for payment will yield a payment of −$8,496, which is machine B's EAC.

Since machine A's EAC is less negative than machine B's, your firm should choose machine A.

Similar to Problems 12-3 to 12-5, self-test problem 3

Notice that, after the initial purchase of the first machine B, the cash flows exhibit a systematic cycle: −$3,500 for two years, followed by −$15,500 for one year (when the next machine B is purchased), repeating this way forever. This systematic cycle, which we don't have a formula for valuing, makes it necessary to convert these cash flows into a perpetuity, which we *can* value.

When we computed the NPV of one iteration of machine B, we basically "squished" that machine's cash flows down to a single lump sum, and when we treated that as the present value of an annuity and solved for the payments we were effectively taking that same value and spreading it evenly across the life of the first machine B. Furthermore, since subsequent machine B purchases will be identical to this first one, we can visualize doing the exact same thing to *every* machine B's cash flow. Turning each machine B's cash flow into an annuity in this manner has the net effect of turning all the machine B's cash flows into a perpetuity, as shown in Figure 12.2.

figure 12.2

Converted Cash Flows of Repeated Purchases of Machine B

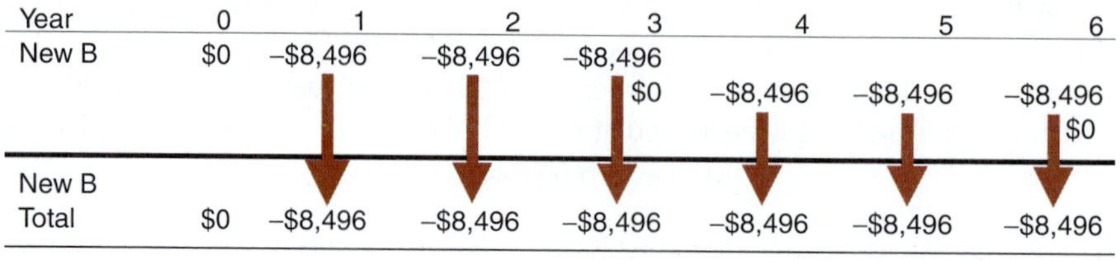

Year 0 1 2 3 4 5 6
New B $0 –$8,496 –$8,496 –$8,496
$0 –$8,496 –$8,496 –$8,496
$0
New B Total $0 –$8,496 –$8,496 –$8,496 –$8,496 –$8,496 –$8,496

In the process, we also turn the repeated purchase of machine A into a perpetuity. We *could* calculate the present values of these two perpetuities and then compare them, which is what we're really interested in doing:

$$PV_{\text{Perpetuity of Infinitely Repeated As}} \text{ vs. } PV_{\text{Perpetuity of Infinitely Repeated Bs}}$$

$$\frac{-\$8{,}048}{0.12} \text{ vs. } \frac{-\$8{,}496}{0.12}$$

But do we really need to? No. The relationship between these two present values of the respective perpetuities is really the same as the relationship between their payment amounts[2] —each machine's respective EAC.

TIME OUT

12-9 Explain how the EAC approach turns uneven cash flows for infinitely repeated asset purchases into perpetuities.

12-10 What if two alternative assets lasted the same length of time: Would the EAC approach still work?

12.7 • Flotation Costs Revisited

LG12-8

In the previous chapter, we talked about how to take flotation costs into account by adjusting the WACC upwards, incorporating flotation costs directly into the issue prices of the securities used to fund projects. Another way that we can account for flotation costs is to adjust the project's initial cash flow so that it will reflect the flotation costs of raising capital for the project as well as the necessary investment in assets.

In this approach, we will:

1. Compute the weighted average flotation cost, f_A, using the firm's target capital weights (because the firm will issue securities in these percentages over the long term):

$$f_A = \frac{E}{E+P+D} f_E + \frac{P}{E+P+D} f_P + \frac{D}{E+P+D} f_D \qquad \textbf{(12-4)}$$

where f_E, f_P, and f_D are the percentage flotation costs for new equity, preferred stock, and debt, respectively.

2. Compute the flotation-adjusted initial investment, CF_0, using:

$$\text{Adjusted } CF_0 = \frac{CF_0}{1 - f_A} \qquad \textbf{(12-5)}$$

EXAMPLE 12-5

LG12-8

Adjusting CF_0 for Flotation Cost

Your company is considering a project that will cost \$1 million. The project will generate after-tax cash flows of \$375,000 per year for five years. The WACC is 15 percent and the firm's target D/A ratio is 0.375. The flotation cost for equity is 5 percent, the flotation cost for debt is 3 percent, and your firm does not plan on issuing any preferred stock within its capital structure. If your firm follows the practice of incorporating flotation costs into the project's initial investment, what will the flotation-adjusted cash flows for this project be?

For interactive versions of this example visit www.mhhe.com/can3e

[2]Because the two perpetuities have the same interest rate and the same periodicity (i.e., length between payments), the only possible source of difference in their present values would be the respective payment amounts.

SOLUTION:

Since the D/A is 0.375, the E/A ratio will be equal to 1 − 0.375 = 0.625, and the weighted-average flotation cost for the firm will be:

$$f_A = \frac{E}{E+P+D} f_E + \frac{P}{E+P+D} f_P + \frac{D}{E+P+D} f_D$$
$$= (0.625 \times 0.05) + (0.375 \times 0.03)$$
$$= 0.0425, \text{ or } 4.25\%$$

Using this, the adjusted CF_0 for the project will be:

$$\text{Adjusted } CF_0 = \frac{CF_0}{1 - f_A}$$
$$= \frac{-\$1{,}000{,}000}{1 - 0.0425}$$
$$= -\$1{,}044{,}386$$

So the flotation-adjusted cash flows for the project will be:

Year	0	1	2	3	4	5
Cash Flow	−$1,044,386	$375,000	$375,000	$375,000	$375,000	$375,000

CALCULATOR HINTS

N = 5
I = 12
PV = 29,012
FV = 0
CPT PMT = −8,048

CALCULATOR HINTS

N = 3
I = 12
PV = 20,406
FV = 0
CPT PMT = 8,496

As we discussed in the previous chapter, this approach to adjusting for flotation costs violates the spirit of the separation principle of capital budgeting, which states that the calculations of cash flows should remain independent of the choice of financing. On the other hand, the approach we used in the last chapter, increasing the project's WACC to incorporate the flotation costs' impact, tends to understate the component cost of new equity. So, which approach is better? Well, even though most practitioners have historically taken the approach of adjusting the WACC upward, it is intuitively a little "distasteful"; it burdens the capital raised to finance a project with a higher required rate of return from then on, even though those flotation costs are actually a one-time thing. So, ideally, we would handle flotation costs as we've done in this chapter, by adjusting the project's initial cash flow to account for them. Pragmatically, however, it is not unusual for firms to use either approach based on what they find the most intuitively appealing.

TIME OUT

12-11 How would you compute the equity flotation cost if a firm were going to use a mixture of retained earnings and new equity to finance a project?

12-12 Why do we divide the initial cash flow by $(1 - f_A)$ instead of multiplying it by $(1 + f_A)$?

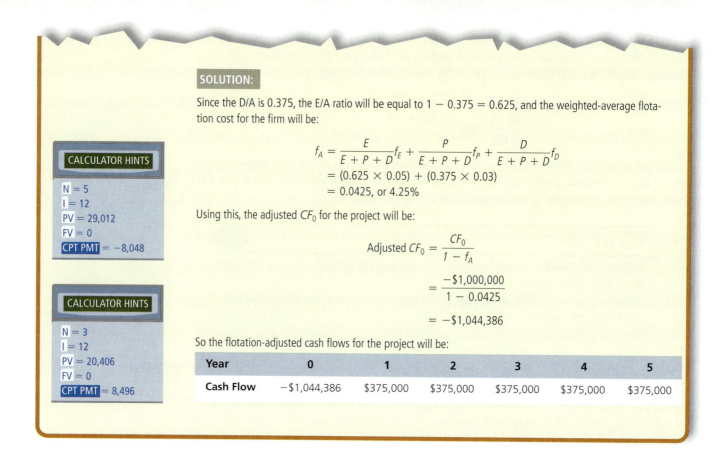

viewpoints REVISITED

Business Application Solution

Based on the given information, the yearly sales, levels of NWC, and resulting changes in NWC for McDonald's will be:

Year	Yearly Sales	Yearly Levels of NWC	Changes in NWC
0	$ 0	$364,000	$364,000
1	2,800,000	937,300	573,300
2	7,210,000	965,900	28,600
3	7,430,000	994,500	28,600
4	7,650,000	512,200	−482,300
5	3,940,000	0	−512,200

OCF calculations, ΔNWC, and ΔFA for each year are shown as follows:

(in millions)	Year 0	Year 1	Year 2	Year 3	Year 4	Year 5
Sales		$2.8000	$7.2100	$7.4300	$7.6500	$3.9400
Less: Variable costs		1.3400	3.5200	3.7000	3.8900	2.0400
Less: Fixed costs		0.0000	0.0000	0.0000	0.0000	0.0000
Less: Depreciation		0.0000	0.0000	0.0000	0.0000	0.0000
Earnings before interest and taxes		$1.4600	$3.6900	$3.7300	$3.7600	$1.9000
Less: Taxes		0.0000	0.0000	0.0000	0.0000	0.0000
Net income		$1.4600	$3.6900	$3.7300	$3.7600	$1.9000
Plus: Depreciation		0.0000	0.0000	0.0000	0.0000	0.0000
Operating cash flow		$1.4600	$3.6900	$3.7300	$3.7600	$1.9000
Δ Fixed assets	$7.0000	$0.0000	$0.0000	$0.0000	$0.0000	$0.0000
Δ Net working capital	0.0000	0.0000	0.0000	0.0000	0.0000	0.0000
Less: Investment in operating capital	$7.0000	0.0000	0.0000	0.0000	0.0000	0.0000
Free cash flow	−$7.0000	$1.4600	$3.6900	$3.7300	$3.7600	$1.9000

Personal Application Solution

Achmed's purchase of a new computer should not be counted as an incremental cash flow to getting an MBA, as he has indicated that he would be getting one anyway. Likewise, the $250 that he paid to take the GMAT is a sunk cost, and should not be counted, either. His tuition payments constitute an annuity due, so his incremental cash flows will equal:

Years	0–3	4–23
FCF	−$15,000	$10,000

summary of learning goals

In this chapter, we discussed how to apply the concept of free cash flow to measure expected cash flows from proposed new projects. The key concept is that only factors that affect a firm's cash flows that are incrementally attributable to the project should be included, and we must also be comprehensive in finding these incrementally attributable cash flows.

LG12-1 Explain why we use pro forma statements to analyze project cash flows. Calculating expected future cash flows for a project is a complex undertaking. Using a systematic approach involving quasi-income statements and other pro forma financial statements ensures that our calculations will be careful and methodical.

LG12-2 Identify which cash flows we can incrementally apply to a project and which ones we cannot. If a particular cash flow effect will take place if the project is undertaken but won't occur if the project is not accepted, then it should be included in the project's cash flows.

LG12-3 Calculate a project's expected cash flows using the free cash flow approach. Free cash flow measures the operating cash flow a project produces minus the necessary investment in operating capital. This concept is as valid for proposed new projects as it is for the firm's current operations.

LG12-4 Explain how accelerated depreciation affects project cash flows. The IRS allows firms to take the same total depreciation amount on an asset regardless of how quickly the firms take it. Since no one gives you any interest or credit for delaying depreciation, time value of money concepts tell us that sooner is always better.

LG12-5 Calculate free cash flows for replacement equipment. New projects and replacement projects differ only in that with replacement projects, we must consider not only the incremental cash flows of purchasing a new asset, but also any cash flows that arise in the process of surrendering old equipment before the end of its usable life.

LG12-6 Calculate cash flows associated with cost-cutting proposals. For cost-cutting proposals, the main benefit comes from cost reductions; often we see no actual change in sales revenues in response to a cost-cutting proposal.

LG12-7 Demonstrate the EAC approach to choosing among alternative cash streams for recurring projects. The EAC approach basically involves taking one iteration of an asset purchase, "squishing it down" to find the present value of all the asset's cash flows at a single point in time, and then spreading them back out "flat"; that is, in the form of an annuity. By conceptualizing doing this for *all* iterations of an infinitely repeated asset purchase, we can turn that infinite series of cash flows into a perpetuity, which we know how to value.

LG12-8 Adjust initial project investments to account for flotation costs. To adjust an initial investment for flotation costs, we simply divide it by one minus the average percentage flotation cost, which gives us the sum of financial securities we must sell in order to raise enough capital to both fund the project and pay underwriting fees.

chapter equations

12-1 $$FCF = \text{Operating cash flow} - \text{Investment in operating capital}$$
$$= [EBIT\,(1 - \text{Tax rate}) + \text{Depreciation}]$$
$$- [\Delta\text{Gross fixed assets} + \Delta\text{Net operating working capital}]$$

12-2 $$\text{Depreciation} = \frac{\text{Depreciable basis} - \text{Ending book value}}{\text{Life of asset}}$$

12-3 $$ATCF = \text{Book value} + (\text{Market value} - \text{Book value}) \times (1 - T_C)$$

12-4 $$f_A = \frac{E}{E + P + D} f_E + \frac{P}{E + P + D} f_P + \frac{D}{E + P + D} f_D$$

12-5 $$\text{Adjusted } CF_0 = \frac{CF_0}{1 - f_A}$$

key terms

depreciable basis, An asset's cost plus the amounts you paid for items such as sales tax, freight charges, and installation and testing fees. *p. 409*

financing costs, Interest paid to debt holders or dividends paid to stockholders. *p. 408*

incremental cash flows, Cash flows directly attributable to the adoption of a new project. *p. 406*

opportunity cost, The dollar cost or forgone opportunity of using an asset already owned by the firm, or a person already employed by the firm, in a new project. *p. 406*

pro forma analysis, Process of estimating expected future cash flows of a project using only the relevant parts of the balance sheet and income statements. *p. 405*

Section 179 deduction, A deduction targeted at small businesses that allows them to immediately expense asset purchases up to a certain limit rather than depreciating them over the assets' useful lives. *p. 414*

substitute and complement, Effects that arise from a new product or service either decreasing or increasing sales, respectively, of the firm's existing products and services. *p. 408*

sunk cost, A cost that has already been incurred and cannot be recovered. *p. 407*

self-test problems with solutions

LG12-3, 12-4

1 Computing FCF for Expansion Project The SCFE Co. wants to add a production line. To do this, the company must spend $200,000 to expand its current building and purchase $1 million in new equipment. The company anticipates moving locations in five years, and it expects to sell its current building and the new equipment at that time. SCFE estimates that the building expansion will add $80,000 to the price the building can be sold for, and that the equipment will have a market value of $290,000 at that time. The new equipment falls into the MACRS five-year class, and the building improvements fall into the "Nonresidential Real Estate" 31.5 years MACRS category.

The new production line is expected to produce 100,000 units per year of a new product, which has a projected sales price of $7.75 per unit and a variable cost of $3.90 a unit. Introducing the new product is expected to cause sales of existing products to decline by $89,000 per year and existing costs to decline by $49,000 per year. Fixed costs of the new line will be $142,000 annually, and the company expects NWC to increase by $1,800,000 when the new line is added.

If the company faces a marginal tax rate of 34 percent, what will be the total expected cash flows for the project?

Solution:

The equipment and the building improvements have to be depreciated separately. The depreciation percentages and the annual dollar depreciation amounts for each year are shown below, along with the remaining book value of both at the end of the project life:

Year	1	2	3	4	5	Remaining Book Value
Equipment MACRS %	20.00%	32.00%	19.20%	11.52%	11.52%	
Depreciation	$200,000	$320,000	$192,000	$115,200	$115,200	$ 57,600
Improvement MACRS %	3.042%	3.175%	3.175%	3.175%	3.175%	
Depreciation	$ 6,084	$ 6,350	$ 6,350	$ 6,350	$ 6,350	$168,516

Calculations of OCF for the five years of the project will be equal to:

	Year 0	Year 1	Year 2	Year 3	Year 4	Year 5
Sales		$775,000	$775,000	$775,000	$775,000	$775,000
Less: Lost sales		89,000	89,000	89,000	89,000	89,000
Less: Variable costs		390,000	390,000	390,000	390,000	390,000
Less: Fixed costs		142,000	142,000	142,000	142,000	142,000
Plus: Lost costs		49,000	49,000	49,000	49,000	49,000
Less: Depreciation		206,084	326,350	198,350	121,550	121,550
Earnings before interest and taxes		−$ 3,084	−$123,350	$ 4,650	$ 81,450	$ 81,450
Less: Taxes		−1,049	−41,939	1,581	27,693	27,693
Net income		−$ 2,035	−$ 81,411	$ 3,069	$ 53,757	$ 53,757
Plus: Depreciation		206,084	326,350	198,350	121,550	121,550
Operating cash flow		$204,049	$244,939	$201,419	$175,307	$175,307

The ATCF from the sale of the two assets will be equal to:

$$ATCF_{\text{Equipment}} = \$57,600 + (\$290,000 - \$57,600)(1 - 0.34)$$
$$= \$210,984$$
$$ATCF_{\text{Improvements}} = \$168,516 + (\$80,000 - \$168,516)(1 - 0.34)$$
$$= \$110,095$$

The levels and changes in NWC will be equal to:

Level of NWC	$1,800,000	$1,800,000	$1,800,000	$1,800,000	$1,800,000	$0
Change in NWC	1,800,000	0	0	0	0	−1,800,000

So the free flows for the project will be equal to:

	Year 0	Year 1	Year 2	Year 3	Year 4	Year 5
Operating cash flow		$204,049	$244,939	$201,419	$175,307	$ 175,307
Less: Δ Fixed Assets	$1,000,000					−210,984
Less: Δ Fixed Assets	200,000					−110,095
Less: Δ Net working capital	1,800,000					−1,800,000
Free cash flow	−$3,000,000	$204,049	$244,939	$201,419	$175,307	$ 2,296,386

LG12-5 **2 Computing FCF for Cost-Cutting Proposal** Your firm is considering the purchase of a new air conditioning unit at a cost of $50,000. It will be straight-line depreciated to zero using a 5-year life with the half-year convention. After five years, you expect that the unit can be sold for a salvage value of $20,000. This air conditioner is more energy efficient than the one it's replacing, so you anticipate saving $2,000 annually in electricity costs. You also anticipate that your workers will be more productive in a cool environment, and you expect to be able to reduce overtime costs by $20,000 per year. If all applicable tax rates are 35 percent, what will be the expected cash flows associated with the purchase of the new air conditioner?

Solution:

	Year 0	Year 1	Year 2	Year 3	Year 4	Year 5
Sales		$ 0	$ 0	$ 0	$ 0	$ 0
Less: Variable costs		−22,000	−22,000	−22,000	−22,000	−22,000
Less: Fixed costs		0	0	0	0	0
Less: Depreciation		5,000	10,000	10,000	10,000	10,000
Earnings before interest and taxes		$17,000	$12,000	$12,000	$12,000	$12,000
Less: Taxes		5,950	4,200	4,200	4,200	4,200
Net income		$11,050	$ 7,800	$ 7,800	$ 7,800	$ 7,800
Plus: Depreciation		5,000	10,000	10,000	10,000	10,000
Operating cash flow		$16,050	$17,800	$17,800	$17,800	$ 17,800
Less: Δ Fixed Assets	$50,000	0	0	0	0	−14,750
Less: Δ Net working capital	0	0	0	0	0	0
Free cash flow	−$50,000	$16,050	$17,800	$17,800	$17,800	$32,550

3 Using EAC Dumb & Dumber Development Company has two mutually exclusive investment projects to evaluate. Assume both projects can be repeated indefinitely. The following cash flows are associated with each project: LG12-3, 12-4

Year	Project A Cash Flow	Project B Cash Flow
0	−$100,000	−$70,000
1	20,000	30,000
2	50,000	30,000
3	50,000	30,000
4	70,000	45,000
5	—	10,000

The project types are equally risky and the firm's cost of capital is 10 percent. Which project should the firm chose?

Solution:

Using the EAC approach:

$NPV_A = \$44{,}880.81$

Solving for the EAC PMT for *A*:

Calculator:

N = 4
I/Y = 10
PV = 44,880.81
CPT PMT = 14,158.59

$NPV_B = \$41{,}550.38$

Solving for the EAC PMT for *B*:

Calculator:

N = 5
I/Y = 10
PV = 41,550.38
CPT PMT = 10,960.89

Which do you choose? Project A, because $14,158.59 > $10,960.89.

questions

1. How is the pro forma statement we used in this chapter for computing OCF different from an accountant's income statement? *(LG12-1)*
2. Suppose you paid your old college finance professor to evaluate a project for you. If you would pay him regardless of your decision concerning whether to proceed with the project, should his fee for evaluating the project be included in the project's incremental cash flows? *(LG12-2)*
3. Why does a decrease in NWC result in a cash inflow to the firm? *(LG12-3)*
4. Everything else held constant, would you rather depreciate a project with straight-line depreciation or with DDB? *(LG12-3)*
5. Everything else held constant, would you rather depreciate a project with DDB depreciation or deduct it under a Section 179 deduction? *(LG12-4)*
6. In a replacement problem, would we ever see changes in NWC? *(LG12-5)*
7. In a replacement problem, will incremental net depreciation always be less than the gross depreciation on the new piece of equipment? *(LG12-5)*
8. In a cost-cutting proposal, what might cause you to sometimes have negative EBIT? *(LG12-6)*
9. How many TVM formulas do you use every time you calculate EAC for a project? *(LG12-7)*
10. Will an increase in flotation costs increase or decrease the initial cash flow for a project? *(LG12-8)*

problems

basic problems

12-1 After-Tax Cash Flow from Sale of Assets Suppose you sell a fixed asset for $109,000 when its book value is $129,000. If your company's marginal tax rate is 39 percent, what will be the effect on cash flows of this sale (i.e., what will be the after-tax cash flow of this sale)? *(LG12-3)*

12-2 PV of Depreciation Tax Benefits Your company is considering a new project that will require $1 million of new equipment at the start of the project. The equipment will have a depreciable life of 10 years and will be depreciated to a book value of $150,000 using straight-line depreciation. The cost of capital is 13 percent, and the firm's tax rate is 34 percent. Estimate the present value of the tax benefits from depreciation. *(LG12-4)*

12-3 EAC Approach You are trying to pick the least-expensive car for your new delivery service. You have two choices: the Scion xA, which will cost $14,000 to purchase and which will have OCF of −$1,200 annually throughout the vehicle's expected life of three years as a delivery vehicle; and the Toyota Prius, which will cost $20,000 to purchase and which will have OCF of −$650 annually throughout that vehicle's expected 4-year life. Both cars will be worthless at the end of their life. If you intend to replace whichever type of car you choose with the same thing when its life runs out, again and again out into the foreseeable future, and if your business has a cost of capital of 12 percent, which one should you choose? *(LG12-7)*

12-4 EAC Approach You are evaluating two different cookie-baking ovens. The Pillsbury 707 costs $57,000, has a 5-year life, and has an annual OCF (after tax) of −$10,000 per year. The Keebler CookieMunster costs $90,000, has a 7-year life, and has an annual OCF (after tax) of −$8,000 per year. If your discount rate is 12 percent, what is each machine's EAC? *(LG12-8)*

12-5 EAC Approach You are considering the purchase of one of two machines used in your manufacturing plant. Machine A has a life of two years, costs $80 initially, and then $125 per year in maintenance costs. Machine B costs $150 initially, has a life of three years, and requires $100 in annual maintenance costs. Either machine must be replaced at the end of its life with an equivalent machine. Which is the better machine for the firm? The discount rate is 12 percent and the tax rate is zero. *(LG12-8)*

intermediate problems

12-6 Project Cash Flows KADS, Inc., has spent $400,000 on research to develop a new computer game. The firm is planning to spend $200,000 on a machine to produce the new game. Shipping and installation costs of the machine will be capitalized and depreciated; they total $50,000. The machine has an expected life of three years, a $75,000 estimated resale value, and falls under the MACRS 7-year class life. Revenue from the new game is expected to be $600,000 per year, with costs of $250,000 per year. The firm has a tax rate of 35 percent, an opportunity cost of capital of 15 percent, and it expects net working capital to increase by $100,000 at the beginning of the project. What will the cash flows for this project be? *(LG12-3)*

12-7 Depreciation Tax Shield Your firm needs a computerized machine tool lathe which costs $50,000 and requires $12,000 in maintenance for each year of its 3-year life. After three years, this machine will be replaced. The machine falls into the MACRS 3-year class life category. Assume a tax rate of 35 percent and a discount rate of 12 percent. Calculate the depreciation tax shield for this project in year 3. *(LG12-4)*

12-8 After-Tax Cash Flow from Sale of Assets If the lathe in the previous problem can be sold for $5,000 at the end of year 3, what is the after-tax salvage value? *(LG12-4)*

12-9 Project Cash Flows You have been asked by the president of your company to evaluate the proposed acquisition of a new special-purpose truck for $60,000. The truck falls into the MACRS 3-year class, and it will be sold after three years for $20,000. Use of the truck will require an increase in NWC (spare parts inventory) of $2,000. The truck will have no effect on revenues, but it is expected to save the firm $20,000 per year in before-tax operating costs, mainly labor. The firm's marginal tax rate is 40 percent. What will the cash flows for this project be? *(LG12-6)*

advanced problems

12-10 Change in NWC You are evaluating a project for The Tiff-any golf club, guaranteed to correct that nasty slice. You estimate the sales price of The Tiff-any to be $400 per unit and sales volume to be 1,000 units in year 1; 1,500 units in year 2; and 1,325 units in year 3. The project has a 3-year life. Variable costs amount to $225 per unit and fixed costs are $100,000 per year. The project requires an initial investment of $165,000 in assets, which will be depreciated straight-line to zero over the 3-year project life. The actual market value of these assets at the end of year 3 is expected to be $35,000. NWC requirements at the beginning of each year will be approximately 20 percent of the projected sales during the coming year. The tax rate is 34 percent and the required return on the project is 10 percent. What change in NWC occurs at the end of year 1? *(LG12-3)*

12-11 Operating Cash Flow Continuing the previous problem, what is the operating cash flow for the project in year 2? *(LG12-3)*

12-12 Project Cash Flows Your highly successful software company is considering adding a new software title to your list. If you add the new product, it will use the full capacity of your disk duplicating machines that you had planned on using for your flagship product, "Battlin' Bobby." You had previously planned on using the unused capacity to start selling "BB" on the west coast in two years. Eventually, you would have had to purchase additional duplicating machines 10 years from today, but since your new product will use up the extra capacity, this will require moving this purchase up to 2 years from today. If the new machines will cost $100,000 and will be depreciated straight-line over a five-year period to a zero salvage value, your marginal tax rate is 32 percent, and your cost of capital is 12 percent, what is the opportunity cost associated with using the unused capacity for the new product? *(LG12-3)*

12-13 Project Cash Flows You are evaluating a project for The Ultimate recreational tennis racket, guaranteed to correct that wimpy backhand. You estimate the sales price of The Ultimate to be $400 per unit and sales volume to be 1,000 units in year 1; 1,250 units in year 2; and 1,325 units in year 3. The project has a 3-year life. Variable costs amount to $225 per unit and fixed costs are $100,000 per year. The project requires an initial investment of $165,000 in assets, which will be depreciated straight-line to zero over the 3-year project life. The actual market value of these assets at the end of year 3 is expected to be $35,000. NWC requirements at the beginning of each year will be approximately 20 percent of the projected sales during the coming year. The tax rate is 34 percent and the required return on the project is 10 percent. What will the cash flows for this project be? *(LG12-3)*

12-14 Project Cash Flows Mom's Cookies, Inc., is considering the purchase of a new cookie oven. The original cost of the old oven was $30,000; it is now five years old, and it has a current market value of $13,333.33. The old oven is being depreciated over a 10-year life toward a zero estimated salvage value on a straight-line basis, resulting in a current book value of $15,000 and an annual depreciation expense of $3,000. The old oven can be used for six more years but has no market value after its depreciable life is over. Management is contemplating the purchase of a new oven whose cost is $25,000 and whose estimated salvage value is zero. Expected before-tax cash savings from the new oven are $4,000 a year over its full MACRS depreciable life. Depreciation is computed using MACRS over a 5-year life, and the cost of capital is 10 percent. Assume a 40 percent tax rate. What will the cash flows for this project be? *(LG12-5)*

12-15 Project Cash Flows Your company is contemplating replacing their current fleet of delivery vehicles with Nissan NV vans. You will be replacing five fully-depreciated vans, which you think you can sell for $3,000 each and which you could probably use for another two years if you chose not to replace them. The NV vans will cost $29,850 each in the configuration you want them and can be depreciated using MACRS over a 5-year life. Expected yearly before-tax cash savings due to acquiring the new vans amounts to about $3,700 each. If your cost of capital is 8 percent and your firm faces a 34 percent tax rate, what will the cash flows for this project be? *(LG12-5)*

research it! Looking up Information on Section 179 Deduction

Go to the IRS's website at **www.irs.gov** and search for information on Section 179 deductions for the current tax year.

What is the maximum Section 179 deduction for the current tax year?

integrated mini-case: Project Cash Flows

Your company, Dawgs "R" Us, is evaluating a new project involving the purchase of a new oven to bake your hotdog buns. If purchased, the new oven will replace your existing oven, which was purchased seven years ago for a total installed price of $1 million.

You have been depreciating the old oven on a straight-line basis over its expected life of 15 years to an ending book value of $250,000, even though you expect it to be worthless at the end of that 15-year period. The new oven will cost $2 million and will fall into the MACRS 5-year depreciation class life. If you purchase the new oven, you expect it to last for eight years. At the end of those eight years, you expect to be able to sell it for $100,000. (Note that both of the ovens, old and new, therefore have an effective remaining life of eight years at the time of your analysis.) If you do purchase the new oven, you estimate that you can sell the old one for its current book value at the same time.

The advantages of the new oven are twofold: Not only do you expect it to reduce the before-tax costs on your current baking operations by $75,000 per year, but you will also be able to produce new types of buns. The sales of the new buns are expected to bring your company $200,000 per year throughout the eight-year life of the new oven, while associated costs of the new buns are only expected to be $80,000 per year.

Since the new oven will allow you to sell these new products, you anticipate that NWC will have to increase immediately by $20,000 upon purchase of the new oven. It will then remain at that increased level throughout the life of the new oven to sustain the new, higher level of operations.

Your company uses a required rate of return of 12 percent for such projects, and your incremental tax rate is 34 percent. What will be the total cash flows for this project?

ANSWERS TO TIME OUT

12-1 You should charge half of her salary and benefits to the new project, and the other half to the existing projects.

12-2 Sure. For example, think about a restaurant chain adding a new item to its menu: say, gourmet coffee. To the extent that some customers who would have bought their current drinks will replace that selection with the new coffee, the coffee is a substitute for those drinks; but, assuming that the coffee will attract some "new" customers, ones who would not have come into the restaurant otherwise, and that those new customers will also buy some of the existing pastry products, then the new coffee is a complement for the pastries.

12-3 Even though we are explicitly keeping track of the level of NWC, what we are really concerned with is the inflow or outflow of cash arising from changes to that level. When we increase NWC, we have to buy inventory, make sales on credit, or tie up cash flow in the form of physical cash, all of which use up cash flow.

12-4 As long as we have any depreciation, OCF will be larger than net income because it reflects the fact that depreciation is not a cash expense.

12-5 Because of the half-year convention, the IRS allows us to take only one-half of the first year's life of the asset during the first calendar year we own it. This, in turn, implies that we will still have the last half of the fifth year of the asset's 5-year life to take during the sixth year that we own it, and so forth.

12-6 They would encourage investment in certain types of assets by putting them into shorter life-class categories. Since the IRS gives you the same total amount of depreciation regardless of the length of depreciable life allowed, the present value of the total tax shields from the depreciation of an asset will be higher if you get to take the depreciation quicker.

12-7 Although a positive investment in operating capital would normally be associated with a purchase of fixed assets, here the positive value was generated by the forgone sale of the old assets: since we sold them at the beginning of the replacement project, we had to give up selling them at the end.

12-8 No. As long as the tax rate is less than 100 percent, the present value of the depreciation tax shields will always be less than the present value of the costs of those assets, implying that net cash flows for such a project would have to be, on average across the life of the project, negative.

12-9 It does so by turning each individual asset purchase not only into an annuity, but into an annuity that is perfectly aligned with the annuities of the identical assets purchased before and after it so as to form a perpetuity.

12-10 Sure. Since the EAC is calculated as the equivalent cost per year, it does not matter if both projects have the same or differing lives.

12-11 Since retained earnings do not have a flotation cost, the average equity flotation cost would simply be a weighted average (where the weights are the relative proportions of retained earnings and new equity) of the flotation cost of the new equity and zero. For example, if a firm was going to use one-third retained earnings and two-thirds new equity, and new equity had a flotation cost of 5 percent, then the weighted average flotation cost of equity would be $1/3 \times 0 + 2/3 \times 0.05 = 0.033$, or 3.33%.

12-12 Multiplying by $(1 + f_A)$ would give us the flotation expense on the initial cash flow itself, but it would not give us the "flotation cost on the flotation cost." If we want to raise both the money needed for a project and the money needed to cover the flotation costs, both entirely from the sale of new securities, we will have to keep in mind that the underwriter will charge us a fee on *all* of the money. Dividing by $(1 - f_A)$ handles this. For example, if we wanted to raise $1 million to buy new assets, and the underwriter was going to charge us a weighted average flotation cost of 5 percent, then we would actually have to sell $1,000,000/(1 − 0.05) = $1,052,631.58 worth of securities, giving $52,631.58 of the proceeds to the underwriter as a fee in order to be able to keep the $1 million we needed.

appendix 12A MACRS Depreciation Tables

	MACRS Depreciation								
								Real Estate	
	Normal Recovery Period						Residential	Nonresidential	
Year	3	5	7	10	15	20	27.5	31.5	39
1	33.33%	20.00%	14.29%	10.00%	5.00%	3.750%	3.485%	3.042%	2.461%
2	44.45	32.00	24.49	18.00	9.50	7.219	3.636	3.175	2.564
3	14.81	19.20	17.49	14.40	8.55	6.677	3.636	3.175	2.564
4	7.41	11.52	12.49	11.52	7.70	6.177	3.636	3.175	2.564
5	0.00	11.52	8.93	9.22	6.93	5.713	3.636	3.175	2.564
6	0.00	5.76	8.92	7.37	6.23	5.285	3.636	3.175	2.564
7	0.00	0.00	8.93	6.55	5.90	4.888	3.636	3.175	2.564
8	0.00	0.00	4.46	6.55	5.90	4.522	3.636	3.175	2.564
9	0.00	0.00	0.00	6.56	5.91	4.462	3.636	3.174	2.564
10	0.00	0.00	0.00	6.55	5.90	4.461	3.637	3.175	2.564
11	0.00	0.00	0.00	3.28	5.91	4.462	3.636	3.174	2.564
12	0.00	0.00	0.00	0.00	5.90	4.461	3.637	3.175	2.564
13	0.00	0.00	0.00	0.00	5.91	4.462	3.636	3.174	2.564
14	0.00	0.00	0.00	0.00	5.90	4.461	3.637	3.175	2.564
15	0.00	0.00	0.00	0.00	5.91	4.462	3.636	3.174	2.564
16	0.00	0.00	0.00	0.00	2.95	4.461	3.637	3.175	2.564
17	0.00	0.00	0.00	0.00	0.00	4.462	3.636	3.174	2.564
18	0.00	0.00	0.00	0.00	0.00	4.461	3.637	3.175	2.564
19	0.00	0.00	0.00	0.00	0.00	4.462	3.636	3.174	2.564
20	0.00	0.00	0.00	0.00	0.00	4.461	3.637	3.175	2.564
21	0.00	0.00	0.00	0.00	0.00	2.231	3.636	3.174	2.564
22	0.00	0.00	0.00	0.00	0.00	0.00	3.637	3.175	2.564
23	0.00	0.00	0.00	0.00	0.00	0.00	3.636	3.174	2.564
24	0.00	0.00	0.00	0.00	0.00	0.00	3.637	3.175	2.564
25	0.00	0.00	0.00	0.00	0.00	0.00	3.636	3.174	2.564
26	0.00	0.00	0.00	0.00	0.00	0.00	3.637	3.175	2.564
27	0.00	0.00	0.00	0.00	0.00	0.00	3.636	3.174	2.564
28	0.00	0.00	0.00	0.00	0.00	0.00	1.970	3.175	2.564
29	0.00	0.00	0.00	0.00	0.00	0.00	0.00	3.174	2.564
30	0.00	0.00	0.00	0.00	0.00	0.00	0.00	3.175	2.564
31	0.00	0.00	0.00	0.00	0.00	0.00	0.00	3.174	2.564
32	0.00	0.00	0.00	0.00	0.00	0.00	0.00	1.720	2.564
33	0.00	0.00	0.00	0.00	0.00	0.00	0.00	0.00	2.564
34	0.00	0.00	0.00	0.00	0.00	0.00	0.00	0.00	2.564
35	0.00	0.00	0.00	0.00	0.00	0.00	0.00	0.00	2.564
36	0.00	0.00	0.00	0.00	0.00	0.00	0.00	0.00	2.564
37	0.00	0.00	0.00	0.00	0.00	0.00	0.00	0.00	2.564
38	0.00	0.00	0.00	0.00	0.00	0.00	0.00	0.00	2.564
39	0.00	0.00	0.00	0.00	0.00	0.00	0.00	0.00	2.564
40	0.00	0.00	0.00	0.00	0.00	0.00	0.00	0.00	0.107
41	0.00	0.00	0.00	0.00	0.00	0.00	0.00	0.00	0.000

SL Depreciation

Year	Normal Recovery Period 2.5	3	3.5	4	5	6	6.5	7	7.5	8	8.5	9
1	20.00%	16.67%	14.29%	12.50%	10.00%	8.33%	7.69%	7.14%	6.67%	6.25%	5.88%	5.56%
2	40.00	33.33	28.57	25.00	20.00	16.67	15.39	14.29	13.33	12.50	11.77	11.11
3	40.00	33.33	28.57	25.00	20.00	16.67	15.38	14.29	13.33	12.50	11.76	11.11
4	0.00	16.67	28.57	25.00	20.00	16.67	15.39	14.28	13.33	12.50	11.77	11.11
5	0.00	0.00	0.00	12.50	20.00	16.66	15.38	14.29	13.34	12.50	11.76	11.11
6	0.00	0.00	0.00	0.00	10.00	16.67	15.39	14.28	13.33	12.50	11.77	11.11
7	0.00	0.00	0.00	0.00	0.00	8.33	15.38	14.29	13.34	12.50	11.76	11.11
8	0.00	0.00	0.00	0.00	0.00	0.00	0.00	7.14	13.33	12.50	11.77	11.11
9	0.00	0.00	0.00	0.00	0.00	0.00	0.00	0.00	0.00	6.25	11.76	11.11
10	0.00	0.00	0.00	0.00	0.00	0.00	0.00	0.00	0.00	0.00	0.00	5.56
11	0.00	0.00	0.00	0.00	0.00	0.00	0.00	0.00	0.00	0.00	0.00	0.00
12	0.00	0.00	0.00	0.00	0.00	0.00	0.00	0.00	0.00	0.00	0.00	0.00
13	0.00	0.00	0.00	0.00	0.00	0.00	0.00	0.00	0.00	0.00	0.00	0.00
14	0.00	0.00	0.00	0.00	0.00	0.00	0.00	0.00	0.00	0.00	0.00	0.00
15	0.00	0.00	0.00	0.00	0.00	0.00	0.00	0.00	0.00	0.00	0.00	0.00
16	0.00	0.00	0.00	0.00	0.00	0.00	0.00	0.00	0.00	0.00	0.00	0.00
17	0.00	0.00	0.00	0.00	0.00	0.00	0.00	0.00	0.00	0.00	0.00	0.00
18	0.00	0.00	0.00	0.00	0.00	0.00	0.00	0.00	0.00	0.00	0.00	0.00
19	0.00	0.00	0.00	0.00	0.00	0.00	0.00	0.00	0.00	0.00	0.00	0.00
20	0.00	0.00	0.00	0.00	0.00	0.00	0.00	0.00	0.00	0.00	0.00	0.00
21	0.00	0.00	0.00	0.00	0.00	0.00	0.00	0.00	0.00	0.00	0.00	0.00
22	0.00	0.00	0.00	0.00	0.00	0.00	0.00	0.00	0.00	0.00	0.00	0.00
23	0.00	0.00	0.00	0.00	0.00	0.00	0.00	0.00	0.00	0.00	0.00	0.00
24	0.00	0.00	0.00	0.00	0.00	0.00	0.00	0.00	0.00	0.00	0.00	0.00
25	0.00	0.00	0.00	0.00	0.00	0.00	0.00	0.00	0.00	0.00	0.00	0.00
26	0.00	0.00	0.00	0.00	0.00	0.00	0.00	0.00	0.00	0.00	0.00	0.00
27	0.00	0.00	0.00	0.00	0.00	0.00	0.00	0.00	0.00	0.00	0.00	0.00
28	0.00	0.00	0.00	0.00	0.00	0.00	0.00	0.00	0.00	0.00	0.00	0.00
29	0.00	0.00	0.00	0.00	0.00	0.00	0.00	0.00	0.00	0.00	0.00	0.00
30	0.00	0.00	0.00	0.00	0.00	0.00	0.00	0.00	0.00	0.00	0.00	0.00
31	0.00	0.00	0.00	0.00	0.00	0.00	0.00	0.00	0.00	0.00	0.00	0.00
32	0.00	0.00	0.00	0.00	0.00	0.00	0.00	0.00	0.00	0.00	0.00	0.00
33	0.00	0.00	0.00	0.00	0.00	0.00	0.00	0.00	0.00	0.00	0.00	0.00
34	0.00	0.00	0.00	0.00	0.00	0.00	0.00	0.00	0.00	0.00	0.00	0.00
35	0.00	0.00	0.00	0.00	0.00	0.00	0.00	0.00	0.00	0.00	0.00	0.00
36	0.00	0.00	0.00	0.00	0.00	0.00	0.00	0.00	0.00	0.00	0.00	0.00
37	0.00	0.00	0.00	0.00	0.00	0.00	0.00	0.00	0.00	0.00	0.00	0.00
38	0.00	0.00	0.00	0.00	0.00	0.00	0.00	0.00	0.00	0.00	0.00	0.00
39	0.00	0.00	0.00	0.00	0.00	0.00	0.00	0.00	0.00	0.00	0.00	0.00
40	0.00	0.00	0.00	0.00	0.00	0.00	0.00	0.00	0.00	0.00	0.00	0.00
41	0.00	0.00	0.00	0.00	0.00	0.00	0.00	0.00	0.00	0.00	0.00	0.00
42	0.00	0.00	0.00	0.00	0.00	0.00	0.00	0.00	0.00	0.00	0.00	0.00
43	0.00	0.00	0.00	0.00	0.00	0.00	0.00	0.00	0.00	0.00	0.00	0.00
44	0.00	0.00	0.00	0.00	0.00	0.00	0.00	0.00	0.00	0.00	0.00	0.00
45	0.00	0.00	0.00	0.00	0.00	0.00	0.00	0.00	0.00	0.00	0.00	0.00
46	0.00	0.00	0.00	0.00	0.00	0.00	0.00	0.00	0.00	0.00	0.00	0.00
47	0.00	0.00	0.00	0.00	0.00	0.00	0.00	0.00	0.00	0.00	0.00	0.00
48	0.00	0.00	0.00	0.00	0.00	0.00	0.00	0.00	0.00	0.00	0.00	0.00
49	0.00	0.00	0.00	0.00	0.00	0.00	0.00	0.00	0.00	0.00	0.00	0.00
50	0.00	0.00	0.00	0.00	0.00	0.00	0.00	0.00	0.00	0.00	0.00	0.00
51	0.00	0.00	0.00	0.00	0.00	0.00	0.00	0.00	0.00	0.00	0.00	0.00
52	0.00	0.00	0.00	0.00	0.00	0.00	0.00	0.00	0.00	0.00	0.00	0.00

SL Depreciation													
	Normal Recovery Period												
Year	9.5	10	10.5	11	11.5	12	12.5	13	13.5	14	15	16	16.5
1	5.26%	5.00%	4.76%	4.55%	4.35%	4.17%	4.00%	3.85%	3.70%	3.57%	3.33%	3.13%	3.03%
2	10.53	10.00	9.52	9.09	8.70	8.33	8.00	7.69	7.41	7.14	6.67	6.25	6.06
3	10.53	10.00	9.52	9.09	8.70	8.33	8.00	7.69	7.41	7.14	6.67	6.25	6.06
4	10.53	10.00	9.53	9.09	8.69	8.33	8.00	7.69	7.41	7.14	6.67	6.25	6.06
5	10.52	10.00	9.52	9.09	8.70	8.33	8.00	7.69	7.41	7.14	6.67	6.25	6.06
6	10.53	10.00	9.53	9.09	8.69	8.33	8.00	7.69	7.41	7.14	6.67	6.25	6.06
7	10.52	10.00	9.52	9.09	8.70	8.34	8.00	7.69	7.41	7.14	6.67	6.25	6.06
8	10.53	10.00	9.53	9.09	8.69	8.33	8.00	7.69	7.41	7.15	6.66	6.25	6.06
9	10.52	10.00	9.52	9.09	8.70	8.34	8.00	7.69	7.41	7.14	6.67	6.25	6.06
10	10.53	10.00	9.53	9.09	8.69	8.33	8.00	7.70	7.40	7.15	6.66	6.25	6.06
11	0.00	5.00	9.52	9.09	8.70	8.34	8.00	7.69	7.41	7.14	6.67	6.25	6.06
12	0.00	0.00	0.00	4.55	8.69	8.33	8.00	7.70	7.40	7.15	6.66	6.25	6.06
13	0.00	0.00	0.00	0.00	0.00	4.17	8.00	7.69	7.41	7.14	6.67	6.25	6.06
14	0.00	0.00	0.00	0.00	0.00	0.00	0.00	3.85	7.40	7.15	6.66	6.25	6.06
15	0.00	0.00	0.00	0.00	0.00	0.00	0.00	0.00	0.00	3.57	6.67	6.25	6.06
16	0.00	0.00	0.00	0.00	0.00	0.00	0.00	0.00	0.00	0.00	3.33	6.25	6.06
17	0.00	0.00	0.00	0.00	0.00	0.00	0.00	0.00	0.00	0.00	0.00	3.12	6.07
18	0.00	0.00	0.00	0.00	0.00	0.00	0.00	0.00	0.00	0.00	0.00	0.00	0.00
19	0.00	0.00	0.00	0.00	0.00	0.00	0.00	0.00	0.00	0.00	0.00	0.00	0.00
20	0.00	0.00	0.00	0.00	0.00	0.00	0.00	0.00	0.00	0.00	0.00	0.00	0.00
21	0.00	0.00	0.00	0.00	0.00	0.00	0.00	0.00	0.00	0.00	0.00	0.00	0.00
22	0.00	0.00	0.00	0.00	0.00	0.00	0.00	0.00	0.00	0.00	0.00	0.00	0.00
23	0.00	0.00	0.00	0.00	0.00	0.00	0.00	0.00	0.00	0.00	0.00	0.00	0.00
24	0.00	0.00	0.00	0.00	0.00	0.00	0.00	0.00	0.00	0.00	0.00	0.00	0.00
25	0.00	0.00	0.00	0.00	0.00	0.00	0.00	0.00	0.00	0.00	0.00	0.00	0.00
26	0.00	0.00	0.00	0.00	0.00	0.00	0.00	0.00	0.00	0.00	0.00	0.00	0.00
27	0.00	0.00	0.00	0.00	0.00	0.00	0.00	0.00	0.00	0.00	0.00	0.00	0.00
28	0.00	0.00	0.00	0.00	0.00	0.00	0.00	0.00	0.00	0.00	0.00	0.00	0.00
29	0.00	0.00	0.00	0.00	0.00	0.00	0.00	0.00	0.00	0.00	0.00	0.00	0.00
30	0.00	0.00	0.00	0.00	0.00	0.00	0.00	0.00	0.00	0.00	0.00	0.00	0.00
31	0.00	0.00	0.00	0.00	0.00	0.00	0.00	0.00	0.00	0.00	0.00	0.00	0.00
32	0.00	0.00	0.00	0.00	0.00	0.00	0.00	0.00	0.00	0.00	0.00	0.00	0.00
33	0.00	0.00	0.00	0.00	0.00	0.00	0.00	0.00	0.00	0.00	0.00	0.00	0.00
34	0.00	0.00	0.00	0.00	0.00	0.00	0.00	0.00	0.00	0.00	0.00	0.00	0.00
35	0.00	0.00	0.00	0.00	0.00	0.00	0.00	0.00	0.00	0.00	0.00	0.00	0.00
36	0.00	0.00	0.00	0.00	0.00	0.00	0.00	0.00	0.00	0.00	0.00	0.00	0.00
37	0.00	0.00	0.00	0.00	0.00	0.00	0.00	0.00	0.00	0.00	0.00	0.00	0.00
38	0.00	0.00	0.00	0.00	0.00	0.00	0.00	0.00	0.00	0.00	0.00	0.00	0.00
39	0.00	0.00	0.00	0.00	0.00	0.00	0.00	0.00	0.00	0.00	0.00	0.00	0.00
40	0.00	0.00	0.00	0.00	0.00	0.00	0.00	0.00	0.00	0.00	0.00	0.00	0.00
41	0.00	0.00	0.00	0.00	0.00	0.00	0.00	0.00	0.00	0.00	0.00	0.00	0.00
42	0.00	0.00	0.00	0.00	0.00	0.00	0.00	0.00	0.00	0.00	0.00	0.00	0.00
43	0.00	0.00	0.00	0.00	0.00	0.00	0.00	0.00	0.00	0.00	0.00	0.00	0.00
44	0.00	0.00	0.00	0.00	0.00	0.00	0.00	0.00	0.00	0.00	0.00	0.00	0.00
45	0.00	0.00	0.00	0.00	0.00	0.00	0.00	0.00	0.00	0.00	0.00	0.00	0.00
46	0.00	0.00	0.00	0.00	0.00	0.00	0.00	0.00	0.00	0.00	0.00	0.00	0.00
47	0.00	0.00	0.00	0.00	0.00	0.00	0.00	0.00	0.00	0.00	0.00	0.00	0.00
48	0.00	0.00	0.00	0.00	0.00	0.00	0.00	0.00	0.00	0.00	0.00	0.00	0.00
49	0.00	0.00	0.00	0.00	0.00	0.00	0.00	0.00	0.00	0.00	0.00	0.00	0.00
50	0.00	0.00	0.00	0.00	0.00	0.00	0.00	0.00	0.00	0.00	0.00	0.00	0.00
51	0.00	0.00	0.00	0.00	0.00	0.00	0.00	0.00	0.00	0.00	0.00	0.00	0.00
52	0.00	0.00	0.00	0.00	0.00	0.00	0.00	0.00	0.00	0.00	0.00	0.00	0.00

SL Depreciation														
	Normal Recovery Period													
Year	17	18	19	20	22	24	25	26.5	28	30	35	40	45	50
1	2.94%	2.78%	2.63%	2.50%	2.273%	2.083%	2.00%	1.887%	1.786%	1.667%	1.429%	1.25%	1.111%	1.00%
2	5.88	5.56	5.26	5.00	4.545	4.167	4.00	3.774	3.571	3.333	2.857	2.50	2.222	2.00
3	5.88	5.56	5.26	5.00	4.545	4.167	4.00	3.774	3.571	3.333	2.857	2.50	2.222	2.00
4	5.88	5.55	5.26	5.00	4.545	4.167	4.00	3.774	3.571	3.333	2.857	2.50	2.222	2.00
5	5.88	5.56	5.26	5.00	4.546	4.167	4.00	3.774	3.571	3.333	2.857	2.50	2.222	2.00
6	5.88	5.55	5.26	5.00	4.545	4.167	4.00	3.774	3.571	3.333	2.857	2.50	2.222	2.00
7	5.88	5.56	5.26	5.00	4.546	4.167	4.00	3.773	3.572	3.333	2.857	2.50	2.222	2.00
8	5.88	5.55	5.26	5.00	4.545	4.167	4.00	3.774	3.571	3.333	2.857	2.50	2.222	2.00
9	5.88	5.56	5.27	5.00	4.546	4.167	4.00	3.773	3.572	3.333	2.857	2.50	2.222	2.00
10	5.88	5.55	5.26	5.00	4.545	4.167	4.00	3.774	3.571	3.333	2.857	2.50	2.222	2.00
11	5.89	5.56	5.27	5.00	4.546	4.166	4.00	3.773	3.572	3.333	2.857	2.50	2.222	2.00
12	5.88	5.55	5.26	5.00	4.545	4.167	4.00	3.774	3.571	3.333	2.857	2.50	2.222	2.00
13	5.89	5.56	5.27	5.00	4.546	4.166	4.00	3.773	3.572	3.334	2.857	2.50	2.222	2.00
14	5.88	5.55	5.26	5.00	4.545	4.167	4.00	3.773	3.571	3.333	2.857	2.50	2.222	2.00
15	5.89	5.56	5.27	5.00	4.546	4.166	4.00	3.774	3.572	3.334	2.857	2.50	2.222	2.00
16	5.88	5.55	5.26	5.00	4.545	4.167	4.00	3.773	3.571	3.333	2.857	2.50	2.222	2.00
17	5.89	5.56	5.27	5.00	4.546	4.166	4.00	3.774	3.572	3.334	2.857	2.50	2.222	2.00
18	2.94	5.55	5.26	5.00	4.545	4.167	4.00	3.773	3.571	3.333	2.857	2.50	2.222	2.00
19	0.00	2.78	5.27	5.00	4.546	4.166	4.00	3.774	3.572	3.334	2.857	2.50	2.222	2.00
20	0.00	0.00	2.63	5.00	4.545	4.167	4.00	3.773	3.571	3.333	2.857	2.50	2.222	2.00
21	0.00	0.00	0.00	2.50	4.546	4.166	4.00	3.774	3.572	3.334	2.857	2.50	2.222	2.00
22	0.00	0.00	0.00	0.00	4.545	4.167	4.00	3.773	3.571	3.333	2.857	2.50	2.222	2.00
23	0.00	0.00	0.00	0.00	2.273	4.166	4.00	3.774	3.572	3.334	2.857	2.50	2.222	2.00
24	0.00	0.00	0.00	0.00	0.000	4.167	4.00	3.773	3.571	3.333	2.857	2.50	2.222	2.00
25	0.00	0.00	0.00	0.00	0.000	2.083	4.00	3.774	3.572	3.334	2.857	2.50	2.222	2.00
26	0.00	0.00	0.00	0.00	0.000	0.000	2.00	3.773	3.571	3.333	2.857	2.50	2.222	2.00
27	0.00	0.00	0.00	0.00	0.000	0.000	0.00	3.774	3.572	3.334	2.857	2.50	2.223	2.00
28	0.00	0.00	0.00	0.00	0.000	0.000	0.00	0.000	3.571	3.333	2.858	2.50	2.222	2.00
29	0.00	0.00	0.00	0.00	0.000	0.000	0.00	0.000	1.786	3.334	2.857	2.50	2.223	2.00
30	0.00	0.00	0.00	0.00	0.000	0.000	0.00	0.000	0.000	3.333	2.858	2.50	2.222	2.00
31	0.00	0.00	0.00	0.00	0.000	0.000	0.00	0.000	0.000	1.667	2.857	2.50	2.223	2.00
32	0.00	0.00	0.00	0.00	0.000	0.000	0.00	0.000	0.000	0.000	2.858	2.50	2.222	2.00
33	0.00	0.00	0.00	0.00	0.000	0.000	0.00	0.000	0.000	0.000	2.857	2.50	2.223	2.00
34	0.00	0.00	0.00	0.00	0.000	0.000	0.00	0.000	0.000	0.000	2.858	2.50	2.222	2.00
35	0.00	0.00	0.00	0.00	0.000	0.000	0.00	0.000	0.000	0.000	2.857	2.50	2.223	2.00
36	0.00	0.00	0.00	0.00	0.000	0.000	0.00	0.000	0.000	0.000	1.429	2.50	2.222	2.00
37	0.00	0.00	0.00	0.00	0.000	0.000	0.00	0.000	0.000	0.000	0.000	2.50	2.223	2.00
38	0.00	0.00	0.00	0.00	0.000	0.000	0.00	0.000	0.000	0.000	0.000	2.50	2.222	2.00
39	0.00	0.00	0.00	0.00	0.000	0.000	0.00	0.000	0.000	0.000	0.000	2.50	2.223	2.00
40	0.00	0.00	0.00	0.00	0.000	0.000	0.00	0.000	0.000	0.000	0.000	2.50	2.222	2.00
41	0.00	0.00	0.00	0.00	0.000	0.000	0.00	0.000	0.000	0.000	0.000	1.25	2.223	2.00
42	0.00	0.00	0.00	0.00	0.000	0.000	0.00	0.000	0.000	0.000	0.000	0.00	2.222	2.00
43	0.00	0.00	0.00	0.00	0.000	0.000	0.00	0.000	0.000	0.000	0.000	0.00	2.223	2.00
44	0.00	0.00	0.00	0.00	0.000	0.000	0.00	0.000	0.000	0.000	0.000	0.00	2.222	2.00
45	0.00	0.00	0.00	0.00	0.000	0.000	0.00	0.000	0.000	0.000	0.000	0.00	2.223	2.00
46	0.00	0.00	0.00	0.00	0.000	0.000	0.00	0.000	0.000	0.000	0.000	0.00	1.111	2.00
47	0.00	0.00	0.00	0.00	0.000	0.000	0.00	0.000	0.000	0.000	0.000	0.00	0.000	2.00
48	0.00	0.00	0.00	0.00	0.000	0.000	0.00	0.000	0.000	0.000	0.000	0.00	0.000	2.00
49	0.00	0.00	0.00	0.00	0.000	0.000	0.00	0.000	0.000	0.000	0.000	0.00	0.000	2.00
50	0.00	0.00	0.00	0.00	0.000	0.000	0.00	0.000	0.000	0.000	0.000	0.00	0.000	2.00
51	0.00	0.00	0.00	0.00	0.000	0.000	0.00	0.000	0.000	0.000	0.000	0.00	0.000	1.00
52	0.00	0.00	0.00	0.00	0.000	0.000	0.00	0.000	0.000	0.000	0.000	0.00	0.000	0.00

PART SIX

13 Weighing Net Present Value and Other Capital Budgeting Criteria

viewpoints

Business Application

ADK Industries, a startup firm in the online social networking industry, has run into capacity constraints with their Internet bandwidth provider. ADK management is considering building their own dedicated Web server farm at a cost of $5 million. In return, the firm expects that the increased bandwidth will generate higher demand for its services, resulting in increased cash flows of $1.2 million in the first year, $1.6 million in the second year, $2.3 million in the third year, and $2.8 million in the fourth year, for a total of $7.9 million over the next four years. At that point, the firm will scrap the server farm as obsolete. If ADK estimates that its target rate of return on such projects is 14 percent, should ADK go ahead with the project? **(See solution on p. 462)**

Personal Application

Letitia Tyler is considering some improvements to her house. The work will take six months to complete, and the contractor has asked for payments of $5,000 at the start, $5,000 after three months, and another $10,000 upon completion. Letitia plans to sell the house in approximately three years and estimates that the work will increase the selling price of her house by approximately $30,000 from its current estimated market price of $124,000. If she must borrow money to pay for the improvements from the bank at an APR (based upon monthly compounding) of 9 percent, should she have the improvements done? **(See solution on p. 462)**

How do interest rates impact Letitia's decision? What does that have to do with the economy?

Learning Goals

LG13-1 Analyze the logic underlying capital budgeting decision techniques.

LG13-2 Calculate and use the payback (PB) and discounted payback (DPB) methods for valuing capital investment opportunities.

LG13-3 Calculate and use the net present value (NPV) method for evaluating capital investment opportunities.

LG13-4 Calculate and use the internal rate of return (IRR) and the modified internal rate of return (MIRR) methods for evaluating capital investment opportunities.

LG13-5 Use NPV profiles to reconcile sources of conflict between NPV and IRR methods.

LG13-6 Compute and use the profitability index (PI).

Once you have calculated the cost of capital for a project and estimated its cash flows, deciding whether to invest in that project basically boils down to asking the question "Is the project worth its projected present value?" To answer this question, we will, not surprisingly, turn once again to the time value of money (TVM) formulas we used to value stocks, bonds, loans, and other marketable securities in Chapters 7 and 8. But first, a caveat: Though the *mechanics* of using the TVM formulas will be the same, the *intuition* underlying our analysis of investment criteria is very different. You will recall that we used the pricing equations for stocks, bonds, and other instruments with an emphasis on equations that had "=" signs. We will see here that most capital budgeting decision rules that we will encounter will have ">" or "<" signs. This difference arises because marketable securities are *financial* assets that trade in competitive financial markets, while capital budgeting projects usually involve the purchase of *real* assets, which typically trade in much less competitive markets. Real assets are considerably less liquid than are financial assets, and firms purchase real assets in the form of capital equipment to create value for their customers. As a result, projects and purchases that involve capital equipment typically convey at least some monopoly power (and the associated monopolistic profits) to the firm purchasing them and adopting them for long-term use. In fact, the reason for the inequality signs in the capital budgeting decision rules we will be examining is that, rather than looking for projects that are worth "enough," we seek projects that are worth "more than enough." That is, capital budgeting equations seek projects that offer more return than they should (sometimes called *economic profits*), even after taking into account their associated risk.

13.1 • The Set of Capital Budgeting Techniques

LG13-1

So, now we are going to apply what we have learned in the preceding two chapters about the cost of capital and cash flows that result from capital budgeting decisions to choose the projects that most deserve the scarce capital—that is, to

table 13.1 | Capital Budgeting Technique Attributes

Technique	Unit of Measurement	Benchmark	Uses TVM	Works Well With Non-Normal Cash Flows	Works Well For Choosing Among Projects
PB (payback)	Time	Varies	No	No	No
DPB (discounted payback)	Time	Varies	Yes	No	No
NPV (net present value)	Dollars	$0	Yes	Yes	Yes
IRR (internal rate of return)	Rate	Cost of capital	Yes	No	No
MIRR (modified internal rate of return)	Rate	Cost of capital	Yes	Yes	No
PI (profitability index)	Rate	1	Yes	Yes	No

determine which projects promise the best returns to the company. No one can predict the future, so these techniques are accompanied by uncertainty. That said, commonly used capital budgeting techniques include:

- NPV (net present value).
- IRR (internal rate of return).
- PB (payback).
- DPB (discounted payback).
- MIRR (modified internal rate of return).
- PI (profitability index).

As we discuss each of these techniques in this chapter, you will find that, while the net present value (NPV) technique is the preferred one for most project evaluations, in some cases using one of the other decision rules, either in lieu of NPV or in conjunction with it, makes sense. For example, a company or person faced with a time constraint to repay the initial capital for a project may be more worried about a project's payback (PB) statistic, while a firm facing capital constraints might prefer to use one of the interest-rate-based decision statistics, such as the profitability index (PI), to prioritize its project choices. How you choose a capital budgeting technique or techniques is affected by five subchoices:

1. The statistical format you choose.
2. The benchmark you compare it to.
3. Whether you compute it with TVM.
4. Whether non-normal cash flows are a factor.
5. What other projects you may or may not have to decide among.

Table 13.1 details the implicit subchoices associated with each of the capital budgeting techniques.

13.2 • The Choice of Decision Statistic Format

Managers tend to focus on three general measurement units for financial decisions: currency, time, and rate of return. Of these three types, rate-based statistics can potentially be the trickiest to use. Computing these statistics usually involves summarizing the relationship between cash inflows and cash outflows across the project's lifetime through the use of a ratio. Any time we use a ratio to create a summary statistic like this, some (crucial) information is lost along the way.

In particular, although rate-based decision statistics tell us the rate of return *per dollar* invested, they don't reflect the *amount* of the investment on which that return is based. To see why this can be a problem, particularly when choosing between two or more projects, ask yourself this question: Would you rather earn a 10 percent rate of return on $100 or a 9 percent rate of return on $1,000?

Despite this tendency to focus on the return per dollar invested while ignoring the number of dollars in question, rate-based decision statistics are actually very popular. Managers appreciate being able to easily compare the expected "earned" rate of return constructed by these decision rules with the "borrowing" rates that potential lenders and the capital markets are quoting to them.

13.3 • Processing Capital Budgeting Decisions

For all of our decision techniques, we need to identify how to calculate a *decision statistic;* decide on an appropriate *benchmark* for comparing the calculated statistic; and define what relationship between the two will dictate project acceptance. When we consider one project at a time, or when we examine each of a group of independent projects, capital budgeting techniques involve two-step decision processes:

1. Compute the statistic.
2. Compare the computed statistic with the benchmark to decide whether to accept or reject the project.

However, when we deal with mutually exclusive projects, we will need to add a new step in the middle of the process:

1. Compute the statistic for each project.
2. *Have a "runoff" between the mutually exclusive projects, choosing the one with the best statistic.*
3. Compare the computed statistic from the runoff winner with the benchmark to decide whether to accept or reject.

As we will see, the presence of this runoff step for mutually exclusive projects, as well as its placement, will create problems when we use decision statistics that either ignore or summarize critical information in the first step.

13.4 • Payback and Discounted Payback

LG13-1

Both the payback and discounted payback rules carry great emotional appeal: If we assume that we are borrowing money to finance a new project, both techniques answer slightly different versions of the question, "How long is it going to take us to recoup our costs?"

So it would seem that these techniques use the same reasoning that banks and other lenders employ when they examine a potential borrower's finances to determine the probability of repayment. While at first this seems like a fairly simple question, it can actually lead to some rather sophisticated insight concerning a project's potential. For example, a project that lasts seven years but is slated to repay its initial investment within the first two years is obviously a stronger candidate than a project that also repays in two years but is slated to last only three years, assuming that the two projects are expected to have the same yearly cash flows once payback is achieved.

LG13-2

Payback Statistic

payback (PB)

A capital budgeting technique that generates decision rules and associated metrics for choosing projects based on how quickly they return their initial investment.

normal cash flows

A set of cash flows with all outflows occurring at the beginning of the set.

The **payback (PB)** statistic remains very popular because it is easy to compute. All we have to do is keep a running subtotal of the cumulative sum of the cash flows up to the point that this sum exactly offsets the initial investment. That is, PB is determined by using this formula:

$$0 = \sum_{n=0}^{PB} CF_n \qquad \textbf{(13-1)}$$

Notice that this computation demands a couple of strong assumptions:

1. The concept of payback rests on the assumption that cash flows are **normal,** with all outflows occurring at the beginning of the project's life, so that we can think of the PB statistic as a type of recovery period for that initial investment. This implies that payback would be meaningless for a set of non-normal cash flows. If, for example, a project required an infusion of cash after it started, such as the cash outflows shown at times 1 and 2 in Example 13-5 (later in the chapter), we could not calculate a payback statistic.
2. Note that PB will not be very likely to occur in an exact, round number of periods, so we will need to make another assumption concerning how cash inflows occur *during* the course of a year. The usual approach to handling this condition is to assume that cash flows arrive smoothly throughout each period, allowing us to count out the months and days to estimate the exact payback statistic.

LG13-2

Payback Benchmark

The payback method shows an additional weakness in that its benchmark must be exogenously specified: In other words, it is not always the same value, nor is it determined by the required rate of return or any other input variable. Ideally, the maximum allowable PB for a project should be set based on some relevant external constraint, such as the number of periods until capital providers need their money back, or the time available until a project would violate a bond issue's protective covenants. As you might suspect, in real life managers often indicate the maximum allowable payback—that is, set the exogenous specification—arbitrarily.

Let us assume that we have been told that the maximum allowable payback for this project is three years. With this decision rule, we want to accept projects that show a calculated statistic less than the benchmark of three years:

Accept project if PB ≤ Maximum allowable PB

Reject project if PB > Maximum allowable PB **(13-2)**

EXAMPLE 13-1

LG13-2

For interactive versions of this example visit www.mhhe.com/can3e

Payback Calculation

Consider the sample project with the cash flows shown in Table 13.2. Should this project be accepted based on payback if the maximum allowable payback period is three years?

table 13.2 | **Payback Calculation on Sample Project with Normal Cash Flows**

Year:	0	1	2	3	4	5
Cash flow	−$10,000	$2,500	$3,500	$5,000	$4,000	$2,000
Cumulative cash flow	−10,000	−7,500	−4,000	1,000		

SOLUTION:

To calculate this project's payback, we would first calculate the cumulative cash flows until they went from negative to positive. From this first step, we know that payback occurs somewhere between periods 2 and 3. To determine the exact statistic, we note that if the magnitude of the last negative cumulative cash flow represents how much cash flow we *need* during year 3 to achieve payback, then the marginal cash flow for year 3 represents how much we will *get* over the course of the entire third year. By linear interpolation, our exact statistic is therefore where we start (year 2) plus what we need (the absolute value of the last negative cumulative cash flow, −$4,000) over what we are going to get during that year:

$$PB = 2 + \frac{\$4{,}000}{\$5{,}000} = 2.8 \text{ years}$$

Since our calculated payback is 2.8 years and the maximum allowable payback period is three years, we should accept the project based on the payback rule.

Similar to Problems 13-5, 13-6, 13-17, 13-23, self-test problem 1

CALCULATOR HINTS

[CF0] = −10000
[CF1] = 2500
[CF2] = 3500
[CF3] = 5000
[CF4] = 4000
[CF5] = 2000
NPV
[I] = 12
CPT [PB] = 2.80

Discounted Payback Statistic

LG13-2

Yet another problem that arises when we use the payback technique is that it does not recognize or incorporate the time value of money. To compensate for this exclusion, we often calculate the **discounted payback (DPB)** statistic instead, using the following formula:

discounted payback (DPB)
A capital budgeting method that generates decision rules and associated metrics that choose projects based on how quickly they return their initial investment plus interest.

$$0 = \sum_{n=0}^{DPB} \frac{CF_n}{(1+i)^n} \qquad \textbf{(13-3)}$$

Notice that all we are doing here is summing the *present values* of the cash flows until we get a cumulative sum of zero, instead of summing the cash flows themselves as we did for the PB statistic. Other than that, we follow all the steps in the computation of DPB just as we did for the PB statistic.

Discounted Payback Benchmark

LG13-2

We may be tempted to assume that we should simply use the same maximum allowable payback benchmark for DPB that we used for PB. If we did so, then we would obviously have to reject this project, since its calculated DPB is 3.56 years (Example 13-2) versus a stated maximum allowable time of only three years. However, we should be very cautious about applying the same benchmark to DPB that we did to PB. To see why, recall that payback calculations only make sense when applied to normal cash flows, so we would assume that we will be dealing with normal cash flows here. But think about *which* cash flows are affected when we switch from calculating payback to discounted payback: Only the ones in the future will fall to lower values, because the present value of the time 0 cash flow will always be the same as its nominal value. And, if the future cash flows are all positive and the initial cash flow is negative, then it is only the positive cash flows that will be affected by switching to cumulative present value for DPB.

In other words, we would expect the calculated DPB statistic to always be larger than the "regular" PB statistic because DPB incorporates the interest you must pay until you reach the benchmark. Said another way, DPB will always take

EXAMPLE 13-2

LG13-2

For interactive versions of this example visit www.mhhe.com/can3e

Discounted Payback Calculation

Consider the same project from Example 13-1. To calculate this project's discounted payback, we would first need to calculate the PV of each cash flow separately. Assuming a 12 percent interest rate, we would calculate these values as shown in Table 13.3.

table 13.3 | **Discounted Payback Calculation: Present Values of Cash Flows**

Year:	0	1	2	3	4	5
Cash flow	−$10,000.00	$2,500.00	$3,500.00	$5,000.00	$4,000.00	$2,000.00
Cash flow present value	−10,000.00	2,232.14	2,790.18	3,558.90	2,542.07	1,134.85

In Table 13.4 we calculate the cumulative present value of the cash flows until they switch from negative to positive:

table 13.4 | **Discounted Payback Calculation on Sample Project with Normal Cash Flows**

Year:	0	1	2	3	4	5
Cash flow	−$10,000.00	$2,500.00	$3,500.00	$5,000.00	$4,000.00	$2,000.00
Cash flow present value	−10,000.00	2,232.14	2,790.18	3,558.90	2,542.07	1,134.85
Cumulative cash flow PV	−10,000.00	−7,767.86	−4,977.68	−1,418.78	1,123.29	

CALCULATOR HINTS

[CF0] = −10000
[CF1] = 2500
[CF2] = 3500
[CF3] = 5000
[CF4] = 4000
[CF5] = 2000
NPV
[I] = 12
CPT [DPB] = 3.56

SOLUTION:

As before, we can stop once the cumulative values go from negative to positive. In this case, linear interpolation will give us a DPB statistic of:

$$DPB = 3 + \frac{\$1,418.78}{\$2,542.07} = 3.56 \text{ years}$$

Similar to Problems 13-7, 13-8, 13-18, 13-24, self-test problem 1

MATH COACH

Payback and Discounted Payback Using Financial Calculators and Spreadsheet Programs

Most financial calculators and spreadsheet programs (with the notable exception of Texas Instrument's BA II Plus Professional) will not compute PB or DPB for you. Instead, you have to go through the process of cumulating cash flows or the PV of cash flows noted in Examples 13-1, 13-2, and 13-3.

longer to achieve payback if you are "chipping away" at the same-sized initial cash outflow with the present values of a bunch of positive cash inflows rather than their simple nominal values. Therefore, it probably is not fair to hold the DPB statistic up to the same benchmark we use for the PB statistic.

What benchmark should we use? Well, as with PB, management will set the DPB maximum allowable payback exogenously and, once again, often arbitrarily. Let us assume that we are told that senior management has set the maximum allowable payback for DPB as 3.5 years.

$$\begin{aligned}&\text{Accept project if calculated DPB} \le \text{Maximum allowable discounted payback} \\ &\text{Reject project if calculated DPB} > \text{Maximum allowable discounted payback}\end{aligned} \quad \textbf{(13-4)}$$

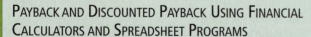

Since our calculated DPB is 3.56 years and the maximum allowable amount is 3.5 years, we should reject the project.

Payback and Discounted Payback Strengths and Weaknesses

LG13-1

A common criticism of PB is that it does not account for the time value of money. The use of PV formulas in computing DPB compensates for TVM, but DPB is not intended to really replace PB, but rather to complement it, providing additional information to analyze capital budgeting decisions.

For example, if we consider a typical, normal payback statistic based on a set of cash flows as a loan problem in which the company borrows the money for the initial investment and then pays it off over time, then PB will intuitively equal the amount of time necessary to repay just principal on the loan, and DPB will indicate the time necessary to repay principal plus interest.

Both PB and DPB have yet another serious flaw. Both decision statistics completely ignore any cash flows that accrue *after* the project reaches its respective payback benchmark. Ignoring this vital information can have serious implications when managers choose between two mutually exclusive projects that have very similar paybacks but very different cash flows after payback is achieved.

EXAMPLE 13-3

LG13-2

Payback Calculation for Alternative Project

For interactive versions of this example visit www.mhhe.com/can3e

Consider once again the sample project shown in Table 13.2. As we calculated in Example 13-1, that project has a PB statistic of 2.8 years. Now, compare that project to the one shown in Table 13.5:

table 13.5 **Payback Calculation on Alternative Sample Project with Normal Cash Flows**

Year:	0	1	2	3	4	5
Cash flow	−$10,000	$2,500	$3,500	$4,000	$104,000	$102,000
Cash flow present value	−10,000	−7,500	−4,000	0	0	0

SOLUTION:

This project would have a slightly higher PB statistic of 3.0. Given that it still achieves payback in exactly the maximum allowable three years, it should be highly favored over the first project due to the large positive cash flows that will accrue in the later years. But managers who ignore this aspect of the PB rule and who focus only on the PB statistics of these two projects will likely incorrectly choose the first project due to its lower PB statistic.

Note that NPV will *not* suffer from this problem. Since the NPV statistic takes all of a project's cash flows into account, there aren't "remaining" cash flows to get left out of the statistic as there are with PB and DPB.

Similar to Problems 13-5, 13-6, 13-17, 13-23

TIME OUT

13-1 Which should we expect to be larger: a project's payback statistic, or its discounted payback statistic?

13-2 If the discount rate is increased, will a project's discounted payback period increase or decrease?

LG13-1

13.5 • Net Present Value

net present value (NPV)

A technique that generates a decision rule and associated metric for choosing projects based on the total discounted value of their cash flows.

At its heart, **net present value (NPV)** represents the "purest" of capital budgeting rules, measuring exactly the value we are interested in: the amount of wealth increase we expect from accepting a project. As we cover in more detail below, the NPV method measures this expected wealth increase by computing the difference between the present values of a project's cash inflows and outflows. Since this calculation includes the necessary capital expenditures and other startup costs of the project as cash outflows, a positive value indicates that the project is desirable—that it more than covers all of the necessary resource costs to do the project.

LG13-3

NPV Statistic

We actually already know how to calculate the NPV statistic. In fact, we used a very similar approach in developing bond and stock pricing equations. The NPV statistic is simply the sum of all the cash flows' present values:

$$NPV = \frac{CF_0}{(1+i)^0} + \frac{CF_1}{(1+i)^1} + \cdots + \frac{CF_N}{(1+i)^N}$$

$$= \sum_{n=0}^{N} \frac{CF_n}{(1+i)^n} \qquad \textbf{(13-5)}$$

EXAMPLE 13-4

LG13-2

For interactive versions of this example visit www.mhhe.com/can3e

NPV for a Normal Set of Cash Flows

A company is evaluating a project with a set of normal cash flows using a risk-appropriate discount rate of 12 percent as shown in Table 13.6. Compute the NPV to determine whether the company should undertake the project.

table 13.6 | **Sample Project with Normal Cash Flows**

Year:	0	1	2	3	4	5
Cash flow	−$10,000	$2,500	$3,500	$5,000	$4,000	$2,000

CALCULATOR HINTS

[CF0] =	−10000
[CF1] =	2500
[CF2] =	3500
[CF3] =	5000
[CF4] =	4000
[CF5] =	2000
NPV	
[I] =	12
CPT [NPV] =	2,258.15

SOLUTION:

The NPV statistic for this project will be:

$$NPV = \frac{-\$10{,}000}{(1.12)^0} + \frac{\$2{,}500}{(1.12)^1} + \frac{\$3{,}500}{(1.12)^2} + \frac{\$5{,}000}{(1.12)^3} + \frac{\$4{,}000}{(12.1)^4} + \frac{\$2{,}000}{(1.12)^5}$$

$$= \$2{,}258.15 > 0$$

The NPV decision will be to *accept* the project.

When you first start calculating NPV, it is easy to miss its deeper meaning. A relatively small NPV, such as the $2,258.15 figure in this example, raises the question of whether $2,258.15 is "worth it," in this sense: Will the project cover the opportunity cost of using the $10,000 of necessary capital? The point, of course, is that the $2,258.15 is above and beyond the recovery of that opportunity cost, so, *yes, it's worth it.*

Similar to Problems 13-1, 13-2, 13-21, 13-27, self-test problem 1

MATH COACH

Financial Calculators versus Spreadsheet Programs

While financial calculators expect to be told CF0 when being asked to compute NPV, the NPV functions in spreadsheet programs such as Microsoft Excel usually *don't* want to be told CF0. Instead, they expect you to handle the inclusion of CF0 in the calculation of the NPV statistic outside the NPV function. For example, if you wanted to find the NPV of the cash flows in Example 13-4 using Excel, the function would look like "=NPV(.12,2500,3500,5000,4000,2000) − 10000".

MATH COACH

Using a Financial Calculator—Part 2 (Revisited)

The TVM worksheet present in most financial calculators has been fine, so far, for the types of TVM problems we've been solving. Sometimes we had to use the worksheet two or three times for a single problem, but that was usually because we needed an intermediate calculation to input into another TVM equation.

In this chapter, we will generally be using simpler TVM equations (i.e., PV and FV), but we'll find ourselves having to use them repeatedly, making only small variations in inputs over and over again within the same problem. We're also going to run up against the problem of cash flow inconsistencies in most projects. If you thought the cash flows of stocks jumped around a lot, wait until you see what project cash flows do! If we stick with the TVM worksheet, these inconsistent cash flows will be a problem for us. If we want to solve for a "common" *i* or *N* value, the TVM worksheet won't let us enter multiple cash flows unless we're solving an annuity problem. (The one notable exception to this has been when we used the TVM worksheet to simultaneously solve the annuity/lump sum problems that arise with bonds. If you recall, those problems require agreement between the inputs to the annuity and the lump sum problems. This kind of agreement is highly unlikely to occur in other circumstances.)

Remember that most financial calculators also have built-in worksheets specifically designed for computing NPV in problems with multiple nonconstant cash flows. In many cases, they will also calculate most of the other decision rule statistics that we're going to be discussing.

Here is what we already know: To make calculator worksheets as flexible as possible, they are usually divided into two parts—one for input, which we'll refer to as the CF (cash flow) worksheet, and one or more for calculating decision statistics. We'll go over the conventions concerning the CF worksheet here. The CF worksheet is usually designed to handle inputting sets of multiple cash flows as quickly as possible. As a result, it normally consists of two sets of variables or cells—one for the cash flows and one to hold a set of frequency counts for the cash flows, so that we can tell it we have seven $1,500 cash flows in a row instead of having to enter $1,500 seven times.

Using the frequency counts to reduce the number of inputs is handy, but you must take care. Frequency counts are only good for embedded annuities of identical cash flows. You have to ensure that you don't mistake another kind of cash flow for an annuity.

Also, using frequency counts will usually affect the way that the calculator counts time periods. As an example, let's talk about how we would put the set of cash flows shown here into a CF worksheet:

Period	0	1	2	3	4	5	6	7	8
	10%								
Cash flow	−$800	$150	$200		$150	$150	$150	$75	$75

To designate which particular value we'll place into each particular cash flow cell in this worksheet, we'll note the value and the cell identifier, such as CF0, CF1, and so forth. We'll do the same for the frequency cells, using F1, F2, etc., to identify which CF cell the frequency cell goes with. (Note that in most calculators, CF0 is treated as a unique value with an unalterable frequency of 1; we're going to make the same assumption here so you'll never see a listing for F0.) For this sample timeline, our inputs would be:

−$800	[CF0]		
$150	[CF1]	1	[F1]
$200	[CF2]	1	[F2]
$0	[CF3]	1	[F3]
$150	[CF4]	3	[F4]
$75	[CF5]	2	[F5]

Then, on the NPV worksheet, you would simply need to enter the interest rate and solve for the NPV:

10%	[I]
[CPT]	[NPV] = −$144.61

Note a few important things about this example:

1. We had to manually enter a value of $0 for CF3: If we hadn't, the calculator wouldn't have known about it and would have implicitly assumed that CF4 came one period after CF2.
2. Once we use a frequency cell for one cash flow, all numbering on any subsequent cash flows that we enter into the calculator is going to be messed up, at least from our point of view. For instance, the first $75 isn't what we would call "CF5," is it? We'd call it "CF7" because it comes at time period 7; but calculators usually treat CF5 as "the fifth set of cash flows," so we'll just have to try to do the same to be consistent.
3. If we really don't need to use frequency cells, we will usually just leave them out of the guidance instructions in this chapter to save space.

LG13-3

NPV Benchmark

NPV analysis includes all of the cash flows—both inflows and outflows. This inclusion implies that any required investment in the project is already factored in, so any NPV greater than zero represents value *above and beyond* that investment. Accordingly, the NPV decision rule is:

$$\text{Accept project if NPV} \geq 0$$
$$\text{Reject project if NPV} < 0 \qquad \textbf{(13-6)}$$

EXAMPLE 13-5

LG13-3

For interactive versions of this example visit www.mhhe.com/can3e

CALCULATOR HINTS

[CF0] = 5000
[CF1] = −10000
[CF2] = −3000
[CF3] = 5000
[CF4] = 4000
[CF5] = 2000
NPV
[I] = 12
CPT [NPV] = 915.67

NPV for a Non-Normal Set of Cash Flows

Note that the NPV rule works equally well with non-normal cash flows, such as those for the project shown in Table 13.7. Compute the NPV for this project to determine whether it should be accepted. Use a 12 percent discount rate.

table 13.7 | **Sample Project with Normal Cash Flows**

Year:	0	1	2	3	4	5
Cash flow	$5,000	−$10,000	−$3,000	$5,000	$4,000	$2,000

SOLUTION:

The NPV statistic will be:

$$NPV = \frac{\$5{,}000}{(1.12)^0} + \frac{-\$10{,}000}{(1.12)^1} + \frac{-\$3{,}000}{(1.12)^2} + \frac{\$5{,}000}{(1.12)^3} + \frac{\$4{,}000}{(12.1)^4} + \frac{\$2{,}000}{(1.12)^5}$$
$$= \$915.67 > 0$$

Based on this NPV, the project should be accepted.

Similar to Problems 13-3, 13-4

NPV Strengths and Weaknesses

LG13-3

One strength of the NPV rule is that the statistic is *not* a ratio as with the rate-based decision statistics. It works equally well for independent projects and for choosing among mutually exclusive projects. In the latter case, the mutually exclusive project with the highest NPV should add the most wealth to the firm, and so management should accept it over any competing projects.

Unfortunately, this ability to choose among projects stems from exactly what gives it its greatest weakness—the format of the statistic. Since the NPV statistic is a dollar figure, it accurately reflects the net effect of any differences in timing or scale of two projects' expected cash flows. It thus allows comparisons of two projects' NPV statistics to fully incorporate those differences. However, this same currency format often results in confusion for uninformed decision makers: Managers not completely familiar with how the NPV statistic works often insist on comparing the NPV to the *cost* of the project, not understanding that the cost is already incorporated into the NPV.

TIME OUT

13-3 Why is a project's cost *not* an appropriate benchmark for its NPV?

13-4 Assuming that it is fairly priced, what should be the NPV of a purchase decision on a corporate bond?

13.6 • Internal Rate of Return and Modified Internal Rate of Return

LG13-1

internal rate of return (IRR)

A capital budgeting technique that generates decision rules and associated metrics for choosing projects based on the implicit expected geometric average of a project's rate of return.

The **internal rate of return (IRR)** technique is, by far, the most popular rate-based capital budgeting technique. The main reason for its popularity is that, if you are considering a project with normal cash flows that is independent of other projects, the IRR statistic will give exactly the same accept/reject decision as the NPV rule does. This is due to the fact that NPV and IRR are very closely related. NPV is the sum of the present values of the cash flows at a particular interest rate (usually the firm's cost of capital), whereas IRR is the interest rate that will cause the NPV to be equal to zero.

Solve for NPV: Solve for IRR:

$$NPV = \sum_{n=0}^{N} \frac{CF_n}{(1+i)^n} \quad \text{versus} \quad 0 = \sum_{n=0}^{N} \frac{CF_n}{(1+IRR)^n} \qquad \textbf{(13-7)}$$

As long as the cash flows of a project are normal, the NPV calculated in the equation on the left will be greater than zero if and only if the IRR calculated in the equation on the right is greater than i.

However, IRR runs into a lot of problems if project cash flows are not normal or if you are using this statistic to decide among mutually exclusive projects. As we will show, we can correct for the non-normal cash flows, but all of the rate-based decision statistics will exhibit the problem of choosing between multiple projects that we discussed above.

EXAMPLE 13-6

LG13-4

IRR Calculation

For interactive versions of this example visit www.mhhe.com/can3e

CALCULATOR HINTS

[CF0] = −10000
[CF1] = 2500
[CF2] = 3500
[CF3] = 5000
[CF4] = 4000
[CF5] = 2000
IRR
[CPT] [IRR] = 20.61

Looking once again at our sample set of normal cash flows from Table 13.6, IRR will be the solution to:

$$0 = \frac{-\$10,000}{(1 + IRR)^0} + \frac{\$2,500}{(1 + IRR)^1} + \frac{\$3,500}{(1 + IRR)^2} + \frac{\$5,000}{(1 + IRR)^3} + \frac{\$4,000}{(1 + IRR)^4} + \frac{\$2,000}{(1 + IRR)^5}$$

$$IRR = 0.2062, \text{ or } 20.62\%$$

Similar to Problems 13-9, 13-10, 13-19, 13-25, self-test problem 1

LG13-4

Internal Rate of Return Statistic

To solve for the IRR statistic, we simply solve the NPV formula for the interest rate that will make NPV equal zero:

$$0 = \sum_{n=0}^{N} \frac{CF_n}{(1 + IRR)^n} \qquad \textbf{(13-8)}$$

Unfortunately, we cannot solve directly for the interest rate that will set NPV equal to zero. We either have to use trial-and-error to determine the appropriate rate, or we have to rely on a calculator or computer, both of which use much the same approach.

LG13-4

Internal Rate of Return Benchmark

Once we calculate the IRR, we must then compare the decision statistic to the relevant cost of capital for the project—the average rate of return necessary to pay back the project's capital providers, given the risk that the project represents:

$$\begin{aligned} &\text{Accept project if IRR} \geq \text{Cost of capital} \\ &\text{Reject project if IRR} < \text{Cost of capital} \end{aligned} \qquad \textbf{(13-9)}$$

At this point, you may find yourself getting a little confused about which rate is *the* interest rate. The IRR statistic will equal the expected rate of return, which incorporates risk (as probabilities). We will compare that expected rate of return to the cost of capital, which is often called the *required rate of return*. Up until this chapter, we have been using all of these phrases interchangeably for "*the*" interest rate. We have been able to get away with doing so to this point because stocks, bonds, and all other types of financial assets trade in relatively liquid, competitive financial markets. In liquid markets, the rate of return you expect to earn is pretty much equal to the rate of return you require for taking on that particular security's risk. In such an environment, it makes sense to assume that we are not going to be able to earn any "extra" return or economic profit above and beyond what is appropriate for the amount of risk we are bearing.

Remember, though, that in this chapter, we are no longer talking about *financial* assets, but *real* assets such as land, factories with inventories, and production lines. These types of assets do not generally trade in perfectly competitive markets. Instead, they trade in quite illiquid markets in which an individual or a firm can gain at least some amount of market or monopoly power by virtue of technological, legal, or marketing expertise.

We noted this difference at the beginning of this chapter when we differentiated between formulas for financial assets such as stocks and bonds and the equations we are using in this chapter to value projects. The formulas we used to value stocks and bonds use "=" signs because those assets trade in nearly perfectly competitive markets, where what you get is (approximately, at least) equal to what you paid for it. Here, on the other hand, we examine situations in which companies seek to choose projects that are worth *more* than what they pay for them—leaving room for economic profit. That is why all of these capital budgeting rules use ">" and "<" signs.

So, when we deal with physical asset projects, we have to expect that two different rates of return will arise. The best way to think of these two rates is as the *expected* rate of return (IRR), and the *required* rate of return (i). We only want to invest in projects where the rate we expect to get (IRR) is larger than the rate investors require (i) based on the project's expected return, including risk.[1]

Problems with Internal Rate of Return

LG13-4

As we mentioned previously, IRR will give the same accept/reject decision as NPV if two conditions hold true:

1. The project has normal cash flows.
2. We are evaluating the project independently of other projects—that is, we are not considering mutually exclusive projects.

NPV profile

A graph of a project's NPV as a function of the cost of capital.

LG13-5

To see the problems that arise if these conditions do *not* hold, we will make use of a tool called the **NPV profile.** This is simply a graph of a project's NPV as a function of possible capital costs. The NPV profile for our sample project with normal cash flows from Table 13.6. appears as Figure 13.1.

figure 13.1

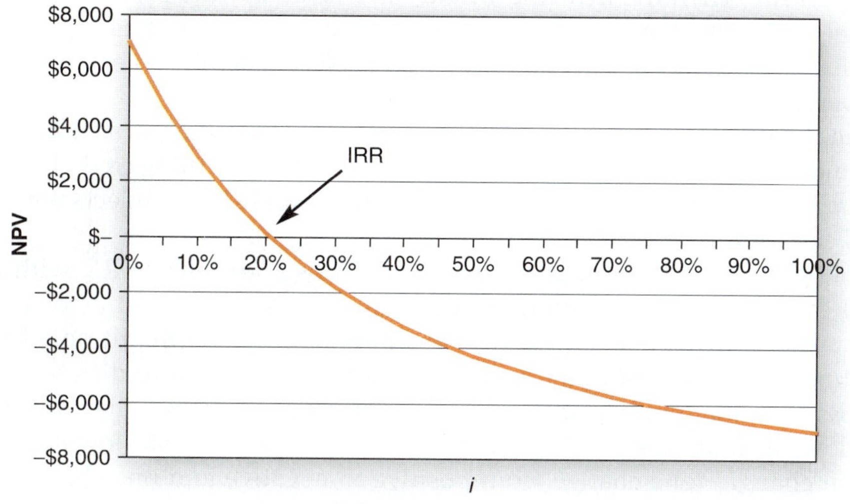

NPV Profile for Sample Normal Cash Flows

This graph presents our sample project's NPV profile, using the normal cash flows listed in Table 13.6.

[1]As explained in earlier chapters, by definition the expected rate of return incorporates risk.

As you can see, the NPV profile for this normal set of cash flows slopes downward. As we noted previously concerning the relationship between the PB and DPB statistics, increasing values of i with a normal set of cash flows affect the present value of positive cash flows, but not that of negative cash flows. All sets of normal cash flows will therefore share this general, downward-sloping shape.

Note that IRR appears on this graph as the intersection of the NPV profile with the x-axis (horizontal)—the intersection will represent the interest rate where NPV equals exactly zero. With normal cash flows such as these, the constant downward slope of the NPV profile dictates that only one such intersection will exist for each project.

TIME OUT

13-5 Is it possible for the NPV profile of a finite set of normal cash flows to never cross the x-axis?

13-6 Suppose a normal set of cash flows has an IRR equal to zero. Would NPV accept or reject such a project?

LG13-5

IRR and NPV Profiles with Non-Normal Cash Flows

But let us revisit what happens to the NPV profile if cash flows are *not* normal. The NPV profile will not necessarily slope continually downward and thus may cross over the x-axis at more than one interest rate. In this case we may find more than one valid IRR for which NPV equals zero. An example of such an NPV profile, constructed from the cash flows in Table 13.7, appears in Figure 13.2.

In this instance, the project shows two valid IRRs: one at 23.62 percent and another at 88.62 percent. Which of these two should we use as "the" statistic? Well, it depends on what the firm pays as the actual cost of capital. If the firm pays 12 percent for capital, then using either of these two IRR values would generate a correct "accept" decision, as the project *does* have a positive NPV at $i = 12$ percent. But what if the firm paid a relatively high cost of capital, for example, 30 percent? Then the IRR rule would have us accept the project if we used the higher value (88.62 percent) as the project's statistic, but reject it if we used the lower IRR (23.62 percent). Of course, since the project generates a negative NPV if i is 30 percent, we would actually want to reject the project.

Using the IRR technique requires a bit more complicated analysis if we come across more than one valid IRR like this. Perhaps the best thing to do in such a situation is to simply use a decision statistic other than IRR on projects with non-normal cash flows.

If you (or, more likely, upper management) insist on using IRR with non-normal cash flows, you are going to need to use some trial and error to find all the possible IRRs. It will help to know how many there might possibly be. According to the Rule of Signs,[2] we can end up with no more different positive IRRs than the number of sign changes in the cash flows—that is, inflows to outflows or outflows to inflows. Since our non-normal cash flow set shows two sign changes (one change from positive to negative and one change from negative to positive), we know that the two IRRs we have found constitute the entire possible set.

[2]First described by René Descartes in his 1637 manuscript *La Geometrie.*

figure 13.2

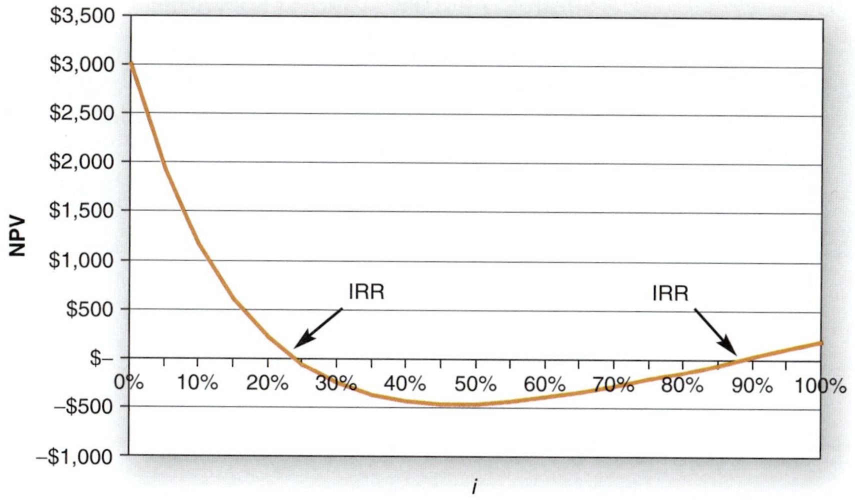

NPV Profile for Sample Non-Normal Cash Flows

Notice how the graph shows two valid IRRs. Which one should you use?

Luckily we can solve IRR's problems associated with non-normal cash flows by using the modified internal rate of return (MIRR), which also accounts for another problem associated with IRR, that of an unrealistic reinvestment rate assumption.

Differing Reinvestment Rate Assumptions of NPV and IRR

LG13-5

In addition to the problems associated with non-normal cash flows and handling mutually exclusive projects discussed above, IRR also has a different assumption than NPV concerning what we do with the cash inflows once we get them back. IRR assumes that any cash inflows will be reinvested in another project with the same earning power as the first project, while NPV assumes that cash inflows will be reinvested at the cost of capital, *i.*

Which assumption is more reasonable? NPV's is, because one way to effectively "earn" the cost of capital is to pay back your capital investors, and all companies have this option. On the other hand, IRR's assumption seems a little far-fetched: If we assume that this project beat out a bunch of other projects at step 2 of the decision process, it must have had the highest possible IRR among all the alternatives, right? But now that the cash flows are rolling in, we find another project with *the same* "highest" possible rate of return? Seems like a little too much to expect, doesn't it?

Modified Internal Rate of Return Statistic

LG13-4

The name **modified internal rate of return** is a little misleading. We are going to calculate IRR the same way we did before, but we are going to *modify* the set of cash flows to account for the cost of capital before we calculate IRR. We first use the cost of capital to "move" all the negative cash flows to the initial project start date (i.e., time 0) and all the positive cash inflows to the project termination date—and only *then* will we use the regular steps to calculate IRR.

modified internal rate of return (MIRR)

A capital budgeting method that converts a project's cash flows using a more consistent reinvestment rate prior to applying the IRR decision rule.

MATH COACH

MIRR Using Financial Calculators and Spreadsheet Programs

Notice that we have assumed that both the positive and negative cash flows get moved using the same interest rate. In many situations, practitioners want to move the negative cash flows using one interest rate and the positive cash flows using another. Because of this, both spreadsheet programs and more advanced financial calculators allow for the use of two interest rates in exactly that way. For now, if you are using a calculator or spreadsheet program that requires two interest rates, just use the cost of capital for both rates.

EXAMPLE 13-7

LG13-4

For interactive versions of this example visit www.mhhe.com/can3e

MIRR Calculation

Turning once again to the sample non-normal project cash flows in Table 13.7, and assuming that the firm still faces a cost of capital of 12 percent, we convert the cash flows as shown in Table 13.8.

table 13.8 MIRR Cash Flow Adjustments for Sample Project with Non-Normal Cash Flows

Year:	0	1	2	3	4	5
Cash flow	$5,000.00	−$10,000.00	−$3,000.00	$5,000.00	$4,000.00	$2,000.00

CALCULATOR HINTS

[CF0] = 5000
[CF1] = −10000
[CF2] = −3000
[CF3] = 5000
[CF4] = 4000
[CF5] = 2000
IRR
[I] = 12
[RI] = 12
[CPT] [MOD] = 13.76

SOLUTION:

Finding the PV of just the negative cash flows:

Year:	0	1	2	3	4	5
Cash flow		−$10,000.00	−$3,000.00			
Present value of cash flows at 12 percent		−8,928.57	−2,391.58			
Sum of PV of cash flows	−11,320.15					

And finding the FV of just the positive cash flows:

Year:	0	1	2	3	4	5
Cash flow	$5,000.00			$5,000.00	$4,000.00	$2,000.00
Future value of cash flows at 12 percent	8,811.71			6,272.00	4,480.00	2,000.00
Sum of FV of cash flows						21,563.71

Gives us the following set of modified cash flows:

Year:	0	1	2	3	4	5
Cash flow	−$11,320.15					$21,563.71

With this new set of modified cash flows, the MIRR is:

$$0 = \frac{-\$11{,}320.15}{(1 + IRR)^0} + \frac{\$21{,}563.71}{(1 + IRR)^5}$$

$$IRR = 0.1376, \text{ or } 13.76\%$$

Since our MIRR decision statistic exceeds the 12 percent cost of capital, we would accept the project under the MIRR method, which uses the same benchmark as the IRR rule. Notice that, regardless of how many possible IRRs a project may have, it will only ever have *one* possible MIRR. When you take a bunch of cash flows and convert them into two cash flows, one negative and one positive, you will only ever see one change in sign.

Similar to Problems 13-11, 13-12, 13-20, 13-26, self-test problem 1

IRRs, MIRRs, and NPV Profiles with Mutually Exclusive Projects

LG13-5

Even if we use the MIRR method for a project with non-normal cash flows, we can still run into problems if we're trying to use it to choose between mutually exclusive projects.

Two (or more) projects are **mutually exclusive** if management can accept one, the other, or neither, but not both, projects. As we will discuss, if we compare two mutually exclusive projects using a rate-based decision statistic, problems can arise if the projects' cash flows exhibit differences in *scale* or *timing* (i.e., the size of the initial investment in each project). Over time, a "large" project that earns a slightly lower rate of return may be a better choice for the firm than a "small" project that earns a higher rate, but we will see that the rate-based decision techniques do not do well in choosing between these types of alternative projects.

mutually exclusive projects
Groups or pairs of projects where you can accept one but not all.

What makes two or more projects mutually exclusive? Generally, mutually exclusive projects either share a common asset or target a common market, but the firm can only spare resources for one of them, or the market may only accept one product. Consider the prototypical example of mutually exclusive projects: A landowner owns two plots of land on either side of a river that people want to cross, and she is considering either building a bridge or operating a ferry for that purpose.

First, let us assume there is enough land on each lot to provide space for bridge footings or for pier pilings, but not for both. In this case, the two plots of land represent assets that the two projects cannot share, which is the first factor making the bridge and the ferry mutually exclusive projects.

Second, even if the land provided enough room to build both ferry landing piers and bridge footings, it stands to reason that no one would take the ferry if they could simply drive across the bridge—so the two projects' inability to share a potential target market provides a second reason why the projects are mutually exclusive.

To see the problems associated with choosing between two mutually exclusive projects using a rate-based decision statistic, let us suppose that we face a choice between two mutually exclusive projects with the cash flows shown in Table 13.9.

Calculating the NPVs for these two projects across a range of possible rates as shown in Table 13.10 will yield the NPV profiles shown in Figure 13.3.

table 13.9 Sample Mutually Exclusive Projects

Year:	0	1	2	3	4	5
Project A cash flows	−$800	$600	$500	$40	$0	$200
Project B cash flows	−400	250	200	250	50	100

table 13.10 NPV Profiles

i	NPV A	NPV B
0%	$540.00	$450.00
2	487.66	409.68
4	439.15	372.48
6	394.07	338.08
8	352.09	306.22
10	312.91	276.63
12	276.27	249.12
14	241.92	223.48
16	209.67	199.54
18	179.33	177.16
20	150.75	156.20
22	123.76	136.54
24	98.25	118.07
26	74.10	100.69
28	51.21	84.32
30	29.47	68.88
32	8.80	54.30
34	−10.86	40.51
36	−29.61	27.45
38	−47.49	15.07
40	−64.56	3.33

figure 13.3

NPV Profiles for Sample Mutually Exclusive Projects

Notice how the two profiles cross each other in the first quadrant. How will this intersection affect how we apply an IRR decision?

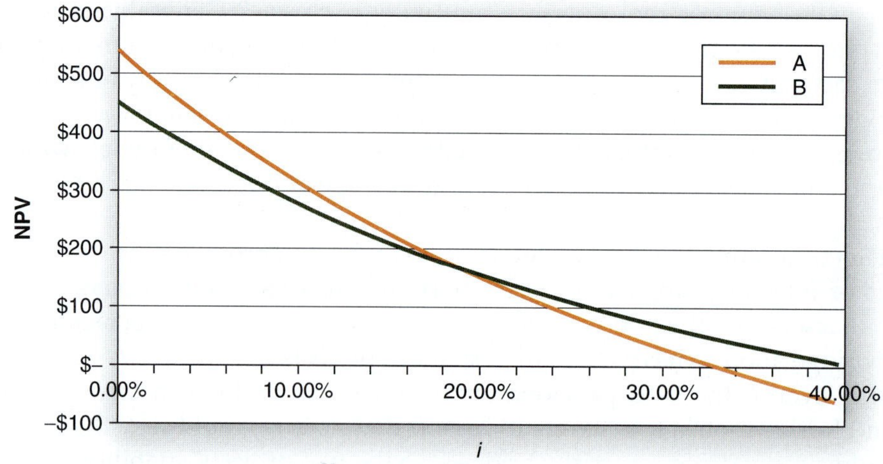

As you can see approximately (and calculate precisely), A's IRR equals 32.88 percent and B's equals 40.59 percent. You will also notice that the two NPV profiles cross each other in the first quadrant, and that intersection is exactly what is going to cause problems for us as we try to apply an IRR decision rule.

table 13.11 | **Decision Process for Projects A and B at $i = 30\%$**

NPV	
1. Compute the statistic for each project.	$NPV_A = \$29.47$ $NPV_B = \$68.88$
2. Have a runoff between the mutually exclusive projects, choosing the one with the best statistic.	$NPV_B > NPV_A$
3. Compare the computed statistic for the winner of the runoff to the benchmark to decide whether to accept or reject.	$\mathbf{NPV_B} > 0$
IRR	
1. Compute the statistic for each project.	$IRR_A = 32.88\%$ $IRR_B = 40.59\%$
2. Have a runoff between the mutually exclusive projects, choosing the one with the best statistic.	$IRR_B > IRR_A$
3. Compare the computed statistic for the winner of the runoff to the benchmark to decide whether to accept or reject.	$\mathbf{IRR_B} > 30\%$

To see why, recall our discussion of the three-step decision process necessary for mutually exclusive projects, and go through that process for both NPV and IRR using a couple of not-so-arbitrary interest rates.

First, let us suppose that the project would be subject to a 30 percent cost of capital. In that case, as per Table 13.11, the NPV for project A would be $29.47 and the NPV for project B would be $68.88. This means that project B would win the runoff. Since its NPV is greater than zero, the NPV decision rule would have us also accept project B.

Likewise, if we were using IRR in the same situation, project B's IRR of 40.59 percent would win the runoff over project A's IRR of 32.88 percent. But since 40.59 percent is greater than the 30 percent cost of capital, IRR would also have us accept project B. These results appear in Table 13.11.

Now let's see what happens if the cost of capital is, say, 10 percent. In that case, as per Table 13.10, the NPV for project A would be $312.91 and the NPV for project B would be $276.63. This means that project A would now win the runoff and, ultimately, would be accepted under the NPV statistic as well.

However, if we were using IRR in the same situation, project B's IRR of 40.59 percent would *still* win the runoff over project A's IRR of 32.88 percent, and, since 40.59 percent is greater than the 30 percent cost of capital, IRR would continue to have us accept project B. These results are summarized in Table 13.12.

table 13.12 | **Decision Process for Projects A and B at $i = 10\%$**

NPV	
1. Compute the statistic for each project.	$NPV_A = \$312.91$ $NPV_B = \$276.63$
2. Have a runoff between the mutually exclusive projects, choosing the one with the best statistic.	$NPV_A > NPV_B$
3. Compare the computed statistic for the winner of the runoff to the benchmark to decide whether to accept or reject.	$\mathbf{NPV_A} > 0$
IRR	
1. Compute the statistic for each project.	$IRR_A = 32.88\%$ $IRR_B = 40.59\%$
2. Have a runoff between the mutually exclusive projects, choosing the one with the best statistic.	$IRR_B > IRR_A$
3. Compare the computed statistic for the winner of the runoff to the benchmark to decide whether to accept or reject.	$\mathbf{IRR_B} > 10\%$

Why is IRR still choosing project B, despite the 30 percent cost of capital? Well, IRR's refusal to "change its mind"[3] arises from a combination of how we calculate the statistic and how we use it in the three-step decision process. Think about it this way: The NPV statistic includes the cost of capital in its calculation, so when we get to the runoff, NPV is able to make an **interest-rate-cognizant** decision. IRR does not incorporate the cost of capital in calculating its statistic. Therefore, when it reaches step 2 it will always be comparing the same two IRRs for two particular projects, no matter what the cost of capital is.

interest-rate cognizant

A decision-making process that includes the cost of capital calculation.

The implication here is that for any interest rate to the right of where the two NPV profiles cross, NPV and IRR will make the same accept/reject decision. For rates to the left of the crossover point, NPV will choose the right project but IRR will chose the wrong project. So, since it is sort of important, how do we calculate the rate at which the two NPV profiles cross? Well, we mathematically manipulate each NPV profile until one comes as close to the x-axis as possible, and then figure out the rate at which they cross each other as the IRR of the other project.

It sounds complicated, but it really is not. All we have to do is subtract one project's cash flows from those of the other, period by period, to get a new set of cash flows that show the differences between the original two projects' cash flows, and then find the IRR of these differences. The values for the cash flows of "A − B," the calculated values for the NPV profile of these differences, and the resulting translated NPV profiles appear in Table 13.13, Table 13.14, and Figure 13.4. Note that A′ will be equal to "A − B," while B′ will be the new, translated, x-axis.

table 13.13 | **Difference in Cash Flows—Sample Mutually Exclusive Projects**

Year:	0	1	2	3	4	5
Project A cash flows	−$800	$600	$500	$ 40	$ 0	$200
Project B cash flows	−400	250	200	250	50	100
A − B	−400	350	300	−210	−50	100

table 13.14 | **NPV Profile, A − B**

i	NPV, A − B
0%	$ 90.00
2	77.98
4	66.67
6	55.99
8	45.88
10	36.28
12	27.15
14	18.45
16	10.13
18	2.17
20	−5.45
22	−12.77
24	− 19.81
26	−26.59
28	−33.12
30	−39.41
32	−45.49
34	−51.37
36	−57.06
38	−62.56
40	−67.89

[3]You will sometimes hear this phenomenon referred to as IRR being "myopic," which is the technical name for nearsightedness.

figure 13.4

Translated NPV Profiles

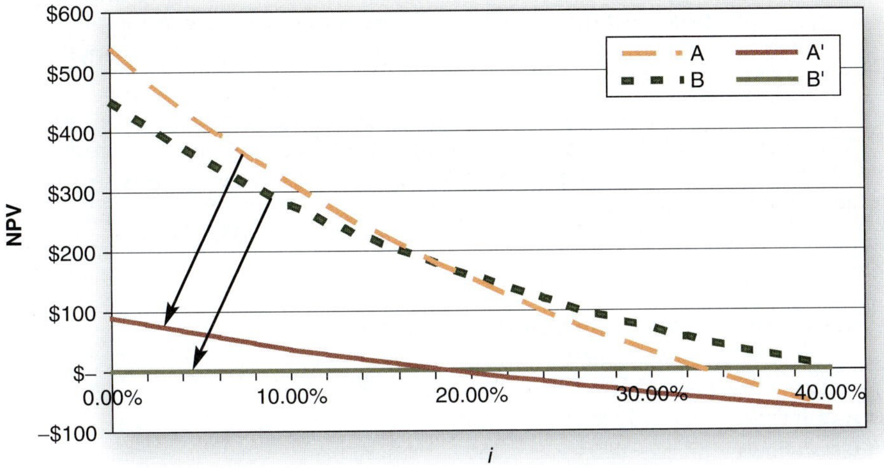

The crossover rate will be equal to the IRR of the "A − B" cash flows:

$$0 = \frac{-\$400}{(1 + IRR)^0} + \frac{\$350}{(1 + IRR)^1} + \frac{\$300}{(1 + IRR)^2} + \frac{-\$210}{(1 + IRR)^3} + \frac{-\$50}{(1 + IRR)^4} + \frac{\$100}{(1 + IRR)^5}$$

$IRR = 0.1856$, or 18.56%

CALCULATOR HINTS

[CF0] = −$400
[CF1] = $350
[CF2] = $300
[CF3] = −$210
[CF4] = −$50
[CF5] = $100
IRR
[CPT] [IRR] = 18.56

So now, IRR will give us the correct answer for these two projects if *i* is greater than 18.56 percent, and will choose exactly the wrong project if *i* is less than 18.56 percent.

You may have noticed that the set of "A − B" cash flows is *not* normal. How, then, can we feel comfortable using IRR to calculate the crossover rate given that we have previously decided not to use IRR with non-normal cash flows? Well, this is a special case: We knew that the two original projects' cash flows *were* normal. So we intuitively understood that their NPV profiles, while not exactly straight lines, at least sloped downward continually. So, if two "almost straight" lines do cross, they are probably only going to cross once. That is, we expect only one solution to the IRR problem for the "A − B" differences in cash flows.

Also notice that we have to worry about IRR giving incorrect decisions only if the NPV profiles cross in the so-called first quadrant of the graph. If they cross outside this quadrant at a rate higher than both projects' IRRs, then we do not have to worry about problems with IRR choosing the wrong project. Any cost of capital high enough for IRR to reject the project at the third step of the IRR decision process will also result in a negative NPV.[4]

[4]Actually, in such cases the IRR rule will still choose the wrong project at step 2 of the decision process, the runoff, but the last step of the decision process, the comparison with the benchmark, will save us. The wrong project may be chosen at the runoff, but if they are both bad projects, they will be rejected anyway.

TIME OUT

13-7 Suppose two projects with normal cash flows, X and Y, have exactly the same required initial investment, but X has a longer payback. Can we say anything about X's IRR versus that of Y?

13-8 Assume you are evaluating a project that requires an initial investment of $5,000 at time zero, then another investment of $4,000 in one year, after which it will have cash inflows of $3,000 per year for five years. How many IRRs could this project possibly have?

table 13.15 | **Sample Mutually Exclusive Projects**

Year:	0	1	2	3	4	5
Project A cash flows	−$800	$600	$500	$ 40	$ 0	$200
Project B cash flows	−400	250	200	250	50	100

LG13-5

MIRR Strengths and Weaknesses

As we have constructed it, the MIRR statistic explicitly corrects IRR's faulty and unreasonable reinvestment rate assumption, implicitly fixing any problems with non-normal cash flows along the way. However, it does not correct the problem of IRR choosing the wrong mutually exclusive project for a particular range of rates. For example, even if we go back to the two sample mutually exclusive projects of Table 13.9 and compute each project's MIRR (using a 12 percent rate to move the cash flows), we will still see that the MIRR of project B (23.39 percent) will *always* be greater than the MIRR of project A (18.85 percent), causing the MIRR to also choose the incorrect project to the left of the crossover rate.

LG13-1

There is an old joke in computer programming that gets reused every time a major software product is revised: "That's not a bug, it's a feature!" Well, this "problem" we are experiencing with IRR and MIRR, as well as NPV, truly *is* a feature. It's a feature of all rate-based decision statistics: They tend to focus on the rate of return *per dollar invested* at the expense of ignoring *how many* dollars are getting invested in each project. IRR and MIRR chose project B all the time because, even though it sometimes had a lower NPV, it was always earning a higher rate of return *per dollar invested.*

What causes this confusion? The two cash flows differ in timing and scale. Looking back at the cash flows associated with our two mutually exclusive projects again (shown again in Table 13.15) we see that project B costs only half as much as project A. Also, project B has a "flatter," less steeply sloped, indifference curve.

TIME OUT

13-9 For a project with normal cash flows, what would you expect the relationship to be between its IRR and its MIRR?

13-10 Describe how you would go about calculating the IRR of a perpetuity.

profitability index (PI)

A decision rule and associated methodology for converting the NPV statistic into a rate-based metric.

13.7 • Profitability Index

Another popular rate-based decision technique is the **profitability index (PI).** PI is based upon NPV, so its results will more closely resemble NPV than will those of IRR or PB/DPB. PI takes the present value of a project's future cash flows and standardizes them by simply dividing by the project's initial investment. The result: We get a decision statistic that measures "bang per buck invested." Such a measure comes in handy when the firm faces resource constraints concerning how much capital is available for new projects.

Profitability Index Statistic

The mathematics of computing the PI are straightforward:

$$PI = \frac{NPV + CF_0}{CF_0} \tag{13-10}$$

EXAMPLE 13-8

LG13-6

Calculation of Profitability Index

Turning yet again to the sample project cash flows in Table 13.6, the PI for that project will be:

$$PI = \frac{\$2{,}258.15 + \$10{,}000}{\$10{,}000} = 1.23$$

Similar to Problems 13-13, 13-14, 13-22, 13-28

For interactive versions of this example visit www.mhhe.com/can3e

Profitability Index Benchmark

Because of its close linkage to the NPV statistic, PI's benchmark is, not surprisingly, identical to that of NPV:

$$\begin{aligned} &\text{Accept project if PI} \geq 1 \\ &\text{Reject project if PI} < 1 \end{aligned} \tag{13-11}$$

Though we might be tempted to assume that, like IRR and MIRR, we should compare the PI to the cost of capital, this is not the case. Remember that the NPV already includes the necessary investment, so any PI above zero is "found money" or the present value of expected economic profits. In this case, the PI of 1.23 is telling us that the project will, roughly speaking, earn the equivalent of a 23 percent return on the initial investment of $10,000 above and beyond the return necessary to repay the initial cost.

TIME OUT

13-11 There is another version of the PI that uses the NPV as its numerator. How would you expect that version's benchmark to change from the version of PI we initially discussed?

13-12 Suppose you have a project whose discounted payback is equal to its termination date. What can you say for sure about its PI? (*Hint:* What will the project's NPV be?)

viewpoints REVISITED

Business Application Solution

ADK's project will have an NPV of:

$$NPV = \frac{-\$5m}{(1.14)^0} + \frac{\$1.2m}{(1.14)^1} + \frac{\$1.6m}{(1.14)^2} + \frac{\$2.3m}{(1.14)^3} + \frac{\$2.8m}{(1.14)^4}$$
$$= \$494{,}038.89 > 0$$

and an IRR of:

$$NPV = \frac{-\$5m}{(1+IRR)^0} + \frac{\$1.2m}{(1+IRR)^1} + \frac{\$1.6m}{(1+IRR)^2} + \frac{\$2.3m}{(1+IRR)^3} + \frac{\$2.8m}{(1+IRR)^4}$$
$$IRR = 18.09\% > 14\%$$

Both the NPV and IRR support accepting the project.

We could also calculate MIRR (16.72 percent) and PI (1.10), and these would provide additional support for accepting the project.

Finally, though we are not given maximum allowable payback or discounted payback, values of 2.96 and 3.70, respectively, would seem to be in an acceptable range, too.

Personal Application Solution

First, we should note that, since cash flows occur every three months, we need to convert the APR of 9 percent to a quarterly rate:

$$i_{qtr} = \left(1 + \frac{0.09}{12}\right)^3 - 1 = 0.0227$$

With these types of cash flows, our choice of decision rules is limited to NPV, MIRR, or PI; we cannot use either the payback rule or IRR because of the non-normality.

The NPV of this project will be:

$$NPV = \frac{-\$5{,}000}{(1.0227)^0} + \frac{-\$5{,}000}{(1.0227)^1} + \frac{-\$10{,}000}{(1.0227)^2} + \frac{\$30{,}000}{(1.0227)^{12}}$$
$$= -\$3{,}473.72 > 0$$

This NPV indicates that the project should be accepted.

summary of learning goals

In this chapter, we apply time value of money (TVM) concepts to project valuation. While the mathematics here are very similar to those used in the valuation of stocks, bonds, and loans, the underlying intuition in valuing capital equipment projects is very different. In project valuation, the main goal is to find projects that convey enough monopoly power to the acquirer that they are worth more than they cost, even taking into account the cost of capital.

Of the capital budgeting techniques we have discussed, NPV is the hands-down winner, working equally well with normal or non-normal cash flows and with independent or mutually exclusive projects. However, the NPV decision technique uses a statistic denominated in currency, which may not be the only pertinent unit of measurement if the firm faces time or resource constraints. In such situations, the additional capital budgeting techniques may provide valuable supplementary guidance in deciding whether to accept a project or not.

A summary of the relevant attributes and strengths and weaknesses of the various capital budgeting techniques is shown in Table 13.16. As we can see, NPV does tend to be the most useful technique, but the others also have their place, particularly for firms facing either time or capital constraints.

Recent surveys asking practitioners which capital budgeting techniques they use in practice tend to support this idea, showing NPV to be the most frequently used technique and that practitioners often use NPV in conjunction with one of the other techniques when making decisions.

However, the choice of other techniques indicates that practitioners tend to favor the conceptually simpler techniques over the more complicated ones. For example, a recent survey by Ryan and Ryan of firms in the Fortune 1000 indicates that, after NPV, IRR and regular payback are next most often used, with discounted payback, profitability index, and modified IRR being used the least. Their results are summarized in Table 13.17.

table 13.16 | **Strengths and Weaknesses of Capital Budgeting Techniques**

Technique	Unit of Measurement	Suitable for Non-Normal Cash Flows	Suitable for Choosing between Mutually Exclusive Projects	Useful for Firms Facing Time Constraints	Useful for Firms Facing Capital Constraints
PB	Time	No	No	Yes	No
DPB	Time	No	No	Yes	No
NPV	Dollars	Yes	Yes	No	Yes
IRR	Rate	No	No	No	Yes
MIRR	Rate	Yes	No	No	Yes
PI	Rate	Yes	No	No	Yes

table 13.17 | **Usage of Capital Budgeting Techniques in Industry**

Capital Budgeting Technique	USAGE INDICATED BY RESPONDENTS				
	Always	Often	Sometimes	Rarely	Never
Net present value	49.8%	35.3%	10.9%	3.0%	1.0%
Internal rate of return	44.6	32.2	15.3	6.4	1.5
Payback	19.4	33.2	21.9	16.8	8.7
Discounted payback	15.5	22.2	19.1	21.1	22.2
Profitability index	5.9	15.5	22.5	21.9	34.2
Modified IRR	2.2	7.1	12.6	27.9	50.3

LG13-1 **Analyze the logic underlying capital budgeting decision techniques.** All capital budgeting techniques attempt to achieve the same thing, but they render different measurement units. Not only do they use different measurement units, but almost all of them exclude some crucial information and may thus give incorrect, inconclusive, or misleading answers.

This kind of "blurry" information with which to make decisions is especially evident when using rate-based decision rules to choose between or among mutually exclusive projects. Rate-based statistics represent summary cash flows, and those summaries tend to lose two important details: The investment size and cash inflows that occur after the rather arbitrary testing period.

LG13-2 **Calculate and use the payback (PB) and discounted payback (DPB) methods for valuing capital investment opportunities.** The payback technique tells us how long it will take the firm to earn back the money invested in a project. Discounted payback tells managers how long it will take to earn back the money invested plus interest at market rates. Management can compute either statistic fairly easily, so PB and DPB remain very popular techniques today. The techniques are particularly useful when firms face time constraints in repaying investors. Managers who are not quite comfortable with TVM principles feel more comfortable with PB than with DPB. Neither method accounts for cash flows that occur after payback. Both methods are subject to managers' sometimes arbitrary maximum payback periods as their benchmarks. Another way to describe these benchmarks is that they are exogenously specified.

LG13-3 **Calculate and use the net present value (NPV) method for evaluating capital investment opportunities.** NPV is the best decision rule we have. This technique handles normal or non-normal cash flows and independent or mutually exclusive projects equally well. Corporate decision makers do, however, need to understand TVM principles thoroughly if they are to calculate decision statistics and then to comprehend exactly what the statistics say or don't say.

LG13-4 **Calculate and use the internal rate of return (IRR) and the modified internal rate of return (MIRR) methods for evaluating capital investment opportunities.** Managers find both the IRR and MIRR methods intuitively appealing, measuring what is best thought of as the "expected" rate of return to be earned from investing in a project. Unfortunately, the basic IRR statistic becomes unreliable when dealing with non-normal cash flows. The method may also choose the wrong project when it is used to compare mutually exclusive projects with marked differences in timing and/or scale of their cash flows. Third, IRR embodies a rather unreasonable assumption about the rate at which cash inflows from the project can be reinvested.

The MIRR decision rule explicitly alters IRR's reinvestment rate assumption, implicitly curing any problems associated non-normal cash flows along the way. But, as a rate-based decision rule, it still suffers from invalidity when it is used to choose between or among mutually exclusive projects.

LG13-5 Use NPV profiles to reconcile sources of conflict between NPV and IRR methods. The main discrepancy between the NPV choice and the IRR's/MIRR's choice between mutually exclusive projects arises because of rate-based decision statistic attributes, which place undue preference for shorter-term, smaller projects rather than longer-term, larger-scale projects that might really give the firm a leg up. Since at times a rate-based decision metric is *desirable* but not necessarily appropriate, we need to be able to explain exactly why the project with the largest IRR isn't necessarily the best project.

LG13-6 Compute and use the profitability index (PI). We presented a simple version of the profitability index that is a simple arithmetic transformation of the NPV into a rate-based decision statistic. Its one important attribute is that, unlike the other rate-based statistics discussed in this chapter, it measures the *gross* return. Consequently, its appropriate benchmark is 1, or anything larger than 1, rather than the cost of capital.

chapter equations

13-1 **Payback Statistic**

$$0 = \sum_{n=0}^{PB} CF_n$$

13-2 **Payback Decision Rule**

Accept project if calculated payback ≤ Maximum allowable payback
Reject project if calculated payback > Maximum allowable payback

13-3 **Discounted Payback Statistic**

$$0 = \sum_{n=0}^{DPB} \frac{CF_n}{(1 + i)^n}$$

13-4 **Discounted Payback Decision Rule**

Accept project if calculated DPB ≤ Maximum allowable discounted payback
Reject project if calculated DPB > Maximum allowable discounted payback

13-5 **NPV Statistic**

$$NPV = \frac{CF_0}{(1 + i)^0} + \frac{CF_1}{(1 + i)^1} + \cdots + \frac{CF_N}{(1 + i)^N}$$

$$= \sum_{n=0}^{N} \frac{CF_n}{(1 + i)^n}$$

13-6 **NPV Decision Rule**

Accept project if NPV ≥ 0
Reject project if NPV < 0

13-7 **Formula Comparison (13-5 to 13-8)**

Solve for NPV versus Solve for IRR

$$NPV = \sum_{n=0}^{N} \frac{CF_n}{(1 + i)^n} \quad \text{versus} \quad 0 = \sum_{n=0}^{N} \frac{CF_n}{(1 + IRR)^n}$$

13-8 IRR Statistic Solve for IRR: $0 = \sum_{n=0}^{N} \frac{CF_n}{(1 + IRR)^n}$

13-9 **IRR Decision Rule**

Accept project if IRR $\geq$ Cost of capital
Reject project if IRR $<$ Cost of capital

13-10 **Profitability Index Statistic**

$$PI = \frac{NPV + CF_0}{CF_0}$$

13-11 **Profitability Index Decision Rule**

Accept project if PI ≥ 1
Reject project if PI < 1

key terms

discounted payback (DPB), A capital budgeting method that generates decision rules and associated metrics that choose projects based on how quickly they return their initial investment plus interest. *p. 443*

interest-rate cognizant, A decision-making process that includes the cost of capital calculation. *p. 458*

internal rate of return (IRR), A capital budgeting technique that generates decision rules and associated metrics for choosing projects based on the implicit expected geometric average of a project's rate of return. *p. 449*

modified internal rate of return (MIRR), A capital budgeting method that converts a project's cash flows using a more consistent reinvestment rate prior to applying the IRR decision rule. *p. 453*

mutually exclusive projects, Groups or pairs of projects where you can accept one but not all. *p. 455*

net present value (NPV), A technique that generates a decision rule and associated metric for choosing projects based on the total discounted value of their cash flows. *p. 446*

normal cash flows, A set of cash flows with all outflows occurring at the beginning of the set. *p. 442*

NPV profile, A graph of a project's NPV as a function of the cost of capital. *p. 451*

payback (PB), A capital budgeting technique that generates decision rules and associated metrics for choosing projects based on how quickly they return their initial investment. *p. 442*

profitability index (PI), A decision rule and associated methodology for converting the NPV statistic into a rate-based metric. *p. 460*

self-test problem with solution

LG13-1 to 13-6

1 Assume you are evaluating two mutually exclusive projects, the cash flows of which appear below, and that your company uses a cost of capital of 8 percent to evaluate projects such as these.

Time	Project A Cash Flow	Project B Cash Flow
0	−$650	−$700
1	100	300
2	250	−200
3	250	550
4	200	200
5	100	80

a. Calculate the payback of Project A.

b. Calculate the discounted payback of Project A.

c. Calculate the IRR of Project A.

d. Calculate the MIRR of Project B.

e. At which rate do these projects' NPV profiles cross?

f. Using the NPV method and assuming a cost of capital of 8 percent, which of these projects should be accepted?

Solution:

a. Calculate the payback of Project A.

Year:	0	1	2	3	4	5
Cash flow	−$650	$100	$250	$250	$200	$100
Cumulative cash flow	−650	−550	−300	−50	150	

$$PB = 3 + \frac{\$50}{\$200} = 3.25 \text{ years}$$

b. Calculate the discounted payback of Project A.

Year:	0	1	2	3	4	5
Cash flow	−$650.00	$100.00	$250.00	$250.00	$200.00	$100.00
Cash flow present value	−650.00	92.59	214.33	198.46	147.01	
Cumulative cash flow PV	−650.00	−557.41	−343.07	−144.61	2.39	

$$DPB = 3 + \frac{\$144.61}{\$147.01} = 3.98 \text{ years}$$

c. Calculate the IRR of Project A.

$$0 = \frac{-\$650}{(1+IRR)^0} + \frac{\$100}{(1+IRR)^1} + \frac{\$250}{(1+IRR)^2} + \frac{\$250}{(1+IRR)^3} + \frac{\$200}{(1+IRR)^4} + \frac{\$100}{(1+IRR)^5}$$

$$IRR = 12.02\%$$

d. Calculate the MIRR of Project B.

Year:	0	1	2	3	4	5
Cash flow	−$700.00	$300.00	−$200.00	$550.00	$200.00	$ 80.00
Present value (if negative)	−700.00		−171.47			
Sum of PVs	−871.47					
Future value (if positive)		408.15		641.52	216.00	80.00
Sum of FVs						1,345.67
Modified CFs	−871.47					1,345.67

With this new set of modified cash flows, the MIRR is:

$$0 = \frac{-\$871.47}{(1+IRR)^0} + \frac{\$1{,}345.67}{(1+IRR)^5}$$

$$IRR = 9.08\%$$

e. At which rate do these projects' NPV profiles cross?

Year:	0	1	2	3	4	5
Project A cash flows	−$650	$100	$250	$250	$200	$100
Project B cash flows	−700	300	−200	550	200	80
A − B	50	−200	450	−300	0	20

$$0 = \frac{\$50}{(1 + IRR)^0} + \frac{-\$200}{(1 + IRR)^1} + \frac{\$450}{(1 + IRR)^2} + \frac{-\$300}{(1 + IRR)^3} + \frac{\$0}{(1 + IRR)^4} + \frac{\$20}{(1 + IRR)^5}$$

$IRR = -12.66\%$

Note: This is outside the first quadrant.

f. Using the NPV method and assuming a cost of capital of 8 percent, which of these mutually exclusive projects should the firm accept?

$$NPV_A = \frac{-\$650}{(1.08)^0} + \frac{\$100}{(1.08)^1} + \frac{\$250}{(1.08)^2} + \frac{\$250}{(1.08)^3} + \frac{\$200}{(1.08)^4} + \frac{\$100}{(1.08)^5} = \$70.45$$

$$NPV_B = \frac{-\$700}{(1.08)^0} + \frac{\$300}{(1.08)^1} + \frac{-\$200}{(1.08)^2} + \frac{\$550}{(1.08)^3} + \frac{\$200}{(1.08)^4} + \frac{\$80}{(1.08)^5} = \$44.37$$

$\text{NPV}_A > \text{NPV}_B$, so Project A should be accepted.

questions

1. Is the set of cash flows depicted below normal or non-normal? Explain. *(LG13-1)*

Time:	0	1	2	3	4	5
Cash flow	−$100	−$50	−$80	$0	$100	$100

2. Derive an accept/reject rule for IRR similar to equation 13-8 that would make the correct decision on cash flows that are non-normal, but which always have one large positive cash flow at time zero followed by a series of negative cash flows. *(LG13-1)*

Time:	0	1	2	3	4	5
Cash flow	+	−	−	−	−	−

3. Is it possible for a company to initiate two products that target the same market that are *not* mutually exclusive? *(LG13-1)*
4. Suppose that your company used "APV," or "All-the-Present Value-Except-CF_0," to analyze capital budgeting projects. What would this rule's benchmark value be? *(LG13-3)*
5. Under what circumstances could payback and discounted payback be equal? *(LG13-2)*
6. Could a project's MIRR ever *exceed* its IRR? *(LG13-4)*

7. If you had two mutually exclusive, normal-cash-flow projects whose NPV profiles crossed at all points, for which range of interest rates would IRR give the right accept/reject answer? *(LG13-5)*
8. Suppose a company wanted to double the firm's value with the next round of capital budgeting project decisions. To what would it set the PI benchmark to make this goal? *(LG13-6)*
9. Suppose a company faced different borrowing and lending rates. How would this range change the way that you would compute the MIRR statistic? *(LG13-4)*

problems

basic problems

13-1 NPV with Normal Cash Flows Compute the NPV for Project M and accept or reject the project with the cash flows shown below if the appropriate cost of capital is 8 percent. *(LG13-3)*

Project M						
Time:	0	1	2	3	4	5
Cash flow	−$1,000	$350	$480	$520	$600	$100

13-2 NPV with Normal Cash Flows Compute the NPV statistic for Project Y and indicate whether the firm should accept or reject the project with the cash flows shown below if the appropriate cost of capital is 12 percent. *(LG13-3)*

Project Y					
Time:	0	1	2	3	4
Cash flow	−$8,000	$3,350	$4,180	$1,520	$300

13-3 NPV with Non-Normal Cash Flows Compute the NPV statistic for Project U and recommend whether the firm should accept or reject the project with the cash flows shown below if the appropriate cost of capital is 10 percent. *(LG13-3)*

Project U						
Time:	0	1	2	3	4	5
Cash flow	−$1,000	$350	$1,480	−$520	$300	−$100

13-4 NPV with Non-Normal Cash Flows Compute the NPV statistic for Project K and recommend whether the firm should accept or reject the project with the cash flows shown below if the appropriate cost of capital is 6 percent. *(LG13-3)*

Project K						
Time:	0	1	2	3	4	5
Cash flow	−$10,000	$5,000	$6,000	$6,000	$5,000	−$10,000

13-5 Payback Compute the payback statistic for Project B and decide whether the firm should accept or reject the project with the cash flows shown below if the appropriate cost of capital is 12 percent and the maximum allowable payback is three years. *(LG13-2)*

Project B						
Time:	0	1	2	3	4	5
Cash flow	−$11,000	$3,350	$4,180	$1,520	$0	$1,000

13-6 **Payback** Compute the payback statistic for Project A and recommend whether the firm should accept or reject the project with the cash flows shown below if the appropriate cost of capital is 8 percent and the maximum allowable payback is four years. *(LG13-2)*

Project A						
Time:	0	1	2	3	4	5
Cash flow	−$1,000	$350	$480	$520	$300	$100

13-7 **Discounted Payback** Compute the discounted payback statistic for Project C and recommend whether the firm should accept or reject the project with the cash flows shown below if the appropriate cost of capital is 8 percent and the maximum allowable discounted payback is three years. *(LG13-2)*

Project C						
Time:	0	1	2	3	4	5
Cash flow	−$1,000	$480	$480	$520	$300	$100

13-8 **Discounted Payback** Compute the discounted payback statistic for Project D and recommend whether the firm should accept or reject the project with the cash flows shown below if the appropriate cost of capital is 12 percent and the maximum allowable discounted payback is four years. *(LG13-2)*

Project D						
Time:	0	1	2	3	4	5
Cash flow	−$11,000	$3,350	$4,180	$1,520	$0	$1,000

13-9 **IRR** Compute the IRR statistic for Project E and note whether the firm should accept or reject the project with the cash flows shown below if the appropriate cost of capital is 8 percent. *(LG13-4)*

Project E						
Time:	0	1	2	3	4	5
Cash flow	−$1,000	$350	$480	$520	$300	$100

13-10 **IRR** Compute the IRR statistic for Project F and note whether the firm should accept or reject the project with the cash flows shown below if the appropriate cost of capital is 12 percent. *(LG13-4)*

Project F					
Time:	0	1	2	3	4
Cash flow	−$11,000	$3,350	$4,180	$1,520	$2,000

13-11 **MIRR** Compute the MIRR statistic for Project I and indicate whether to accept or reject the project with the cash flows shown below if the appropriate cost of capital is 12 percent. *(LG13-4)*

Project I					
Time:	0	1	2	3	4
Cash flow	−$11,000	$5,330	$4,180	$1,520	$2,000

13-12 MIRR Compute the MIRR statistic for Project J and advise whether to accept or reject the project with the cash flows shown below if the appropriate cost of capital is 10 percent. *(LG13-4)*

Project J						
Time:	0	1	2	3	4	5
Cash flow	−$1,000	$350	$1,480	−$520	$300	−$100

13-13 PI Compute the PI statistic for Project Z and advise the firm whether to accept or reject the project with the cash flows shown below if the appropriate cost of capital is 8 percent. *(LG13-6)*

Project Z						
Time:	0	1	2	3	4	5
Cash flow	−$1,000	$350	$480	$650	$300	$100

13-14 PI Compute the PI statistic for Project Q and indicate whether you would accept or reject the project with the cash flows shown below if the appropriate cost of capital is 12 percent. *(LG13-6)*

Project Q					
Time:	0	1	2	3	4
Cash flow	−$11,000	$3,350	$4,180	$1,520	$2,000

13-15 Multiple IRRs How many possible IRRs could you find for the following set of cash flows? *(LG13-1)*

Time:	0	1	2	3	4
Cash flow	−$11,000	$3,350	$4,180	$1,520	$2,000

13-16 Multiple IRRs How many possible IRRs could you find for the following set of cash flows? *(LG13-1)*

Time:	0	1	2	3	4
Cash flow	−$211,000	−$39,350	$440,180	$217,520	−$2,000

intermediate problems

Use this information to answer the next six questions. If a particular decision method should not be used, indicate why.

Suppose your firm is considering investing in a project with the cash flows shown below, that the required rate of return on projects of this risk class is 8 percent, and that the maximum allowable payback and discounted payback statistics for the project are 3.5 and 4.5 years, respectively.

Time:	0	1	2	3	4	5	6
Cash flow	−$5,000	$1,200	$2,400	$1,600	$1,600	$1,400	$1,200

13-17 Payback Use the payback decision rule to evaluate this project; should it be accepted or rejected? *(LG13-2)*

13-18 Discounted Payback Use the discounted payback decision rule to evaluate this project; should it be accepted or rejected? *(LG13-2)*

13-19 IRR Use the IRR decision rule to evaluate this project; should it be accepted or rejected? *(LG13-4)*

13-20 MIRR Use the MIRR decision rule to evaluate this project; should it be accepted or rejected? *(LG13-4)*

13-21 NPV Use the NPV decision rule to evaluate this project; should it be accepted or rejected? *(LG13-3)*

13-22 PI Use the PI decision rule to evaluate this project; should it be accepted or rejected? *(LG13-6)*

Use this information to answer the next six questions. If you should not use a particular decision technique, indicate why.

Suppose your firm is considering investing in a project with the cash flows shown below, that the required rate of return on projects of this risk class is 11 percent, and that the maximum allowable payback and discounted payback statistics for your company are 3 and 3.5 years, respectively.

Time:	0	1	2	3	4	5
Cash flow	−$235,000	$65,800	$84,000	$141,000	$122,000	$81,200

13-23 Payback Use the payback decision rule to evaluate this project; should it be accepted or rejected? *(LG13-2)*

13-24 Discounted Payback Use the discounted payback decision rule to evaluate this project; should it be accepted or rejected? *(LG13-2)*

13-25 IRR Use the IRR decision rule to evaluate this project; should it be accepted or rejected? *(LG13-4)*

13-26 MIRR Use the MIRR decision rule to evaluate this project; should it be accepted or rejected? *(LG13-4)*

13-27 NPV Use the NPV decision rule to evaluate this project; should it be accepted or rejected? *(LG13-3)*

13-28 PI Use the PI decision rule to evaluate this project; should it be accepted or rejected? *(LG13-6)*

advanced problems

Use the project cash flows for the two mutually exclusive projects shown below to answer the following two questions.

Time	Project A Cash Flow	Project B Cash Flow
0	−$725	−$850
1	100	200
2	250	200
3	250	200
4	200	200
5	100	200
6	100	200
7	100	200

13-29 NPV Profiles Graph the NPV profiles for both projects on a common chart, making sure that you identify all of the "crucial" points. *(LG13-5)*

13-30 IRR Applicability For what range of possible interest rates would you want to use IRR to choose between these two projects? For what range of rates would you NOT want to use IRR? *(LG13-5)*

13-31 Multiple IRRs Construct an NPV profile and determine EXACTLY how many nonnegative IRRs you can find for the following set of cash flows: *(LG13-5)*

Time:	0	1	2	3	4	5	6	7
Cash flow	−$200	$400	$150	−$100	−$100	−$300	$200	−$300

13-32 Multiple IRRs Construct an NPV profile and determine EXACTLY how many nonnegative IRRs you can find for the following set of cash flows: *(LG13-5)*

Time:	0	1	2	3	4	5	6	7
Cash flow	−$150	$275	$150	−$100	$300	−$300	$200	−$300

research it! Business Valuation

The capital budgeting decision techniques that we have discussed all have strengths and weaknesses, but they do comprise the most popular rules for valuing projects. Valuing entire businesses, on the other hand, requires that some adjustments be made to various pieces of these methodologies. For example, one alternative to NPV used quite frequently for valuing firms is called adjusted present value (APV).

To explore these alternative decision rules, do a Web search on Google **(www.google.com)** for APV and answer the following questions:

1. What is APV, and how does it differ from NPV?
2. What other business valuation models seem to be popular?

integrated mini-case Project Valuation

Suppose your firm is considering investing in a project with the accompanying cash flows, that the required rate of return on projects of this risk class is 11 percent, and that the maximum allowable payback and discounted payback statistics for your company are 3 and 3.5 years, respectively.

Time:	0	1	2	3	4	5
Cash flow	−$175,000	−$65,800	$94,000	$41,000	$122,000	$81,200

Using every one of the capital budgeting decision methods discussed in this chapter, evaluate this project, indicating whether each decision rule would call for acceptance or rejection of the project.

ANSWERS TO TIME OUT

13-1 Given that we are only going to be working with projects with normal sets of cash flows, the discounted payback will always be larger, as it will take longer for the present values of the future, positive cash flows to sum to the initial cost than it will for the cash flows themselves to do so.

13-2 If the discount rate is increased, the PVs of the cash inflows will decrease causing the discounted payback period to increase.

13-3 Because the cost is already included in the NPV; using it as the benchmark, also, would involve double-counting it.

13-4 It should be equal to zero, because the cost of the bond to the purchaser should be exactly equal to the sum of the present values of the coupons and the face value.

13-5 No: If the cash flows are normal, some large interest rate has to exist at which the size of the present value of the future, positive cash flows becomes less than the initial, negative cash flow.

13-6 It should reject: Such a project would have the sums of the positive cash flows equal to the negative, initial cash flow, which would have to result in a negative NPV given any positive interest rate.

13-7 The project with the longer payback will have the lower IRR, as its cash flows will, on average, be later than the other project's.

13-8 Only one, because there is only one change in sign of the cash flows—from negative to positive between years 1 and 2.

13-9 Assuming the IRR exceeds the cost of capital, the MIRR should be less than the IRR because the MIRR uses a lower reinvestment rate assumption.

13-10 You would solve the perpetuity formula for the interest rate by dividing the cash flow by the initial cost.

13-11 It would use a benchmark of 1 instead of zero.

13-12 It will have a PI and an NPV of zero.

PART SEVEN

14 Working Capital Management and Policies

viewpoints

Business Application

Chewbacca Manufacturing expects sales of $32 million next year. CM's cost of goods sold normally runs at 55 percent of sales; inventory requirements are usually 10 percent of annual sales; the average accounts receivable balance is one-sixth of annual sales; and the average accounts payable balance is 5 percent of sales. If all sales are on credit, what will Chewbacca's level of net working capital and its cash cycle be? **(See solution on p. 494)**

Personal Application

Wanda has saved enough money to go back to grad school. She is planning to put the money in a money market account where it will earn 3.5 percent. If she anticipates slowly drawing the money out over the course of her time in grad school at a constant rate of $25,000 per year but is charged a commission of $9.95 every time she sells shares, how much should she take out of the mutual fund at a time? **(See solution on p. 494)**

Where else can you park your money . . . for less?

Learning Goals

LG14-1 Set overall objectives of a good working capital policy.

LG14-2 Discuss how net working capital serves the firm.

LG14-3 Analyze the firm's operating and cash cycles to determine what funding for current assets the firm needs.

LG14-4 Model the optimal trade-off between carrying costs and shortage costs that dictates the firm's current asset investment.

LG14-5 Compare the flexible and restrictive approaches to financing current assets.

LG14-6 Differentiate among sources of short-term financing available for funding current assets.

LG14-7 Justify the firm's need to hold cash.

LG14-8 Use the Baumol and Miller-Orr models for determining cash policy.

LG14-9 Identify sources of float and show how to control float for the firm's disbursement and collection functions.

LG14-10 Identify firms' choices for using excess cash.

LG14-11 Connect the firm's credit terms and collection policy and the amount of capital the firm has invested in accounts receivable.

In this chapter, we focus on the major trade-off implicit in funding net working capital. By and large, the trade-off involves comparing how much it costs the firm to carry an investment in current assets with the **shortage costs** associated with the firm not having enough cash, inventory, or accounts receivable.

As we'll see, the firm's ideal solution to providing net working capital would be to get someone else to foot the bill. Though this may be a valid approach to fund *some* of the firm's current assets, it's usually difficult to get someone else to cover the *entire* amount of net working capital necessary to run the firm efficiently. We will, however, discuss how to shift those costs elsewhere as much as possible in this chapter by covering the following topics:

1. How to determine the optimal amount of investment in current assets.
2. How to measure the portion of current assets that the firm is responsible for funding.
3. How to choose the source of funding for that portion of current assets.

LG14-1, 14-2

Depending on the firm's line of business and the extent to which it provides physical goods versus services, the management of portions of the current assets may come under a specialized department responsible for the firm's **operations management.** Though beyond the scope of this book, if you ever get a chance to read about the models used in operations management, you'll notice that many of the concepts we'll discuss are directly related to inventory management models. For example, our discussion of flexible, restrictive, and compromise financing of current assets would fit right in with the concept of "**just in time**" (**JIT**) inventory management, while the Baumol

shortage costs

Costs associated with not having sufficient cash, inventory, or accounts receivable.

operations management

The area of management concerned with designing and overseeing the process of production.

just in time (JIT)

A production strategy that attempts to improve a firm's return on investment by reducing in-process inventory and associated carrying costs as much as possible.

Barabas Economic Order Quantity (EOQ)

The inventory order quantity that minimizes total holding and ordering costs.

opportunity cost

The cost or forgone opportunity of using an asset already in use by the firm, or a person already employed by the firm, in a new project.

operating cycle

The time required to acquire raw materials and to produce, sell, and receive payment for the finished goods.

cash cycle

The operating cycle minus the average payment period.

table 14.1 | **The Basic Balance Sheet**

Total Assets		Total Liabilities and Equity
Current assets:	Net working capital	Current liabilities:
Cash and marketable securities		Accrued wages and taxes
Accounts receivable		Accounts payable
Inventory		Notes payable
Fixed assets:		Long-term debt
Gross plant and equipment		Stockholders' equity:
Less: Depreciation		Preferred stock
Net plant and equipment		Common stock and paid-in surplus
Other long-term assets		Retained earnings

model for determining the target cash balance is a simple extension of the **Barabas Economic Order Quantity (EOQ)** model for minimizing total inventory holding and ordering costs.

14.1 • Revisiting the Balance-Sheet Model of the Firm

Recall our discussion of the balance sheet in Chapter 2. At a glance, the balance sheet brings together the firm's assets or sources of financing and its liabilities, or investments, as Table 14.1 shows. Net working capital reflects the need for the firm to generate funds to stay in business and maximize profit.

Earlier in the text, we discussed the fact that the current assets, while the most liquid, are also usually less profitable than fixed assets. This explains why some managers like to think of net working capital as *"the net amount of current assets that the firm has to fund, above and beyond those that someone else funds for us."*

To put it bluntly, net working capital is a necessary evil: Most firms can't sell finished goods without inventory to display, or without offering to sell to customers on credit, and so forth. Firms incur costs associated with keeping inventory on hand and with selling to customers on credit.

But just because a firm has to fund *some* net working capital does not mean that it should fund all of it or even a large portion of it. Instead, the firm should, to the best of its ability, ensure that the marginal benefit of each dollar tied up in net working capital equals the marginal **opportunity cost** of not having that dollar invested in fixed assets with positive net present value (NPV).

TIME OUT

14-1 Why might a firm's creditors *not* think of net working capital as a necessary evil, but rather as a good thing?

14-2 If demand for a firm's products suddenly slows down so that inventory increases while sales decrease, how will the firm's needs for net working capital react?

14.2 • Tracing Cash and Net Working Capital

To trace cash flows through the firm's operations, we must measure the **operating cycle**—the time necessary to acquire raw materials, turn them into finished goods, sell them, and receive payment for them—as well as the firm's **cash cycle.**

Let's think of net working capital as the portion of current assets that the firm must fund (above and beyond those assets funded by current liabilities). Then we can similarly think of the firm's cash cycle as the portion of the operating cycle that the firm must finance. LG14-3

The Operating Cycle

To measure the firm's operating cycle, we need to turn to some of the ratios that we discussed in Chapter 3:

$$\text{Operating cycle} = \text{Days' sales in inventory} + \text{Average collection period} \quad \textbf{(14-1)}$$

$$= \frac{\text{Inventory} \times 365}{\text{Cost of goods sold}} + \frac{\text{Accounts receivable} \times 365}{\text{Credit sales}}$$

EXAMPLE 14-1

LG14-3

Calculation of Operating Cycle

Suppose that MMK Industries has annual sales of $1 million, cost of goods sold of $650,000, average inventories of $116,000, and average accounts receivable of $150,000. Assuming that all MMK's sales are on credit, what will be the firm's operating cycle?

For interactive versions of this example visit www.mhhe.com/can3e

SOLUTION:

The operating cycle will be equal to:

$$\text{Operating cycle} = \frac{\text{Inventory} \times 365}{\text{Cost of goods sold}} + \frac{\text{Accounts receivable} \times 365}{\text{Credit sales}}$$

$$= \frac{\$116{,}000 \times 365}{\$650{,}000} + \frac{\$150{,}000 \times 365}{\$1{,}000{,}000}$$

$$= 65.14 \text{ days} + 54.75 \text{ days}$$

$$= 119.89 \text{ days}$$

So it will take MMK almost 120 days from the time it receives raw materials to produce, market, sell, and collect the cash for the finished goods.

Similar to Problems 14-13, 14-14

The Cash Cycle

The firm's cash cycle will simply be the operating cycle minus the average payment period as shown in Figure 14.1:

$$\text{Cash cycle} = \text{Operating cycle} - \text{Average payment period} \quad \textbf{(14-2)}$$

$$= \text{Operating cycle} - \frac{\text{Accounts payable} \times 365}{\text{Cost of goods sold}}$$

Note that even though it will take MMK almost 120 days to turn the raw materials into cash, the cash cycle indicates that the firm will have to foot the bill for its

figure 14.1

Relationship between Operating and Cash Cycles
The firm's cash cycle will simply be the operating cycle minus the average payment period.

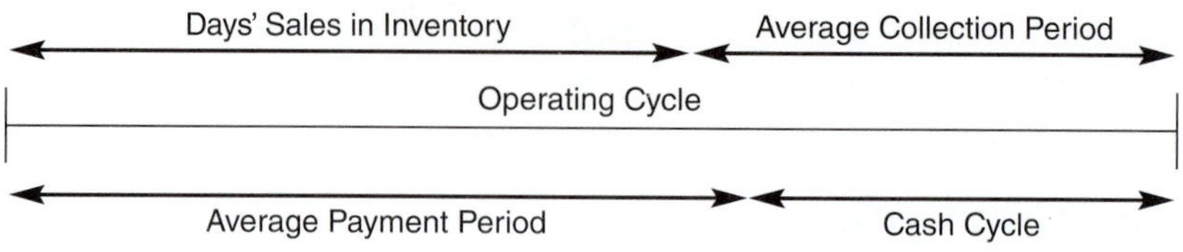

EXAMPLE 14-2

LG14-3

For interactive versions of this example visit www.mhhe.com/can3e

Calculation of Cash Cycle

Extending the previous example, assume that MMK's average accounts payable balance is \$120,000. What will be the firm's cash cycle?

SOLUTION:

The cash cycle will be equal to:

$$\begin{aligned}\text{Cash cycle} &= \text{Operating cycle} - \frac{\text{Accounts payable} \times 365}{\text{Cost of goods sold}}\\ &= 119.89 \text{ days} - \frac{\$120{,}000 \times 365}{\$650{,}000}\\ &= 119.89 \text{ days} - 67.38 \text{ days}\\ &= 52.50 \text{ days}\end{aligned}$$

Similar to Problems 14-15, 14-16

production cycle for only 52.50 days of that time. This is the crux of managing the firm's operating and cash cycles: Minimize the number of days that the firm has to pay for its production cycle.

TIME OUT

14-3 How will a firm affect its operating cycle if it can reduce inventory on hand?

14-4 When we compare two firms, will the one with the longer cash cycle tend to have more or less net working capital requirements than the one with a shorter cash cycle, everything held equal? Why?

LG14-4 14.3 • Some Aspects of Short-Term Financial Policy

In the last section, we derived the cash cycle by first determining the operating cycle and then subtracting the payment cycle. This derivation suggests two obvious ways that firms can reduce their net working capital needs.

1. They can manage their need for current assets.
2. They can seek to obtain as many current liabilities as economically feasible to fund the current assets that they do need.

finance at work — global

KAIZEN (改善)

Kaizen is a Japanese approach to productivity improvement that aims to eliminate waste through just-in-time delivery, standardized work and equipment, and so on. The five basic elements of kaizen are:

1. Teamwork
2. Personal discipline
3. Improved morale
4. Quality circles
5. Suggestions for improvement

Studies show that the kaizen approach can reduce (sometimes dramatically) net working capital requirements, with businesses adopting the approach reporting reductions in finished-goods and in-process inventory of anywhere from 10 to 30 percent.

want to know more?

Key Words to Search for Updates: The article "Off the shelf: low inventories drove down working capital last year. But will that continue as the economy improves?" (www.cfo.com)

The Size of the Current Assets Investment

Choosing the optimal level of investment in each current asset type involves a trade-off between carrying costs and shortage costs.

Carrying costs are associated with having current assets and fall into two general categories:

carrying costs
The opportunity costs associated with having capital tied up in current assets instead of more productive fixed assets and explicit costs necessary to maintain the value of the current assets.

1. The opportunity costs associated with having capital tied up in current assets instead of more productive fixed assets.
2. Explicit costs necessary to maintain the value of the current assets.

For example, a car dealer who purchases used vehicles and keeps them in inventory would incur the opportunity cost of not being able to invest the money paid for the used vehicles in a more lucrative opportunity, such as new hybrid vehicles. Our car dealer will also have to pay rental or lease payments on the piece of property where the used cars are on display and any maintenance costs necessary to keep the cars ready to sell.

Shortage costs are the costs associated with not having enough current assets and can include opportunity costs such as sales lost due to not having enough inventory on hand, as well as any explicit transaction fees paid to replenish the particular type of current asset. For example, consider a camera shop that has a reorder policy to reorder particular lenses from its supplier only if a customer comes in asking for them, and even then to order only one at a time. In today's business environment, most customers who are seeking an item want it *now*. If that item is out of stock at one store, the customer will probably buy it either at another store or online, resulting in lost sales to the store. If, in addition, we assume that stores pays a shipping fee for every order placed—or if they get quantity discounts if they order in bulk—then their policy will probably result in higher shipping fees. Stores may also face higher costs of goods sold than they would if they ordered in quantity.

Carrying costs will increase, and shortage costs will decrease, as a firm buys more of any particular asset. Therefore, firms should ideally try to choose the point of an asset's lowest total cost, which occurs where marginal carrying and shortage costs are equal. This level is identified as CA* in Figure 14.2.

figure 14.2

Carrying and Shortage Costs

The point at which marginal carrying and shortage costs are equal (CA) is the optimal level of investment for each current asset category.

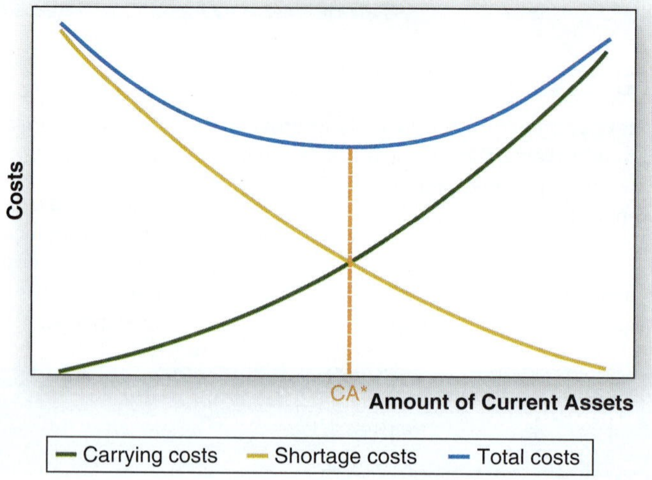

LG14-5

Alternative Financing Policies for Current Assets

In a perfect world, a firm would use long-term debt and equity to finance long-term (i.e., fixed) assets and short-term debt to finance current assets. Such an approach would allow the firm to maturity-match assets with their corresponding liabilities, resulting in a low or nonexistent level for net working capital. As we have previously discussed, in the real world, net working capital is usually positive for most firms. The implication: At least some portion of current assets must be financed with long-term debt, equity, or a mixture of both.

Assuming that most firms can expect to have some steady, stable need for current assets throughout their calendar year and additional demand for current assets that fluctuates on some seasonal cycle, a growing firm's total demand for assets would resemble that shown in Figure 14.3.

So, a firm in such a situation faces the basic question of whether it should finance the peaks or the valleys of total asset demand (or somewhere in between) using long-term financing. Figure 14.4, Figure 14.5, and Figure 14.6 illustrate some of these choices.

We usually refer to the decision to finance the peaks of asset demand with long-term debt and equity, shown in Figure 14.4, as a *flexible financing policy*. It provides the firm with a surplus of cash and marketable securities most of the time—except during peak asset demand.

figure 14.3

Components of Current Assets

A firm makes long- or short-term financing decisions by examining the peaks and valleys of total asset demand.

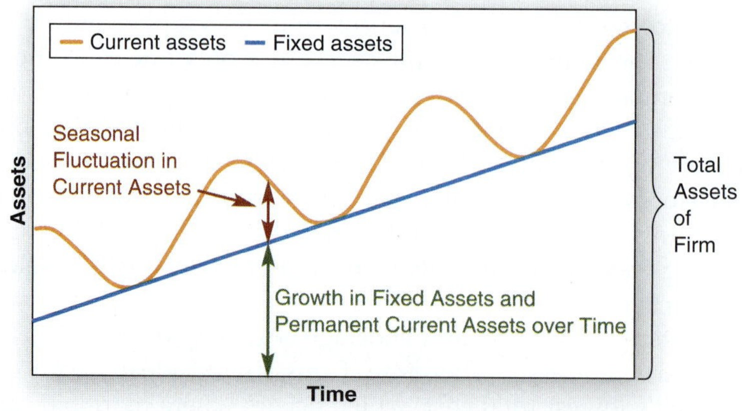

figure 14.4

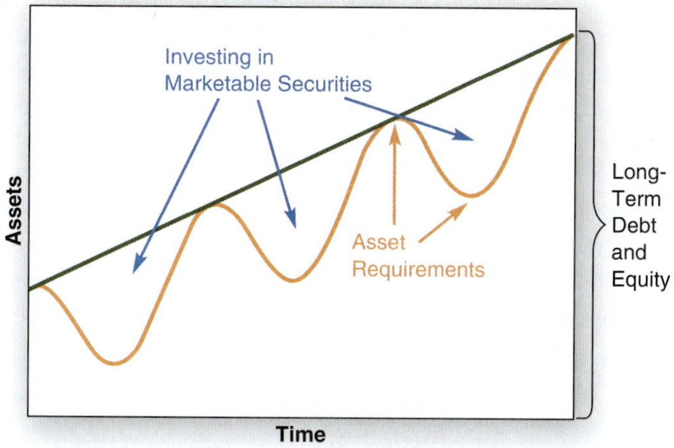

Flexible Financing of CA
Flexible financing policy reflects the decision to finance the peaks of asset demand with long-term debt and equity.

figure 14.5

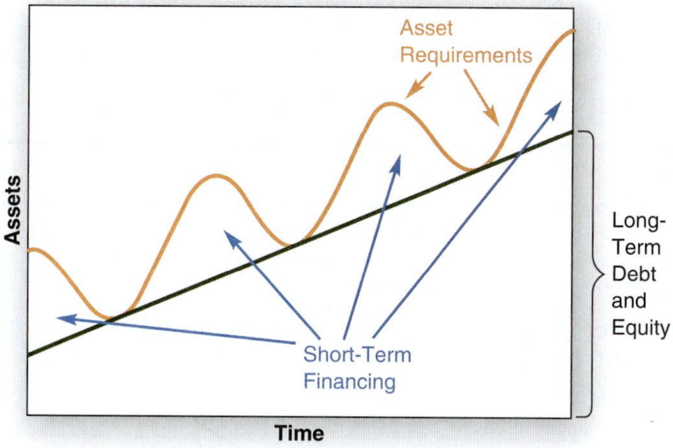

Restrictive Financing of CA
Restrictive financing policy reflects the decision to finance the troughs of asset demand with long-term debt and equity.

figure 14.6

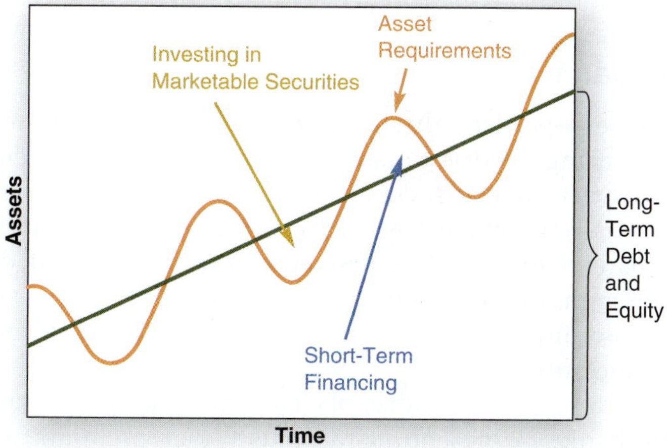

Compromise Financing of CA
Compromise financing policy reflects the decision to finance the seasonally adjusted average level of asset demand with long-term debt and equity.

On the opposite side of the continuum, we refer to a decision to finance the troughs or valleys of asset demand with long-term debt and equity, shown in Figure 14.5, as a *restrictive financing policy.* Under this policy, the firm will have to seek short-term financing for all peak demand fluctuations for current assets, as well as for in-between demand situations. In some ways, this policy is the most "conservative"; on the other hand, it's also the least convenient for the firm, as it involves seeking some level of short-term financing almost all of the time.

A third choice is to follow a *compromise financing policy,* wherein the firm finances the seasonally adjusted average level of asset demand with long-term debt and equity. The firm uses both short-term financing and short-term investing as needed. Figure 14.6 illustrates such a policy. Which approach works best? As is the case with almost all working capital decisions, it depends on several factors:

- Current and future expected interest rate levels. If we expect rates to rise in the future, the firm may want to lock in fixed rates for a longer time by shifting toward a flexible financing policy. With falling rates, the opposite would of course hold true.
- The spread between short- and long-term rates. Long-term borrowing usually costs more than short-term financing, but the "gap" (called the *spread*) between the two terms may be historically small or large, encouraging firms to shift to a more flexible or restrictive policy, respectively.
- Alternative financing availability and costs, discussed in the following sections. Firms with easy and sustained access to alternative sources will want to shift toward more restrictive policies.

TIME OUT

14-5 Suppose that the gap between short-term rates and long-term rates increases. Would firms tend to shift more toward flexible current asset financing policies or toward more restrictive policies?

14-6 If a firm offers longer credit terms to its customers, what will happen to its carrying costs?

LG14-6

14.4 • The Short-Term Financial Plan

Firms that follow any financing policy other than a flexible financing plan will find themselves forced to seek short-term financing at times. Depending on their industry, they may find themselves using unsecured loans, secured loans, or other sources of short-term financing.

Unsecured Loans

For most businesses—particularly smaller ones—the most common way to cover a short-term financing need is to apply at a bank for a commercial loan. The company may expect to need such short-term loans repeatedly in the future—perhaps because it is following a restrictive financing policy but faces seasonal fluctuations in asset demand, as discussed previously. If the bank deems the firm creditworthy enough, the bank will usually grant the firm a *line of credit,* upon which the firm can draw and then pay off repeatedly as the firm goes through those seasonal fluctuations.

compensating balance

Amount of money required to be kept in a firm's deposit accounts with a lender according to a lending arrangement.

Fees for lines of credit can be both explicit (usually taking the form of an interest rate equal to the bank's prime lending rate plus a small premium) and implicit (as a compensating balance requirement and/or a bank's up-front commitment fee). A **compensating balance** is a percentage of the borrowed money (usually

5 to 10 percent) that the bank requires the firm to keep on deposit in the firm's bank accounts. In return, the bank agrees to lend money to the firm.[1]

Commitment fees, if charged, are usually calculated as a flat percentage of the credit line. But banks also charge commitment fees based on the portion of the line of credit "taken down" (i.e., used by the firm) or even of the portion *not* taken down. The amount of fees the bank charges for a line of credit and their type will depend on whether the bank is trying to encourage the use of the line of credit or not.

Secured Loans

Asset-based loans are short-term loans secured by a company's assets. Secured loans carry lower interest rates than unsecured loans, so it is usually in the firm's best interest to provide security (or collateral) when it can. Though real estate, accounts receivable, inventory, and equipment are all sometimes used to back asset-based loans, most firms seeking such a loan to finance seasonal fluctuations in current assets will typically prefer to use inventory or accounts receivable as security for the loan, as they won't wish to encumber long-term assets such as real estate or equipment.

asset-based loans
Short-term loans secured by a company's assets.

Accounts receivable can either be sold outright to a factor or assigned. A **factor** is an entity who will buy accounts receivable on a discounted basis before they are due, with the spread between the discounted price and the receivable's face value providing the factor with expected compensation for both the time value of money and the expected level of defaults among the accounts receivable. **Assignment** is a process whereby the firm borrows money from another entity, providing in return a lien on the accounts receivable as well as the right of **recourse** (i.e., the legal right to hold the firm responsible for payment of the debt if the accounts receivable debtors do not repay as promised).

factor
An entity that will buy accounts receivable from a firm before they are due on a discounted basis.

assignment
A process whereby the firm borrows money from another entity, providing in return both a lien on the accounts receivable and the right of recourse.

recourse
The legal right to hold a firm responsible for payment of a debt if the debtors do not repay as promised.

Firms can also use their inventory as collateral for an inventory loan, a secured short-term loan used to purchase that inventory. Inventory loans include blanket inventory liens, trust receipts, and field warehousing financing. The major difference between the three lies with the question of who owns and keeps the inventory in question:

- Under a blanket inventory lien, the lender gets a lien against all the firm's inventory, but the firm retains ownership and possession.
- When the borrower holds the inventory in trust for the lender, with any proceed from the sale of the inventory being the property of that lender, the document acknowledging this loan commitment is referred to as the *trust receipt.*
- In field warehousing financing, a public warehouse company takes possession and supervises the inventory for the lender.

Other Sources

Two other primary sources of short-term financing are commercial paper issues and financing through banker's acceptances. **Commercial paper,** which we explore in depth in Chapter 18, is a money-market security, issued by large banks and medium-to-large corporations, that matures in nine months or less. Since these issues have such short durations, and since firms use the proceeds only for current transactions, commercial paper (or simply *paper*) is exempt from registering as a security with the SEC. The corresponding lack of paperwork and

commercial paper
A money-market security, issued by large banks and medium-to-large corporations, that matures in nine months or less.

[1]If you are sitting there wondering why the bank doesn't just lend only 95 percent or 90 percent of the money, instead of lending it all and then asking for part of it back, the answer has to do with bank regulations. Though it's too complicated to go into great detail, the simple answer is that bank regulators see a difference between a $900,000 loan and a $1,000,000 loan with a 10 percent compensating balance requirement, though they may sound the same to us.

regulations to issue short-term debt, along with the fact that commercial paper is usually issued only by firms with very high credit rankings, makes commercial paper cheaper than using a bank line of credit.

banker's acceptance (BA)

A short-term promissory note issued by a corporation, bearing the unconditional guarantee (*acceptance*) of a major bank.

A **banker's acceptance** (**BA**) is a short-term promissory note issued by a corporation, bearing the unconditional guarantee (*acceptance*) of a major bank. The bank guarantee makes them very safe, and the rates are usually roughly equivalent to those charged on commercial paper.

TIME OUT

14-7 If its bank started charging fees to a firm based upon the portion of a line of credit not taken down, how would the firm's financing policy for current assets likely change? Why would a bank take such a stance?

14-8 If a firm starts selling its accounts receivable to a factor, how will the firm's cash cycle change?

LG14-7

14.5 • Cash Management

One confusing distinction in this class is the difference between a *cash flow* and a *cash account*. Cash flows, which we have discussed in a number of contexts within this book, such as estimating cash flows for proposed new projects in Chapter 12, are a good thing. A cash account, on the other hand, is a current asset account just like all the other current asset accounts we have been discussing, and it has exactly the same attributes of high liquidity and low profitability that inventory and accounts receivable accounts have. Sure, cash may be a bit more liquid than inventory or money tied up in accounts receivable, but it's not really any more profitable.[2]

Reasons for Holding Cash

A firm may keep part of its capital tied up in cash for three primary reasons:

transaction facilitation

The use of cash to pay employees' wages, taxes, suppliers' bills, interest on debts, and dividends on stock.

1. **Transaction facilitation:** Firms need cash to pay employees' wages, taxes, suppliers' bills, interest on debts, and stock dividends. Though the firm will have cash coming in from day-to-day operations and any financing activities, the inflows and outflows are not usually perfectly synchronized, so the firm will need to keep enough cash on hand to meet reasonable transaction demands.
2. Compensating balances: As we previously discussed, firms must often keep a certain percentage of borrowed funds in their checking accounts with their lending institution. Since lenders are exempt from paying interest on corporate checking accounts, compensating balances become a cheap source of funds for the lender and represent opportunity costs for borrowing firms.
3. Investment opportunities: In some industries, investment opportunities come and go very quickly. Sometimes, this happens even too quickly for the firm to arrange a loan or seek other financing, so having excess cash on hand may allow the firm to take advantage of investment opportunities that would otherwise be impossible to transact.

[2]Most students realize that cash held in the form of currency does not earn any interest, but they are usually surprised to learn that, by law, corporate checking accounts at commercial banks are not allowed to earn interest, either. Though firms find legal ways around that restriction, we'll leave that discussion to a more advanced text on financial institutions.

To determine how much cash to keep on hand, firms must trade off the opportunity costs associated with holding too much cash against the shortage costs of not holding enough. The two standard models for calculating the trade-offs are the Baumol Model and the Miller-Orr Model.

TIME OUT

14-9 In what types of industries would firms need more cash on hand for transaction facilitation? In what industries might firms need less?

14-10 If a firm is going to take a loan with a bank that has a compensating balance requirement, how does that affect the amount of money the firm must borrow?

Determining the Target Cash Balance: The Baumol Model

LG14-8

An economist named William Baumol developed the first model designed to minimize the sum of the opportunity costs associated with holding cash and the trading costs associated with converting other assets to cash.[3] Baumol's model is intuitively appealing, and analysts still use it in industries for which cash outflows are fairly predictable. For other industries, its use is more problematic due to the model's rather unrealistic assumptions:

- The model assumes that the firm has a constant, perfectly predictable disbursement rate for cash. In reality, disbursement rates are much more variable and unpredictable.
- The model assumes that no cash will come in during the period in question. Since most firms hope to make more money than they pay out, and usually have cash inflows at all times, this assumption is obviously at odds with what we usually see.
- The model does not allow for any **safety stock** of extra cash to buffer the firm against an unexpectedly high demand for cash.

safety stock

Excess amounts of a current asset kept on hand to meet unexpected shocks in demand.

In Baumol's model, cash is assumed to start from a **replenishment level,** C, and then decline smoothly to a value of zero. When cash declines to zero, it can be immediately replenished by selling another C worth of marketable securities, for which the firm has to pay a trading cost of F.

replenishment level

The level to which the cash account is "refilled" when marketable securities are sold to recapitalize it.

Thus the model implies that cash levels will follow a cyclical pattern throughout the year. For example, if a firm sells \$20,000 worth of marketable securities each time it needs to replenish cash and disburses \$5,000 in cash each week, then the cash balance would cycle every four weeks, as shown in Figure 14.7.

Notice another implication of the cash being disbursed at a constant rate. The average cash level should equal one-half of the replenishment level, $C/2$. If the firm can earn an interest rate i on marketable securities, then keeping an average cash balance of $C/2$ will impose an opportunity cost on the firm of:

$$\text{Opportunity cost} = \frac{C}{2} \times i \qquad \textbf{(14-3)}$$

If we also assume that a particular firm faces an annual demand for cash of T, then the firm will need to sell marketable securities T/C times during the year, incurring in the process annual trading costs of:

$$\text{Trading cost} = \frac{T}{C} \times F \qquad \textbf{(14-4)}$$

[3]See W. S. Baumol, "The Transactions Demand for Cash: An Inventory Theoretic Approach," *Quarterly Journal of Economics* 66, no. 4 (November 1952), pp. 545–556.

figure 14.7

Cash Flow Patterns of the Baumol Model

In this model, when cash declines to zero, it can be immediately replenished by selling marketable securities.

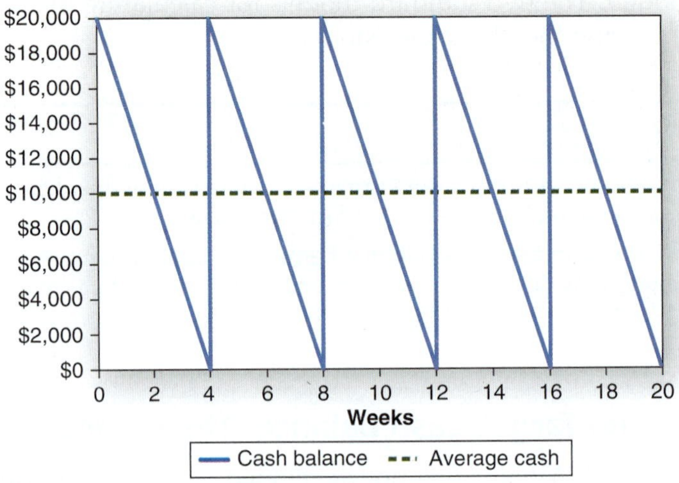

The firm's total annual costs associated with its cash management policy will therefore be:

$$\text{Total cost} = \frac{C}{2} \times i + \frac{T}{C} \times F \qquad \textbf{(14-5)}$$

Solving this for the value of C that minimizes annual costs, C^*, yields:

$$C^* = \sqrt{2TF/i} \qquad \textbf{(14-6)}$$

EXAMPLE 14-3

LG14-8

For interactive versions of this example visit www.mhhe.com/can3e

Optimal Cash Replenishment under Baumol Model

Suppose that AFS Industries faces an annual demand for cash of $2 million, incurs transaction costs of $150 every time it sells marketable securities, and can earn 6 percent on its marketable securities. What will be the firm's optimal cash replenishment level?

SOLUTION:

The optimal cash replenishment level will be:

$$\begin{aligned} C^* &= \sqrt{2TF/i} \\ &= \sqrt{2(\$2{,}000{,}000)(\$150)/0.06} \\ &= \$100{,}000 \end{aligned}$$

Similar to Problems 14-19, 14-20, self-test problem 4

Determining the Target Cash Balance: The Miller-Orr Model

The Miller-Orr model takes a different approach to calculating the optimal cash management strategy.[4] It assumes that daily net cash flows are normally

[4]See M. H. Miller and D. Orr, "A Model of the Demand for Money by Firms," *Quarterly Journal of Economics* 80, no. 3 (August 1966), pp. 413–435.

distributed and allows for both cash inflows and outflows. This model bases its computations on information about:

- The lower control limit, L.
- The trading cost for marketable securities per transaction, F.
- The standard deviation in net daily cash flows, σ.
- The daily interest rate on marketable securities, i_{day}.

Using their model, Miller and Orr show that the optimal cash return point, Z^*, and upper limit for cash balances, H^*, are equal to:

$$Z^* = \sqrt[3]{3F\sigma^2/4i_{day}} + L \qquad \textbf{(14-7)}$$

$$H^* = 3Z^* - 2L \qquad \textbf{(14-8)}$$

Note that the firm determines L, and that the firm can set it to a non-zero number to recognize the use of safety stock.

The optimal cash return point, Z^*, is analogous to the replenishment level, C^*, in Baumol's model, but with one key difference. Since Baumol's model only allowed for cash disbursements, C^* was always "replenished to" from a level of zero. In the Miller-Orr model, Z^* will be the replenishment level to which cash is replenished when the cash level hits L, but it will also be the return level that cash is brought back *down* to when cash hits H^*.

LG14-8

EXAMPLE 14-4

Calculation of Optimal Return Point and Upper Limit for the Miller-Orr Model

For interactive versions of this example visit www.mhhe.com/can3e

Suppose that Dandy Candy, Inc., would like to maintain its cash account at a minimum level of $100,000 but expects the standard deviation in net daily cash flows to be $5,000; the effective annual rate on marketable securities will be 8 percent per year, and the trading cost per sale or purchase of marketable securities will be $200 per transaction. What will be Dandy Candy's optimal cash return point and upper limit?

SOLUTION:

The daily interest rate on marketable securities will equal:

$$i_{day} = \sqrt[365]{1.08} - 1 = 0.000211$$

And the optimal cash return point and upper limit will equal:

$$\begin{aligned} Z^* &= \sqrt[3]{3F\sigma^2/4i_{day}} + L \\ &= \sqrt[3]{3(\$200)(\$5{,}000)^2/(4 \times 0.000211)} + \$100{,}000 \\ &= \$126{,}101.72 \\ H^* &= 3Z^* - 2L \\ &= \$178{,}305.16 \end{aligned}$$

Assuming the random cash balances shown below, Dandy Candy would buy or sell securities to make adjustments as indicated:

Day	Cash Balance before Adjustment	Adjustment	Cash after Adjustment
1	$177,025.21		$177,025.21
2	$158,965.54		$158,965.54
3	$162,488.16		$162,488.16
4	$183,466.74	−$57,365.02	$126,101.72
5	$132,548.06		$132,548.06
6	$129,816.11		$129,816.11
7	$103,709.38		$103,709.38
8	$77,229.23	$48,872.49	$126,101.72
9	$121,483.60		$121,483.60
10	$109,309.78		$109,309.78
11	$81,609.28	$44,492.44	$126,101.72
12	$128,636.69		$128,636.69
13	$102,121.84		$102,121.84
14	$125,376.66		$125,376.66
15	$145,025.00		$145,025.00
16	$142,320.22		$142,320.22
17	$166,501.15		$166,501.15
18	$191,226.65	−$65,124.93	$126,101.72
19	$119,127.54		$119,127.54
20	$109,377.65		$109,377.65
21	$80,841.15	$45,260.57	$126,101.72
22	$125,476.90		$125,476.90
23	$114,416.24		$114,416.24

Similar to Problems 14-21, 14-22, 14-23, 14-24, self-test problem 5

As Figure 14.8 shows, the firm will reduce cash to $126,101.72 by buying marketable securities when the cash balance gets up to $178,305.16, and it will increase cash to $126,101.72 by selling marketable securities when the cash balance gets down to $100,000.

figure 14.8

Cash Flow Patterns of the Miller-Orr Model

The model assumes that the distribution of daily net cash flows is normally distributed and allows for both cash inflows and outflows.

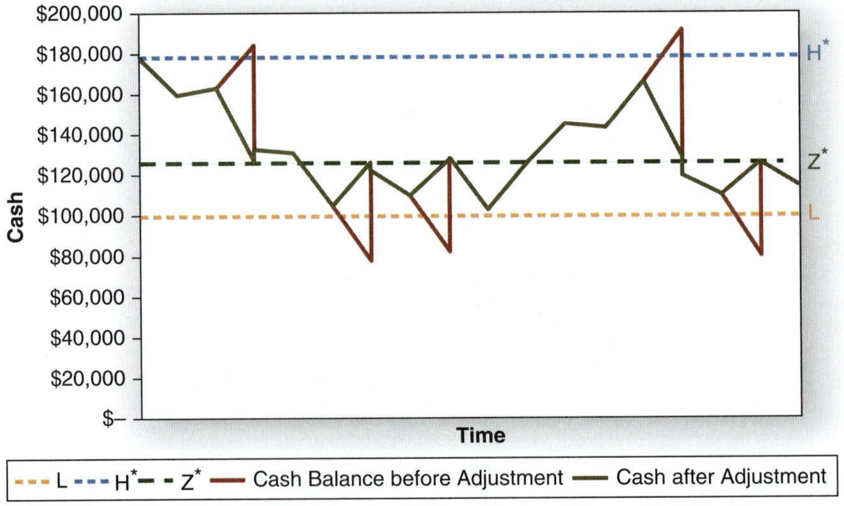

Other Factors Influencing the Target Cash Balance

Even the Miller-Orr model, the more realistic of the two models because it deals with both cash inflows and outflows, still ignores fundamental factors that influence firms' cash management practices. First, firms also have the option of borrowing short-term to meet unexpected demands for cash. Though the short-term borrowing rate faced by the firm is likely to be more expensive than the opportunity cost incurred by selling marketable securities,[5] this isn't necessarily the comparison that matters. If the probability of an unexpected demand for cash causing a firm to borrow in the short term is low enough, or if the amount of interest to be earned by investing in longer-term securities is sufficiently higher than that to be earned on marketable securities, then it might be worth it for the firm to risk occasionally paying a relatively high interest rate on short-term borrowing if it can earn a substantially higher return by investing the funds that would have been tied up in marketable securities in something more lucrative.

Second, the authors of both models developed their ideas when buying and selling marketable securities was a relatively expensive and time-consuming proposition. The costs and delays of trading securities have fallen dramatically since the advent of the Internet. The cost has fallen so much that many large firms habitually use all or the majority of their available cash to purchase overnight securities. If trading costs are low enough that it makes sense for the firm to incur at least two sets of trading costs each day—one for selling enough marketable securities in the morning to make it through the day, and another for purchasing marketable securities at the end of the business day—then it's also probable that any unforeseen demand for cash *during* the day can probably be met fairly cheaply by selling marketable securities as needed. Or, put another way, the transactions costs associated with trading securities have fallen so dramatically relative to the opportunity costs of not having cash invested in marketable securities that keeping any "extra" money idle in cash just doesn't make sense.

Finally, both models ignore the fact that many firms must keep compensating balances in their deposit accounts as part of borrowing agreements with their banks. If the compensating balance requirement was a constant amount or percentage, then we could adjust the Miller-Orr model so that L included the compensating balance, but many firms must only keep a certain minimum compensating balance *on average*. This implies that an unforeseen demand for cash that causes a firm's deposit account to temporarily dip below the minimum compensating balance can be offset by keeping a corresponding amount of excess cash in the account in a later period. Even the more modern Miller-Orr model does not allow for that.

TIME OUT

14-11 What effect does increasing the standard deviation in daily cash flows have on the cash return point in the Miller-Orr model?

14-12 If you were asked to adjust the Baumol model to reflect the need to keep a minimum cash balance, how would you go about doing so?

[5] To see why, go down to your local bank or savings and loan and see which is higher: The rate it pays on savings accounts or the rate it charges on short-term borrowing.

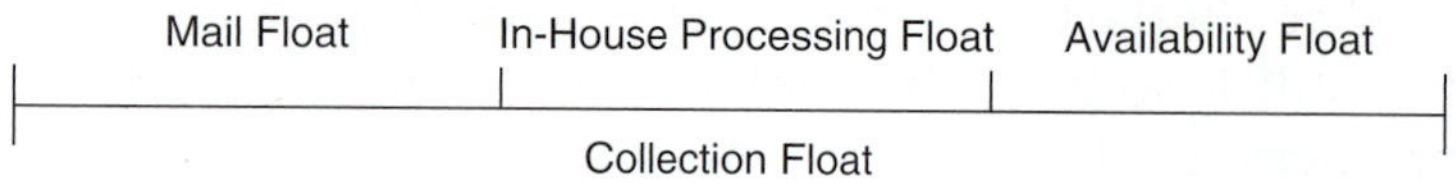

figure 14.9

Components of Collection Float

Cash is not always liquid due to collection float.

LG14-9

14.6 • Float Control: Managing the Collection and Disbursement of Cash

The economic definition of cash includes undeposited checks, but as we all know, an undeposited check is not as liquid as the same amount of cash sitting inside your checking account. So another component of a good cash management policy involves making sure that checks clear in a timely manner.

Accelerating Collections

float

The period of time between when a payment is sent out and when the money is actually received by the collecting firm.

The period of time between when a check is written and when it clears and the funds are available for use is referred to as **float.** The checks sent to a firm experience three different types of collection float, illustrated in Figure 14.9:

1. Mail float is the length of time that checks are en route to the firm, either through the postal system or through some sort of electronic transfer.
2. In-house processing float is the length of time needed for the firm to process and deposit check payments from its customers once they have been received.
3. Availability float is the length of time necessary for a check to clear through the banking system once it has been deposited.

Together, these three types of float span the entire length of time between the customer sending a payment and the firm receiving cash in its account.

Several different techniques can help firms reduce collection float:

- A lockbox system is a collection of geographically dispersed post office boxes, each maintained for the firm by a bank local to the respective box. For firms with hundreds or thousands of customers spread across a large region, the ideal situation is to have enough locations so that no customer is more than a couple of hundred miles from one of the firm's post office boxes. By having customers send their payments to the closest post office box, and then having the local bank pick up and handle the payment processing several times a day, the firm can reduce both mail float and in-house processing float.
- Concentration banking accelerates cash collections from customers by having funds sent to several geographically situated regional banks and then transferred to a main concentration account in another bank. The funds can be transferred through depository transfer checks and electronic transfers.
- Wire transfers are the fastest way of transmitting money from a local bank into the concentration bank. Banks within the United States utilize the Society for Worldwide Interbank Financial Telecommunication (SWIFT) system to make payments to banks in countries outside of the United States. Bank-to-bank transfers conducted within the United States take place over the Fedwire system, which uses the Federal Reserve System and its assignment of bank routing numbers.

Delaying Disbursements

Disbursement float is the delay between the firm sending out a payment and the money being taken out of the firm's bank account. Two legal ways to increase

finance at work — global

CULTURAL DIFFERENCES IN PREFERENCES FOR PAYING BILLS

Japan's Postal Savings Bank, the world's largest bank, has long been used as an example of the efficiencies available to both individuals and businesses of electronic transactions. Electronic transactions are instantaneous transactions that use security authentication rather than conventional check-clearing processes to transfer funds from a buyer to the seller.

However, in 2006, one of the Nikkei trade papers summarized the results of a survey among Japanese women regarding payment methods used for Internet shopping. Not surprisingly, the vast majority (56 percent) of respondents purchasing goods over the Internet reported that they used credit cards for their transactions. However, the distribution of the rest of the responses illustrates a vast difference between alternative payment pipelines that American and Japanese consumers use.

For example, 17.6 percent of Japanese respondents ordered online, then paid in cash at their local convenience store; 13.1 percent paid COD when the mailman delivered the goods; and 4.3 percent paid using electronic transfers from their post office savings accounts.

What implications does this have for the money management policies of firms doing business in Japan? Well, given that a far larger percentage of Americans probably pay for their online purchases with credit cards, and that the alternative methods of payment listed previously could be expected to have different clearing times than do payments received through a merchant's credit card account, it's something that firms seeking to do business in Japan should consider.

want to know more? **Key Words to Search for Updates:** "Marketing Tip: Payment Methods" (see the Japan Marketing News blog at www.japanmarketingnews.com/consumer_industry_data/index.html).

disbursement float involve keeping the cash available to the firm until the very last moment:

- A **zero-balance account** is a checking account that the firm sets up so that the bank agrees to automatically transfer funds from an interest-bearing account to pay off any checks presented. Since zero-balance accounts never contain excess cash, they represent one way that firms can get around regulations against corporations having interest-bearing checking accounts.
- **Drafts** resemble checks, but differ in that they are payable by the firm issuing them rather than payable by a bank. When a draft is sent to the firm's bank for payment, the bank must present the draft to the firm *before* disbursing the funds.

zero-balance account A corporate checking account which keeps a zero balance, automatically transferring in just enough funds to cover any checks received on the account from another interest-bearing account.

draft Similar to a check, but payable by the issuing firm rather than by its bank.

Ethical and Legal Questions

Using collected cash before actually receiving it, or continuing to use disbursed cash after you have sent a check out, can earn your firm higher returns, but this practice is illegal. The most extreme form of taking illegal advantage of disbursement float is a practice called *check kiting,* which is any sort of fraud that involves drawing out money from a bank account with insufficient funds to cover the check.

The Check Clearing for the 21st Century Act, which allows for transmitting electronic images of checks rather than the physical paper checks themselves, has greatly reduced the incidence of check kiting by substantially shortening the time required for a check to be cleared from one bank to another.

TIME OUT

14-13 In Japan, many consumers pay their bills by electronic deduction from their checking accounts instead of using paper checks. What effect do you think this has on the collection float of Japanese firms versus that of American firms?

14-14 What's the difference between a lockbox system and concentration banking?

LG14-10

14.7 • Investing Idle Cash

As both the Baumol and Miller-Orr models imply, firms habitually move cash into and out of marketable securities in order to partially offset the opportunity costs of having capital tied up in current assets. Most large firms will manage their marketable securities investments themselves. Smaller firms will typically invest through an independently managed money-market fund or by letting their bank transfer all available excess funds at the end of each business day into a sweep account, which will then be invested on their behalf.

Why Firms Have Surplus Cash

Firms tend to have surplus cash available either due to seasonal fluctuations in their cash flow patterns, or in preparation for planned expenditures. Seasonal fluctuations in the amount of cash on hand can occur as a result of either cyclical sales or cyclical purchases of raw materials. For example, a firm that produces swimming pool accessories will obviously experience higher sales from spring through late fall, and a firm that distributes fresh vegetables purchased on the spot market will have higher cash outflows during the harvest season.

Firms' cash balances may also temporarily increase immediately prior to a planned expenditure, either because they have been "saving up" for the expenditure, or because they issued stocks or bonds in advance of the expenditure but need someplace to "park" the funds until they are needed.

What to Do with Surplus Cash

As mentioned, firms usually put surplus cash into money-market securities. As discussed in Chapter 18, these include Treasury bills, federal funds and repurchase agreements, commercial paper, negotiable certificates of deposit, and banker's acceptances.

TIME OUT

14-15 Should a firm with nonseasonal cash flows that lacks any good prospective investments keep excess cash on hand? Why or why not?

14-16 Suppose a firm has a temporary surplus of cash meant to fund an upcoming expansion project. Why might it not wish to invest these funds in capital-market (as opposed to money-market) securities?

LG14-11

14.8 • Credit Management

As is the case with the firm's cash management policy, the firm's optimal credit policy will trade off the opportunity cost of lost sales (if the firm does not grant credit or is too conservative in terms of the credit it does grant) against the carrying costs associated with funding the accounts receivable plus the expected costs of default on the accounts receivable.

credit terms
A listing of the credit period, the cash discount, and the type of credit instrument to be used.

Credit Policy: Terms of the Sale

As a minimum, the **credit terms** of sale usually contain at least the credit period, the cash discount, and a description of the type of credit instrument. The credit period is the maturity of the credit that the firm is willing to extend, which varies based on attributes of the goods being sold and the customer purchasing the goods. For example, perishable goods will usually carry a lower credit period, regardless of who is purchasing them. Creditworthy, established customers will probably be given better credit terms than customers the firm has not dealt with before.

To encourage early repayment, firms will often offer a percentage discount if the bill is paid within a certain time period. For example, a firm that quotes customers terms of "2/10, net 30" is offering them the choice between paying the entire bill within 30 days or taking a 2 percent discount off the invoiced price if they pay within 10 days.

For most trade credit, the invoice is the only type of credit instrument involved. When the customer signs a copy upon receipt of the goods, the customer makes an implicit promise to pay under the terms listed on the invoice. If a firm wishes for a customer to make a more explicit acknowledgment of its ability and obligation to pay, a firm can ask the customer to sign a promissory note upon delivery of the goods or to furnish a commercial draft or banker's acceptance in advance of the delivery of the goods.

Credit Analysis

Before granting a customer credit, the firm may wish to engage in **credit analysis.** Such analysis involves a systematic determination of the potential borrower's ability and willingness to pay for the goods being provided on credit. A thorough credit analysis will look at the potential borrower's past record and its present and forecasted future financial condition, which generally involves examining the "five C's":

credit analysis
A systematic determination of a borrower's ability and willingness to repay a potential loan.

1. *Capacity:* Does the borrower have the legal and economic ability to pay?
2. *Character:* Does the borrower's reputation indicate a willingness to settle debt obligations?
3. *Capital:* Having assets at risk makes it more likely that the borrower will repay as promised.
4. *Collateral:* Goods that can be seized and sold, with the proceeds being used to pay the firm in the event of bankruptcy by the borrower, also makes it more likely that the customer will repay as promised.
5. *Conditions:* Any economic conditions that may affect the borrower's ability to repay the loan should also be taken into account.

Collection Policy

The firm's collection policy is aimed at collecting past-due debts from customers. The usual procedure for collecting follows a typical path of:

1. Sending one or more delinquency letters informing the customer of the past-due status of the account, asking the customer to contact the firm to discuss alternative means of repayment and pointing out what legal recourse the firm has.
2. Initiating telephone calls conveying the same information as above.
3. Employing a collection agency.
4. Taking legal action against the customer if all else fails.

To monitor and control this process, firms use a tool called an *aging schedule,* which stratifies a firm's accounts receivable by the age of each account. For example, a firm that offers terms of 2/10, net 60 to its customers might want to measure the age of accounts receivable using the categories shown in Table 14.2.

table 14.2 Sample Aging Schedule

Age Bracket	Percentage of AR in Bracket
0–10 days	10%
11–30 days	35
31–60 days	45
61–90 days	7
Over 90 days	3
	100

Such an aging schedule would allow the firm to see what percentage of its customers are still eligible to take the discount (i.e., those in the "0–10 days" category), how many are past due by less than 30 days (i.e., those in the "61–90 days" category), and how many are over 30 days past due (i.e., those in the "Over 90 days" category).

Firms often link their collection policies to their aging schedules. For example, the customers in Table 14.2 that fall into the "61–90 days" category might be sent a delinquency letter, while those in the "Over 90 days" category might be phoned.

TIME OUT

14-17 Why do firms offer customers discounts for paying early?

14-18 Should a firm always turn far-overdue bills from customers over to a collection agency or sue the customers? Why or why not?

viewpoints REVISITED

Business Application Solution

Chewbacca's operating cycle will be equal to:

$$\text{Operating cycle} = \frac{0.1 \times 365}{0.55} + \frac{0.1667 \times 365}{1}$$
$$= 127.20 \text{ days}$$

Their cash cycle will be equal to:

$$\text{Cash cycle} = 127.20 - \frac{0.05 \times 365}{0.55}$$
$$= 94.02 \text{ days}$$

Absent any other information about current assets or current liabilities, Chewbacca's net working capital will be:

$$(0.10 + 0.1667 - 0.05) \times \$32 \text{ million}$$
$$= \$6.93 \text{ million}$$

Personal Application Solution

Since Wanda will be drawing out the money smoothly from the account, she can use the Baumol model to determine the optimal replenishment level for her personal stock of cash:

$$C^* = \sqrt{2(\$25{,}000)(\$9.95)/0.035}$$
$$= \$3{,}770.18$$

summary of learning goals

In this chapter, we discussed the firm's working capital policy, focusing on how we can determine the optimal amount to be invested in current assets, the portion of that amount to be provided by the firm, and sources of funding for that portion.

LG14-1 **Set overall objectives of a good working capital policy.** A good working capital policy has the firm providing enough net working capital, but not too much.

LG14-2 **Discuss how net working capital serves the firm.** Net working capital measures the portion of current assets that are not funded by current liabilities, but which must be funded by other sources of capital.

LG14-3 **Analyze the firm's operating and cash cycles to determine what funding for current assets the firm needs.** The cash cycle is basically the operating cycle minus the average payment period and represents the funding need.

LG14-4 **Model the optimal trade-off between carrying costs and shortage costs that dictates the firm's current asset investment.** Ideally, the firm will have just enough current assets so that the marginal carrying costs and marginal shortage costs are equal, thereby minimizing total cost.

LG14-5 **Compare the flexible and restrictive approaches to financing current assets.** A flexible financing policy has the firm funding short-term fluctuations in the amount of current assets with long-term debt; a restrictive policy has the firm funding those fluctuations with short-term debt.

LG14-6 **Differentiate among sources of short-term financing available for funding current assets.** The firm can use unsecured loans, secure loans, commercial paper, or banker's acceptances.

LG14-7 **Justify the firm's need to hold cash.** The three main reasons for holding cash are to facilitate transactions, to provide for compensating balances for loan agreements, and to take advantage of short-lived investment opportunities.

LG14-8 **Use the Baumol and Miller-Orr models for determining cash policy.** The Baumol model was designed to help determine a firm's cash policy under conditions of certain cash demand, while the Miller-Orr model is designed for conditions of stochastic cash demand.

LG14-9 **Identify sources of float and show how to control float for the firm's disbursement and collection functions.** Float stems from delays in physically sending or receiving a payment and from processing delays either by the receiving firm or by the check-clearing process. To the extent that it is legally and ethically possible, firms will attempt to increase disbursement float and reduce collection float so as to reduce the amount of cash they have to keep on hand.

LG14-10 **Identify firms' choices for using excess cash.** Excess cash is generally invested in money-market instruments or marketable securities.

LG14-11 **Connect the firm's credit terms and collection policy and the amount of capital the firm has invested in accounts receivable.** The more generously the firm grants credit, the more its customers will take advantage of that generosity and the longer the firm will have to pay for producing and selling its product without collecting any money for it, so generous credit terms will result in the firm requiring a larger investment in net working capital than would otherwise be the case.

chapter equations

$$\text{14-1}\quad \text{Operating cycle} = \text{Days' sales in inventory} + \text{Average collection period}$$
$$= \frac{\text{Inventory} \times 365}{\text{Cost of goods sold}} + \frac{\text{Accounts receivable} \times 365}{\text{Credit sales}}$$

$$\text{14-2}\quad \text{Cash cycle} = \text{Operating cycle} - \text{Average payment period}$$
$$= \text{Operating cycle} - \frac{\text{Accounts payable} \times 365}{\text{Cost of goods sold}}$$

$$\text{14-3}\quad \text{Opportunity cost} = \frac{C}{2} \times i$$

$$\text{14-4}\quad \text{Trading cost} = \frac{T}{C} \times F$$

$$\text{14-5}\quad \text{Total cost} = \frac{C}{2} \times i + \frac{T}{C} \times F$$

$$\text{14-6}\quad C^* = \sqrt{2TF/i}$$

$$\text{14-7}\quad Z^* = \sqrt[3]{3F\sigma^2/4i_{day}} + L$$

$$\text{14-8}\quad H^* = 3Z^* - 2L$$

key terms

asset-based loans, Short-term loans secured by a company's assets. *p. 483*

assignment, A process whereby the firm borrows money from another entity, providing in return both a lien on the accounts receivable and the right of **recourse.** *p. 483*

banker's acceptance (BA), A short-term promissory note issued by a corporation, bearing the unconditional guarantee (*acceptance*) of a major bank. *p. 484*

Barabas Economic Order Quantity (EOQ), The inventory order quantity that minimizes total holding and ordering costs. *p. 476*

carrying costs, The opportunity costs associated with having capital tied up in current assets instead of more productive fixed assets and explicit costs necessary to maintain the value of the current assets. *p. 479*

cash cycle, The operating cycle minus the average payment period. *p. 476*

commercial paper, A money-market security, issued by large banks and medium-to-large corporations, that matures in nine months or less. *p. 483*

compensating balance, Amount of money required to be kept in a firm's deposit accounts with a lender according to a lending arrangement. *p. 482*

credit analysis, A systematic determination of a borrower's ability and willingness to repay a potential loan. *p. 493*

credit terms, A listing of the credit period, the cash discount, and the type of credit instrument to be used. *p. 492*

draft, Similar to a check, but payable by the issuing firm rather than by its bank. *p. 491*

factor, An entity that will buy accounts receivable from a firm before they are due on a discounted basis. *p. 483*

float, The period of time between when a payment is sent out and when the money is actually received by the collecting firm. *p. 490*

just in time (JIT), A production strategy that attempts to improve a firm's return on investment by reducing inprocess inventory and associated carrying costs as much as possible. *p. 475*

operating cycle, The time required to acquire raw materials and to produce, sell, and receive payment for the finished goods. *p. 476*

operations management, The area of management concerned with designing and overseeing the process of production. *p. 475*

opportunity cost, The cost or forgone opportunity of using an asset already in use by the firm, or a person already employed by the firm, in a new project. *p. 476*

recourse, The legal right to hold a firm responsible for payment of a debt if the debtors do not repay as promised. *p. 483*

replenishment level, The level to which the cash account is "refilled" when marketable securities are sold to recapitalize it. *p. 485*

safety stock, Excess amounts of a current asset kept on hand to meet unexpected shocks in demand. *p. 485*

shortage costs, Costs associated with a firm's not having sufficient cash, inventory, or accounts receivable. *p. 475*

transaction facilitation, The use of cash to pay employees' wages, taxes, suppliers' bills, interest on debts, and dividends on stock. *p. 484*

zero-balance account, A corporate checking account which keeps a zero balance, automatically transferring in just enough funds to cover any checks *received* on the account from another interest-bearing account. *p. 491*

self-test problems with solutions

1 Computing Operating Cycle and Cash Cycle Your firm currently has an operating cycle of 73 days. You are analyzing some operational changes that are expected to decrease the average collection period by five days and decrease the days' sales in inventory by three days. The average payment period is expected to decrease by 10 days. If all of these changes are adopted, what will your firm's new operating cycle be? LG14-3

Solution:

Since the operating cycle is equal to days' sales in inventory plus the average collection period, the operating cycle of the firm will decrease to $73 - 5 - 3 = 65$ days. The change in the average payment period has no effect on the operating cycle.

2 Minimizing Carrying and Shortage Costs Suppose that your firm is seeking a five-year, amortizing \$500,000 loan with annual payments and your bank is offering you the choice between a \$600,000 loan with a \$100,000 compensating balance and a \$500,000 loan without a compensating balance. If the interest rate on the \$500,000 loan is 9 percent, how low would the interest rate on the loan with the compensating balance have to be in order for you to choose it? LG14-4

Solution:

The payments on the \$500,000 loan would be equal to \$128,546.23. To pay less on the \$600,000 loan, you would have to have an interest rate lower than 2.34 percent.

3 Flexible versus Restrictive Financing If your firm faces a long-term borrowing rate of 8 percent, a short-term borrowing rate of 10 percent, can earn 7 percent when investing marketable securities, and needs to fund \$3 million in permanent current assets and \$1 million in seasonal current assets (for six months out of the year), what would be the cost difference between using a flexible and a restrictive financing policy? LG14-5

Solution:

Under either policy, you will be funding the $3 million in permanent current assets with long-term debt, so you can ignore this as an incremental difference between the two policies. If you use long-term debt, you will be paying $1 million × 8 percent = $80,000 per year in interest, but earning $1 million × 7 percent × 0.5 = $35,000 in interest for the half year that you get to invest the money in marketable securities, for a net cost of $80,000 − $35,000 = $45,000 for the flexible financing policy. With the restrictive financing policy, you will be paying $1 million × 10 percent × 0.5 = $50,000 per year, so your net costs will be lower if you follow the flexible financing policy.

LG14-8

4 Baumol Model Suppose that Overton, Inc., faces an annual demand for cash of $17 million, incurs transaction costs of $200 every time it sells marketable securities, and can earn 7.3 percent on its marketable securities. What will be its optimal cash replenishment level?

Solution:

The optimal cash replenishment level will be:

$$\begin{aligned} C^* &= \sqrt{2TF/i} \\ &= \sqrt{2(\$17{,}000{,}000)(\$200)/0.073} \\ &= \$305{,}205.97 \end{aligned}$$

LG14-8

5 Miller-Orr Model GenCo would like to maintain its cash account at a minimum level of $250,000, but management expects the standard deviation in net daily cash flows to be $15,000, the effective annual rate on marketable securities to be 5 percent per year, and the trading cost per sale or purchase of marketable securities to be $110 per transaction. What will be GenCo's optimal cash return point and upper limit?

Solution:

The daily interest rate on marketable securities will be equal to:

$$i_{day} = \sqrt[365]{1.05} - 1 = 0.000134$$

And the optimal cash return point and upper limit will be equal to:

$$\begin{aligned} Z^* &= \sqrt[3]{3F\sigma^2/4i_{day}} + L \\ &= \sqrt[3]{3(\$110)(\$15{,}000)^2/(4 \times 0.000134)} + \$250{,}000 \\ &= \$301{,}783.25 \\ H^* &= 3(\$301{,}783.25) - 2(\$250{,}000) \\ &= \$405{,}349.76 \end{aligned}$$

LG14-9

6 Float Calculation AFS, Inc., estimates that it takes, on average, three days for customers' payments to arrive, two days for the payments to be processed and deposited by AFS's bookkeeping department, and three more days for checks to clear once they are deposited. What is AFS's collection float?

Solution:

The collection float will be 3 + 2 + 3 = 8 days.

7 Aging Schedule OTK Sports has constructed the aging schedule shown in the following table. If the company offers terms of 2/10, net 30 to its customers, and if its collection policy is to send a letter on bills more than 30 days overdue and to call on bills more than 60 days overdue, how many letters will it need to print? LG14-11

Age Bracket	Number of Customers in Bracket
0–10 days	25
11–30 days	78
31–60 days	17
61–90 days	3
Over 90 days	1

Solution:

OTK will need to print 17 letters.

questions

1. Is it possible for a firm to have negative net working capital? How? *(LG14-1)*
2. Would it be possible for a decision to deny credit to your customers to be value maximizing? How? *(LG14-1)*
3. Which of the following will result in an increase in net working capital? *(LG14-2)*
   a. An increase in cash.
   b. A decrease in accounts payable.
   c. An increase in notes payable.
   d. A decrease in accounts receivable.
   e. An increase in inventory.
4. Would it be possible for a firm to have a negative cash cycle? How? *(LG14-3)*
5. If a firm's inventory turnover ratio increases, what will happen to the firm's operating cycle? *(LG14-3)*
6. If a firm's inventory turnover ratio increases, what will happen to the firm's cash cycle? *(LG14-3)*
7. Everything else held constant, will an increase in the amount of inventory on hand increase or decrease the firm's profitability? *(LG14-4)*
8. Would a firm ever use short-term debt to finance permanent current assets? Why or why not? *(LG14-5)*
9. Suppose that short-term borrowing actually becomes more expensive than long-term borrowing: How would this affect the firm's choice between a flexible financing policy and a restrictive policy? *(LG14-5)*
10. If asset-backed loans are cheaper than unsecured loans, what is the disadvantage to the firm in using an asset-backed loan? *(LG14-6)*
11. Is an increase in the cash account a source of funds or a use of funds? *(LG14-7)*
12. What will be the carrying cost associated with a compensating balance requirement? *(LG14-7)*

13. What will be the shortage cost associated with a compensating balance requirement? *(LG14-7)*

14. What would be the shortage costs associated with a restaurant not having enough cash on hand to make change? *(LG14-7)*

15. If a firm needs to keep a minimum cash balance on hand and faces both cash inflows and outflows, which of the cash management models discussed in this chapter would be more appropriate for the firm to use? *(LG14-8)*

16. What effect will increasing the trading costs associated with selling marketable securities have on the optimal replenishment level in the Baumol Model? Why? *(LG14-8)*

17. What effect will an increase in the standard deviation of daily cash flows have on the return point in the Miller-Orr model? Why? *(LG14-8)*

18. Could a firm ever have negative collection float? Why or why not? *(LG14-9)*

19. Could a firm ever have negative disbursement float? Why or why not? *(LG14-9)*

20. Would a draft have availability float? Why or why not? *(LG14-9)*

21. From our discussion of capital markets elsewhere in this book, why would you expect a firm to have a time delay between raising funds to finance a project and the expenditure of those funds on that project? *(LG14-9)*

22. What purpose does a discount on credit terms serve? What is the cost of such a discount to the offering firm? *(LG14-9)*

basic problems

problems

14-1 Net Working Capital Requirements JohnBoy Industries has a cash balance of $45,000, accounts payable of $125,000, inventory of $175,000, accounts receivable of $210,000, notes payable of $120,000, and accrued wages and taxes of $37,000. How much net working capital does the firm need to fund? *(LG14-2)*

14-2 Net Working Capital Requirements Dandee Lions, Inc., has a cash balance of $105,000, accounts payable of $220,000, inventory of $203,000, accounts receivable of $319,000, notes payable of $65,000, and accrued wages and taxes of $75,000. How much net working capital does the firm need to fund? *(LG14-2)*

14-3 Days' Sales in Inventory Dabble, Inc., has sales of $980,000 and cost of goods sold of $640,000. The firm had a beginning inventory of $36,000 and an ending inventory of $46,000. What is the length of the days' sales in inventory? *(LG14-3)*

14-4 Days' Sales in Inventory Sow Tire, Inc., has sales of $1,450,000 and cost of goods sold of $980,000. The firm had a beginning inventory of $97,000 and an ending inventory of $82,000. What is the length of the days' sales in inventory? *(LG14-3)*

14-5 Average Payment Period If a firm has a cash cycle of 67 days and an operating cycle of 104 days, what is its average payment period? *(LG14-3)*

14-6 Average Payment Period If a firm has a cash cycle of 45 days and an operating cycle of 77 days, what is its average payment period? *(LG14-3)*

14-7 Payables Turnover If a firm has a cash cycle of 73 days and an operating cycle of 127 days, what is its payables turnover? *(LG14-3)*

14-8 Payables Turnover If a firm has a cash cycle of 54 days and an operating cycle of 77 days, what is its payables turnover? *(LG14-3)*

14-9 Compensating Balance Would it be worthwhile to incur a compensating balance of $10,000 in order to get a 1 percent lower interest rate on a 1-year, pure discount loan of $225,000? *(LG14-7)*

14-10 Compensating Balance Would it be worthwhile to incur a compensating balance of $7,500 in order to get a 0.65 percent lower interest rate on a two-year, pure discount loan of $150,000? *(LG14-7)*

14-11 Collection Float CM Enterprises estimates that it takes, on average, three days for customers' payments to arrive, one day for the payments to be processed and deposited by the bookkeeping department, and two more days for the checks to clear once they are deposited. What is CM's collection float? *(LG14-9)*

14-12 Collection Float Smelpank, Inc., estimates that it takes, on average, four days for customers' payments to arrive, three days for the payments to be processed and deposited by the bookkeeping department, and three more days for the checks to clear once they are deposited. What is the firm's collection float? *(LG14-9)*

intermediate problems

14-13 Operating Cycle Suppose that Dunn Industries has annual sales of $2.3 million, cost of goods sold of $1,650,000, average inventories of $1,116,000, and average accounts receivable of $750,000. Assuming that all of Dunn's sales are on credit, what will be the firm's operating cycle? *(LG14-3)*

14-14 Operating Cycle Suppose that LilyMac Photography has annual sales of $230,000, cost of goods sold of $165,000, average inventories of $4,500, and average accounts receivable of $25,000. Assuming that all of LilyMac's sales are on credit, what will be the firm's operating cycle? *(LG14-3)*

14-15 Cash Cycle Suppose that LilyMac Photography has annual sales of $230,000, cost of goods sold of $165,000, average inventories of $4,500, average accounts receivable of $25,000, and an average accounts payable balance of $7,000. Assuming that all of LilyMac's sales are on credit, what will be the firm's cash cycle? *(LG14-3)*

14-16 Cash Cycle Suppose that Ken-Z Art Gallery has annual sales of $870,000, cost of goods sold of $560,000, average inventories of $244,500, average accounts receivable of $265,000, and an average accounts payable balance of $79,000. Assuming that all of Ken-Z's sales are on credit, what will be the firm's cash cycle? *(LG14-3)*

14-17 Compensating Balance Interest Rate Suppose your firm is seeking an eight-year, amortizing $800,000 loan with annual payments, and your bank is offering you the choice between an $850,000 loan with a $50,000 compensating balance and an $800,000 loan without a compensating balance. If the interest rate on the $800,000 loan is 8.5 percent, how low would the interest rate on the loan with the compensating balance have to be for you to choose it? *(LG14-4)*

14-18 Compensating Balance Interest Rate Suppose your firm is seeking a four-year, amortizing $200,000 loan with annual payments and your bank is offering you the choice between a $205,000 loan with a $5,000 compensating balance and a $200,000 loan without a compensating balance. If the interest rate on the $200,000 loan is 9.8 percent, how low would the interest rate on the loan with the compensating balance have to be for you to choose it? *(LG14-4)*

14-19 Optimal Cash Replenishment Level Rose Axels faces a smooth annual demand for cash of $5 million, incurs transaction costs of $275 every time the company sells marketable securities, and can earn 4.3 percent on its marketable securities. What will be its optimal cash replenishment level? *(LG14-8)*

14-20 Optimal Cash Replenishment Level Watkins Resources faces a smooth annual demand for cash of $1.5 million, incurs transaction costs of $75 every time the firm sells marketable securities, and can earn 3.7 percent on its marketable securities. What will be its optimal cash replenishment level? *(LG14-8)*

14-21 Optimal Cash Return Point HotFoot Shoes would like to maintain its cash account at a minimum level of $25,000, but expects the standard deviation in net daily cash flows to be $4,000, the effective annual rate on marketable securities to be 6.5 percent per year, and the trading cost per sale or purchase of marketable securities to be $200 per transaction. What will be its optimal cash return point? *(LG14-8)*

14-22 Optimal Cash Return Point Veggie Burgers, Inc., would like to maintain its cash account at a minimum level of $245,000 but expects the standard deviation in net daily cash flows to be $12,000, the effective annual rate on marketable securities to be 4.7 percent per year, and the trading cost per sale or purchase of marketable securities to be $27.50 per transaction. What will be its optimal cash return point? *(LG14-8)*

14-23 Optimal Upper Cash Limit Veggie Burgers, Inc., would like to maintain its cash account at a minimum level of $245,000 but expects the standard deviation in net daily cash flows to be $12,000, the effective annual rate on marketable securities to be 3.7 percent per year, and the trading cost per sale or purchase of marketable securities to be $27.50 per transaction. What will be its optimal upper cash limit? *(LG14-8)*

14-24 Optimal Upper Cash Limit HotFoot Shoes would like to maintain its cash account at a minimum level of $25,000 but expects the standard deviation in net daily cash flows to be $2,000, the effective annual rate on marketable securities to be 3.5 percent per year, and the trading cost per sale or purchase of marketable securities to be $200 per transaction. What will be its optimal upper cash limit? *(LG14-8)*

research it! Looking Up Information on a Firm's Cash Cycle

Go to the SEC's Edgar site at **www.sec.gov/edgar/quickedgar.htm** and download the latest annual (10-K) report for the firm of your choice. Use the financial statements in the report to calculate the firm's cash cycle.

integrated mini-case Line of Credit

Your bank offers you a $140,000 line of credit with an interest rate of 2.30 percent per quarter. The loan agreement also requires that 7 percent of the unused portion of the credit line be deposited in a non-interest-bearing account as a compensating balance. Your short-term investments are paying 1.55 percent per quarter.

1. What is your effective annual interest rate if you borrow the whole $140,000 for the entire year?
2. What will be the carrying cost in this problem?
3. What will be the shortage cost in this problem?

ANSWERS TO TIME OUT

14-1 A creditor might think of net working capital as a buffer, in that it represents the amount of short-term capital slated to come into the firm above and beyond the amount that the creditor is owed. The larger the amount of the net working capital is, the greater is the chance that the creditor will get paid back.

14-2 Everything else held constant, we would normally expect net working capital to increase in such a situation: Inventory would increase and accounts receivable might also increase if the firm offered better credit terms to try to stimulate sales.

14-3 Reducing inventory on hand would reduce days' sales in inventory, which would cause the operating cycle to decrease.

14-4 The firm with a longer cash cycle will tend to have more net working capital requirements, as the firm will have to fund current assets for a longer period of time.

14-5 As the relative cost of long-term debt increased, firms would tend to shift toward more restrictive policies.

14-6 Carrying costs will increase, because the firm will have to fund a longer collection cycle.

14-7 The firm would be less likely to ask for an excessive amount when it requested a line of credit, implying that the firm's use of such a line of credit would tend to decrease slightly. A bank might adopt such a policy if it wanted to encourage firms to ask for only as much credit as they intended to use.

14-8 Since the firm would not have to wait on collection of the accounts receivable, the cash cycle would decrease.

14-9 Retail firms, which involve a lot of customer transactions, would probably need more cash on hand; industries where direct customer interaction is rare, such as utilities, would need less.

14-10 The firm will need to borrow more money than it really needs, so that both its needs and the compensating balance requirement are met.

14-11 It will cause the cash return point to increase.

14-12 Add the minimum cash balance to C*.

14-13 Since mail float will be eliminated, collection float should decrease.

14-14 In a lockbox system, customers' payments are physically collected close to them, but not necessarily processed close to them; in concentration banking, both the physical collection and much of the processing takes place close to the customer, speeding up the firm's receipt of funds.

14-15 No, they should not keep excess cash on hand, as it is costing the firm interest to raise the money but the firm is not earning any interest on spare cash that is just sitting around.

14-16 Investing money in long-term capital-market funds could expose the firm to the risk that the invested principal might be worth less when the firm needs the money. For example, if a firm bought bonds that were longer term than its time horizon for investing in an expansion project, it could see its investment value go down if interest rates went up.

14-17 If customers pay early, the firm's cash cycle is shortened.

14-18 Not necessarily. If the amount due is small enough, it probably is not worth pursuing the overdue bill. However, if a collection agency is willing to work for a percentage of the amount recovered, the firm might as well turn collection over to the agency regardless of the size involved because the firm incurs no out-of-pocket cost.

appendix 14A The Cash Budget

14A.1 • The Cash Budget

Learning Goal

LG14-12 Be able to create and interpret a cash budget.

The production and sales in many firms vary over the year. For example, a toy retailer will have many more sales in November and December than in March and April. On the other hand, consider the manufacturer of toys. That company would have to manufacture most of the toys it will sell to the retail stores before November. For the most part, all businesses have some seasonality in their sales and/or production cycle. This seasonality creates periods during the year in which the firm will generate large cash surpluses and other periods in which it will generate large cash deficits. Financial managers must plan ahead for such times so that the firm always has adequate cash to pay its liabilities. The **cash budget** is the instrument they use.

cash budget

A calculation of the estimated cash flow from receipts and disbursements over a specific time period.

Consider the example of Yellow Jacket, Inc., a manufacturer of coats and jackets that has decided to operate its factory at a constant pace all year. Thus, inventory builds up until early fall, when it ships large amounts of its product to retailers. The coats are mostly sold in the fall, depleting inventory. This strategy allows the company to keep a few full-time workers instead of hiring many seasonal employees and then laying them off during the slow times of the year. However, incurring costs during most of the year with few sales and then selling the coats in the fall creates a serious cash flow problem that the financial manager is responsible for resolving.

Cash budgets can be created for daily, monthly, or quarterly time periods. Given the severe seasonality of Yellow Jacket's sales, its cash budget is done monthly. The cash budget begins with a projection of sales for the year. In this case, Yellow Jacket is projecting a 10 percent increase in sales each month from the same month of the previous year. The top of Table 14A.1 shows these monthly projected sales, which are quite seasonal. Many companies have sales terms like 2/10 net 45, which means that customers must pay within 45 days of the sale—but if they pay within 10 days they can take a 2 percent discount. Even with terms like this, Yellow Jacket has found that its customers take the 2 percent discount if they pay in the same month of the sale, which 30 percent do. Then 50 percent pay in the month after the sale, leaving the final 20 percent to pay in the following month. This is illustrated in the cash collection row of the table. Note that the firm collects only \$1 million in cash payments in July while it collects as much as \$26.4 million in November.

The total sales for the year are \$125 million. If the company pursues the level production strategy, then it needs to produce the coats at a sale value rate of \$10.42 million per month (= \$125 million ÷ 12). Table 14A.2 shows the cash disbursements per month. The manufacturing costs are assumed to be materials at 50 percent of sales, while wages are 15 percent of sales. Thus, material cost payments are \$5.2 million per month (= \$10.42 million × 50%) and wage payments

table 14A.1 | **Cash Collection**

	A	B	C	D	E	F	G	H	I	J	K	L	M
1	($ millions)	**Jan**	**Feb**	**Mar**	**Apr**	**May**	**Jun**	**Jul**	**Aug**	**Sep**	**Oct**	**Nov**	**Dec**
2													
3	Sales	10	10	5	2	1	1	1	5	20	30	25	15
4													
5	Cash Collection	14.3	10.7	8.5	5.1	2.3	1.2	1.0	2.2	8.6	19.8	26.4	22.9
6													
7													
8	Assumptions												
9	Collection:												
10	Month 0, 30% pay with 2% discount												
11	Month 1, 50% pay												
12	Month 2, 20% pay												
13													
14	10% increase in sales from previous year												
15													

October cash collection comes from:

30% × October sales after 2% discount = 0.3 × 0.98 × $30
plus 50% × September sales = 0.5 × $20
plus 20% × August sales = 0.2 × $5

Total = $19.8

table 14A.2 | **Cash Disbursement**

	A	B	C	D	E	F	G	H	I	J	K	L	M
1	($ millions)	**Jan**	**Feb**	**Mar**	**Apr**	**May**	**Jun**	**Jul**	**Aug**	**Sep**	**Oct**	**Nov**	**Dec**
2													
3	Sales	10	10	5	2	1	1	1	5	20	30	25	15
4													
5	Cash Collection	14.3	10.7	8.5	5.1	2.3	1.2	1.0	2.2	8.6	19.8	26.4	22.9
6													
7	Disbursements												
8	Materials	5.2	5.2	5.2	5.2	5.2	5.2	5.2	5.2	5.2	5.2	5.2	5.2
9	Wages, Salaries & Other	1.6	1.6	1.6	1.6	1.6	1.6	1.6	1.6	1.6	1.6	1.6	1.6
10	Taxes	0	0	2.7	0	0	2.7	0	0	2.7	0	0	2.7
11	Capital Projects	0	0	0	0	0	15.0	0	0	0	0	0	0
12	Long-Term Financing	0	1.0	5.0	0	1.0	0	0	1.0	5.0	0	1.0	0
13	(interest & dividends)												
14	Total Cash Disbursement	6.8	7.8	14.5	6.8	7.8	24.5	6.8	7.8	14.5	6.8	7.8	9.5
15													
16													
17													
18	Assumptions												
19	Disbursement:												
20	Material is 50% of sales												
21	Wages, etc. are 15% of sales												
22	$15 million factory upgrade in June												
23	$5 million in interest, twice per year												
24	$1 million in dividends, quarterly												
25	$2.7 million in taxes, quarterly												

November cash disbursement comes from:

$5.2 million in materials purchased
+ $1.6 million in wages
+ $2.7 million in quarterly taxes paid
+ $5.0 million in semiannual interest payment on debt

$14.5 million

are $1.6 million per month (= $10.42 million × 15%). Other payments predicted throughout the year are those for capital investments, interest payments, and dividend payments. Yellow Jacket plans to invest in some factory upgrades for which it will pay $15 million in June. Interest payments on its bonds are semiannual (March and September), while quarterly dividends are paid in February, May, August, and November. Notice that the total cash disbursements have a high degree of variability over time. In addition, the payments do not align well with the cash collection. For example in June, the firm receives only $1.2 million in cash and expects to pay $24.5 million. On the other hand, it expects to collect $26.4 million in November and pay only $7.8 million.

table 14A.3 | **Cash Budget**

	A	B	C	D	E	F	G	H	I	J	K	L	M
1	($ millions)	**Jan**	**Feb**	**Mar**	**Apr**	**May**	**Jun**	**Jul**	**Aug**	**Sep**	**Oct**	**Nov**	**Dec**
2													
3	Sales	10	10	5	2	1	1	1	5	20	30	25	15
4													
5	Cash Collection	14.3	10.7	8.5	5.1	2.3	1.2	1.0	2.2	8.6	19.8	26.4	22.9
6													
7	Disbursements												
8	Materials	5.2	5.2	5.2	5.2	5.2	5.2	5.2	5.2	5.2	5.2	5.2	5.2
9	Wages, Salaries & Other	1.6	1.6	1.6	1.6	1.6	1.6	1.6	1.6	1.6	1.6	1.6	1.6
10	Taxes	0	0	2.7	0	0	2.7	0	0	2.7	0	0	2.7
11	Capital Projects	0	0	0	0	0	15.0	0	0	0	0	0	0
12	Long-Term Financing	0	1.0	5.0	0	1.0	0	0	1.0	5.0	0	1.0	0
13	(interest & dividends)												
14	Total Cash Disbursement	6.8	7.8	14.5	6.8	7.8	24.5	6.8	7.8	14.5	6.8	7.8	9.5
15													
16	Net Cash Flow	7.5	2.9	–6.0	–1.7	–5.5	–23.3	–5.8	–5.6	–5.9	13.0	18.6	13.4
17													
18	Cumulative Net Cash Flow	7.5	10.4	4.4	2.7	–2.8	–26.1	–31.9	–37.5	–43.4	–30.4	–11.8	1.6
19													
20	Minimum Cash Balance	2.0	2.0	2.0	2.0	2.0	2.0	2.0	2.0	2.0	2.0	2.0	2.0
21													
22	Cash Surplus or Deficit	5.5	8.4	2.4	0.7	–4.8	–28.1	–33.9	–39.5	–45.4	–32.4	–13.8	–0.4
23													
24	Assumptions												
25	Minimum cash balance of $2 million												
26													
27													
28													
29													
30													

Net cash flow = Cash collection – Total cash disbursement

Cumulative net cash flow = Last month's cumulative cash flow + This month's net cash flow

Cash surplus or deficit = Cumulative net cash flow – Minimum cash balance

The cash budget can now be completed. Table 14A.3 shows that the next step is to compute the net cash flow generated each month. This is simply the cash collection for that month minus that month's disbursement. Note that Yellow Jacket has seven months in a row (March through September) in which it generates a negative cash flow. The cumulative net cash flow row shows that the surplus of cash generated in January and February helps with the deficits from March and April. However, by May, Yellow Jacket enters a cash deficit situation that lasts the rest of the year. The deficit is increased by the fact that the firm likes to have a cash balance minimum of $2 million at all times. Finally, the cash budget shows the cash account surplus or deficit during the year. It is apparent that Yellow Jacket will need to obtain a bank loan or line of revolving credit that can handle a maximum of $45.4 million (September's deficit is the highest).

Note that Yellow Jacket is a profitable firm. Yet, the seasonality in the sales of coats and jackets causes severe cash deficit problems during the year. If financial managers do not plan ahead for this situation, then the firm will experience significant financial stresses that can damage its reputation and relationship with suppliers and customers. The value of building the cash budget on a spreadsheet (as shown in these tables) is that sensitivity analysis and what-if scenarios can easily be implemented.

TIME OUT

14A-1 Should all cash payments and receipts made by the firm be included in the cash budget?

14A-2 Due to the nature of Yellow Jacket's business, they are likely to experience significant cash deficits each year. How is their bank likely to view this situation?

summary of learning goal

LG14-12 **Be able to create and interpret a cash budget.** Creating a cash budget involves recording estimates of the cash collected and cash disbursed during each period (e.g., daily, monthly, or quarterly). These estimates are then used to determine the net cash surplus or deficit each period. Over the year, large cash deficits may accumulate. Planning ahead for these situations allows the firm to operate smoothly through them.

key term

cash budget A calculation of the estimated cash flow from receipts and disbursements over a specific time period. *p. 505*

self-test problem with solution

LG14-12 **1 Sensitivity Analysis** The cash budget for Yellow Jacket was created starting with the assumption that sales would grow by 10 percent in the coming months compared to that month the previous year. What would the accumulated deficits look like with just 5 percent growth? Assume the disbursements on interest payments, dividends, and capital spending are not changed. Also assume tax payments are reduced by \$0.1 million per quarter.

Solution:

First adjust each sales estimate by multiplying by (1.05/1.10) to remove the ten percent growth and create five percent growth. In this scenario, the total sales for the year will be \$119.3 million. The reduced sales will decrease the cash collection, but they will also reduce the disbursement for materials, wages, and other costs directly related to the production of coats. The new cash budget is:

	A	B	C	D	E	F	G	H	I	J	K	L	M
1	($ millions)	**Jan**	**Feb**	**Mar**	**Apr**	**May**	**Jun**	**Jul**	**Aug**	**Sep**	**Oct**	**Nov**	**Dec**
2													
3	Sales	9.5	9.5	4.8	1.9	1.0	1.0	1.0	4.8	19.1	28.6	23.9	14.3
4													
5	Cash Collection	14.2	10.3	8.1	4.9	2.2	1.1	0.9	2.1	8.2	18.9	25.2	21.9
6													
7	Disbursements												
8	Materials	5.0	5.0	5.0	5.0	5.0	5.0	5.0	5.0	5.0	5.0	5.0	5.0
9	Wages, Salaries & Other	1.5	1.5	1.5	1.5	1.5	1.5	1.5	1.5	1.5	1.5	1.5	1.5
10	Taxes	0	0	2.6	0	0	2.6	0	0	2.6	0	0	2.6
11	Capital Projects	0	0	0	0	0	15.0	0	0	0	0	0	0
12	Long-Term Financing	0	1.0	5.0	0	1.0	0	0	1.0	5.0	0	1.0	0
13	(interest & dividends)												
14	Total Cash Disbursement	6.5	7.5	14.1	6.5	7.5	24.1	6.5	7.5	14.1	6.5	7.5	9.1
15													
16	Net Cash Flow	7.7	2.8	−6.0	−1.6	−5.3	−22.9	−5.5	−5.4	−5.9	12.5	17.7	12.8
17													
18	Cumulative Net Cash Flow	7.7	10.6	4.6	3.0	−2.3	−25.2	−30.7	−36.1	−42.0	−29.6	−11.9	1.1
19													
20	Minimum Cash Balance	2.0	2.0	2.0	2.0	2.0	2.0	2.0	2.0	2.0	2.0	2.0	2.0
21													
22	Cash Surplus or Deficit	5.7	8.6	2.6	1.0	−4.3	−27.2	−32.7	−38.1	−44.0	−31.6	−13.9	−1.1

Notice the change to a 5 percent growth rate does not impact this cash budget much. For example, the cash account deficit still starts in May and lasts throughout the year. In addition, the worst deficit (in September) is actually \$1.3 million smaller than before.

problems

basic problems

14A-1 Cumulative Net Cash Flow The net cash flow for a firm in January, February, and March is −\$2.5 million, −\$3.0 million, and \$2.4 million, respectively. What is the cumulative net cash flow for March? *(LG14-12)*

14A-2 Cumulative Net Cash Flow The net cash flow for a firm in January, February, and March is \$3.5 million, −\$1.0 million, and \$1.4 million, respectively. What is the cumulative net cash flow for March? *(LG14-12)*

14A-3 Cash Disbursement The Hug-a-Bear company makes its teddy bears the month before they are sold and pays for all materials in the month of purchase. If sales of \$2.5 million are expected in November and the firm pays 50 percent of sales in material costs, then what is the materials cash disbursement in October? *(LG14-12)*

14A-4 Cash Disbursement The Snow Adventures company makes its snowboards the month before they are sold and pays for all materials in the month of purchase. If sales of \$7.8 million are expected in November and the firm pays 65 percent of sales in material costs, then what is the materials cash disbursement in October? *(LG14-12)*

intermediate problems

14A-5 Cash Collection Consider a company that has sales in May, June, and July of $10 million, $12 million, and $9 million, respectively. The firm is paid by 35 percent of its customers in the month of the sale, 40 percent in the following month, and 22 percent in the next month *(3 percent are bad sales and never pay)*. What is the cash collected in July? *(LG14-12)*

14A-6 Cash Collection Consider a company that has sales in May, June, and July of $11 million, $10 million, and $12 million, respectively. The firm is paid by 25 percent of its customers in the month of the sale, 50 percent in the following month, and 23 percent in the next month *(2 percent are bad sales and never pay)*. What is the cash collected in July? *(LG14-12)*

14A-7 Cash Surplus or Deficit A firm has estimated the 2-month cash budget below. What is the cash surplus or deficit for these two months? *(LG14-12)*

($ in millions)	MAR	APR
Sales	120.0	130.0
Cash collection	84.0	90.0
Total cash disbursement	90.0	85.0
Net cash flow	−6.0	5.0
Cumulative net cash flow	−15.0	?
Minimum cash balance	10.0	10.0
Cash surplus or deficit	?	?

14A-8 Cash Surplus or Deficit A firm has estimated the two-month cash budget below. What is the cash surplus or deficit for these two months? *(LG14-12)*

($ in millions)	MAR	APR
Sales	75.0	68.0
Cash collection	63.0	65.0
Total cash disbursement	60.0	57.0
Net cash flow	3.0	8.0
Cumulative net cash flow	11.0	?
Minimum cash balance	3.0	3.0
Cash surplus or deficit	?	?

advanced problems

14A-9 Cash Budget Spreadsheet Problem The company from the text, Yellow Jacket, has decided to change its production strategy. Instead of a steady production throughout the year, they will produce the coats they estimate to sell in the month prior. This will impact the materials and wage disbursements of the cash budget. *(For the December computation, assume that the following January sales will increase by 10 percent from the prior year.)* Build this cash budget. How does this impact the cash surplus/deficit of the firm? *(LG14-12)*

ANSWERS TO TIME OUT

14A-1 All cash flows that can be estimated or predicted ahead of time should be included. For example, if the firm expects to make a payment from a legal judgment on a certain date, that cash disbursement should be included so that it can be planned for.

14A-2 Banks understand the seasonality of some businesses. As long as the firm can show that it will be able to pay back the loan at the end of the cycle, banks are happy to loan money and collect fees and interest payments. The cash budget can be used not only to plan ahead by the financial manager, but it can also be used when negotiating with the bank to show the dynamics of the cash flow cycle.

PART SEVEN

15 Financial Planning and Forecasting

viewpoints

Business Application

Riada Industries has had sales of $1 million, $1.3 million, and $1.7 million in the last three years and expects this trend to continue into the future. The company currently has the capacity in its $1.5 million of fixed assets to handle sales of $2 million per year and has $500,000 in current assets supporting the latest year's sales. If current liabilities are $300,000 and the firm has a profit margin of 5 percent and a retention ratio of 70 percent, how much external funding will Riada need to raise to support next year's sales? **(See solution on p. 532)**

Personal Application

Kamala starts college next month. She will be working a part-time job where she will earn $300 a month, and she has a partial scholarship, which will reduce her out-of-pocket expenses associated with going back to school (including room and board) to $10,000 per year. Assuming that Kamala has $5,000 saved up for college, how much will she need to borrow this year? **(See solution on p. 532)**

What will Kamala's future cash flows look like and when will she need the loan?

What key elements does a firm need to analyze in order to plan its future? Sales are crucial, both in projected volume and in resources for support. In previous chapters, we've shown you how to do quite a lot of analysis, but there's always been an underlying assumption that external guidance is available. In other words, you've known where to find how many units you expect to sell, the prices at which you expect to sell, what types of assets you would need to support those sales, how much assistance you would get from suppliers and employees (in the form of accounts payable and accrued wages, respectively), and how much capital you would need to raise from external sources. When you answer these questions, you are able to form a financial plan for the firm. To form a plan, we will start with the idea of forecasting expected future sales. Then we will cover the use of those forecasted sales to estimate what level of assets will be needed to support them. We will find the "spontaneous" sources of funds that can be expected to help fund the necessary assets, determine how much of the net required assets can be funded internally through retained earnings, and then see how much will need to be funded through external sources.

Learning Goals

LG15-1 Describe the process of financial planning in the context of the firm and how base case projections are used in the strategic planning process.

LG15-2 Identify how forecasting sales supports the process of financial planning.

LG15-3 Compare and contrast the naïve, average, and seasonality- and trend-adjusted approaches to forecasting sales and how they are implemented.

LG15-4 Explain and demonstrate the additional funds needed (AFN) approach to estimating a firm's need to seek external financing.

LG15-5 Use pro forma financial statements to estimate additional funds needed.

15.1 • Financial Planning

LG15-1

When most of us hear the term **financial planning,** we think of its meaning in the context of investments, where financial planners help individuals set and achieve their long-term financial goals. Your personal financial planner can provide advice on investments, tax planning, asset allocation, risk management, retirement planning, and estate planning. The financial planning process of a firm pretty much involves the same types of activities, although in a slightly more

financial planning

The process of mapping out the future cash inflows and outflows of the firm.

strategic planning

The process of determining where a firm is going over the next year or more, how it is going to get there, and how it will know if it gets there or not.

base case

The set of assumptions underlying the firm's financial plan.

LG15-2

base case projections

The projected financial statements associated with the base case.

complex environment. In this process, each operating division of a firm normally creates a pro forma set of financial statements depicting its expected financial situation in the foreseeable future. Managers use the most reasonable set of assumptions concerning relevant factors such as demand and prices for their products, costs of raw materials and labor, and expected future tax rates. The pro forma financial statements from all of the firm's divisions are then combined in a set of master pro forma statements for the entire firm, which form the basis for the firm's *financial plan.*

The financial plan is an important element in the process of *strategic planning,* which involves formulating, implementing, and evaluating cross-functional decisions that will enable a firm to achieve its long-term objectives. Put more simply, **strategic planning** is the process of determining where a firm is going over the next year or more, how it is going to get there, and how it will know if it gets there or not.

The set of assumptions underlying the firm's financial plan is normally referred to as the **base case,** and the resulting projected financial statements are referred to as **base case projections.** These projections are useful in the strategic planning process for setting internal goals, for providing information to shareholders and other external stakeholders concerning the firm's future expectations, and for estimating the firm's future needs for internal and external financing.

In order to construct the pro forma statements in the financial plan, we need a methodology for consistently estimating values for the financial statements. The most logical way to proceed is to assume that every balance sheet and income statement item will be a function of the firm's sales. So if we can predict future sales, that will give us a starting point for predicting everything else.

As we will see, predicting future sales can be as simple as assuming they will be equal to current sales (appropriate when the firm's sales are stable over time), or as complicated as adjusting for seasonality and time trends. However, once we have calculated a forecast for sales that we are comfortable with, we can then use that forecast to determine how much external financing the firm will need to raise.

LG15-2

15.2 • Forecasting Sales

The Naïve Approach

LG15-3

naïve approach

Assuming that future sales will be equal to the latest period's sales.

The simplest approach to estimating a future period's sales is to *assume that they will be equal to those of the latest observed period.* In statistics, this is often simply referred to as the **naïve approach,** as it would have us use the latest observed sales figure as the expected value for the sales at any future period:

$$E(Sales_{t+j}) = Sales_t \text{ for all } j > 0 \qquad \textbf{(15-1)}$$

How well does the naïve approach work? To find out, we need to examine how much error may be in its forecasts. There are several commonly used statistics for measuring the amount of forecast error produced by a particular estimation strategy. One of the most popular, and the one we will use in this chapter, is the *mean absolute percentage error,* or **MAPE,** which is calculated across the n forecasts of a *testing period* as:

MAPE

Mean absolute percentage error, a measurement of a forecast's accuracy.

$$MAPE = \frac{\sum_{t=1}^{n} \left| \frac{Actual_t - Forecast_t}{Actual_t} \right|}{n} \qquad \textbf{(15-2)}$$

MAPE measures the efficiency of a forecast developed using *one set* of historic, observed data on *another set* that is held "out-of-sample" during the formulation of the forecast. Or, put another way, MAPE measures how well a forecasting technique works when using one set of historic data to forecast another later (but still historic) set of "testing data." As such, it measures how well your forecasting technique would have worked in the past, but that does not necessarily mean that it will work equally as well going into the future.

As long as sales remain fairly stable over time for a company, the naïve approach may actually be an appropriate estimation method. However, if there *is* reason to expect that sales either will systematically change over time or will exhibit large period-to-period variation, we may wish to use a more sophisticated estimation method.

EXAMPLE 15-1

LG15-3

Estimation of Future Sales Using the Naïve Approach

For interactive versions of this example visit www.mhhe.com/can3e

A survey of the monthly sales reports for Target Corporation, publicly available on the company's investor information page at investors.target.com, yields the monthly sales figures for January 2010 through December 2012 shown in Table 15.1. Assuming you were at the beginning of January 2012 and were going to use the naïve approach, what would be your best estimates of the anticipated sales for each month of 2012? Using those estimates and the actual realized monthly sales figures for 2012, what would be the MAPE of the naïve forecasts for 2012?

table 15.1 | **Target Corporation Monthly Sales (in millions) for January 2010–December 2012**

Month	2010	2011	2012
January	$4,289	$ 4,383	$ 4,608
February	$4,637	$ 4,750	$ 5,132
March	$6,233	$ 5,955	$ 6,427
April	$4,288	$ 4,874	$ 4,978
May	$4,622	$ 4,799	$ 5,038
June	$5,918	$ 6,256	$ 6,419
July	$4,585	$ 4,840	$ 4,995
August	$5,023	$ 5,292	$ 5,543
September	$5,562	$ 5,923	$ 6,075
October	$4,641	$ 4,839	$ 4,982
November	$6,012	$ 6,191	$ 6,183
December	$9,882	$10,138	$10,214

SOLUTION:

Using the naïve approach, the expected sales for each month of 2012 will be equal to the December 2011 sales figure, $10,138 million, resulting in a MAPE of:

$$MAPE = \frac{\sum_{t=1}^{n}\left|\frac{Actual_t - Forecast_t}{Actual_t}\right|}{n}$$

$$= \frac{\left(\begin{aligned}&\left|\frac{4{,}608 - 10{,}138}{4{,}608}\right| + \left|\frac{5{,}132 - 10{,}138}{5{,}132}\right| + \left|\frac{6{,}427 - 10{,}138}{6{,}427}\right| + \left|\frac{4{,}978 - 10{,}138}{4{,}978}\right|\\ &+\left|\frac{5{,}038 - 10{,}138}{5{,}038}\right| + \left|\frac{6{,}419 - 10{,}138}{6{,}419}\right| + \left|\frac{4{,}995 - 10{,}138}{4{,}995}\right| + \left|\frac{5{,}543 - 10{,}138}{5{,}543}\right|\\ &+\left|\frac{6{,}075 - 10{,}138}{6{,}075}\right| + \left|\frac{4{,}982 - 10{,}138}{4{,}982}\right| + \left|\frac{6{,}183 - 10{,}138}{6{,}183}\right| + \left|\frac{10{,}214 - 10{,}138}{10{,}214}\right|\end{aligned}\right)}{12}$$

$$= 0.7992, \text{ or } 79.92\%$$

This is a very high forecast error.

Similar to Problems 15-1, 15-2, self-test problem 1

LG15-3

The Average Approach

average approach

Assuming that future sales will be equal to the average historical value across some relevant period.

One of the basic principles of statistics is that when you are using a sample to estimate something about the population it is taken from, more observations are always better. This principle is based on the idea that observation-specific, idiosyncratic errors (errors that apply only to a single sample) are likely to cancel out as a sample gets larger and larger. This idea holds true when using historic sales figures to predict future sales estimates, as well. The naïve approach that we discussed above can be thought of as using a sample size of one to predict future sales, with the associated risk that any particular error in the last observed period's sales will be included in the prediction of future sales. We can improve the accuracy of this prediction in the face of assumed idiosyncratic errors by taking the mean of multiple historic observations as our predictor:

$$E(Sales_{n+j}) = \frac{\sum_{i=1}^{n} Sales_t}{n} \text{ for all } j > 0 \qquad \textbf{(15-3)}$$

The question here, though, is, "How far back do we go when computing the average?" Well, it basically depends upon how stable you think the sales figures have been and will be going forward in time: More observations are better *if the sample is representative of the population.* However, to the extent that sales may be expected to occasionally shift to a new level, historic sales figures from before the point in time where such a shift occurs may be "stale," or not truly representative of the new level of sales. If we knew for sure that such a shift had not happened, then the best estimator for future expected sales would simply be an average of *all* available historic sales figures.

However, if we were to take a look at the historic sales figures for 2010 and 2011 as shown in Figure 15.1, we might notice that average sales seemed to be consistently higher during 2011 than they were during 2010, implying that perhaps just such a shift *had* occurred.

figure 15.1

Target Historic Sales versus Average Annual Sales, 2010 and 2011

Focus on the yearly average line in the graph. What can you conclude?

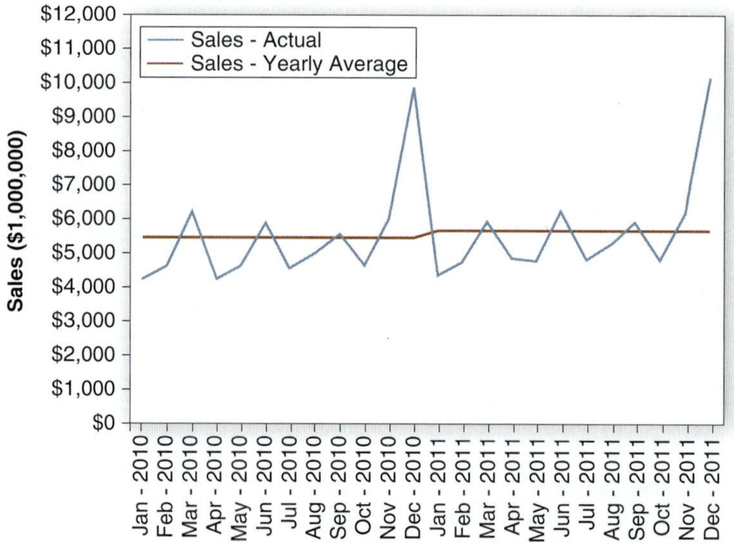

Note two important facts here. First, using an average as our predictor greatly reduced the MAPE compared to the naïve forecasts, regardless of which average was chosen. This implies that there apparently was a great deal of idiosyncratic "incorrectness" induced when we simply used the December 2011 monthly sales figure as our naïve forecast for all of the 2012 monthly sales figures; this incorrectness was greatly reduced when we used an average of multiple monthly sales figures instead.

Second, note that the MAPE was actually a little bit better (i.e., lower) when we used all available historic data rather than just the last historic year's average monthly sales figure. This may be an artifact of our MAPE statistic[1] or it might imply that what we thought was a systematic shift in monthly sales between 2010 and 2011 either did not persist or was not strong enough to matter to our MAPE statistic in 2011. Or it simply may not have been statistically significant enough to take into account. Either way, we should take this example as a cautionary tale concerning the possible risks of discarding a subset of our historic data due to a perceived structural shift.

LG15-3

EXAMPLE 15-2

Estimation of Future Sales Using the Historic Average Approach

For interactive versions of this example visit www.mhhe.com/can3e

Assume once again that you were at the beginning of January 2012 and wanted to estimate Target's upcoming sales for 2012 using a historic average approach. Compare and contrast the estimates and the associated MAPE figures from using all 24 months of historic data for 2010 and 2011 with those obtained by using only the 12 months of historic data from 2011 to compute your average.

SOLUTION:

Using all two years' worth of historic data, the average monthly sales figure would be \$5,581 million, and the resulting MAPE for the 2012 forecasts would be:

$$MAPE = \frac{\sum_{t=1}^{n}\left|\frac{Actual_t - Forecast_t}{Actual_t}\right|}{n}$$

$$= \frac{\left(\begin{array}{l}\left|\frac{4,608-5,581}{4,608}\right| + \left|\frac{5,132-5,581}{5,132}\right| + \left|\frac{6,427-5,581}{6,427}\right| + \left|\frac{4,978-5,581}{4,978}\right| \\ + \left|\frac{5,038-5,581}{5,038}\right| + \left|\frac{6,419-5,581}{6,419}\right| + \left|\frac{4,995-5,581}{4,995}\right| + \left|\frac{5,543-5,581}{5,543}\right| \\ + \left|\frac{6,075-5,581}{6,075}\right| + \left|\frac{4,982-5,581}{4,982}\right| + \left|\frac{6,183-5,581}{6,183}\right| + \left|\frac{10,214-5,581}{10,214}\right|\end{array}\right)}{12}$$

$$= 0.1388, \text{ or } 13.88\%$$

Using just the historic monthly sales data from 2011, the average monthly sales figure would be \$5,687 million, and the resulting MAPE for the 2012 forecasts would be:

$$MAPE = \frac{\sum_{t=1}^{n}\left|\frac{Actual_t - Forecast_t}{Actual_t}\right|}{n}$$

[1]MAPE has several quirks that are well-documented in statistical literature, but an in-depth discussion of the associated problems is outside the scope of this book.

$$
= \frac{\left(\begin{array}{l} \left|\frac{4{,}608 - 5{,}687}{4{,}608}\right| + \left|\frac{5{,}132 - 5{,}687}{5{,}132}\right| + \left|\frac{6{,}427 - 5{,}687}{6{,}427}\right| + \left|\frac{4{,}978 - 5{,}687}{4{,}978}\right| \\ + \left|\frac{5{,}038 - 5{,}687}{5{,}038}\right| + \left|\frac{6{,}419 - 5{,}687}{6{,}419}\right| + \left|\frac{4{,}995 - 5{,}687}{4{,}995}\right| + \left|\frac{5{,}543 - 5{,}687}{5{,}543}\right| \\ + \left|\frac{6{,}075 - 5{,}687}{6{,}075}\right| + \left|\frac{4{,}982 - 5{,}687}{4{,}982}\right| + \left|\frac{6{,}183 - 5{,}687}{6{,}183}\right| + \left|\frac{10{,}214 - 5{,}687}{10{,}214}\right| \end{array}\right)}{12}
$$

$$= 0.1447, \text{ or } 14.47\%$$

Similar to Problems 15-3, 15-4, self-test problem 2

LG15-3

Estimating Sales with Systematic Variations: Adjusting for Trends and Seasonality

A close examination of the sales data in Table 15.1 shows us that several strong patterns emerge that would be evident even if we were just looking at the 2010 and 2011 monthly sales figures:

1. There definitely seems to be a quarterly pattern, with sales figures being highest during the third month of each quarter.
2. This pattern is greatly exaggerated in the fourth quarter of each year, when the company experiences holiday sales.
3. There does seem to be a slight upward trend in sales across time.

deseasonalize

To remove the effects of seasonality from historic data.

To more accurately predict future sales, you must make adjustments for such patterns in sales. One common method for doing so, and the one that we will use, is to **deseasonalize** the historic sales figures by dividing each month's actual sales by a *seasonal index,* calculated by dividing the month's sales by a *moving average* around that month of annual sales. Then, calculate the trend using linear regression on the deseasonalized figures. Finally, use the seasonal indexes and regression parameters we have developed to predict future sales.

EXAMPLE 15-3

LG15-3

For interactive versions of this example visit www.mhhe.com/can3e

Estimation of Future Sales by Adjusting for Seasonality and Trend

Using Target Corporation's historic monthly sales figures for 2010 and 2011 (see Table 15.1) to compute monthly seasonal and trend adjustments, estimate the monthly sales figures for 2012 and then compute the MAPE for these forecasts across 2012.

centered moving average

A moving average created to put a specific observation exactly in the center of the period over which the moving average is calculated.

SOLUTION:

To compute the monthly seasonal indexes, we need to compute a **centered moving average** for the year's worth of monthly sales surrounding each historic monthly sales figure. If we had an odd number of months in a year, this would be pretty straightforward: We would simply have to average the month's sales with an equal amount of monthly sales from before and after that month to construct a centered moving average. However, since a year has an even number of months, the year "centered" around a particular month must either include five months before and six months after the month in question, or six months before and five months after; obviously, neither of these averages will be exactly centered around the month in question. The easiest way to handle this is to compute both of these "centered" averages and then take an average of them, in turn. This approach is shown below:

1. The column "12-CMA" is a 12-month centered moving average where the sales figure it will be associated with (which, as we will discuss, is actually the actual sales figure from the *next* row) is the seventh of 12 months used in the computation of the average. This means that the *next* 12-CMA figure treats the associated monthly sales figure as the sixth of 12 monthly sales figures included in its average, and so forth.

   For example, the first figure in the 12-CMA column, $5,474, is a 12-month average where the July 2010 actual sales figure of $4,585 is the seventh of 12 included in the average (meaning that it has 6 other months before it and 5 months after it in that average). The second figure in the 12-CMA column, $5,482, includes the July 2010 actual sales figure of $4,585 as the sixth of 12 (meaning that it has 5 before it and 6 after it). The first figure in the 2-CMA column is therefore an average of these two 12-CMA figures, $5,474 and $5,482, which together "bracket" the month of July. By taking an average like this, we wind up with an average that is centered smack-dab over the month of July.
2. The July 2010 actual sales figure, $4,585, is then divided by this 2-CMA to get a seasonal index for the month of July of approximately 0.8369, meaning that this month's actual sales figures are 83.69 percent of the average sales figure for the year exactly surrounding it. This process is then repeated for all of the other months of the calendar, resulting in the (raw) seasonal indexes shown.
3. As a final step before using the seasonal indexes to deseasonalize the historic monthly sales figures, note that the seasonal indexes are summed directly below their calculation. Theoretically, this sum should be 12, but rounding and other statistical artifacts have caused it to actually be approximately 11.99. To keep this "statistical drift" from unduly influencing the rest of our problem, we renormalize all of the seasonal indexes by multiplying each value by 12 and dividing by their sum, so that the new sum (shown at the bottom of the "Adj. Seas. Index" column) sums to exactly 12.
4. Finally, to deseasonalize the monthly historic sales figures, we divide the actual sales figure for each month by the appropriate seasonal index calculated for that month of the year, which are shown in the table as "Deseas. Sales."

Date	Observation	Month	Sales - Actual	12-CMA	2-CMA	Seas.-Irreg.	Seas. Index	Adj. Seas. Index	Deseas. Sales
Jan - 2010	1	1	$ 4,289						$ 4,374.08
Feb - 2010	2	2	$ 4,637						$ 5,651.56
Mar - 2010	3	3	$ 6,233						$ 5,644.73
Apr - 2010	4	4	$ 4,288						$ 5,595.59
May - 2010	5	5	$ 4,622						$ 5,498.25
Jun - 2010	6	6	$ 5,918	$ 5,474					$ 5,595.87
Jul - 2010	7	7	$ 4,585	$ 5,482	$ 5,478	0.836946	0.836946105	0.837471342	$ 5,544.66
Aug - 2010	8	8	$ 5,023	$ 5,492	$ 5,487	0.915457	0.915457341	0.916031849	$ 5,755.24
Sep - 2010	9	9	$ 5,562	$ 5,468	$ 5,480	1.014964	1.014963504	1.015600457	$ 5,559.52
Oct - 2010	10	10	$ 4,641	$ 5,517	$ 5,493	0.844919	0.844919137	0.845449377	$ 5,624.69
Nov - 2010	11	11	$ 6,012	$ 5,532	$ 5,525	1.088219	1.088218657	1.088901583	$ 5,786.27
Dec - 2010	12	12	$ 9,882	$ 5,560	$ 5,546	1.781798	1.781797966	1.782916157	$ 5,295.89
Jan - 2011	13	1	$ 4,383	$ 5,581	$ 5,571	0.786782	0.78678225	0.787276005	$ 4,469.94
Feb - 2011	14	2	$ 4,750	$ 5,604	$ 5,593	0.849333	0.849332827	0.849865837	$ 5,789.28
Mar - 2011	15	3	$ 5,955	$ 5,634	$ 5,619	1.059821	1.059820694	1.060485798	$ 5,392.97
Apr - 2011	16	4	$ 4,874	$ 5,650	$ 5,642	0.863853	0.863852539	0.864394661	$ 6,360,28
May - 2011	17	5	$ 4,799	$ 5,665	$ 5,658	0.848198	0.848198308	0.848730606	$ 5,708.81
Jun - 2011	18	6	$ 6,256	$ 5,687	$ 5,676	1.102185	1.102184637	1.102876328	$ 5,915.47
Jul - 2011	19	7	$ 4,840				11.99247396	12	$ 5,853.04
Aug - 2011	20	8	$ 5,292						$ 5,063.45
Sep - 2011	21	9	$ 5,923						$ 5,920.35
Oct - 2011	22	10	$ 4,839						$ 5,864.66
Nov - 2011	23	11	$ 6,191						$ 5,958.55
Dec - 2011	24	12	$ 10,138						$ 5,433.08

Similar to Problems 15-7, 15-8, 15-11, 15-12, self-test problem 3

Summary Output	
Regression Statistics	
Multiple R	0.624095866
R Square	0.38949565
Adjusted R Square	0.361745452
Standard Error	150.470127
Observations	24

Anova	DF	SS	MS	F	Significance F
Regression	1	317787.7149	317787.7	14.03578	0.001117156
Residual	22	498107.7005	22641.26		
Total	23	815895.4153			

	Coefficients	Standard Error	T-Stat	P-Value	Lower 95%	Upper 95%
Intercept	5365.659759	63.4006611	84.63097	3.74E-29	5234.174836	5497.14468
X Variable 1	16.62339145	4.437121973	3.746436	0.001117	7.421363693	25.8254192

Now that we have the deseasonalized sales figures, we can regress them against the time period (the column titled "Observation") to get parameters for estimating the historic trend. The results of this regression are shown in the preceding tables, with the intercept and slope coefficients that we will need for estimating future sales highlighted.

Finally, we reverse the process, using the parameters of the regression to estimate still-seasonally-adjusted monthly sales figures for 2012 and then "de-adjusting" them by multiplying them by the respective monthly seasonal index. For example, the seasonally adjusted forecast for January of 2012 (month 25 in our time series) would be computed as $5,365.659759 + ($16.62339145 × 25) = $5,781.244546, which would then in turn be multiplied by the seasonal index for January to yield $5,781.244546 × 0.787276005 = $4,551.44. Forecasted values for all months of 2012 would be as shown below:

Date	Observation	Month	Deseas. Sales	Forecast (S. Adj.)	Sales Forecast
Jan-2012	25	1	$5,853.09	$5,781.244546	$ 4,551.44
Feb-2012	26	2	$6,038.60	5,797.867937	$ 4,927.41
Mar-2012	27	3	$6,060.43	5,814.491329	$ 6,166.19
Apr-2012	28	4	$5,758.94	5,831.11472	$ 5,040.38
May-2012	29	5	$5,935.92	5,847.738111	$ 4,963.15
Jun-2012	30	6	$5,820.24	5,864.361503	$ 6,467.67
Jul-2012	31	7	$5,964.38	5,880.984894	$ 4,925.16
Aug-2012	32	8	$6,051.10	5,897.608286	$ 5,402.40
Sep-2012	33	9	$5,981.68	5,914.231677	$ 6,006.50
Oct-2012	34	10	$5,892.72	5,930.855069	$ 5,014.24
Nov-2012	35	11	$5,678.20	5,947.47846	$ 6,476.22
Dec-2012	36	12	$5,728.82	5,964.101852	$10,633.49

These forecasts, when compared to the actual monthly sales results for 2012, yield a MAPE of only 0.0228, or 2.28 percent. Apparently, deseasonalizing and adjusting for the trend in this manner greatly increases the forecast accuracy over the use of either the naïve or average approach.

TIME OUT

15-1 What would be an appropriate way to forecast sales for a firm that has stable year-to-year sales, but seasonally fluctuating month-to-month sales?

15-2 Suppose you were forecasting sales for a firm that exhibited a cyclical pattern within each week. How would you go about forecasting sales for this firm?

15.3 • External Financing

The Simple Approach to Estimating Necessary External Financing: Additional Funds Needed

LG15-4

If sales are expected to increase in the future, that increase must be supported by an accompanying increase in assets. Of the funds necessary to finance an increase in assets, some will be provided by increases in liabilities that will occur as direct reactions to the increase in sales. For example, if a company sells more product, it will have to order more raw materials. Assuming that the company's supplier offers it **trade credit,** then ordering more materials means that the amount of accounts payable increases, too. Such corresponding increases in liabilities are referred to as *spontaneous* increases.

trade credit

The practice of one firm selling to another on credit terms.

In most lines of business, the spontaneous increases in liabilities will not be enough, by themselves, to fund the necessary increases in assets. Even if we make the logical assumption that as sales increase the firm will also experience a corresponding increase in retained earnings, most firms will still have a portion of the necessary increase in assets that will need to be funded from external capital. We call this portion the **additional funds needed (AFN),** and it can be computed as:

additional funds needed (AFN)

The amount of external financing a firm must seek in order to change the asset base as necessary to support a different level of sales.

$$\begin{aligned} AFN = &\text{ Necessary increase in assets} \\ &- \text{Spontaneous increase in liabilities} \\ &- \text{Projected increase in retained earnings} \end{aligned} \qquad \textbf{(15-4)}$$

The necessary increase in assets can usually be computed by dividing the amount of assets tied directly to sales (A^*) by the amount of current sales (S_0) to get the **capital intensity ratio,** and then multiplying the capital intensity ratio by the projected increase in sales (ΔS):

capital intensity ratio

Relevant assets divided by current sales.

$$\text{Necessary increase in assets} = \frac{A^*}{S_0} \times \Delta S \qquad \textbf{(15-5)}$$

The spontaneous increase in liabilities can be computed by dividing the amount of liabilities tied directly to sales (L^*) by the amount of current sales to get the **spontaneous liabilities ratio,** and then multiplying the spontaneous liabilities ratio by the projected increase in sales:

spontaneous liabilities ratio

Relevant liabilities divided by current sales.

$$\text{Spontaneous increase in liabilities} = \frac{L^*}{S_0} \times \Delta S \qquad \textbf{(15-6)}$$

And the projected increase in retained earnings can be calculated by multiplying the profit margin (M) by the projected sales in the coming period (S_1), and then in turn multiplying this by the retention ratio (RR):

$$\text{Projected increase in retained earnings} = M \times S_1 \times RR \qquad \textbf{(15-7)}$$

EXAMPLE 15-4

LG15-4

For interactive versions of this example visit www.mhhe.com/can3e

Calculation of AFN

Suppose that Dandy Candy, Inc., currently has the following balance sheet and that sales for the year just ended were \$8 million. The firm also has a profit margin of 20 percent, a retention ratio of 40 percent, and expects sales of \$10 million next year. If all assets and current liabilities are expected to grow with sales, how much in additional funds will Dandy Candy need from external sources to fund the expected growth?

Assets		**Liabilities and Equity**	
Current assets	\$1,000,000	Current liabilities	\$ 500,000
Fixed assets	5,000,000	Long-term debt	2,500,000
		Equity	3,000,000
Total assets	\$6,000,000	Total liabilities and equity	\$6,000,000

SOLUTION:

Since it is stated that all assets are expected to grow with sales, A^* is \$6,000,000, and the necessary increase in assets will be:

$$\begin{aligned}\text{Necessary increase in assets} &= \frac{A^*}{S_0} \times \Delta S \\ &= \frac{\$6{,}000{,}000}{\$8{,}000{,}000} \times (\$10{,}000{,}000 - \$8{,}000{,}000) \\ &= 0.75 \times \$2{,}000{,}000 \\ &= \$1{,}500{,}000\end{aligned}$$

The spontaneous increase in liabilities will be expected to be:

$$\begin{aligned}\text{Spontaneous increase in liabilities} &= \frac{L^*}{S_0} \times \Delta S \\ &= \frac{\$500{,}000}{\$8{,}000{,}000} \times (\$10{,}000{,}000 - \$8{,}000{,}000) \\ &= \$125{,}000\end{aligned}$$

And the projected increase in retained earnings will be:

$$\begin{aligned}\text{Projected increase in retained earnings} &= M \times S_1 \times RR \\ &= 0.20 \times \$10{,}000{,}000 \times 0.40 \\ &= \$800{,}000\end{aligned}$$

So the amount of AFN will be equal to \$1,500,000 − \$125,000 − \$800,000 = \$575,000.

Similar to Problems 15-5, 15-6, self-test problem 4

LG15-4

AFN WITH UNUSED CAPACITY ASSETS In the previous example, we assumed that all assets would need to grow proportionately with sales. While this may be the case if a firm is currently fully utilizing its fixed assets, most firms will probably have some unused capacity that could be used to support the increase in sales. In such a situation, A^* would not be equal to total assets, but instead would be equal to the portion of assets that *would* need to change to support the anticipated growth in sales. In most cases, and for most firms, this would make A^* equal to current assets (CA); remember that CA are those assets that are most liquid, implying both that they can be easily acquired when needed, and that a firm probably won't keep "spare" CA on hand until they are needed to support the increase in sales.

EXAMPLE 15-5

LG15-4

Calculation of AFN with Excess Capacity

Amending the previous example, suppose that Dandy Candy, Inc., expects only current assets and current liabilities to grow with sales because the firm has enough unused fixed asset capacity to support the new, high level of expected sales. In this situation, how much in additional funds will Dandy Candy need from external sources to fund the expected growth?

For interactive versions of this example visit www.mhhe.com/can3e

SOLUTION:

In this case, A^* will be equal to CA, \$1,000,000, and the necessary increase in assets will be:

$$\begin{aligned}\text{Necessary increase in assets} &= \frac{A^*}{S_0} \times \Delta S \\ &= \frac{\$1{,}000{,}000}{\$8{,}000{,}000} \times (\$10{,}000{,}000 - \$8{,}000{,}000) \\ &= 0.125 \times \$2{,}000{,}000 \\ &= \$250{,}000\end{aligned}$$

The spontaneous increase in liabilities will still be expected to be:

$$\begin{aligned}\text{Spontaneous increase in liabilities} &= \frac{L^*}{S_0} \times \Delta S \\ &= \frac{\$500{,}000}{\$8{,}000{,}000} \times (\$10{,}000{,}000 - \$8{,}000{,}000) \\ &= \$125{,}000\end{aligned}$$

And the projected increase in retained earnings will still be:

$$\begin{aligned}\text{Projected increase in retained earnings} &= M \times S_1 \times RR \\ &= 0.20 \times \$10{,}000{,}000 \times 0.40 \\ &= \$800{,}000\end{aligned}$$

So the amount of AFN will be equal to \$250,000 − \$125,000 − \$800,000 = −\$675,000. This negative AFN implies that the firm can actually expect to generate more money internally from the increase in sales than it needs to support the higher level of sales.

Similar to Problem 15-9

AFN WITH "LUMPY" ASSETS The previous example begs the question of exactly *why* a firm would be sitting around with unused fixed-asset capacity. While there are several possible reasons for this, the most common is that fixed assets usually are not **infinitely divisible;** that is, you can not buy just one-fourth of a nuclear power plant or three-fourths of a bridge now and then buy the rest when demand grows to the point where you need it. For most fixed assets, when demand starts to outstrip the capacity of any machines already in use, the company adds another machine to cover the incremental amount of demand, even though the change in demand may not be large enough to use the new machine's entire capacity.

LG15-4

infinitely divisible
The ability to divide a given amount into as small a portion as needed.

So, when Dandy Candy is expecting an increase in sales in the coming year, it's very likely that the reason the company has unused fixed-asset capacity available to help support the new sales is because a previous increase in sales caused it to go from $X - 1$ machines to X machines, and the available unused capacity is all from that last machine. A company that is currently fully utilizing its fixed assets and expecting an increase in sales will have to consider buying one more machine—and that one more machine may actually have more capacity than is needed for the increase in sales expected next year. You will often hear this situation referred to as fixed assets being "chunky" or "lumpy," since they have to be bought in discrete, nondivisible, integer-based quantities. Obviously, the decision to go ahead and purchase this not-soon-to-be-used excess fixed-asset capacity will depend upon a number of factors: How much of the machine's capacity will "go to waste" in the near term, what kind of profit margin the firm will make on the portion of the new machine's capacity that *is* used, whether further increases in sales are expected in subsequent years, and so on. But let's suppose that a careful analysis of all the relevant factors causes the firm to proceed with such a purchase of excess fixed-asset capacity: Then the necessary increase in assets to support the new level of sales must include not only the capital intensity ratio based on current assets, but also the entirety of the fixed assets purchased.

EXAMPLE 15-6

LG15-4

For interactive versions of this example visit www.mhhe.com/can3e

Calculation of AFN with Lumpy Assets

Once again continuing with our Dandy Candy example, suppose that, instead of having excess fixed-asset capacity available, the firm will have to purchase an additional \$2.5 million in fixed assets to support the expected increase in sales, in addition to having to finance a proportionate increase in current assets. In this situation, how much in additional funds will Dandy Candy need from external sources to fund the expected growth?

SOLUTION:

In this case, A^* will still be equal to CA, \$1,000,000, but the necessary increase in assets will also have to include the required \$2,500,000 increase in fixed assets, and so will be:

$$\begin{aligned}\text{Necessary increase in assets} &= \$2{,}500{,}000 + \frac{A^*}{S_0} \times \Delta S \\ &= \$2{,}500{,}000 + \frac{\$1{,}000{,}000}{\$8{,}000{,}000} \times (\$10{,}000{,}000 - \$8{,}000{,}000) \\ &= \$2{,}500{,}000 + 0.125 \times \$2{,}000{,}000 \\ &= \$2{,}750{,}000\end{aligned}$$

The spontaneous increase in liabilities will still be expected to be:

$$\begin{aligned}\text{Spontaneous increase in liabilities} &= \frac{L^*}{S_0} \times \Delta S \\ &= \frac{\$500{,}000}{\$8{,}000{,}000} \times (\$10{,}000{,}000 - \$8{,}000{,}000) \\ &= \$125{,}000\end{aligned}$$

And the projected increase in retained earnings will still be:

$$\begin{aligned}\text{Projected increase in retained earnings} &= M \times S_1 \times RR \\ &= 0.20 \times \$10{,}000{,}000 \times 0.40 \\ &= \$800{,}000\end{aligned}$$

So the amount of AFN will be equal to \$2,750,000 − \$125,000 − \$800,000 = \$1,825,000. Note that this amount of AFN is almost as large as the expected increase in sales and is driven largely by the need to increase fixed assets so much.

Similar to Problem 15-10

TIME OUT

15-3 Which liabilities would tend to spontaneously increase with sales, and why?

15-4 Some firms can sometimes lease a portion of an asset (e.g., think about firms that share a lease on a corporate jet). How would the ability to lease portions of assets affect the problem with lumpy assets discussed in this section?

Forecasting Financial Statements

LG15-5

Calculating AFN using the formula in equation 15-4 has a couple of problems: First, this approach involves an inherent assumption that any balance sheet or income statement items that change in response to a change in sales *will do so as a linear function of sales.* In other words, it assumes that everything that changes with sales does so by remaining a fixed percentage of (changing) sales. While this assumption will probably make sense for many of the balance sheet and income statement items, there is no reason that it should hold true for *all* of them; and even if a particular balance sheet or income statement entry *does* change with sales, that change will not necessarily be a linear function of the change in sales. For example, many formulas used in production management for determining the optimal amount of inventory to keep on hand in response to an anticipated doubling of sales would have inventory go up at only the square root of the rate of change in sales.

The second problem with the way that we have been calculating AFN so far is that it only accounts for what we might call the **first order effects** to the income statement and balance sheet. That is, this approach ignores the fact that interest on debt, and therefore taxes, net income, dividends, and retained earnings, will be a function of how the AFN is raised. And, since AFN is itself partially a function of the amount of retained earnings. . . . You see the problem? A more complete calculation of AFN should involve *circular references,* where AFN is a function of retained earnings, but where retained earnings is also a function of AFN.

first order effects

The immediately observable effects of changing one item on another. Usually contrasted with *higher order effects,* which are the subsequent, less observable effects of the change.

To come up with a more realistic estimate for AFN, therefore, we are going to need to construct a more flexible depiction of what is happening to each of the balance sheet and income statement items in response to both the anticipated change in sales *and* in response to the resulting changes in all of the other balance sheet and income statement items, as well. To do so, we will once again make use of pro forma statements, as introduced in Chapter 12. Given the necessity for including the circular references discussed above, the only feasible way to construct these pro forma statements will be by using a spreadsheet program such as Microsoft Excel.

LG15-5

AFN USING PRO FORMA STATEMENTS In order to compute AFN using pro forma statements, we need to:

1. Identify and compute the balance sheet and income statement items that would logically change either directly proportionately with sales or indirectly as a function of those items. (For most firms, this will normally include all balance sheet and income statement items *except* notes payable, long-term debt, owners' equity, and, depending upon the relative divisibility of the firm's fixed assets as discussed previously, possibly some portion of the fixed assets.)
2. Use amounts for these items adjusted for the impact of the change in sales to calculate a first pass at AFN.
3. Determine a strategy for changing the items that do not vary proportionately with sales. For example, if we assume that externally obtained notes payable, long-term debt, and equity will be used to cover the AFN, we need to specify what relationship should exist *between* the additions to these accounts. Should we keep the debt-to-equity and short-term to long-term-debt ratios constant at their current values, or is there some other strategy that should be pursued? Also, what will be our *plug variable,* the balance sheet or income statement item that will ultimately bear the responsibility for balancing the balance sheet?
4. Allow our spreadsheet program to solve for the value for our plug variable that allows the balance sheet to balance.

Notice that although Example 15-7 keeps notes payable constant when forecasting into the future, other strategies may include changing it, too, in order to fund the AFN.

EXAMPLE 15-7

LG15-5

For interactive versions of this example visit www.mhhe.com/can3e

Calculation of AFN using Pro Forma Financial Statements

Suppose that the 2013 actual and 2014 projected financial statements for Dandy Candy are initially as shown in Tables 15.2 and 15.3. In these tables, sales are projected to rise by 25 percent in the coming year, and the components of the income statement and balance sheet that are expected to increase at the same 25 percent rate as sales are indicated in green type. Assuming that Dandy Candy wants to cover the AFN by selling equal amounts of common stock and long-term debt while keeping notes payable fixed at $75,000, how much in additional funds will Dandy Candy need to raise by selling new debt and shares of equity if debt carries a 10 percent interest rate?

table 15.2 | Dandy Candy Income Statements

	A	B	C
1		2013 Actual	2014 Forecast
2	Sales	$ 8,000,000	$10,000,000
3	Less: Costs except depreciation	6,000,000	7,500,000
4	Less: Depreciation	1,000,000	1,250,000
5	EBIT	$ 1,000,000	$ 1,250,000
6	Less: Interest	257,500	257,500
7	EBT	$ 742,500	$ 992,500
8	Less: Taxes (40%)	297,000	397,000
9	Net income	$ 445,500	$ 595,500
10	Common dividends	$ 267,300	$ 267,300
11	Addition to retained earnings	$ 178,200	$ 328,200

table 15.3 | Dandy Candy Balance Sheets

	A	B	C
1		2013 Actual	2014 Forecast
2	Assets		
3	Cash	$ 250,000	$ 312,500
4	Accounts receivable	250,000	312,500
5	Inventories	500,000	625,000
6	Total current assets	$ 1,000,000	$ 1,250,000
7	Net plant and equipment	5,000,000	6,250,000
8	Total assets	$ 6,000,000	$ 7,500,000
9	Liabilities and Equity		
10	Accounts payable	$ 125,000	$ 156,250
11	Notes payable	75,000	75,000
12	Accruals	50,000	62,500
13	Total current liabilities	$ 250,000	$ 293,750
14	Long-term debt	2,500,000	2,500,000
15	Total debt	$ 2,750,000	$ 2,793,750
16	Common stock	$ 3,000,000	$ 3,000,000
17	Retained earnings	250,000	578,200
18	Total common equity	$ 3,250,000	$ 3,578,200
19	Total liabilities and equity	$ 6,000,000	$ 6,371,950
20	Necessary increase in assets		$ 1,500,000
21	Spontaneous increase in liabilities		43,750
22	Projected increase in retained earnings		328,200
23	Additional funds needed Change in (NP + LTD + Common stock)		$ 1,128,050

SOLUTION:

In Table 15.3, the usual items used to cover AFN are indicated in red type. We are told that notes payable will remain at $75,000, which means that only the other two red items, long-term debt and common stock, will be adjusted to cover the AFN. One additional point to note is that we're also told that debt carries a 10 percent interest rate, meaning that the interest charges of $257,500 shown in Table 15.2 are calculated as $0.10 \times (\$75{,}000 + \$2{,}500{,}000) = \$257{,}500$.

The first pass at calculating AFN has therefore already been done for us: Table 15.3 shows that, at this point, we need to cover an AFN of $1,128,050. Using the strategy of raising the money to cover AFN equally from long-term debt and common stock described in the problem, the next logical step would seem to be to split the $1,128,050 in two and add each half to the 2014 forecasted long-term debt and common stock accounts as shown in Table 15.4. The relevant formulas used for doing so are associated with the cell that the formula is actually in by enclosing both in a light blue box. For example, notice that both the forecasted long-term debt and common stock accounts for 2014 are calculated by taking the corresponding value from 2013 and adding one-half of $1,128,050.

table 15.4 | **First Stab at Covering AFN using Pro Forma Financial Statements**

	A	B	C		D	E	F	
1	Percentage sales growth	25%						
2		2013 Actual	2014 Forecast			2013 Actual	2014 Forecast	
3	Sales	$ 8,000,000	$ 10,000,000		Assets			
4	Costs except depreciation	6,000,000	7,500,000		Cash	$ 250,000	$ 312,500	
5	Depreciation	1,000,000	1,250,000		Accounts receivable	250,000	312,500	
6	EBIT	$ 1,000,000	$ 1,250,000		Inventories	500,000	625,000	
7	Interest	257,500	313,903	= 0.1* (I15 + I18)	Total current assets	$ 1,000,000	$ 1,250,000	
8	EBT	$ 742,500	$ 936,098		Net plant and equipment	5,000,000	6,250,000	
9	Taxes (40%)	297,000	374,439		Total assets	$ 6,000,000	$ 7,500,000	
10	Net income	$ 445,500	$ 561,659		Liabilities and Equity			
11	Common dividends	$ 267,300	$ 267,300		Accounts payable	$ 125,000	$ 156,250	
12	Addition to retained earnings	$ 178,200	$ 294,359		Notes payable	75,000	75,000	
13					Accruals	50,000	62,500	
14					Total current liabilities	$ 250,000	$ 293,750	
15					Long-term debt	2,500,000	3,064,025	= G18 + 1128050/2
16					Total debt	$ 2,750,000	$ 3,357,775	
17					Common stock	$ 3,000,000	$ 3,564,025	= G20 + 1128050/2
18					Retained earnings	250,000	544,359	
19					Total common equity	$ 3,250,000	$ 4,108,384	
20					Total liabilities and equity	$ 6,000,000	$ 7,466,159	
21					Necessary increase in assets		$ 1,500,000	
22					Spontaneous increase in liabilities		43,750	
23					Projected increase in retained earnings		294,359	
24					Additional funds needed		$ 1,161,892	
25					Change in (NP + LTD + Common Stock)		$ 1,128,050	

This should cause the 2014 forecasted balance sheet to balance, right? Well, not quite: Notice that the AFN shown near the bottom of Table 15.4 has increased. Why? Because, since we increased the amount of forecasted debt, the amount of forecasted interest (the formula for which is highlighted in the 2014 forecasted income statement) went up, too, causing the amount of retained earnings to go down, and the amount of AFN to increase. So, we're trying to hit what is effectively a moving target here.

If we change the formulas for long-term debt and common stock to get the amount of AFN from the bottom of the worksheet (instead of passing each "$1,128,050/2") as shown in Table 15.5, then we get a warning from Excel about a circular reference error, and are offered guidance on "Make a circular reference work by changing the number of times that Excel iterates formulas."

table 15.5 | Making AFN using Pro Forma Financial Statements Self-Referential

	A	B	C		D	E	F	
1	Percentage sales growth	25%						
2		2013 Actual	2014 Forecast			2013 Actual	2014 Forecast	
3	Sales	$ 8,000,000	$ 10,000,000		Assets			
4	Costs except depreciation	6,000,000	7,500,000		Cash	$ 250,000	$ 312,500	
5	Depreciation	1,000,000	1,250,000		Accounts receivable	250,000	312,500	
6	EBIT	$ 1,000,000	$ 1,250,000		Inventories	500,000	625,000	
7	Interest	257,500	313,903	= 0.1* (I15 + I18)	Total current assets	$ 1,000,000	$ 1,250,000	
8	EBT	$ 742,500	$ 936,098		Net plant and equipment	5,000,000	6,250,000	
9	Taxes (40%)	297,000	374,439		Total assets	$ 6,000,000	$ 7,500,000	
10	Net income	$ 445,500	$ 561,659		Liabilities and Equity			
11	Common dividends	$ 267,300	$ 267,300		Accounts payable	$ 125,000	$ 156,250	
12	Addition to retained earnings	$ 178,200	$ 294,359		Notes payable	75,000	75,000	
13					Accruals	50,000	62,500	
14					Total current liabilities	$ 250,000	$ 293,750	
15					Long-term debt	2,500,000		= G18 + I28/2
16					Total debt	$ 2,750,000	$ 3,357,775	
17					Common stock	$ 3,000,000		= G20 + I28/2
18					Retained earnings	250,000	544,359	
19					Total common equity	$ 3,250,000	$ 4,108,384	
20					Total liabilities and equity	$ 6,000,000	$ 7,466,159	
21					Necessary increase in assets		$ 1,500,000	
22					Spontaneous increase in liabilities		43,750	
23					Projected increase in retained earnings		294,359	
24					Additional funds needed		$ 1,161,892	
25					Change in (NP + LTD + Common Stock)		$ 1,128,050	

To fix this, we are directed "Enable **iterative calculation,**" as Figure 15.2 on page 530 shows. Upon doing so, Excel iteratively adjusts down to an AFN $1,162,938, as shown in Table 15.6, at which value the effects of both the sources of funding chosen and the resulting amount of interest/retained earnings are included.

iterative calculation

The practice of letting a spreadsheet program or calculator repeatedly compute an answer so as to take into account circular dependency in a system of equations.

table 15.6 | **AFN Calculation using Pro Forma Financial Statements that are Iteratively Self-Referential**

	A	B	C		D	E	F	
1	Percentage sales growth	25%						
2		**2013 Actual**	**2014 Forecast**			**2013 Actual**	**2014 Forecast**	
3	Sales	$ 8,000,000	$ 10,000,000		Assets			
4	Costs except depreciation	6,000,000	7,500,000		Cash	$ 250,000	$ 312,500	
5	Depreciation	1,000,000	1,250,000		Accounts receivable	250,000	312,500	
6	EBIT	$ 1,000,000	$ 1,250,000		Inventories	500,000	625,000	
7	Interest	257,500	315,647	= 0.1* (I15 + I18)	Total current assets	$ 1,000,000	$ 1,250,000	
8	EBT	$ 742,500	$ 934,353		Net plant and equipment	5,000,000	6,250,000	
9	Taxes (40%)	297,000	373,741		Total assets	$ 6,000,000	$ 7,500,000	
10	Net income	$ 445,500	$ 560,612		Liabilities and Equity			
11	Common dividends	$ 267,300	$ 267,300		Accounts payable	$ 125,000	$ 156,250	
12	Addition to retained earnings	$ 178,200	$ 293,312		Notes payable	75,000	75,000	
13					Accruals	50,000	62,500	
14					Total current liabilities	$ 250,000	$ 293,750	
15					Long-term debt	2,500,000	3,081,469	= G18 + I28/2
16					Total debt	$ 2,750,000	$ 3,375,219	
17					Common stock	$ 3,000,000	$ 3,581,469	= G20 + I28/2
18					Retained earnings	250,000	543,312	
19					Total common equity	$ 3,250,000	$ 4,124,781	
20					Total liabilities and equity	$ 6,000,000	$ 7,500,000	
21					Necessary increase in assets		$ 1,500,000	
22					Spontaneous increase in liabilities		43,750	
23					Projected increase in retained earnings		293,312	
24					Additional funds needed		$ 1,162,938	
25					Change in (NP + LTD + Common Stock)		$ 1,162,938	

figure 15.2

Making AFN using Pro Forma Financial Statements Self-Referential

When you are working in Excel and are warned about a circular reference error, fix the problem by checking the "Enable iterative calculations box" under Options, Formulas.

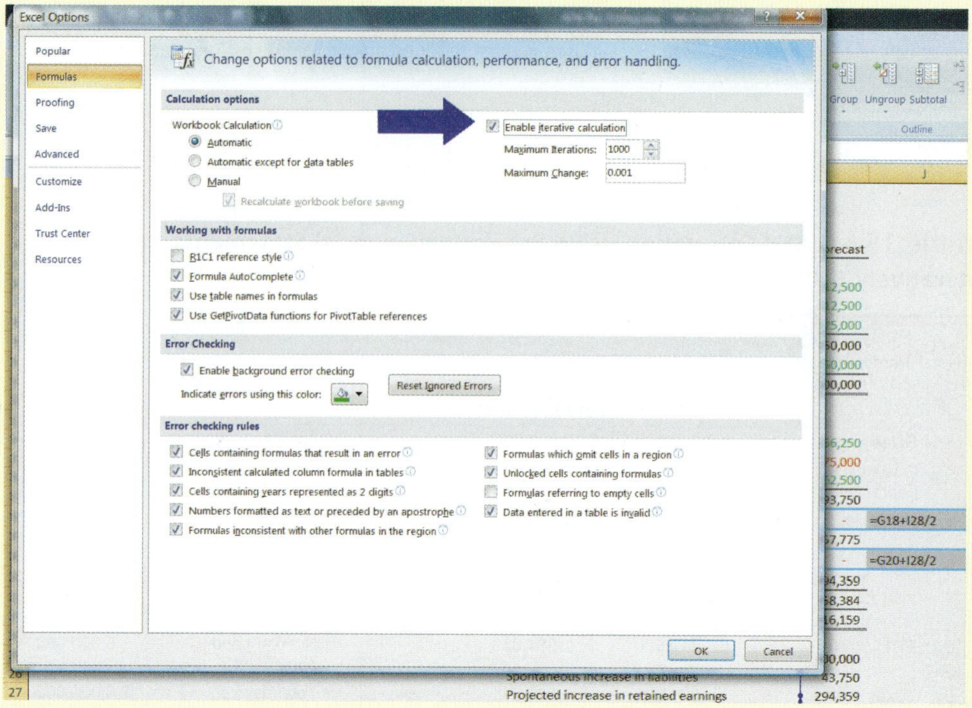

Similar to Problems 15-13, 15-14, self-test problem 5

EXAMPLE 15-8

LG15-5

For interactive versions of this example visit www.mhhe.com/can3e

Calculation of AFN using Pro Forma Financial Statements Constructed using Ratios

Continuing our previous example, let's suppose that we believed that the anticipated increase in sales was going to be due to a change in Dandy Candy's credit policy toward its customers. Specifically, let's suppose that all Dandy Candy's sales were credit sales, and that the firm was going to offer to lengthen the term of credit it offered to its customers. In 2013, Dandy Candy's average collection period (ACP) was:

$$ACP = \frac{\text{Accounts receivable} \times 365 \text{ days}}{\text{Credit sales}}$$

$$= \frac{\$250{,}000 \times 365 \text{ days}}{\$8{,}000{,}000}$$

$$= 11.41 \text{ days}$$

Also assume that Dandy Candy had analyzed the new credit policy and had determined that it could be expected to increase sales by the 25 percent amount we had already discussed, but that it could also be expected to change the ACP to 25 days. What would this do to the AFN for 2014?

SOLUTION:

We can "reverse engineer" the ACP formula to determine what the expected new value for accounts receivable will be in 2014:

$$ACP = \frac{\text{Accounts receivable} \times 365 \text{ days}}{\text{Credit sales}}$$

$$25 = \frac{\text{Accounts receivable} \times 365 \text{ days}}{\$10{,}000{,}000}$$

$$\frac{\$250{,}000{,}000}{365} = \text{Accounts receivable}$$

$$\$684{,}932 = \text{Accounts receivable}$$

Substituting this as our expected accounts receivable figure for 2014 causes a change in our AFN to $1,546,888, as shown in Table 15.7. As we would expect, this figure is higher than the one calculated in the previous section because now we are assuming that accounts receivable is increasing at a rate of ($684,932 − $250,000)/$250,000 = 174 percent, which is much faster than the 25 percent growth we were using in the previous section. If we are assuming that one of the portions of current assets is increasing at a faster rate than sales, of course we are going to need more external financing.

table 15.7 Dandy Candy Balance Sheets

	A	B	C		D	E	F	
1	Percentage sales growth	25%						
2		2013 Actual	2014 Forecast			2013 Actual	2014 Forecast	
3	Sales	$ 8,000,000	$ 10,000,000		Assets			
4	Costs except depreciation	6,000,000	7,500,000		Cash	$ 250,000	$ 312,500	
5	Depreciation	1,000,000	1,250,000		Accounts receivable	250,000	684,932	
6	EBIT	$ 1,000,000	$ 1,250,000		Inventories	500,000	625,000	
7	Interest	257,500	334,844	= 0.1* (I15 + I18)	Total current assets	$ 1,000,000	$ 1,622,432	
8	EBT	$ 742,500	$ 915,156		Net plant and equipment	5,000,000	6,250,000	
9	Taxes (40%)	297,000	366,062		Total assets	$ 6,000,000	$ 7,872,432	
10	Net income	$ 445,500	$ 549,093		Liabilities and Equity			
11	Common dividends	$ 267,300	$ 267,300		Accounts payable	$ 125,000	$ 156,250	
12	Addition to retained earnings	$ 178,200	$ 281,793		Notes payable	75,000	75,000	
13					Accruals	50,000	62,500	
14					Total current liabilities	$ 250,000	$ 293,750	
15					Long-term debt	2,500,000	3,273,444	= G18 + I28/2
16					Total debt	$ 2,750,000	$ 3,567,194	
17					Common stock	$ 3,000,000	$ 3,773,444	= G20 + I28/2
18					Retained earnings	250,000	531,793	
19					Total common equity	$ 3,250,000	$ 4,305,237	
20					Total liabilities and equity	$ 6,000,000	$ 7,872,432	
21					Necessary increase in assets		$ 1,872,432	
22					Spontaneous increase in liabilities		43,750	
23					Projected increase in retained earnings		281,793	
24					Additional funds needed		$ 1,546,888	
25					Change in (NP + LTD + Common Stock)		$ 1,546,888	

Similar to Problems 15-13, 15-14

LG15-5

AFN USING PRO FORMA STATEMENTS BASED ON RATIO ANALYSIS Finally, there's often reason to expect that some of the balance sheet and income statement items that we have been continuing to treat as linear functions of sales might not grow proportionately with sales. In fact, it's pretty easy to imagine that the expected change in sales might even be based on some fundamental underlying change in the company's business policies or in the surrounding macroeconomic environment, and that such a change might be reflected in or signaled by changes to a specific subset of the balance sheet and income statement items that have a particular underlying relationship.

Such underlying relationships were the focus of our discussion of ratios back in Chapter 3 and, just as we impose structure on the combination of external funding sources to be used, we can use those ratios to guide us in changing the relevant balance sheet or income statement items.

TIME OUT

15-5 When would iterative calculation not be necessary to find the AFN using pro forma financial statements?

15-6 Suppose a firm was planning to greatly reduce its raw materials inventory next year by introducing just-in-time inventory control procedures. Assuming no other changes to the firm's operations, what would this do to AFN?

viewpoints REVISITED

Business Application Solution

Using regression, the intercept and slope for Riada's sales as a function of time are \$633,333.33 and \$350,000, respectively, implying that Riada's expected sales in year 4 will be \$633,333.33 + \$350,000 × 4 = \$2,033,333. This will be a ΔS of \$2,033,333 − \$1,700,000 = \$333,333. The necessary increase in current assets will be \$500,000/\$1,700,000 × \$333,333 = \$98,039. Since we are told that there are enough fixed assets to support \$2 million in sales, the necessary increase in fixed assets will be \$1,500,000/\$2,000,000 × \$33,333 (sales in excess of \$2 million) = \$25,000, for a total necessary increase in assets of \$98,039 + \$25,000 = \$123,039. The spontaneous increase in liabilities will be \$300,000/\$1,700,000 × \$333,333 = \$58,824, and the projected increase in retained earnings will be 0.05 × \$2,033,333 × 0.7 = \$71,167, resulting in an AFN of:

$$AFN = \$123{,}039 - \$58{,}824 - \$71{,}167$$
$$= -\$6{,}952$$

Personal Application Solution

Since Kamala earns \$300 per month, she will earn \$300 × 12 = \$3,600 over the course of the year. Since she needs \$10,000 to fund college this year, she will need to borrow \$10,000 − \$3,600 − \$5,000 = \$1,400.

summary of learning goals

This chapter has covered the concepts involved in developing a financial plan for the firm: forecasting sales, translating this into required changes in assets and expected changes in liabilities and retained earnings, and then calculating the iterative solution for the amount of external funding needed.

LG15-1 Describe the process of financial planning in the context of the firm and how base case projections are used in the strategic planning process. Financial planning involves estimating projected cash flows, which are useful for setting internal goals, for providing information to shareholders and other external stakeholders concerning the firm's future expectations, and for estimating the firm's future needs for internal and external financing.

LG15-2 Identify how forecasting sales supports the process of financial planning. Forecasted sales drives the amount of assets needed, the liabilities used to help fund those assets, and the amount of external funds needed.

LG15-3 Compare and contrast the naïve, average, and seasonality- and trend-adjusted approaches to forecasting sales and how they are implemented. The naïve approach is appropriate when sales are stable over time; the average approach is appropriate when there is a possibility of large, random variations over time; and the seasonality- and trend-adjusted approaches are appropriate when sales are systematically changing over time.

LG15-4 Explain and demonstrate the additional funds needed (AFN) approach to estimating a firm's need to seek external financing. The additional funds needed by the firm can be calculated by assuming that much of the firm's balance sheet will grow proportionately with projected changes in sales and then extrapolating the amount of additional capital needed.

LG15-5 Use pro forma financial statements to estimate additional funds needed. Pro forma statements can be used to iteratively refine the amount of additional funds needed.

chapter equations

15-1 $E(Sales_{t+j}) = Sales_t \text{ for all } j > 0$

15-2 $$MAPE = \frac{\sum_{t=1}^{n} \left| \dfrac{Actual_t - Forecast_t}{Actual_t} \right|}{n}$$

15-3 $$E(Sales_{n+j}) = \frac{\sum_{i=1}^{n} Sales_t}{n} \text{ for all } j > 0$$

15-4 $AFN = \text{Necessary increase in assets}$
$- \text{Spontaneous increase in liabilities}$
$- \text{Projected increase in retained earnings}$

15-5 $$\text{Necessary increase in assets} = \frac{A^*}{S_0} \times \Delta S$$

15-6 $$\text{Spontaneous increase in liabilities} = \frac{L^*}{S_0} \times \Delta S$$

15-7 $\text{Projected increase in retained earnings} = M \times S_1 \times RR$

key terms

additional funds needed (AFN), The amount of external financing a firm must seek in order to change the asset base as necessary to support a different level of sales. *p. 521*

average approach, Assuming that future sales will be equal to the average historical value across some relevant period. *p. 516*

base case, The set of assumptions underlying the firm's financial plan. *p. 514*

base case projections, The projected financial statements associated with the base case. *p. 514*

capital intensity ratio, Relevant assets divided by current sales. *p. 521*

centered moving average, A moving average created to put a specific observation exactly in the center of the period over which the moving average is calculated. *p. 518*

deseasonalize, To remove the effects of seasonality from historic data. *p. 518*

financial planning, The process of mapping out the future cash inflows and outflows of the firm. *p. 513*

first order effects, The immediately observable effects of changing one item on another. Usually contrasted with *higher order effects,* which are the subsequent, less observable effects of the change. *p. 525*

infinitely divisible, The ability to divide a given amount into as small a portion as needed. *p. 523*

iterative calculation, The practice of letting a spreadsheet program or calculator repeatedly compute an answer so as to take into account circular dependency in a system of equations. *p. 529*

MAPE, Mean absolute percentage error, a measurement of a forecast's accuracy. *p. 514*

naïve approach, Assuming that future sales will be equal to the latest period's sales. *p. 514*

spontaneous liabilities ratio, Relevant liabilities divided by current sales. *p. 521*

strategic planning, The process of determining where a firm is going over the next year or more, how it is going to get there, and how it will know if it gets there or not. *p. 514*

trade credit, The practice of one firm selling to another on credit terms. *p. 521*

self-test problems with solutions

LG15-3

1 Naïve Approach June Bug, Inc., has had sales of \$25 million, \$28 million, and \$23 million for each of the last three years. Using the naïve approach, what would be the forecast for next year's sales, and what would be the MAPE if the actual sales were \$26 million?

Solution:

The naïve approach would be to take the last historic period's sales, \$23 million, as the forecast for next year. This would result in a MAPE of:

$$MAPE = \frac{\sum_{t=1}^{n} \left| \frac{Actual_t - Forecast_t}{Actual_t} \right|}{n}$$

$$= \frac{\left| \frac{\$26{,}000{,}000 - \$23{,}000{,}000}{\$26{,}000{,}000} \right|}{1}$$

$$= 0.1154, \text{ or } 11.54\%$$

LG15-3

2 Average Approach Using the average of the three historic sales figures in the previous problem, what would be the forecast for next year and the MAPE of that forecast?

Solution:

The average sales figure would be:

$$E(Sales_{n+j}) = \frac{\sum_{i=1}^{n} Sales_t}{n} \text{ for all } j > 0$$

$$= \frac{\$25{,}000{,}000 + \$28{,}000{,}000 + \$23{,}000{,}000}{3}$$

$$= 25{,}333{,}333$$

And the MAPE would be:

$$MAPE = \frac{\sum_{t=1}^{n} \left| \frac{Actual_t - Forecast_t}{Actual_t} \right|}{n}$$

$$= \frac{\left| \frac{\$26{,}000{,}000 - \$25{,}333{,}333}{\$26{,}000{,}000} \right|}{1}$$

$$= 0.0256, \text{ or } 2.56\%$$

3 Adjusting for Seasonality American Food Services has detected a strong weekly cyclicality in its food sales, but the firm does not believe that there is any consistent trend across time. Management is attempting to forecast next week's daily sales figures using the historic figures for the last four weeks shown below. If they are somewhat worried about the possibility of large, random variations in their historic data, what should their forecasts be? LG15-3

Solution:

The firm should calculate seasonal (i.e., daily) adjustment indexes, deseasonalize the historic sales figures, take their average, and then use the re-seasonalized average to produce forecasts for each day of the week. Please refer to Example 15-3 for a detailed guide to the steps involved. The results will be as shown below:

Observation	Day	Sales - Actual		7-CMA	*(1)	*(2)	Adj. Seas. Index	Deseas. Sales	*(3)
1	1	$ 41,028						$ 34,983.07	
2	2	23,724						48,411.85	
3	3	34,820						50,459.74	
4	4	32,735		$ 46,551	0.703209			42,946.78	
5	5	32,373		49,057	0.659906			61,124.64	
6	6	70,698		49,735	1.421482			50,854.47	
7	7	90,478		48,926	1.849266			46,043.46	
8	1	58,571		49,106	1.192757	1.167272014	1.172795784	49,941.35	
9	2	28,473		47,900	0.594426	0.487737264	0.490045336	58,102.79	
10	3	29,157		48,109	0.606065	0.686804915	0.690055017	42,253.15	
11	4	33,989		48,146	0.705953	0.758632382	0.762222385	44,591.97	
12	5	23,934		48,019	0.498425	0.527128272	0.52962275	45,190.66	
13	6	72,159		47,052	1.533615	1.383654456	1.390202192	51,905.40	
14	7	90,741		48,023	1.889543	1.955801284	1.965056535	46,177.30	
15	1	57,682		50,129	1.150678	6.967030588	7	49,183.33	
16	2	21,699		49,741	0.436236			44,279.58	
17	3	35,955		48,011	0.748891			52,104.54	
18	4	48,731		50,390	0.967069			63,932.79	
19	5	21,223		50,166	0.423054			40,071.92	
20	6	60,046		50,211	1.195867			43,192.28	
21	7	107,397		50,454	2.128594			54,653.39	
22	1	56,112		48,440	1.158382			47,844.65	
23	2	22,015		50,896	0.43255			44,924.41	
24	3	37,657		53,379	0.705459			54,571.01	
25	4	34,630		52,605	0.658299			45,432.93	
26	5	38,414						72,530.87	
27	6	77,431						55,697.65	
28	7	101,978						51,895.71	
	1								$ 58,359.23
	2								24,385.04
	3								34,337.67
	4								37,928.78
	5								26,354.44
	6								69,177.54
	7								97,782.74

*(1) = Actual sales for day j / 7-CMA for day j
*(2) = Average of Seas. Irreg. values for day j
(Ex: (1.192757 + 1.150678 + 1.158382) / 3 = 1.16727014
*(3) = Average of 28 days of Deseas. Sales × Adj. Seas. Index for day j

LG15-4

4 Estimating AFN Using Simple Approach Jon Buoys currently has the following balance sheet. Sales for the year just ended were $23 million, and the firm expects sales next year of $25 million. The firm has a profit margin of 15 percent, a retention ratio of 10 percent, and unused fixed-asset capacity sufficient to cover the projected $25 million in sales. Using the simple approach to calculating AFN, how much in external funds will Jon Buoys require?

Assets		Liabilities and Equity	
Current assets	$ 10,000,000	Current liabilities	$ 3,500,000
Fixed assets	35,000,000	Long-term debt	11,500,000
		Equity	30,000,000
Total assets	$45,000,000	Total liabilities and equity	$45,000,000

Solution:

Since it is stated that there is sufficient existing fixed asset capacity to cover the projected sales, A^* is $10 million and the necessary increase in assets will be:

$$\begin{aligned}\text{Necessary increase in assets} &= \frac{A^*}{S_0} \times \Delta S \\ &= \frac{\$10{,}000{,}000}{\$23{,}000{,}000} \times (\$25{,}000{,}000 - \$23{,}000{,}000) \\ &= \$869{,}565\end{aligned}$$

The spontaneous increase in liabilities is expected to be:

$$\begin{aligned}\text{Spontaneous increase in liabilities} &= \frac{L^*}{S_0} \times \Delta S \\ &= \frac{\$3{,}500{,}000}{\$23{,}000{,}000} \times (\$25{,}000{,}000 - \$23{,}000{,}000) \\ &= \$304{,}348\end{aligned}$$

And the projected increase in retained earnings will be:

$$\begin{aligned}\text{Projected increase in retained earnings} &= M \times S_1 \times RR \\ &= 0.15 \times \$25{,}000{,}000 \times 0.10 \\ &= \$375{,}000\end{aligned}$$

So the amount of AFN will be equal to $869,565 − $304,348 − $375,000 = $190,217.

LG15-4

5 Estimating AFN Using Pro Forma Statements Suppose that the 2013 actual and 2014 projected financial statements for Krazy Krackers are initially as shown in the following table. In these tables, sales are projected to rise by 15 percent in the coming year, and the components of the income statement and balance sheet that are expected to increase at the same 15 percent rate as sales are indicated by green type. Assuming that Krazy Krackers wants to cover the AFN with only long-term debt, how much in additional funds will Krazy Krackers need to raise if debt carries a 10 percent interest rate?

Solution:

The answer is shown in the following table:

	A	B	C	D	E	F
1		2013 Actual	2014 Forecast		2013 Actual	2014 Forecast
2	Sales	$ 6,000,000	$ 6,900,000	Assets		
3	Costs except depreciation	3,400,000	3,910,000	Cash	$ 400,000	$ 460,000
4	Depreciation	500,000	575,000	Accounts receivable	245,000	281,750
5	EBIT	$ 2,100,000	$ 2,415,000	Inventories	1,200,000	1,380,000
6	Interest	200,000	200,000	Total current assets	$ 1,845,000	$ 2,121,750
7	EBT	$ 1,900,000	$ 2,215,000	Net plant and equipment	5,000,000	5,750,000
8	Taxes (40%)	760,000	886,000	Total assets	$ 6,845,000	$ 7,871,750
9	Net income	$ 1,140,000	$ 1,329,000			
10				Liabilities and Equity		
11	Common dividends	$ 570,000	$ 570,000	Accounts payable	$ 179,000	$ 205,850
12	Addition to retained earnings	$ 570,000	$ 759,000	Notes payable	1,000,000	1,000,000
13				Accruals	350,000	402,500
14				Total current liabilities	$ 1,529,000	$ 1,608,350
15				Long-term debt	1,000,000	1,000,000
16				Total debt	$ 2,529,000	$ 2,608,350
17				Common stock	$ 4,100,000	$ 4,100,000
18				Retained earnings	216,000	975,000
19				Total common equity	$ 4,316,000	$ 5,075,000
20				Total liabilities and equity	$ 6,845,000	$ 7,683,350

	A	B	C	D	E	F
1		2013 Actual	2014 Forecast		2013 Actual	2014 Forecast
2	Sales	$ 6,000,000	$ 6,900,000	Assets		
3	Costs except depreciation	3,400,000	3,910,000	Cash	$ 400,000	$ 460,000
4	Depreciation	500,000	575,000	Accounts receivable	245,000	281,750
5	EBIT	$ 2,100,000	$ 2,415,000	Inventories	1,200,000	1,380,000
6	Less interest	200,000	220,043	Total current assets	$ 1,845,000	$ 2,121,750
7	EBT	$ 1,900,000	$ 2,194,957	Net plant and equipment	5,000,000	5,750,000
8	Taxes (40%)	760,000	877,983	Total assets	$ 6,845,000	$ 7,871,750
9	Net income	$ 1,140,000	$ 1,316,974	Liabilities and Equity		
10	Common dividends	$ 570,000	$ 570,000	Accounts payable	$ 179,000	$ 205,850
11	Addition to retained earnings	$ 570,000	$ 746,974	Notes payable	1,000,000	1,000,000
12				Accruals	350,000	402,500
13				Total current liabilities	$ 1,529,000	$ 1,608,350
14				Long-term debt	1,000,000	1,200,426
15				Total debt	$ 2,529,000	$ 2,808,776
16				Common stock	$ 4,100,000	$ 4,100,000
17				Retained earnings	216,000	962,974
18				Total common equity	$ 4,316,000	$ 5,062,974
19				Total liabilities and equity	$ 6,845,000	$ 7,871,750
20				Necessary increase in assets		$ 1,026,750
21				Spontaneous increase in liabilities		79,350
22				Projected increase in retained earnings		746,974
22				Additional funds needed		$ 200,426
24				Change in (NP + LTD + Common Stock)		$ 200,426

questions

1. Compare and contrast the use of pro forma financial statements in corporate financial planning with their use in accounting. *(LG15-1)*
2. Why might current liabilities be considered a spontaneous source of funding for a firm? *(LG15-2)*
3. What approach should be used to forecast sales if a firm believes that sales will be stable over time? *(LG15-3)*
4. What approach should be used to forecast sales if a firm believes that sales will increase over time? *(LG15-3)*
5. What is the optimal length of time over which to take an average of historic sales when using the average approach? *(LG15-3)*
6. What is the theoretical minimum value for MAPE? *(LG15-3)*
7. If a firm needs to keep a minimum cash balance on hand and faces both cash inflows and outflows, which of the cash management models discussed in this chapter would be more appropriate for it to use? *(LG15-3)*
8. Can the procedure described in this chapter for adjusting for seasonality apply to periods longer than a year? How? *(LG15-3)*
9. Everything else held constant, which will be greater: AFN for a firm with excess fixed-asset capacity, or AFN for a firm with no excess fixed-asset capacity? Why? *(LG15-4)*
10. What does a negative value for AFN mean? *(LG15-4)*
11. Which specific item of a pro forma income statement should be most expected to vary proportionately with sales? Why? *(LG15-5)*
12. Explain why we need to use the iterative calculation approach described in the text to get a complete solution for AFN. *(LG15-5)*

problems

basic problems

15-1 Naïve Sales Forecast Suppose a firm has had the following historic sales figures. What would be the forecast for next year's sales using the naïve approach? *(LG15-3)*

Year:	2009	2010	2011	2012	2013
Sales	$1,500,000	$1,750,000	$1,400,000	$2,000,000	$1,600,000

15-2 Naïve Sales Forecast Suppose a firm has had the following historic sales figures. What would be the forecast for next year's sales using the naïve approach? *(LG15-3)*

Year:	2009	2010	2011	2012	2013
Sales	$2,500,000	$3,750,000	$2,400,000	$2,000,000	$2,600,000

15-3 Average Sales Forecast Suppose a firm has had the following historic sales figures. What would be the forecast for next year's sales using the average approach? *(LG15-3)*

Year:	2009	2010	2011	2012	2013
Sales	$1,500,000	$1,750,000	$1,400,000	$2,000,000	$1,600,000

15-4 Average Sales Forecast Suppose a firm has had the following historic sales figures. What would be the forecast for next year's sales using the average approach? *(LG15-3)*

Year:	2009	2010	2011	2012	2013
Sales	$2,500,000	$3,750,000	$2,400,000	$2,000,000	$2,600,000

15-5 Additional Funds Needed Suppose that Gyp Sum Industries currently has the following balance sheet, and that sales for the year just ended were $10 million. The firm also has a profit margin of 25 percent, a retention ratio of 30 percent, and expects sales of $8 million next year. If all assets and current liabilities are expected to shrink with sales, what amount of additional funds will Gyp Sum need from external sources to fund the expected growth? *(LG15-4)*

Assets		Liabilities and Equity	
Current assets	$2,000,000	Current liabilities	$1,500,000
Fixed assets	4,000,000	Long-term debt	1,500,000
		Equity	3,000,000
Total assets	$6,000,000	Total liabilities and equity	$6,000,000

intermediate problems

15-6 Additional Funds Needed Suppose that Wind Em Corp. currently has the following balance sheet, and that sales for the year just ended were $7 million. The firm also has a profit margin of 27 percent, a retention ratio of 20 percent, and expects sales of $8 million next year. If all assets and current liabilities are expected to grow with sales, what amount of additional funds will Wind Em need from external sources to fund the expected growth? *(LG15-4)*

Assets		Liabilities and Equity	
Current assets	$2,000,000	Current liabilities	$2,500,000
Fixed assets	5,000,000	Long-term debt	1,500,000
		Equity	3,000,000
Total assets	$7,000,000	Total liabilities and equity	$7,000,000

15-7 Regression Sales Forecast Suppose a firm has had the following historic sales figures. What would be the forecast for next year's sales using regression to estimate a trend? *(LG15-3)*

Year:	2009	2010	2011	2012	2013
Sales	$1,500,000	$1,750,000	$1,700,000	$2,000,000	$1,800,000

15-8 Regression Sales Forecast Suppose a firm has had the following historic sales figures. What would be the forecast for next year's sales using regression to estimate a trend? *(LG15-3)*

Year:	2009	2010	2011	2012	2013
Sales	$2,500,000	$3,750,000	$4,400,000	$5,000,000	$5,600,000

15-9 AFN with Excess Capacity Suppose that Psy Ops Industries currently has the following balance sheet, and that sales for the year just ended were $5 million. The firm also has a profit margin of 25 percent, a retention ratio of 30 percent, and expects sales of $8 million next year. If fixed assets have enough capacity to cover the increase in sales and all other assets and current liabilities are expected to increase with sales, what amount of additional funds will Psy Ops need from external sources to fund the expected growth? *(LG15-4)*

Assets		Liabilities and Equity	
Current assets	$2,000,000	Current liabilities	$1,500,000
Fixed assets	4,000,000	Long-term debt	1,500,000
		Equity	3,000,000
Total assets	$6,000,000	Total liabilities and equity	$6,000,000

15-10 AFN with Lumpy Assets Suppose that Wall-E Corp. currently has the following balance sheet, and that sales for the year just ended were $7 million. The firm also has a profit margin of 27 percent, a retention ratio of 20 percent, and expects sales of $9 million next year. Fixed assets are currently fully utilized, and the nature of Wall-E's fixed assets is such that they must be added in $1 million increments. If current assets and current liabilities are expected to grow with sales, what amount of additional funds will Wall-E need from external sources to fund the expected growth? *(LG15-4)*

Assets		Liabilities and Equity	
Current assets	$2,000,000	Current liabilities	$2,500,000
Fixed assets	5,000,000	Long-term debt	1,500,000
		Equity	3,000,000
Total assets	$7,000,000	Total liabilities and equity	$7,000,000

advanced problems

15-11 Seasonal and Trend Estimated Sales John's Bait and Fish Shop has had the monthly sales amounts listed below for the last four years. Assuming that there is both seasonality and a trend, estimate monthly sales for each month of the coming year. *(LG15-2)*

Year:	2010	2011	2012	2013
January	$ 417,812	$ 585,558	$ 334,336	$ 587,080
February	113,240	138,414	165,492	113,788
March	139,815	177,676	86,015	137,015
April	428,157	392,734	512,061	457,425
May	436,880	926,046	534,007	851,622
June	743,947	1,084,321	597,606	741,444

Year:	2010	2011	2012	2013
July	$ 1,449,280	$ 1,249,470	$ 1,564,939	$ 1,579,376
August	1,428,123	1,794,586	1,849,585	1,590,067
September	1,178,795	1,022,538	683,038	724,279
October	368,475	465,971	483,142	651,824
November	257,638	389,276	261,309	309,872
December	321,208	386,377	234,736	371,721

15-12 Seasonal and Trend Estimated Sales Sara's Ice Cream Shop is closed for six months out of the year but has had the monthly sales amounts listed below for the last four years. Assuming that there is both seasonality and a trend, estimate monthly sales for each month of the coming year. *(LG15-3)*

Year:	2010	2011	2012	2013
May	$ 436,880	$ 926,046	$ 534,007	$ 851,622
June	743,947	1,084,321	597,606	741,444
July	1,449,280	1,249,470	1,564,939	1,579,376
August	1,428,123	1,794,586	1,849,585	1,590,067
September	1,178,795	1,022,538	683,038	724,279
October	368,475	465,971	483,142	651,824

15-13 Pro Forma Additional Funds Needed Suppose that the 2013 actual and 2014 projected financial statements for Comfy Corners Catbeds are initially as shown. In these tables, sales are projected to rise by 22 percent in the coming year, and the components of the income statement and balance sheet that are expected to increase at the same 22 percent rate as sales are indicated by green type. Assuming that Comfy Corners Catbeds wants to cover the AFN with half equity, 25 percent long-term debt, and the remainder from notes payable, what amount of additional funds will be needed if debt carries a 10 percent interest rate? *(LG15-3)*

	A	B	C	D	E	F
1		Income Statement			Balance Sheet	
2		2013 Actual	2014 Forecast		2013 Actual	2014 Forecast
3	Sales	$ 4,000,000	$ 4,880,000	Assets		
4	Costs except depreciation	2,600,000	3,172,000	Cash	$ 600,000	$ 732,000
5	Depreciation	1,000,000	1,220,000	Accounts receivable	137,000	167,140
6	EBIT	$ 400,000	$ 488,000	Inventories	1,013,000	1,235,860
7	Interest	198,000	198,000	Total current assets	$ 1,750,000	$ 2,135,000
8	EBT	$ 202,000	$ 290,000	Net plant and equipment	5,000,000	6,100,000
9	Taxes (40%)	80,800	116,000	Total assets	$ 6,750,000	$ 8,235,000
10	Net income	$ 121,200	$ 174,000			
11				Liabilities and Equity		
12	Common dividends	$ 60,600	$ 60,600	Accounts payable	$ 179,000	$ 218,380
13	Addition to retained earnings	$ 60,600	$ 113,400	Notes payable	980,000	980,000
14				Accruals	375,000	457,500
15				Total current liabilities	$ 1,534,000	$ 1,655,880
16				Long-term debt	1,000,000	1,000,000
17				Total debt	$ 2,534,000	$ 2,655,880
18				Common stock	$ 4,000,000	$ 4,000,000
19				Retained earnings	216,000	329,400
20				Total common equity	$ 4,216,000	$ 4,329,400
21				Total liabilities and equity	$ 6,750,000	$ 6,985,280

15-14 Pro Forma Additional Funds Needed Suppose that the 2013 actual and 2014 projected financial statements for AFS are initially as shown. In these tables, sales are projected to rise by 14 percent in the coming year, and the components of the income statement and balance sheet that are expected to increase at the same 14 percent rate as sales are indicated by green type. Assuming that AFS wants to cover the AFN with half equity and half long-term debt, what amount of additional funds will be needed if debt carries a 9 percent interest rate? *(LG15-3)*

	A	B	C	D	E	F
1	Income Statement			Balance Sheet		
2		2013 Actual	2014 Forecast		2013 Actual	2014 Forecast
3	Sales	$ 5,500,000	$ 6,270,000	Assets		
4	Costs except depreciation	3,000,000	3,420,000	Cash	$ 750,000	$ 855,000
5	Depreciation	1,200,000	1,368,000	Accounts receivable	140,000	159,600
6	EBIT	$ 1,300,000	$ 1,482,000	Inventories	800,000	912,000
7	Interest	153,000	153,000	Total current assets	$ 1,690,000	$ 1,926,600
8	EBT	$ 1,147,000	$ 1,329,000	Net plant and equipment	5,000,000	5,700,000
9	Taxes (40%)	458,800	531,600	Total assets	$ 6,690,000	$ 7,626,600
10	Net income	$ 688,200	$ 797,400			
11				Liabilities and Equity		
12	Common dividends	$ 344,100	$ 344,100	Accounts payable	$ 350,000	$ 399,000
13	Addition to retained earnings	$ 344,100	$ 453,300	Notes payable	500,000	500,000
14				Accruals	375,000	427,500
15				Total current liabilities	$ 1,225,000	$ 1,326,500
16				Long-term debt	1,200,000	1,200,000
17				Total debt	$ 2,425,000	$ 2,526,500
18				Common stock	$ 4,000,000	$ 4,000,000
19				Retained earnings	265,000	718,300
20				Total common equity	$ 4,265,000	$ 4,718,300
21				Total liabilities and equity	$ 6,690,000	$ 7,244,800

research it! Looking Up Sales Information

Go to the Johnson & Johnson's investor relations sales and earnings page at **www.investor.jnj.com/sales-earnings.cfm.** The company reports sales on a quarterly basis, so download all available sales reports and set the last four quarters' sales figures aside as an "out-of-sample" test group. Use the rest of the "worldwide" historical sales figures to forecast what the last four quarters' sales figures would have been expected to be, and then perform a MAPE analysis on your forecasts. How accurate was your forecast, and do you think you could have been more accurate if you had calculated forecasts for each component of worldwide sales ("U.S. consumer sales," "international pharmaceutical sales," etc.) separately?

integrated mini-case Effect of Capital Structure on AFN

Suppose that the 2013 actual and 2014 projected financial statements for your firm are initially as shown in the following table. Sales are projected to rise by 18 percent in the coming year, and the components of the income statement and balance sheet that are expected to increase at the same 18 percent rate as sales are indicated by green type. Assuming that your firm has to pay 9 percent interest on debt, what would the AFN be if needed capital was to be raised entirely from equity?

How would your answer change if the entire AFN was to be raised from long-term debt? And what does this imply about the relationship between the sources of AFN funding and the amount needed?

	A	B	C	D	E	F
1	Income Statement				Balance Sheet	
2		2013 Actual	2014 Forecast		2013 Actual	2014 Forecast
3	Sales	$ 10,000,000	$ 11,800,000	Assets		
4	Costs except depreciation	5,200,000	6,136,000	Cash	$ 540,000	$ 637,200
5	Depreciation	800,000	944,000	Accounts receivable	800,000	944,000
6	EBIT	$ 4,000,000	$ 4,720,000	Inventories	1,600,000	1,888,000
7	Interest	181,530	181,530	Total current assets	$ 2,940,000	$ 3,469,200
8	EBT	$ 3,818,470	$ 4,538,470	Net plant and equipment	7,500,000	8,850,000
9	Taxes (40%)	1,527,388	1,815,388	Total assets	$ 10,440,000	$ 12,319,200
10	Net income	$ 2,291,082	$ 2,723,082			
11				Liabilities and Equity		
12	Common dividends	$ 2,000,000	$ 2,000,000	Accounts payable	$ 557,000	$ 657,260
13	Addition to retained earnings	$ 291,082	$ 723,082	Notes payable	750,000	750,000
14				Accruals	1,200,000	1,416,000
15				Total current liabilities	$ 2,507,000	$ 2,823,260
16				Long-term debt	2,017,000	2,017,000
17				Total debt	$ 4,524,000	$ 4,840,260
18				Common stock	$ 5,250,000	$ 5,250,000
19				Retained earnings	666,000	1,389,082
20				Total common equity	$ 5,916,000	$ 6,639,082
21				Total liabilities and equity	$ 10,440,000	$ 11,479,342

ANSWERS TO TIME OUT

15-1 Forecasts would need to be adjusted for seasonality, but would not need a regression to adjust for a trend, since none exists.

15-2 You would need to compute day-of-the-week indexes centered on the seven days around each day of the week and then use these indexes to deseasonalize the historic observations, just as we did with the monthly seasonal indexes in this section.

15-3 Accounts payable and accrued wages would be most likely to spontaneously increase with sales. If you are making more stuff, you will buy more raw material from your suppliers (and, presumably, therefore buy more on credit from them), and you will use your workers' labor more, too.

15-4 The firm would not need to add an entire new machine to increase fixed assets capacity, but only the larger of either the portion required to support sales or the minimum portion that can be leased.

15-5 If a firm was planning on using only external equity to raise needed assets, and if there was no resulting forecasted change on retained earnings, then there would be no feedback effect from increasing interest on debt, and iterative calculations would not be needed.

15-6 This would reduce AFN by reducing the amount of current assets.

PART EIGHT

16 Assessing Long-Term Debt, Equity, and Capital Structure

viewpoints

Business Application

Suppose that Kieran has decided that it's time to take her photography business, currently run on an all-equity basis, and leverage it so that it's funded with 50 percent debt. The business currently has $30,000 worth of assets and a 15 percent marginal tax rate. Kieran has in hand a bank quote at an interest rate of 9.5 percent on an interest-only loan. As long as Kieran doesn't anticipate any chance that the firm won't be able to cover the required interest payments on the loan, or that the bank won't renew the loan at the end of its term, what economic benefits will accrue to Kieran by re-leveraging the firm? **(See solution on p. 566)**

Personal Application

Gunter has just graduated from college and started a new job. He's thinking about buying a townhouse for $150,000 but doesn't have a down payment. His bank has offered to lend him 80 percent of the money—a 30-year mortgage at a rate of 5.875 percent. Further, the bank will lend Gunter the other $30,000 through a home equity loan at a rate of 7.90 percent. His applicable tax rate is 25 percent. If he accepts the bank's offer, what weighted-average after-tax interest rate will Gunter pay for the purchase of the townhouse? **(See solution on p. 566)**

What other options does Gunter have for financing his home purchase?

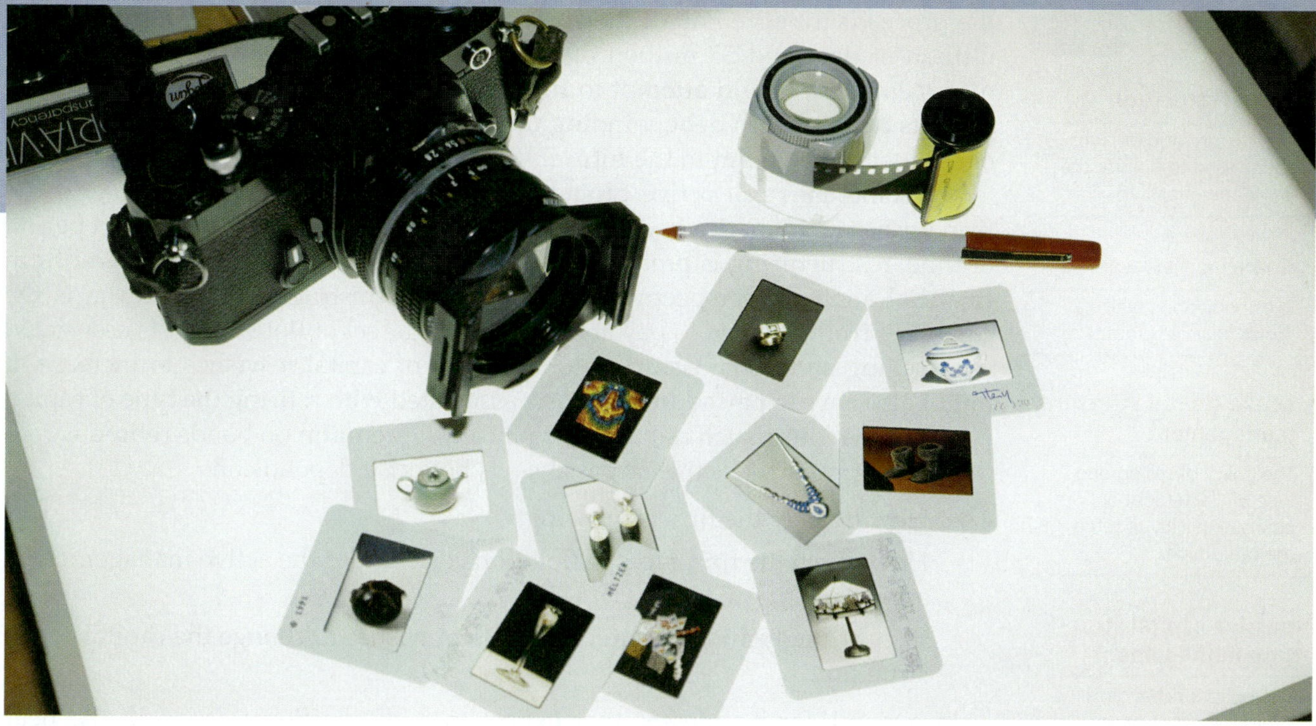

So far, we've assumed that a firm's **capital structure**—the mix of debt and equity the firm uses to finance its operations—is either given or irrelevant to the decisions we've been making. Although this assumption works well in the short term, firms can and do change their capital structures in the longer term. Therefore, we need to analyze factors that affect the firm's decision to change its funding mix.

As we'll see, two main factors come into play: (1) whether debt interest payments are tax deductible and (2) how increased debt might affect the likelihood of the firm either going bankrupt or entering into **financial distress** (i.e., approaching bankruptcy). Financial managers carefully choose a capital structure that sets these two factors' marginal effects equal to one another. By doing so, they simultaneously maximize firm value and minimize any new project's financing costs.

Learning Goals

LG16-1 Differentiate between active and passive changes to capital structure.

LG16-2 Explain why finance professionals refer to debt as "leverage."

LG16-3 Show how the firm apportions risk and return among stockholders and bondholders in a "perfect world."

LG16-4 Describe how the optimal capital structure changes under corporate taxation.

LG16-5 Demonstrate how individual shareholders can affect capital structure by borrowing and lending on their own account.

LG16-6 Calculate the EBIT and EPS levels at which shareholders become indifferent when choosing between two capital structures.

LG16-7 Describe how the firm's choice of optimal capital structure changes under the possibility of bankruptcy.

LG16-8 Analyze whether real-world business practices reflect the theoretical basis for optimal capital structure.

16.1 • Active versus Passive Capital Structure Changes

In theory, firms seeking to change their capital structure can take one of two approaches. The first approach is to immediately sell additional claims of one type of capital and use the proceeds to retire other kinds of claims. This is a strategy of **active management.** The second approach is to simply wait until the firm requires additional capital to cover capital budgeting needs and then sell more of the type of claims it wishes to increase in its capital structure. This is a strategy of **passive management.**

For example, suppose that Kennemore Corp. currently has $10 million in assets, financed entirely with equity. The firm has decided to switch to a 50 percent debt/50 percent equity structure. With *active* capital structure management, it would sell $5 million of debt and use

LG16-1

capital structure The mixture of debt and equity used to finance the firm's operations.

financial distress The condition in which a firm is near bankruptcy.

active capital structure management The policy of selling one type of claim (debt or equity) explicitly to retire the other type.

passive capital structure management The policy of changing the capital structure gradually over time by funding new capital projects disproportionately with the type of capital you want to increase in the capital structure.

the proceeds to retire half of the equity. Thus Kennemore will wind up with $5 million of debt and $5 million of equity today. With passive capital structure management, it would attempt to fund the next $10 million of assets for future projects entirely with debt, winding up with $10 million of debt and $10 million of equity at some point in the future.

We sometimes call active capital structure management *restructuring*. If the firm wishes to dramatically change its capital structure in a relatively short period of time, restructuring is preferable, both from the firm's point of view and from financial analysts' perspective. The downside to restructuring, however, is the cost. The firm will need to pay at least one "extra" set of flotation costs associated with selling additional securities of the type of capital it wishes to increase. It might also have to pay additional costs associated with retiring the type of capital it wishes to reduce, such as having to pay a call premium on bonds retired early.

Which approach—active or passive—is better? It depends on:

- How quickly the firm is growing.
- How much the firm faces in flotation costs under the active management approach.
- How strongly and how quickly the firm wishes to change the capital structure.

In general, for businesses that expect to add significant assets in the near future (either due to growth or by replacing existing assets), the passive management approach works best. Such firms will be able to alter their structure relatively quickly without incurring the additional costs of active management.

TIME OUT

16-1 Which strategy, active or passive capital structure management, would make the process of changing the firm's capital structure a longer-term proposition? Why?

16-2 Suppose that a firm was simultaneously evaluating the addition of a new capital budgeting project and a proposed capital structure change: Should the old capital structure or the proposed new capital structure be used in determining the WACC for the new project?

Having said that, in this chapter we focus on active capital structure management. This focus will allow us to examine the benefits of a proposed capital structure change without having to separate out the additional impacts of capital budgeting decisions. Passive capital structure management must account for capital budgeting as the firm increases its capital on an as-needed basis.

LG16-2

16.2 • Capital Structure Theory: The Effect of Financial Leverage

financial leverage Another name for debt in the capital structure.

In finance, we refer to using debt within a firm's capital structure as **financial leverage.**[1] Why? Because just as a physical lever magnifies force in one direction and movement in another, the force of debt on one side magnifies the effect of potential expected return on the other. It also magnifies variability, or risk, around that return. To see why it does so, we first need to tie up some theoretical loose ends.

[1] In addition to financial leverage, firms also make use of operating leverage, which refers to the use of fixed versus variable expenses to potentially magnify the firm's earnings. Together, these two types of leverage are often referred to as total leverage.

Modigliani and Miller's "Perfect World"

The basic tool for examining various variables' effects on the firm's choice of optimal capital structure is the **Modigliani-Miller (M&M) theorem,** named after its authors, Franco Modigliani and Merton Miller, who completed the theorem in 1958. The full development of the M&M theorem starts with a "perfect world," one that features:

Modigliani–Miller (M&M) theorem

In an efficient market without taxes and bankruptcy costs, the value of a firm does not depend upon the firm's capital structure.

- No taxes.
- No chance of bankruptcy.
- Perfectly efficient markets.
- Symmetric information sets for all participants.

In this perfect world, the M&M theorem's two main propositions are:

Proposition I (perfect world): $V_L = V_U$ **(16-1)**

where

V_U is the value of an unleveraged, or all-equity-financed, firm.

V_L is the value of a leveraged firm (i.e., one whose capital structure contains debt).

Proposition II (perfect world): $i_E = i_{E,0} + \frac{D}{E}(i_{E,0} - i_D)$ **(16-2)**

where

$iE_{,0}$ is the cost of capital for an all-equity firm.

i_E and i_D are the costs of equity and debt in a leveraged firm.

Both of these propositions reflect a common underlying intuition, which we sometimes refer to as the **capital structure irrelevance assertion.** Merton Miller, in his testimony in Glendale Federal Bank's lawsuit against the U.S. government in December 1997, probably put it best:

capital structure irrelevance assertion

Another name for the Modigliani-Miller theorem.

> *I have a simple explanation [for the first Modigliani-Miller proposition]. It's after the ball game, and the pizza man comes up to Yogi Berra and he says, "Yogi, how do you want me to cut this pizza, into quarters?" Yogi says, "No, cut it into eight pieces, I'm feeling hungry tonight." Now when I tell that story, the usual reaction is, "And you mean to say that they gave you a [Nobel] prize for that?"*

In terms of Proposition I, what Miller is saying is that, in this perfect world, the firm will be worth the same no matter how it is financed. However, if we were to think of the risk of the firm as the toppings of the pizza, having those toppings distributed unevenly would imply that slices with more toppings (risk) would be expected to offer more "taste sensation" (i.e., rate of return). To see why, let's take a closer look at Proposition II.

THE EFFECT OF LEVERAGE ON THE COST OF EQUITY Even Proposition II, which explicitly deals with the cost increase of equity capital as a function of the firm's D/E ratio, stems from this same argument of capital structure irrelevance. To see this, we need to combine a couple of observations from earlier chapters with a new bit of information:

1. First, think back to our previous discussion of WACC in Chapter 11. From this, we know that WACC will have to be equal to $iE_{,0}$ for an all-equity firm, as equity will be the only component cost of capital with any weight in the WACC:

$$WACC = \frac{E}{E+0} i_{E,0} + \frac{0}{E+D} i_D \times (1 - T_C)$$
$$= i_{E,0} \text{ for an all-equity firm}$$

2. Second, think back to the IRR rule discussed in Chapter 13. If firms will only accept projects for which the expected rate of return is at least as large as the required, or target, rate of return, then we can think of the WACC not only as the *average* rate that the firm will *pay* to capital providers but also as the minimum average expected rate of return on the firm's asset investments that must be *earned* if the firm wants to be able to pay back the capital providers.

$$IRR \geq i_{E,0} \Rightarrow i_{E,0} = \text{Minimum acceptable expected rate of return}$$

3. Finally, let's address the question of what will happen to a firm's WACC in M&M's perfect world as the capital structure changes. Irving Fisher's seminal work on the theory of investment[2] included the **separation principle,** which states that, with a well-functioning capital market, the firm's capital budgeting decisions are separate from its capital structure decisions. That is, *what you do* with the money and *where you get it* are two distinctly separate decisions. So changing the firm's capital structure in our perfect world should not affect the group of projects chosen, or the minimum acceptable rate of return dictated by those projects' lower boundary of expected returns.

separation principle

The assumption that decisions about *which* projects to fund are separate from the decisions about *how* to fund them.

$$WACC = i_{E,0} \forall \frac{D}{E}$$

Putting all of this together with a simplified[3] version of the formula for WACC from Chapter 11 allows us to solve the WACC formula for i_E:

$$WACC = \frac{E}{E+D} i_E + \frac{D}{E+D} i_D$$

$$i_{E,0} = \frac{E}{E+D} i_E + \frac{D}{E+D} i_D$$

$$\Rightarrow$$

$$i_E = \frac{E+D}{E}\left[i_{E,0} - \frac{D}{E+D} i_D\right]$$

$$= \frac{E+D}{E} i_{E,0} - \left(\frac{E+D}{E} \times \frac{D}{E+D}\right) i_D$$

$$= \left(\frac{E}{E} + \frac{D}{E}\right) i_{E,0} - \frac{D}{E} i_D$$

$$= i_{E,0} + \frac{D}{E} i_{E,0} - \frac{D}{E} i_D$$

$$i_E = i_{E,0} + \frac{D}{E}(i_{E,0} - i_D)$$

This derivation shows that the firm's cost of equity increases with the use of debt in the capital structure. But the fact that WACC, $i_{E,0}$, is constant in the D/E ratio implies that a positive relationship between the cost of equity capital and the use of debt in the capital structure is solely due to reapportioning the expected

[2]See Irving Fisher, *The Theory of Interest, as Determined by Impatience to Spend Income and Opportunity to Invest It* (New York: Macmillan, 1930).

[3]The two simplifications that we have made are that we can use the before-tax cost of debt instead of the after-tax cost (as we are operating in a world without taxes for right now), and we have left out any consideration of preferred stock so as to make our analysis a little more succinct. Given preferred stock's aspect as a hybrid form of debt and equity, leaving it in wouldn't really add any intuition to the subsequent discussion, but would instead merely make it needlessly more complex.

rate of return to the firm's assets among claimholders. It does not imply any addition or subtraction of the total amount of return available. That is, the cost of equity goes up as the amount of debt increases, but the WACC stays the same.

THE EFFECT OF LEVERAGE ON THE WACC Since debt is cheaper than equity, the firm uses less expensive equity and more relatively cheap debt at a rate that just offsets the effect on WACC of the increased cost of equity. This leads us to what we will call Proposition IIa, which M&M's theorem implies (but to which we don't usually refer so formally):

$$\text{Proposition IIa (perfect world): } WACC = i_{E,0} = \frac{E}{E+D}i_E + \frac{E}{E+D}i_D \quad \textbf{(16-3)}$$

$$\text{which will be constant in } \frac{D}{E}$$

Let's extend Merton Miller's pizza analogy and turn that pizza into a two-layer cake, dividing up the two layers among a group of people on the TV show *Survivor.* If you have ever seen this show, you are probably aware that it consists of following the day-to-day activities of groups of people "stranded" in some exotic locale with very few resources. The survivors usually have access to some plentiful staple food source, but the participants all get rather sick of this plain fare after the first couple of weeks. Periodic infusions of small delicacies, either as prizes in a game or simply to stave off a rebellion, go a long way toward making the winners more satisfied with their participation.

Assume that one such group has been given the task of eating the two-layered cake. If it's a cake that everyone likes, then the most basic logical distribution of the finished product would be to give each person a proportionate share of the cake. However, show producers are rarely nice enough to just drop off delicacies for no reason at all. So let's assume that, while one layer of this cake *is* filled with some savory delight that everyone likes, the other layer is filled with exotic cockroaches, which all group members loathe, albeit to different degrees. Furthermore, let's assume that the show's producers have dictated that the group must finish off the entire cake in a certain amount of time, or someone will be "kicked off the island."

You can see that this situation might prompt the group to make some very interesting allotment decisions concerning who gets to/has to eat how much of the cake. The group might decide that the people who agree to take more of the cockroach layer get a larger, proportionate share of the enjoyable layer, too. Or the group may decide that people who eat a slight majority of the disgusting layer get virtually *all* of the enjoyable layer.

These two allocation schemes correspond exactly to the situation seen in all-equity and mixed debt/equity capital structures, respectively. If we logically assume that all humans are risk averse, then any financial claim against a firm comes with some of the layer that everyone wants—returns. But any financial claim will also come with some less desirable layer that everyone loathes—risks. In an all-equity firm, the equity holders share the firm's expected return and expected risk in strictly proportional amounts. Someone who has put in one-fourth of the equity, thereby buying one-fourth of the firm's shares, can in return expect to receive one-fourth of the firm's returns on its assets. That investor has at risk the money paid for those shares. Someone who put in twice as much money would expect twice as much in return, but would also run the risk of losing twice as much money, and so forth.

In a firm that employs a mixture of debt and equity, however, the parties have implicitly agreed to a disproportionate sharing of the risk and return layers of the firm. The debt holders have put in a certain portion of the firm's capital and thereby expect exactly the return (and the return of their capital) as spelled out in the bond indenture. Their expected returns will never change; they will get exactly what they signed up for, with no business risk on the line. The equity holders, in accepting for themselves a residual claim on the company's future proceeds, have agreed to accept more than their fair share of the risk layer—they take on both business and financial risk. In return, they also expect a disproportionately large share of the expected return layer.

This is what we are seeing in equation 16-2. The reason that i_E increases as D/E increases is to compensate stockholders for bearing more and more residual risk as the number of stockholders declines.

EXAMPLE 16-1

LG16-3

For interactive versions of this example visit www.mhhe.com/can3e

Impact on Expected Return and Volatility of Increasing Leverage in a Perfect World

Suppose we are in M&M's perfect world, and we have a firm with $100 million in assets, currently financed entirely with equity. Equity is worth $100 per share, and book value of equity is equal to market value of equity.[4] Also, let's assume that the firm's expected EBIT values depend on which state of the economy occurs this year, with the possible values of EBIT and their associated probabilities as shown below:

State	Recession	Average	Boom
Probability of state	0.2	0.6	0.2
Expected EBIT in state	$10 million	$25 million	$35 million

The firm is considering switching to either a 30-percent- or 60-percent-debt capital structure and has determined that it would have to pay an 8 percent yield on perpetual debt in either event.[5] What will be the effect on expected EPS and the volatility of that EPS if the firm stays with its current capital structure or switches to either of the two proposed structures?

SOLUTION:

If the firm stays with its all-equity structure, it will have $100 million/$100 = 1 million shares outstanding, and the EPS under each state of nature will be:

State	Recession	Average	Boom
EBIT	$10,000,000	$25,000,000	$35,000,000
Less: Interest	0	0	0
EBT	$10,000,000	$25,000,000	$35,000,000
Less: Taxes	0	0	0
Net income	$10,000,000	$25,000,000	$35,000,000
EPS	$ 10.00	$ 25.00	$ 35.00

The expected EPS and standard deviation of the EPS will be:

$$E(EPS) = 0.2 \times \$10.00 + 0.6 \times \$25.00 + 0.2 \times \$35.00 = \$24.00$$

$$\sigma_{EPS} = \sqrt{0.2(\$10.00 - \$24.00)^2 + 0.6(\$25.00 - \$24.00)^2 + 0.2(\$35.00 - \$24.00)^2} = \$8.00$$

[4]Please note that this assumption is made purely to simplify the math. Having the market and book values of equity differ would add to the complexity of this example, but would not change the basic intuition.

[5]This assumption is also made to simplify the calculations. We could consider a situation in which debt had a finite maturity, but to the extent that a firm would want to stick with a particular capital structure, any retirement of debt would have to be perfectly offset with an equivalent issue of new debt, which would add much numerical complexity of the example, but nothing to the intuition.

If the firm refinances 30 percent of the capital by selling \$30 million in debt and uses the proceeds to retire \$30 million in equity, the interest on the debt will amount to 0.08 × \$30 million = \$2.4 million, and the firm will have \$70 million/\$100 = 700,000 shares outstanding, and the EPS under each state of nature will be:

State	Recession	Average	Boom
EBIT	\$10,000,000	\$25,000,000	\$35,000,000
Less: Interest	2,400,000	2,400,000	2,400,000
EBT	\$ 7,600,000	\$22,600,000	\$32,600,000
Less: Taxes	0	0	0
Net income	\$ 7,600,000	\$22,600,000	\$32,600,000
EPS	\$ 10.86	\$ 32.29	\$ 46.57

The expected EPS and standard deviation of the EPS will be:

$$E(EPS) = 0.2 \times \$10.86 + 0.6 \times \$32.29 + 0.2 \times \$46.57 = \$30.86$$

$$\sigma_{EPS} = \sqrt{0.2(\$10.86 - \$30.86)^2 + 0.6(\$32.29 - \$30.86)^2 + 0.2(\$46.57 - \$30.86)^2} = \$11.43$$

If the firm refinances 60 percent of the capital by selling \$60 million in debt and using the proceeds to retire \$60 million in equity, the interest on the debt will amount to 0.08 × \$60 million = \$4.8 million, and it will have \$40 million/\$100 = 400,000 shares outstanding, and the EPS under each state of nature will be:

State	Recession	Average	Boom
EBIT	\$10,000,000	\$25,000,000	\$35,000,000
Less: Interest	4,800,000	4,800,000	4,800,000
EBT	\$ 5,200,000	\$20,200,000	\$30,200,000
Less: Taxes	0	0	0
Net income	\$ 5,200,000	\$20,200,000	\$30,200,000
EPS	\$ 13.00	\$ 50.50	\$ 75.50

The expected EPS and standard deviation of the EPS will be:

$$E(EPS) = 0.2 \times \$13.00 + 0.6 \times \$50.50 + 0.2 \times \$75.50 = \$48.00$$

$$\sigma_{EPS} = \sqrt{0.2(\$13.00 - \$48.00)^2 + 0.6(\$50.50 - \$48.00)^2 + 0.2(\$75.50 - \$48.00)^2} = \$20.00$$

Similar to Problems 16-5, 16-6, 16-7, 16-8, self-test problem 1

As this example shows, increasing the amount of debt in the capital structure will increase the expected EPS level, but it will also increase the variation—also known as risk—that we can expect around that expected EPS. This basic intuition is driven by the fact that stockholders hold the residual claim to earnings. Thus they bear more of the business risk, also known as the state-of-nature-induced volatility, than debt holders do. In fact, as long as EBIT is large enough to ensure that debt holders receive their promised interest payments even in the worst state of nature, and even under all three levels of debt considered in this problem, equity holders bear *all* of the risk once debt is introduced into a firm's capital structure.

M&M with Corporate Taxes

LG16-4

The value of the M&M theorem does not really lie in the wisdom of their two propositions, which are driven by the very unrealistic set of "perfect world" assumptions listed previously. Instead, the value lies in examining what happens to these two propositions when we relax the unrealistic assumptions and move closer to what we see in real life.

For example, if we slightly relax the assumptions above and allow ourselves to assume that corporations are taxed, that corporate debt is perpetual, and that interest is tax deductible, then the main propositions of the M&M theorem become:[6]

$$\text{Proposition I (with corporate taxes): } V_L = V_U + DT_C \qquad \textbf{(16-4)}$$

where

V_U is the value of an unleveraged firm.

V_L is the value of a leveraged firm.

D is the level of perpetual firm debt.

T_C is the applicable coporate tax rate.

$$\text{Proposition II (with corporate taxes): } i_E = i_{E,0} + \frac{D}{E}(i_{E,0} - i_D) \times (1 - T_C) \qquad \textbf{(16-5)}$$

where

$i_{E,0}$ is the cost of capital of capital for an all-equity firm.

i_E and i_D are the costs of equity and debt in a leveraged firm.

$$\text{Proposition IIa (with corporate taxes): } WACC = \frac{E}{E + D} i_E + \frac{D}{E + D} i_D(1 - T_C)$$

$$\text{which will be decreasing in } \frac{D}{E} \qquad \textbf{(16-6)}$$

We often refer to this situation as the "The More Debt, the Better" condition. Under this condition implied by M&M, the firm's value forever increases (and the WACC forever decreases) as the firm takes on larger and larger amounts of debt, as implied in Proposition I.

Note how a relatively minor change in our assumptions has dramatically altered the firm's suggested capital structure strategy. In the perfect world, capital structure did not matter, so the firm was free to choose whichever level of debt it preferred. In this slightly more realistic world with corporate taxes, managers can maximize the firm's value by taking on as much debt as possible. Thus the firm should try to be as close to 100 percent debt-financed as possible.

What caused this change in optimal strategy? It's not so much that we have added taxation, but that we have added it *differentially:* any money paid out to stockholders is taxable, so that a dollar paid in dividends actually means removing $1.00/(1 − T_C) in company earnings. On the other hand, paying a dollar in interest to service debt carries no equivalent tax "surcharge."

However, though adding corporate taxes to our environment changes the firm's optimal strategy, it does not really change the effect that an increase in leverage has on the stockholders' expected returns and the volatility of those returns.

EXAMPLE 16-2

LG16-4

For interactive versions of this example visit www.mhhe.com/can3e

Impact of Leverage on Shareholders' Expected Return and Volatility with Corporate Taxes

Reexamine the situation we described in Example 16-1. Now suppose that the firm faces a 35 percent tax rate. What will be the effect on expected EPS and the volatility of that EPS if the firm stays with its current capital structure or switches to either of the two proposed structures?

[6]The assumption of perpetual debt makes the mathematical expressions for Propositions I and II concise: with perpetual debt, the present value of the tax shields to interest on debt are the present value of the perpetuity, $PV = [(D \times i_D) \times T_C]/i_D$, which simplifies to DT_C.

SOLUTION:

If the firm stays with its all-equity structure, it will have $100 million/$100 = 1 million shares outstanding, and the EPS under each state of nature will be:

State	Recession	Average	Boom
EBIT	$10,000,000	$25,000,000	$35,000,000
Less: Interest	0	0	0
EBT	$10,000,000	$25,000,000	$35,000,000
Less: Taxes (35%)	3,500,000	8,750,000	12,250,000
Net income	$ 6,500,000	$16,250,000	$22,750,000
EPS	$ 6.50	$ 16.25	$ 22.75

The expected EPS and standard deviation of the EPS will be:

$$E(EPS) = 0.2 \times \$6.50 + 0.6 \times \$16.25 + 0.2 \times \$22.75 = \$15.60$$

$$\sigma_{EPS} = \sqrt{0.2(\$6.50 - \$15.60)^2 + 0.6(\$16.25 - \$15.60)^2 + 0.2(\$22.75 - \$15.60)^2} = \$5.20$$

If the firm refinances 30 percent of the capital by selling $30 million in debt and using the proceeds to retire $30 million in equity, the interest on the debt will amount to 0.08 × $30 million = $2.4 million, and the firm will have $70 million/$100 = 700,000 shares outstanding, and the EPS under each state of nature will be:

State	Recession	Average	Boom
EBIT	$10,000,000	$25,000,000	$ 35,000,000
Less: Interest	2,400,000	2,400,000	2,400,000
EBT	$ 7,600,000	$22,600,000	$ 32,600,000
Less: Taxes (35%)	2,660,000	7,910,000	11,410,000
Net income	$ 4,940,000	$14,690,000	$ 21,190,000
EPS	$ 7.06	$ 20.99	$ 30.27

The expected EPS and standard deviation of the EPS will be:

$$E(EPS) = 0.2 \times \$7.06 + 0.6 \times \$20.99 + 0.2 \times \$30.27 = \$20.06$$

$$\sigma_{EPS} = \sqrt{0.2(\$7.06 - \$20.06)^2 + 0.6(\$20.99 - \$20.06)^2 + 0.2(\$30.27 - \$20.06)^2} = \$7.43$$

If the firm refinances 60 percent of the capital by selling $60 million in debt and using the proceeds to retire $60 million in equity, the interest on the debt will amount to 0.08 × $60 million = $4.8 million, and the firm will have $40 million/$100 = 400,000 shares outstanding, and the EPS under each state of nature will be

State	Recession	Average	Boom
EBIT	$10,000,000	$25,000,000	$35,000,000
Less: Interest	4,800,000	4,800,000	4,800,000
EBT	$ 5,200,000	$20,200,000	$30,200,000
Less: Taxes (35%)	1,820,000	7,070,000	10,570,000
Net income	$ 3,380,000	$13,130,000	$19,630,000
EPS	$ 8.45	$ 32.83	$ 49.08

The expected EPS and standard deviation of the EPS will be:

$$E(EPS) = 0.2 \times \$8.45 + 0.6 \times \$32.83 + 0.2 \times \$49.08 = \$31.20$$

$$\sigma_{EPS} = \sqrt{0.2(\$8.45 - \$31.20)^2 + 0.6(\$32.83 - \$31.20)^2 + 0.2(\$49.08 - \$31.20)^2} = \$13.00$$

Similar to Problems 16-9, 16-10, 16-11, 16-12, self-test problem 2

finance at work — corporate

LEVERAGED BUYOUTS (LBOs)

One of the most extreme examples of firm re-leveraging occurs when someone uses a firm's debt capacity to buy out the majority of the firm's equity holders. Such a *leveraged buyout* is designed to allow the acquirer to gain control of a firm without having to commit a lot of capital.

A typical LBO uses a ratio of 70 percent debt to 30 percent equity, although debt can reach as high as 90 percent to 95 percent of the target company's total capitalization. In fact, when LBOs first became popular back in the 1960s, they were originally known as *bootstrap* transactions, a reference to the expression "pulling yourself up by your own bootstraps," which reflected the general consensus that the firm was, more or less, paying for its own acquisition.

want to know more? **Key Words to Search for Updates:** syndicated loan, management buyout, LBO

table 16.1 | **Expected EPS and Volatility in EPS in Examples 16-1 and 16-2**

E(EPS)	0% Debt	30% Debt	60% Debt
Perfect world	$24.00	$30.86	$48.00
With corporate taxes	15.60	20.06	31.20
EPS S.D.	**0% Debt**	**30% Debt**	**60% Debt**
Perfect world	$ 8.00	$11.43	$20.00
With corporate taxes	5.20	7.43	13.00

To summarize, the expected EPS and volatility in EPS for the three different proposed capital structures in Examples 16-1 and 16-2 are shown in Table 16.1. As we can see, adding corporate taxes to the mix reduces both the level and volatility of EPS, but increasing leverage still magnifies the expected EPS and its volatility.

A casual glance at the two versions of Proposition I that we have encountered so far, the one in equation 16-1 for the perfect world and the one in equation 16-4 for the world with corporate taxes, would probably lead one to believe that it's better to be a leveraged firm in a world with taxes: After all, $V_L = V_U + DT_C$ sounds like a good deal compared to $V_L = V_U$, right? Well, not really: We have to remember that V_U in a world with taxes is going to be less than V_U in a world without taxes, so the equations for V_L in these two versions of Proposition I really are not comparable.

Or, returning once more to our cake analogy, in this with-tax world, the cake starts out the same size as it did in the world without taxes, but the taxman gets to take a bite before the bondholders or the stockholders get their portions. Most important, the size of the bite that the taxman gets is based on how the rest of the cake will be divided between the bondholders and stockholders: If we can precommit to giving the bondholders as much cake as possible (and the stockholders as little as possible), then the taxman will not take anything—that is, then the value of the firm that goes to the bondholders and stockholders (considered as one single group) is maximized.

The Choice to Re-Leverage

In both of the worlds we have talked about so far, we have seen that increasing the amount of firm debt increases both the expected cash flows to equity holders and the volatility of those cash flows. Considering our discussion of the CAPM and the SML in Chapter 10, we should probably be wondering what happens to the firm's investors if it decides to change its capital structure. If they were happiest with the mix of risk and expected return the firm was offering before, are they going to be upset if they are "booted" off their optimal mix to something that has a different mixture of risk and expected return?

EXAMPLE 16-3

LG16-5

Undoing a Change in Leverage

For example, let's suppose that an investor originally owned 100 shares in the unleveraged firm that we started with in Example 16-2, but that the firm switched to the proposed 30 percent debt level in its capital structure. How could the investor change her holdings so that they could return to exactly the same combination of expected return and risk that they had before the change?

For interactive versions of this example visit www.mhhe.com/can3e

SOLUTION:

Owning 100 shares in the original unleveraged firm, the shareholder would expect to receive total earnings of $650, $1,625, or $2,275 on those 100 shares, depending on the state of the economy that occurred:

State	Recession	Average	Boom
EBIT	$10,000,000	$ 25,000,000	$ 35,000,000
Less: Interest	0	0	0
EBT	$10,000,000	$ 25,000,000	$ 35,000,000
Less: Taxes (35%)	3,500,000	8,750,000	12,250,000
Net income	$ 6,500,000	$ 16,250,000	$ 22,750,000
EPS	$ 6.50	$ 16.25	$ 22.75
Average EPS	$ 15.60		
EPS S.D.	$ 5.20		
Shareholder earnings	$ 650	$ 1,625	$ 2,275
Average earnings	$ 1,560		
Earnings S.D.	$ 520		

Once the firm re-leveraged, that same shareholder would face a stream of earnings that would be, on average, higher than before, but also more volatile:

State	Recession	Average	Boom
EBIT	$10,000,000	$ 25,000,000	$ 35,000,000
Less: Interest	$ 2,400,000	$ 2,400,000	$ 2,400,000
EBT	$ 7,600,000	$ 22,600,000	$ 32,600,000
Less: Taxes (35%)	$ 2,660,000	$ 7,910,000	11,410,000
Net income	$ 4,940,000	$ 14,690,000	$ 21,190,000
EPS	$ 7.06	$ 20.99	$ 30.27
Average EPS	$ 20.06		
EPS S.D.	$ 7.43		
Shareholder earnings	$ 705.71	$ 2,098.57	$ 3,027.14
Average earnings	$ 2,005.71		
Earnings S.D.	$ 742.86		

To undo the firm's "leveraging up" move, the shareholder would need to "leverage down." That is, since the firm borrowed 30 percent of its capital structure, the shareholder would need to lend 30 percent of her own personal investment portfolio to counter that borrowing. To do so, she would sell 30 of her 100 shares, which would yield 30 × $100 per share = $3,000. She would then turn around and invest this

$3,000 in the firm's bonds. The bonds would earn a before-tax return of $\$3,000 \times 0.08 = \$240$ per year, or $\$240 \times (1 - 0.35) = \$156$ per year after taxes. Combining these after-tax earnings with the after-tax earnings on the 70 shares of stock she still owned would give her the exact same distribution of total earnings she would have earned if the firm had not leveraged up:

State	Recession	Average	Boom
After-tax earnings on 3 bonds	$156	$ 156	$ 156
After-tax earnings on 70 shares	494	1,469	2,119
Total after-tax earnings	$650	$1,625	$2,275

Similar to self-test problem 3

So far, the answer is no. Remember that the worlds we have been working in so far assume perfectly efficient capital markets, implying that any investors who were unhappy with a change in the firm's capital structure would be able to costlessly undo any changes inflicted upon them.

EXAMPLE 16-4

LG16-5

For interactive versions of this example visit www.mhhe.com/can3e

Exceeding the Firm's Leverage

Assume that the firm in the previous example decided not to add debt to its capital structure, but one of its investors, who currently owns 50 shares in the company, has decided that she would like to have the same risk/expected return combination that she would have had if the firm had adopted a capital structure that was 60 percent debt. What could this investor do?

SOLUTION:

Since she currently owns 50 shares in the unleveraged firm, her "starting" wealth will be equal to $50 \times \$100 = \$5,000$, and she is facing a distribution of total earnings per period, dependent on the state of the economy, that look like this:

State	Recession	Average	Boom
EBIT	$10,000,000	$ 25,000,000	$35,000,000
Less: Interest	0	0	0
EBT	$ 10,000,000	$ 25,000,000	$35,000,000
Less: Taxes (35%)	3,500,000	8,750,000	12,250,000
Net income	$ 6,500,000	$ 16,250,000	$22,750,000
EPS	$ 6.50	$ 16.25	$ 22.75
Average EPS	$ 15.60		
EPS S.D.	$ 5.20		
Shareholder earnings	$ 325.00	$ 812.50	$ 1,137.50
Average earnings	$ 780.00		
Earnings S.D.	$ 260.00		

She would rather have a distribution that looks like this:

State	Recession	Average	Boom
EBIT	$10,000,000	$ 25,000,000	$35,000,000
Less: Interest	4,800,000	4,800,000	4,800,000
EBT	$ 5,200,000	$ 20,200,000	$30,200,000
Less: Taxes (35%)	1,820,000	7,070,000	10,570,000
Net income	$ 3,380,000	$ 13,130,000	$19,630,000
EPS	$ 8.45	$ 32.83	$ 49.08
Average EPS	$ 31.20		
EPS S.D.	$ 13.00		
Shareholder earnings	**$ 422.50**	**$ 1,641.25**	**$ 2,453.75**
Average earnings	$ 1,560.00		
Earnings S.D.	$ 650.00		

To replicate this distribution of earnings across the possible states of the economy, she will need to borrow enough money, *B,* so that the borrowed money will be 60 percent of the total amount and that her initial capital will be 1 − 0.60 = 40% of the total amount she will invest in the stock:

$$\$5{,}000 = 0.4(\$5{,}000 + B)$$
$$\frac{\$5{,}000}{0.4} - \$5{,}000 = B$$
$$\$12{,}500 - \$5{,}000 = B$$
$$\$7{,}500 = B$$

If she follows this strategy, borrowing $7,500 and putting the entire $12,500 into the stock of the nonleveraged firm, then she will have to pay 0.08 × $7,500 × (1 − 0.35) = $390 in after-tax interest no matter what the state of the economy is, and her distribution of net payoffs will be exactly the same as if she had been able to buy shares in a leveraged firm:

State	Recession	Average	Boom	
After-tax payments on $7,500 loan	−$390.00	−$ 390.00	−$ 390.00	
After-tax earnings on 125 shares	812.50	2,031.25	2,843.75	(= 125 × $22.75)
Total after-tax earnings	**$422.50**	**$1,641.25**	**$2,453.75**	

Similar to Problems 16-3, 16-9, 16-10

Note that investors could also leverage themselves *more* than the firm if they wished to. All they would have to do is to borrow enough money and invest it in stock along with the money they started with, so that the ratio of borrowed money to their initial money was set equal to the D/E ratio that they wished the firm had chosen.

Break-Even EBIT and EBIT Expectations

The last few examples have had us examining what we expect the distribution of EPS to look like, given a particular choice of capital structure. It's also possible to analyze this issue "backwards," solving for a particular expected EPS level that would make investors indifferent between two proposed capital structures. To do so, we simply need to express EPS for each capital structure as a function of EBIT, set the two EPS expressions equal to one another, and then solve for the EBIT level that will solve the equality, called the **break-even EBIT.**

break-even EBIT

The level of EBIT at which EPS will be equal for two different capital structures.

EXAMPLE 16-5

LG16-6

For interactive versions of this example visit www.mhhe.com/can3e

Calculating Break-Even EBIT

Calculate the break-even EBIT between the all-equity and 30-percent-debt capital structures for the firm used in the previous examples.

SOLUTION:

Remember that the formula for EPS is net income divided by the number of shares, and that, for an all-equity firm, EBIT will be the same as EBT. Then EPS for the all-equity firm can be written as:

$$EPS_{All\text{-}equity} = \frac{EBIT(1 - T_C)}{\text{Number of shares}}$$

$$= \frac{EBIT(1 - 0.35)}{1{,}000{,}000}$$

For the capital structure with 30 percent debt, EPS can be expressed as:

$$EPS_{30\%\text{Debt}} = \frac{(EBIT - \text{Interest})(1 - T_C)}{\text{Number of shares}}$$

$$= \frac{(EBIT - \$2{,}400{,}000)(1 - 0.35)}{700{,}000}$$

Setting these two equations equal to one another and solving for EBIT will give us the break-even EBIT:

$$EPS_{30\%\text{Debt}} = EPS_{All\text{-}equity}$$

$$\frac{(EBIT - \$2{,}400{,}00)(1 - 0.35)}{700{,}000} = \frac{EBIT(1 - 0.35)}{1{,}000{,}000}$$

$$\frac{0.65EBIT - \$1{,}560{,}000}{700{,}000} = \frac{0.65EBIT}{1{,}000{,}000}$$

$$650{,}000EBIT - \$1{,}560{,}000{,}000{,}000 = 455{,}000EBIT$$

$$195{,}000EBIT = \$1{,}560{,}000{,}000{,}000$$

$$EBIT = \frac{\$1{,}560{,}000{,}000{,}000}{195{,}000}$$

$$EBIT = \$8{,}000{,}000$$

To show that this level of EBIT really will set EPS equal for the two alternative capital structures, we can compute the two EPS figures and compare:

$$EPS_{All\text{-}equity} = \frac{EBIT(1 - 0.35)}{1{,}000{,}000}$$

$$= \frac{\$8{,}000{,}000(1 - 0.35)}{1{,}000{,}000}$$

$$= \$5.20$$

versus

$$EPS_{30\%\text{Debt}} = \frac{(EBIT - \$2{,}400{,}000)(1 - 0.35)}{700{,}000}$$

$$= \frac{(\$8{,}000{,}000 - \$2{,}400{,}000)(1 - 0.35)}{700{,}000}$$

$$= \$5.20$$

Similar to Problems 16-13, 16-14, self-test problem 4

TIME OUT

16-3 Why does the optimal capital structure shift from "debt doesn't matter" to "the more debt, the better" when we add corporate taxation to our assumptions?

16-4 If a firm increases its leverage and one of its shareholders doesn't like the EPS impact of the change, how can the firm undo the effects of the change?

16.3 • M&M with Corporate Taxes and Bankruptcy

LG16-7

We can relax the final M&M unrealistic assumption even more by allowing for the possibility that the firm may go bankrupt. By doing this, we imply that the firm's debt holders will have to allow for the possibility that they might not receive everything they have been promised. In this more realistic type of situation, bondholders will be asked to bear some firm risk. Debt holders will thus ask for a little more compensation than they would if our "perfect world" assumptions held true.

As we will discuss, it turns out that a firm does not actually have to go bankrupt for the costs of financial distress to start affecting firm value.

Types of Bankruptcies in the United States

The United States' Bankruptcy Code allows for two types of bankruptcy for which most businesses can file. We generally refer to the two types by the chapter of that code that describes the procedure for each—Chapter 7 and Chapter 11 bankruptcies.

Chapter 7 bankruptcy involves a business liquidation. When the firm files for Chapter 7, it must immediately cease operations, and the bankruptcy court will very quickly appoint a trustee whose primary responsibility will be to sell the firm's assets and use the proceeds to pay off as many claimants as possible.

Chapter 7 bankruptcy
Form of bankruptcy in which the firm is liquidated, with the assets sold off to satisfy the claims of the capital providers.

These claimants are paid according to the absolute priority rule in the following order:

1. *Secured lenders,* including bondholders where the bonds give them liens on specific assets.
2. *Lawyers,* primarily those handling the bankruptcy for the company.
3. *Employees.*
4. *Government.*
5. *Unsecured debt holders.*
6. *Equity holders.*

Depending on the size and number of claims above them, unsecured debt holders (such as those who hold debentures) rarely receive all the money owed them in a Chapter 7 liquidation. Stockholders seldom receive much at all.

A **Chapter 11 bankruptcy,** on the other hand, involves an attempt to allow the firm to reorganize the business under court supervision. When a firm files for Chapter 11, it is allowed to remain in operation, but its creditors must refrain from contacting the company about debts due except through the bankruptcy court. This explains why you will sometimes hear a Chapter 11 filing referred to as the company seeking *protection.*

Chapter 11 bankruptcy
Form of bankruptcy in which the firm seeks to reorganize, restructuring debt claims to remain viable.

Once a company files for Chapter 11, all of its creditors must register with the bankruptcy court and may file informational briefs concerning their preferences for the form that the firm reorganization will take. The court will consider this input and will try to come up with a reorganized capital structure for the firm that follows the guidelines in Section 507 of the bankruptcy code. In general, such reorganizations usually involve maintaining (in some form) any higher claimants' stake in the firm, but it is not unusual for the process to result in a reorganization plan that involves canceling unsecured debt.

Within a period of a few months to several years, companies that file for Chapter 11 may "emerge" from bankruptcy if a proposed reorganization plan gains approval by a sufficient majority[7] of the firm's debt holders. The firm may also find its bankruptcy converted to a Chapter 7 filing if the court feels that the firm is not viable or if a sufficient majority of the firm's debt holders cannot agree on a reorganization plan.

Costs of Financial Distress

A firm filing for bankruptcy will most certainly incur some substantial costs, such as fees to lawyers, consultants, and accountants, in addition to the reorganization or restructuring costs. However, a long list of costs is incurred if a firm even *gets close* to bankruptcy—a situation called *financial distress.*

When firms come close to bankruptcy (or if they are *perceived* as being close to bankruptcy), many groups start treating those troubled firms differently:

- Customers may be leery of buying from them, especially if buyers are concerned about post-sales support.
- Suppliers will be concerned about selling to the firm, particularly on credit, so sellers will start to tighten the credit terms they offer the firm.
- Other firms will be less likely to offer the firm valuable partnering opportunities, decreasing the number of wealth-enhancing projects the firm might be able to choose from.
- The firm's better employees may decide to look elsewhere for jobs, resulting in a loss of efficiency in the firm's operations.

EQUITY AS A CALL OPTION ON THE VALUE OF THE FIRM If the firm gets close enough to bankruptcy that the equity market value is close to worthless, even the equity holders may start treating the firm differently. To see why, let's envision what the payoff diagram for equity in a leveraged firm looks like.

In an all-equity firm, the total value of equity will simply equal the firm value. Thus if we graph the value of the equity holders' claims against the firm, value will simply be a 45-degree line, as illustrated in Figure 16.1.

However, if we allow debt holders into the firm, the bondholders' claims will take precedence over those of equity holders, up to the amount of promised repayment. So the *debt holders'* claims will be equal to that shown by the yellow line in Figure 16.2. In such a situation, the equity holders will receive a residual claim, equal to the amount left over after debt holders have been paid. The size of this claim is represented by the area highlighted in Figure 16.3.

Taking the absolute magnitude of this portion of the equity holders' claim, along with the minimum equity value of zero implied by equity's limited liability attribute, the payoff to the entire claim of the equity holders will appear as shown in Figure 16.4.

As you can see, the size of the equity holders' claim if the firm were not leveraged would be divided into two parts—a debt holders' portion and an equity holders' portion—if the firm became leveraged. This payoff diagram is interesting because this payoff diagram for equity holders looks exactly like the payoff to

[7]Proposed reorganization plans must meet with approval of two-thirds of outstanding claimants in terms of dollars due and one-half of claimants by numbers.

figure 16.1

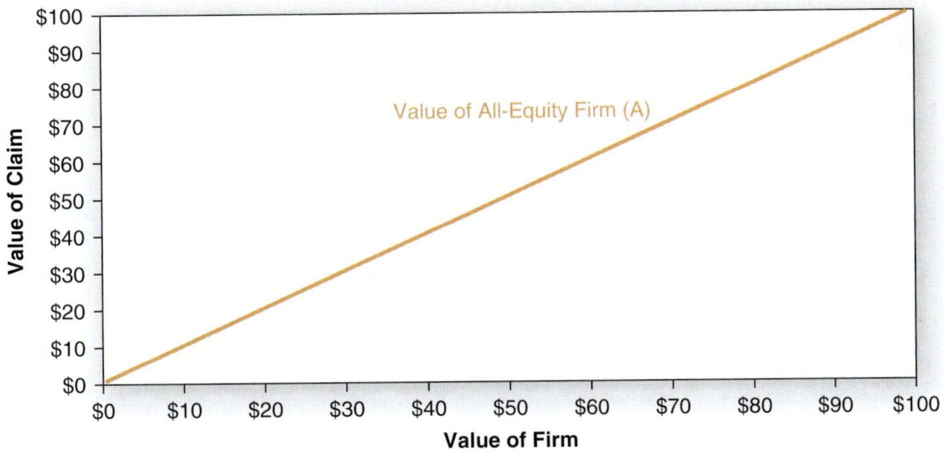

Total Value of Equity in an All-Equity Firm

In an all-equity firm, the total value of equity simply equals the firm value, shown in the graph as a 45-degree line.

figure 16.2

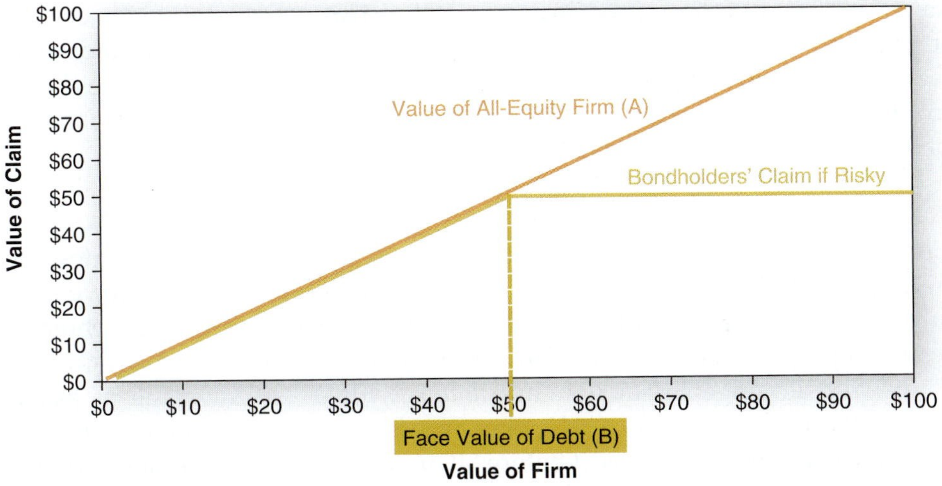

Value of Bondholders' Claim against Firm

Bondholders claims take precedence over those of equity holders, so the face value of debt will be equal to that shown by the yellow line.

figure 16.3

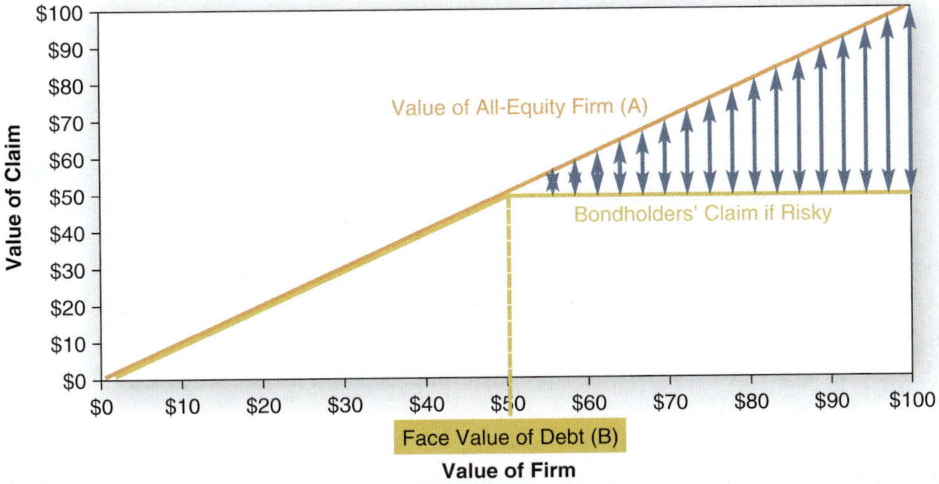

Residual Value of Equity in Firm

Equity holders receive a residual claim, one equal to the amount left over after debt holders have been paid. The shaded area shows the size of this claim.

figure 16.4

Stockholders' Claim with Debt in the Firm

If the firm is *not* leveraged, the size of the equity holders' claim is divided into two parts—a debt holders' portion and an equity holders' portion.

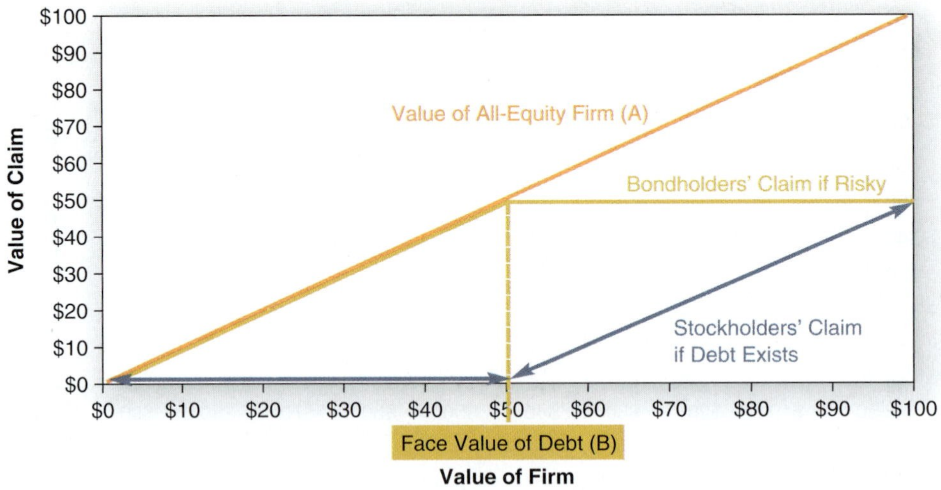

long position

The position of buying and owning a particular security, which will show a profit if the security increases in value.

call option

A derivative instrument that grants the holder the right, but not the obligation, to buy the underlying asset at some prespecified price for a finite length of time.

overinvestment problem

A situation that arises when a firm's equity is close to worthless, equity holders will prefer to invest in overly risky projects with a small chance of success rather than simply paying debt holders their regularly scheduled payments.

someone who owns a **long position** on a **call option.** A call option is a contract that gives the owner the right, but not the obligation, to purchase an underlying asset at a certain price. In this case, the equity in a leveraged firm has the right to "buy" the firm back from the debt holders by paying them an amount, *B,* that the debt holders are due under the debt contract.

THE OVERINVESTMENT AND UNDERINVESTMENT PROBLEMS More important, equity actually represents a very special case of a long call position, one in which the call owners (the equity holders) presumably also have some control over the potential value of the underlying asset through their choice of investment projects between now and when the debt is due.

Envision a leveraged firm that has assets with a current value of exactly ($B − $1,000,000), all currently held in cash. Also assume that the firm has one more chance to invest in a project before $B are due to the debt holders, and that management is trying to choose between two projects, both of which will cost the entire ($B − $1,000,000) stock of cash. Project X will return $B with no risk. Project Y will return ($B + $5,000,000) with a probability of 1 percent and $0 with a probability of 99 percent.

If we ignore TVM, project X's NPV will be $B − ($B − $1,000,000) = $1,000,000, while project Y's expected NPV will be 0.01 × [($B + $5,000,000) − ($B − $1,000,000)] + 0.99 × [$0 − ($B − $1,000,000)] = $60,000 − 0.99 × ($B − $1,000,000). As long as $B is greater than $50,505.05 (which seems likely, given that project X is offering a risk-free return of $1,000,000), project X's NPV will be greater than project Y's expected NPV, and we would expect the firm to chose project X, right?

Wrong. If stockholders have their way, the firm will choose project Y every time. Why? Because on the slim chance that it pays off, they will have $5 million above what they need to pay to the debt holders. In the very probable event that the project fails to return any money, thereby losing the entire investment . . . well, it was not like the equity holders were ever going to get any of that money, anyway, because they would just have had to pay it out to the debt holders if they had not invested it in this project.

We call this tendency on stockholders' part in leveraged firms—where equity is close to being worthless—to invest in arguably bad projects "gambling with other people's money" or, more formally, the **overinvestment problem.** Equity

figure 16.5

Value of a Leveraged Firm: Taxes but No Bankruptcy

The slope is equal to the tax rate, which reflects the linear relationship of the impact of debt on firm value.

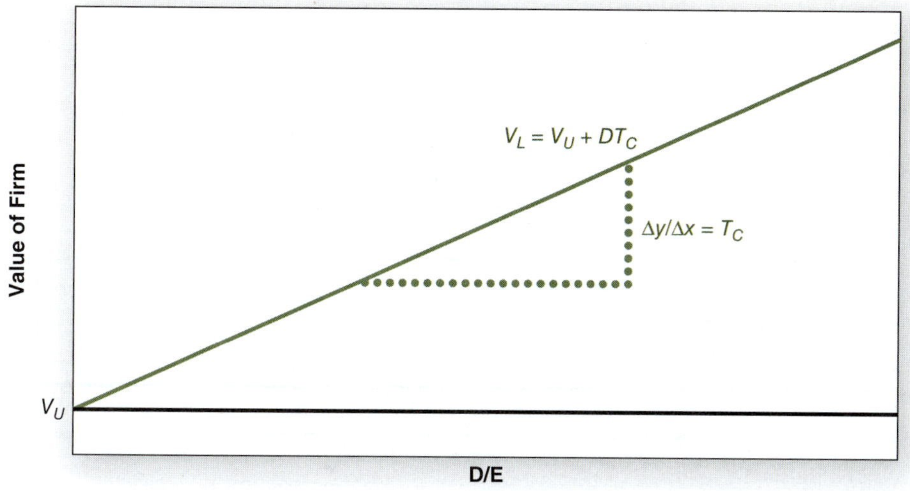

holders' associated decision not to invest in the safe project X—because the resulting increase in wealth from ($B − $1,000,000) to $B would simply go to the debt holders—the **underinvestment problem.**

underinvestment problem

The situation that arises when a firm's equity is close to worthless, equity holders will prefer not to invest in safe projects.

The Value of the Firm with Taxes *and* Bankruptcy

We modeled the functional relationship between the impact of debt on firm value and the tax rate in the previous section under the assumption that debt was perpetual. This impact of debt on firm value represents a fairly well-known linear relationship, with the slope being equal to the tax rate, as shown in Figure 16.5.

The relationship between the amount of debt and the expected costs of bankruptcy or financial distress is not as well known. We have discussed some of the factors that we believe can reasonably affect this relationship. In light of that discussion, we are going to assume that the relationship between the amount of debt and the expected costs of bankruptcy or financial distress is nonlinear and convex in the amount of debt, as shown in Figure 16.6.

figure 16.6

Financial Distress Costs as a Function of D/E

Let's start with the assumption that the relationship between the amount of debt and the expected costs of bankruptcy or financial distress is nonlinear, creating a convex debt curve.

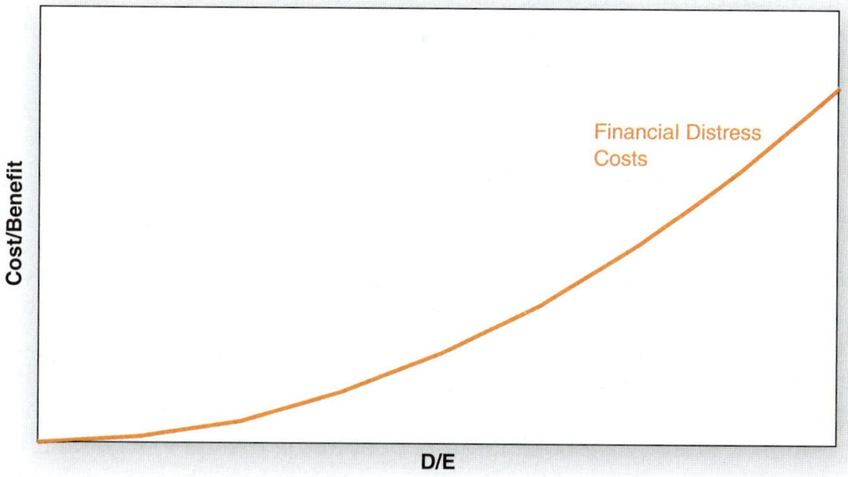

figure 16.7

Value of Leveraged Firm: Taxes and Bankruptcy

Exactly where the D/E level will be optimal for a firm depends on the firm's tax rate and how quickly the costs of financial distress increase as a function of debt.

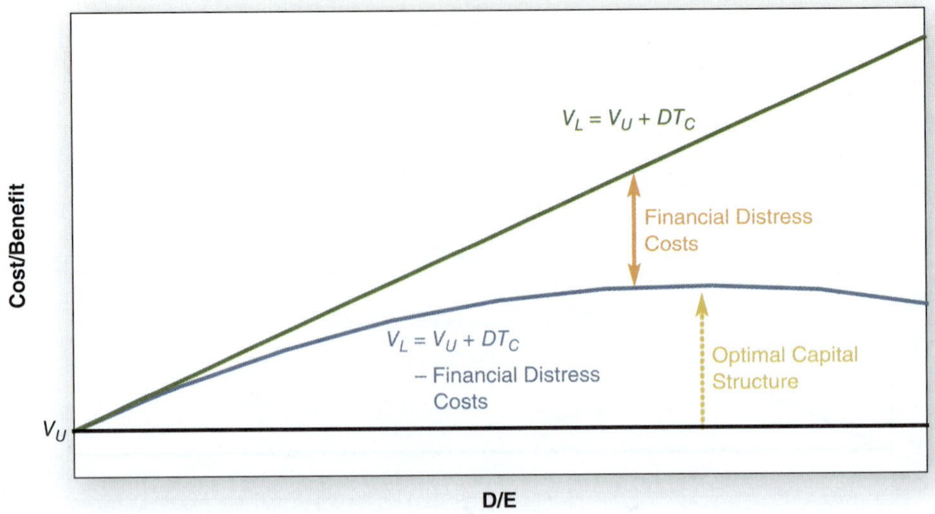

So let's combine the linearly increasing benefits of debt created by the interest tax shield with nonlinearly increasing costs of debt posed by the potential costs of financial distress. Doing so, we will eventually come to a point where we are increasing the D/E ratio of the firm beyond which the marginal costs of financial distress starts to outweigh the marginal benefits of the interest tax shield. Such a situation is shown in Figure 16.7.

Exactly which D/E level will be optimal for a particular firm will depend on both the firm's tax rate and how quickly the potential costs of financial distress increase as a function of debt. For example, a firm with a very low marginal tax rate would have the financial distress costs offsetting the tax deductibility of interest very quickly (i.e., at a low level of D/E), while a firm with a large debt capacity/high marginal tax rate would find a higher level of D/E optimal.

In this world (as opposed to M&M's ideal world), we can write a version of M&M's Proposition I as long as we are willing to be rather vague about the functional relationship between debt and the costs of financial distress. However, we really cannot formulate an analogous form of Proposition II because doing so would require us to come up with a more specific function of the costs of financial distress than we are capable of.

Proposition I (with corporate taxes and bankruptcy):

$$V_L = V_U + DT_C - PV\text{ (costs of financial distress)} \quad \textbf{(16-7)}$$

where

V_U is the value of an unleveraged firm.

V_L is the value of a leveraged firm.

D is the level of perpetual firm debt.

T_C is the applicable corporate tax rate.

Simply put, in this world, Proposition I is effectively saying, "The more debt the better, but only up to a certain point."

If we could write a nice, concise functional form for Proposition II in this world, it would still have i_E increasing in the D/E ratio. But the rate of increase would be nonlinear since, as the amount of debt in the firm got larger and larger, making the probability/costs of bankruptcy increasingly higher, the debt holders would have to bear some of that risk.

figure 16.8

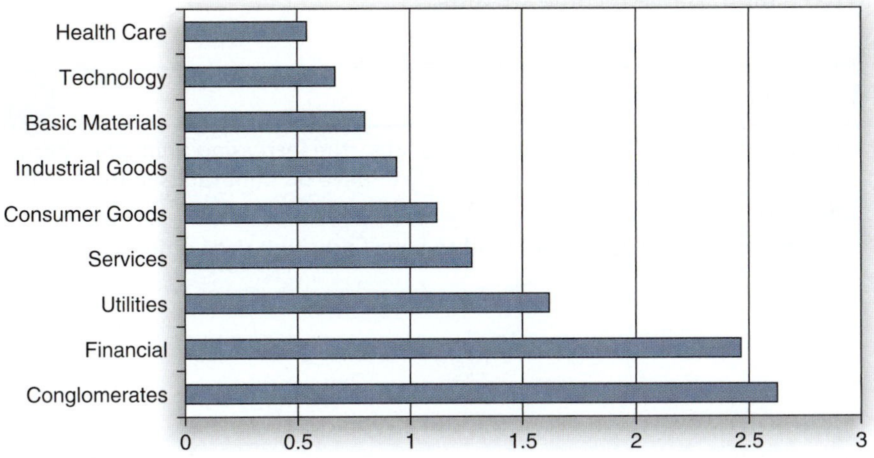

Average D/E Ratios for Major Sectors of U.S. Economy

Sectors with the lowest D/E ratios tend to have low or quite variable income streams, while sectors with the highest D/E ratios tend to have high, stable income streams.

Source: *Yahoo!* http://biz.yahoo.com/p/sectors.html

Likewise, a form of Proposition IIa would have the WACC decreasing up until the optimal debt level was achieved, but increasing past that point. In effect, the WACC would initially be decreasing as the firm switched from the "expensive" capital (i.e., equity) to the "cheap" capital (debt). But in this world the debt would not stay cheap but would itself get more and more expensive as the firm used more of it because the debt holders would ask for a higher and higher rate of return to compensate them for the increasingly higher chance of bankruptcy. Past the optimal debt level, it would just be too expensive to use more of it.

TIME OUT

16-5 What causes the overinvestment problem discussed in this section?

16-6 If the bondholders of a firm in financial distress felt that they could recoup more of their investment by renegotiating their claims with the firm and allowing it to continue to operate, what type of bankruptcy would they probably push for?

16.4 • Capital Structure Theory versus Reality

LG16-8

Optimal Theoretical Capital Structure

Based on our discussions of M&M's theory of optimal capital structure, we cannot develop a closed-end formula that will tell us how much debt a particular firm should have in its capital structure. Instead, we can do the next best thing: we can list the factors that should affect firms' capital structures:

- Firms facing relatively high tax rates should make more use of debt.
- Firms with stable, predictable income streams should be able to make more use of debt than would otherwise be the case.

Observed Capital Structures

Though debt levels vary, the general levels of debt we see across segments of our economy do tend to follow these rough rules. As shown in Figure 16.8, the sectors of the U.S. economy with the lowest D/E ratios—health care and technology—both tend to have low or quite variable income streams, and the sectors with the highest D/E ratios—utilities, financial, and conglomerates—tend to have high, stable income streams.

TIME OUT

16-7 What effect is the "graying of America" (i.e., the increasing number of baby boomers reaching retirement age) likely to have on debt ratios in the health care industry? Why?

16-8 Explain why utility companies tend to have fairly high debt ratios.

viewpoints REVISITED

Business Application Solution

If she re-leverages, Kieran will be financing 50 percent of the assets, or $15,000, with debt. The tax savings per year will be equal to:

$$\$15{,}000 \times 0.095 \times 0.15 = \$213.75$$

And the present value of those tax savings, assuming that they continue on indefinitely, will be:

$$\frac{\$213.75}{0.095} = \$2{,}250$$

Personal Application Solution

Since both the first mortgage and the home-equity loan would be tax deductible under current IRS guidelines, Gunter's weighted-average after-tax interest rate will be equal to $0.8 \times 0.05875 \times (1 - 0.25) + 0.2 \times 0.079 \times (1 - 0.25) = 4.71\%$.

summary of learning goals

This chapter has explored the concept of the firm's optimal capital structure. While we were not able to construct a closed-form equation to tell us exactly how much debt a particular firm should take on, we were able to identify the attributes of the firm that should affect such a decision.

LG16-1 Differentiate between active and passive changes to capital structure. When firms wish to change their capital structure, they will often do so by raising capital for new projects gradually to minimize underwriting costs. This passive approach is in contrast with the firm actively selling one type of financial claim (usually debt) and using the proceeds to retire another type of capital (usually equity).

LG16-2 Explain why finance professionals refer to debt as "leverage." Debt in the firm's capital structure magnifies both the potential earning power of equity and its volatility or risk.

LG16-3 Show how the firm apportions risk and return among stockholders and bondholders in a "perfect world." In such a world, the entire "layers" of risk and return are split between the equity holders and the debt holders, but they are not split proportionately. Equity holders, in agreeing to take more than their fair share of the risk of the firm, also get a disproportionately larger portion of the return, too.

LG16-4 Describe how the optimal capital structure changes under corporate taxation. With corporate taxation, the tax deductibility of the interest payments to debt holders means that such payments are partially subsidized by the taxing authority, making them more attractive. Since we have not yet relaxed the assumption of no chance of bankruptcy, this attractiveness applies no matter how much debt is used, so a capital structure that is as close as possible to all-debt will maximize the subsidy and minimize the firm's WACC.

LG16-5 Demonstrate how individual shareholders can affect capital structure by borrowing and lending on their own account. Individual shareholders can choose to borrow part of their investment in the firm's stock if they wish to increase their own personal leverage, or they can choose to lend part of their personal wealth if they wish to reduce their personal leverage.

LG16-6 Calculate the EBIT and EPS levels at which shareholders become indifferent when choosing between two capital structures. We can calculate the break-even EBIT by setting EPS as a function of the firm's EBIT at two different capital structures equal to one another and then solving for the level of EBIT that makes this equality hold.

LG16-7 Describe how the firm's choice of optimal capital structure changes under the possibility of bankruptcy. Once we relax the "no possibility of bankruptcy" assumption from M&M's perfect world, increasing the firm's debt level increases both this probability and the expected costs of financial distress. Past a certain level of debt, increasing the debt further will cause the expected costs of financial distress to outweigh the benefits of the tax-deductibility of interest.

LG16-8 Analyze whether real-world business practices reflect the theoretical basis for optimal capital structure. As observed from real data, firms that have higher chances of financial distress tend to use less debt, while those firms for whom the tax benefits are substantial tend to use more. This more or less confirms the theory derived from M&M's work.

chapter equations

16-1 Proposition I (perfect world): $V_L = V_U$

16-2 Proposition II (perfect world): $i_E = i_{E,0} + \frac{D}{E}(i_{E,0} - i_D)$

16-3 Proposition IIa (perfect world): $WACC = i_{E,0} = \frac{E}{E+D}i_E + \frac{D}{E+D}i_D$

16-4 Proposition I (with corporate taxes): $V_L = V_U + DT_C$

16-5 Proposition II (with corporate taxes): $i_E = i_{E,0} + \frac{D}{E}(i_{E,0} - i_D) \times (1 - T_C)$

16-6 Proposition IIa (with corporate taxes):

$$WACC = \frac{E}{E+D}i_E + \frac{D}{E+D}i_D(1 - T_C)$$

16-7 Proposition I (with corporate taxes and bankruptcy):

$V_L = V_U + DT_C - PV$ (costs of financial distress)

key terms

active capital structure management, The policy of selling one type of claim (debt or equity) explicitly to retire the other type. *p. 545*

break-even EBIT, The level of EBIT at which EPS will be equal for two different capital structures. *p. 557*

call option, A derivative instrument that grants the holder the right, but not the obligation, to buy the underlying asset at some prespecified price for a finite length of time. *p. 562*

capital structure, The mixture of debt and equity used to finance the firm's operations. *p. 545*

capital structure irrelevance assertion, Another name for the Modigliani-Miller theorem. *p. 547*

Chapter 7 bankruptcy, Form of bankruptcy in which the firm is liquidated, with the assets sold off to satisfy the claims of the capital providers. *p. 559*

Chapter 11 bankruptcy, Form of bankruptcy in which the firm seeks to reorganize, restructuring debt claims to remain viable. *p. 559*

financial distress, The condition in which a firm is near bankruptcy. *p. 545*

financial leverage, Another name for debt in the capital structure. *p. 546*

long position, The position of buying and owning a particular security, which will show a profit if the security increases in value. *p. 562*

Modigliani–Miller (M&M) theorem, In an efficient market without taxes and bankruptcy costs, the value of a firm does not depend upon the firm's capital structure. *p. 547*

overinvestment problem, A situation that arises when a firm's equity is close to worthless, equity holders will prefer to invest in overly risky projects with a small chance of success rather than simply paying debt holders their regularly scheduled payments. *p. 562*

passive capital structure management, The policy of changing the capital structure gradually over time by funding new capital projects disproportionately with the type of capital you want to increase in the capital structure. *p. 545*

separation principle, The assumption that decisions about *which* projects to fund are separate from the decisions about *how* to fund them. *p. 548*

underinvestment problem, The situation that arises when a firm's equity is close to worthless, equity holders will prefer not to invest in safe projects. *p. 563*

self-test problems with solutions

LG16-2, 16-3

1 Computing Expected Return and Standard Deviation in a Perfect World ILKD, Inc., doesn't face any taxes or chance of bankruptcy and has $50 million in assets, currently financed entirely with equity. Equity is worth $80 per share, and book value of equity is equal to market value of equity. Also, let's assume that the firm's expected values for EBIT depend on which state of the economy occurs this year, with the possible values of EBIT and their associated probabilities shown as follows:

State	Recession	Average	Boom
Probability of state	0.15	0.55	0.30
Expected EBIT in state	$2 million	$15 million	$25 million

The firm is considering switching to a 30-percent-debt capital structure and has determined that it would have to pay a 10 percent yield on perpetual debt whether or not it changed the capital structure. What will be the effect on expected EPS and the volatility of that EPS if the firm switches to the proposed capital structure?

Solution:

Expected values and standard deviations of EPS will be as shown:

EPS without Debt

State	Recession	Average	Boom
EBIT	$2,000,000	$15,000,000	$25,000,000
Less: Interest	0	0	0
EBT	$2,000,000	$15,000,000	$25,000,000
Less: Taxes	0	0	0
Net income	$2,000,000	$15,000,000	$25,000,000
EPS	$ 3.20	$ 24.00	$ 40.00
Average EPS	$ 25.68		
EPS S.D.	$ 11.78		

EPS with 30% Debt

State	Recession	Average	Boom
EBIT	$2,000,000	$15,000,000	$25,000,000
Less: Interest	1,500,000	1,500,000	1,500,000
EBT	$ 500,000	$13,500,000	$23,500,000
Less: Taxes	0	0	0
Net income	$ 500,000	$13,500,000	$23,500,000
EPS	$ 1.14	$ 30.86	$ 53.71
Average EPS	$ 33.26		
EPS S.D.	$ 16.83		

As expected, the expected average EPS is larger if the firm is leveraged, but so is the standard deviation of EPS.

LG16-4

2 Impact of Leverage on Expected Return and Volatility with Corporate Taxes Reexamine the situation described in Problem ST-1, but now suppose that the firm faces a 34 percent tax rate. What will be the effect on expected EPS and the volatility of that EPS if the firm stays with its current capital structure or switches to a 30-percent-debt capital structure?

Solution:

The expected values and standard deviations for EPS will be as follows:

EPS without Debt

State	Recession	Average	Boom
EBIT	$ 2,000,000	$15,000,000	$25,000,000
Less: Interest	0	0	0
EBT	$ 2,000,000	$15,000,000	$25,000,000
Less: Taxes (34%)	680,000	5,100,000	8,500,000
Net income	$ 1,320,000	$ 9,900,000	$16,500,000
EPS	$ 2.11	$ 15.84	$ 26.40
Average EPS	$ 16.95		
EPS S.D.	$ 7.78		

EPS with 30% Debt

State	Recession	Average	Boom
EBIT	$ 2,000,000	$ 15,000,000	$25,000,000
Less: Interest	1,500,000	1,500,000	1,500,000
EBT	$ 500,000	$ 13,500,000	$23,500,000
Less: Taxes (34%)	170,000	4,590,000	7,990,000
Net income	$ 330,000	$ 8,910,000	$15,510,000
EPS	$ 0.75	$ 20.37	$ 35.45
Average EPS	$ 21.95		
EPS S.D.	$ 11.11		

LG16-5

3 Undoing a Change in Leverage Let's suppose that investors originally owned 100 shares each in the unleveraged firm that we started with in Problem ST-2, but that the firm switched to the proposed 30 percent debt level in its capital structure. How could the investors change their holdings to return themselves to exactly the same combination of expected return and risk that they had before the change?

Solution:

Owning 100 shares in the original, unleveraged firm, the shareholders would expect to receive total earnings of $211.20, $1,584.00, or $2,640.00 on those 100 shares, depending on the state of the economy that occurred.

EPS without Debt

State	Recession	Average	Boom
EBIT	$2,000,000	$15,000,000	$25,000,000
Less: Interest	0	0	0
EBT	$2,000,000	$15,000,000	$25,000,000
Less: Taxes (35%)	680,000	5,100,000	8,500,000
Net income	$1,320,000	$ 9,900,000	$16,500,000
EPS	$ 2.11	$ 15.84	$ 26.40
Average EPS	$ 16.95		
EPS S.D.	$ 7.78		
Shareholder earnings	$ 211.20	$ 1,584.00	$ 2,640.00
Average earnings	$ 1,694.88		
Earning S.D.	$ 777.77		

Once the firm re-leveraged, those same shareholders would face a stream of earnings that would be, on average, higher than before, but also more volatile:

EPS with 30% Debt

State	Recession	Average	Boom
EBIT	$2,000,000	$15,000,000	$ 25,000,000
Less: Interest	1,500,000	1,500,000	1,500,000
EBT	$ 500,000	$13,500,000	$ 23,500,000
Less: Taxes (35%)	170,000	4,590,000	7,990,000
Net income	$ 330,000	$ 8,910,000	$ 15,510,000
EPS	$ 0.75	$ 20.37	$ 35.45
Average EPS	$ 21.95		
EPS S.D.	$ 11.11		
Shareholder earnings	$ 75.43	$ 2,036.57	$ 3,545.14
Average earnings	$ 2,194.97		
Earning S.D.	$ 1,111.11		

To undo the firm "leveraging up," the shareholders would need to "leverage down"; that is, since the firm borrowed 30 percent of its capital structure, the shareholders would need to lend 30 percent of their own personal investment portfolio to counter that out. To do so, they would sell 30 of their 100 shares, which would yield 30 × $80 per share = $2,400. They would then turn around and invest this $2,400 in the firm's bonds, which would earn a before-tax return of $2,400 × 0.10 = $240 per year, or $240 × (1 − 0.34) = $158.40 per year after taxes. Combining these after-tax earnings with the after-tax earnings on the 70 shares of stock they still owned would give them the exact same distribution of total earnings they would have earned if the firm had not leveraged up.

After-tax earnings on $2,400 invested in bonds	$158.40	$ 158.40	$ 158.40
After-tax earnings on 70 shares	52.80	1,425.60	2,481.60
Total after-tax earnings	$211.20	$ 1,584.00	$2,640.00

4 Calculating Break-Even EBIT: Calculate the break-even EBIT between the all-equity and 30-percent-debt capital structures for the firm used in the previous problems. LG16-6

Solution:

EPS for the all-equity firm can be written as:

$$EPS_{All\text{-}equity} = \frac{EBIT(1 - T_C)}{\text{Number of shares}}$$

$$= \frac{EBIT(1 - 0.34)}{625{,}000}$$

For the capital structure with 30 percent debt, EPS can be expressed as:

$$EPS_{30\%\text{Debt}} = \frac{(EBIT - \text{Interest})(1 - T_C)}{\text{Number of shares}}$$

$$= \frac{(EBIT - \$1{,}500{,}000)(1 - 0.34)}{437{,}500}$$

Setting these two equations equal to one another and solving for EBIT will give us the break-even EBIT:

$$EPS_{30\%\text{Debt}} = EPS_{All\text{-}equity}$$

$$\frac{(EBIT - \$1{,}500{,}000)(1 - 0.34)}{437{,}500} = \frac{EBIT(1 - 0.34)}{625{,}000}$$

$$\frac{0.66EBIT - \$990{,}000}{437{,}500} = \frac{0.66EBIT}{625{,}000}$$

$$412{,}500EBIT - \$618{,}750{,}000{,}000 = 288{,}750EBIT$$

$$123{,}750EBIT = \$618{,}750{,}000{,}000$$

$$EBIT = \frac{\$618{,}750{,}000{,}000}{123{,}750}$$

$$EBIT = \$5{,}000{,}000$$

questions

1. How will passive and active capital structure changes differ? *(LG16-1)*
2. Why is debt often referred to as *leverage* in finance? *(LG16-2)*
3. In M&M's perfect world, will the debt holders ever bear any of the risk of the firm? *(LG16-3)*
4. Why does allowing for the existence of corporate taxation cause firms to prefer the maximum amount of debt possible? *(LG16-4)*
5. If a firm increased the amount of debt in its capital structure, but a shareholder wanted to switch back to the mixture of expected return and risk she had before the switch, how would she go about doing so? *(LG16-5)*

6. If an investor wanted to reduce the risk of a leveraged stock in his portfolio, how could he go about doing so while still retaining shares in the company? *(LG16-5)*

7. Suppose you were the financial manager for a firm and were considering a proposed increase in the amount of debt in the firm's capital structure. If you thought the firm was going to consistently earn a level of EBIT above its break-even level of EBIT (based on the current and proposed new capital structures), would this cause you to prefer leveraging the firm up or staying at your current capital structure? *(LG16-6)*

8. Explain why, in a world with both corporate taxes and the chance of bankruptcy, a small firm with volatile EBIT is unlikely to have much debt. *(LG16-7)*

9. If the U.S. government completely eliminated taxation at the corporate level, how would this influence the capital structures of firms in a world with bankruptcy? *(LG16-7)*

10. Would you expect a utility company to have high or low debt levels? Why? *(LG16-8)*

problems

basic problems

16-1 **Capital Structure Weights** Suppose that Lil John Industries' equity is currently selling for $37 per share and that 2 million shares are outstanding. If the firm also has 30,000 bonds outstanding, and they are selling at 103 percent of par, what are the firm's current capital structure weights? *(LG16-3)*

16-2 **Capital Structure Weights** Suppose that Papa Bell, Inc.'s, equity is currently selling for $55 per share, with 4 million shares outstanding. If the firm also has 17,000 bonds outstanding, and they are selling at 94 percent of par, what are the firm's current capital structure weights? *(LG16-3)*

16-3 **Restructuring Strategy** Suppose that Lil John Industries' equity is currently selling for $27 per share and that 2 million shares are outstanding. The firm also has 50,000 bonds outstanding, which are selling at 103 percent of par. If Lil John was considering an active change to its capital structure so that the firm would have a D/E of 1.4, which type of security *(stocks or bonds)* would it need to sell to accomplish this, and how much would the firm have to sell? *(LG16-1)*

16-4 **Capital Structure Weights** Suppose that Papa Bell, Inc.'s, equity is currently selling for $45 per share, with 4 million shares outstanding. The firm also has 7,000 bonds outstanding, which are selling at 94 percent of par. If Papa Bell was considering an active change to its capital structure so as to have a D/E of 0.4, which type of security *(stocks or bonds)* would the firm need to sell to accomplish this, and how much would it have to sell? *(LG16-1)*

intermediate problems

16-5 **Expected EPS after Leveraging** Daddi Mac, Inc., doesn't face any taxes and has $290 million in assets, currently financed entirely with equity. Equity is worth $37 per share, and book value of equity is equal to market value of equity. Also, let's assume that the firm's expected values for EBIT depend upon which state of the economy occurs this year, with the possible values of EBIT and their associated probabilities shown as follows:

State	Recession	Average	Boom
Probability of state	0.25	0.55	0.20
Expected EBIT in state	$5 million	$10 million	$17 million

The firm is considering switching to a 20-percent-debt capital structure and has determined that it would have to pay an 8 percent yield on perpetual debt in either event. What will be the level of expected EPS if the firm switches to the proposed capital structure? *(LG16-3)*

16-6 Expected EPS after Leveraging HiLo, Inc., doesn't face any taxes and has $150 million in assets, currently financed entirely with equity. Equity is worth $7 per share, and book value of equity is equal to market value of equity. Also, let's assume that the firm's expected values for EBIT depend upon which state of the economy occurs this year, with the possible values of EBIT and their associated probabilities shown as follows:

State	Pessimistic	Optimistic
Probability of state	0.45	0.55
Expected EBIT in state	$5 million	$19 million

The firm is considering switching to a 40-percent-debt capital structure, and has determined that it would have to pay a 12 percent yield on perpetual debt in either event. What will be the level of expected EPS if the firm switches to the proposed capital structure? *(LG16-3)*

16-7 Standard Deviation in EPS after Leveraging Daddi Mac, Inc., doesn't face any taxes and has $350 million in assets, currently financed entirely with equity. Equity is worth $37 per share, and book value of equity is equal to market value of equity. Also, let's assume that the firm's expected values for EBIT depend upon which state of the economy occurs this year, with the possible values of EBIT and their associated probabilities shown as follows:

State	Recession	Average	Boom
Probability of state	0.25	0.55	0.20
Expected EBIT in state	$5 million	$10 million	$17 million

The firm is considering switching to a 20-percent-debt capital structure, and has determined that it would have to pay an 8 percent yield on perpetual debt regardless of whether it changes the capital structure. What will be the standard deviation in EPS if the firm switches to the proposed capital structure? *(LG16-3)*

16-8 Standard Deviation in EPS after Leveraging HiLo, Inc., doesn't face any taxes and has $100 million in assets, currently financed entirely with equity. Equity is worth $7 per share, and book value of equity is equal to market value of equity. Also, let's assume that the firm's expected values for EBIT depend upon which state of the economy occurs this year, with the possible values of EBIT and their associated probabilities shown as follows:

State	Pessimistic	Optimistic
Probability of state	0.45	0.55
Expected EBIT in state	$5 million	$19 million

The firm is considering switching to a 40-percent-debt capital structure, and has determined that it would have to pay a 12 percent yield on perpetual debt in either event. What will be the standard deviation in EPS if the firm switches to the proposed capital structure? *(LG16-3)*

advanced problems

16-9 Expected EPS after Leveraging with Taxes NoNuns Cos. has a 25 percent tax rate and has $350 million in assets, currently financed entirely with equity. Equity is worth $37 per share, and book value of equity is equal to market value of equity. Also, let's assume that the firm's expected values for EBIT depend upon which state of the economy occurs this year, with the possible values of EBIT and their associated probabilities shown as follows:

State	Recession	Average	Boom
Probability of state	0.25	0.55	0.20
Expected EBIT in state	$5 million	$10 million	$17 million

The firm is considering switching to a 20-percent-debt capital structure, and has determined that it would have to pay an 8 percent yield on perpetual debt in either event. What will be the level of expected EPS if the firm switches to the proposed capital structure? *(LG16-4)*

16-10 Expected EPS after Leveraging with Taxes GTB, Inc., has a 34 percent tax rate and has $100 million in assets, currently financed entirely with equity. Equity is worth $7 per share, and book value of equity is equal to market value of equity. Also, let's assume that the firm's expected values for EBIT depend upon which state of the economy occurs this year, with the possible values of EBIT and their associated probabilities shown as follows:

State	Pessimistic	Optimistic
Probability of state	0.45	0.55
Expected EBIT in state	$5 million	$19 million

The firm is considering switching to a 40-percent-debt capital structure, and has determined that it would have to pay a 12 percent yield on perpetual debt in either event. What will be the level of expected EPS if GTB switches to the proposed capital structure? *(LG16-4)*

16-11 Standard Deviation in EPS after Leveraging with Taxes NoNuns Cos. has a 25 percent tax rate and has $350 million in assets, currently financed entirely with equity. Equity is worth $37 per share, and book value of equity is equal to market value of equity. Also, let's assume that the firm's expected values for EBIT depend upon which state of the economy occurs this year, with the possible values of EBIT and their associated probabilities shown as follows:

State	Recession	Average	Boom
Probability of state	0.25	0.55	0.20
Expected EBIT in state	$5 million	$10 million	$17 million

The firm is considering switching to a 20-percent-debt capital structure, and has determined that it would have to pay an 8 percent yield on perpetual debt in either event. What will be the standard deviation in EPS if NoNuns switches to the proposed capital structure? *(LG16-4)*

16-12 Standard Deviation in EPS after Leveraging with Taxes GTB, Inc., has a 34 percent tax rate and has $100 million in assets, currently financed entirely with equity. Equity is worth $7 per share, and book value of equity is equal to market value of equity. Also, let's assume that the firm's expected values for EBIT depend upon which state of the economy occurs this year, with the possible values of EBIT and their associated probabilities shown as follows:

State	Pessimistic	Optimistic
Probability of state	0.45	0.55
Expected EBIT in state	$5 million	$19 million

The firm is considering switching to a 40-percent-debt capital structure, and has determined that it would have to pay a 12 percent yield on perpetual debt in either event. What will be the standard deviation in EPS if it switches to the proposed capital structure? *(LG16-4)*

16-13 Break-Even EBIT with Taxes NoNuns Cos. has a 25 percent tax rate and has $350 million in assets, currently financed entirely with equity. Equity is worth $37 per share, and book value of equity is equal to market value of equity. Also, let's assume that the firm's expected values for EBIT depend upon which state of the economy occurs this year, with the possible values of EBIT and their associated probabilities shown as follows:

State	Recession	Average	Boom
Probability of state	0.25	0.55	0.20
Expected EBIT in state	$5 million	$10 million	$17 million

The firm is considering switching to a 20-percent-debt capital structure, and has determined that it would have to pay an 8 percent yield on perpetual debt in either event. What will be the break-even level of EBIT? *(LG16-6)*

16-14 Break-Even EBIT with Taxes GTB, Inc., has a 34 percent tax rate and has $100 million in assets, currently financed entirely with equity. Equity is worth $7 per share, and book value of equity is equal to market value of equity. Also, let's assume that the firm's expected values for EBIT depend upon which state of the economy occurs this year, with the possible values of EBIT and their associated probabilities shown as follows:

State	Pessimistic	Optimistic
Probability of state	0.45	0.55
Expected EBIT in state	$5 million	$19 million

The firm is considering switching to a 40-percent-debt capital structure, and has determined that it would have to pay a 12 percent yield on perpetual debt in either event. What will be the break-even level of EBIT? *(LG16-6)*

research it! Investigating Firms' Debt Ratios

Go to the Yahoo! Industry Center at **http://biz.yahoo.com/ic/,** choose an industry from among the "Top Industries" listed in the left column, and choose three of the leading firms for that industry.

What are these firms' debt ratios? Investigate each firm's background to try to determine whether the factors we discussed in this chapter are driving any differences in the amount of debt that they each have in their capital structures.

integrated mini-case: Change in Equity Ownership

The CEO of JJJ, Inc., owns 27 percent of his currently all-equity-financed firm worth $100 million. He has proposed splitting off one of the divisions (worth $25 million) of his company to let it operate as an independent firm. Existing shareholders will not get shares in the new firm; instead, the new firm is expected to raise $25 million through an IPO, the proceeds from which are to be used to repurchase shares in JJJ.

Assuming that the CEO does not participate in the stock buyback, what will his percentage ownership be after the division is split off?

ANSWERS TO TIME OUT

16-1 Passive capital management would take longer, as the firm would have to wait until new capital budgeting projects required funds before altering the capital structure.

16-2 The new capital structure should be used. As pointed out in Chapter 11, new projects should be evaluated using the capital structure that will actually be used to fund them.

16-3 With interest on debt being tax deductible, the government essentially picks up part of the tab for debt. This makes it even cheaper, so firms maximize their use of debt so as to maximize the interest tax shield.

16-4 The firm can unleverage, or lend, part of its portfolio.

16-5 When stockholders' equity stake is close to worthless, they can gamble on risky projects without any risk to themselves but with the opportunity of regaining some value if such projects earn a high rate of return. Given this, they will tend to actually prefer such projects in this type of situation.

16-6 They would prefer a Chapter 11 reorganization.

16-7 Given that the health care industry will likely experience higher, more stable revenues and profits, we should expect that the industry will be able to support higher debt ratios.

16-8 Utility companies have fairly high debt ratios because they have relatively high, stable cash flows, both due to the nature of their product and due to the barriers to entry represented by the large initial capital investment necessary to build a power plant and a power distribution infrastructure.

PART EIGHT

17 Sharing Firm Wealth: Dividends, Share Repurchases, and Other Payouts

viewpoints

Business Application

Suppose that SWV Corp. has consistently followed the pure residual dividend policy in the past, but is considering switching to a "smoothed" residual dividend policy, where dividends would be set at a level that management feels they could comfortably maintain for the foreseeable future. If SWV does have a considerable amount of excess cash, it will consider either issuing an extraordinary dividend or buying back some of its stock. What would be the probable impact on the firm's stock price if it does adopt this new policy? **(See solution on p. 594)**

Personal Application

Assume that personal tax rates on dividends and capital gains have shifted back so that the rate on dividends is significantly higher than that on capital gains. Marc is considering buying stock to put into his Roth IRA, a type of retirement account established by U.S. tax law that allows individuals to deposit funds into an account up to a certain maximum each year. Contributions are taxed before they are deposited, but all deposits plus any earnings can be withdrawn tax-free after the individual reaches 59.5 years of age. Marc is interested in two stocks. One pays returns primarily as a dividend yield, and the other returns primarily a capital gains yield. If he can't buy both stocks under the annual contribution limit, which should he choose for his Roth IRA? **(See solution on p. 594)**

Pay taxes now (Roth IRA) or pay them later (Traditional IRA)? Check out the dynamics.

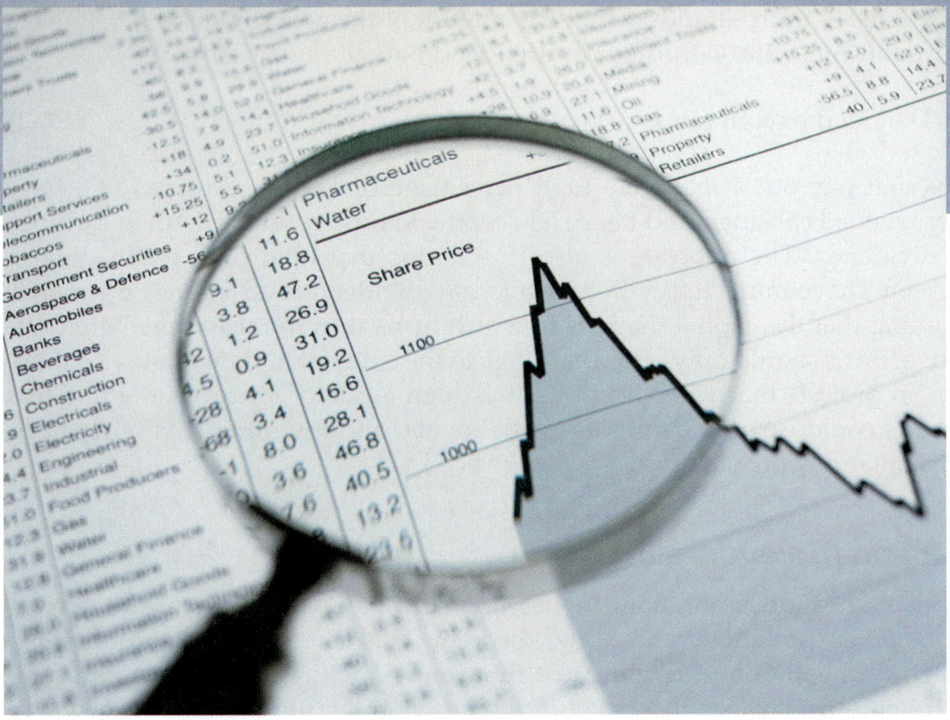

Thus far, we've examined the firm's investment and financing decisions. Both kinds of decisions are vitally important for the firm to achieve its primary goal: maximizing shareholder wealth. But few shareholders would be satisfied with maximized share value if they didn't get to benefit from that share value. The firm also needs to get that wealth back into shareholders' pockets. That's what this chapter is all about.

In a theoretically perfect world without any taxes, or where all of the firm's cash disbursements were taxed equally (whether capital gains, regular interest payments, or dividends), distributing capital to shareholders would be a simple proposition. It would be based entirely upon the firm's available opportunities for investment in prospective projects. In the real world, though, it's not so straightforward. As we'll discuss, the U.S. government treats dividends and interest payments differently than it does capital gains for individual tax returns. Further, potentially varying personal tax rates throughout a shareholder's investment horizon dictate that firms will confront varying bondholder and shareholder preferences when the firms design their payout strategies.

Learning Goals

LG17-1 Identify factors that affect a firm's payout policies.

LG17-2 Discuss how investors' preferences regarding differential tax rates and timing can guide the firm's policies on the distribution of dividends and capital gains.

LG17-3 Summarize the information effect, the clientele effect, and other corporate control issues.

LG17-4 Analyze a firm's decision to distribute constant ordinary dividends or extraordinary dividends.

LG17-5 Explain the effect that cash dividend payment procedures have on stock prices.

LG17-6 Differentiate between a stock dividend's impact and a stock split's impact on the firm's books.

LG17-7 Note the advantages and disadvantages of a firm's stock repurchases.

17.1 • Dividends versus Capital Gains

We can see the basic choice between a firm paying out money in the form of a cash dividend or using the money to repurchase shares of stock by examining the formula for a constant-growth stock we used in Chapter 8:

$$P_0 = \frac{D_1}{i - g} \qquad \textbf{(17-1)}$$

LG17-1

LG17-2

You will recall from Chapter 8 that the amount of the next dividend, D_1, links to the capital gains rate, g, through the dividend payout ratio, defined as

$$\text{Dividend payout ratio} = \frac{\text{Dividends}}{\text{Net income}} \quad \textbf{(17-2)}$$

Firms that pay out a relatively high percentage of current earnings will have fewer retained earnings, and hence less capital to fund future growth in earnings and dividends. The opposite is also true: Firms that hold onto retained earnings won't have much left with which to pay dividends and interest payments. Assuming that the capital markets to which firms turn to raise capital are competitive, firms should only retain earnings to the extent that they can invest those funds in projects that will earn at least as high a rate of return as the rate that investors could earn by taking the same money and investing it in other firms with similar risk profiles.

Dividend Irrelevance Theorem

The idea that it does not matter whether a firm pays dividends or not derives from another Modigliani and Miller theorem. This is referred to, appropriately enough, as the **dividend irrelevance theorem.** As with their theory about capital structure irrelevance discussed in the last chapter, the dividend irrelevance theorem is set in a perfect world, one that features:

dividend irrelevance theorem

A theorem showing that, in M&M's perfect world, it doesn't matter if a firm pays out funds through dividends or capital gains.

- No taxes.
- No transaction costs (including trading commissions).
- Perfectly efficient markets.
- Completely rational investors.

In such an environment, M&M show that the decision to pay or not to pay dividends doesn't matter. If a firm pays dividends, doing so will simply reduce the value of each share by the amount paid in dividends. If shareowners don't want the value of their shares reduced by dividends, they can simply turn around and buy additional shares in the company with the dividend proceeds. Doing so will keep the total amount of wealth they have invested in the firm constant. Similarly, if a firm chooses not to pay dividends, but investors wish that the firm would pay out regularly, then they can simply sell enough shares to reap the same dollars of income that they would have gotten if the firm had paid dividends.

Of course, just as with the capital structure irrelevance theorems discussed in the last chapter, relaxing the "no taxes" assumption substantially changes the implications concerning optimal firm dividend policy. Until fairly recently, the capital gains tax rate was substantially lower than was the tax rate on dividends, which were taxed as normal income. This inequality led some firms to prefer to pay out lower dividends/retain higher levels of earnings than probably would have been the case otherwise.

However, the **Jobs and Growth Tax Relief Reconciliation Act (JGTRRA)** of 2003 (Public Law 108-27) changed the general tax rate applicable to net capital gains for individuals to 15 percent or 5 percent (depending on the taxpayer's total taxable income). The new capital gains rates also apply to most dividends paid from domestic corporations and certain qualified foreign corporations. The upshot: Investors find that dividends are much more attractive relative to capital gains than they have been in the past, when dividends were taxed at a higher rate than capital gains income.

Jobs and Growth Tax Relief Reconciliation Act (JGTRRA)

A 2003 law that lowered the rate on both dividends and capital gains for individual investors in most situations.

For most investors, this equalization of the tax rates on capital gains and dividends has moved the real world *closer* to the concept of dividend irrelevance embodied in M&M's perfect world, but additional factors might give investors strong preferences for or against dividends.

Why Some Investors Favor Dividends

Gordon and Lintner proposed one of the strongest arguments for dividends, sometimes referred to as the **bird-in-the-hand theory.** This theory argues that dividends that the firm has committed to pay are less risky (and hence more attractive) to risk-averse investors than are potential future capital gains. Allowing the firm to retain "extra" earnings increases the risk that the firm will spend those earnings on non-value-maximizing investments.

bird-in-the-hand theory

The argument that receiving a dividend today is preferable to letting management have the chance to spend or waste the money between now and the future.

M&M refer to this argument as the *bird-in-the-hand fallacy,* claiming that many, if not most, investors will reinvest their dividends in the same or similar firms anyway. Further, the long-run riskiness of the firm's cash flows to investors is determined only by the riskiness of the firm's asset cash flows and not by its dividend payout policy.

Why Some Investors Favor Capital Gains

Even if the tax rates on capital gains and dividends are identical, some investors may prefer capital gains over dividends because capital gains may offer them more choice concerning the timing of cash flows.

When a firm pays out dividends, all stockholders share in the dividend distribution, and all must therefore pay taxes on those dividends in that period. If, instead, the firm retains earnings, consequently causing share price to increase, then only shareholders who sell shares of stock will experience a capital gain, and so only those shareholders will have to pay taxes.

Investors who don't need or want any cash will not sell their stock and they therefore will not incur any obligation to pay taxes on capital gains until they choose to do so. Note that this ability to "time" tax assessments will be especially attractive for investors who expect their capital gains tax rate to decline over time. Not only will these investors be able to push the tax bill off into later in the future, they may also be able to reduce the total tax in doing so.

EXAMPLE 17-1

LG17-2

Dividend Preference

For interactive versions of this example visit www.mhhe.com/can3e

Suppose that a firm has a retention ratio of 45 percent and net income of $9 million. The firm's investors are currently subject to a 15 percent tax rate on both dividends and capital gains, but everyone expects the tax rate on capital gains to increase to 35 percent over the next year. If the firm is considering temporarily suspending the dividend in order to fund a new, one-year project, and both the firm and investors face an 11 percent interest rate, what rate of return on the project would be necessary for the firm to retain the money, considering only the tax implications for its shareholders?

SOLUTION:

The firm is currently paying out $(1-.45) \times \$9{,}000{,}000 = \$4{,}950{,}000$ in dividends. At the current tax rate, investors get to keep $(1-.15) \times \$4{,}950{,}000 = \$4{,}207{,}500$ of this after taxes. If the firm were to stop paying dividends and instead put this $4,950,000 into new projects, the new projects would return an expected future value of $\$4{,}950{,}000 \times (1 + r)$ in one year, which, assuming that the new tax rate goes into effect, would increase the shareholders' after-tax wealth by $\$4{,}950{,}000 \times (1 + r) \times (1 - 0.35)$. The firm should only retain the money if the present value of the after-tax increase in shareholder wealth would be larger than the present value of the after-tax increase in shareholder wealth due to the dividend:

$$\text{If } \frac{\$4{,}950{,}000 \times (1 + r) \times (1 - 0.35)}{1.11} > \$4{,}207{,}500$$

$$\$2{,}898{,}648.65 \times (1 + r) > \$4{,}207{,}500$$

$$(1 + r) > \frac{\$4{,}207{,}500}{\$2{,}898{,}648.65}$$

$$(1 + r) > 1.4515$$

$$r > 0.4515$$

Unless the firm expects to earn a 45.15 percent return on the project, the tax implications rule against retaining the money.

Similar to Problems 17-3, 17-4

TIME OUT

17-1 Why should increasing a firm's dividend payout ratio cause the future dividend growth rate to decrease?

17-2 Would dividends truly be irrelevant in a more realistic world that features trading costs?

LG17-3

17.2 • Other Dividend Policy Issues

Risks, taxation, and cash flow timing, which we discussed in the previous section, are all fairly tangible. Managers must also consider some additional factors in setting the firm's optimal dividend payout policy.

The Information Effect

Managers hate to cut dividends—and investors hate to have them cut—so firms do not do so except in very dire circumstances. Along the same lines, managers will hesitate to raise dividends unless they feel that the firm can maintain dividends at the new, higher level for the foreseeable future. Because of management's hesitation to ever cut dividends, if a firm announces an increase in the next dividend, analysts often see such announcements as a very positive signal concerning the firm's performance and its expected future cash flow levels.

The Clientele Effect

clientele effect

The tendency of investors to find a payout policy that they prefer and stick with it.

The **clientele effect** refers to the fact that, in real life, investors do *not* have identical desires about the taxability and timing of firm payouts. Different groups of investors, or clienteles, will be attracted to different firms based on those firms' varying payout policies.

Shareholders who desire a particular mix of dividend policy attributes will invest in firms with dividend policies that have those particular attributes. If firms then change their dividend policy, the investors who desired the previous policy will sell their shares to reinvest in another firm with a policy closer to that which they desire. New investors who were previously uninterested in the stock may be attracted to it because of the policy change.

If we assume that investors face no transaction fees for buying or selling stock, and that unlimited demand exists for both old and new dividend policies, then a firm changing its policy in this manner would not see any effect on its stock price. However, investors *do* incur transaction fees for trading shares, and some evidence suggests that changes in tax laws or in the macroeconomic environment result in a demand shift from one dividend policy type to another. If demand for a certain dividend policy increases enough, then a firm changing to that dividend policy might actually see its demand for its stock increase enough to positively affect its stock price, even though investors will have to pay transaction fees to switch into the stock.

For example, Microsoft's September 2003 announcement that it would double its dividend was particularly well received. The dividend change occurred approximately four months after JGTRRA made dividends more attractive for most investors.

Corporate Control Issues

While the clientele effect implies a rather passive role for shareholders—one in which they are forced either to accept a company's dividend policy or leave to look for one more to their liking—firms that have shareholders with significant stakes in the firm may actually find those shareholders *dictating* the dividend payout policy. For example, in Germany, where banks are allowed to have sizable equity investments in firms to which they lend, recent studies[1] show that bank-controlled firms pay out lower dividends and are much more likely to omit dividends than any other type of firm.

Similar research also shows this tendency in closely held corporations, where owners have historically sought to avoid double taxation by leaving the profits in the corporation as accumulated earnings.[2] As long as the firm can justify accumulating earnings as necessary to the business's reasonable needs, such as funding a possible expansion or similar activity, then shareholders will have at least some latitude in determining when they wish to pay the earnings out.

TIME OUT

17-3 What type of clientele would you expect to prefer dividends over capital gains? Why?

17-4 When might raising a firm's dividend payout ratio be seen as a negative signal?

17.3 • Real-World Dividend Policy

LG17-4

Taking into account all of the factors noted previously, it would still seem intuitive that the firm's basic dividend policy should be to pay out as dividends any cash flow that is surplus after the firm has invested in all available positive net present value projects:

$$\text{Dividends} = \text{Net income} - \text{Retained earnings necessary to fund positive NPV projects} \quad \textbf{(17-3)}$$

[1]See, for example, Luis Correia da Silva et al., *Dividend Policy and Corporate Governance* (New York: Oxford University Press, 2004).

[2]In fact, many recent tax court cases related to closely held C corporations involve the nonpayment of sufficient dividends relative to profits, which subjects the C corporation to the accumulated earnings tax.

figure 17.1 General Electric Company's Dividend and EPS History

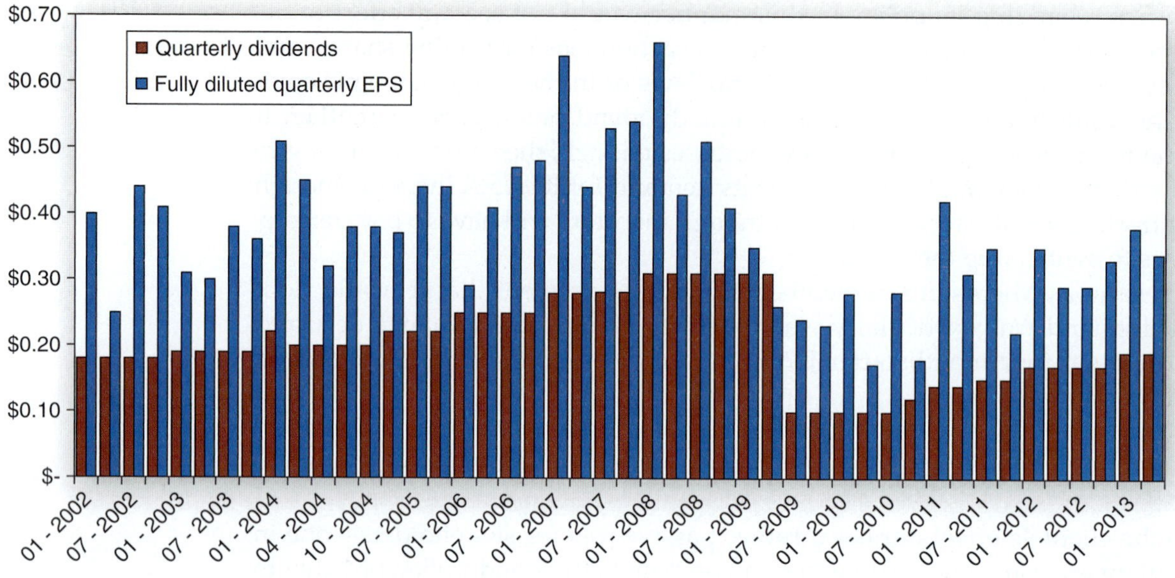

The Residual Dividend Model

residual dividend model

The policy of a firm paying out only funds that are left over after all positive-NPV projects are funded.

free cash flow theory of dividends

Another name for the residual dividend model.

We generally refer to this dividend policy approach as the **residual dividend model,** or the **free cash flow theory of dividends.** Though we would expect that the firm might respond to the factors discussed previously and thus to deviate somewhat from this ideal, the current low tax rates on dividends would seem to be a prime environment for it to apply.

However, the residual dividend model doesn't really seem to explain the observed dividend policies of real-world companies. Most companies pay relatively consistent dividends from one year to the next, and managers seem to prefer paying a steadily increasing dividend rather than paying a dividend that fluctuates dramatically from one year to the next. For example, consider the dividends and EPS figures for General Electric Co. (GE) shown in Figure 17.1.

GE has very consistently kept the dividend for all four quarters stable when possible, raising the dividend smoothly from year to year when circumstances allowed. However, EPS was quite volatile throughout this time period, and in 2009 GE decided to revise its quarterly dividend from $.31 per quarter to $.10 per quarter in response to prevailing economic conditions. Since then, GE's dividend has once again been increasing steadily from year to year.

Many companies follow an approach similar to GE's. The general consensus about why firms follow this approach seems to be that managers at these firms feel that their investors value dependability and stability in their personal dividend streams more than investors resent the burden that such a strategy places on the firm's cash flows.

Paying a constant yet steadily increasing dividend *does* impose a burden on the firm, for several different reasons. For exmple, firms in this situation frequently find themselves simultaneously issuing new equity (and paying the associated underwriting fees for doing so) and paying dividends to existing equity holders.

Probably the most compelling reason that most firms have for paying a consistent dividend like this is that most investors are very risk averse, so they actually prefer a slightly lower, consistent dividend stream to one that is, on average, higher but more volatile.

Extraordinary Dividends

To minimize the burden of stable dividends, some firms divide dividends into two classes: ordinary and extraordinary. By setting the ordinary dividends relatively low, the firm signals the minimum expected payout level that investors can count on. Because the ordinary dividends are set fairly low, the firms supplement small payments with periodic extraordinary dividends, such as those shown for Bassett Furniture in Figure 17.2.

Bassett Furniture, like GE, chose to revise its dividend during 2009 in response to economic conditions. However, Bassett went even further, suspending its dividend for over two years until conditions improved. When the dividend was reinstated, Bassett chose to set the new ordinary dividend at a much lower rate, supplementing it with sizeable extraordinary dividends from time-to-time as had been their pattern in the past.

The firm gains at least one advantage from this strategy. During periods when the firm really needs retained earnings for various projects, the firm simply forgoes the extraordinary dividend but continues to pay the ordinary one.

EXAMPLE 17-2

LG17-4

Dividend Policy

The annual dividends and EPS figures for Kellogg Company for the five-year period from 2006 through 2010 are shown in the following figure. Does Kellogg appear to be following a residual dividend policy? Have any extraordinary dividends been paid during this period?

For interactive versions of this example visit www.mhhe.com/can3e

Kellogg Company Total Annual EPS and Dividends

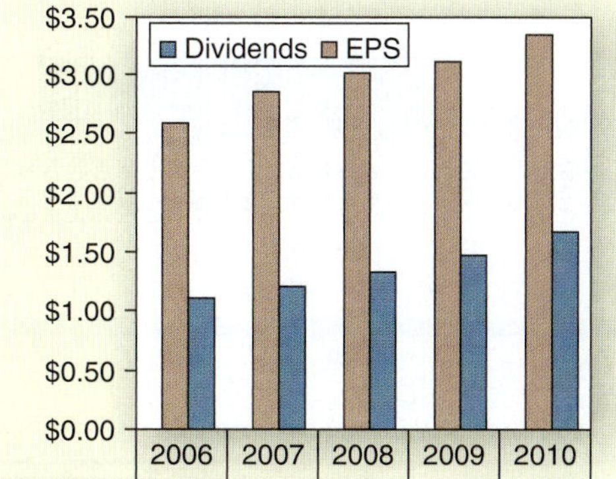

	2006	2007	2008	2009	2010
Dividends	1.138	1.202	1.30	1.43	1.605
EPS	2.51	2.76	2.99	3.16	3.30

SOLUTION:

Over the five-year period, Kellogg's EPS has increased by ($3.30 − $2.51)/$2.51 = 31.47%. At the same time, dividends have increased by ($1.605 − $1.138)/$1.138 = 41.04%, so Kellogg does not appear to be following a residual dividend policy. (If they were following a residual dividend policy, we would expect dividends, on average, to increase at a lower rate than EPS.) Instead, they seem to be following the policy of maintaining a steady state of increase. Likewise, they do not appear to have paid any extraordinary dividends during this period.

finance at work — corporate

MICROSOFT'S EXTRAORDINARY DIVIDEND

In 2004, Microsoft amassed a cash balance of nearly $60 billion. It then announced that it would pay out more than $32 billion of that war chest as a one-time, extraordinary dividend. This was one of the largest extraordinary dividend payments in history and came about because of a confluence of several different factors.

First, Microsoft had been enjoying monopoly-like profits on its software products for quite a few years, which allowed it to amass a large amount of cash. Second, the JGTRRA had just been passed, making the payment of such a large dividend less burdensome to investors from a tax standpoint. Third, Microsoft's opportunities for new products, and hence the need for capital investment in new projects, didn't seem to be keeping up with the accumulation of cash.

want to know more? **Key Words to Search for Updates:** The article "Microsoft Announces Payouts to Investors" (www.washingtonpost.com)

figure 17.2

Recent Dividend History for Bassett Furniture

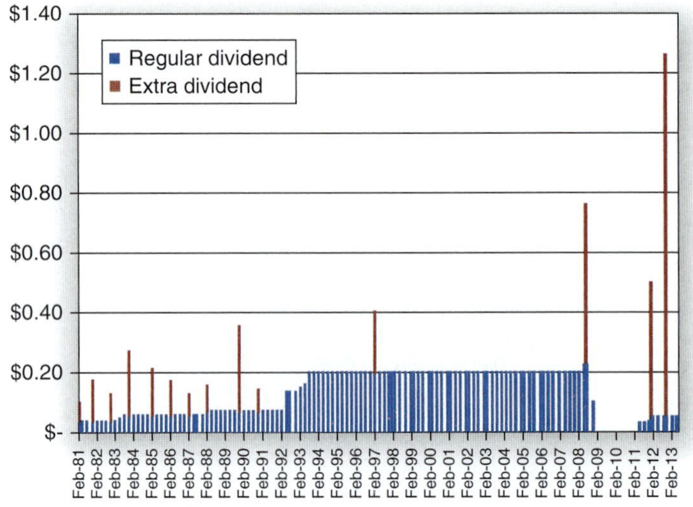

TIME OUT

17-5 What would prompt a firm like GE to start paying out a much higher percentage of its earnings as dividends?

17-6 Would extraordinary dividends be more likely to be used by a firm with cyclical sales or by one with stable sales?

LG17-5 17.4 • Dividend Payment Logistics

Technically, dividends do not become firm obligations until the firm declares them. The firm must allow itself some lead time between announcing the dividend and actually paying it. The firm must also allow time to determine the owner of record for each share as well as provide processing time between determining owners of record and actually mailing the checks. These different tasks require corporations to establish a definitive set of dates associated with paying out a dividend:

- The declaration date.
- The ex-dividend date.
- The record date.
- The payment date.

Payment Procedures

The board of directors announces its intention to pay a dividend on the **declaration date.** On the declaration date, that specific dividend becomes a firm liability, and the company records that liability on its books accordingly. On the declaration date, the Board will also announce a date of record and a payment date.

The **ex-dividend date** is the first day that the shares will trade without the dividend attached. Prior to that date, anyone purchasing a share of the firm's stock can claim the right to receive the dividend. So the stock is said to trade *cum dividend* (or, with dividend) until the ex-dividend date; subsequent to the ex-dividend date, anyone purchasing the share will purchase the share ex-dividend and can no longer claim the right to the dividend. On the **record date,** the firm will look on its books to find the registered owners of record so that it can start addressing payments. The record date is usually set at least a couple of business days after the ex-dividend date to allow time for shares purchased before the ex-dividend date to be properly registered.[3] The firm sends dividends out on the **payment date.**

declaration date
The date the board of directors announces its intention to pay a dividend.

ex-dividend date
The first day that shares will trade without the purchaser receiving an upcoming dividend.

record date
The day that the firm will determine the owner-of-record for the purposes of an upcoming dividend payment.

payment date
The actual date that a dividend will be sent out.

Effect of Dividends on Stock Prices

As you will recall from Chapter 8, a stock share's price should equal the present value of its expected future dividends. If dividends were paid as a continuous, steady stream at every instant through time, then we wouldn't expect dividend payment procedures to have much impact on the stock's price. But the fact that firms pay dividends as discrete cash flows received at certain intervals implies that the price of a share of stock will appreciate as the next, and every subsequent, dividend gets closer, and then fall precipitously once that dividend no longer accompanies the stock.

For example, consider a stock that is expected to pay a $1.00 per year dividend forever and that the next dividend is expected exactly one year from now. If the appropriate rate of return on this share of stock is 10 percent, then the stock price should simply be set as the present value of the perpetuity:

$$P_0 = \frac{D}{i} \quad \textbf{(17-4)}$$

$$= \frac{\$1}{0.1}$$

$$= \$10$$

[3]In most countries, registration is essentially automatic for shares purchased before the ex-dividend date, so the likelihood of people who bought the shares prior to the ex-dividend date not receiving the dividends they are due is pretty small.

Now, to see what's going to happen as we get closer to the dividend payment date, let's express this as the sum of the present value of the next dividend (D_1) and the present value of the perpetuity of all subsequent dividends (starting with D_2):

$$P_0 = \frac{D_1}{1+i} + \left(\frac{D_2}{i} \times \frac{1}{1+i}\right) \tag{17-5}$$

We can also express the lump sum portions of this formula in terms of a daily interest rate so that we can examine what happens as the number of days until the next dividend payment approaches zero:

$$\begin{aligned} P_0 &= \frac{D_1}{(1+i_{daily})^n} + \left(\frac{D_2}{i_{yearly}} \times \frac{1}{(1+i_{daily})^n}\right) \\ &= \frac{\$1}{(1+0.000261)^{365}} + \left(\frac{\$1}{0.10} \times \frac{1}{(1+0.000261)^{365}}\right) \\ &= \$0.9091 + \$9.0909 \\ &= \$10 \end{aligned} \tag{17-6}$$

Note that the daily interest rate in this problem can be computed as shown in Chapter 5:

$$\begin{aligned} i_{daily} &= \sqrt[365]{1+i_{yearly}} - 1 \\ &= \sqrt[365]{1.10} - 1 \\ &= 0.000261 \end{aligned} \tag{17-7}$$

As the number of days until the next dividend decreases, the present value will increase. For example, when there are only 200 days left, the present value will become:

$$\begin{aligned} P_0 &= \frac{D_1}{(1+i_{daily})^n} + \left(\frac{D_2}{i_{yearly}} \times \frac{1}{(1+i_{daily})^n}\right) \\ &= \frac{\$1}{(1+0.000261)^{200}} + \left(\frac{\$1}{0.10} \times \frac{1}{(1+0.000261)^{200}}\right) \\ &= \$0.9491 + \$9.4912 \\ &= \$10.44 \end{aligned}$$

If we temporarily ignore the difference between the ex-dividend date and the payment date, then the present value upon payment will become:

$$\begin{aligned} P_0 &= \frac{D_1}{(1+i_{daily})^n} + \left(\frac{D_2}{i_{yearly}} \times \frac{1}{(1+i_{daily})^n}\right) \\ &= \frac{\$1}{(1+0.000261)^{0}} + \left(\frac{\$1}{0.10} \times \frac{1}{(1+0.000261)^{0}}\right) \\ &= \$1 + \$10 \\ &= \$11 \end{aligned}$$

This pattern in the present value of the dividends leading up to the next dividend is shown in Figure 17.3.

After that next dividend has been paid, the stock once again becomes a perpetuity for which the next cash flow is one year away, so the price will immediately fall back to \$10. This process of a buildup in price followed by a precipitous

figure 17.3

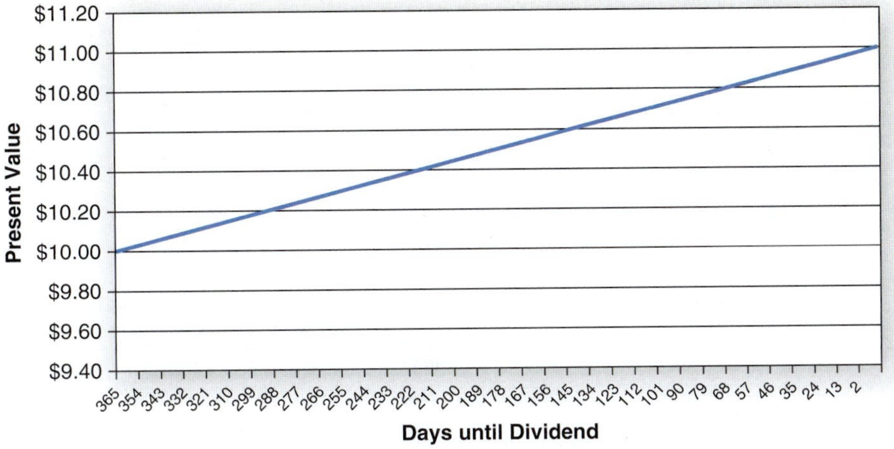

Price Path of Stock Approaching Dividend Payment

drop once the next dividend is paid will continue through time as shown in Figure 17.4.

Adding back in the gap between the ex-dividend date and the payment date causes the present value both to peak at a lower value (the present value of $11 on the ex-dividend date instead of the explicit value of the $11 on the payment date itself). Then the present value falls a little further after the ex-dividend date. For example, taking the hypothetical stock discussed previously and further assuming a 30-day gap between the ex-dividend date and the payment date, the price will hit its highest value one day before the ex-dividend day:

$$P_0 = \frac{D_1}{(1 + i_{daily})^n} + \left(\frac{D_2}{i_{yearly}} \times \frac{1}{(1 + i_{daily})^n}\right)$$

$$= \frac{\$1}{(1 + 0.000261)^{31}} + \left(\frac{\$1}{0.10} \times \frac{1}{(1 + 0.000261)^{31}}\right) = \$0.9919 + \$9.9194 = \$10.91$$

figure 17.4

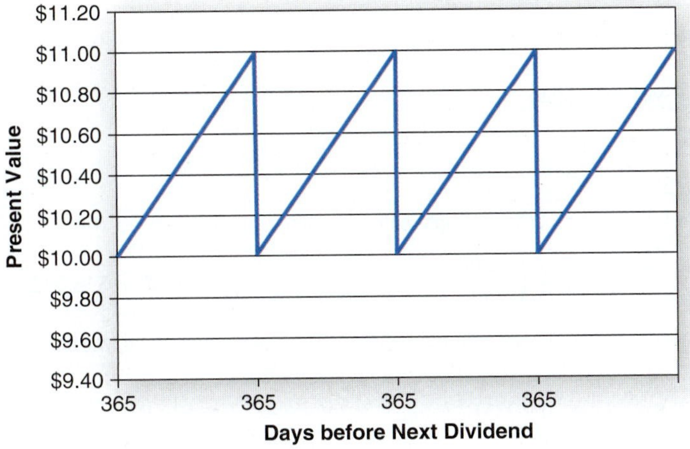

Price Pattern in Response to Repeated Dividends

figure 17.5

Price Pattern Taking into Account Ex-Dividend Days

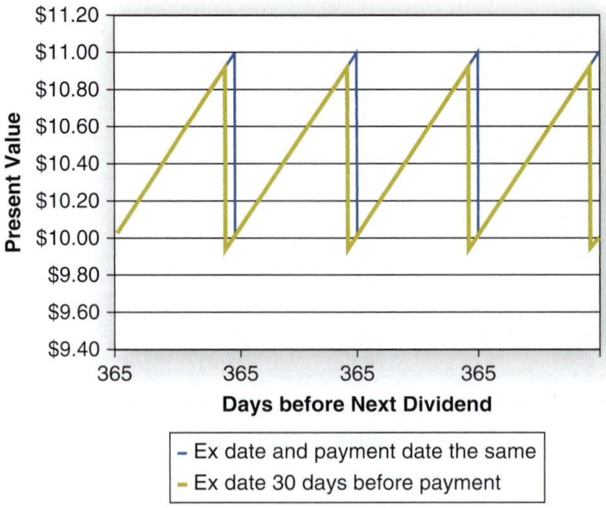

After the stock goes ex-dividend, the first dividend to be received will then be D_2, which will still be 365 + 30 = 395 days away at that point, so the price will drop to:

$$P_0 = \left(\frac{\$1}{0.10} \times \frac{1}{(1 + 0.000261)^{30}}\right) = \$9.92$$

This will cause the price path of the stock to follow the red path shown in Figure 17.5.

Though this example has been a little simplistic, the basic intuition—that stock prices should increase as the next dividend approaches and then fall by the present value of that dividend once the stock goes ex-dividend—has been shown repeatedly.

EXAMPLE 17-3

LG17-5

For interactive versions of this example visit www.mhhe.com/can3e

Price Patterns in Response to Dividends

KAD, Inc., is expected to pay a dividend of $2.00 per year indefinitely. If the appropriate rate of return on this stock is 13 percent per year, and the stock consistently goes ex-dividend 55 days before dividend payment date, what will be the expected minimum and maximum prices in light of the dividend payment logistics?

SOLUTION:

The daily interest rate will be equal to:

$$i_{daily} = \sqrt[365]{1.13} - 1$$
$$= .0335\%$$

So the maximum stock price, which will occur right before the stock goes ex-dividend, will be:

$$P_0 = \frac{\$2.00}{(1 + .000335)^{56}} + \left(\frac{\$2.00}{.13} \times \frac{1}{(1 + .000335)^{56}}\right) = \$1.9628 + \$15.0988 = \$17.06$$

And the minimum stock price, which will occur right after the stock goes ex-dividend, will be:

$$P_0 = \left(\frac{\$2.00}{.13} \times \frac{1}{(1 + .000335)^{55}}\right) = \$15.10$$

Similar to Problems 17-11, 17-12, self-test problem 1

TIME OUT

17-7 Most firms set the ex-dividend date one month in advance of the payment date. Why?

17-8 Suppose that the gap between the ex-dividend date and the payment date was eliminated. What effect would you expect that to have on the pattern of stock prices leading up to the dividend payment?

17.5 • Stock Dividends and Stock Splits

LG17-6

In addition to disbursing cash through the dividend payment system as described previously, firms may also distribute additional shares of stock through either a **stock dividend** or a **stock split.** Though the mechanics and accounting treatments of these two approaches are different, they both have the end result of increasing the number of shares outstanding without changing the total market value of owner's equity. So either a stock dividend or a stock split will decrease the stock price.

stock dividend
A pro-rata distribution of additional shares of stock to the current owners of the stock.

stock split
An exchange of existing shares for a different (usually large) number of "new" shares, with proportionately different par and market values.

Stock Dividends

When they wish to distribute a stock dividend, companies perform a pro rata distribution of additional shares of stock to the current owners of the stock. For example, a 20 percent stock dividend would increase the number of shares held by each stockholder by 20 percent, so an investor who owned 100 shares before the dividend would own 120 afterwards. For accounting purposes, the fair market value of these shares is transferred from retained earnings to the common stock and paid-in-surplus accounts, meaning that no change occurs in the share's par value.

Stock Splits

In a stock split, the company exchanges new shares for old shares in the firm. A split usually involves converting each old share into more than one new share, which increases the shares outstanding. Sometimes you will also hear of "reverse" stock splits, in which stockholders trade in multiple shares for fewer new shares. For example, if you owned 250 shares in a firm and it announced a 2-for-1 stock split, you would receive $2 \times 250 = 500$ new shares of stock. If, instead, it announced a 1-for-5 reverse split, you would receive $250/5 = 50$ new shares once you turned in your original 250 shares (likely held in street name).

Although a stock split will alter the par value of a firm's stock on the company's books, it will not cause any shift in money among the owner's equity accounts.

Effect of Splits and Stock Dividends on Stock Prices

The purpose of either a stock dividend or stock split is to lower (or, in the case of a reverse split, raise) the share's market price proportionately. For example, in a 3-for-1 split, you should expect to see the post-split shares trading at approximately one-third of the presplit price.

Why do firms do this? The general consensus seems to be that firms like to have their shares trade in a particular price range. If their share price moves outside that range, then the firms split their shares or announce a stock dividend to move their share price back into the desired range. Given investors' preference to trade in "round lots" (i.e., in increments of 100 shares), as well as the fact that many brokers' commission schedules encourage trading in round lots, this strategy of keeping the price within a certain range may not be a bad one. If typical investors invest in "chunks" of $10,000 or less, then they'll find it more cost-effective to buy 100 shares of a $75 stock (100 × $75 = $7,500) rather than investing in an odd lot of a $150 stock.

EXAMPLE 17-4

LG17-6

For interactive versions of this example visit www.mhhe.com/can3e

Stock Split versus Stock Dividend

Suppose that LilyMac Industries currently has 50,000 shares outstanding, which are selling for $37.00 per share, and that the current values of the common stock, paid-in-surplus, and retained earnings accounts are $100,000, $1,000,000, and $2,500,000, respectively. If LilyMac performs a 50 percent stock dividend, how would these accounts and the current market price be affected? How would the accounts and the share price be affected if LilyMac instead chose to perform a 3-for-2 stock split?

SOLUTION:

Under a 50 percent stock dividend, the number of shares would increase by 0.50 × 50,000 = 25,000, and the current market value of those 25,000 shares, 25,000 × $37 = $925,000 would be transferred out of retained earnings into the common stock and paid-in-surplus accounts. Since, by inference from the current number of shares outstanding and the current balance of the common stock account, the par value per share is $100,000/50,000 = $2.00 per share, $2.00 × 25,000 = $50,000 of the $925,000 would go into the common stock account, and the remainder of the $925,000, $925,000 − $50,000 = $875,000 would go into the paid-in-surplus account. In summary, the stock dividend would not affect the share price, but would cause retained earnings to decrease by $925,000 to $2,500,000 − $925,000 = $1,575,000, paid-in-surplus to increase to $1,000,000 + $875,000 = $1,875,000, and the common stock account to increase to $100,000 + $50,000 = $150,000, and would cause the number of shares outstanding to increase to 50,000 + 25,000 = 75,000.

The 3-for-2 stock split, on the other hand, would also cause the number of shares to increase to 3/2 × 50,000 = 75,000 and the current market price to decrease to 2/3 × $37 = $24.67, but the current balances of the common stock, paid-in-surplus, and retained earnings accounts would remain unchanged (though the par value per share would have to be adjusted to $100,000/75,000 = $1.33 per share).

Similar to Problems 17-7, 17-8

LG17-7

17.6 • Stock Repurchases

repurchase or buyback

The firm buys back shares of its own stock.

Firms sometimes use another method to return capital to shareholders: They engage in a stock **repurchase** or **buyback**. In the United States, the most common method to do this is through an open-market stock repurchase. In such a repurchase, the firm simply buys shares of its own stock on the stock market just like any other investor. The firm may or may not publicly announce its intention to buy back shares, but any such announcement is not binding. Open market repurchases can span months or even years, allowing the firm to choose to repurchase only when the price is within a particular range or when it feels the advantages outweigh the disadvantages.

fixed-price tender offer

A repurchase offer specifying a single purchase price.

Prior to 1981, all repurchases were carried out using a **fixed-price tender offer**. Such an offer is announced publicly and specifies in advance a single purchase price, the number of shares sought, and the duration of the offer. The offer may allow tendered shares to be withdrawn prior to the offer's expiration date and may also be made conditional upon receiving tender offers for a minimum acceptable number of shares. If the number of shares tendered exceeds the number sought, then the company usually purchases shares from those tendered on a pro rata basis. For example, if a company is seeking to repurchase 1 million shares of stock but shareholders offer 2 million shares, then it would buy half of the offered shares from each seller. If the number of shares tendered is less than the number sought, then the company might choose to extend the offer's expiration date.

Since 1981, firms have been increasingly using an alternative form of tender offer, the *Dutch auction share repurchase.* A Dutch auction offer specifies a price range within which the shares will ultimately be purchased and the number of shares desired by the company, and shareholders are invited to offer their shares for sale at any price within that stated range. At the close of the auction, the firm then analyzes all submitted sale offers to choose the lowest purchase price that allows the firm to buy the number of shares it is seeking. The firm pays that price to all investors who tendered at or below that price but does not purchase any shares that are offered at higher prices. If too few shares are tendered, then the firm either cancels the offer (provided it had been made conditional on a minimum acceptance), or it buys back all tendered shares at the maximum price bid by the shareholders who chose to participate in the auction.

Dutch auction share repurchases have increased in popularity for several reasons. First, the Dutch auction process relies on the company's shareholders to value the stock rather than an independent valuation assessment. To the extent that such valuations are often inaccurate or result in an offer price that the shareholders find unsatisfactory, this seems to be a more efficient, market-driven approach to coming up with a bid price. Second, the Dutch auction process offers at least the possibility that the firm will pay less than the maximum price of the specified range, implying that the stock is less likely to be overvalued in the offer. Finally, since Dutch auctions increase the uncertainty concerning the final price at which a repurchase may take place, they tend to discourage arbitrageurs, who often drive up the price in fixed-price tender offers, from participating.

Advantages of Repurchases

Under tax structures in which capital gains rates are significantly less than dividend tax rates, repurchases can offer the firm a very efficient way to return money to shareholders. Even if capital gains aren't preferentially taxed relative to dividends, shareholders' choice of whether to participate in a buyback implies that capital gains taxes can be deferred until the shareholder wishes to incur them.

Stock repurchases offer another advantage in that reductions in or cessations of repurchase programs don't seem to be perceived as a negative informational signal in the same way that reduced dividends are. So starting a buyback program doesn't imply the same kind of long-term commitment on the firm's part that increasing the dividend would.

Finally, though the cessation of a repurchase program isn't perceived negatively, the announcement of the *initiation* of a stock repurchase program *is* usually viewed as a *positive* signal. The reasoning here: If management, who knows the firm's prospects better than anyone, thinks that the shares are worth buying, then the stock is probably underpriced.

Disadvantages of Repurchases

As you might suspect, repurchases also pose several potential disadvantages. First, that very same positive informational effect that a share repurchase announcement gives may actually be a double-edged sword. Say a shareholder sells shares to the firm in a repurchase. Subsequently, the shareholder finds out that management had information about good future prospects for the firm that was not publicly announced prior to the repurchase. Such a situation will make the firm vulnerable to litigation.

A stock repurchase announcement may even be viewed as a negative signal if investors perceive the repurchase as a signal that the firm doesn't have enough attractive capital budgeting projects available to use the cash used for the repurchase. Even if the announcement is perceived as a positive signal, that isn't necessarily a good thing if it results in the firm paying more for the shares than they are worth. Doing so will result in share dilution, which basically involves a transfer of wealth from the shareholders staying in the firm (i.e., those not tendering their shares) to those leaving it.

Finally, the IRS may impose penalties on the firm if tax authorities can show that the repurchase was performed primarily to avoid dividend taxation. This possibility makes the attractiveness/legality of using a repurchase in lieu of a cash dividend questionable.

Effect of Repurchases on Stock Prices

A large body of evidence supports the idea that, on average, the advantages of share repurchases outweigh the disadvantages. For example, Josef Lakonishok and Theo Vermaelen[4] have shown that repurchasing companies experience economically and statistically significant abnormal returns in the two years after the repurchase. The upward price drift seems to be mainly caused by the behavior of the small firms in their sample.

TIME OUT

17-9 If the par value of stock might represent a superior claim in the event of bankruptcy, would stockholders profit more from a stock dividend or stock split? Why?

17-10 Explain why shareholders who do not participate in a firm's stock repurchase will normally see a concentration of their equity stake.

viewpoints REVISITED

Business Application Solution

If SWV does adopt the new payout policy, the firm should probably expect its stock price to benefit (i.e., go up) because of it. Since investors are risk averse, they will value the increased certainty in the "promised" dividend.

To the extent that it can disburse any extra funds in a stock repurchase instead of an extraordinary dividend, SWV should probably be able to increase the stock price even more by doing so.

Personal Application Solution

Marc should think in terms of leaving the stock for which he will face the lowest tax rate for gains outside the Roth account, which means that he should put the high-dividend-yield stock in the Roth.

[4]See Josef Lakonishok and Theo Vermaelen, "Anomalous Price Behavior around Repurchase Tender Offers," *The Journal of Finance* 45, no. 2 (June 3 1990), pp. 455–477.

summary of learning goals

In this chapter, we've explored major factors affecting the firm's decisions about how much cash to pay out to shareholders and what form this payout should take. We've seen that tax considerations stemming from differential taxation of dividends and capital gains must be a significant consideration in these decisions. Firms should also be concerned with the signaling aspect of changes in the firm's dividend stream. Finally, managers must remain conscious of their investors' timing preferences.

LG17-1 **Identify factors that affect a firm's payout policies.** Factors include the impact of differential investor tax rates on dividends and capital gains, information effects of changes to a firm's dividend policy, the shareholders' preference for a particular payout policy, and the impact on corporate control issues of a change in the firm's dividend payout policy.

LG17-2 **Discuss how investors' preferences regarding differential tax rates and timing can guide the firm's policies on the distribution of dividends and capital gains.** Capital gains are normally taxed at a lower rate than are dividends for the firm's investors. Investors may choose to some extent when they incur capital gains taxes but don't have that freedom with dividends. Both of these factors tend to make capital gains the preferred method for firms to disseminate excess cash. However, some regulatory restrictions against doing so too often will tend to mitigate this tendency.

LG17-3 **Summarize the information effect, the clientele effect, and other corporate control issues.** Dividends act as signals, not just of management's opinion concerning the firm's short-term prospects, but also of the firm's perceived ability to maintain that level of dividends for the foreseeable future. So a relatively small change in a firm's dividend payout can have a relatively large impact on the stock price. Similarly, investors will find it relatively expensive to change their investments due to a change in the company's payout policy, so firms will tend to exhibit "inertia" with regard to their payout policy, if for no other reason than to placate the clientele that they've managed to attract while using past and current payout policies.

LG17-4 **Analyze a firm's decision to distribute constant ordinary dividends or extraordinary dividends.** Analysts tend to see dividend changes as signals about persistent changes in the firm's future prospects. Therefore, managers are loathe to either lower dividends or increase them unless they are fairly confident that the new level can be sustained into the foreseeable future. The residual dividend policy lets managers commit to a fairly conservative dividend payout policy in that they don't raise the "normal" dividend without very good cause, but they can and do issue extraordinary dividends to share occasional "windfalls" with equity holders without fear of such extraordinary dividends committing them to continued higher payouts in the future.

LG17-5 **Explain the effect that cash dividend payment procedures have on stock prices.** Firms delay between the last date that a dividend accompanies a share of stock (i.e., the day before the ex-dividend date) and the actual payment date. Because of this delay, stock prices will get larger and larger as the front end of the infinite stream of dividends approaches, but will peak and decline on the ex-dividend date by the present value of the dividend.

LG17-6 **Differentiate between a stock dividend's impact and a stock split's impact on the firm's books.** Stock dividends involve a transfer from the retained earnings account into the common stock and paid-in-surplus accounts but do not cause any change in par value per share. Stock splits do not involve a transfer of funds between any of the company's bookkeeping accounts, but the increase in the number of shares dictates that the amounts in each account must be shared over a new, different number of shares than was previously the case, so a stock split does change both the par value and book value per share.

LG17-7 **Note the advantages and disadvantages of a firm's stock repurchases.** The primary advantage of a stock repurchase arises when capital gains are taxed at a significantly lower rate than dividends, while the primary disadvantage of a repurchase is the potential for the dilution of existing owners' value if the firm pays too much for the repurchased shares.

chapter equations

$$\text{17-1} \quad P_0 = \frac{D_1}{i - g}$$

$$\text{17-2} \quad \text{Dividend payout ratio} = \frac{\text{Dividends}}{\text{Net income}}$$

17-3 Dividends = Net income − Retained earnings necessary to fund positive NPV projects

$$\text{17-4} \quad P_0 = \frac{D}{i}$$

$$\text{17-5} \quad P_0 = \frac{D_1}{1 + i} + \left(\frac{D_2}{i} \times \frac{1}{1 + i}\right)$$

$$\text{17-6} \quad P_0 = \frac{D_1}{(1 + i_{daily})^n} + \left(\frac{D_2}{i_{yearly}} \times \frac{1}{(1 + i_{daily})^n}\right)$$

$$\text{17-7} \quad i_{daily} = \sqrt[365]{1 + i_{yearly}} - 1$$

key terms

bird-in-the-hand theory, The argument that receiving a dividend today is preferable to letting management have the chance to spend or waste the money between now and the future. *p. 581*

clientele effect, The tendency of investors to find a payout policy that they prefer and stick with it. *p. 582*

declaration date, The date the board of directors announces its intention to pay a dividend. *p. 587*

dividend irrelevance theorem, A theorem showing that, in M&M's perfect world, it doesn't matter if a firm pays out funds through dividends or capital gains. *p. 580*

ex-dividend date, The first day that shares will trade without the purchaser receiving an upcoming dividend. *p. 587*

fixed-price tender offer, A repurchase offer specifying a single purchase price. *p. 592*

free cash flow theory of dividends, Another name for the residual dividend model. *p. 584*

Jobs and Growth Tax Relief Reconciliation Act (JGTRRA), A 2003 law that lowered the rate on both dividends and capital gains for individual investors in most situations. *p. 580*

payment date, The actual date that a dividend will be sent out. *p. 587*

record date, The day that the firm will determine the owner-of-record for the purposes of an upcoming dividend payment. *p. 587*

repurchase or buyback, The firm buys back shares of its own stock. *p. 592*

residual dividend model, The policy of a firm paying out only funds that are left over after all positive-NPV projects are funded. *p. 584*

stock dividend, A pro-rata distribution of additional shares of stock to the current owners of the stock. *p. 591*

stock split, An exchange of existing shares for a different (usually large) number of "new" shares, with proportionately different par and market values. *p. 591*

self-test problems with solutions

1 Computing Pattern of Stock Prices Due to Dividend Payments Stone Woof Beds is expected to pay a dividend of \$2.25 per year, indefinitely. If the appropriate rate of return on this stock is 12 percent per year, and the stock consistently goes ex-dividend 25 days before the dividend payment date, what will be the expected minimum and maximum prices in light of the dividend payment logistics? LG17-5

Solution:

The daily interest rate will be equal to:

$$i_{daily} = \sqrt[365]{1.12} - 1$$
$$= 0.000311$$

As with the example in the chapter, the stock will hit its highest value one day before its ex-dividend date:

$$P_0 = \frac{D_1}{(1 + i_{daily})^n} + \left(\frac{D_2}{i_{yearly}} \times \frac{1}{(1 + i_{daily})^n}\right)$$
$$= \frac{\$2.25}{(1 + 0.000311)^{26}} + \left(\frac{\$2.25}{0.12} \times \frac{1}{(1 + 0.000311)^{26}}\right)$$
$$= \$2.2319 + \$18.5992 = \$20.83$$

and it will hit its lowest value on the ex-dividend date:

$$P_0 = \frac{D_1}{(1 + i_{daily})^n} + \left(\frac{D_2}{i_{yearly}} \times \frac{1}{(1 + i_{daily})^n}\right)$$
$$= \frac{\$2.25}{(1 + 0.000311)^{390}} + \left(\frac{\$2.25}{0.12} \times \frac{1}{(1 + 0.000311)^{390}}\right)$$
$$= \$1.9934 + \$16.6116 = \$18.61$$

2 Calculating shares in a stock split. You own 300 shares in a firm that are selling for \$20 per share. The firm has just announced a 5-for-4 stock split. How many shares will you have after the split, and what do you expect them to be selling for? LG17-6

Solution:

You should wind up with $300 \times \frac{5}{4} = 375$ shares, and each share should sell for $\$20 \times \frac{4}{5} = \$16$.

questions

1. Why might a firm's investors wish to delay receiving cash from the firm? *(LG17-1)*
2. Why might the government actually want the capital gains tax rate to be lower than the dividend tax rate? *(LG17-2)*

3. What condition would be necessary in order for the riskiness of the firm's cash flows to investors to be affected by the firm's dividend payout policy? *(LG17-2)*
4. Explain how an announced increase in a firm's dividend payout might be perceived as either a good or a bad information signal. *(LG17-3)*
5. We talked about how a firm might attract a different clientele by switching dividend payout policies. Might a particular clientele change its preference for dividends versus capital gains through no action of the firm? Explain. *(LG17-3)*
6. Suppose that federal banking regulators in the United States announced that they are going to allow banks to take on significant equity investments in firms to which they have lent. What would you expect, on average, to happen to those firms' dividend payout ratios over time? *(LG17-4)*
7. If a firm follows the modified residual dividend model discussed in this chapter, are extraordinary dividends paid out of residual net income? *(LG17-4)*
8. Suppose a firm announces a new dividend amount every year with the first quarterly dividend declaration, but never explicitly states that the dividend will be continued for the other three quarters of the year. However, in the past the firm has always continued the first quarter's dividend into the other three quarters of the year. How much would you expect this firm's share price to react when it announced the new, first-quarter dividend at the beginning of a new year? *(LG17-4)*
9. Could the record date ever be before the ex-dividend date? Why or why not? *(LG17-5)*
10. Suppose a firm managed to consistently lower the length of time between the ex-dividend date and the payment date. On average, how would this affect the firm's stock price? *(LG17-5)*
11. If a firm announces a dividend decrease, would you expect the stock price to go down more or less than the present value of that decrease? Why? *(LG17-5)*
12. How big of a stock dividend would a firm have to announce for the stock price to be affected as much as it would through a 3-for-1 stock split? *(LG17-6)*
13. Why might a firm announce a reverse stock split? *(LG17-6)*
14. Would it be possible for a firm to announce a "reverse stock dividend"? *(LG17-6)*
15. Why might firms prefer to conduct stock repurchases through open-market operations rather than through fixed-price tender offers? *(LG17-7)*

problems

basic problems

17-1 Payout Ratio Suppose a firm pays total dividends of $500,000 out of net income of $2 million. What would the firm's payout ratio be? *(LG17-2)*

17-2 Payout Ratio Suppose a firm pays total dividends of $750,000 out of net income of $5 million. What would the firm's payout ratio be? *(LG17-2)*

17-3 Total Dividend Amount Suppose a firm has a retention ratio of 35 percent and net income of $5 million. How much does it pay out in dividends? *(LG17-2)*

17-4 **Total Dividend Amount** Suppose a firm has a retention ratio of 56 percent and net income of $9 million. How much does it pay out in dividends? *(LG17-2)*

17-5 **Dividend per Share** Suppose a firm has a retention ratio of 40 percent, net income of $17 million, and 10 million shares outstanding. What would be the dividend per share paid out on the firm's stock? *(LG17-2)*

17-6 **Dividend per Share** Suppose a firm has a retention ratio of 60 percent, net income of $35 million, and 140 million shares outstanding. What would be the dividend per share paid out on the firm's stock? *(LG17-2)*

17-7 **Stock Dividend Effects** If a firm has retained earnings of $3 million, a common shares account of $5 million, and additional paid-in capital of $10 million, how would these accounts change in response to a 10 percent stock dividend? Assume market value of equity is equal to book value of equity. *(LG17-6)*

17-8 **Stock Dividend Effects** If a firm has retained earnings of $23 million, a common shares account of $275 million, and additional paid-in capital of $100 million, how would these accounts change in response to a 20 percent stock dividend? Assume market value of equity is equal to book value of equity. *(LG17-6)*

intermediate problems

17-9 **Extraordinary Dividend** JBK, Inc., normally pays an annual dividend. The last such dividend paid was $2.50, all future dividends are expected to grow at 5 percent, and the firm faces a required rate of return on equity of 11 percent. If the firm just announced that the next dividend will be an extraordinary dividend of $17 per share that is not expected to affect any other future dividends, what should the stock price be? *(LG17-4)*

17-10 **Extraordinary Dividend** MMK Cos. normally pays an annual dividend. The last such dividend paid was $2.25, all future dividends are expected to grow at a rate of 7 percent per year, and the firm faces a required rate of return on equity of 13 percent. If the firm just announced that the next dividend will be an extraordinary dividend of $25 per share that is not expected to affect any other future dividends, what should the stock price be? *(LG17-4)*

17-11 **Effects of Dividends on Stock Prices** Gen Corp. is expected to pay a dividend of $3.50 per year indefinitely. If the appropriate rate of return on this stock is 11 percent per year, and the stock consistently goes ex-dividend 35 days before dividend payment date, what will be the expected minimum and maximum prices in light of the dividend payment logistics? *(LG17-5)*

17-12 **Effects of Dividends on Stock Prices** Kenzie Cos. is expected to pay a dividend of $2.75 per year indefinitely. If the appropriate rate of return on this stock is 16 percent per year, and the stock consistently goes ex-dividend 40 days before dividend payment date, what will be the expected minimum and maximum prices in light of the dividend payment logistics? *(LG17-5)*

advanced problems

17-13 **Dividends versus Capital Gains** Show mathematically that, with a tax rate on both dividends and capital gains of 5 percent, it doesn't matter whether earnings are paid out as dividends or kept in the firm to cause g to grow for a constant-dividend stock. *(LG17-2)*

17-14 **Dividends versus Capital Gains** Show mathematically that, with a tax rate on both dividends and capital gains of 15 percent, it doesn't matter whether earnings are paid out as dividends or kept in the firm to cause g to grow for a constant-dividend stock. *(LG17-2)*

17-15 **Dividends Set Annually** Suppose that a firm always announces a yearly dividend at the end of the first quarter of the year, but then pays the dividend out as four equal quarterly payments. If the next such "annual" dividend has been announced as \$4, it is exactly one quarter until the first quarterly dividend from that \$4, the effective annual required rate of return on the company's stock is 13 percent, and all future "annual" dividends are expected to grow at 3 percent per year indefinitely, how much will this stock be worth? *(LG17-4)*

17-16 **Dividends Set Annually** Suppose that a firm always announces a yearly dividend at the end of the first quarter of the year, but then pays the dividend out as four equal quarterly payments. If the next such "annual" dividend has been announced as \$6, it is exactly one quarter until the first quarterly dividend from that \$6, the effective annual required rate of return on the company's stock is 17 percent, and all future "annual" dividends are expected to grow at 6 percent per year indefinitely, how much will this stock be worth? *(LG17-4)*

17-17 **Change in Lead Time of Dividend Announcement** Everything else held constant, if a firm announces that it will double the length of time between its ex-dividend date and its payment date, what should be the effect on the stock price? *(LG17-5)*

17-18 **Change in Lead Time of Dividend Announcement** Everything else held constant, if a firm announces that it will halve the length of time between its ex-dividend date and its payment date, what should be the effect on the stock price? *(LG17-5)*

research it! Identifying a Firm's Dividend Policy

Go to Ford Motor Company's Investor Relations website and download the dividend history from **www.corporate-ir.net/ireye/ir_site.zhtml?ticker=F&script=11909&layout=-6&item_id='96topresent.htm**. Adjust the dividends for stock splits and graph them; identify any trends in dividends you see. Does Ford seem to follow a residual dividend policy or another policy?

integrated mini-case Investor Perceptions of Dividend Growth

Your firm currently pays a quarterly dividend of \$1.35. You are planning on doubling this dividend but then keeping it flat for the next three years, after which it is expected to increase at the industry standard rate of 4 percent per year indefinitely. Your required rate of return on your company's stock is 12.5 percent, and the last \$1.35 dividend was just paid.

What will be the time value of money impact on your stock price if investors are fully informed concerning your future intentions for all dividends? What will be the present value of all expected future dividends if you don't tell the investors that you will be keeping the quarterly dividend constant for the first three years, and they assume after the fifth coming dividend that dividends will remain at \$2.70 indefinitely?

ANSWERS TO TIME OUT

17-1 Increasing the dividend payout ratio will reduce the amount of retained earnings, which therefore reduces the amount of money that can be invested in projects that would cause future earnings (and dividends) to grow.

17-2 No. Having to pay trading costs when selling shares would cause investors to increase their preference for dividends, which don't involve trading costs.

17-3 Investors who need a stable payment stream over time and for whom the tax burden of dividends wouldn't be very large prefer dividends over capital gains. The typical example of this is a retiree.

17-4 Raising a firm's dividend payout ratio might be seen as a negative signal if investors interpret it as indicating that the firm has run out of good investment opportunities.

17-5 In general, a firm would increase its payout ratio if earnings became more stable or if commitments on earnings (such as future investments in projects) decrease.

17-6 A firm with cyclical sales would be more likely to use extraordinary dividends, as it would be unwilling to commit to a higher, fixed dividend amount.

17-7 A firm sets the ex-dividend date one month in advance of the dividend payment date to give itself plenty of time to determine the owner of record for each share and to provide ample processing time between determining owners of record and actually mailing the checks.

17-8 Stock prices would peak higher, following the blue path shown in Figure 17.5.

17-9 It would be more to stockholders' advantage for the firm to pay a stock dividend, as this would give shareholders more shares while keeping the par value of each share constant.

17-10 The shareholders who do not participate will see their equity stake stay more-or-less constant on a dollar basis, but that constant dollar amount will represent a larger proportion of the firm's equity because the shareholders who do participate are taking their money out of the firm.

PART EIGHT

18 Issuing Capital and the Investment Banking Process

viewpoints

Business Application

ADK Industries, a publicly traded firm in the online social networking industry, is considering building its own dedicated Web server firm at a cost of $5 million. The firm currently has $20 million of assets on its balance sheet, financed with $6 million in debt and $14 million in equity. Firm managers are considering options about how to finance the $5 million. What types of issues do managers need to consider as they make their decisions? **(See solution on p. 621)**

Personal Application

After spending several years raising her children, Marge Upton has decided to reopen her bicycle repair shop. Prior to the time away, Marge operated a successful bicycle repair business in her hometown. Marge remained involved in civic activities while she was raising her children and has maintained her relations with local bankers and other businesspeople. To get the business up and running again, Marge will need to rent a building for the repair shop and purchase equipment and supplies. She estimates that she will need $25,000 to get started. Marge has $5,000 in savings to invest in the business. She also has friends and relatives who will invest another $5,000. What can Marge do to get the remaining funds needed to reopen her bicycle repair shop? **(See solution on p. 621)**

What if Marge found a business partner? Things to consider. . .

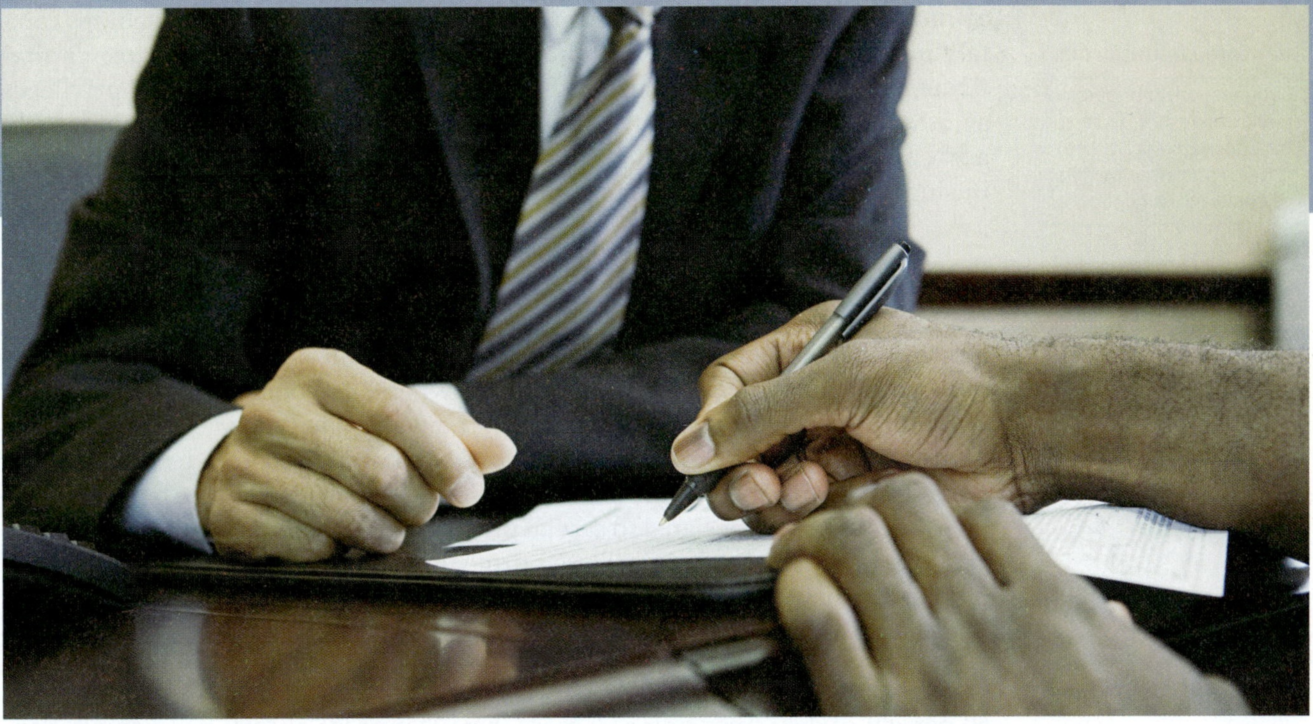

Firms finance their existing and new assets with capital. Some capital used to finance assets comes from retained earnings—the profits that firms retain and reinvest. In addition, firms use debt financing (borrowed funds, usually loans or bonds) and equity financing (ownership shares that the firm sells). A firm will choose its preferred type of capital funding depending upon its size, its stage in its life cycle, and, as a related issue, its prospects for future growth.

In this chapter, we describe the decisions that firms face when they raise capital. We first look at small firms in their early operating stages. Small firms that are just getting started depend mainly on banks and venture capital firms for their capital funding. We then look at the process of going public, as well as publicly traded firms' subsequent issues of debt and equity. Then we describe the types of securities that public firms issue and explore the role that investment banks play in the process. As we go through the chapter, note how important financial institutions become in raising capital funds to finance a firm's assets. For example, banks and institutions known as *venture capital firms* provide short- and medium-term financing to small and newer firms, while investment banks assist publicly traded firms to arrange new securities issues.

Learning goals

LG18-1 Evaluate different methods for small firms to get funding.

LG18-2 Appreciate what venture capital is and entrepreneurship.

LG18-3 Differentiate among sources of capital funding for public firms.

LG18-4 Trace the process by which securities are underwritten.

18.1 • Sources of Capital for New and Small Firms

LG18-1

Most new and small firms finance their business assets by borrowing funds from private or public sources. Private capital fund suppliers fall into two basic categories: suppliers of debt financing and suppliers of equity financing. Debt financing includes capital funds borrowed from personal savings, friends or relatives, financial institutions such

venture capital firms

Organizations that purchase equity interests in firms and have the same rights and privileges as other owners of equity investments.

as commercial bank loans, or venture capitalists. Equity financing includes capital funds invested by venture capitalists. Venture capitalists, or **venture capital firms,** purchase equity interests in firms and have the same rights and privileges as other owners of equity investments. Public sources of capital include debt and equity financing provided by government agencies such as the U.S. Small Business Administration (SBA).

Debt Financing

Debt financing includes personal capital (loans from friends and relatives) or external capital (loans from banks or venture capitalists). Most new businesses use personal capital. So often, the firm's owners' personal wealth ties directly to the firm's success. However, almost all new and small business owners must borrow capital from external sources. Most external capital providers require that a significant percentage of the firm owners' funds be invested in the business. This investment serves as a signal to capital providers that the firm's owners, with a lot at stake, will work hard to make the firm succeed. Work generally increases the probability that the loan will be paid back in full.

BANK LOANS Most new and small firms rely on bank loans as a major part of their capital funding. Bank loans, including mortgages, represent more than 60 percent of debt financing and more than 20 percent of total financing in non-publicly traded firms. However, the financial crisis of 2008 and 2009 had a huge impact on small firms' abilities to get bank loans. Extraordinary changes in the lending environment developed after August 2008 as the financial health of major financial institutions deteriorated. Further, the collapse of the financial markets, in the fall of 2008, dramatically disrupted the availability of loans to small businesses. Between June 30, 2008, and June 30, 2009, outstanding small business loans declined by more than $14 billion. In addition to supply-side changes in bank loan availability, demand for credit by small firms fell precipitously. The most severe recession since the Great Depression hit the United States. The historic economic slowdown resulted in high levels of unemployment and consequently reduced demand for goods and services produced by all businesses, including small firms. Because of reluctance to make new investments in this economic environment, demand for loans by small businesses declined. Small business bank lending continued to suffer even as the U.S. economy slowly recovered. Outstanding small business loans at banks decreased by over $47 billion from 2007 levels. Further, 87 percent of loan applications filed by small businesses were rejected. Many small businesses stopped even trying to get bank loans. According to a poll conducted by the New York Federal Reserve Banks in 2012, 59 percent of small businesses in the New York area did not apply for loans in 2011; half of these stated that they did not apply because they felt they would not be approved.

Commercial banks find small-business loans to be complicated and risky propositions because the bank is frequently asked to assume the credit risk of an individual whose business cash flows require considerable analysis, often with incomplete accounting information available to the credit officer. The payoff for these loans is also small, by definition, because loan principal amounts are usually small. A $50,000 loan with 3 percent interest spread over the cost of funds provides only $1,500 of gross revenues before loan loss provisions, monitoring costs, and allocation of overheads. Low profitability has caused many banks to build small business scoring models similar to, but more sophisticated than, those used for mortgage loans and consumer credit. Small business models often combine computer-based financial analysis of borrower financial statements with behavioral analysis of the owner of the new and/or small business.

figure 18.1 Credit Process Flow Chart

Follow the two indicated lines to trace information flow and cash flow.

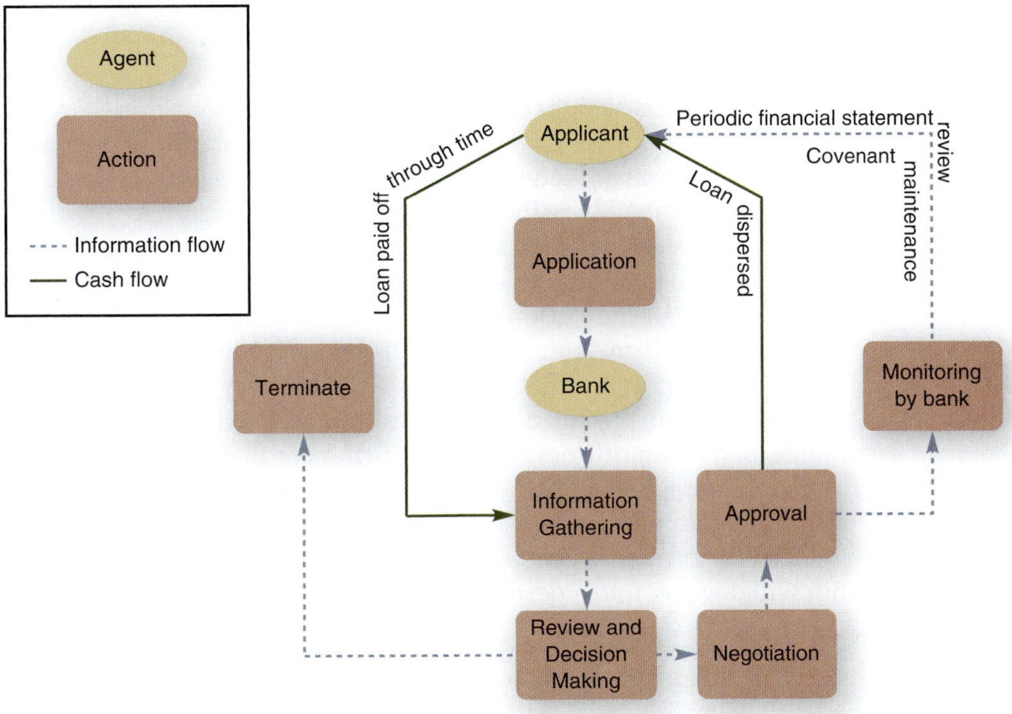

Midmarket business firms also rely heavily on banks for their capital needs. Although definitions of midmarket firms vary, they typically have sales revenues from $5 million to $100 million a year and have a recognizable corporate structure (unlike many small businesses). However, midmarket firms are not publicly traded. Thus, they do not have ready access to deep, liquid capital markets (as do large corporations). Midmarket firms require credit analysis different from the kinds of analysis used for new or small businesses because, while still assessing the character of the firm's management, the main focus is on the business itself.

Figure 18.1 illustrates the credit process for a hypothetical small or midmarket business loan, the Applicant. The credit process begins with a loan officer, the Bank, gathering information on the firm. Having gathered information about the firm, the loan officer will decide whether pursuing the new business is worthwhile, given the firm's needs, the bank's credit policies, the current economy, and the competitive lending environment. If loan officers decide that midmarket firms are worth the investment, they structure and price agreements as laid out in the bank's credit-granting policy and then negotiate with the firm. The bank's credit-granting policy will include several areas of analysis, including cash flow analysis, ratio analysis, and financial statement comparisons (as described in Chapters 2 and 3). At any time in this process, conditions could change or new information could be revealed, significantly changing the firm's situation and forcing the account officer to begin the process again.

Once the firm owners and loan officer tentatively agree on a loan, the loan officer must obtain internal approval from the bank's credit risk management team. Generally, even for the smallest midmarket credit, at least two officers must approve a new loan customer. Larger credit requests must be presented formally (either in hard copy or through a computer network) to a credit approval officer and/or committee before they can be signed.

Having reviewed the financial and other applicant conditions, the bank can include loan covenants (similar to bond covenants discussed in Chapter 7) as a part of the loan agreement. Loan covenants reduce the bank's risk of granting and carrying the loan. Covenants can include a variety of conditions, such as ratio maintenance at or within stated ranges or key-person insurance policies on employees critical to the business' success.

The credit process does not end when the applicant signs the loan agreement. Before allowing the loan to be finalized, the account officer must make sure that any conditions that are required for the loan have been cleared, i.e., "clearing conditions precedent." These include various searches, registration of collateral, and confirmation of the officer's authority to borrow. Credit must then be monitored throughout the loan's life to ensure that the borrower is living up to its commitments and to detect deterioration should it occur to protect the bank's interest.

Typically, the firm's credit needs will change from time to time. A growing firm will have expanding credit needs. A firm moving into the international arena will need foreign exchange. Further, even if the credit agreements offered do not change, bank loan officers review the firm's credit needs annually to ensure that the firm complying with the original credit agreement terms. Banks typically wish to maintain close contact with new and small firms to meet their ongoing financial service requirements—both credit and noncredit—so that the relationship will develop into a permanent, mutually beneficial one as the firm grows.

spot loan

A loan in which the firm receives the funds as soon as the loan is approved.

take down

Borrowing against a line of credit or loan commitment.

loan commitment agreement

A contractual commitment by a bank to loan a firm a certain maximum amount at given interest rate terms for a stated length of time over which the firm has the option to take down this loan.

up-front (or facility) fee

A fee charged by a bank for making funds available through a loan commitment.

back-end (or commitment) fee

A fee charged by a bank on any unused balances of a loan commitment line at the end of the loan commitment period.

Loan Commitments In the past, businesses borrowed **spot loans,** in which the firm would receive the funds as soon as the bank approved the loan. These days, most business loans are made as firms **"take down"** (or borrow against) pre-negotiated lines of credit or loan commitments. Banks make **loan commitment agreements**—contractual commitments to loan the firm a certain maximum amount (say, $10 million)—at given interest rate terms (say, 12 percent). The loan commitment agreement also defines the length of time over which the borrower may take down this loan. In return for making the loan commitment, the bank may charge an **up-front** (or **facility**) **fee** of, say, ⅛ of 1 percent of the commitment size, or $12,500 in this example. In addition, the bank must stand ready to supply the full $10 million at any time over the commitment period—for example, one year. Meanwhile, the firm has a valuable option to take down any amount between $0 and $10 million. The bank may also charge the borrower a **back-end** (or **commitment**) **fee** on any unused balances on the commitment line at the end of the period. In this example, if the firm takes down only $8 million in funds over the year and the fee on *unused* commitments is ¼ percent, the firm must pay an additional expense of ¼ percent times $2 million, or $5,000.

EXAMPLE 18-1

LG18-1

Calculating Fees on a Loan Commitment

For interactive versions of this example visit www.mhhe.com/can3e

Calculate the total fees a firm would have to pay if its bank offers the firm the following loan commitment: A loan commitment of $1 million with an up-front fee of 1 percent and a back-end fee of 50 basis points (0.5 percent). The take down on the loan is 85 percent.

SOLUTION:

Up-front fee	$= \$1{,}000{,}000 \times 0.0100$	$= \$10{,}000$
Back-end fee	$= \$1{,}000{,}000 \times 0.0050 \times (1 - 0.85)$	$= 750$
Total		$= \$10{,}750$

Similar to Problems 18-1, 18-2, self-test problem 1

During the financial crisis of 2008 and 2009, loan commitments set up prior to the market meltdown proved to be a lifeline for many businesses. During the crisis, financial markets (including loan markets) dried up. Banks that held illiquid loans, mortgage-backed securities, and asset-backed securities at the start of the crisis tended to increase holdings of liquid assets and decrease investments in loans and new commitments to lend. At the same time, loan requests by businesses increased not only because these firms needed a substitute in the absence of market liquidity, but also to meet increased precautionary demands for cash. Because of concern about the liquidity of their existing loans and securitized assets, the banks rationally protected themselves by hoarding liquidity, to the detriment of their customers and markets. Unable to get new loans, businesses that had existing loan commitments were able to draw on them to meet their funding needs. In fact, some firms drew funds from existing loan commitments simply due to fears about disturbances in the credit markets. To take one example, American Electric Power (AEP) drew down $3 billion from an existing credit line issued by J.P. Morgan and Barclays. According to its SEC filing, "AEP took this proactive step to increase its cash position while there are disruptions in the debt markets. The borrowing provides AEP flexibility and will act as a bridge until the capital markets improve."

Fixed- versus Floating-Rate Loans Banks make loans (both spot loans and loan commitments) available to firms at either (1) fixed interest rates as fixed-rate loan commitments or (2) floating (or variable) rates as variable-rate loans. With **fixed-rate loans,** the firm makes fixed interest payments over the life of the loan. With **variable-rate loans** the loan's interest rate (and thus the interest payments the firm must make) changes over the loan's life. A floating rate is set at a fixed spread over a prevailing benchmark rate, such as a Treasury-bill rate, the federal funds rate, or a prime rate. If the benchmark rate rises during the loan period, so does the firm's loan cost. The floating interest rate is specified in the loan contract. The spread is also stated in the loan contract; the bank sets the spread as a function of the firm's credit risk and the owners' credit history.

fixed-rate loan

A loan on which the interest payments the firm must make cannot change over the life of the loan.

variable-rate loan

A loan on which the interest rate on the loan (and thus the interest payments the firm must make) can change over the life of the loan.

SMALL BUSINESS ADMINISTRATION The U.S. Congress created the Small Business Administration (SBA) on July 30, 1953, to "aid, counsel, assist and protect, insofar as is possible, the interests of small business concerns." For qualified new and small firms that cannot obtain long-term financing on reasonable terms from banks or other financial institutions, the SBA offers a basic loan guarantee program. Through this program, the SBA can guarantee up to $3.75 million (representing 75 percent of the loan value) at an interest rate not to exceed 2.75 percent more than the prime lending rate. Maturities on these loans can extend up to 10 years for working-capital loans and 25 years for fixed-asset loans.

While the SBA's primary function is to guarantee loans made to new and small businesses by private financial institutions (such as banks), the SBA offers direct loan programs as well. The SBA's Certified Development Company Loan Program provides long-term, fixed-rate capital funding to small businesses that use the funds to purchase real estate, machinery, or equipment for expansion or modernization. Private, nonprofit corporations called *certified development companies* offer these loans to contribute to communities' or regions' economic development. The SBA funds the loans via a 100 percent SBA-guaranteed debenture and a bank generally secures the loans. SBA loans require an investment of at least 10 percent owner's equity. The SBA's Microloan Loan Program provides up to $50,000 in short-term loans to small businesses to fund working-capital purchases. Through this program the SBA makes or guarantees a loan to a bank, which then makes the microloan to the firm. The bank also provides the fledgling firm with management and technical assistance.

LG18-2

Equity Financing and Expertise

New and small firms have difficulty obtaining debt financing from banks because banks are generally not willing or able to make loans to new companies with no assets and little or no business history. In these cases, new and small firms often turn to venture capital firms to get capital financing as well as advice. **Venture capital** is a professionally managed pool of money used to finance new and often high-risk firms. Venture capital is generally provided by investment institutions or private individuals willing to back an untried company and its managers in return for an equity investment in the firm.

venture capital

A professionally managed pool of money used to finance new and often high-risk firms.

Venture capital firms do not make outright loans. Rather, they purchase equity interests in firms that give the venture capitalists the same rights and privileges associated with equity investments made by the firm's other owners. As equity holders, venture capital firms are *not* generally passive investors. Rather, they provide valuable expertise to the firm's managers and sometimes even help in recruiting senior managers for the firm. They also generally expect to be kept fully informed about the firm's operations, any problems, and whether all firm owners' joint goals are being met.

Many types of venture capital firms have sprung up, especially since 1980. **Institutional venture capital firms'** sole purpose is to find and fund the most promising new firms. Private-sector institutional venture capital firms include venture capital limited partnerships (that are established by professional venture capital firms, acting as general partners in the firm: organizing and managing the firm and eventually liquidating their equity investment); financial venture capital firms (subsidiaries of banks); and corporate venture capital firms (subsidiaries of nonfinancial corporations that generally specialize in making start-up investments in high-tech firms). Limited partner venture capital firms dominate the industry.

institutional venture capital firms

Business entities whose sole purpose is to find and fund the most promising new firms.

In addition to private sector institutional venture capital firms, the federal government, through the SBA, operates Small Business Investment Companies (SBICs). SBICs are privately organized venture capital firms licensed by the SBA to make equity investments (as well as loans) to entrepreneurs for start-up activities and expansions. As federally sponsored entities, SBICs rely on their unique opportunity to obtain investment funds from the U.S. Treasury at very low rates relative to private-sector institutional venture capital firms. In contrast to institutional venture capital firms, **angel venture capitalists** (or **angels**) are wealthy individuals who make equity investments. Angel venture capitalists have invested much more in new and small firms than institutional venture capital firms have.

angel venture capitalists (or angels)

Wealthy individuals who make equity investments.

Venture capital firms receive many unsolicited proposals of funding from new and small firms. The venture capital firms reject the majority of these requests. Venture capital firms look for two things in making their decisions to invest in a firm. The first is a high return. Venture capital firms are willing to invest in high-risk new and small firms. However, they require high levels of returns (sometimes as high as 700 percent within five to seven years) to take on these risks. The second is an easy exit. Venture capital firms realize a profit on their investments by eventually selling their firm interests. They want a quick and easy exit opportunity when it comes time to sell. Basically, venture capital firms provide equity funds to new, unproven, and young firms. This willingness separates venture capital firms from commercial banks and investment firms, which prefer to invest in existing, financially secure businesses.

TIME OUT

18-1 What sources of debt financing are available to new and small firms?

18-2 What is venture capital?

The Choice to Go Public

If they succeed, at some point new and small firms grow until they need more capital than they can raise on their own and do not want or need to pay to get additional funds from banks and venture capitalists. At this point, the firm decides to make an **initial public offering (IPO)** of stock. That is, the firm allows its equity, some of which was held privately by managers and venture capital investors, to be *publicly* traded in stock markets for the first time. The number of IPOs in the United States averages about 200 deals per year. However, the financial crisis brought about a drought in these firm events. For a 10-week period, starting in August 2008, no firm conducted an IPO, the longest stretch of inactivity since IPO data began to be tracked in 1980. Even through 2012, the IPO market had not recovered. For the year, 128 companies undertook an IPO. This was up 2.4 percent from 2010 and is four times the number of deals in 2008. However, the number of deals in 2012 was down from the 154 IPOs in 2011 and was still far below the long-term average.

initial public offerings (IPOs)

A first-time issue of stock by a private firm going public (e.g., allowing its equity, some of which was held privately by managers and venture capital investors, to be *publicly* traded in stock markets for the first time).

The technical details associated with the sale of public stock appear below. However, in making the decision to go from a private to a public firm, managers must consider the benefits versus the costs of doing so. As mentioned previously, a major benefit of going public is that the firm will have a new, larger pool of equity capital than is available from any previous source (bank or venture capitalist). This new equity allows a firm to undertake new and profitable investment opportunities that it could not undertake as a private firm. The market provides a market value for the firm's common stock, which is really a readily available measure of firm performance (another advantage of going public). Such a transparent measure of firm performance can attract even more stockholders and can provide a tool that can be used to reward firm managers (i.e., through stock or option payments as part of compensation packages). Finally, as private firms, managers generally must invest much of their personal wealth and human capital in the firm. From Chapters 9 and 10, we know that this results in a poorly diversified portfolio for the firm's original owners. By going public, the original owners can reallocate their personal wealth away from the firm and into more diversified portfolios.

However, some significant costs are attached to the decision to become a public firm. First and foremost is the direct financial cost of an IPO. Cash expenses associated with an IPO (e.g., legal services, printing) can sometimes total as much as $1 million. These expenses must be paid regardless of whether the IPO succeeds or not. Additionally, underwriters charge a discount (on average about 7 percent) to sell the stock and IPOs are typically underpriced (on average about 15 percent) to ensure a successful sale. Thus, a significant amount of the issue proceeds do not actually become available to the newly public firm.

Add to these financial costs a substantial demand for time from the firm's owners during the IPO process. That is, the firm's owners and top managers must spend a significant amount of time with the investment bankers to discuss all aspects of the firm and with major potential stockholders before the IPO is completed. These time demands grow even more significantly as the offering date approaches. Further, throughout the IPO process, managers must disclose firm details that may be valuable to competitors. Further, shareholders of a public firm have the right to a great deal of information about the firm. The release of this information to stockholders also releases it to competitors.

Finally, the firm is exposed to reputational costs if the IPO is unsuccessful or is beset with problems. Such was the case with the Facebook IPO in 2012. The IPO was touted as one of the largest IPOs of a technology firm, with a market capitalization of over $104 billion at its peak. For many years, Mark Zuckerberg, Facebook's founder and chief executive, resisted taking the firm public. However, as the number of private shareholders exceeded 500, the firm was required to go public. With great anticipation, the IPO occurred on May 18, 2012. However, as described in the Finance at Work box, the event was plagued by a series of missteps and technical issues, including the last minute increase in the number of shares issued and a computer malfunction on the NASDAQ exchange during the first hours of trading. Facebook's shares lost over a half of their initial value in less than three months of the IPO and brought doubt to the firm's reputation as the leader in social networking.

Two newer methods of going public include a Dutch auction IPO and a direct IPO. A Dutch auction IPO uses a bidding process to discover the highest price at which the issuing company can sell shares to the public. The company announces the number of shares being sold, and then investors submit their bids, stating the number of shares they want and at what price. The lowest successful bid, which allows the firm to sell all of the shares, becomes the price for all bidders, even those who bid a higher price. The Dutch auction method guarantees that the initial offering price is set so that all of the shares are sold at a price that reflects market demand. Further, unlike the traditional IPO (which gives an advantage to larger investors and investment banks), this method gives individual investors a chance to buy shares at the IPO price. Finally, this method of IPO allocation allows young and growing companies to raise as much cash as the market is willing to afford it.

The drawback of a Dutch auction IPO is that if the initial market demand is not sufficient, a company using a Dutch auction rather than an investment bank to issue and sell its shares may not raise the funds it needs. One of the more notable Dutch auction IPOs was Google's $2.7 billion initial public offering in August 2004. Google's initial price range for the stocks was between $108 and $135 per share. Several well-publicized problems with the IPO caused that price to drop. When the Dutch auction finished, the price was $85 per share.

A direct IPO involves the issuance of stock directly to investors without using an investment bank as an intermediary. Direct IPOs allow a firm to avoid various costs associated with a traditional IPO. For example, the average commission charged by IPO underwriters is 13 percent of the proceeds of the securities sale: A direct IPO involves costs that are, on average, 3 percent. Further, direct IPOs are exempt from many of the Securities and Exchange Commission's registration and reporting requirements. Direct IPOs can also be completed within a shorter time frame and without extensive disclosure of firm-sensitive information. Finally, because only a limited number of investors may buy stock in a direct IPO they tend to have a long-term investment horizon. Thus, the pressure for the newly public firm to produce short-term profits is reduced.

A disadvantage of a direct IPO, however, is that the amount that a company can raise through a direct IPO over a 12-month period is limited. In addition, to ensure that all shares are sold, the stock must generally be offered at a price that is lower than might be achieved through a traditional IPO. Finally, since shares are sold through exempt offerings, shares are not generally freely traded. Thus, no market price is established for the shares.

finance at work — markets

INSIDE THE FUMBLED FACEBOOK OFFERING

Less than three days before Facebook Inc.'s initial public offering, Chief Financial Officer David Ebersman decided to boost the number of shares the company would offer investors by 25 percent. His main adviser at lead underwriter Morgan Stanley assured him there was plenty of demand. That decision by the 41-year-old Facebook executive may have doomed any real chance the social-networking company had that its stock would jump on its first day of trading—a hallmark of successful IPOs. On Tuesday, the second full day of trading, Facebook shares fell $3.03, or 8.9 percent, to $31, after falling 11 percent on Monday. Investors are blaming the downdraft on the last-moment expansion of the offering.

Securities and Exchange Commission Chairman Mary Schapiro said Tuesday that her agency will examine "issues" surrounding the IPO in an effort to ensure confidence in public markets. Adding to the tumult on Tuesday was news that analysts at Morgan Stanley and another underwriter, Goldman Sachs Group Inc., had told clients earlier this month that they were reducing their earnings estimates for Facebook following a filing that said the company's ad-sales growth isn't keeping up with expansion of its user base.

Also on Tuesday, NASDAQ OMX Group Inc. said that if it had fully realized the extent of the technical problems that hampered the first day of trading, it would have delayed the IPO. Facebook's offering was one of the most widely anticipated in recent memory. In terms of the company's fundraising goals, it was a success. It raised $16 billion for Facebook and some early investors and valued the company at $104 billion. The offering, the biggest ever for a U.S. Internet company, has thus far left many investors with losses. It remains to be seen whether that will matter to Facebook over the long term. . . . The outcome has the potential to dent the reputation of Morgan Stanley, long considered the marquee bank for technology offerings. The company announced on April 23 that its revenue and profit had declined in the first quarter, from the fourth quarter of 2011. The news came two weeks before Facebook kicked off its "roadshow" on May 7 to pitch its shares to large investors. One week into the roadshow, the company raised its price range for the share sale, to between $34 and $38, from $28 to $35.

On May 15, *The Wall Street Journal* reported that General Motors Co. planned to stop advertising with Facebook after deciding that paid ads on the site have little impact on consumers' car purchases. The move fueled questions about whether Facebook's business prospects could support its valuation. Then came word that Facebook was expanding the deal by asking private investors to sell more shares. Mr. Ebersman insisted that the lead three banks on the deal—Morgan Stanley, JPMorgan Chase & Co., and Goldman Sachs—get regular and equal access to the so-called "book" showing investor orders, which generally was updated about every six hours during the roadshow. As word spread that the deal would be growing, investors got nervous that demand would be sated before the shares even began to trade. At the same time, some bankers felt ill-prepared to manage investors' questions about the change in size. Many learned of the growth in the deal's size after the change was filed Wednesday morning with regulators. One person said decisions were kept close to the vest to prevent leaks. Another person said that, after the disclosure, underwriters made "hundreds of calls" to investors explaining the move.

By Thursday morning, there was one big decision left: the share price. Early Thursday morning, Mr. Ebersman and Mr. Grimes talked on the phone and "directionally agreed" that the offer price should be $38 a share. Soon after, Mr. Ebersman called bankers at JPMorgan and Goldman Sachs to get their opinions on the price. After some discussion, there was agreement about the $38. Around 1:30 p.m. Eastern time, Facebook's "pricing committee" of board members dialed onto a conference call and were informed by Mr. Ebersman that he intended to go with a $38 share price. Nobody voiced objections and the call was quick, the person said. The shares did open around $42. "Good karma," one thought. Then shares promptly fell.

Source: Shayndi Raice, Anupreeta Das, and Gina Chon, "Inside Fumbled Facebook Offering," *The Wall Street Journal* Online, May 3, 2012. Used with permission of Dow Jones & Company, Inc. via Copyright Clearance Center, Inc.

want to know more? Key Words to Search for Updates: Facebook IPO, largest tech IPOs

18.2 • Public Firms' Capital Sources

LG18-3

In contrast to small and new firms that can only get capital funding from mainly private sources, public firms raise the majority of their capital funds from public debt and equity markets. Public firms raise large amounts of short-term debt in the money market, primarily as commercial paper. Further, public firms raise long-term capital by issuing securities in the public debt and equity markets.

figure 18.2

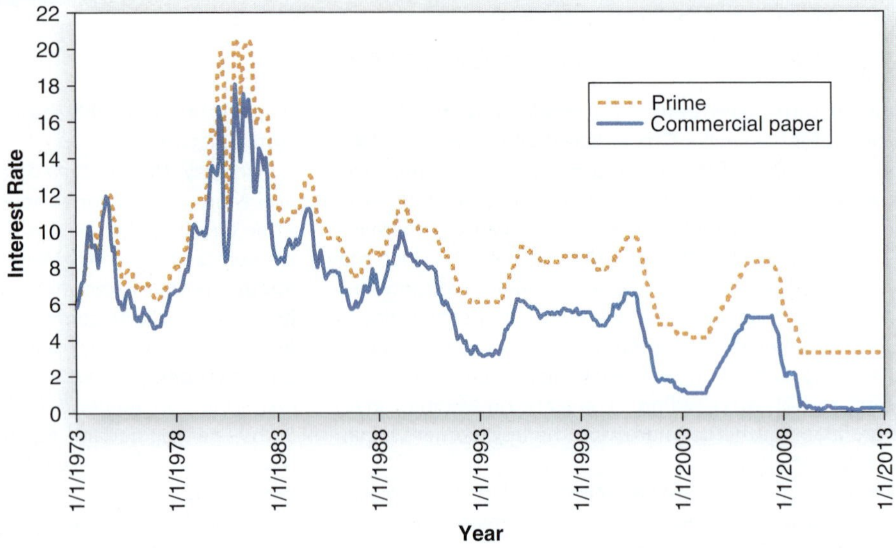

Commercial Paper and Prime Rates

Notice the cohesive relationship between the prime rate and the commercial paper rate over time.

Debt Financing

Public firms or corporations obtain debt financing to meet their capital needs in two major ways: commercial paper and corporate bonds. As we noted in Chapter 6, both of these types of debt financing trade in the financial markets. Commercial paper is short-term debt sold and traded in the money markets, while long-term debt is sold and traded in the capital markets.

commercial paper

An unsecured short-term promissory note issued by a public firm to raise short-term cash, often to finance working capital requirements.

COMMERCIAL PAPER **Commercial paper** is an unsecured short-term promissory note issued by a public firm to raise short-term cash, often to finance working-capital requirements. Commercial paper is one of the largest (in terms of dollar value outstanding) of the money market instruments, with $0.95 trillion outstanding as of 2013. One reason that so much commercial paper is outstanding is that companies with strong credit ratings can generally borrow money at a lower interest rate by issuing commercial paper than by directly borrowing (via loans) from banks. Indeed, although business loans were the major asset on bank balance sheets between 1965 and 1990, they have dropped in importance since 1990. This trend reflects the growth of the commercial paper market.

Figure 18.2 illustrates the difference between commercial paper rates and the prime rate for borrowing from banks from 1973 through 2013. Notice that in the late 1990s, as the U.S. economy thrived and default risk on the highest quality borrowers decreased, the spread between the prime rate and the commercial paper rate increased. Further, during the latter part of and following the financial crisis, commercial paper rates fell to near zero, falling as low as 0.13 percent in January 2010. Despite these low rates, the commercial paper market shrank in size, from over $2.2 trillion in August 2007 to as low as $0.95 trillion in April 2013, for two reasons. First, while commercial paper rates were historically low from 2009 through 2013, so were long-term bond rates. Wanting to lock in to low rates for the long run, firms issued and used debt with longer maturity and less short-term commercial paper financing. Second, at the height of the financial crisis there was a run on money market mutual funds. Money market mutual funds invested heavily in the commercial paper market. As investors pulled their money from

figure 18.3

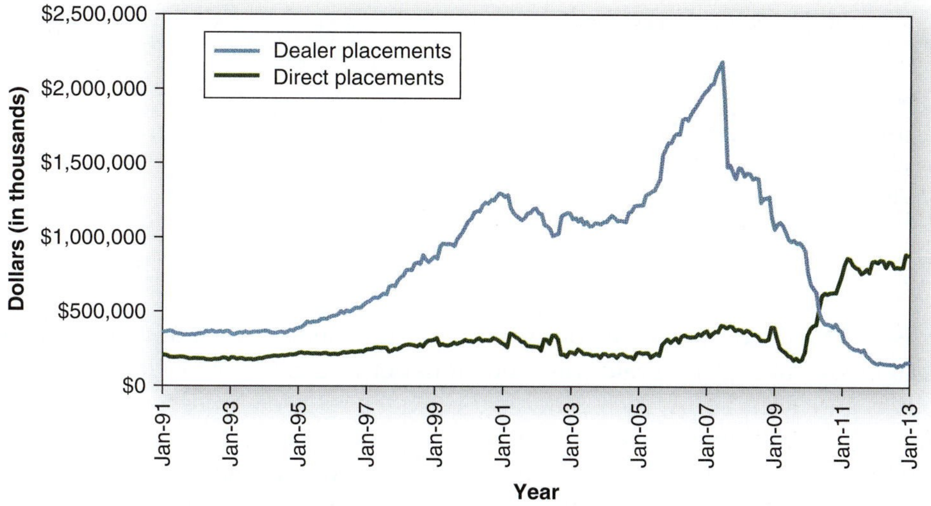

Direct versus Dealer Placements of Commercial Paper

A huge price spread between direct purchases of commercial paper and purchases through dealers or brokers occurred during the financial crisis of 2008 and 2009.

these funds, the commercial paper market shrank by $52.1 billion. In response to the commercial paper crisis, the Federal Reserve Board announced the creation of the Commercial Paper Funding Facility (CPFF), a facility that complemented the Federal Reserve's existing credit facilities to help provide liquidity to short-term funding markets.

LG18-4

Trading Process for Commercial Paper Commercial paper is sold to investors either directly (about 84 percent of all issues in 2013—see Figure 18.3), using the issuers' own sales force (e.g., GMAC), or indirectly through brokers and dealers (about 16 percent of all issues in 2013), such as commercial banks and investment banks underwriting the issues. Commercial paper underwritten and issued through brokers and dealers is more expensive to the issuer, usually increasing the cost of the issue by $\frac{1}{10}$ to $\frac{1}{8}$ of a percent, reflecting an underwriting cost. In return, the dealer guarantees the sale of the whole issue. To help achieve this goal, the dealer contacts prospective buyers of the commercial paper, determines the appropriate discount rate on the commercial paper, and relays any special requests in terms of specific quantities and maturities to the issuer. If a potential investor (such as a money market mutual fund) issues commercial paper through a dealer and makes a request at the beginning of the day for a particular maturity, the request is often completed by the end of the day.

When a firm issues commercial paper directly to a buyer, the company saves the cost of the dealer (and the underwriting services). This became the dominant method of commercial paper placement in 2010. However, with a direct placement, the issuing firm must find appropriate investors and determine the appropriate discount rate that will place the complete paper issue. When the firm decides how much commercial paper it wants to issue, it posts offering rates to potential buyers based on its own estimates of investor demand. The firm then monitors the flow of money during the day and adjusts its commercial paper rates depending on investor demand.

Because commercial paper is unsecured debt, the issuing company's credit rating is of particular importance in determining how marketable a commercial paper issue will be. Credit ratings provide potential investors with information regarding the ability of the issuing firm to repay the borrowed funds as

table 18.1 **Commercial Paper Credit Ratings as Assigned by Major Rating Agencies**

	Moody's	S&P	Fitch
Superior	P1	A1+ or A1	F1+ or F1
Satisfactory	P2	A2	F2
Adequate	P3	A3	F3
Speculative	NP	B or C	F4
Defaulted	NP	D	F5

promised and to compare the commercial paper issues of different companies. Several credit rating firms rate commercial paper issues (e.g., Standard & Poor's, Moody's, and Fitch ICBA, Inc.). Standard & Poor's rates commercial paper from A1 for highest quality issues to D for lowest quality issues, Moody's rates commercial paper from P1 for highest quality issues to "NP, not prime," for lowest quality issues, and Fitch rates issues from F1 to F5. Table 18.1 summarizes the credit ratings assigned to commercial paper by Standard & Poor's, Moody's, and Fitch. Only the top three of the five categories are relevant because issuers usually will not attempt to market lower grade commercial paper. Virtually all companies that issue commercial paper obtain ratings from at least one rating services company, and most obtain two rating evaluations. The better the credit rating on a commercial paper issue, the lower the interest rate (or discount from par) on the issue.

Commercial paper issuers with lower than prime credit ratings often back their commercial paper issues with lines of credit from commercial banks. In these cases, banks agree to make the promised payment on the commercial paper if the issuer cannot pay off the debt at maturity. Thus, a letter of credit backing commercial paper effectively substitutes the credit rating of the issuing firm with the credit rating of the bank. This reduces the paper purchasers' risk and results in a lower interest rate (and higher credit rating) on the commercial paper.

LONG-TERM DEBT As Chapter 7 described in detail, corporate bonds are long-term debt securities issued by public corporations ($10,754.6 billion outstanding in 2013; approximately 22 percent of all outstanding long-term bonds). The minimum denomination on publicly traded corporate bonds is $1,000, and coupon-paying corporate bonds generally pay interest semiannually.

LG18-4 **The Trading Process for Corporate Bonds** The initial or primary sale of corporate bond issues occurs either through a public offering, using an investment bank serving as a security underwriter, or through a private placement to a small group of investors (often financial institutions). Generally, when a firm issues bonds to the public, many investment banks are interested in underwriting the bonds. The bonds can generally be sold in a national market. Total dollar volume of new debt issues was $1,240.3 billion in 2012, up from $748.0 billion in 2011. Table 18.2 lists the activity of the top 10 bond underwriters in 2012. Most bonds issued by smaller firms are underwritten by small regional investment banks located in the immediate area of the municipal issuer (e.g., Bernardi Securities located in Chicago). The high cost of gathering information about smaller corporate bond issuers limits smaller investors' interest in the sales of these issues.

Most often, corporate bonds are offered publicly through investment banking firms acting as underwriters. Normally, the investment bank facilitates this

table 18.2 | **Top Underwriters of Domestic Debt (in billions of dollars)**

Manager	Amount	2012 Market Share	Number of Deals	2011 Market Share
JPMorgan	$149.6	15.0%	485	15.4%
Bank of America Merrill Lynch	110.8	11.1	416	12.6
Citigroup	104.7	10.5	386	9.9
Morgan Stanley	80.7	8.1	272	8.3
Goldman Sachs	70.7	7.1	223	8.2
Barclays Capital	68.6	6.9	251	7.6
Deutsche Bank AG	54.9	5.5	207	5.5
Wells Fargo	54.8	5.5	239	3.9
Royal Bank of Scotland Group	39.9	4.0	150	4.6
HSBC Holdings	39.2	3.9	124	4.0
Top ten total	$773.9	77.6%	2,753	80.0%
Industry total	$999.5	100.0%	1,129	$748.0

Source: Thomson Reuters website 2013. www.thompsonreuters.com

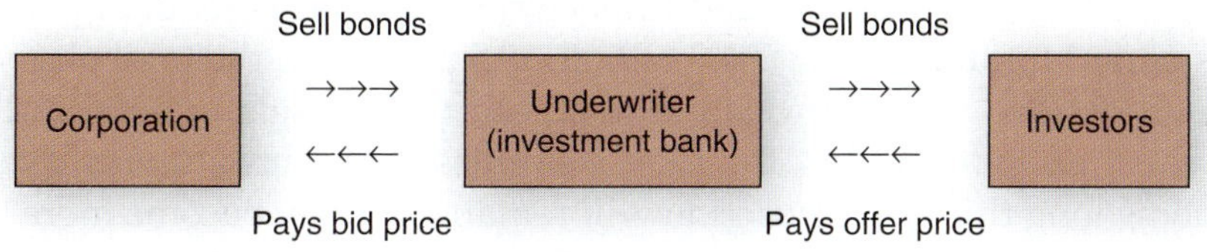

figure 18.4

Firm Commitment Underwriting of a Corporate Bond Issue

Two-way arrows show the interdependence between participants.

transaction using a **firm commitment underwriting,** illustrated in Figure 18.4. The investment bank guarantees the firm a price for newly issued bonds by buying the whole issue at a fixed price from the bond-issuing firm at a discount from par. The investment bank then seeks to resell these securities to investors at a higher price. As a result, the investment bank takes a risk that it may not be able to resell the securities to investors at a higher price. This may occur if a firm's bond value suddenly falls due to an unexpected change in interest rates or negative information being released about the issuing firm. If this occurs, the investment bank takes a loss on its security underwriting. However, the bond *issuer* is protected by being able to sell the whole issue.

firm commitment underwriting

A security issue in which the investment bank guarantees the issuer a price for newly issued securities by buying the whole issue at a fixed price from the security issuer (the bid price). The investment bank then seeks to resell the securities to investors at a higher price (the offer price).

The investment bank can purchase the bonds through competitive bidding against other investment bankers or by directly negotiating with the issuer. In a **competitive sale,** the bond-issuing firm invites bids from a number of underwriters. The investment bank that submits the highest bid to the bond issuer wins the bid. The underwriter may use a syndicate of other underwriters and investment banks to distribute (sell) the issue to the public. With a **negotiated sale,** a single investment bank obtains the exclusive right to originate, underwrite, and distribute the new bonds through a one-on-one negotiation process. With a negotiated sale, the investment bank provides the origination and advising services to the issuers.

competitive sale

A sale of securities in which the issuing firm invites bids from a number of underwriters. The investment bank that submits the highest bid to the issuer wins the bid. The winning bid underwriter then distributes (sells) the issue to the public.

Some corporate securities are offered on a **best efforts underwriting** basis, in which the underwriter does not guarantee a firm price to the issuer (as with a firm commitment offering). Here, the underwriter acts more as a placing or distribution agent for a fee. Unlike firm commitment underwriting, with best efforts underwriting, the investment bank incurs no risk of mispricing the security since it simply seeks to sell the securities at the best market price it can get for the issuing firm.

negotiated sale

A sale of securities in which the investment bank obtains the exclusive right to originate, underwrite, and distribute the new securities through a one-on-one negotiation process. With a negotiated sale, the investment bank provides the origination and advising services to the issuers.

best efforts underwriting

A security issue in which the underwriter does not guarantee a firm price to the issuer (as with a firm commitment offering) and acts more as a placing or distribution agent for a fee.

In a private placement, a public firm (sometimes with an investment bank's help) seeks to find a large institutional buyer or group of buyers (usually fewer than 10) to purchase the whole issue. To protect smaller individual investors against a lack of disclosure, the Securities Exchange Act of 1934 requires publicly traded securities to be registered with the Securities and Exchange Commission (SEC). Private placements, on the other hand, can be unregistered and can only be resold to large, financially sophisticated investors. These large investors supposedly possess the resources and expertise to analyze a security's risk.

Privately placed bonds (and stocks) have traditionally been among the most illiquid securities, with only the very largest financial institutions or institutional investors being able or willing to buy and hold them without an active secondary market. In April 1990, however, the Securities and Exchange Commission (SEC) amended its Regulation 144A. The amendment allowed large investors to begin trading privately placed securities among themselves even though, in general, privately placed securities do not satisfy the stringent disclosure and informational requirements that the SEC imposes on approved publicly registered issues. Rule 144A private placements may now be underwritten by investment banks on a firm commitment basis. Of the total $960.8 billion in private debt and equity placements in 2012, $896.2 billion (93 percent) were Rule 144A placements. JPMorgan was the lead underwriter of Rule 144A debt placements over this period (underwriting $94.0 billion, 10.5 percent of the total placements).

The SEC defined "large investors" as those with assets of $100 million or more—which excludes all but the very wealthiest household savers. We might well ask how long this size restriction will remain. As they become more sophisticated and information acquisition costs fall, savers will increasingly demand access to the private placement market. In such a world, savers would have a choice not only between the secondary securities from financial institutions and the primary securities publicly offered by public firms, but also between publicly offered (registered) securities and privately offered (unregistered) securities.

The secondary market for corporate bonds is thin (i.e., trades are relatively infrequent). Thin trading is mainly a result of a lack of information on bond issuers, as well as special features (such as covenants) that are built into those bonds' contracts. Information on corporate bond issuers (particularly smaller firms) is generally more costly to obtain and evaluate, although this is in part offset by bond rating agencies (see Chapter 7).

Equity Financing

Public firms can also issue corporate stock or equity as another major source of capital financing. As Chapter 8 described in detail, corporate stock represents ownership shares in a public corporation. In exchange for funds, the firm gives the stockholders ownership rights in the firm, as well as cash flows in the form of dividends. Further, common stockholders have voting privileges on major issues in the firm, such as the election of the board of directors, which oversees the day-to-day operations of the firm.

Before a corporation can issue common stock, a majority of both the board of directors and the firm's existing common stockholders must authorize the sale of shares. In the 1990s, the market value of corporate stock outstanding increased faster than any other type of financial security. From 1994 through 2000, stock values increased over 200 percent, from $6,333.3 billion to $19,522.8 billion outstanding. A slow U.S. economy saw market values fall to a low of $11,900.5 billion at the end of 2002, but by 2007 stock market values had rebounded to $25,577.3 billion. The period of the financial crisis and the worldwide recession saw equity values fall 45 percent, to $13,965.7 billion, in March 2009 before rebounding to

figure 18.5

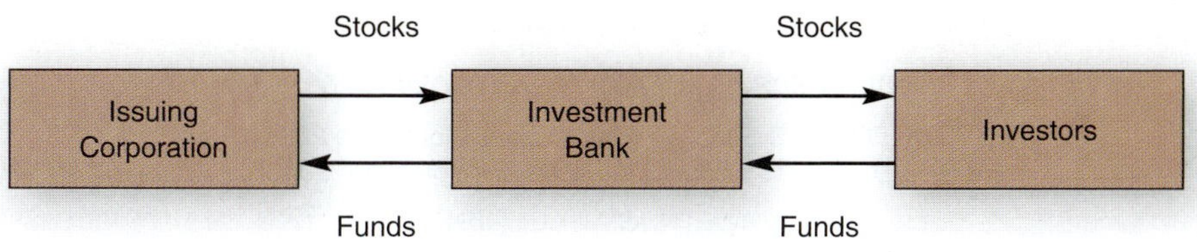

Primary Market Stock Transaction
Investment banks are intermediaries between fund users and fund suppliers.

table 18.3 | **Top Underwriters of Domestic Equity (in billions of dollars)**

Manager	Amount	2012 Market Share	Number of Deals	2011 Market Share
Citigroup	$30.4	12.4%	201	10.4%
Bank of America Merrill Lynch	27.3	11.2	203	11.2
Goldman Sachs	26.1	10.7	148	11.3
Barclays Capital	25.9	10.6	160	8.6
JPMorgan	25.6	10.5	191	12.5
Morgan Stanley	25.4	10.4	156	10.7
Credit Suisse	19.2	7.8	150	8.2
Deutsche Bank AG	18.6	7.6	144	6.4
UBS	10.6	4.3	107	5.3
Wells Fargo	10.3	4.2	126	4.6
Top ten total	$219.4	89.7	1,586	89.2%
Industry total	$244.5	100.0%	795	$182.0

Source: Thomson Reuters website 2013. www.thompsonreuters.com

$20,008.5 at the end of that year. Equity values finally surpassed their pre-crisis levels in 2012, rising to $25,905.9 by year's end.

LG18-4

THE TRADING PROCESS FOR CORPORATE EQUITY **Primary markets** are markets in which corporations raise funds through *new* stock issues. Initial investors (fund suppliers) buy new stock securities in exchange for funds (money) that the issuer (user of funds) needs. A primary market sale may be a first-time issue by a private firm going public (i.e., an IPO). Alternatively, a primary market sale may be a seasoned offering, in which the firm already has shares of the stock trading in the secondary markets. In both cases, the issuer receives the sale proceeds and the primary market investors receive the securities.

primary markets
Markets in which corporations raise funds through *new* issues of securities.

As illustrated in Figure 18.5, most primary securities market transactions go through investment banks (e.g., Goldman Sachs or Morgan Stanley), which serve as intermediaries between the issuing firms (fund users) and ultimate investors (fund suppliers). Total dollar volume of new equity issues was $244.5 billion in 2012, up from $182.0 billion in 2011. Table 18.3 lists the activity of the top 10 equity underwriters in 2012.

As with the primary sales of bonds (discussed previously), investment banks can conduct a primary sale of stock using a firm commitment underwriting or on a best efforts underwriting basis. In a firm commitment underwriting, the investment bank purchases stock from the issuing firm for a guaranteed price (called the bid price or **net proceeds**) and resells the stock to investors at a higher price (called the offer price or **gross proceeds**). The difference between the gross proceeds and the net proceeds on an issue (called the **underwriter's spread**) is compensation for the expenses and risks incurred by the investment bank. In the 2000s, underwriter's gross spread on first-time equity issues

net proceeds
The guaranteed price at which the investment bank purchases the stock from the issuing firm in a firm commitment underwriting.

gross proceeds
The higher price at which the investment bank resells the stock to investors in a firm commitment underwriting.

underwriter's spread
The difference between the gross proceeds and the net proceeds.

figure 18.6

Debt Issue Announcement

This debt issue announcement clearly spells out all details and serves as a reference point.

New Issue of Debt

VIRGINIA ELECTRIC AND POWER COMPANY

$250,000,000 2013 Series A 1.20% Senior Notes due 2018
$500,000,000 2013 Series B 4.0% Senior Notes due 2043

UNDERWRITING AGREEMENT

January 3, 2013

Pricing Term Sheet

Title of Senior Notes:

- 2013 Series A 1.20% Senior Notes due 2018
- 2013 Series B 4.0% Senior Notes due 2043

Aggregate Principal Amount:

- Series A Senior Notes: $250,000,000
- Series B Senior Notes: $500,000,000

Initial Price to Public:

- Series A Senior Notes: 99.738% of the principal amount of the Series A Senior Notes plus accrued interest, if any, from the date of issuance
- Series B Senior Notes: 99.600% of the principal amount of the Series B Senior Notes plus accrued interest, if any, from the date of issuance

Initial Purchase Price to be paid by Underwriters:

- Series A Senior Notes: 99.138% of the principal amount of the Series A Senior Notes
- Series B Senior Notes: 98.725% of the principal amount of the Series B Senior Notes

Time of Delivery: January 8, 2013, 10:00 A.M.

Closing Location: One James Center
901 East Cary Street
Richmond, Virginia 23219

The Senior Notes will be available for inspection by the Representatives at:

One James Center
901 East Cary Street
Richmond, Virginia 23219

Underwriter	Principal Amount of Series A Senior Notes to be Purchased	Principal Amount of Series B Senior Notes to be Purchased
Citigroup Global Markets Inc.	$ 62,500,000	$ 125,000,000
Goldman, Sachs & Co.	$ 62,500,000	$ 125,000,000
Merrill Lynch, Pierce, Fenner & Smith Incorporated	$ 62,500,000	$ 125,000,000
Scotia Capital (USA) Inc.	$ 62,500,000	$ 125,000,000
Total:	$ 250,000,000	$ 500,000,000

(i.e., private firms going public—the initial public offering, or IPO) averaged 7.23 percent and on seasoned equity issues (i.e., publicly traded firms issuing additional shares) averaged 4.86 percent.

EXAMPLE 18-2

LG18-4

For interactive versions of this example visit www.mhhe.com/can3e

Calculating Costs of Issuing Stock

Renee's, Inc., needs to raise $100 million to finance firm expansion. In discussions with its investment bank, Renee's learns that the bankers recommend a gross proceeds price of $40 per share, and they will charge an underwriter's spread of 6.5 percent of the gross price.

Calculate the net proceeds to Renee's from the sale of stock. How many shares of stock will Renee's need to sell in order to receive the $100 million needed?

SOLUTION:

$$\text{Net proceeds} = \text{Gross proceeds} - \text{Underwriter's spread}$$
$$= \$40 - (0.065 \times \$40) = \$37.40$$
$$\text{Funds needed} = \$100 \text{ million} = \$37.40 \times \text{Number of shares sold}$$
$$\text{Number of shares sold} = \$100 \text{ million}/\$37.40 = 2{,}673{,}797 \text{ shares}$$

Similar to Problems 18-3, 18-4, self-test problem 2

figure 18.7

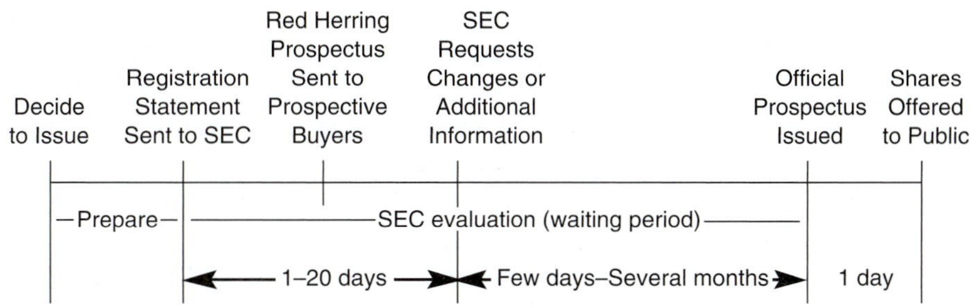

Getting Shares of Stock to the Investing Public

Steps in the process of issuing shares to the public must pass through an SEC evaluation period.

Often, investment banks will bring in a number of other investment banks to help sell and distribute a new security issue. Such a group of sellers is called a **syndicate.** For example, Figure 18.6 describes the offering of two issues of senior debt by Virginia Electric and Power Company, including a list of the syndicate of four investment banks involved in the initial issue. The investment banks are listed according to their degree of participation in new share sales. The lead bank(s) in the syndicate (Citigroup Global Markets), who directly negotiate with the issuing firm on behalf of the syndicate, are called the **originating house(s).** Once an issue is arranged and its terms set, each syndicate member is assigned a given number of shares in the issue it is responsible for selling. Shares of stock issued through a syndicate of investment banks spread the risk associated with the stock sale among several investment banks. A syndicate also results in a larger pool of potential outside investors, widening the scope of the investor base and increasing the probability of a successful sale.

syndicate
The group of investment banks used to help sell and distribute a new security issue.

originating house(s)
The lead bank(s) in a syndicate, who directly negotiate with the issuing firm on behalf of the syndicate.

Just as with primary sales of corporate bond issues, firms may initially issue corporate stocks through public sales (wherein the stock issue is offered to the general investing public). New stock issues may also be sold by private placement (wherein stock is sold privately to a limited number of large investors). In a public sale of stock, once the issuing firm and the investment bank have agreed on the stock issue details, the investment bank must get SEC approval in accordance with the Securities Exchange Act of 1934. Stock registration can be a lengthy process. We illustrate the process in Figure 18.7. The process starts with the preparation of the registration statement to be filed with the SEC. The registration statement includes:

- Information about the issuing firm's business.
- The key provisions and features of the security to be issued.
- The risks involved with the security.
- Managements' background.

figure 18.8

Getting Shelf Registrations to the Investing Public

The process of getting shelf registrations to the public can occur over two years.

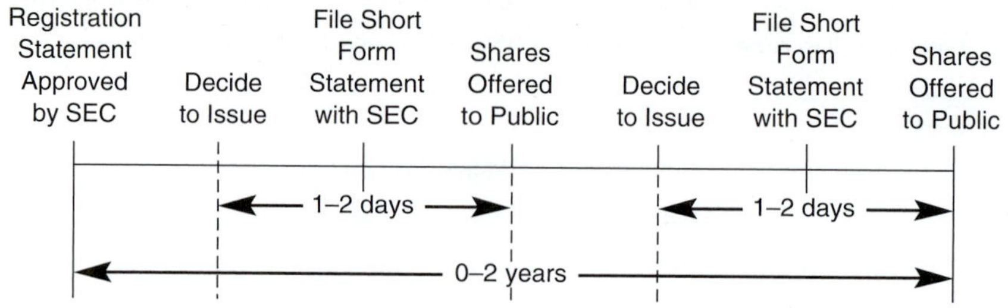

red herring prospectus

A preliminary registration statement filed with the SEC.

prospectus

Official document in which the issuing firm (along with its investment bankers) sets the final selling price on the securities and describes the issue.

shelf registration

A method of registering securities that allows firms that plan to offer multiple issues of the security over a two-year period to submit one registration statement.

The focus of the registration statement is to fully disclose information about the firm and the securities issued to the public at large. At the same time that the issuing firm and its investment bank prepare the registration statement to be filed with the SEC, they must also prepare a preliminary version of the public offering's prospectus called the **red herring prospectus.** The red herring prospectus is similar to the registration statement, but is distributed to potential equity buyers. Once the SEC registers the issue, the red herring prospectus is replaced with the official or final prospectus.

After the firm submits the registration statement, the SEC has 20 days to request additional information or changes to the registration statement. This review period is called the waiting period, during which the SEC works through the new security issue approval process. First-time or infrequent issuers can sometimes wait up to several months for SEC registration, especially if the SEC keeps requesting additional information and revised red herring prospectuses. However, companies that know the registration process well can generally obtain registration in a few days.

Once the SEC is satisfied with the registration statement, it registers the issue. At this point, the issuing firm (along with its investment bankers) sets the final share selling price, prints the official **prospectus** describing the issue, and sends it to all potential buyers of the issue. Upon issuance of the prospectus (generally the day following SEC registration), the firm may sell the shares.

To reduce registration time and costs, yet still protect the public by requiring issuers to disclose information about the firm and the security to be issued, the SEC passed a rule in 1982 allowing for "shelf registration." As illustrated in Figure 18.8, **shelf registration** allows firms that plan to offer multiple issues of stock over a two-year period to submit one registration statement as described above (called a *master registration statement*). The registration statement summarizes the firm's financing plans for the two-year period. Thus, the securities are shelved for up to two years until the firm is ready to issue them. Once the issuer and its investment bank decide to issue shares during the two-year shelf registration period, they prepare and file a short-form statement with the SEC. Upon SEC approval, the shares can be priced and offered to the public usually within one or two days of deciding to take the shares "off the shelf."

Thus, shelf registration allows a firm to get stocks into the market quickly (e.g., in one or two days) if the firm feels conditions (especially the price it can get for the new stock) are right, without the time lag generally associated with full SEC registration. For example, in March 2013, Two Harbors Investment Corp. announced a public offering of 50 million shares of its common stock under its shelf registration filed with the SEC. Credit Suisse Securities led the underwriting of shares that were sold just days after this announcement.

TIME OUT

18-3 What sources of debt and equity financing are available to public firms?

18-4 What is the difference between a public firm's commercial paper and its long-term debt?

viewpoints REVISITED

Business Application Solution

Because ADK Industries is a publicly traded firm, the managers need to consider several factors as they decide how to finance the $5 million needed for firm expansion. The first issue managers must consider is whether to finance the $5 million with debt, equity, or a combination of the two forms of capital. Public firms obtain debt financing in two major ways: commercial paper and corporate bonds. Commercial paper is sold to investors either directly or indirectly through brokers and dealers. The initial or primary corporate bond issue sales occur either through a public offering, using an investment bank serving as a security underwriter, or through a private placement to small groups of investors. ADK Industries could also raise capital by selling corporate stock or equity. Like the primary sale of corporate bonds, corporate stocks may initially be issued through either a public sale or a private placement. In a public sale of stock, once the issuing firm and the investment bank have agreed on the details of the stock issue, the investment bank must get SEC approval in accordance with the Securities Exchange Act of 1934.

Personal Application Solution

Marge Upton has to consider several issues as she seeks to find the $15,000 she needs to reopen her bicycle repair shop. Marge will want to consider borrowing funds from private or public sources. Private debt financing includes capital funds borrowed from personal savings, friends or relatives, financial institutions such as commercial bank loans, or venture capitalists. Private equity financing includes capital funds invested by venture capitalists. Public sources of capital include debt and equity financing provided by government agencies such as the U.S. Small Business Administration (SBA).

summary of learning goals

This chapter presented an overview of the decisions firms face when they raise capital. The chapter noted the important role that financial institutions play in this process.

LG18-1 Evaluate different methods for small firms to get funding. Most new and small firms finance their assets by borrowing funds from private or public sources. Private debt financing includes capital funds borrowed from friends or relatives, financial institutions such as commercial bank loans, or venture capitalists. Private equity financing includes capital funds invested by venture capitalists. Public sources of capital include debt and equity financing provided by government agencies such as the U.S. Small Business Administration.

LG18-2 Appreciate what venture capital is and how it encourages entrepreneurship. Venture capital is a professionally managed pool of money used to finance new and often high-risk firms. Venture capital is generally provided by investment institutions or private individuals willing to back an untried company and its managers in return for an equity investment in the firm.

LG18-3 Differentiate among sources of capital funding for public firms. The initial or primary sale of corporate bond or stock issues occurs through either a public offering or a private placement. In a public offering, an investment bank facilitates this transfer using a firm commitment underwriting. The investment bank guarantees the firm a price for newly issued bonds or stock by buying the whole issue at a fixed price from the issuing firm. The investment bank then seeks to resell these securities to investors at a higher price. In a private placement, the issuing firm seeks to find a large institutional buyer to purchase the whole issue.

LG18-4 Trace the process by which securities are underwritten. The process starts with the preparation of the registration statement to be filed with the SEC. At the same time that the issuing firm and its investment bank prepare the registration statement to be filed, they must also prepare a preliminary version of the public offering's prospectus, called the red herring prospectus. Once the SEC registers the issue, the red herring prospectus is replaced with the official or final prospectus. After the firm submits the registration statement, the SEC has 20 days to request additional information or changes to the registration statement. This review period is called the waiting period, during which the SEC works through the new security issue approval process. Once the SEC is satisfied with the registration statement, it registers the issue. At this point, the issuing firm (along with its investment bankers) sets the final share selling price, prints the official prospectus describing the issue, and sends it to all potential buyers of the issue. Upon issuance of the prospectus (generally the day following SEC registration), the firm may sell the shares.

key terms

angel venture capitalists (or **angels**), Wealthy individuals who make equity investments. *p. 608*

back-end (or **commitment**) **fee,** A fee charged by a bank on any unused balances of a loan commitment line at the end of the loan commitment period. *p. 606*

best efforts underwriting, A security issue in which the underwriter does not guarantee a firm price to the issuer (as with a firm commitment offering) and acts more as a placing or distribution agent for a fee. *p. 615*

commercial paper, An unsecured short-term promissory note issued by a public firm to raise short-term cash, often to finance working capital requirements. *p. 612*

competitive sale, A sale of securities in which the issuing firm invites bids from a number of underwriters. The investment bank that submits the highest bid to the issuer wins the bid. The winning bid underwriter then distributes (sells) the issue to the public. *p. 615*

firm commitment underwriting, A security issue in which the investment bank guarantees the issuer a price for newly issued securities by buying the whole issue at a fixed price from the security issuer (the bid price). The investment bank then seeks to resell the securities to investors at a higher price (the offer price). *p. 615*

fixed-rate loan, A loan on which the interest payments the firm must make cannot change over the life of the loan. *p. 607*

gross proceeds, The higher price at which the investment bank resells the stock to investors in a firm commitment underwriting. *p. 617*

initial public offerings (IPO), A first-time issue of stock by a private firm going public (e.g., allowing its equity, some of which was held privately by managers and venture capital investors, to be *publicly* traded in stock markets for the first time). *p. 609*

institutional venture capital firms, Business entities whose sole purpose is to find and fund the most promising new firms. *p. 608*

loan commitment agreement, A contractual commitment by a bank to loan a firm a certain maximum amount at given interest rate terms for a stated length of time over which the firm has the option to take down this loan. *p. 606*

negotiated sale, A sale of securities in which the investment bank obtains the exclusive right to originate, underwrite, and distribute the new securities through a one-on-one negotiation process. With a negotiated sale, the investment bank provides the origination and advising services to the issuers. *p. 615*

net proceeds, The guaranteed price at which the investment bank purchases the stock from the issuing firm in a firm commitment underwriting. *p. 617*

originating house(s), The lead bank(s) in a syndicate, who directly negotiate with the issuing firm on behalf of the syndicate. *p. 619*

primary markets, Markets in which corporations raise funds through *new* issues of securities. *p. 617*

prospectus, Official document in which the issuing firm (along with its investment bankers) sets the final selling price on the securities and describes the issue. *p. 620*

red herring prospectus, A preliminary registration statement filed with the SEC. *p. 620*

shelf registration, A method of registering securities that allows firms that plan to offer multiple issues of the security over a two-year period to submit one registration statement. *p. 620*

spot loan, A loan in which the firm receives the funds as soon as the loan is approved. *p. 606*

syndicate, The group of investment banks used to help sell and distribute a new security issue. *p. 619*

take down, Borrowing against a line of credit or loan commitment. *p. 606*

underwriter's spread, The difference between the gross proceeds and the net proceeds. *p. 617*

up-front (or facility) fee, A fee charged by a bank for making funds available through a loan commitment. *p. 606*

variable-rate loan, A loan on which the interest rate on the loan (and thus the interest payments the firm must make) can change over the life of the loan. *p. 607*

venture capital, A professionally managed pool of money used to finance new and often high-risk firms. *p. 608*

venture capital firms, Organizations that purchase equity interests in firms and have the same rights and privileges as other owners of equity investments. *p. 604*

self-test problems with solutions

1 Calculating Fees on a Loan Commitment Sandy's Bed and Breakfast has been approved for a $125,000 loan commitment from its local bank. The bank has offered the following terms: term = one year, up-front fee = 45 basis points, back-end fee = 65 basis points, and rate on the loan = 8.25 percent. Sandy's expects to immediately take down $110,000 and no more during the year unless there is some unforeseen need. Calculate the total interest and fees Sandy's Bed and Breakfast can expect to pay on this loan commitment.

LG18-1

Solution:

Up-front fee	= $125,000 × 0.0045	= $ 562.50
Back-end fee	= ($125,000 − $110,000) × 0.0065	= 97.50
Interest	= $110,000 × 0.0825	= 9,075.00
Total		= $9,735.00

2 Calculating Costs of Issuing Stock Jerry's Bait & Tackle Corp. recently went public with an initial public offering of 3.75 million shares of stock. The underwriter used a firm commitment offering in which the net proceeds were $13.875 per share and the underwriter's spread was 7.5 percent of the gross proceeds. Jerry's also paid legal and other administrative costs of $850,000 for the IPO. Calculate the gross proceeds and the total funds received by Jerry's Bait & Tackle Corp. from the sale of the 3.75 million shares of stock.

LG18-4

Solution:

$$\text{Net proceeds} = \$13.875 = \text{Gross proceeds} - \text{Underwriter's spread}$$
$$= \text{Gross proceeds} - (0.075 \times \text{Gross proceeds})$$
$$= (1 - 0.075) \times \text{Gross proceeds}$$
$$\text{Gross proceeds} = \$13.875/(1 - 0.075) = \$15.00$$

$$\text{Total funds received by Jerry's Bait \& Tackle} = (\$13.875 \times 3{,}750{,}000) - \$850{,}000$$
$$= \$51{,}181{,}250$$

questions

1. Describe the various sources of capital funding available to new and small firms. *(LG18-1)*
2. What processes do banks use to evaluate bank loans to small versus midmarket business firms? *(LG18-1)*
3. What is the difference between a spot loan and a loan commitment? *(LG18-1)*
4. Why do banks charge up-front fees and back-end fees on loan commitments? *(LG18-1)*
5. What is the difference between a fixed-rate and a floating-rate loan? *(LG18-1)*
6. What types of programs does the Small Business Administration offer to new and small businesses? Under what conditions would a new or small firm use each program? *(LG18-1)*
7. What is venture capital? *(LG18-2)*
8. What are the different types of venture capital firms? How do institutional venture capital firms differ from angel venture capital firms? *(LG18-2)*
9. What are the advantages and disadvantages to a new or small firm of getting capital funding from a venture capital firm? *(LG18-2)*
10. As a new or small firm considers going public what must the owners consider? *(LG18-1)*
11. Describe the various sources of capital funding available to public firms. *(LG18-3)*
12. What is the difference between a direct and an indirect placement of commercial paper? *(LG18-3)*
13. Can a public firm with a lower-than-prime credit rating issue commercial paper? *(LG18-3)*
14. How does a best efforts underwriting differ from a firm commitment underwriting? If you operated a company issuing stock for the first time, which type of underwriting would you prefer? Why might you still choose the alternative? *(LG18-4)*
15. How does a competitive sale of corporate bonds differ from a negotiated sale? Which type of underwriting would you prefer? Why might you still choose the alternative? *(LG18-4)*
16. How does a public offering of debt or equity securities issued by a public firm differ from a private placement? *(LG18-4)*

17. What are the net proceeds, gross proceeds, and underwriter's spread? How does each affect the funds received by a public firm when debt or equity securities are issued? *(LG18-4)*

18. Why would an investment bank use a syndicate to assist in underwriting debt or equity securities? *(LG18-4)*

19. What is the difference between a prospectus and a red herring prospectus? *(LG18-4)*

20. What is a shelf registration? Why would a public firm want to issue securities using a shelf registration? *(LG18-4)*

problems

basic problems

18-1 Calculating Fees on a Loan Commitment You have approached your local bank for a start-up loan commitment for $250,000 needed to open a computer repair store. You have requested that the term of the loan be one year. Your bank has offered you the following terms: size of loan commitment = $250,000, term = one year, up-front fee = 50 basis points, back-end fee = 75 basis points. If you take down 80 percent of the total loan commitment, calculate the total fees you will pay on this loan commitment. *(LG18-1)*

18-2 Calculating Fees on a Loan Commitment Calculate the total fees a firm would have to pay when its bank offers the firm the following loan commitment: A loan commitment of $4.25 million with an up-front fee of 75 basis points and a back-end fee of 25 basis points. The take down on the loan is 50 percent. *(LG18-1)*

18-3 Calculating Costs of Issuing Stock Husker's Tuxedo's, Inc., needs to raise $250 million to finance its plan for nationwide expansion. In discussions with its investment bank, Husker's learns that the bankers recommend an offer price (or gross price) of $35 per share and they will charge an underwriter's spread of $1.75 per share. Calculate the net proceeds to Husker's from the sale of stock. How many shares of stock will Husker's need to sell in order to receive the $250 million needed? *(LG18-4)*

18-4 Calculating Costs of Issuing Stock Don's Captain Morgan, Inc., needs to raise $12.5 million to finance plant expansion. In discussions with its investment bank, Don's learns that the bankers recommend an offer price (or gross proceeds) of $25.50 per share and Don's will receive $23.75 per share. Calculate the underwriter's spread on the issue. How many shares of stock will Don's need to sell in order to receive the $12.5 million it needs? *(LG18-4)*

18-5 Calculating Costs of Issuing Debt The Fitness Studio, Inc., with the help of its investment bank, recently issued $43.125 million of new debt. The offer price (and face value) on the debt was $1,000 per bond and the underwriter's spread was 7 percent of the gross proceeds. Calculate the amount of capital funding The Fitness Studio raised through this debt offering. *(LG18-4)*

18-6 Calculating Costs of Issuing Debt Harper's Dog Pens, Inc., with the help of its investment bank, recently issued $191.5 million of new debt. The offer price on the debt was $1,000 per bond and the underwriter's spread was 5 percent of the gross proceeds. Calculate the amount of capital funding Harper's Dog Pens raised through this bond issue. *(LG18-4)*

intermediate problems

18-7 **Calculating Fees on a Loan Commitment** You have approached your local bank for a start-up loan commitment for $250,000 needed to open a computer repair store. You have requested that the term of the loan be one year. Your bank has offered you the following terms: size of loan commitment = $250,000, term = one year, up-front fee = 50 basis points, back-end fee = 75 basis points, and rate on the loan = 8 percent. If you immediately take down $150,000 and no more during the year, calculate the total interest and fees you will pay on this loan commitment. *(LG18-1)*

18-8 **Calculating Fees on a Loan Commitment** Casey's One Stop has been approved for a $127,500 loan commitment from its local bank. The bank has offered the following terms: term = one year, up-front fee = 85 basis points, back-end fee = 35 basis points, and rate on the loan = 7.75 percent. Casey's expects to immediately take down $119,000 and no more during the year unless there is some unforeseen need. Calculate the total interest and fees Casey's One Stop can expect to pay on this loan commitment. *(LG18-1)*

18-9 **Calculating Costs of Issuing Debt** DiPitro's Paint and Wallpaper, Inc., needs to raise $1 million to finance plant expansion. In discussions with its investment bank, DiPitro's learns that the bankers recommend a debt issue with gross proceeds of $1,000 per bond and they will charge an underwriter's spread of 6.5 percent of the gross proceeds. How many bonds will DiPitro's Paint and Wallpaper need to sell in order to receive the $1 million it needs? *(LG18-4)*

18-10 **Calculating Costs of Issuing Debt** Renee's Boutique, Inc., needs to raise $58 million to finance firm expansion. In discussions with its investment bank, Renee's learns that the bankers recommend a debt issue with an offer price of $1,000 per bond and they will charge an underwriter's spread of 5 percent of the gross price. Calculate the net proceeds to Renee's from the sale of the debt. How many bonds will Renee's Boutique need to sell in order to receive the $58 million it needs? *(LG18-4)*

18-11 **Calculating Costs of Issuing Stock** The Fitness Studio, Inc., with the help of its investment bank, recently issued 2.5 million shares of new stock. The offer price on the stock was $20.50 per share and The Fitness Studio received a total of $48,687,500 through this stock offering. Calculate the net proceeds and the underwriter's spread on the stock offering. What percentage of the gross price is the investment bank charging The Fitness Studio for underwriting the stock issue? *(LG18-4)*

18-12 **Calculating Costs of Issuing Stock** Harper's Dog Pens, Inc., with the help of its investment bank, recently issued 8.5 million shares of new stock. The offer price on the stock was $12.00 per share and Harper's received a total of $97.75 million from the stock offering. Calculate the net proceeds and the underwriter's spread charged by the underwriter to Harper's Dog Pens, Inc. What percentage of the gross proceeds is the investment bank charging Harper's Dog Pens for underwriting the stock issue? *(LG18-4)*

18-13 **Calculating Costs of Issuing Stock** Zimba Technology Corp. recently went public with an initial public offering of 2.5 million shares of stock. The underwriter used a firm commitment offering in which the net proceeds was $8.05 per share and the underwriter's spread was 8 percent of the gross proceeds. Zimba also paid legal and other administrative costs of $250,000 for the IPO. Calculate the gross proceeds and the total funds received by Zimba from the sale of the 2.5 million shares of stock. *(LG18-4)*

18-14 Calculating Costs of Issuing Stock Howett Pockett, Inc., plans to issue 10 million new shares of its stock. In discussions with its investment bank, Howett Pocket learns that the bankers recommend a net proceed of $33.80 per share and they will charge an underwriter's spread of 5.5 percent of the gross proceeds. In addition, Howett Pockett must pay $3.4 million in legal and other administrative expenses for the seasoned stock offering. Calculate the gross proceeds and the total funds received by Howett Pockett from the sale of the 10 million shares of stock. *(LG18-4)*

advanced problems

18-15 Calculating Fees on a Loan Commitment During the last year, you have had a loan commitment from your bank to fund inventory purchases for your small business. The total line available was $500,000, of which you took down $400,000. It is now the end of the loan commitment period and your bank had you pay the back-end fees. You have misplaced the paperwork that listed the terms of the commitment, but you know you paid total fees (this does not include any interest paid to borrow the $400,000) of $3,250 on this loan commitment. You remember that the up-front fee was 50 basis points. Calculate the back-end fee on this loan commitment. *(LG18-1)*

18-16 Calculating Fees on a Loan Commitment During the last year, you have had a loan commitment from your bank to fund working capital for your business. The total line available was $17 million, of which you took down $13 million. It is now the end of the loan commitment period and your bank had you pay the back-end fees. You have misplaced the paperwork that listed the terms of the commitment, but you know you paid total fees (this does not include any interest paid to borrow the $13 million) of $72,500 on this loan commitment. You remember that the back-end fee was 75 basis points. Calculate the up-front fee on this loan commitment. *(LG18-1)*

18-17 Calculating Costs of Issuing Stock DiPitro's Paint and Wallpaper, Inc., needs to raise $1 million to finance plant expansion. In discussions with its investment bank, DiPitro's learns that the bankers recommend a gross price of $25 per share and that 45,000 shares of stock be sold. If the net proceeds on the stock sale leaves DiPitro's with $1 million, calculate the underwriter's spread on the stock issue. *(LG18-4)*

18-18 Calculating Costs of Issuing Stock Renee's Boutique, Inc., needs to raise $58 million to finance firm expansion. In discussions with its investment bank, Renee's learns that the bankers recommend an offer price of $33.75 per share and that 1.8 million shares of stock be sold. If the net proceeds on the stock sale leaves Renee's with $58 million, calculate the underwriter's spread on the stock issue. *(LG18-4)*

18-19 Calculating Costs of Issuing Stock Hughes Technology Corp. recently went public with an initial public offering in which it received a total of $60 million in new capital funding. The underwriter used a firm commitment offering in which the offer price was $10 and the underwriter's spread was $0.75. Hughes also paid legal and other administrative costs of \$1.05 million for the IPO. Calculate the number of shares issued through this IPO. *(LG18-4)*

18-20 **Calculating Costs of Issuing Stock** Howett Pockett, Inc., needs to raise \$12 million in new capital funding from a seasoned equity offering. In discussions with its investment bank, Howett Pockett learns that the bankers recommend a gross price of \$13.50 per share and they will charge an underwriter's spread of \$1.00 per share. In addition, Howett Pockett must pay \$500,000 in legal and other administrative expenses for the seasoned stock offering. Calculate the number of shares of stock that Howett Pockett will need to sell to raise the \$12 million. *(LG18-4)*

research it! Underwriters

Go to the Thomson Financial—Investment Banking and Capital Markets Group website at **www.thomsonreuters.com/DealsIntelligence** and find the latest information available for debt and equity securities underwriting. Click on "QUARTERLY REVIEWS." Under "Select Category," select "Debt & Equity." Click on the latest quarter for "Global Equity Capital Markets." This will download a file onto your computer that will contain the most recent information on top underwriters for equity securities. Go back and repeat the last step, clicking on "Global Debt Capital Markets." What is the most recent dollar value of global debt and equity underwritten by investment banks? Who are the top underwriters of debt and equity? How have the top writers' market shares changed in the last year?

integrated mini-case Capital Funding in a Public Firm

Nuran Security Systems, Inc., needs to raise \$150 million for asset expansion. As it raises the capital funding, Nuran wants to maintain its current debt ratio of 60 percent. Nuran has been approved for a loan commitment from its local bank. The bank has offered the following terms: term = one year, up-front fee = 60 basis points, back-end fee = 90 basis points. Nuran expects it will take down 90 percent of the loan commitment.

Nuran's will also issue new shares of stock to support this asset growth. Nuran's investment bank will use a firm commitment offering in which the net proceeds are \$23.875 per share and the underwriter's spread is 7 percent of the gross proceeds. Nuran Security Systems will also pay legal and other administrative costs of \$750,000 for the stock issue.

Calculate the amount of debt and equity funding Nuran Security Systems will need to keep its current debt ratio constant and the number of shares of stock the firm must issue to raise the needed funds. What can Nuran Security Systems, Inc., expect to pay for fees on this loan commitment and stock issue?

ANSWERS TO TIME OUT

18-1 Most new and small firms finance their business assets by borrowing funds from private or public sources. Private capital fund suppliers fall into two basic categories: suppliers of debt financing and suppliers of equity financing. Debt financing includes capital funds borrowed from friends or relatives, financial institutions such as commercial bank loans, or venture capitalists. Equity financing includes capital funds invested by venture capitalists. Public sources of capital include debt and equity financing provided by government agencies such as the U.S. Small Business Administration (SBA).

18-2 Venture capital is a professionally managed pool of money used to finance new and often high-risk firms.

18-3 In contrast to small and new firms that can only get capital funding from mainly private sources, public firms raise the majority of their capital funds from public debt and equity markets. Public firms raise large amounts of short-term debt in the money market, primarily as commercial paper. Further, public firms raise long-term capital by issuing securities in the public debt and equity markets.

18-4 Commercial paper is short-term debt sold and traded in the money markets, while long-term debt is sold and traded in the capital markets.

PART NINE

19 International Corporate Finance

viewpoints

Business Application

A firm's CEO is investigating the possibility of building its first overseas production facility. As the financial manager, Andres must report on the financial risks of building a factory in Mexico.

Because the firm has experienced only domestic operations to date, the managers aren't familiar with the potential problems that conducting international operations entail. Andres must educate the other managers not only about these potential problems, but also about the additional steps in their capital budgeting process to account for the international aspects of this project. What topics does Andres need to address with the management team? **(See solution on p. 648)**

Personal Application

Juliana is studying at a U.S. university and has been accepted into a study abroad program for a semester in Switzerland. This program will begin in six months. She has been advised that she will probably spend $10,000 during the semester abroad.

Juliana will need to convert her dollars to Swiss francs (Switzerland is not a member of the EU and does not use the euro as its currency, in keeping with the country's traditional neutrality). How many francs will her $10,000 purchase, and should she buy them now or wait for six months? Has she any other strategies to keep her costs as low as possible? **(See solution on p. 648)**

How DO you convert currency, anyway?

We work and live today in a global business and financial environment. Consider Starbucks Coffee Company. Starbucks operates in more than 50 countries, including the United States, its home country. Starbucks buys coffee beans from countries all over the world. To provide the exotic blends that customers have come to expect, company employees travel to many of these countries with agriculturally based, small economies like Colombia, Ethiopia, Guatemala, Kenya, Papua New Guinea, and Yemen. After blending and processing, the coffee is then sold in stores (on virtually any corner) in large-economy countries like the United States, Australia, Canada, China, Germany, United Kingdom, to name a few.

Consider the financial transactions that Starbucks must process to enable these business activities. Financial managers need to assess the risks of investing in property and buildings in less-developed countries. They must plan for currency exchange between the U.S. dollar and foreign currencies—no small feat today with the large changes in the value of the dollar—to pay for labor, beans, and capital investments in other countries and return shareholder profits in U.S. dollars. Exchange rates between currencies change over time. Such fluctuations can change the value of foreign investments and future cash flows. Especially today, managers must plan to counteract exchange rate uncertainty or risk. Starbucks uses techniques like hedging to reduce these risks.

In general, we can say that all of the typical opportunities and risks we've discussed so far are magnified and complicated in the global environment. In this chapter, we'll describe these complications and provide background and tools to help address them.

Learning Goals

LG19-1 Gauge the dynamics of the global economy and recognize potential international opportunities.

LG19-2 Recognize patterns of increasing capital involvement as the firm seeks to expand business internationally.

LG19-3 Compute currency exchanges.

LG19-4 Recognize situations that evoke exchange rate risk and develop tools to manage those risks.

LG19-5 Apply theories of how interest rates and inflation influence forward exchange rates and future spot rates.

LG19-6 Anticipate political risks when investing internationally.

LG19-7 As a financial manager, plan to work through capital budgeting issues for international investments.

LG19-1

19.1 • Global Business

International Opportunities

The United States has the largest economy in the world. Table 19.1 shows many other very large economies too. In fact, some large economies are experiencing faster growth rates than the United States. While the U.S. economy grows at a level close to the world average rate, countries like China and India have a lot of catching up to do—they have been experiencing much faster growth. It's no wonder that firms around the world are interested in the opportunities these developing economies represent.

How does a business decide how best to operate in the global economy? Most firms start out slowly, minimizing their risk should something not work out. The most basic level of participation is to either import foreign goods, export goods overseas, or both. Figure 19.1 shows that the United States actively imports and exports many goods. Canada (27.2 percent), Mexico (19.1 percent), China (10.1 percent), and Japan (6.4 percent) are the United States' favorite export destinations. In a different order—China (25.0 percent), Canada (19.8 percent), Mexico (16.5 percent), and Japan (8.1 percent)—the same four nations provide the United States with the most imports. In 2011, the United States imported $457 billion more in products from these countries than it exported. The figure shows why there is so much interest in China—trade with China represents more than half of this overall trade imbalance.

Two factors that affect the trading activity between countries are restrictions on the kinds of products that may enter a country and tariffs charged for transporting goods across borders. To protect domestic firms (often agricultural businesses) from foreign competition, some countries' governments pass laws restricting trade. Such laws may prohibit or limit importation of certain products or place a tax, or tariff, on imported goods. Trade barriers enacted by one country often lead to retaliatory barriers by other countries, so that both countries face about the same restrictions. The resultant trade war usually harms all economies involved.

North American Free Trade Agreement (NAFTA)
The trading block consisting of Canada, Mexico, and the United States.

Central American Free Trade Agreement
A free trade agreement between the Central American countries and the United States.

Mercosur
The Southern Common Market of South America.

European Union (EU)
A political and economic union of 27 European countries.

To facilitate trade between countries, several international trade agreements have been enacted in the past two decades. Trade agreements seek to reduce, or even eliminate, trade restrictions and tariffs to ease trade between the countries. For example, in 1988, Canada and the United States agreed to form a free-trade zone for unrestricted trade. In 1994, they expanded the free-trade zone to include Mexico in the **North American Free Trade Agreement (NAFTA)**. In 2003 and 2004, respectively, the United States signed a bilateral trade pact with Chile and a regional deal with Costa Rica, the Dominican Republic, El Salvador, Guatemala, Honduras, and Nicaragua, known as the **Central American Free Trade Agreement**. South American countries created their own free-trade zone called the **Mercosur** (Argentina, Brazil, Paraguay, Uruguay, and Venezuela) starting in 1998.

Other regions of the world have also formed trading zones or are in the process of doing so. One of the largest, oldest, and most important is the **European Union (EU)**. The current 27 members include the original western European countries (except Switzerland) and, more recently, eastern European countries such as the Czech Republic, Hungary and Poland (added in 2004), and Bulgaria and Romania (added in 2007). The EU creates an open marketplace where goods and services can easily cross borders. Taken together, the EU rivals the United States' economic power. In addition to this economic cooperation between European countries, many of the countries have formed a monetary union. Sixteen countries use a single currency called the *euro* (€). The euro was created on January 1, 1999, but was not available as coins and notes until 2002.

table 19.1 Gross Domestic Product in the Largest Economies around the World

Global growth has been lower since the financial crisis.

		Average Annual GDP Growth (%)		
Country	**2011 GDP ($ billions)**	**1998–2002**	**2003–2007**	**2008–2011**
United States	14,991	3.3	2.8	0.2
China	7,318	8.2	11.7	9.6
Japan	5,867	0.2	1.9	−0.7
Germany	3,600	1.7	1.7	0.8
France	2,773	2.6	2.0	0.1
Brazil	2,477	1.7	4.0	3.8
United Kingdom	2,445	3.2	3.1	−0.6
Italy	2,194	1.8	1.3	−1.1
Russia	1,857	4.2	7.5	1.5
India	1,848	5.5	8.8	7.2
Canada	1,736	3.9	2.6	0.9
Spain	1,477	4.1	3.5	−0.7
Australia	1,379	3.8	3.5	2.4
Mexico	1,153	3.2	3.4	1.2
South Korea	1,116	4.5	4.3	3.1
Indonesia	846	0.1	5.5	5.8
Netherlands	836	2.9	2.4	0.2
Turkey	775	1.2	6.9	3.4
Switzerland	659	1.8	2.5	1.3
Saudi Arabia	576	1.5	4.8	3.9
Average	**2,796**	**3.0**	**4.2**	**2.1**

Source: World Development Indicators 2012, World Bank

figure 19.1 Exports from and Imports to the United States by Country, 2011

The United States imports far more from China than it exports to China.

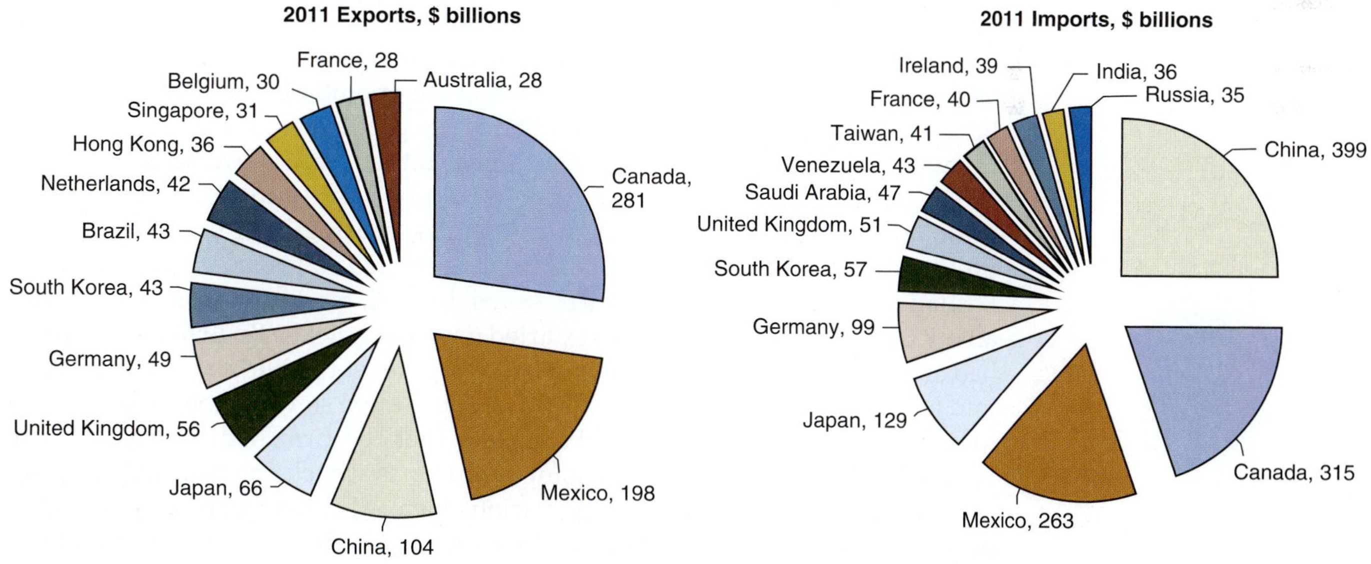

Source: U.S. Department of Commerce: Bureau of Economic Analysis

The former country currencies, like the French franc and the German mark, are no longer legal tender. European micro states like Monaco and Vatican City also use the euro. Estonia joined the monetary union in 2011.

World Trade Organization (WTO)

An international organization that deals with international trade rules and helps settle disputes between its member governments.

In addition to free-trade zones, international organizations promote and facilitate unrestricted trade globally. For example, the **World Trade Organization (WTO)**, located in Geneva, Switzerland, has 159 country signatories. Its goals are to increase international trade by promoting lower trade barriers and providing a platform for negotiations and disputes. Also, the **International Monetary Fund (IMF)**, an organization of 188 countries (located in Washington, D.C.), monitors currency exchange, examines financial stability, and watches the overall global financial system.

LG19-2

Corporate Expansion into Other Countries

International Monetary Fund (IMF)

An international organization that monitors exchange rates and balance of payments and oversees the global financial system.

Seattle, Washington, coffee giant Starbucks provides an illustration of how firms evolve from doing business locally or domestically to expanding their operations across nations and, eventually, overseas. Firms typically become active internationally in steps, with different levels of involvement.

Probably the lowest level of involvement is the simple import and export operation. Say that Starbucks simply bought coffee beans from farmers in other countries, that is, it imported coffee beans. Indeed, this was exactly what Starbucks' mission was at its founding in 1971. After processing the imported beans in the United States, the three founders focused on providing fellow coffee lovers in the Seattle area with the best coffee available. At this stage in its development, the company risked only the hazards of importing the beans. By 1981, Starbucks had expanded to four coffee shops and a coffee roasting plant outside of Seattle. Likewise, many firms expand into international markets with simple, relatively low-risk import/export operations. But remaining simple import/export operations with this low involvement level seems to "leave money on the table"—that is, companies miss out on serving potential customers with higher levels of service. In Starbucks' case, it could glean profits from coffee lovers across the United States.

To increase the level of involvement, firms often partner with other firms using licenses, franchising, or sales subsidiary arrangements. Starbucks did exactly that. By 1991, Starbucks had worked out licensing operations in U.S. airports and began selling mail-order coffee. Its risks at this point were still minimal—the licensees took on all of the risk, and Starbucks profited from the licensing fees. Many firms follow this same low-risk, higher return pattern overseas.

The next logical step for most firms would be joint ventures, with domestic companies partnering with foreign companies, sharing both the risks and the profits. By 1987, Starbucks had plans in place for 125 coffee stores in Vancouver, Portland, and Chicago—up from 17 stores. In 1992, Starbucks went public with an initial public offering (IPO) and started growing quickly. By 1997, the company had 10 times as many stores as it had had when it went public and had expanded into Japan and Singapore in addition to opening more stores in the United States. Moving into new countries quickly meant that the firm had to leave foreign operations to local managers via joint ventures. Starbucks had started courting customers across the world, selling various blended coffee beans as well as the beverages themselves. By doing so, the coffee giant risked its own capital for a chance of much greater profits. Starbucks chose locations carefully, in politically stable, relatively wealthy countries.

The last stage of international operations involves direct capital involvement. Starbucks embarked upon this stage in Japan and Singapore—operating directly in foreign countries by opening and operating stores itself. In this case, Starbucks faces all the risks of operating a business in the foreign country, but also reaps

figure 19.2

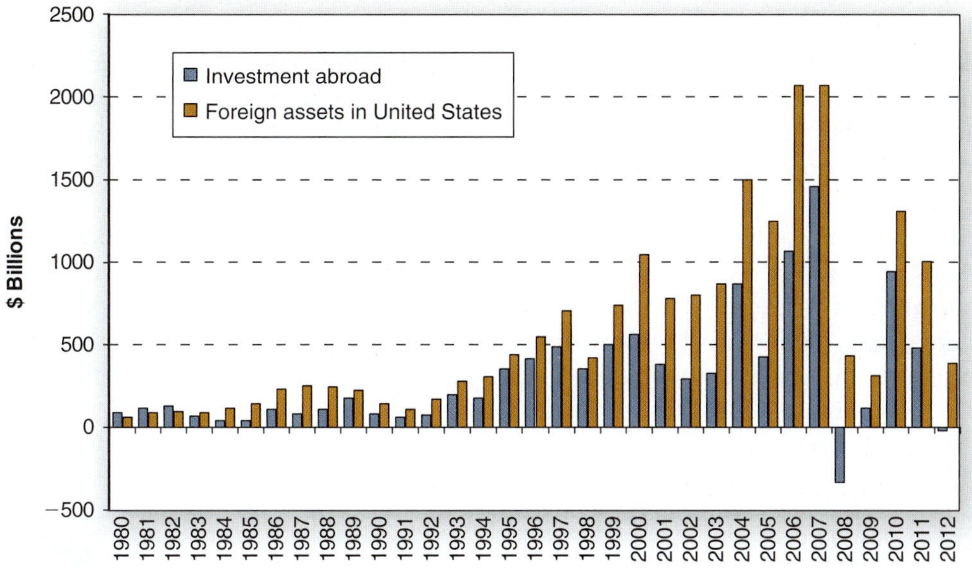

Foreign Direct Investment Abroad and into the United States

International investment nearly stopped during the global financial crisis.

Source: U.S. Department of Commerce: Bureau of Economic Analysis

all the potential rewards. In summary, firms can expand internationally through several methods that require increasingly higher participation in capital at risk and potential for profits. These levels are:

- Import/export
- Partnering
  - Sales subsidiary
  - Licensing/franchising
  - Joint venture
- Direct ownership

Multinational corporations (MNCs) invest their capital for direct ownership of assets to produce products and services in multiple countries. For example, Starbucks now owns and operates in 61 countries. Companies like Nike find it less expensive to manufacture their product in low labor–cost countries like China and Vietnam. In other cases, companies have found that it is more efficient to manufacture the products they sell within the countries where they want to sell those products. For example, Toyota has invested $23 billion in manufacturing and sales operations in North America. Some of these multinational corporations often become truly global firms, producing and selling many products all over the world.

multinational corporation (MNC)

A company that operates production and/or sales facilities in multiple countries.

The capital spent to run overseas operations is called **foreign direct investment**. The direct investment of U.S. firms abroad and the investment of foreign firms in the United States have substantially increased recently. Figure 19.2 shows the direct investment each year since 1980. With all of the political talk about U.S. jobs being outsourced overseas, you may be surprised to see that direct foreign investment by foreign firms into the United States is higher than that of U.S. firms investing abroad.

foreign direct investment

A long-term investment of capital in a business operation located in an economy other than that in which the company is based.

As a multinational corporation, Starbucks Coffee invests its capital in operations overseas. By the end of 2012, Starbucks owned and operated or licensed more than 5,100 stores outside the United States in more than 60 countries. The majority of foreign company–owned stores are in Canada, Singapore, and the United Kingdom. In addition to this direct capital invested, Starbucks also enters into joint ventures and licensing operations with international partners. Most of these are in Japan, China, Taiwan, and South Korea. These international operations accounted for nearly 25 percent of Starbucks' total revenue in 2012.

Firms commonly start international business through simple import and export operations. As firms gain experience, they escalate their international commitment through partnering. Finally, the firms gain enough knowledge to make direct ownership investments in other countries. In the end, many firms employ a variety of import/export operations, partnership arrangements, and direct ownership—just like Starbucks has!

TIME OUT

19-1 What motivates the governments of countries to create free-trade zones?

19-2 What does the large amount of foreign direct investment coming into the United States mean for U.S. workers?

19.2 • Foreign Currency Exchange

exchange rate
Specifies how much one currency is worth in terms of the other.

spot transaction
An exchange of one currency for another today.

The first challenge that managers face when they seek to conduct business internationally is that different countries, or monetary unions, use different currencies. Selling products internationally requires conversion of one currency into another. The foreign exchange (or forex) market, by which traders convert one foreign currency into another, is one of the largest financial markets in the world. Currency trading entails no specific physical location; instead, it's an over-the-counter market whose main participants are commercial and investment banks, and foreign exchange dealers and brokers around the world. They communicate using electronic networks. Any firm's bank, or experts within the firm, can access this market to exchange one currency for another.

LG19-3

Exchange Rates

indirect quote
The amount of foreign currency needed to buy one unit of domestic currency.

direct quote
The amount of domestic currency needed to buy one unit of foreign currency.

To buy products internationally, a U.S. firm must buy foreign currency with U.S. dollars. We call the price of one currency in terms of another an **exchange rate**. If we're exchanging one currency for another immediately, we participate in a **spot transaction**. Table 19.2 shows quotes from the exchange market. A currency's price can appear in either domestic currency units or foreign currency units. An **indirect quote** lists the amount of foreign currency it takes to buy one unit of domestic currency. Table 19.2 shows that on this day in April 2013, it cost 96.290 Japanese yen to purchase one U.S. dollar. It also cost 0.7669 euro to buy one dollar, denoted as $1 = €0.7669. A **direct quote** expresses the exchange rate as the amount of domestic currency needed to buy one unit of foreign currency. So Table 19.2 also shows that one yen will purchase 0.010385 U.S. dollar. One euro buys 1.3039 dollars, denoted as €1 = $1.3039. Note that a direct quote is simply the inverse of an indirect quote: Direct quote = 1 ÷ Indirect quote.

table 19.2 | Currency Exchange Rates, April 15, 2013

U.S. $1 will buy	Indirect Quote
Yen ¥	96.290
Euro €	0.7669
Canada $	1.0250
United Kingdom £	0.6541
Australian $	0.9707
Swiss Franc	1.0739
One of the following will buy U.S. dollar	**Direct Quote**
Yen, ¥	$0.010385
Euro, €	1.3039
Canada, $	0.9756
United Kingdom, £	1.5288
Australian, $	1.0302
Swiss Franc	0.9312

Data Source: http://finance.yahoo.com/currency

cross rates

The currency exchange rate between two foreign currencies, each of which is not the currency of the domestic country.

EXAMPLE 19-1

LG19-3

Exchanging Currency

Erin has been invited to go on a ski vacation in Canada over the holiday break. She figures that she will need 1,500 Canadian dollars for the trip. How many U.S. dollars does Erin need to convert to Canadian dollars?

For interactive versions of this example visit www.mhhe.com/can3e

SOLUTION:

Using the currency exchange rates in Table 19.2, observe that US$1 = CA$1.0250. Therefore, Erin will need US$1,463 as shown:

$$\text{CA\$1,500} \times \frac{\text{US\$1}}{\text{CA\$1.0250}} = \text{US\$1,463}$$

Similar to Problems 19-1, 19-2, 19-3, 19-4, self-test problem 1

Of course, some U.S. firms may want to exchange two non-dollar currencies. So cross-currency quotes are useful. Table 19.3 shows the **cross rates** on this day in April 2013. The table shows that ¥1 = €0.00796 and €1 = ¥125.5574. Again, all of these rates are inverses of each other.[1] If an exchange rate quote between two currencies isn't available, you can derive it as a cross rate through two exchange rates with a third currency. For example, the direct quote exchange rate between U.S. dollars and euros is €1 = $1.3039 and between U.S. dollars and yen is ¥1 = $0.010385. We can then compute the cross rate between yen and euros as

$$\frac{€\,1}{\$1.3039} \times \frac{\$0.010385}{¥1} = \frac{€\,0.00796}{¥1}$$

MATH COACH

CONVERTING CURRENCY

When you're determining how much of one currency results from a sum of another currency, which exchange rate quote to use (direct or indirect) and how to use it may get confusing. You can use either quote. The trick is to make sure the right currency label is canceled out, to leave the desired currency label. See that in the previous example, Erin is using the indirect quote. She places the desired currency in the numerator and the currency to be converted in the denominator so that CA$ can be canceled out, leaving US$. She could have solved the problem using the direct quote, CA$1 = US$0.9756. All she needed to do was to make sure that her desired currency is in the numerator and the other is in the denominator, like:

$$\text{CA\$1,500} \times \frac{\text{US\$0.9756}}{\text{CA\$1}} = \text{US\$1,463}$$

[1]Any differences are simply the result of rounding the rate quotes.

table 19.3 | **Cross Rates, April 15, 2013**

	Yen ¥	Euro €	Canadian $	U.K. £	Australian $	Swiss Franc
1 Yen ¥	1	0.007964	0.010645	0.006793	0.010081	0.011153
1 Euro €	125.5574	1	1.3365	0.8529	1.2657	1.4003
1 Canadian $	93.9415	0.7482	1	0.6381	0.9470	1.0477
1 U.K. £	147.2099	1.1725	1.5670	1	1.4840	1.6418
1 Australian $	99.1965	0.7900	1.0559	0.6738	1	1.1063
1 Swiss Franc	89.6638	0.7141	0.9545	0.6091	0.9039	1

The result, ¥1 = €0.007964, is the cross rate shown in Table 19.3.

In fact, some people intentionally look for exchange rate mispricings by comparing direct quote exchange rates between two currencies with cross rates determined through a third currency. If direct quotes and cross rates differ, **arbitrage**—a form of buying low and selling high—is possible. For example, suppose that the yen-to-euro exchange rate was ¥1 = €0.007970. Obviously, this rate is higher than the cross rate of ¥1 = €0.007964, so a profitable arbitrage exists. To earn the profit, make the three simultaneous trades:

1. Trade $1,000,000 for ¥96,292,729.90 (= $1,000,000 × ¥1 ÷ $0.010385).
2. Trade ¥96,292,729.90 for €767,453.06 (= ¥96,292,729.90 × €0.007970 ÷ ¥1).
3. Trade €767,453.06 for $1,000,682.04 (=€767,453.06 × $1.3039 ÷ €1).

Notice that the beginning $1 million has become $1,000,682.04. Because the exchange rate is mispriced, a trader made a $682.04 profit! Because three exchange rates are necessary to profit from a mispricing, this process is sometimes called *triangular* arbitrage and a person doing it is called an **arbitrageur**.

arbitrage

The practice of simultaneously purchasing and selling an asset in different forms or markets to take advantage of an imbalance in price.

arbitrageur

A trader who engages in arbitrage.

LG19-4

Exchange Rate Risk

Corporations easily exchange one currency for another. The problem that firms face is that exchange rates change over time. Consider a company that invests $100 million in projects in Europe when the exchange rate to euros was €1 = $1.15. The company would be investing €86.96 million (= $100 million × €1 ÷ $1.15). Say that two years later, the investment had increased by 10 percent to €95.65 million. But when the company sells the projects and converts the euros back to dollars, it finds that the exchange rate changed unfavorably to €1 =$0.85. The exchange to dollars results in $81.3 million (= €95.65 × $0.85 ÷ €1). Even though the investment earned a 10 percent return in the foreign market, the company lost money on it because the exchange rate moved in the wrong direction. Specifically, the loss was due to the 26 percent decline [(= $1.15 − $0.85) ÷ 1.15] in the value of the euro. The potential for exchange rates to change (unfavorably) over time is called **exchange rate risk**.

The exchange rates between most major world currencies have a **freely floating regime**. That is, the exchange rates are free to change according to supply and demand for the currencies. Governments sometimes try to influence exchange rates by buying or selling their currency to change supply or demand. Such an attempt to manipulate the exchange rate through the currency exchange market indicates a **managed-floating regime**.

The dramatic dollar/euro exchange rate change shown in Figure 19.3 actually occurred in January of 1999 and 2001. Right after the decline in the value of the euro, the euro's value rallied strongly. In two and half years, the euro's value increased more than 50 percent. This large change in the exchange rate significantly affected importing, exporting, and foreign direct investment. When

exchange rate risk

The possibility that the spot currency exchange rate will change and reduce the value of foreign assets and cash flows.

freely floating regime

An exchange rate regime where the currency is completely determined by the foreign-exchange market through supply and demand.

managed-floating regime

An exchange rate regime where the country's central bank allows its currency price to float freely between an upper and lower bound and may buy or sell large amounts of it in order to provide price support or resistance.

finance at work — personal

EXCHANGING CURRENCY FOR YOUR TRIP

One ramification of a global economy is that many people travel to foreign countries for business or pleasure. How do you get foreign currency for your trip? Currency exchange rates vary from place to place and day to day. You can find exchange bureaus at airports and banks. You can even exchange currency in the lobby of your five-star hotel! But retail exchange services are costly. You will find that where and how you exchange currency can make a big difference in how much you'll have to spend.

You'll get the best exchange rate if you let your bank make your transactions for you. Banks frequently participate in the currency exchange market and earn the best exchange rates. Your bank converts the currency for you when you use your credit card or ATM card in a foreign country. The cost of using credit cards issued in the United States to make purchases internationally has risen in recent years because some banks have added a *currency-conversion fee* of up to 2 percent. Credit card companies charge this fee in addition to the standard 1 percent fee that they charge for foreign purchases. Credit cards should work well for most purchases. But you will still need cash for the little things like taxis, tips, and a coffee at Starbucks. ATM networks have proliferated globally, so you can use your ATM or debit card to get foreign currency almost anywhere in the world. But again, be aware of the fees. Some banks charge 1 to 3 percent of the withdrawal as a conversion fee for foreign ATM use. Others impose a flat fee of up to $5 per withdrawal. Check your bank's website to find out which ATM brands are in your bank's network and how much your bank will charge you for transactions.

Even with fees imposed on credit card and ATM use, they are still a better deal than the exchange bureaus found at airports and hotels. A 2005 *Consumer Reports* survey of transaction costs found that converting dollars into euros at an exchange bureau cost 10 percent more than using a Visa with a 3 percent conversion fee. Exchanging dollars at a five-star hotel costs even more! It's good to know the exchange rate before you leave so that you will know whether you are getting ripped-off or not!

want to know more? Key Words to Search for Updates: exchange rates, currency-conversion fee

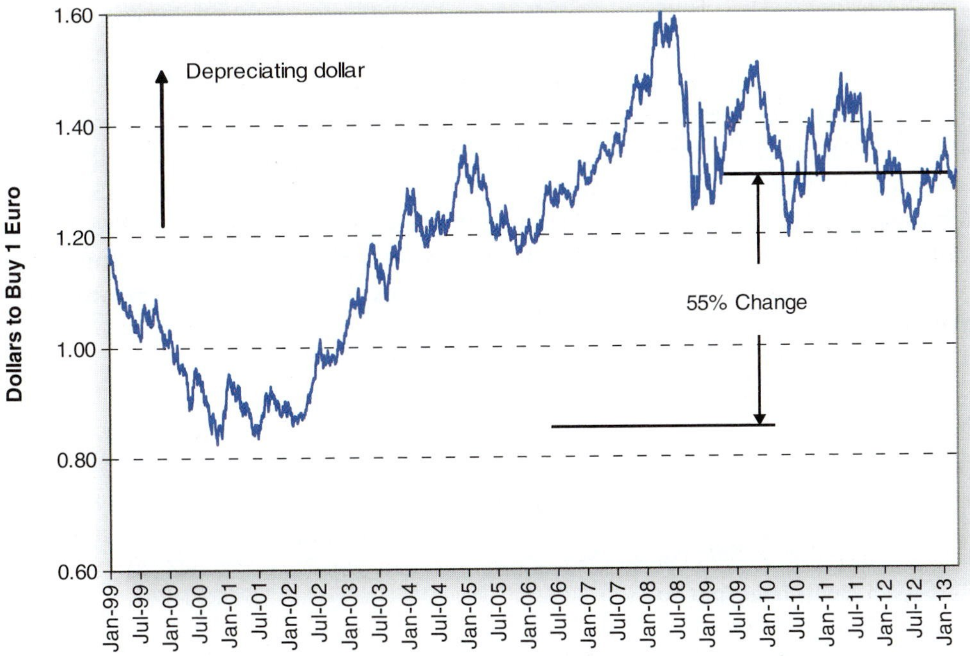

figure 19.3

Number of U.S. Dollars to Purchase 1 Euro, Exchange Rates January 1999 to April 2013

Currency exchange rates can dramatically change over time.

Data Source: Board of Governors of the Federal Reserve System

more dollars are needed to buy a foreign currency than before, we say that the dollar is *weakening*. If, fewer dollars are needed to buy the foreign currency, then the dollar is *strengthening*. The euro remains strong today, especially relative to the dollar.

fixed peg arrangement

An exchange rate regime where a currency's price is fixed to the value of another currency or to a basket of other currencies.

In some cases, a government fixes, or *pegs,* its currency's value to another currency. For nearly seven years, China's currency was pegged at 8.28 yuan to the U.S. dollar. Then, on July 21, 2005, China changed its exchange rate to a **fixed peg arrangement** to a basket of world currencies. This change effectively meant that the new rate became 8.11 yuan per U.S. dollar. The People's Republic of China stated that the foreign currency basket is dominated by the U.S. dollar, euro, Japanese yen, and South Korean won, with a smaller proportion made up of the British pound, Thai baht, Russian ruble, Australian dollar, Canadian dollar, and Singapore dollar. Since China changed its pegging standard, the yuan has strengthened to 6.1914 yuan per dollar (April 16, 2013).

LG19-4

The Forward Exchange Rate and Hedging

forward exchange rate

A contractual arrangement that states the exchange rate to be used at a future exchange date.

premium

The case when the forward rate indicates a stronger currency over the spot rate.

discount

The case when the forward rate indicates a weaker currency over the spot rate.

hedging

A strategy used to minimize exposure to an unwanted business or financial risk, while still allowing the business to profit.

futures

A standardized contract traded in a futures exchange market designed to buy (or sell) the underlying asset at a specific price on a certain future date.

option

A standardized contract in which the buyer has the right (but not the obligation) to buy (or sell) an asset at a set price by a future date.

currency swap

A foreign exchange agreement to exchange a given amount of one currency for another and then later return the original amounts swapped.

Financial managers can manage exchange rate risk to some extent by using **forward exchange rates**. While spot exchange rates hold for transactions occurring right now, traders quote forward rates for transactions to be completed in 30, 90, or 180 days. Companies can negotiate an exchange rate in advance for currency that they will exchange months in the future. Table 19.4 shows spot and forward rates for converting Swiss francs and U.K. pounds sterling to U.S. dollars. The table shows that over the next six months, you would be able to buy fewer Swiss francs with one dollar than you could today. The spot rate is US$1 = 0.9312 francs and the six-month forward rate is US$1 = 0.9284 franc. In this circumstance, we say that the forward Swiss franc is selling at a **premium** to the spot rate. The opposite is occurring with the exchange for U.K. pounds sterling. One dollar will buy more pounds in the forward market, so we say that the forward pound is selling at a **discount** to the spot rate.

Financial managers implement **hedging** strategies to reduce exchange rate risks. First, they can minimize the amount of foreign currency that the firm needs to exchange. For example, consider a case in which money is borrowed in the United States, converted to euros, and invested in Europe. As the project earns cash flows each year, the cash flows are converted back to dollars to pay interest and principal on the loan. An alternative is to borrow euros with a loan from a European bank. Then the loan can be repaid with the project cash flows without currency exchange. A second strategy is to lock in the exchange rates by negotiating currency trades that will occur in the future using forward rates. Last, financial derivative securities can be used for hedging. To hedge currency risks, companies use **futures** contracts, **options**, and **currency swaps**.

table 19.4 | **Spot and Forward Exchange Rates**

Exchange Rate Per U.S. $1	
Swiss franc spot rate	0.9312
1-month forward	0.9307
3-month forward	0.9298
6-month forward	0.9284
U.K. pound spot rate	0.6541
1-month forward	0.6543
3-month forward	0.6547
6-month forward	0.6552

Companies can agree to exchange currency in the future using forward rates.

Starbucks operates on a large scale in Canada, the United Kingdom, and Japan, and thus has large exchange rate exposure risk. To manage these risks, Starbucks implements all three strategies just mentioned:

1. It has acquired Japanese yen-denominated bank loans to support Japanese operations.
2. It has forward rate contracts in yen, the Canadian dollar, and the pound to hedge its investments and exchange rate exposures in Starbucks Japan and the Canadian and U.K. subsidiaries.
3. It claims in its annual report that it "may engage in transactions involving various derivative instruments, with maturities generally not exceeding five years, to hedge assets, liabilities, revenues and purchases denominated in foreign currencies."

EXAMPLE 19-2

LG19-4

Currency Exchange Risk

For interactive versions of this example visit www.mhhe.com/can3e

Starbucks Coffee begins some international activities by entering into partnership agreements with companies already operating in the country. Sometimes, Starbucks purchases 100 percent ownership of the foreign business. For example, in early 2007, Starbucks announced a deal to purchase 18 percent of Marinopolus Romania B.V., a coffee business in Romania. Although the specifics of the deal were not announced, imagine negotiating a \$20 million deal with a Romanian firm when the Romanian currency, the leu, is under distress. In fact, a new leu replaced the old one in late 2006. The old leu required 3,333 to exchange for one dollar. The new leu needs only 2.57 per dollar. If Starbucks invests \$20 million in Romania, how many new lei (plural of leu) are they investing? If the exchange rate changes to 3.15, how much value has Starbucks' investment lost?

SOLUTION:

\$20 million will purchase 51.4 million lei (= \$20 million × \$2.57 lei/\$). If the exchange rate changes, then the 51.4 million lei will be worth only \$16.3 million (= 51.4 million lei ÷ 3.15 lei/\$). This weakening of the leu would cause an 18.5 percent reduction in the value of the investment in Romania.

Similar to Problems 19-5, 19-6, 19-7, 19-8, 19-15, 19-16, 19-21, 19-22, self-test problem 1

Interest Rate Parity

LG19-5

Why do spot exchange rates and forward rates differ? Table 19.4 shows that forward rates can be either higher or lower then the spot rate. What factors affect the forward rate? The answer lies in comparing interest rates in the two countries. Say that you hear about an interest rate available in another country—say South Africa—that is higher than any available in your country, the United States. If you want to earn the higher rate for six months, you would need to convert your dollars to South African rands at the spot rate, earn the high return, and then convert the money back to your own currency in six months. In order to lock in your future exchange rate and thus your profit, you could use a forward rate contract. As long as the forward rate is the same as the spot rate, you would earn a higher interest rate on the South African investment than is available domestically.

Unfortunately, the financial markets have already thought this one through. The concept of **interest rate parity** suggests that the forward rate will be such

interest rate parity
A theory that the difference in interest rates between two countries is equal to the difference between the forward currency exchange rate and the spot exchange rate.

that the total return earned (interest rate and changes in exchange rate) will be the same between the two countries. In other words, the difference between the spot and forward rates arises precisely because of the difference in the interest rates available in the two countries. If i_d is the interest rate available in your home (domestic) country and i_f is the rate in the foreign country, then the interest rate parity relationship is expressed as

$$\frac{\text{Forward exchange rate}}{\text{Spot exchange rate}} = \frac{1 + i_d}{1 + i_f} \qquad \textbf{(19-1)}$$

The forex market requires that both the forward and spot rates be expressed as direct quotes. The direct quote is the amount of domestic currency received per unit of foreign currency. Consider that the U.S. risk-free rate is at historically low levels. While we always express interest rates in annualized terms, the actual investment problem and thus our equation requires us to express the interest rates for the same period as the forward exchange rate.

The spot and forward rates in Table 19.4 are indirect quotes. The direct quote for the United Kingdom spot rate would be 1.5288 (= 1 ÷ 0.6541) and for the six-month forward rate 1.5263 (= 1 ÷ 0.6552). Given interest rate parity, what should the forward rate be? Use a six-month interest rate for the United States of 0.18 percent and for the United Kingdom of 0.34 percent. Rearranging equation 19–1 means that the forward rate should be:

$$\frac{1 + 0.0018}{1 + 0.0034} \times 1.5288 = 1.5263$$

Note how the equation implies that when the foreign interest rate is higher, then the forward rate will indicate a weakening of the foreign currency. When the foreign interest rate is lower than the domestic rate, the forward exchange rate will indicate a strengthening of the foreign currency. Thus, the difference in spot and forward rates is directly a result of the difference in interest rates in the two countries. If the forward rate is not consistent with interest rate parity, then an arbitrage is possible. Arbitrageurs could (1) borrow in one low-rate country, (2) exchange the money to another currency and deposit it to earn the higher rate, (3) enter into a forward rate contract to guarantee the future exchange rate, and at the end (4) repay the loan. The money left over would be the arbitrage profit.

LG19-5 Purchasing Power Parity and Future Exchange Rates

Interest rate parity describes why spot and forward rates differ. But why do exchange rates change over time—even from one day to the next? Why has the exchange rate between two major currencies like the dollar and euro changed so much, as shown in Figure 19.3? In short, the answer is inflation. The concept of **purchasing power parity (PPP)** illustrates how inflation causes exchange rates to change.

purchasing power parity (PPP)

A theory relating the expected adjustment needed in the future spot exchange rate between countries to the inflation rate in each economy.

The idea of purchasing power parity stems from a concept known as the **law of one price**. Essentially, the law of one price dictates that identical products should have the same price, adjusted for currency exchange, no matter where in the world they sell. The law of one price seems reasonable when we consider an item like an ounce of gold. Denote the price in the domestic country as P_d and the price in the foreign country is P_f. Then the PPP relationship is shown as:

law of one price

An economic principle that states all identical goods in different markets must have the same price.

$$P_d = P_f \times \text{Spot rate} \qquad \textbf{(19-2)}$$

Note that we must denote the spot rate as the amount of domestic currency exchanged for one unit of foreign currency. So, if gold is selling in the United States for $1,400 per ounce and Table 19.2 shows that $1.5288 = £1, then gold should sell for £915.75 (= $1,400 ÷ $1.5288/£) in the United Kingdom. If gold sold for only £900 per ounce, then you could buy gold in the United Kingdom and sell it in the United States for a profit, acting as an arbitrageur. Large players in the gold market are very happy to make a profit through buying in one market and selling in another. Their buying in the United Kingdom will boost the price and their selling in the United States will apply downward pressure on prices, thus moving prices to the appropriate levels as shown in PPP. In this way, opportunities for arbitrage eliminate different prices and ensure that the law of one price holds.

PPP may not hold exactly because of transaction costs that may include shipping, insurance, trading costs, and so on. Trade restrictions and tariffs may also inhibit the law of one price. Finally, many products and services are not reasonably transportable, so the law of one price may not apply. For example, you may not expect the law of one price to hold for a haircut in London as it would in a small Midwestern town in the United States.

So, even though the PPP doesn't work perfectly, the concept can illustrate why exchange rates can—must—change over time. Imagine that the price level of goods did not change in the United States, but the overall price index increased by 10 percent in Argentina. This is one way of saying that the inflation rate was zero in the United States and 10 percent in Argentina. In order for PPP to hold at the end of the year, the current spot exchange rate of 1 peso = $0.2520 would have to change by the end of the year, or arbitrage becomes possible. Since inflation in Argentina was 10 percent higher than in the United States, then the peso must decrease in value (purchasing power) by 10 percent in order for PPP to hold. This relationship is shown in the *relative* form of the PPP equation. The new exchange rate will be:

$$\underset{\substack{\text{(domestic amount per}\\\text{unit of foreign currency)}}}{\text{Expected exchange}} = \underset{\substack{\text{(domestic amount per}\\\text{unit of foreign currency)}}}{\text{Current spot rate}} \times (1 + \text{Domestic inflation rate} - \text{Foreign inflation rate}) \tag{19-3}$$

Using this relative PPP equation, we expect the Argentinean peso exchange rate at the end of the year to be $0.2268 (= $0.2520 × {1 + 0 − 0.10}). If inflation in Argentina went even higher, its currency would depreciate further. Of course, many other factors could change worldwide in the course of the year to impact both exchange rates in either or both countries. Further, PPP adjustments don't take place on a particular day at the end of the year. Rather, the forex and other markets adjust minute-by-minute to take new information into account. However, because it takes all current information about the future into account, we consider the relative PPP estimate to be the best forecast of future exchange rates between countries.

Interest rate parity describes the relationship between the current spot rate and the forward rate. Purchasing power parity describes how the current spot rate will likely change in the future. Your intuition likely tells you that the two parity concepts are related. Chapter 6 shows how expected inflation is one component of a country's current and future interest rates through the Fisher effect. High interest rates tend to go with and to predict high inflation. So both the forward rate from interest rate parity and the expected future spot rate from PPP should be consistent in indicating either a weakening or strengthening of a particular country's currency.

finance at work — markets

QUANTITATIVE EASING AND EXCHANGE RATES

The global financial crisis has caused central banks around the world to take unprecedented actions. In order to stabilize the financial system, central banks infused economies with money. To do this, central banks create new money and then purchase assets in the economy. They hold the assets while the new money circulates through the economy. The most common assets purchased are bonds. The Japanese central bank was the first to implement this "quantitative easing" strategy in the early 2000s to cope with Japan's deflation problem. The bank's hope was that it would cause some inflation.

The U.S. Federal Reserve embarked on a quantitative easing program in 2008 that resulted in an extraordinary $1.5 trillion of new money. The Fed mostly purchased risky mortgage-backed securities from banks. Many economists worry that pumping such a large amount of money into the economy will result in inflation. After all, when you create more of something, its value declines. If the value of the dollar declines, then you would need more dollars to buy goods and services. This is inflation. Although many people may call this "printing money," central banks don't really deal with paper money anymore. They just create electronic money in their accounts and transfer it to banks.

Consider the purchasing power parity equation. Note that if the inflation rate in the United States increases, then the U.S. dollar will weaken against foreign currency. Indeed, this inflation was expected, as Figure 19.3 shows a spike in the depreciating dollar against the euro during 2008. However, struggling economies in Europe caused European banks to also follow the Fed's actions with their own quantitative easing. Thus, their new higher inflation expectations caused a devaluation of the British pound and the euro (as seen in the figure) versus the U.S. dollar.

In 2010, the U.S. Fed announced a second quantitative easing program (called QE2) to pump more than another half trillion dollars into the economy. Then in 2012, the Fed announced that it would continue purchasing bonds at a rate of $85 billion per month for the foreseeable future. The various policy announcements of central banks have created quite volatile currency exchange markets in the past few years. But so far, currencies have not been affected on the inflation expectations these programs have created. Time will tell what actual inflation occurs.

want to know more? Key Words to Search for Updates: quantitative easing, inflation, dollar exchange rate

EXAMPLE 19-3

LG19-5

For interactive versions of this example visit www.mhhe.com/can3e

Expected Exchange Rates

You know that your firm will want to convert 25 million Brazilian real to U.S. dollars in six months. The current exchange rate is $0.4766 = 1 real. The inflation rates in Brazil and in the United States are expected to be 7 percent and 3.5 percent, respectively. You need to estimate the likely exchange rate in six months and how many dollars your firm will likely realize in the transaction.

SOLUTION:

Inflation is stated in annual terms, so you will have to use six-month values of 3.5 percent and 1.75 percent for Brazil and the United States. Using the relative form of PPP, compute that the expected exchange rate is:

$$\$0.4766 \times (1 + 0.0175 - 0.035) = \$0.4683 \text{ per real}$$

If this turns out to be the spot rate in six months, then the 25 million real will be exchanged for $11.7 million (= 25 million real × $0.4683/real). Thus, your firm will want to use some kind of exchange risk management tool to lock in a better real-to-dollar value. What might your firm do to protect itself from foreign exchange risk?

Similar to Problems 19-19, 19-20

TIME OUT

19-3 Why is currency exchange risky for a multinational firm? What can be done to reduce the risk?

19-4 Describe how arbitrage works and how it reinforces the relationship between exchange rates and cross rates.

19-5 Explain why currency exchange rates change over time and how to forecast those changes.

19.3 • Political Risks

LG19-6

Multinational corporations face uncertainty in addition to foreign currency risks. These firms also face uncertainty about foreign and domestic government actions. **Political risk** refers to the possibility that a country's political decisions or events will adversely affect the business climate so that the MNC's investment might fall in value or even completely lose its value.

political risk

The possibility that changes in the political environment will occur that reduce the profitability of doing business in that country.

Sometimes governments change suddenly and violently. A new government typically will not honor the agreements and policies of the former government unless the country or government will profit handsomely for doing so. Although revolution is an extreme case of a change in government, even publicly elected governments may change at each election. In a two-party system like the one in the United States, one administration may create certain trade, tax, and labor policies and the next administration may change those policies. Some political risks to the assets and cash flows of MNCs are:

- Government seizure of a company's assets in the country.
- Expropriation with minimal compensation (the government demanding specific cash flows).
- Enactment of new taxation.
- Limiting or blocking the conversion of local currency to the MNC's domestic currency.

Consider how quickly a country can change from foreign-investment-friendly to hostile. Venezuela has immense oil reserves. For many years Venezuela did not have the capital to fully develop these resources. Consequently, the country entered into service contracts with numerous foreign oil companies to invest in and operate Venezuela's oil fields. In the 1990s, several dozen foreign companies participated in the Venezuelan oil sector at the government's invitation. But Venezuela's hospitality toward foreign companies did not last long. In the 2000s, the Venezuelan government under Hugo Chavez sought to force the renegotiation of contracts and nationalized (seized) entire companies and industries. Venezuela also began nationalizing companies in vitally important industries, including energy and telecommunications. In the Spring of 2007, Verizon was forced to sell its stake in CANTV to the Venezuelan government for \$572 million—about \$100 million less than a previously agreed-to sale price that was awaiting Venezuelan regulatory approval. Since then, the government has nationalized the cement industry, rice processing and packaging, oil rigs, glass-manufacturing plants, and a French firm's supermarkets.

Some countries seem to require payments to various government officials as a condition of doing business in the country. While some countries consider such payments simply part of doing business, the Western world considers such

figure 19.4

Political Stability and Control of Corruption Rankings, World Bank, 2011

The higher the index, the more political stability and less corruption.

Source: Worldwide Governance Indicators, World Bank, http://info.worldbank.org/governance/wgi/index.asp, April 2013.

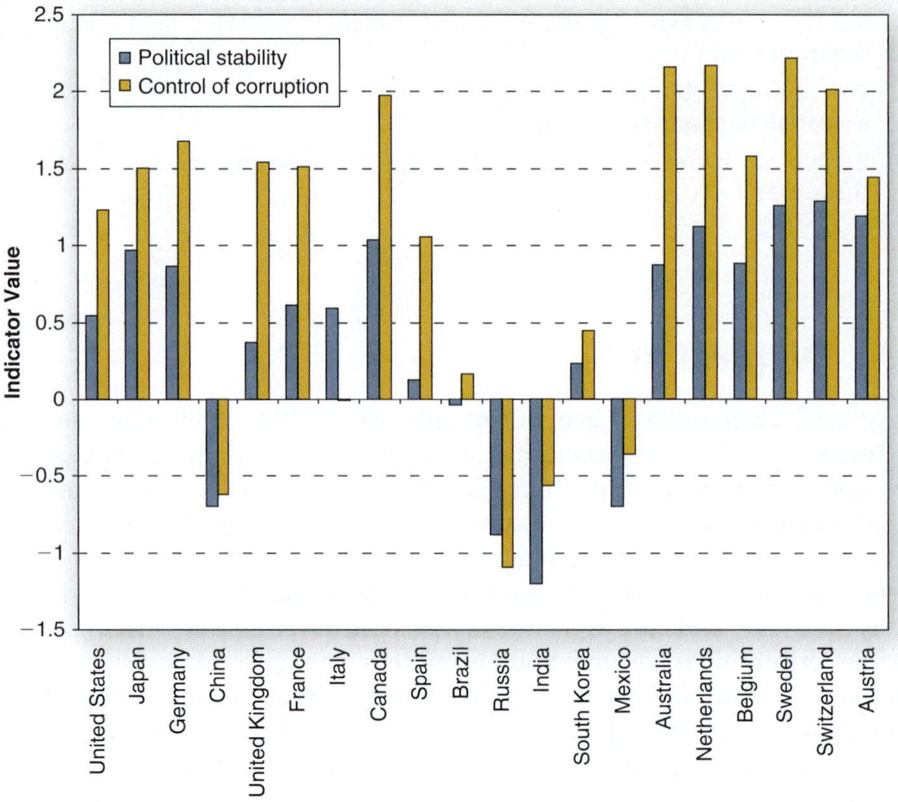

practices corrupt and illegal. This corruption and bribery is banned by the agreement signed by countries in the World Trade Organization. Nevertheless, it likely still occurs, especially in smaller, less developed countries. Each year, the World Bank reports on various country governance indicators. Figure 19.4 shows the index values of the *political stability* indicator and the *control of corruption* indicator. Political stability measures the likelihood of government destabilization or significant policy change. A higher value indicates a more stable government. A higher control of corruption ranking means the bribery and other forms of corruption are minimal. Of these countries, Switzerland has the highest political stability and high control of corruption values, while Russia and India have the lowest values.

Companies can minimize the impact of political risk. Remember that acquiring the capital from inside the foreign country can reduce the need for currency exchange. Similarly, using local financing may reduce losses from a confiscation of assets. If the assets are seized by the government, then the company can refuse to pay back the financing obtained within the country. Another strategy is to purchase country risk insurance from private insurance companies or from the U.S. government sponsored Overseas Private Investment Corporation. Some political risks must be borne by the MNCs as a cost of doing business internationally. Presumably, the opportunities are valuable enough to compensate for these risks.

TIME OUT

19-6 Give some examples of how an MNC can lose assets or cash flow because of political risk.

19-7 Describe some strategies for dealing with political risk.

19.4 • International Capital Budgeting

LG19-7

Great business opportunities arise globally every day. But we have also demonstrated that the opportunities come with significant financial and political risks when the firm does business internationally. Financial managers can use strategies like hedging to minimize some of these risks. Managers need to look at global opportunities with their eyes wide open, recognizing all of the potential risks as well as the opportunities for above-average profits as they evaluate foreign opportunities.

Managers may begin their evaluation of possible foreign projects with regular capital budgeting processes, but the global component adds several complications. Recall that assessing the net present value of a project requires that we estimate the value of future cash flows and that we establish a discount rate that's consistent with project risk. Estimating future cash flows is difficult in a domestic analysis, so we can only imagine the problems with estimating direct and indirect costs and future revenues in unfamiliar territory. We should also use a high discount rate that will account for the added exchange and political risk that the project may incur.

Note that the cash flows of a foreign project will be in the foreign currency, while the discount rate is usually evaluated from the domestic country perspective. A financial manager has two alternative methods for resolving this problem. First, all incremental cash flows can be converted to the domestic currency, which requires exchange rate estimates for each year. We estimate the exchange rate from estimates of how the spot rate will change using PPP. Once the cash flows have been translated into the domestic currency, the regular NPV computation can proceed. The second possibility is to convert the domestic discount rate to an equivalent rate in the foreign country. You would need to use different discount rates in two countries because the two countries will likely experience different inflation rates, which affects PPP. So analysts will have to adjust the discount rate by the difference in the inflation rates between the two countries. The resulting NPV will be denoted in the foreign currency and should be converted back into the domestic currency using the current spot rate. Since both methods rely on some inflation rate estimates, they should produce the same NPV.

TIME OUT

19-8 Explain why the two methods for applying the NPV analysis in an international context should produce the same result.

viewpoints REVISITED

Business Application Solution

Andres should discuss the dynamics of foreign currency exchange. The current spot rate between the dollar and the Mexican peso is $1 = 11.13 pesos. However, the exchange rate has been volatile over the past five years and has varied from 9 pesos to the dollar to 13 pesos to the dollar. Thus, managers should know how a weakening or strengthening dollar will affect the value of the assets invested in Mexico and the cash flow earned from those operations.

The managers should also be aware of the political risks that could impact investment in Mexico. Mexico does not rate highly in political stability or control of corruption (see Figure 19.4), but political policy decisions in the United States can also impact the trade and investment between the two countries.

Andres must account for the increased risks of this project by increasing the discount rate in the NPV analysis. Also, he will have to estimate the future exchange rates in order to translate future cash flows in pesos to dollars.

Personal Application Solution

Juliana can see from Table 19.4 that the exchange rate between the Swiss franc and the U.S. dollar is $1 = 0.9312 franc. Therefore, if she buys the currency now, she will receive 9,312 francs (=$10,000 × 0.9312 franc/$).

Juliana can also see from the six-month forward rate that the dollar is expected to weaken compared to the Swiss franc. Therefore, she may be tempted to exchange the currency now. However, the interest rate parity concept suggests that she will likely end up with the same amount of francs in six months if she either buys the francs now and deposits them in a Swiss bank to earn interest, or keeps the $10,000 deposited in a U.S. bank and exchanges for francs in six months. Therefore, she should do whichever is more convenient for her.

summary of learning goals

International business opportunities have substantially increased over the past few decades. Multinational corporations like Starbucks can produce and sell products in whichever countries maximize their firms' values. In this chapter, we've explored the risks associated with international business operations and how to ameliorate those risks.

LG19-1 **Gauge the dynamics of the global economy and recognize potential international opportunities.** Many large economies in the world trade extensively among themselves. In addition, many smaller developing economies provide investment and trading opportunities. Although the United States has the largest economy by far, the combined economies of the European countries in the European Union creates a marketplace nearly as big as the United States. Other trading zones have also formed in other parts of the world. These zones voluntarily reduce trading restrictions and tariffs. The World Trade Organization and the International Monetary Fund also promote free trade globally.

LG19-2 **Recognize patterns of increasing capital involvement as the firm seeks to expand business internationally.** Firms typically take a step-by-step approach to expanding their business overseas, taking on increasing risks with each step they take. The low-risk (but low-reward) approach is simple importing and exporting. Domestic firms can also partner with in-country firms through sales subsidiaries, licensing arrangements, and joint ventures. The MNC invests capital directly into projects in multiple countries. This foreign direct investment in the United States by foreign MNCs has reached a trillion dollars annually in the last few years. U.S. MNCs invested less then half of that into foreign countries recently.

LG19-3 **Compute currency exchanges.** To buy and sell products internationally, you will need to exchange one currency for another to pay for foreign goods. The direct quote spot currency exchange rate determines how much of your domestic currency you will need for each unit of the foreign currency. You can also determine the cross rate between two foreign currencies if you know the two exchange rates between the domestic currency and each foreign currency. If the relationship between the currency exchange rates and cross rate between the three currencies does not hold, then triangular arbitrage may be possible.

LG19-4 **Recognize situations that evoke exchange rate risk and develop tools to manage those risks.** Currency exchange rates change over time. This is a financial risk for firms doing business overseas because the firms are exposed to the risk that future foreign or domestic cash flows will be adversely affected by a drastic change in exchange rates. Most currency exchange rates either freely float over time or are managed by a government via a pegging system. When it takes more dollars over time to buy a unit of foreign currency, the dollar is said to be weakening. If fewer dollars will buy a unit of foreign currency, then the dollar is strengthening.

Financial managers can cope with the exchange rate risk by forming contracts in the forward market or through hedging in the derivative markets. In addition, managers can minimize the need for exchanging currencies by obtaining capital within the country where the investment is to be made.

LG19-5 **Apply theories of how interest rates and inflation influence forward exchange rates and future spot rates.** The relationship between the spot rate and the forward exchange rate is established by the level of interest rates in the two countries as specified by interest rate parity. An expected change in the spot exchange rates is described by purchasing power parity. It shows the difference in expected inflation rates between the two countries, which determines the exchange rates. The country with the higher inflation rate will see a weakening of its currency.

LG19-6 **Anticipate political risks when investing internationally.** Governments can suddenly change in terms of who has power and in terms of political ideology. New governments may make new and different demands on international firms' assets and cash flows invested in the country. This political risk can also occur when stable governments change trade restrictions, tariffs, taxes, and other trade policies. Some political risks can be managed through country risk insurance and through raising capital within the country where the firm is operating.

LG19-7 **As a financial manager, plan to work through capital budgeting issues for international investments.** The presence of exchange rate risk and political risk increase the overall risk of investing in new projects in foreign countries. Financial managers need to adjust for this increased risk by evaluating projects using higher discount rates in the NPV analysis. For capital budgeting, either future foreign currency cash flows need to be converted to domestic currency or the discount rate needs to be translated from the domestic country to the foreign country.

chapter equations

19-1 $$\frac{\text{Forward exchange rate}}{\text{Spot exchange rate}} = \frac{1 + i_d}{1 + i_f}$$

19-2 $P_d = P_f \times \text{Spot rate}$

19-3 $$\underset{\text{(domestic amount per unit of foreign currency)}}{\text{Expected exchange}} = \underset{\text{(domestic amount per unit of foreign currency)}}{\text{Current spot rate}} \times (1 + \text{Domestic inflation rate} - \text{Foreign inflation rate})$$

key terms

arbitrage, The practice of simultaneously purchasing and selling an asset in different forms or markets to take advantage of an imbalance in price. *p. 638*

arbitrageur, A trader who engages in arbitrage. *p. 638*

Central American Free Trade Agreement, A free trade agreement between the Central American countries and the United States. *p. 632*

cross rates, The currency exchange rate between two foreign currencies, each of which is not the currency of the domestic country. *p. 637*

currency swap, A foreign exchange agreement to exchange a given amount of one currency for another and then later return the original amounts swapped. *p. 640*

direct quote, The amount of domestic currency needed to buy one unit of foreign currency. *p. 636*

discount, The case when the forward rate indicates a weaker currency over the spot rate. *p. 640*

European Union (EU), A political and economic union of 27 European countries. *p. 632*

exchange rate, Specifies how much one currency is worth in terms of the other. *p. 636*

exchange rate risk, The possibility that the spot currency exchange rate will change and reduce the value of foreign assets and cash flows. *p. 638*

fixed peg arrangement, An exchange rate regime where a currency's price is fixed to the value of another currency or to a basket of other currencies. *p. 640*

foreign direct investment, A long-term investment of capital in a business operation located in an economy other than that in which the company is based. *p. 635*

forward exchange rate, A contractual arrangement that states the exchange rate to be used at a future exchange date. *p. 640*

freely floating regime, An exchange rate regime where the currency is completely determined by the foreign-exchange market through supply and demand. *p. 638*

futures, A standardized contract traded in a futures exchange market designed to buy (or sell) the underlying asset at a specific price on a certain future date. *p. 640*

hedging, A strategy used to minimize exposure to an unwanted business or financial risk, while still allowing the business to profit. *p. 640*

indirect quote, The amount of foreign currency needed to buy one unit of domestic currency. *p. 636*

interest rate parity, A theory that the difference in interest rates between two countries is equal to the difference between the forward currency exchange rate and the spot exchange rate. *p. 641*

International Monetary Fund (IMF), An international organization that monitors exchange rates and balance of payments and oversees the global financial system. *p. 634*

law of one price, An economic principle that states all identical goods in different markets must have the same price. *p. 642*

managed-floating regime, An exchange rate regime where the country's central bank allows its currency price to float freely between an upper and lower bound and may buy or sell large amounts of it in order to provide price support or resistance. *p. 638*

Mercosur, The Southern Common Market of South America. *p. 632*

multinational corporation (MNC), A company that operates production and/or sales facilities in multiple countries. *p. 635*

North American Free Trade Agreement (NAFTA), The trading block consisting of Canada, Mexico, and the United States. *p. 632*

option, A standardized contract in which the buyer has the right (but not the obligation) to buy (or sell) an asset at a set price by a future date. *p. 640*

political risk, The possibility that changes in the political environment will occur that reduce the profitability of doing business in that country. *p. 645*

premium, The case when the forward rate indicates a stronger currency over the spot rate. *p. 640*

purchasing power parity (PPP), A theory relating the expected adjustment needed in the future spot exchange rate between countries to the inflation rate in each economy. *p. 642*

spot transaction, An exchange of one currency for another today. *p. 636*

World Trade Organization (WTO), An international organization that deals with international trade rules and helps settle disputes between its member governments. *p. 634*

self-test problems with solutions

1 Exchange Rate Risk Your firm has invested \$150 million in projects in Europe and \$250 million in Japan. The current spot exchange rates are \$1 = €0.7623 and \$1 = ¥118.04. Consider that over this year, these investments appreciate by 10 percent each, as measured in the foreign currency. However, the spot rates also change to \$1 = €0.7563 and \$1 = ¥124.66. You need to determine the value of the projects in dollars and their appreciation for the year. LG19-4

Solution:

First compute the starting values of the projects in Europe and Japan:

In Europe: \$150 million × €0.7623/\$ = €114.345 million
In Japan: \$250 million × ¥118.04/\$ = ¥29,510 million

Next, compute the value after the 10 percent appreciation:

In Europe: €114.345 million × (1 + 0.1) = €125.780 million
In Japan: ¥29,510 million × (1 + 0.1) = ¥32,461 million

Last, compute the dollar value using the new spot rates:

In Europe: €125.780 million ÷ €0.7563/\$ = \$166.31 million
In Japan: ¥32,461 million ÷ ¥124.66/\$ = \$260.4 million

Note that while both project values increased 10 percent in their own markets, the change in exchange rates made the value changes 10.9 percent [= (\$166.31m − \$150m) ÷ \$150m] in Europe and 4.2 percent [= (\$260.4m − \$250m) ÷ \$250m] in Japan.

2 Interest Rate Parity Arbitrage You believe that you have found a small mispricing between the spot exchange rate and the forward rate between the Japanese yen and the British pound. Consider the following information: LG19-5

Spot rate: £1 = ¥229.02
6-month forward rate: £1 = ¥227.01
Interest rate in Japan: 0.5 percent
Interest rate in the United Kingdom: 5.25 percent

You want to verify that a mispricing exists and determine the profit (in pounds) of a £10 million arbitrage.

Solution:

You can use the interest rate parity equation 19-1 to verify a mispricing in the forward rate. First, you need to convert these exchange rates and interest rate for use in the equation. From the perspective of the British pound, these are indirect quotes and need to be direct quotes. Also, the forward rate is for six months, thus a 6-month interest rate must be used. The recomputed exchange rates and interest rates are:

Direct quote spot rate: ¥1 = £0.004366431
Direct quote 6-month forward rate: ¥1 = £0.004405092
6-month interest rate in Japan: 0.25 percent
6-month interest rate in the United Kingdom: 2.625 percent

Given the current spot rate and interest rates, the forward rate should be

$$\text{Forward rate} = \frac{1 + 0.02625}{1 + 0.0025} \times 0.004366431 = 0.00469875£/¥$$

Since this is different from the forward rate quote, an arbitrage is possible. You want to borrow enough Japanese yen to deposit £ 10 million. So, you should conduct the following trades:

- Borrow ¥2,290.2 million (= £10 million ÷ 0.004366431 ¥/£) at the annual 0.5 percent interest rate
- Convert the yen to £10 million and make a deposit to earn a 5.25 percent rate
- Enter into a forward contract for the amount that will be owed, ¥2,295.9255 million (= ¥2,290.2 million × 1.0025)

After six months:

- The deposit will result in £10.2625 million (= £10 *million* × 1.02625)
- Convert £10.113764 million (= ¥2,295.9255 million × 0.004405092 £/¥) into yen using the forward contract to repay the loan
- You keep the difference of £148,736 (= £10.2625 million − £10.113764 million)

questions

1. What do global organizations like the World Trade Organization and the International Monetary Fund do? *(LG19-1)*
2. What is the purpose of trading zones? What are some of the most important zones for world trade? *(LG19-1)*
3. Explain how a country's import trade limitations and tariffs influence MNCs' foreign direct investment. *(LG19-1)*
4. What are the risks of foreign direct investment into the United States? What does new FDI into the United States mean for firms already operating in that industry in the United States? *(LG19-2)*
5. Describe the similarities and the differences of exchange rate/cross rate arbitrage and spot rate/forward rate arbitrage. *(LG19-3, LG19-5)*
6. What is meant when it is said that the U.S. dollar is strengthening? How would it impact your vacation abroad and foreign visitors to the United States? *(LG19-4)*
7. Describe the difference between a forward rate selling at a discount and selling at a premium. If the spot rate between the U.S. dollar and the Brazilian real is $1 = 2.0875 real and the 3-month forward rate is $1 = 2.1025 real, is the forward real selling at a discount or a premium? *(LG19-4)*
8. What is meant by hedging exchange rate risk and what are some ways it is done? *(LG19-4)*
9. What are the advantages of borrowing money in the country you plan to invest it in? *(LG19-4, LG19-6)*

10. If a Sony television costs $500 in the United States, what do you think it should cost in Japan? What are some reasons that your price might not be right? *(LG19-5)*

11. What happens to a country's currency over time when it has a high inflation rate? What will that mean for the country's exports and imports? *(LG19-5)*

12. What forces are at work that cause the price of wheat per bushel to be the same in most every country of the world? *(LG19-5)*

13. If the spot exchange rate between the U.S. dollar and the Singapore dollar is $1 = SG$1.5266 and the 3-month expected exchange rate is $1 = SG$1.5305, then what is the expected inflation relationship between the two countries? *(LG19-5)*

14. Over the past decade, China has acquired hundreds of billions of U.S. dollars because of the trade imbalance between the two countries. Many of these dollars were used to purchase U.S. Treasury bonds. What would likely happen to the dollar's value, and interest rates and inflation in the United States, if China decided to suddenly sell the Treasury bonds and exchange the dollars for other currencies? *(LG19-5)*

15. Can a U.S. firm experience political risk problems in its overseas projects because of the U.S. government? Give examples. *(LG19-6)*

16. Give some examples of the financial complications that occur when evaluating a capital budgeting project in a foreign country. *(LG19-7)*

problems

basic problems

19-1 Exchange Rate Quote Convert each of the following direct quotes to dollar indirect quotes *(LG19-3)*:

a. 1 Danish krone = $0.170

b. 1 Indian rupee = $0.0184

c. 1 Israeli shekel = $0.2751

19-2 Exchange Rate Quote Convert each of the following direct quotes to dollar indirect quotes *(LG19-3)*:

a. 1 Korean won = $0.0009

b. 1 Malaysian ringgit = $0.3238

c. 1 Thai baht = $0.0331

19-3 Exchange Rate Quote Convert each of the following indirect quotes to dollar direct quotes *(LG19-3)*:

a. $1 = 20,864 Vietnamese dong

b. $1 = 6.300 Venezuelan bolivar fuerte

c. $1 = 9.175 South African rand

19-4 Exchange Rate Quote Convert each of the following indirect quotes to dollar direct quotes *(LG19-3)*:

a. $1 = 3.7497 Saudi Arabian riyal

b. $1 = 44.15 Philippine peso

c. $1 = 0.5409 Latvian lat

19-5 **Currency Exchange** Compute the amount of each foreign currency that can be purchased for $500,000 *(LG19-3):*

a. 1 Danish krone = $0.170

b. 1 Indian rupee = $0.0184

c. 1 Israeli shekel = $0.2751

19-6 **Currency Exchange** Compute the amount of each foreign currency that can be purchased for $1 million *(LG19-3):*

a. 1 Korean won = $0.0009

b. 1 Malaysian ringgit = $0.3238

c. 1 Thai baht = $0.0331

19-7 **Currency Exchange** Compute the number of dollars that can be bought with 2 million of each foreign currency units *(LG19-3):*

a. $1 = 20,864 Vietnamese dong

b. $1 = 6.300 Venezuelan bolivar

c. $1 = 9.175 South African rand

19-8 **Currency Exchange** Compute the number of dollars that can be bought with 1 million of each foreign currency units *(LG19-3):*

a. $1 = 3.7497 Saudi Arabian riyal

b. $1 = 44.15 Philippine peso

c. $1 = 0.5409 Latvian lat

19-9 **Law of One Price** If the price of silver in England is £15.23 per ounce, what is the expected price of silver in the United States if the spot exchange rate is $1 = £0.6535? *(LG19-5)*

19-10 **Law of One Price** If the price of copper in Europe is €2.12 per ounce, what is the expected price of copper in the United States if the spot exchange rate is $1 = £0.7623? *(LG19-5)*

19-11 **Discount Rates** A financial manager has determined that the appropriate discount rate for a foreign project is 12 percent. However, that discount rate applies in the United States using dollars. What discount rate should be used in the foreign country using the foreign currency? The inflation rate in the United States and in the foreign country is expected to be 3 percent and 6 percent, respectively. *(LG19-7)*

19-12 **Discount Rates** A financial manager has determined that the appropriate discount rate for a foreign project is 16 percent. However, that discount rate applies in the United States using dollars. What discount rate should the manager use in the foreign country using the foreign currency? The inflation rate in the United States and in the foreign country is expected to be 5 percent and 4 percent, respectively. *(LG19-7)*

intermediate problems

19-13 **Cross Rate** Given these two exchange rates, $1 = 12.268 Mexican pesos and $1 = €0.7624, compute the cross rate between the Mexican peso and the euro. State this exchange rate in pesos and in euros. *(LG19-3)*

19-14 **Cross Rate** Given these two exchange rates, $1 = 0.9952 Australian dollars and $1 = £0.6476, compute the cross rate between the Australian dollars and the pound. State this exchange rate in Australian dollars and in pounds. *(LG19-3)*

19-15 Exchange Rate Risk In 1997, many East Asian currencies suddenly and dramatically devalued. What is the percentage change in value of a $50 million investment in Indonesia when the exchange rate changes from $1 = 2,000 rupiah to $1 = 10,000 rupiah? *(LG19-4)*

19-16 Exchange Rate Risk The Russian financial crisis of 1998 caused its currency to be dramatically devalued. What is the percentage change in value of a $100 million investment in Russia when the exchange rate changes from $1 = 6 rubles to $1 = 21 rubles? *(LG19-4)*

19-17 Interest Rate Parity The spot rate between the U.S. dollar and the New Zealand dollar is $1 = NZD1.1867. If the interest rate in the United States is 5 percent and in New Zealand is 4 percent, then what should be the 3-month forward exchange rate? *(LG19-5)*

19-18 Interest Rate Parity The spot rate between the U.S. dollar and the Taiwan dollar is $1 = TWD29.905. If the interest rate in the United States is 5 percent and in Taiwan is 3 percent, then what should be the 1-month forward exchange rate? *(LG19-5)*

19-19 Purchasing Power Parity The current spot rate between the U.S. dollar and the Swedish krona is $1 = 6.5228 krona. If the inflation rate in the United States is 4 percent and in Sweden is 2 percent, then what is the expected spot rate in one year? *(LG19-5)*

19-20 Purchasing Power Parity The current spot rate between the U.S. dollar and the Netherland Antilles guilder is $1 = 1.7915 guilder. If the inflation rate in the United States is 3 percent and in the Netherland Antilles is 7 percent, then what is the expected spot rate in one year? *(LG19-5)*

advanced problems

19-21 Exchange Rate Risk A U.S. firm is expecting cash flows of 25 million Mexican pesos and 35 million Indian rupees. The current spot exchange rates are $1 = 12.268 pesos and $1 = 45.204 rupees. If these cash flows are not received for one year and the expected spot rates at that time will be $1 = 11.118 pesos and $1 = 44.075 rupees, then what is the difference in dollars received that was caused by the delay? *(LG19-4)*

19-22 Exchange Rate Risk A U.S. firm is expecting to pay cash flows of 15 million Egyptian pounds and 25 million Qatar rials. The current spot exchange rates are: $1 = 5.725 pounds and $1 = 3.639 rials. If these cash flows are delayed one year and the expected spot rates at that time will be $1 = 5.892 pounds and $1 = 3.988 rials, what is the difference in dollars paid that was caused by the delay? *(LG19-4)*

19-23 Triangular Arbitrage The U.S. dollar spot exchange rate with the Canadian dollar is $1 = CA$1.18. The U.S. dollar and Swiss franc exchange rate is $1 = 1.219 francs. If the cross rate between the franc and Canadian dollar is 1 franc = CA$0.9750, then show that an arbitrage is possible. What positions should be taken to profit from the mispricing? *(LG19-3)*

19-24 Triangular Arbitrage The U.S. dollar spot exchange rate with the Australian dollar is $1 = AU$1.2697. The U.S. dollar and euro exchange rate is $1 = €0.7559. If the cross rate between the euro and Australian dollar is €1 = AU$1.598, then show that an arbitrage is possible. What positions should be taken to profit from the mispricing? *(LG19-3)*

19-25 Spreadsheet Problem Below are the Consumer Price Index inflation rates each year for the United States and Japan. Also shown is the spot exchange rate for the beginning of each year.

a. Using PPP (equation 19-3), compute what the 1-year forward exchange rate should be each year.

b. Compare the forward rates computed in part (a) to the actual exchange rate at the beginning of the next year. How well does PPP predict the future exchange rate? Is it biased too high or too low, or is it about right?

Year	Beginning of Year Exchange Rate (Yen Per $)	U.S. CPI Inflation Rate	Japan CPI Inflation Rate
1990	146.25	6.1	3.1
1991	134.60	3.1	3.3
1992	124.50	2.9	1.6
1993	125.40	2.8	1.1
1994	112.50	2.7	0.5
1995	100.52	2.5	−0.3
1996	103.92	3.3	0.0
1997	115.49	1.7	1.6
1998	132.40	1.6	0.7
1999	112.15	2.7	−0.4
2000	101.70	3.4	−0.9
2001	114.73	1.6	−0.9
2002	132.02	2.4	−1.1
2003	119.86	1.9	−0.3
2004	106.95	3.3	0.0
2005	102.83	3.4	−0.4
2006	116.34	2.5	0.3
2007	118.83	4.1	−0.4
2008	109.70	0.0	1.4
2009	91.12	2.6	1.3
2010	92.55	1.6	0.1
2011	81.56	2.9	−0.2
2012	76.67	1.6	−0.1
2013	87.10		

research it! Find Currency Exchange Rates

Currency spot exchange rates are widely available on the Web. For example, at Yahoo! Finance **(http://finance.yahoo.com/currency)** you can find the exchange rates between more than 150 currencies. The calculator the site provides computes the amount of one currency resulting from converting money in another currency. You can also see a graph of the desired exchange rate for a history of up to five years. Daily and monthly historical data for the dollar exchange rates are available at the Federal Reserve website **(http://research.stlouisfed.org/fred2/).** Many of the exchange rate data are available for more than 30 years. See how exchange rates have changed over the years.

integrated mini-case: Assessing Exchange Rate Risk

Imagine that you are a financial manager of a multinational corporation, like Starbucks Coffee, in charge of determining the impact of exchange rate changes on the firm. Changes in currency exchange affect both the balance sheet and the income statement. The balance sheet impact occurs when the values of international assets are translated to U.S. dollars. The values of those assets change as the exchange rate changes. The value of costs, revenue, and profit also impact the income statement because of exchange rate risk. Consider that your firm has the following investments in coffee bean production and processing:

Country	Value ($ millions)
Colombia	$ 75
Kenya	100
Papua New Guinea	80

The expense of all the labor, production, and beans will require the following exchanges to the foreign currency:

Country	Cash Flow (millions)
Colombia	78,180 pesos
Kenya	3,200 shilling
Papua New Guinea	100 kina

Your firm has also invested in store facilities to sell the coffee products. The countries and the value of the investments are:

Country	Value ($ millions)
Canada	$200
Japan	100
United Kingdom	150

The net profit from these countries next year is projected to be:

Country	Cash Flow (millions)
Canada	CA$80
Japan	¥7,200
United Kingdom	£30

Current spot exchange rates are:

$1 = 2,204.5 Colombian pesos
$1 = 69.480 Kenyan shilling
$1 = 3.0189 Papua New Guinea kina
$1 = 1.1690 Canadian dollars
$1 = 117.04 Japanese yen
$1 = 0.5182 British pound

Your task is to determine the following:

a. What is the impact on the value of the international assets and the cash flow if the dollar were to devalue by 10 percent against each currency *(one at a time)*?

b. What is the overall impact of a 10 percent dollar devaluation against every currency?

c. What is the impact on the value of the international assets and the cash flow if the dollar were to strengthen by 10 percent against each currency *(one at a time)*?

d. What is the overall impact of a 10 percent strengthening against every currency?

e. What can be done to hedge this risk?

ANSWERS TO TIME OUT

19-1 Free-trade zones are motivated by the idea that when trade between multiple countries is unencumbered by tariffs, restrictions, and quotas, then more trade will occur. An increase in trade benefits all countries involved. Thus, the wealth of all countries increases in a free-trade zone. This free trade is perceived as fair only when the same laws (labor, pollution, etc.) apply to all countries involved.

19-2 Capital that flows into the United States winds itself through the economy and increases the investment in new business projects, factories, technology, and so on. In short, capital coming into the United States will lead to more jobs for U.S. workers. In addition, capital usually buys factories and technology, so those jobs will be higher-quality ones.

19-3 Multinational firms make investments in foreign countries. One risk is that the value of these investments changes as the exchange rates between the home countries and the foreign countries change. A second risk involves the payment and receipt of cash flows. In business, payment and receipt of cash flows is contracted for the future. But the value of those payments can change before they are made because of the change in exchange rates. To reduce the risks, firms can hedge their investments and cash flows through contracts in the forward markets, futures, options, and currency swaps.

19-4 Arbitrage seeks to find two different avenues to buy and sell the same assets at different prices. When arbitrageurs find this case to occur, they buy the low-price assets and sell the high-price asset to capture the difference as profit. For currency exchange rates, an arbitrage opportunity exists when the price of U.S. to a foreign currency is different from the price through a third currency using cross rates. The buying of the low-priced exchange rate and the selling of the high-price rate causes prices to adjust so that the opportunity disappears.

19-5 The difference in interest rates and inflation between two countries drives the changes in the exchange rate between the currencies. The difference in interest rates impacts the forward exchange rates. This can be seen through the interest rate parity equation. When inflation differs between two countries, the change in prices of goods directly leads to changes in the exchange rate as seen in the purchasing power parity equation. These changes can be forecasted using estimates of inflation and interest rates, and the forward rate.

19-6 Multinational companies can lose assets invested in a country when civil war breaks out and those assets get destroyed. Assets can also be lost when the government decides to seize the firm's assets. Cash flow of the firm can be reduced when the government enacts new taxes or new tariffs or limits the conversion of the local currency into the MNC's home country currency.

19-7 MNCs should acquire some capital from within the countries in which they operate. This will allow for less currency exchange to be needed because some of the capital to be repaid will occur within the foreign countries. In addition, governments may be less likely to seize assets when those assets are partially owned by local investors. Finally, insurance can be purchased to protect against some political risks.

19-8 The NPV method requires cash flows and a discount rate. Whether the cash flows are in domestic currency or in the foreign currency, they are equivalent if they are converted using the PPP equation in the future and estimates of future inflation. The discount rates will also be equivalent if they are adjusted by the inflation rates too. Since both the cash flows and the discount rates are equivalent in the two currencies, the NPV analysis conducted in each currency will provide the same outcome.

PART NINE

20 Mergers and Acquisitions and Financial Distress

viewpoints

Business Application

BSW Corporation has approached MHM Production, Inc., for a possible merger. The cash flows of MHM Production are projected to be $5.5 million in the coming year and are expected to grow by 3 percent annually in years 2 through 6. After the first six years, cash flows are expected to remain constant. Managers of BSW estimate that, because of synergies, the merged firm's cash flows would increase by $6 million in the first year after the merger and that these cash flows will grow by 3 percent in years 2 through 6 following the merger. After the first six years, they expect incremental cash flows from synergies to be $2 million annually. BSW Corp.'s management expects the WACC for the merged firms over the foreseeable future to be 9 percent. Managers of MHM Production are asking $90 million for the firm. Should BSW Corporation acquire MHM Production at this price? **(See solution on p. 683)**

Personal Application

James Upton holds $25,000 in subordinated debentures of Jaylon's Jazz Music Production, Inc. The firm has just announced that it will file Chapter 7 bankruptcy. The firm's assets have a book value of $500,000. The liquidated assets produce $250,000. Administrative expenses associated with the bankruptcy, unpaid wages, employee benefits, and taxes total $10,000. The firm has debt owed to secured creditors of $175,000, accounts payable of $25,000, notes payable to banks of $120,000, and total subordinated (to notes payable) debt outstanding of $100,000. How much of the total $25,000 in subordinated debentures in Jaylon's Jazz Music Production, Inc., can James Upton expect to recover? **(See solution on p. 683)**

Vulture investors buy distressed debt before and during the bankruptcy process. Think you have what it takes to be a vulture?

Learning Goals

LG20-1 Differentiate among types of and address motives for mergers and acquisitions.

LG20-2 Mathematically value mergers.

LG20-3 Suggest methods by which a firm can informally resolve severe financial distress.

LG20-4 Differentiate between Chapter 7 and Chapter 11 bankruptcy.

LG20-5 Build and use statistical models to predict bankruptcy.

You may recall that as we discussed various organizational structures in Chapter 1, we stated that one advantage of corporate organization is that the expected life of a corporation can be unlimited. But no corporation can expect to go on forever despite all circumstances. In this chapter, we look at two situations that may cause corporations to cease to exist—mergers and acquisitions or financial distress.

First, we look at mergers and acquisitions, in which two firms combine assets, liabilities, and equity. In this case, the target firm becomes part of the bidder firm and ceases to exist as an independent entity. We then look at a second way that firms cease to exist—through financial distress. In the most extreme cases of financial distress, firms go out of business and another firm buys their assets or everything is liquidated to pay off creditors and, possibly, the firms' stockholders. However, financial distress can involve much less devastating circumstances, consisting of events like a manufacturing plant fire that stops production for a week. Firms can usually recover quickly from these types of financially distressing events.

20.1 • Mergers and Acquisitions

A **merger** is a transaction in which two firms combine to form a single firm. An **acquisition** is the purchase of one firm by another. Despite these two distinct definitions, the terms mergers and acquisitions, are often used interchangeably. From this definition of acquisition, we can see a clear distinction between the buyer (or bidder firm) and the seller (or target firm). Likewise, but perhaps a bit less clear, in mergers we can classify the acquiring firm (the bidder, who initiates the transaction) and the seller (or target, who receives the offer). Typically, in a merger or acquisition the acquiring firm retains its identity, while the target firm ceases to exist. A **consolidation** is another type of merger in which an entirely new firm is created. A consolidation absorbs both the bidder and target firms into this new firm and the old firms cease to exist as separate entities. Table 20.1 lists the largest mergers as of 2013.

merger

A transaction in which two firms combine to form a single firm.

acquisition

The purchase of one firm by another.

consolidation

A type of merger in which an entirely new firm is created. Both the bidder and target firms are absorbed into this new firm and cease to exist as separate entities.

Figure 20.1 shows the total value of mergers and acquisitions between 1990 and 2012. For most of this period, the mergers and acquisitions business boomed as firms sought to combine with like firms to make the most of their economic clout.

table 20.1 | **Largest Mergers and Acquisitions**

Bidder	Target	Transaction Value	Year Announced
America Online, Inc.	Time Warner, Inc.	$164,747m	2000
Verizon/AT&T	Vodafone	130,000m	2013
Pfizer, Inc.	Warner-Lambert Co.	90,000m	1999
Exxon Corp.	Mobil Corp.	77,200m	1988
Citicorp	Travelers Group	73,000m	1998
AT&T	BellSouth	72,671m	2006
Comcast	AT&T Broadband	72,041m	2001
Pfizer	Wyeth	67,286m	2009
Bank of America	NationsBank	64,000m	1998
SBC Communications, Inc.	Ameritech Corp.	63,000m	1998

figure 20.1

Total Values of Mergers and Acquisitions Managed by Investment Banks, 1990–2012 (in billions of dollars)

M&A activity flows with the economy.

Source: Thomson Reuters Financial website, www.thomsonreuters.com

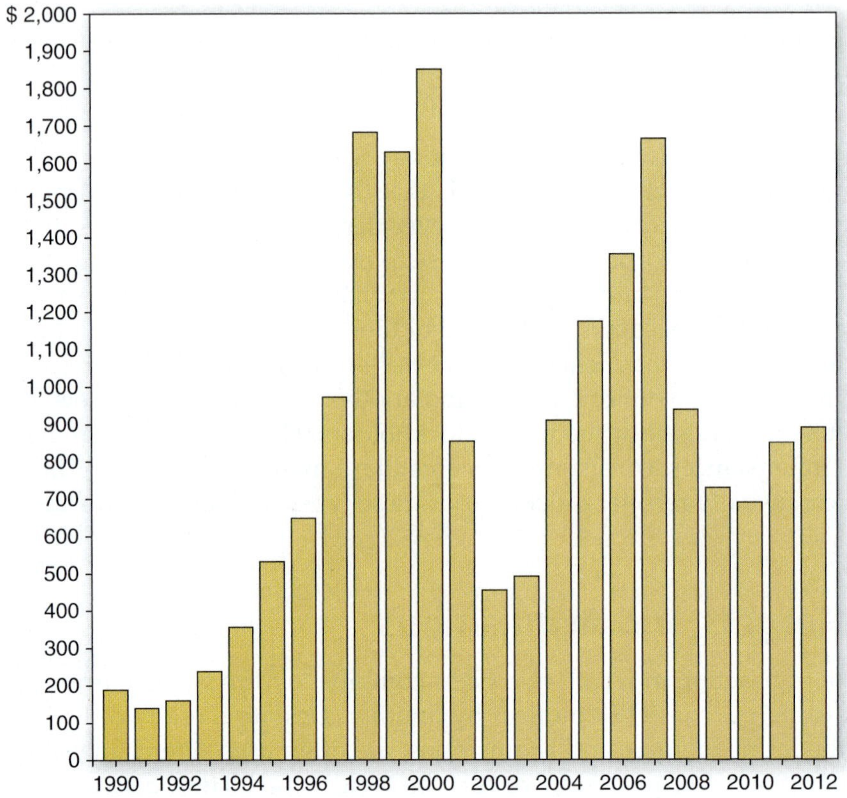

Total dollar volume (measured by market value of the target firm; i.e., the transaction value) of domestic mergers and acquisitions increased from less than $200 billion in 1990 to $1.83 *trillion* in 2000. Nevertheless, as the U.S. economy experienced falling economic activity in the early 2000s, merger and acquisition activity fell 53 percent in 2001 to $819 billion. Domestic M&A activity bottomed out at $458 billion in 2002 before recovering, topping $1.7 trillion in 2007. During the financial crisis, domestic M&A activity fell to $903 billion in 2008, $713 billion in 2009, and $687 billion in 2010. Note that while this period included the worst financial crisis since the Great Depression, M&A activity remained at higher levels than those experienced in the early 2000s. As the U.S. economy recovered in 2011 and 2012, M&A activity rose as well (to $861 billion and $882 billion, respectively).

Types of Mergers

LG20-1

The general expression *merger and acquisition* encompasses many specific types of financial combinations. For example, a **horizontal merger** combines two companies in the same industry, such as the merger between Pfizer and Wyeth listed in Table 20.1. A **market extension merger,** a type of horizontal merger, combines two firms that sell the same products in different market areas. As we will discuss, forming a larger firm may create beneficial economies of scale. The impact on an industry of a horizontal merger of two small competitors is generally minimal. However, the horizontal merger of two industry leaders, such as Pfizer and Wyeth, can restrict competition within the firms' industry. Federal Trade Commission (FTC) regulators (a branch of the Justice Department) scrutinize any merger that involves industry leaders for any negative impact on the industry before the merger is approved. Horizontal mergers are regulated by the government for possible negative effects on competition. They decrease the number of firms in an industry, possibly making it easier for the industry members to go into cartels for monopoly profits.

horizontal merger

The merger of two companies in the same industry.

market extension merger

A type of horizontal merger that combines two firms that sell the same products in different market areas.

A **vertical merger** combines a firm with a supplier or distributor, such as the merger of Barnes & Noble (the nation's largest book retailer) and Ingram Book Group (the nation's largest book wholesaler). Vertical mergers occur between firms in different stages of production operation for many reasons such as avoidance of fixed costs, the elimination of costs of searching for prices, contracting, payment collection, communication, advertising and coordination, and better planning for inventory.

vertical merger

A combination of a firm with a supplier or distributor.

A **conglomerate merger** combines two companies that have no related products or markets. For example, the $164.7 billion merger of Internet titan America Online (AOL) and media conglomerate Time Warner in 2000 represents not just a conglomerate merger but one of the largest mergers of all time. The merger combined Time Warner's more traditional lines of business (print publications and cable TV) with AOL's newer lines of business (online and interactive services). Conglomerate mergers were very popular in the 1960s and 1970s. The motive for these mergers comes from portfolio theory. That is, the merger combines two companies that operate in businesses so different that if an event has a negative effect on one business, the other business and the overall cash flows of the firm will be minimally affected. Thus, these mergers are intended to make earnings and cash flows less volatile. However, it turned out that many conglomerate mergers resulted in decreased market values and were dismantled in the 1980s and 1990s. This type of merger is seen infrequently in the 2000s.

conglomerate merger

A merger that combines two firms that have no related products or markets.

A **product extension merger** is a combination of firms that sell different, but somewhat related, products. For example, the merger of Bank of America and Merrill Lynch in 2008 combined two types of financial institutions: a commercial bank and an investment bank. Product extension mergers are something of a hybrid classification—crossing a horizontal merger and a conglomerate merger. That is, these mergers are not horizontal in that they do not combine firms that compete directly for business customers for a single product, and they are not conglomerate mergers in that they do not combine firms in two completely different lines of business. Rather, the firms involved in a product extension merger produce different products and sell them with greater success to the already common set of customers that the two separate companies share.

product extension merger

A merger that combines two firms that sell different, but somewhat related products.

Motives for Mergers and Acquisitions

LG20-1

The main motivation for a merger or acquisition is **synergy,** the working together of the two firms to produce a combined value that is greater than the sum of their individual values. Thus, managers merge firms to maximize the value of the

synergy

The value of the combined firms is greater than the sum of the value of the two firms individually.

firms to the shareholders. The sources of value-enhancing synergy in a merger come from four areas: revenue enhancement, cost reduction, tax considerations, and lower cost of capital. However, there are also some non-value-maximizing motives behind a merger. These include managers' personal incentives that may destroy firm value and the misallocation of capital between the merged firms.

REVENUE ENHANCEMENT The revenue synergies argument has three dimensions. First, acquiring a firm in a growing market may enhance revenues. For example, while the merger of J.P. Morgan and Chase Manhattan to form JPMorgan Chase was estimated to produce a cost savings of $1.5 billion, the CEOs of both companies stated that the success of the merger was pinned on revenue growth. The merger combined JPMorgan's greater array of products with Chase's broad client base. The merger added substantially to many businesses (such as equity underwriting and asset management) that Chase had been trying to build on its own through smaller deals and gave it a bigger presence in Europe where investment and corporate banking were fast-growing businesses. When JPMorgan Chase then acquired Bank One, analysts praised the combination as one that offered revenue growth potential, the result of the combination of two different business models as well as expense reduction.

Second, the acquiring firm's revenue stream may become more stable if the asset and liability portfolio of the target institution exhibits credit, interest rate, and liquidity risk characteristics that differ from those of the acquirer. Indeed, managers often cite diversification as the reason for a merger, stating that diversification of risk helps to stabilize the firm's earnings, which benefits owners. For example, real estate loan portfolios of commercial banks have shown very strong cycles. Specifically, in the late 2000s, U.S. subprime real estate mortgage defaults hit record highs, while high-grade mortgages experienced much smaller default rates. Thus, a diversified real estate portfolio (including both subprime and high-grade mortgages), and, consequently, the cash and revenue streams of the merged banks, may be far less risky than one in which both acquirer and target specialize in a single type of mortgage.

Third, expanding into markets that are less than fully competitive offers an opportunity for revenue enhancement. That is, firms may be able to identify and expand geographically into those markets in which *economic rents* potentially exist, but in which regulators will not view such entry as potentially anticompetitive. Indeed, to the extent that geographic expansions are viewed as enhancing a firm's monopoly power by generating excessive rents, regulators may act to prevent a merger unless it produces potential efficiency gains that cannot be reasonably achieved by other means. In recent years, the ultimate enforcement of antimonopoly laws and guidelines has fallen to the U.S. Department of Justice. In particular, the Department of Justice has established guidelines regarding the acceptability or unacceptability of acquisitions based on the potential increase in concentration in the market in which an acquisition takes place with the cost-efficiency exception just noted (see below).

COST REDUCTION A reason frequently given for a merger is the potential cost synergies that may result from economies of scale, economies of scope, or managerial efficiency sources (often called *X-efficiencies* because they are difficult to specify in a quantitative fashion).

economies of scale

A merged firm has an advantage over smaller firms if cuts associated with the merger lower the firm's operating costs of production.

Economies of Scale As firms become larger through a merger, the increase in size allows for the reduction or elimination of overlapping resources. If these cuts lower the firm's operating costs of production, merged firms may have an **economy of scale** advantage over smaller firms. Economies of scale imply that the unit or average cost of producing goods and services falls as the size of the firm expands.

An example of a merger that was intended to take advantage of economies of scale is that of Exxon Corporation and Mobil Corporation. With a larger production base, the oil companies were able to gain greater economies of scale as they were able to pursue new policies in upstream exploration and production of oil. As a result, the ExxonMobil merger was expected to save $2.8 billion in costs over a period of three years. A second example is the merger of AT&T and BellSouth. This merger produced cost synergies totaling $2 billion in the first year of operations, increasing to $3 billion by 2010. The cost cuts were principally related to economies of scale in network operations and information technology.

Figure 20.2 depicts economies of scale for three firms of different size. The average cost of production is:

$$AC_i = \frac{TC_i}{S_i} \quad \textbf{(20-1)}$$

where

AC_i = Average costs of the ith firm

TC_i = Total costs of the ith firm

S_i = Size of the firm measured by sales

The average production cost to the largest (merged) firm in Figure 20.2 (size C) is lower than the cost to smaller (nonmerged) firms B and A. This means that at any given price for the firm's products, firm C can make a higher profit than either B or A. Alternatively, firm C can undercut B and A in price and potentially gain a larger market share. For example, AOL's acquisition of Time Warner was billed as a cost-savings acquisition. Because of overlapping savings from lower overhead, technical costs, and marketing expenses, the firms said they expected $1 billion in cost savings during the first year. In the framework of Figure 20.2, AOL, firm A, might be operating at AC_A and Time Warner might be represented as firm B operating at AC_B. Savings on overhead, technology, and marketing would lower the average costs for the combined (larger) firm to point C in Figure 20.2, operating at AC_C.

The long-term implication of economies of scale for a firm is that the larger and most cost-efficient firms will drive out smaller, less cost-efficient firms, leading to increased large-firm dominance and concentration in production.

figure 20.2

Economies of Scale in Mergers

Shown here are cost data for three firms of different sizes, A, B, and C.

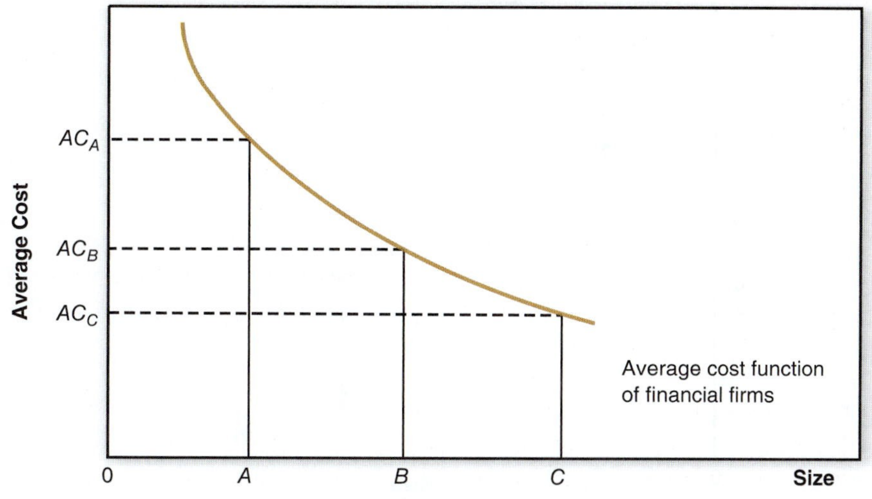

Such an implication is reinforced if time-related operating improvements increasingly benefit large firms more than small firms. For example, satellite technology and supercomputers, in which enormous operating or technological advances are being made, may be available to only the largest firms in an industry. The effect of improving operations over time, which is biased toward larger projects, is to shift the *AC* curve downward over time but with a larger downward shift for large, merged firms; see Figure 20.3. AC_1 is the hypothetical *AC* curve prior to cost-reducing innovations. AC_2 reflects the cost-lowering effects of technology and consolidation on firms of all sizes but with the greatest benefit accruing to those of the largest size.

Economies of Scope The simple economy of scale concept ignores the interrelationships among products and the "jointness" in the costs of producing them. In particular, merged firms' abilities to generate synergistic cost savings through the joint use of inputs in producing multiple products are called **economies of scope** as opposed to economies of scale.

economies of scope

A merged firm's ability to generate synergistic cost savings through the joint use of inputs in producing multiple products.

The mergers and acquisitions in the banking industry in recent years (a result of the loosening of federal regulations) provide numerous examples of attempts to take advantage of economies of scope. For example, in 1997 Travelers Group acquired Salomon Brothers for $9 billion. Then in 1998 Travelers and Citicorp announced an $83 billion merger. Travelers' chairman, Sanford I. Weill, decided to build the largest financial services company in the United States. Travelers had long been involved in the insurance and mutual fund business before the acquisition of Salomon (it already owned Smith Barney), but it had lacked foreign influence and recognition as well as respect on Wall Street. The Salomon Brothers acquisition and the Citicorp merger were attempts to alleviate these deficiencies. Another example is Lincoln National Corp. (an Indiana-based insurance company), which became one of the nation's premier sellers of life insurance, annuities, mutual funds, and 401(k) retirement plans through a series of acquisitions of firms such as Delaware Management Holdings (for $510 million) and Voyageur Fund Management (for $70 million), both mutual fund companies. Technology played a particularly large role in Lincoln National's plans as it committed major resources to technology purchases needed to support late-night calls from mutual fund, 401(k), and variable annuity customers who expect to be able to make investment selections 24 hours a day.

figure 20.3

Long-Term Effect of Economies of Scale

Long-term implications of economies of scale indicate that larger, more cost-efficient firms will drive out smaller, less cost-efficient firms.

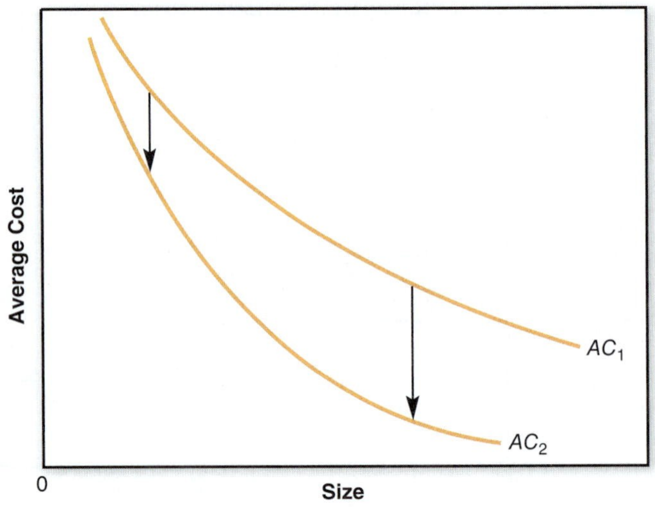

Mergers may allow two firms to jointly use their input resources such as capital and labor to produce a set of goods or services at a lower cost than if the two firms operated independently of one another. Specifically, let X_1 and X_2 be two products; each is produced by one firm as a specialized producer. That is, firm *A* produces only X_1, but no X_2, and firm *B* produces only X_2, but no X_1. The average cost functions (*AC*) of these firms are: LG20-2

$$AC_A[X_1, 0] \text{ and } AC_B[0, X_2]$$

Economies of scope exist if these firms merge and jointly produce X_1 and X_2, resulting in:

$$AC_{A+B}[X_1, X_2] < AC_A[X_1, 0] + AC_B[0, X_2] \quad \textbf{(20-2)}$$

That is, the cost of joint production via cost synergies is less than the separate and independent production of these services.

Formally, if AC_{FS} is the total average cost of a nonspecialized firm, economies of scope would imply that:

$$AC_{FS} < TAC \quad \textbf{(20-3)}$$

That is, the average cost to jointly produce goods or services may be less than the average cost to produce these products separately.

EXAMPLE 20-1

LG20-2

Calculation of Average Costs with Economies of Scope

Let TC_I be a specialized firm's total cost to produce Internet services to retail customers. Suppose that the total operating costs of producing these services (TC_I) is $2.5 million for a sales volume (S_I) of $10 million. Thus, the average cost (AC_I) of Internet service production for the firm is:

$$AC_I = \frac{TC_I}{S_I} = \frac{\$2{,}500{,}000}{\$10{,}000{,}000} = 0.25 = 25\%$$

At the same time, a specialized cable network provider is selling its service to the same retail customers. The firm's total cost (TC_C) to run the operation is $500,000 ($TC_C$) for $1 million in sales ($S_C$).

$$AC_C = \frac{TC_C}{S_C} = \frac{\$500{,}000}{\$1{,}000{,}000} = 0.50 = 50\%$$

Consequently, the total average cost (*TAC*) for the Internet provider to produce Internet services and the cable network firm to produce cable TV is:

$$TAC = \frac{\$3{,}000{,}000}{\$11{,}000{,}000} = 0.2727 = 27.27\%$$

Suppose, instead, that a single firm acting as a provider of Internet and cable TV services (*IC*) produces both $10 million of Internet services and $1 million cable programming (i.e., S_{IC} = $11,000,000). For the single firm to provide both Internet and cable services requires very similar overhead and marketing services. Further, common technologies in the Internet and cable service production functions suggest that a single firm, simultaneously (or jointly) producing both Internet and cable services at a total cost TC_{IC}, should be able to do this at a lower average cost than could the specialized firms that separately produce these services. That is, the single firm should be able to produce the $11,000,000 ($S_{IC}$) of Internet and cable services at a lower cost (say TC_{IC} = $2,550,000) than should two specialized firms.

$$AC_{IC} = \frac{TC_{IC}}{S_{IC}} = \frac{\$2{,}550{,}000}{\$11{,}000{,}000} = 23.18\% < 27.27\%$$

Similar to Problems 20-1, 20-2, self-test problem 1

For interactive versions of this example visit www.mhhe.com/can3e

X-efficiencies

Cost savings not directly due to economies of scope or economies of scale.

X-Efficiencies **X-efficiencies** are those cost savings not directly due to economies of scope or economies of scale. As such, they are usually attributed to superior management skills and other difficult-to-measure managerial factors. For example, a change in management can cause the value of merged firms to be greater than the sum of the value of the two individual firms. New, better managers may be able to force necessary cuts or realign the firm's operations where incumbent managers were not. The motive for these acquisitions does not come from the combining of the two firms. Rather, the merger is the mechanism that allows new managers to replace old inefficient managers. To date, the explicit identification of what composes these efficiencies remains to be established in the empirical finance literature.

Herfindahl-Hirschman Index (HHI)

An index or measure of market concentration based on the squared market shares of market participants.

MERGER GUIDLINES FOR ACCEPTABILITY To the extent that mergers are viewed as enhancing the monopoly power of a firm in its industry, regulators may act to prevent a merger unless the merger produces potential efficiency gains that cannot be reasonably achieved by other means.[1] In recent years, the ultimate enforcement of antimonopoly laws and guidelines has fallen to the U.S. Department of Justice. In particular, the Department of Justice has laid down guidelines regarding the acceptability or unacceptability of acquisitions based on the potential increase in concentration in the market in which an acquisition takes place, with the cost efficiency exception just noted. These merger guidelines are based on a measure of market concentration called the **Herfindahl-Hirschman Index (HHI)**. This index is created by taking the percentage market shares of each firm in a market, squaring them, and then adding the squared shares. Thus, in a market where a single firm had a 100 percent market share, the HHI would be:

$$HHI = (100)^2 = 10{,}000$$

Alternatively, in a market in which there are an infinitely large number of firms of equal size, then:

$$HHI = 0$$

Thus, the HHI must lie between 0 and 10,000.

Whether a merger will be challenged under the Department of Justice guidelines depends on the postmerger HHI level. As you can see in Table 20.2, the Department of Justice defines a *concentrated* market as having a postmerger HHI ratio of greater than 2,500, a moderately concentrated market as having a ratio of 1,500 to 2,500, and an unconcentrated market as having a ratio of less than 1,500. In a moderately concentrated market, postmerger HHI increases of 100 or more are likely to be challenged, while in a highly concentrated market, postmerger HHI increases of 200 or more are likely to be challenged.

table 20.2 | **2010 Department of Justice Horizontal Merger Guidelines**

Postmerger Market Concentration	Level of Herfindahl-Hirschman Index	Change in Herfindahl-Hirschman Index and Likelihood of a Challenged Merger
Highly concentrated	Greater than 2,500	Greater than 200—likely to be challenged 100 to 200—depends on other factors* Less than 100—unlikely to be challenged
Moderately concentrated	1,500–2,500	Greater than 100—likely to be challenged; other factors considered* Less than or equal to 100—unlikely to be challenged
Unconcentrated	Less than 1,500	Any increase—unlikely to be challenged

*In addition to the postmerger concentration of the market and the size of the resulting increase in concentration, the department will consider the presence of the following factors in deciding whether to challenge a merger: ease of entry; the nature of the product and its terms of sale; market information about specific transactions; buyer market characteristics; conduct of firms in the market; and market performance. [For a detailed explanation of these factors see Sections III(B) and III(C) of the 2010 Department of Justice Merger Guidelines.]

Source: Department of Justice, Merger Guidelines, 2010.

[1]U.S. Department of Justice, "Horizontal Merger Guidelines," August 19, 2010.

EXAMPLE 20-2

LG20-2

Calculation of Change in the HHI Associated with a Merger

For interactive versions of this example visit www.mhhe.com/can3e

Consider a market that has three firms with the following market shares:

Bank A = 50%
Bank B = 46%
Bank C = 4%

The premerger HHI for the market is:

$$HHI = (50)^2 + (46)^2 + (4)^2 = 2{,}500 + 2{,}116 + 16 = 4{,}632$$

Thus, the market is highly concentrated, according to the Department of Justice guidelines.

Suppose firm A wants to acquire firm C so that the post-acquisition market would exhibit the following shares:

A + C = 54%
B = 46%

The postmerger HHI would be:

$$HHI = (54)^2 + (46)^2 = 2{,}916 + 2{,}116 = 5{,}032$$

Thus, the increase or change in the HHI (ΔHHI) postmerger is:

$$\Delta HHI = 5{,}032 - 4{,}632 = 400$$

Since the increase is 400 points, which is more than the 200-point benchmark defined in the Department of Justice guidelines, the market is heavily concentrated and the merger could be challenged.

Similar to Problems 20-3, 20-4, self-test problem 2

TAX CONSIDERATIONS Tax considerations have been the motive for many mergers. Tax gains with an acquisition can result from the ability to use net operating losses to reduce taxes, tax gains from unused debt capacity, and tax gains from the use of surplus funds.

Tax Gains from Net Operating Losses Profitable firms in a high tax bracket can merge with a firm with large accumulated tax losses. When the firms merge, losses of the unprofitable firm can be used to offset taxes of the profitable firm rather than being carried forward and used in the future to offset possible profits.

Tax Gains from Unused Debt Capacity Tax savings arise when mergers result in an increase in debt. Mergers typically result in increased leverage for the merged firm. As discussed in Chapter 16, because interest on debt is tax deductible, firms experience a tax gain with the increased leverage after a merger. Of course, remember that the increased leverage increases firm value only if the marginal tax benefit from additional debt is greater than or equal to the marginal increase in the financial distress costs from the additional debt. This is true if the merged firm is better diversified than the two independent firms and the cost of financial distress is less for the merged firm.

Tax Gains from Surplus Funds Mergers can reduce taxes by disposing of surplus cash. That is, if a firm has free cash flow (i.e., the firm has cash available after all taxes have been paid and after all positive net present value projects have been purchased), it has several ways to use this free cash flow. It could pay extra dividends, invest in marketable securities, repurchase its stock, or acquire another firm. However, an extra dividend will increase the income tax paid by some of the firm's stockholders. Marketable securities, while a reasonable short-term use of funds, earn a rate of return less than that required by the firm's stockholders. Like a cash dividend, a stock repurchase can result in a capital gain and more tax payments for stockholders. However, when the firm makes an acquisition with surplus cash it avoids these problems.

LOWERING THE COST OF CAPITAL A merger can often result in a lower cost of capital because the costs of issuing securities are subject to economies of scale. However, diversification resulting from a merger also results in a lower cost of capital. That is, stabilization of earnings can make the debt of the merged firm less risky than that of the two independent firms. As a result, lenders demand a lower interest rate on the debt of the merged firm.

MANAGERS' PERSONAL INCENTIVES Unfortunately, business decisions are sometimes based on managers' personal incentives rather than on economic analysis. Managers expand through mergers to get personal benefits from building and managing large corporations. Academic research has documented this motive, finding that mergers are often positively related to sales and asset growth and do not always result in increased stock prices. For example, in order to build corporate empires from which they get personal benefits, managers use free cash flows to acquire a firm that may have a negative net present value. This is particularly true for poorly monitored managers who merge to maximize their corporation's asset size because managers' compensation is based on firm size. Likewise, unmonitored managers can try to build corporate empires through the pursuit of negative NPV mergers to entrench themselves. That is, because of its greater size and the managers' supposed expertise in managing the large company, managers make themselves indispensable to the firm. Finally, some managers overestimate their own managerial abilities and merge with the belief that they can manage the takeover target better than the target's current management. Acquiring managers then overbid for the target and fail to realize the gains expected from the merger in the post-merger period. Thus, the stock price and stockholders' wealth fall.

MISALLOCATION OF CAPITAL If managers of the merged firm use the merger to transfer resources between the two firms to subsidize negative NPV projects that would otherwise be rejected, a merger destroys value. This occurs if the firm's managers are reluctant to cut jobs or have other reasons to keep a losing business in operation.

LG20-2

Valuing a Merger

The net present value (NPV) or discounted cash flow (DCF) method discussed in Chapter 13 is the most accurate and reliable tool used to evaluate whether a merger will be a profitable one. The NPV method allows bidder and target firm managers to predict pro forma cash flows of the merged firm. These forecasted cash flows are then discounted to a present value based on the merged firm's weighted average cost of capital (WACC) to determine the merged firm's present value. Finally, the present value of the merged firm is compared with the asking price of the target firm to determine whether the merger is profitable.

The valuation process starts with estimates of the expected future cash flows and the WACC for the bidder and target firms' cash flows. Managers then must value the synergies resulting from the merger. This requires estimates of the cash flows generated by synergies. To simplify the analysis managers generally assume that some synergies are more certain while others are less predictable. For example, synergies resulting from tax savings or fixed cost reductions are easier to predict, while those related to increased sales or reductions in production costs are less certain.

EXAMPLE 20-3

LG20-2

Calculating the Net Present Value of a Merger

The 2015 cash flows of a target firm being considered for a merger bid are $800,000 and are expected to grow by 4 percent annually for the next five years. Managers estimate that because of synergies the merged firm's cash flows will increase by an additional $315,000 in the first year after the merger and that these cash flows will grow by 5 percent in years 2 through 5 following the merger. After the first five years, all incremental cash flows are expected to grow at a rate of 3 percent annually. The WACC for the merged firms over the foreseeable future is expected to be 10 percent. Managers of the target firm are asking a price of $15 million for the firm. Is this merger a positive NPV project for the bidding firm?

For interactive versions of this example visit www.mhhe.com/can3e

SOLUTION:

table 20.3 **Projected Post-Merger Incremental Cash Flows for Merged Firm (in millions of dollars)**

	2016	2017	2018	2019	2020
Cash flows from target firm	$0.8(1.04)	$ $0.8(1.04)^2$	$ $0.8(1.04)^3$	$ $0.8(1.04)^4$	$ $0.8(1.04)^5$
	= $0.832	= $0.865	= $0.900	= $0.936	= $0.973
Cash flows from synergies		$0.315(1.05)^1$	$0.315(1.05)^2$	$0.315(1.05)^3$	$0.315(1.05)^4$
	= $0.315	= $0.331	= $0.347	= $0.365	= $0.383
Incremental cash flows	$1.147	$ 1.196	$ 1.247	$ 1.301	$ 1.356

Table 20.3 shows the projected incremental cash flow for the bidder firm for the first five years after the merger. After the first five years, cash flows will grow at a rate of 3 percent. Thus, the value of cash flows after year 5 can be looked at as a constant growth problem similar to that used to value stocks, discussed in Chapter 8. That is, managers first calculate the value of the firm's incremental cash flows received after year 5 at the end of year 5 (the end of the super-normal growth period) as:

$$\text{Value of incremental cash flows received after year 5} = \frac{\text{Incremental cash flow in year 6}}{(WACC - \text{Growth rate) in cash flows after year 5}}$$

$$= \frac{\$1.356\text{m}(1 + 0.03)}{(0.10 - 0.03)} = \$19.956\text{m as of the end of year 5}$$

To find the present value of the total incremental cash flows, managers next discount the projected incremental cash flows by the WACC as follows:

$$\text{Present value of incremental cash flows from the merger} = \frac{\$1.147\text{m}}{(1.10)^1} + \frac{\$1.196\text{m}}{(1.10)^2} + \frac{\$1.247\text{m}}{(1.10)^3} + \frac{\$1.301\text{m}}{(1.10)^4} + \frac{\$1.356\text{m}}{(1.10)^5} + \frac{\$19.956\text{m}}{(1.10)^5}$$

$$= 17.09\text{m}$$

Finally, the NPV of the merger is calculated by subtracting the price of the target firm from the present value of the cash flows from the merger:

$$NPV = \$17.09\text{m} - \$15\text{m} = \$2.09\text{m}$$

This merger would be beneficial for the stockholders of the bidder firm. Their wealth would increase by $2.09 million as a result of the merger.

Similar to Problems 20-13, 20-14, self-test problem 3

TIME OUT

20-1 What is the difference between a vertical merger and a horizontal merger?

20-2 What are economies of scale and scope?

LG20-3

20.2 • Financial Distress

Types and Causes of Financial Distress

business failure

A type of financial distress in which a firm no longer stays in business.

economic failure

A type of financial distress in which the return on a firm's assets is less then the firm's cost of capital.

technical insolvency

A type of financial distress in which a firm's operating cash flows are not sufficient to pay its liabilities as they come due.

A firm in financial distress can mean many things. At the extreme, **business failure** is a type of financial distress in which a firm no longer stays in business. However, financial distress does not automatically mean the end of the firm. Other levels of financial distress exist as well. For example, **economic failure** is a type of financial distress in which the return on a firm's assets is less then the firm's cost of capital. Thus, the firm is not earning enough on its assets to pay the fund suppliers their promised payments. **Technical insolvency** is a type of financial distress in which a firm's operating cash flows are not sufficient to pay its liabilities as they come due. In both cases, the firm can continue as a going concern and even eventually a thriving firm. However, if not addressed, these types of financial distress can lead to dividend cuts, plant closings, layoffs, and, eventually, a possible business failure or merger or acquisition by another firm.

Financial distress can be the result of one or several factors, some of which are firm specific, while others are more market specific. A firm's financial leverage can cause financial distress. Large amounts of debt, such as bonds and loans, increase the firm's interest charges and pose a significant claim on its cash flows. Relatively low debt-to-equity ratios may not significantly impact the probability of debt repayment. Yet beyond some point, the risk of financial distress increases, as does the probability of some loss of interest or principal for the firm's creditors. Figure 20.4 shows defaulted debt issues as a percentage of all debt outstanding from 1990 through 2012.

As with leverage, a highly volatile earnings stream increases the probability that a firm cannot meet its fixed interest and principal charges for any capital structure and thus will experience financial distress. Volatility in earnings can be the result of production issues (such as input price volatility or volatility in the availability of inputs) or sales issues (such as changing needs of the firm's customers or reduced creditworthiness of the firm's customers).

Another firm-specific factor that can cause financial distress is bad or poor management. For example, management may not be skilled at production, marketing, finance, or the building of an effective organization. Further, management may fail to put credible and sensible accounting, budgeting, and control

figure 20.4

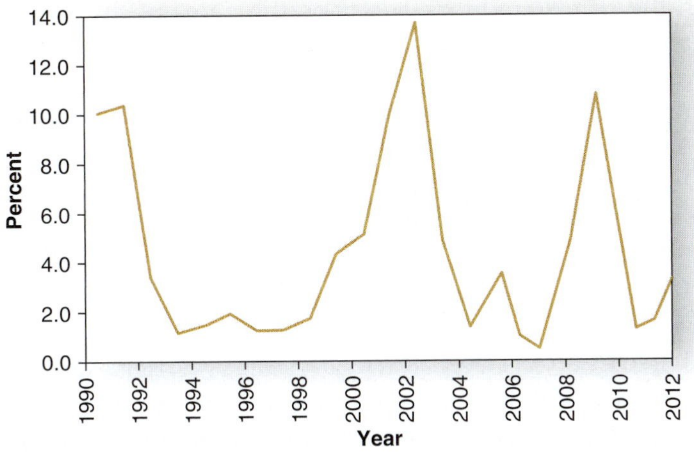

Default Rates on Outstanding Debt

Some ingredients of financial distress are firm-specific, while others are market-specific.

systems in place. Finally, the firm may lose one or a few key players on which production or management depends.

Market-specific factors such as fluctuations in the business cycle can cause financial distress in a firm as well. For example, during recessions, firms in the consumer durable goods sector that produce autos, refrigerators, or houses do poorly compared to those in the nondurable goods sector producing foods and clothing. People cut back on luxuries during a recession but are less likely to cut back on necessities such as food. Thus, firms in the consumer durable goods sectors of the economy are especially prone to financial distress. Likewise, the level of interest rates can cause financial distress. High interest rates indicate restrictive monetary policy actions by the Federal Reserve (see Chapter 6). High interest rate levels may encourage firms to take excessive risks, thus increasing the probability of financial distress.

The challenge for the manager and creditors of a financially distressed firm is to decide whether the situation is temporary and the firm can recover over the long run, or whether the problem is permanent and endangers the firm's existence. Further, the managers and/or creditors must decide whether the situation can be handled with an informal resolution of the financial distress or a formal filing of bankruptcy.

Informal Resolutions of Financial Distress

LG20-3

Informal resolutions of financial distress include the voluntary restructuring of debt agreements or the complete liquidation of the firm's assets. When financial distress appears to be temporary, the firm's creditors will generally work to restructure the firm to help it recover and reestablish itself as a viable entity. If, however, it is determined that the firm cannot recover from the financial distress, the firm and its creditors may agree to a liquidation of the firm's assets.

RESTRUCTURING A FIRM'S DEBT AGREEMENTS If financial distress in a firm is judged to be temporary, the firm and its creditors will generally agree to restructure the firm. That is, the creditors and the firm will restructure the debt agreements. In this case, the firm arranges a voluntary settlement or **workout** with its creditors. By keeping the firm alive through a workout, the creditors

workout

A voluntary settlement in which a firm's creditors will arrange with the firm to help it recover and reestablish itself as a viable entity.

extension

An arrangement in which the firm's creditors postpone the dates of the required interest and/or principal payments.

composition

An agreement in which creditors voluntarily reduce their claims on the firm, receiving only a partial payment for their claims, by reducing the principal amount or the interest rate on the debt, or by taking equity in exchange for debt.

liquidation

The termination of the firm as a going concern in which assets are sold or liquidated and any proceeds go to pay off the firm's creditors.

assignment

A voluntary liquidation proceeding that passes the liquidation of the firm's assets to a third party that is designated as the assignee or trustee.

assignee or trustee

The assignee liquidates the firm's assets through a private sale or a public auction and then distributes any proceeds from the sale to the firms' creditors and stockholders.

can continue to receive payments from the firm. Restructuring typically takes the form of an extension and/or a composition. An **extension** is an arrangement in which the firm's creditors postpone the dates of the required interest and/or principal payments. With an extension, eventually creditors receive their promised payments in full. Creditors will agree to an extension rather than force a firm to file for bankruptcy if the expected payoff from this voluntary negotiation is higher than their expected payoff after legal bankruptcy proceedings. In a **composition,** creditors voluntarily reduce their claims on the firm, receiving only a partial payment for their claims. This is accomplished by reducing the principal amount or the interest rate on the debt, or by taking equity in exchange for debt.

INFORMAL LIQUIDATION OF A FIRM'S ASSETS After examining a firm's situation, the firm's creditors may determine that the only acceptable course of action is to liquidate the firm. **Liquidation** results in the termination of the firm as a going concern. In a voluntary liquidation, the firm's assets are sold or liquidated and any proceeds go to pay off the firm's creditors. The goal of the voluntary liquidation is to recover the maximum amount through the sale of the firm's assets per dollar owed. An **assignment** is a type of informal liquidation that generally yields the firm's creditors a larger amount than they would get through formal bankruptcy liquidation. An assignment passes the liquidation of the firm's assets to a third party that is designated as the **assignee** or **trustee.** The assignee liquidates the firm's assets through a private sale or a public auction. The assignee then distributes any proceeds from the sale to the firms' creditors and stockholders (if any funds are left after all creditors are paid). Once all assets are sold and creditors are paid the proceeds, the assignee has the creditors sign a release acknowledging the full settlement of the claim.

Assignments are most feasible for small firms or firms whose situation is not too complex. This method of resolving financial distress saves all parties in terms of time, legal formality, and expense compared to liquidation in a formal bankruptcy court proceeding. For example, an assignee is more flexible in its ability to sell assets than a federal bankruptcy trustee. Thus, asset sales can take place faster, before plant and equipment or inventory becomes obsolete or ruined. However, an assignment does not necessarily result in a full and legal discharge of all the firm's liabilities and does not protect the firm's creditors against fraud. These problems are resolved only by formal liquidation in bankruptcy.

LG20-4

Federal Bankruptcy Laws

If a firm in financial distress cannot agree on an informal restructuring or liquidation with its creditors, the creditors can force the firm into bankruptcy. Likewise, a firm can voluntarily file for bankruptcy protection with a federal court. Like informal resolutions of financial distress, bankruptcy can result in either a restructuring (or reorganization) or a liquidation of the firm. Table 20.4 lists the biggest bankruptcies of U.S.-based firms through 2012. Note that 7 of the 15 largest bankruptcies occurred during the financial crisis of 2008–2009, for example, Lehman Brothers and Washington Mutual.

Chapter 11

A formal bankruptcy proceeding involving the reorganization of the corporation with some provision for repayment to the firm's creditors.

The Bankruptcy Reform Act of 1978 is the governing bankruptcy legislation in the United States. The two key parts of this law for firms in financial distress are Chapters 7 and 11, which cover bankruptcy liquidation and reorganization of a failing firm. Chapter 11 outlines the process for reorganization of a failing firm. The goal of a **Chapter 11** proceeding is to plan a reorganization of the corporation with some provision for repayment to the firm's creditors. The Chapter 11 reorganization process allows a firm in temporary financial distress to continue

table 20.4 Largest U.S. Bankruptcies

Firm	Bankruptcy Date	Total Assets Prebankruptcy
Lehman Brothers	09/15/2008	$691,063m
Washington Mutual	09/26/2008	327,900m
WorldCom, Inc.	07/21/2002	103,914m
General Motors	06/04/2009	82,300m
CIT Group	11/01/2009	71,019m
Enron Corp.	12/02/2001	63,392m
Conseco, Inc.	12/18/2002	61,392m
Chrysler	04/30/2009	39,300m
Thornburg Mortgage	05/01/2009	36,521m
Pacific Gas and Electric	04/06/2001	36,152m
Texaco, Inc.	04/12/1987	35,892m
Financial Corp. of America	09/09/1988	33,864m
Refco Inc.	10/17/2005	33,333m
IndyMac	07/31/2008	32,734m
Global Crossing Ltd.	01/28/2002	30,185m

Source: BankruptcyData.com website 2013. www.BankruptcyData.com

operating while the creditors' claims are settled using a collective procedure. **Chapter 7** outlines the process to be followed for liquidating a failed firm. Chapter 7 is generally only used if reorganization under Chapter 11 is determined to be infeasible.

Chapter 7

A formal bankruptcy proceeding which outlines the process to be followed for liquidating a failed firm.

When a firm files for bankruptcy with a federal court it is officially considered to be bankrupt. At this point, a collective legal procedure begins in which all claims against the firm are resolved. These formal proceedings are designed to protect both the failed firm and its creditors. Specifically, at this time, bankruptcy law takes precedence over commercial and tax laws that normally govern firms. Thus, individual creditors are prohibited from beginning or proceeding with lawsuits against the firm. Further, if the situation is considered to be temporary, the firm may use the time during the bankruptcy proceedings to solve its cash flow problems without fear of asset seizure by its creditors. On the other hand, if the firm is truly bankrupt in the sense that its liabilities exceed its assets, the creditors can use bankruptcy procedures to stop the firm's managers from continuing to operate, lose more money, and thus deplete assets that should go to creditors. Bankruptcy law allows for and even encourages negotiations between a firm, its creditors, and its stockholders.

REORGANIZATION PROCEDURES IN BANKRUPTCY The procedures for corporate reorganization under Chapter 11 include several steps. First, a firm must voluntarily file a reorganization petition or the firm's creditors can file an involuntary petition of reorganization under Chapter 11 in a federal bankruptcy court. With an involuntary reorganization, three or more creditors (or one creditor if there are fewer than 12 total creditors) of the firm can file a petition alleging that the corporation is not paying its debts. Next, a federal judge reviews the petition. If the petition is approved, a time for filing proof of claims of creditors and shareholders is set and the corporation is given 120 days to submit a reorganization plan. At this point, the firm, now the debtor in possession (DIP) of the firm's assets, continues to run the business. The U.S. Bankruptcy Code assigns the debtor in possession as a fiduciary position, with the rights and powers of a Chapter 11 trustee. The firm, as debtor in possession, performs all but the investigative functions and duties of a trustee. Duties include accounting for property, examining and objecting to claims, filing informational reports such as monthly operating reports, and filing tax returns and reports which are either necessary finance at work | markets

AMERICAN LANDS IN BANKRUPTCY

The parent of American Airlines filed for bankruptcy protection, an abrupt course change by one of the country's largest carriers that caps a decade of restructurings that are helping revive the long-troubled industry. AMR Corp. said its filing on Tuesday in New York would help it cut costs and emerge more competitive after losing more than $10 billion since 2001. The Fort Worth, Texas, company for years has resisted the type of court-protected restructuring that allowed other big carriers including United Continental Holdings Inc.'s United Airlines and Delta Air Lines Inc. to realign costs and find merger partners. AMR said its annual labor costs, including pensions, are about $800 million more than rivals, a figure unions dispute. Its financial woes have grown in recent months as contract talks with its pilots fizzled and fuel prices rose.

AMR's longtime Chairman and Chief Executive Gerard J. Arpey opted to retire. The board appointed AMR President Thomas Horton, age 50, to succeed him. In an interview, Mr. Horton said the cost gap with rivals "was widening" for a variety of reasons "and we didn't see a clear line of sight in closing it." The move set off a scramble by creditors owed some $29.6 billion, according to its bankruptcy petition, and raises uncertainty over how its multibillion dollar pension obligations will be handled.

Analysts viewed AMR's filing as broadly positive for the airline industry, in part because American is expected to reduce excess capacity that has led to unprofitable routes. "Assuming a successful reorganization, we would envision a smaller AMR with a cost structure that could stand profitably next to its peers." AMR is third among U.S. and global airline companies by traffic, behind United Continental and Delta. The company, which has roughly $25 billion in assets, made a bankruptcy filing that ranks as the 24th-largest since 1980 and the second-largest airline bankruptcy behind United Airlines parent UAL. The airline enters bankruptcy protection with more than $4 billion in cash on hand, a decision that surprised some industry observers but drew praise from bankruptcy experts, who said troubled companies often wait too long to file. They also said AMR will likely benefit from the experience of its competitors in bankruptcy. AMR's filing appears to have been "very well planned," said Eric Schaffer, a partner in Reed Smith's bankruptcy practice who has worked on past airline restructurings.

Labor groups that have long been at odds with management will now have to vie with bondholders, leasing firms and others for position on the creditors' committee during the bankruptcy process, with the panel ultimately appointed by a Justice Department representative. One airline-industry expert said the filing isn't likely to end the battle with unions, which will fight management efforts to curb wages, benefits and pensions.

On November 15 and 16, AMR's board convened for half-day meetings in Fort Worth. After the meetings, directors asked bankers and lawyers to prepare detailed presentations on an AMR bankruptcy filing: The effect on employees and relationships with unions and what steps could be taken under bankruptcy protection to better the company's finances. Directors also wanted to hear how their bankruptcy case might compare with past proceedings involving United Airlines, Delta, and other competitors. Tom Roberts, an attorney for AMR, said the airline's cash position was key to the timing of the bankruptcy filing. "Cash is critical to a successful restructuring in bankruptcy," he said. "Problem is, if we waited any longer, we may have adversely affected our ability to successfully restructure this company."

Source: Doug Cameron, Mike Spector, and Jack Nicas, "American Lands in Bankruptcy," *The Wall Street Journal* Online, November 30, 2011. Used with permission of Dow Jones & Company, Inc. via Copyright Clearance Center, Inc.

want to know more? Key Words to Search for Updates: American Airlines, bankruptcy, pensions

or ordered by the court. The debtor in possession also may, with the court's approval, employ attorneys, accountants, appraisers, auctioneers, or other professional persons to assist the debtor in the bankruptcy proceedings. Further, the court appoints creditor committees to represent the creditors' interests.

Within the stated time period, the firm must submit its reorganization plan to the court. The key section of the plan generally involves the firm's capital structure. As stated above, financial distress generally results from the firm's inability to pay its debt. Thus with a reorganization, the firm's capital structure is generally restructured to reduce the debt obligations. This restructuring of debt often occurs through a cramdown, in which the court modifies terms of the bankrupt firm's debt over the objection of the debt holders, i.e., the modification is "crammed down" on the debt holders. Restructuring the debt through cramdown allows the bankruptcy courts to modify loan terms so that all parties come out better than they would have without the modifications. The goal of the court is to restructure the debt in such a way that the new terms are fair and equitable to all parties involved. Along with a determination of the new capital structure, the firm must outline a plan for payment of the remaining and new debt securities and for exchanging any outstanding debt for new securities.

Under the Bankruptcy Reform Act of 1978, creditors and stockholders are separated into groups, or classes, with similar priority claims on the assets of the firm. Creditors with substantially the same priority claim are placed in the same class to ensure that they receive similar treatment under the reorganization plan. Senior debt holders, with higher legal priority, are generally paid in full before junior debt holders can receive any payment. Common stockholders are the last to receive any payment or new securities and often receive nothing. Each class of claimants votes to accept or reject the reorganization plan. A class of creditors accepts the plan if two-thirds of the class in dollar amount and one-half the class in number vote for approval. After the creditors have voted to accept the reorganization plan, it is confirmed by the bankruptcy courts. Once approved by all parties, any payments or exchange of securities written into the plan are made.

Chapter 11 bankruptcy does not always mean that a firm survives. Successful firms use the period of reorganization bankruptcy to cut costs, renegotiate contracts, remove debt from their balance sheets, and eventually emerge from bankruptcy. Indeed, Chapter 11 businesses sometimes end up with competitive advantages over competitors thanks to their ability to restructure the company. The Finance at Work selection discusses some of the issues associated with the Chapter 11 bankruptcy of American Airlines.

A new method of reorganization that combines the informal workout and the formal Chapter 11 reorganization is a **prepackaged bankruptcy.** In a prepackaged bankruptcy the firm and its creditors agree to a private reorganization outside the formal bankruptcy process. After the private reorganization is arranged or prepackaged, the firm files for formal Chapter 11 bankruptcy. Prepackaged bankruptcies are attractive in that they shorten and simplify the bankruptcy process. This means they can save the firm money in the form of legal and other fees and often generate more funds available for the creditors. Further, prepackaged bankruptcies generally result in less disruption to the firm's business and less damage to its goodwill. For example, in June 2009, General Motors (GM) filed a prepackaged bankruptcy. The deal slashed the firm's debt and health care obligations by about $48 billion and GM emerged from bankruptcy in 40 days.

prepackaged bankruptcy

A bankruptcy in which the firm and its creditors agree to a private reorganization outside the formal bankruptcy process. After the private reorganization is arranged or prepackaged, the firm files for formal Chapter 11 bankruptcy.

LIQUIDATION PROCEDURES IN BANKRUPTCY If a firm is too financially distressed to be reorganized, it is liquidated via a Chapter 7 bankruptcy. A firm is liquidated once the bankruptcy courts determine that reorganization is not feasible. At this point, the judge appoints a trustee-in-bankruptcy to take over the firm's property and protect the creditors' interests. The trustee is responsible for liquidating the firm's assets, examining the creditors' claims, keeping records, disbursing funds, furnishing information to involved parties as requested, and making final reports on the liquidation. Bankruptcy courts have established a specific priority of claims in a liquidation or an absolute priority rule. Specifically, the distribution of the funds from asset liquidation occurs according to the following priority of claims:

1. Property taxes past due.
2. Claims of secured creditors, who receive the proceeds from the sale of specific collateral as stated in a lien or mortgage.
3. Administrative expenses associated with the bankruptcy proceedings.
4. Unpaid expenses incurred after the filing of the bankruptcy petition but before the trustee is appointed.

5. Wages due to employees in the 90 days immediately preceding the start of the bankruptcy proceedings (limited to $2,000 per employee).
6. Unpaid employee benefit plan contributions that should have been paid in the six months prior to the bankruptcy filing (limited to $2,000 per employee).
7. Unsecured customer claims (limited to $900 per customer).
8. Taxes due to federal, state, and other governmental agencies.
9. Unsecured creditor claims including any unsatisfied amounts of secured creditors' claims.
10. Preferred stockholders (up to the par value of the preferred stock).
11. Common stockholders receive any remaining funds.

Distributions to priority and secured creditors must be paid in full before unsecured creditors receive any funds from asset liquidation. If, after the priority and secured creditors are paid in full, there are insufficient funds to pay the unsecured creditors in full, funds remaining are distributed on a pro rata basis. Further, as funds are distributed to unsecured creditors, senior status unsecured creditors must be paid in full before subordinate creditors receive any funds.

EXAMPLE 20-4

LG20-4

For interactive versions of this example visit www.mhhe.com/can3e

Calculating Creditor and Stockholder Payoffs in a Chapter 7 Bankruptcy

Lucky Dog, Inc., declared bankruptcy on August 20, 2015 through a Chapter 7 filing. Lucky Dog's balance sheet at the time of the bankruptcy filing is listed below.

LUCKY DOG, INC.
Balance Sheet as of August 20, 2015
(in millions of dollars)

Assets		**Liabilities and Equity**	
Current assets:		Current liabilities:	
Cash and marketable securities	$ 42	Accrued wages (1,500 employees)	$ 4
		Unpaid employee benefits	2
Accounts receivable	110	Unsecured customer deposits	1
Inventory	177	Accrued taxes	8
Total	$329	Accounts payable	55
		Notes payable to banks	136
Fixed assets:		Total	$206
Gross plant and equipment	$670	Long-term debt:	
Less: Depreciation	84	First mortgage	$100
Net plant and equipment	$586	Subordinate debentures	209
		Total	$309
		Stockholders' equity:	
		Preferred stock (2.5 million shares)	$ 6
		Common stock and paid-in surplus (20 million shares)	64
		Retained earnings	33
		Total	$ 40
Total assets	$915	Total liabilities and equity	$915

The accrued wages were earned within the last 90 days prior to filing for bankruptcy. The unpaid employee benefits were due in the six months prior to the filing for bankruptcy. The unsecured customer deposits are for less than $900 each. Lucky Dog, Inc., has no property taxes past due. The first mortgage is secured against the fixed assets of the firm. The debentures are subordinate to the notes payable to banks. The liquidation of the firm's current assets produced $140 million and of the firm's fixed assets produced $275 million for a total of only $415 million in funds to distribute to the creditors and stockholders of the firm.

The administrative expenses associated with the bankruptcy totaled $0.75 million and unpaid expenses incurred after the filing of the bankruptcy petition but before the trustee was appointed totaled $0.25 million. Show how the trustee will distribute the $415 million of funds among Lucky Dog's creditors and stockholders.

SOLUTION:

The distribution of the $415 million of funds is as follows:

Proceeds from liquidation of assets:	$415.00m
Administrative expenses associated with the bankruptcy proceedings	0.75m
Unpaid expenses incurred after the filing of the bankruptcy petition but before the trustee is appointed	0.25m
Wages due to employees (1,500 employees × $2,000 maximum)	3.00m
Unpaid employee benefit plan contributions	2.00m
Unsecured customer claims	1.00m
Taxes due to federal, state, and other governmental agencies	8.00m
Funds available for secured creditors:	$400.00m
First mortgage	100.00m
Funds available for unsecured creditors:	$300.00m

Note that the employees received only $3 million of the $4 million, or 75 percent, of the wages due to them. This is because payment of wages due are capped at $2,000 per employee. The remaining $300 million is distributed to the unsecured creditors on a pro rata basis, with senior creditors paid in full before subordinate creditors. The following table shows the distribution to unsecured creditors:

Unsecured Creditors	Amount	Settlement at 75%[a]	Distribution after Subordinate Adjustment	Percent of Claim Received
Accounts payable	$ 55m	$ 41.25m	$ 41.25m	75.00%
Notes payable to banks	136m	102.00m	136.00m[b]	100.00
Subordinate debentures	209m	156.75m	122.75m[b]	58.73
Total	$400m	$300.00m	$300.00m	

[a] $300 million is available to pay 400 million in unsecured creditors. Thus, the pro rata settlement rate is $300m/$400m = 75%.

[b] Notes payable to banks must be paid in full before subordinate debenture holders can be paid anything. Thus, $34 million ($136m − $102m) of the original settlement amount is moved from subordinate debentures to notes payable to banks; subordinate debenture holders receive only $122.75 million ($156.75m − $34m), or 58.73 percent of the amount owed to them.

Similar to Problems 20-15, 20-16, self-test problem 4

Predicting Bankruptcy

LG20-5

Managers, creditors, and stockholders can use many models to predict bankruptcy. These vary from relatively qualitative to highly quantitative models. These models are not mutually exclusive. A manager or creditor may use more than one model to reach a borrowing and/or lending decision. Indeed, a great deal of time and effort has recently been expended by financial institutions in building highly technical bankruptcy risk evaluation models. We discuss just a few of the models, so-called credit-scoring models, here.

credit-scoring models

Quantitative models that use data on observed firm characteristics either to sort firms into different bankruptcy risk classes or to calculate the probability of bankruptcy.

Credit-scoring models are quantitative models that use data on observed firm characteristics either to sort firms into different bankruptcy risk classes or to calculate the probability of bankruptcy. These models use past data, such as financial ratios, as inputs to explain repayment experiences on old debt. The relative importance of the factors used to explain past repayment performance then forecasts repayment performance on new debt. By selecting and combining different economic and financial firm characteristics, managers or creditors may be able to:

1. Numerically establish which factors are important in explaining bankruptcy risk.
2. Evaluate the relative degree or importance of these factors.
3. Improve the pricing of bankruptcy risk.
4. Screen high-risk firms.

The primary benefit from credit scoring is that creditors can more accurately predict a firm's performance without having to use more resources. With an average accuracy rate of 85 percent, the use of these models means fewer defaults and write-offs for lenders. Indeed, many commercial credit grantors are implementing credit-scoring models as a way to come into accordance with the Sarbanes-Oxley Act of 2002, which sets guidelines for corporate governance in several areas, including risk management and control assessment.

To use credit-scoring models, managers and creditors must identify objective economic and financial measures of risk for any particular class of borrower. For corporate debt, cash flow information and financial ratios such as the debt-to-equity ratio are usually key factors. After data are identified, a statistical technique quantifies or scores the bankruptcy risk probability or classification. Credit-scoring models include three broad types: (1) linear discriminant models, (2) linear probability models, and (3) logit models.

LINEAR DISCRIMINANT MODELS Linear discriminant models divide firms into high or low bankruptcy risk classes based on their observed financial characteristics (X_j). A widely used discriminant model is the *Z-score* model developed by Edward Altman.[2] The indicator variable Z is an overall measure of a firm's bankruptcy risk classification. This classification, in turn, depends on the values of various financial ratios of the firm (X_j) and the weighted importance of these ratios based on the observed experience of bankrupt versus nonbankrupt firms derived from a discriminant analysis model.

Altman's credit-scoring model takes the following form:

$$Z = 1.2X_1 + 1.4X_2 + 3.3X_3 + 0.6X_4 + 1.0X_5 \qquad \textbf{(20-4)}$$

where

X_1 = Net working capital/Total assets

X_2 = Retained earnings/Total assets

X_3 = Earnings before interest and taxes/Total assets

X_4 = Market value of equity/Book value of long-term debt

X_5 = Sales/Total assets ratio

[2]E. I. Altman, "Managing the Commercial Lending Process," in *Handbook of Banking Strategy*, ed. R. C. Aspinwall and R. A. Eisenbeis (New York: John Wiley & Sons, 1985), pp. 473–510.

The lower (higher) the value of Z, the higher (lower) is a firm's bankruptcy risk classification. Specifically, a Z-score of less than 1.81 indicates high risk of bankruptcy within the next year, a Z-score of greater than 2.99 indicates low risk of bankruptcy within the next year, and a Z-score between 1.81 and 2.99 is indeterminate.

EXAMPLE 20-5

LG20-5

Calculation of Altman's *Z*-Score

For interactive versions of this example visit www.mhhe.com/can3e

Suppose that the financial ratios of a potential borrowing firm took the following values:

$$X_1 = 0.2$$
$$X_2 = 0$$
$$X_3 = -0.20$$
$$X_4 = 0.10$$
$$X_5 = 2.0$$

The ratio X_2 is zero and X_3 is negative, indicating that the firm has had negative earnings or losses in recent periods. Also, X_4 indicates that the firm is highly leveraged. However, the net working capital ratio (X_1) and the sales/total assets ratio (X_5) indicate that the firm is reasonably liquid and is maintaining its sales volume. The Z-score provides an overall score or indicator of the firm's credit risk since it combines and weights these five factors according to their past importance in explaining borrower default.

SOLUTION:

For the borrower in question:

$$Z = 1.2(0.2) + 1.4(0) + 3.3(-0.20) + 0.6(0.10) + 1.0(2.0)$$
$$Z = 0.24 + 0 - 0.66 + 0.06 + 2.0$$
$$Z = 1.64$$

According to the Altman's Z-score, this firm should be placed in the high bankruptcy risk class. A creditor should not lend to this firm until it improves its financial condition.

Similar to Problems 20-5, 20-6, self-test problem 5

Use of the Z-score model to make credit risk evaluations has a number of problems. The first problem is that this model usually discriminates only between two extreme cases of firm behavior: bankruptcy and no bankruptcy. In the real world various gradations of bankruptcy risk exist, from nonpayment or delay of interest payments (nonperforming assets) to outright default on all promised interest and principal payments. This problem suggests that a more accurate or finely calibrated sorting among firms may require defining more classes in the scoring model.

The second problem is that there is no obvious economic reason to expect that the weights in the Z-score model—or, more generally, the weights in any credit-scoring model—will be constant over any but very short periods. The same concern also applies to the scoring model's explanatory variables (X_j). Specifically, due to changing financial and market conditions, other firm-specific financial ratios may come to be increasingly relevant in explaining bankruptcy risk.

The third problem is that these models ignore important, hard-to-quantify factors that may play a crucial role in the bankruptcy/no-bankruptcy decision.

For example, the reputation of the firm and the managers' backgrounds could be important firm-specific characteristics, as could macro factors such as the phase of the business cycle. Credit-scoring models often ignore these variables. Moreover, traditional credit-scoring models rarely use publicly available information, such as the prices of the outstanding public debt and equity of the borrower.

A fourth problem relates to the availability of bankruptcy records. Currently, no centralized, publicly available database on defaulted loans or bankruptcies for proprietary or other reasons exists. Some task forces by consortiums of commercial banks and consulting firms are currently seeking to construct such databases, but it may well be many years before they are fully developed. This constrains the ability of many creditors to use credit-scoring models for larger business loans.

linear probability and logit models

Models that produce a value for the expected probability of bankruptcy.

LINEAR PROBABILITY MODELS AND LOGIT MODELS While linear discriminant models divide firms into high or low bankruptcy risk classes, **linear probability** and **logit models** produce a value for the expected probability of bankruptcy. That is, factors explaining past repayment performance (or bankruptcy) can be used to assess the probability of future bankruptcy, called the *probability of default (PD)* in these models.

Briefly, these models divide firms into two groups: those that defaulted (or declared bankruptcy) over some past period of time ($PD = 1$) and those that did not default (or declare bankruptcy) over that period ($PD = 0$). They then relate these observations by linear regression to a set of j causal variables (X_{ij}) that reflect financial information about the ith firm, such as leverage or earnings. The models take the following form:

$$PD_i = \sum_{j=1}^{n} \beta_j X_{ij} + \text{Error} \qquad \textbf{(20-5)}$$

where β_j is the estimated weight of the jth variable (for example, the debt ratio) in explaining past defaults. These variables, X_{ij}, derived from past experience, can then be used to find default (or bankruptcy) probabilities on future debt instruments.

EXAMPLE 20-6

LG20-5

For interactive versions of this example visit www.mhhe.com/can3e

Calculation of Bankruptcy Probability Using Linear Probability Models

Suppose a linear probability model you have developed finds there are two factors influencing the past bankruptcy behavior of firms: the debt-to-equity ratio and the sales-to-total assets ratio. Based on past bankruptcy experience, the linear probability model is estimated as:

$$PD_i = 0.5\ (\text{Debt/Equity}) - 0.1\ (\text{Sales/Total assets})$$

SOLUTION:

A firm you are thinking of investing in has a debt-to-equity ratio of 30 percent and a sales-to-asset ratio of 1.2. Its expected probability of default, or bankruptcy, is estimated as:

$$PD_i = 0.5\ (0.30) - 0.1\ (1.2) = 0.03, \text{ or } 3\%$$

Similar to Problems 20-7, 20-8, self-test problem 6

While linear probability models are straightforward as long as current financial information is available on a firm, their major weakness is that the estimated probabilities of bankruptcy can lie outside the interval of 0 to 1. The logit model overcomes this weakness by restricting the estimated range of bankruptcy probabilities from the linear regression model to lie between 0 and 1.[3]

TIME OUT

20-3 What is the difference between a restructuring (or reorganization) and a liquidation of a financially distressed firm?

20-4 What is Altman's *Z*-score?

[3]Essentially this is done by plugging the estimated value of PD_i from the linear probability model (in our example, $PD_i = 0.03$) into the following formula:

$$F(PD_i) = \frac{1}{1 + e^{-PD_i}}$$

where e is the exponential (equal to 2.718) and $F(PD_i)$ is the logistically transformed value of PD_i. In our example,

$$F(PD_i) = \frac{1}{1 + e^{-0.03}} = 0.5075, \text{ or } 50.75\%$$

viewpoints REVISITED

Business Application Solution

MHM Production, Inc., is asking a price of $90 million to be purchased by BSW Corporation. The cash flows for MHM Production are projected to be $5.5 million in the coming year and are expected to grow at 3 percent annually in years 2 through 6. After the first six years, cash flows are expected to remain constant. Managers at BSW estimate that because of synergies, the merged firm's cash flows will increase by $6 million in the first year and that these cash flows will increase by 3 percent in years 2 through 6 following the merger. After the first six years incremental cash flows from synergies are expected to be $2 million annually (for a total increase of $\$5.5\text{m}(1.03)^5 + \$2\text{m}$, or $8.376 million annually). Thus, the value of incremental cash flows after year 6 can be looked at as a perpetuity

(continued)

Personal Application Solution

James Upton holds $25,000 in subordinate debentures of Jaylon's Jazz Music Production, Inc. The firm has just announced that it will file Chapter 7 bankruptcy. The firm's assets have a book value of $500,000. The liquidated assets produce $250,000. Administrative expenses associated with the bankruptcy, unpaid wages, employee benefits, and taxes total $10,000. The firm has debt owed to secured creditors of $175,000, accounts payable of $25,000, notes payable to banks of $120,000, and total subordinate (to notes payable) debt outstanding of $100,000.

The distribution of the $250,000 of funds is as follows:

(continued)

viewpoints REVISITED

Business Application Solution (concluded)

problem. The WACC for the merged firms is 9 percent. Thus, first calculate the value of the incremental firm's cash flows received after year 6 as:

Value of incremental cash flows received after year 6

$$= \frac{\text{Annual incremental cash flow 7}}{WACC}$$

$$= \frac{\$8.376\text{m}}{0.09}$$

$$= \$93.07\text{m as of the end of year 6}$$

To find the present value of the total incremental cash flows to BSW Corp., managers next discount the projected cash flows by the WACC as follows:

Present value of incremental cash flows from the merger:

$$= \frac{\$11.5\text{m}}{(1.09)^1} + \frac{\$11.5\text{m}(1.03)}{(1.09)^2} + \frac{\$11.5\text{m}(1.03)^2}{(1.09)^3}$$

$$+ \frac{\$11.5\text{m}(1.03)^3}{(1.09)^4} + \frac{\$11.5\text{m}(1.03)^4}{(1.09)^5} + \frac{\$11.5\text{m}(1.03)^5}{(1.09)^6}$$

$$+ \frac{\$93.07\text{m}}{(1.09)^6} = \$110.70\text{m}$$

Finally, the NPV of the merger is calculated by subtracting the price of the MHM from the present value of the cash flows from the merger.

$$NPV = \$110.70\text{m} - \$90\text{m} = \$20.70\text{m}$$

This merger would be beneficial for the stockholders of BSW Corporation. Their wealth would increase by $20.70 million as a result of the merger.

Personal Application Solution (concluded)

Proceeds from liquidation of assets:	$250,000
Administrative expenses associated with the bankruptcy proceedings, wages due to employees, unpaid employee benefit plan contributions, taxes due to federal, state, and other governmental agencies	10,000
Funds available for secured creditors:	240,000
Payments to secured creditors	175,000
Funds available for unsecured creditors:	$ 65,000

The remaining $65,000 is distributed to the unsecured creditors on a pro rata basis, with senior creditors paid in full before subordinate creditors. See the table below.

Unsecured Creditors	Amount	Settlement at 26.53%[a]	Distribution after Subordinate Adjustment	Percent of Claim Received
Accounts payable	$ 25,000	$ 6,632.65	$ 6,632.65	26.53%
Notes payable to banks	120.000	31,836.74	58,367.35[b]	48.64
Subordinate debentures	100,000	26,530.61	0.00[b]	0.00
Total	$245,000	$ 65,000.00	$65,000.00	

[a] $65,000 is available to pay $245,000 in unsecured creditors. Thus, the pro rata settlement rata is $65,000/$245,000 = 26.53%.

[b] Notes payable to banks must be paid in full before subordinate debenture holders can be paid anything. Thus, the $26,530.61 of the original settlement amount assigned to the subordinate debenture holders is moved to notes payable to banks; subordinate debenture holders receive none of the amount owed to them.

summary of learning goals

LG20-1 Differentiate among types of and address motives for mergers and acquisitions. A merger is a transaction in which two firms combine to form a single firm. An acquisition is the purchase of one firm by another. Despite these two distinct definitions, the two terms, mergers and acquisitions, are often used interchangeably. A consolidation is a type of merger in which an entirely new firm is created. A horizontal merger combines two companies in the same industry. A vertical merger combines a firm with a supplier or distributor. A conglomerate merger combines two companies that have no related products or markets. A product extension merger is a combination of firms that sell different, but somewhat related products.

LG20-2 Mathematically value mergers. The net present value (NPV) or discounted cash flow (DCF) method is the most accurate and reliable tool used to evaluate whether a merger will be a profitable one. The NPV method allows bidder and target firm managers to predict pro forma cash flows of the merged firm. The valuation process starts with estimates of the expected future cash flows and the WACC for the bidder and target firm's cash flows. Managers then must value the synergies resulting from the merger. This requires estimates of the cash flows generated by synergies. These forecasted incremental cash flows are then discounted to a present value based on the firm's weighted average cost of capital (WACC) to determine the merger's present value. Finally, the present value of the merger is compared with the asking price of the target firm to determine whether the merger is profitable.

LG20-3 Suggest methods by which a firm can informally resolve severe financial distress. Informal resolutions of financial distress include the voluntary restructuring of debt agreements or the complete liquidation of the firm's assets. When financial distress appears to be temporary, the firm's creditors will generally work to restructure the firm to help it recover and reestablish itself as a viable entity. If, however, it is determined that the firm cannot recover from the financial distress, the firm and its creditors may agree to a liquidation of the firm's assets.

LG20-4 Differentiate between Chapter 7 and Chapter 11 bankruptcy. The Bankruptcy Reform Act of 1978 is the governing bankruptcy legislation in the United States. The two key parts of this law for firms in financial distress are Chapters 7 and 11, which cover bankruptcy liquidation and reorganization of a failing firm. Chapter 11 outlines the process for reorganization of a failing firm. The goal of a Chapter 11 proceeding is to plan a reorganization of the corporation with some provision for repayment to the firm's creditors. The Chapter 11 reorganization process allows a firm in temporary financial distress to continue operating while the creditors' claims are settled using a collective procedure. Chapter 7 outlines the process to be followed for liquidating a failed firm. Chapter 7 is generally only used if it has been determined that reorganization under Chapter 11 is infeasible.

LG20-5 Build and use statistical models to predict bankruptcy. Credit-scoring models are quantitative models that use data on observed firm characteristics either to sort firms into different bankruptcy risk classes or to calculate the probability of bankruptcy. These models use past data, such as financial ratios, as inputs to explain repayment experiences on old debt. The relative importance of the factors used to explain past repayment performance then forecasts repayment performance on new debt. By selecting and combining different economic and financial firm characteristics, managers or creditors may be able to: (1) numerically establish which factors are important in explaining bankruptcy risk; (2) evaluate the relative degree or importance of these factors; (3) improve the pricing of bankruptcy risk; and (4) screen high-risk firms. The primary benefit from credit scoring is that creditors can more accurately predict a firm's performance without having to use more resources.

chapter equations

$$\textbf{20-1} \quad AC_i = \frac{TC_i}{S_i}$$

$$\textbf{20-2} \quad AC_A + {}_B[X_1, X_2] < AC_A[X_1, 0] + AC_B[0, X_2]$$

$$\textbf{20-3} \quad AC_{FS} < TAC$$

$$\textbf{20-4} \quad Z = 1.2X_1 + 1.4X_2 + 3.3X_3 + 0.6X_4 + 1.0X_5$$

$$\textbf{20-5} \quad PD_i = \sum_{j=1}^{n} \beta_j X_{ij} + \text{Error}$$

key terms

acquisition, The purchase of one firm by another. *p. 661*

assignee or **trustee,** The assignee liquidates the firm's assets through a private sale or a public auction and then distributes any proceeds from the sale to the firms' creditors and stockholders. *p. 674*

assignment, A voluntary liquidation proceeding that passes the liquidation of the firm's assets to a third party that is designated as the assignee or trustee. *p. 674*

business failure, A type of financial distress in which a firm no longer stays in business. *p. 672*

Chapter 7, A formal bankruptcy proceeding which outlines the process to be followed for liquidating a failed firm. *p. 675*

Chapter 11, A formal bankruptcy proceeding involving the reorganization of the corporation with some provision for repayment to the firm's creditors. *p. 674*

composition, An agreement in which creditors voluntarily reduce their claims on the firm, receiving only a partial payment for their claims, by reducing the principal amount or the interest rate on the debt, or by taking equity in exchange for debt. *p. 674*

conglomerate merger, A merger that combines two firms that have no related products or markets. *p. 663*

consolidation, A type of merger in which an entirely new firm is created. Both the bidder and target firms are absorbed into this new firm and cease to exist as separate entities. *p. 661*

credit-scoring models, Quantitative models that use data on observed firm characteristics either to sort firms into different bankruptcy risk classes or to calculate the probability of bankruptcy. *p. 680*

economic failure, A type of financial distress in which the return on a firm's assets is less then the firm's cost of capital. *p. 672*

economies of scale, A merged firm has an advantage over smaller firms if cuts associated with the merger lower the firm's operating costs of production. *p. 664*

economies of scope, A merged firm's ability to generate synergistic cost savings through the joint use of inputs in producing multiple products. *p. 666*

extension, An arrangement in which the firm's creditors postpone the dates of the required interest and/or principal payments. *p. 674*

Herfindahl-Hirschman Index (HHI), An index or measure of market concentration based on the squared market shares of market participants. *p. 668*

horizontal merger, The merger of two companies in the same industry. *p. 663*

linear probability and **logit models,** Models that produce a value for the expected probability of bankruptcy. *p. 682*

liquidation, The termination of the firm as a going concern in which assets are sold or liquidated and any proceeds go to pay off the firm's creditors. *p. 674*

market extension merger, A type of horizontal merger that combines two firms that sell the same products in different market areas. *p. 663*

merger, A transaction in which two firms combine to form a single firm. *p. 661*

prepackaged bankruptcy, A bankruptcy in which the firm and its creditors agree to a private reorganization outside the formal bankruptcy process. After the private reorganization is arranged or prepackaged, the firm files for formal Chapter 11 bankruptcy. *p. 677*

product extension merger, A merger that combines two firms that sell different, but somewhat related products. *p. 663*

synergy, The value of the combined firms is greater than the sum of the value of the two firms individually. *p. 663*

technical insolvency, A type of financial distress in which a firm's operating cash flows are not sufficient to pay its liabilities as they come due. *p. 672*

vertical merger, A combination of a firm with a supplier or distributor. *p. 663*

workout, A voluntary settlement in which a firm's creditors will arrange with the firm to help it recover and reestablish itself as a viable entity. *p. 673*

X-efficiencies, Cost savings not directly due to economies of scope or economies of scale. *p. 668*

self-test problems with solutions

LG20-2

1 Calculation of Average Costs with Economies of Scope A specialized firm's (P) total cost to produce printers for sales to retail customers is TC_P. The total operating costs of producing printers is \$5.5 million for a sales volume (S_P) of \$20 million. At the same time, a specialized printer ink provider (I) is selling its products to the same retail customers. The firm's total cost (TC_I) to run the operation is \$780,000 for \$1.2 million in sales (S_I).

Suppose, instead, that a single firm acting as a producer of printers and printer ink (PI) produces both \$20 million of printers and \$1.2 million of printer ink (i.e., S_{PI} = \$21,200,000). For the single firm to provide both printers and printer ink requires very similar overhead and marketing services. Thus, a single firm, simultaneously (or jointly) producing both printers and printer ink at a total cost TC_{PI}, should be able to do this at a lower average cost than could the specialized firms that separately produce these services. That is, the single firm should be able to produce the \$21,200,000 (S_{PI}) of printers and printer ink at a lower cost of TC_{PI} = \$5,180,000 than the two specialized firms.

Calculate the average cost (AC_P) of printer production for firm P, the average cost (AC_I) of printer ink production for firm I. Calculate the total average cost (TAC) for the printer provider to produce printers and the printer ink firm to produce printer ink. Calculate the total average cost (AC_{PI}) for the single firm to produce printers and printer ink.

Solution:

The average cost (AC_P) of printer production for firm P is:

$$AC_P = \frac{TC_P}{S_P} = \frac{\$5{,}500{,}000}{\$20{,}000{,}000} = 0.275 = 27.50\%$$

The average cost (AC_I) of printer ink production for firm I is:

$$AC_I = \frac{TC_I}{S_I} = \frac{\$780{,}000}{\$1{,}200{,}000} = 0.65 = 65.00\%$$

The total average cost (TAC) for the printer producer to produce printers and the printer ink firm to produce printer ink is:

$$TAC = \frac{\$6{,}280{,}000}{\$21{,}200{,}000} = 0.2962 = 29.62\%$$

The total average cost (AC_{PI}) for the single firm acting as producer of both printers and printer ink is:

$$AC_{PI} = \frac{TC_{PI}}{S_{PI}} = \frac{\$5{,}180{,}000}{\$21{,}200{,}000} = 24.43\% < 29.62\%$$

LG20-2

2 Calculation of Change in the HHI Associated with a Merger Consider a market that has three firms with the following market shares:

Bank A = 45%

Bank B = 39%

Bank C = 16%

Suppose firm B wants to acquire firm C so that the post-acquisition market would exhibit the following shares:

B + C = 55%

A = 45%

Calculate the pre- and postmerger HHI and the change in the HHI resulting from the merger. According to Department of Justice guidelines, is this merger likely to be challenged?

Solution:

The premerger HHI for the market is:

$$HHI = (45)^2 + (39)^2 + (16)^2 = 2{,}025 + 1{,}521 + 256 = 3{,}802$$

Thus, the market is highly concentrated according to the Department of Justice guidelines. The postmerger HHI would be:

$$HHI = (55)^2 + (45)^2 = 3{,}025 + 2{,}025 = 5{,}050$$

Thus, the increase or change in the HHI (ΔHHI) postmerger is:

$$\Delta HHI = 5{,}050 - 3{,}802 = 1{,}248$$

Since the increase is 1,248 points, which is more than the 200-point benchmark defined in the Department of Justice guidelines, the market is heavily concentrated and the merger could be challenged.

LG20-2

3 Valuation of a Merger Tater Bug, Inc., is asking a price of $45 million to be purchased by BSW Corporation. Tater Bug currently has total cash flows of $3 million, that are expected to grow indefinitely at 2 percent annually. Managers at BSW estimate that, because of synergies, the merged firm's cash flows will increase by $400,000 in the first year after the merger and that these cash flows will grow by an additional 4 percent in years 2 through 4 following the merger. After the first four years, these incremental cash flows will grow at a rate of 2 percent indefinitely. The WACC for the merged firms is 9 percent. Calculate the NPV of the merger. Should BSW Corporation agree to acquire Tater Bug for the asking price of $45 million?

Solution:

The incremental cash flows for the first four years after the merger are:

Year after merger:	1	2	3	4
Cash flows from Tater Bug	\$3.0m(1.02) = \$3.060m	\$3.0m$(1.02)^2$ = \$3.121m	\$3.0m$(1.02)^3$ = \$3.184m	\$3.0m$(1.02)^4$ = \$3.247m
Cash flows from synergies	= \$0.400m	\$0.4m$(1.04)^1$ = \$0.416m	\$0.4m$(1.04)^2$ = \$0.433m	\$0.4m$(1.04)^3$ = \$0.450m
Incremental cash flows	\$3.460m	\$3.537m	\$3.616m	\$3.697m

The value of incremental cash flows after year 4 is:

$$\text{Value of incremental cash flows received after year 4 at end of year 4} = \frac{\text{Incremental cash flow in year 5}}{\text{WACC} - \text{Growth rate in cash flows after year 4}}$$

$$= \frac{\$3.697m(1 + 0.02)}{(0.09 - 0.02)} = \$53.874m$$

To find the present value of the total incremental cash flows, managers next discount the projected cash flows by the WACC as follows:

$$\text{Present value of cash flows from the merger} = \frac{\$3.460m}{(1.09)^1} + \frac{\$3.537m}{(1.09)^2} + \frac{\$3.616m}{(1.09)^3} + \frac{\$3.697m}{(1.09)^4} + \frac{\$53.874m}{(1.09)^4} = \$49.729m$$

Finally, the NPV of the merger is calculated by subtracting the price of the target firm from the present value of the incremental cash flows from the merger.

$$NPV = \$49.729m - \$45m = \$4.729m$$

This merger would be beneficial for the stockholders of the bidder firm. Their wealth would increase by $4.729 million as a result of the merger.

4 Calculating Creditor and Stockholder Payoffs in a Chapter 7 Bankruptcy LG20-3

Big Roo Hen House, Inc., declared bankruptcy on August 20, 2015 through a Chapter 7 filing. Big Roo's balance sheet at the time of the bankruptcy filing is listed below.

Big Roo Hen House, Inc.
Balance Sheet as of August 20, 2015
(in millions of dollars)

Assets	2015	Liabilities & Equity	2015
Current assets:		Current liabilities:	
Cash and marketable securities	$ 12	Accrued wages (1,000 employees)	$ 1
		Unpaid employee benefits	1
Accounts receivable	32	Unsecured customer deposits	1
Inventory	52	Accrued taxes	2
Total	$ 96	Accounts payable	12
		Notes payable to banks	38
		Total	$ 55
Fixed assets:			
Gross plant and equipment	$176	Long-term Debt:	
Less: Depreciation	22	First mortgage	$ 60
Net plant and equipment	$154	Subordinate debentures	25
		Total	$ 85
		Stockholders' equity:	
		Preferred stock (2 million shares)	$ 2
		Common stock and paid-in surplus (10 million shares)	20
		Retained earnings	88
		Total	$110
Total assets	$250	Total liabilities and equity	$250

The accrued wages were earned within the last 90 days prior to filing for bankruptcy. The unpaid employee benefits were due in the 6 months prior to the filing for bankruptcy. The unsecured customer deposits are for less than $900 each. Big Roo Hen House, Inc., has no property taxes past due. The first mortgage is secured against the fixed assets of the firm. The debentures are subordinate to the notes payable to banks. The liquidation of the firm's current assets produced $40 million and, of the firm's fixed assets, produced $70 million for a total of only $110 million in funds to distribute to the creditors and stockholders of the firm.

The administrative expenses associated with the bankruptcy totaled \$0.25 million, and unpaid expenses incurred after the filing of the bankruptcy petition but before the trustee was appointed totaled \$0.25 million.

Show how the trustee will distribute the \$110 million of funds among the Big Roo Hen House's creditors and stockholders. Report both dollar values and percent of claim recovered.

Solution:

The distribution of the \$110 million of funds is as follows:

Proceeds from liquidation of assets:	\$110.00m
Administrative expenses associated with the bankruptcy proceedings	0.25m
Unpaid expenses incurred after the filing of the bankruptcy petition but before the trustee is appointed	0.25m
Wages due to employees (1,000 employees × \$2,000 maximum)	1.00m
Unpaid employee benefit plan contributions	1.00m
Unsecured customer claims	1.00m
Taxes due to federal, state, and other governmental agencies	2.00m
Funds available for secured creditors:	\$104.50m
First mortgage	60.00m
Funds available for unsecured creditors:	\$ 44.50m

The remaining \$44.5 million is distributed to the unsecured creditors on a pro rata basis, with senior creditors paid in full before subordinate creditors. Thus:

Unsecured Creditors	Amount	Settlement at 59.33333%[a]	Distribution after subordinate adjustment	Percent of claim received
Accounts payable	\$12m	\$ 7.12m	\$ 7.12m	59.33%
Notes payable to banks	38m	22.55m	37.38m[b]	98.37
Subordinate debentures	25m	14.83m	0.00m[b]	0.00
Total	\$75m	\$44.50m	\$44.50m	

[a] \$44.5 million is available to pay \$75 million in unsecured creditors. Thus, the pro rata settlement rate is \$44.5m/\$75m = 59.33333%.
[b] Notes payable to banks must be paid in full before subordinate debenture holders can be paid anything. Thus, \$15.45 million (\$38m − \$22.55m) of the original settlement amount would be moved from subordinate debentures to notes payable to banks. However, subordinate debenture holders only have \$14.83 million available to transfer. Thus, notes payable get \$37.38 million (\$22.55m – \$14.83m) and subordinate debenture holders receive nothing.

LG20-5

5 Calculating Bankruptcy Class Suppose that the financial ratios of a potential borrowing firm took the following values:

X_1 = Net working capital/Total assets = 0.15
X_2 = Retained earnings/Total assets = 0.10
X_3 = Earnings before interest and taxes/Total assets = 0.12
X_4 = Market value of equity/Book value of long-term debt = 0.80
X_5 = Sales/Total assets ratio = 1.90

Calculate and interpret the Altman's *Z*-score for this firm.

Solution:

For the borrower in question

$$Z = 1.2(0.15) + 1.4(0.1) + 3.3(0.12) + 0.6(0.80) + 1.0(1.90)$$
$$Z = 0.18 + 0.14 + 0.396 + 0.48 + 1.9$$
$$Z = 3.096$$

According to the Altman's *Z*-score, this firm should be placed in the low bankruptcy risk class. A creditor should lend to this firm with a high probability that the investment will be paid back as promised.

6 Calculation of Bankruptcy Probability Using Linear Probability Models Suppose a linear probability model you have developed finds there are two factors influencing the past bankruptcy behavior of firms: the debt-to-equity ratio and the profit margin. Based on past bankruptcy experience, the linear probability model is estimated as: LG20-5

$$PD_i = 0.25(\text{Debt/Equity}) - 3.56(\text{Profit margin})$$

A firm you are thinking of investing in has a debt-to-equity ratio of 75 percent and a profit margin of 4.5 percent. Calculate the expected probability of default for this firm.

Solution:

The firm's expected probability of default, or bankruptcy, is estimated as:

$$PD_i = 0.25(0.75) - 3.56(0.045) = 0.0273, \text{ or } 2.73\%$$

questions

1. Describe the difference between a merger and an acquisition. *(LG20-1)*
2. Describe the difference between a horizontal merger and a vertical merger. *(LG20-1)*
3. Classify each of the following as a horizontal merger, a vertical merger, a market extension merger, a conglomerate merger, or a product extension merger. *(LG20-1)*
   a. Walmart acquires Kmart.
   b. Kroger grocery stores acquires Bunny Bread.
   c. Schnucks grocery stores headquartered in St. Louis and operating in the Midwest acquires FoodLand headquartered and operating in Hawaii.
   d. Bank of America acquires Aflac.
   e. Ford Motors buys the St. Louis Rams.
4. What is synergy and how does it apply to mergers? *(LG20-1)*
5. Describe the three dimensions of revenue synergies that may be achieved in a merger. *(LG20-1)*
6. What is the difference between economies of scope and economies of scale? Can two firms involved in a merger benefit from both economies of scale and economies of scope? *(LG20-1)*
7. What is the Herfindahl-Hirschman Index? How is it calculated and interpreted? *(LG20-2)*
8. How can managers' personal incentives result in value-destroying mergers and acquisitions? *(LG20-1)*
9. Why is NPV valuation an appropriate tool to use in the evaluation of a merger target? *(LG20-2)*
10. What is the difference between business failure, economic failure, and technical insolvency? *(LG20-3)*
11. A firm is experiencing a temporary period of financial distress as the result of a hurricane that has hit its local area. Because many of the firm's customers have been severely hurt by the hurricane, they are unable to pay their debts to the firm. This stoppage of cash inflows has left the firm temporarily unable to pay its own bills. What options do the firm's creditors have with respect to getting paid? *(LG20-3)*

12. What is the job of the trustee in an informal liquidation of a firm's assets? *(LG20-3)*
13. What is the difference between a Chapter 11 and a Chapter 7 bankruptcy? *(LG20-4)*
14. Does a Chapter 7 bankruptcy increase the probability that creditors will be paid in full more than a Chapter 11 bankruptcy? *(LG20-4)*
15. What is the order of payment to a firm's creditors in a Chapter 7 bankruptcy? *(LG20-4)*
16. To what extent are employees of a bankrupt firm paid their wages and benefits due? *(LG20-4)*
17. What is a credit-scoring model? *(LG20-5)*
18. What is the difference between a linear discriminant and a linear probability credit-scoring model? *(LG20-5)*
19. A firm has an Altman's *Z*-score of 1.76. What does this mean? *(LG20-5)*
20. The Altman's *Z*-score model has several weaknesses. What are they? *(LG20-5)*
21. A linear probability model you have developed finds that a firm has a PD of 0.16. What does this mean? *(LG20-5)*

problems

basic problems

20-1 Calculation of Average Costs with Economies of Scope Peter's TV Supplies is considering a merger with Jan's Radio Supply Stores. Peter's total operating costs of producing services are $250,000 for a sales volume (S_P) of $4.5 million. Jan's total operating costs of producing services are $50,000 for a sales volume (S_J) of $550,000. *(LG20-2)*

- **a.** Calculate the average cost of production for the two firms.
- **b.** If the two firms merge, calculate the total average cost (*TAC*) for the merged firm assuming no synergies.
- **c.** Suppose, instead, that synergies in the production process result in a cost of production for the merged firms totaling $270,000 for a sales volume of $5,050,000. Calculate the total average cost ($AC_{PeterJan}$) for the merged firm.

20-2 Calculation of Average Costs with Economies of Scope Cindy's Computer Corp. is considering a merger with Bobby's Hard Drive, Inc. Cindy's total operating costs of producing services are $3.4 million for a sales volume (S_C) of $16 million. Bobby's total operating costs of producing services are $2.5 million for a sales volume (S_B) of $8 million. *(LG20-2)*

- **a.** Calculate the average cost of production for the two firms.
- **b.** If the two firms merge, calculate the total average cost (*TAC*) for the merged firm assuming no synergies.
- **c.** Suppose, instead, that synergies in the production process result in a cost of production for the merged firms totaling $5.3 million for a sales volume of $24 million. Calculate the total average cost ($AC_{CindyBobby}$) for the merged firm.

20-3 Calculation of Change in the HHI Associated with a Merger Consider a market that has three firms with the following market shares:

Firm A = 35%
Firm B = 41%
Firm C = 24%

Suppose firm B wants to acquire firm C so that the post-acquisition market would exhibit the following shares:

B + C = 65%
A = 35%

Calculate the pre- and postmerger HHI and the change in the HHI resulting from the merger. According to Department of Justice guidelines, is this merger likely to be challenged? *(LG20-2)*

20-4 **Calculation of Change in the HHI Associated with a Merger** Consider a market that has three firms with the following market shares:

Firm A = 35%
Firm B = 41%
Firm C = 24%

Suppose firm A wants to acquire firm C so that the post-acquisition market would exhibit the following shares:

A + C = 76%
B = 24%

Calculate the pre- and postmerger HHI and the change in the HHI resulting from the merger. According to Department of Justice guidelines, is this merger likely to be challenged? *(LG20-2)*

20-5 **Calculation of Altman's Z-Score** Suppose that the financial ratios of a potential borrowing firm take the following values: X_1 = Net working capital/Total assets = 0.10, X_2 = Retained earnings/Total assets = 0.20, X_3 = Earnings before interest and taxes/Total assets = 0.22, X_4 = Market value of equity/Book value of long-term debt = 0.60, X_5 = Sales/Total assets ratio = 0.90. Calculate and interpret the Altman's Z-score for this firm. *(LG20-5)*

20-6 **Calculation of Altman's Z-Score** Suppose that the financial ratios of a potential borrowing firm take the following values: X_1 = Net working capital/Total assets = 0.27, X_2 = Retained earnings/Total assets = 0.37, X_3 = Earnings before interest and taxes/Total assets = 0.44, X_4 = Market value of equity/Book value of long-term debt = 1.25, X_5 = Sales/Total assets ratio = 2.75. Calculate and interpret the Altman's Z-score for this firm. *(LG20-5)*

20-7 **Calculation of Bankruptcy Probability** Suppose a linear probability model you have developed finds there are two factors influencing the past bankruptcy behavior of firms: the debt ratio and the profit margin. Based on past bankruptcy experience, the linear probability model is estimated as:

$$PD_i = 0.15 \text{ (Debt ratio)} - 0.10 \text{ (Profit margin)}$$

A firm you are thinking of lending to has a debt ratio of 45 percent and a profit margin of 6 percent. Calculate the firm's expected probability of default, or bankruptcy. *(LG20-5)*

20-8 **Calculation of Bankruptcy Probability** A linear probability model you have developed finds there are two factors influencing the past bankruptcy behavior of firms: the equity multiplier and the total asset turnover ratio. Based on past bankruptcy experience, the linear probability model is estimated as:

$$PD_i = 0.02 \text{ (Equity multiplier)} - 0.01 \text{ (Total asset turnover)}$$

A firm you are thinking of lending to has an equity multiplier of 2.75 times and a total asset turnover ratio of 1.8. Calculate the firm's expected probability of default, or bankruptcy. *(LG20-5)*

intermediate problems

20-9 Calculation of Average Costs with Economies of Scope George's Dry Cleaning is considering a merger with Weezzie's Laundry Supply Stores. George's total operating costs of producing services are $550,000 for sales volume *(SG)* of $4.5 million. Weezzie's total operating costs of producing services are $185,000 for a sales volume (S_W) of $2 million. *(LG20-2)*

a. Calculate the average cost of production for the two firms.

b. For a sales volume of $6.5 million, calculate the reduction in production costs the merged firms need to experience such that the total average cost ($AC_{GeorgeWeezzie}$) for the merged firms is equal to 10 percent.

20-10 Calculation of Average Costs with Economies of Scope Jenny's Day Care is considering a merger with Lionel's Diaper Manufacturers. Jenny's total operating costs of producing services are $595,000 for sales volume (S_j) of $2.4 million. Lionel's total operating costs of producing services are $340,000 for a sales volume (S_L) of $1,400,000. *(LG20-2)*

a. Calculate the average cost of production for the two firms.

b. For a sales volume of $3.8 million, calculate the reduction in production costs the merged firms need to experience such that the total average cost ($AC_{JennyLionel}$) for the merged firms is equal to 20 percent.

20-11 Calculation of Change in the HHI Associated with a Merger The Justice Department has been asked to review a merger request for a market with the following four firms. *(LG20-2)*

Firm	Assets
A	$12 million
B	25 million
C	102 million
D	3 million

a. What is the HHI for the existing market?

b. If Firm A acquires Firm D, what will be the impact on the market's level of concentration?

c. If Firm C acquires Firm D, what will be the impact on the market's level of concentration?

d. What is likely to be the Justice Department's response to the two merger applications?

20-12 Calculation of Change in the HHI Associated with a Merger The Justice Department has been asked to review a merger request for a market with the following four firms. *(LG20-2)*

Firm	Assets
A	$156 million
B	130 million
C	45 million
D	100 million

a. What is the HHI for the existing market?

b. If Firm B acquires Firm D, what will be the impact on the market's level of concentration?

c. If Firm C acquires Firm D, what will be the impact on the market's level of concentration?

d. What is likely to be the Justice Department's response to the two merger applications?

20-13 Valuation of a Merger Stubborn Motors, Inc., is asking a price of $75 million to be purchased by Rubber Tire Motor Corp. Stubborn Motors currently has total cash flows of $2 million that are expected to grow indefinitely by 1 percent annually. Managers estimate that, because of synergies, the merged firm's cash flows will increase by $4 million in the first year after the merger and that these cash flows will grow by an additional 4 percent in years 2 through 4 following the merger. After the first four years, these incremental cash flows will grow at a rate of 1 percent annually. The WACC for the merged firms is 10 percent. Calculate the NPV of the merger. Should Rubber Tire Motor Corporation agree to acquire Stubborn Motors for the asking price of $75 million? *(LG20-2)*

20-14 Valuation of a Merger You own stock in Make-UP-Artists, Inc., which has just made a bid of $30 million to purchase MHM Corporation. MHM Corp. currently has total cash flows of $2.5 million that are expected to grow indefinitely by 2 percent annually. Managers estimate that, because of synergies, the merged firm's cash flows will increase by $500,000 in the first year after the merger and that these cash flows will grow by an additional 4 percent in years 2 through 5 following the merger. After the first five years, these incremental cash flows will grow at a rate of 2 percent annually. The merged firms are expected to have a beta = 1.2, the risk free rate is 4.5 percent, and the market risk premium is currently 5.5 percent. Calculate the NPV of the merger. Will you vote in favor of the merger? *(LG20-2)*

20-15 Calculating Creditor and Stockholder Payoffs in a Chapter 7 Bankruptcy You own $25,000 in subordinated debt of Local Crossings, Inc., which declared bankruptcy on May 15, 2015, through a Chapter 7 filing. Local Crossings' balance sheet at the time of the bankruptcy filing is listed below.

LOCAL CROSSINGS, INC.
Balance Sheet as of May 15, 2015
(in millions of dollars)

Assets		**Liabilities and Equity**	
Current assets:		Current liabilities:	
Cash and marketable securities	$ 406	Accrued wages (10,500 employees)	$ 20
Accounts receivable	978	Unpaid employee benefits	15
Inventory	1,038	Unsecured customer deposits	50
Total	$2,422	Accrued taxes	375
		Accounts payable	841
		Notes payable to banks	1,518
Fixed assets:		Total	$2,819
Gross plant and equipment	$7,253	Long-term debt:	
Less: Depreciation	1,050	First mortgage	$1,200
Net plant and equipment	$6,203	Subordinate debentures	2,018
		Total	$3,218
		Stockholders' equity:	
		Preferred stock (100 million shares)	$ 100
		Common stock and paid-in surplus (200 million shares)	1,500
		Retained earnings	988
		Total	$2,588
Total assets	$8,625	Total liabilities and equity	$8,625

www.mhhe.com/can3e

The accrued wages were earned within the last 90 days prior to filing for bankruptcy. The unpaid employee benefits were due in the six months prior to the filing for bankruptcy. The unsecured customer deposits are for less than $900 each. Local Crossings, Inc., has no property taxes past due. The first mortgage is secured against the fixed assets of the firm. The debentures are subordinate to the notes payable to banks. The liquidation of the firm's current assets produced $1,298 million and of the firm's fixed assets produced $3,552 million for a total of only $4,850 million in funds to distribute to the creditors and stockholders of the firm.

The administrative expenses associated with the bankruptcy totaled $15 million and unpaid expenses incurred after the filing of the bankruptcy petition but before the trustee was appointed totaled $10 million. Show how the trustee will distribute the $4,850 million of funds among the Local Crossings' creditors and stockholders. How much of the $25,000 debt you own will you recover? *(LG20-4)*

20-16 Calculating Creditor and Stockholder Payoffs in a Chapter 7 Bankruptcy WorldGone, Inc., declared bankruptcy on September 25, 2015, through a Chapter 7 filing. WorldGone's balance sheet at the time of the bankruptcy filing is listed below.

WORLDGONE, INC.
Balance Sheet as of September 25, 2015
(in millions of dollars)

Assets		**Liabilities and Equity**	
Current assets:		Current liabilities:	
Cash and marketable securities	$ 263	Accrued wages (10,000 employees)	$ 18
Accounts receivable	1,428	Unpaid employee benefits	15
Inventory	2,100	Unsecured customer deposits	69
Total	$ 3,791	Accrued taxes	252
		Accounts payable	711
		Notes payable to banks	1,975
Fixed assets:		Total	$ 3,040
Gross plant and equipment	$ 7,752	Long-term debt:	
Less: Depreciation	1,248	First mortgage	$ 1,232
Net plant and equipment	$ 6,504	Subordinate debentures	2,214
		Total	$ 3,446
		Stockholders' equity:	
		Preferred stock (100 million shares)	$ 100
		Common stock and paid-in surplus (200 million shares)	2,500
		Retained earnings	1,209
		Total	$ 3,809
Total assets	$10,295	Total liabilities and equity	$10,295

The accrued wages were earned within the last 90 days prior to filing for bankruptcy. The unpaid employee benefits were due in the six months prior to the filing for bankruptcy. The unsecured customer deposits are for less than $900 each. WorldGone, Inc., has no property taxes past due. The first mortgage is secured against the fixed assets of the firm. The debentures are subordinate to the notes payable to banks. The liquidation of the firm's current assets produced $2,263 million and of the firm's fixed assets produced $3,722 million for a total of only $5,985 million in funds to distribute to the creditors and stockholders of the firm.

The administrative expenses associated with the bankruptcy totaled $25 million and unpaid expenses incurred after the filing of the bankruptcy petition but before the trustee was appointed totaled $10 million. Show how the trustee will distribute the $5,985 million of funds among the WorldGone's creditors and stockholders. *(LG20-4)*

20-17 Calculation of Altman's *Z*-Score Use the following financial statements for Lake of Egypt Marina to calculate and interpret the Altman's *Z*-score for this firm as of 2015. *(LG20-5)*

LAKE OF EGYPT MARINA, INC.
Balance Sheet as of December 31, 2015 and 2014
(in millions of dollars)

Assets	**2015**	**2014**	**Liabilities and Equity**	**2015**	**2014**
Current assets:			Current liabilities:		
Cash and marketable securities	$ 75	$ 65	Accrued wages and taxes	$ 40	$ 43
Accounts receivable	115	110	Accounts payable	90	80
Inventory	200	190	Notes payable	80	70
Total	$390	$365	Total	$210	$193
Fixed assets:			Long-term debt:	$300	$280
Gross plant and equipment	$580	$471	Stockholders' equity:		
Less: Depreciation	110	100	Preferred stock (5 million shares)	$ 5	$ 5
Net plant and equipment	$470	$371	Common stock and paid-in surplus (65 million shares)	65	65
Other long-term assets	50	49	Retained earnings	330	242
Total	$520	$420	Total	$400	$312
Total assets	$910	$785	Total liabilities and equity	$910	$785

LAKE OF EGYPT MARINA, INC.
Income Statement for Years Ending December 31, 2015 and 2014
(in millions of dollars)

	2015	**2014**
Net sales (all credit)	$ 515	$ 432
Less: Cost of goods sold	260	200
Gross profits	$ 255	$ 232
Less: Depreciation and other operating expenses	22	20
Earnings before interest and taxes (EBIT)	$ 233	$ 212
Less: Interest	33	30
Earnings before taxes (EBT)	$ 200	$ 182
Less: Taxes	57	55
Net income	$ 143	$ 127
Less: Preferred stock dividends	$ 5	$ 5
Net income available to common stockholders	$ 138	$ 122
Less: Common stock dividends	65	65
Addition to retained earnings	$ 73	$ 57
Per (common) share data:		
Earnings per share (EPS)	$ 2.123	$ 1.877
Dividends per share (DPS)	$ 1.000	$ 1.000
Book value per share (BVPS)	$ 6.077	$ 4.723
Market value (price) per share (MVPS)	$14.750	$12.550

20-18 Calculation of Altman's *Z*-Score Use the following financial statements for Garners' Platoon Mental Health Care, Inc., to calculate and interpret the Altman's *Z*-score for this firm. *(LG20-5)*

GARNERS' PLATOON MENTAL HEALTH CARE, INC.
Balance Sheet as of December 31, 2015
(in millions of dollars)

Assets		**Liabilities and Equity**	
Current assets:		Current liabilities:	
Cash and marketable securities	$ 247	Accrued wages and taxes	$ 186
Accounts receivable	652	Accounts payable	510
Inventory	1,035	Notes payable	513
Total	$1,934	Total	$1,209
Fixed assets:		Long-term debt:	$1,818
Gross plant and equipment	$3,419	Stockholders' equity:	
Less: Depreciation	494	Preferred stock (35 million shares)	$ 35
Net plant and equipment	$2,925	Common stock and paid-in surplus (375 million shares)	375
Other long-term assets	525	Retained earnings	1,947
Total	$3,450	Total	$2,357
Total assets	$5,384	Total liabilities and equity	$5,384

GARNERS' PLATOON MENTAL HEALTH CARE, INC.
Income Statement for Years Ending December 31, 2015
(in millions of dollars)

Net sales (all credit)	$ 2,964
Less: Cost of goods sold	1,420
Gross profits	$ 1,544
Less: Depreciation and other operating expenses	120
Earnings before interest and taxes (EBIT)	$ 1,424
Less: Interest	187
Earnings before taxes (EBT)	$ 1,237
Less: Taxes	456
Net income	$ 781
Less: Preferred stock dividends	$ 35
Net income available to common stockholders	$ 746
Less: Common stock dividends	375
Addition to retained earnings	$ 371
Per (common) share data:	
Earnings per share (EPS)	$ 1.989
Dividends per share (DPS)	$ 1.000
Book value per share (BVPS)	$ 6.192
Market value (price) per share (MVPS)	$ 8.420

20-19 Calculation of Bankruptcy Probability Suppose a linear probability model you have developed finds there are two factors influencing the past bankruptcy behavior of firms: the debt ratio and the profit margin. Based on past bankruptcy experience, the linear probability model is estimated as:

$$PD_i = 0.15\ (\text{Debt ratio}) - 0.5\ (\text{Profit margin})$$

You know a particular firm has a debt ratio of 55 percent and a probability of default of 5 percent. Calculate the firm's profit margin. *(LG20-5)*

20-20 Calculation of Bankruptcy Probability A linear probability model you have developed finds there are two factors influencing the past bankruptcy behavior of firms: the equity multiplier and the total asset turnover ratio. Based on past bankruptcy experience, the linear probability model is estimated as:

$$PD_i = 0.02 \text{ (Equity multiplier)} - 0.01 \text{ (Total asset turnover)}$$

A firm has an equity multiplier of 1.8 times and a probability of default of 2.2 percent. Calculate the firm's total asset turnover ratio. *(LG20-5)*

advanced problems

20-21 Economies of Scope A survey of a local market has provided the following average cost data: Johnson Construction Corp. (JCC) has assets of $3 million and an average cost of 20 percent. Anderson Architects (AA) has assets of $4 million and an average cost of 30 percent. Cole Home Builders (CHB) has assets of $4 million and an average cost of 25 percent. For each firm, average costs are measured as a proportion of assets. JCC is planning to acquire AA and CHB with the expectation of reducing overall average costs by eliminating the duplication of services. *(LG20-2)*

a. What should the average cost after the acquisition be for JCC to justify this merger?

b. If JCC plans to reduce operating costs by $500,000 after the merger, what will the average cost be for the new firm?

20-22 Economies of Scope A survey of a national market has provided the following average cost data: Jackson County Construction (JCC) has assets of $2.55 million and an average cost of 30 percent. Arkansas Architects (AA) has assets of $1.7 million and an average cost of 25 percent. Colorado Home Builders (CHB) has assets of $1 million and an average cost of 15 percent. For each firm, average costs are measured as a proportion of assets. JCC is planning to acquire AA and CHB with the expectation of reducing overall average costs by eliminating the duplication of services. *(LG20-2)*

a. What should the average cost after the acquisition be for JCC to justify this merger?

b. If JCC plans to reduce operating costs by $425,000 after the merger, what will the average cost be for the new firm?

20-23 Calculation of Change in the HHI Associated with a Merger Cakes Corp. currently has a 60 percent market share in banking services, followed by Cookies, Inc., with 20 percent and Dippen Dough with 20 percent. *(LG20-2)*

a. What is the concentration ratio as measured by the Herfindahl-Hirschman Index (HHI)?

b. If Cakes Corp. acquires Cookies, Inc., what will be the new HHI?

c. Assume the Justice Department will allow mergers as long as the changes in HHI do not exceed 1,400. What is the minimum amount of assets that Cakes Corp. will have to divest after it merges with Cookies, Inc.?

20-24 Calculation of Change in the HHI Associated with a Merger Tractor Supply Corp. currently has a 50 percent market share in banking services, followed by Farm Equipment, Inc., with 30 percent and Plow Mart with 20 percent. *(LG20-2)*

a. What is the concentration ratio as measured by the Herfindahl-Hirschman Index (HHI)?

b. If Tractor Supply Corp. acquires Plow Mart, Inc., what will be the new HHI?

c. Assume the Justice department will allow mergers as long as the changes in HHI do not exceed 1,500. What is the minimum amount of assets that Tractor Supply Corp. will have to divest after it merges with Plow Mart, Inc.?

20-25 Valuation of a Merger The managers of BSW, Inc., have approached KCMP about a possible merger. KCMP Corp. is asking a price of $72 million to be purchased by BSW, Inc. KCMP Corp. currently has total cash flows of $6 million that are expected to grow by 2 percent annually for the next two years. Managers are uncertain of the growth in KCMP Corp's cash flows in year 3. Managers estimate that, because of synergies, the merged firm's cash flows will increase by $1 million in the first year after the merger and that these cash flows will grow by an additional 3 percent in years 2 and 3 following the merger. Managers have estimated that the present value of any incremental cash flows received after year 3 is $54.09 million. The WACC for the merged firms is 10 percent. Calculate KCMP Corp.'s minimum incremental cash flow needed in year 3 after the merger such that BSW, Inc., would see this merger as a positive NPV project. *(LG20-2)*

20-26 Valuation of a Merger The managers of State Bank have been approached by City Bank about a possible merger. State Bank is asking a price of $205 million to be purchased by City Bank. State Bank currently has total cash flows of $15 million that are expected to grow by 1 percent annually for the next two years. Managers are uncertain of the growth in State Bank's cash flows in year 3. Managers estimate that because of synergies the merged firm's cash flows will increase by $1.5 million in the first year after the merger and that these cash flows will grow by an additional 5 percent in years 2 and 3 following the merger. Managers have estimated that the present value of any incremental cash flows received after year 3 is $158.75 million. The WACC for the merged firms is 8 percent. Calculate State Bank's minimum incremental cash flow needed in year 3 after the merger such that City Bank would see this merger as a positive NPV project. *(LG20-2)*

20-27 Calculating the Probability of Bankruptcy A linear probability model you have developed finds there are two factors influencing the past bankruptcy behavior of firms: the debt-to-equity ratio and the sales-to-total assets ratio. Based on past bankruptcy experience, the linear probability model is estimated as:

$$PD_i = 0.5\,(\text{Debt/Equity}) - 0.01\,(\text{Sales/Total assets})$$

A firm you are thinking of lending to has a sales-to-asset ratio of 2.0 and its expected probability of default, or bankruptcy, is estimated to be 8 percent. Calculate the firm's debt ratio. *(LG20-5)*

20-28 Calculating the Probability of Bankruptcy A linear probability model you have developed finds there are two factors influencing the past bankruptcy behavior of firms: the debt-to-equity ratio and the profit margin. Based on past bankruptcy experience, the linear probability model is estimated as:

$$PD_i = 0.1\ (\text{Debt/Equity}) - 1.5\ (\text{Profit margin})$$

A firm you are thinking of lending to has a debt-to-equity ratio of 110 percent and its expected probability of default, or bankruptcy, is estimated to be 5 percent. If sales are $1.5 million, calculate the firm's net income. *(LG20-5)*

research it! Mergers and Acquisitions

Go to the Thomson Financial—Investment Banking and Capital Markets Group website at **www.thomsonreuters.com/DealsIntelligence** and find the latest information available for the dollar value of mergers and acquisition activity using the following steps. Click on "Quarterly Reviews." Under "Mergers & Acquisitions," click on "Global M&A Financial Advisory" for the most recent quarter. This will download a file to your computer that will contain the most recent information on merger and acquisition activity. What is the most recent dollar value of global merger and acquisition activity undertaken? Who are the top advisors on these merger and acquisition deals? How has the top advisor market share changed in the last year?

integrated mini-case Capital Funding in a Public Firm

Disaster Airlines is a firm in severe financial distress. The firm can no longer pay its bills on time and it is far behind on payments to its banks and long-term debt holders. The firm has decided to either be purchased by another air carrier or liquidate its assets and close. The managers have approached Altruistic Airlines about being acquired. After examining Disaster's financial statements, looking at the routes owned by Disaster, and looking at the condition of the fixed assets, Altruistic Airlines has offered to pay the stockholders of Disaster Airlines $8 million to be acquired. Disaster Airlines covers flights to both areas in which Altruistic already flies, but also has routes in areas into which Altruistic is interested in expanding. As part of the analysis, Altruistic determined that the additional cash flows resulting from the acquisition would total $500,000 this year and would grow at a rate of 4 percent for the next three years. After this time, the cash flows would grow at a rate of 2 percent annually. The WACC of Altruistic Airlines would be 8 percent after the merger.

If, instead, Disaster Airlines decides to liquidate its assets, it will pay off its debt and give any remaining funds to the firm's stockholders. Disaster Airlines' balance sheet is listed below.

DISASTER AIRLINES, INC.
Balance Sheet as of June 25, 2015
(in millions of dollars)

Assets		**Liabilities and Equity**	
Current assets:		Current liabilities:	
Cash and marketable securities	$ 63	Accrued wages (2,500 employees)	$ 4
Accounts receivable	28	Unpaid employee benefits	3
Inventory	100	Unsecured customer deposits	6
Total	$ 191	Accrued taxes	22
		Accounts payable	157
		Notes payable to banks	211
Fixed assets:		Total	$ 403
Gross plant and equipment	$1,152	Long-term debt:	
Less: Depreciation	248	First mortgage	$ 160
Net plant and equipment	$ 904	Subordinate debentures	412
		Total	$ 572
		Stockholders' equity:	
		Common stock and paid-in surplus (100 million shares)	$ 100
		Retained earnings	20
		Total	$ 120
Total assets	$ 1,095	Total liabilities and equity	$ 1,095

The accrued wages were earned within the last 90 days prior to filing for bankruptcy. The unpaid employee benefits were due in the six months prior to the filing for bankruptcy. The unsecured customer deposits are for less than $900 each. Disaster Airlines has no property taxes past due. The first mortgage is secured against the fixed assets of the firm. The debentures are subordinate to the notes payable to banks. The liquidation of the firm's current assets produced $186 million and of the firm's fixed assets produced $800 million for a total of only $986 million in funds to distribute to the creditors and stockholders of the firm. The administrative expenses associated with the bankruptcy totaled $1 million and unpaid expenses incurred after the filing of the bankruptcy petition but before the trustee was appointed totaled $5 million.

Show which method of dissolution, an acquisition by Altruistic Airlines or a liquidation of assets, is more beneficial for the creditors and stockholders of Disaster Airlines and the stockholders of Altruistic Airlines.

ANSWERS TO TIME OUT

20-1 A vertical merger combines a firm with a supplier or distributor. Vertical mergers occur between firms in different stages of production operation for many reasons such as avoidance of fixed costs, the elimination of costs of searching for prices, contracting, payment collection, communication, advertising and coordination, and better planning for inventory. A horizontal merger combines two companies in the same industry. Forming a larger firm may create beneficial economies of scale.

20-2 With economies of scale, a merged firm has an advantage over smaller firms if cuts associated with the merger lower the firm's operating costs of production. With economies of scope, merged firms are able to generate synergistic cost savings through the joint use of inputs in producing multiple products.

20-3 Chapter 11 outlines the process for reorganization of a failing firm. The goal of a Chapter 11 proceeding is to plan a reorganization of the corporation with some provision for repayment to the firm's creditors. The Chapter 11 reorganization process allows a firm in temporary financial distress to continue operating while the creditors' claims are settled using a collective procedure. Chapter 7 outlines the process to be followed for liquidating a failed firm. Liquidation results in the termination of the firm as a going concern. If a firm is too financially distressed to be reorganized, it is liquidated via a Chapter 7 bankruptcy. A firm is liquidated once the bankruptcy courts determine that reorganization is not feasible.

20-4 A widely used discriminant model is the *Z*-score model developed by Edward Altman. The indicator variable Z is an overall measure of a firm's bankruptcy risk classification. This classification, in turn, depends on the values of various financial ratios of the firm (X_j) and the weighted importance of these ratios based on the observed experience of bankrupt versus nonbankrupt firms derived from a discriminant analysis model. The lower (higher) the value of Z, the higher (lower) is a firm's bankruptcy risk classification. Specifically, a *Z*-score of less than 1.81 indicates high risk of bankruptcy within the next year, a *Z*-score of greater than 2.99 indicates low risk of bankruptcy within the next year, and a *Z*-score between 1.81 and 2.99 is indeterminate.

appendix A Present Value and Future Value Tables

appendix table a–1 | Future value of \$1 after N years = $(1 + i)^N$

	INTEREST RATE PER YEAR														
Number of Years	1%	2%	3%	4%	5%	6%	7%	8%	9%	10%	11%	12%	13%	14%	15%
1	1.0100	1.0200	1.0300	1.0400	1.0500	1.0600	1.0700	1.0800	1.0900	1.1000	1.1100	1.1200	1.1300	1.1400	1.1500
2	1.0201	1.0404	1.0609	1.0816	1.1025	1.1236	1.1449	1.1664	1.1881	1.2100	1.2321	1.2544	1.2769	1.2996	1.3225
3	1.0303	1.0612	1.0927	1.1249	1.1576	1.1910	1.2250	1.2597	1.2950	1.3310	1.3676	1.4049	1.4429	1.4815	1.5209
4	1.0406	1.0824	1.1255	1.1699	1.2155	1.2625	1.3108	1.3605	1.4116	1.4641	1.5181	1.5735	1.6305	1.6890	1.7490
5	1.0510	1.1041	1.1593	1.2167	1.2763	1.3382	1.4026	1.4693	1.5386	1.6105	1.6851	1.7623	1.8424	1.9254	2.0114
6	1.0615	1.1262	1.1941	1.2653	1.3401	1.4185	1.5007	1.5869	1.6771	1.7716	1.8704	1.9738	2.0820	2.1950	2.3131
7	1.0721	1.1487	1.2299	1.3159	1.4071	1.5036	1.6058	1.7138	1.8280	1.9487	2.0762	2.2107	2.3526	2.5023	2.6600
8	1.0829	1.1717	1.2668	1.3686	1.4775	1.5938	1.7182	1.8509	1.9926	2.1436	2.3045	2.4760	2.6584	2.8526	3.0590
9	1.0937	1.1951	1.3048	1.4233	1.5513	1.6895	1.8385	1.9990	2.1719	2.3579	2.5580	2.7731	3.0040	3.2519	3.5179
10	1.1046	1.2190	1.3439	1.4802	1.6289	1.7908	1.9672	2.1589	2.3674	2.5937	2.8394	3.1058	3.3946	3.7072	4.0456
11	1.1157	1.2434	1.3842	1.5395	1.7103	1.8983	2.1049	2.3316	2.5804	2.8531	3.1518	3.4785	3.8359	4.2262	4.6524
12	1.1268	1.2682	1.4258	1.6010	1.7959	2.0122	2.2522	2.5182	2.8127	3.1384	3.4985	3.8960	4.3345	4.8179	5.3503
13	1.1381	1.2936	1.4685	1.6651	1.8856	2.1329	2.4098	2.7196	3.0658	3.4523	3.8833	4.3635	4.8980	5.4924	6.1528
14	1.1495	1.3195	1.5126	1.7317	1.9799	2.2609	2.5785	2.9372	3.3417	3.7975	4.3104	4.8871	5.5348	6.2613	7.0757
15	1.1610	1.3459	1.5580	1.8009	2.0789	2.3966	2.7590	3.1722	3.6425	4.1772	4.7846	5.4736	6.2543	7.1379	8.1371
16	1.1726	1.3728	1.6047	1.8730	2.1829	2.5404	2.9522	3.4259	3.9703	4.5950	5.3109	6.1304	7.0673	8.1372	9.3576
17	1.1843	1.4002	1.6528	1.9479	2.2920	2.6928	3.1588	3.7000	4.3276	5.0545	5.8951	6.8660	7.9861	9.2765	10.7613
18	1.1961	1.4282	1.7024	2.0258	2.4066	2.8543	3.3799	3.9960	4.7171	5.5599	6.5436	7.6900	9.0243	10.5752	12.3755
19	1.2081	1.4568	1.7535	2.1068	2.5270	3.0256	3.6165	4.3157	5.1417	6.1159	7.2633	8.6128	10.1974	12.0557	14.2318
20	1.2202	1.4859	1.8061	2.1911	2.6533	3.2071	3.8697	4.6610	5.6044	6.7275	8.0623	9.6463	11.5231	13.7435	16.3665

	INTEREST RATE PER YEAR														
Number of Years	16%	17%	18%	19%	20%	21%	22%	23%	24%	25%	26%	27%	28%	29%	30%
1	1.1600	1.1700	1.1800	1.1900	1.2000	1.2100	1.2200	1.2300	1.2400	1.2500	1.2600	1.2700	1.2800	1.2900	1.3000
2	1.3456	1.3689	1.3924	1.4161	1.4400	1.4641	1.4884	1.5129	1.5376	1.5625	1.5876	1.6129	1.6384	1.6641	1.6900
3	1.5609	1.6016	1.6430	1.6852	1.7280	1.7716	1.8158	1.8609	1.9066	1.9531	2.0004	2.0484	2.0972	2.1467	2.1970
4	1.8106	1.8739	1.9388	2.0053	2.0736	2.1436	2.2153	2.2889	2.3642	2.4414	2.5205	2.6014	2.6844	2.7692	2.8561
5	2.1003	2.1924	2.2878	2.3864	2.4883	2.5937	2.7027	2.8153	2.9316	3.0518	3.1758	3.3038	3.4360	3.5723	3.7129
6	2.4364	2.5652	2.6996	2.8398	2.9860	3.1384	3.2973	3.4628	3.6352	3.8147	4.0015	4.1959	4.3980	4.6083	4.8268
7	2.8262	3.0012	3.1855	3.3793	3.5832	3.7975	4.0227	4.2593	4.5077	4.7684	5.0419	5.3288	5.6295	5.9447	6.2749
8	3.2784	3.5115	3.7589	4.0214	4.2998	4.5950	4.9077	5.2389	5.5895	5.9605	6.3528	6.7675	7.2058	7.6686	8.1573
9	3.8030	4.1084	4.4355	4.7854	5.1598	5.5599	5.9874	6.4439	6.9310	7.4506	8.0045	8.5948	9.2234	9.8925	10.6045
10	4.4114	4.8068	5.2338	5.6947	6.1917	6.7275	7.3046	7.9259	8.5944	9.3132	10.0857	10.9153	11.8059	12.7614	13.7858
11	5.1173	5.6240	6.1759	6.7767	7.4301	8.1403	8.9117	9.7489	10.6571	11.6415	12.7080	13.8625	15.1116	16.4622	17.9216
12	5.9360	6.5801	7.2876	8.0642	8.9161	9.8497	10.8722	11.9912	13.2148	14.5519	16.0120	17.6053	19.3428	21.2362	23.2981
13	6.8858	7.6987	8.5994	9.5964	10.6993	11.9182	13.2641	14.7491	16.3863	18.1899	20.1752	22.3588	24.7588	27.3947	30.2875
14	7.9875	9.0075	10.1472	11.4198	12.8392	14.4210	16.1822	18.1414	20.3191	22.7374	25.4207	28.3957	31.6913	35.3391	39.3738
15	9.2655	10.5387	11.9737	13.5895	15.4070	17.4494	19.7423	22.3140	25.1956	28.4217	32.0301	36.0625	40.5648	45.5875	51.1859
16	10.7480	12.3303	14.1290	16.1715	18.4884	21.1138	24.0856	27.4462	31.2426	5.5271	40.3579	45.7994	51.9230	58.8079	66.5417
17	12.4677	14.4265	16.6722	19.2441	22.1861	25.5477	29.3844	33.7588	38.7408	44.4089	50.8510	58.1652	66.4614	75.8621	86.5042
18	14.4625	16.8790	19.6733	22.9005	26.6233	30.9127	35.8490	41.5233	48.0386	55.5112	64.0722	73.8698	85.0706	97.8622	112.4554
19	16.7765	19.7484	23.2144	27.2516	31.9480	37.4043	43.7358	51.0737	59.5679	69.3889	80.7310	93.8147	108.8904	126.2422	146.1920
20	19.4608	23.1056	27.3930	32.4294	38.3376	45.2593	53.3576	62.8206	73.8641	86.7362	101.7211	119.1446	139.3797	162.8524	190.0496

appendix table a–2 | Discount factors: Present value of $1 to be received after *N* years = $1/(1 + i)^N$

Number of Years	INTEREST RATE PER YEAR 1%	2%	3%	4%	5%	6%	7%	8%	9%	10%	11%	12%	13%	14%	15%
1	0.9901	0.9804	0.9709	0.9615	0.9524	0.9434	0.9346	0.9259	0.9174	0.9091	0.9009	0.8929	0.8850	0.8772	0.8696
2	0.9803	0.9612	0.9426	0.9246	0.9070	0.8900	0.8734	0.8573	0.8417	0.8264	0.8116	0.7972	0.7831	0.7695	0.7561
3	0.9706	0.9423	0.9151	0.8890	0.8638	0.8396	0.8163	0.7938	0.7722	0.7513	0.7312	0.7118	0.6931	0.6750	0.6575
4	0.9610	0.9238	0.8885	0.8548	0.8227	0.7921	0.7629	0.7350	0.7084	0.6830	0.6587	0.6355	0.6133	0.5921	0.5718
5	0.9515	0.9057	0.8626	0.8219	0.7835	0.7473	0.7130	0.6806	0.6499	0.6209	0.5935	0.5674	0.5428	0.5194	0.4972
6	0.9420	0.8880	0.8375	0.7903	0.7462	0.7050	0.6663	0.6302	0.5963	0.5645	0.5346	0.5066	0.4803	0.4556	0.4323
7	0.9327	0.8706	0.8131	0.7599	0.7107	0.6651	0.6227	0.5835	0.5470	0.5132	0.4817	0.4523	0.4251	0.3996	0.3759
8	0.9235	0.8535	0.7894	0.7307	0.6768	0.6274	0.5820	0.5403	0.5019	0.4665	0.4339	0.4039	0.3762	0.3506	0.3269
9	0.9143	0.8368	0.7664	0.7026	0.6446	0.5919	0.5439	0.5002	0.4604	0.4241	0.3909	0.3606	0.3329	0.3075	0.2843
10	0.9053	0.8203	0.7441	0.6756	0.6139	0.5584	0.5083	0.4632	0.4224	0.3855	0.3522	0.3220	0.2946	0.2697	0.2472
11	0.8963	0.8043	0.7224	0.6496	0.5847	0.5268	0.4751	0.4289	0.3875	0.3505	0.3173	0.2875	0.2607	0.2366	0.2149
12	0.8874	0.7885	0.7014	0.6246	0.5568	0.4970	0.4440	0.3971	0.3555	0.3186	0.2858	0.2567	0.2307	0.2076	0.1869
13	0.8787	0.7730	0.6810	0.6006	0.5303	0.4688	0.4150	0.3677	0.3262	0.2897	0.2575	0.2292	0.2042	0.1821	0.1625
14	0.8700	0.7579	0.6611	0.5775	0.5051	0.4423	0.3878	0.3405	0.2992	0.2633	0.2320	0.2046	0.1807	0.1597	0.1413
15	0.8613	0.7430	0.6419	0.5553	0.4810	0.4173	0.3624	0.3152	0.2745	0.2394	0.2090	0.1827	0.1599	0.1401	0.1229
16	0.8528	0.7284	0.6232	0.5339	0.4581	0.3936	0.3387	0.2919	0.2519	0.2176	0.1883	0.1631	0.1415	0.1229	0.1069
17	0.8444	0.7142	0.6050	0.5134	0.4363	0.3714	0.3166	0.2703	0.2311	0.1978	0.1696	0.1456	0.1252	0.1078	0.0929
18	0.8360	0.7002	0.5874	0.4936	0.4155	0.3503	0.2959	0.2502	0.2120	0.1799	0.1528	0.1300	0.1108	0.0946	0.0808
19	0.8277	0.6864	0.5703	0.4746	0.3957	0.3305	0.2765	0.2317	0.1945	0.1635	0.1377	0.1161	0.0981	0.0829	0.0703
20	0.8195	0.6730	0.5537	0.4564	0.3769	0.3118	0.2584	0.2145	0.1784	0.1486	0.1240	0.1037	0.0868	0.0728	0.0611

Number of Years	INTEREST RATE PER YEAR 16%	17%	18%	19%	20%	21%	22%	23%	24%	25%	26%	27%	28%	29%	30%
1	0.8621	0.8547	0.8475	0.8403	0.8333	0.8264	0.8197	0.8130	0.8065	0.8000	0.7937	0.7874	0.7813	0.7752	0.7692
2	0.7432	0.7305	0.7182	0.7062	0.6944	0.6830	0.6719	0.6610	0.6504	0.6400	0.6299	0.6200	0.6104	0.6009	0.5917
3	0.6407	0.6244	0.6086	0.5934	0.5787	0.5645	0.5507	0.5374	0.5245	0.5120	0.4999	0.4882	0.4768	0.4658	0.4552
4	0.5523	0.5337	0.5158	0.4987	0.4823	0.4665	0.4514	0.4369	0.4230	0.4096	0.3968	0.3844	0.3725	0.3611	0.3501
5	0.4761	0.4561	0.4371	0.4190	0.4019	0.3855	0.3700	0.3552	0.3411	0.3277	0.3149	0.3027	0.2910	0.2799	0.2693
6	0.4104	0.3898	0.3704	0.3521	0.3349	0.3186	0.3033	0.2888	0.2751	0.2621	0.2499	0.2383	0.2274	0.2170	0.2072
7	0.3538	0.3332	0.3139	0.2959	0.2791	0.2633	0.2486	0.2348	0.2218	0.2097	0.1983	0.1877	0.1776	0.1682	0.1594
8	0.3050	0.2848	0.2660	0.2487	0.2326	0.2176	0.2038	0.1909	0.1789	0.1678	0.1574	0.1478	0.1388	0.1304	0.1226
9	0.2630	0.2434	0.2255	0.2090	0.1938	0.1799	0.1670	0.1552	0.1443	0.1342	0.1249	0.1164	0.1084	0.1011	0.0943
10	0.2267	0.2080	0.1911	0.1756	0.1615	0.1486	0.1369	0.1262	0.1164	0.1074	0.0992	0.0916	0.0847	0.0784	0.0725
11	0.1954	0.1778	0.1619	0.1476	0.1346	0.1228	0.1122	0.1026	0.0938	0.0859	0.0787	0.0721	0.0662	0.0607	0.0558
12	0.1685	0.1520	0.1372	0.1240	0.1122	0.1015	0.0920	0.0834	0.0757	0.0687	0.0625	0.0568	0.0517	0.0471	0.0429
13	0.1452	0.1299	0.1163	0.1042	0.0935	0.0839	0.0754	0.0678	0.0610	0.0550	0.0496	0.0447	0.0404	0.0365	0.0330
14	0.1252	0.1110	0.0985	0.0876	0.0779	0.0693	0.0618	0.0551	0.0492	0.0440	0.0393	0.0352	0.0316	0.0283	0.0254
15	0.1079	0.0949	0.0835	0.0736	0.0649	0.0573	0.0507	0.0448	0.0397	0.0352	0.0312	0.0277	0.0247	0.0219	0.0195
16	0.0930	0.0811	0.0708	0.0618	0.0541	0.0474	0.0415	0.0364	0.0320	0.0281	0.0248	0.0218	0.0193	0.0170	0.0150
17	0.0802	0.0693	0.0600	0.0520	0.0451	0.0391	0.0340	0.0296	0.0258	0.0225	0.0197	0.0172	0.0150	0.0132	0.0116
18	0.0691	0.0592	0.0508	0.0437	0.0376	0.0323	0.0279	0.0241	0.0208	0.0180	0.0156	0.0135	0.0118	0.0102	0.0089
19	0.0596	0.0506	0.0431	0.0367	0.0313	0.0267	0.0229	0.0196	0.0168	0.0144	0.0124	0.0107	0.0092	0.0079	0.0068
20	0.0514	0.0433	0.0365	0.0308	0.0261	0.0221	0.0187	0.0159	0.0135	0.0115	0.0098	0.0084	0.0072	0.0061	0.0053

appendix table a–3 | Annuity table: Present value of $1 per year for each of *N* years = $1/i - 1/[i(1 + i)^N]$

	INTEREST RATE PER YEAR														
Number of Years	1%	2%	3%	4%	5%	6%	7%	8%	9%	10%	11%	12%	13%	14%	15%
1	0.9901	0.9804	0.9709	0.9615	0.9524	0.9434	0.9346	0.9259	0.9174	0.9091	0.9009	0.8929	0.8850	0.8772	0.8696
2	1.9704	1.9416	1.9135	1.8861	1.8594	1.8334	1.8080	1.7833	1.7591	1.7355	1.7125	1.6901	1.6681	1.6467	1.6257
3	2.9410	2.8839	2.8286	2.7751	2.7232	2.6730	2.6243	2.5771	2.5313	2.4869	2.4437	2.4018	2.3612	2.3216	2.2832
4	3.9020	3.8077	3.7171	3.6299	3.5460	3.4651	3.3872	3.3121	3.2397	3.1699	3.1024	3.0373	2.9745	2.9137	2.8550
5	4.8534	4.7135	4.5797	4.4518	4.3295	4.2124	4.1002	3.9927	3.8897	3.7908	3.6959	3.6048	3.5172	3.4331	3.3522
6	5.7955	5.6014	5.4172	5.2421	5.0757	4.9173	4.7665	4.6229	4.4859	4.3553	4.2305	4.1114	3.9975	3.8887	3.7845
7	6.7282	6.4720	6.2303	6.0021	5.7864	5.5824	5.3893	5.2064	5.0330	4.8684	4.7122	4.5638	4.4226	4.2883	4.1604
8	7.6517	7.3255	7.0197	6.7327	6.4632	6.2098	5.9713	5.7466	5.5348	5.3349	5.1461	4.9676	4.7988	4.6389	4.4873
9	8.5660	8.1622	7.7861	7.4353	7.1078	6.8017	6.5152	6.2469	5.9952	5.7590	5.5370	5.3282	5.1317	4.9464	4.7716
10	9.4713	8.9826	8.5302	8.1109	7.7217	7.3601	7.0236	6.7101	6.4177	6.1446	5.8892	5.6502	5.4262	5.2161	5.0188
11	10.3676	9.7868	9.2526	8.7605	8.3064	7.8869	7.4987	7.1390	6.8052	6.4951	6.2065	5.9377	5.6869	5.4527	5.2337
12	11.2551	10.5753	9.9540	9.3851	8.8633	8.3838	7.9427	7.5361	7.1607	6.8137	6.4924	6.1944	5.9176	5.6603	5.4206
13	12.1337	11.3484	10.6350	9.9856	9.3936	8.8527	8.3577	7.9038	7.4869	7.1034	6.7499	6.4235	6.1218	5.8424	5.5831
14	13.0037	12.1062	11.2961	10.5631	9.8986	9.2950	8.7455	8.2442	7.7862	7.3667	6.9819	6.6282	6.3025	6.0021	5.7245
15	13.8651	12.8493	11.9379	11.1184	10.3797	9.7122	9.1079	8.5595	8.0607	7.6061	7.1909	6.8109	6.4624	6.1422	5.8474
16	14.7179	13.5777	12.5611	11.6523	10.8378	10.1059	9.4466	8.8514	8.3126	7.8237	7.3792	6.9740	6.6039	6.2651	5.9542
17	15.5623	14.2919	13.1661	12.1657	11.2741	10.4773	9.7632	9.1216	8.5436	8.0216	7.5488	7.1196	6.7291	6.3729	6.0472
18	16.3983	14.9920	13.7535	12.6593	11.6896	10.8276	10.0591	9.3719	8.7556	8.2014	7.7016	7.2497	6.8399	6.4674	6.1280
19	17.2260	15.6785	14.3238	13.1339	12.0853	11.1581	10.3356	9.6036	8.9501	8.3649	7.8393	7.3658	6.9380	6.5504	6.1982
20	18.0456	16.3514	14.8775	13.5903	12.4622	11.4699	10.5940	9.8181	9.1285	8.5136	7.9633	7.4694	7.0248	6.6231	6.2593

	INTEREST RATE PER YEAR														
Number of Years	16%	17%	18%	19%	20%	21%	22%	23%	24%	25%	26%	27%	28%	29%	30%
1	0.8621	0.8547	0.8475	0.8403	0.8333	0.8264	0.8197	0.8130	0.8065	0.8000	0.7937	0.7874	0.7813	0.7752	0.7692
2	1.6052	1.5852	1.5656	1.5465	1.5278	1.5095	1.4915	1.4740	1.4568	1.4400	1.4235	1.4074	1.3916	1.3761	1.3609
3	2.2459	2.2096	2.1743	2.1399	2.1065	2.0739	2.0422	2.0114	1.9813	1.9520	1.9234	1.8956	1.8684	1.8420	1.8161
4	2.7982	2.7432	2.6901	2.6386	2.5887	2.5404	2.4936	2.4483	2.4043	2.3616	2.3202	2.2800	2.2410	2.2031	2.1662
5	3.2743	3.1993	3.1272	3.0576	2.9906	2.9260	2.8636	2.8035	2.7454	2.6893	2.6351	2.5827	2.5320	2.4830	2.4356
6	3.6847	3.5892	3.4976	3.4098	3.3255	3.2446	3.1669	3.0923	3.0205	2.9514	2.8850	2.8210	2.7594	2.7000	2.6427
7	4.0386	3.9224	3.8115	3.7057	3.6046	3.5079	3.4155	3.3270	3.2423	3.1611	3.0833	3.0087	2.9370	2.8682	2.8021
8	4.3436	4.2072	4.0776	3.9544	3.8372	3.7256	3.6193	3.5179	3.4212	3.3289	3.2407	3.1564	3.0758	2.9986	2.9247
9	4.6065	4.4506	4.3030	4.1633	4.0310	3.9054	3.7863	3.6731	3.5655	3.4631	3.3657	3.2728	3.1842	3.0997	3.0190
10	4.8332	4.6586	4.4941	4.3389	4.1925	4.0541	3.9232	3.7993	3.6819	3.5705	3.4648	3.3644	3.2689	3.1781	3.0915
11	5.0286	4.8364	4.6560	4.4865	4.3271	4.1769	4.0354	3.9018	3.7757	3.6564	3.5435	3.4365	3.3351	3.2388	3.1473
12	5.1971	4.9884	4.7932	4.6105	4.4392	4.2784	4.1274	3.9852	3.8514	3.7251	3.6059	3.4933	3.3868	3.2859	3.1903
13	5.3423	5.1183	4.9095	4.7147	4.5327	4.3624	4.2028	4.0530	3.9124	3.7801	3.6555	3.5381	3.4272	3.3224	3.2233
14	5.4675	5.2293	5.0081	4.8023	4.6106	4.4317	4.2646	4.1082	3.9616	3.8241	3.6949	3.5733	3.4587	3.3507	3.2487
15	5.5755	5.3242	5.0916	4.8759	4.6755	4.4890	4.3152	4.1530	4.0013	3.8593	3.7261	3.6010	3.4834	3.3726	3.2682
16	5.6685	5.4053	5.1624	4.9377	4.7296	4.5364	4.3567	4.1894	4.0333	3.8874	3.7509	3.6228	3.5026	3.3896	3.2832
17	5.7487	5.4746	5.2223	4.9897	4.7746	4.5755	4.3908	4.2190	4.0591	3.9099	3.7705	3.6400	3.5177	3.4028	3.2948
18	5.8178	5.5339	5.2732	5.0333	4.8122	4.6079	4.4187	4.2431	4.0799	3.9279	3.7861	3.6536	3.5294	3.4130	3.3037
19	5.8775	5.5845	5.3162	5.0700	4.8435	4.6346	4.4415	4.2627	4.0967	3.9424	3.7985	3.6642	3.5386	3.4210	3.3105
20	5.9288	5.6278	5.3527	5.1009	4.8696	4.6567	4.4603	4.2786	4.1103	3.9539	3.8083	3.6726	3.5458	3.4271	3.3158

appendix table a–4 | Annuity table: Future value of \$1 per year for each of N years = $[(1 + i)^N - 1]/i$

	INTEREST RATE PER YEAR														
Number of Years	1%	2%	3%	4%	5%	6%	7%	8%	9%	10%	11%	12%	13%	14%	15%
1	1.0000	1.0000	1.0000	1.0000	1.0000	1.0000	1.0000	1.0000	1.0000	1.0000	1.0000	1.0000	1.0000	1.0000	1.0000
2	2.0100	2.0200	2.0300	2.0400	2.0500	2.0600	2.0700	2.0800	2.0900	2.1000	2.1100	2.1200	2.1300	2.1400	2.1500
3	3.0301	3.0604	3.0909	3.1216	3.1525	3.1836	3.2149	3.2464	3.2781	3.3100	3.3421	3.3744	3.4069	3.4396	3.4725
4	4.0604	4.1216	4.1836	4.2465	4.3101	4.3746	4.4399	4.5061	4.5731	4.6410	4.7097	4.7793	4.8498	4.9211	4.9934
5	5.1010	5.2040	5.3091	5.4163	5.5256	5.6371	5.7507	5.8666	5.9847	6.1051	6.2278	6.3528	6.4803	6.6101	6.7424
6	6.1520	6.3081	6.4684	6.6330	6.8019	6.9753	7.1533	7.3359	7.5233	7.7156	7.9129	8.1152	8.3227	8.5355	8.7537
7	7.2135	7.4343	7.6625	7.8983	8.1420	8.3938	8.6540	8.9228	9.2004	9.4872	9.7833	10.0890	10.4047	10.7305	11.0668
8	8.2857	8.5830	8.8923	9.2142	9.5491	9.8975	10.2598	10.6366	11.0285	11.4359	11.8594	12.2997	12.7573	13.2328	13.7268
9	9.3685	9.7546	10.1591	10.5828	11.0266	11.4913	11.9780	12.4876	13.0210	13.5795	14.1640	14.7757	15.4157	16.0853	16.7858
10	10.4622	10.9497	11.4639	12.0061	12.5779	13.1808	13.8164	14.4866	15.1929	15.9374	16.7220	17.5487	18.4197	19.3373	20.3037
11	11.5668	12.1687	12.8078	13.4864	14.2068	14.9716	15.7836	16.6455	17.5603	18.5312	19.5614	20.6546	21.8143	23.0445	24.3493
12	12.6825	13.4121	14.1920	15.0258	15.9171	16.8699	17.8885	18.9771	20.1407	21.3843	22.7132	24.1331	25.6502	27.2707	29.0017
13	13.8093	14.6803	15.6178	16.6268	17.7130	18.8821	20.1406	21.4953	22.9534	24.5227	26.2116	28.0291	29.9847	32.0887	34.3519
14	14.9474	15.9739	17.0863	18.2919	19.5986	21.0151	22.5505	24.2149	26.0192	27.9750	30.0949	32.3926	34.8827	37.5811	40.5047
15	16.0969	17.2934	18.5989	20.0236	21.5786	23.2760	25.1290	27.1521	29.3609	31.7725	34.4054	37.2797	40.4175	43.8424	47.5804
16	17.2579	18.6393	20.1569	21.8245	23.6575	25.6725	27.8881	30.3243	33.0034	35.9497	39.1899	42.7533	46.6717	50.9804	55.7175
17	18.4304	20.0121	21.7616	23.6975	25.8404	28.2129	30.8402	33.7502	36.9737	40.5447	44.5008	48.8837	53.7391	59.1176	65.0751
18	19.6147	21.4123	23.4144	25.6454	28.1324	30.9057	33.9990	37.4502	41.3013	45.5992	50.3959	55.7497	61.7251	68.3941	75.8364
19	20.8109	22.8406	25.1169	27.6712	30.5390	33.7600	37.3790	41.4463	46.0185	51.1591	56.9395	63.4397	70.7494	78.9692	88.2118
20	22.0190	24.2974	26.8704	29.7781	33.0660	36.7856	40.9955	45.7620	51.1601	57.2750	64.2028	72.0524	80.9468	91.0249	102.4436

	INTEREST RATE PER YEAR														
Number of Years	16%	17%	18%	19%	20%	21%	22%	23%	24%	25%	26%	27%	28%	29%	30%
1	1.0000	1.0000	1.0000	1.0000	1.0000	1.0000	1.0000	1.0000	1.0000	1.0000	1.0000	1.0000	1.0000	1.0000	1.0000
2	2.1600	2.1700	2.1800	2.1900	2.2000	2.2100	2.2200	2.2300	2.2400	2.2500	2.2600	2.2700	2.2800	2.2900	2.3000
3	3.5056	3.5389	3.5724	3.6061	3.6400	3.6741	3.7084	3.7429	3.7776	3.8125	3.8476	3.8829	3.9184	3.9541	3.9900
4	5.0665	5.1405	5.2154	5.2913	5.3680	5.4457	5.5242	5.6038	5.6842	5.7656	5.8480	5.9313	6.0156	6.1008	6.1870
5	6.8771	7.0144	7.1542	7.2966	7.4416	7.5892	7.7396	7.8926	8.0484	8.2070	8.3684	8.5327	8.6999	8.8700	9.0431
6	8.9775	9.2068	9.4420	9.6830	9.9299	10.1830	10.4423	10.7079	10.9801	11.2588	11.5442	11.8366	12.1359	12.4423	12.7560
7	11.4139	11.7720	12.1415	12.5227	12.9159	13.3214	13.7396	14.1708	14.6153	15.0735	15.5458	16.0324	16.5339	17.0506	17.5828
8	14.2401	14.7733	15.3270	15.9020	16.4991	17.1189	17.7623	18.4300	19.1229	19.8419	20.5876	21.3612	22.1634	22.9953	23.8577
9	17.5185	18.2847	19.0859	19.9234	20.7989	21.7139	22.6700	23.6690	24.7125	25.8023	26.9404	28.1287	29.3692	30.6639	32.0150
10	21.3215	22.3931	23.5213	24.7089	25.9587	27.2738	28.6574	30.1128	31.6434	33.2529	34.9449	36.7235	38.5926	40.5564	42.6195
11	25.7329	27.1999	28.7551	30.4035	32.1504	34.0013	35.9620	38.0388	40.2379	42.5661	45.0306	47.6388	50.3985	53.3178	56.4053
12	30.8502	32.8239	34.9311	37.1802	39.5805	42.1416	44.8737	47.7877	50.8950	54.2077	57.7386	61.5013	65.5100	69.7800	74.3270
13	36.7862	39.4040	42.2187	45.2445	48.4966	51.9913	55.7459	59.7788	64.1097	68.7596	73.7506	79.1066	84.8529	91.0161	97.6250
14	43.6720	47.1027	50.8180	54.8409	59.1959	63.9095	69.0100	74.5280	80.4961	86.9495	93.9258	101.4654	109.6117	118.4108	127.9125
15	51.6595	56.1101	60.9653	66.2607	72.0351	78.3305	85.1922	92.6694	100.8151	109.6868	119.3465	129.8611	141.3029	153.7500	167.2863
16	60.9250	66.6488	72.9390	79.8502	87.4421	95.7799	104.9345	114.9834	126.0108	138.1085	151.3766	165.9236	181.8677	199.3374	218.4722
17	71.6730	78.9792	87.0680	96.0218	105.9306	116.8937	129.0201	142.4295	157.2534	173.6357	191.7345	211.7230	233.7907	258.1453	285.0139
18	84.1407	93.4056	103.7403	115.2659	128.1167	142.4413	158.4045	176.1883	195.9942	218.0446	242.5855	269.8882	300.2521	334.0074	371.5180
19	98.6032	110.2846	123.4135	138.1664	154.7400	173.3540	194.2535	217.7116	244.0328	273.5558	306.6577	343.7580	385.3227	431.8696	483.9734
20	115.3797	130.0329	146.6280	165.4180	186.6880	210.7584	237.9893	268.7853	303.6006	342.9447	387.3887	437.5726	494.2131	558.1118	630.1655

appendix B Selected Answers to End-of-Chapter Problems

Chapter 2

2-1. $1,800,000

2-5. The change in capital structure would decrease the stockholders' EPS by $0.21875.

2-9. $4,650,000

2-13. Year-end balance = $274m

2-17. $31.75m

2-21. $350,000

2-25. a. Tax Liability = $8,781,500

b. Average Tax Rate = 35.00%; Marginal Tax Rate = 35.00%

2-29. $68m

2-33. $169m

2-37. Accounts Payable: $56m; Total current assets: $118m; Long-term debt: $195m

Chapter 3

3-1. Current ratio = 1.95 times

Quick ratio = 0.84 times

Cash ratio = 0.21 times

3-5. $14.29m

3-9. Book value per share = $3.50 per share

Earnings per share = $0.70 per share

Market-to-book ratio = 2.57 times

PE ratio = 12.86 times

3-13. 5.96%

3-17. $11.43m

3-21. 12.22%

3-25. $1,518,750

3-35.

Cash	Step 4	$ 103m			
Accounts receivable	Step 2	197m	Current liabilities		$ 500m
Inventory	Step 3	800m	Long-term debt	Step 9	460m
Current assets	Step 1	$1,100m	Total debt	Step 7	$ 960m
Fixed assets	Step 6	500m	Stockholders' equity	Step 8	640m
Total assets		$1,600m	Total liabilities and equity	Step 5	$1,600m

3-39. Current sustainable growth rate = 19.51%

New sustainable growth rate = 20.69%

An increase of 1.18%

Chapter 4

4-3. $540

4-7. $422.72

4-11. $750.37

4-15. ≈ 10.29 years

4-19. 28.57%

4-23. \$625 today because PV = \$510.19

4-27. \$1,828.04

4-31. 13 years, 6.5 months

4-35. −25% (first year return), 33.33% (second year return needed)

4-39. \$3,944.31

Chapter 5

5-3. \$5,279.94

5-7. \$3,593.44

5-11. \$6,987.50

5-15. 10.47%

5-19. \$1,211,611.28

5-23. \$67,662.70

5-27. \$222.22, the value decreased

5-31. 177,077%

5-35. 1.37%

5-39. Monthly payments: \$622.13; Interest only: \$187.50

5-45. 12 monthly payments: \$183.33; EAR: 19.53%

5-51. \$280.76

5-53. \$4,209.64

5-57. Amount at 65: \$1,618,027.66; Annual payment: \$135,688.06

Combined Chapters 4 and 5 Problems

4&5-1. \$949,039.23

4&5-5. \$2,715.08, \$119.11

4&5-9. \$2,125.70

Chapter 6

6-1. 8.35%

6-5. ${}_1R_1 = 6\%$
${}_1R_2 = 6.50\%$
${}_1R_3 = 6.83\%$
${}_1R_4 = 7.09\%$

6-9. 3.58%

6-13. 0.55%

6-17. 0.1536%

6-21. 8.15%

6-25. 14.27%

Chapter 7

7-3. 84 years and 6 months

7-7. Par value: \$1,136.46; interest payment: \$15.63

7-11. \$471.01

7-15. 5.22%

7-19. \$32.87; 3.15%

7-23. \$1,072.91; premium bond

7-27. 5.35%

7-31. 7.38%; the municipal bond will give more profit after taxes

7-35. −\$2.90, −0.26%

7-39. −\$104.22, −11.13%

Chapter 8

8-1. 0.89%

8-5. $3,886.00

8-9. $930.00

8-13. $50.67

8-17. 5.18%

8-21. 15.69%

8-25. $43.42; $38.59

8-29. $68.93

8-33. $48.13

Chapter 9

9-3. $25; 2.56%

9-7. Rail Haul, Poker-R-Us, Idol Staff

9-11. Adobe Systems: 0.3750; Dow Chemical: 0.3125; Office Depot: 0.3125

9-15. 2.548%

9-19.

Decade	CoV
1950s	NA
1960s	3.88
1970s	1.19
1980s	1.12
1990s	1.35
2000s	1.29

9-23. Alaska Air: 0.299; Best Buy: 0.627; Ford Motor: 0.074

9-27.

	Portfolio Return
2000	4.08%
2001	−3.78%
2002	−4.02%
2003	15.27%
2004	8.67%
2005	5.37%
2006	9.11%
2007	6.11%
2008	−8.52%
2009	6.87%
2010	11.28%
2011	13.03%
2012	9.43%
Average =	5.6%
Std dev =	7.1%

9-31. $2,168.00; 5.27%

9-35. A.

	All Ordinaries (Australia)	Nikkei 225 (Japan)	FTSE 100 (England)
Average =	−0.31%	−0.22%	0.10%
Std dev =	4.78%	6.77%	4.82%

B. Correlations

	All Ordinaries (Australia)	Nikkei 225 (Japan)	FTSE 100 (England)
All Ordinaries (Australia)	1		
Nikkei 225 (Japan)	0.721	1	
FTSE 100 (England)	0.874	0.725	1

Chapter 10

10-3. 8%

10-7. 8.55%

10-11. 1.26

10-15. 10.46%

10-19. 16%, over-valued

10-23. 20%, 29.99%

10-27. 1.42, 15.57%

10-29. US Bancorp: 18.8%; Praxair: 23.9%; Eastman Kodak: 7.75%

Chapter 11

11-3. 8.71%

11-7. 8.25%

11-11. 12.52%

11-15. 10.30%

11-19. 11.57%

11-23. 7.36%

11-27. Division A = 9.3%; Division B = 10.5%; Division C = 11.4%; Division D = 12.3%

Chapter 12

12-3. The Scion xA, because it has an EAC of −$7,028.89.

12-7. $2,591.75

12-11. $125,950

Chapter 13

13-3. NPV = $293.45, so this project should be accepted.

13-7. 2.35 years, so this project should be accepted.

13-11. MIRR = 10.56% and since it is less than the 12 percent cost of capital, this project should be rejected.

13-15. One IRR

13-19. IRR = 22.69% and since IRR > i, this project should be accepted.

13-23. PB = 2.60 years, so this project should be accepted.

13-27. NPV = $124,106.98 and since NPV > 0, this project should be accepted.

13-31. There appears to be only one nonnegative IRR for the set of cash flows.

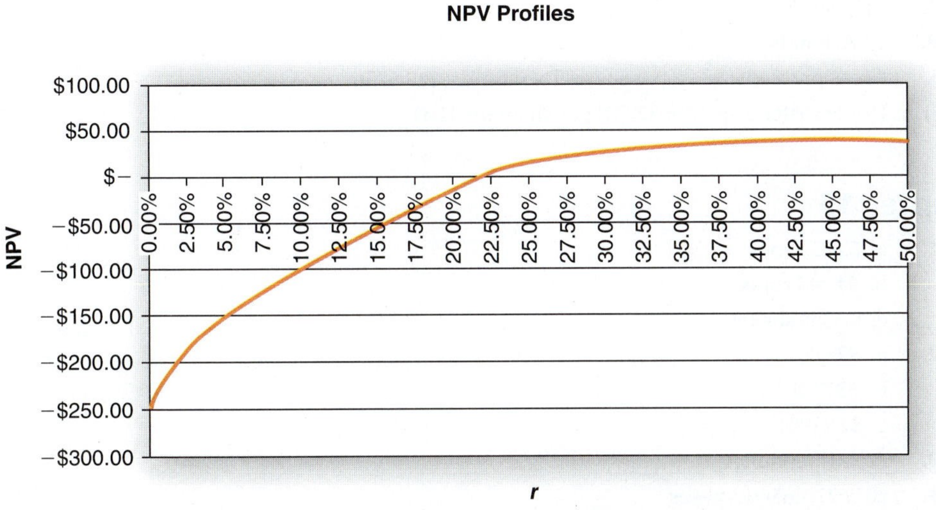

Chapter 14

14-3. 26.23 days
14-7. 6.76 times
14-11. 6 days
14-15. 34.14 days
14-20. \$77,981.29
14-24. \$80,599.43

Chapter 15

15-1. \$1,600,000
15-5. −\$1,500,000
15-9. −\$300,000

Chapter 16

16-1. 0.7054; 0.2946
16-5. \$0.88
16-9. \$0.45
16-13. \$28,000,050

Chapter 17

17-1. 0.25
17-5. \$1.02 per share
17-9. \$56.70
17-13. $P_0(1 - t_c) = \dfrac{D_1(1 - t_c)}{i}$

17-17. The stock should have a new maximum value of

$$P_0 = \frac{D_1}{(1 + i_{daily})^{2N}} + \left(\frac{D_2}{i_{yearly}} \times \frac{1}{(1 + i_{daily})^{2N}}\right)$$ and a new minimum

value of $P_0 = \left(\dfrac{D_2}{i_{yearly}} \times \dfrac{1}{(1 + i_{daily})^{2N}}\right)$.

Chapter 18

18-1. \$1,625
18-5. \$40,106,250
18-9. 1,070 bonds
18-13. Gross proceeds: \$8.75 per share; Total funds: \$19.875m.
18-17. Underwriter's spread: \$2.778 per share (or 11.11%)

Chapter 19

19-1. a. 5.882 krone
b. 54.348 rupee
c. 3.6350 shekel
19-7. a. \$95.86
b. \$317,460
c. \$217,984
19-9. \$23.31 per ounce
9-13. €0.0621; 16.0913 pesos

19-17. \$0.8448 per NZD

19-21. The firm would get \$0.23 million more in one year.

19-23. The inferred cross-rate is 1 franc = 1 franc × (\$1 / 1.219 francs) × (CA\$1.18 / \$1) = CA\$0.9680. Starting with U.S. dollars, buy francs and convert them to Canadian dollars and then back to U.S. dollars.

Chapter 20

20-1. a. $AC_{Peter} = 5.56\%$

$AC_{Jan} = 9.09\%$

b. $TAC = 5.94\%$

c. $TAC = 5.35\%$

20-5. 2.39

According to the Altman's Z-score, the firm should be placed in the indeterminant bankruptcy class.

20-9. a. $AC_{George} = 12.22\%$; $AC_{Weezzie} = 9.25\%$.

b. \$85,000

20-13. NPV = −\$4.67m

This merger would not be beneficial for the stockholders of the bidder firm.

20-17. Z-score = 4.07

According to the Altman's Z-score, this firm should be placed in the low bankruptcy risk class.

20-21. a. The average cost after merger = \$2,800,000/\$11,000,000 = 25.45%. If Johnson Construction can lower its average costs to less than 25.45%, it should go ahead with the merger.

b. The average cost after merger = \$2,300,000/\$11,000,000 = 20.91%.

20-25. \$6.16m

photo credits

Page 3: John Lamb/Photodisc/Getty Images RF.
Page 33: Photographer's Choice/Getty Images RF.
Page 76: © Pixtal/age fotostock RF.
Page 119: Ryan McVay/Getty Images RF.
Page 149: © Royalty-Free/Corbis RF.
Page 189: © Brand X Pictures/ PunchStock RF.
Page 233: © Royalty-Free/Corbis RF.
Page 273: Getty Images.
Page 307: © Purestock/SuperStock RF.
Page 339: © Ingram Publishing RF.
Page 373: Photodisc/Getty Images RF.
Page 405: Antenna/Getty Images RF.
Page 439: Photodisc/Getty Images RF.
Page 474: Stockbyte/Getty Images RF.
Page 512: © Blend Images/Jetta Productions/Getty Images RF.
Page 545: © Royalty-Free/Corbis.
Page 579: Adam Gault/Getty Images RF.
Page 603: Image Source/Getty Images RF.
Page 631: © McGraw-Hill Education/Chris Kerrigan.
Page 661: © McGraw-Hill Education/Lars A. Niki.

index

Note: Page numbers followed by n refer to footnotes.

a

Accelerated depreciation, 413–414
  impact of, 415–416
Accounting, finance vs., 11
Accounting methods
  fixed asset depreciation, 36
  GAAP, 45
Accounts payable management, 81
Accounts payable turnover, 81, 83, 92, 101
Accounts receivable management, 80–81
Accounts receivable turnover, 83, 92, 101
Acid-test ratio, 78–79, 92, 101
Acquisitions, 661; *see also* Mergers and acquisitions
Active capital structure management, 546
Active management, 545
Add-on interest, 171
Additional funds needed (AFN), 521
  calculation of, 522
  with excess capacity, 523
  with lumpy assets, 523–524
  pro forma statements and, 525–532
  with unused capacity, 522
Adjustable rate mortgages (ARMs), 202
Agency bonds, 237
Agency problem, 17
Agency relationship, 3, 17, 20
Agency theory, 17–20
Agent, 17
Aging schedule, 494
Altman, E. I., 680–681
American Airlines, 676
American Recovery and Reinvestment Act, 23
American Stock Exchange (AMEX), 275
Amortization schedule, 168
Amortized loan, 167
Angel investors, 13
Angel venture capitalist (or angels), 608
Anginer, Deniz, 351
Annual percentage rate (APR), 164
Annuity, 151–152
Annuity cash flow analysis
  future value of multiple cash flows, 152–153
  ordinary annuities vs. annuities due, 160–162
  present value of multiple annuities, 159–160
Annuity date, 160
Annuity due, 160–161
Annuity loans, 166–171
  add-on interest, 171
  amortization schedule, 168–169
  interest rates on, 166
  payment on amortized loan, 167–168
  time period, 170
Apple Computer, 21
Arbitrage/arbitrageur, 638
Arpey, Gerard J., 676
Ask, 280
Aspinwall, R. C., 680
Asset-backed commercial paper (ABCP), 201
Asset-backed securities, 238
Asset-based loans, 483
Asset classes, 10, 34
  performance of, 310–311
  risk of, 314–315
Asset management ratios, 79–83, 92
  accounts payable, 81
  accounts receivable, 80–81
  calculation of, 82–83
  fixed asset and working capital management, 81–82
  inventory management, 79–80
  total asset management, 82–83
Asset pricing, 343
Asset transformer, 200, 220
Assets
  on balance sheet, 34
  current assets, 34
  fixed assets, 34
Assignee or trustee, 674
Assignment, 483, 674
Auditor, 19
Availability float, 490
Average approach, 516–518
Average collection period (ACP), 80, 83, 92, 101
Average payment period (APP), 81, 83, 92, 101
Average returns, 309
Average tax rate, 42

b

Back-end (or commitment) fee, 606
Balance sheet, 34–38
  assets, 34–35
  example of, 35
  liabilities and stockholders' equity, 35–36
Balance sheet management, 36–38, 476
  accounting method for fixed asset depreciation, 36
  book value vs. market value, 37–38
  debt vs. equity financing, 37
  liquidity, 34, 36–37
  net working capital, 36
Bank loans, 604–606
Banker's acceptances (BA), 193, 484
Bankruptcy; *see also* Financial distress
  federal laws, 674–675
  firm value with taxes and, 563–565
  largest U.S., 675
  liquidation procedures, 677–678
  prediction of, 679–683
  priority of claimants, 559
  reorganization procedures, 675–677
  types of, 559–560
Bankruptcy Reform Act of 1978, 674, 677
Barabas Economic Order Quantity (EOQ), 476
Base case, 514
Base case projections, 514
Basic earnings power (BEP), 87–88, 93, 102
Baumol, William S., 485
Baumol model, 476, 485–486
  optimal cash replenishment, 486
Bearer bonds, 234
Behavioral finance, 351, 355
Benartzi, Shlomo, 319
Best efforts underwriting, 616
Beta, 345
  concerns about, 350–352
  DJIA stock betas, 346
  finding, 349
  as measure of market risk, 345–347
  portfolio's beta, 348–349
  proxy betas, 381
  security market line and, 347
  spreadsheet computation, 350

Bid, 279
Bird-in-the-hand theory, 581
Blinder, Meyer, 352
Board of directors, 19
Bond market, 256–258
capital gains in, 246–247
major indexes, 258
overview of, 233–241
Bond price, 234–235
interest rate risk and, 243–247
Bond quotes, 239–241
Bond rating, 253–254
Bond valuation, 242–247
interest rate risk and, 245–246
prices and interest rate risk, 243–247
PV of bond cash flows, 242–243
Bond yields, 247–253
credit risk and, 255–256
current yield, 247–248
municipal bonds and, 251
summary of, 252–253
yield to call, 249–250
yield to maturity, 247–248
Bonds, 233–234; *see also* Bond valuation; Corporate bonds
bond-based securities, 236–237
bond quotes, 239–241
corporate bonds, 236, 614–616
features of, 234–235
investment grade, 253
issuers of, 235–236
municipal bonds, 236, 241
premium/discount, 240
Treasury bonds, 235–236
zero coupon bond, 242
Book value, 37
Book value per share (BVPS), 40
Break-even EBIT, 557–558
Brokers, 275
Bubbles, stock market, 356
Budgeting; *see* Capital budgeting
Business environment
finance in, 4
variables in, 3
Business failure, 672
Business functions, finance in, 11–12
Business organizations, 13–15
characteristics of, 14
forms of, 3
types, 13–15
Business ownership, 273
Business risk, 381
Buy-side analysts, 287
Buyback, 592

C

C corporations, 583
Call, 234–235
Call option, 562
Call premium, 234
Callability, 209
Cameron, Doug, 676
Campbell, John Y., 319
Capital
cost of; *see* Cost of capital
misallocation of, 670
return to investors, 7
Capital asset pricing model (CAPM), 343–344
under- or overvalued stock and, 347–348
Capital budgeting
cash budgets, 505–507
cash flow estimation, 406–408
choice of, 440
decision statistic format, 440–441
discounted payback (DPB), 440, 443–445
internal rate of return, 449–460
with mutually exclusive projects, 455–460
international capital budgeting, 647
IRR (internal rate of return), 440
modified internal rate of return (MIRR), 440
with mutually exclusive projects, 455–460
net present value, 419–421, 440, 446–449
payback (PB), 440–442
profitability index (PI), 440
techniques for, 439–440
Capital budgeting projects
depreciation calculation, 408–409
guiding principles for, 406–408
operating cash flow calculation, 409–410
opportunity costs, 406–407
stock dividends and bond interest, 408
substitutionary and complementary effects, 407–408
total project cash flow, 408–413
Capital flow, 6
Capital gains
dividends vs., 579–582
investor preference for, 581
Capital intensity, 82–83, 93, 101
Capital intensity ratio, 521
Capital market efficiency, 352–355
Capital market instruments, 193–195
Capital market line (CML), 344
Capital markets, 192–193
Capital projects; *see* Cash flow estimation
Capital sources; *see also* Debt financing; Equity financing
debt financing, 604–607
for new and small firms, 603–610
for public firms, 611–620
Small Business Administration (SBA), 607–608
Capital structure, 37, 44, 84, 545–546; *see also* Capital sources; Dividends; Modigliani-Miller (M&M) theorem
active vs. passive changes, 545–546
capital structure weights and WACC, 378–379
debt vs. equity financing, 37, 41, 44, 84
financial leverage and, 546–559
firm's EPS, 41, 551
observed capital structure, 565–566
optimal theoretical structure, 565
theory vs. reality, 565–566
Capital structure irrelevance assertion, 547
CAPM; *see* Capital asset pricing model
Carroll, Archie B., 30n
Carrying costs, 479
shortage costs and, 480
Cash account, 484
Cash budget, 505–507
Cash coverage, 85–86, 93, 101
Cash cycle, 476–478
calculation of, 478
Cash flow, 484
Cash flow(s); *see also* Cash flow estimation; Statement of cash flows
defined, 3
of finance, 7, 9
of financial institutions, 22
from financing activities, 47–48
from investing activities, 46–47
from operations, 46
moving, 130–131
organizing, 120
PV of bond cash flows, 242–243
stock valuation and, 281–283
total project cash flow, 408–413
Cash flow estimation
accelerated depreciation, 413–416
complementary effects, 407–408
depreciation calculation, 408–409
EAC approach, 418–421
gross fixed asset changes, 410
guiding principles for, 406–408
MACRS depreciation, 414
net working capital changes, 411–412
operating cash flow calculation, 409–410
opportunity costs, 406–407
Section 179 deduction, 414
special cases, 416–418
stock dividends and bond interest, 408
substitutionary effects, 407–408
sunk costs, 407
total project cash flow, 408–413
Cash flows from financing activities, 47–48
Cash flows from investment activities, 46
Cash flows from operations, 46
Cash management, 484–489
Baumol model, 485–486
cash and net working capital, 476–477
float control, 490–492
investing idle cash, 492
Miller-Orr model, 486–488
reasons for holding cash, 484–485
target cash balances, 489
Cash ratio, 78–79, 92, 101
Centered moving average, 518
Central American Free Trade Agreement, 632
Certified development companies, 607

Chapter 7 bankruptcy, 559, 675, 677
creditor/stockholder payoffs, 678–679
Chapter 11 bankruptcy, 559, 674, 677
Check Clearing for the 21st Century Act, 491
Chief executive officer (CEO), 17, 20
Chief financial officer (CFO), 11
Chon, Gina, 611
Clientele effect, 582–583
Coefficient of variation, 315
Colgate-Palmolive Company, 34
Collection policy, 493–494, 506
Commercial paper, 193, 483, 612
credit ratings, 614
direct vs. dealer placements, 613
prime rates and, 612
trading process for, 613–614
Commercial Paper Funding Facility (CPFF), 613
Commitment fee, 606
Common-size financial statements, 94
Common stock, 36, 274
Compensating balances, 482, 484
Competitive sale, 615
Complement, 408
Component costs, 374
Composition, 674
Compounding, 121
at different interest rates over time, 125–126
EARs and APRs, 164–165
effect of compounding frequency, 162–164
interest rates, 133–134
power of, 123–124
Rule of 72, 132
Compounding frequency, 162–164
Compromise financing policy, 482
Concentration banking, 490
Conglomerate merger, 663
Consolidation, 661
Consols, 160
Constant-growth model, 284, 357–358
Coca-Cola example, 285
for required return, 357–358
Consumer price index (CPI), 205
Control of corruption indicator, 646
Convertibility feature, 209
Convertible bonds, 209, 238
Corporate bonds, 193–194, 236
credit ratings on, 253–255
default risk premium, 208
top underwriters of domestic debt, 615
trading process for, 614–616
Corporate control issues, 583
Corporate goals, 16–17
Corporate governance, 18–19
monitors of, 19
Corporate income taxes, 41–44
Corporate stocks, 193–194
Corporate taxes
calculation of, 42–43
firm value with bankruptcy and, 563–565
with interest and dividend income, 43
M&M theorem with, 551–554, 559
tax rates, 42, 377
Corporations, 14; *see also* Capital sources; Cost of capital
agency problem, 17
interest/dividends received/paid by, 43–44
Correia da Silva, Luis, 583
Correlation, 322
Cost of capital; *see also* Capital budgeting
cost of equity, 374–375, 547
cost of preferred stock, 376
divisional WACC, 383–388
firm WACC vs. project WACC, 379–383, 385
flotation-adjusted cost of equity, 389–390
mergers and, 670
WACC formula, 374–379
Cost reduction, by M&A, 664
Costs
carrying costs, 479
currency conversion, 638
financing, 408
flotation, 389–390, 421–422
historical, 37
minimizing costs, 17
opportunity, 406–407
shortage, 480
sunk, 407
Coupon rate, 234–235, 252
Covenants, 209, 606
Coverage ratios, 85–86
Credit analysis, 493
Credit analysts, 19
Credit management, 492–494
collection policy, 493–494
credit analysis, 493
credit policy, 492–493
Credit policy, 492–493
Credit process flow chart, 605
Credit quality risk, 253
Credit ratings, on commercial paper, 614
Credit risk, 207, 253–256
bond ratings, 253–255
yield and, 255–256
Credit risk premium, 207
Credit-scoring models, 680
Credit terms, 492
Cross rates, 637
Cross-sectional analysis, 96
Currency-conversion fees, 638
Currency swap, 640
Current assets, 34, 37
alternative financing for, 480–482
components of, 480
size of, 479
Current liabilities, 34–35
Current ratio, 78–79, 92, 101
Current yield, 247, 252

d

Das, Anupreeta, 611
Days' sales in inventory, 80, 83, 92, 101
Dealers, 276
Debentures, 254
Debt
cost of, 376–377
default rates, 673
restructuring, 673–674
Debt capacity, tax gains from unused, 669
Debt financing, 604–607
bank loans, 604–606
commercial paper, 612–614
credit process flow chart, 605
debt issue announcement, 618
equity financing vs., 37, 41, 44, 84
fixed vs. floating rate loans, 607
loan commitments, 606–607
long-term debt, 614–616
for new and small firms, 603–604
for public firms, 612–616
Small Business Administration (SBA), 607
top underwriters, 615
Debt holders, 560
Debt management ratios, 84–86, 93
calculation of, 86
cash coverage, 85
coverage ratios, 85
debt vs. equity financing, 84–85
fixed-charge coverage, 85
times interest earned, 85
Debt ratio, 84, 86, 93, 101
Debt-to-equity, 93, 101
Debt-to-equity ratio, 84, 86
Decision statistic format, 440–441
Declaration date, 587
Default risk, 205, 207
Default risk premium, 207
corporate bonds, 208
Defined benefit plan, 12
Defined contribution plan, 12
Delegated monitor, 200
Demyanyk, Yuliya, 239
Depreciable basis, 406
Depreciation
accelerated depreciation, 413–414
cash flows calculation and, 408–409
fixed asset depreciation, 36
half-year convention and, 413–414
MACRS, 36, 414
MACRS depreciation tables, 434–437
straight-line method, 36
Derivative security, 196
Deseasonalize, 518
Dimon, James, 197
Direct IPO, 610
Direct quote, 636
Direct transfer, 198
Discount, 640
Discount bond, 240
Discount rate, 128
Discounted payback (DPB), 440, 443
calculation, 444
strengths and weaknesses, 445
Discounted payback (DPB) benchmark, 443–445
Discounted payback (DPB) statistic, 443
Discounting, 128
multiple rates, 130
over multiple periods, 128

Diversifiable risk, 317
Diversification, 316, 321–323
asset class risk and, 314–315
international opportunities for, 323
investor diversification problems, 319
Dividend discount model, 283–284
Dividend irrelevance theorem, 580
Dividend payout, 87–88, 93, 102
Dividend payout ratio, 580
Dividend yield, 285
Dividends
capital gains vs., 579–582
clientele effect, 582–583
corporate control issues, 583
corporate taxes and, 43
effect on stock prices, 587–590
extraordinary dividends, 585
free cash flow theory, 584
information effect, 582
investor preference for, 581–582
irrelevance theory, 580–581
paid/received by corporations, 43–44
payment logistics, 586–590
payment procedures, 587
policy issues, 582–586
real-world policy, 583–586
residual dividend model, 584
stock dividends, 591
stock splits, 591–592
Dividends per share (DPS), 39
Divisional WACC, 383–388
example decisions using, 387
pros and cons of, 383–386
subjective vs. objective approaches, 386–388
WACC errors, 386
Dollar return, 307–308
Double taxation, 14
Dow Jones Industrial Average (DJIA), 194, 277
required returns for DJIA stocks, 348
stock betas, 346
Drafts, 491
DuPont analysis, 90–94
application of, 93–94
DuPont Corporation, 90
Dutch auction IPO, 610
Dutch auction share repurchase, 593

e

EAC approach, 418–421
Earnings management, 52–53
Earnings per share (EPS), 39, 41, 554
Ebersman, David, 611
EBIT (earnings before interest and taxes), 39
break-even EBIT, 557–558
EBI expectations, 558
EBITDA (earnings before interest, taxes, depreciation, and amortization), 39
EBT (earnings before taxes), 39
Economic environment, participants in, 6
Economic failure, 672
Economic profits, 439
Economic rents, 664
Economies of scale, 18, 664–665
long-term effect of, 666
Economies of scope, 666–667
average costs calculation, 667
EE savings bonds, 238
Effective annual rate (EAR), 164
Efficient frontier, 320
Efficient market, 352
conditions needed for, 352
Efficient market hypothesis (EMH), 353–354
semistrong-form efficiency, 353
strong-form efficiency, 353
weak-form efficiency, 353
Efficient portfolios, 320
Eisenbeis, R. A., 680
Electronic transactions, 491
Employee stock option plan (ESOP), 18
Equipment trust certificates, 255
Equity, 13, 273
as call option on value of firm, 560–562
cost of, 374–375
trading process for, 617–620
Equity financing, 608, 616–620
cost of issuing stock, 619
debt financing vs., 37, 41, 84
initial public offering (IPO), 609–611
primary market stock transaction, 617
top underwriters of, 617
Equity multiplier, 84, 86, 93, 101
Ethics, 3
role of, 20–21
European Union (EU), 632
Ex-dividend date, 587
Exchange rate risk, 638–640
Exchange rates, 636–638
expected exchange rates, 644
forward rate and hedging, 640–642
future exchange rates, 642–653
quantitative easing, 644
Executive compensation, 20
Executive stock options, 357
Expected returns, 286, 340–343
leverage impact on, 552–553
maximization of, 344
risk and, 340–342
risk premiums, 342–343
Extension, 674
External financing, 521–524
additional funds needed (AFN), 521
Extraordinary dividends, 585–586

f

Facebook IPO, 611
Facility fee, 606
Factor, 483
Fallen angels, 255
Fannie Mae, 238
Federal bankruptcy laws, 674–675
Federal funds, 193
Federal Reserve
CPFF and, 613
federal funds rate and, 193
Federal Reserve Board, 613
Federal Trade Commission (FTC), 663
Fiduciary, 20
FIFO (first-in, first out), 97
Finance, 4
accounting vs., 11
in business and life, 4–11
defined, 3–6
in other business functions, 11–12
in personal life, 12
subareas of, 6–9
Financial analysts, 287
Financial asset, 10
Financial calculator, 126–127
Financial crisis of 2008, 22–23
mortgage-backed securities and, 239
overview of, 5
public sector and, 23
recovery of, 23–24
risk measurement and management, 201–203
source and implications of, 3
start and worsening of, 22–23
Financial decisions, application and theory for, 9–10
Financial distress, 545–546, 672–683
bankruptcy laws, 674–675
costs of, 560–563
equity as call option on value of firm, 560–562
firm value with taxes and bankruptcy, 563–565
informal resolutions of, 673–674
liquidation procedures, 677–678
overinvestment/underinvestment problems, 562–563
prediction of, 679–683
reorganization procedures, 675–677
types and causes of, 672–673
Financial institutions, 197–203
cash flows of, 22
economic functions performed by, 199–200
financial crisis, 201–202
financial markets and, 9
liquidity and price risk, 200–201
monitoring costs of, 200
risk measurement and management, 201–203
types of, 199
Financial intermediaries, 21
Financial leverage, 37, 345, 546
debt vs. equity financing, 37
Financial management and managers, 4, 7–9, 11
agency theory, 17–20
decisions for, 8–9
defined, 3
firm goals, 16–17
risk and return implications, 355–356
Financial markets, 4, 9, 21, 189–190
derivative securities, 196–197
financial institutions and, 9
foreign exchange, 195–196

intermediaries and the firm, 21–22
money markets vs. capital markets, 192–195
primary vs. secondary markets, 190–192
Financial planning, 513–514
sales forecasts
average approach, 516–518
naïve approach, 514–515
systematic variations, 518–520
short-term, 478–484
Financial risk, 381
Financial statement analysis
asset management ratios, 79–83, 92
cautions in using ratios, 97–98
cross-sectional analysis, 96–97
debt management ratios, 84–86
DuPont analysis, 90–94
internal and sustainable growth rates, 95–96
liquidity ratios, 78, 92
market value ratios, 89–90
profitability ratios, 86, 88, 93
ratio analysis for, 77–78
spreading financial statements, 94
time series analysis, 96–97
Financial statements, 32–34
balance sheet, 34–38
common size-financial statements, 94–96
forecasting of, 525–532
free cash flow, 49–51
income statement, 39–44
interpretation cautions, 52–55
pro forma statements, 525–530
statement of cash flows, 45–49
statement of retained earnings, 51–52
Financial theories, 4
Financing costs, 408
Firm commitment underwriting, 615
Firm goals, 16–17
Firm-specific risk, 316
Firm WACC
incorrect decisions by, 385
project WACC vs., 379–383
First order effects, 525
Fisher, Irving, 206, 548
Fisher, Kenneth, 351
Fisher Effect, 206
Fitzpatrick, Dan, 197
Fixed asset turnover, 81, 83, 92, 101
Fixed asset and working capital management, 81
Fixed assets, 34
capital budgeting projects, 410
depreciation method for, 36
Fixed-charge coverage, 85–86, 93, 101
Fixed-income securities, 233–234
Fixed peg arrangement, 640
Fixed-price tender offer, 592
Fixed-rate loan, 607
Flexible financing policy, 480
Float, 490
Float control, 490–491
accelerating collections, 490
delaying disbursements, 490–491
ethical and legal questions, 491
Flotation costs, 389–390, 421–422
flotation-adjusted cost of equity, 389–390
Forecasting, financial statements, 525–532
Forecasting sales, 514–520
average approach, 516–518
historic average approach, 517
naïve approach, 514–515
systematic variations, 518–520
trends and seasonality, 518–520
Foreign currency exchange, 636–644
exchange rate risk, 638–640
exchange rates, 636–638
forward exchange rate, 640–641
future exchange rates, 642–644
hedging, 640–641
interest rate parity, 641–642
purchasing power parity, 642–644
Foreign direct investment, 635
Foreign exchange markets, 195–196
Foreign exchange risk, 195
Forward exchange rate, 640
hedging and, 640–641
Forward P/E ratio, 292
Forward rate, 217
estimation of, 218
401k plan, 12
Freddie Mac, 238
Free cash flow (FCF), 49–51
calculation of, 49–50
Free cash flow theory of dividends, 584
Freely floating regime, 638
Future value (FV), 120–127
of an annuity due, 161
compounding and, 121–127
of level cash flows, 151–152
of multiple cash flows, 149–154
several cash flows, 150
in single period, 121
tables, 704–707
use of, 130–133
Futures, 640
FV; *see* Future value

g

GAAP accounting principles, 45, 98
Gates, Bill, 273
General partners, 15
General partnership, 13
Geometric mean return, 310
Global business, 632–636
control of corruption, 646
corporate expansion, 634–636
GDP in largest economies, 633
international opportunities, 632–634
multinational corporations (MNCs), 635
political risks, 645–646
trade agreements, 632
U.S. exports/imports, 633
U.S. foreign direct investment, 635
Google, 15, 273
Gordon, Myron J., 284
Gordon growth model, 284
Greek debt crisis, 256
Gross domestic product, 633
Gross fixed assets, 410
Gross proceeds, 617
Gross profit, 39
Gross profit margin, 87–88, 93, 101
Growth rates, 95–96
calculation of, 96
internal growth rate, 95–96
sustainable growth rate, 95–96
Growth stocks, 286

h

Half-year convention, 413–414
Hedging, 640
Herfindahl-Hirschman Index (HHI), 668
calculation of change in, 669
High-yield bonds, 255
Historical cost, 37
Historical returns, 307–311
computing returns, 307–310
Historical risks, 311–316
computing volatility, 312–314
risk of asset classes, 314–315
risk vs. return, 315–316
Horizontal merger, 663
Human resource managers, 11–12
Hybrid organizations, 14–15

i

Illiquid asset, 37
In-house processing float, 490
Income statement, 39–44
corporate income taxes, 41–42
debt vs. equity financing, 41
example of, 40
noncash entries, 45–46
Incremental cash flows, 406
Indenture agreement, 233–234
Indirect quote, 636
Indirect transfer, 199
Individual Retirement Account (IRA), 12
Individual securities, interest rate influences on
default or credit risk, 205, 207–208
inflation, 205
liquidity risk, 205, 208–209
real interest rates, 205–207
special provisions or covenants, 205, 209
term to maturity, 205, 209–211
Infinity divisible, 523
Inflation, 205–206
definition, 205
Fisher effect and, 206
nominal interest rate, 205, 207
Inflow, 120
Information effect, 582
Initial public offerings (IPOs), 190, 609–611
Institutional venture capital firms, 608

Interest
  bond, 408
  corporate taxes and, 43
  paid/received by corporations, 43–44
  simple interest, 122
Interest rate, 120
Interest-rate cognizant, 458
Interest rate parity, 641–642
Interest rate risk, 245–247
  bond prices and, 243–247
Interest rates, 203–218
  compounding and, 125–126
  computation of, 133–134
  Fisher effect and, 206
  forecasting, 217–218
  influencing factors for
    default or credit risk, 205, 207–208
    inflation, 205
    liquidity risk, 208–209
    nominal interest rates, 205
    real risk-free rate, 205–207
    special provisions or covenants, 205, 209
    term to maturity, 205, 209–211
  key rates (1972–2013), 204–205
  nominal, 203
  prime, 612
Internal growth rate, 95, 102
Internal rate of return (IRR), 440, 449–460
  benchmark, 450–451
  IRR statistic, 450
  modified internal rate of return, 453–455
  mutually exclusive projects, 455–460
  non-normal cash flows, 452–453
  NPV profile, 451
  problems with, 451–452
  reinvestment rate assumptions, 453
  strengths and weaknesses, 460
Internal Revenue Service (IRS), 19
Internal Revenue Service (IRS) Publication 946, 409
International capital budgeting, 647
International finance, 9–10
International investments, 323
International Monetary Fund (IMF), 634
International opportunities, 632–634
Inventory management, 79–80
Inventory turnover, 79, 83, 92, 101
Investment analyst, 19
Investment banks, 19, 190
Investment grade, 253
Investment in operating capital (IOC), 49
Investment opportunities, 484
Investments, 6–8
Investor psychology, 280
Investors, 5; *see also* Shareholders
  return of capital to, 7
Invisible hand, 16
Iterative calculation, 528

j

Jobs and Growth Tax Relief Reconciliation Act (JGTRRA) of 2003, 580
Jobs, Steven, 21
JPMorgan, 197
Junk bonds, 254
Just in time (JIT), 475–476

k

Kaizen, 479

l

Law of one price, 642
Leverage
  break-even EBIT, 557–558
  choice to re-leverage, 554–557
  effect on cost of equity, 547–549
  effect on WACC, 549–551
  exceeding firm's leverage, 556–557
  expected return, 550–553
  financial leverage, 345
  shareholders' expected return, 552–553
  undoing a change in, 555
Leveraged buyouts (LBOs), 554
Liabilities, 35
LIFO (last-in, first-out), 97
Limit order, 280
Limited liability, 14
Limited liability companies (LLCs), 13, 15
Limited liability partnerships (LLPs), 15
Limited partners, 15
Limited partnerships (LPs), 15
Line of credit, 482
Linear discriminant models, 680–682
Linear probability, 682
Lintner, John, 344
Liquidation, 674, 677–678
Liquidity, 34, 36–37, 198
Liquidity premium theory, 214–216
  calculation of yield curves, 215
Liquidity ratios, 78, 92
  calculation of, 78–79
Liquidity risk, 205, 208
Loan commitment, calculating fees on, 606
Loan commitment agreement, 606
Loan covenants, 606
Loan principal, 168
Loans, fixed vs. floating rate, 607
Lockbox system, 490
Logit models, 682
Long position, 562
Long-term assets, 34
Long-term debt, 35, 614–616

m

M&M theorem; *see* Modigliani-Miller (M&M) theorem
MACRS (modified accelerated cost recovery system), 36, 52, 414
MACRS (modified accelerated cost recovery system) depreciation tables, 434–437
Mail float, 490
Managed-floating regime, 638
Management, personal incentives for mergers, 670
MAPE (mean absolute percentage error), 514
Marginal tax rate, 42
Market bubbles, 356
Market capitalization, 278
Market extension merger, 663
Market interest rate, 252
Market makers, 276
Market order, 280
Market portfolio, 343–345
Market risk, 317, 343–352
  beta and, 345–352
  market portfolio, 343–345
  portfolio beta, 348
  security market line, 346–348
Market risk premium, 343
Market segmentation theory, 216–217
Market-to-book ratio, 89–90, 93, 102
Market value, 37
Market value per share (MVPS), 40
Market value ratios, 89–90, 93
  calculation of, 90
Marketable securities, 34, 48
Marketing managers, 11
Markkula, Mike, 21
Markowitz, Harry, 318
Master registration statement, 620
Maturity date, 233–234
Maturity premium (MP), 209
Maximization of shareholder wealth, 16–17
Mean absolute percentage error (MAPE), 514
Mercosur, 632
Mergers and acquisitions, 661–671
  guidelines for acceptability, 668
  largest, 662
  motives for, 663–670
    capital cost reductions, 670
    capital misallocation, 670
    cost reduction, 664–667
    managers' personal incentives, 670
    revenue enhancement, 664
    tax considerations, 669–670
  types, 663
  valuation of, 670–671
Microsoft, 273
Miller, Merton, 486, 547
Miller-Orr model, 486–488
  optimal return point, 487
  patterns of, 488
  upper limit, 487
MIRR; *see* Modified internal rate of return
Modern portfolio theory (MPT), 318–324
  CAPM and, 344
  efficient frontier, 320
  efficient portfolio, 320
  optimal portfolio, 318
Modified internal rate of return (MIRR), 440, 449–460
  MIRR calculation, 454–455
  modified internal rate of return statistic, 453

mutually exclusive projects, 455–460
strengths and weaknesses, 460
Modigliani-Miller (M&M) theorem, 547–558
assumptions for, 547
bird-in-the-hand fallacy, 581
break-even EBIT, 557–558
capital structure irrelevance assertion, 547
corporate taxes, 551–554
corporate taxes and bankruptcy, 559–565
dividend irrelevance theorem, 580
leverage effect on cost of equity, 547–549
leverage effect WACC, 549–550
Proposition I (perfect world), 547, 564
Proposition I (with corporate taxes), 552
Proposition II (perfect world), 547
Proposition II (with corporate taxes), 552
Proposition IIa (perfect world), 549, 552, 565
Money market instruments, 193–194
Money markets, 192
Moody's Investors Service, 208, 253
Mortgage-backed securities, 23, 193–194, 238
financial crisis and, 239
Mortgage bonds, 255
Mortgages, 193–194
amortization schedules, 168–169
subprime mortgage crisis, 22
Moving average, 518
Multinational corporation (MNC), 635
Municipal bonds, 236, 241
taxable equivalent yield, 251
yield and, 251
Mutually exclusive projects, 455–460

n

Naïve approach, 514–515
estimate of future sales, 515
NASDAQ, 191
NASDAQ Composite Index, 277
NASDAQ Stock Market, 276
Negotiable certificates of deposit, 193
Negotiated sale, 616
Net change in cash and marketable securities, 48
Net income, 17, 39
Net operating losses, tax gains from, 669
Net operating profit after taxes (NOPAT), 49
Net present value (NPV), 440, 446–449
benchmark, 448
capital budgeting decisions, 419–421
of a merger, 671
mutually exclusive projects, 455–456
normal set of cash flows, 446
NPV statistic, 446
reinvestment rate assumptions, 453
strengths and weaknesses, 449
Net present value (NPV) profiles, 451–452
with mutually exclusive projects, 455–460
non-normal cash flows, 452–453
Net proceeds, 617
Net working capital, 36, 476
calculation changes in, 411–412
tracing cash and, 476–478
New York Stock Exchange (NYSE), 274
Nicas, Jack, 676
Nominal interest rates, 203
factors affecting, 205
inflation vs., 207
Nondiversifiable risk, 318
Normal cash flows, 442
North American Free Trade Agreement (NAFTA), 632
NYSE (New York Stock Exchange), as secondary market, 191

o

Operating cash flow (OCF), 49
calculation of, 409–410
Operating cycle, 476–477
calculation of, 477
Operating profit margin, 87–88, 93, 101
Operational managers, 11
Operations management, 475–476
Opportunity cost, 406–407, 476
Optimal portfolio, 318
Option, 18, 640
Ordinary dividends, 585
Organizational form, 3
Originating house(s), 618
Orol, Ronald D., 161
Orr, D., 486
Outflow, 120
Over-the-counter market, 192
Overconfidence, 355
Overinvestment problem, 562

p

Page, Larry, 273
Paid-in surplus, 36
Par value, 233–234
Partnerships, 13–14
Passive capital structure management, 546
Passive management, 545
Patriot Bonds, 238
Payback (PB), 440–442
alternative project, 445
strengths and weaknesses of, 445
Payback (PB) benchmark, 442
Payment date, 587
Penny stocks, 352
Percentage return, 308
Perks (perquisites), 18
Perpetuity, 160
PITI (principal, interest, taxes, and insurance), 169
Political risk, 645–646
Political stability, 646
Polkovichenko, Valery, 319
Portfolio beta, 348
Portfolio return, 323–324
Portfolios, 316
diversifying to reduce risk, 316–318, 321–324
efficient portfolios, 320
formation of, 316–324
modern portfolio theory, 318–321
optimal portfolio, 318
Preferred stock, 36, 284–286
cost of capital, 376
Premium, 640
Premium bond, 240
Prepackaged bankruptcy, 677
Present value (PV), 10, 121, 128–130; *see also* Net present value (NPV)
of an annuity due, 161–162
bond cash flows, 242–243
discounting and, 128–130
of level cash flows, 155–158
moving cash flows, 130–132
of multiple annuities, 159–160
of multiple cash flows, 155–160
of next period's cash flow, 128
of several cash flows, 155
tables, 704–707
use of, 130–133
Price-earnings (P/E) ratio, 89–90, 93, 102, 291
Price risk, 198
Primary markets, 190–191, 617
Prime rate, 612
Principal, 17, 233–234
Private placement, 616
Privately held information, 353
Pro forma analysis, 405–406
Pro forma statements
AFN and, 525–530
ratio analysis and, 532
Probability, 340
Probability of default (PD), 682
Probability distribution, 341
Producer price index (PPI), 205
Product extension merger, 663
Profit margin, 87–88, 90, 93, 101
Profitability index (PI), 440, 460–461
benchmark, 461
calculation of, 461
index statistic, 461
Profitability ratios, 86–88, 93
calculation of, 88
Project budgets; *see* Capital budgeting
Project cash flow estimates; *see* Cash flow estimation
Project WACC
business risks, 381
calculation of, 382–383
firm WACC vs., 379–383, 385
pure-play approach, 381–383
risk-sensitive WACC vs., 384
Prospectus, 620
Proxy beta, 381
Public corporation, 14
Public information, 353

Public sector, financial crisis of 2008, 23
Purchasing power parity (PPP), 642–643
future exchange rates, 642–643
PV; *see* Present value

q

Quick ratio, 78–79, 92, 101

r

Raice, Shayndi, 611
Rajan, Raghuram, 18n
Rappaport, Liz, 197
Rate of return, 133
Ratio analysis, 77–78
AFN using pro forma statements, 532
asset management ratios, 79–83
cautions in using, 97–98
debt management ratios, 84–86
DuPont analysis, 90–94
liquidity ratios, 78–79
market value ratios, 89–90
profitability ratios, 86–88
Real assets, 10
Real markets, 10
Real risk-free rate, 205–206
calculation of, 206
Record date, 587
Recourse, 483
Red herring prospectus, 620
Reinvestment rate risk, 245
Relative value, 291
Reorganization procedures, 675–677
Replenishment level, 485
Repurchase, 592
Repurchase agreements (repos), 193
Required return, 342
constant-growth model for, 357–358
Residual claimants, 274
Residual dividend model, 584
Restricted stock, 21, 357
Restrictive financing policy, 482
Restructuring, 546
Retained earnings, 6–7, 36
statement of, 51–52
Retention ratio (RR), 95, 102
Return on assets (ROA), 87–88, 90–93, 102
Return of capital to investors, 7
Return on equity (ROE), 87–93, 102
Returns; *see also* Expected return; Internal rate of return (IRR); Risk and return
average, 309
computing, 307–310
dollar returns, 307–310
geometric mean return, 310
percentage return, 308–309
performance of asset classes, 310–311
portfolio return, 323–324
return asymmetries, 134
risk vs., 315–316
Revenue enhancement, by M&A, 664
Risk, 9–10; *see also* Historical risks; Risk and return
asset classes, 314–315
business, 381
currency exchange risk, 641
default or credit, 208
diversifiable risk, 317
diversifying to reduce, 316–318
exchange rate, 638–640
expected return and, 340–342
financial, 381
firm-specific, 316
foreign exchange, 638–640
historical risks, 311–316
interest rate, 245
liquidity, 209
market risk, 317, 345–346
nondiversifiable, 318
political, 645–646
price risk, 198
reinvestment rate, 245
return vs., 315–316
total, 312
Risk-free rate (RFR), 206, 343
Risk management, 201
Risk measurement, 201
Risk premiums, 342–343
market risk premium, 343
Risk and return
capital market efficiency, 352–355
expected returns, 340–342
financial manager implications, 355–356
historical returns, 307–311
historical risks, 311–316
market risk
beta and, 345–347
market portfolio, 343–345
security market line, 347
portfolios, diversification, 314–315
Rule of 72, 132

s

S corporations, 15
Safety stock, 485
Sales forecasts
average approach, 516–518
naïve approach, 514–515
systematic variations, 518–520
Sales to working capital, 81, 83, 92, 101
Sample project description, 405–406
Sarbanes-Oxley Act of 2002, 20n, 52–53, 680
Savings bonds, 238
Scott, Mike, 21
Sculley, John, 21
Seasonal index, 518
Secondary markets, 191–192, 202
Secondary securities, 200
Section 179 deduction, 414
Secured loans, 483
Securities, 6
Securities and Exchange Act of 1934, 619
Securities and Exchange Commission (SEC), 19, 33, 611
new security issues, 190
private placement rules, 616
Regulation 144A, 616
shelf registration, 620
Securitization, 23
Security market line (SML), 346–348
beta as risk measure, 347
Sell-side analysts, 287
Semistrong-form efficiency, 353
Senior bonds, 254
Separation principle, 389, 548
Shapiro, Mary, 611
Shareholders, 14
clientele effect on, 582–583
dividends preference by, 581–582
wealth maximization of, 16–17
Sharpe, William, 344
Shelf registration, 620
Short-term financial plan, 478–484
current assets policy, 479–482
secured loans, 483
unsecured loans, 482–483
Shortage costs, 475–476
carrying costs and, 480
Simple interest, 122
Small Business Administration (SBA), 607
Smith, Adam, 16
Smoothing earnings, 52
Social responsibility, 16
Sole proprietorship, 13–14
Sources and uses of cash, 46–49
cash flow from financing activities, 47–48
cash flows from investing activities, 46–47
cash flows from operations, 46–47
net change in cash and marketable securities, 48–49
Special provisions, 205, 209
Special purpose vehicles (SPVs), 201
Spector, Mike, 676
Spontaneous liabilities ratio, 521
Spot loan, 606
Spot transaction, 636
Spread, 482
Spreading the financial statements, 94
Stakeholder, 16
Standard & Poor's 500 Index (S&P 500), 277
Standard & Poor's Corporation, 208, 253
bond credit ratings, 254
commercial paper ratings, 614
Standard deviation, 312, 341
Starbucks Coffee Company, 631, 634, 636, 641
State and local government agency bonds, 193–194
Statement of cash flows, 45–49
GAAP accounting principles, 45
noncash entries, 45–46
sources and uses of cash, 46–49
Statement of retained earnings, 51–52
Statman, Meir, 351
Stock dividend, 408, 591
Stock indexes, 277
Stock market bubble, 355

Stock markets, 274–281; *see also* Market risk
delisting letters, 53
tracking of, 277–279
Stock quote, 276
Stock repurchases, 592–594
advantages of, 593
disadvantages of, 593–594
stock price and, 594
Stock split, 591
stock dividends vs., 592
Stock valuation, 281–287
cash flows, 281–283
Coca-Cola example, 282
constant-growth model, 284
dividend discount models, 283–284
estimating future stock prices, 293–294
expected return, 286
P/E model, 291–293
preferred stock, 284–286
variable-growth techniques, 287–290
Stockholders; *see* Shareholders
Stockholders' equity, 34, 36
Stocks; *see also* Dividends
common stock, 274
cost of issuing, 619
dividends and stock prices, 587–590
preferred, 35
repurchases, 592–594
splits and, 591
trading process, 279–281
Straight-line depreciation, 36
Strategic planning, 514
Strong-form efficiency, 353–354
Structured investment vehicles (SIVs), 201
Subprime market, 202–203
Subprime mortgage borrowers, 22
Substitute, 408
Sunk costs, 407
Sunstein, Cass, 319
Surplus cash, 492
Surplus funds, tax gains from, 670
Sustainable growth rate, 95, 102
SWIFT system, 490
Syndicate, 618
Synergy, 663

t

Take down, 606
Taxable equivalent yield, 251–252
Taxes, 6–7
corporate income taxes, 41–44
merger motives and, 669–670
net operating losses, 669
surplus funds, 670
unused debt capacity, 669
WACC and tax rates, 377–378
Technical analysis, 353
Technical insolvency, 672
Term structure of interest rates, 209
liquidity premium theory, 211
market segmentation theory, 211
unbiased expectations theory, 211–213
Thaler, Richard, 319
Ticker symbol, 275
Time line, 120
Time series analysis, 96
Time to maturity, 205, 234
Time value of money (TVM), 10, 119; *see also* Annuity cash flow analysis; Single cash flow analysis
cash flows for, 120
decision factors for, 119
solving for time, 135
Times interest earned, 85–86, 93, 101
Total asset management, 82
Total asset turnover, 82–83, 93, 101
Total risk, 312
Trade credit, 521
Trading posts, 275
Trading volume, 192
Trailing P/E ratio, 291
Transaction facilitation, 484
Treasurer, 11
Treasury bills, 193
Treasury bonds, 235–236
Treasury Inflation-Protected Securities (TIPS), 236–237
Treasury notes and bonds, 193–194

u

Unbiased expectations theory, 212–213
Underinvestment problem, 563
Underwriter's spread, 617
U.S. Department of Commerce, 205
U.S. Department of Justice, 663–664
merger guidelines, 668–669
U.S. government agency securities, 237
Unlimited liability, 13
Unsecured corporate bonds, 254
Unsecured loans, 482
Up-front (or facility) fee, 606
Utkus, Stephen, 319

v

Valuation; *see* Bond valuation; Future value (FV); Present value (PV); Stock valuation
Value stocks, 292
Van Hemert, Otto, 239
Variable growth rate, 287
Variable-growth techniques, 287–290
McDonald's example, 290
Variable-rate loan, 607
Venture capital, 608
Venture capital firms, 604
Venture capitalists, 13
Vertical merger, 663
Vidal, David, 30

w

WACC; *see* Weighted average cost of capital (WACC)
Weak-form efficiency, 353
Weighted average cost of capital (WACC), 374
cost of debt, 376–377
cost of equity, 374–375
cost of preferred stock, 376–377
divisional WACC, 383–388
firm WACC vs. project WACC, 379–380
flotation costs, 389–390
formula for, 374–379
leverage effect, 549–551
merger valuation and, 670–671
project cost numbers, 380–383
pure play approach, 381–383
risk-appropriate, 381
tax rates and, 377–378
weight calculation, 378–379
Weill, Sanford I., 666
Window dressing, 98
Wire transfers, 490
Workout, 673
World Trade Organization (WTO), 634
Wozniak, Stephen, 21
Wulf, Julie, 18n

x

X-efficiencies, 664, 668

y

Yield curves
calculation of, 213
common shapes for, 210
market segmentation, 216
unbiased expectation vs. liquidity premium, 214
Yield to call, 249–250, 252
Yield to maturity, 247–248, 252
YouTube, 15

z

Z-score, 681
Zero-balance account, 491
Zero coupon bond, 242
Zuckerman, Gregory, 197